Perspectives from the Past

PRIMARY SOURCES IN WESTERN CIVILIZATIONS

VOLUME 1

From the Ancient Near East through
the Age of Absolutism

JAMES M. BROPHY · STEVEN EPSTEIN · CAT NILAN

JOHN ROBERTSON · THOMAS MAX SAFLEY

W · W · NORTON & COMPANY NEW YORK · LONDON

Library of Congress Cataloging-in-Publication Data
Perspectives from the past : primary sources in Western civilizations /
James M. Brophy [et al.]—2nd ed.
    p.   cm.
    Contents: v. 1. From the ancient Near East through the age of absolutism
—v. 2. From early modern era through contemporary times.
    ISBN 0-393-97821-4 (v. 1: pbk.) — ISBN 0-393-97822-2 (v. 2: pbk.)
    1. Civilization, Western—History—Sources. I. Brophy, James M.
CB245 .P45   2002
909'.09812—dc21

                                                                    2001055859

ISBN 0-393-97821-4 (pbk.)

W. W. Norton & Company, Inc., 500 Fifth Avenue, New York, N.Y. 10110
http://www.wwnorton.com

W. W. Norton & Company Ltd., Castle House, 75/76 Wells Street, London W1T 3QT

1 2 3 4 5 6 7 8 9 0

ABOUT THE AUTHORS

JAMES M. BROPHY is associate professor of modern European history at the University of Delaware. He received his B.A. from Vassar College and did his graduate training at the Universität Tübingen and Indiana University, where he specialized in the social and political history of nineteenth-century Europe. He is the author of *Capitalism, Politics, and Railroads in Prussia, 1830–1870* (1998) and has published numerous articles on nineteenth-century German history. He regularly teaches the Western civilization survey as well as specialized courses and seminars on historiography, modern European history, modern German history, and European nationalisms.

STEVEN EPSTEIN teaches history at the University of Colorado-Boulder. He was educated at Swarthmore College, St John's College Cambridge, and Harvard, where he developed his interests in medieval social and economic history. He is the author of *Speaking of Slavery: Color, Ethnicity, and Human Bondage in Italy* (2001), *Genoa and the Genoese 958–1528* (1996), *Wage Labor and Guilds in Medieval Europe* (1991), and other works on medieval history. He has taught the first half of the Western civilizations survey for over fifteen years.

CAT NILAN earned her undergraduate degree in French studies and Ph.D. in western European history at Yale University and holds an M.A. in women's history from Sarah Lawrence College.

She has taught a wide range of survey courses in European and world history, as well as seminars on the history of women, the family, the working classes, and crime and the prison system. Her research and writing focuses on the social and cultural history of childhood in Romantic-era France, with an emphasis on the problems of juvenile delinquency and child abuse.

JOHN ROBERTSON received both his M.A. (1976) and his Ph.D. (1981) in ancient history from the University of Pennsylvania. A specialist in the social and economic history of the ancient Near East, Professor Robertson has published several articles in major scholarly journals and contributed articles to such major reference works as the *Anchor Bible Dictionary* and the recently published *Civilizations of the Ancient Near East*. He has also participated in archaeological excavations in Syria and Greece as well as the American Southwest. Since 1982, Professor Robertson has been a member of the faculty of the department of history at Central Michigan University, where he has taught the history of Western civilization for both the department of history and the university honors program, as well as more specialized courses in the history of the ancient Near East and the Islamic and modern Middle East.

THOMAS MAX SAFLEY teaches the history of early modern Europe at the University of Pennsylvania. A specialist in economic and social history, his particular research interests include the history of marriage and the family, of poverty and charity, and of labor and business. In addition to numerous articles and reviews, Professor Safley is the author of *Let No Man Put Asunder: The Control of Marriage in the German Southwest, 1550–1620* (1984), *Charity and Economy in the Orphanages of Early Modern Augsburg* (1996), and *Matheus Miller's Memoir: A Merchant's Life in the Seventeenth Century* (2000). He is also co-editor of *The Workplace before the Factory: Artisans and Proletarians, 1500–1800* (1993) and serves on the editorial board of the *Sixteenth Century Journal.* At the University of Pennsylvania, Professor Safley regularly teaches the introductory survey of European history and advanced lecture courses on the early modern period. He also offers a broad array of undergraduate and graduate seminars.

CONTENTS

CHAPTER 2 ❧ THE GROWTH OF EMPIRES IN THE ANCIENT NEAR EAST 48

CHAPTER 3 ❧ GODS AND EMPIRES: THE IRON AGE NEAR EAST 86

CHAPTER 6   ROMAN CIVILIZATION   228

CHAPTER 7   CHRISTIANITY AND THE TRANSFORMATION OF THE ROMAN WORLD   276

CHAPTER 8 ✑ ROME'S THREE HEIRS: THE BYZANTINE, ISLAMIC, AND EARLY MEDIEVAL WORLDS   319

CHAPTER 9 ✑ THE EXPANSION OF EUROPE: ECONOMY, SOCIETY, AND POLITICS IN THE HIGH MIDDLE AGES, 1000–1300   358

CHAPTER **12** ☙ COMMERCE, CONQUEST, AND COLONIZATION, 1300–1600   502

CHAPTER **13** ☙ THE CIVILIZATION OF THE RENAISSANCE, C. 1350–1550   547

CHAPTER 16 ❧ THE ECONOMY AND SOCIETY OF EARLY MODERN EUROPE 680

CHAPTER 17 ☙ THE AGE OF ABSOLUTISM, 1660–1789   735

PREFACE FOR INSTRUCTORS

The authors of this text are very pleased to have been afforded the opportunity to design and compile this reader, which is the outgrowth of approximately seventy-five years of combined experience teaching the history of Western civilization. In the course of acquiring that experience, the authors were frustrated by what we perceived as serious shortcomings in most of the available supplementary readers. Among the more notable deficiencies are a frequent overemphasis on political and intellectual history at the expense of social and economic history and on elite culture at the expense of sources relating to the experiences of people of lesser socioeconomic station and, especially, of women. There is also an underinclusion of sources representative of the experiences and perspectives of European societies east of what is today Germany and a focus on Western civilization that often has neglected to address the West's important interactions with, and development of attitudes toward, non-Western peoples and civilizations. Some texts, in a laudable attempt to be more inclusive, incorporate more selections to serve up a veritable smorgasbord of thematically unlinked snippets, many of them so abbreviated or cited so disjointedly that the student can hardly gain a proper appreciation of their context or of the nature and structure of the documents from which they are derived. For ancient and medieval sources, this problem is all too often compounded by the use of translations that are either obsolete (from the standpoint of recent advances in philology) or rendered in an antiquated idiom that is hardly conducive to engaging students' interest. Finally, many readers are compiled by only one editor, who, whatever his or her experience and scholarly credentials, may understandably be hard pressed to command adequately the range and variety of primary sources available for examining the diverse aspects of Western civilization.

We by no means have the hubris to believe that what we have assembled will satisfy all the desiderata of every instructor. Nonetheless, to address the concerns noted above, and others, we have endeavored to produce a text that incorporates, as much as possible, the following features:

- Selections that consist of complete texts or lengthy excerpts of primary-source documents, ranging from one to eight pages in length and rendered in authoritative and eloquent, yet idiomatic, translations.

- Recognition that visual artifacts are also meaningful primary sources. Each chapter of this edition contains two visual features (photographs, paintings, posters, cartoons, sculptures, etc.), intended to help students learn how to analyze and interpret visual sources.

- An appropriate balance of primary sources from the Western canon, works that are illustrative of the origins and development of Western political institutions, intellectual life, and high culture or that illustrate aspects of social and economic history as well as more mundane aspects of life in Western societies. In other words, we have strived to provide selections pertinent to the lives, roles, achievements, and contributions of elite and commoner, ruler and ruled, master and servant, man and woman.

- Selections that reflect the experiences and perspectives of women and the dynamics of gender relations, including family and household structure.

- Selections that attempt to place a focus on the western European experience within a broader, even global perspective, by including selections relating to eastern Europe, the ancient and Islamic Middle East, Africa, Asia, and the Western Hemisphere. Thus, interspersed among the works of Western authors are excerpts from ancient Egyptian and Babylonian literature and private letters, the Quran, and works of such figures as Ibn Khaldun, Ibn Battuta, Bernal Diaz de Castillo, Edward Morel, Mohandas Ghandi, Frantz Fanon, Chai Ling, and the Ayatollah Ruhollah Khomeini. Readings such as these are intended to help students trace the evolution of the concept of the West and its relations with the non-West—matters of immense significance as an increasingly global society stands at the beginning of the twenty-first century.

- The incorporation of several unifying questions and issues to link documents both within and among chapters in a coherent, pedagogically useful internal framework. The documents in this reader have been chosen with an overarching purpose of interweaving a number of thematic threads that compose vital elements in the colorful fabrics of Western civilization: What are the status, responsibilities, and rights of the individual within the local community and broader society, and how have they changed over time? How have people defined their own communities, and how have they viewed outsiders? Who should have power within and over the community and society, and why? How have people responded to changes in the material world around them? Who or what controls the cosmos, and how have humankind's perceptions of its appropriate role and function within the cosmos changed?

The pedagogical and critical apparatus provided in this reader has been designed to guide the student to an appreciation of the sources but without imparting too much in the way of historical interpretation. For each chapter we have supplied an introduction that provides an historical context for the readings and alerts the student to the thematic threads that link them. Each reading in turn has an introduction that supplies an even more specific context and alerts the student to issues of interpretation or biased perspective. Finally, each selection is accompanied by several questions intended to stimulate analysis and discussion. The placement of these questions after each selection is quite intentional, as it is our hope that students will engage each document without a preconceived or predetermined sense of why it may be important and will instead learn to trust their own critical capacities and discern the significance of a reading on their own.

Obviously, to organize a project as complex as a reader of this kind and to bring it to a successful and timely fruition require the skills, support, inspiration, and dedication of many people other than the authors. We wish to express our admiration and profound gratitude to the editorial and marketing staff of W. W. Norton, especially to Kate Nash, Sarah Caldwell, Susan Upson, Jane Carter, Aaron Javsicas, and, most especially, to Jon Durbin, who assembled the team, helped us to define and refine our work, organized the project, offered useful insight and judicious criticism, and kept all of us on task and on time. The credit for this reader is surely as much his, and theirs, as ours.

PREFACE FOR STUDENTS

The purpose of this collection of illustrations and documents is to provide the student with the raw materials of history, the sources, in the form of the objects and written words that survive from the past. Your textbook relies on such documents, known as primary sources, as well as on the works of many past and present historians who have analyzed and interpreted these sources—the secondary literature. In some cases the historians were themselves sources, eyewitnesses to the events they recorded. Authors of textbooks select which facts and interpretations you should know, and so the textbook filters what you think about the human past by limiting the information available to you. Textbooks are useful because they provide a coherent historical narrative for students of history, but it is important to remember that they are only an introduction to the rich complexity of human experience over time.

A collection of historical documents and artifacts provides a vital supplement to the textbook, but it also has problems. First, the sources, mostly not intended for us to read and study, exist for the reasons that prompted some people to create them and others to preserve them. These reasons may include a measure of lies, self-deception, or ignorance about what was really happening and being recorded. So we must ask the following questions about any document or object—a treaty, contract, painting, photograph, poem, newspaper article, or sculpture: Why does it exist? What specific purpose did it serve when it was done? Who is its author? What motives prompted the creator to produce this material in this form?

The second major problem is that we, the editors of this collection, have selected, from millions of possible choices, these particular documents and objects, and not others. Even in this process, because of the limitations of space and our own personal experiences, we present a necessarily partial and highly selective view of Western civilization (also because of space limitations, it has been necessary to delete portions from some of the longer sections*). Our purpose is not to repeat what you can find in the textbook but to give you the opportunity to see and discuss how historians, now including you, make history out of documents and objects, and their understanding of why people behave the way they do.

The illustrations in this collection provide a glimpse at the millions of material objects that survive from the past. These churches, buildings, paintings, mosaics, sculptures, photographs, and other items make up an important set of sources for the historian to consider about the past. It is certainly difficult to appreciate an immense building or a small manuscript painting from a photograph. Nevertheless, the editors of this collection added illustrations to the Second Edition in order to make clear the full range of sources historians utilize. Also, the illustrations in many cases complement the written documents and in every case provide opportunities for a broader discussion of historical questions and the variety of sources that can help answer them.

Before exploring in more detail what documents are, we should be clear about what history is. Simply put, history is what we can say about the human past, in this case about the vast area of Western civilization from its origins to the most recent past. We can say, or write, things about the past because people left us their words, in the form of documents, and we can, like detectives, question these sources and then try to understand what happened. Before the written word, there is no history in the strictest sense; instead there are preliterate societies and the tens of thousands of years for which we know only what the anthropologists and archeologists can tell us from the physical remains of bodies and objects made by human hands. And yet during this time profoundly important human institutions like language, the family, and religion first appeared. History begins with writing because that is when the documentation starts.

Although history cannot exist without written documents, we must remember that this evidence is complex and ambiguous. In the first place, it first appears in ancient languages, and the majority of documents in this book were not originally in English. The act of translating the documents into modern English raises another barrier or filter, and we must use our imaginations to recreate the past worlds in which modern words like *liberty, race,* or *sin* had different meanings. One job of the historian is to understand the language of the documents in their widest possible contexts. All the authors intended their

---

* We indicate omissions, no matter how brief, with three spaced asterisks (* * *), running them in when the opening, middle, or closing of a paragraph has been deleted and centering them between lines when a full paragraph is dropped. Why asterisks, when ellipsis dots are the standard? Because authors use ellipsis dots, and we want to distinguish our deletions from theirs.

documents to communicate something, but as time passes, languages and contexts change, and so it becomes more difficult for us to figure out what a document meant then and may mean now. Language is an imperfect way to communicate, but we must make the best of what we have. If we recollect how difficult it is sometimes to understand the events we see and experience, then we can perhaps understand how careful we must be when we interpret someone else's report about an event in the past, especially when that past is far removed in space and time from our experience.

The documents give us the language, or testimony, of witnesses, observers, or people with some point to make. This evidence, like any other, must be examined for flaws, contradictions, lies, and what it tells us that the writer did not necessarily intend to reveal. Like a patient detective, we must question our witnesses with a full awareness of their limited and often-biased perception, piecing together our knowledge of their history with the aid of multiple testimonies and a broad context. Consider the document, whatever it is, as testimony and a piece of a bigger puzzle, many of the remaining pieces of which are missing or broken. It is useful at the beginning to be clear about the simple issues—What type of document is this evidence? Who wrote it? Where and when was it written? Why does it exist? Try to understand the context of the document by relating it to the wider world—how do words by Plato or about the Nazi Party fit with what you already know about ancient Greece or twentieth-century Germany?

When the document, or witness, has been correctly identified and placed in some context, we may then interrogate it further by asking questions about the words before us. Not all documents suggest the same questions, but there are some general questions that apply to nearly every document. One place to begin is to ask, Who or what is left out? Once you see the main point, it is interesting to ask what the documents tell us about people and subjects often left out of the records—women, children, or religious or ethnic minorities, for example. Or, if the document is about a religious minority, we can ask what it tells us about the majority. Take the document and try to turn it inside out by determining the basic assumptions or biases of its author, and then explore what has been intentionally or unintentionally left out. Another way to ask a fresh question of an old witness is to look beneath the surface and see what else is there. For example, if the document in question seems mainly to offer evidence on religion, ask what it tells us about the economy or contemporary eating habits or whatever else might occur to you. Documents frequently reveal excellent information on topics far from their ostensible subjects, if we remember to ask.

Every document in this collection is some kind of story, either long or short. The stories are almost all nonfiction, at least in theory, but they all have characters; a plot, or story line; and above all a point to the story, the meaning.

We have suggested some possible meanings in the sample questions at the end of each document, but these questions are just there to help your thinking or get a discussion going, about the many possible meanings of the documents. You can ask what the meaning was in the document's own time, as well as what we might now see as a meaning that makes sense to us of some pieces of the past. The point of the story in a document may often concern a central issue in history, the process of change. If history is what we can say about the human past, then the most important words describe how change occurs, for example, rapidly, as in revolutions and wars, or more slowly, as in marriage or family life. Every document casts some light on human change, and the meaning of the story often relates to why something changed.

History is often at its dullest when a document simply describes a static situation, for example, a law or farming. However, even a good description reveals choices and emphasis. If you ask, Why this law now? Why farm in this way? How did these activities influence human behavior? you can see that the real subject of nearly all documents is human change, on some level. You will find that people can and will strongly disagree about the meaning of a story: they can and will use the same evidence from a document to draw radically different meanings. This is one of the challenges of history and what makes it fun, for some explanations and meanings make more sense than others in the broader context of what you know about an episode or period of history. Argue about meaning, and you will learn something about not only your own biases and values but also the process of sifting facts for good arguments and answers. These skills have a value well beyond the study of history.

The documents and objects in this collection, even the most general works of philosophy or social analysis, reveal the particular and contingent aspects of history. Even the most abstract of these documents and objects comes from a specific time, place, and person and sheds some light on a unique set of circumstances. When history is like the other social sciences (economics, sociology, political science, and others), it tries to deal with typical or average people, societies, or behavior. When history is like the other humanities (literature, religion, art, and others), it stresses individual people, their quirks and uniqueness. The documents and objects also illustrate the contingent aspect of history, which unlike the social or natural sciences but like the humanities, appears to lack rules or laws. History depends on what people did, subject to the restrictions of their natures, resources, climate, and other natural factors—people with histories of their own! Rerunning this history is not like a movie, and it would never turn out the same way twice, for it is specific and contingent to the way it turned out this time. The documents and objects do not tell a story of an orderly progression from simple to complex societies or from bad to good ones. Instead, history continues, and people cope, or not, with the issues of religious faith, family life, making a living, and creating artifacts and documents. These documents and objects collectively provide perspectives on how experiments in living succeeded or failed. We invite you to use them to learn more about the people of the past than the textbooks can say and to use your imaginations to get these witnesses to answer your questions about the process and meaning of human change.

WHERE TO BEGIN?

This checklist is a series of questions that can be used to analyze most of the documents and objects in this reader.

✔ What type of document or object is this evidence?

✔ Why does the document or object exist? What motives prompted the author to create the material in this form?

✔ Who created this work?

✔ Who or what is left out—women, children, minorities, members of the majority?

✔ In addition to the main subject, what other kinds of information can be obtained?

✔ How do the subjects of the document or object relate to what we know about broader society?

✔ What was the meaning of the document or object in its own time? What is its meaning for the audience?

✔ What does the document or object tell us about change in society?

1 ❧ THE ORIGINS OF WESTERN CIVILIZATIONS IN THE ANCIENT NEAR EAST

In the history of humankind's sojourn on this planet, no development has been more momentous or more fraught with consequence than the emergence of civilization. Just what constitutes civilization has been and will continue to be debated by scholars for years. But as evidenced by the appearance of states, cities, complex economies, and writing, among other characteristics, civilizations can be said to have arisen independently in several areas across the globe. By far the earliest of them, however, arose in that region of Southwestern Asia and northern Africa that we today refer to as the Middle East.

By about 5000 B.C.E., in what is now eastern Iraq, a Neolithic people whom archaeologists refer to as the Samarrans began to establish villages where rainfall alone could not support agriculture.¹ Their pioneering efforts in the technology of canal irrigation paved the way for the emergence of cities and, with them, the civilization of ancient Sumer. The world's first cities arose in the floodplain of Lower Mesopotamia, the land between the Tigris and Euphrates rivers (modern-day southern Iraq), more than 5,000 years ago, as large population centers governed by administrators powerful enough to organize and direct the construction of large architectural complexes, quite likely temples. These efforts were fueled by agricultural production on an unprecedentedly massive scale, entailing the cultivation of thousands of acres of wheat, barley, and other foodstuffs. The floodplain's wondrous fertility could be unleashed only by the profuse application of irrigation water brought from the Euphrates and (perhaps to a lesser extent) the Tigris. Organizing the digging and maintaining of irrigation canals, the plowing, sowing, and harvesting of the fields, and the maintaining of huge flocks of livestock was a truly formidable task.

By about 3200 B.C.E., the size and scope of the administration of these great estates necessitated the creation of a new technology that itself shaped the future

---

¹B.C.E. means "before the common era." [Editor.]

of civilization: writing. Incised on clay tablets, the early pictographs evolved into a system, which we refer to as cuneiform (literally, "wedge shaped"), that spread throughout the ancient Near East and remained in use for almost 3,000 years. The cuneiform scribes of ancient Mesopotamia (and Anatolia, Syria, Iran, and even Egypt) bequeathed to us a remarkably durable legacy of tens of thousands of records—mostly clay tablets but also inscriptions on stone monuments and objects. The majority of the tablets are detailed accounts of the administration of temples, palaces, and public institutions, tediously dry in themselves but, when reconstructed into coherent archives, crucial evidence of social and economic organization. The remaining records—among them, royal inscriptions, letters, poems, hymns, prayers, law "codes," contracts, and a variety of literary works—provide, at best, tantalizing samples from what was once an undoubtedly vast corpus. Enough remains to us, nonetheless, to reconstruct a fairly complex outline of the sequence of dynasties and political configurations in the history of Mesopotamia and the Near East. But perhaps more appealing to our common humanity, these records allow us at least some limited insight into the enduring structures of the lives and the everyday concerns of people who seem to have believed that their fortune and existence depended on ensuring the continued favor of their gods. Those gods might bestow on them benevolence and plenty or, just as likely, abandon them to destitution and catastrophe, the latter all too often brought by the rampages of "barbarian" invaders or the no less destructive rampages of the normally life-sustaining rivers.

Civilization arose in Egypt somewhat later but developed a unique form and identity. According to their later traditions, the Egyptians believed that, in their remote past, a king named Menes had been the first to unite the two rival kingdoms of Upper Egypt and Lower Egypt. From our modern vantage point, we detect only scant traces of a ruler named Menes in the earliest Egyptian records, and most scholars are convinced that the unification of Egypt was rather more complicated than the pulling together of two kingdoms. Nonetheless, by around 3100 B.C.E. there was created what some have recognized as the world's first unified nation-state. For the next 3,000 years the people of Egypt regarded the absolute rule of a divine king (who by the middle of the second millennium B.C.E. came to be known as pharaoh) as the only desirable state of affairs. On his shoulders fell the responsibility of preserving the stability of the cosmos (what the Egyptians called ma'at), which included the unity of the Two Lands of Upper and Lower Egypt. Only through the king's vigorous stewardship might chaos and calamity be averted. Over time, there developed around the king's person a royal court and a highly hierarchical administration which were served by a class of professional (and mostly male) scribes, highly trained in the hieroglyphic script and its derivatives. Through their efforts, the people and resources of the kingdom could be marshaled to ensure the king's success, both in this world and the next. It is from the records they have left us—inscribed and painted on *temple and tomb walls, or written on papyrus or even flakes of stone—that we glean our hard-won knowledge of ancient Egyptian history and culture.*

Neither the grandeur of Egyptian kingship nor the king's preservation of cosmic harmony would have been possible, of course, without the Nile River. As the Greek "father of history" Herodotus so succinctly put it, Egypt is "the river's gift." Until the completion of the Aswan High Dam in the early 1970s, every year between July and October the Nile overflowed its banks, bringing life-giving water and rich silt which, together with the generative power of the sun, literally resurrected the black land of the Nile Valley. It may well be that in this annual resurrection of the land was born the Egyptian concept of a resurrection and continued existence after death (though only if proper preparations were made and precautions taken). Often, modern observers tend to focus on the Egyptians' supposed morbid preoccupation with death and the hereafter. In part, that perception stems from the accidents of archaeological preservation. Millennia of flooding and silt deposits, combined with continued human occupation of town and village sites, have largely obliterated the towns and villages of the ancient Egyptians. Most of what has been left to us are the remains of temples and tombs, built in the low desert where the Nile's floods did not reach; that the remaining records say so much about kings, gods, and death should hardly surprise us. As some of the documents in this chapter make clear, however, the ancient Egyptians did not while away their lives dreamily pining for death.

FROM *Atrahasis:* An Account
of the Great Flood

The theme of a great flood appears in several works of ancient Mesopotamian literature, including the Sumerian King List, The Epic of Gilgamesh, and the following work, the earliest known example of which dates to about 1700 B.C.E. Its hero, Atrahasis (literally, "exceedingly wise"), is a figure of great antiquity who reappears under different names in later flood stories (including Ut-napishtim in the Epic of Gilgamesh); some scholars have traced versions of his name into later Greek, Roman, and Arabic tales. As will become apparent, however, this is much more than a flood story, for it also gives us one version of why and how, according to ancient Mesopotamian belief, humans came into being.

From *Myths from Mesopotamia: Creation, the Flood, Gilgamesh, and Others,* translated by Stephanie Dalley (Oxford, Eng.: Oxford University Press, 1989).

When the gods instead of man
Did the work, bore the loads,
The gods' load was too great,
The work too hard, the trouble too much,
The great Anunnaki made the Igigi
Carry the workload sevenfold.
Anu their father was king,
Their counsellor warrior Ellil,
Their chamberlain was Ninurta,
Their canal-controller Ennugi.
They took the box (of lots)
Cast the lots; the gods made the division.
Anu went up to the sky,
[And Ellil (?)] took the earth for his people.
The bolt which bars the sea
Was assigned to far-sighted Enki.
When Anu had gone up to the sky,
[And the gods of] the Apsu had gone below,
The Anunnaki of the sky
Made the Igigi bear the workload.
The gods had to dig out canals,
Had to clear channels, the lifelines of the land,
The Igigi had to dig out canals,
Had to clear channels, the lifelines of the land.
The gods dug out the Tigris river (bed)
And then dug out the Euphrates.

*   *   *

They were counting the years of loads.
For 3,600 years they bore the excess,
Hard work, night and day.
They groaned and blamed each other,
Grumbled over the masses of excavated soil:
"Let us confront our [   ] the chamberlain,
And get him to relieve us of our hard work!
Come, let us carry the Lord,
The counsellor of gods, the warrior, from his
    dwelling.
Come, let us carry Ellil,
The counsellor of gods, the warrior, from his
    dwelling."
Then [ ] made his voice heard
And spoke to the gods his brothers,
"Come! Let us carry
The counsellor of gods, the warrior, from his
    dwelling.

Come! Let us carry Ellil,
The counsellor of gods, the warrior, from his
    dwelling.
Now, cry battle!
Let us mix fight with battle!"
The gods listened to his speech,
Set fire to their tools,
Put aside their spades for fire,
Their loads for the fire-god,
They flared up. When they reached
The gate of warrior Ellil's dwelling,
It was night, the middle watch,
The house was surrounded, the god had not
    realized.
It was night, the middle watch,
Ekur was surrounded, Ellil had not realized.
Yet Kalkal was attentive, and had it closed,
He held the lock and watched the gate.
Kalkal roused Nusku.
They listened to the noise of the Igigi.
Then Nusku roused his master,
Made him get out of bed:
"My lord, your house is surrounded,
A rabble is running around your door!
Ellil, your house is surrounded,
A rabble is running around your door!"
Ellil had weapons brought to his dwelling.
Ellil made his voice heard
And spoke to the vizier Nusku,
"Nusku, bar your door,
Take up your weapons and stand in front of
    me."
Nusku barred his door,
Took up his weapons and stood in front of Ellil.
Nusku made his voice heard
And spoke to the warrior Ellil,
"O my lord, your face is sallow as tamarisk!
Why do you fear your own sons?
O Ellil, your face is sallow as tamarisk!
Why do you fear your own sons?
Send for Anu to be brought down to you,
Have Enki fetched into your presence."
He sent for Anu to be brought down to him,
Enki was fetched into his presence,
Anu king of the sky was present,
Enki king of the Apsu attended.

The great Anunnaki were present.
Ellil got up and the case was put.
Ellil made his voice heard
And spoke to the great gods,
"Is it against me that they have risen?
Shall I do battle . . . ?
What did I see with my own eyes?
A rabble was running around my door!"
Anu made his voice heard
And spoke to the warrior Ellil,
"Let Nusku go out
And find out word of the Igigi
Who have surrounded your door. * * *"
Ellil made his voice heard
And spoke to the vizier Nusku,
"Nusku, open your door,
Take up your weapons and stand before
     me.
In the assembly of all the gods,
Bow, then stand and tell them,
'Your father Anu,
Your counsellor warrior Ellil,
Your chamberlain Ninurta
And your canal-controller Ennugi
Have sent me to say,
Who is in charge of the rabble?
Who is in charge of the fighting?
Who declared war?
Who ran to the door of Ellil?' "
Nusku opened his door,
Took up his weapons, went before Ellil
In the assembly of all the gods
He bowed, then stood and told the message.
"Your father Anu,
Your counsellor warrior Ellil,
Your chamberlain Ninurta
And your canal-controller Ennugi
Have sent me to say,
'Who is in charge of the rabble?
Who is in charge of the fighting?
Who declared war?
Who ran to the door of Ellil?' "

                *   *   *

"Every single one of us gods declared war!
We have put a stop to the digging.

The load is excessive, it is killing us!
Our work is too hard, the trouble too
     much!
So every single one of us gods
Has agreed to complain to Ellil."
Nusku took his weapons,
Went [and returned to Ellil] * * *

                *   *   *

Ellil listened to that speech.
His tears flowed.
Ellil spoke guardedly,
Addressed the warrior Anu,
"Noble one, take a decree
With you to the sky, show your strength—
While the Anunnaki are sitting before you
Call up one god and let them cast him for
     destruction!"
Anu made his voice heard
And spoke to the gods his brothers,
"What are we complaining of?
Their work was indeed too hard, their trouble
     was too much.
Every day the earth resounded
The warning signal was loud enough, we kept
     hearing the noise. * * *
While the Anunnaki are sitting before you,
And while Belet-ili the womb-goddess is present,
Call up one and cast him for destruction!"
Anu made his voice heard and spoke to Nusku,
"Nusku, open your door, take up your weapons,
Bow in the assembly of the great gods, then
     stand
And tell them
'Your father Anu, your counsellor warrior
     Ellil,
Your chamberlain Ninurta and your canal-
     controller Ennugi
Have sent me to say,
Who is in charge of the rabble? Who will be in
     charge of battle?
Which god started the war?
A rabble was running around my door!' "
When Nusku heard this,
He took up his weapons,

Bowed in the assembly of the great gods, then
    stood
And told them,
"Your father Anu, your counsellor warrior Ellil,
Your chamberlain Ninurta and your canal-
    controller Ennugi
Have sent me to say,
'Who is in charge of the rabble? Who is in
    charge of the fighting?
Which god started the war?
A rabble was running around Ellil's
    door.' " * * *
(The god Enki) made his voice heard
And spoke to the gods his brothers,
"Why are we blaming them?
Their work was too hard, their trouble was too
    much.
Every day the earth resounded.
The warning signal was loud enough. * * *"

       *   *   *

"Belet-ili the womb-goddess is present,
Let the womb-goddess create offspring,
And let man bear the load of the gods!"
They called up the goddess, asked
The midwife of the gods, wise Mami,
"You are the womb-goddess (to be the) creator
    of mankind!
Create a mortal, that he may bear the yoke!
Let him bear the yoke, the work of Ellil,
Let man bear the load of the gods!"
Nintu made her voice heard
And spoke to the great gods,
"It is not proper for me to make him.
The work is Enki's;
He makes everything pure!
If he gives me clay, then I will do it."
Enki made his voice heard
And spoke to the great gods,
"On the first, seventh, and fifteenth of the
    month
I shall make a purification by washing.
Then one god should be slaughtered.
And the gods can be purified by immersion.
Nintu shall mix clay

With his flesh and his blood.
Then a god and a man
Will be mixed together in clay.
Let us hear the drumbeat forever after,
Let a ghost come into existence from the god's
    flesh,
Let her proclaim it as his living sign,
And let the ghost exist so as not to forget."
They answered "Yes!" in the assembly,
The great Anunnaki who assign the fates.

On the first, seventh, and fifteenth of the month
He made a purification by washing.
Geshtu-e, a god who had intelligence,
They slaughtered in their assembly.
Nintu mixed clay
With his flesh and blood.
They heard the drumbeat forever after.
A ghost came into existence from the god's
    flesh,
And she proclaimed it as his living sign.
The ghost existed so as not to forget the slain
    god.
After she had mixed that clay,
She called up the Anunnaki, the great gods.
The Igigi, the great gods,
Spat spittle upon the clay.
Mami made her voice heard
And spoke to the great gods,
"I have carried out perfectly
The work that you ordered of me.
You have slaughtered a god together with his
    intelligence.
I have relieved you of your hard work,
I have imposed your load on man.
You have bestowed noise on mankind.
I have undone the fetter and granted freedom."
They listened to this speech of hers,
And were freed from anxiety, and kissed her
    feet:
"We used to call you Mami
But now your name shall be Mistress of All
    Gods."

       *   *   *

600 years, less than 600, passed,
And the country became too wide, the people
    too numerous.
The country was as noisy as a bellowing bull.
The God grew restless at their racket,
Ellil had to listen to their noise.
He addressed the great gods,
"The noise of mankind has become too much,
I am losing sleep over their racket.
Give the order that šuruppu-disease shall break
    out . . ."

*   *   *

Now there was one Atrahasis
Whose ear was open to his god Enki.
He would speak with his god
And his god would speak with him.
Atrahasis made his voice heard
And spoke to his lord,
"How long will the gods make us suffer?
Will they make us suffer illness forever?"
Enki made his voice heard
And spoke to his servant:
"Call the elders, the senior men!
Start an uprising in your own house,
Let heralds proclaim . . .
Let them make a loud noise in the land:
Do not revere your gods,
Do not pray to your goddesses,
But search out the door of Namtara.
Bring a baked loaf into his presence.
May the flour offering reach him,
May he be shamed by the presents
And wipe away his 'hand.' "
Atrahasis took the order,
Gathered the elders to his door.
Atrahasis made his voice heard
And spoke to the elders,
"I have called the elders, the senior men!
Start an uprising in your own house,
Let heralds proclaim . . .
Let them make a loud noise in the land:
Do not revere your gods!
Do not pray to your goddesses!
Search out the door of Namtara.

Bring a baked loaf into his presence.
May the flour offering reach him;
May he be shamed by the presents
And wipe away his 'hand.' "
The elders listened to his speech;
They built a temple for Namtara in the city.
Heralds proclaimed . . .
They made a loud noise in the land.
They did not revere their god,
Did not pray to their goddess,
But searched out the door of Namtara,
Brought a baked loaf into his presence.
The flour offering reached him.
And he was shamed by the presents.
And wiped away his "hand."
The šuruppu-disease left them,
The gods went back to their regular offerings.

*   *   *

600 years, less than 600, passed
And the country became too wide, the people
    too numerous.
The country was as noisy as a bellowing bull.
The God grew restless at their clamour,
Ellil had to listen to their noise.
He addressed the great gods,
"The noise of mankind has become too much.
I am losing sleep over their racket.
Cut off food supplies to the people!
Let the vegetation be too scant for their hunger!
Let Adad wipe away his rain.
Below let no flood-water flow from the springs.
Let wind go, let it strip the ground bare,
Let clouds gather but not drop rain,
Let the field yield a diminished harvest,
Let Nissaba stop up her bosom.
No happiness shall come to them.
Let their [ ] be dejected."

*   *   *

"Call the elders,
Start an uprising in your house,
Let heralds proclaim . . .
Let them make a loud noise in the land:
Do not revere your gods!

Do not pray to your goddess!
Search out the door of Adad,
Bring a baked loaf into his presence.
May the flour offering reach him,
May he be shamed by the presents
And wipe away his 'hand.' "
Then he will make a mist form in the morning
And in the night he will steal out and make dew
    drop,
Deliver the field of its produce ninefold, like a
    thief.
They built a temple for Adad in the city,
Ordered heralds to proclaim
And make a loud noise in the land.
They did not revere their gods,
Did not pray to their goddess,
But searched out the door of Adad,
Brought a baked loaf into his presence.
The flour offering reached him;
He was shamed by the presents
And wiped away his "hand."
He made mist form in the morning
And in the night he stole out and made dew drop,
Delivered the field of its produce ninefold, like a
    thief.
The drought left them,
The gods went back to their regular offerings.

*   *   *

600 years, less than 600 years, passed.
The country became too wide, the people too
    numerous.
He grew restless at their noise.
Sleep could not overtake him because of their
    racket.
Ellil organized his assembly,
Addressed the gods his sons,
"The noise of mankind has become too much.
I have become restless at their noise.
Sleep cannot overtake me because of their racket.
Give the order that šuruppu-disease shall break
    out,
Let Namtar put an end to their noise straight
    away!
Let sickness: headache, šuruppu, ašakku,

Blow in to them like a storm."
They gave the order, and šuruppu-disease did
    break out.
Namtar put an end to their noise straight away.
Sickness: headache, šuruppu, ašakku,
Blew into them like a storm.
The thoughtful man, Atrahasis
Kept his ear open to his master Ea (Enki);
He would speak with his god,
And his god Ea would speak with him.
Atrahasis made his voice heard and spoke,
Said to Ea his master,
"Oh Lord, people are grumbling!
Your sickness is consuming the country!
Oh Lord Ea, people are grumbling!
Sickness from the gods is consuming the country!
Since you created us
You ought to cut off sickness: headache, šuruppu
    and ašakku."
Ea made his voice heard and spoke,
Said to Atrahasis,
"Order the heralds to proclaim,
To make a loud noise in the land:
Do not revere your gods,
Do not pray to your goddesses! * * *"
Ellil organized his assembly,
Addressed the gods his sons,
"You are not to inflict disease on them again,
Even though the people have not diminished—
    they are more than before!
I have become restless at their noise,
Sleep cannot overtake me because of their racket!
Cut off food from the people,
Let vegetation be too scant for their stomachs!
Let Adad on high make his rain scarce,
Let him block below, and not raise flood-water
    from the springs!
Let the field decrease its yield,
Let Nissaba turn away her breast,
Let the dark fields become white,
Let the broad countryside breed alkali
Let earth clamp down her womb
So that no vegetation sprouts, no grain grows.
Let ašakku be inflicted on the people,
Let the womb be too tight to let a baby out!"

They cut off food for the people,
Vegetation . . . became too scant for their
    stomachs.
Adad on high made his rain scarce,
Blocked below, and did not raise flood-water from
    the springs.
The field decreased its yield,
Nissaba turned away her breast,
The dark fields became white,
The broad countryside bred alkali.
Earth clamped down her womb:
No vegetation sprouted, no grain grew.
Ašakku was inflicted on the people.
The womb was too tight to let a baby out.
Ea kept guard over the bolt that bars the sea,
Together with his *lahmu*-heroes.
Above, Adad made his rain scarce,
Blocked below, and did not raise flood-water from
    the springs.
The field decreased its yield,
Nissaba turned away her breast,
The dark fields became white,
The broad countryside bred alkali.
Earth clamped down her womb:
No vegetation sprouted, no grain grew.
Ašakku was inflicted on the people,
The womb was too tight to let a baby out. ✴ ✴ ✴
When the second year arrived
They had depleted the storehouse.
When the third year arrived
The people's looks were changed by starvation.
When the fourth year arrived
Their upstanding bearing bowed,
Their well-set shoulders slouched,
People went out in public hunched over.
When the fifth year arrived,
A daughter would eye her mother coming in;
A mother would not even open her door to her
    daughter.
A daughter would watch the scales at the sale of
    her mother,
A mother would watch the scales at the sale of her
    daughter.
When the sixth year arrived
They served up a daughter for a meal,

Served up a son for food. ✴ ✴ ✴
Only one or two households were left.
Their faces were covered with scabs like malt.
People stayed alive by . . . . . . life.
The thoughtful man Atrahasis
Kept his ear open to his master Ea.
He would speak with his god,
And his god Ea would speak with him.
He left the door of his god,
Put his bed right beside the river,
For even the canals were quite silent.

                    ✴   ✴   ✴

They were furious with each other, Enki and Ellil.
"We, the great Anunna, all of us,
Agreed together on a plan.
Anu and Adad were to guard above,
I was to guard the earth below.
Where you went,
You were to undo the chain and set us free!
You were to release produce for the people!

                    ✴   ✴   ✴

You imposed your loads on man,
You bestowed noise on mankind,
You slaughtered a god together with his
    intelligence,
You must . . . and create a flood.
It is indeed your power that shall be used against
    your people!
You agreed to the wrong plan!
Have it reversed!
Let us make far-sighted Enki swear . . . an oath."
Enki made his voice heard
And spoke to his brother gods,
"Why should you make me swear an oath?
Why should I use my power against my people?
The flood that you mention to me—
What is it? I don't even know!
Could I give birth to a flood?
That is Ellil's kind of work!"

                    ✴   ✴   ✴

Atrahasis made his voice heard
And spoke to his master,

"Indicate to me the meaning of the dream. ✳ ✳ ✳"
Enki made his voice heard
And spoke to his servant,
"You say, 'I should find out in bed.'
Make sure you attend to the message I shall tell
  you!
Wall, listen constantly to me!
Reed hut, make sure you attend to all my words!
Dismantle the house, build a boat,
Reject possessions, and save living things.
The boat that you build ✳ ✳ ✳
Roof it like the Apsu
So that the Sun cannot see inside it!
Make upper decks and lower decks.
The tackle must be very strong,
The bitumen strong, to give strength.
I shall make rain fall on you here,
A wealth of birds, a hamper of fish."
He opened the sand clock and filled it,
He told him the sand needed for the Flood was
Seven nights' worth.
Atrahasis received the message.
He gathered the elders at his door.
Atrahasis made his voice heard
And spoke to the elders,
"My god is out of favour with your god.
Enki and Ellil have become angry with each other.
They have driven me out of my house.
Since I always stand in awe of Enki,
He told me of this matter.
I can no longer stay in,
I cannot set my foot on Ellil's territory again.
I must go down to the Apsu and stay with my
  god.
This is what he told me."

   ✳ ✳ ✳

The carpenter brought his axe,
The reed worker brought his stone,
A child brought bitumen.
The poor fetched what was needed. ✳ ✳ ✳
He selected and put on board,
The birds that fly in the sky,
Cattle of Shakkan,
Wild animals of open country,

he put on board. ✳ ✳ ✳
He put his family on board.
They were eating, they were drinking.
But he went in and out,
Could not stay still or rest on his haunches,
His heart was breaking and he was vomiting bile.
The face of the weather changed.
Adad bellowed from the clouds.
When he heard his noise,
Bitumen was brought and he sealed his door.
While he was closing up his door
Adad kept bellowing from the clouds.
The winds were raging even as he went up
And cut through the rope, he released the boat.

   ✳ ✳ ✳

Anzu was tearing at the sky with his talons, ✳ ✳ ✳
The *kašušu*-weapon went against the people like
  an army.
No one could see anyone else,
They could not be recognized in the catastrophe.
The Flood roared like a bull,
Like a wild ass screaming the winds howled.
The darkness was total, there was no sun. ✳ ✳ ✳
As for Nintu the Great Mistress,
Her lips became encrusted with rime.
The great gods, the Anunna,
Stayed parched and famished.
The goddess watched and wept,
Midwife of the gods, wise Mami: ✳ ✳ ✳
"However could I, in the assembly of gods,
Have ordered such destruction with them?
Ellil was strong enough to give a wicked order.
Like Tiruru he ought to have cancelled that wicked
  order!
I heard their cry levelled at me,
Against myself, against my person.
Beyond my control my offspring have become like
  white sheep.
As for me, how am I to live in a house of
  bereavement?
My noise has turned to silence.
Could I go away, up to the sky
And live as in a cloister?
What was Anu's intention as decision-maker?

It was his command that the gods his sons
    obeyed,
He who did not deliberate, but sent the Flood,
He who gathered the people to catastrophe." * * *
Nintu was wailing,
"Would a true father have given birth to the
    rolling sea
So that they could clog the river like
    dragonflies?
They are washed up like a raft on a bank,
They are washed up like a raft on a bank in open
    country!
I have seen, and wept over them!
Shall I ever finish weeping for them?"
She wept, she gave vent to her feelings,
Nintu wept and fuelled her passions.
The gods wept with her for the country.
She was sated with grief, she longed for beer in
    vain.
Where she sat weeping, there the great gods sat
    too,
But, like sheep, could only fill their windpipes with
    bleating.
Thirsty as they were, their lips
Discharged only the rime of famine.
For seven days and seven nights
The torrent, storm and flood came on.
    (Atrahasis offers sacrifice to the gods.)

       *   *   *

The gods smelt the fragrance,
Gathered like flies over the offering.
When they had eaten the offering,
Nintu got up and blamed them all,
"Whatever came over Anu who makes the
    decisions?
Did Ellil dare to come for the smoke
    offering?
Those two who did not deliberate, but sent the
    Flood,
Gathered the people to catastrophe—
You agreed the destruction.
Now their bright faces are dark forever."
Then she went up to the big flies

Which Anu had made, and declared before the
    gods,
"His grief is mine! My destiny goes with his!
He must deliver me from evil, and appease
    me! * * *
Let these flies be the lapis lazuli of my necklace
By which I may remember it daily forever!"
The warrior Ellil spotted the boat
And was furious with the Igigi.
"We, the great Anunna, all of us,
Agreed together on an oath!
No form of life should have escaped!
How did any man survive the catastrophe?"
Anu made his voice heard
And spoke to the warrior Ellil,
"Who but Enki would do this?
He made sure that the reed hut disclosed the
    order."
Enki made his voice heard
And spoke to the great gods,
"I did it, in defiance of you!
I made sure life was preserved. * * *"

       *   *   *

Ellil made his voice heard
And spoke to far-sighted Enki,
"Come, summon Nintu the womb-goddess!
Confer with each other in the assembly."
Enki made his voice heard
And spoke to the womb-goddess Nintu,
"You are the womb-goddess who decrees
    destinies. * * *
In addition let there be one-third of the
    people,
Among the people the woman who gives birth
    yet does
Not give birth successfully;
Let there be the *pašittu*-demon among the
    people,
To snatch the baby from its mother's lap.
Establish *ugbabtu, entu, egiṣītu*-women:
They shall be taboo, and thus control
    childbirth."

       *   *   *

REVIEW QUESTIONS

1. According to this account of the great flood, why were humans created?
2. Why did the gods decide to send a flood on humankind?
3. What does this myth suggest about the proper relationship between gods and humankind and, by extension, about the place of humans in the cosmos?
4. Does Atrahasis's role parallel that of a well-known figure from the Hebrew Bible's Book of Genesis?

FROM *The Epic of Gilgamesh*

With the exception of the Hebrew Bible, the Epic of Gilgamesh is the most celebrated literary work of the ancient Near East. Although Gilgamesh almost certainly was an actual ruler of the Sumerian city of Uruk in the early third millennium B.C.E., the Akkadian epic that developed around him (elements of which can be found in even earlier Sumerian stories about him) is most prized today not as a historical source for his era but as one of world literature's earliest and most profound statements on the human condition, and especially on the inescapability of human mortality. And, although it is not included in the excerpt that follows, the epic also contains by far the most-detailed account of the Flood that is to be found in Mesopotamian literature. (In fact, the discovery of a cuneiform tablet containing this story, with its obvious parallels to the story of Noah and the Flood in the biblical Book of Genesis, helped to foster continued archeological expeditions to Iraq in the late nineteenth and early twentieth centuries.)

From *Myths from Mesopotamia: Creation, the Flood, Gilgamesh, and Others*, translated by Stephanie Dalley (Oxford, Eng.: Oxford University Press, 1989), pp. 50–120.

FROM **Tablet I**

Of him who found out all things, I shall tell the land,
Of him who experienced everything, I shall teach the whole.
He searched lands everywhere.
He who experienced the whole gained complete wisdom.
He found out what was secret and uncovered what was hidden,
He brought back a tale of times before the Flood.
He had journeyed far and wide, weary and at last resigned.
He engraved all toils on a memorial monument of stone.
He had the wall of Uruk built, the sheepfold
Of holiest Eanna, the pure treasury.
See its wall, which is like a copper band,
Survey its battlements, which nobody else can match,

Take the threshold, which is from time
   immemorial,
Approach Eanna, the home of Ishtar,
Which no future king nor any man will ever
   match!
Go up on to the wall of Uruk and walk
   around!
Inspect the foundation platform and scrutinize
   the brickwork!
Testify that its bricks are baked bricks,
And that the Seven Counsellors must have laid
   its foundations!
One square mile is city, one square mile is
   orchards,
one square mile is claypits, as well as the open
   ground of Ishtar's temple.
Three square miles and the open ground
   comprise Uruk.
Look for the copper tablet-box,
Undo its bronze lock,
Open the door to its secret,
Lift out the lapis lazuli tablet and read it,
The story of that man, Gilgamesh, who went
   through all kinds of sufferings.
He was superior to other kings, a warrior lord of
   great stature,
A hero born of Uruk, a goring wild bull.
He marches at the front as leader,
He goes behind, the support of his brothers,
A strong net, the protection of his men,
The raging flood-wave, which can destroy even a
   stone wall.
Son of Lugalbanda, Gilgamesh, perfect in
   strength,
Son of the lofty cow, the wild cow Ninsun.
He is Gilgamesh, perfect in splendour,
Who opened up passes in the mountains,
Who could dig pits even in the mountainside,
Who crossed the ocean, the broad seas, as far as
   the sunrise.
Who inspected the edges of the world, kept
   searching for eternal life,
Who reached Ut-napishtim the far-distant, by
   force.

Who restored to their rightful place cult centres
   which the Flood had ruined.
There is nobody among the kings of teeming
   humanity
Who can compare with him,
Who can say "I am king" beside Gilgamesh.
Gilgamesh was named from birth for fame.
Two-thirds of him was divine, and one-third
   mortal.
Belet-ili designed the shape of his body,
Made his form perfect, * * *
In Uruk the Sheepfold he would walk about,
Show himself superior, his head held high like a
   wild bull.
He had no rival, and at his *pukku*
His weapons would rise up, his comrades have
   to rise up.
The young men of Uruk became dejected in
   their private quarters.
Gilgamesh would not leave any son alone for his
   father.
Day and night his behaviour was overbearing.
   * * *
Powerful, superb, knowledgeable and expert,
Gilgamesh would not leave young girls alone,
The daughters of warriors, the brides of young
   men.
The gods often heard their complaints.

   *   *   *

They called upon great Aruru:
"You, Aruru, you created mankind!
Now create someone for him, to match the
   ardour of his energies!
Let them be regular rivals, and let Uruk be
   allowed peace!"
When Aruru heard this, she created inside
   herself the word of Anu.
Aruru washed her hands, pinched off a piece of
   clay, cast it out into open country.
She created a primitive man, Enkidu the warrior:
   offspring of silence, sky-bolt of Ninurta.
His whole body was shaggy with hair, he was
   furnished with tresses like a woman,
His locks of hair grew luxuriant like grain.

He knew neither people nor country; he was
      dressed as cattle are.
With gazelles he eats vegetation,
With cattle he quenches his thirst at the watering
      place.
With wild beasts he satisfies his need for water.
A hunter, a brigand,
Came face to face with him beside the watering
      place.
He saw him on three successive days beside the
      watering place.
The hunter looked at him, and was dumbstruck
      to see him.
In perplexity he went back into his house
And was afraid, stayed mute, was silent,
And was ill at ease, his face worried.
[   ] The grief in his innermost being.
His face was like that of a long-distance traveller.

                    *   *   *

The hunter went off to see Gilgamesh.
He took the road, set his face towards Uruk,
Entered the presence of Gilgamesh:
"There was a young man who came from the
      mountain,
On the land he was strong, he was powerful.
His strength is very hard, like a sky-bolt of Anu.
He walks about on the mountain all the time,
All the time he eats vegetation with cattle,
All the time he puts his feet in the water at the
      watering place.
I am too frightened to approach him.
He kept filling in the pits that I dug,
He kept pulling out the traps that I laid.
He kept helping cattle, wild beasts of open
      country, to escape my grasp.
He did not allow me to work in the open
      country."
Gilgamesh spoke to him, to the hunter,
"Go, hunter, lead forth the harlot Shamhat,
And when he approaches the cattle at the
      watering place,
She must take off her clothes and reveal her
      attractions.
He will see her and go close to her.

Then his cattle, who have grown up in open
      country with him, will become alien to
      him."
The hunter went; he led forth the harlot
      Shamhat with him,
And they took the road, they made the journey.
In three days they reached the appointed place.
Hunter and harlot sat down in their hiding place.
For one day, then a second, they sat at the
      watering place.
Then cattle arrived at the watering place; they
      drank.
Then wild beasts arrived at the water; they
      satisfied their need.
And he, Enkidu, whose origin is the mountain,
Who eats vegetation with gazelles,
Drinks at the watering place with cattle,
Satisfied his need for water with wild beasts.
Shamhat looked at the primitive man,
The murderous youth from the depths of open
      country.
"Here he is, Shamhat, bare your bosom,
Open your legs and let him take in your
      attractions!
Do not pull away, take wind of him!
He will see you and come close to you.
Spread open your garments, and let him lie
      upon you,
Do for him, the primitive man, as women do.
Then his cattle, who have grown up in open
      country with him, will become alien to him.
His love-making he will lavish upon you!"
Shamhat loosened her undergarments, opened
      her legs and he took in her attractions.
She did not pull away. She took wind of him,
Spread open her garments, and he lay upon her.
She did for him, the primitive man, as women do.
His love-making he lavished upon her.
For six days and seven nights Enkidu was
      aroused and poured himself into Shamhat.
When he was sated with her charms,
He set his face towards the open country of his
      cattle.
The gazelles saw Enkidu and scattered,
The cattle of open country kept away from his
      body.

For Enkidu had stripped; his body was too clean.
His legs, which used to keep pace with his cattle,
    were at a standstill.
Enkidu had been diminished, he could not run
    as before.
Yet he had acquired judgement, had become
    wiser.
He turned back, he sat at the harlot's feet.
The harlot was looking at his expression,
And he listened attentively to what the harlot
    said.
The harlot spoke to him, to Enkidu,
"You have become profound Enkidu, you have
    become like a god.
Why should you roam open country with wild
    beasts?
Come, let me take you into Uruk the Sheepfold,
To the pure house, the dwelling of Anu and
    Ishtar,
Where Gilgamesh is perfect in strength,
And is like a wild bull, more powerful than any
    of the people."

                    *   *   *

Let me show you Gilgamesh, a man of joy and
    woe!
Look at him, observe his face,
He is beautiful in manhood, dignified,
His whole body is charged with seductive charm.
He is more powerful in strength of arms than you!
He does not sleep by day or night.
O Enkidu, change your plan for punishing him!
Shamash loves Gilgamesh,
And Anu, Ellil, and Ea made him wise!
Before you came from the mountains,
Gilgamesh was dreaming about you in Uruk.
Gilgamesh arose and described a dream, he told
    it to his mother,
"Mother, I saw a dream in the night.
There were stars in the sky for me.
And something like a sky-bolt of Anu kept
    falling upon me!
I tried to lift it up, but it was too heavy for me.
I tried to turn it over, but I couldn't budge it.
The countrymen of Uruk were standing over it.
The countrymen had gathered over it,

The men crowded over it,
The young men massed over it,
They kissed its feet like very young children.
I loved it as a wife, doted on it,
I carried it, laid it at your feet,
You treated it as equal to me."
The wise mother of Gilgamesh, all-knowing,
    understood,
She spoke to her lord.
The wise wild cow Ninsun all-knowing,
    understood,
She spoke to Gilgamesh,
"When there were stars in the sky for you,
And something like a sky-bolt of Anu kept
    falling upon you,
You tried to lift it up, but it was too heavy for
    you,
You tried to turn it over, but you couldn't
    budge it,
You carried it, laid it at my feet,
I treated it as equal to you,
And you loved it as a wife, and doted on it:
It means a strong partner shall come to you,
    one who can save the life of a friend,
He will be the most powerful in strength of
    arms in the land.
His strength will be as great as that of a sky-bolt
    of Anu.
You will love him as a wife, you will dote upon
    him.
And he will always keep you safe.
That is the meaning of your dream."
Gilgamesh spoke to her, to his mother.
"Mother, I have had a second dream.
An axe was thrown down in the street of
Uruk the Sheepfold and they gathered over it,
The countrymen of Uruk stood over it.
The land gathered together over it,
The men massed over it.
I carried it, laid it at your feet.
I loved it as a wife, doted upon it.
And you treated it as equal to me."
The wise mother of Gilgamesh, all-knowing,
understood, she spoke to her son.
The wise wild cow Ninsun, all-knowing,
    understood, she spoke to Gilgamesh,

"The copper axe which you saw is a man.
You will love it as a wife, you will dote upon it,
And I shall treat it as equal to you.
A strong partner will come to you, one who can
 save the life of a comrade.
He will be the most powerful in strength of
 arms in the land.
His strength will be as great as that of a sky-bolt
 of Anu."
Gilgamesh spoke to his mother,
"Let it fall, then, according to the word of Ellil
 the great counsellor.
I shall gain a friend to advise me."
Ninsun retold his dreams.
Thus Shamhat heard the dreams of Gilgamesh
 and told them to Enkidu.
"The dreams mean that you will love one
 another."[1]

   * * *

FROM **Tablet VIII**

When the first light of dawn appeared
Gilgamesh said to his friend,
"Enkidu, my friend, your mother a gazelle,
And your father a wild donkey sired you,
Their milk was from onagers; they reared
 you,
And cattle made you familiar with all the
 pastures.

---

[1]Eventually, Enkidu confronts Gilgamesh in Uruk; they fight; and they become fast friends and companions in fantastic adventures. They journey to the Pine Mountain to fell the trees there, but must first slay Humbaba, the terrifying monster who guards the forest. Afterwards, Ishtar, the goddess of love and sex, is smitten with Gilgamesh and offers to marry him, but, knowing the fate of her previous lovers, Gilgamesh spurns her. Grievously insulted, Ishtar approaches her father, Anu, the chief of the gods, to ask for the Bull of Heaven to send against Gilgamesh and Enkidu. At first reluctant, Anu eventually agrees, but the two heroes kill the Bull of Heaven as well and insult Ishtar with part of its carcass. The gods then decide that one of them must die: Enkidu. As Enkidu grows progressively more ill, Gilgamesh begins to mourn. [Editor.]

Enkidu's paths led to the Pine Forest.
They shall weep for you night and day, never fall
 silent,
Weep for you, the elders of the broad city, of
 Uruk the Sheepfold.
The summit will bless us after our death,
They shall weep for you, the * * * of the
 mountains,
They shall mourn * * *
The open country as if it were your father, the
 field as if it were your mother.
They shall weep for you, myrtle, cypress, and
 pine,
In the midst of which we armed ourselves in our
 fury.
They shall weep for you, the bear, hyena,
 leopard, tiger, stag, cheetah,
Lion, wild bulls, deer, mountain goat, cattle, and
 other wild beasts of open country.
It shall weep for you, the holy river Ulaya, along
 whose bank
We used to walk so proudly.
It shall weep for you, the pure Euphrates,
With whose water in waterskins we used to
 refresh ourselves.
They shall weep for you, the young men of the
 broad city, of Uruk the Sheepfold,
Who watched the fighting when we struck down
 the Bull of Heaven.
He shall weep for you, the ploughman at his
 plough
Who extols your name with sweet Alala.
He shall weep for you, * * * of the
broad city, of Uruk the Sheepfold,
Who will extol your name in the first . . .
He shall weep for you, the shepherd, the
 herdsman,
Who used to make the beer mixture for your
 mouth.
She shall weep for you, the wet-nurse
Who used to put butter on your lower parts.
He shall weep for you, the elder
Who used to put ale to your mouth.
She shall weep for you, the harlot

By whom you were anointed with perfumed oil.
They shall weep for you, parents-in-law
Who comfort the wife . . . of your loins
They shall weep for you, the young men, like
     brothers
They shall weep for you and tear out their hair
     over you.
For you, Enkidu, I, like your mother, your
     father,
Will weep on your plains. ✶ ✶ ✶
Listen to me, young men, listen to me!
Listen to me, elders of Uruk, listen to me!
I myself must weep for Enkidu my friend,
Mourn bitterly, like a wailing woman.
As for the axe at my side, spur to my arm,
The sword in my belt, the shield for my front,
My festival clothes, my manly sash:
Evil rose up and robbed me of them.
My friend was the hunted mule, wild ass of the
     mountains, leopard of open country.
Enkidu the strong man was the hunted wild ass
     of the mountains, leopard of open country.
We who met, and scaled the mountain,
Seized the Bull of Heaven and slew it,
Demolished Humbaba the mighty one of the
     Pine Forest,
Now, what is the sleep that has taken hold of you?
Turn to me, you! You aren't listening to me!
But he cannot lift his head.
I touch his heart, but it does not beat at all.
My friend has covered his face like a
daughter-in-law."
He circled over him like an eagle,
Like a lioness whose cubs are trapped in a pit,
He paced back and forth.
He tore out and spoilt well-curled hair,
He stripped off and threw away finery as if it
     were taboo.
When the first light of dawn appeared,
     Gilgamesh
sent out a shout through the land.
The smith, ✶ ✶ ✶ the coppersmith,
the silversmith, the jeweller were summoned.
He made a likeness of his friend, he fashioned
a statue of his friend.

The four limbs of the friend were made of ✶ ✶ ✶
his chest was of lapis lazuli,
His skin was of gold.

✶   ✶   ✶

"I will lay you to rest on a bed of loving care
And will let you stay in a restful dwelling, a
     dwelling of the left
Princes of the earth will kiss your feet.
I will make the people of Uruk weep for you,
     mourn for you.
I will fill the proud people with sorrow for you.
And I myself will neglect my appearance after
     your death
Clad only in a lionskin, I will roam the open
     country."

✶   ✶   ✶

FROM **Tablets IX and X**

Gilgamesh mourned bitterly for Enkidu his
     friend,
And roamed open country.
"Shall I die too? Am I not like Enkidu?
Grief has entered my innermost being,
I am afraid of Death, and so I roam open
     country.
I shall take the road and go quickly
To see Ut-napishtim, son of Ubara-Tutu."[2]

✶   ✶   ✶

Ut-napishtim spoke to him, to Gilgamesh,
"Why are your cheeks wasted, your face
     dejected,
Your heart so wretched, your appearance worn
     out,
And grief in your innermost being?

---

[2]To reach Ut-napishtim, who corresponds to Atrahasis
in the first reading in this chapter, Gilgamesh must
undertake a dangerous journey that culminates in a
voyage by boat across a sea of lethal water. Finally, he
reaches the far shore, where an amazed Ut-napishtim
has watched him coming. [Editor.]

Your face is like that of a long-distance
   traveller.
Your face is weathered by cold and heat . . .
Clad only in a lionskin you roam open
   country."
Gilgamesh spoke to him, to Ut-napishtim,
"How would my cheeks not be wasted, nor my
   face dejected,
Nor my heart wretched, nor my appearance
   worn out,
Nor grief in my innermost being,
Nor my face like that of a long-distance traveller,
Nor my face weathered by cold and heat . . .
Nor roaming open country clad only in a
   lionskin?
My friend was the hunted mule, wild ass of the
   mountain, leopard of open country,
Enkidu my friend was the hunted mule, wild ass
   of the mountain, leopard of open country.
We who met and scaled the mountain,
Seized the Bull of Heaven and slew it,
Demolished Humbaba who dwelt in the Pine
   Forest,
Killed lions in the passes of the mountains,
My friend whom I love so much, who
   experienced every hardship with me,
Enkidu my friend whom I love so much, who
   experienced every hardship with me—
The fate of mortals conquered him! For six days
   and seven nights I wept over him,
I did not allow him to be buried
Until a worm fell out of his nose.
I was frightened. I am afraid of Death, and so I
   roam open country.
I roam open country for long distances;
The words of my friend weigh upon me.
The words of Enkidu my friend weigh upon
   me.
I roam the open country on long journeys.
How, O how could I stay silent, how, O how
   could I keep quiet?
My friend whom I love has turned to clay:
Enkidu my friend whom I love has turned to
   clay.
Am I not like him? Must I lie down too,
Never to rise, ever again?"

Gilgamesh spoke to him, to Ut-napishtim,
"So I thought I would go to see Ut-napishtim
   the far-distant, of whom people speak.
I searched, went through all countries,
Passed through and through difficult lands,
And crossed to and fro all seas.
My face never had enough of sweet sleep,
My fibre was filled with grief.
I made myself over-anxious by lack of sleep.
What did I gain from my toils?
I did not make a good impression on the
   alewife, for my clothes were finished.
I killed a bear, hyena, lion, leopard, tiger, deer,
   mountain goat, cattle, and other wild beasts of
   open country.
I ate meat from them, I spread out their skins.
Let her door be bolted against grief with pitch
   and bitumen!
Because of me, games are spoiled, * * *
My own misfortunes have reduced me to misery."
Ut-napishtim spoke to him, to Gilgamesh,
"Why do you prolong grief, Gilgamesh?
Since the gods made you from the flesh of gods
   and mankind,
Since the gods made you like your father and
   mother,
Death is inevitable at some time, both for
   Gilgamesh and for a fool. * * *

     *   *   *

You have made yourself weary for lack of sleep,
You only fill your flesh with grief,
You only bring the distant days of reckoning
   closer.
Mankind's fame is cut down like reeds in a
   reed-bed.
A fine young man, a fine girl, * * *
Nobody sees Death,
Nobody sees the face of Death,
Nobody hears the voice of Death.
Savage Death just cuts mankind down.
Sometimes we build a house, sometimes we
   make a nest,
But then brothers divide it upon inheritance.
Sometimes there is hostility in the land,
But then the river rises and brings flood-water.

Dragonflies drift on the river,
Their faces look upon the face of the Sun,
But then suddenly there is nothing.
The sleeping and the dead are just like each
    other,
Death's picture cannot be drawn.
The primitive man is as any young man.
When they blessed me,
The Anunnaki, the great gods, assembled;
Mammitum who creates fate decreed destinies
    with them.
They appointed death and life.
They did not mark out days for death,
But they did so for life."[3]

        *   *   *

FROM **Tablet XI**

"So now, who can gather the gods on your
    behalf,
That you too may find eternal life which you
    seek?
For a start, you must not sleep for six days and
    seven nights."
As soon as he was sitting, his head between his
    knees,
Sleep breathed over him like a fog.
Ut-napishtim spoke to her, to his wife,
"Look at the young man who wants eternal life!
Sleep breathes over him like a fog!"
His wife spoke to him, to Ut-napishtim the far-
    distant,
"Touch him, and let the man wake up.
Let him go back in peace the way he came,
Go back to his country through the great gate,
    through which he once left."

---

[3]Gilgamesh asks Ut-napishtim how he "came to stand in the gods' assembly and sought eternal life." Ut-napishtim tells him the story of how, long ago, the gods had decided to send a great flood to destroy human-kind, but how, at the instruction of Ea (Enki), he had built a great boat and had brought aboard it all manner of living things to survive the flood. After the flood subsided, Ut-napishtim and his wife were granted im-mortality. Ut-napishtim now addresses Gilgamesh. [Editor.]

Ut-napishtim spoke to her, to his wife,
"Man behaves badly: he will behave badly
    towards you.
For a start, bake a daily portion for him, put it
    each time by his head,
And mark on the wall the days that he sleeps."
She baked a daily portion for him, put it each
    time by his head,
And marked on the wall for him the days that
    he slept.
His first day's portion was dried out,
The second was going bad, the third was soggy,
The fourth had white mould on,
The fifth had discoloured,
The sixth was stinking,
The seventh—at that moment he touched him
    and the man woke up.
Gilgamesh spoke to him, to Ut-napishtim the
    far-distant,
"No sooner had sleep come upon me
Than you touched me, straight away, and roused
    me!"
Ut-napishtim spoke to him, to Gilgamesh,
"Look, Gilgamesh, count your daily portions,
That the number of days you slept may be
    proved to you.
Your first day's ration is dried out,
The second is going bad, the third is soggy,
The fourth has white mould on,
The fifth has discoloured, the sixth is stinking,
The seventh—at that moment you woke up."
Gilgamesh spoke to him, to Ut-napishtim the
    far-distant,
"How, O how could I have done it, Ut-
    napishtim?
Wherever can I go?
The Snatchers have blocked my routes:
Death is waiting in my bedroom,
And wherever I set my foot, Death is there too."
Ut-napishtim spoke to him, to Ur-shanabi the
    boatman,
"Ur-shanabi, the quay will cast you out, the
    ferry will reject you.
Be deprived of her side, at whose side you once
    went.

The man whom you led: filthy hair fetters his
body,
Skins have ruined the beauty of his flesh.
Take him, Ur-shanabi, bring him to a wash-
bowl,
And let him wash in water his filthy hair, as
clean as possible.
Let him throw away his skins, and let the sea
carry them off.
Let his body be soaked until it is fresh.
Put a new headband on his head.
Have him wear a robe as a proud garment
Until he comes to his city,
Until he reaches his journey's end.
The garment shall not discolour, but stay
absolutely new."
Ur-shanabi took him and brought him to a
wash-bowl,
And he washed in water his filthy hair, as clean
as possible.
He threw away his skins, and the sea carried
them off.
His body was soaked until it was fresh.
He put a new headband on his head.
He wore a robe as a proud garment
Until he came to his city,
Until he reached his journey's end.
The garment would not discolour, and stayed
absolutely new.
Gilgamesh and Ur-shanabi embarked on the
boat.
They cast off the *magillu*-boat and sailed away.
His wife spoke to him, to Ut-napishtim the far-
distant,
"Gilgamesh came, weary, striving,
What will you give him to take back to his
country?"
And Gilgamesh out there raised the pole,
He brought the boat near the shore.
Ut-napishtim spoke to him, to Gilgamesh,
"Gilgamesh, you came, weary, striving,
What can I give you to take back to your
country?
Let me reveal a closely guarded matter,
Gilgamesh,
And let me tell you the secret of the gods.

There is a plant whose root is like camel-thorn,
Whose thorn, like a rose's, will spike your
hands.
If you yourself can win that plant, you will find
rejuvenation."
When Gilgamesh heard this, he opened the pipe,
He tied heavy stones to his feet.
They dragged him down into the Apsu, and he
saw the plant.
He took the plant himself: it spiked his hands.
He cut the heavy stones from his feet.
The sea threw him up on to its shore.
Gilgamesh spoke to him, to Ur-shanabi the
boatman,
"Ur-shanabi, this plant is a plant to cure a crisis!
With it a man may win the breath of life.
I shall take it back to Uruk the Sheepfold; I shall
give it to an elder to eat, and so try out the
plant.
Its name shall be: 'An old man grows into a
young man.'
I too shall eat it and turn into the young man
that I once was."
At twenty leagues they ate their ration.
At thirty leagues they stopped for the night.
Gilgamesh saw a pool whose water was cool,
And went down into the water and washed.
A snake smelt the fragrance of the plant.
It came up silently and carried off the plant.
As it took it away, it shed its scaly skin.
Thereupon Gilgamesh sat down and wept.
His tears flowed over his cheeks.
He spoke to Ur-shanabi the boatman,
"For what purpose, Ur-shanabi, have my arms
grown weary?
For what purpose was the blood inside me so
red?
I did not gain an advantage for myself,
I have given the advantage to the 'lion of the
ground.'
Now the current will carry twenty leagues away.
While I was opening the pipe, arranging the
gear,
I found a door-thong which must have
been set there as an omen for me. I shall give
up.

TWO IMAGES OF SUMERIAN RULERSHIP (C. 2480 B.C.E.)

The first image (top) is a plaque of Ur-Nanshe, who ruled the Sumerian city-state of Lagash around 2480 B.C.E. He is shown both as a builder carrying a basket of bricks, with his family facing him (above), and enthroned (below). The second image (bottom), from a limestone monument known as the Vulture Stela, depicts Ur-Nanshe's successor Eannatum leading the troops of Lagash to victory against the rival city-state of Umma. The inscriptions on the stela record Lagash's victory and the terms it imposed on Umma. What do these images suggest about the status and responsibilities of Sumerian rulers? What do they suggest about the uses of cuneiform writing during the mid–third millennium B.C.E.?

And I have left the boat on the shore."
At twenty leagues they ate their ration.
At thirty leagues they stopped for the night.
They reached Uruk the Sheepfold.
Gilgamesh spoke to him, to Ur-shanabi the
  boatman,
"Go up on to the wall of Uruk, Ur-shanabi, and
  walk around,
Inspect the foundation platform and scrutinize
  the
brickwork! Testify that its bricks are baked
  bricks,
And that the Seven Counsellors must have laid
  its foundations!
One square mile is city, one square mile is
orchards, one square mile is claypits, as well as

the open ground of Ishtar's temple.
Three square miles and the open ground
  comprise Uruk."

*   *   *

Review Questions

1. What kind of figure is Gilgamesh?
2. What becomes of his quest in this epic, and why?
3. What roles do the gods play in the story?
4. When his quest is completed, what is Gilgamesh's view of his fate?

FROM *The Cursing of Akkad*

The earliest surviving examples of this literary work date to shortly before 2000 B.C.E.; in other words, several generations after the fall of the dynasty of Akkad, the events surrounding which it supposedly relates. Clearly, it is intended to show how catastrophic the consequences might be when a ruler commits a sacrilege against a god, in this instance, Enlil (or Ellil), the most powerful of the gods of Sumer, whose great temple was Ekur, in the city of Nippur. According to this text, Naram-Sin, grandson of the great conqueror Sargon of Akkad and himself one of the great kings of the Akkad dynasty, proceeded to begin to rebuild Ekur without Enlil's permission, with disastrous results.

From *The Harps That Once . . . : Sumerian Poetry in Translation*, by Thorkild Jacobsen (New Haven, Conn.: Yale University Press, 1987), pp. 360–74.

*   *   *

When Enlil's frowning brow
had killed Kishi,
  as were it the bull of heaven,
had felled the house of Uruk land
  down in the dust,

  as one would a great ox,
and Enlil then and there
  had given Sargon, king of Akkadê,
lordship and kingship
from south to north—
in those days holy Inanna
  was building

Akkadê's temple close
    to be her august home,
set up the throne
    in Ulmash,

Like a young married man
    building a house
    for the first time,
like a young daughter
    setting up a home,
holy Inanna
    went without sleep
to provision the storehouses
    with things,
furnish that city with
    dwellings and building plots,
feed its people superb food,
give its people superb water
    to drink,
have the courtyard joyful
    with celebrants with
    rinsed heads,
have the people sit down
    in festival grounds,
have acquaintances eat together
and outsiders circle around
    like strange birds in the sky,
have Marhashi put back
    in the rolls,
have monkeys, huge elephants,
    water buffaloes, beasts
    of faraway places,
jostle each other in the wide streets,
and dogs, panthers, mountain goats,
    and *alum* sheep full of long wool.

In those days she filled
    Akkadê's stores for emmer wheat
    with gold,
filled its stores for white emmer wheat
    with silver,
had copper, tin, and slabs of lapis lazuli
    regularly delivered
    into its barns for grain,

while she plastered its grain piles
    over with mud-plaster outside.

She gave its old women
    the gift of counsel,
gave its old men
    the gift of just testimony,
to its maidens
    she gave playgrounds,
to its young men she gave
    arms worthy of weapons,
to its little ones
    she gave a merry heart.
Hand-holding nursing mothers,
    daughters of generals,
were dancing to the *algasurrû* lyre;
the heart of the city
    was one of *tigi*-harps,
    its outskirts of reed pipes
    and tambourines,
its quay, where the boats moored,
    was resounding with jocund shouts.

All lands lay
    in safe pastures,
Akkadê's people looked out
    over pleasant tracts,
its king, the shepherd Naram-Suen,
radiated light flamelike
    on Akkadê's holy throne dais.
Its city wall—like a great mountain range—
    abutted heaven,
in its city-gates—like unto the Tigris
    going to the sea—
Inanna opened up the gateways.
From Sumer's own stores
    barges were towed upstream.
The Mardu bedouins of the highland,
    men who knew not grain,
were coming in to her with perfect bulls,
    perfect kids,
the Meluhhans, men of the black mountains,
were bringing down
    strange goods to her from them,
the Elamites and Subareans

were toting things to her
  as were they packasses.
All the city rulers, the heads of temples,
and the surveyors of the desert fringe,
were bringing in punctually
  their monthly and new year
  food offerings.
O how it caused vexation
  in Akkadê's city gate!
Holy Inanna just didn't know
  how to receive all those food portions,
but like the citizens she did not tire
  of the pleasure of finding
  storehouses and storage plots
  to keep up with them.

Upon this fell—as an ominous silence—
  the matter of Ekur.
Akkadê became to her
  fraught with shuddering,
fear befell her in Ulmash,
she took her seat out of the city.
Like a maiden who decides
  to abandon home
holy Inanna abandoned Akkadê's
  temple close,
like a warrior going up against armed might,
she brought the forces for
  fight and battle
  out of the city,
confronted with them
  murderous foes.

Not five days it was, not ten days it was
before Ninurta had the ornament of lordship,
  the crown of kingship,
the podium, and the throne
  granted to kingship,
fetched into his temple Eshumesha.
Utu took advisement
  away from the city,
Enki took away its wits.
Its halo, that abutted heaven,
An drew up
  into heaven's inside.
Its holy mooring stakes,

that were firmly driven in,
Enki pulled down
  into the Apsû.
Its weapons Inanna
  had carried off.
Akkadê's temple close
  ended its life
  as were it but
  a little carp in the deep.
The city's enemies appeared
  in front of it;
like a huge elephant
  it put the neck down,
like a huge bull
  it lifted the horns,
like a raging basilisk
  it slithered the head
  from side to side,
and, heavy-weight that it was,
  it went pillaging
  instead of in combat.

That Akkadê's royalty
  was not to occupy a good steady seat,
that nothing whatever
  that was in store for it
  was propitious,
that the house would be shaken,
  the treasuries dispersed,
which Naram-Suen had seen
  in a dream vision,
he let only his heart know,
  put it not on his tongue,
  spoke of it with no man.

Because of Ekur
  he dressed in mourning
covered his chariot over
  with a cargo mat,
took down the cabin
  from his barge,
cut down on his royal
  requirements.
For all of seven years
  Naram-Suen persevered,
—who ever saw a king

holding his head
  in his hands for all of seven years?

When in his seeking an omen
  about the temple,
building the temple
  was not in the omen,
and a second time
  seeking an omen
  about the temple,
building the temple
  was not in the omen:
he, to change
  what had been
  entrusted to him,
denied, O Enlil!
  what had been told him,
scattered
  what had been
  put together for him.
He called up his troops
and like a bruiser
  entering the main courtyard,
he balled the hands at Ekur;
like one having strong knees
  bending down to wrestle,
he counted the *gigunu*
  worth but thirty shekel;
like a marauder raiding a town,
he set up big storm ladders
  against the house.

To dismantle Ekur as were it
  a great ship,
to remove earth from it
  like one mining a silver mountain,
to cleave it as were it a
  lapis lazuli range,
to make it collapse
  like a city Ishkur has flooded,
he had great copper axes
  cast for the temple.
Though verily it was not
  the cedar mountains,
both edges he sharpened
  on the *agasiliqqu* axes.

To its socle he put copper mattocks,
—and the ground settled
  in the country's foundations.

to its top he put copper axes,
—and with that the temple
  let the neck sink to the ground
  like a young man who is killed,
and with it the necks of all lands
  were let sink to the ground.
Its rain-gutters he peeled off,
—and the rains vanished in the sky.
Its doorsills he took down,
  —and the decorum of the country
  changed.
In its "gate in which the grain
  is not to be cut"
  he cut the grain,
—and with that, grain was cut off
  from the country's lands.
Into its "gate of peace"
  he had pickaxes strike,
—and for all lands
  their peace became hostility.

In the "grand arch," like a heavy spring flood,
he made Ekur's wooden posts into splinters
  like firewood.
Into its holy of holies,
  the house knowing not daylight,
  looked the nation,
and upon the gods' holy bath vessels
  looked men of Uri.
Its *lahamu* figures standing
  along the great supporting terrace
  and the house,
although they were not men
  who had committed sacrilege,
Naram-Suen threw into the fire;
and for the cedars, cypresses, *supālus*,
  and boxwoods,
its trees of the *gigunu*
  he cast lots.

Its gold he did up in crates,
its silver he did up in leather packs,

with its copper he filled the harbor quay
  like grain brought en masse.
Its silver the silversmith was reshaping,
its precious stones the jeweler was reshaping,
its copper the metal-caster
  was pounding into scrap.
Though it was not the goods of a sacked city,
he had big boats moor at the quay
  by the house,
he had big boats moor at the quay
  toward Enlil's temple,
and the goods leave the city.
As he made the goods leave the city
Akkadê's sense left it.
He was letting the boats pitch
  in taking off,
  and Akkadê's judgment wavered.

The roaring storm,
  hushing the people one and all,
the risen floodstorm,
  having none that could oppose,
Enlil,
  in considering
  what he would lay waste
  because his beloved Ekur
  had been laid waste,
decided to lift his eyes
  unto the mountains of Gubin,
decided to bring down from it as one
  the widespread foothill tribes.
No likes of the nation,
  not counted with the country,
  the Gutians,
  knowing no restraints,
of human face, dogs' cunning, monkey's build,
Enlil decided to bring out
  of the mountains.
Numerous like locusts
  they came striding,
stretched out their arms in the desert for him
  like gazelle and wild-ass snares,
nothing escaped their arms,
nobody did their arms leave.
No envoy traveled the road.

No ambassador's boat was passing by
  on the river.
Enlil's yellow goats had been driven as spoil
  from the fold,
  their herdsmen made to follow them.
The cows had been driven as spoil
  from their pen,
  their cowherders made to follow them.
The watch was put in neck-stocks,
footpads sat in ambush on the roads,
in the country's city gates
  the doorleaves were stuck in the mud,
in all lands on the walls of their cities
  they were crying sore cries,
inside the city, not in the wide desert outside,
  they had the gardens.

It being like the days when cities
  were first built,
the great fields carried no grain,
the flooded tracts carried no fish,
the gardens' irrigation beds carried no
  sirop and wine,
for long days rain rained not,
  no underbrush grew up.

In those days oil for one silver shekel
  was half a quart,
barley for one shekel
  was half a quart,
wool for one shekel
  was half a mina,
fish for one shekel
  filled a ten-quart measure.
Thus they bought at the
  market rate of their cities.
He who lay down ill on the roof
  died on the roof.
He who lay down ill in the house
  was not buried.
The people from their hunger
  were coming to blows
  among themselves.
At Kiur, Enlil's great place,
dogs banded together;

in the silent streets,
in these dogs would devour
    men walking by twos,
dogs would devour men walking by threes,
numerous teeth were strewn about
    numerous heads tossed around,
teeth were strewn
    heads sown as seedcorn
decent heads were exchanged
    for crooked heads,
men lay on top of men,
crooks bled from above
    on blood of decent men.

In those days Enlil built
    out of scraps from his great sanctuaries
a small reed sanctuary,
between sunrise and sunset
    its stores dwindled.
Old women who were left over
    from that day,
old men who were left over
    from that day,
and the chief elegist who was left over
    from that year,
set up, for seven days and seven nights,
seven harps toward him on the ground,
    like the firm base of heaven,
and played within them also
    tambourine, sistron and kettledrum for him
    thunderously like Ishkur.
The old women held not back
    cries of: "Woe, my city!"
The old men held not back
    cries of: "Woe, its men!"
The elegist held not back
    cries of: "Woe, Ekur!"
Its maidens held not back from
    pulling out their hair,
its lads held not back
    the pointed knives lacerating themselves.
Weeping, Enlil's ancestors
    were placing their supplications
on Enlil's holy knees
    in Duku, laden with holy dread,

and so Enlil entered the holy "holy of holies"
    and lay down eschewing food.

At that time Suen, Enki, Inanna, Ninurta,
    Ishkur, Utu, Nusku, Nidaba,
    and the great gods
were trying to calm Enlil's heart,
    were making pleas saying:
"Enlil, may the city that sacked your city
    be done to as your city was,
that defiled your *gigunu*
    be done to as Nippur was.
May the one who knew the city
    turn the head unto
    the clay-pit left of it,
and may the men who knew men there
    not find them in it,
may a brother not recognize his brother,
may its maiden be wickedly killed
    in her home,
may its father cry out bitterly
    in his house where the wife was killed,
may its doves mourn in their crannies,
may things be thrown at its sparrows
    in their hiding places,
may it be wary like a frightened dove!"

A second time Suen, Enki, Inanna, Ninurta,
    Ishkur, Utu, Nusku, and heavenly Nidaba
    verily spoke,
set their face toward the city,
and were bitterly cursing Akkadê saying:
"O city, you rushed at Ekur"
—O Enlil, may it come to be!—
"Akkadê, you rushed at Ekur"
—O Enlil, may it come to be!—
"May at your holy city wall,
    as high as it is,
    laments be sent up,
may your *gigunus*
    be heaped up like dust,
may the standing *lahamus*
    of the upper terrace
pitch from it to earth
    like huge lads drunk with wine!

May your clay return to its Apsû,
be clay cursed by Enki!
May your grain return to its furrow,
be grain cursed by the grain goddess!
May your wood return to its forests,
be wood cursed by the carpenter god!
May the bull-butcher butcher the spouse!
May your sheep-slaughterer slaughter the son!
May the waters wash away your pauper
   as he finds children to sell for money!
May your harlot hang herself
in the gate of her hostel!
May your hierodule who is a mother,
   and your courtesan who is a mother,
    stab the child!
May your gold have the purchasing power of
   silver,
May your silver be priced as . . . ,
May your copper be priced as lead!
Akkadê, may your strong one
   be cut off from his strength,
may he not manage to lift
   the provision sack onto his saddle,
may his arms not enjoy controlling
   your choice chariot donkeys,
   may he lie ill into evening.
May that city die in famine,
may your patrician, who eats finest bread,
   lie down hungry,
may your man who used to get up from
   firstfruits
eat cutting from his beams,
may he grind with his teeth the leather fittings
of "the great door of the leather fittings" of his
   father's
house,
into your palace built in joy of heart
   may anguish be cast,
may the "badman" of the deserts of silent tracts
   howl, howl, and howl from it.

"Over your consecrated grounds
   where ritual handwashings are established,
may the fox of the ruined mounds
    sweep its tail,

in your "gate of the country" that was
   established
may the sleeper-bird,
   the bird foreboder of anguish
   place its nest.
In your city that,
   celebrating with *tigi*-harps,
   does not sleep,
that for merriness of heart
   lies not down,
may Nanna's bull Turesi
bellow as were it roaming
   a desert of silent tracts.
May long grass grow
   on your canal banks
   where the boats were hauled,
and may grass, lamentably,
   grow on your road
   laid down for chariots.
Moreover, may no man pass
   along your canal banks
   where boats are hauled,
   places where in future
   water is to be drawn
by splay-horned mouflons
   and fleet snakes of the mountains
   only.
May your central plain growing fine grass
   grow reeds for lament.
Akkadê, may your waters pouring sweet
   pour as saline waters.
May one who has said:
   "Let me settle in that city!"
   not have pleasant residence there,
who has said:
   'Let me lie down in Akkadê'
   not have pleasant resting place there!"

Presently under the sun of that day
   thus it verily came to be,
long grass grew up on its canal banks
   where the boats were hauled.
grass, lamentably, grew up on its road
   laid down for chariots,
moreover, no man passed along
   on its canal banks

where boats were hauled,
  places where water was now drawn
by splay-horned mouflons and fleet
  snakes of the mountains only.
Its central plain growing fine grass
  grew reeds of lament,
Akkadè's water flowing sweet
  flowed as saline waters.
For who had said:
"Let me settle in that city!"
  residence was not pleasant,
for who had said:
"Let me lie down in Akkadè!"
  the resting place was not pleasant,
Akkadè was destroyed!

A praise hymn for Inanna.

REVIEW QUESTIONS

1. Other historical evidence makes it clear that no disaster of the kind described in the hymn befell either Naram-Sin or the city of Akkad during his reign. Why, then, might such a work have been composed?
2. In the hymn, what are the interrelations among divine favor (or lack thereof), a ruler's actions, and the fate of a city and its people?
3. What does the hymn suggest about the Sumerian view regarding historical causation?

"Hymn to the Nile"

No less than Mesopotamian civilization, the ancient Egyptians were completely dependent on the water of a life-sustaining river. Whereas the ancient Sumerians and Babylonians feared the destructive potential of Tigris and Euphrates flooding, the Egyptians' perception of the Nile seems to have been rather different.

From *Ancient Near Eastern Texts Relating to the Old Testament*, edited by James B. Pritchard (Princeton, N.J.: Princeton University Press, 1983), pp. 372–73.

Hail to thee, O Nile, that issues from the earth and comes to keep Egypt alive! Hidden in his form of appearance, a darkness by day, *to whom minstrels have sung*. He that waters the meadows which Re created, in order to keep every kid alive. He that makes to drink the desert and the place distant *from water: that is his dew* coming down (*from*) heaven. The beloved of Geb, the one who controls Nepri, and the one who makes the craftsmanship of Ptah to flourish.

THE LORD OF FISHES, HE WHO MAKES the marsh-birds TO GO UPSTREAM. There are no birds which come down *because of the hot winds*. He who makes barley and brings emmer into being, that he may make the temples festive. If he is sluggish, then nostrils are stopped up, and everybody is poor. If there be (thus) a cutting down in the food-offerings of the gods, then a million men perish among mortals, covetousness is practised, the entire land *is in a fury*, and great and small *are on the execution-block*. (But) people *are different when he approaches*. Khnum constructed him. When he rises, then the land is in jubilation, then every belly is in joy, every *backbone* takes on laughter, and every tooth is exposed.

THE BRINGER OF FOOD, rich in provisions, creator of all good, lord of majesty, sweet of fragrance. *What is in him is satisfaction.* He who brings grass into being for the cattle and (thus) gives sacrifice to every god, *whether he be* in the underworld, heaven, or earth, *him who is* under his authority. He who takes in possession the Two Lands, fills the magazines, makes the granaries wide, and gives things (to) the poor.

He who makes *every beloved* TREE TO GROW, without *lack* of them. He who brings a ship into being by his strength, without hewing in stone. *The enduring image with* the White Crown. He cannot be seen; (*he has*) no taxes; he has no *levies;* no one *can read of* the mystery; no one knows the place where he is; he cannot be found *by the power* of writing. (*HE HAS*) NO SHRINES; HE HAS NO PORTION. *He has no service of (his) desire.* (But) generations of thy children jubilate for thee, and men give the greeting as a king, stable of laws, coming forth (at) his season and filling Upper and Lower Egypt. (Whenever) water is drunk, every eye is in him, who gives an excess of his good

He who was sorrowful is come forth gay. Every heart is gay. Sobek, the child of Neith, *laughs,* and the Ennead, *in which thou art, is exalted.* Vomiting forth and making the field to drink. Anointing the whole land. Making one man rich and slaying another, (but) there is no *coming to trial* with him, who makes satisfaction without *being thwarted,* for whom no boundaries are made.

A MAKER OF LIGHT when issuing from darkness, a fat for his cattle. His limits are all that is created. There is no district which can live without him. Men are clothed with flax from his meadows, for (he) made Hedj-hotep for his service. (He) made *anointing* with his unguents, being the *associate* of Ptah in his nature, bringing into being all service *in* him, all writings and divine words, his *responsibility* in Lower Egypt.

ENTERING INTO THE UNDERWORLD AND COMING FORTH ABOVE, loving to come forth as a mystery. If thou art (too) heavy (to rise), the people are few, and one begs for the water *of the year.* (Then) the rich man looks like him who is worried, and every man is seen (to be) carrying his

weapons. There is no companion *backing up* a companion. There are no garments for clothing; there are no ornaments for the children of nobles. There is no *listening at night, that one may answer with coolness.* There is no anointing for anybody.

HE WHO ESTABLISHES TRUTH in the heart of men, for it is said: "Deceit *comes after* poverty." *If one compares thee* with the great green sea, *which does not control the Grain-God,* whom all the gods praise, there are no birds coming down from his desert. His hand does not *beat with* gold, *with* making ingots of silver. No one can eat genuine lapis lazuli. (But) barley is foremost and lasting.

MEN BEGAN to sing TO THEE with the harp, and men sing to thee with the hand. The generations of thy children jubilate for thee. Men equip messengers for thee, who come (back) bearing treasures (to) ornament this land. He who makes a ship to prosper *before* mankind; he who sustains hearts in pregnant women; he who loves a multitude of all (kinds of) his cattle.

WHEN THOU RISEST IN THE CITY OF THE RULER, then men are satisfied with the goodly produce of the meadows. *Oh for* the little lotus-blossoms, everything that *pours forth* upon earth, all (kinds of) herbs *in the hands of* children! *They have (even) forgotten how to* eat. Good things are strewn about the houses. The land comes down *frolicking.*

WHEN THE NILE FLOODS, offering is made to thee, oxen are sacrificed to thee, great oblations are made to thee, birds are fattened for thee, lions are hunted for thee in the desert, fire is provided for thee. And offering is made to every (other) god, as is done for the Nile, with *prime* incense, oxen, cattle, birds, and flame. The Nile has made his cavern in Thebes, and his name is no (longer) known in the underworld. Not a god will come forth *in his form, if the plan is ignored.*

O ALL MEN who uphold the Ennead, fear ye the majesty which his son, the All-Lord, *has* made, (by) *making verdant* the two banks. So it is "Verdant art thou!" So it is "Verdant art thou!" So it is "O Nile, *verdant art thou,* who makest man and cattle to live!"

THE NARMER PALETTE (C. 3100 B.C.E.)

Found at Hierakonpolis in Upper Egypt and dating to around 3100 B.C.E., this schist palette bears images of a king named Narmer, whom some scholars identify with the king Menes that later Egyptian tradition identified as the first king to unify Upper and Lower Egypt. On one side of the palette (left), Narmer, wearing the crown of Upper Egypt, wields a mace against a captive. On the other side (right), where he wears the crown of Lower Egypt, Narmer inspects the aftermath of battle. Below, we see two animals with intertwined necks, a motif borrowed from the art of Iran and Mesopotamia. What images here suggest that Narmer claims to rule a unified Egypt? Was the process of unification peaceful? Do aspects of this image indicate the king's higher status? Is there evidence of Egyptian contact with Southwest Asia? How might that contact have been achieved?

REVIEW QUESTIONS

1. What kinds of abundance does this hymn attribute to the Nile?

2. Does the hymn communicate a sense of dependency?

3. If so, are the overtones more optimistic or pessimistic?

FROM *Songs to Senusert III*

Egypt's life and prosperity were directly linked to the power of the king and to his efficacy as protector, steward, and provider. Much of Egyptian literature is dedicated to glorifying the king, although little of it has survived from the Old Kingdom. The following text proclaims the greatness of Senusert III, a Middle Kingdom ruler under whom a highly centralized and unified Egyptian state thrived only a few centuries after the end of the Old Kingdom.

From *Hymns, Prayers, and Songs: An Anthology of Ancient Egyptian Lyric Poetry*, translated by John L. Foster (Atlanta, Ga.: Scholars Press, 1995), pp. 102–7.

For the Horus, Netcherkheperu, the Two Ladies, Netchermesut, the Golden Horus, Kheper, King of Upper and Lower Egypt, Khakaurê, son of Rê, Senusert—who takes the Two Lands in triumph:

Greetings to you, Khakaurê,
    our Horus who embodies the divine,
Protects the land, widens its borders,
    and conquers foreign countries by power of
      his crown,
Uniting the Two Lands through his mighty arm,
    subduing the foreign lands by his own hand;
Who can slaughter bowmen without striking a
      blow
    and shoot an arrow without drawing the
      bowstring;
Who instills the tribesmen in their lands with
      terror
    and slays the Nine Peoples by means of fear;
Whose slaughters cause the deaths of thousands
    among those tribes who try to cross his
      borders,

Shooting arrows like Sakhmet,
    overthrowing thousands who ignore his
      might—
The tongue of his Majesty overawes Nubia,
    his very words scatter the Asiatics.

Sole Horus, youth divine,
    who keeps watch over his borders,
Who does not allow his servants to weary
    but lets the people rest till dawn
While his young folk take their sleep—
    his heart is their protector;
His decrees have marked out his boundaries,
    his word has gathered the Two Banks
      together. ✶ ✶ ✶

How happy are the gods,
    for you have maintained their offerings!
How happy are your children,
    for you have established their domain!
How happy are your fathers who were before,
    for you have increased their portion!
How happy are Egyptians in your strength,

for you have protected the ancient heritage!

How happy is mankind under your governing,
  for your mighty power has received their lives
    unto itself!

How happy are the Two Banks in awe of you,
  for you have increased their possessions!

How happy are your young men of the army,
  for you have allowed them to prosper!

How happy are the old and venerable,
  for you have caused them to feel young again!

How happy are the Two Lands in your strength,
  for you have protected their citadels!

Refrain: O Horus who broadens his borders, may
  you go on forever. ✶ ✶ ✶

How great is the Lord of his city!
  He is exalted a thousand times over; other
    persons are small.

How great is the Lord of his city!
  He is a dike which holds back the River,
    restraining its flood
      of water.

How great is the Lord of his city!
  He is a cool room which lets each man sleep
    until dawn.

How great is the Lord of his city!
  He is a rampart with walls of copper from
    Sinai.

How great is the Lord of his city!
  He is a refuge which does not lack his helping
    hand.

How great is the Lord of his city!
  He is a fort which rescues the fearful man
    from his enemy.

How great is the Lord of his city!
  He is a sunshade to help keep cool in
    summer.

How great is the Lord of his city!

He is a warm dry nook in winter.

How great is the Lord of his city!
  He is the mountain which blocks the storm in
    a time of raging sky.

How great is the Lord of his city!
  He is Sakhmet against the enemies who test
    his borders. ✶ ✶ ✶

He came to us to seize the Southland,
  and the Double Crown was firm on his head.

He came, he united the Two Lands,
  he mingled the Sedge and the Bee.

He came, he ruled the Egyptians,
  he placed the desert under his control.

He came, he protected the Two Lands,
  he pacified the Two Banks.

He came, he nourished the Egyptians,
  he dispelled their troubles.

He came, he saved the nobles,
  he let the throats of the commoners breathe.

He came, he trampled the foreigners,
  he struck down the tribes who did not fear
    him.

He came, he descended to his frontiers,
  he rescued those who had been injured.

He came, his arms received the veneration
  for what his power had brought to us.

He came, he helped us raise our children,
  we have buried our elders with his blessing.

✶   ✶   ✶

REVIEW QUESTIONS

1. What kinds of power are attributed to the king?
2. How far does that power extend?
3. How does the king deal with foreigners (i.e., non-Egyptians)?

FROM The Instructions of Ptah-hotep

In contrast to ancient Mesopotamia, no ancient Egyptian law code has survived, although various texts suggest that laws did indeed exist. This document, however, provides an excellent description of proper behavior in personal relations and, implicitly, a sense of Egyptian social values, at least among the elite. Dating perhaps as early as the late Old Kingdom, this text is presented as the instructions of the vizier (the most important royal official under the king himself), Ptah-hotep, to his son.

From *Ancient Egyptian Literature,* volume 1, *The Old and Middle Kingdoms,* by Miriam Lichtheim (Berkeley: University of California Press, 1973), pp. 205–9.

Instruction of the Mayor of the city, the Vizier Ptahhotep, under the Majesty of King Isesi, who lives for all eternity. The mayor of the city, the vizier Ptahhotep, said:

O king, my lord!
Age is here, old age arrived,
Feebleness came, weakness grows,
Childlike one sleeps all day.
Eyes are dim, ears deaf,
Strength is waning through weariness,
The mouth, silenced, speaks not,
The heart, void, recalls not the past,
The bones ache throughout.
Good has become evil, all taste is gone,
What age does to people is evil in everything.
The nose, clogged, breathes not,
Painful are standing and sitting.

May this servant be ordered to make a staff of old
    age,
So as to tell him the words of those who heard,
The ways of the ancestors,
Who have listened to the gods.
May such be done for you,
So that strife may be banned from the people,
And the Two Shores may serve you!
Said the majesty of this god:
Instruct him then in the sayings of the past,
May he become a model for the children of the
    great,
May obedience enter him,

And the devotion of him who speaks to him,
No one is born wise.

Beginning of the formulations of excellent discourse spoken by the Prince, Count, God's Father, God's beloved, Eldest Son of the King, of his body, Mayor of the city and Vizier, Ptahhotep, in instructing the ignorant in knowledge and in the standard of excellent discourse, as profit for him who will hear, as woe to him who would neglect them. He spoke to his son:

1. Don't be proud of your knowledge,
    Consult the ignorant and the wise;
    The limits of art are not reached,
    No artist's skills are perfect;
    Good speech is more hidden than greenstone,
    Yet may be found among maids at the
        grindstones.

2. If you meet a disputant in action,
    A powerful man, superior to you,
    Fold your arms, bend your back,
    To flout him will not make him agree with you.
    Make little of the evil speech
    By not opposing him while he's in action;
    He will be called an ignoramus,
    Your self-control will match his pile of words.

3. If you meet a disputant in action
    Who is your equal, on your level,
    You will make your worth exceed his by
        silence,

While he is speaking evilly,
There will be much talk by the hearers,
Your name will be good in the mind of the
    magistrates.

4. If you meet a disputant in action,
A poor man, not your equal,
Do not attack him because he is weak,
Let him alone, he will confute himself.
Do not answer him to relieve your heart,
Do not vent yourself against your opponent,
Wretched is he who injures a poor man,
One will wish to do what you desire,
You will beat him through the magistrates'
    reproof.

5. If you are a man who leads,
Who controls the affairs of the many,
Seek out every beneficent deed,
That your conduct may be blameless.
Great is justice, lasting in effect,
Unchallenged since the time of Osiris.
One punishes the transgressor of laws,
Though the greedy overlooks this;
Baseness may seize riches,
Yet crime never lands its wares;
In the end it is justice that lasts,
Man says: "It is my father's ground."

6. Do not scheme against people,
God punishes accordingly:
If a man says: "I shall live by it,"
He will lack bread for his mouth.
If a man says: "I shall be rich,"
He will have to say: "My cleverness has
    snared me."
If he says: "I will snare for myself,"
He will be unable to say: "I snared for my
    profit."
If a man says: "I will rob someone,"
He will end being given to a stranger.
People's schemes do not prevail,
God's command is what prevails;
Live then in the midst of peace,
What they give comes by itself.

7. If you are one among guests
At the table of one greater than you,

Take what he gives as it is set before you;
Look at what is before you,
Don't shoot many glances at him,
Molesting him offends the *ka*.
Don't speak to him until he summons,
One does not know what may displease;
Speak when he has addressed you,
Then your words will please the heart.
The nobleman, when he is behind food,
Behaves as his *ka* commands him;
He will give to him whom he favors,
It is the custom when night has come.
It is the *ka* that makes his hands reach out,
The great man gives to the chosen man;
Thus eating is under the counsel of god,
A fool is who complains of it.

8. If you are a man of trust,
Sent by one great man to another,
Adhere to the nature of him who sent you,
Give his message as he said it.
Guard against reviling speech,
Which embroils one great with another;
Keep to the truth, don't exceed it,
But an outburst should not be repeated.
Do not malign anyone,
Great or small, the *ka* abhors it.

9. If you plow and there's growth in the field,
And god lets it prosper in your hand,
Do not boast at your neighbors' side,
One has great respect for the silent man:
Man of character is man of wealth.
If he robs he is like a crocodile in court.
Don't impose on one who is childless,
Neither decry nor boast of it;
There is many a father who has grief,
And a mother of children less content than
    another;
It is the lonely whom god fosters,
While the family man prays for a follower.

10. If you are poor, serve a man of worth,
That all your conduct may be well with the
    god.
Do not recall if he once was poor,
Don't be arrogant toward him

For knowing his former state;
Respect him for what has accrued to him,
For wealth does not come by itself.
It is their law for him whom they love,
His gain, he gathered it himself;
It is the god who makes him worthy
And protects him while he sleeps.

11. Follow your heart as long as you live,
    Do no more than is required,
    Do not shorten the time of "follow-the-
       heart,"
    Trimming its moment offends the *ka*.
    Don't waste time on daily cares
    Beyond providing for your household;
    When wealth has come, follow your heart,
    Wealth does no good if one is glum!

12. If you are a man of worth
    And produce a son by the grace of god,
    If he is straight, takes after you,
    Takes good care of your possessions,
    Do for him all that is good,
    He is your son, your *ka* begot him,
    Don't withdraw your heart from him.
    But an offspring can make trouble:
    If he strays, neglects your counsel,
    Disobeys all that is said,
    His mouth spouting evil speech,
    Punish him for all his talk!
    They hate him who crosses you,
    His guilt was fated in the womb;
    He whom they guide can not go wrong,
    Whom they make boatless can not cross.

13. If you are in the antechamber,
    Stand and sit as fits your rank,
    Which was assigned you the first day.
    Do not trespass—you will be turned back,
    Keen is the face to him who enters announced,
    Spacious the seat of him who has been called.
    The antechamber has a rule,
    All behavior is by measure;
    It is the god who gives advancement,
    He who uses elbows is not helped.

14. If you are among the people,
    Gain supporters through being trusted;

The trusted man who does not vent his
   belly's speech,
He will himself become a leader.
A man of means—what is he like?
Your name is good, you are not maligned,
Your body is sleek, your face benign,
One praises you without your knowing.
He whose heart obeys his belly
Puts contempt of himself in place of love,
His heart is bald, his body unanointed;
The great-hearted is god-given,
He who obeys his belly belongs to the
   enemy.

15. Report your commission without faltering,
    Give your advice in your master's council.
    If he is fluent in his speech,
    It will not be hard for the envoy to report,
    Nor will he be answered, "Who is he to
       know it?"
    As to the master, his affairs will fail
    If he plans to punish him for it,
    He should be silent upon hearing: "I have
       told."

16. If you are a man who leads,
    Whose authority reaches wide,
    You should do outstanding things,
    Remember the day that comes after.
    No strife will occur in the midst of honors,
    But where the crocodile enters hatred arises.

17. If you are a man who leads,
    Listen calmly to the speech of one who
       pleads;
    Don't stop him from purging his body
    Of that which he planned to tell.
    A man in distress wants to pour out his heart
    More than that his case be won.
    About him who stops a plea
    One says: "Why does he reject it?"
    Not all one pleads for can be granted,
    But a good hearing soothes the heart.

18. If you want friendship to endure
    In the house you enter
    As master, brother, or friend,
    In whatever place you enter,

Beware of approaching the women!
Unhappy is the place where it is done,
Unwelcome is he who intrudes on them.
A thousand men are turned away from their
  good:
A short moment like a dream,
Then death comes for having known them.
Poor advice is "shoot the opponent,"
When one goes to do it the heart rejects it.
He who fails through lust of them,
No affair of his can prosper.

19. If you want a perfect conduct,
    To be free from every evil,
    Guard against the vice of greed:
    A grievous sickness without cure,
    There is no treatment for it.
    It embroils fathers, mothers,
    And the brothers of the mother,
    It parts wife from husband;
    It is a compound of all evils,
    A bundle of all hateful things.
    That man endures whose rule is rightness,
    Who walks a straight line;
    He will make a will by it,
    The greedy has no tomb.

20. Do not be greedy in the division,
    Do not covet more than your share;
    Do not be greedy toward your kin,
    The mild has a greater claim than the harsh.
    Poor is he who shuns his kin,
    He is deprived of interchange.
    Even a little of what is craved
    Turns a quarreler into an amiable man.

21. When you prosper and found your house,
    And love your wife with ardor,
    Fill her belly, clothe her back,
    Ointment soothes her body.
    Gladden her heart as long as you live,
    She is a fertile field for her lord.
    Do not contend with her in court,
    Keep her from power, restrain her—
    Her eye is her storm when she gazes—
    Thus will you make her stay in your
      house. * * *

22. Sustain your friends with what you have,
    You have it by the grace of god;
    Of him who fails to sustain his friends
    One says, "a selfish *ka*."
    One plans the morrow but knows not what
      will be,
    The right *ka* is the *ka* by which one is
      sustained.
    If praiseworthy deeds are done,
    Friends will say, "welcome!"
    One does not bring supplies to town,
    One brings friends when there is need.

23. Do not repeat calumny,
    Nor should you listen to it,
    It is the spouting of the hot-bellied.
    Report a thing observed, not heard,
    If it is negligible, don't say anything,
    He who is before you recognizes worth.
    If a seizure is ordered and carried out,
    Hatred will arise against him who seizes;
    Calumny is like a dream against which one
      covers the face.

24. If you are a man of worth
    Who sits in his master's council,
    Concentrate on excellence,
    Your silence is better than chatter.
    Speak when you know you have a solution,
    It is the skilled who should speak in council;
    Speaking is harder than all other work,
    He who understands it makes it serve.

25. If you are mighty, gain respect through
      knowledge
    And through gentleness of speech.
    Don't command except as is fitting,
    He who provokes gets into trouble.
    Don't be haughty, lest you be humbled,
    Don't be mute, lest you be chided.
    When you answer one who is fuming,
    Avert your face, control yourself.
    The flame of the hot-heart sweeps across,
    He who steps gently, his path is paved.
    He who frets all day has no happy
      moment,
    He who's gay all day can't keep house. * * *

26. Don't oppose a great man's action,
    Don't vex the heart of one who is burdened;
    If he gets angry at him who foils him,
    The *ka* will part from him who loves him.
    Yet he is the provider along with the god,
    What he wishes should be done for him.
    When he turns his face back to you after
        raging,
    There will be peace from his *ka;*
    As ill will comes from opposition,
    So goodwill increases love.

27. Teach the great what is useful to him,
    Be his aid before the people;
    If you let his knowledge impress his lord,
    Your sustenance will come from his *ka.*
    As the favorite's belly is filled,
    So your back will be clothed by it,
    And his help will be there to sustain you.
    For your superior whom you love
    And who lives by it,
    He in turn will give you good support.
    Thus will love of you endure
    In the belly of those who love you,
    He is a *ka* who loves to listen.

28. If you are a magistrate of standing,
    Commissioned to satisfy the many,
    Hew a straight line.
    When you speak don't lean to one side,
    Beware lest one complain:
    "Judges, he distorts the matter!"
    And your deed turns into a judgment of you.

29. If you are angered by a misdeed,
    Lean toward a man on account of his
        rightness;
    Pass it over, don't recall it,
    Since he was silent to you the first day.

30. If you are great after having been humble,
    Have gained wealth after having been poor
    In the past, in a town which you know,
    Knowing your former condition,
    Do not put trust in your wealth,
    Which came to you as gift of god;
    So that you will not fall behind one like you,
    To whom the same has happened.

31. Bend your back to your superior,
    Your overseer from the palace;
    Then your house will endure in its wealth,
    Your rewards in their right place.
    Wretched is he who opposes a superior,
    One lives as long as he is mild,
    Baring the arm does not hurt it.
    Do not plunder a neighbor's house,
    Do not steal the goods of one near you,
    Lest he denounce you before you are heard.
    A quarreler is a mindless person,
    If he is known as an aggressor
    The hostile man will have trouble in the
        neighborhood.

*   *   *

33. If you probe the character of a friend,
    Don't inquire, but approach him,
    Deal with him alone,
    So as not to suffer from his manner.
    Dispute with him after a time,
    Test his heart in conversation;
    If what he has seen escapes him,
    If he does a thing that annoys you,
    Be yet friendly with him, don't attack,
    Be restrained, don't let fly,
    Don't answer with hostility,
    Neither part from him nor attack him;
    His time does not fail to come,
    One does not escape what is fated.

34. Be generous as long as you live,
    What leaves the storehouse does not
        return;
    It is the food to be shared which is coveted,
    One whose belly is empty is an accuser;
    One deprived becomes an opponent,
    Don't have him for a neighbor.
    Kindness is a man's memorial
    For the years after the function.

35. Know your helpers, then you prosper,
    Don't be mean toward your friends,
    They are one's watered field,
    And greater then one's riches,
    For what belongs to one belongs to another.

The character of a son-of-man is profit to
    him;
Good nature is a memorial.

36.   Punish firmly, chastise soundly,
    Then repression of crime becomes an
       example;
    Punishment except for crime
    Turns the complainer into an enemy.

37.   If you take to wife a *špnt*
    Who is joyful and known by her town,
    If she is fickle and likes the moment,
    Do not reject her, let her eat,
    The joyful brings happiness.

Epilogue

If you listen to my sayings,
All your affairs will go forward;
In their truth resides their value,
Their memory goes on in the speech of men,
Because of the worth of their precepts;
If every word is carried on,
They will not perish in this land.
If advice is given for the good,
The great will speak accordingly;
It is teaching a man to speak to posterity,
He who hears it becomes a master-hearer;
It is good to speak to posterity,
It will listen to it.

If a good example is set by him who leads,
He will be beneficent for ever,
His wisdom being for all time.
The wise feeds his *ba* with what endures,
So that it is happy with him on earth.
The wise is known by his wisdom,
The great by his good actions;
His heart matches his tongue,
His lips are straight when he speaks;
He has eyes that see,
His ears are made to hear what will profit his son,
Acting with truth he is free of falsehood.
Useful is hearing to a son who hears;
If hearing enters the hearer,
The hearer becomes a listener,

Hearing well is speaking well.
Useful is hearing to one who hears,
Hearing is better than all else,
It creates good will.
How good for a son to grasp his father's words,
He will reach old age through them.

He who hears is beloved of god,
He whom god hates does not hear.
The heart makes of its owner a hearer or non-hearer,
Man's heart is his life-prosperity-health!
The hearer is one who hears what is said,
He who loves to hear is one who does what is said.
How good for a son to listen to his father,
How happy is he to whom it is said:
"The son, he pleases as a master of hearing."
The hearer of whom this is said,
He is well-endowed
And honored by his father;
His remembrance is in the mouth of the living,
Those on earth and those who will be.

If a man's son accepts his father's words,
No plan of his will go wrong.
Teach your son to be a hearer,
One who will be valued by the nobles;
One who guides his speech by what he was told,
One regarded as a hearer.
This son excels, his deeds stand out,
While failure follows him who hears not.
The wise wakes early to his lasting gain,
While the fool is hard pressed.

The fool who does not hear,
He can do nothing at all;
He sees knowledge in ignorance,
Usefulness in harmfulness.
He does all that one detests
And is blamed for it each day;
He lives on that by which one dies,
His food is distortion of speech.
His sort is known to the officials,
Who say: "A living death each day."
One passes over his doings,
Because of his many daily troubles.

A son who hears is a follower of Horus,
It goes well with him when he has heard.

When he is old, has reached veneration,
He will speak likewise to his children,
Renewing the teaching of his father.
Every man teaches as he acts,
He will speak to the children,
So that they will speak to their children:
Set an example, don't give offense,
If justice stands firm your children will live.

*   *   *

Conceal your heart, control your mouth,
Then you will be known among the officials;
Be quite exact before your lord,
Act so that one will say to him: "He's the son of
    that one."
And those who hear it will say:
"Blessed is he to whom he was born!"
Be deliberate when you speak,
So as to say things that count;
Then the officials who listen will say:
"How good is what comes from his mouth!"
Act so that your lord will say of you:
"How good is he whom his father taught;
When he came forth from his body,
He told him all that was in his mind,
And he does even more than he was told."

Lo, the good son, the gift of god,
Exceeds what is told him by his lord,
He will do right when his heart is straight.
As you succeed me, sound in your body,
The king content with all that was done,
May you obtain many years of life!
Not small is what I did on earth,
I had one hundred and ten years of life
As gift of the king,
Honors exceeding those of the ancestors,
By doing justice for the king,
Until the state of veneration!

*   *   *

REVIEW QUESTIONS

1. According to Ptah-hotep, what are the most important virtues in proper human relations?
2. Are those virtues to be applied differently to people of different rank and social class?
3. How much importance is ascribed to the ability to fight physically?

FROM "Songs of the Birdcatcher's Daughter"

The following Egyptian love poem was quite likely composed and set down in writing by a man, as the vast majority of Egyptian scribes were male. It provides another uniquely human insight into the relationships between ancient Egyptian men and women.

From *Hymns, Prayers, and Songs: An Anthology of Ancient Egyptian Lyric Poetry,* translated by John L. Foster (Atlanta, Ga.: Scholars Press, 1995), pp. 163–66.

* * *

i

HE SPEAKS:

What is my love trying to do to me?
    Am I to keep quiet about it?
Making me stand at the door of her house
    while she gets herself inside!
Not even saying, "Have a nice trip home!"
    Why, she dammed up her ears the whole
        night!

* * *

HE SPEAKS:

My love is one alone, without her equal,
    beautiful above all women.
See her, like the goddess of the morning star in
        splendor
    at the beginning of a happy year.

With dazzling presence and a fair complexion,
    with lovely watching eyes,
With lips that are sweet in speaking,
    and not a word too much;
Straight her neck and white her breast,
    and her tresses gleam like lapis lazuli;
Her arms are more precious than gold,
    her fingers like lotus blossoms,
With curving hips and a trim waist,
    and thighs that only heighten her beauty.
Her step is pleasing as she treads upon earth;
    and she fastens my heart in her embrace.
She makes the necks of the young men
    swing round about to see her.
Happy is he who can fully embrace her—
    he is first of all the young lovers!
Just look at her as she walks along,
    like that goddess beyond, One alone!

SHE SPEAKS:

My heart was intending to go and see Nefrus
    and sit awhile at her house;
But I found Mehy riding down the road
    along with his band of young men.
I did not know how to escape him
    in order to get by him unhindered.
Oh look! the path is like the River—
    there is no place to put my feet!

My heart is so foolish:
    "Why avoid Mehy?"
Oh, if I go near him
    I shall tell him my wavering heart.
"I am yours!" I would say to him.
    And he would shout out my name
And put me away in the finest
        harem
    of all those meant for his servants.

* * *

ii

SHE SPEAKS:

The voice of the wild goose cries out,
    caught by his bait-worm;
And love of you ensnares me—
    I do not know how to work free.
I must gather my nets;
    but what in the world shall I tell mother,
Returning to her each day
    loaded down with my catch?
I shall be setting no trap today;
    I am taken myself—by love of you.

* * *

vi

SHE SPEAKS:

The voice of the swallow is calling,
    saying, "Land is alight. What is your path?"
O little bird, cease your chattering,

for I found my love in his bed;
And my heart was overjoyed
　　when he said to me, "I shall never be far;
But hand in hand we shall walk,
　　and I shall be with you in each happy place."
He put me first of his favorite girls!
　　—he would never injure my heart.

REVIEW QUESTIONS

1. In this poem, what kinds of feelings characterize the intimate relationships between men and
   women?
2. Do the lovers appear to be equals?
3. If these poems were composed mostly by male
   scribes, what do they communicate about an
   ancient Egyptian man's conception of the ideal
   woman?

FROM *The Book of the Dead*

*Beginning in the late Old Kingdom, there were inscribed on the walls of the interior
chambers of pyramids magical texts that were intended to ensure that the deceased
king passed successfully into the next life. In the following centuries, these so-called
Pyramid Texts were developed further, and the possibility of proceeding into the
next world became less exclusively focused on the king and his immediate family
and more inclusive of Egyptians of lesser rank (what some scholars have referred to
as the "democratization of death"). From this process emerged the collection of texts
that has come to be known (erroneously) as* The Book of the Dead. *The following
selection has been referred to as the "Protestation of Guiltlessness" or the "Negative
Confession." It was to be recited by the deceased as he or she appeared for judgment before the god Osiris and his entourage.*

From *Ancient Near Eastern Texts Relating to the Old Testament,* edited by James B. Pritchard,
translated by H. L. Ginsberg (3d ed.; Princeton, N.J.: Princeton University Press, 1983).

*　　*　　*

What is said on reaching the Broad-Hall of
the Two Justices, absolving X [the deceased] of
every sin which he has committed, and seeing
the faces of the gods:

Hail to thee, O great god, lord of the Two
Justices! I have come to thee, my lord, I have been
brought that I might see thy beauty. I know thee;
I know thy name and the names of the forty-
two gods who are with thee in the Broad-Hall
of the Two Justices, who live on them who *preserve* evil and who drink their blood on that
day of reckoning up character in the presence of
Wennofer. Behold, "*Sati-mertifi,* Lord of Justice,"
is thy name. I have come to thee; I have brought
thee justice; I have expelled deceit for thee.

I have not committed evil against men.

I have not mistreated cattle.

I have not committed sin in the place of truth.

I have not known that which is not.

I have not seen evil. . . .

My name has not reached the Master of the Barque.

I have not blasphemed a god.

I have not *done violence to* a poor man.

I have not done that which the gods abominate.

I have not defamed a slave to his superior.

I have not made anyone sick.

I have not made anyone weep.

I have not killed.

I have given no order to a killer.

I have not caused anyone suffering.

I have not cut down on the food-income in the temples.

I have not damaged the bread of the gods.

I have not taken the loaves of the blessed dead.

I have not had sexual relations with a boy.

I have not defiled myself.

I have neither increased or diminished the grain-measure.

I have not diminished the *aroura*.

I have not falsified a half-*aroura* of land.

I have not added to the weight of the balance.

I have not *weakened* the plummet of the scales.

I have not taken milk from the mouths of children.

I have not driven cattle away from their pasturage.

I have not snared the birds *of* the gods.

I have not caught fish in their marshes.

I have not held up the water in its season.

I have not built a dam against running water.

I have not quenched a fire at its proper time.

I have not neglected the appointed times and their meat-offerings.

I have not driven away the cattle of the god's property.

I have not stopped a god on his procession.

I am pure!—four times. My purity is the purity of that great *benu*-bird which is in Herakleopolis, because I am really that nose of the Lord of Breath, who makes all men to live, on that day of filling out the Eye of Horus in Heliopolis, in the second month of the second season, the last day, in the presence of the lord of this land. I am the one who has seen the filling out of the Eye in Heliopolis. Evil will never happen to me in this land or in this Broad-Hall of the Two Justices, because I know the names of these gods who are in it, the followers of the great god.

O Wide-of-Stride, who comes forth from Heliopolis, I have not committed evil.

O Embracer-of-Fire, who comes forth from Babylon, I have not stolen.

O Nosey, who comes forth from Hermopolis, I have not been covetous.

O Swallower-of-Shadows, who comes forth from the pit, I have not robbed.

O Dangerous-of-Face, who came forth from *Rostau,* I have not killed men.

O *Ruti,* who comes forth from heaven, I have not damaged the grain-measure.

O His-Eyes-are-of-Flint, who comes forth from the shrine, I have not caused *crookedness.*

O Flamer, who comes forth *backward,* I have not stolen the property of a god.

O Breaker-of-Bones, who comes forth from Herakleopolis, I have not told lies.

O *Commander-of-Fire,* who comes forth from Memphis, I have not taken away food.

O Dweller-in-the-Pit, who comes forth from the west, I have not been contentious.

O White-of-Teeth, who comes forth from the Faiyum, I have not trespassed.

O Eater-of-Blood, who comes forth from the execution-block, I have not slain the cattle of the god.

O Eater-of-Entrails, who comes forth from the Thirty, I have not *practised usury.*

O Lord-of-Justice, who comes forth from *Ma'ati,* I have not stolen the *bread-ration.*

O Wanderer, who comes forth from Bubastis, I have not *gossiped.*

O *Aadi,* who comes forth from Heliopolis, my mouth has not gone on unchecked.

O *Djudju*-serpent, who comes forth from Busiris, I have not argued with *some one summoned because of* his property.

O *Wamemti*-serpent, who comes forth from the place of judgment, I have not committed adultery.

O *Maa-Intef,* who comes forth from the Temple of Min, I have not defiled myself.

O Superior-of-the-Nobles, who comes forth from *Imau,* I have not caused terror.

O Wrecker, who comes forth from *the Saite Nome,* I have not trespassed.

O Mischief-Maker, who comes forth from the sanctuary, I have not been overheated.

O Child, who comes forth from the Heliopolitan Nome, I have not been unresponsive to a matter of justice.

O *Ser-kheru,* who comes forth from *Wensi,* I have not been quarrelsome.

O Bastet, who comes forth from the sanctum, I have not winked.

O His-Face-Behind-Him, who comes forth from *Tep-het-djat*; I have not *been perverted*; I have not had sexual relations with a boy.

O Hot-of-Leg, who comes forth from the twilight, I have not swallowed my heart.

O Dark-One, who comes forth from the darkness, I have not been abusive.

O Bringer-of-His-Peace, who comes forth from Sais, I have not been overenergetic.

O Lord-of-Faces, who comes forth from the Heroonpolite Nome, my heart has not been hasty.

O Plan-Maker, who comes forth from *Utenet,* I have not transgressed my color; I have not washed the god.

O Lord-of-Horns, who comes forth from Siut, my voice is not too much about matters.

O *Nefer-tem,* who comes forth from Memphis, I have not committed sins; I have not done evil.

O *Tem-sep,* who comes forth from Busiris, I have not been abusive against a king.

O Acting-with-His-Heart, who comes forth from *Tjebu,* I have not waded in water.

O Flowing-One, who comes forth from Nun, my voice has not been loud.

O Commander-of-the-People, who comes forth from *his shrine,* I have not been abusive against a god.

O *Neheb-nefert,* who comes forth from *the Saite Nome,* I have never made puffings-up.

O *Neheb-kau,* who comes forth from the town, I have not made *discriminations for* myself.

O High-of-Head serpent, who comes forth from the cavern, my portion has not been too large, *not even* in my own property.

O *In-af* serpent, who comes forth from the cemetery, I have not blasphemed against my local god.

WORDS TO BE SPOKEN BY X [the deceased]:

Hail to you, ye gods who are in this Broad-Hall of the Two Justices! I know you; I know your names. I shall not fall for dread of you. Ye have not reported guilt of mine up to this god in whose retinue ye are; no deed of mine has come *from* you. Ye have spoken truth about me in the presence of the All-Lord, because I acted justly in Egypt. I have not been abusive to a god. No deed of mine has come *from* a king who is in his day.

Hail to you who are in the Broad-Hall of the Two Justices, who have no deceit in your bodies, who live on truth and who eat of truth in the presence of Horus, who is in his sun disc. May ye rescue me from Babi, who lives on the entrails *of elders* on that day of the great reckoning. Behold me—I have come to you without sin, without guilt, without evil, without a witness against me, without one against whom I have taken action. I live on truth, and I eat of truth. I have done that which men said and that with which gods are content. I have satisfied a god with that which he desires. I have given bread to the hungry, water to the thirsty, clothing to the naked, and a ferry-boat to him who was marooned. I have provided divine offerings for the gods and mortuary offerings for the dead. So rescue me, you; protect me, you. Ye will not make report against me in the presence of the great god. I am one pure of mouth and pure of hands, one to whom "Welcome, welcome, in peace!" is said by those who see him, because I have heard those great words which the ass discussed with the cat in the house of *the hippopotamus,* when the witness was His-Face-Behind-Him and he gave out a cry. I have seen the splitting of the *ished*-tree in *Rostau.* I am one who has a concern for the gods, who knows the *nature* of their bodies. I have come here to testify to justice and to bring the scales to their proper position in the cemetery.

O thou who art high upon his standard, Lord

of the *Atef*-Crown, whose name has been made "Lord of Breath," mayest thou rescue me from thy messengers who give forth uncleanliness and create *destruction,* who have no covering up of their faces, because I have effected justice for the Lord of Justice, being pure—my front is pure, my rear is clean, my middle is in the flowing water of justice; there is no part of me free of justice. . . .

. . . "I will not announce thee," says the door-keeper of the Broad-Hall of the Two Justices, "unless thou tellest my name." "Understander of Hearts, Searcher of Bodies is thy name." "Then to whom should I announce thee?" "To the god who is in his hour of service." "Thou shouldst tell it to the interpreter of the Two Lands." "Well, who is the interpreter of the Two Lands?" "It is Thoth."

"Come," says Thoth, "why hast thou come?" "I have come here to be announced." "What is thy condition?" "I am pure of sin. I have protected myself from the strife of those who are in their days. I am not among them." "Then to whom shall I announce thee? I shall announce thee to him whose ceiling is of fire, whose walls are living serpents, and whose pavement is water. Who is he?" "He is Osiris." "Then go thou. Behold, thou art announced. Thy bread is the Restored Eye; thy beer is the Restored Eye. Thou hast invocation-offerings upon earth in the Restored Eye." So spoke Osiris to *X,* the deceased.

Instructions for the Use of the Spell

TO BE DONE IN CONFORMANCE WITH WHAT TAKES PLACE IN THIS BROAD-HALL OF THE TWO JUS-TICES. THIS SPELL IS TO BE RECITED WHEN ONE IS CLEAN AND PURE, CLOTHED IN FRESH GARMENTS, SHOD WITH WHITE SANDALS, PAINTED WITH STIBIUM, AND ANOINTED WITH MYRRH, TO WHOM CATTLE, FOWL, INCENSE, BREAD, BEER, AND VEGETABLES HAVE BEEN OFFERED. THEN MAKE THOU THIS TEXT IN WRITING ON A CLEAN PAVEMENT WITH *OCHRE* SMEARED WITH EARTH UPON WHICH PIGS AND OTHER SMALL CATTLE HAVE NOT TRODDEN. AS FOR HIM ON WHOSE BEHALF THIS BOOK IS MADE, HE SHALL BE PROSPEROUS AND HIS CHILDREN SHALL BE PROSPEROUS, WITHOUT *GREED,* BECAUSE HE SHALL BE A TRUSTED MAN OF the king AND HIS COURTIERS. LOAVES, JARS, BREAD, AND JOINTS OF MEAT SHALL BE GIVEN TO HIM FROM THE ALTAR OF the great god. HE CANNOT BE HELD BACK AT ANY DOOR OF THE WEST, BUT HE SHALL BE USHERED IN WITH the Kings of Upper and Lower Egypt, and he shall be in the retinue of Osiris.

Right and true a million times.

REVIEW QUESTIONS

1. What does this text reveal about the Egyptians' concept of the next life and in particular, about the individual's eligibility for it? Can you detect any parallels in the beliefs of later religious systems?
2. How, ideally, was one to conduct oneself in order to appear blameless before the gods?
3. What does this text have to say about Egyptian social values?

Harper's Songs

The ancient Egyptians have often been characterized as morbidly fascinated by death and eagerly anticipating the next life, an attitude distinctly in contrast with that of most of modern Western society. The next readings are from a very unusual genre in Egyptian literature and present somewhat contrasting views of the afterlife. They may give us pause to reconsider.

From *Hymns, Prayers, and Songs: An Anthology of Ancient Egyptian Lyric Poetry,* translated by John L. Foster (Atlanta, Ga.: Scholars Press, 1995), pp. 168–69.

From the Tomb of King Intef

Song in the tomb of King Intef, vindicated, in front of the singer with the harp:

> He is prospering, this fine prince;
> death is a happy ending.

i

One generation passes, another stays behind—
such has it been since the men of ancient times.
The gods of long ago rest in their pyramids,
and the great and blessed likewise lie buried in
  their tombs.
Yet those who built great mansions, their places
  are no more.
What has become of them all?

I have heard the words of Imhotep, and Hordjedef
  too,
retold time and again in their narrations.
Where are their dwellings now?
Their walls are down,
Their places gone,
like something that has never been.

There is no return for them
to explain their present being,
To say how it is with them,
to gentle our hearts
until we hasten to the place where they have gone.

ii

So, let your heart be strong,
let these things fade from your thoughts.
Look to yourself,
and follow your heart's desire while you live!

Put myrrh on your head,
be clothed in fine linen,
Anoint yourself with the god's own perfumes,
heap up your happiness,
and let not your heart become weary.

Follow your heart's desire and what you find
  good;
act on your own behalf while on earth!
And let not your heart be troubled—
that day of mourning for you must come;
And Osiris, the Weary-Hearted, will not hear their
  wailing,
weeping does not save the heart from the grave.
So spend your days joyfully
and do not be weary with living!
No man takes his things with him,
and none who go can come back again.

*   *   *

From the Tomb of Neferhotep

Chanted by the singer with the harp for the God's Father of Amun, Neferhotep, vindicated:

O all you excellent eminent dead, O Ennead, O
    Lady of Life
    in the West,
hear what has been composed
To sing the praises of the God's Father in
    honoring his soul,
what is helpful for the excellent dead man
Now that he is a living god for eternity,
elevated in the West.
May these words become a memorial in future
to anyone who passes by.

I have heard those songs in the tombs of ancient
    days
and what they say, exalting life on earth
and belittling the city of the dead.
Why is this, acting this way against the land of
    eternity
which is just and without terror?
It loathes disorder;
and no one arms himself against a neighbor
in this land without a rebel.

All our ancestors have come to rest within it
since the wastes at the beginning of time;
And those who shall come to be, millions on
    millions,
all go there.
There is no lingering in our Beloved Land,
not one fails to arrive there;
And the span of what was done on earth is the
    flicker of a dream
when they say, "Welcome, safe and sound!"
to the one who reaches the West.

*   *   *

REVIEW QUESTIONS

1. According to the harper's songs, how ought
   one to spend this life?
2. Do you believe that the ancient Egyptians were
   obsessed with death?

2 ∾ THE GROWTH OF EMPIRES IN THE ANCIENT NEAR EAST

To the people who lived then, our designations second millennium or 2000 B.C.E. would have been, of course, absolutely meaningless. From our vantage point, however, 2000 B.C.E. is a significant temporal marker in the history of the ancient Near East and Egypt. By that time, essential structures of both Sumerian/Mesopotamian and Egyptian civilization had been well and long established. The foundations of those structures were now to be subjected to major tremors. Their superstructures would sustain some damage, but their foundations would largely endure.

By 2000 B.C.E., the imperial dynasties established by Sargon and then by the kings of the Third Dynasty of Ur had come and gone, although the idealized memory of Sargon's rulership would inspire future Mesopotamian kings for the next 1,500 years. The decline of the Ur III empire had been sealed by the cataclysm of invasion and destruction, memorialized in a literary work known as the "Lamentation over the Destruction of Sumer and Ur." The next 400 years were to be inaugurated by fragmentation as chieftains of recently arrived Amorite tribal groups established themselves in small kingdoms in the urbanized regions of Sumer and Akkad. In time, one of those minor kingdoms, Babylon, was to establish itself, and its god Marduk, as supreme. The ascent of the great Amorite king Hammurabi saw Babylon take center stage in Lower Mesopotamia (henceforth Babylonia), not to relinquish it until the era of Alexander the Great's successors. But Babylon's rise was possible only because Hammurabi proved himself (as thousands of cuneiform tablets from the palace of Mari on the Euphrates testify for us) a master player in an era when power politics, trade and diplomacy, and competition for resources encompassed an arena extending from Anatolia to the Persian Gulf and from Iran to the Mediterannean as far as Crete. His dynasty's fall, around 150 years later, came at the hands of a relatively new *player, the Hittite kingdom of Anatolia, whose rise ushered onto the ancient Near Eastern stage speakers and writers of a language that we can identify as Indo-European, related to the later languages of western Europe. When the curtain eventually lifts again in Babylonia, another new ruling group from the outside, the Kassites, is in charge. Yet, like the Akkadian kings and then the Amorites before them, the Kassites are captured—or, perhaps, captivated—by the enduring traditions and structures of Sumerian civilization.*

By 2000 B.C.E., Egypt had been rocked by its own cataclysm: the breakdown of the Old Kingdom and, for the first time, of the divinely ordained, cosmic stability of ma'at *that was the underpinning of Egypt's civilization. The reunification established by the rulers of Thebes (whose god Amun, like Babylon's Marduk, would soon emerge supreme) during the Middle Kingdom brought renewed strength and cultural vitality, as well as the assertion of Egypt's interests and power as far away as Nubia to the south, Crete to the north, and Palestine to the east. The Middle Kingdom also saw a reassertion of royal traditions and absolutism, though they seem punctuated by the lingering remembrance of the threat posed by discord and societal breakdown. In time, that threat became real enough, as "vile Asiatics" recently arrived from Palestine into the Nile Delta asserted their own power as the Hyksos dynasties of Lower Egypt. Egypt was once again divided, but, for the first time, by the abomination of "barbarian" invasion. Once again, it was a royal family from Amun's city Thebes that restored the unity of the Two Lands of Upper and Lower Egypt, this time by expelling the invaders, chasing them back into Palestine, and subsequently, perhaps as insurance against a repetition of such an abomination, conquering and ruling most of the eastern Mediterranean seaboard from the Sinai to Syria, as well as the region of Nubia into the interior of Africa.*

The zenith of Egypt's New Kingdom empire coincides with the era of the Late Bronze Age, an age of unprecedented internationalism. As reflected vividly in the diplomatic correspondence of the Amarna letters and, more recently, in the preserved cargo of a shipwreck discovered off the coast of Turkey at Ulu Burun, kings from Babylonia to Cyprus negotiated favors and offered their daughters in marriage, while maritime traders plied the sea routes of the Aegean and eastern Mediterranean, carrying wares such as ingots of bronze, tusks of ivory, disks of blue glass, and pottery containers filled with valuable oils and resins. Envoys and ambassadors trudged well-worn caravan tracks, bearing messages from kings offering alliances to other kings or from local princes offering supplication to pharaoh or informing him of depredations by hapiru *outlaws. At the top of royal wish lists was the gold of Nubia, which was in the power of pharaoh to dispense to royal "brothers" in Babylonia, Assyria, Hatti, Mitanni, Alashiya (Cyprus), or Ahhiyawa (perhaps Mycenaean Greece). Many pounds of that same gold were expended on the burial of a short-lived pharaoh named Tutankhamun, whose abandoned birth name of Tutankhaten testifies to the genius (or madness) of his predecessor, regarded by some experts as the first to espouse monotheism, a religious system based on a single God (in this instance, the sun as personified in its disk, or aten). Later Egyptians would condemn Akhenaten's "revolution" as heresy and attempt to eradicate his memory. Only well after the internationalism of the Late Bronze Age had been disrupted and Egypt itself had become a broken reed would the Hebrews (perhaps not totally unrelated to those* hapiru *outlaws of the Amarna letters) develop the concept of monotheism, a concept that was to eventually become one of the most central and enduring structures of civilization throughout the West and the world.*

Laws from Ancient Mesopotamia

Dating to the reign of Hammurabi of Babylon (the conventional dates for which are 1795–1750 B.C.E.), the Laws of Hammurabi are not the earliest Mesopotamian compilation of legal rulings known to us. They are, however, the longest and most diverse collection and undoubtedly constitute the single most informative document yet discovered regarding concepts of justice and social regulation in Mesopotamian society. Hammurabi's laws also provide extremely important evidence about the status and rights of women of various social classes in Babylonian society in the early second millennium B.C.E. The treatment of women according to those laws can be usefully compared to the treatment accorded them in a later body of legal rulings, the Middle Assyrian Laws, which date to a period roughly 500 years after Hammurabi's reign.

From *Law Collections from Mesopotamia and Asia Minor*, edited by Martha T. Roth, SBL Writings from the Ancient World Series, vol. 6 (Atlanta, Ga.: Scholars Press, 1995), pp. 76–135.

FROM The Laws of Hammurabi

When the august god Anu, king of the Anunnaku deities, and the god Enlil, lord of heaven and earth, who determines the destinies of the land, allotted supreme power over all peoples to the god Marduk, the firstborn son of the god Ea, exalted him among the Igigu deities, named the city of Babylon with its august name and made it supreme within the regions of the world, and established for him within it eternal kingship whose foundations are as fixed as heaven and earth,

at that time, the gods Anu and Enlil, for the enhancement of the well-being of the people, named me by my name: Hammurabi, the pious prince, who venerates the gods, to make justice prevail in the land, to abolish the wicked and the evil, to prevent the strong from oppressing the weak, to rise like the sun-god Shamash over all humankind, to illuminate the land.

I am Hammurabi, the shepherd, selected by the god Enlil, he who heaps high abundance and plenty, who perfects every possible thing for the city Nippur, the city known as band-of-heaven-and-earth, the pious provider of the Ekur temple;

the capable king, the restorer of the city Eridu, the purifier of the rites of the Eabzu temple;

the onslaught of the four regions of the world, who magnifies the reputation of the city Babylon, who gladdens the heart of his divine lord Marduk, whose days are devoted to the Esagil temple;

*   *   *

When the god Marduk commanded me to provide just ways for the people of the land in order to attain appropriate behavior, I established truth and justice as the declaration of the land, I enhanced the well-being of the people.

*   *   *

1. If a man accuses another man and charges him with homicide but cannot bring proof against him, his accuser shall be killed.

2. If a man charges another man with practicing witchcraft but cannot bring proof against him, he who is charged with witchcraft shall go to the divine River Ordeal, he shall indeed submit to the divine River Ordeal; if the divine River Ordeal should overwhelm him, his accuser shall take full legal possession of his estate; if the divine River Ordeal should clear that man and should he survive, he who made the charge of witchcraft against him shall be killed; he who submitted to the divine River Ordeal shall take full legal possession of his accuser's estate.

3. If a man comes forward to give false testimony in a case but cannot bring evidence for his accusation, if that case involves a capital offense, that man shall be killed.

*   *   *

6. If a man steals valuables belonging to the god or to the palace, that man shall be killed, and also he who received the stolen goods from him shall be killed.

7. If a man should purchase silver, gold, a slave, a slave woman, an ox, a sheep, a donkey, or anything else whatsoever, from a son of a man or from a slave of a man without witnesses or a contract—or if he accepts the goods for safekeeping—that man is a thief, he shall be killed.

8. If a man steals an ox, a sheep, a donkey, a pig, or a boat—if it belongs either to the god or to the palace, he shall give thirtyfold; if it belongs to a commoner, he shall replace it tenfold; if the thief does not have anything to give, he shall be killed.

*   *   *

15. If a man should enable a palace slave, a palace slave woman, a commoner's slave, or a commoner's slave woman to leave through the main city-gate, he shall be killed.

16. If a man should harbor a fugitive slave or slave woman of either the palace or of a commoner in his house and not bring him out at the herald's public proclamation, that householder shall be killed.

17. If a man seizes a fugitive slave or slave woman in the open country and leads him back to his owner, the slave owner shall give him 2 shekels of silver.

18. If that slave should refuse to identify his owner, he shall lead him off to the palace, his circumstances shall be investigated, and they shall return him to his owner.

19. If he should detain that slave in his own house and afterward the slave is discovered in his possession, that man shall be killed.

20. If the slave should escape the custody of the one who seized him, that man shall swear an oath by the god to the owner of the slave, and he shall be released.

21. If a man breaks into a house, they shall kill him and hang him in front of that very breach.

22. If a man commits a robbery and is then seized, that man shall be killed.

*   *   *

53. If a man neglects to reinforce the embankment of the irrigation canal of his field and does not reinforce its embankment, and then a breach opens in its embankment and allows the water to carry away the common irrigated area, the man in whose embankment the breach opened shall replace the grain whose loss he caused.

54. If he cannot replace the grain they shall sell him and his property, and the residents of the common irrigated area whose grain crops the water carried away shall divide (the proceeds).

55. If a man opens his branch of the canal for irrigation and negligently allows the water to carry away his neighbor's field, he shall measure and deliver grain in accordance with his neighbor's yield.

*   *   *

102. If a merchant should give silver to a trading agent for an investment venture, and he incurs a loss on his journeys, he shall return silver to the merchant in the amount of the capital sum.

103. If enemy forces should make him abandon whatever goods he is transporting while on his business trip, the trading agent shall swear an oath by the god and shall be released.

104. If a merchant gives a trading agent grain, wool, oil, or any other commodity for local transactions, the trading agent shall return to the merchant the silver for each transaction; the trading agent shall collect a sealed receipt for each payment in silver that he gives to the merchant.

105. If the trading agent should be negligent and not take a sealed receipt for each payment in silver that he gives to the merchant, any silver that is not documented in a sealed receipt will not be included in the final accounting.

*   *   *

108. If a woman innkeeper should refuse to accept grain for the price of beer but accepts only silver measured by the large weight, thereby reducing the value of beer in relation to the value of grain, they shall charge and convict that woman innkeeper and they shall cast her into the water.

109. If there should be a woman innkeeper in whose house criminals congregate, and she does not seize those criminals and lead them off to the palace authorities, that woman innkeeper shall be killed.

*   *   *

117. If an obligation is outstanding against a man and he sells or gives into debt service his wife, his son, or his daughter, they shall perform service in the house of their buyer or of the one who holds them in debt service for three years; their release shall be secured in the fourth year.

118. If he should give a male or female slave into debt service, the merchant may extend the term beyond the three years, he may sell him; there are no grounds for a claim.

119. If an obligation is outstanding against a man and he therefore sells his slave woman who has borne him children, the owner of the slave woman shall weigh and deliver the silver which the merchant weighed and delivered as the loan and he shall thereby redeem his slave woman.

*   *   *

128. If a man marries a wife but does not draw up a formal contract for her, she is not a wife.

129. If a man's wife should be seized lying with another male, they shall bind them and throw them into the water; if the wife's master allows his wife to live, then the king shall allow his subject (i.e., the other male) to live.

130. If a man pins down another man's virgin wife who is still residing in her father's house, and they seize him lying with her, that man shall be killed; that woman shall be released.

131. If her husband accuses his own wife of adultery, although she has not been seized lying with another male, she shall swear to her innocence by an oath by the god, and return to her house.

132. If a man's wife should have a finger pointed against her in accusation involving another male, although she has not been seized lying with another male, she shall submit to the divine River Ordeal for her husband.[1]

*   *   *

134. If a man should be captured and there are not sufficient provisions in his house, his wife may enter another's house; that woman will not be subject to any penalty.

135. If a man should be captured and there are not sufficient provisions in his house, before his return his wife enters another's house and bears children, and afterwards her husband returns and gets back to his city, that woman shall return to her first husband; the children shall inherit from their father.

136. If a man deserts his city and flees, and after his departure his wife enters another's house—if that man then should return and seize his wife, because he repudiated his city and fled, the wife of the deserter will not return to her husband.

*   *   *

138. If a man intends to divorce his first-ranking wife who did not bear him children, he shall give her silver as much as was her bridewealth and restore to her the dowry that she brought from her father's house, and he shall divorce her.

139. If there is no bridewealth, he shall give her 60 shekels of silver as a divorce settlement.

140. If he is a commoner, he shall give her 20 shekels of silver.

141. If the wife of a man who is residing in the man's house should decide to leave, and she appropriates goods, squanders her household possessions, or disparages her husband, they shall charge and convict her; and if her husband should declare his intention to divorce her, then he shall divorce her; neither her travel expenses, nor her divorce settlement, nor anything else shall be given to her. If her husband should not declare his intention to divorce her, then her husband may marry another woman and that first woman shall reside in her husband's house as a slave woman.

142. If a woman repudiates her husband, and declares, "You will not have marital relations with me"—her circumstances shall be investigated by the authorities of her city quarter, and if she is circumspect and without fault, but her husband is wayward and disparages her greatly, that woman will not be subject to any penalty; she shall take her dowry and she shall depart for her father's house.

143. If she is not circumspect but is wayward, squanders her household possessions, and disparages her husband, they shall cast that woman into the water.

*   *   *

150. If a man awards to his wife a field, orchard, house, or movable property, and makes out a sealed document for her, after her husband's death her children will not bring a claim against her; the mother shall give her estate to whichever of her children she loves, but she will not give it to an outsider.

151. If a woman who is residing in a man's house should have her husband agree by binding contract that no creditor of her husband shall seize her for his debts—if that man has a debt incurred before marrying that woman, his creditors will not seize his wife; and if that woman has a debt incurred before entering the man's house, her creditors will not seize her husband.

*   *   *

153. If a man's wife has her husband killed on account of (her relationship with) another male, they shall impale that woman.

154. If a man should carnally know his daughter, they shall banish that man from the city.

155. If a man selects a bride for his son and his son carnally knows her, after which he himself then lies with her and they seize him in the act,

---

[1]The woman would take an oath swearing to her innocence before the river god. She then would be required to plunge into the river. If she survived, she was deemed innocent; if she drowned, it was deemed the punishment of the river god, in whose name she had falsely sworn. [Editor.]

they shall bind that man and cast him into the water.

156. If a man selects a bride for his son and his son does not yet carnally know her, and he himself then lies with her, he shall weigh and deliver to her 30 shekels of silver; moreover, he shall restore to her whatever she brought from her father's house, and a husband of her choice shall marry her.

157. If a man, after his father's death, should lie with his mother, they shall burn them both.

158. If a man, after his father's death, should be discovered in the lap of the father's principal wife who had borne children, that man shall be disinherited from the paternal estate.

*   *   *

162. If a man marries a wife, she bears him children, and that woman then goes to her fate, her father shall have no claim to her dowry; her dowry belongs only to her children.

163. If a man marries a wife but she does not provide him with children, and that woman goes to her fate—if his father-in-law then returns to him the bridewealth that that man brought to his father-in-law's house, her husband shall have no claim to that woman's dowry; her dowry belongs only to her father's house.

*   *   *

169. If he should be guilty of a grave offense deserving the penalty of disinheritance by his father, they shall pardon him for his first one; if he should commit a grave offense a second time, the father may disinherit his son.

*   *   *

188. If a craftsman takes a young child to rear and then teaches him his craft, he will not be reclaimed.

189. If he should not teach him his craft, that rearling shall return to his father's house.

190. If a man should not reckon the young child whom he took and raised in adoption as equal with his children, that rearling shall return to his father's house.

191. If a man establishes his household by reckoning as equal with any future children the young child whom he took and raised in adoption, but afterwards he has children of his own and then decides to disinherit the rearling, that young child will not depart empty-handed; the father who raised him shall give him a one-third share of his property as his inheritance and he shall depart; he will not give him any property from field, orchard, or house.

*   *   *

195. If a child should strike his father, they shall cut off his hand.

196. If an *awīlu* should blind the eye of another *awīlu*, they shall blind his eye.[2]

197. If he should break the bone of another *awīlu*, they shall break his bone.

198. If he should blind the eye of a commoner or break the bone of a commoner, he shall weigh and deliver 60 shekels of silver.

199. If he should blind the eye of an *awīlu*'s slave or break the bone of an *awīlu*'s slave, he shall weigh and deliver one-half of his value in silver.

200. If an *awīlu* should knock out the tooth of another *awīlu* of his own rank, they shall knock out his tooth.

201. If he should knock out the tooth of a commoner, he shall weigh and deliver 20 shekels of silver.

202. If an *awīlu* should strike the cheek of an *awīlu* who is of status higher than his own, he shall be flogged in the public assembly with 60 stripes of an ox whip.

203. If a member of the *awīlu*-class should strike the cheek of another member of the *awīlu*-class who is his equal, he shall weigh and deliver 60 shekels of silver.

204. If a commoner should strike the cheek of another commoner, he shall weigh and deliver 10 shekels of silver.

---

[2] The most basic meaning of *awīlu* is "man." In this context it seems to represent a free man, probably an owner of private land and with a status higher than that of a "commoner." [Editor.]

209. If an *awīlu* strikes a woman of the *awīlu*-class and thereby causes her to miscarry her fetus, he shall weigh and deliver 10 shekels of silver for her fetus.
210. If that woman should die, they shall kill his daughter.
211. If he should cause a woman of the commoner-class to miscarry her fetus by the beating, he shall weigh and deliver 5 shekels of silver.
212. If that woman should die, he shall weigh and deliver 30 shekels of silver.

*   *   *

218. If a physician performs major surgery with a bronze lancet upon an *awīlu* and thus causes the *awīlu*'s death, or opens an *awīlu*'s temple with a bronze lancet and thus blinds the *awīlu*'s eye, they shall cut off his hand.
219. If a physician performs major surgery with a bronze lancet upon a slave of a commoner and thus causes the slave's death, he shall replace the slave with a slave of comparable value.
220. If he opens his (the commoner's slave's) temple with a bronze lancet and thus blinds his eye, he shall weigh and deliver silver equal to half his value.

*   *   *

226. If a barber shaves off the slave-hairlock of a slave not belonging to him without the consent of the slave's owner, they shall cut off that barber's hand.
227. If a man misinforms a barber so that he then shaves off the slave-hairlock of a slave not belonging to him, they shall kill that man and hang him in his own doorway; the barber shall swear, "I did not knowingly shave it off," and he shall be released.

*   *   *

These are the just decisions which Hammurabi, the able king, has established and thereby has di-

rected the land along the course of truth and the correct way of life.

I am Hammurabi, noble king. I have not been careless or negligent toward humankind, granted to my care by the god Enlil, and with whose shepherding the god Marduk charged me. I have sought for them peaceful places, I removed serious difficulties, I spread light over them. With the mighty weapon which the gods Zababa and Ishtar bestowed upon me, with the wisdom which the god Ea allotted to me, with the ability which the god Marduk gave me, I annihilated enemies everywhere, I put an end to wars, I enhanced the well-being of the land, I made the people of all settlements lie in safe pastures, I did not tolerate anyone intimidating them. The great gods having chosen me, I am indeed the shepherd who brings peace, whose scepter is just. My benevolent shade is spread over my city, I held the people of the lands of Sumer and Akkad safely on my lap. They prospered under my protective spirit, I maintained them in peace, with my skillful wisdom I sheltered them.

In order that the mighty not wrong the weak, to provide just ways for the waif and the widow, I have inscribed my precious pronouncements upon my stela and set it up before the statue of me, the king of justice, in the city of Babylon, the city which the gods Anu and Enlil have elevated, within the Esagil, the temple whose foundations are fixed as are heaven and earth, in order to render the judgments of the land, to give the verdicts of the land, and to provide just ways for the wronged.

*   *   *

FROM Middle Assyrian Laws

*   *   *

4. If either a slave or a slave woman should receive something from a man's wife, they shall cut off the slave's or slave woman's nose and ears; they shall restore the stolen goods; the man shall cut

off his own wife's ears. But if he releases his wife and does not cut off her ears, they shall not cut off the nose and ears of the slave or slave woman, and they shall not restore the stolen goods.

*   *   *

7. If a woman should lay a hand upon a man and they prove the charges against her, she shall pay 1,800 shekels of lead; they shall strike her 20 blows with rods.

8. If a woman should crush a man's testicle during a quarrel, they shall cut off one of her fingers. And even if the physician should bandage it, but the second testicle then becomes infected along with it and becomes . . . , or she should crush the second testicle during the quarrel—they shall gouge out both her * * *

9. If a man lays a hand upon a woman, attacking her like a rutting bull, and they prove the charges against him and find him guilty, they shall cut off one of his fingers. If he should kiss her, they shall draw his lower lip across the blade of an ax and cut it off.

*   *   *

12. If a wife of a man should walk along the main thoroughfare and should a man seize her and say to her, "I want to have sex with you!"—she shall not consent but she shall protect herself; should he seize her by force and fornicate with her—whether they discover him upon the woman or witnesses later prove the charges against him that he fornicated with the woman—they shall kill the man; there is no punishment for the woman.

13. If the wife of a man should go out of her own house, and go to another man where he resides, and should he fornicate with her knowing that she is the wife of a man, they shall kill the man and the wife.

14. If a man should fornicate with another man's wife either in an inn or in the main thoroughfare, knowing that she is the wife of a man, they shall treat the fornicator as the man declares he wishes his wife to be treated. If he should fornicate with her without knowing that she is the wife of a man,

the fornicator is clear; the man shall prove the charges against his wife and he shall treat her as he wishes.

15. If a man should seize another man upon his wife and they prove the charges against him and find him guilty, they shall kill both of them; there is no liability for him. If he should seize him and bring him either before the king or the judges, and they prove the charges against him and find him guilty—if the woman's husband kills his wife, then he shall also kill the man; if he cuts off his wife's nose, he shall turn the man into a eunuch and they shall lacerate his entire face; but if he wishes to release his wife, he shall release the man.

16. If a man should fornicate with the wife of a man . . . by her invitation, there is no punishment for the man; the husband shall impose whatever punishment he chooses upon his wife. If he should fornicate with her by force and they prove the charges against him and find him guilty, his punishment shall be identical to that of the wife of the man.

*   *   *

23. If a man's wife should take another man's wife into her house and give her to a man for purposes of fornication, and the man knows that she is the wife of a man, they shall treat him as one who has fornicated with the wife of another man; and they treat the female procurer just as the woman's husband treats his fornicating wife. And if the woman's husband intends to do nothing to his fornicating wife, they shall do nothing to the fornicator or to the female procurer; they shall release them. But if the man's wife does not know what was intended, and the woman who takes her into her house brings the man in to her by deceit, and he then fornicates with her—if, as soon as she leaves the house, she should declare that she has been the victim of fornication, they shall release the woman, she is clear; they shall kill the fornicator and the female procurer. But if the woman should not so declare, the man shall impose whatever punishment on his wife he wishes; they shall kill the fornicator and the female procurer.

24. If a man's wife should withdraw herself from her husband and enter into the house of another Assyrian, either in that city or in any of the nearby towns, to a house which he assigns to her, residing with the mistress of the household staying overnight three or four nights, and the householder is not aware that it is the wife of a man who is residing in his house, and later that woman is seized, the householder whose wife withdrew herself from him shall mutilate his wife and not take her back. As for the man's wife with whom his wife resided, they shall cut off her ears; if he pleases, her husband shall give 12,600 shekels of lead as her value, and, if he pleases, he shall take back his wife. However, if the householder knows that it is a man's wife who is residing in his house with his wife, he shall give "triple." And if he should deny that he knew of her status, he shall declare, "I did not know," they shall undergo the divine River Ordeal. And if the man in whose house the wife of a man resided should refuse to undergo the divine River Ordeal, he shall give "triple"; if it is the man whose wife withdrew herself from him who should refuse to undergo the divine River Ordeal, he in whose house she resided is clear; he shall bear the expenses of the divine River Ordeal. However, if the man whose wife withdrew herself from him does not mutilate his wife, he shall take back his wife; no sanctions are imposed.

*   *   *

37. If a man intends to divorce his wife, if it is his wish, he shall give her something; if that is not his wish, he shall not give her anything, and she shall leave emptyhanded.

*   *   *

40. Wives of a man, or widows, or any Assyrian women who go out into the main thoroughfare shall not have their heads bare. Daughters of a man with either a cloth or garments shall veil their heads. When they go about in the main thoroughfare during the daytime, they shall be veiled. A concubine who goes about in the main thoroughfare with her mistress is to be veiled. A married *qadiltu*-woman is to be veiled when she goes about in the main thoroughfare, but an unmarried one is to leave her head bare in the main thoroughfare, she shall not be veiled. A prostitute shall not be veiled, her head shall be bare. Whoever sees a veiled prostitute shall seize her, secure witnesses, and bring her to the palace entrance. They shall not take away her jewelry, but he who has seized her takes her clothing; they shall strike her 50 blows with rods; they shall pour hot pitch over her head. And if a man should see a veiled prostitute and release her, and does not bring her to the palace entrance, they shall strike that man 50 blows with rods; the one who informs against him shall take his clothing; they shall pierce his ears, thread them on a cord, tie it at his back; he shall perform the king's service for one full month. Slave women shall not be veiled, and he who should see a veiled slave woman shall seize her and bring her to the palace entrance; they shall cut off her ears; he who seizes her shall take her clothing. If a man should see a veiled slave woman but release her and not seize her, and does not bring her to the palace entrance, and they then prove the charges against him and find him guilty, they shall strike him 50 blows with rods; they shall pierce his ears, thread them on a cord, tie it at his back; the one who informs against him shall take his garments; he shall perform the king's service for one full month.

*   *   *

53. If a woman aborts her fetus by her own action and they then prove the charges against her and find her guilty, they shall impale her, they shall not bury her. If she dies as a result of aborting her fetus, they shall impale her, they shall not bury her. If any persons should hide that woman because she aborted her fetus * * *

*   *   *

55. If a man forcibly seizes and rapes a maiden who is residing in her father's house, who is not betrothed, whose womb is not opened, who is not married, and against whose father's house there is

no outstanding claim—whether within the city or in the countryside, or at night whether in the main thoroughfare, or in a granary, or during the city festival—the father of the maiden shall take the wife of the fornicator of the maiden and hand her over to be raped; he shall not return her to her husband, but he shall take (and keep) her; the father shall give his daughter who is the victim of fornication into the protection of the household of her fornicator. If he, the fornicator, has no wife, the fornicator shall give "triple" the silver as the value of the maiden to her father; her fornicator shall marry her; he shall not reject her. If the father does not desire it so, he shall receive "triple" silver for the maiden, and he shall give his daughter in marriage to whomever he chooses.

56. If a maiden should willingly give herself to a man, the man shall so swear; they shall have no claim to his wife; the fornicator shall pay "triple" the silver as the value of the maiden; the father shall treat his daughter in whatever manner he chooses.

*   *   *

59. In addition to the punishments for a man's wife that are written on the tablet, a man may whip his wife, pluck out her hair, mutilate her ears, or strike her, with impunity.

REVIEW QUESTIONS

1. Of the hundreds of records of litigation that exist from the era of Hammurabi and his successors, not one specifically states that a dispute was resolved in accordance with Hammurabi's laws; some, in fact, record rulings that directly contradict those laws. This has caused some scholars to question why Hammurabi had these laws compiled in the first place. Why do you think Hammurabi had his laws compiled? (Do the prologue and epilogue to the laws provide any clues?)

2. What principles of justice and compensation are evident in these laws, and what kinds of recourse did society have against wrongdoers?

3. What evidence of social classes in Babylonian society do they provide?

4. How did women's rights compare with those of men?

5. What do these laws tell us about Mesopotamian views about responsibility for sexual activity?

6. What do they tell us about power and authority within Mesopotamian families?

FROM *The Righteous Sufferer*

More properly known from its actual title, "I will praise the Lord of Wisdom," this great work of Mesopotamian literature has inspired much comparison with the biblical Book of Job with its story of long suffering at the hands of inscrutable divine power. The sufferer, revealed relatively late in the poem to be a man named Shubshi-meshre-Shakkan, is buffeted by many misfortunes and brought low, even to the brink of death, for reasons he cannot fathom. Eventually, perhaps with the intercession of the goddess Sarpanitum, he is forgiven and his health restored by Marduk, her husband and the most powerful of the Babylonian deities. Evident throughout is the utter helplessness of human beings in the face of divine anger and their utter dependence on a hardly foreseeable divine forgiveness.

From *From Distant Days,* translated by B. R. Foster (Bethesda, Md.: CDL Press, 1995), pp. 300–13.

Tablet I

I will praise the lord of wisdom, solicitous god,
Furious in the night, calming in the daylight:
Marduk! lord of wisdom, solicitous god,
Furious in the night, calming in the daylight:
Whose anger engulfs like a tempest,
Whose breeze is sweet as the breath of morn,
In his fury not to be withstood, his rage the
  deluge,
Merciful in his feelings, his emotions relenting.
The skies cannot sustain the weight of his hand,
His gentle palm rescues the moribund.
Marduk! The skies cannot sustain the weight of
  his hand,
His gentle palm rescues the moribund.
When he is angry, graves are dug,
His mercy raised the fallen from disaster.
When he glowers, protective spirits take
  flight,
He has regard for and turns to the one whose
  god has forsaken him.
Harsh is his punishment, he . . . in battles,
When moved to mercy,
he quickly feels pain like a mother in labor.
He is bull-headed in his love of mercy,
Like a cow with a calf, he keeps turning around
  watchfully.
His scourge is barbed and punctures the body,
His bandages are soothing, they heal the
  doomed.
He speaks and makes one incur many sins,
On the day of his justice sin and guilt are
  dispelled.
He is the one who makes shivering and
  trembling,
Through his sacral spell chills and shivering are
  relieved.
Who raises the flood of Adad, the blow of Erra,

Who reconciles the wrathful god and goddess,
The Lord divines the gods' inmost thoughts,
But no god understands his behavior.
Marduk divines the gods' inmost thoughts,
But no god understands his behavior!
As heavy his hand, so compassionate his heart,
As brutal his weapons, so life-sustaining his
  feelings.
Without his consent, who could cure his blow?
Against his will, who could sin and escape?
I will proclaim his anger, which runs deep, like a
  fish.
He punished me abruptly, then granted life.
I will teach the people, I will instruct the land to
  fear,
To be mindful of him is propitious for ＊ ＊ ＊
After the Lord changed day into night,
And the warrior Marduk became furious with
  me,
My own god threw me over and disappeared,
My goddess broke rank and vanished.
He cut off the benevolent angel who walked
  beside me,
My protecting spirit was frightened off,
to seek out someone else.
My vigor was taken away,
my manly appearance became gloomy,
My dignity flew off, my cover leaped away.
Terrifying signs beset me:
I was forced out of my house. I wandered
  outside.
My omens were confused, they were abnormal
  every day,
The prognostication of diviner and dream
  interpreter could not explain what I was
  undergoing.
What was said in the street portended ill for me,
When I lay down at night, my dream was
  terrifying.

The king, incarnation of the gods, sun of his
    peoples,
His heart was enraged with me
and appeasing him was impossible.
Courtiers were plotting hostile action against me,
They gathered themselves to instigate base deeds:
If the first "I will make him end his life"
Says the second "I ousted him from his
    command!"
So likewise the third "I will get my hands on his
    post!"
"I'll force his house!" vows the fourth
As the fifth pants to speak
Sixth and seventh follow in his train!
The clique of seven have massed their forces,
Merciless as fiends, equal to demons.
So one is their body, united in purpose,
Their hearts fulminate against me, ablaze like
    fire.
Slander and lies they try to lend credence against
    me.
My mouth, once proud, was muzzled like a . . . ,
My lips, which used to discourse,
    became those of a deaf man.
My resounding call struck dumb,
My proud head bent earthward,
My stout heart turned feeble for terror,
My broad breast brushed aside by a novice,
My far-reaching arms pinned by flimsy matting,
I, who walked proudly, learned slinking,
I, so grand, became servile.
To my vast family I became a loner,
As I went through the streets,
    ears were pricked up at me,
I would enter the palace, eyes would squint at
    me,
My city was glowering at me like an enemy,
Belligerent and hostile would seem my land!
My brother became my foe,
My friend became a malignant demon,
My comrade would denounce me savagely,
My colleague was constantly keeping the taint to
    his weapons,
My best friend would pinch off my life.
My slave cursed me openly in the assembly of
    gentlefolk,

My slavegirl defamed me before the rabble.
An acquaintance would see me and make
    himself scarce,
My family disowned me.
A pit awaited anyone speaking well of me,
While he who was uttering defamation of me
    forged ahead.
One who relayed base things about me
    had a god for his help,
For the one who said "What a pity about him!"
    death came early,
The one of no help, his life became charmed,
I had no one to go at my side, nor saw I a
    champion.
They parceled my possessions among the riffraff,
The sources of my watercourses they blocked
    with muck,
They chased the harvest song from my fields,
They left my community deathly still,
    like that of a ravaged foe.
They let another assume my duties,
They appointed an outsider to my prerogatives.
By day sighing, by night lamentation,
Monthly, trepidation, despair the year.
I moaned like a dove all my days,
I let out groans as my song.
My eyes are forced to look through constant
    crying,
My eyelids are smarting through ✳ ✳ ✳ of tears.
My face is darkened from the apprehensions of
    my heart,
Terror and panic have jaundiced my face.
The . . . of my heart is quaking in ceaseless
    apprehension.
✳ ✳ ✳ Like a burning fire,
Like the bursting of a flame falsehood beset me,
✳ ✳ ✳ Lamentation, my imploring!
The speech of my lips was senseless, like a
    moron's,
When I tried to talk, my conversation was
    gibberish.
I watch, that in daylight good will come upon
    me!
The moon will change, the sun will shine!

Tablet II

One whole year to the next! The normal time
   passed.
As I turned around, it was more and more
   terrible.
My ill luck was on the increase, I could find no
   good fortune.
I called to my god, he did not show his face,
I prayed to my goddess, she did not raise her
   head.
The diviner with his inspection
did not get to the bottom of it,
Nor did the dream interpreter with his incense
   clear up my case.
I beseeched a dream spirit, but it did not
   enlighten me,
The exorcist with his ritual did not appease
   divine wrath.
What bizarre actions everywhere!
I looked behind: persecution, harassment!
Like one who had not made libations to his god,
Nor invoked his goddess with a food offering,
Who was not wont to prostrate, nor seen to bow
   down,
From whose mouth supplication and prayer were
   wanting,
Who skipped holy days, despised festivals,
Who was neglectful, omitted the gods' rites,
Who had not taught his people reverence and
   worship,
Who did not invoke his god, but ate his food
   offering,
Who snubbed his goddess, brought her no flour
   offering,
Like one possessed, who forgot his lord,
Who casually swore a solemn oath by his god:
   I, indeed, seemed such a one!
I, for my part, was mindful of supplication and
   prayer,
Prayer to me was the natural recourse, sacrifice
   my rule.
The day for reverencing the gods was a source
   of satisfaction to me,
The goddess's procession day was my profit and
   return.

Praying for the king, that was my joy,
His sennet was as if for my own good omen.
I instructed my land to observe the god's rites,
The goddess's name did I drill my people to
   esteem.
I made my praises of the king like a god's,
And taught the populace reverence for the
   palace.
I wish I knew that these things were pleasing to
   a god!
What seems good to one's self could be an
   offense to a god,
What in one's own heart seems abominable
   could be good to one's god!
Who could learn the reasoning of the gods in
   heaven?
Who could grasp the intentions of the gods of
   the depths?
Where might human beings have learned the
   way of a god?
He who lived by his brawn died in confinement.
Suddenly one is downcast, in a trice full of
   cheer,
One moment he sings in exaltation,
In a trice he groans like a professional mourner.
People's motivations change in a twinkling!
Starving, they become like corpses,
Full, they would rival their gods.
In good times, they speak of scaling heaven,
When it goes badly, they complain of going
   down to hell.
I have pondered these things;
I have made no sense of them.
But as for me, in despair, a whirlwind is driving
   me!
Debilitating disease is let loose upon me:
An evil vapor has blown against me from the
   ends of the earth,
Head pain has surged up upon me from the
   breast of hell,
A malignant spectre has come forth from its
   hidden depth,
A relentless ghost came out of its dwelling place.
A she-demon came down from the mountain,
Ague set forth with the flood and sea.

Debility broke through the ground with the
  plants.
They assembled their host, together they came
  upon me:
They struck my head, they closed around my
  pate,
My features were gloomy, my eyes ran a flood,
They wrenched my muscles, made my neck
  limp,
They thwacked my chest, pounded my breast,
They affected my flesh, threw me into
  convulsions,
They kindled a fire in my epigastrium,
They churned up my bowels, they twisted my
  entrails,
Coughing and hacking infected my lungs,
They infected my limbs, made my flesh pasty,
My lofty stature they toppled like a wall,
My robust figure they flattened like a bulrush,
I was dropped like a dried fig, I was tossed on
  my face.
A demon has clothed himself in my body for a
  garment,
Drowsiness smothers me like a net,
My eyes stare, they cannot see,
My ears prick up, they cannot hear.
Numbness has spread over my whole body,
Paralysis has fallen upon my flesh.
Stiffness has seized my arms,
Debility has fallen upon my loins,
My feet forgot how to move.
A stroke has overcome me, I choke like one
  fallen,
Signs of death have shrouded my face!
If someone thinks of me, I can't respond to the
  inquirer,
"Alas!" they weep, I have lost consciousness.
A snare is laid on my mouth,
And a bolt bars my lips.
My way in is barred, my point of slaking
  blocked,
My hunger is chronic, my gullet constricted.
If it be of grain, I choke it down like stinkweed,
Beer, the sustenance of mankind, is sickening to
  me.
Indeed, the malady drags on!

For lack of food my features are unrecognizable,
My flesh is waste, my blood has run dry,
My bones are loose, covered only with skin,
My tissues are inflamed, afflicted with gangrene.
I took to bed, confined, going out was
  exhaustion,
My house turned into my prison.
My flesh was a shackle, my arms being useless,
My person was a fetter, my feet having given
  way.
My afflictions were grievous, the blow was
  severe!
A scourge full of barbs thrashed me,
A crop lacerated me, cruel with thorns.
All day long tormentor would torment me,
Nor at night would he let me breathe freely a
  moment.
From writhing, my joints were separated,
My limbs were splayed and thrust apart.
I spent the night in my dung like an ox,
I wallowed in my excrement like a sheep.
The exorcist recoiled from my symptoms,
While my omens have perplexed the diviner.
The exorcist did not clarify the nature of my
  complaint,
While the diviner put no time limit on my
  illness.
No god came to the rescue, nor lent me a hand,
No goddess took pity on me, nor went at my
  side.
My grave was open, my funerary goods ready,
Before I had died, lamentation for me was done.
All my country said, "How wretched he was!"
When my ill-wisher heard, his face lit up,
When the tidings reached her, my ill-wisher,
  her mood became radiant.
The day grew dim for my whole family,
For those who knew me, their sun grew dark.

Tablet III

Heavy was his hand upon me, I could not bear
  it!
Dread of him was oppressive.
His fierce punishment ∗ ∗ ∗, the deluge,
His stride was . . . , it . . .

Harsh, severe illness does not . . . my person,
I lost sight of alertness, ✶ ✶ ✶ make my mind
  stray.
I groan day and night alike,
Dreaming and waking I am equally wretched.
A remarkable young man of extraordinary
  physique,
Magnificent in body, clothed in new
  garments,
Because I was only half awake, his features
  lacked form.
He was clad in splendor, robed in dread—
He came in upon me, he stood over me.
When I saw him, my flesh grew numb.
✶ ✶ ✶ "The Lady has sent me, ✶ ✶ ✶
A second time I saw a dream.
In the dream I saw at night,
A remarkable purifier, [   ]
Holding in his hand a tamarisk rod of
  purification,
"Laluralimma, resident of Nippur,
"Has sent me to cleanse you."
He was carrying water, he poured it over me,
He pronounced the resuscitating incantation,
he massaged my body.
A third time I saw a dream.
In my dream I saw at night:
A remarkable young woman of shining
  countenance,
Clothed like a person, being like a god,
A queen among peoples
She entered upon me and sat down . . .
She ordered my deliverance. ✶ ✶ ✶
"Fear not," she said . . .
She ordered my deliverance, "Most wretched
  indeed is he,
"Whoever he might be,
  the one who saw the vision at night."
In the dream was Ur-Nintinugga, a
  Babylonian . . .
A bearded young man wearing a tiara,
He was an exorcist, carrying a tablet,
"Marduk has sent me!
"To Shubshi-meshre-Sakkan I have brought a
  swathe,
"From his pure hands I have brought a swathe."

He has entrusted me into the hands of my
  ministrant.
In waking hours he sent a message,
He revealed his favorable sign to my people.
I was awake in my sickness, a healing serpent
  slithered by.
My illness was quickly over, my fetters were
  broken.
After my lord's heart had quieted,
And the feelings of merciful Marduk were
  appeased,
And he had accepted my prayers,
His sweet relenting ✶ ✶ ✶,
He applied to me his spell
  which binds debilitating disease,
He drove back the evil vapor to the ends of the
  earth,
He bore off the head pain to the breast of hell,
He sent down the malignant spectre to its
  hidden depth,
The relentless ghost he returned to its dwelling,
He overthrew the she-demon, sending it off to a
  mountain,
He replaced the ague in flood and sea.
He eradicated debility like a plant,
Uneasy sleep, excessive drowsiness,
He dissipated like smoke filling the sky.
The turning towards people with "Woe!" and
  "Alas!"
  he drove away like a cloud. ✶ ✶ ✶
The tenacious disease in the head,
  which was heavy as a millstone,
He raised like dew of night, he removed it from
  me.
My beclouded eyes,
  which were wrapped in the shroud of death,
He drove the cloud a thousand leagues away,
  he brightened my vision.
My ears, which were stopped
  and clogged like a deaf man's,
He removed their blockage, he opened my
  hearing.
My nose, whose breathing was choked
  by symptoms of fever,
He soothed its affliction so I could breathe
  freely.

My babbling lips, which had taken on a hard
      crust,
He wiped away their distress
      and undid their deformation.
My mouth, which was muffled,
      so that proper speech was difficult,
He scoured like copper and removed its filth.
My teeth, which were clenched
      and locked together firmly,
He opened their fastening, freed the jaws.
My tongue, which was tied and could not
      converse,
He wiped off its coating
      and its speech became fluent.
My windpipe, which was tight and choking,
      as though on a gobbet,
He made well and let it sing its songs like a
      flute.
My gullet, which was swollen so it could not
      take food,
Its swelling went down and he opened its
      blockage. * * *

FROM Tablet IV

The Lord took hold of me,
The Lord set me on my feet,
The Lord revived me,
He rescued me from the pit,
He summoned me from destruction,
He pulled me from the river of death.
He took my hand.
He who smote me,
Marduk, he restored me!
He smote the hand of my smiter,
It was Marduk who made him drop his weapon.

*   *   *

With prostration and supplication to Esagila[1]
I who went down to the grave
      have returned to the "Gate of Sunrise."
In the "Gate of Prosperity" prosperity was given
      me.[2]

In the "Gateway of the Guardian Spirit" a
      guardian spirit
      drew nigh to me.
In the "Gate of Well-being" I beheld well-
      being.
In the "Gate of Life" I was granted life.
In the "Gate of Sunrise" I was reckoned among
      the living.
In the "Gate of Splendid Wonderment"
      my signs were plain to see.
In the "Gate of Release from Guilt"
      I was released from my bond.
In the "Gate of Petition" my mouth made
      inquiry.
In the "Gate of Release from Sighing" my sighs
      were released.
In the "Gate of Pure Water"
      I was sprinkled with purifying water.
In the "Gate of Conciliation" I appeared with
      Marduk,
In the "Gate of Joy" I kissed the foot of
      Sarpanitum.
I was assiduous in supplication and prayer
      before them,
I placed fragrant incense before them,
An offering, a gift, sundry donations I
      presented,
Many fatted oxen I slaughtered, butchered
      many . . . ,
Honey-sweet beer and pure wine I repeatedly
      libated.
The protecting genius, the guardian spirit,
      divine attendants of the fabric of Esagila,
I made their feelings glow with libation,
I made them exultant with lavish meals.
To the threshold, the bolt socket, the bolt, the
      doors
I offered oil, butterfat, and choicest grain. * * *

*   *   *

I proceeded along Kunush-kadru Street in a state
      of redemption.
He who has done wrong by Esagila, let him
      learn from me.
It was Marduk who put a muzzle on the mouth
      of the lion

---

[1]Esagila was the temple of Marduk in Babylon. [Editor.]
[2]The gates mentioned here and in the following lines
were gates in Babylon. [Editor.]

that was devouring me.
Marduk took away the sling of my pursuer
and deflected his slingstone. ✳ ✳ ✳
The Babylonians saw how Marduk can restore to
   life,
And all mouths proclaimed his greatness,
"Who would have said he would see his sun?
"Who would have imagined
   that he would pass through his street?
"Who but Marduk revived him as he was dying?
"Besides Sarpanitum, which goddess
   bestowed his breath of life?
"Marduk can restore to life from the grave,
"Sarpanitum knows how to rescue from
   annihilation.
"Wherever earth is founded, heavens are
   stretched wide,
"Wherever sun shines, fire blazes,

"Wherever water runs, wind blows,
"Those whose bits of clay Aruru pinched off to
   form them,
"Those endowed with life, who walk upright,
"Teeming mankind, as many as they be,
give praise to Marduk!"

✳   ✳   ✳

REVIEW QUESTIONS

1. What does this text suggest about the values of Babylonian society?
2. What kinds of events counted as misfortune?
3. To what methods might people appeal as recourse against misfortune?

Letters of Royal Women of the Old Babylonian Period

Women's voices, though not completely silent, are all too infrequently heard in the documents of ancient Mesopotamia. Excavations earlier in this century recovered major portions of the palace archives (dating to the early second millennium B.C.E.) of the northern Mesopotamian cities of Mari and Karana, including cuneiform tablets containing letters to and from women of the royal houses of both places.

From *Mari and Karana: Two Old Babylonian Cities,* by Stephanie Dalley (Glenview, Ill.: Addison-Wesley Longman, 1984), pp. 104–9.

✳   ✳   ✳

Speak to Iltani, thus Yasitna-abum your son. May Shamash and Marduk grant that my mother live forever for my sake. My mother called my name, and my heart came alive. Now, do send me a letter saying how you are, and give me new life. Whenever I reread your letter, the dust-storms of Adad are forgotten; my heart is replenished with life. The servant boy whom my mother sent to me is far too young. For that servant boy does not keep *me* regularly supplied; it is I who have to keep *him* regularly supplied! Whenever I go on a journey, not even so much as 2 litres of bread for my ration is carried behind me. May my mother send me another servant boy who will be able to carry 10 litres of bread for my ration behind me, and who will be able really to help.

*   *   *

Speak to my lady; thus Belassunu. Ever since the harvest I have written frequently to you, but you have never sent me a reply of any kind. The king had spoken to me saying, "Stay in Zarbat. As soon as I come, Usi-nawir will come with me, and he will let you plead your innocence." Now, why are you silent? He neither lets me plead my innocence nor lets me go. You are near the ruler where you are: write, that they may take me back to the ruler. What have I done wrong? Why have you frowned upon me, and not pleaded my cause? Who will deal with the matter, and who has turned to help me?

*   *   *

Speak to my lord; thus Iltani thy servant. My lord wrote to me about letting go the oxen, sheep and donkeys belonging to Tazabru, saying: "If you do not let them go, I shall cut you into twelve pieces." That is what my lord wrote to me. Why has my lord written my death sentence to me? Only yesterday I spoke to my lord saying it was his own shepherd who had in the past kept his oxen and his sheep; he was pasturing them in Yashibatum. That is what I told my lord. Now, let my lord simply write that they are to take his oxen and sheep away from Yashibatum. If I have taken any of his oxen or sheep, may my lord inflict the punishment on me. Would I, without my lord's permission, would I have laid hands on and taken anything? Why then has my lord written my death sentence?

*   *   *

Speak to Iltani, my sister; thus Lamassani. I am well. The caravan comes regularly. You have never written to me to say how you are. I am still looking for a necklace of lapis lazuli, for which you wrote to me, and I shall send you a serving woman with it, but until now I have not found what you wrote for, and so I have not yet sent a slavegirl. Are you not aware that I am receiving short rations of barley? For in the city of Ashur, barley is expensive and linseed oil is expensive. Your son

Sin-rimeni often comes and goes, but you have never mentioned me to him; you have not heaped honour on my head in the household where I am staying. As you must be aware, I am receiving short rations: please provide me with barley and linseed oil.

*   *   *

Speak to Iltani my sister, thus Amat-Shamash your sister. May my divine lord and lady grant that you live forever for my sake. Previously when Aqba-hammu came to Sippar I gave him cause to honour my priesthood, and he honoured me greatly, for he said to me: "When I go back to Karana, write to me and I shall send you a boat full of whatever you need. Offer a prayer for me to your divine lord." Now, I have written, and he has provided me with two servants. But you have not recalled my name; you never even sent me so much as a single jar of perfume; you never said: "Approach and offer a prayer for me to your divine lady." Instead you say: "What do you think I am for?" Apart from you, does a girl who has washed her husband's feet for one day not send her own sister provisions from then onwards? And the slaves whom my father gave me have grown old. Now, I have sent half a mina of silver to the king. Allow me my claim, and let him send to me slaves that have been captured recently, and who are trustworthy. Now, in recollection of you, I have sent to you five minas of first-rate wool and a basket of "shrimps."

*   *   *

Speak to the lady my mother, thus Erishti-Aya your daughter. May my divine lord and lady grant you long life for my sake. Why didn't you ever wear my dress, but sent it back to me, and made me dishonoured and accursed? I am your daughter, and you are the wife of a king. . . . Your husband and you put me into the cloister; but the soldiers who were taken captive pay me more respect than you! You should pay me respect, and then my divine lord and lady will honour you with the good opinion of the city and its inhabitants. I am sending you a nanny. Do send me something to make me happy, and then I will be happy. Don't neglect me.

*　　*　　*

Speak to my star, my father and my lord, thus your daughter Kiru. It really was a sign when I spoke to you in the courtyard saying: "You are going away, and so you will not be able to direct the country; the country will become hostile behind you." That is what I said to my father and lord, but he didn't listen to me. . . . Now, if I am truly a woman, may my lord and father pay heed to my words—I am always writing the words of the gods to my father!

*　　*　　*

About my worries I have written twice to my lord, and my lord has written to me saying: "Go into Ashlakka and don't cry." My lord wrote that to me, and now I have entered Ashlakka and my worries have been fully justified! The wife of Ibal-Addu is queen all right; that woman takes it upon herself to receive personally every delivery for Ashlakka city and its towns. She made me sit in a corner holding my head in my hands like any idiot woman. Food and drink were regularly put in front of her, while my eyes envied and my mouth watered. She put a strong guard on me, and took no notice at all of appeals in my lord's name. So my fears have been fulfilled here . . . May my lord send someone to fetch me back to my lord, that I may look upon my lord's face.

*　　*　　*

REVIEW QUESTIONS

1. What kinds of roles and responsibilities did these women have?
2. What were their relationships with the other members of their families and households?

The Story of Sinuhe

This Middle Kingdom novel was one of the most popular works of Egyptian literature. It tells the tale of an Egyptian official named Sinuhe who became fearful in the wake of the king's assassination and fled into self-imposed exile in Asia where, despite much success, he finds himself longing for his homeland.

From *Ancient Egyptian Literature*, vol. 1, *The Old and Middle Kingdoms*, by Miriam Lichtheim (Berkeley: University of California Press, 1973), pp. 62–76.

The Prince, Count, Governor of the domains of the sovereign in the lands of the Asiatics, true and beloved Friend of the King, the Attendant Sinuhe, says:

I was an attendant who attended his lord, a servant of the royal harem, waiting on the Princess, the highly praised Royal Wife of King Sesostris in Khenemsut, the daughter of King Amenemhet in Kanefru, Nefru, the revered.

Year 30, third month of the inundation, day 7: the god ascended to his horizon. The King of Upper and Lower Egypt, *Sehetepibre*, flew to heaven and united with the sun-disk, the divine body merging with its maker. Then the residence was hushed; hearts grieved; the great portals were shut; the courtiers were head-on-knee; the people moaned.

His majesty, however, had despatched an army

to the land of the Tjemeh, with his eldest son as its commander, the good god Sesostris. He had been sent to smite the foreign lands and to punish those of Tjehenu. Now he was returning, bringing captives of the Tjehenu and cattle of all kinds beyond number. The officials of the palace sent to the western border to let the king's son know the event that had occurred at the court. The messengers met him on the road, reaching him at night. Not a moment did he delay. The falcon flew with his attendants, without letting his army know it.

But the royal sons who had been with him on this expedition had also been sent for. One of them was summoned while I was standing there. I heard his voice, as he spoke, while I was in the near distance. My heart fluttered, my arms spread out, a trembling befell all my limbs. I removed myself in leaps, to seek a hiding place. I put myself between two bushes, so as to leave the road to its traveler.

I set out southward. I did not plan to go to the residence. I believed there would be turmoil and did not expect to survive it. I crossed Maaty near Sycamore; I reached Isle-of-Snefru. I spent the day there at the edge of the cultivation. Departing at dawn I encountered a man who stood on the road. He saluted me while I was afraid of him. At dinner time I reached "Cattle-Quay." I crossed in a barge without a rudder, by the force of the westwind. I passed to the east of the quarry, at the height of "Mistress of the Red Mountain." Then I made my way northward. I reached the "Walls of the Ruler," which were made to repel the Asiatics and to crush the Sand-farers. I crouched in a bush for fear of being seen by the guard on duty upon the wall.

I set out at night. At dawn I reached Peten. I halted at "Isle-of-Kem-Wer." An attack of thirst overtook me; I was parched, my throat burned. I said, "This is the taste of death." I raised my heart and collected myself when I heard the lowing sound of cattle and saw Asiatics. One of their leaders, who had been in Egypt, recognized me. He gave me water and boiled milk for me. I went with him to his tribe. What they did for me was good.

Land gave me to land. I traveled to Byblos; I returned to Qedem. I spent a year and a half there. Then Ammunenshi, the ruler of Upper Retenu, took me to him, saying to me: "You will be happy with me; you will hear the language of Egypt." He said this because he knew my character and had heard of my skill, Egyptians who were with him having borne witness for me. He said to me: "Why have you come here? Has something happened at the residence?" I said to him: "King Sehetepibre departed to the horizon, and one did not know the circumstances." But I spoke in half-truths: "When I returned from the expedition to the land of the Tjemeh, it was reported to me and my heart grew faint. It carried me away on the path of flight, though I had not been talked about; no one had spat in my face; I had not heard a reproach; my name had not been heard in the mouth of the herald. I do not know what brought me to this country; it is as if planned by god. As if a Delta-man saw himself in Yebu, a marsh-man in Nubia."

Then he said to me: "How then is that land without that excellent god, fear of whom was throughout the lands like Sakhmet in a year of plague?" I said to him in reply: "Of course his son has entered into the palace, having taken his father's heritage.

He is a god without peer,
No other comes before him;
He is lord of knowledge, wise planner, skilled
    leader,
One goes and comes by his will.

He was the smiter of foreign lands,
While his father stayed in the palace,
He reported to him on commands carried out.

He is a champion who acts with his arm,
A fighter who has no equal,
When seen engaged in archery,
When joining the melee.

Horn-curber who makes hands turn weak,
His foes can not close ranks;
Keen-sighted he smashes foreheads,
None can withstand his presence.

Wide-striding he smites the fleeing,
No retreat for him who turns him his back;
Steadfast in time of attack,
He makes turn back and turns not his back.

Stouthearted when he sees the mass,
He lets not slackness fill his heart;
Eager at the sight of combat,
Joyful when he works his bow.

Clasping his shield he treads under foot,
No second blow needed to kill;
None can escape his arrow,
None turn aside his bow.

The Bowmen flee before him,
As before the might of the goddess;
As he fights he plans the goal,
Unconcerned about all else.

Lord of grace, rich in kindness,
He has conquered through affection;
His city loves him more than itself,
Acclaims him more than its own god.

Men outdo women in hailing him,
Now that he is king;
Victor while yet in the egg,
Set to be ruler since his birth.

Augmenter of those born with him,
He is unique, god-given;
Happy the land that he rules!

Enlarger of frontiers,
He will conquer southern lands,
While ignoring northern lands,
Though made to smite Asiatics and tread on Sand-
  farers!

"Send to him! Let him know your name as one who inquires while being far from his majesty. He will not fail to do good to a land that will be loyal to him."

He said to me: "Well then, Egypt is happy knowing that he is strong. But you are here. You shall stay with me. What I shall do for you is good."

He set me at the head of his children. He married me to his eldest daughter. He let me choose for myself of his land, of the best that was his, on his border with another land. It was a good land called Yaa. Figs were in it and grapes. It had more wine than water. Abundant was its honey, plentiful its oil. All kinds of fruit were on its trees. Barley was there and emmer, and no end of cattle of all kinds. Much also came to me because of the love of me; for he had made me chief of a tribe in the best part of his land. Loaves were made for me daily, and wine as daily fare, cooked meat, roast fowl, as well as desert game. For they snared for me and laid it before me, in addition to the catch of my hounds. Many sweets were made for me, and milk dishes of all kinds.

I passed many years, my children becoming strong men, each a master of his tribe. The envoy who came north or went south to the residence stayed with me. I let everyone stay with me. I gave water to the thirsty; I showed the way to him who had strayed; I rescued him who had been robbed. When Asiatics conspired to attack the Rulers of Hill-Countries, I opposed their movements. For this ruler of Retenu made me carry out numerous missions as commander of his troops. Every hill tribe against which I marched I vanquished, so that it was driven from the pasture of its wells. I plundered its cattle, carried off its families, seized their food, and killed people by my strong arm, by my bow, by my movements and my skillful plans. I won his heart and he loved me, for he recognized my valor. He set me at the head of his children, for he saw the strength of my arms.

There came a hero of Retenu,
To challenge me in my tent.
A champion was he without peer,
He had subdued it all.
He said he would fight with me,
He planned to plunder me,
He meant to seize my cattle
At the behest of his tribe.

The ruler conferred with me and I said: "I do not know him; I am not his ally, that I could walk about in his camp. Have I ever opened his back rooms or climbed over his fence? It is envy, because he sees me doing your commissions. I am indeed like a stray bull in a strange herd, whom the bull of the herd charges, whom the longhorn attacks. Is an inferior beloved when he becomes a superior? No Asiatic makes friends with a Delta-man. And what would make papyrus cleave to the mountain? If a bull loves combat, should a champion bull retreat for fear of being equaled? If he wishes to fight, let him declare his wish. Is there a god who does not know what he has ordained, and a man who knows how it will be?"

At night I strung my bow, sorted my arrows, practiced with my dagger, polished my weapons. When it dawned Retenu came. It had assembled its tribes; it had gathered its neighboring peoples; it was intent on this combat.

He came toward me while I waited, having placed myself near him. Every heart burned for me; the women jabbered. All hearts ached for me thinking: "Is there another champion who could fight him?" He raised his battle-axe and shield, while his armful of missiles fell toward me. When I had made his weapons attack me, I let his arrows pass me by without effect, one following the other. Then, when he charged me, I shot him, my arrow sticking in his neck. He screamed; he fell on his nose; I slew him with his axe. I raised my war cry over his back, while every Asiatic shouted. I gave praise to Mont, while his people mourned him. The ruler Ammunenshi took me in his arms.

Then I carried off his goods; I plundered his cattle. What he had meant to do to me I did to him. I took what was in his tent; I stripped his camp. Thus I became great, wealthy in goods, rich in herds. It was the god who acted, so as to show mercy to one with whom he had been angry, whom he had made stray abroad. For today his heart is appeased.

> A fugitive fled his surroundings—
>   I am famed at home.
> A laggard lagged from hunger—
>   I give bread to my neighbor.
> A man left his land in nakedness—
>   I have bright clothes, fine linen.
> A man ran for lack of one to send—
>   I am rich in servants.

> My house is fine, my dwelling spacious—
>   My thoughts are at the palace!

Whichever god decreed this flight, have mercy, bring me home! Surely you will let me see the place in which my heart dwells! What is more important than that my corpse be buried in the land in which I was born! Come to my aid! What if the happy event should occur! May god pity me! May he act so as to make happy the end of one whom he punished! May his heart ache for one whom he forced to live abroad! If he is truly appeased today, may he hearken to the prayer of one far away! May he return one whom he made roam the earth to the place from which he carried him off!

May Egypt's king have mercy on me, that I may live by his mercy! May I greet the mistress of the land who is in the palace! May I hear the commands of her children! Would that my body were young again! For old age has come; feebleness has overtaken me. My eyes are heavy, my arms weak; my legs fail to follow. The heart is weary; death is near. May I be conducted to the city of eternity! May I serve the Mistress of All! May she speak well of me to her children; may she spend eternity above me!

Now when the majesty of King Kheperkare was told of the condition in which I was, his majesty sent word to me with royal gifts, in order to gladden the heart of this servant like that of a foreign ruler. And the royal children who were in his palace sent me their messages. Copy of the decree brought to this servant concerning his return to Egypt:

Horus: Living in Births; the Two Ladies: Living in Births; the King of Upper and Lower Egypt; *Kheperkare*; the Son of Re: *Sesostris*, who lives forever. Royal decree to the Attendant Sinuhe:

This decree of the King is brought to you to let you know: That you circled the foreign countries, going from Qedem to Retenu, land giving you to land, was the counsel of your own heart. What had you done that one should act against you? You had not cursed, so that your speech would be reproved. You had not spoken against the counsel of the nobles, that your words should have been rejected. This matter—it carried away your heart. It was not in my heart against you. This your heaven in the palace lives and prospers to this day. Her head is adorned with the kingship of the land; her children are in the palace. You will store riches which they give you; you will live on their bounty. Come back to Egypt! See the residence in which you lived! Kiss the ground at the great portals, mingle with the courtiers! For today you have begun to age. You have lost a man's strength. Think of the day of burial, the passing into reveredness.

A night is made for you with ointments and wrappings from the hand of Tait. A funeral procession is made for you on the day of burial; the mummy case is of gold, its head of lapis lazuli. The sky is above you as you lie in the hearse, oxen drawing you, musicians going before you. The dance of the *mww*-dancers is done at the door of your tomb; the offering-list is read to you; sacrifice is made before your offering-stone. Your tomb-pillars, made of white stone, are among those of the royal children. You shall not die abroad! Not shall Asiatics inter you. You shall not be wrapped in the skin of a ram to serve as your coffin. Too long a roaming of the earth! Think of your corpse, come back!

This decree reached me while I was standing in the midst of my tribe. When it had been read to me, I threw myself on my belly. Having touched the soil, I spread it on my chest. I strode around my camp shouting: "What compares with this which is done to a servant whom his heart led astray to alien lands? Truly good is the kindness that saves me from death! Your *ka* will grant me to reach my end, my body being at home!"

Copy of the reply to this decree:

The servant of the Palace, Sinuhe, says: In very good peace! Regarding the matter of this flight which this servant did in his ignorance. It is your *ka*, O good god, lord of the Two Lands, which Re loves and which Mont lord of Thebes favors; and Amun lord of Thrones-of-the-Two-Lands, and Sobk-Re lord of Sumenu, and Horus, Hathor, Atum with his Ennead, and Sopdu-Neferbau-Semseru the Eastern Horus, and the Lady of Yemet—may she enfold your head—and the conclave upon the flood, and Min-Horus of the hill-countries, and Wereret lady of Punt, Nut, Haroeris-Re, and all the gods of Egypt and the isles of the sea—may they give life and joy to your nostrils, may they endue you with their bounty, may they give you eternity without limit, infinity without bounds! May the fear of you resound in lowlands and highlands, for you have subdued all that the sun encircles! This is the prayer of this servant for his lord who saves from the West.

The lord of knowledge who knows people knew in the majesty of the palace that this servant was afraid to say it. It is like a thing too great to repeat. The great god, the peer of Re, knows the heart of one who has served him willingly. This servant is in the hand of one who thinks about him. He is placed under his care. Your Majesty is the conquering Horus; your arms vanquish all lands. May then your Majesty command to have brought to you the prince of Meki from Qedem, the mountain chiefs from Keshu, and the prince of Menus from the lands of the Fenkhu. They are rulers of renown who have grown up in the love of you. I do not mention Retenu—it belongs to you like your hounds.

Lo, this flight which the servant made—I did not plan it. It was not in my heart; I did not devise it. I do not know what removed me from my place. It was like a dream. As if a Delta-man saw himself in Yebu, a marsh-man in Nubia. I was not afraid; no one ran after me. I had not heard a reproach; my name was not heard in the mouth of the herald. Yet my flesh crept, my feet hurried, my heart drove me; the god who had willed this flight dragged me away. Nor am I a haughty man. He who knows his land respects men. Re has set the fear of you throughout the land, the dread of you in every foreign country. Whether I am at the residence, whether I am in this place, it is you who covers this horizon. The sun rises at your pleasure. The water in the river is drunk when you wish. The air of heaven is breathed at your bidding. This servant will hand over to the brood which this servant begot in this place. This servant has been sent for! Your Majesty will do as he wishes! One lives by the breath which you give. As Re, Horus, and Hathor love your august nose, may Mont lord of Thebes wish it to live forever!

I was allowed to spend one more day in Yaa, handing over my possessions to my children, my eldest son taking charge of my tribe; all my possessions became his—my serfs, my herds, my fruit, my fruit trees. This servant departed southward. I halted at Horusways. The commander in charge of the garrison sent a message to the residence to let it be known. Then his majesty sent a trusted overseer of the royal domains with whom were loaded ships, bearing royal gifts for the Asiatics who had come with me to escort me to Horusways. I called each one by his name, while every butler was at his task. When I had started and set sail, there was kneading and straining beside me, until I reached the city of Itj-tawy.

When it dawned, very early, they came to summon me. Ten men came and ten men went to usher me into the palace. My forehead touched the ground between the sphinxes, and the royal children stood in the gateway to meet me. The courtiers who usher through the forecourt set me on the way to the audience-hall. I found his majesty on the great throne in a kiosk of gold. Stretched out on my belly, I did not know myself before him, while this god greeted me pleasantly. I was like a man seized by darkness. My *ba* was gone, my limbs trembled; my heart was not in my body, I did not know life from death.

His majesty said to one of the courtiers: "Lift him up, let him speak to me." Then his majesty said: "Now you have come, after having roamed foreign lands. Flight has taken its toll of you. You have aged, have reached old age. It is no small matter that your corpse will be interred without being escorted by Bowmen. But don't act thus, don't act thus, speechless though your name was called!" Fearful of punishment I answered with the answer of a frightened man: "What has my lord said to me, that I might answer it? It is not disrespect to the god! It is the terror which is in my body, like that which caused the fateful flight! Here I am before you. Life is yours. May your Majesty do as he wishes!"

Then the royal daughters were brought in, and his majesty said to the queen: "Here is Sinuhe, come as an Asiatic, a product of nomads!" She uttered a very great cry, and the royal daughters shrieked all together. They said to his majesty: "Is it really he, O king, our lord?" Said his majesty: "It is really he!" Now having brought with them their necklaces, rattles, and sistra, they held them out to his majesty.

Your hands upon the radiance, eternal king,
Jewels of heaven's mistress!
The Gold gives life to your nostrils,
The Lady of Stars enfolds you!

Southcrown fared north, northcrown south,
Joined, united by your majesty's word.
While the Cobra decks your brow,
You deliver the poor from harm.
Peace to you from Re, Lord of Lands!
Hail to you and the Mistress of All!

Slacken your bow, lay down your arrow,
Give breath to him who gasps for breath!
Give us our good gift on this good day,
Grant us the son of northwind, Bowman born in
    Egypt!

He made the flight in fear of you,
He left the land in dread of you!
A face that sees you shall not pale,
Eyes that see you shall not fear!

His majesty said: "He shall not fear, he shall not dread!" He shall be a Companion among the nobles. He shall be among the courtiers. Proceed to the robing-room to wait on him!"

I left the audience-hall, the royal daughters giving me their hands. We went through the great portals, and I was put in the house of a prince. In it were luxuries: a bathroom and mirrors. In it were riches from the treasury; clothes of royal linen, myrrh, and the choice perfume of the king and of his favorite courtiers were in every room. Every servant was at his task. Years were removed from my body. I was shaved; my hair was combed. Thus was my squalor returned to the foreign land, my dress to the Sand-farers. I was clothed in fine linen; I was anointed with fine oil. I slept on a bed. I had returned the sand to those who dwell in it, the tree-oil to those who grease themselves with it.

I was given a house and garden that had belonged to a courtier. Many craftsmen rebuilt it, and all its woodwork was made anew. Meals were brought to me from the palace three times, four times a day, apart from what the royal children gave without a moment's pause.

A stone pyramid was built for me in the midst of the pyramids. The masons who build tombs constructed it. A master draughtsman designed in it. A master sculptor carved in it. The overseers of construction in the necropolis busied themselves with it. All the equipment that is placed in a tomb-shaft was supplied. Mortuary priests were given

me. A funerary domain was made for me. It had fields and a garden in the right place, as is done for a Companion of the first rank. My statue was overlaid with gold, its skirt with electrum. It was his majesty who ordered it made. There is no commoner for whom the like has been done. I was in the favor of the king, until the day of landing came.

REVIEW QUESTIONS

1. What kind of image of the king does this story present?
2. What is the story's view of non-Egyptians?
3. What are the chief reasons why Sinuhe, as he grows older, wishes to return home?

"The Hymn of Victory of Thutmose III"

The following hymn, which was inscribed in the temple of the god Amun (or Amon) at Karnak (in Thebes), glorifies the conquests of Thutmose III, perhaps the greatest of all the warrior pharaohs of the New Kingdom, whose many victorious campaigns into Palestine and Syria established Egypt's empire there. Later pharaohs, including Ramesses III of Dynasty 20, borrowed freely from it in their own compositions. Evident throughout is the nature of the relationship between Amun and the king, as well as the Egyptian view of the king's appropriate attitude and actions toward outsiders. (As you read, be aware of the following probable identifications: Naharin, a region of Syria/Mesopotamia; Djahi, roughly the coast of modern Syria and Lebanon; Retenu, the Syria-Palestine highlands; Keftiu, Crete; Isy, Cyprus; the Tehenu, Libyans; the Utentiu, perhaps people south of Egypt; and Shat-Djeba, somewhere in Nubia.)

Ancient Near Eastern Texts Relating to the Old Testament, edited by James B. Pritchard (Princeton, N. J.: Princeton University Press, 1950), pp. 373–375.

Words spoken by Amon-Re, Lord of the Thrones of the Two Lands:

Welcome to me, as thou exultest at the sight of my beauty, my son and my avenger, Men-kheper-Re, living forever! I shine forth for

love of thee, and my heart is glad at thy good comings into my temple, while my hands endow thy body with protection and life. How sweet is thy graciousness toward my breast!

I establish thee in my dwelling place. I *work a*

wonder for thee: I give thee valor and victory over all foreign countries; I set the glory of thee and the fear of thee in all lands, the terror of thee as far as the four supports of heaven. I magnify the awe of thee in all bodies. I set the battle cry of thy majesty throughout the Nine Bows.

The great ones of all foreign countries are gathered together in thy grasp. I stretch out my own arms, and I tie them up for thee; I bind the barbarians of Nubia by ten-thousands and thousands, the northerners by hundred-thousands as living captives. I cause thy opponents to fall beneath thy sandals, so that thou crushest the quarrelsome and the disaffected of heart, according as I have commended to thee the earth in its length and its breadth, so that westerners and easterners are under thy oversight.

Thou treadest all foreign countries, thy heart glad. There is none who can thrust himself into the vicinity of thy majesty, while I am thy guide, (but) thou reachest them (thyself). Thou hast crossed the waters of the Great Bend of Naharin [the Euphrates] by the victory and by the power which I have decreed to thee. They hear thy battle cry, having entered into caves. I have cut their nostrils off from the breath of life, so that I might set the dread of thy majesty throughout their hearts. My serpent-diadem which is upon thy head, she consumes them; she makes a speedy prey among *those twisted of nature;* she devours those who are in their islands by her flame; she cuts off the heads of the Asiatics. There is none of them missing, (but they are) fallen and *in travail* because of her might.

I cause thy victories to circulate in all lands. The gleaming (serpent), she who is upon my brow, is thy servant, (so that) there shall arise none rebellious to thee as far as that which heaven encircles. They come, bearing tribute upon their backs, bowing down to thy majesty, as I decree. I have made the aggressors who come near thee grow weak, for their hearts are burned up and their bodies are trembling.

I have come,
    That I may cause thee to trample down the
        great ones of Djahi;

I spread them out under thy feet throughout
    their countries.
I cause them to see thy majesty as the lord of
    radiance,
    So that thou shinest into their faces as my
        likeness.
I have come,
    That I may cause thee to trample down those
        who are in Asia;
    Thou smitest the heads of the Asiatics of Retenu.
I cause them to see thy majesty equipped with thy
    adornment,
    As thou takest the weapons of war in the
        chariot.
I have come,
    That I may cause thee to trample down the
        eastern land;
    Thou treadest upon those who are in the
        regions of God's Land.
I cause them to see thy majesty as a *shooting* star,
    Sowing its fire in a flame, as it gives off its
        steam.
I have come,
    That I may cause thee to trample down the
        western land;
    Keftiu and Isy are under the awe (of thee).
I cause them to see thy majesty as a young bull,
    Firm of heart, sharp of horns, who cannot be
        felled.
I have come,
    That I may cause thee to trample down those
        who are in their islands;
    The lands of Mitanni are trembling under the
        fear of thee,
I cause them to see thy majesty as a crocodile,
    The lord of fear in the water, who cannot be
        approached.
I have come,
    That I may cause thee to trample down those
        who are in the islands;
    They who are in the midst of the Great Green
        Sea [the Mediterranean] are under thy battle
        cry.
I cause them to see thy majesty as the Avenger
    Appearing in glory on the back of his sacrifice.
I have come,

THE EGYPTIAN KING AND SUBJECT PEOPLES (C. 1380 B.C.E.)

The New Kingdom was a period of Egyptian domination in Syria-Palestine and in the Nubian regions of Africa south of Egypt. This image from a Dynasty 18 tomb painting from Thebes shows the pharoah Amunhotep III and his queen, Tiye, seated on thrones in their palace. The dais on which their thrones sit is decorated with scenes of foreigners from Egypt's imperial dominions, bound and kneeling. The images on the king's footstool likewise are of foreigners. What do these images suggest about the Egyptian view of the relationship between king and empire? How are the foreigners depicted as different from Egyptians? How are they distinguished from each other?

That I may cause thee to trample down the
Tehenu;
The Utentiu belong to the might of thy glory.
I cause them to see thy majesty as a fierce lion,
As thou makest them corpses throughout their
valleys.
I have come,
That I may cause thee to trample down the ends
of the lands;
That which the Ocean encircles is enclosed
within thy grasp.
I cause them to see thy majesty as a lord of the
wing,
Taking possession of what he sees as he wishes.
I have come,
That I may cause thee to trample down the
front of the land;
Thou bindest the Sand-Dwellers as living
captives.
I cause them to see thy majesty like a jackal of the
Southland,
The lord of speed, the runner coursing the Two
Lands.
I have come,
That I may cause thee to trample down the bar-
barians of Nubia;
As far as *Shat-Djeba* is in thy grip.
I cause them to see thy majesty like thy two broth-
ers;

I have joined their hands together for thee in
victory.

Thy two sisters (also), I have set them in protection behind thee, while the arms of my majesty
are uplifting, warding off evil. I give thy protection, my son, my beloved, Horus: Mighty Bull,
Appearing in Thebes, whom I begot in the divine
[body], Thutmose, living forever, who has done
for me all that my *ka* desires.

Thou hast erected my dwelling place as the
work of eternity, made longer and wider than that
which had been before, and the very great gateway
(named) [*Men-kheper-Re*], *whose Beauty Makes
Festive the [House of] Amon.* Thy monuments are
greater than (those of) any king who has been. I
commanded thee to make them, and I am satisfied
with them. I have established thee upon the throne
of Horus for millions of years, that thou mightest
lead the living for eternity.

REVIEW QUESTIONS

1. What does this document reveal about pharaoh's relationship with the god Amun and
about the nature of ancient Egyptian kingship?
2. What does it show about the Egyptians' attitude toward the conquered people of their
empire?

Akhenaton's "Hymn to the Aton"

*The nature of the relationship between the king and the gods and the religious focus
of the Egyptian royal court took on a significant (though short-lived) new direction
during the reign of the New Kingdom pharaoh Amunhotep IV, better known to history by the name he assumed, Akhenaton ("Beloved of the Aton"). Referred to by
some today as the heretic pharaoh, Akhenaton tried to redirect worship in the Egyptian royal court to an almost exclusive focus on the Aton, the personification of the
sun's power as manifested in the sun disk. Many have seen in this an important
precursor of the Hebrews' monotheism centered on their god, Yahweh; some, in fact,
have claimed that the Hebrews derived their monotheism from learning of Akhena-*

ton's reform during their captivity in Egypt (as described in the Hebrew Bible's Book of Exodus). The following hymn is generally ascribed to Akhenaton himself and shows some interesting parallels to Psalm 104 in the Hebrew Bible.

From *Hymns, Prayers, and Songs: An Anthology of Ancient Egyptian Lyric Poetry,* translated by John L. Foster, SBL Writings from the Ancient World Series, vol. 8 (Atlanta, Ga.: Scholars Press, 1995), pp. 154–58.

In Praise of the living Horakhty who rejoices in the Horizon in his Name of the divine Light which is in the Sundisk, living eternally and forever, the living Aton, Great One who is in the Festival, Lord of all the sundisk circles, Lord of Heaven, Lord of Earth, Living on Maat, Lord of the Two Lands, Nefer-kheper-rê Wa-en-rê, Son of the Sun, Who lives on Maat, Lord of Appearances, Akhenaton, One Great in his Time; and the Great Royal Wife, whom he loves, Mistress of the Two Lands, Nefer-neferu-aten Nefertiti, living, healthy, flourishing forever and eternity. He says:

i

May you always appear thus gloriously in the
    horizon of the sky,
  O living Aton, origin of life!
Arisen from the eastern horizon,
  you have filled all earth with your splendor;
You are beautiful, great, dazzling, exalted above
    each land,
    yet your rays encompass the lands
      to the limits of all which you have created;
There in the Sun, you reach to their boundaries,
  making them bow to your Son, whom you
    love;
And though you are far, your rays are over the
    earth,
  and you are in the faces of those who watch
    your journeying.

ii

You go to rest in the western horizon,
  and earth is in a darkness like death,

With the sleepers in bedchambers, heads
    covered—
    the eye cannot discern its companion;
All their goods might be carried off—
  though they are near—without their knowing.
Every lion comes forth from his doorway,
  insects and snakes bite and sting;
Darkness shrouds, earth is silent—
  he who created them is at rest in his tomb.

iii

Dawn rises shining on the horizon,
  gleams from the sundisk as day.
You scatter the darkness, bestow your sunbeams,
  and the Two Lands offer thanksgiving.
The Sunfolk awaken and stand on their feet,
  for you have raised them up;
Their bodies are bathed, they put on their
    clothing,
  their arms raised in praise at your appearing.
Throughout the land
  they take up their work.

iv

The herds are at peace in their meadows,
  trees and the vegetation grow green,
Birds fly from their nests,
  their wings spread wide in praise of your
    Person;
All the small beasts leap about on their feet,
  and all who fly up or settle to rest
    live because you have shone upon them.
Ships go downstream or upstream as well,
  each path lies open because of your
    presence;

The fish in the River dart about in your sight,
and your beams are deep in the Great Green
Sea.

v

It is you who create the seed in women,
shape the fluids into human beings,
Make the son alive in the womb of his mother,
soothe him, ending his tears,
Nurturer from the womb to those given breath
to bring into life all that he has created.
He descends from the womb to breathe
on the day of his birth,
And you open his mouth, determine his nature,
and minister to his needs.

vi

The fledgling in the egg speaks in the shell,
so you give him breath within it to succor
him;
And you have given to him his allotted time
so that he might break out from the egg
To come forth peeping at that time
and move about upon his own two feet
when he emerges from it.

vii

How various are the things you have created,
and they are all mysterious to the sight!
O sole God, without another of your kind,
you created the world according to your
desire,
while you were alone,
With mankind and cattle and every sort of small
beast,
all those upon land, those who go upon feet,
Those who are on high soaring upon their
wings,
the foreign lands of Khor and Kush,
and all that belongs to Egypt.

viii

You give each person his place in life,
and you provide for his needs;
Each one has his sustenance,
and his lifetime is reckoned for him.
Tongues are separated by words,
the natures of persons as well;
And their skins are made different
so you can distinguish the peoples.

ix

You create Hapy, the Nile, in the Underworld
to bring him, at your desire, to nourish the
people,
Just as you create them for yourself,
Lord of them all, who is weary for them,
O Lord of all earth, who shines for them,
O Aton of day, awesome in majesty.
All the foreign lands are far away,
yet you make their lives possible,
For you have placed a Hapy in the sky
that he might come down upon them—
Making waves upon the mountains like those of
the Great Green Sea
to water the fields in their villages.

x

How well ordered it is, your governing,
O Lord of Eternity, Hapy in heaven!
You belong to the foreign peoples,
to the small beasts of each land who go upon
feet.
And Hapy comes from Below to beloved Egypt
as well,
while your rays are nursing each meadow.
You shine, and they live,
they grow strong for you;
You fashion the seasons to make all your
creation flourish—
the winter for cooling
and the heat which ripens;
And you have made the sky far off

in order to shine down from it,
  to watch over all you have created.

xi

You are one alone,
  shining forth in your visible Form as the
    living Aton,
Glorious, giving light,
  far-off yet approaching nearby.
You create the numberless visible forms from
    yourself—
  you who are one alone—
Cities, towns, fields, the road, the River;
  and each eye looks to you as its shining
    example:
You are in the sun-disk of day,
  overseer of wherever you go and whatever
    shall be;
For you fashion their sight so that you may be
    complete—
  as they celebrate with one voice your creation.

xii

And you are in my heart;
  there is no other who knows you
Except for your son, Akhenaton,
  Nefer-kheper-rê Wa-en-rê.
Let him be wise with your counsel, your
    strength,
  that the world may approach your condition

just as when you created it.
You have risen, and they are alive;
  you go to rest, and they die.
For you are the measure of Time itself,
  one lives by means of you.
Eyes shall be filled with beauty until your
    setting;
  all labor is set aside when you go to rest in
    the West.
Then rise! Let the creatures of earth thrive for
    the king!
  And let me hasten on with every footstep
    as I have since you founded the world.
And raise them up for your son
  who came forth from your very body.

The King of Upper and Lower Egypt, who lives
on Truth, Lord of the Two Lands, Nefer-Kheper-
Rê Wa-en-rê, son of the Sun, who lives on Truth,
Lord of Appearances, Akhenaton, one exalted in
his own lifetime; and the Great Royal Wife, whom
he loves, Nefer-neferu-aton Nefertiti, who lives
and flourishes for eternity and everlasting.

REVIEW QUESTIONS

1. What kinds of powers does this hymn ascribe
   to the Aton?
2. What is the king's relationship to his newly elevated god?

A Letter from Tell el-Amarna

Eager to establish firmly the supremacy of the Aton, Akhenaton decided to move his court to a virgin site. He built there a new capital that he named Akhetaton, the remains of which are located at Tell el-Amarna. In the early 1880s, Egyptian fella-heen (laborers) digging for decayed mud brick (an excellent fertilizer) in the tell came across a collection of clay tablets, inscribed in cuneiform, that turned out to be a portion of the diplomatic correspondence addressed to the Egyptian royal court. Written in the Akkadian language of Mesopotamia, most of these letters were from

Egypt's vassals in Palestine and Syria, but many are letters from the kings of the other great powers of the ancient Near East during the mid-fourteenth century B.C.E. The following letter to pharaoh is from the king of Mittani, a Hurrian state in northern Syria and Mesopotamia which, until the then-recent reemergence of the Hittites, had been Egypt's chief rival for control of Syria and Palestine.

From *The Amarna Letters,* edited and translated by William L. Moran (Baltimore: Johns Hopkins University Press, 1992), pp 43–45.

Say to Nimmureya, Great King, the king of Egypt, my brother, my son-in-law, who loves me, and whom I love: Message of Tušratta, Great King, your father-in-law, who loves you, the king of Mittani, your brother. For me all goes well. For you may all go well. For your household, for my sister, for the rest of your wives, for your sons, for your chariots, for your horses, for your *warriors,* for your country, and for whatever else belongs to you, may all go very, very well.

As far back as the time of your ancestors, they always showed love to my ancestors. You yourself went even further and showed very great love to my father. Now, in keeping with our constant and mutual love, you have made it ten times greater than the love shown my father. May the gods grant it, and may Teššup, my lord, and Aman make *flour[ish]* for evermore, just as it is now, this mutual love of ours.

When my brother sent Mane, his messenger, saying, "Send your daughter here to be my wife and the mistress of Egypt," I caused my brother no distress and *immediately* I said, "Of course!" The one whom my brother requested I showed to Mane, and he saw her. When he saw her, he praised her greatly. I will *lead* her in safety to my brother's country. May Šauška and Aman make her the image of my brother's desire.

Keliya, my messenger, *brought* my brother's words to me, and when I heard them, they were very pleasing, and I rejoiced very, very much, saying, "*Certainly* there is this between us: we love each other." Now, with such words let us love each other forevermore.

When I wrote to my brother, I said, "Let us love each other very, very much, and between us let there be friendship." I also said to my brother, "May my brother treat me ten times better than he did my father."

I also asked my brother for much gold, saying, "May my brother grant me more than he did to my father and send it to me. You sent my father much gold. You sent him large gold jars and gold jugs. You sent him gold bricks as if they *were just the equivalent of* copper."

When I sent Keliya to my brother, I asked for much gold, saying, "May my brother treat me ten times better than he did my father, and may he send much gold that has not been worked."

May my brother send me much more than he did to my father. Thus did I say to my brother: "I am going to build a *mausoleum* for my grandfather." I also said, "In accordance with a favorable *answer,* I am going to make the paraphernalia." And thus did I also say: "The gold that my brother sends me may he send for the bride-price as well."

Now my brother has sent the gold. I say, "It may be little or not, not a little but much. Still, it has been worked. But though it has been worked, I rejoiced over it much, and whatever it was my brother sent, I am happy about it."

I now hereby write to my brother, and may my brother show me much more love than he did to my father. I hereby ask for gold from my brother, and the gold that I ask for from my brother is meant for a double purpose: one, for the *mausoleum,* and the other, for the bride-price.

May my brother send me in very great quantities gold that has not been worked, and may my brother send me much more gold than he did to my father. In my brother's country, gold is as plentiful as dirt. May the gods grant that, just as now gold is plentiful in my brother's country, he make it even ten times more plentiful than now. May the gold that I ask for not become a source of distress to my brother, and may my brother not cause me distress. May my brother send me in very large quantities gold that has not been worked. Whatever my brother needs for his house, let him write and take it. I will give ten times more than what my brother asks for. This country is my brother's country, and this house is my brother's house.

I herewith send my messenger, Keliya, to my brother, and may my brother not detain him. May he let him go promptly so that he may be on his way and I hear my brother's greeting and rejoice exceedingly. Forevermore may I constantly hear the greeting of my brother. May Teššup, my lord, and Aman grant that these words that we shall be constantly writing achieve their *purpose,* and may they be, as long as they exist, just as they are now. Just as we love each other now, exactly as now, so may we love each other forevermore.

I herewith send as my brother's greeting-gift:

1 gold goblet, with inlays of genuine lapis lazuli in its handle, 1 *maninnu*-necklace, with a *counterweight,* 20 pieces of genuine lapis lazuli, and 19 pieces of gold, its centerpiece being of genuine lapis lazuli set in gold; 1 *maninnu*-necklace, with a *counterweight,* 42 genuine *hulalu*-stones, and 40 pieces of gold shaped like *arzallu*-stones, its centerpiece being of genuine *hulalu*-stone set in gold; 10 teams of horses; 10 wooden-chariots along with everything belonging to them; and 30 women (and) men.

REVIEW QUESTIONS

1. How does the king of Mittani address the pharaoh, and what does that imply about the nature of their relationship?
2. How does that compare to the view of Asiatics encountered in the preceding readings?
3. How were relations solidified between the great powers of the fourteenth century B.C.E.?
4. In particular, what is the role of royal women in international diplomacy?

FROM The Letters of Deir el-Medina

Tomb and temple inscriptions, as well as the more formal works of Egyptian literature, communicate an idealized view of authority, social values, and correct behavior. To that idealized perspective we can compare the straightforward, unvarnished, often emotionally charged letters recovered from the site of Deir el-Medina, near Thebes, where lived several generations of the foremen, artists, and artisans responsible for constructing and decorating the magnificent New Kingdom royal tombs in the Valley of the Kings.

From *Letters from Ancient Egypt,* translated by Edward Wente, SBL Writings from the Ancient World Series, vol. 1 (Atlanta, Ga.: Scholars Press, 1990), pp. 140–49.

On Fortunetelling

Kenhikhopeshef addresses the woman Inerwau:

What means your failing to go to the woman diviner on account of the two infants who died while in your charge? Inquire of the woman diviner about the death of the two infants, whether it was their fate or their destiny. And you shall inquire about them for me and get a view of my own life and their mother's life. As for whatever god shall be mentioned to you afterwards, you shall write me concerning his identity. You will be rendering service for one who knows her occupation.

On Illness

Addressed by the draftsman Pay to his son, the draftsman Preemhab:

Don't turn your back on me, for I'm not well. Don't be sparing in tears for me because I am in this darkness and my lord Amon has turned his back on me.

May you bring me a bit of honey for my eyes as well as ochre that has been freshly molded into sticks and genuine galena. . . . Be to it! Be to it! Am I not your father? Now I am incapacitated. I am searching for my eyesight, but it no longer exists.

*   *   *

". . . in Hikuptah . . . reached me," so you said. . . . You made for him good plans, and all that you said was heeded. And you caused there to be released . . . and said to me, "You should go to our house and enter a stall, being the one where the two boxes are standing next to the pigsty. Look opposite those two millstones, and you will find those two pits with the copper tools lying within them."

I did accordingly while I myself was with the . . . : 500 copper spikes, 30 large copper hoes, 50 large copper chisels, 60 large copper spikes for splitting stone, 25 copper adzes, 30 copper double-edged knives, and 40 copper. . . . And I discovered a jar of Coptos ware, which was capped with gypsum and sealed with two seal impressions and which was inscribed with a list of what was in it: 10 *deben*-weights of silver, 2 *mine*-weights of gold, 7 heart amulets, 7 chains of gold, and 20 gold signet rings. And Mose said to me, "Let the jar be opened, and we shall divide the items that are in it between the two of us, for no one knows of it, and you shall not inform your father about it." But I replied to him, "In no way! I will not break the seal," so I told him.

A further matter: Now when I withdrew the copper objects belonging to Pharaoh, l.p.h., saying, "I shall take them to the overseer of the treasury of Pharaoh, l.p.h., and cause the servants to be released," the deputy officer of the northern quarter came and apprehended me.[1] And he said to me, "You discovered some . . . which were registered in the house of the master of works and were issued to the necropolis. Have them handed over so that I may take them to Pharaoh, l.p.h., namely, the things that were discovered and you appropriated. But I replied to him, "In no way! They are the tools of work which used to be under my grandfather's supervision. One came to look for them, but they couldn't be found. So our twelve servants were taken away in place of them. My father appealed to Pharaoh, and he had me set free, for I am a native of the necropolis community, who is enlisted at the place where they are. I shall take them (the copper objects) to the overseer of the treasury of Pharaoh, l.p.h., and our servants, whom they seized, shall be set free," so I said to him. And he caused it to be accomplished.

On Family

The scribe Turo greets his mother, the chantress of Amon [name lost]: In life, prosperity and health

---

[1]In this and other letters, "l.p.h." is an abbreviation of the translation ("life, prosperity, health" for the king) of a standard formula that appears next to references to him in many Egyptian texts. [Editor.]

and in the favor of Amon-Re, King of the Gods! And further:

How are you? Further, I am calling upon Amon, Mut, Khonsu, and all the gods of Southern Heliopolis (Thebes) and upon Pre when he rises each day to keep you healthy, to keep you in the favor of the deified Western Promontory, the mistress, and to let me see you healthy each and every day. And further:

I am being sent as far as the east side to the vizier in order to collect dues of his agents who are in the fields. And . . . as last year's balance due. Now there is no loincloth for my rear, for my loincloth has been taken away. . . . apportioned to the granary of Pharaoh. Please give your personal attention and have me provided that I may cause. . . . Don't make me walk helpless, or you will be made helpless, because . . .

Now as soon as I return from the errand, I will deliver his goods in grain. . . . Don't listen to what Wadjmose has said, or you may have to serve as a member of the crew!

*   *   *

The workman Horemwia, he addresses the citizeness Tanetdjesere, his daughter:

You are my good daughter. If the workman Baki throws you out of the house, I will take action! As for the house, it is what belongs to(?) Pharaoh, l.p.h., but you may dwell in the anteroom to my storehouse because it is I who built it. Nobody in the world shall throw you out of there.

*   *   *

Addressed by Takhentyshepse to her sister Iye: In life, prosperity and health! And further:

I shall send you the barley, and you shall have it ground for me and add emmer to it. And you shall make me bread with it, for I have been quarreling with Merymaat my husband. "I will divorce you," he keeps saying when he quarrels with me on account of my mother in questioning the amount of barley required for bread. "Now your mother does nothing for you," he keeps telling me

and says, "Although you have brothers and sisters, they don't take care of you," he keeps telling me in arguing with me daily, "Now look, this is what you have done to me ever since I've lived here, whereas all people furnish bread, beer, and fish daily to their family members. In short, should you say anything, you will have to go back down to the Black Land." It is good if you take note.

*   *   *

I have written to you. It's none of my wife's business.

On Personal Relations

The draftsman Prehotep communicates to his superior, the scribe of the Place of Truth Kenhikhopeshef: In life, prosperity and health!

What's the meaning of this negative attitude that you are adopting toward me? I'm like a donkey to you. If there is work, bring the donkey! And if there is fodder, bring the ox! If there is beer, you never ask for me. Only if there is work to be done, will you ask for me.

Upon my head, if I am a man who is bad in his behavior with beer, don't ask for me. It is good for you to take notice in the Estate of Amon-Re, King of the Gods, l.p.h.

I am a man who is lacking beer in his house. I am seeking to fill my stomach by my writing to you.

*   *   *

To the scribe Nekhemmut: In life, prosperity and health and in the favor of your august god, Amon-Re, King of the Gods, your good lord, every day! And further:

What's the meaning of your getting into such a bad mood as you are in that nobody's speech can enter your ears as a consequence of your inflated ego? You are not a man since you are unable to make your wives pregnant like your fellowmen.

A further matter: You abound in being exceedingly stingy. You give no one anything. As for him who has no children, he adopts an orphan instead to bring him up. It is his responsibility to pour water onto your hands as one's own eldest son.

REVIEW QUESTIONS

1. What kinds of concerns appear in these letters?
2. How do these documents differ from those presented earlier in this chapter?
3. What kinds of roles did women play in the village society of Deir el-Medina?

CARGO FROM THE ULU BURUN SHIPWRECK (C. 1300 B.C.E.)

In 1982, the wreck of a fourteenth-century B.C.E. merchant ship, possibly of Canaanite origin, was discovered off the southwestern coast of Turkey at Ulu Burun. Its cargo included thousands of items representing as many as seven civilizations of the Late Bronze Age, including more than 200 four-handled ("oxhide") ingots of copper like the one shown above as well as many tools. The items shown are of copper and bronze and reflect designs originating in Egypt, Canaan, Cyprus, and Mycenaean Greece. What does this suggest about the nature of Late Bronze Age trade? What kinds of metal implements might be traded, and why?

3 ✦ GODS AND EMPIRES: THE IRON AGE NEAR EAST

Once again using our advantage of hindsight, we can identify the period 1200–1100 B.C.E. as a watershed in the history of the ancient Near East. Before 1200, the region enjoyed a vibrant internationalism and interaction set against the backdrop of competing great kingdoms, some of them with substantial empires. By 1100, most of those great kingdoms had disappeared, in some instances suddenly, even catastrophically. Among them were the Hittite kingdom of Anatolia, the Kassites of Babylonia, the kingdom of Alashiya on Cyprus, and Mycenaean Greece. Others were in decline, most notably, New Kingdom Egypt, whose empire in Syria and Palestine had waned and whose dynastic unity was dissolving. Scholars today still debate the impact of the invasion of the Sea Peoples on these events. In one prominent view, their invasions were the most catastrophic event to befall the ancient Near East prior to the arrival of Alexander's armies. Others see their arrival, though certainly shattering, as but one event in a concatenation of causes, both external and internal, that brought down the great Late Bronze Age kingdoms, ushered in a new configuration of states and peoples, and led to the ascendancy of iron over bronze as the preferred metal of technology.

Within the new configuration emerged peoples whose contributions to later Western and world civilizations were both profound and enduring. Among the Sea Peoples, it is the Philistines whose memory has endured the longest, if for no other reason than the region in which they settled took on their name, as Palestine. The Hebrew Bible depicts them as a potent and incorrigible threat to the early Israelites, and the ensuing animosity undoubtedly has contributed to the modern (and surely unjustified) connotation of philistine as crude and unsophisticated. To their north, the long-established Canaanite craftsmen and traders of Tyre, Sidon, and Beirut, who came to be identified as Phoenicians, established far-flung commercial routes and colonies that carried their goods and reputation to the Straits of Gibraltar and beyond. As part of their enterprise they refined and disseminated a new technology that eventually would revolutionize both lit-

eracy and society—alphabetic writing. Meanwhile, to the west of the Phoenicians there soon emerged several tribal kingdoms of the Aramaeans, perhaps the most powerful of which was centered on the ancient city of Damascus. In time, Aramaean peoples spread across the Middle Eastern landscape, as far away as Babylonia, bringing with them their language, Aramaic, and an alphabetic writing system whose use would eventually supplant the ancient cuneiform system. Aramaic became the official language of the Persian empire, it was the language spoken by Jesus Christ, and it remained the dominant spoken language throughout the Middle East until supplanted by Arabic in the wake of the Arab/Islamic conquests many centuries later.

The ancient Hebrews, or Israelites, had an impact on the shaping of Western civilization that dwarfs their impact on the history and culture of their own time. They emerge from almost total obscurity late during the second millennium B.C.E., in circumstances about which historians and archaeologists have yet to reach consensus and are continually struggling to understand. According to the (hardly objective or verifiable) accounts in the Hebrew Bible, they came to dominate the area of modern Israel and Palestine under two great kings, David and Solomon, whose reigns together encompass less than a century (approximately 1000–920 B.C.E.). The civil war that erupted on Solomon's death left the previously united Hebrew monarchy irreparably divided into its two constituent parts, Israel in the north and Judah in the south.

Within a few centuries, however, both of these kingdoms, and most of the rest of the Middle East as well, were overcome by the reasserted might of Mesopotamian and then Persian Empires. The Assyrians destroyed Israel in 722 and by 650 had conquered virtually all of the Middle East; their kings celebrated their brutal conquests in vivid accounts that shock twenty-first-century sensibilities. One of their successors to imperial dominion, the Chaldaean king Nebuchadnezzar of Babylonia, captured the Judahite capital, Jerusalem, in 587 and deported much of its population to Babylon—an event that began the Diaspora, the "dispersion" that has so dominated the experience of the Jewish people since that time. With Cyrus and his successors came the greatest of all ancient Near Eastern empires, that of the Achaemenid Persians, under whom developed a system and mentality of universal dominion that later empires emulated for centuries to come.

It was probably during the "captivity" in Babylon that the displaced Judahites (in Hebrew, yehudim—the word came to be jews) began in earnest the process of compiling and editing their ancient laws and traditions. The body of writings that was developed over the next several centuries—the Hebrew Bible, condescendingly known in Christian tradition as the Old Testament—is, along with the New Testament, arguably the most influential corpus of literature in human history. Without a doubt, it is the ancient Near East's most significant contribution to the shaping of Western civilization, and its impact on the formation of later Islamic civilization worldwide, through its contribution to the teachings of the prophet Muhammad as recorded in the Quran, is likewise beyond measuring. Furthermore, for the nearly two millennia before the archaeological rediscovery of ancient Mesopotamian civilization in the mid-nineteenth century and the decipherment of the cuneiform and hieroglyphic scripts, the Bible was the chief fount of knowledge of human history from the creation of the world (which some scholars, using Biblical evidence, dated to exactly 4004 B.C.) to the rise of the Greeks.

The theory of evolution and the modern discoveries of historians and archaeologists have undermined the historical value of much of the Bible's narrative. Obviously, then, it is not in the accuracy of their historical accounts that the Hebrews have had their greatest influence on later civilization. Rather, their singular contribution lies in the unique perspective that dominated their sense of their own history: their special relationship with a divine being who chose them as his own people and established with them a covenant that promised them his support and protection. In return, they pledged to accept only him as their exclusive deity and to govern their behavior, both cultic and social, in accordance with a body of explicitly defined regulations handed down by him, and him alone. The working out of this covenant in the historical experience of the Hebrew people provided the developmental context for concepts that became central to the tradition of Western civilization: divinely revealed law as the basis of the relationship between God and humankind, and a monotheism founded on humankind's exclusive acceptance of a single, universal supreme being and creator who demands justice and righteousness. These concepts today remain at the heart of the faiths of the children of Abraham—the shared monotheistic tradition of Judaism, Christianity, and Islam.

"The Journey of Wen-Amon to Phoenicia"

After the Sea Peoples' invasions of the thirteenth and twelfth centuries B.C.E., Egypt's New Kingdom empire in Syria and Palestine waned, and the breakdown of Egypt's unity was imminent. Egypt's influence and prestige in Syria and Palestine suffered accordingly. The following story relates the adventures of an Egyptian official sent to Phoenicia to procure cedar wood for the temple of Amun (spelled "Amon" here).

From Ancient Near Eastern Texts Relating to the Old Testament, edited by James B. Pritchard, 3d ed.; (Princeton, N.J.: Princeton University Press, 1950), pp. 25–29.

EGYPTIAN BATTLE WITH THE SEA PEOPLES (C. 1150 B.C.E.)

This scene from a monumental relief at Medinet Habu in Thebes purports to depict the Egyptian defeat of the Sea Peoples' fleet in a battle that evidently was fought near the Nile Delta. Do the Egyptians seem in command of the situation? What kinds of weapons do they use? Do you see evidence of distinctive modes of dress and headgear? What do you believe is the intended effect on someone viewing this relief?

Year 5, 4th month of the 3rd season, day 16: the day on which Wen-Amon, the Senior of the Forecourt of the House of Amon, [Lord of the Thrones] of the Two Lands, set out to fetch the woodwork for the great and august barque of Amon-Re, King of the Gods, which is on [the River and which is named:] "User-het-Amon." On the day when I reached Tanis, the place [where Ne-su-Ba-neb]-Ded and Ta-net-Amon were, I gave them the letters of Amon-Re, King of the Gods, and they had them read in their presence. And they said: "Yes, I will do as Amon-Re, King of the Gods, our [lord], has said!" I SPENT UP TO THE 4TH MONTH OF THE 3RD SEASON in Tanis. And Ne-su-Ba-neb-Ded and Ta-net-Amon sent me off with the ship captain Mengebet, and I embarked on the great Syrian sea IN THE 1ST MONTH OF THE 3RD SEASON, DAY 1.

I reached Dor, a town of the Tjeker, and Beder, its prince, had 50 loaves of bread, one jug of wine, and one leg of beef brought to me. And a man of my ship ran away and stole one [vessel] of gold, [amounting] to 5 deben, four jars of silver, amounting to 20 deben, and a sack of 11 deben of silver. [Total of what] he [stole]: 5 deben of gold and 31 deben of silver.

I got up in the morning, and I went to the place where the Prince was, and I said to him: "I have been robbed in your harbor. Now you are the prince of this land, and you are its investigator who should look for my silver. Now about this silver—it belongs to Amon-Re, King of the Gods, the lord of the lands; it belongs to Ne-su-Ba-neb-Ded; it belongs to Heri-Hor, my lord, and the other great men of Egypt! It belongs to you; it belongs to Weret: it belongs to Mekmer; it belongs to Zakar-Baal, the Prince of Byblos!"

And he said to me: "Whether you are important or whether you are eminent—look here, I do not recognize this accusation which you have made to me! Suppose it had been a thief who belonged to my land who went on your boat and stole your silver, I should have repaid it to you from my treasury, until they had found this thief of yours—whoever he may be. Now about the

thief who robbed you—he belongs to you! He belongs to your ship! Spend a few days here visiting me, so that I may look for him."

I spent nine days moored (in) his harbor, and I went (to) call on him, and I said to him: "Look, you have not found my silver. [Just let] me [go] with the ship captains and with those who go (to) sea!" But he said to me: "Be quiet! . . ." . . . I went out of Tyre at the break of dawn. . . . Zakar-Baal, the Prince of Byblos, . . . ship." I found 30 deben of silver in it, and I seized upon it. [And I said to the Tjeker: "I have seized upon] your silver, and it will stay with me [until] you find [my silver or the thief] who stole it! Even though you have not stolen, I shall take it. But as for you, . . ." So they went away, and I enjoyed my triumph [in] a tent (on) the shore of the [sea], (in) the harbor of Byblos. And [I hid] Amon-of-the-Road, and I put his property inside him.

And the [Prince] of Byblos sent to me, saying: "Get [out of my] harbor!" And I sent to him, saying: "Where should [I go to]? . . . If [you have a ship] to carry me, have me taken to Egypt again!" So I spent twenty-nine days in his [harbor, while] he [spent] the time sending to me every day to say: "Get out (of) my harbor!"

NOW WHILE HE WAS MAKING OFFERING to his gods, the god seized one of his youths and made him possessed. And he said to him: "Bring up [the] god! Bring the messenger who is carrying him! Amon is the one who sent him out! He is the one who made him come!" And while the possessed (youth) was having his frenzy on this night, I had (already) found a ship headed for Egypt and had loaded everything that I had into it. While I was watching for the darkness, thinking that when it descended I would load the god (also), so that no other eye might see him, the harbor master came to me, saying: "Wait until morning—so says the Prince." So I said to him: "Aren't you the one who spends the time coming to me every day to say: 'Get out (of) my harbor'? Aren't you saying 'Wait' tonight in order to let the ship which I have found get away—and (then) you will come again (to) say: 'Go away!'?" So he went and told it to the Prince. And the Prince sent to the captain of the ship to say: "Wait until morning—so says the Prince!"

When MORNING CAME, he sent and brought me up, but the god stayed in the tent where he was, (on) the shore of the sea. And I found him sitting (in) his upper room, with his back turned to a window, so that the waves of the great Syrian sea broke against the back of his head.

So I said to him: "*May* Amon *favor you!*" But he said to me "How long, up to today, since you came from the place where Amon is?" So I said to him: "Five months and one day up to now." And he said to me: "Well, you're truthful! Where is the letter of Amon which (should be) in your hand? Where is the dispatch of the High Priest of Amon which (should be) in your hand?" And I told him: "I gave them to Ne-su-Ba-neb-Ded and Ta-net-Amon." And he was very, very angry, and he said to me: "Now see—neither letters nor dispatches are in your hand! Where is the cedar ship which Ne-su-Ba-neb-Ded gave to you? Where is its Syrian crew? Didn't he turn you over to this foreign ship captain to have him kill you and throw you into the sea? (Then) with whom would they have looked for the god? And you too—with whom would they have looked for you too?" So he spoke to me.

BUT I SAID TO HIM: "Wasn't it an Egyptian ship? Now it is Egyptian crews which sail under Ne-su-Ba-neb-Ded! He has no Syrian crews." And he said to me: "Aren't there twenty ships here in my harbor which are in commercial relations with Ne-su-Ba-neb-Ded? As to this Sidon, the other (place) which you have passed, aren't there fifty more ships there which are in commercial relations with Werket-El, and which are drawn up to his house?" And I was silent in this great time.

And he answered and said to me: "On what business have you come?" So I told him: "I have come after the woodwork for the great and august barque of Amon-Re, King of the Gods. Your father did (it), your grandfather did (it), and you will do it too!" So I spoke to him. But he said to me: "To be sure, they did it! And if you give me

(something) for doing it, I will do it! Why, when my people carried out this commission, Pharaoh —life, prosperity, health!—sent six ships loaded with Egyptian goods, and they unloaded them into their storehouses! You—what is it that you're bringing me—me also?" And he had the journal rolls of his fathers brought, and he had them read out in my presence, and they found a thousand *deben* of silver and all kinds of things in his scrolls.

So he said to me: "If the ruler of Egypt were the lord of mine, and I were his servant also, he would not have to send silver and gold, saying: 'Carry out the commission of Amon!' There would be no carrying of a royal-gift, such as they used to do for my father. As for me—me also— I am not your servant! I am not the servant of him who sent you either! If I cry out to the Lebanon, the heavens open up, and the logs are here lying (on) the shore of the sea! Give me the sails which you have brought to carry your ships which would hold the logs for (Egypt)! Give me the ropes [which] you have brought [*to lash the cedar*] logs which I am to cut down to make you . . . which I shall make for you (as) the sails of your boats, and the *spars* will be (too) heavy and will break, and you will die in the middle of the sea! See, Amon made thunder in the sky when he put Seth near him. Now when Amon founded all lands, in founding them he founded first the land of Egypt, from which you come; for craftsmanship came out of it, to reach the place where I am, and learning came out of it, to reach the place where I am. What are these silly trips which they have had you make?"

And I said to him: "(That's) not true! What I am on are no 'silly trips' at all! There is no ship upon the River which does not belong to Amon! The sea is his, and the Lebanon is his, of which you say: 'It is mine!' It forms the *nursery* for User-het-Amon, the lord of [every] ship! Why, he spoke—Amon-Re, King of the Gods—and said to Heri-Hor, my master: 'Send me forth!' So he had me come, carrying this great god. But see, you have made this great god spend these twenty-nine days moored (in) your harbor, although you did not know (it). Isn't he here? Isn't he the (same) as he was? You are stationed (here) to carry on the commerce of the Lebanon with Amon, its lord. As for your saying that the former kings sent silver and gold—suppose that they had life and health; (then) they would not have had such things sent! (But) they had such things sent to your fathers in place of life and health! Now as for Amon-Re, King of the Gods—he is the lord of this life and health, and he was the lord of your fathers. They spent their lifetimes making offering to Amon. And you also—you are the servant of Amon! If you say to Amon: 'Yes, I will do (it)!' and you carry out his commission, you will live, you will be prosperous, you will be healthy, and you will be good to your entire land and your people! (But) don't wish for yourself anything belonging to Amon-Re, (King of) the Gods. Why, a lion wants his own property! Have your secretary brought to me, so that I may send him to Ne-su-Ba-neb-Ded and Ta-net-Amon, the *officers* whom Amon put in the north of his land, and they will have all kinds of things sent. I shall send him to them to say: 'Let it be brought until I shall go (back again) to the south, and I shall (then) have every bit of the debt still (due to you) brought to you.'" So I spoke to him.

So he entrusted my letter to his messenger, and he loaded in the *keel,* the bow-post, the stern-post, along with four other hewn timbers—seven in all—and he had them taken to Egypt. And in the first month of the second season his messenger who had gone to Egypt came back to me in Syria. And Ne-su-Ba-neb-Ded and Ta-net-Amon sent: 4 jars and 1 *kak-men* of gold; 5 jars of silver; 10 pieces of clothing in royal linen; 10 *kherd* of good Upper Egyptian linen; 500 (rolls of) finished papyrus; 500 cowhides; 500 ropes; 20 sacks of lentils; and 30 baskets of fish. And she sent to me (personally): 5 pieces of clothing in good Upper Egyptian linen; 5 *kherd* of good Upper Egyptian linen; 1 sack of lentils; and 5 baskets of fish.

And the Prince was glad, and he detailed three hundred men and three hundred cattle, and he put supervisors at their head, to have them cut

down the timber. So they cut them down, and they spent the second season lying there.

In the third month of the third season they dragged them (to) the shore of the sea, and the Prince came out and stood by them. And he sent to me, saying: "Come!" Now when I presented myself near him, the shadow of his lotus-blossom fell upon me. And Pen-Amon, a butler who belonged to him, cut me off, saying: "The shadow of Pharaoh— life, prosperity, health!—your lord, has fallen on you!" But he was angry at him, saying: "Let him alone!"

So I presented myself near him, and he answered and said to me: "See, the commission which my fathers carried out formerly, I have carried it out (also), even though you have not done for me what your fathers would have done for me, and you too (should have done)! See, the last of your woodwork has arrived and is lying (here). Do as I wish, and come to load it in—for aren't they going to give it to you? Don't come to look at the terror of the sea! If you look at the terror of the sea, you will see my own (too)! Why, I have not done to you what was done to the messengers of Kha-em-Waset, when they spent seventeen years in this land—they died (where) they were!" And he said to his butler: "Take him and show him their *tomb* in which they are lying."

But I said to him: "Don't show it to me! As for Kha-em-Waset—they were men whom he sent to you as messengers, and he was a man himself. You do not have one of his messengers (here in me), when you say: 'Go and see your companions!' Now, shouldn't you rejoice and have a stela [made] for yourself and say on it: 'Amon-Re, King of the Gods, sent to me Amon-of-the-Road, his messenger—[life], prosperity, health!—and Wen-Amon, his human messenger, after the woodwork for the great and august barque of Amon-Re, King of the Gods. I cut it down. I loaded it in. I provided it (with) my ships and my crews. I caused them to reach Egypt, in order to ask fifty years of life from Amon for myself, over and above my fate.' And it shall come to pass that, after another time, a messenger may come from the land of

Egypt who knows writing, and he may read your name on the stela. And you will receive water (in) the West, like the gods who are here!"

And he said to me: "This which you have said to me is a great testimony of words!" So I said to him: "As for the many things which you have said to me, if I reach the place where the High Priest of Amon is and he sees how you have (carried out this) commission, it is your (carrying out of this) commission (which) will *draw out* something for you."

And I went (to) the shore of the sea, to the place where the timber was lying, and I spied eleven ships belonging to the Tjeker coming in from the sea, in order to say: "Arrest him! Don't let a ship of his (go) to the land of Egypt!" Then I sat down and wept. And the letter scribe of the Prince came out to me, and he said to me: "What's the matter with you?" And I said to him: "Haven't you seen the birds go down to Egypt a second time? Look at them—how they travel to the cool pools! (But) how long shall I be left here! Now don't you see those who are coming again to arrest me?"

So he went and told it to the Prince. And the Prince began to weep because of the words which were said to him, for they were painful. And he sent out to me his letter scribe, and he brought to me two jugs of wine and one ram. And he sent to me Ta-net-Not, an Egyptian singer who was with him, saying: "Sing to him! Don't let his heart take on cares!" And he sent to me, to say: "Eat and drink! Don't let your heart take on cares, for to-morrow you shall hear whatever I have to say."

When morning came, he had his assembly summoned, and he stood in their midst, and he said to the Tjeker; "What have you come (for)?" And they said to him: "We have come after the *blasted* ships which you are sending to Egypt with our opponents!" But he said to them: "I cannot arrest the messenger of Amon inside my land. Let

me send him away, and you go after him to arrest him."

So he loaded me in, and he sent me away from there at the harbor of the sea. And the wind cast me on the land of Alashiya. And they of the town came out against me to kill me, but I *forced my way* through them to the place where Heteb, the princess of the town, was. I met her as she was going out of one house of hers and going into another of hers.

So I greeted her, and I said to the people who were standing near her: "Isn't there one of you who understands Egyptian?" And one of them said: "I understand (it)." So I said to him: "Tell my lady that I have heard, as far away as Thebes, the place where Amon is, that injustice is done in every town but justice is done in the land of Ala-shiya. Yet injustice is done here every day!" And she said: "Why, what do you (mean) by saying it?" So I told her: "If the sea is stormy and the wind casts me on the land where you are, you should not let them take me *in charge* to kill me. For I am a messenger of Amon. Look here—as for me, they will search for me all the time! As to this crew of the Prince of Byblos which they are bent on killing, won't its lord find ten crews of yours, and he also kill them?"

So she had the people summoned, and they stood (there). And she said to me: "Spend the night . . ."

REVIEW QUESTIONS

1. What kind of treatment had Egyptian officials come to expect from the ruler of Byblos? What kind of treatment did Wen-Amun receive at his hands? Do you see evidence for a change in Egypt's prestige?
2. What does this document reveal about the customs and protocol of trade and diplomacy?

FROM The Book of Ezekiel:
Phoenician Trade in the Hebrew Bible

The documentary record that the Phoenicians left to us about their history and trade is frustratingly scant. Historians necessarily have had to rely on descriptions provided by other sources, most notably, the accounts of ancient Greek historians like Herodotus; later Roman authors' accounts of the Carthaginians, whose origins were Phoenician (which is why, in Latin, the Carthaginians are referred to as Poeni, or Punic); and references to the Phoenicians in the Hebrew Bible. As you might expect, none of these sources tends to be impartial. The following selection from the Book of Ezekiel (27: 1–33) is drawn from one of several prophecies against foreign nations and culminates in the prophesied destruction of the Phoenician city of Tyre, whose wealth and fame are described vividly.

The Oxford Study Bible, edited by M. Jack Suggs, Katharine Doob Sakenfeld, and James R. Mueller (Oxford, Eng.: Oxford University Press, 1992).

*   *   *

27

This word of the LORD came to me: O man, raise a dirge over Tyre and say to her who is enthroned at the gateway to the sea, who carries the trade of the nations to many coasts and islands: These are the words of the Lord GOD:

Tyre, you declared,
"I am perfect in beauty."
Your frontiers were on the high seas,
your builders made your beauty perfect;
they used pine from Senir
to fashion all your ribs;
they took a cedar from Lebanon
to set up a mast for you.
They made your oars of oaks from Bashan;
for your deck they used cypress
from the coasts of Kittim.
Your canvas was linen,
patterned linen from Egypt
to serve you for sails;

your awnings were violet and purple
from the coasts of Elishah.
Men from Sidon and Arvad served as
    your oarsmen;
you had skilled men among you, Tyre,
acting as your helmsmen.
You had skilled veterans from Gebal
to caulk your seams.

Every fully manned seagoing ship
    visited your harbour
to traffic in your wares;
Persia, Lydia, and Put
supplied mercenaries for your army;
they arrayed shield and helmet in you,
and it was they who gave you your splendour.
Men of Arvad and Cilicia manned your
    walls on every side.
Men of Gammad were posted on your towers:
they arrayed their bucklers around your
    battlements,
making your beauty perfect.

Tarshish was a source of your commerce, from its abundant resources offering silver, iron, tin, and lead as your staple wares. Javan, Tubal, and Meshech dealt with you, offering slaves and bronze utensils as your imports. Men from Togarmah offered horses, cavalry steeds, and mules as your wares. Rhodians dealt with you; many islands were a source of your commerce, paying their dues to you in ivory tusks and ebony. Edom was a source of your commerce, so many were your undertakings, and offered purple garnets, brocade and fine linen, black coral and red jasper, for your wares. Judah and Israel traded with you, offering wheat from Minnith, and meal, grape-syrup, oil, and balm as your imports. Damascus was a source of your commerce, so many were your undertakings, from its abundant resources offering Helbon wine and Suhar wool, and casks of wine from Izalla, in exchange for your wares; wrought iron, cassia, and sweet cane were among your imports. Dedan traded with you in coarse woollens for saddlecloths. Arabia and all the rulers of Kedar traded with you; they were the source of your commerce in lambs, rams, and goats. Merchants from Sheba and Raamah traded with you, offering all the choicest spices, every kind of precious stone, and gold as your wares. Harran, Kanneh, and Eden, merchants from Asshur and all Media, traded with you; they were your dealers in choice stuffs: violet cloths and brocades, in stores of coloured fabric rolled up and tied with cords.

Ships of Tarshish were the caravans for your imports;
you were deeply laden with full cargoes
on the high seas.
Your oarsmen brought you into many
waters. * * *
When your wares were unloaded off the seas
you met the needs of many nations;
with your vast resources and your imports
you enriched the kings of the earth. * * *"

*   *   *

REVIEW QUESTIONS

1. How well constructed were the ships of Tyre?
2. What commodities and goods traded at Tyre? How farflung were Tyre's trade connections?

FROM The Book of I Kings: Solomon's Construction of Yahweh's Temple in Jerusalem

As recounted in the following selection from the First Book of Kings, 5–8, in the Hebrew Bible, the crowning achievement of the reign of the Israelite king Solomon was the building of the great temple of Yahweh in Jerusalem, perhaps sometime during the later tenth century B.C.E. That temple was part of a larger palace complex, no archaeological evidence of which has yet been recovered. This helps explain why modern historians have been compelled to reassess the biblical accounts of the great power and extent of David's and Solomon's kingdom. Nonetheless, Solomon's First Temple, later destroyed by the Babylonians under Nebuchadnezzar in the sixth century B.C.E. (the Second Temple, rebuilt by Herod the Great in the first century B.C.E., was also destroyed by the Romans in the first century C.E.[1]), became the central

*locus of ritual and worship in early Judaism and is an overriding reason for modern
Israel's adamant refusal to restore Jerusalem to Arab control today.*

The Oxford Study Bible, edited by M. Jack Suggs, Katharine Doob Sakenfeld, and James R.
Mueller (Oxford, Eng.: Oxford University Press, 1992).

*   *   *

When Hiram king of Tyre heard that Solomon
had been anointed king in his father's place, he
sent envoys to him, because he had always been
friendly with David. Solomon sent this message to
Hiram: "You know that my father David could
not build a house for the name of the LORD his
God, because of the armed nations surrounding
him until the LORD made them subject to him.
But now on every side the LORD my God has given
me peace; there is no one to oppose me, I fear no
attack. So I propose to build a house for the name
of the LORD my God, following the promise given
by the LORD to my father David: 'Your son whom
I shall set on the throne in your place will build
the house for my name.' If therefore you will now
give orders that cedars be felled and brought from
Lebanon, my men will work with yours, and I
shall pay you for your men whatever sum you fix;
for, as you know, we have none so skilled at felling
trees as your Sidonians."

Hiram was greatly pleased to receive Solomon's message, and said, "Blessed be the LORD
today who has given David a wise son to rule over
this great people." He sent Solomon this reply: "I
have received your message. In this matter of timber, both cedar and pine, I shall do all you wish.
My men will bring down the logs from Lebanon
to the sea and I shall make them up into rafts to
be floated to the place you appoint; I shall have
them broken up there and you can remove them.
You, for your part, will meet my wishes if you
provide the food for my household." So Hiram
kept Solomon supplied with all the cedar and pine
that he wanted, and Solomon supplied Hiram with
twenty thousand kor of wheat as food for his

household and twenty kor of oil of pounded olives; Solomon gave this yearly to Hiram. The LORD
bestowed wisdom on Solomon as he had promised
him; there was peace between Hiram and Solomon and they concluded a treaty.

King Solomon raised a forced levy from the
whole of Israel amounting to thirty thousand men.
He sent them to Lebanon in monthly relays of ten
thousand, so that the men spent one month in
Lebanon and two at home; Adoniram was super-
intendent of the levy. Solomon had also seventy
thousand hauliers and eighty thousand quarry-
men, apart from the three thousand three hundred
foremen in charge of the work who superintended
the labourers. By the king's orders they quarried
huge, costly blocks for laying the foundation of
the LORD's house in hewn stone. The builders supplied by Solomon and Hiram, together with the
Gebalites, shaped the blocks and prepared both
timber and stone for the building of the house.

It was in the four hundred and eightieth year after
the Israelites had come out of Egypt, in the fourth
year of Solomon's reign over Israel, in the second
month of that year, the month of Ziv, that he began to build the house of the LORD.

The house which King Solomon built for the
LORD was sixty cubits long by twenty cubits broad,
and its height was thirty cubits. The vestibule in
front of the sanctuary was twenty cubits long,
spanning the whole breadth of the house, while it
projected ten cubits in front of the house; and he
fitted the house with embrasures. Then he built a
terrace against its wall round both the sanctuary
and the inner shrine. He made arcades all round:
the lowest arcade was five cubits in depth, the
middle six, and the highest seven; for he made
rebatements all round the outside of the main wall
so that the bearer beams might not be fixed into

---

[1]C.E. means "common era." [Editor.]

the walls. In the building of the house, only blocks of stone dressed at the quarry were used; no hammer or axe or any iron tool whatever was heard in the house while it was being built.

The entrance to the lowest arcade was in the right-hand corner of the house; there was access by a spiral stairway from that to the middle arcade, and from the middle arcade to the highest. So Solomon built the house and finished it, having constructed the terrace five cubits high against the whole building, braced the house with struts of cedar, and roofed it with beams and coffering of cedar.

Then the word of the LORD came to Solomon, saying, "As for this house which you are building, if you are obedient to my ordinances and conform to my precepts and loyally observe all my commands, then I will fulfil my promise to you, the promise I gave to your father David, and I will dwell among the Israelites and never forsake my people Israel."

So Solomon built the LORD's house and finished it. He panelled the inner walls of the house with cedar boards, covering the interior from floor to rafters with wood; the floor he laid with boards of pine. In the innermost part of the house he partitioned off a space of twenty cubits with cedar boards from floor to rafters and made of it an inner shrine, to be the Most Holy Place. The sanctuary in front of this was forty cubits long. The cedar inside the house was carved with open flowers and gourds; all was cedar, no stone was left visible.

He prepared an inner shrine in the farthest recesses of the house to receive the Ark of the Covenant of the LORD. This inner shrine was twenty cubits square and it stood twenty cubits high; he overlaid it with red gold and made an altar of cedar. Solomon overlaid the inside of the house with red gold and drew a veil with golden chains across in front of the inner shrine. The whole house he overlaid with gold until it was all covered; and the whole of the altar by the inner shrine he overlaid with gold.

In the inner shrine he carved two cherubim of wild olive wood, each ten cubits high. Each wing of the cherubim was five cubits long, and from wingtip to wingtip was ten cubits. Similarly, the second cherub measured ten cubits; the two cherubim were alike in size and shape, and each ten cubits high. He put the cherubim within the inner shrine and their wings were spread, so that a wing of one cherub touched the wall on one side and a wing of the other touched the wall on the other side, and their other wings met in the middle; he overlaid the cherubim with gold.

Round all the walls of the house he carved figures of cherubim, palm trees, and open flowers, both in the inner chamber and in the outer. The floor of the house he overlaid with gold, both in the inner chamber and in the outer. At the entrance to the inner shrine he made a double door of wild olive wood; the pilasters and the doorposts were pentagonal. The doors were of wild olive, and he carved cherubim, palms, and open flowers on them, overlaying them with gold and hammering the gold upon the cherubim and the palms. Similarly for the doorway of the sanctuary he made a square frame of wild olive and a double door of pine, each leaf having two swivel-pins. On them he carved cherubim, palms, and open flowers, overlaying them evenly with gold over the carving.

He built the inner court with three courses of dressed stone and one course of lengths of cedar.

In the fourth year of Solomon's reign, in the month of Ziv, the foundation of the house of the LORD was laid; and in the eleventh year, in the month of Bul, which is the eighth month, the house was finished in all its details according to the specification. It had taken seven years to build.

By the time he had finished, Solomon had been engaged on building for thirteen years. He built the House of the Forest of Lebanon, a hundred cubits long, fifty broad, and thirty high, constructed of four rows of cedar columns, on top of which were laid lengths of cedar. It had a cedar roof, extending over the beams, which rested on the columns, fifteen in each row; and the number of the beams was forty-five. There were three rows of window-frames, and the windows corresponded to each other at three levels. All the doorways and the windows had square frames, and window corresponded to window at three levels.

Solomon made also the portico, fifty cubits long and thirty broad, with a cornice above.

He built the Portico of Judgement, the portico containing the throne where he was to give judgement; this was panelled in cedar from floor to rafters.

His own house where he was to reside, in another courtyard set back from the portico, and the house he made for Pharaoh's daughter whom he had married, were constructed like this portico.

All these were made of costly blocks of stone, hewn to measure and trimmed with the saw on the inner and outer sides, from foundation to coping and from the court of the house as far as the great court. At the base were costly stones, huge blocks, some ten and some eight cubits in size, and above were costly stones dressed to measure, and cedar. The great court had three courses of dressed stone all around and a course of lengths of cedar; so had the inner court of the house of the LORD, and so had the vestibule of the house.

King Solomon fetched from Tyre Hiram, the son of a widow of the tribe of Naphtali. His father, a native of Tyre, had been a worker in bronze, and he himself was a man of great skill and ingenuity, versed in every kind of craftsmanship in bronze. After he came to King Solomon, Hiram carried out all his works.

He cast in a mould the two bronze pillars. One stood eighteen cubits high and it took a cord of twelve cubits long to go round it; it was hollow, and the metal was four fingers thick. The second pillar was the same. He made two capitals of solid bronze to set on the tops of the pillars, each capital five cubits high. He made two bands of ornamental network, in festoons of chain-work, for the capitals on the tops of the pillars, a band of network for each capital. He made pomegranates in two rows all round on top of the ornamental network of the one pillar; he did the same with the other capital. The capitals at the tops of the pillars in the vestibule were shaped like lilies and were four cubits high. On the capitals at the tops of the

two pillars, immediately above the cushion, extending beyond the network upwards, were two hundred pomegranates in rows all round on the two capitals. Then he erected the pillars at the vestibule of the sanctuary. When he had erected the pillar on the right side, he named it Jachin; and when he had erected the one on the left side, he named it Boaz. On the tops of the pillars was lily-work. Thus the work of the pillars was finished.

He made the Sea of cast metal; it was round in shape, the diameter from rim to rim being ten cubits; it stood five cubits high, and it took a line thirty cubits long to go round it. All round the Sea on the outside under its rim, completely surrounding the thirty cubits of its circumference, were two rows of gourds, cast in one piece with the Sea itself. It was mounted on twelve oxen, three facing north, three west, three south, and three east, their hindquarters turned inwards; the Sea rested on top of them. Its thickness was a hand's breadth; its rim was made like that of a cup, shaped like the calyx of a lily; it held two thousand bath.

Hiram also made the ten trolleys of bronze; each trolley was four cubits long, four wide, and three high. This was the construction of the trolleys: they had panels set in frames; on these panels were portrayed lions, oxen, and cherubim, and the same on the frames; above and below the lions, oxen, and cherubim were fillets of hammered work of spiral design. Each trolley had four bronze wheels with bronze axles; it also had four flanges and handles beneath the laver, and these handles were of cast metal with a spiral design on their sides. The opening for the basin was set within a crown which projected one cubit; the opening was round with a level edge, and it had decorations in relief. The panels of the trolleys were square, not round. The four wheels were beneath the panels, and the wheel-forks were made in one piece with the trolleys; the height of each wheel was one and a half cubits. The wheels were constructed like those of a chariot, their axles, hubs, spokes, and felloes being all of cast metal. The four handles were at the four corners of each trolley, of one piece with the trolley. At the top of the trolley there was a circular band half a cubit high; the struts and panels on the trolley were of one piece with it. On the plates, that is on the panels, he carved cherubim, lions, and palm trees, wherever there was a blank space, with spiral work all round it. This is how the ten trolleys were made; all of them were cast alike, having the same size and the same shape.

Hiram then made ten bronze basins, each holding forty bath and measuring four cubits; there was a basin for each of the ten trolleys. He put five trolleys on the right side of the house and five on the left side; and he placed the Sea in the south-east corner of it.

Hiram made the pots, the shovels, and the tossing-bowls. With them he finished all the work which he had undertaken for King Solomon in the house of the LORD: the two pillars; the two bowl-shaped capitals on the tops of the pillars; the two ornamental networks to cover the two bowl-shaped capitals on the tops of the pillars; the four hundred pomegranates for the two networks, two rows of pomegranates for each network, to cover the bowl-shaped capitals on the two pillars; the ten trolleys and the ten basins on the trolleys; the one Sea and the twelve oxen which supported it; the pots, the shovels, and the tossing-bowls—all these objects in the house of the LORD which Hiram made for King Solomon being of burnished bronze. The king cast them in the foundry between Succoth and Zarethan in the plain of the Jordan.

Solomon put all these objects in their places; so great was the quantity of bronze used in their making that the weight of it was beyond all reckoning. He made also all the furnishings for the house of the LORD: the golden altar and the golden table upon which was set the Bread of the Presence; the lampstands of red gold, five on the right side and five on the left side of the inner shrine; the flowers, lamps, and tongs of gold; the cups, snuffers, tossing-bowls, saucers, and firepans of red gold; and the panels for the doors of the inner sanctuary, the Most Holy Place, and for the doors of the house, of gold.

When all the work which King Solomon did for the house of the LORD was completed, he brought in the sacred treasures of his father David, the silver, the gold, and the vessels, and deposited them in the treasuries of the house of the LORD.

Then Solomon summoned to him at Jerusalem the elders of Israel, all the heads of the tribes who were chiefs of families in Israel, in order to bring up the Ark of the Covenant of the LORD from the City of David, which is called Zion. All the men of Israel assembled in King Solomon's presence at the pilgrim-feast in the month Ethanim, the seventh month. When the elders of Israel had all arrived, the priests lifted the Ark of the LORD and carried it up; the Tent of Meeting and all the sacred furnishings of the Tent were carried by the priests and the Levites. King Solomon and the whole congregation of Israel assembled with him before the Ark sacrificed sheep and oxen in numbers past counting or reckoning.

The priests brought in the Ark of the Covenant of the LORD to its place in the inner shrine of the house, the Most Holy Place, beneath the wings of the cherubim. The cherubim, whose wings were spread over the place of the Ark, formed a canopy above the Ark and its poles. The poles projected, and their ends were visible from the Holy Place immediately in front of the inner shrine, but from nowhere else outside; they are there to this day. There was nothing inside the Ark but the two stone tablets which Moses had deposited there at Horeb, when the LORD made the covenant with the Israelites after they left Egypt.

The priests came out of the Holy Place, since the cloud was filling the house of the LORD, and they could not continue to minister because of it, for the glory of the LORD filled his house. Then Solomon said:

"The LORD has caused his sun to shine in the
  heavens,
but he has said he would dwell in thick darkness.
I have built you a lofty house,
a dwelling-place for you to occupy for ever."

While the whole assembly of Israelites stood, the king turned and blessed them: "Blessed be the

LORD the God of Israel who spoke directly to my father David and has himself fulfilled his promise. For he said, 'From the day when I brought my people Israel out of Egypt, I chose no city out of all the tribes of Israel where I should build a house for my name to be, but I chose Jerusalem where my name should be, and David to be over my people Israel.'

"My father David had it in mind to build a house for the name of the LORD the God of Israel, but the LORD said to him, 'You purposed to build a house for my name, and your purpose was good. Nevertheless, you are not to build it; but the son who is to be born to you, he is to build the house for my name.' The LORD has now fulfilled his promise: I have succeeded my father David and taken his place on the throne of Israel as the LORD promised; and I have built the house for the name of the LORD the God of Israel. I have assigned a place in it for the Ark containing the covenant of the LORD, which he made with our forefathers when he brought them out of Egypt."

Standing in front of the altar of the LORD in the presence of the whole assembly of Israel, Solomon spread out his hands towards heaven and said, "LORD God of Israel, there is no God like you in heaven above or on earth beneath, keeping covenant with your servants and showing them constant love while they continue faithful to you with all their hearts. You have kept your promise to your servant David my father; by your deeds this day you have fulfilled what you said to him in words. Now, therefore, LORD God of Israel, keep this promise of yours to your servant David my father, when you said: 'You will never want for a man appointed by me to sit on the throne of Israel, if only your sons look to their ways and walk before me as you have done.' God of Israel, let the promise which you made to your servant David my father be confirmed.

"But can God indeed dwell on earth? Heaven itself, the highest heaven, cannot contain you; how much less this house that I have built! Yet attend, LORD my God, to the prayer and the supplication of your servant; listen to the cry and the prayer which your servant makes before you this day, that

your eyes may ever be on this house night and day, this place of which you said, 'My name will be there.' Hear your servant when he prays towards this place. Hear the supplication of your servant and your people Israel when they pray towards this place. Hear in heaven your dwelling and, when you hear, forgive.

"Should anyone wrong a neighbour and be adjured to take an oath, and come to take the oath before your altar in this house, then hear in heaven and take action: be your servants' judge, condemning the guilty person and bringing his deeds on his own head, acquitting the innocent and rewarding him as his innocence may deserve.

"Should your people Israel be defeated by an enemy because they have sinned against you, and then turn back to you, confessing your name and making their prayer and supplication to you in this house, hear in heaven; forgive the sin of your people Israel and restore them to the land which you gave to their forefathers.

"Should the heavens be shut up and there be no rain, because your servant and your people Israel have sinned against you, and they then pray towards this place, confessing your name and forsaking their sin when they feel your punishment, hear in heaven and forgive their sin; so teach them the good way which they are to follow, and grant rain on your land which you have given to your people as their own possession.

"Should there be famine in the land, or pestilence, or blight either black or red, or locusts developing or fully grown, or should their enemies besiege them in any of their cities, or plague or sickness befall them, then hear the prayer or supplication of everyone among your people Israel, as each, prompted by the remorse of his own heart, spreads out his hands towards this house: hear it in heaven your dwelling-place, forgive, and take action. As you know a person's heart, reward him according to his deeds, for you alone know the hearts of all; and so they will fear you throughout their lives in the land you gave to our forefathers.

"The foreigner too, anyone who does not belong to your people Israel, but has come from a distant land because of your fame (for your great fame and your strong hand and outstretched arm will be widely known), when such a one comes and prays towards this house, hear in heaven your dwelling-place and respond to the call which the foreigner makes to you, so that like your people Israel all the peoples of the earth may know your fame and fear you, and learn that this house which I have built bears your name.

"When your people go to war against an enemy, wherever you send them, and when they pray to the LORD, turning towards this city which you have chosen and towards this house which I have built for your name, then hear in heaven their prayer and supplication, and maintain their cause.

"Should they sin against you (and who is free from sin?) and should you in your anger give them over to an enemy who carries them captive to his own land, far or near, and should they then in the land of their captivity have a change of heart and make supplication to you there and say, 'We have sinned and acted perversely and wickedly,' and turn back to you wholeheartedly in the land of their enemies who took them captive, and pray to you, turning towards their land which you gave to their forefathers and towards this city which you chose and this house which I have built for your name, then in heaven your dwelling-place hear their prayer and supplication, and maintain their cause. Forgive your people their sins and transgressions against you; put pity for them in their captors' hearts. For they are your possession, your people whom you brought out of Egypt, from the smelting furnace. Let your eyes be ever open to the entreaty of your servant and of your people Israel, and hear whenever they call to you. You yourself have singled them out from all the peoples of the earth to be your possession; so, Lord GOD, you promised through your servant Moses when you brought our forefathers from Egypt."

As Solomon finished all this prayer and supplication to the LORD, he rose from before the altar of the LORD, where he had been kneeling with his hands spread out to heaven; he stood up and in a loud voice blessed the whole assembly of Israel: "Blessed be the LORD who has given his people Israel rest, as he promised: not one of the promises he made through his servant Moses has failed. May the LORD our God be with us as he was with our forefathers; may he never leave us or forsake us. May he turn our hearts towards him, so that we may conform to all his ways, observing his commandments, statutes, and judgements, as he commanded our forefathers. And may the words of my supplication to the LORD be with the LORD our God day and night, that, as the need arises day by day, he may maintain the cause of his servant and of his people Israel. So all the peoples of the earth will know that the LORD is God, he and no other, and you will be perfect in loyalty to the LORD our God as you are this day, conforming to his statutes and observing his commandments."

The king and all Israel with him offered sacrifices before the LORD; Solomon offered as shared-offerings to the LORD twenty-two thousand oxen and a hundred and twenty thousand sheep. Thus the king and the Israelites dedicated the house of the LORD. On that day also the king consecrated the centre of the court which lay in front of the house of the LORD; there he offered the whole-offering, the grain-offering, and the fat portions of the shared-offerings, because the bronze altar which stood before the LORD was too small to accommodate the whole-offering, the grain-offering, and the fat portions of the shared-offerings.

So Solomon and with him all Israel, a great assembly from Lebo-hamath to the wadi of Egypt, celebrated the pilgrim-feast at that time before the LORD our God for seven days. On the eighth day he dismissed the people; and they blessed the king, and went home happy and glad at heart for all the prosperity granted by the LORD to his servant David and to his people Israel.

*   *   *

REVIEW QUESTIONS

1. How are the wealth, skills, and products of the cities of Phoenicia represented in this selection?
2. Why did Solomon cause the temple to be built?
3. How is the temple intended to serve as a link between Yahweh and his people?

FROM *The Annals of Ashurnasirpal II of Assyria*

The ninth century B.C.E. witnessed the reemergence of Assyria under two powerful kings, Ashurnasirpal II and Shalmaneser III. Both kings waged farflung military campaigns, the efficiency and brutality of which set the tone for the next 250 years of Assyrian conquest and empire. Ashurnasirpal's new capital city at Kalhu (Nimrud) on the Tigris River included a magnificent palace, the construction of which incorporated long cuneiform inscriptions celebrating his conquests and proclaiming his majesty and that of the chief Assyrian god, Ashur. The following selection includes the prologue to Ashurnasirpal's annals, followed by an account of his first year's campaign. As you read, you may find reason to agree with the assessment of the historian A. T. Olmstead, who characterized Ashurnasirpal's career as one of "calculated frightfulness."

From *Ancient Records of Assyria and Babylonia,* vol. I, by D. D. Luckenbill (Chicago: University of Chicago Press, 1926), pp. 138–45.

*   *   *

Unto Ninurta, the powerful, the almighty, the exalted, the chief of the gods, the valiant, the gigantic, the perfect, whose onslaught in battle cannot be equaled, the first(born) son, the destroyer of opposition, the first-born of Nudimmud, the hero of the Igigi, the powerful, the prince of the gods, the offspring of E-kur, who holds the bolt of heaven and earth, who opens the depths, who treads the broad earth, the god without whom the decisions of heaven and earth are not decided, the destroyer, the mighty one, the command of whose mouth is not void, pre-eminent in the (four) quarters (of the world), who gives scepter and law unto all cities, the impetuous ruler, the word of whose lips is not altered, (of) boundless strength, the master of the gods, the exalted, Utgallu, the lord of lords, whose hand controls the ends of heaven and earth, the king of battle, the strong one who conquers opposition, the triumphant, the perfect, the lord of the nether waters and of the oceans, the terrible, the merciless one whose onslaught is a storm (deluge), who overwhelms the land of enemies, who strikes down the wicked, the powerful god whose counsel is not void, the light of heaven and earth, who gives light unto the midst of the deep, who destroys the wicked, who brings to subjection the disobedient, who overthrows foes, whose name in the assembly of the gods no god can humble, the giver of life, the god Ab-u, to whom it is good to pray (?), who dwells in the city of Calah, the great lord, my lord, (I) Assur-nâsir-pal (do pray); the mighty king, king of the universe, the king without a rival, the king of the whole of the four quarters (of the world), the Sun of all peoples, favorite of Enlil and Ninurta, the beloved of Anu and Dagan, the worshiper of the great gods, the submissive one who is dear unto thy heart, the prince, the favorite of Enlil, whose priesthood is pleasing unto thy great godhead so that thou hast established his reign, the valiant hero who goes hither and yon trusting in Assur, his lord, and who is without a rival among the princes of the four quarters (of the world), the wonderful shepherd, who fears not opposition, the mighty flood who has no conqueror, the king who has brought into subjection those that were not submissive to him, who has brought under his sway the totality of all peoples, the mighty hero who treads on the neck of his foe, who tramples all enemies under foot, who shatters the might of the haughty, who goes about trusting in the great gods, his lords, whose hand has conquered all the countries, who has brought under his sway all the mountain (regions) and has received their tribute, who has taken hostages, and who has established might over all lands.

When Assur, the lord, who called me by my name and has made great my kingdom, intrusted his merciless weapon unto my lordly hand, (I) Assur-nâsir-pal, the exalted prince, who fears the great gods, the powerful despot, conqueror of cities and mountains to their farthest borders, the king of rulers, who consumes the wicked, who is crowned with glory, who fears not opposition, the strong, the exalted, the unsparing, who destroys opposition, the king of all princes, the lord of lords, the shepherd(?), the king of kings, the exalted priest, the chosen of the hero Ninurta, the worshiper of the great gods, the avenger (of his fathers), the king who trusting in Assur and Shamash, the gods, his helpers, walks righteously and has cut down haughty mountain(eers) and princes who were his enemies, like reeds of the marsh, bringing all lands into subjection under his feet, who provides the offerings for the great gods, the rightful prince who has been permanently intrusted (with the task) of maintaining the cults(?) of the temples of his land, the work of whose hands and the offering of whose sacrifices the great gods of heaven and earth love, and whose priesthood in the temples they have established for all time,—their weapons they presented as my (*v.*, his) royal gift,—the radiance of whose arms and the awe-inspiring splendor of whose rule have made him supreme over the kings of the four quarters (of the world), who has battled with all the enemies of Assur north and south and has laid tribute and tax upon them, conqueror of the foes of Assur; son of Tukulti-Ninurta, priest of Assur, who overcame all his enemies and fixed the bodies of his foes upon stakes; grandson of Adad-Nirâri, the priest, the viceroy of the great gods, who brought about the overthrow of those that did not obey him and established his sway over all; the descendant of Assur-dân, who freed(?) cities and founded temples. And now at the command of the great gods my sovereignty, my dominion, and my power are manifesting themselves; I am regal, I am lordly, I am exalted, I am mighty, I am honored, I am glorified, I am pre-eminent, I am powerful, I am valiant, I am lion-brave, and I am heroic! (I), Assur-nâsir-pal, the mighty king, the king of Assyria, chosen of Sin, favorite of Anu, beloved of Adad, mighty one among the gods, I am the merciless weapon that strikes down the land of his enemies; I am a king, mighty in battle, destroying cities and highlands, first in war, king of the four quarters (of the world), who has conquered his foes, destroyed all his enemies, king of all the regions (of earth), of all princes, every one of them, the king who has trampled down all who were not submissive to him, and who has brought under his sway the totality of all peoples. These decrees of destiny came forth at the word of the great gods, and for my destiny they duly ordained them. In (every) desire of my heart and undertaking of my hand, Ishtar, the lady, who loves my priesthood, was gracious unto me and her heart prompted to the waging of war and battle.

At that time Assur-nâsir-pal, the exalted prince, who fears the great gods, the desire of whose heart Enlil has caused him to attain, and whose mighty hand has conquered all princes who were disobedient unto him, conqueror of his foes, who shattered the power of the mighty in difficult regions,—when Assur, my great lord, who called me by name and made great my kingship over the kings of the four quarters (of the world), had made my name exceeding great, and had intrusted his merciless weapon unto my lordly power, and in his wrath had commanded me to conquer, to subdue and to rule; trusting in Assur, my lord, I marched by difficult roads over steep mountains with the hosts of my army, and there was none who opposed me.

In the beginning of my kingship, in the first year of my reign, when Shamash the judge of the (four) regions (of the world) had spread his kindly shadow over me, and I had seated myself upon the royal throne in might, and (when) he had placed in my hand the scepter, which rules the peoples, I mobilized my chariots and armies, crossed over steep mountains by difficult roads which had not been prepared for the passage of chariots and troops, and marched to the land of Tumme. Libê, their fortified city, and the cities of Surra, Abuku, Arura, and Arubê, which lie among the mountains of Urini, Aruni and Etini, fortified cities, I captured. I slew great numbers of them; their spoil, their possessions and their cattle I carried off. The men escaped, and occupied a steep mountain; the mountain was exceeding steep and I did not go after them. The peak of the mountain rose like the point of an iron dagger, and no bird of heaven that flies comes to it. Like the nest of the eagle (vulture) their stronghold was situated within the mountain, whereinto none of the kings, my fathers, had penetrated. For three days the warrior searched out the mountain, his stout heart urging to battle; he climbed up on foot, he cast down the mountain, he destroyed their nest, he shattered their host. Two hundred of their fighting men I cut down with the sword; their heavy booty I carried off like a flock of sheep; with their blood I dyed the mountain red like wool; with the rest of them I darkened(?) the gullies and precipices of the mountain; their cities I destroyed, I devastated, I burned with fire. From the land of Tumme I departed, to the land of Kirruri I went down. Tribute from the lands of Kirruri, Simesi, Simera, Ulmania, Adaush, (from) the Hargeans and Harmaseans, —horses, mules, cattle, sheep, wine, vessels of copper, I received as their tribute and I imposed the carrying of the headpad(?) upon them.

While I was staying in the land of Kirruri, the awe-inspiring splendor of Assur, my lord, overwhelmed the men of the lands of Gilzani and Hubushkia; horses, silver, gold, lead, copper and vessels of copper they brought to me as their tribute. From the land of Kirruri I departed, and I entered by the pass of Hulun into the land of Kirhi, which lies inside. The cities of Hatu, Hataru, Nishtun, Irbidi, Mitkia, Arsania, Téla, and Halua, cities of the land of Kirhi which lie among the mighty mountains of Usu, Arua, and Arardi, I captured. Great numbers of them I slew, their spoil and their possessions I carried away. The

men escaped and occupied a lofty mountain peak which was over against the city of Nishtun and which was suspended like a cloud from heaven. Against these men, unto whom none among the kings my fathers had come near, my warriors flew like birds. 260 of their fighting men I cut down with the sword, I cut off their heads, and I formed them into pillars. The rest of them built a nest on the rocks of the mountain like a bird. Their spoil and their possessions I brought down from the mountain, and the cities which were in the midst of the mighty ranges, I destroyed, I devastated, I burned with fire. All the men who had fled from before my arms came down and embraced my feet. Tribute and tax, and the carrying of the headpad(?) I imposed upon them. Bûbu, son of Bubâ, the governor of the city of Nishtun, I flayed in the city of Arbela and I spread his skin upon the city wall. At that time I fashioned an image of my own likeness, the glory of my power I inscribed thereon, and in the mountain of Eki, in the city of Assur-nâsir-pal, at the (river) source, I set it up.

In this (same) eponymy, on the twenty-fourth day of the month *Abu*, at the word of Assur and Ishtar, the great gods, my lords, I departed from Nineveh, against the cities which lie at the foot of the mighty mountains of Nipur and Pasate I marched. I captured the cities of Arkun, Ushhu and Pilazi and twenty cities of their neighborhood. Great numbers (of the inhabitants) I slew, their spoil and their possessions I carried off, their cities I burned with fire. All the men who had fled from before my arms, came down and embraced my feet, and I imposed forced labor upon them. From the cities at the foot of the mountains of Nipur and Pasate I departed, the Tigris I crossed, and I drew near to the land of Kutmuhi, I received tribute from the lands of Kutmuhi and Mushki—vessels of copper, cattle, sheep, and wine.

While I was staying in the land of Kutmuhi, they brought me the word: "The city of Sûru of Bît-Halupê has revolted, they have slain Hamatai, their governor, and Ahia-baba, the son of a nobody, whom they brought from Bît-Adini, they have set up as king over them." With the help of Adad and the great gods who have made great my kingdom, I mobilized (my) chariots and armies and marched along the bank of the Habur. During my advance I received much tribute from Shulmanu-haman-ilâni of the city of Gardiganni, from Ilu-Adad of the city of Katna—silver, gold, lead, vessels of copper, and garments of brightly colored wool, and garments of linen. To the city of Sûru of Bît-Halupê I drew near, and the terror of the splendor of Assur, my lord, overwhelmed them. The chief men and the elders of the city, to save their lives, came forth into my presence and embraced my feet, saying: "If it is thy pleasure, slay! If it is thy pleasure, let live! That which thy heart desireth, do!" Ahiababa, the son of nobody, whom they had brought from Bît-Adini, I took captive. In the valor of my heart and with the fury of my weapons I stormed the city. All the rebels they seized and delivered them up. My officers I caused to enter into his palace and his temples. His silver, his gold, his goods and his possessions, copper, iron, lead, vessels of copper, cups of copper, dishes of copper, a great hoard of copper, alabaster, tables with inlay, the women of his palaces, his daughters, the captive rebels together with their possessions, the gods together with their possessions, precious stone from the mountains, his chariot with equipment, his horses, broken to the yoke, trappings of men and trappings of horses, garments of brightly colored wool and garments of linen, goodly oil, cedar, and fine sweet-scented herbs, panels(?) of cedar, purple and crimson wool, his wagons, his cattle, his sheep, his heavy spoil, which like the stars of heaven could not be counted, I carried off. Azi-ilu I set over them as my own governor. I built a pillar over against his city gate, and I flayed all the chief men who had revolted, and I covered the pillar with their skins; some I walled up within the pillar, some I impaled upon the pillar on stakes, and others I bound to stakes round about the pillar; many within the border of my own land I flayed, and I spread their skins upon the walls; and I cut off the limbs of the officers, of the royal officers who had rebelled. Ahiababa I took to Nineveh, I flayed him, I spread his skin upon the wall of Nineveh. My power and might I established over the land of Lakê. While I was staying in the city of Sûru, (I received) tribute from all the kings of the land of Lakê,—silver, gold, lead, copper, vessels of copper, cattle, sheep, garments of brightly colored wool, and garments of linen, and I increased the tribute and taxes and imposed them upon them. At that time, the tribute of Haiâni of the city of Hindani,—silver, gold, lead, copper, *umu*-stone, alabaster, purple wool, and (Bactrian) camels I received from him as tribute. At that time I fashioned a heroic image of my royal self, my power and my glory I inscribed thereon, in the midst of his palace I set it up. I fashioned memorial steles and inscribed thereon my glory and my prowess, and I set them up by his city gate.

*　　*　　*

REVIEW QUESTIONS

1. What is the relationship between the king and the gods? Do the king's conquests appear to be divinely sanctioned?
2. Would you characterize the Assyrians' attitude toward conquered peoples as benevolent?
3. To what kinds of techniques did the Assyrians resort in order to ensure their control?
4. What were the motives that underlay Ashurnasirpal's conquests?

THE ASSYRIAN ATTACK ON LACHISH (701 B.C.E.)

The Assyrian onslaught at the Israelite city of Lachish is depicted on a portion of a wall relief in the palace of the Assyrian king Sennacherib at Nineveh. What kinds of military technology did the Assyrian army employ? Can you see evidence of one fate of the vanquished? What might be the practical uses of images such as these?

Letters from Diviners to the Assyrian King

Very firmly entrenched in the Mesopotamian mentality (at least to the extent that we can discern it in their literature) was the belief that the gods determined human destinies and that no human endeavor could succeed without divine permission. (Indeed, that point of view is perhaps echoed in the modern Arabs' habit of liberally sprinkling everyday conversation with the expression insh'allah, *"if God wills.") Fortunately for humans, the gods might reveal their intentions through physical phenomena, or omens. Omens could either occur naturally (such as dreams, abnormal births, celestial events, or the movement of animals) or be induced by human agency (very commonly, by extispicy, examining the entrails of a ritually killed sheep). There accordingly developed early on in Mesopotamian civilization specialized diviners, scholar-technicians who were trained to perform the rituals of inducing the appropriate phenomena, interpret the results, and thereby divine the gods' intentions or decisions. Over time, there developed a vast omen literature that set down in a fairly systematic fashion the correlations between omens and subsequent events.*

The following letters from diviners to the Assyrian kings Esarhaddon and Ashurbanipal report on their findings.

From *Letters from Mesopotamia,* translated by A. Leo Oppenheim (Chicago: University of Chicago Press, 1967), pp. 157–58.

To my lord, the king of all countries (Assurbanipal), from your servant Bēl-u[. . .]:

May the gods Bēl, Nabû, and Šamas bless Your Majesty.

If an eclipse occurs, but it is not observed in the capital, such an eclipse is considered not to have occurred. "The capital" means the city in which the king happens to be staying. Now, there were clouds everywhere; we thus do not know whether the eclipse did or did not occur. The lord of all kings should write to Assur and to all cities such as Babylon, Nippur, Uruk, and Borsippa. Possibly it was observed in these cities. The king should also watch out for the regular reports . . . I have already written everything to Your Majesty concerning the portent of an eclipse that occurred in the months Addaru and Nisannu. And as to the apotropaic rites for the eclipse which they have already performed, what harm can be done (even if the eclipse did not take place)? It is advantageous to perform the rites; the king should therefore not send the experts away.

The great gods who live in the city of Your Majesty have covered the sky and have thus not shown the eclipse. This is what the king should know: to wit, that this eclipse has no relation to Your Majesty or his country. On this account the king should be happy.

PS: If the storm god Adad thunders in the month of Nisannu, it means the "small barley" crop will diminish.

*   *   *

To the king, my lord (Esarhaddon), from your servant Balasī:

Good health to Your Majesty! May the gods Nabû and Marduk bless Your Majesty.

As to Your Majesty's writing me about the

wording of the omen prediction as follows: "What is the meaning of 'The king will come to naught together with his powerful officials'?" Experts must be put to work on this problem. Predictions in omens depend on the months of the year; thus, one is not like the other; they take their meanings from their contexts. In this case the prediction of the omen means actually, "He will come to naught."

As to that earthquake which occurred recently: there is nothing to it. One should however perform the ritual for an earthquake and thus your gods will make the bad portent by-pass you (to wit the ritual called) "Ea-has-done-it-Ea-has-removed-it," because he (the god Ea) who caused the quake has also created the relevant (apotropaic) *namburbi*-ritual against it. There were no earthquakes in the times of the king's father and even his grandfathers, and I myself have not experienced earthquakes because I am too young. But this god (i.e., Ea) has given a warning to the king. The king should pray to the god with uplifted hands and recite the (apotropaic) *namburbi*-ritual and—I say—the evil will be averted.

*   *   *

To the king, my lord (Esarhaddon), from your servant Balasī:

Good health to Your Majesty! May the gods Nabû and Marduk bless Your Majesty.

As to Your Majesty's request addressed to me concerning the incident with the ravens, here are the relevant omens: "If a raven brings something into a person's house, this man will obtain something that does not belong to him. If a falcon or a raven drops something he is carrying upon a person's house or in front of a man, this house will have much traffic—traffic means profit. If a bird carries meat, another bird, or anything else, and drops it upon a person's house, this man will obtain a large inheritance."

May the gods Nabû and Marduk bless Your Majesty. May they give Your Majesty long-lasting life, old age, extremely old age.

*   *   *

REVIEW QUESTIONS

1. According to these letters, what kinds of natural occurrences might be perceived as ominous?
2. How important were omens in the conduct of the royal court?
3. Might one be able to regard Mesopotamian divination as a science?

The Cylinder Inscription of Cyrus

The rise of the Persians under Cyrus the Great from obscurity as subjects of the Medes to imperial dominion over the entire Middle East is one of the more-compelling stories of ancient history. Between 550 and 539 B.C.E., Cyrus gained control, successively, of the empires of the Medes of Iran, the Lydians of Anatolia, and the Chaldaeans of Babylonia, to create the largest empire ever seen to that time. Discovered at Babylon in 1879, the following inscription celebrates Cyrus's taking possession of Babylon from Nabonidus, the last Chaldaean king, and his restoration of the cult of Marduk—a magnanimous act paralleled by his granting of permission for the rebuilding of Yahweh's temple in Jerusalem (as recorded in the Bible).

From *The Context of Scripture,* vol. 2, *Monumental Inscriptions from the Biblical World,* edited by William W. Hallo (Leiden, Neth.: Brill, 2000), pp. 315–16.

* * *

An incompetent person was installed to exercise lordship over his country. [. . .] he imposed upon them. An imitation of Esagila he ma[de ?], for Ur and the rest of the sacred centers, improper rituals [ ] daily he recited. Irreverently, he put an end to the regular offerings; he [ ], he established in the sacred centers. By his own plan, he did away with the worship of Marduk, the king of the gods; he continually did evil against his (Marduk's) city. Daily, [without interruption . . .], he [imposed] the corvée upon its inhabitants unrelentingly, ruining them all.

Upon (hearing) their cries, the lord of the gods became furiously angry [and he left] their borders; and the gods who lived among them forsook their dwellings, angry that he had brought (them) into Babylon. Marduk [ ] turned (?) towards all the habitations that were abandoned and all the people of Sumer and Akkad who had become corpses; [he was recon]ciled and had mercy (upon them). He surveyed and looked throughout all the lands, searching for a righteous king whom he would support. He called out his name: Cyrus, king of Anshan; he pronounced his name to be king over all (the world). He (Marduk) made the land of Gutium and all the Umman-manda bow in submission at his feet. And he (Cyrus) shepherded with justice and righteousness all the black-headed people, over whom he (Marduk) had given him victory. Marduk, the great lord, guardian (?) of his people, looked with gladness upon his good deeds and upright heart. He ordered him to march to his city Babylon. He set him on the road to Babylon and like a companion and friend, he went at his side. His vast army, whose number, like the water of the river, cannot be known, marched at his side fully armed. He made him enter his city Babylon without fighting or battle; he saved Babylon from hardship. He delivered Nabonidus, the king who did not revere him, into his hands. All the people of Babylon, all the land of Sumer and Akkad, princes and governors, bowed to him and kissed his feet. They rejoiced at his kingship and their faces shone. Ruler by whose aid the dead were revived and who had all been redeemed from hardship and difficulty, they greeted him with gladness and praised his name.

I am Cyrus, king of the world, great king, mighty king, king of Babylon, king of Sumer and Akkad, king of the four quarters, son of Cambyses, great king, king of Anshan, grandson of Cyrus, great king, king of Anshan, descendant of Teispes, great king, king of Anshan, (of an) eternal line of kingship, whose rule Bel (i.e., Marduk) and Nabu love, whose kingship they desire for their hearts' pleasure.

When I entered Babylon in a peaceful manner, I took up my lordly reign in the royal palace amidst rejoicing and happiness. Marduk, the great lord, caused the magnanimous people of Babylon [to . . .] me, (and) I daily attended to his worship. My vast army moved about Babylon in peace; I did not permit anyone to frighten (the people of) [Sumer] and Akkad. I sought the welfare of the city of Babylon and all its sacred centers. As for the citizens of Babylon, upon whom he imposed corvée which was not the god's will and not befitting them, I relieved their weariness and freed them from their service (?). Marduk, the great lord, rejoiced over my [good] deeds. He sent gracious blessings upon me, Cyrus, the king who worships him, and upon Cambyses, the son who is [my] offspring, [and upo]n all my army, and in peace, before him, we move [about].

By his exalted [word], all the kings who sit upon thrones throughout the world, from the Upper Sea to the Lower Sea, who live in the dis[tricts far-off], the kings of the West, who dwell in tents, all of them brought their heavy tribute before me and in Babylon they kissed my feet. From [Ninev]eh (?), Ashur and Susa, Agade, Eshnunna, Zamban, Meturnu, Der, as far as the region of Gutium, I returned the (images of) the gods to the sacred centers [on the other side of] the Tigris whose sanctuaries had been abandoned for a long time, and I let them dwell in eternal abodes. I gathered all their inhabitants and returned (to them) their dwellings. In addition, at the command of Marduk, the great lord, I settled in their habitations, in pleasing abodes, the gods of Sumer and Akkad, whom Nabonidus, to the anger of the lord of the gods, had brought into Babylon. May all the gods whom I settled in their sacred centers ask daily of Bel and Nabu that my days be long and may they intercede for my welfare. May they say to Marduk, my lord: "As for Cyrus, the king who reveres you, and Cambyses, his son, [   ] a reign." I settled all the lands in peaceful abodes.

*   *   *

REVIEW QUESTIONS

1. How would you assess Cyrus's policy toward the newly conquered city of Babylon?
2. Do you see any contrasts between Cyrus's treatment of the city of Babylon and Ashurnasirpal's treatment of the cities and towns he conquered?

HERODOTUS

FROM *The Histories:* Customs of the Persians

The Greek historian Herodotus, who wrote during the fifth century B.C.E., has long been lauded as the father of history (although some would call him the grandfather and accord Thucydides the appellation father). Although modern historians are quite aware of Herodotus's own prejudices and gullibility, his The Histories nonetheless remains our most important source for the history of the Persian invasions of Greece in 490 and 480–479 B.C.E. As background for that story, Herodotus also furnished a virtual travelogue of the peoples, places, and customs of the fifth century B.C.E. world. (In fact, his description of Egyptian customs remains an often-cited source on techniques of mummification.) In the following selection, Herodotus reports his knowledge of the customs of the Persians.

From *Herodotus: The Histories,* edited by Walter Blanco and Jennifer Tolbert Roberts, translated by Walter Blanco (New York: Norton, 1992), pp. 48–50.

*   *   *

These are the customs I know the Persians to observe. They are not allowed to build statues, temples, and altars, and in fact they accuse those who do of silliness, in my opinion because unlike the Greeks, they don't think of the gods as having human form. It is their custom to climb to the mountaintops and sacrifice to Zeus, which is the name they give to the full circle of the sky. They sacrifice to the sun and the moon and the earth, as well as to fire, water, and air. At first, they sacrificed only to these, but they later learned to sacrifice to the Heavenly Aphrodite—they learned this from the Assyrians and the Arabians. The Assyrians call Aphrodite Mylitta, the Arabians call her Alilat, and the Persians call her Mitra.

This is the way the Persians sacrifice to the above-mentioned gods: they make no altars and light no fires when they are about to sacrifice. They don't pour libations or play the flute or wear garlands or sprinkle barley on their victims. Whenever someone wants to sacrifice to one of the gods, he leads the victim to a ritually pure place and invokes the god while wearing his turban wreathed, preferably, with myrtle. It is not allowed for the sacrificer to pray, in private, for good things for himself. Instead, he prays for the well-being of all the Persians and of the king, for the sacrificer, after all, is included among all the Persians. When he has cut up the sacrificial victim into pieces and then boiled the meat, he spreads out the tenderest grass—preferably clover—and then places all of the meat on top of it. When he has arranged the meat piece by piece, a Magus stands near and chants a hymn on the origin of the gods—anyway, that's the kind of hymn they say it is. It is not their custom to perform a sacrifice without a Magus. The sacrificer waits a little while, then carries away the meat and does whatever he wants with it.

The day of all days they celebrate the most is their own birthday. On that day, the right thing to do is to serve a bigger meal than on any other day. On that day, their rich people serve up oxen, horses, camels, and donkeys that have been roasted whole in ovens, while their poor people serve smaller cattle, like sheep and goats. They eat few main dishes, but lots of appetizers, one after another, and for this reason the Persians say that the Greeks eat a main course and then stop when they are still hungry since after dinner nothing worth mentioning is brought out, though they wouldn't stop eating if it was. They love wine, but they are not allowed to vomit or to urinate in front of someone else. But though they have to be careful about that, they are accustomed to deliberate about their most important affairs when they are drunk, and then, on the next day, when they are sober, the master of the house they have been deliberating in proposes the decision that pleased them most. If they like it even when they are sober, they adopt it, but if not, they let it go. If they ever come to a provisional decision while sober, though, they then get drunk and reconsider it.

This is how you can tell if people who happen to meet each other on the street are social equals: instead of a verbal greeting, they kiss each other on the lips. If one is of slightly lower rank, they kiss each other's cheeks. If one is of a much lower rank, though, he prostrates himself and pays homage to the other. After themselves, Persians have the highest respect for the people who live closest to them, and next highest for those next closest, and so on. In accordance with this principle, they have the least respect for those who live farthest away. They consider themselves to be the best of people by far and others to share worth proportionally, so the people who live the farthest away are the worst. Subject nations ruled each other even under Median rule. That is, the Medes ruled over everything, but especially over those nearest to them, while those, in turn, ruled their neighbors, and so on. The Persians rank nations according to the same principle, by which each nation has a surrogate rule over the next one.

Nevertheless, the Persians are more inclined than other people to adopt foreign customs. For example, they wear Median clothes in the belief that they are more attractive than their own, and they wear Egyptian breastplates into war. They seek out and learn about all kinds of delights, and they even learned from the Greeks to have sex with boys. Each Persian man has many lawfully wedded wives, but many more mistresses.

Second only to being brave in battle, a man is considered manly if he has many sons to show for himself, and every year the king sends gifts to the man who shows off the most sons. They believe that there is strength in numbers. They educate their sons from the age of five to the age of twenty in only three things: horseback riding, archery, and telling the truth. The boy does not come into the presence of his father until he is five years old—until then he lives with the women. This is done so that if he should die while he is growing up he won't cause any grief to his father.

I approve of that custom, and I also approve of the one that forbids even the king to put someone to death on the basis of only one charge, and that forbids any Persian to do any of his household slaves any irreparable harm on the basis of one charge either. If, however, he finds on review that there are more and greater offenses than services, then he may give way to anger.

They say that no one has yet killed his own father or mother. It is inevitable, they say, that any such child who has ever been born will be found on investigation to have been either a changeling or a bastard. They say that it just isn't likely that a true parent will be killed by his own child.

Whatever they are not allowed to do, they are also not allowed to talk about. They consider lying to be the most disgraceful of all things. After that, it is owing money—for many reasons, but mostly, they say, because it is necessary for somebody who owes money to tell lies.

No citizen who is an albino or who has leprosy is allowed into the city or to mingle with other Persians. They say that he has committed some offense against the sun. Foreigners who catch these diseases are driven out of the country by posses. Even white doves are driven out, charged with the same offense.

They don't spit, urinate, or wash their hands in rivers, or allow anyone else to, for they especially revere rivers.

The Persians don't notice it, though we do, but this also happens to be true of them: their names, which refer to their physical characteristics or to their social importance, all end in the same letter, which the Dorians call san and which the Ionians call sigma. If you look into it, you will find that Persian names end in this letter—not some here and some there, but *all* of them.

I am able to say these things with certainty because I know them for a fact. There are things about the dead, though, which are concealed or referred to obliquely—for example that the corpse of a Persian man is not buried until it has been torn at by a bird or a dog. I know for sure, though, that the Magi practice this—because they do it openly—and that the Persians cover a corpse with wax before putting it in the ground. The Magi are very different from other people, including the Egyptian priests. The Egyptian priests refrain from killing any living thing, except what they ritually sacrifice. The Magi, however, will kill everything but dogs and people with their own hands. In fact, they make a point of killing things, and go around killing ants and snakes and anything else that creeps, crawls, and flies. Well, that's how they've been practicing this custom since the beginning, so let it stay that way.

*   *   *

REVIEW QUESTIONS

1. How would you judge Herodotus's general opinion of Persian customs and values? Does he find things to admire about them?

2. Do any of his observations suggest to you that he might have been taken in by someone else's stories?

FROM **The Book of Genesis:**
Noah and the Flood

The Hebrew Bible shows many parallels to ancient Mesopotamian literature. Perhaps the most famous is the shared story of a great flood designed to exterminate all human beings. In both stories, however, one man is instructed to build a great vessel and to bring aboard it "all manner of living things."

From *The Oxford Study Bible,* edited by M. Jack Suggs, Katharine Doob Sakenfeld, and James R. Mueller (Oxford, Eng.: Oxford University Press, 1992).

*   *   *

When the LORD saw how great was the wickedness of human beings on earth, and how their every thought and inclination were always wicked, he bitterly regretted that he had made mankind on earth. He said, "I shall wipe off the face of the earth this human race which I have created—yes, man and beast, creeping things and birds. I regret that I ever made them." Noah, however, had won the LORD's favour.

This is the story of Noah. Noah was a righteous man, the one blameless man of his time, and he walked with God. He had three sons: Shem, Ham, and Japheth. God saw that the world was corrupt and full of violence; and seeing this corruption, for the life of everyone on earth was corrupt, God said to Noah, 'I am going to bring the whole human race to an end, for because of them the earth is full of violence. I am about to destroy them, and the earth along with them. Make yourself an ark with ribs of cypress; cover it with reeds and coat it inside and out with pitch. This is to be its design: the length of the ark is to be three hundred cubits, its breadth fifty cubits, and its height thirty cubits. You are to make a roof for the ark, giving it a fall of one cubit when complete; put a door in the side of the ark, and build three decks, lower, middle, and upper. I am about to bring the waters of the flood over the earth to destroy from under heaven every human being that has the spirit of life; everything on earth shall

perish. But with you I shall make my covenant, and you will go into the ark, you with your sons, your wife, and your sons' wives. You are to bring living creatures of every kind into the ark to keep them alive with you, two of each kind, a male and a female; two of every kind of bird, beast, and creeping thing are to come to you to be kept alive. See that you take and store by you every kind of food that can be eaten; this will be food for you and for them.' Noah carried out exactly all God had commanded him.

The LORD said to Noah, "Go into the ark, you and all your household; for you alone in this generation have I found to be righteous. Take with you seven pairs, a male and female, of all beasts that are ritually clean, and one pair, a male and female, of all beasts that are not clean; also seven pairs, males and females, of every bird—to ensure that life continues on earth. For in seven days' time I am going to send rain on the earth for forty days and forty nights, and I shall wipe off the face of the earth every living creature I have made." Noah did all that the LORD had commanded him. He was six hundred years old when the water of the flood came on the earth.

So to escape the flood Noah went into the ark together with his sons, his wife, and his sons' wives. And to him on board the ark went one pair, a male and a female, of all beasts, clean and unclean, of birds, and of everything that creeps on the ground, two by two, as God had commanded. At the end of seven days the water of the flood came over the earth. In the year when Noah was six hundred years old, on the seventeenth day of the second month, that very day all the springs of the great deep burst out, the windows of the heavens were opened, and rain fell on the earth for forty days and forty nights. That was the day Noah went into the ark with his sons, Shem, Ham, and Japheth, his own wife, and his three sons' wives. Wild animals of every kind, cattle of every kind, every kind of thing that creeps on the ground, and winged birds of every kind—all living creatures came two by two to Noah in the ark. Those which came were one male and one female of all living things; they came in as God had commanded Noah, and the LORD closed the door on him.

The flood continued on the earth for forty days, and the swelling waters lifted up the ark so that it rose high above the ground. The ark floated on the surface of the swollen waters as they increased over the earth. They increased more and more until they covered all the high mountains everywhere under heaven. The water increased until the mountains were covered to a depth of fifteen cubits. Every living thing that moved on earth perished: birds, cattle, wild animals, all creatures that swarm on the ground, and all human beings. Everything on dry land died, everything that had the breath of life in its nostrils. God wiped out every living creature that existed on earth, man and beast, creeping thing and bird; they were all wiped out over the whole earth, and only Noah and those who were with him in the ark survived.

When the water had increased over the earth for a hundred and fifty days, God took thought for Noah and all the beasts and cattle with him in the ark, and he caused a wind to blow over the earth, so that the water began to subside. The springs of the deep and the windows of the heavens were stopped up, the downpour from the skies was checked. Gradually the water receded from the earth, and by the end of a hundred and fifty days it had abated. On the seventeenth day of the sev-enth month the ark grounded on the mountains of Ararat. The water continued to abate until the tenth month, and on the first day of the tenth month the tops of the mountains could be seen.

At the end of forty days Noah opened the hatch that he had made in the ark, and sent out a raven; it continued flying to and fro until the water on the earth had dried up. Then Noah sent out a dove to see whether the water on the earth had subsided. But the dove found no place where she could settle because all the earth was under water, and so she came back to him in the ark. Noah reached out and caught her, and brought her into the ark. He waited seven days more and again sent out the dove from the ark. She came back to him towards evening with a freshly plucked olive leaf in her beak. Noah knew then that the water had subsided from the earth's surface. He waited yet another seven days and, when he sent out the dove, she did not come back to him. So it came about that, on the first day of the first month of his six hundred and first year, the water had dried up on the earth, and when Noah removed the hatch and looked out, he saw that the ground was dry.

By the twenty-seventh day of the second month the earth was dry, and God spoke to Noah. "Come out of the ark together with your wife, your sons, and their wives," he said. "Bring out every living creature that is with you, live things of every kind, birds, beasts, and creeping things, and let them spread over the earth and be fruitful and increase on it." So Noah came out with his sons, his wife, and his sons' wives, and all the animals, creeping things, and birds; everything that moves on the ground came out of the ark, one kind after another.

Noah built an altar to the LORD and, taking beasts and birds of every kind that were ritually clean, he offered them as whole-offerings on it. When the LORD smelt the soothing odour, he said within himself, "Never again shall I put the earth under a curse because of mankind, however evil their inclination may be from their youth upwards, nor shall I ever again kill all living creatures, as I have just done.

"As long as the earth lasts,
seedtime and harvest, cold and heat,
summer and winter, day and night,
they will never cease."

GOD blessed Noah and his sons; he said to them, "Be fruitful and increase in numbers, and fill the earth. Fear and dread of you will come on all the animals on earth, on all the birds of the air, on everything that moves on the ground, and on all fish in the sea; they are made subject to you. Every creature that lives and moves will be food for you; I give them all to you, as I have given you every green plant. But you must never eat flesh with its life still in it, that is the blood. And further, for your life-blood I shall demand satisfaction; from every animal I shall require it, and from human beings also I shall require satisfaction for the death of their fellows.

Anyone who sheds human blood,
for that human being his blood will be shed;
because in the image of God
has God made human beings.

Be fruitful, then, and increase in number; people the earth and rule over it."

God said to Noah and his sons: "I am now establishing my covenant with you and with your descendants after you, and with every living creature that is with you, all birds and cattle, all the animals with you on earth, all that have come out of the ark. I shall sustain my covenant with you: never again will all living creatures be destroyed by the waters of a flood, never again will there be a flood to lay waste the earth."

God said, "For all generations to come, this is the sign which I am giving of the covenant between myself and you and all living creatures with you:

"My bow I set in the clouds
to be a sign of the covenant
between myself and the earth.
When I bring clouds over the earth,
the rainbow will appear in the clouds.

"Then I shall remember the covenant which I have made with you and with all living creatures, and never again will the waters become a flood to destroy all creation. Whenever the bow appears in the cloud, I shall see it and remember the everlasting covenant between God and living creatures of every kind on earth." So God said to Noah, "This is the sign of the covenant which I have established with all that lives on earth."

The sons of Noah who came out of the ark were Shem, Ham, and Japheth; Ham was the father of Canaan. These three were the sons of Noah, and their descendants spread over the whole earth.

*   *   *

REVIEW QUESTIONS

1. According to the Book of Genesis, why does God decide to visit a flood on humankind?
2. Does God intend to destroy all of his creation?
3. Why does God decide to spare Noah and his family?
4. Can you identify any parallels or contrasts between the Genesis version of the flood story and the version in the Mesopotamian story of Atrahasis in Chapter 1?

FROM The Torah: Laws

Modern scholars question the historicity of the Bible's account of the Hebrew Exodus, when thousands supposedly migrated from Egypt under the leadership of a man named Moses. The Egyptian records make no mention of such an event, nor is there any other evidence of it outside the biblical account. The impact of the Exodus story on the self-concept of the early Jewish people as a people who are chosen by God (who has identified himself by then as Yahweh) and whose fate is bound to their acceptance of him, is, however, immeasurable. As they made their way through the barren wilderness of the Sinai Desert, the Hebrews received from Yahweh a set of laws, the Decalogue or Ten Commandments. These laws were to govern both their relationship with him and their behavior among themselves. In subsequent books of the Pentateuch (the first five books of the Hebrew Bible, the authorship of which was traditionally ascribed to Moses), these laws were expanded and elaborated on to form the basis of the Torah, the corpus of biblical law. The Torah remains today the very core of Judaism and of Jewish self-identity as a people chosen by God.

From *The Oxford Study Bible*, edited by M. Jack Suggs, Katharine Doob Sakenfeld, and James R. Mueller (Oxford, Eng.: Oxford University Press, 1992).

FROM The Book of Exodus

*   *   *

Moses brought the people out from the camp to meet God, and they took their stand at the foot of the mountain. Mount Sinai was enveloped in smoke because the LORD had come down on it in fire; the smoke rose like the smoke from a kiln; all the people trembled violently, and the sound of the trumpet grew ever louder. Whenever Moses spoke, God answered him in a peal of thunder. The LORD came down on the top of Mount Sinai and summoned Moses up to the mountaintop. The LORD said to him, "Go down; warn the people solemnly that they must not force their way through to the LORD to see him, or many of them will perish. Even the priests, who may approach the LORD, must hallow themselves, for fear that the LORD may break out against them." Moses answered the LORD, "The people cannot come up Mount Sinai, because you solemnly warned us to set bounds to the mountain and keep it holy." The

LORD said, "Go down; then come back, bringing Aaron with you, but let neither priests nor people force their way up to the LORD, for fear that he may break out against them." So Moses went down to the people and spoke to them.

God spoke all these words:

I am the LORD your God who brought you out of Egypt, out of the land of slavery.

You must have no other god besides me.

You must not make a carved image for yourself, nor the likeness of anything in the heavens above, or on the earth below, or in the waters under the earth.

You must not bow down to them in worship; for I, the LORD your God, am a jealous God, punishing the children for the sins of the parents to the third and fourth generation of those who reject me. But I keep faith with thousands, those who love me and keep my commandments.

You must not make wrong use of the name of the LORD your God; the LORD will not leave unpunished anyone who misuses his name.

Remember to keep the sabbath day holy. You have six days to labour and do all your work; but the seventh day is a sabbath of the LORD your God; that day you must not do any work, neither you, nor your son or your daughter, your slave or your slave-girl, your cattle, or the alien residing among you; for in six days the LORD made the heavens and the earth, the sea, and all that is in them, and on the seventh day he rested. Therefore the LORD blessed the sabbath day and declared it holy.

Honour your father and your mother, so that you may enjoy long life in the land which the LORD your God is giving you.

Do not commit murder.

Do not commit adultery.

Do not steal.

Do not give false evidence against your neighbour.

Do not covet your neighbour's household: you must not covet your neighbour's wife, his slave, his slave-girl, his ox, his donkey, or anything that belongs to him.

*   *   *

The LORD said to Moses, Say this to the Israelites: You know now that I have spoken from heaven to you. You must not make gods of silver to be worshipped besides me, nor may you make yourselves gods of gold. The altar you make for me is to be of earth, and you are to sacrifice on it both your whole-offerings and your shared-offerings, your sheep and goats and your cattle. Wherever I cause my name to be invoked, I will come to you and bless you. If you make an altar of stones for me, you must not build it of hewn stones, for if you use a tool on them, you profane them. You must not mount up to my altar by steps, in case your private parts are exposed over against it.

These are the laws you are to set before them:

When you purchase a Hebrew as a slave, he will be your slave for six years; in the seventh year he is to go free without paying anything.

If he comes to you alone, he is to go away alone; but if he is already a married man, his wife is to go away with him.

If his master gives him a wife, and she bears him sons or daughters, the woman with her children belongs to her master, and the man must go away alone. But if the slave should say, 'I am devoted to my master and my wife and children; I do not wish to go free,' then his master must bring him to God: he is to be brought to the door or the doorpost, and his master will pierce his ear with an awl; the man will then be his slave for life.

When a man sells his daughter into slavery, she is not to go free as male slaves may. If she proves unpleasing to her master who had designated her for himself, he must let her be redeemed; he has treated her unfairly, and therefore he has no right to sell her to foreigners. If he assigns her to his son, he must allow her the rights of a daughter. If he takes another woman, he must not deprive the first of meat, clothes, and conjugal rights; if he does not provide her with these three things, she is to go free without payment.

Whoever strikes another man and kills him must be put to death. But if he did not act with intent, but it came about by act of God, the slayer may flee to a place which I shall appoint for you. But if a man wilfully kills another by treachery, you are to take him even from my altar to be put to death.

Whoever strikes his father or mother must be put to death.

Whoever kidnaps an Israelite must be put to death, whether he has sold him, or the man is found in his possession.

Whoever reviles his father or mother must be put to death.

When men quarrel and one hits another with a stone or with his fist, and the man is not killed but takes to his bed, and if he recovers so as to walk about outside with his staff, then the one who struck him has no liability, except that he must pay compensation for the other's loss of time and see that his recovery is complete.

When a man strikes his slave or his slave-girl with a stick and the slave dies on the spot, he must be punished. But he is not to be punished if the slave survives for one day or two, because the slave is his property.

When, in the course of a brawl, a man knocks against a pregnant woman so that she has a miscarriage but suffers no further injury, then the offender must pay whatever fine the woman's husband demands after assessment. But where injury ensues, you are to give life for life, eye for eye, tooth for tooth, hand for hand, foot for foot, burn for burn, bruise for bruise, wound for wound.

When a man strikes his slave or slave-girl in the eye and destroys it, he must let the slave go free in compensation for the eye. When he knocks out the tooth of a slave or a slave-girl, he must let the slave go free in compensation for the tooth.

When an ox gores a man or a woman to death, the ox must be put to death by stoning, and its flesh is not to be eaten; the owner of the ox will be free from liability. If, however, the ox has for some time past been a vicious animal, and the owner has been duly warned but has not kept it under control, and the ox kills a man or a woman, then the ox must be stoned to death, and the owner put to death as well. If, however, the penalty is commuted for a money payment, he must pay in redemption of his life whatever is imposed upon him. If the ox gores a son or a daughter, the same ruling applies. If the ox gores a slave or slave-girl, its owner must pay thirty shekels of silver to their master, and the ox must be stoned to death.

*   *   *

When a man borrows a beast from his neighbour and it is injured or dies while its owner is not present, the borrower must make full restitution; but if the owner is with it, the borrower does not have to make restitution. If it was hired, only the hire is due.

When a man seduces a virgin who is not yet betrothed, he must pay the bride-price for her to be his wife. If her father refuses to give her to him, the seducer must pay in silver a sum equal to the bride-price for virgins.

You must not allow a witch to live.

Whoever has sexual intercourse with a beast must be put to death.

Whoever sacrifices to any god but the LORD must be put to death under solemn ban.

You must not wrong or oppress an alien; you were yourselves aliens in Egypt.

You must not wrong a widow or a fatherless child. If you do, and they appeal to me, be sure that I shall listen; my anger will be roused and I shall kill you with the sword; your own wives will become widows and your children fatherless.

If you advance money to any poor man amongst my people, you are not to act like a moneylender; you must not exact interest from him.

If you take your neighbour's cloak in pawn, return it to him by sunset, because it is his only covering. It is the cloak in which he wraps his body; in what else can he sleep? If he appeals to me, I shall listen, for I am full of compassion.

You must not revile God, nor curse a chief of your own people.

You must not hold back the first of your harvest, whether grain or wine. You must give me your firstborn sons. You must do the same with your oxen and your sheep. They should stay with the mother for seven days; on the eighth day you are to give them to me.

You must be holy to me: you are not to eat the flesh of anything killed by beasts in the open country; you are to throw it to the dogs.

You must not spread a baseless rumour, nor make common cause with a wicked man by giving malicious evidence.

You must not be led into wrongdoing by the majority, nor, when you give evidence in a lawsuit, should you side with the majority to pervert justice; nor should you show favouritism to a poor person in his lawsuit.

Should you come upon your enemy's ox or donkey straying, you must take it back to him. Should you see the donkey of someone who hates you lying helpless under its load, however unwilling you may be to help, you must lend a hand with it.

You must not deprive the poor man of justice in his lawsuit. Avoid all lies, and do not cause the death of the innocent and guiltless; for I the LORD will never acquit the guilty. Do not accept a bribe, for bribery makes the discerning person blind and the just person give a crooked answer.

Do not oppress the alien, for you know how it feels to be an alien; you yourselves were aliens in Egypt.

For six years you may sow your land and gather its produce; but in the seventh year you must let it lie fallow and leave it alone. Let it provide food for the poor of your people, and what they leave the wild animals may eat. You are to do likewise with your vineyard and your olive grove.

For six days you may do your work, but on the seventh day abstain from work, so that your ox and your donkey may rest, and your home-born slave and the alien may refresh themselves.

*　　*　　*

FROM The Book of Leviticus

*　　*　　*

When anyone reviles his father and his mother, he must be put to death. Since he has reviled his father and his mother, let his blood be on his own head. If a man commits adultery with another's wife, that is with the wife of a fellow-countryman, both adulterer and adulteress must be put to death. The man who has intercourse with his father's wife has brought shame on his father. Both must be put to death; their blood be on their own heads! If a man has intercourse with his daughter-in-law, both must be put to death. Their deed is a violation of nature; their blood be on their own heads! If a man has intercourse with a man as with a woman, both commit an abomination. They must be put to death; their blood be on their own heads! If a man takes both a woman and her mother, that is lewdness. Both he and they must be burnt, so that there may be no

lewdness in your midst. A man who has sexual intercourse with an animal must be put to death, and you are to kill the beast. If a woman approaches an animal to mate with it, you must kill both woman and beast. They must be put to death; their blood be on their own heads! If a man takes his sister, whether his father's daughter or his mother's daughter, and they see one another naked, it is an infamous disgrace. They are to be cut off in the presence of their people. The man has had intercourse with his sister and he must be held responsible. If a man lies with a woman during her monthly period, uncovering her body, he has exposed her discharge and she has uncovered the source of her discharge; they are both to be cut off from their people. You must not have intercourse with your mother's sister or your father's sister: it is the exposure of a blood relation. Both must accept responsibility. A man who has intercourse with his uncle's wife has brought shame on his uncle. They must accept responsibility for their sin and be proscribed and put to death. If a man takes his brother's wife, it is impurity. He has brought shame on his brother; they are to be proscribed.

You are to observe my statutes and my laws and carry them out, so that the land into which I am bringing you to live may not spew you out. You must not conform to the institutions of the nations whom I am driving out before you: they did all these things and I abhorred them, and I told you that you should occupy their land, and I would give you possession of it, a land flowing with milk and honey. I am the LORD your God: I have made a clear separation between you and the nations, and you are to make a clear separation between clean beasts and unclean beasts and between unclean and clean birds. You must not contaminate yourselves through beast or bird or anything that creeps on the ground, for I have made a clear separation between them and you, declaring them unclean. You must be holy to me, because I the LORD am holy. I have made a clear separation between you and the heathen, that you may belong to me. Any man or woman among you who calls up ghosts or spirits must be put to death. The people are to stone them; their blood be on their own heads.

*　　*　　*

If your fellow-countryman is reduced to poverty and sells himself to you, you must not use him to work for you as a slave. His status will be that of a hired man or a stranger lodging with you; he will work for you only until the jubilee year. He will then leave your service, with his children, and go back to his family and to his ancestral property: because they are my slaves whom I brought out of Egypt, they must not be sold as slaves are sold. You must not work him ruthlessly, but you are to fear your God. Such slaves as you have, male or female, should come from the nations round about you; from them you may buy slaves. You may also buy the children of those who have settled and lodge with you and such of their family as are born in your land. These may become your property, and you may leave them to your sons after you; you may use them as slaves permanently. But your fellow-Israelites you must not work ruthlessly.

*　　*　　*

If you conform to my statutes, if you observe and carry out my commandments, I shall give you rain at the proper season; the land will yield its produce and the trees of the countryside their fruit. Threshing will last till vintage, and vintage till sowing; you will eat your fill and live secure in your land.

I shall give peace in the land, and you will lie down to sleep with none to terrify you. I shall rid the land of beasts of prey and it will not be ravaged by the sword. You will put your enemies to flight and they will fall in battle before you. Five of you will give chase to a hundred and a hundred of you chase ten thousand; so will the enemy fall by your sword. I shall look upon you with favour, making you fruitful and increasing your numbers; I shall give full effect to my covenant with you. Your harvest will last you in store until you have to clear out the old to make room for the new. I

shall establish my Tabernacle among you and never spurn you. I shall be ever present among you; I shall become your God and you will become my people. I am the LORD your God who brought you out of Egypt to be slaves there no longer; I broke the bars of your yoke and enabled you to walk erect.

But if you do not listen to me, if you fail to keep all these commandments, if you reject my statutes, spurn my judgements, and fail to obey all my commandments, and if you break my covenant, then assuredly this is what I shall do to you: I shall bring upon you sudden terror, wasting disease, recurrent fever, and plagues that dim the sight and cause the appetite to fail. You will sow your seed to no purpose, for your enemies will eat the crop. I shall set my face against you, and you will be routed by your enemies. Those that hate you will hound you, and you will run when there is no one pursuing.

*　　*　　*

If in spite of this you do not listen to me and still oppose me, I shall oppose you in anger, and I myself shall punish you seven times over for your sins. Instead of meat you will eat your sons and your daughters. I shall destroy your shrines and demolish your incense-altars. I shall pile your corpses on your lifeless idols, and I shall spurn you. I shall make your cities desolate and lay waste your sanctuaries; I shall not accept the soothing odour of your offerings. I shall destroy your land, and the enemies who occupy it will be appalled. I shall scatter you among the heathen, pursue you with drawn sword; your land will be desert and your cities heaps of rubble. Then, all the time that it lies desolate, while you are in exile among your enemies, your land will enjoy its sabbaths to the full. All the time of its desolation it will have the sabbath rest which it did not have while you were living there. And I shall make those of you who are left in the land of your enemies so fearful that, when a leaf rustles behind them in the wind, they will run as if it were a sword after them; they will fall with no one in pursuit. Though no one pursues them they will stumble over one another, as if a sword were after them, and you will be helpless to make a stand against the enemy. You will meet your end among the heathen, and your enemies' land will swallow you up. Those who survive will pine away in an enemy land because of their iniquities, and also because of their forefathers' iniquities they will pine away just as they did.

But though they confess their iniquity, their own and that of their forefathers, their treachery and their opposition to me, I in my turn shall oppose them and carry them off into their enemies' land. If then their stubborn spirit is broken and they accept their punishment in full, I shall remember my covenant with Jacob, my covenant also with Isaac, and my covenant with Abraham, and I shall remember the land. The land, deserted by its people, will enjoy in full its sabbaths while it lies desolate; they will pay the penalty in full because they rejected my judgements and spurned my statutes. Yet even then while they are in their enemies' land, I shall not have so rejected and spurned them as to bring them to an end and break my covenant with them, because I am the LORD their God. I shall remember on their behalf the covenant with the former generation whom I brought out of Egypt in full sight of the nations, that I might be their God. I am the LORD.

*   *   *

FROM The Book of Deuteronomy

*   *   *

When a man takes a wife and, after intercourse, turns against her and brings trumped-up charges against her, giving her a bad name and saying, "I took this woman and slept with her and did not find proof of virginity in her," then the girl's father and mother should take the proof of her virginity to the elders of the town at the town gate. The girl's father will say to the elders, "I gave my daughter in marriage to this man, and he has turned against her. He has trumped up a charge and said, 'I have not found proofs of virginity in your daughter.' Here are the proofs." They must then spread the cloth before the elders of the town. The elders must take the man and punish him: they are to fine him a hundred pieces of silver because he has given a bad name to a virgin of Israel, and the money is to be handed over to the girl's father. She will remain his wife: he will not be free to divorce her all his days.

If, on the other hand, the accusation turns out to be true, no proof of the girl's virginity being found, then they must bring her out to the door of her father's house and the men of her town will stone her to death. She has committed an outrage in Israel by playing the prostitute in her father's house: you must rid yourselves of this wickedness.

When a man is discovered lying with a married woman, both are to be put to death, the woman as well as the man who lay with her: you must purge Israel of this wickedness.

When a virgin is pledged in marriage to a man, and another man encounters her in the town and lies with her, bring both of them out to the gate of that town and stone them to death; the girl because, although she was in the town, she did not cry for help, and the man because he violated another man's wife: you must rid yourselves of this wickedness.

But if it is out in the country that the man encounters and rapes such a girl, then the man alone is to be put to death because he lay with her. Do nothing to the girl; no guilt deserving of death attaches to her: this case is like that of a man who attacks another and murders him: the man came upon her in the country and, though the girl may have cried for help, there was no one to come to her rescue.

When a man encounters a virgin who is not yet betrothed and forces her to lie with him, and they are discovered, then the man who lies with her must give the girl's father fifty pieces of silver, and she will be his wife because he has violated her. He is not free to divorce her all his days.

A man must not take his father's wife: he must not bring shame on his father.

REVIEW QUESTIONS

1. In the Torah, what is Yahweh's relationship to his chosen people?
2. How are these chosen people to set themselves apart from other peoples, and how are they to relate to them?
3. As reflected in these laws, what are the principal values and modes of acceptable behavior in Hebrew society?
4. What kinds of principles of compensation do these laws reflect, and how do they compare with the principles of compensation reflected in the laws of Hammurabi (see Chapter 1)?
5. What kinds of attitudes toward sexual behavior do these laws reflect, and how is that behavior regulated?
6. What status and rights do women possess in the context of these laws?
7. What does Yahweh promise in return for obedience to his laws? For disobedience to them?

FROM The Book of Amos: Prophecies

The works of the so-called literary prophets announced a new phase in the history of the covenant between Yahweh and his chosen people. Amos, a Judahite shepherd and fig grower who marks the first of this series of prophets, brought his message to the northern kingdom of Israel around 750 B.C.E., denouncing the sinfulness of that society and predicting its destruction. In the following selection, Amos reveals his visions that foretell Israel's doom.

From *The Oxford Study Bible*, edited by M. Jack Suggs, Katharine Doob Sakenfeld, and James R. Mueller (Oxford, Eng.: Oxford University Press, 1992).

*   *   *

Amaziah, the priest of Bethel, reported to King Jeroboam of Israel: "Amos has conspired against you here in the heart of Israel; the country cannot tolerate all his words. This is what he is saying: 'Jeroboam will die by the sword, and the Israelites will assuredly be deported from their native land.'" To Amos himself Amaziah said, "Seer, go away! Off with you to Judah! Earn your living and do your prophesying there. But never prophesy again at Bethel, for this is the king's sanctuary, a royal shrine." "I was no prophet," Amos replied to Amaziah, "nor was I a prophet's son; I was a herdsman and fig-grower. But the LORD took me

as I followed the flock and it was the LORD who said to me, 'Go and prophesy to my people Israel.' So now listen to the word of the LORD. You tell me I am not to prophesy against Israel or speak out against the people of Isaac. Now these are the words of the LORD: Your wife will become a prostitute in the city, and your sons and daughters will fall by the sword. Your land will be parcelled out with a measuring line, you yourself will die in a heathen country, and Israel will be deported from their native land."

This was what the Lord GOD showed me: it was a basket of summer fruit. "What is that you are looking at, Amos?" he said. I answered, "A basket of ripe summer fruit." Then the LORD said to me, "The time is ripe for my people Israel. Never again shall I pardon them. On that day, says the Lord GOD, the palace songs will give way to lamentation: 'So many corpses, flung out everywhere! Silence!'"

Listen to this, you that grind the poor and suppress the humble in the land while you say, "When will the new moon be over so that we may sell grain? When will the sabbath be past so that we may expose our wheat for sale, giving short measure in the bushel and taking overweight in the silver, tilting the scales fraudulently, and selling the refuse of the wheat; that we may buy the weak for silver and the poor for a pair of sandals?" The LORD has sworn by the arrogance of Jacob: I shall never forget any of those activities of theirs.

Will not the earth quake on account of this?
Will not all who live on it mourn?
The whole earth will surge and seethe like the Nile
and subside like the river of Egypt.

On that day, says the Lord GOD,
I shall make the sun go down at noon
and darken the earth in broad daylight.
I shall turn your pilgrim-feasts into mourning
and all your songs into lamentation.
I shall make you all put sackcloth round your
    waists
and have everyone's head shaved.
I shall make it like mourning for an only son
and the end of it like a bitter day.

The time is coming, says the Lord GOD,
when I shall send famine on the land,
not hunger for bread or thirst for water,
but for hearing the word of the LORD.
People will stagger from sea to sea,
they will range from north to east,
in search of the word of the LORD,
but they will not find it.
On that day fair maidens and young men
will faint from thirst;
all who take their oath by Ashimah, goddess of
    Samaria,

all who swear, "As your god lives, Dan,"
and, "By the sacred way to Beersheba,"
they all will fall to rise no more.

I saw the Lord standing by the altar, and he said:

Strike the capitals so that the whole porch is
    shaken;
smash them down on the heads of the people,
and those who are left I shall put to the sword.
No fugitive will escape,
no survivor find safety.
Though they dig down to Sheol,
from there my hand will take them;
though they climb up to the heavens,
from there I shall bring them down.
If they hide on the summit of Carmel,
there I shall hunt them out and take them;
if they conceal themselves from my sight in the
    depths of the sea,
there at my command the sea serpent will bite
    them.
If they are herded off into captivity by their
    enemies,
there I shall command the sword to slay them;
I shall fix my eye on them
for evil, and not for good.

The LORD the God of Hosts—
at his touch the earth heaves,
and all who live on it mourn,
while the whole earth surges like the Nile
and subsides like the river of Egypt;
he builds his upper chambers in the heavens
and arches the vault of the sky over the earth;
he summons the waters of the sea
and pours them over the earth—
his name is the LORD.

Are not you Israelites like the Cushites to me?
says the LORD.
Did I not bring Israel up from Egypt,
and the Philistines from Caphtor, the Aramaeans
    from Kir?
Behold, I, the Lord GOD,
have my eyes on this sinful kingdom,
and I shall destroy it from the face of the earth.

Yet I shall not totally destroy Jacob's posterity,
says the LORD.
No; I shall give the command,
and shake Israel among all the nations,
as a sieve is shaken to and fro
without one pebble falling to the ground.
They will die by the sword, all the sinners of my
    people,
who say, "You will not let disaster approach
or overtake us."
On that day I shall restore
David's fallen house;
I shall repair its gaping walls and restore its ruins;
I shall rebuild it as it was long ago,
so that Israel may possess what is left of Edom
and of all the nations who were once named as
    mine.

This is the word of the LORD, who will do this.

A time is coming, says the LORD,
when the ploughman will follow hard on the
    reaper,
and he who treads the grapes after him who sows
    the seed.

The mountains will run with fresh wine,
and every hill will flow with it.

I shall restore the fortunes of my people Israel;
they will rebuild their devastated cities and live in
    them,
plant vineyards and drink the wine,
cultivate gardens and eat the fruit.
Once more I shall plant them on their own soil,
and never again will they be uprooted
from the soil I have given them.
It is the word of the LORD your God.

*   *   *

REVIEW QUESTIONS

1. According to Amos, why has Yahweh decided
   to punish Israel?
2. How thorough will that destruction be?
3. Does Yahweh offer any hope of salvation?

FROM The Book of Jeremiah: Prophecies

Given the resurgence of the great Mesopotamian powers of Assyria and then, follow-
ing Assyria's demise, Babylon, it was perhaps inevitable that Israel and then Judah
would be conquered. There emerged in Judah during the late seventh century B.C.E.
one of the greatest of the Hebrew prophets, Jeremiah, who foretold the destruction of
Judah as God's punishment of its people, who had failed to live up to their cove-
nant with him. Jeremiah, however, goes on to extend hope to the people of Judah in
the form of a new covenant that will focus, not on the unity and collective obedi-
ence of the Hebrew people but on the heartfelt commitment and renewal of the in-
dividual. Such a change in the focus of the covenant was to serve Judaism well in
the coming years of the Diaspora.

From *The Oxford Study Bible*, edited by M. Jack Suggs, Katharine Doob Sakenfeld, and
James R. Mueller (Oxford, Eng.: Oxford University Press, 1992).

        *   *   *

This word came from the LORD to Jeremiah. Stand at the gate of the LORD's house and there make this proclamation: Hear the word of the LORD, all you of Judah who come in through these gates to worship him. These are the words of the LORD of Hosts the God of Israel: Amend your ways and your deeds, that I may let you live in this place. You keep saying, "This place is the temple of the LORD, the temple of the LORD, the temple of the LORD!" This slogan of yours is a lie; put no trust in it. If you amend your ways and your deeds, deal fairly with one another, cease to oppress the alien, the fatherless, and the widow, if you shed no innocent blood in this place and do not run after other gods to your own ruin, then I shall let you live in this place, in the land which long ago I gave to your forefathers for all time.

You gain nothing by putting your trust in this lie. You steal, you murder, you commit adultery and perjury, you burn sacrifices to Baal, and you run after other gods whom you have not known; will you then come and stand before me in this house which bears my name, and say, "We are safe"? Safe, you think to indulge in all these abominations! Do you regard this house which bears my name as a bandits' cave? I warn you, I myself have seen all this, says the LORD.

Go to my shrine at Shiloh, which once I made a dwelling for my name, and see what I did to it because of the wickedness of my people Israel. Now you have done all these things, says the LORD; though I spoke to you again and again, you did not listen, and though I called, you did not respond. Therefore what I did to Shiloh I shall do to this house which bears my name, the house in which you put your trust, the place I gave to you and your forefathers; I shall fling you away out of my presence, as I did with all your kinsfolk, all Ephraim's offspring.

Offer up no prayer for this people, Jeremiah, raise no plea or prayer on their behalf, and do not intercede with me, for I shall not listen to you. Do you not see what they are doing in the towns of Judah and in the streets of Jerusalem?

Children are gathering wood, fathers lighting the fire, women kneading dough to make crescent-cakes in honour of the queen of heaven: and drink-offerings are poured out to other gods—all to grieve me. But is it I, says the LORD, whom they grieve? No; it is themselves, to their own confusion. Therefore, says the Lord GOD, my anger and my fury will pour out on this place, on man and beast, on trees and crops, and it will burn unquenched.

These are the words of the LORD of Hosts the God of Israel: Add your whole-offerings to your sacrifices and eat the flesh yourselves. For when I brought your forefathers out of Egypt, I gave them no instructions or commands about whole-offering or sacrifice. What I did command them was this: Obey me, and I shall be your God and you will be my people. You must conform to all my commands, if you are to prosper.

But they did not listen; they paid no heed, and persisted in their own plans with evil and stubborn hearts; they turned their backs and not their faces to me, from the day when your forefathers left Egypt until now. Again and again I sent to them all my servants the prophets; but instead of listening and paying heed to me, they in their stubbornness proved even more wicked than their forefathers. Tell them all this, but they will not listen to you; call them, but they will not respond. Then say to them: This is the nation who did not obey the LORD their God or accept correction. Truth has perished; it is heard no more on their lips.

        *   *   *

So the corpses of this people will become food for the birds of the air and the wild beasts, with none to scare them away. From the towns of Judah and the streets of Jerusalem I shall banish all sounds of joy and gladness, the voices of bridegroom and bride; for the whole land will become desert.

At that time, says the LORD, the bones of the kings of Judah, of the officers, priests, and prophets, and of all who have lived in Jerusalem, will be brought out from their graves. They will be exposed to the sun, the moon, and all the host of heaven, which they loved and served and adored, from which they sought guidance and to which they bowed in worship. Those bones will not be gathered up and reburied; they will be dung spread over the ground. All the survivors of this wicked race, wherever I have banished them, would rather die than live. This is the word of the LORD of Hosts.

*   *   *

Woe betide the shepherds who let the sheep of my flock scatter and be lost! says the LORD. Therefore these are the words of the LORD the God of Israel to the shepherds who tend my people: You have scattered and dispersed my flock. You have not watched over them; but I am watching you to punish you for your misdeeds, says the LORD. I myself shall gather the remnant of my sheep from all the lands to which I have dispersed them. I shall bring them back to their homes, and they will be fruitful and increase. I shall appoint shepherds who will tend them, so that never again will they know fear or dismay or punishment. This is the word of the LORD.

The days are coming, says the LORD,
when I shall make a righteous Branch spring from
    David's line,
a king who will rule wisely,
maintaining justice and right in the land.
In his days Judah will be kept safe,
and Israel will live undisturbed.
This will be the name to be given to him:
The LORD our Righteousness.

Therefore the time is coming, says the LORD, when people will no longer swear 'by the life of the LORD who brought the Israelites up from Egypt'; instead they will swear 'by the life of the LORD who brought the descendants of the Israelites back from a northern land and from all the lands to which he had dispersed them'; and they will live on their own soil.

Of the prophets:

Within my breast my heart gives way,
there is no strength in my bones;
because of the LORD, because of his holy
    words,
I have become like a drunken man,
like one overcome by wine.
For the land is full of adulterers,
and because of them the earth lies parched,
the open pastures have dried up.
The lives they lead are wicked,
and the powers they possess are misused.
For prophet and priest alike are godless;
even in my house I have witnessed their evil
    deeds.
This is the word of the LORD.
Therefore their path will turn slippery beneath
    their feet;
they will be dispersed in the dark and fall
    headlong,
for I shall bring disaster on them,
their day of reckoning.
This is the word of the LORD.
Among the prophets of Samaria
I found a lack of sense:
they prophesied in Baal's name
and led my people Israel astray.
Among the prophets of Jerusalem
I see a thing most horrible:
adulterers and hypocrites.
They encourage evildoers,
so that no one turns back from sin;
to me all her inhabitants
are like those of Sodom and Gomorrah.

These then are the words of the LORD of
Hosts about the prophets:

I shall give them wormwood to eat
and bitter poison to drink;
for from the prophets of Jerusalem
a godless spirit has spread to the whole country.

These are the words of the LORD of Hosts:

Do not listen to what is prophesied to you by the
    prophets,
who buoy you up with false hopes;
they give voice to their own fancies;

it is not the LORD's words they speak.
They say to those who spurn the word of the
    LORD,
"Prosperity will be yours";
and to all who follow their stubborn hearts they
    say,
"No harm will befall you."
For which of them has stood in the council of the
    LORD,
has been aware of his word and listened to it?
Which of them has heeded his word and obeyed?
See what a scorching wind has gone from the
    LORD,
a furious whirlwind
which whirls round the heads of the wicked.
The LORD's anger is not to be turned aside,
until he has fully accomplished his purposes.
In days to come you will truly understand.
I did not send these prophets,
yet they went in haste;
I did not speak to them,
yet they prophesied.
But if they had stood in my council,
they would have proclaimed my words to my
    people
and turned them from their evil ways and their
    evil doings.
Am I a God near at hand only, not a God when
    far away?
Can anyone hide in some secret place and I not
    see him?
Do I not fill heaven and earth?
This is the word of the LORD.

          *   *   *

But do not be afraid, Jacob my servant;
Israel, do not despair, says the LORD.
For I shall bring you back safe from afar,
and your posterity from the land where they are
    captives.
Jacob will be at rest once more,
secure and untroubled.
For I am with you to save you, says the LORD.
I shall make an end of all the nations
among whom I have dispersed you,
but I shall not make an end of you.

I shall discipline you only as you deserve,
I shall not leave you wholly unpunished.

For these are the words of the LORD to Zion:

Your wound is past healing;
the blow you suffered was cruel.
There can be no remedy for your sore;
the new skin cannot grow.
All your friends have forgotten you;
they look for you no longer.
I have struck you down as an enemy strikes,
and have punished you cruelly,
because of your great wickedness, your flagrant
    sins.
Why complain of your injury,
that your sore cannot be healed?
Because of your great wickedness, your flagrant
    sins,
I have done this to you.
Yet all who devoured you will themselves be
    devoured;
all your oppressors will go into captivity;
those who plunder you will be plundered,
and those who despoil you I shall give up to be
    spoiled.
I shall cause the new skin to grow
and heal your wounds, says the LORD,
although you are called outcast, Zion,
forsaken by all.

These are the words of the LORD:

I shall restore the fortunes of Jacob's clans
and show my love for his dwellings.
Every city will be rebuilt on its own mound,
every mansion will occupy its traditional site.
From them praise will be heard
and sounds of merrymaking.
I shall increase them, they will not diminish;
I shall raise them to honour,
no longer to be despised.
Their children will be what once they were,
and their community will be established in my
    sight.
I shall punish all their oppressors.
A ruler will appear, one of themselves;

a governor will arise from their own number.
I shall myself bring him near and let him
   approach me,
for who dare risk his life by approaching me?
says the LORD.
So you will be my people,
and I shall be your God.
See what a scorching wind has gone out from
   the LORD,
a sweeping whirlwind
which whirls round the heads of the wicked.
The LORD's fierce anger is not to be turned aside
until he has fully accomplished his purposes.
In days to come you will understand.

At that time, says the LORD, I shall be the God of
all the families of Israel, and they will be my people. These are the words of the LORD:

A people that escaped the sword
found favour in the wilderness.
The LORD went to give rest to Israel;
from afar he appeared to them:
I have dearly loved you from of old,
and still I maintain my unfailing care for you.
Virgin Israel, I shall build you up again,
and you will be rebuilt.
Again you will provide yourself with tambourines,
and go forth with the merry throng of dancers.
Again you will plant vineyards on the hills of
   Samaria,
and those who plant them will enjoy the fruit;
for a day will come when the watchmen
cry out on Ephraim's hills,
"Come, let us go up to Zion,
to the LORD our God."

For these are the words of the LORD:

Break into shouts of joy for Jacob's sake,
lead the nations, crying loud and clear,
sing out your praises and say:
"The LORD has saved his people;
he has preserved a remnant of Israel."
See how I bring them from a northern land;

I shall gather them from the far ends of the earth,
among them the blind and lame,
the woman with child and the woman in labour.
A vast company, they come home,
weeping as they come,
but I shall comfort them and be their escort.
I shall lead them by streams of water;
their path will be smooth, they will not stumble.
For I have become a father to Israel,
and Ephraim is my eldest son.
Listen to the word of the LORD, you nations,
announce it, make it known to coastlands far
   away:
He who scattered Israel will gather them again
and watch over them as a shepherd watches his
   flock.
For the LORD has delivered Jacob
and redeemed him from a foe too strong for him.
They will come with shouts of joy to Zion's height,
radiant at the bounty of the LORD:
the grain, the new wine, and the oil,
the young of flock and herd.
They will be like a well-watered garden
and never languish again.
Girls will then dance for joy,
and men young and old will rejoice;
I shall turn their grief into gladness,
comfort them, and give them joy after sorrow.
I shall satisfy the priests with the fat of the land
and my people will have their fill of my bounty.
This is the word of the LORD.

*   *   *

REVIEW QUESTIONS

1. According to Jeremiah, what is God's opinion
   of the kings of Judah and the priests and
   prophets of Jerusalem?
2. What punishments does God promise?
3. Does God offer a promise of redemption?
4. Who will bring that redemption?

FROM **The Book of Isaiah: Prophecies**

The Book of Isaiah contains the writings of at least two different authors separated in time by about 150 years: a prophet named Isaiah, from Jerusalem, whose career spanned the latter half of the eighth century B.C.E., and an unknown prophet, referred to now as the Second Isaiah, whose writings are included here. The Second Isaiah's career was in Babylon and dates to the later part of the exile there (587–39 B.C.E.). In the Second Isaiah's writings, Yahweh has assumed a role much larger than that of the exclusive God of a chosen people.

From *The Oxford Study Bible,* edited by M. Jack Suggs, Katharine Doob Sakenfeld, and James R. Mueller (Oxford, Eng.: Oxford University Press, 1992).

*   *   *

Hear me now, Jacob my servant;
Israel, my chosen one, hear me.
Thus says the LORD your maker,
your helper, who fashioned you from birth:
Have no fear, Jacob my servant,
Jeshurun whom I have chosen,
for I shall pour down rain on thirsty land,
showers on dry ground.
I shall pour out my spirit on your offspring
and my blessing on your children.
They will grow up like a green tamarisk,
like willows by flowing streams.
This person will say, "I am the LORD's";
that one will call himself a son of Jacob;
another will write the LORD's name on his hand
and the name of Israel will be added to his
    own.

Thus says the LORD, Israel's King,
the LORD of Hosts, his Redeemer:
I am the first and I am the last,
and there is no god but me.
Who is like me? Let him speak up;
let him declare his proof and set it out for me:
let him announce beforehand things to come,
let him foretell what is yet to be.
Take heart, have no fear.
Did I not tell you this long ago?

I foretold it, and you are my witnesses.
Is there any god apart from me,
any other deity? I know none!

Those who make idols are all less than nothing;
their cherished images profit nobody:
their worshippers are blind;
their ignorance shows up their foolishness.
Whoever makes a god or casts an image,
his labour is wasted.
All the votaries are put to shame;
the craftsmen are but mortals.
Let them all assemble and confront me;
they will be afraid and utterly shamed.

*   *   *

Jacob, remember all this;
Israel, remember, for you are my servant:
I have fashioned you, and you are in my service;
Israel, never forget me.
I have swept away your transgressions like mist,
and your sins are dispersed like clouds;
turn back to me, for I have redeemed you.
Shout in triumph, you heavens, for it is the LORD's
    doing;
cry out for joy, you lowest depths of the earth;
break into songs of triumph, you mountains,
you forest and all your trees;
for the LORD has redeemed Jacob
and through Israel he wins glory.

Thus says the LORD, your Redeemer,
who formed you from birth:
I am the LORD who made all things,
by myself I stretched out the heavens,
alone I fashioned the earth.
I frustrate false prophets and their omens,
and make fools of diviners;
I reverse what wise men say
and make nonsense of their wisdom.
I confirm my servants' prophecies
and bring about my messengers' plans.
Of Jerusalem I say, "She will be inhabited once
    more,"
and of the towns of Judah, "They will be rebuilt;
I shall restore their ruins."
I say to the deep waters, "Be dried up;
I shall make your streams run dry."
I say to Cyrus, "You will be my shepherd
to fulfil all my purpose,
so that Jerusalem may be rebuilt
and the foundations of the temple be laid."

Thus says the LORD to Cyrus his anointed,
whom he has taken by the right hand,
subduing nations before him
and stripping kings of their strength;
before whom doors will be opened
and no gates barred;
I myself shall go before you
and level the swelling hills;
I shall break down bronze gates
and cut through iron bars.
I shall give you treasures from dark vaults,
and hoards from secret places,
so that you may know that I am the LORD,
Israel's God, who calls you by name.
For the sake of Jacob my servant
and Israel my chosen one
I have called you by name
and given you a title, though you have not known
    me.
I am the LORD, and there is none other;
apart from me there is no god.
Though you have not known me I shall strengthen
    you,
so that from east to west

all may know there is none besides me:
I am the LORD, and there is none other;
I make the light, I create the darkness;
author alike of wellbeing and woe,
I, the LORD, do all these things. . . .

*   *   *

Will the pot contend with the potter,
or the earthenware with the hand that shapes it?
Will the clay ask the potter what he is making
or his handiwork say to him, "You have no skill"?
Will the child say to his father, "What are you
    begetting?"
or to his mother, "What are you bringing to
    birth?"
Thus says the LORD, Israel's Holy One, his Maker:
Would you dare question me concerning my
    children,
or instruct me in my handiwork?
I alone made the earth
and created mankind upon it.
With my own hands I stretched out the heavens
and directed all their host.
With righteous purpose I have roused this man,
and I shall smooth all his paths;
he it is who will rebuild my city
and set my exiles free—
not for a price nor for a bribe,
says the LORD of Hosts.

*   *   *

All the makers of idols are confounded and
    brought to shame,
they perish in confusion together.
But Israel has been delivered by the LORD,
a deliverance for all time to come;
they will never be confounded, never put to
    shame.

Thus says the LORD, the Creator of the heavens,
he who is God,
who made the earth and fashioned it
and by himself fixed it firmly,
who created it not as a formless waste
but as a place to be lived in:
I am the LORD, and there is none other.

I did not speak in secret, in realms of darkness;
I did not say to Jacob's people,
"Look for me in the formless waste.
I the LORD speak what is right, I declare what is
  just.

Gather together, come, draw near,
you survivors of the nations,
who in ignorance carry wooden idols in
  procession,
praying to a god that cannot save.
Come forward and urge your case, consult
  together:
who foretold this in days of old,
who stated it long ago?
Was it not I, the LORD?
There is no god but me,
none other than I, victorious and able to save.

From every corner of the earth
turn to me and be saved;
for I am God, there is none other.
By my life I have sworn,
I have given a promise of victory,
a promise that will not be broken;
to me every knee will bow,
by me every tongue will swear,
saying, "In the LORD alone
are victory and might.
All who defy him
will stand ashamed in his presence,
but all Israel's descendants will be victorious
and will glory in the LORD."

*   *   *

Come down and sit in the dust,
virgin daughter of Babylon.
Descend from your throne and sit on the ground,
daughter of the Chaldaeans;
never again will you be called
tender and delicate.
Take the handmill, grind meal, remove your
  veil;
strip off your skirt, bare your thighs, wade through
  rivers,
so that your nakedness may be seen,
your shame exposed.

I shall take vengeance and show clemency to
  none,
says our Redeemer, the Holy One of Israel,
whose name is the LORD of Hosts.

Daughter of the Chaldaeans,
go into the darkness and sit in silence;
for never again will you be called
queen of many kingdoms.
I was angry with my people;
I dishonoured my own possession
and surrendered them into your power.
You showed them no mercy;
even on the aged you laid a very heavy yoke.
You said, "I shall reign a queen for ever";
you gave no thought to your actions,
nor did you consider their outcome.

Now listen to this,
you lover of luxury, carefree on your throne,
saying to yourself,
"I am, and there is none other.
I shall never sit in widow's mourning,
never know the loss of children."
Yet suddenly, in a single day,
both these things will come upon you;
they will both come upon you in full measure:
loss of children and widowhood,
despite your many sorceries, all your countless
  spells.
Secure in your wicked ways
you thought, "No one can see me."
It was your wisdom and knowledge
that led you astray.
You said to yourself,
"I am, and there is none other."
Therefore evil will overtake you,
and you will not know how to conjure it away;
disaster will befall you,
and you will not be able to avert it;
ruin all unforeseen
will suddenly come upon you.
Persist in your spells and your many sorceries,
in which you have trafficked all your life.
Maybe you can get help from them!
Maybe you will yet inspire terror!

In spite of your many wiles you are powerless.
Let your astrologers, your star-gazers
who foretell your future month by month,
persist, and save you!
But they are like stubble
and fire burns them up;
they cannot snatch themselves from the flame.
It is not a glowing coal to warm them,
not a fire for them to sit by!
So much for your magicians
with whom you have trafficked all your life:
they have wandered off, each his own way,
and there is not one to save you.

Hear this, you house of Jacob,
who are called by the name of Israel,
and have sprung from the seed of Judah;
who swear by the name of the Lord
and invoke the God of Israel,
but not with honesty and sincerity,
though you call yourselves citizens of the Holy
    City
and lean for support on the God of Israel,
whose name is the Lord of Hosts:
Long ago I announced what would first happen,
I revealed it with my own mouth;
suddenly I acted and it came about.
Knowing your stubbornness,
your neck being as stiff as iron, your brow like
    brass,
I told you of these things long ago,
and declared them to you before they happened,
so that you could not say, "They were my idol's
    doing;
my image, the god that I fashioned, ordained
    them."
You have heard what I said; consider it well,
and admit the truth of it.

*   *   *

Thus says the Lord your Redeemer, the Holy One
    of Israel:
I am the Lord your God:
I teach you for your own wellbeing
and lead you in the way you should go.

If only you had listened to my commands,
your prosperity would have rolled on like a river,
your success like the waves of the sea;
your children would have been like the sand in
    number,
your descendants countless as its grains;
their name would never be erased or blotted from
    my sight.

Go out from Babylon, hasten away from the
    Chaldaeans;
proclaim it with joyful song,
sending out the news to the ends of the earth;
tell them, "The Lord has redeemed his servant
    Jacob."
Though he led them through desert places,
they suffered no thirst;
he made water flow for them from the rock,
for them he split the rock and streams gushed
    forth.

There is no peace for the wicked,
says the Lord.

Listen to me, you coasts and islands,
pay heed, you peoples far distant:
the Lord called me before I was born,
he named me from my mother's womb.
He made my tongue a sharp sword
and hid me under the shelter of his hand;
he made me into a polished arrow,
in his quiver he concealed me.
He said to me, "Israel, you are my servant
through whom I shall win glory."
Once I said, "I have toiled in vain;
I have spent my strength for nothing,
and to no purpose."
Yet my cause is with the Lord
and my reward with my God.
The Lord had formed me in the womb to be his
    servant,
to bring Jacob back to him
that Israel should be gathered to him,
so that I might rise to honour in the Lord's sight
and my God might be my strength.
And now the Lord has said to me:

"It is too slight a task for you, as my servant,
to restore the tribes of Jacob,
to bring back the survivors of Israel:
I shall appoint you a light to the nations
so that my salvation may reach earth's farthest
  bounds."

These are the words of the Holy One,
the Lord who redeems Israel,
to one who is despised,
and whom people abhor,
the slave of tyrants:
Kings will rise when they see you,
princes will do homage,
because of the Lord who is faithful,
because of Israel's Holy One who has chosen you.

These are the words of the Lord:
In the time of my favour I answered you;
on the day of deliverance I came to your aid.
I have formed you, and destined you
to be a light for peoples,
restoring the land
and allotting once more its desolate holdings.
I said to the prisoners, "Go free,"
and to those in darkness, "Come out into the
  open."
Along every path they will find pasture
and grazing in all the arid places.
They will neither hunger nor thirst,
nor will scorching heat or sun distress them;
for one who loves them will guide them
and lead them by springs of water.
I shall make every hill a path
and raise up my highways.
They are coming: some from far away,
some from the north and the west,
and others from the land of Syene.
Shout for joy, you heavens; earth, rejoice;
break into songs of triumph, you mountains,
for the Lord has comforted his people
and has had pity on them in their distress.

But Zion says,
"The Lord has forsaken me;
my Lord has forgotten me."

Can a woman forget the infant at her breast,
or a mother the child of her womb?
But should even these forget,
I shall never forget you.
I have inscribed you on the palms of my hands;
your walls are always before my eyes.
Those who rebuild you make better speed
than those who pulled you down,
while those who laid you waste leave you and go.
Raise your eyes and look around:
they are all assembling, flocking back to you.
By my life I, the Lord, swear it:
you will wear them as your jewels,
and adorn yourself with them like a bride;
I did indeed make you waste and desolate,
I razed you to the ground,
but now the land is too small for its inhabitants,
while they who made you a ruin are far away.
Children born during your bereavement will say,
"Make room for us to live here,
the place is too cramped."
Then you will say to yourself,
Who bore these children for me,
bereaved and barren as I was?
Who reared them
when I was left alone, left by myself;
where did I get them?'

These are the words of the Lord God:
I shall beckon to the nations
and hoist my signal to the peoples,
and they will bring your sons in their arms
and your daughters will be carried on their
  shoulders;
kings will be your foster-fathers,
their princesses serve as your nurses.
They will bow to the earth before you
and lick the dust from your feet.
You will know that I am the Lord;
none who look to me will be disappointed.

*   *   *

Who could have believed what we have heard?
To whom has the power of the Lord been
  revealed?

He grew up before the LORD like a young plant
whose roots are in parched ground;
he had no beauty, no majesty to catch our eyes,
no grace to attract us to him.
He was despised, shunned by all,
pain-racked and afflicted by disease;
we despised him, we held him of no account,
an object from which people turn away their eyes.
Yet it was our afflictions he was bearing,
our pain he endured,
while we thought of him as smitten by God,
struck down by disease and misery.
But he was pierced for our transgressions,
crushed for our iniquities;
the chastisement he bore restored us to health
and by his wounds we are healed.
We had all strayed like sheep,
each of us going his own way,
but the LORD laid on him
the guilt of us all.
He was maltreated, yet he was submissive
and did not open his mouth;
like a sheep led to the slaughter,
like a ewe that is dumb before the shearers,
he did not open his mouth.
He was arrested and sentenced and taken away,
and who gave a thought to his fate—
how he was cut off from the world of the living,
stricken to death for my people's transgression?
He was assigned a grave with the wicked,
a burial-place among felons,
though he had done no violence,
had spoken no word of treachery.

Yet the LORD took thought for his oppressed
    servant
and healed him who had given himself as a
    sacrifice for sin.
He will enjoy long life and see his children's
    children,
and in his hand the LORD's purpose will prosper.
By his humiliation my servant will justify many;
after his suffering he will see light and be satisfied;
it is their guilt he bears.

Therefore I shall allot him a portion with the
    great,
and he will share the spoil with the mighty,
because he exposed himself to death
and was reckoned among transgressors,
for he bore the sin of many
and interceded for transgressors.

*   *   *

REVIEW QUESTION

1. According to the Second Isaiah, what now is
   the dominion of the Hebrews' God?
2. What role has Israel now assumed in relation
   to the other nations of the earth?
3. Does a messiah figure emerge in this document?
4. What is God's view of Babylon?

An Aramaic Letter from Elephantine

*The exile of the Jews of Jerusalem to Babylon in 587 B.C.E. marked the beginning of
the Diaspora, the dispersion of the Jewish people from Judah throughout the Near
East and, in time, the globe. By the period of the Achaemenid Persian Empire, a
Jewish community had established itself at Elephantine in southern Egypt, where the*

following letter was recovered. Written on papyrus in the Aramaic script and dating to 410 B.C.E., it is addressed to the Persian governor of Judah from the Jewish community.

From *Ancient Near Eastern Texts Relating to the Old Testament,* edited by James B. Pritchard (Princeton, N.J.: Princeton University Press, 1983).

To our lord Bagoas, governor of Judah, your servants Yedoniah and his colleagues, the priests who are in the fortress of Elephantine. May the God of Heaven seek after the welfare of our lord exceedingly at all times and give you favor before King Darius and the nobles a thousand times more than now. May you be happy and healthy at all times. Now, your servant Yedoniah and his colleagues depose as follows: In the month of Tammuz in the 14th year of King Darius, when Arsames departed and went to the king, the priests of the god Khnub, who is in the fortress of Elephantine, conspired with Vidaranag, who was commander-in-chief here, to wipe out the temple of the god Yaho from the fortress of Elephantine. So that wretch Vidaranag sent to his son Nefayan, who was in command of the garrison of the fortress of Syene, this order, "The temple of the god Yaho in the fortress of Yeb is to be destroyed." Nefayan thereupon led the Egyptians with the other troops. Coming with their weapons to the fortress of Elephantine, they entered that temple and razed it to the ground. The stone pillars that were there they smashed. Five "great" gateways built with hewn blocks of stone which were in that temple they demolished, but their doors *are standing,* and the hinges of those doors are of bronze; and *their* roof of cedarwood, all of it, with the . . . and whatever else was there, everything they burnt with fire. As for the basins of gold and silver and other articles that were in that temple, they carried all of them off and made them their own.—Now, our forefathers built this temple in the fortress of Elephantine back in the days of the kingdom of Egypt, and when Cambyses came to Egypt he found it built. They knocked down all the temples of the gods of Egypt, but no one did any damage to this temple. But when this hap-

pened, we and our wives and our children wore sackcloth, and fasted, and prayed to Yaho the Lord of Heaven, who has let us see our desire upon that Vidaranag. The dogs took the fetter out of his feet, and any property he had gained was lost; and any men who have sought to do evil to this temple have all been killed and we have seen our desire upon them.—We have also sent a letter before now, when this evil was done to us, to our lord and to the high priest Johanan and his colleagues the priests in Jerusalem and to Ostanes the brother of Anani and the nobles of the Jews. Never a letter have they sent to us. Also, from the month of Tammuz, year 14 of King Darius, to this day, we have been wearing sackcloth and fasting, making our wives as widows, not anointing ourselves with oil or drinking wine. Also, from then to now, in the year 17 of King Darius, no meal-offering, incense, nor burnt offering have been offered in this temple. Now your servants Yedoniah, and his colleagues, and the Jews, the citizens of Elephantine, all say thus: If it please our lord, take thought of this temple to rebuild it, since they do not let us rebuild it. Look to your well-wishers and friends here in Egypt. Let a letter be sent from you to them concerning the temple of the god Yaho to build it in the fortress of Elephantine as it was built before; and the meal-offering, incense, and burnt offering will be offered in your name, and we shall pray for you at all times, we, and our wives, and our children, and the Jews who are here, all of them, if you do thus, so that that temple is rebuilt. And you shall have a merit before Yaho the God of Heaven more than a man who offers to him burnt offering and sacrifices worth a thousand talents of silver and because of gold. Because of this we have written to inform you. We have also set the whole matter forth in a letter in our name to Delaiah and Shelemiah, the sons of Sanballat the governor of Samaria. Also, Arsames knew nothing of all that was done to us. On the 20th of Marheshwan, year 17 of King Darius.

REVIEW QUESTIONS

1. Why was this letter written? Does it provide any evidence of a relationship between the Elephantine community and that in Jerusalem?
2. What does it suggest about the conditions of the Jews living in the Diaspora (the Jewish communities outside Palestine) at this time?

4 ❧ THE GREEK EXPERIMENT

By the time that the uncharacteristically allied city-states of Hellas (Greece) had to face invasion by the massive forces of the Achaemenid Persian emperor Darius in 490 B.C.E., the much more ancient civilizations of Mesopotamia and Egypt (not to mention India and China) had been thriving for thousands of years. By 500 B.C.E., both Babylon and Egypt—in fact, the entire Near East—had fallen under the sway of the Persian Empire, which could boast of one of the more-sophisticated imperial systems of antiquity and resources vastly superior to those of the upstarts from the Aegean, located on the empire's far western periphery. The Greeks themselves, from the Persian perspective, undoubtedly seemed to be a disorganized, belligerent, even barbarian people who represented no real threat to continued Persian dominion.

Nonetheless, only eleven years after the Persians' first invasion, the Greeks had vanquished and expelled not only the invasion of Darius but also a second, even more massive invasion under the son and successor of Darius, Xerxes. The Greeks' improbable success came to be seen as one of the first events in the process by which the West, over many centuries, defined itself as an entity distinct from and, in its eyes, generally superior to the East.

Scholars today recognize (as did ancient Greek writers) the tremendous debt the early Greeks owed to the older civilizations of the ancient Near East and Egypt. Indeed, to be aware of that debt, one need look no further than early Greek statuary and temple architecture, with their obviously Egyptian inspiration, or the Greek alphabet, borrowed from the Phoenicians, with whom the Greeks traded. However, within the unique context of early Greek society, political development, and culture, there emerged a number of concepts and issues that have remained at the heart of the ongoing development of Western civilization and have had significant impact on the non-Western civilizations that, in the past two centuries, have increasingly been confronted with the ideas and values of the West. What are the appropriate roles and rights of the individual in society? To what does the individual owe primary allegiance, the dictates of conscience or the laws of the state? How should a state be properly organized and governed, and by whom? What ought to be the respective roles of men and women in society? Do divine forces govern natural phenomena and human history? Indeed, do gods/or a god even exist? Some have claimed that much of the history of Western culture subsequent to the era of the Greek city-states has centered on the continuing endeavor to answer these and other questions that the Greeks raised.

The Greeks took some giant steps in addressing these questions. In fact, they made perhaps their most significant contributions to that endeavor during the relatively brief "golden age" that accompanied Athens's rise to preeminence among the city-states after the defeat of the Persians. Classical Greek civilization achieved its loftiest heights in Athens during the decades prior to Athens's disastrous defeat by Sparta and its allies at the end of the Peloponnesian War. Less than seventy years later, Athens, Sparta, and the other previously independent city-states were compelled to cede their autonomy to the hegemony of the Macedonian King Philip II, whose son Alexander would inaugurate a new era during which the affairs of those city-states would take a back seat to the Hellenistic kingdoms. Nonetheless, the relatively brief zenith of the classical Greek city-states would, in time, be recognized as vastly out of proportion to their influence on the later course of Western civilization.

HOMER

FROM *The Iliad*

The existence of the poet named Homer is still debated among scholars. The influence of the epic poems, The Iliad *and* The Odyssey, *that the later Greeks attributed to him, is not. For the warrior aristocracy whose interests these poems reflected and for whom they were recited as entertainment, Homer's tales of the Greeks' siege of Troy and of the exploits of Odysseus and his men on their way home after that siege provided a vivid model of heroic values and behavior in a world where the gods intruded their designs regularly into human affairs. The plot of* The Iliad *centers on the anger of the greatest of the Greek heroes, Achilles, which causes him first to withdraw from the combat after a perceived insult from the Greeks' leader, Agamemnon, only to return wrathfully to avenge his friend Patroclus, who has been killed while wearing Achilles' armor in an attempt to inspire his comrades. Achilles vents his wrath on the Trojans' greatest hero, Hector, whom he challenges and kills,*

PROTO-CANAANITE	EARLY LETTER NAMES AND MEANINGS	PHOENICIAN	EARLY GREEK	EARLY MONUMENTAL LATIN	MODERN ENGLISH CAPITALS
𐤀	*alp* oxhead				A
	bêt house			B	B
	gaml throwstick				C
	digg fish			D	D
	hô(?) man calling				E
	wô (waw) mace				F
	zê(n) ?				
	ḥê(t) fence?			H	H
	ṭê(t) spindle?				
	yad arm				I
	kapp palm			K	K
	lamd ox-goad				L
	mêm water				M
	naḥš snake				N
	cên eye			O	O
	pi't corner?				P
	sa(d) plant				
	qu(p) ?				Q
	ra'š head of man			R	R
	tann composite bow				S
	tô (taw) owner's mark			T	T

ORIGINS OF THE GREEK ALPHABET (C. 500 B.C.E.)

This chart illustrates the evolution of the writing system that we refer to as the alphabet. How great is the Greek (and later Roman) debt to the Phoenicians and earlier Canaanites? Can you identify the origin of the word alphabet?

and then drags his mangled corpse behind his chariot around Troy's walls. In the selection below, from an earlier part of the poem, Hector has momentarily withdrawn from the fighting and encounters his wife, Andromache, and infant son, Astyanax, for what will be, unbeknownst to them but surely known to the audience hearing the poem, the last time.

From *The Iliad of Homer,* translated by Richmond Lattimore (Chicago: University of Chicago Press, 1951).

*　　*　　*

FROM Book VI

So speaking Hektor of the shining helm departed
and in speed made his way to his own well-
    established dwelling,
but failed to find in the house Andromache of
    the white arms;
for she, with the child, and followed by one fair-
    robed attendant,
had taken her place on the tower in lamentation,
    and tearful.
When he saw no sign of his perfect wife within
    the house, Hektor
stopped in his way on the threshold and spoke
    among the handmaidens:
"Come then, tell me truthfully as you may,
    handmaidens:
where has Andromache of the white arms gone?
    Is she
with any of the sisters of her lord or the wives
    of his brothers?
Or has she gone to the house of Athene, where
    all the other
lovely-haired women of Troy propitiate the grim
    goddess?"
    Then in turn the hard-working housekeeper
    gave him an answer:
"Hektor, since you have urged me to tell you
    the truth, she is not
with any of the sisters of her lord or the wives
    of his brothers,
nor has she gone to the house of Athene, where
    all the other

lovely-haired women of Troy propitiate the grim
    goddess,
but she has gone to the great bastion of Ilion,
    because she heard that
the Trojans were losing, and great grew the
    strength of the Achaians.
Therefore she has gone in speed to the wall, like
    a woman
gone mad, and a nurse attending her carries the
    baby."
    So the housekeeper spoke, and Hektor
    hastened from his home
backward by the way he had come through the
    well-laid streets. So
as he had come to the gates on his way through
    the great city,
the Skaian gates, whereby he would issue into
    the plain, there
at last his own generous wife came running to
    meet him,
Andromache, the daughter of high-hearted
    Eëtion;
Eëtion, who had dwelt underneath wooded
    Plakos,
in Thebe below Plakos, lord over the Kilikian
    people.
It was his daughter who was given to Hektor of
    the bronze helm.
She came to him there, and beside her went an
    attendant carrying
the boy in the fold of her bosom, a little child,
    only a baby,
Hektor's son, the admired, beautiful as a star
    shining,
whom Hektor called Skamandrios, but all of the
    others

Astyanax—lord of the city; since Hektor alone
saved Ilion.

Hektor smiled in silence as he looked on his
son, but she,

Andromache, stood close beside him, letting her
tears fall,

and clung to his hand and called him by name
and spoke to him: "Dearest,

your own great strength will be your death, and
you have no pity

on your little son, nor on me, ill-starred, who
soon must be your widow;

for presently the Achaians, gathering together,

will set upon you and kill you; and for me it
would be far better

to sink into the earth when I have lost you, for
there is no other

consolation for me after you have gone to your
destiny—

only grief; since I have no father, no honoured
mother.

It was brilliant Achilleus who slew my father,
Eëtion,

when he stormed the strong-founded citadel of
the Kilikians,

Thebe of the towering gates. He killed Eëtion

but did not strip his armour, for his heart
respected the dead man,

but burned the body in all its elaborate war-gear

and piled a grave mound over it, and the
nymphs of the mountains,

daughters of Zeus of the aegis, planted elm trees
about it.

And they who were my seven brothers in the
great house all went

upon a single day down into the house of the
death god,

for swift-footed brilliant Achilleus slaughtered all
of them

as they were tending their white sheep and their
lumbering oxen;

and when he had led my mother, who was
queen under wooded Plakos,

here, along with all his other possessions,
Achilleus

released her again, accepting ransom beyond
count, but Artemis

of the showering arrows struck her down in the
halls of her father.

Hektor, thus you are father to me, and my
honoured mother,

you are my brother, and you it is who are my
young husband.

Please take pity upon me then, stay here on the
rampart,

that you may not leave your child an orphan,
your wife a widow,

but draw your people up by the fig tree, there
where the city

is openest to attack, and where the wall may be
mounted.

Three times their bravest came that way, and
fought there to storm it

about the two Aiantes and renowned Idomeneus,

about the two Atreidai and the fighting son of
Tydeus.

Either some man well skilled in prophetic arts
had spoken,

or the very spirit within themselves had stirred
them to the onslaught."

Then tall Hektor of the shining helm
answered her: "All these

things are in my mind also, lady; yet I would
feel deep shame

before the Trojans, and the Trojan women with
trailing garments,

if like a coward I were to shrink aside from the
fighting;

and the spirit will not let me, since I have
learned to be valiant

and to fight always among the foremost ranks of
the Trojans,

winning for my own self great glory, and for my
father.

For I know this thing well in my heart, and my
mind knows it:

there will come a day when sacred Ilion shall
perish,

and Priam, and the people of Priam of the
strong ash spear.

But it is not so much the pain to come of the
Trojans
that troubles me, not even of Priam the king nor
Hekabe,
not the thought of my brothers who in their
numbers and valour
shall drop in the dust under the hands of men
who hate them,
as troubles me the thought of you, when some
bronze-armoured
Achaian leads you off, taking away your day of
liberty,
in tears; and in Argos you must work at the
loom of another,
and carry water from the spring Messeis or
Hypereia,
all unwilling, but strong will be the necessity
upon you;
and some day seeing you shedding tears a man
will say of you:
'This is the wife of Hektor, who was ever the
bravest fighter
of the Trojans, breakers of horses, in the days
when they fought about Ilion.'
So will one speak of you; and for you it will be
yet a fresh grief,
to be widowed of such a man who could fight
off the day of your slavery.
But may I be dead and the piled earth hide me
under before I
hear you crying and know by this that they drag
you captive."
So speaking glorious Hektor held out his arms
to his baby,
who shrank back to his fair-girdled nurse's
bosom
screaming, and frightened at the aspect of his
own father,
terrified as he saw the bronze and the crest with
its horse-hair,
nodding dreadfully, as he thought, from the peak
of the helmet.
Then his beloved father laughed out, and his
honoured mother,
and at once glorious Hektor lifted from his head
the helmet

and laid it in all its shining upon the ground.
Then taking
up his dear son he tossed him about in his arms,
and kissed him,
and lifted his voice in prayer to Zeus and the
other immortals:
"Zeus, and you other immortals, grant that this
boy, who is my son,
may be as I am, pre-eminent among the Trojans,
great in strength, as am I, and rule strongly over
Ilion;
and some day let them say of him: 'He is better
by far than his father,'
as he comes in from the fighting; and let him
kill his enemy
and bring home the blooded spoils, and delight
the heart of his mother."
So speaking he set his child again in the arms
of his beloved
wife, who took him back again to her fragrant
bosom
smiling in her tears; and her husband saw, and
took pity upon her,
and stroked her with his hand, and called her by
name and spoke to her:
"Poor Andromache! Why does your heart
sorrow so much for me?
No man is going to hurl me to Hades, unless it
is fated,
but as for fate, I think that no man yet has
escaped it
once it has taken its first form, neither brave
man nor coward.
Go therefore back to our house, and take up
your own work,
the loom and the distaff, and see to it that your
handmaidens
ply their work also; but the men must see to the
fighting,
all men who are the people of Ilion, but I
beyond others."
So glorious Hektor spoke and again took up
the helmet
with its crest of horse-hair, while his beloved
wife went homeward,

turning to look back on the way, letting the live
    tears fall.
And as she came in speed into the well-settled
    household
of Hektor the slayer of men, she found numbers
    of handmaidens
within, and her coming stirred all of them into
    lamentation.
So they mourned in his house over Hektor while
    he was living
still, for they thought he would never again
    come back from the fighting
alive, escaping the Achaian hands and their
    violence.

*   *   *

REVIEW QUESTION

1. What does this selection reveal about the Greek view of ideal heroic behavior?
2. Does it assume that humans are able to resist the dictates of fate?
3. What does this selection say about the respective roles of men and women?

HESIOD

FROM *Works and Days*

The partly autobiographical Works and Days *of Hesiod (ca. 700 B.C.E.) reflects a world quite different from that of Homer's heroes. Indeed, in one part of this work Hesiod describes five ages of mankind that begin with a golden age of men who "lived like gods" but that decline thereafter, culminating in an age of bronze that coincides with the Homeric heroes ("a god-like race of hero-men") and then his own age, that of a race of iron, oppressed by hard labor and sorrow. As the following readings suggest, humankind's lot and the values of the time are in many ways quite different from those of Homer's world.*

From *Works and Days,* translated by Hugh G. Evelyn-White in *Homeric Hymns and Homerica,* (Cambridge, Mass.: Harvard University Press, 1936), pp. 361–362.

*   *   *

From "On Work and Wealth"

To you, foolish Perses, I will speak good sense. Badness can be got easily and in shoals: the road to her is smooth, and she lives very near us. But between us and Goodness the gods have placed the sweat of our brows: long and steep is the path that leads to her, and it is rough at the first; but when a man has reached the top, then indeed she is easy, though before that she was hard.

That man is altogether best who considers all things himself and marks what will be better afterwards and at the end; and he, again, is good who listens to a good adviser; but whoever neither thinks for himself nor keeps in mind what another man tells him, he is an unprofitable man. But do you at any rate, always remembering my charge, work, well-born Perses, that Hunger may hate you, and venerable Demeter richly crowned may love you and fill your barn with food; for Hunger is altogether a meet comrade for the sluggard. Both gods and men are angry with a man who lives idle, for in nature he is like the stingless drones who waste the labor of the bees, eating without working; but let it be your care to order your work properly, that in the right season your barns may be full of victual. Through work men grow rich in flocks and substance, and working they are much better loved by the immortals. Work is no disgrace: it is idleness which is a disgrace. But if you work, the idle will soon envy you as you grow rich, for fame and renown attend on wealth. And whatever be your lot, work is best for you, if you turn your misguided mind away from other men's property to your work and attend to your livelihood as I bid you. An evil shame is the needy man's companion, shame which both greatly harms and prospers men: shame is with poverty, but confidence with wealth.

Wealth should not be seized: god-given wealth is much better; for if a man take great wealth violently and perforce, or if he steal it through his tongue, as often happens when gain deceives men's sense and dishonor tramples down honor, the gods soon blot him out and make that man's house low, and wealth attends him only for a little time. Alike with him who does wrong to a suppliant or a guest, or who goes up to his brother's bed and commits unnatural sin in lying with his wife, or who infatuately offends against fatherless children, or who abuses his old father at the cheerless threshold of old age and attacks him with harsh words, truly Zeus himself is angry, and at the last lays on him a heavy requital for his evildoing. But do you turn your foolish heart altogether away from these things, and, as far as you are able, sacrifice to the deathless gods purely and cleanly, and burn rich meats also, and at other times propitiate them with libations and incense, both when you go to bed and when the holy light

has come back, that they may be gracious to you in heart and spirit, and so you may buy another's holding and not another yours.

. . . He who adds to what he has, will keep off bright-eyed hunger; for if you add only a little to a little and do this often, soon that little will become great. What a man has by him at home does not trouble him: it is better to have your stuff at home, for whatever is abroad may mean loss. It is a good thing to draw on what you have; but it grieves your heart to need something and not to have it, and I bid you mark this. Take your fill when the cask is first opened and when it is nearly spent, but midways be sparing: it is poor saving when you come to the lees.

Let the wage promised to a friend be fixed; even with your brother smile—and get a witness; for trust and mistrust, alike ruin men.

Do not let a flaunting woman coax and cozen and deceive you: she is after your barn. The man who trusts womankind trusts deceivers.

There should be an only son, to feed his father's house, for so wealth will increase in the home; but if you leave a second son you should die old. Yet Zeus can easily give great wealth to a greater number. More hands mean more work and more increase.

If your heart within you desires wealth, do these things and work with work upon work.

*   *   *

"Pandora"

For the gods have hidden and keep hidden what
    could be men's livelihood.
It could have been that easily in one day you
    could work out
enough to keep you for a year, with no more
    working.
Soon you could have hung up your steering oar
    in the smoke of the fireplace,

From *Work and Days,* translated by Richard Lattimore, (Ann Arbor, Mich.: University of Michigan Press, 1959).

and the work the oxen and patient mules do
    would be abolished,
but Zeus in the anger of his heart hid it away
because the devious-minded Prometheus had
    cheated him;
and therefore Zeus thought up dismal sorrows
    for mankind.
He hid fire; but Prometheus, the powerful son of
    Iapetos,
stole it again from Zeus of the counsels, to give
    to mortals.
He hid it out of the sight of Zeus who delights
    in thunder
in the hollow fennel stalk. In anger the cloud-
    gatherer spoke to him:
"Son of Iapetos, deviser of crafts beyond all
    others,
you are happy that you stole the fire, and
    outwitted my thinking;
but it will be a great sorrow to you, and to men
    who come after.
As the price of fire I will give them an evil, and
    all men shall fondle
this, their evil, close to their hearts, and take
    delight in it."
    So spoke the father of gods and mortals; and
    laughed out loud.
He told glorious Hephaistos to make haste, and
    plaster
earth with water, and to infuse it with a human
    voice
and vigor, and make the face like the immortal
    goddesses,
the bewitching features of a young girl;
    meanwhile Athene
was to teach her her skills, and how to do the
    intricate weaving,
while Aphrodite was to mist her head in golden
    endearment
and the cruelty of desire and longings that wear
    out the body,
but to Hermes, the guide, the slayer of Argos, he
    gave instructions
to put in her the mind of a hussy, and a
    treacherous nature.

So Zeus spoke. And all obeyed Lord Zeus, the
    son of Kronos.
The renowned strong smith modeled her figure
    of earth, in the likeness
of a decorous young girl, as the son of Kronos
    had wished it.
The goddess gray-eyed Athene dressed and
    arrayed her; the Graces,
who are goddesses, and hallowed Persuasion put
    necklaces
of gold upon her body, while the Seasons, with
    glorious tresses,
put upon her head a coronal of spring flowers,
and Pallas Athene put all decor upon her body.
But into her heart Hermes, the guide, the slayer
    of Argos,
put lies, and wheedling words of falsehood, and
    a treacherous nature,
made her as Zeus of the deep thunder wished,
    and he, the gods' herald,
put a voice inside her, and gave her the name of
    woman,
Pandora, because all the gods who have their
    homes on Olympos
had given her each a gift, to be a sorrow to men
who eat bread. Now when he had done with this
    sheer, impossible
deception, the Father sent the gods' fleet
    messenger, Hermes,
to Epimetheus, bringing her, a gift, nor did
    Epimetheus
remember to think how Prometheus had told
    him never
to accept a gift from Olympian Zeus, but always
    to send it
back, for fear it might prove to be an evil for
    mankind.
He took the evil, and only perceived it when he
    possessed her.
    Since before this time the races of men had
    been living on earth
free from all evils, free from laborious work, and
    free from
all wearing sicknesses that bring their fates down
    on men

(for men grow old suddenly in the midst of
    misfortune;)
but the woman, with her hands lifting away the
    lid from the great jar,
scattered its contents, and her design was sad
    troubles for mankind.
Hope was the only spirit that stayed there in the
    unbreakable
closure of the jar, under its rim, and could not
    fly forth
abroad, for the lid of the great jar closed down
    first and contained her;
this was by the will of cloud-gathering Zeus of
    the aegis;
but there are other troubles by thousands that
    hover about men,
for the earth is full of evil things, and the sea is
    full of them;

there are sicknesses that come to men by day,
    while in the night
moving of themselves they haunt us, bringing
    sorrow to mortals,
and silently, for Zeus of the counsels took the
    voice out of them.

So there is no way to avoid what Zeus has
    intended.

REVIEW QUESTIONS

1. What kind of society does Hesiod's writing reflect?
2. How might one succeed in it?
3. According to Hesiod, what is the underlying
   cause of man's misery, and what is the relationship of women to it?

Poems of Sappho of Lesbos and Semonides of Amorgos

*Although we have but a portion of her work and much of that only in fragments,
Sappho has justifiably been referred to as the greatest female poet ever. She lived at
the end of the seventh century B.C.E. on the island of Lesbos, where she possibly
served as a teacher in a school for girls. By and large, her poems reflect the intimate
feelings and relationships of young women. The poet Semonides lived and wrote on
the Aegean island of Amorgos during the seventh century B.C.E., which makes him
roughly contemporary with Sappho. The selection by him is one of our few sources
concerning the Greek male's view of women during this early period.*

Sappho of Lesbos
FROM Poems

1
"Honest, I want to die," she said to me.
She was in tears when she went away,

From *Poems by Sappho*, translated by Bernard Knox, in
The Norton Book of Classical Literature, and *Poem on
Women* by Semonides (New York: Norton, 1993), pp.
227–29.

Said to me not once but many times:
"Sappho, why must we suffer so?
It's not by choice; I don't want to leave you
    here."

And I, this is what I said to answer her:
"Farewell. Go in peace. But remember me.
Don't ever forget how well I took care of you.

If you do, let me recall to you

All the good days we had together,
The wreathes you wore, of roses and violets

As we lay side by side, the necklaces
Woven from flowers to drape your soft
    shoulders,

The perfume, precious, fit for royalty
. . .
How much you used, to anoint yourself!

The soft bed where you would satisfy . . .
    desire . . .

         *   *   *

2
Some there are who say that the fairest thing seen
on the black earth is an array of horsemen;
some, men marching; some would say ships; but
    I say she whom one loves best

is the loveliest. Light were the work to make this
plain to all, since she, who surpassed in beauty
all mortality, Helen, once forsaking her
    lordly husband,

fled away to Troy-land across the water.
Not the thought of child nor beloved parents
was remembered, after the Queen of Cyprus
    won her at first sight.

Since young brides have hearts that can be
    persuaded
easily, light things, palpitant to passion
as am I, remembering Anaktória who has gone
    from me

and whose lovely walk and the shining pallor
of her face I would rather see before my
eyes than Lydia's chariots in all their glory
    armored for battle.

Like the very gods in my sight is he who
sits where he can look in your eyes, who listens
close to you, to hear the soft voice, its sweetness
    murmur in love and

laughter, all for him. But it breaks my spirit;
underneath my breast all the heart is shaken.
Let me only glance where you are, the voice
    dies, I can say nothing,

but my lips are stricken to silence, underneath my skin the tenuous flame suffuses;
nothing shows in front of my eyes, my ears are
    muted in thunder.

And the sweat breaks running upon me, fever
shakes my body, paler I turn than grass is;
I can feel that I have been changed, I feel that
    death has come near me.

         *   *   *

Semonides of Amorgos
Poem on Women

In the beginning the god made the female mind separately. One he made from a long-bristled sow. In her house everything lies in disorder, smeared with mud, and rolls about the floor; and she herself unwashed, in clothes unlaundered, sits by the dungheap and grows fat.

Another he made from a wicked vixen; a woman who knows everything. No bad thing and no better kind of thing is lost on her; for she often calls a good thing bad and a bad thing good. Her attitude is never the same.

Another he made from a bitch, vicious, own daughter of her mother, who wants to hear everything and know everything. She peers everywhere and strays everywhere, always yapping, even if she sees no human being. A man cannot stop her by threatening, nor by losing his temper and knocking out her teeth with a stone, nor with honeyed words, not even if she is sitting with friends,

From *Females of the Species: Semonides on Women*, by Hugh Lloyd-Jones (Park Ridge, N.J.: Noyes Press, 1975), pp. 30, 32, 34, 38.

but ceaselessly she keeps up a barking you can do nothing with.

Another is from a bee; the man who gets her is fortunate, for on her alone blame does not settle. She causes his property to grow and increase, and she grows old with a husband whom she loves and who loves her, the mother of a handsome and reputable family. She stands out among all women, and a godlike beauty plays about her. She takes no pleasure in sitting among women in places where they tell stories about love. Women like her are the best and most sensible whom Zeus bestows on men.

Zeus has contrived that all these tribes of women are with men and remain with them. Yes, this is the worst plague Zeus has made—women; if they seem to be some use to him who has them, it is to him especially that they prove a plague. The man who lives with a woman never goes through all his day in cheerfulness; he will not be quick to push out of his house Starvation, a housemate who is an enemy, a god who is against us. Just when a man most wishes to enjoy himself at home, through the dispensation of a god or the kindness of a man, she finds a way of finding fault with him and lifts her crest for battle. Yes, where

there is a woman, men cannot even give hearty entertainment to a guest who has come to the house; and the very woman who seems most respectable is the one who turns out guilty of the worst atrocity; because while her husband is not looking . . . and the neighbours get pleasure in seeing how he too is mistaken. Each man will take care to praise his own wife and find fault with the other's; we do not realize that the fate of all of us is alike. Yes, this is the greatest plague that Zeus has made, and he has bound us to them with a fetter that cannot be broken. Because of this some have gone to Hades fighting for a woman. . . .

REVIEW QUESTIONS

1. What kinds of love do Sappho's poems celebrate?
2. How does the image of women as conveyed in her poetry compare with that in other selections in this chapter?
3. According to Semonides, how do women differ from men?
4. In general, are women assets or problems as far as Semonides is concerned?
5. Which qualities does he believe distinguish a good woman?

Spartan Society and Values

Among all the Greek city-states, Sparta was distinguished by the military ethic that governed virtually every aspect of its society. The life of the Spartan citizen was geared toward maintaining a constant state of military preparedness. For this achievement no sacrifice was too great, as was heroically demonstrated by the Spartans who defended the pass at Thermopylae against the Persians in 480 B.C.E. The following selections shed light on the values and organization of Spartan society. The first, "The Spartan Creed," is the work of the Spartan poet Tyrtaeus, whose poetry continued to inspire Spartan warriors long after his death. The second selection is a description of Spartan laws and customs by Xenophon, an Athenian follower of the philosopher Socrates. Xenophon is known best for his work, the Anabasis, *which de-*

scribes the retreat, led by him, of a mercenary army stranded in Persian territory ca. 400 B.C.E.

Tyrtaeus
"The Spartan Creed"

I would not say anything for a man nor take
  account of him
for any speed of his feet or wrestling skill he
  might have,
not if he had the size of a Cyclops and strength
  to go with it,
not if he could outrun Bóreas, the North Wind
  of Thrace,
not if he were more handsome and gracefully
  formed than Tithónos,
or had more riches than Midas had, or Kínyras
  too,
not if he were more of a king than Tantalid
  Pelops,
or had the power of speech and persuasion
  Adrastos had,
not if he had all splendors except for a fighting
  spirit.
For no man ever proves himself a good man in
  war
unless he can endure to face the blood and the
  slaughter,
go close against the enemy and fight with his
  hands.
Here is courage, mankind's finest possession,
  here is
the noblest prize that a young man can endeavor
  to win,
and it is a good thing his city and all the people
  share with him
when a man plants his feet and stands in the
  foremost spears
relentlessly, all thought of foul flight completely
  forgotten,

and has well trained his heart to be steadfast and
  to endure,
and with words encourages the man who is
  stationed beside him.
Here is a man who proves himself to be valiant
  in war.
With a sudden rush he turns to flight the rugged
  battalions
of the enemy, and sustains the beating waves of
  assault.
And he who so falls among the champions and
  loses his sweet life,
so blessing with honor his city, his father, and
  all his people,
with wounds in his chest, where the spear that
  he was facing has transfixed
that massive guard of his shield, and gone
  through his breastplate as well,
why, such a man is lamented alike by the young
  and the elders,
and all his city goes into mourning and grieves
  for his loss.

His tomb is pointed to with pride, and so are
  his children,
and his children's children, and afterward all the
  race that is his.
His shining glory is never forgotten, his name is
  remembered,
and he becomes an immortal, though he lies
  under the ground,
when one who was a brave man has been killed
  by the furious War God
standing his ground and fighting hard for his
  children and land.
But if he escapes the doom of death, the
  destroyer of bodies,
and wins his battle, and bright renown for the
  work of his spear,
all men give place to him alike, the youth and
  the elders,

From *Greek Lyrics,* translated by Richmond Lattimore
(Chicago: University of Chicago Press, 1960).

and much joy comes his way before he goes
    down to the dead.
Aging, he has reputation among his citizens. No
    one
tries to interfere with his honors or all he
    deserves;
all men withdraw before his presence, and yield
    their seats to him,
the youth, and the men his age, and even those
    older than he.
Thus a man should endeavor to reach this high
    place of courage
with all his heart, and, so trying, never be
    backward in war.

Xenophon
FROM "The Laws and Customs of the Spartans"

*   *   *

But reflecting once how Sparta, one of the least populous of states, had proved the most powerful and celebrated city in Greece, I wondered by what means this result had been produced. When I proceeded, however, to contemplate the institutions of the Spartans, I wondered no longer.

Lycurgus, who made the laws for them, by obedience to which they have flourished, I not only admire, but consider to have been in the fullest sense a wise man; for he rendered his country preëminent in prosperity, not by imitating other states, but by making ordinances contrary to those of most governments.

With regard, for example, to the procreation of children, that I may begin from the beginning, other people feed their young women, who are about to produce offspring, and who are of the class regarded as well brought up, on the most moderate quantity of vegetable food possible, and on the least possible quantity of meat, while they either keep them from wine altogether, or allow

From *Xenophon's Minor Works,* trans. J. S. Watson (Bell, Bohn Classical Library, 1878).

them to use it only when mixed with water; and as the greater number of the men engaged in trades are sedentary, so the rest of the Greeks think it proper that their young women should sit quiet and spin wool. But how can we expect that women thus treated should produce a vigorous progeny? Lycurgus, on the contrary, thought that female slaves were competent to furnish clothes; and, considering that the production of children was the noblest duty of the free, he enacted, in the first place, that the female should practice bodily exercises no less than the male sex; and he thus appointed for the women contests with one another, just as for the men, expecting that when both parents were rendered strong a stronger offspring would be born from them.

Observing, too, that the men of other nations, when women were united to husbands, associated with their wives during the early part of their intercourse without restraint, he made enactments quite at variance with this practice; for he ordained that a man should think it shame to be seen going in to his wife, or coming out from her. When married people meet in this way, they must feel stronger desire for the company of one another, and whatever offspring is produced must thus be rendered far more robust than if the parents were satiated with each other's society.

In addition to these regulations, he also took from the men the liberty of marrying when each of them pleased, and appointed that they should contract marriages only when they were in full bodily vigour, deeming this injunction also conducive to the production of an excellent offspring. Seeing also that if old men chanced to have young wives, they watched their wives with the utmost strictness, he made a law quite opposed to this feeling; for he appointed that an old man should introduce to his wife whatever man in the prime of life he admired for his corporeal and mental qualities, in order that she might have children by him. If, again, a man was unwilling to associate with his wife, and yet was desirous of having proper children, he made a provision also with respect to him, that whatever women he saw likely to have offspring, and of good disposition, he

ter taking food,
complexioned,
who are inactiv
feeble, he did n
point; and as he
gages in labou
proves himself
dition, he order
exercise should
it should never
food. With rega
to have been b
would easily fin
bodied, than th
selves alike in
their shoulders.

From acqui
prohibited then
He instituted,
money, that, e
house, it could
masters or of s
room, and a c
place, gold and
they are disco
them is punish
be an object of
session of mor
use of it afford
That at Sp
obedience to
know. I suppo:
attempt to est
things, until h
men in the st
regard to it. I
eration, that, i
men are not
magistrates, bu
ing free men
men not only
trates, but eve
themselves bel
are called upo

might, on obtaining the consent of her husband, have children by her. Many similar permissions he gave; for the women are willing to have two families, and the men to receive brothers to their children, who are equal to them in birth and standing, but have no claim to share in their property.

Let him who wishes, then, consider whether Lycurgus, in thus making enactments different from those of other legislators, in regard to the procreation of children, secured for Sparta a race of men eminent for size and strength.

Having given this account of the procreation of children, I wish also to detail the education of those of both sexes. Of the other Greeks, those who say that they bring up their sons best set slaves over them to take charge of them, as soon as the children can understand what is said to them, and send them, at the same time, to schoolmasters, to learn letters, and music, and the exercises of the palaestra. They also render their children's feet delicate by the use of sandals, and weaken their bodies by changes of clothes; and as to food, they regard their appetite as the measure of what they are to take. But Lycurgus, instead of allowing each citizen to set slaves as guardians over his children, appointed a man to have the care of them all, one of those from whom the chief magistrates are chosen; and he is called the paedonomus. He invested this man with full authority to assemble the boys, and, if he found that any one was negligent of his duties, to punish him severely. He assigned him also some of the grown-up boys as whip-carriers, that they might inflict whatever chastisement was necessary; so that great dread of disgrace, and great willingness to obey, prevailed among them.

Instead, also, of making their feet soft with sandals, he enacted that they should harden them by going without sandals; thinking that, if they exercised themselves in this state, they would go up steep places with far greater ease, and descend declivities with greater safety; and that they would also leap, and skip, and run faster unshod, if they had their feet inured to doing so, than shod. Instead of being rendered effeminate, too, by a variety of dresses, he made it a practice that they

should accustom themselves to one dress throughout the year; thinking that they would thus be better prepared to endure cold and heat.

As to food, he ordained that they should exhort the boys to take only such a quantity as never to be oppressed with overeating, and not to be strangers to living somewhat frugally; supposing that, being thus brought up, they would be the better able, if they should be required, to support toil under a scarcity of supplies, would be the more likely to persevere in exertion, should it be imposed on them, on the same quantity of provisions, and would be less desirous of sauces, more easily satisfied with any kind of food, and pass their lives in greater health. He also considered that the fare which rendered the body slender would be more conducive to increasing its stature than that which expanded it with nutriment. Yet that the boys might not suffer too much from hunger, Lycurgus, though he did not allow them to take what they wanted without trouble, gave them liberty to steal certain things to relieve the cravings of nature; and he made it honourable to steal as many cheeses as possible. That he did not give them leave to form schemes for getting food because he was at a loss what to allot them, I suppose no one is ignorant; as it is evident that he who designs to steal must be wakeful during the night, and use deceit, and lay plots; and, if he would gain anything of consequence, must employ spies. All these things, therefore, it is plain that he taught the children from a desire to render them more dexterous in securing provisions, and better qualified for warfare.

Some one may say, "Why, then, if he thought it honourable to steal, did he inflict a great number of whiplashes on him who was caught in the act?" I answer, that in other things which men teach, they punish him who does not follow his instructions properly; and that the Spartans accordingly punished those who were detected as having attempted to steal in an improper manner. These boys he gave in charge to others to whip them at the altar of Diana Orthia; designing to show by this enactment that it is possible for a person, after enduring pain for a short time, to

enjoy pleasur
also shown b
is need of acti
the least, and

In order,
donomus bei
a president, l
izens may ha
assume the d
ever he may
punish them
this, Lycurgu
boys much
men respect
that if, on a
pen to be pr
case be witl
most active
mand of ea
never witho

It appea
also of the b
likewise son
other Greek
as among t
or, as amon
of the you
upon them;
prohibit th
having the
curgus, act
thought pr
he ought
youth, and
faultless fri
praise upo
excellent I
showed th
bodily attr
ing this a
Lacedaem(
abstain fr
less strictl
course wit
family fro
state of tl

though he himself couldn't go home honorably. He would stay to leave eternal fame behind him, and see to it that Sparta's prosperity was not snuffed out. You see, the Spartans had consulted the Delphic oracle as soon as the war broke out, and the Pythian priestless had prophesied that either the Lacedaemonian people would be uprooted by the barbarians or their king would die. She uttered the prophecy in the following hexameter verses:

But for you, O dwellers in Sparta's wide land,
Either your glorious city shall be sacked by the
    men of Persia
Or, if not, she will mourn the action of Heracles,
The dead ruler over all the land of Lacedaemon.
The strength of bulls and lions cannot resist the
    foe,
For he has the strength of Zeus. No, he will not
    leave off,
I say, until he tears city or king limb from limb.

Leonidas dismissed the allies with this prophecy in mind, and because he wanted to be the only Spartan to win such fame; they did not go home in disarray over a difference of opinion.

For me, not the least evidence for this view is the well-known fact that Leonidas also tried to dismiss the army seer I mentioned—Megistias the Acarnanian, who they say descended from Melampus, and who foretold the future from his sacrificial animals. But although he had been dismissed to keep him from being killed with everyone else, he didn't leave; instead, he sent home his only son, who had gone to war with him.

The allies who had been dismissed obeyed Leonidas and left. Only the Thespians and the Thebans stayed with the Lacedaemonians. The Thebans remained without wanting to because Leonidas, regarding them as hostages, held them against their will. The Thespians, on the other hand, were very willing to stay. Refusing to abandon Leonidas or desert his men, they stayed behind and died along with them. The Thespian commander was Demophilus, son of Diadromes.

Xerxes poured out drink offerings at sunrise. He waited until about midmorning and then be-

gan the attack. This plan had been arranged in advance with Ephialtes, because the descent from the mountain would be much quicker, with much less ground to cover, than the march around and the climb up had been. The barbarians under Xerxes moved forward while the Greeks under Leonidas advanced like men who are going out to their deaths; and this time they went much farther out into the wider part of the pass than they had at first. In the first days of battle, concerned with protecting the defending wall, they would only make forays into the narrowest part and fight there. This time, as the two sides grappled with each other beyond the narrow neck of the pass, very many barbarians fell while their company commanders whipped each and every man, driving them constantly forward. Many of them fell into the sea and drowned; many others trampled each other alive; no one cared about the dying. And because they knew that death was coming from the troops who had circled the mountain, the Greeks fought the barbarians with all the strength they had, fought recklessly out of their minds.

Most of their spears were broken by now, so they slaughtered Persians with their swords. That brave man Leonidas fell in the struggle, and other renowned Spartans along with him. I have learned the names of these noble men, as I have learned the names of all the three hundred Spartans who perished. And, indeed, many brave Persians died there, too, two sons of Darius among them—Abrocomes and Hyperanthes, Darius' children by Phratagune, daughter of Artanes. This Artanes was the brother of King Darius, and the son of Hystaspes, son of Arsames. When he married his daughter to Darius, Artanes gave up his whole estate along with her since she was his only child.

Thus two brothers of Xerxes died in the battle.

There was a tremendous crush of Persians and Lacedaemonians around the body of Leonidas, until by sheer courage the Greeks dragged him away after beating back the enemy four times. The fight continued until Ephialtes arrived. The nature of the battle changed as soon as the Greeks realized that he was there. They fell back to the narrow part of the pass and, after ducking behind the wall, massed together on the hillock behind it and dug in—all except the Thebans. This mound is in the pass where the stone lion now stands in honor of Leonidas. The men defended themselves on this hillock with daggers, if they still had them, or with their hands and teeth, while some of the Persians came at them head-on after pulling down and demolishing the wall and others surrounded them and stood there burying them under arrows, spears, and stones.

They say that Dieneces the Spartan stood out even in this company of Lacedaemonians and Thespians. Just before the battle with the Persians, he heard some Trachinian say that when the barbarians shot their arrows the sky was so full of them that the sun was blotted out—that's how many Persians there were. Dieneces wasn't fazed at all. He pooh-poohed the Persian numbers, and is reported to have said that his Trachinian friend had brought good news, because if the Persians blotted out the sun they could have their battle in the shade rather than in the sunlight. They say Dieneces the Spartan left this and other witticisms to be remembered by. After him, they say, two Lacedaemonian brothers, Alpheus and Maron, sons of Orsiphantus, distinguished themselves. The most outstanding Thespian was named Dithyrambus, son of Harmatides.

The men were buried where they fell, along with those who had died before the departure of the men Leonidas had dismissed. There is an epitaph over the mass grave which says:

IN THIS PLACE FOUR THOUSAND
PELOPONNESIANS FOUGHT
FOUR MILLION MEN

That epitaph was for all the men. These words commemorate the Spartans alone:

STRANGER GO TELL THE
LACEDAEMONIANS THAT WE WHO LIE
HERE OBEYED THEIR ORDERS

*   *   *

REVIEW QUESTIONS

1. According to Herodotus, why does Xerxes decide to invade Greece? Do he or his generals fear the Greeks at all?
2. What special attributes of the Greeks make it possible for them to resist and eventually defeat the Persian forces?
3. Do the Persians, and Xerxes specifically, possess any flaws that ensure their eventual defeat?
4. How does Herodotus's account of the Spartans at Thermopylae compare with the readings preceding this one?

THUCYDIDES

FROM *The Peloponnesian Wars*

The costly Peloponnesian War of 431–404 B.C.E. was the culmination of years of growing tension between Sparta and its allies, and the Athenian empire. The Athenian historian Thucydides, who was scrupulously rigorous in his assessment and use of historical evidence, offered a version of the speech given by the Athenian leader Pericles to honor those Athenians who fell in battle during the war's first year. It has come to be regarded as one of the classic statements of the values of a democracy.

From *Thucydides: The Peloponnesian Wars,* translated by Benjamin Jowett, revised by P. A. Brunt (New York: Washington Square Press, 1991).

Pericles' Funeral Speech

During the same winter, in accordance with traditional custom, the funeral of those who first fell in this war was celebrated by the Athenians at the public charge. The ceremony is as follows: Three days before the celebration they erect a tent in which the bones of the dead are laid out, and every one brings to his own dead any offering which he pleases. At the time of the funeral, the bones are placed in chests of cypress wood, which are conveyed on hearses; there is one chest for each tribe. They also carry a single empty litter decked with a pall for all whose bodies had not been found and recovered. The procession is accompanied by anyone who chooses, whether citizen or foreigner; and the female relatives of the deceased are present at the funeral and make lamentation. The public sepulcher is situated in the most beautiful suburb of the city; there they always bury those who fall in war; only after the battle of Marathon, in recognition of their pre-eminent valor, the dead were interred on the field. When the remains have been laid in the earth, a man, chosen by the city for his reputed sagacity of judgment and eminent prestige, delivers the appropriate eulogy over them; after which the people depart. This is the manner of interment, and the ceremony was repeated from time to time throughout the war. Over the first who were buried, Pericles was chosen to speak. At the fitting moment he advanced from the sepulcher to a lofty stage, which had been erected in order that he might be heard as far away as possible by the crowd, and spoke somewhat as follows:

"Most of those who have spoken here before me commend the law-giver who added this oration to our other funeral customs, thinking it right for an oration to be delivered at the funeral of those killed in wars. But I would have thought it enough that when men have been brave in action, they should also be publicly honored in action, and with such a ceremony as this state funeral, which you are now witnessing. Then the reputation of many would not have been imperiled by one man and their merits believed or not, as he speaks well or ill. For it is difficult to say neither too little nor too much when belief in the truth is hard to confirm. The friend of the dead who knows the facts may well think that the words of the speaker fall short of his wishes and knowledge; another who is not well informed, when he hears of anything which surpasses his own nature, may be envious and suspect exaggeration. Mankind is tolerant of the praises of others so long as each hearer thinks himself capable of doing anything he has heard; but when the speaker rises above this, jealousy and incredulity are at once aroused. However, since our ancestors have set the seal of their approval upon the practice, I must obey the law and, to the utmost of my power, endeavor to satisfy the wishes and beliefs of you all.

"I will speak of our ancestors first, for it is right and seemly that on such an occasion as this we should also render this honor to their memory. Men of the same stock, ever dwelling in this land, in successive generations to this very day, by their valor handed it down as a free land. They are worthy of praise, and still more are our fathers, who added to their inheritance, and after many a struggle bequeathed to us, their sons, the great empire we possess. Most of it those of our own number who are still in the settled time of life have strengthened further and have richly endowed our city in every way and made her most self-sufficient for both peace and war. Of the military exploits by which our various possessions were acquired or of the energy with which we or our fathers resisted the onslaught of barbarians or Hellenes I will not speak, for the tale would be long and is familiar to you. But before I praise the dead, I shall first proceed to show by what kind of practices we attained to our position, and under what kind of institutions and manner of life our empire became great. For I conceive that it would not be unsuited to the occasion that this should be told, and that this whole assembly of citizens and foreigners may profitably listen to it.

"Our institutions do not emulate the laws of others. We do not copy our neighbors: rather, we are an example to them. Our system is called a democracy, for it respects the majority and not the few; but while the law secures equality to all alike in their private disputes, the claim of excellence is also recognized; and when a citizen is in any way distinguished, he is generally preferred to the public service, not in rotation, but for merit. Nor again is there any bar in poverty and obscurity of rank to a man who can do the state some service. It is as free men that we conduct our public life, and in our daily occupations we avoid mutual suspicions; we are not angry with our neighbor if he does what he likes; we do not put on sour looks at him which, though harmless, are not pleasant. While we give no offense in our private intercourse, in our public acts we are prevented from doing wrong by fear; we respect the authorities and the laws, especially those which are ordained for the protection of the injured as well as those unwritten laws which bring upon the transgressor admitted dishonor.

"Furthermore, none have provided more relaxations for the spirit from toil; we have regular games and sacrifices throughout the year; our homes are furnished with elegance; and the delight which we daily feel in all these things banishes melancholy. Because of the greatness of our city, the fruits of the whole earth flow in upon us so that we enjoy the goods of other countries as freely as our own.

"Then, again, in military training we are superior to our adversaries, as I shall show. Our city is thrown open to the world, and we never expel a foreigner or prevent him from seeing or learning anything which, if not concealed, it might profit an enemy to see. We rely not so much upon preparations or stratagems, as upon our own courage in action. And in the matter of education, whereas from early youth they are always undergoing laborious exercises which are to make them brave, we live at ease and yet are equally ready to face perils to which our strength is equal. And here is the evidence. The Lacedæmonians march against our land not by themselves, but with all their allies: we invade a neighbor's country alone; and although our opponents are fighting for their homes and we are on a foreign soil, we seldom have any difficulty in overcoming them. Our enemies have never yet felt our strength in full; the care of a navy divides our attention, and on land we are obliged to send our own citizens to many parts. But if they meet and defeat some part of our army, they boast of having routed us all, and when defeated, of having been vanquished by our whole force.

"If then we prefer to meet danger with a light heart but without laborious training and with a courage which is instilled by habit more than by laws, we are the gainers; we do not anticipate the pain, although, when the hour comes, we show ourselves no less bold than those who never allow themselves to rest. Nor is this the only cause for marveling at our city. We are lovers of beauty without extravagance and of learning without loss of vigor. Wealth we employ less for talk and ostentation than when there is a real use for it. To avow poverty with us is no disgrace: the true disgrace is in doing nothing to avoid it. The same persons attend at once to the concerns of their households and of the city, and men of diverse employments have a very fair idea of politics. If a man takes no interest in public affairs, we alone do not commend him as quiet but condemn him as useless; and if few of us are originators, we are all sound judges of a policy. In our opinion action does not suffer from discussion but, rather, from the want of that instruction which is gained by discussion preparatory to the action required. For we have an exceptional gift of acting with audacity after calculating the prospects of our enterprises, whereas other men are bold from ignorance but hesitate upon reflection. But it would be right to esteem those men bravest in spirit who have the clearest understanding of the pains and pleasures of life and do not on that account shrink from danger. In doing good, again, we are unlike others; we make our friends by conferring, not by receiving favors. Now a man who confers a favor is the firmer friend because he would keep alive the memory of an obligation by kindness to the recipient; the man who owes an obligation is colder in his feelings because he knows that in recruiting the service, he will not be winning gratitude but only paying a debt. We alone do good to our neighbors, not so much upon a calculation of interest, but in the fearless confidence of freedom.

"To sum up, I say that the whole city is an education for Hellas and that each individual in our society would seem to be capable of the greatest self-reliance and of the utmost dexterity and grace in the widest range of activities. This is no passing boast in a speech, but truth and fact, and verified by the actual power of the city which we have won by this way of life. For when put to the test, Athens alone among her contemporaries is superior to report. No enemy who comes against her is indignant at the reverses which he sustains at the hands of such men; no subject complains that his masters do not deserve to rule. And we shall assuredly not be without witnesses; there are mighty monuments of our power which will make us the wonder of this and of succeeding ages; we shall not need the praises of Homer or of any other whose poetry will please for the moment, but whose reconstruction of the facts the truth will damage. For we have compelled every land and sea to open a path to our daring and have everywhere planted eternal memorials of our triumphs and misfortunes. Such is the city these men fought and died for and nobly disdained to lose, and every one of us who survive would naturally wear himself out in her service.

"This is why I have dwelt upon the greatness of Athens, showing you that we are contending for a higher prize than those who enjoy no like advantages, and establishing by manifest proof the merit of these men whom I am now commemorating. Their loftiest praise has been already spoken; for in descanting on the city, I have honored the qualities which earned renown for them and for men such as they. And of how few Hellenes can it be said as of them, that their deeds matched their fame! In my belief an end such as theirs proves a man's worth; it is at once its first revelation and final seal. For even those who come short in other ways may justly plead the valor with which they have fought for their country; they have blotted out evil with good, and their public services have outweighed the harm they have done in their private actions. None of these men were enervated by wealth or hesitated to resign the pleasures of life; none of them put off the evil day in the hope, natural to poverty, that a man, though poor, may yet become rich. But deeming that vengeance on their enemies was sweeter than any of these things and that they could hazard their lives in no nobler cause, they accepted the risk and resolved on revenge in preference to every other aim. They resigned to hope the obscure chance of success, but in the danger already visible they thought it right to act in reliance upon themselves alone. And when the moment for fighting came, they held it nobler to suffer death than to yield and save their lives; it was the report of dishonor from which they fled, but on the battlefield their feet stood fast; and while for a moment they were in the hands of fortune, at the height, less of terror than of glory, they departed.

"Such was the conduct of these men; they were worthy of Athens. The rest of us must pray for a safer issue to our courage and yet disdain to show any less daring towards our enemies. We must not consider only what words can be uttered on the utility of such a spirit. Anyone might discourse to you at length on all the advantages of resisting the enemy bravely, but you know them just as well yourselves. It is better that you should actually gaze day by day on the power of the city until you are filled with the love of her; and when you are convinced of her greatness, reflect that it was acquired by men of daring who knew their duty and feared dishonor in the hour of action, men who if they ever failed in an enterprise, even then disdained to deprive the city of their prowess but offered themselves up as the finest contribution to the common cause. All alike gave their lives and received praise which grows not old and the most conspicuous of sepulchers—I speak not so much of that in which their remains are laid as of that in which their glory survives to be remembered forever, on every fitting occasion in word and deed. For every land is a sepulcher for famous men; not only are they commemorated by inscriptions on monuments in their own country, but even in foreign lands there dwells an unwritten memorial of them, graven not so much on stone as in the hearts of men. Make them your examples now; and, esteeming courage to be freedom and freedom to be happiness, do not weigh too nicely the perils of war. It is not the unfortunate men with no hope of blessing, who would with best reason be unsparing of their lives, but the prosperous, who, if they survive, are always in danger of a change for the worse, and whose situation would be most transformed by any reverse. To a man of spirit it is more painful to be oppressed like a weakling than in the consciousness of strength and common hopes to meet a death that comes unfelt.

"Therefore I do not now commiserate the parents of the dead who stand here; I shall rather comfort them. They know that their life has been passed amid manifold vicissitudes and that those men may be deemed fortunate who have gained most honor, whether an honorable death, like the men we bury here, or an honorable sorrow like yours, and whose days have been so measured that the term of their happiness is likewise the term of their life. I know how hard it is to make you feel this when the good fortune of others will often remind you of the happiness in which you, like them, once rejoiced. Sorrow is felt at the want not of those blessings which a man never knew, but

of those which were a part of his life before they were taken from him. Some of you are of an age at which you may have other children, and that hope should make you bear your sorrow better; not only will the children who may hereafter be born make you forget those you have lost, but the city will be doubly a gainer; she will not be left desolate, and she will be safer. For a man's counsel cannot have equal weight or worth when he has no children like the rest to risk in the general danger. To those of you who have passed their prime, I say: 'Congratulate yourselves that you have been happy during the greater part of your days; remember that what remains will not last long, and let it be lightened by the glory of these men.' For only the love of honor is ever young; and it is not so much profit, as some say, but honor which is the delight of men when they are old and useless.

"To you who are the sons and brothers of the departed, I see that the struggle to emulate them will be arduous. For all men praise the dead; and, however pre-eminent your virtue may be, you would hardly be thought their equals, but somewhat inferior. The living have their rivals and detractors; but when a man is out of the way, the honor and good will which he receives is uncontested. And, if I am also to speak of womanly virtues to those of you who will now be widows, let me sum them up in one short admonition: 'Your glory will be great if you show no more than the infirmities of your nature, a glory that consists in being least the subjects of report among men, for good or evil.'

"I have spoken in obedience to the law, making use of such fitting words as I had. The tribute of deeds has been paid in part, for the dead have been honorably interred; it remains only that their children shall be maintained at the public charge until they are grown up: this is the solid prize with which, as with a garland, Athens crowns these men and those left behind after such contests. For where the rewards of virtue are greatest, there men do the greatest services to their cities. And now, when you have duly lamented, everyone his own dead, you may depart."

Such was the order of the funeral celebrated in this winter, with the end of which ended the first year of this war.

*   *   *

REVIEW QUESTIONS

1. What, in Pericles' estimation, are the benefits of democracy?
2. What are the reasons for Athens's greatness?
3. How do the values of Athenian democracy compare with those of Spartan society?

XENOPHON

FROM *Oeconomicus*

While the modern democracies of the early twenty-first century C.E. rightfully trace their pedigrees back to classical Athens, it bears remembering that participation in Athenian democracy was restricted to male citizens of that polis. Resident aliens, women, and slaves had no voice. That women were excluded from political activity is hardly surprising given the social restrictions that were placed on them, not to mention the inferior status they had within their own households. In the following reading, the philosopher Socrates (of whom Xenophon was a student) questions one of his students, Ischomachos, about how he has educated his wife.

From *Xenophon's Socratic Discourse: An Interpretation of the Oeconomicus*, edited by Leo Strauss (Ithaca, N.Y.: Cornell University Press, 1970), pp 32–38.

*   *   *

" 'As to what you asked me, Socrates,' he said, 'I never spend time indoors. Indeed,' he said, 'my wife is quite able by herself to manage the things within the house.'

" 'It would please me very much, Ischomachos,' I said, 'if I might also inquire about this—whether you yourself educated your wife to be the way she ought to be, or whether, when you took her from her mother and father, she already knew how to manage the things that are appropriate to her.'

" 'How, Socrates,' he said, 'could she have known anything when I took her, since she came to me when she was not yet fifteen, and had lived previously under diligent supervision in order that she might see and hear as little as possible and ask the fewest possible questions? Doesn't it seem to you that one should be content if she came knowing only how to take the wool and make clothes, and had seen how the spinning work is distributed among the female attendants? For as to matters of the stomach, Socrates,' he said, 'she came to me very finely educated; and to me, at any rate, that seems to be an education of the greatest importance both for a man and a woman.'

" 'By the gods, Ischomachos,' I said, 'relate to

me what you first began teaching her. I'd listen to you relating these things with more pleasure than if you were telling me about the finest contest in wrestling or horsemanship.'

"And Ischomachos replied: 'Well, Socrates,' he said, 'when she had gotten accustomed to me and had been domesticated to the extent that we could have discussions, I questioned her somewhat as follows. "Tell me, woman, have you thought yet why it was that I took you and your parents gave you to me? That it was not for want of someone else to spend the night with—this is obvious, I know, to you too. Rather, when I considered for myself, and your parents for you, whom we might take as the best partner for the household and children, I chose you, and your parents, as it appears, from among the possibilities chose me. Should a god grant us children, we will then consider, with respect to them, how we may best educate them; for this too is a good common to us —to obtain the best allies and the best supporters in old age; but for the present this household is what is common to us. As to myself, everything of mine I declare to be in common, and as for you, everything you've brought you have deposited in common. It's not necessary to calculate which of us has contributed the greater number of things, but it is necessary to know this well, that which ever of us is the better partner will be the one to contribute the things of greater worth." To this, Socrates, my wife replied: "What can I do to help you?" she said. "What is my capacity? But everything depends on you: my work, my mother told me, is to be moderate." "By Zeus, woman," I said "my father told me the same thing. But it's for moderate people—for man and woman alike —not only to keep their substance in the best condition but also to add as much as possible to it by fine and just means." "Then what do you see," said my wife, "that I might do to help in increasing the household?" "By Zeus," I said, "just try to do in the best manner possible what the gods have brought you forth to be capable of and what the law praises." "And what are these things?" she said. . . . "Since, then, work and diligence are needed both for the indoor and for the outdoor

things, it seems to me," ' he had said, ' "that the god directly prepared the woman's nature for indoor works and indoor concerns. For he equipped the man, in body and in soul, with a greater capacity to endure cold and heat, journey and expeditions, and so has ordered him to the outdoor works; but in bringing forth, for the woman, a body that is less capable in these respects," ' he said that he had said, ' "the god has, it seems to me, ordered her to the indoor works. But knowing that he had implanted in the woman, and ordered her to, the nourishment of newborn children, he also gave her a greater affection for the newborn infants than he gave to the man. Since he had also ordered the woman to the guarding of the thing brought in, the god, understanding that a fearful soul is not worse at guarding, also gave the woman a greater share of fear than the man. And knowing too that the one who had the outdoor works would need to defend himself should someone act unjustly, to him he gave a greater share of boldness. But because it's necessary for both to give and to take, he endowed both with memory and diligence in like degree, so that you can't distinguish whether the male or the female kind has the greater share of these things. As for self-control in the necessary things, he endowed both with this too in like degree; and the god allowed the one who proved the better, whether the man or the woman, to derive more from this good. Since, then, the nature of each has not been brought forth to be naturally apt for all of the same things, each has need of the other, and their pairing is more beneficial to each, for where one falls short the other is capable. Now," I said, "O woman, as we know what has been ordered to each of us by the god, we must, separately, do what's appropriate to each. The law too praises these things," ' he said that he had said, ' "in pairing man and woman; and as the god made them partners in children, so too does the law appoint them partners. . . . It will be necessary," I said, "for you to remain indoors and to send out those of the servants whose work is outside; as for those whose work is to be done inside, these are to be in your charge; you must receive what is brought in and distribute what needs to be expended, and as for what needs to be set aside, you must use forethought and guard against expending in a month what was intended to last a year. When wool is brought to you, it must be your concern that clothes be made for whoever needs them. And it must be your concern that the dry grain be fine and fit for eating. There is one thing, however," I said, "among the concerns appropriate to you, that will perhaps seem less agreeable: whenever any of the servants become ill, it must be your concern that all be attended." "By Zeus," said my wife, "that will be most agreeable, at least if those who have been well tended are going to be grateful and feel more good will than before." I admired her reply,' said Ischomachos, 'and spoke: "Isn't it through this kind of forethought that the leader of the hive so disposes the other bees to her that when she leaves the hive, not one of the bees supposes they must let her go, but rather they all follow? . . . But the most pleasant thing of all: if you look to be better than I and make me your servant, you will have no need to fear that with advancing age you will be honored any less in the household, and you may trust that as you grow older, the better a partner you prove to be for me, and for the children the better a guardian of the household, by so much more will you be honored in the household. . . ." I seem to remember saying such things to her, Socrates, at the time of our first discussion.' "

" 'Did you notice, Ischomachos,' I said, 'that she was stirred to diligence by these things?'

" 'Yes, by Zeus,' said Ischomachos. 'I know she once became very upset, and blushed deeply, when she was unable to give me one of the things I had brought in when I asked for it. Seeing she was irritated, I spoke. "Don't be discouraged, woman," I said, "because you can't give me what I happen to ask for. It is indeed clear poverty not to have a thing to use when it's needed; at the same time our present want—to look for something and be unable to find it—is certainly a less painful thing than not to look for it at all, knowing it's not there. But you aren't at fault in this," I

said; "rather I am, since I handed over these things to you without giving orders as to where each kind of thing should be put, so that you would know where to put them and where to find them again. There is nothing, woman, so useful or fine for human beings as order. . . . That an ordered arrangement of implements is a good, then, and that it is easy to find in the house an advantageous place for each kind of thing, has been established. But how fine it looks, too, when shoes of any kind are set out in a regular manner; it is fine to see clothes of any kind when they are sorted, as also bedcovers, bronze kettles, and things pertaining to the table, and—what of all things would be most ridiculed, not indeed by the solemn man but by the wit—even pots have a graceful look when distinctly arranged." ' "

" 'What then, Ischomachos?' I said. 'Did your wife seem to listen at all to what you were trying so seriously to teach her?'

" 'What else did she do if not promise to be diligent, manifest her very great pleasure, as though she had found some easy means out of a difficulty, and ask me to order things separately as quickly as possible in the way I had stated?'

" 'How, then, Ischomachos,' I said, 'did you separately order them for her?'

" 'What else seemed best to me if not to show her first the capacity of the house? For it is not adorned with decorations, Socrates; the rooms were planned and built simply with a view to their being the most advantageous receptacles for the things that would be in them, so that each calls for what is suitable to it. The bedroom, being in an interior part of the house, invites the most valuable bedcovers and implements; the dry parts of the dwelling, the grain; the cool places, the wine; and the well-lighted places, the works and implements that need light. And I displayed to her the areas for the daily use of human beings, furnished so as to be cool in summer and warm in winter. And I displayed to her the house as a whole, and how it lies open to the south—obviously, so as to be well exposed to the sun in winter and well shaded in summer. Then I pointed out to her the women's apartments, separated from the men's by a bolted door, so that nothing may be taken out that shouldn't be and so that the servants may not produce offspring without our knowledge. For the useful ones, for the most part, feel even more good will once they have had children, but when wicked ones are paired together, they become only more resourceful in their bad behavior. When we had gone through these things,' he said, 'we then proceeded to separate our belongings according to tribes. We began first,' he said, 'by collecting whatever we use for sacrifices. After this we distinguished the woman's ornaments for festivals, the man's dress for festivals and war, bedcovers for the women's apartments, bedcovers for the men's apartments, shoes for women, shoes for men. Another tribe consisted of arms, another of instruments for spinning, another of instruments for breadmaking, another of instruments for cooking, another of the things for bathing, another of the things for kneading bread, another of the things for the table; and all these things were further divided according to whether they were used every day or only for festivals. We also set apart the expenses for each month from the amount that had been calculated and reserved for the whole year; for in this way we could better see how things would come out at the end. And when we had sorted our belongings according to tribes, we took each kind of thing to its appropriate place. After this, as to the implements the servants use from day to day—those for the making of bread, for cooking, for spinning, and others of this sort—we pointed out to those who would be using them where each must go, handed them over, and gave orders that they be kept secure. Those we use for festivals, for entertaining foreigners, or only from time to time we handed over to the housekeeper, and after pointing out to her their places and counting and making lists of the various kinds of things, we told her to give each what he needed of them, to remember what she had given someone, and when she had got it back, to return it to the place she had taken it from. We chose as housekeeper the one who upon examination

seemed to us the most self-controlled as regards food, wine, sleep, and intercourse with men, and who, in addition, seemed to have a good memory and the forethought to avoid punishment for negligence and to consider how, by gratifying us in some way, she might be honored by us in return. We taught her also to feel good will toward us, sharing our delights when we were delighted in some way, and when there was something painful, inviting her aid. We further educated her to be eager to increase the household, making her thoroughly acquainted with it and giving her a share in its prosperity. And we inspired justice in her, honoring the just more than the unjust and displaying to her that they live richer and freer lives than the unjust. We then installed her in the place. But in addition to all these things, Socrates,' he said, 'I told my wife that there would be no benefit in any of this unless she herself was diligent in seeing that the order is preserved in each thing. I taught her that in the cities subject to good laws the citizens do not think it enough merely to have fine laws, but in addition choose guardians of the laws to examine them, to praise the one who acts lawfully, and to punish the one who acts contrary to the laws. Then,' he said 'I suggested that my wife consider herself a guardian of the laws regarding the things in the house; that she inspect the implements whenever it seems best to her, just as a garrison commander inspects his guards; that she test the fitness of each thing, just as the council tests the fitness of horses and horsemen; and that, like a queen, she praise and honor the deserving, to the limit of her capacity, and rebuke and punish the one who needs such things. In addition,' he said, 'I taught her that she could not be justly annoyed if I gave her many more orders in regard to our possessions than I gave to the servants, displaying to her that the servants share in their master's wealth only to the extent that they carry it, attend to it, or guard it, and that no one of them is allowed to use it unless the lord gives it to him, whereas everything is the master's to use as he wishes. To the one deriving the greatest benefit from its preservation and the greatest harm from its destruction belongs the greatest concern for a thing—this I declared to her.'

" 'What then?' I said. 'After your wife had heard these things, Ischomachos, did she at all obey you?'

" 'What else did she do,' he said, 'if not tell me I didn't understand her correctly if I supposed that in teaching her to be concerned with our substance I had ordered her to do something hard. For as she told me,' he said, 'it would have been much harder if I had ordered her to neglect her own things than if she were required to concern herself with the goods of the household. For just as it seems natural,' he said, 'for a sensible woman to be concerned for her offspring rather than to neglect them, so, she said, it's more pleasant for a sensible woman to be concerned for those of the possessions that delight her because they are her own than to neglect them.' "

"On hearing that his wife had replied to him in this way," said Socrates, "I spoke. 'By Hera, Ischomachos,' I said, 'you display your wife's manly understanding.'

" 'There are other instances of her high-mindedness that I am willing to relate to you,' said Ischomachos, 'instances of her obeying me quickly in some matter after hearing it only once.'

" 'In what sort of thing?' I said. 'Speak; for to me it is much more pleasant to learn of the virtue of a living woman than to have had Zeuxis display for me the fine likeness of a woman he had painted.'

"Ischomachos then speaks. 'And yet once, Socrates,' he said, 'I saw she had applied a good deal of white lead to her face, that she might seem to be fairer than she was, and some dye, so that she would look more flushed than was the truth, and she also wore high shoes, that she might seem taller than she naturally was. "Tell me, woman," I said, "would you judge me more worthy to be loved as a partner in wealth if I showed you our substance itself, didn't boast of having more substance than is really mine, and didn't hide any part of our substance, or if instead I tried to deceive you by saying I have more substance than is really mine and by displaying to you counterfeit money,

necklaces of gilt wood, and purple robes that lose their color, and asserting they are genuine?" She broke in straightway. "Hush," she said; "don't you become like that; if you did, I could never love you from my soul." "Haven't we also come together, woman," I said, "as partners in one another's bodies?" "Human beings say so, at least," she said. "Would I then seem more worthy to be loved," I said, "as a partner in the body, if I tried to offer you my body after concerning myself that it be healthy and strong, so that I would really be well complexioned, or if instead I smeared myself with vermilion, applied flesh color beneath the eyes, and then displayed myself to you and embraced you, all the while deceiving you and offering you vermilion to see and touch instead of my own skin?" "I wouldn't touch vermilion with as much pleasure as I would you," she said, "or see flesh color with as much pleasure as your own, or see painted eyes with as much pleasure as your healthy ones." "You must believe, woman," ' Ischomachos said that he had said, " 'that I too am not more pleased by the color of white lead or dye than by your color, but just as the gods have made horses most pleasant to horses, oxen to oxen, and sheep to sheep, so human beings suppose the pure body of a human being is most pleasant. Such deceits may in some way deceive outsiders and go undetected, but when those who are always together try to deceive one another they are necessarily found out. For either they are found out when they rise from their beds and before they have prepared themselves, or they are detected by their sweat or exposed by tears, or they are genuinely revealed in bathing." '

" 'By the gods,' I said, 'what did she reply to this?'

" 'What else,' he said, 'was her reply, if not that she never did anything of the sort again and tried always to display herself suitably and in a pure state. At the same time she asked me if I could not advise her how she might really come to sight as fine and not merely seem to be. I advised her, Socrates,' he said, 'not always to sit about like a slave but to try, with the gods' help, to stand at the loom like a mistress, to teach others what she knew better than they, and to learn what she did not know as well; and also to examine the breadmaker, to watch over the housekeeper in her distribution of things, and to go about and investigate whether each kind of thing is in the place it should be. In this way, it seemed to me, she could both attend to her concerns and have the opportunity to walk about. And I said it would be good exercise to moisten and knead the bread and to shake out and fold the clothes and bedcovers. I said that if she exercised in this way, she would take more pleasure in eating, would become healthier, and so would come to sight as better complexioned in truth. And a wife's looks, when in contrast to a waiting maid she is purer and more suitably dressed, become attractive, especially when she gratifies her husband willingly instead of serving him under compulsion. On the other hand, women who always sit about in pretentious solemnity lend themselves to comparison with those who use adornments and deceit. And

now, Socrates,' he said, 'know well, my wife still arranges her life as I taught her then and as I tell you now.' "

*   *   *

REVIEW QUESTIONS

1. What kinds of attitudes toward women underlie Ischomachos's treatment of his wife?
2. How do women and men differ, in his eyes?
3. What are her responsibilities in the household?
4. What can you deduce from this reading about the internal configuration of a Greek dwelling (at least, that of someone of Ischomachos's social standing)?
5. Can you discern any contrasts between the role of women as presented here and their role in Spartan society as described in the earlier selection by Xenophon?

SOPHOCLES

FROM *Antigone*

One of the foremost features of the culture of classical Athens was its focus on the rights, responsibilities, and potential of the individual and its celebration of human intellect and personality. Nowhere is this more evident than in the surviving works of the greatest of the Athenian tragedians, Aeschylus, Sophocles, and Euripides. Sophocles wrote his play Antigone, *from which the following excerpts are taken, shortly before 441 B.C.E. Like so many of the plays of this era,* Antigone *focuses on the nobility of spirit of the human being when faced with terrible conflict. Indeed, one well-known analysis of its impact characterizes it as the only work of literature that expresses "all the principal constants of conflict in the condition of man . . . : the confrontation of men and women; of age and of youth; of society and of the individual; of the living and the dead; of men and of god(s)."*

From *The Antigone of Sophocles,* translated by George Herbert Palmer (Boston: Houghton Mifflin, 1927).

THE PERSONS

CREON, King of Thebes
EURYDICE, his wife
HAEMON, his son, betrothed to Antigone
ANTIGONE, } his nieces, daughters of Oedipus and
ISMENE, } Jocasta, former King and Queen of
{ Thebes
WATCHMAN
MESSENGER
SECOND MESSENGER
BOY AND GUARDS, silent persons
CHORUS OF THEBAN ELDERS

The Scene throughout is at Thebes, in front of the palace. The Play begins at daybreak.

ANTIGONE: Ismene, my own sister, of all the woes begun in Oedipus can you imagine any that Zeus will not complete within our lives? There is no grief or crime, no degradation or dishonor, not to be found among the woes of you and me. And what is this new edict issued lately by our captain, people say, to the whole city? Do you know, and did you hear? Or have you failed to learn how on our friends fall evils from our foes?

ISMENE: To me, Antigone, have come no tidings of our friends, for good or ill, since we two lost two brothers, slain in mutual strife the self-same day. I know the Argive host retreated this last night, but I know nothing further—whether we gain or lose.

ANTIGONE: I guessed as much, and therefore brought you here alone outside the gate to learn the truth.

ISMENE: What is it, then? You seem to hint at some dark tale.

ANTIGONE: Yes. In his order for the burial of our brothers has not Creon honored the one, outraged the other? To Eteocles, they say, he paid each proper rite and custom and laid him in the ground, to be in honor with the dead below. But as for poor dead Polynices' body, they say he has proclaimed among our people that none shall hide it in a grave and mourn, but let it lie unwept, unburied, welcome provision for the birds who watch for such-like prey. These are, they say, the orders our good Creon has proclaimed for you and me—yes, even for me!—and now comes hither to make plain his will to such as do not know. Nor does he treat the matter lightly. But let one do what he forbids, and death by public stoning shall await him in the city. So it stands now, and you must quickly show if you are rightly born or the base child of noble parents.

ISMENE: But, my poor sister, if it has come to this, what further can I do to help or hinder?

ANTIGONE: Think, will you share my toil and strife?

ISMENE: In what bold deed? What is your plan?

ANTIGONE: To try if you with this hand's help will raise that body.

ISMENE: What! Bury him? In opposition to the State?

ANTIGONE: My brother, though, and yours. If you refuse, I will be found no traitor.

ISMENE: Reckless! When Creon too forbids?

ANTIGONE: 'T is not for him to keep me from my own.

ISMENE: Alas! consider, sister, how our father died, hated and scorned, because of self-exposed offences doing his eyes a violence with his own hand. And then his mother and his wife—ah, double title!—with twisted cord ended her life in shame. A third disaster came. Our pair of brothers in a single day, like wretched suicides, wrought out one common ruin by each other's hand. And now once more, when we are the only ones still left, think what a far worse fate we two shall meet if we, defying law, transgress our rulers' will and power. Nay, rather let us bear in mind that we are women, so not fit to strive with men. Moreover, since we are the subjects of those stronger than ourselves, we must obey these orders and orders harsher still. I, then, beseeching those beneath the earth to grant me pardon, seeing I am compelled, will bow to those in power. To act beyond one's sphere shows little wisdom.

ANTIGONE: I will not urge you. No! Nor if hereafter you desire, shall you with my consent give any aid. Be what you will, and I will bury him. Good it would be to die in doing so. Dearly shall I lie with him, with my dear, after my pious sin. And longer must I satisfy those there below than people here, for there I shall lie ever. But you, if you think well, keep disregarding what the gods regard!

ISMENE: I mean no disregard. But to defy the State—it is not in me.

ANTIGONE: Make that, then, your excuse! I will go raise a grave over my dearest brother.

ISMENE: O my poor sister, how I fear for you!

ANTIGONE: Be not disturbed for me. Let your own course be true.

ISMENE: At least do not reveal what you have done. Keep it a secret. I will hide it too.

ANTIGONE: Ha? Speak it out! Far more my enemy if silent than if telling it to all!

ISMENE: Hot heart and chilling deeds!

ANTIGONE: I know I please those I most ought to please.

ISMENE: If you succeed. But you desire what cannot be.

ANTIGONE: Why, then, when strength shall fail me, I will cease.

ISMENE: Best not pursue at all what cannot be.

ANTIGONE: Speak thus, and I shall hate you. And he who died will hate you,—rightly too. Nay, leave me and my rash design to meet our doom, for I shall meet none equal to not dying nobly.

ISMENE: Go, then, if go you must. And yet of this be sure, that mad as is your going, dearly are you loved by those you love.

*   *   *

[*Enter* CREON.]

CREON: Sirs, our city's welfare, though shaken in a heavy surge, the gods have safely righted. Therefore by mandate I have brought you hither, parted from all the rest, because I know full well how in the time of Laïus you steadily respected the power of the throne. So also in the days when Oedipus upheld the State. And even when he fell, you stood around the children of his house with faithful hearts. Since, then, these two have fallen in one day by double doom, smiting and smitten in their own hand's guilt, I take possession of all power

and of the throne through being next of kin to the two dead.

It is impossible fully to learn what a man is in heart and mind and judgment until he proves himself by test of office and of laws. For to my thinking he who ordering a great state catches at plans not through their being best, and then through fear holds his lips locked, appears and ever has appeared most base. Him who regards his friend more than his land I count no man at all. I therefore,—all-seeing Zeus bear witness!—never shall keep silence when I see woe coming on my citizens instead of weal. Nor would I ever make that man my friend who is my country's foe; because I know how it is she who saves us, and when we sail with her secure we find true friends.

Such are the principles by which I make this city prosper. And in accord herewith I now have issued public edict touching the sons of Oedipus: ordering that Eteocles, who fell fighting for this city after winning all distinction with his spear, be laid within a grave and given whatever honors meet the brave dead below. But for his brother Polynices, who coming back from exile tried by fire utterly to destroy his native land and his ancestral gods, tried even to taste the blood of his own kin or force them into bondage—this man we have proclaimed throughout the city none shall honor with a grave and none lament, but that his corpse be left unburied, for the birds and dogs to eat, disgraced for all to see. Such is my will. Never by act of mine shall bad men have more honor than the just. But he who is well minded toward this state alike in life or death by me is honored.

*   *   *

CREON: You there, now turning to the ground your face, do you acknowledge or deny you did this thing?

ANTIGONE: I say I did it. I deny not that I did.

CREON: (*To Watchman.*) Then go your way, clear of a heavy charge. [*Exit.*] (*To Antigone.*) Tell me, not at full length but briefly, did you know my edict against doing this?

ANTIGONE: I did. How could I help it? It was plain.

CREON: Yet you presumed to transgress laws?

ANTIGONE: Yes, for it was not Zeus who gave this edict; nor yet did Justice, dwelling with the gods below, make for men laws like these. I did not think such force was in your edicts that the unwritten and unchanging laws of God you, a mere man, could traverse. These are not matters of to-day or yesterday, but are from everlasting. No man can tell at what time they appeared. In view of them I would not, through fear of human will, meet judgment from the gods. That I shall die, I knew,—how fail to know it?—though you had never made an edict. And if before my time I die, I count it gain. For he who lives like me in many woes, how can he fail to find in death a gain? So then for me to meet this doom is not a grief at all. But when my mother's child had died if I had kept his corpse unburied, then I should have grieved. For this I do not grieve. And if I seem to you to have been working folly, it may be he who charges folly is the fool.

CHORUS: Plain is the headstrong temper of this child of headstrong father. She knows not how to bend in times of ill.

CREON: Yet know that spirits very stiff may soonest fail. The strongest iron, baked in the fire overhard, you may see oftenest snap and break. By a little bit, I find, high-mettled steeds are managed. There is no place for pride in one who is dependent. She first set out in crime when she transgressed the established laws; and after that comes further crime in boasting here, laughing at having done so. I am no longer man, she is the man, if such power rests in her unchallenged. Be she my sister's child, or closer to my blood than all who bow before our household Zeus, she and her kin shall not escape the direst doom.

Yes, for I count her sister an equal plotter of this burial. Summon her hither! Even now I saw her in the house raving and uncontrolled. It often happens that the stealthy heart is caught before the act, when in the dark men fashion crooked deeds. But it is hateful, too, when one found out in wrong will give his guilt fine names.

ANTIGONE: Do you desire more than having caught to kill me?

CREON: No, nothing. Having that, I have the whole.

ANTIGONE: Then why delay? For nothing in your words can give me pleasure—and may they never please! So also you mine naurally displease. Yet how could I have gained glory more glorious than by now laying my own brother in the grave? All here would speak approval, did not terror seal their lips. Rulers, so fortunate in much besides, have this advantage too—that they can do and say whatever they may please.

CREON: Of all the race of Cadmus you alone see it so.

ANTIGONE: These also do, but curb their tongues through fear of you.

CREON: And are you not ashamed to act so unlike them?

ANTIGONE: 'T is no disgrace to honor one's own kin.

CREON: Was not he also of your blood who fell, his rival?

ANTIGONE: Mine, by one mother and one father too.

CREON: Why then pay honors which dishonor him?

ANTIGONE: He who is dead would not describe it so.

CREON: Yes, if you give like honor to his impious foe.

ANTIGONE: It was no slave who died. It was his brother.

CREON: Wasting the land. And he defending it.

ANTIGONE: But these are rites called for by Death itself.

CREON: The good and bad should not be like in lot.

ANTIGONE: Who knows if that is pity below?

CREON: A hated man is not beloved, though dead.

ANTIGONE: I take no part in hate. 'T is mine to love.

CREON: Down to the grave, then, if you needs must love, and love those there! But while I live, no woman masters me.

*   *   *

CHORUS: But here is Haemon, the youngest of your sons. Does he come grieving for the fate of his intended bride Antigone, vexed at his vanished nuptials?

[*Enter* HAEMON.]

*   *   *

CREON: Soon we shall know, better than seers could say. My son, because you heard the immutable decree passed on your promised bride, you are not here incensed against your father? Are we not dear to you, do what we may?

HAEMON: My father, I am yours; and with just judgment you may direct, and I shall follow. No marriage shall be counted greater gain than your wise guidance.

CREON: Yes, so it should be settled in your heart, my son, always to take your stand behind your father's judgment. Therefore men pray to rear obedient children and to have them in their homes, to recompense the foe with ill and honor as their father does the friend. If one begets unprofitable children, what shall we say but that he breeds pains for himself, loud laughter for his foes? Do not, my son, at pleasure's bidding, give up your wits for any woman. But know embraces soon grow cold when she who shares the home is false. What ulcer can be worse than the false friend? Then spurn the girl as if she were your foe, and let her seek a husband in the house of Hades. For having found her only, out of all the State, openly disobedient, recreant to that State I will not be, but I will have her life.

Let her appeal to Zeus, the god of kindred; but if I train my kin to be disorderly, I surely shall all those outside my kin. He who in private matters is a faithful man will prove himself upright in public too. But one who wantonly forces the law, and thinks to dictate to the rulers, wins no praise from me. No, whosoever is established by the State should be obeyed, in matters trivial and just or in their opposites. And the obedient man, I should be confident, would govern well and easily be governed, and posted in the storm of spears would hold his ground, a true and loyal comrade. Than lawlessness there is no greater ill. It ruins states, overturns homes, and joining with the spear-thrust breaks the ranks in rout. But in the steady lines what saves most lives is discipline. Therefore we must defend the public order and not at all subject it to a woman. Better be pushed aside, if need be, by a man than to be known as women's subjects.

CHORUS: Unless through age we are at fault, you seem to say with reason what you say.

HAEMON: Father, the gods plant wisdom in mankind, which is of all possessions highest. In what respects you have not spoken rightly I cannot say, and may I never learn; and still it may be possible for some one else to be right too. I naturally watch in your behalf all that men do or say or find to blame. For your eye terrifies the common man and checks the words you might not wish to hear; but it is mine to hear things uttered in the dark. I know how the whole city mourns this maid, as one who of all women least deservedly for noblest deeds meets basest death. "She who, when her brother had fallen in the fight and lay unburied, did not leave him to be torn by savage dogs and birds, is she not worthy to receive some golden honor?" Such guarded talk runs covertly about.

For me, my father, nothing I possess is dearer than your welfare. For what can bring to children greater glory than a successful father's noble name, or to a father than his son's renown? Do not then carry in your heart one fixed belief that what you say and nothing else is right. For he who thinks that he alone is wise, or that he has a tongue and mind no other has, will when laid open be found empty. However wise a man may be, it is no shame to learn, learn much, and not to be too firm. You see along the streams in winter how many trees bend down and save their branches; while those that stand up stiff go trunk and all to ruin. So he who tightly draws his vessel's sheet and will not slack, upsets the boat and ends his course with benches upside down. Be yielding, then, and admit change. For if from me, though younger, an opinion be allowed, I count it best that man should be by nature wise. But if that cannot be, —and usually the scale does not incline so—then it is well to learn from good advisers.

CHORUS: My lord, you ought, when Haemon speaks aright, to learn of him; and Haemon, you of him. For both have spoken well.

CREON: At our age shall we learn from one so young?

HAEMON: Only the truth. Young though I am, do not regard my years more than the facts.

CREON: The fact, you mean, of being gentle to the unruly.

HAEMON: I would not ask for gentleness to wicked persons.

CREON: But is not she tainted with some such ill?

HAEMON: With one accord the men of Thebes say no.

CREON: And shall the city tell me how to rule?

HAEMON: Surely you see how childish are such words!

CREON: Govern this land for others than myself?

HAEMON: No city is the property of one alone.

CREON: Is not the city reckoned his who rules?

HAEMON: Excellent ruling,—you alone, the land deserted!

CREON: He fights, it seems, the woman's battle.

HAEMON: If you are she. Indeed my care is all for you.

CREON: Perverted boy, pressing a cause against your father!

HAEMON: Because I see you causelessly do wrong.

CREON: Do I do wrong in reverencing my office?

HAEMON: It is not reverence to trample on the rights of gods.

CREON: A hateful heart that bends before a woman!

HAEMON: But never will you find me subservient to the base.

CREON: Why, all your argument is urged for her.

HAEMON: Yes, and for you and me, and for the gods below.

CREON: You shall not marry her this side the grave.

HAEMON: So then she dies; but if she dies, destroys another.

CREON: Will you assail me with your threats, audacious boy?

HAEMON: Is it a threat to combat silly schemes?

CREON: To your sorrow you shall teach, while yourself in need of teaching.

HAEMON: But that you are my father, I had counted you ill-taught.

CREON: Be a plaything for your mistress, but trifle not with me!

HAEMON: Will you then speak, and when you speak not listen?

CREON: And has it come to this? But, by Olympus, you shall not lightly heap reproach on insult. Bring me that piece of malice, straightway to die before my eyes in presence of her bridegroom!

HAEMON: Not in my precence. Do not think it! She shall not die while I am near. And you youself shall see my face no more. Rave on then here with those who will submit!
[*Exit.*]

*   *   *

CHORUS: So you will put them both to death?

CREON: Not her who had no finger in the business. You say well.

CHORUS: And by what doom do you intend to slay the other?

CREON: Leading her where the ways are clear of humankind, I will shut her up alive in a stone cell, allowing only so much food for expiation that the whole city may escape the stain. And if she calls upon the Grave,—the only god she honors —she may obtain deliverance from death; or else will learn, though late, that honor done the Grave is labor lost.
[*Exit.*]

*   *   *

ANTIGONE: Men of my land, you see me taking my last walk here, looking my last upon the sunshine—never more. No, Hades, who brings all to bed, leads me alive along the strand of Acheron, missing my part in wedding song. Never did bridal hymn hymn me. But I shall be the bride of Acheron.

CHORUS: And yet you will in glory and with praise pass to the secret places of the dead. Not smitten with slow disease, nor meeting the sword's portion, but self-possessed, alone among mankind you go to the Grave alive.

ANTIGONE: I have heard of the pitiful end of the stranger from Phrygia, the daughter of Tantalus, on Mount Sipylus; o'er whom like clinging ivy a rocky growth would creep, and from her wasting form the showers and snow, 't is said, are never absent, but drop upon her neck down from her weeping brows. Most like to her, God brings me to my rest.

CHORUS: Nay, nay! She was a god and sprung from gods. But we are mortals and of human birth. Yet for a mortal maid to win a godlike lot is high renown, whether one live or die.

ANTIGONE: Ah, I am mocked! Why, by our country's gods, taunt me when not yet gone but here before you? O thou my city, and ye great ones of my city, thou spring of Dircé, and thou grove of charioted Thebes, I call on you to witness how all unwept of friends and by what cruel laws I go to that sepulchral mound for an unheard-of burial. Ah, poor me! Having no home with mankind or with corpses, with living or with dead!

CHORUS: Onward pressing to the utmost verge of daring, on the deep foundation stone of Right you fell, my child,—a grievous fall. A father's penalty you pay.

ANTIGONE: Ah, there you touched my bitterest pang, my father's thrice-told woe, and all the doom of the great line of Labdacus. Alas, the horrors of my mother's bed! And the embraces—his very self begetting—of that father and that hapless mother from whom I here, distracted, once was born! To them I go, accursed, unwedded, now to dwell. Alas for you, my brother, who made an ill-starred marriage and in your death stripped me, alive, of all.

CHORUS: In pious actions there is piety. Yet

power, when his whose right it is, may nowise be transgressed. Your self-willed temper slew you.

ANTIGONE: Unwept, unfriended, with no bridal song, poor I am led along the appointed way. Never again that sacred ball of fire may I, alas! behold. Yet for my tearless lot not a friend grieves.

CREON: Do you not know that groans and dirges before death would never cease, were it allowed to voice them? Away with her forthwith! And when, as I commanded, you have shut her in the vaulted tomb, leave her alone in solitude, to die if so she must, or let her live her life prisoned in such a home. Thus we are clear of what befalls the maid. Only from dwelling in the light above shall she be hindered.

ANTIGONE: O grave! O bridal chamber! Hollow home, forever holding me! whither I go to join my own; for far the greater number Persephassa has received among the dead, all gone! Last of them I, and most unhappy far, now go below before I reach the limit of my life; yet going, dearly cherish it among my hopes to have my coming welcome to my father, welcome to you, my mother, welcome too to you, my brother. When you all died, with my own hand I washed you, did you service, and poured libations at your graves. But, Polynices, for ministering to your corpse this is my recompense.

Rightly I honored you, the wise will think. Yet had I children, or were my husband mouldering in death, I might not in defiance of my townsmen have taken up the task. And wherefore so? I might have had another husband, had mine died, a child too by another man when I had lost my own; but mother and father hidden in the grave, there is no brother ever to be born. Yet when upon such grounds I held you first in honor, to Creon's eye I seemed to sin and to be over-bold, my brother dear. And now he leads me forth, a captive, deprived of bridal bed and song,—without experience of marriage or the rearing of a child,—that so poor I, cut off from friends but still alive, enter the caverned chambers of the dead.

What ordinance of heaven have I transgressed? Yet why in misery still look to gods or call on them for aid, when even this name of impious I got by piety! No, if such acts are pleasing to the gods, I may by suffering come to know my sin. But if these others rather sin, may they not suffer greater ill than they now wrongly wreak on me.

CHORUS: Still the same winds' same blasts of passion sway her.

CREON: Therefore her guards shall smart for their delay.

ANTIGONE: Ah me! The signal comes that death is nigh!

CHORUS: I cannot bid you hope it will not follow.

ANTIGONE: O city in the land of Thebes! Home of my fathers! And ye, ancestral gods! Men seize me and I cannot stay. Behold, O lords of Thebes, how I, last remnant of the royal line, now suffer, and from whom—I who revered the right.
[ANTIGONE *is led away.*

*   *   *

[*Enter a messenger.*]

MESSENGER: Ye dwellers at the palace of Cadmus and Amphion, there is no human life, however placed, that I can praise or blame. For fortune raises, fortune overthrows, him who is now in good or evil fortune. No seer can tell the destinies of man. Creon was enviable once, I thought, through having saved this land of Cadmus from its foes. Winning full sovereignty he ruled the land, blest too in noble issue. Now all is gone. For when man parts with happiness, I count him not alive, but a mere breathing corpse. Let him have riches in his house, great riches if you will, and live in royal state; if happiness be absent, I would not pay a puff of smoke for all the rest, when weighed with joy.

CHORUS: What new disaster to our kings come you to tell?

MESSENGER: Dead! And the living caused the death.

CHORUS: Who is the slayer? Who has fallen? Speak!

MESSENGER: Haemon is gone. With violence his blood is shed.

CHORUS: What? By his father's hand, or by his own?

MESSENGER: His own, incensed against his father for the murder.

*   *   *

CHORUS: But lo! Our lord himself draws near, bringing in his arms clear proof—if we may say so—of wrong not wrought by others but by his erring self.
[*Enter* CREON, *bearing the body of* HAEMON.]

*   *   *

CREON: Alas, the sins of a presumptuous soul, stubborn and deadly! Ah, ye who see slayers and slain of kindred blood! Woe for my ill-starred plans! Alas, my boy, so young in life and young in sorrow! Woe! Woe! Thou, dead and gone? And by my folly, not thy own!

CHORUS: Ah me! It seems you see the right too late!

CREON: Unhappy I have learned it now. But then some god possessed me, smote on my head a heavy blow, drove me along a brutish path, and so—alas!—o'erthrew my joy and trampled it. Woe, woe, for the wearisome works of man!
[*Enter a second messenger.*]

SECOND MESSENGER: My lord, 't is having and still getting. You bear one sorrow in your arms; enter the house, and there you soon should see another.

CREON: What is there yet more sorrowful than this?

SECOND MESSENGER: The queen is dead, true mother of the dead here. Poor lady, she has fallen by wounds dealt even now.

CREON: Alas, alas! Insatiate gulf of death! Why, why thus cause my ruin? And cruel messenger, speeding my pain, what is the tale you tell? Why, one already dead you slay anew! What say you, boy? What tidings do you bring? Ah, must the slaughterous ending of my wife follow the death of him?
[*The Scene opens, and the body of* EURYDICE *is disclosed.*]

CHORUS: Here you may see! It shall be hid no longer.

CREON: Ah me! A fresh, a second grief poor I behold. What more has fate in waiting? Just now I took my child in my arms—alas!—and face to face behold another corse. Woe! Woe! unhappy mother! Woe, my child!

SECOND MESSENGER: Crazed, clinging to the altar, and closing her dark eyes, she fist bemoaned the glorious grave of Megareus who died before, then this one's end; and with her last breath called down ill on you, the murderer of your children.

CREON: Alas! Alas! Fear thrills me. Will none strike home with two-edged sword? Poor I am steeped in sore distress.

SECOND MESSENGER: You were accused by her who died of causing both the deaths.

CREON: And by what sort of violence did she depart?

SECOND MESSENGER: Her own hand smote herself below the heart, soon as she learned the lamentable ending of her son.

CREON: Ah me! To no one else can this be shifted from my guilty self. 'T was I indeed that killed thee, wretched I! I say the truth, 't was I. Take me, my servants, take me straightway hence, to be no more than nothing.

CHORUS: Wise wishes these, if any way is wise in evil. Briefest is best, when evil clogs our feet.

CREON: Come, then, appear, fairest of fates that brings my final day! O come, best boon, and let me never see another day!

CHORUS: Time will determine that. The present needs our care. Let them whose right it is direct the rest!

CREON: All I desire is summed up in that prayer.

CHORUS: Pray no more now. From his appointed woe man cannot fly.

CREON: Then take away the useless man who by no will of his killed thee, my child, and thee too lying here. Alas poor me, who know not which to look on, where to turn! All in my hands was at cross purposes, and on my head fell fate I could not guide.

CHORUS: Wisdom is far the greater part of peace. The gods will have their dues. Large language, bringing to the proud large chastisement, at last brings wisdom.

*   *   *

REVIEW QUESTIONS

1. What is the dilemma with which Antigone is confronted?
2. Where, in her eyes, must her principal allegiance lie?
3. How does the fact that Antigone is a woman affect her treatment by Creon?
4. How do you think this play would have been received by a Spartan audience?

VASE DEPICTING A SLAVE, PERHAPS IN A SCENE FROM A GREEK PLAY (C. 450 B.C.E.).

Slaves at Athens included a variety of nationalities and were at the bottom of the socio-economic hierarchy. What does the depiction in this vase painting suggest about attitudes toward slaves? How do the physical features and clothing of this slave differ from what you have observed in other works of classical Greek art?

PLATO

FROM "Apology"

Our knowledge of the life, personality, and teachings of the late-fifth-century B.C.E.
Athenian philosopher and social critic Socrates is derived almost entirely from the
dialogues composed by his most famous student, Plato. In them, Plato recreates Soc-
rates' method of using questions and answers (what today we still refer to as the
"Socratic method") to examine and test commonly held opinions. In the following
excerpt from the "Apology" (a word that in ancient Greek referred to a defense of
one's actions or beliefs, not an expression of contrition or regret), Socrates, on trial
before an Athenian jury for allegedly subverting the youth of Athens by converting
them to gods of his own invention, defends his career as a teacher. (His eloquence
and intellect, in the end, did not save him from condemnation and subsequent exe-
cution in 399 B.C.E.*)*

From *The Last Days of Socrates,* translated by Hugh Tredennick (New York: Penguin Books, 1969), pp. 48–52, 72–76.

*   *   *

Here perhaps one of you might interrupt me and say "But what is it that you do, Socrates? How is it that you have been misrepresented like this? Surely all this talk and gossip about you would never have arisen if you had confined yourself to ordinary activities, but only if your behaviour was abnormal. Tell us the explanation, if you do not want us to invent it for ourselves. "This seems to me to be a reasonable request, and I will try to explain to you what it is that has given me this false notoriety; so please give me your attention. Perhaps some of you will think that I am not being serious; but I assure you that I am going to tell you the whole truth.

I have gained this reputation, gentlemen, from nothing more or less than a kind of wisdom. What kind of wisdom do I mean? Human wisdom, I suppose. It seems that I really am wise in this limited sense. Presumably the geniuses whom I mentioned just now are wise in a wisdom that is more than human; I do not know how else to account for it. I certainly have no knowledge of such wisdom, and anyone who says that I have is a liar and wilful slanderer. Now, gentlemen, please do not interrupt me if I seem to make an extravagant claim; for what I am going to tell you is not my own opinion; I am going to refer you to an unimpeachable authority. I shall call as witness to my wisdom (such as it is) the god at Delphi.

You know Chaerephon, of course. He was a friend of mine from boyhood, and a good democrat who played his part with the rest of you in the recent expulsion and restoration. And you know what he was like; how enthusiastic he was over anything that he had once undertaken. Well, one day he actually went to Delphi and asked this question of the god—as I said before, gentlemen, please do not interrupt—he asked whether there was anyone wiser than myself. The priestess replied that there was no one. As Chaerephon is dead, the evidence for my statement will be supplied by his brother, who is here in court.

Please consider my object in telling you this. I want to explain to you how the attack upon my reputation first started. When I heard about the oracle's answer, I said to myself "What does the god mean? Why does he not use plain language? I am only too conscious that I have no claim to wisdom, great or small; so what can he mean by asserting that I am the wisest man in the world? He cannot be telling a lie; that would not be right for him."

After puzzling about it for some time, I set myself at last with considerable reluctance to check the truth of it in the following way. I went to interview a man with a high reputation for wisdom, because I felt that here if anywhere I should succeed in disproving the oracle and pointing out to my divine authority "You said that I was the wisest of men, but here is a man who is wiser than I am."

Well, I gave a thorough examination to this person—I need not mention his name, but it was one of our politicians that I was studying when I had this experience—and in conversation with him I formed the impression that although in many people's opinion, and especially in his own, he appeared to be wise, in fact he was not. Then when I began to try to show him that he only thought he was wise and was not really so, my efforts were resented both by him and by many of the other people present. However, I reflected as I walked away: "Well, I am certainly wiser than this man. It is only too likely that neither of us has any knowledge to boast of; but he thinks that he knows something which he does not know, whereas I am quite conscious of my ignorance. At any rate it seems that I am wiser than he is to this small extent, that I do not think that I know what I do not know."

After this I went on to interview a man with an even greater reputation for wisdom, and I formed the same impression again; and here too I incurred the resentment of the man himself and a number of others.

From that time on I interviewed one person after another. I realized with distress and alarm that I was making myself unpopular, but I felt compelled to put my religious duty first; since I was trying to find out the meaning of the oracle, I was bound to interview everyone who had a reputation for knowledge. And by Dog, gentlemen! (for I must be frank with you) my honest impression was this: it seemed to me, as I pursued my investigation at the god's command, that the people with the greatest reputations were almost entirely deficient, while others who were supposed to be their inferiors were much better qualified in practical intelligence.

I want you to think of my adventures as a sort of pilgrimage undertaken to establish the truth of the oracle once for all. After I had finished with the politicians I turned to the poets, dramatic, lyric, and all the rest, in the belief that here I should expose myself as a comparative ignoramus. I used to pick up what I thought were some of their most perfect works and question them closely about the meaning of what they had written, in the hope of incidentally enlarging my own knowledge. Well, gentlemen, I hesitate to tell you the truth, but it must be told. It is hardly an exaggeration to say that any of the bystanders could have explained those poems better than their actual authors. So I soon made up my mind about the poets too: I decided that it was not wisdom that enabled them to write their poetry, but a kind of instinct or inspiration, such as you find in seers and prophets who deliver all their sublime messages without knowing in the least what they mean. It seemed clear to me that the poets were in much the same case; and I also observed that the very fact that they were poets made them think that they had a perfect understanding of all other subjects, of which they were totally ignorant. So I left that line of inquiry too with the same sense of advantage that I had felt in the case of the politicians.

Last of all I turned to the skilled craftsmen. I knew quite well that I had practically no technical qualifications myself, and I was sure that I should find them full of impressive knowledge. In this I was not disappointed; they understood things which I did not, and to that extent they were wiser than I was. But, gentlemen, these professional experts seemed to share the same failing which I had noticed in the poets; I mean that on the strength of their technical proficiency they claimed a perfect understanding of every other subject, however important; and I felt that this error more than outweighed their positive wisdom. So I made myself spokesman for the oracle, and asked myself whether I would rather be as I was—neither wise with their wisdom nor stupid with their stupidity —or possess both qualities as they did. I replied through myself to the oracle that it was best for me to be as I was.

The effect of these investigations of mine, gentlemen, has been to arouse against me a great deal of hostility, and hostility of a particularly bitter and persistent kind, which has resulted in various malicious suggestions, including the description of me as a professor of wisdom. This is due to the fact that whenever I succeed in disproving another person's claim to wisdom in a given subject, the bystanders assume that I know everything about that subject myself. But the truth of the matter, gentlemen, is pretty certainly this: that real wisdom is the property of God, and this oracle is his way of telling us that human wisdom has little or no value. It seems to me that he is not referring literally to Socrates, but has merely taken my name as an example, as if he would say to us "The wisest of you men is he who has realized, like Socrates, that in respect of wisdom he is really worthless."

That is why I still go about seeking and searching in obedience to the divine command, if I think that anyone is wise, whether citizen or stranger; and when I think that any person is not wise, I try to help the cause of God by proving that he is not. This occupation has kept me too busy to do much either in politics or in my own affairs; in fact, my service to God has reduced me to extreme poverty.

*   *   *

Well, gentlemen, for the sake of a very small gain in time you are going to earn the reputation—and the blame from those who wish to disparage our city—of having put Socrates to death, "that wise man"—because they will say I am wise even if I am not, these people who want to find fault with you. If you had waited just a little while, you would have had your way in the course of nature. You can see that I am well on in life and near to death. I am saying this not to

all of you but to those who voted for my execution, and I have something else to say to them as well.

No doubt you think, gentlemen, that I have been condemned for lack of the arguments which I could have used if I had thought it right to leave nothing unsaid or undone to secure my acquittal. But that is very far from the truth. It is not a lack of arguments that has caused my condemnation, but a lack of effrontery and impudence, and the fact that I have refused to address you in the way which would give you most pleasure. You would have liked to hear me weep and wail, doing and saying all sorts of things which I regard as unworthy of myself, but which you are used to hearing from other people. But I did not think then that I ought to stoop to servility because I was in danger, and I do not regret now the way in which I pleaded my case; I would much rather die as the result of this defence than live as the result of the other sort. In a court of law, just as in warfare, neither I nor any other ought to use his wits to escape death by any means. In battle it is often obvious that you could escape being killed by giving up your arms and throwing yourself upon the mercy of your pursuers; and in every kind of danger there are plenty of devices for avoiding death if you are unscrupulous enough to stick at nothing. But I suggest, gentlemen, that the difficulty is not so much to escape death; the real difficulty is to escape from doing wrong, which is far more fleet of foot. In this present instance, I, the slow old man, have been overtaken by the slower of the two, but my accusers, who are clever and quick, have been overtaken by the faster: by iniquity. When I leave this court I shall go away condemned by you to death, but they will go away convicted by Truth herself of depravity and wickedness. And they accept their sentence even as I accept mine. No doubt it was bound to be so, and I think that the result is fair enough.

Having said so much, I feel moved to prophesy to you who have given your vote against me; for I am now at that point where the gift of prophecy comes most readily to men: at the point of death. I tell you, my executioners, that as soon as I am

5 ❧ THE EXPANSION OF GREECE

While Aristotle was composing his works Ethics *and* Politics, *his former pupil Alexander, the young king of Macedonia, was in the process of rendering his former tutor's discourse on the proper structure of the polis somewhat obsolete. Between 336 and his death in 322 B.C.E., Alexander achieved success almost beyond imagining: the subjugation of the vast Persian Empire, followed by further conquests that took his armies as far east as India. Yet, almost immediately on Alexander's death, his empire began to fragment, and in less than 300 years the Ptolemid, Seleucid, and Antigonid kingdoms all had succumbed to the ascending empires of the Romans from the west and the Parthians from the east. Political and military dominion, then, proved to be ephemeral. Not so fleeting, however, were the influence of Greek culture and urban institutions on the Near East (and the reciprocal influence of Near Eastern and Egyptian cultures on the Greeks) and the devastating impact of the invaders from the west on the previously established state structures of the areas they conquered.*

Historians, and the times during which they write, create history as much as do the great figures and civilizations about which they write. Nowhere is this more evident than in the history of Western perceptions of both Alexander and the new world order that he is claimed to have inaugurated. Until relatively recently, the West has made itself quite comfortable with an idealized image of Alexander the Great as a heroic figure whose conquests were aimed at harmoniously fusing Greek culture with the cultures of the Persian Empire. Likewise, Hellenistic civilization was regarded as mixed, essentially Greek in its inspiration but enriched by its contact with the older Near Eastern cultures. The rise of this point of view, understandably enough, coincided largely with the European colonial ascendancy over the Near and Far East and Africa that began during the nineteenth century C.E. With the disappearance of that colonialism over the past few decades, however, and as previously subject peoples have raised their own voices, there has come a dramatic reevaluation of Hellenistic civilization. The idealized image of a cultural fusion has been replaced with an image of that civilization as more emphatically Greek and of the Greek ruling class of the Hellenistic kingdoms as a colonial presence that was quite determined to maintain its superiority and preserve a large degree of separation from the indigenous peoples. Meanwhile, the political traditions of the regions over which the Greeks ruled continued largely as they had for centuries.

As the Hellenistic world order of large kingdoms took shape, it is not surprising that the traditional institutions and parochial perspectives of the polis were found wanting. This is nowhere more evident than in the development of religion and philosophy in the Hellenistic era. Much of Greek religion had been bound directly to formal cult and ritual within the polis. As the expansion of Greek colonization into the Near Eastern world began to sever the links to the traditional religion of the polis, another kind of religious experience, the mystery religions, became increasingly popular because of their more universal appeal and their promise of salvation and mystical union with a divine presence. In many ways, the spread of these mystery religions established a milieu that later promoted the spread of Christianity in the eastern Mediterranean.

Much of the philosophical thought of Plato and Aristotle had resonated greatest within the political context of the traditional city-state. Although much of the thought of the great Hellenistic philosophers derived from their classical predecessors, it also liberated itself from the confines of the city-state, developing an increasingly universal appeal. Long after the absorption of the Hellenistic kingdoms into the Roman and Parthian empires, the Hellenistic schools of philosophy, and in particular, the Stoic teachings of a divine, universal natural law and the basic brotherhood of human beings, provided rich intellectual capital for the continued development of the legal, political, and spiritual traditions of the West.

In both the broad sweep of its cultural expansion and the increasingly universal appeal of the philosophical doctrines and systems of religious belief of the time, the new world order of the Hellenistic period can justifiably be regarded as the first truly cosmopolitan age. The widespread Greek cultural legacy endowed to the Near East set the stage for the eventual success, during the subsequent era of the Roman Empire, of what became the most successful of the cosmopolitan religions: Christianity.

PLATO

FROM *The Republic*

After the death of his teacher, Socrates, Plato established the Academy, a school of philosophical instruction in an olive grove on the outskirts of Athens. (The fame of this school is apparent in the modern application of the terms academy *and* academic *to institutions of higher learning.) Among the works that Plato produced there was* The Republic, *commonly regarded as one of the most influential works of political philosophy ever written. Perhaps the central problem that Plato addresses is how to achieve a just society within the framework of the city-state. The following selection, which includes his famous Allegory of the Cave, offers some of his ideas on how to achieve that end.*

From *The Republic*, by Plato, translated by Richard W. Sterling and William C. Scott (New York: Norton, 1985), pp. 146–151, 209–115.

*   *   *

Book V

*   *   *

Now, then, can you think of any of the human arts in which men do not generally excel women? Let's not make a long story out of it by bringing up weaving and baking cakes and boiling vegetables, matters in which women take pride and would be mortified should a man best them in these skills.

You are surely correct in saying that the one sex excels the other in every respect. But it is also true that individually many women are more skilled than many men, even if your general proposition is true.

Then we must conclude that sex cannot be the criterion in appointments to government positions. No office should be reserved for a man just because he is a man or for a woman just because she is a woman. All the capabilities with which nature endows us are distributed among men and women alike. Hence women will have the rightful opportunity to share in every task, and so will men, even though women are the weaker of the two sexes.

Agreed.

Could we then assign all the tasks to the men and none to the women?

How could we propose such thing as that?

Well, then, we shall want to say instead that one woman has the capacity to be a doctor and another not, that one woman is naturally musical and another is unmusical.

Certainly.

Could we deny that there are some women who are warlike and natural athletes while others love neither war nor gymnastic?

I don't think we can.

Again, are there not women who love wisdom and those who do not? Are not some women high-spirited and some not?

There are all these kinds of women, too.

Hence it must also be true that one woman is fit to be a guardian and another unfit. For these are the same criteria we used when we were selecting men as guardians, are they not?

Yes.

As guardians of the state, then, women and men are naturally the same, except that one is weaker and the other stronger.

Apparently.

It follows that women with the requisite qualities must be chosen to live and guard together with men of like qualities since they have the necessary competence and are naturally kin.

By all means.

And the same natures ought to perform the same functions?

Yes.

So we have closed the circle. We agree that we do nothing against nature by educating the guardians' wives in music and gymnastic.

We are agreed.

Since we have legislated in harmony with nature, we have not proposed anything impractical or unattainable. On the contrary, we may say that if anything contradicts nature, it is the way things are done today.

So it appears.

Now we designed our inquiry to test whether our proposals would turn out to be both possible and desirable?

Yes.

Well, I take it we have just established that they are possible.

Yes.

Then we must see if we can agree that they are also desirable.

Clearly.

In preparing a woman to be a guardian, then, we won't prescribe one kind of education for women guardians and another for the men because their natures are the same.

No. There should be no differentiation.

Let me ask you a question.

About what?

About men. Do you think some are better and some worse, or are all alike?

They are certainly not all alike.

Then which do you think will become the better men in the city we are building: the guardians who are being educated in the manner we have prescribed or the cobblers who received instruction in the cobbler's art?

An absurd question.

I understand your answer. You mean that the guardians are the best of our citizens.

By far.

And will not the women guardians be the best of the women?

Yes.

And can we wish for the state anything better than that it should nurture the best possible men and women?

Nothing.

And the education we have prescribed in music and gymnastic will produce this outcome?

Without fail.

Therefore the institutions we have proposed for the state are not only possible, they are the best possible.

Quite so.

Then wearing virtue as a garment, the guardians' wives must go naked and take part alongside their men in war and the other functions of government, and no other duties will be required of them. Owing to the weakness of their gender, however, they shall perform the less burdensome tasks. When they are at their exercises for the body's benefit, any man who laughs at their nakedness will be "gathering unripe fruit," for he does not know what he ridicules nor where his laughter leads. He is ignorant of the fairest words ever spoken: what is beneficial must be beautiful; only the harmful is ugly.

You are right.

Having successfully reached this point in our legislation for women, we could compare ourselves with a swimmer who has surmounted a wave without being drowned by it. Our argument that men and women guardians should pursue all things in common turns out to be consistent in itself, since we have found our proposals to be both possible and beneficial.

That was no small wave, either.

You won't think it was so big when you see what the next one looks like.

Go ahead, then, and let me see.

Here it is. I think that everything we have said so far leads up to the following law.

What law?

That all the women shall belong to all the men and that none shall cohabit privately; that the children should also be raised in common and no child should know its parent nor the parent its child.

A far greater wave, indeed. Your proposal raises questions about both practicability and utility that will provoke the greatest misgivings.

I shouldn't think anyone would want to debate its utility. The desirability of having wives and children in common, were it possible, ought to be self-evident. But I suppose the main subject of dispute would be whether or not it would be possible to establish such a community.

I expect both aspects of the proposal will produce plenty of debate.

I see that you want to entangle me in both questions at once. I hoped for your consent in the matter of utility, so that I could escape from having to discuss it. Then I would only have to consider the question of feasibility.

Your escape efforts have been detected. You won't be allowed to run away, and you will be obliged to defend your case on both counts.

I will pay your penalty. But first, relent a little. Let me go on holiday, like men with lazy minds are wont to do, so that they may entertain themselves with their own thoughts as they walk alone. These men pursue their desires without pausing to inquire how they might be achieved. All such considerations they dismiss in order to spare themselves the trouble of weighing the possible against the impossible. They assume that what they wish is already at hand, giving their imaginations free rein in concocting the details and relishing in advance what they will do when everything is in place. So do idle minds become more idle still. I now yield to this same weakness. I would like to postpone the feasibility issue for later consideration. With your permission, I shall assume the feasibility of my proposal and proceed to inquire how the rulers will arrange the partic-

ulars in practice. At the same time, I shall seek to demonstrate that nothing could be more beneficial to our city and its guardians than a successful implementation of our proposal. Let us consider this first, and then we can address the other issue.

Permission granted. Proceed as you suggest.

I suppose that worthy rulers will be prepared to command and worthy helpers ready to obey. In some of their commands the rulers will obey the laws. In those matters of detail that we have left to their discretion their commands will imitate the spirit of the laws.

Presumably they will.

As their lawgiver, you will have selected these men. You will apply the same criteria to select women whose natures are as similar as possible to those of the men. They will live in common houses and eat at common meals. There will be no private property. They will live together, learn together, and exercise together. The necessities of nature, I presume, would see to it that they will also mate with one another. Or is necessity too strong a word?

Not if you mean the necessities of love. They attract and compel most people with far greater force than all geometric necessities posited by the mathematicians.

You are right, Glaucon. But irregularity in sexual relations or in any other matters has no place in a happy city; the rules will not tolerate it.

They would be right.

Then it is evident that we must make marriage a sacred relationship, so far as may be. And those marriages that attain the highest degree of sanctity will produce the best results.

Agreed.

What will produce the best results? You can help me, Glaucon, for I have seen hunting dogs and a number of pedigreed cocks at your house. Have you noticed something about how they mate and breed?

What?

Well, first of all, even though all of them are thoroughbreds, some prove out better than others?

True.

So are you indiscriminate in how you breed them, or do you breed from the best?

From the best.

And which age do you select for the breeding? The young or the old or, so far as possible, those in their prime?

Those in their prime.

And if you failed to supervise the breeding in this way, you would have to expect that the quality of your stock of birds and hounds would deteriorate?

Certainly.

Would it be the same with horses and other animals?

Without doubt.

Well, then, old friend, if the same holds true for human beings, we can see how urgent is our need for rulers with the highest skills.

It does hold true, but what of it?

I say this because the rulers will have to employ many of the kinds of drugs we spoke of earlier. Remember we said that those who can be healed by submitting their bodies to diet and regimen do not need drugs and can be attended by an ordinary doctor. But we know that where it is necessary to prescribe drugs, a physician with greater imagination and audacity will be indispensable.

True, but what is your point?

I mean that the rulers will probably have to resort to frequent doses of lies and mystifications for the benefit of their subjects. You will recall that we said these kinds of lies could be advantageous if used after the manner of medical remedies.

And we were right.

And the right use of this sort of medicine will very often be imperative in matters of marriage and the begetting of children.

How so?

It follows necessarily from the conclusion we reached a moment ago. The best of the men must mate with the best of the women as often as possible. Inferior should mate with inferior as seldom as possible. In order to safeguard the quality of the stock the children of the best unions must be retained for nurture by the rulers, but the others not. And how all this will be managed must be known to none but the rulers, so that the guardian flock will not be divided by dissension.

*   *   *

Book VII

Here allegory may show us best how education—or the lack of it—affects our nature. Imagine men living in a cave with a long passageway stretching between them and the cave's mouth, where it opens wide to the light. Imagine further that since childhood the cave dwellers have had their legs and necks shackled so as to be confined to the same spot. They are further constrained by blinders that prevent them from turning their heads; they can see only directly in front of them. Next, imagine a light from a fire some distance behind them and burning at a higher elevation. Between the prisoners and the fire is a raised path along whose edge there is a low wall like the partition at the front of a puppet stage. The wall conceals the puppeteers while they manipulate their puppets above it.

So far I can visualize it.

Imagine, further, men behind the wall carrying all sorts of objects along its length and holding them above it. The objects include human and animal images made of stone and wood and all other material. Presumably, those who carry them sometimes speak and are sometimes silent.

You describe a strange prison and strange prisoners.

Like ourselves. Tell me, do you not think those men would see only the shadows cast by the fire on the wall of the cave? Would they have seen anything of themselves or of one another?

How could they if they couldn't move their heads their whole life long?

Could they see the objects held above the wall behind them or only the shadows cast in front?

Only the shadows.

If, then, they could talk with one another,

don't you think they would impute reality to the passing shadows?

Necessarily.

Imagine an echo in their prison, bouncing off the wall toward which the prisoners were turned. Should one of those behind the wall speak, would the prisoners not think that the sound came from the shadows in front of them?

No doubt of it.

By every measure, then, reality for the prisoners would be nothing but shadows cast by artifacts.

It could be nothing else.

Imagine now how their liberation from bondage and error would come about if something like the following happened. One prisoner is freed from his shackles. He is suddenly compelled to stand up, turn around, walk, and look toward the light. He suffers pain and distress from the glare of the light. So dazzled is he that he cannot even discern the very objects whose shadows he used to be able to see. Now what do you suppose he would answer if he were told that all he had seen before was illusion but that now he was nearer reality, observing real things and therefore seeing more truly? What if someone pointed to the objects being carried above the wall, questioning him as to what each one is? Would he not be at a loss? Would he not regard those things he saw formerly as more real than the things now being shown him?

He would.

Again, let him be compelled to look directly at the light. Would his eyes not feel pain? Would he not flee, turning back to those things he was able to discern before, convinced that they are in every truth clearer and more exact than anything he has seen since?

He would.

Then let him be dragged away by force up the rough and steep incline of the cave's passageway, held fast until he is hauled out into the light of the sun. Would not such a rough passage be painful? Would he not resent the experience? And when he came out into the sunlight, would he not be dazzled once again and unable to see what he calls realities?

He could not see even one of them, at least not immediately.

Habituation, then, is evidently required in order to see things higher up. In the beginning he would most easily see shadows; next, reflections in the water of men and other objects. Then he would see the objects themselves. From there he would go on to behold the heavens and the heavenly phenomena—more easily the moon and stars by night than the sun by day.

Yes.

Finally, I suppose, he would be able to look on the sun itself, not in reflections in the water or in fleeting images in some alien setting. He would look at the sun as it is, in its own domain, and so be able to see what it is really like.

Yes.

It is at this stage that he would be able to conclude that the sun is the cause of the seasons and of the year's turning, that it governs all the visible world and is in some sense also the cause of all visible things.

This is surely the next step he would take.

Now, supposing he recalled where he came from. Supposing he thought of his fellow prisoners and of what passed for wisdom in the place they were inhabiting. Don't you think he would feel pity for all that and rejoice in his own change of circumstance?

He surely would.

Suppose there had been honors and citations those below bestowed upon one another. Suppose prizes were offered for the one quickest to identify the shadows as they go by and best able to remember the sequence and configurations in which they appear. All these skills, in turn, would enhance the ability to guess what would come next. Do you think he would covet such rewards? More, would he envy and want to emulate those who hold power over the prisoners and are in turn reverenced by them? Or would he not rather hold fast to Homer's words that it is "better to be the poor servant of a poor master," better to endure anything, than to believe those things and live that way?

I think he would prefer anything to such a life.

Consider, further, if he should go back down again into the cave and return to the place he was before, would not his eyes now go dark after so abruptly leaving the sunlight behind?

They would.

Suppose he should then have to compete once more in shadow watching with those who never left the cave. And this before his eyes had become accustomed to the dark and his dimmed vision still required a long period of habituation. Would he not be laughed at? Would it not be said that he had made the journey above only to come back with his eyes ruined and that it is futile even to attempt the ascent? Further, if anyone tried to release the prisoners and lead them up and they could get their hands on him and kill him, would they not kill him?

Of course.

Now, my dear Glaucon, we must apply the allegory as a whole to all that has been said so far. The prisoners' cave is the counterpart of our own visible order, and the light of the fire betokens the power of the sun. If you liken the ascent and exploration of things above to the soul's journey through the intelligible order, you will have understood my thinking, since that is what you wanted to hear. God only knows whether it is true. But, in any case, this is the way things appear to me: in the intelligible world the last thing to be seen—and then only dimly—is the idea of the good. Once seen, however, the conclusion becomes irresistible that it is the cause of all things right and good, that in the visible world it gives birth to light and its sovereign source, that in the intelligible world it is itself sovereign and the author of truth and reason, and that the man who will act wisely in private and public life must have seen it.

I agree, insofar as I can follow your thinking.

Come join me, then, in this further thought. Don't be surprised if those who have attained this high vision are unwilling to be involved in the affairs of men. Their souls will ever feel the pull from above and yearn to sojourn there. Such a preference is likely enough if the assumptions of our allegory continue to be valid.

Yes, it is likely.

By the same token, would you think it strange if someone returning from divine contemplation to the miseries of men should appear ridiculous? What if he were still blinking his eyes and not yet readjusted to the surrounding darkness before being compelled to testify in court about the shadows of justice or about the images casting the shadows? What if he had to enter into debate about the notions of such matters held fast by people who had never seen justice itself?

It would not be strange.

Nonetheless, a man with common sense would know that eyesight can be impaired in two different ways by dint of two different causes, namely, transitions from light into darkness and from darkness into light. Believing that the soul also meets with the same experience, he would not thoughtlessly laugh when he saw a soul perturbed and having difficulty in comprehending something. Instead he would try to ascertain whether the cause of its faded vision was the passage from a brighter life to unaccustomed darkness or from the deeper darkness of ignorance toward the world of light, whose brightness then dazzled the soul's eye. He will count the first happy, and the second he will pity. Should he be minded to laugh, he who comes from below will merit it more than the one who descends from the light above.

A fair statement.

If this is true, it follows that education is not what some professors say it is. They claim they can transplant the power of knowledge into a soul that has none, as if they were engrafting vision into blind eyes.

They do claim that.

But our reasoning goes quite to the contrary. We assert that this power is already in the soul of everyone. The way each of us learns compares with what happens to the eye: it cannot be turned away from darkness to face the light without turning the whole body. So it is with our capacity to know; together with the entire soul one must turn away from the world of transient things toward the world of perpetual being, until finally one learns to endure the sight of its most radiant manifestation. This is what we call goodness, is it not?

Yes.

Then there must be some art that would most easily and effectively turn and convert the soul in the way we have described. It would lay no claim to produce sight in the soul's eye. Instead it would assume that sight is already there but wrongly directed; wrongly the soul is not looking where it should. This condition it would be the purpose of the art to remedy.

Such an art might be possible.

Wisdom, then, seems to be of a different order than those other things that are also called virtues of the soul. They seem more akin to the attributes of the body, for when they are not there at the outset, they can be cultivated by exercise and habit. But the ability to think is more divine. Its power is constant and never lost. It can be useful and benign or malevolent and useless, according to the purposes toward which it is directed. Or have you never observed in men who are called vicious but wise how sharp-sighted the petty soul is and how quickly it can pick out those things toward which it has turned its attention? All this shows that we have to do not with poor eyesight but with a soul under compulsion of evil, so that the keener his vision, the more harm he inflicts.

I have seen these things.

Consider then what would happen if such a soul had been differently trained from childhood or had been liberated early from the love of food and similar pleasures that are attached to us at birth like leaden weights. Supposing, I say, he were freed from all these kinds of things that draw the soul's vision downward. If he were then turned and converted to the contemplation of real things, he would be using the very same faculties of vision and be seeing them just as keenly as he now sees their opposites.

That is likely.

And must we not draw other likely and nec-essary conclusions from all that has been said so far? On the one hand, men lacking education and experience in truth cannot adequately preside over a city. Without a sense of purpose or duty in life they will also be without a sense of direction to govern their public and private acts. On the other hand, those who prolong their education endlessly are also unfit to rule because they become incapable of action. Instead, they suffer themselves to believe that while still living they have already been transported to the Islands of the Blessed.

So our duty as founders is to compel the best natures to achieve that sovereign knowledge we described awhile ago, to scale the heights in order to reach the vision of the good. But after they have reached the summit and have seen the view, we must not permit what they are now allowed to do.

What is that?

Remain above, refusing to go down again among those prisoners to share their labors and their rewards, whatever their worth may be.

Must we wrong them in this way, making them live a worse life when a better is possible?

My friend, you have forgotten again that the law is concerned not with the happiness of any particular class in the city but with the happiness of the city as a whole. Its method is to create harmony among the citizens by persuasion and compulsion, making them share the benefits that each is able to bestow on the community. The law itself produces such men in the city, not in order to let them do as they please but with the intention of using them to bind the city together.

True, I did forget.

Consider further, Glaucon, that in fact we won't be wronging the philosophers who come among us. When we require them to govern the city and be its guardians, we shall vindicate our actions. For we shall say to them that it is quite understandable that men of their quality do not participate in the public life of other cities. After all, there they develop autonomously without favor from the government. It is only just that self-educated men, owing nothing to others for their enlightenment, are not eager to pay anyone for it. But you have been begotten by us to be like kings and leaders in a hive of bees, governing the city for its good and yours. Your education is better and more complete, and you are better equipped to participate in the two ways of life. So down you must go, each in turn, to where the others live and habituate yourselves to see in the dark. Once you have adjusted, you will see ten thousand times better than those who regularly dwell there. Because you have seen the reality of beauty, justice, and goodness, you will be able to know idols and shadows for what they are. Together and wide awake, you and we will govern our city, far differently from most cities today whose inhabitants are ruled darkly as in a dream by men who will fight with each other over shadows and use faction in order to rule, as if that were some great good. The truth is that the city where those who rule are least eager to do so will be the best governed and the least plagued by dissension. The city with the contrary kind of rulers will be burdened with the contrary characteristics.

I agree.

When we tell them this, will our students disobey us? Will they refuse to play their role in the affairs of state even when they know that most of the time they will be able to dwell with one another in a better world?

Certainly not. These are just requirements, and they are just men. Yet they will surely approach holding office as an imposed necessity, quite in the opposite frame of mind from those who now rule our cities.

Indeed, old friend. A well-governed city becomes a possibility only if you can discover a better way of life for your future rulers than holding office. Only in such a state will those who rule be really rich, not in gold but with the wealth that yields happiness: a life of goodness and wisdom. But such a government is impossible if men behave like beggars, turning to politics because of

what is lacking in their private lives and hoping to find their good in the public business. When office and the power of governing are treated like prizes to be won in battle the result must be a civil war that will destroy the city along with the office seekers.

True.

Is there any life other than that of true philosophers that looks with scorn on political office?

None, by Zeus.

That is why we require that those in office should not be lovers of power. Otherwise there will be a fight among rival lovers.

Right.

Who else would you compel to guard the city? Who else than those who have the clearest understanding of the principles of good government and who have won distinction in another kind of life preferable to the life of politics?

No one else.

*　　*　　*

REVIEW QUESTIONS

1. In Plato's view, to whom ought the governing of the state be entrusted?
2. How were they to be educated for such responsibility?
3. Were women to have any possible role in directing the state? How do Plato's views in this regard contrast with the attitudes expressed in Xenophon's *Oeconomicus*?
4. How do Plato's ideas compare with the values underlying the democratic system of Athens?
5. Do you see any influence of the Spartan system in Plato's ideas?
6. Does Plato draw any contrasts between the material and immaterial realms?

ARISTOTLE

FROM *Politics*

After twenty years as a student of Plato at the Academy and a subsequent three-year stint as a tutor for Alexander, the young son of King Philip II of Macedonia, Aristotle established his own school, the Lyceum, at Athens and taught there until almost the end of his life. Much of his work is a continuation of Plato's, although, in contrast to Plato's emphasis on the primacy of a world of universal forms or ideas, Aristotle asserted that those ideal forms could not exist independently of the world of matter that could be directly experienced and observed by human senses. His two most important surviving works are the Ethics *and the* Politics. *The* Ethics *is his investigation of human character in order to determine what produces a good character and, therefore, happiness. Aristotle also believed, however, that the greatest degree of human happiness could be achieved only in the context of a properly ordered and governed city-state, the formation and characteristics of which are the focus of the* Politics.

From *The Politics of Aristotle,* edited by H. W. C. Davis, translated by Benjamin Jowett (Oxford, Eng.: Oxford University Press, 1905), pp. 258–61, 264–68.

*　　*　　*

He who thus considers things in their first growth and origin, whether a state or anything else, will obtain the clearest view of them. In the first place (1) there must be a union of those who cannot exist without each other; for example, of male and female, that the race may continue; and this is a union which is formed, not of deliberate purpose, but because, in common with other animals and with plants, mankind have a natural desire to leave behind them an image of themselves. And (2) there must be a union of natural ruler and subject, that both may be preserved. For he who can foresee with his mind is by nature intended to be lord and master, and he who can work with his body is a subject, and by nature a slave; hence master and slave have the same interest. . . .

Of household management we have seen that there are three parts—one is the rule of a master

over slaves, which has been discussed already, another of a father, and the third of a husband. A husband and father rules over wife and children, both free, but the rule differs, the rule over his children being a royal, over his wife a constitutional rule. For although there may be exceptions to the order of nature, the male is by nature fitter for command than the female, just as the elder and full-grown is superior to the younger and more immature. . . .

Now it is obvious that the same principle applies generally, and therefore almost all things rule and are ruled according to nature. But the kind of rule differs; the freeman rules over the slave after another manner from that in which the male rules over the female, or the man over the child; although the parts of the soul are present in all of them, they are present in different degrees. For the slave has no deliberative faculty at all; the woman has, but it is without authority, and the child has, but it is immature. So it must necessarily be with the moral virtues also; all may be supposed to partake of them, but only in such manner and degree as is required by each for the fulfillment of his duty. . . . The courage of a man is shown in commanding, of a woman in obeying. . . . All classes must be deemed to have their special attributes; as the poet says of women, "Silence is a woman's glory," but this is not equally the glory of man. . . .

*   *   *

Next let us consider what should be our arrangements about property; should the citizens of the perfect state have possessions in common or not? . . .

There is always a difficulty in men living together and having things in common, but especially in their having common property. . . . The present arrangement, if improved as it might be by good customs and laws, would be far better, and would have the advantages of both systems. Property should be in a certain sense common, but, as a general rule, private. For when everyone has his separate interest, men will not complain of one another, and they will make more progress, because everyone will be attending to his own business. Yet among good men, and as regards use, "friends," as the proverb says, "will have all things common." . . . For although every human has his own property, some things he will place at the disposal of his friends, while of others he shares the use of them. . . .

Again, how immeasurably greater is the pleasure, when a man feels a thing to be his own! For love of self is a feeling implanted by nature and not given in vain, although selfishness is rightly condemned. This, however is not mere love of self, but love of self in excess, like the miser's love of money; for all, or almost all, men love money, and other such objects in a measure. Furthermore, there is the greatest pleasure in doing a kindness or service to friends or guests or companions, which can only be done when a man has private property. These advantages are lost by the excessive unification of the state. . . . No one, when men have all things in common, will any longer

set an example of liberality or do any liberal action; for liberality consists in the use a man makes of his own property.

Such legislation may have a specious appearance of benevolence. Men readily listen to it, and are easily induced to believe that in some wonderful manner everybody will become everybody's friend, especially when someone is heard denouncing the evils now existing in states, suits about contracts, convictions for perjury, flatteries of rich men, and the like, which are said to arise out of the possession of private property. These evils, however, are due to a very different cause— the wickedness of human nature. Indeed, we see that there is much more quarreling among those who have all things in common, though there are not many of them when compared with the vast numbers who have private property.

Again, we ought to reckon, not only the evils from which the citizens will be saved, but also the advantages which they will lose. The life which they are to lead appears to be quite impracticable. The error of Socrates must be attributed to the false notion of unity from which he starts. Unity there should be, both of the family and of the state, but in some respects only. For there is a point at which a state may attain such a degree of unity as to be no longer a state, or at which, without actually ceasing to exist, it will become an inferior state, like harmony passing into unison, or rhythm which has been reduced to a single foot. The state, as I was saying, is a plurality, which should be united and made into a community by education. . . . Let us remember that we should not disregard the experience of ages. . . .

*   *   *

. . . We have next to consider whether there is only one form of government or many; and if many, what they are, and how many; and what are the differences between them.

A constitution is the arrangement of powers in a state, especially of the supreme power, and the constitution is the government. For example, in democracies the people are supreme, but in oligarchies, the few; therefore, we say that the two constitutions are different; and so in other cases.

First let us consider what is the purpose of a state and how many forms of government there are by which human society is regulated. We have already said, earlier in this treatise, when drawing a distinction between household management and the rule of a governor, that man is by nature a political animal. And therefore men, even when they do not require one another's help, desire to live together all the same, and are in fact brought together by their common interests in proportion as they severally attain to any measure of well-being. Well-being is certainly the chief end of individuals and of states. . . .

The conclusion is evident: governments which have a regard to the common interest are constituted in accordance with strict principles of justice, and are therefore true forms; but those which regard only the interest of the rulers are all defective and perverted forms. For they are despotic, whereas a state is a community of free men.

Having determined these points, we have next to consider how many forms of constitution there are, and what they are; and in the first place what are the true forms, for when they are determined the perversions of them will at once be apparent. The words constitution and government have the same meaning; and the government, which is the supreme authority in states, is necessarily in the hands either of one, or of a few, or of many. The true forms of government, therefore, are those in which the one, or the few, or the many, govern with a view to the common interest; but governments which rule with a view to the private interest, whether of the one, or of the few, or of the many, are perversions. For citizens, if they are truly citizens, ought all to participate in the advantages of a state. We call that form of government in which one rules, and which regards the common interest, kingship or royalty; that in which more than one, but not many, rule, aristocracy. It is so called, either because the rulers are the best men, or because they have at heart the best interest of the state and of the citizens. But when the citizens at large administer the state

for the common interest, the government is called by the generic name—constitutional government. And there is a reason for this use of language. One man or a few may excel in virtue; but of virtue there are many kinds. As the number of rulers increases it becomes more difficult for them to attain perfection in every kind, though they may in military virtue, for this is found in the masses. Hence, in a constitutional government the fighting men have the supreme power, and those who possess arms are citizens.

Of the above-mentioned forms, the perversions are as follows: of royalty, tyranny; of aristocracy, oligarchy; of constitutional government, democracy. For tyranny is a kind of monarchy which has in view the interest of the monarch only; oligarchy has in view the interest of the wealthy; democracy, of the needy; none of them the common good of all.

*   *   *

. . . But a state exists for the sake of a good life, and not for the sake of life only. If life only were the object, slaves and brute animals might form a state, but they cannot, for they have no share in happiness or in a life of free choice. Nor does a state exist merely for the sake of alliance and security from injustice, nor yet for the sake of trade and mutual intercourse; for then the Tyrrhenians and the Carthaginians, and all who have commercial treaties with one another, would be citizens of one state. . . . Those who care for good government take into consideration the larger questions of virtue and vice in states. Whence it may be further inferred that virtue must be the serious care of a state which truly deserves the name. Otherwise the community becomes a mere alliance, which differs only in place from alliances of which the members live apart. And law is only a convention, "a surety to one another of justice," as the sophist Lycophron says, and has no real power to make the citizens good and just. . . .

Clearly then a state is not a mere society, having a common place, established for the prevention of crime and for the sake of trade. These are conditions without which a state cannot exist; but all of them together do not constitute a state, which is a community of families and aggregations of families in well-being for the sake of a perfect and self-sufficing life. Such a community can only be established among those who live in the same place and intermarry. Hence arise in states family connections, brotherhoods, common sacrifices, amusements which draw men together. They are created by friendship, for friendship is the motive of society. The end is the good life, and these are the means towards it. And the state is the union of families and villages having for an end a perfect and self-sufficing life, by which we mean a happy and honorable life.

Our conclusion, then, is that political society exists for the sake of noble actions, and not of mere companionship. And they who contribute most to such a society have a greater share in it than those who have the same or a greater freedom or nobility of birth but are inferior to them in political virtue; or than those who exceed them in wealth but are surpassed by them in virtue. . . .

We maintain that the true forms of government are three, and that the best must be that which is administered by the best, and in which there is one man, or a whole family, or many persons, excelling in virtue, and both rulers and subjects are fitted, the one to rule, the others to be ruled, in such a manner as to attain the most eligible life. We showed at the commencement of our inquiry that the virtue of the good man is necessarily the same as the virtue of the citizen of the perfect state. Clearly then in the same manner, and by the same means through which a man becomes truly good, he will frame a state which will be truly good whether aristocratical, or under kingly rule, and the same education and the same habits will be found to make a good man a good statesman and king. . . .

*   *   *

We have now to inquire what is the best constitution for most states, and the best life for most men, neither assuming a standard of virtue which is above ordinary persons, nor an education which is exceptionally favored by nature and circumstances, nor yet an ideal state which is an inspiration only, but having regard to the life in which the majority are able to share, and to the form of government which states in general can attain. . . . If it was truly said in the *Ethics* that the happy life is the life according to unimpeded virtue and that virtue is a mean, then the life which is a mean and a mean attainable by everyone must be best. And the same criteria of virtue and vice are characteristic of cities and of constitutions; for the constitution is in pattern the life of the city.

Now in all states there are three elements; one class is very rich, another very poor, and a third in the mean. It is admitted that moderation and the mean are best, and therefore it will clearly be best to possess the gifts of fortune in moderation; for in that condition of life men are most ready to listen to reason. . . . Those who have too much of the goods of fortune, strength, wealth, friends, and the like, are neither willing nor able to submit to authority. The evil begins at home; for when they are boys, by reason of the luxury in which they are brought up, they never learn, even at school, the habit of obedience. On the other hand, the very poor, who are in the opposite extreme, are too degraded. So that the one class cannot obey, and can only rule despotically; the other knows not how to command and must be ruled like slaves. Thus arises a city, not of freemen, but of masters and slaves, the one despising, the other envying. Nothing can be more fatal to friendship and good fellowship in states than this; for good fellowship starts from friendship. When men are at enmity with one another, they would rather not even share the same path.

But a city ought to be composed, as far as possible, of equals and similars; and these are generally the middle classes. Wherefore a city which is composed of middle-class citizens is necessarily best constituted with respect to what we call the natural elements of a state. And this class of citizens is most secure in a state, for they do not, like the poor, covet their neighbors' goods; nor do others covet theirs, as the poor covet the goods of the rich. And as they neither plot against others nor are themselves plotted against, they pass through life safely. . . .

Thus it is manifest that the best political community is formed by citizens of the middle class, and that those states are likely to be well administered in which the middle class is large, and if possible larger than both the other classes, or at any rate than either singly, for the addition of the middle class turns the scale and prevents either of the extremes from being dominant. Great then is the good fortune of a state in which the citizens have a moderate and sufficient property. For where some possess much and the rest nothing, there may arise an extreme democracy, or a pure oligarchy; or a tyranny may grow out of either extreme—out of either the most rampant democracy or out of an oligarchy. But it is not so likely to arise out of a middle and nearly equal condition.

Democracies are safer and more permanent than oligarchies, because they have a middle class which is more numerous and has a greater share in the government. For when there is no middle class and the poor greatly exceed in number, troubles arise and the state soon comes to an end. A proof of the superiority of the middle class is that the best legislators have been of a middle rank; for

example, Solon, as his own verses testify, and Lycurgus, for he was not a king. . . .

What then is the best form of government, and what makes it the best is evident. Of other states, since we say there are many kinds of democracy and oligarchy, it is not difficult to see which has the first and which the second or any other place in the order of excellence, now that we have determined which is best. For that which is nearest to the best must of necessity be the better, and that which is furthest from it the worse, if we are judging absolutely and not with reference to given conditions. I say "with reference to given conditions," since a particular government may be preferable for some, but another form may be better for others.

*   *   *

REVIEW QUESTIONS

1. In Aristotle's view, what constitutes a state?
2. What is the purpose of the state?
3. Ought women to have any role in the governing of the state?
4. What is Aristotle's view of democracy?
5. Do you find any of Aristotle's views pertinent to government and society of the late twentieth and early twenty-first century C.E.?

PLUTARCH

FROM *"Life of Alexander"*

The biographies produced by Plutarch are an important (though by no means entirely objective or accurate) source of knowledge of the lives of many great figures of the Greek and Roman past. The following selections reveal something of ancient opinion concerning Alexander's character amd intentions. To a great extent, they also communicate a view of him that dominated much thinking until relatively recent times.

* * *

Philonicus the Thessalian brought the horse Bucephalus to Philip, offering to sell him for thirteen talents; but when they went into the field to try him, they found him so very vicious and unmanageable, that he reared up when they endeavored to mount him, and would not so much as endure the voice of any of Philip's attendants. Upon which, as they were leading him away as wholly useless and untractable, Alexander, who stood by, said, "What an excellent horse do they lose, for want of skill and boldness to manage him!" Philip at first took no notice of what he said; but when he heard him repeat the same thing several times, and saw he was very frustrated to see the horse sent away, "Do you criticize," said Philip, "those who are older than yourself, as if you knew more, and were better able to manage him then they?" "I could manage this horse," replied Alexander, "better than others do." "And if you do not," said Philip, "what will you forfeit for your rashness?" "I will pay," answered Alexander, "the whole price of the horse." At this the whole company fell laughing; and as soon as the wager was settled among them, he immediately ran to the horse, and, taking hold of the bridle, turned him directly towards the sun, having, it seems, observed that he was disturbed at and afraid of the motion of his own shadow; then letting him go forward a little, still keeping the reins in his hand, and stroking him gently when he began to grow eager and fiery, . . . with one nimble leap, Alexander securely mounted him, and when he was seated, by little and little drew in the bridle, and curbed him without either striking or spurring him. Presently, when he found him free from all rebelliousness, and only impatient for the course, he let him go at full speed, inciting him now with a commanding voice, and urging him also with his heel. Philip and his friends looked on at first

in silence and anxiety for the result, but when he came back rejoicing and triumphing for what he had performed, they all burst out into acclamations of applause; and his father, shedding tears, it is said, for joy, kissed him as he came down from his horse, and in his transport said, "O my son, carve out a kingdom equal to and worthy of yourself, for Macedonia is too small for you."

* * *

After the company had drunk a good deal somebody began to sing the verses of a man named Pranichus . . . which had been written to humiliate and make fun of some Macedonian commanders who had recently been defeated by the barbarians. The older members of the party took offense at this and showed their resentment of both the poet and the singer, but Alexander and those sitting near him listened with obvious pleasure and told the man to continue. Thereupon Cleitus, who had already drunk too much and was rough and hot-tempered by nature, became angrier than ever and shouted that it was not right for Macedonians to be insulted in the presence of barbarians and enemies, even if they had met with misfortune, for they were better men than those who were laughing at them. Alexander retorted that if Cleitus was trying to disguise cowardice as misfortune, he must be pleading his own case. At this Cleitus sprang to his feet and shouted back, "Yes, it was my cowardice that saved your life, you who call yourself the son of the gods, when you were turning your back to Spithridates' sword. And it is the blood of these Macedonians and their wounds which have made you so great that you disown your father Philip and claim to be the son of Ammon!"

These words made Alexander furious. "You scum," he cried out, "do you think that you can

From *Readings in Ancient History,* vol. 1, edited by William S. Davis (Boston: Allyn and Bacon, 1912).

From *The Age of Alexander,* translated by Ian Scott-Kilvert (New York: Penguin Books, 1973), pp. 257–58, 307–9.

keep on speaking of me like this, and stir up trouble among the Macedonians and not pay for it?" "Oh, but we Macedonians do pay for it," Cleitus retorted. "Just think of the rewards we get for all our efforts. It's the dead ones who are happy, because they never lived to see Macedonians being beaten with Median rods, or begging the Persians for an audience with our own king." Cleitus blurted out all this impulsively, whereupon Alexander's friends jumped up and began to abuse him, while the older men tried to calm down both sides. . . . But Cleitus refused to take back anything and he challenged Alexander to speak out whatever he wished to say in front of the company, or else not invite to his table freeborn men who spoke their minds: it would be better for him to spend his time among barbarians and slaves, who would prostrate themselves before his white tunic and his Persian girdle. At this Alexander could no longer control his rage: he hurled one of the apples that lay on the table at Cleitus, hit him, and then looked around for his dagger. One of his bodyguards, Aristophanes, had already moved it out of harm's way, and the others crowded around him and begged him to be quiet. But Alexander leaped to his feet and shouted out in the Macedonian tongue for his bodyguard to turn out, a signal that this was an extreme emergency. . . . As Cleitus still refused to give way, . . . Alexander seized a spear from one of his guards, faced Cleitus as he was drawing aside the curtain of the doorway, and ran him through. With a roar of pain and a groan, Cleitus fell, and immediately the king's anger left him. When he came to himself and saw his friends standing around him speechless, he snatched the weapon out of the dead body and would have plunged it into his own throat if the guards had not forestalled him by seizing his hands and carrying him by force to his chamber.

There he spent the rest of the night and the whole of the following day sobbing in an agony of remorse. At last he lay exhausted by his grief, uttering deep groans but unable to speak a word, until his friends, alarmed at his silence, forced their way into his room. He paid no attention to what any of them said, except that when Aristander the diviner reminded him . . . that these events had long ago been ordained by fate, he seemed to accept this assurance.

*   *   *

Now Fortune argues that Alexander belongs to her and to her alone. However, this ought to be denied in the name of philosophy and even more so because of the wrath and indignation of Alexander at the notion that he received as a gift of Fortune that empire which he purchased with a copious expenditure of his blood and repeated wounds,

And many sleepless nights he spent
And bloody days consumed while making war,

contending with invincible forces, nations without number, impassable rivers, and rocks above the range of bow and arrow, helped only by good judgment, perseverance, courage and self-control.

And I imagine he might address Fortune when she claimed these deeds for herself in these words: "Do not depreciate my honor, or strip me of my fame . . . my body bears many indications that Fortune was my adversary, not my ally. First I was struck in the head by a stone and clubbed on the neck in the Illyrian land. Later, at the Granicus, my head was broken by the lone knife of a barbarian, and at Issus my thigh was gashed with a sword. Before Gaza my ankle was pierced by an arrow, when I fell heavily, dislocating my shoulder. At Maracanda my shin was broken by an arrow. Then came blows and the ravages of famine in the Indian lands. Among the Aspasians I was shot in the shoulder by an arrow; in the land of the Gandridae in the leg; among the Malli a missile from a bow reached me, burying its iron point in my breast, and when I had also been struck by a club along the neck, the ladders that had been raised against the walls gave way, and Fortune, taking delight in such a deed, penned me up there

From *De Alexandri Magni Fortuna aut Virtute*, Oration I, in *Sources in Western Civilization: Ancient Greece*, translated by Truesdell S. Brown (New York: Free Press, 1965).

alone, not to contend with famous adversaries but with unknown barbarians. And if Ptolemy had not covered me with his shield and if Limnaeus had not died in front of me after intercepting countless missiles, and if the Macedonians had not torn down the walls in their rage, then that nameless barbarian village would have been Alexander's tomb."

And in this same expedition gales, droughts, deep rivers, rocks higher than a bird can fly, monstrous beasts, savage customs, a succession of petty rulers and constant betrayals were also encountered. But even before the expedition itself, Greece fought back after the ways of Philip. The Thebans shook the dust of Chaeronea from their weapons, rising up after disaster while Athens extended a helping hand. All Macedon was ripe for rebellion, looking secretly to Amyntas and the sons of Aeropus. The Illyrians erupted and the state of affairs in Scythia threatened her troubled neighbors. Persian gold, diffused in every direction by popular orators, stirred up the Peloponnese. Philip's treasury was empty and there was even a deficit of two hundred talents, as Onesicritus relates. With such an appalling lack of money and with the government still in confusion a young man just barely beyond boyhood had the audacity to entertain thoughts of Babylon and Susa, and even of an empire embracing all mankind—and this, mind you, with thirty thousand foot and four thousand horse. Those at least are the figures given by Aristobulus; according to King Ptolemy there were thirty thousand foot and five thousand horse, while Anaximenes gives 43,500 foot and 5,500 horse. The great and magnificent sum which Fortune had provided for his traveling chest was seventy talents, as Aristobulus tells it, but Duris says he had only supplies for thirty days.

Then Alexander must have been an unthinking hothead to challenge such a formidable power with his meager resources? Not at all. Did anyone ever start out for war with greater or better preparation for succeeding than nobility of character, intelligence, self-mastery and courage—with which philosophy had equipped him for his journey? He crossed over against the Persians with

greater resources furnished by his teacher Aristotle than by his father Philip. In fact there are writers who allege that Alexander once said that he had brought the *Iliad* and the *Odyssey* along as a provision for the army; and we believe them, honoring Homer. And if anyone maintains that he only used Homer for relaxation after toil and as a pleasant way of diverting his leisure moments, but that his real provision for the journey lay in the philosophic doctrines, in discourses on fearlessness and valor, on self-mastery and on high-mindedness we look on this with scorn. For obviously Alexander wrote nothing about syllogisms or propositions, and he never held forth in the Lyceum or presented a thesis for debate in the Academy, while such a view would restrict philosophy to things of this sort as though it were made up of words rather than deeds. Yet there were famous philosophers like Pythagoras, or Socrates, or Arcesilaus or Carneades who wrote nothing. And these men were not occupied with such great wars, or civilizing barbarian princes, or establishing Greek cities among savage peoples, nor did they continue pressing on against lawless and ignorant tribes in order to instruct them in law and peace. Instead, though they did have the time, they abandoned writing to the sophists. Then why are they believed to have been philosophers? Because of what they said, how they lived and what they taught. Then let Alexander be judged on the same basis and he will be revealed as a philosopher by what he said, by what he did and by what he taught.

But first and, if you will, most surprising, look at Alexander's pupils and compare them with those of Socrates and Plato. Now they were teaching adaptable scholars who spoke the same language, for even if they knew nothing else they all understood Greek. Despite this, there were many of them whom they failed to convince: the Critiases, Alcibiadeses and Clitophons went astray, spitting out their doctrines as a horse gets rid of a bit. But then look at Alexander's instruction: he taught marriage to the Hyrcanians, he showed the Arachosians how to farm, he persuaded the Sogdianians to support their fathers instead of killing them, and induced the Persians to respect their mothers and not to marry them. What an admirable philosophy, which caused the Indians to bow down before the gods of Greece, the Scythians to bury their dead instead of devouring them! We are astonished at the ability of Carneades if he hellenizes Clitomachus, who was a Carthaginian by birth formerly named Hasdrubal, and we also admire Zeno for his skill if he induces Diogenes of Babylon to become a philosopher. But thanks to Alexander Homer was read in Asia, and the sons of Persia, Susiana, and Gedrosia sang the choruses of Euripides and Sophocles. Now Socrates was brought to judgment for introducing foreign gods by informers in Athens, but Alexander caused Bactra and the Caucasus to worship the gods of Greece. While Plato drew up a single form of government which was so strict he could induce no one to adopt it, Alexander, by founding more than seventy cities among the barbarian tribes, and seeding Asia with Greek outposts, suppressed their savage and uncivilized customs. Although a few of us read about the laws of Plato, countless numbers have adopted and continue to use the laws of Alexander. Those whom Alexander conquered were more fortunate than those who escaped, because there was no one to correct their foolish way of life, while the conquerer forced his subjects to live in prosperity. Therefore Themistocles' remark when he received munificent gifts from the [Persian] king during his exile and obtained three tribute-paying cities—one to furnish him with grain, one with wine and the other with condiments: "Oh, my children, had we not been ruined, we would have been ruined indeed!"—was a remark that might have been made even more appropriately by those whom Alexander conquered. For they would not have been civilized unless they had been conquered. And Egypt would not have had its Alexandria, or Mesopotamia its Seleuceia, or India its Bucephalia, nor would the Caucasus have had a Greek city founded there, yet it is by means of such cities that savagery is gradually extinguished and bad customs changed into good ones. Now if philosophers really set such store by refining and altering rough and ignorant dispositions, then Alexander, who is seen transforming

countless races and natural savages, ought truly to be regarded as a very great philosopher.

Now the much-admired *Republic* of Zeno, the founder of the Stoic school, adds up to this one thing: that we ought not to live in cities or in demes, each distinguished by its own regulations, but we should look on all men as fellow citizens and demesmen, having one life and one world, feeding together like a single herd sharing a common pasture. Zeno, however, wrote this as a dream, a philosophic image of a well-governed state, while Alexander expressed his views by deeds. He did not follow Aristotle's advice to treat the Greeks as a leader, the barbarians as a master, cultivating the former as friends and kinsmen, and treating the latter as animals or plants. Had he done so his kingdom would have been filled with warfare, banishments and secret plots, but he regarded himself as divinely sent to mediate and govern the world. And those whom he failed to win over by persuasion he overpowered in arms, bringing them together from every land, combining, as it were in a loving cup, their lives, customs, marriages and manner of living; he bade them all look on the inhabited world as their native land, on his camp as their citadel and protection, on good men as their kinsmen and evildoers as aliens, and not to distinguish Greek from barbarian by the chlamys, or the shield, or the sword, or the sleeved tunic but to associate Hellenism with virtue and barbarism with evildoing; and to regard their clothing, food, marriages and manners as common to all, blended together by their blood and their children.

Now Demaratus of Corinth, the mercenary and a friend of Philip's, wept tears of joy when he saw Alexander in Susa, exclaiming that those Greeks who had died earlier had been robbed of great happiness since they had not seen Alexander sitting on Darius' throne. But I, by Zeus, do not envy those who saw a spectacle which is associated with Fortune and lesser kings, but I think I would have been more pleased at the fair and blessed sight of the marriage procession when, bringing together one hundred Persian brides and one hundred Greek and Macedonian grooms into a single tent bedecked with gold, with a single hearth and a single table, he was the first, crowned with flowers, to raise the hymeneal song, singing as it were a song of friendship, while he joined together the greatest and most powerful peoples into one community by wedlock: the bridegroom of one, but for everyone at once a bride-giver, a father and a sponsor. I would gladly have said: "O barbarous and foolish Xerxes, your great efforts in putting a bridge across the Hellespont were wasted, for intelligent rulers do not join Asia to Europe in this way with planks, or floats or lifeless and unfeeling fetters; but they unite the races by true laws, and chaste marriages and common offspring." . . .

. . . For he did not cross Asia like a robber, nor did he have it in mind to ravage and despoil it for the booty and loot presented by such an unheard-of stroke of fortune—the way Hannibal treated Italy later on, or the way the Treres acted earlier in Ionia or the Scythians in Media. Instead he conducted himself as he did out of a desire to subject all the races in the world to one rule and one form of government, making all mankind a single people. Had not the divinity that sent Alexander recalled his soul so soon, there would have been a single law, as it were, watching over all mankind, and all men would have looked to one form of justice as their common source of light. But now, that portion of the world that never beheld Alexander has remained as if deprived of the sun.

Now, at the outset, the very purpose of his expedition commends the man as a philosopher for aiming not at wealth and luxury for himself but at bringing peace, harmony and mutual fellowship to all men. Secondly, let us examine what he said, since other kings and rulers reveal their character by the spirit of their pronouncements. . . . When he talked to Diogenes himself, in Corinth, he was so captivated and overwhelmed by the man's way of life and reputation that he would often refer to him later, saying: "If I were not Alexander, I would like to be Diogenes!" By this he meant: . . . "If I did not intend to blend the customs of the Greeks and the barbarians; to cross

every continent and tame it; to search out the farthest points of land and sea; to make Ocean the boundary of Macedon; and if I did not mean to transplant the peace and the justice of Greece to every people, even then I would not waste my energies in useless luxury, but I would emulate the frugality of Diogenes. But now, Diogenes, excuse me. I am imitating Heracles, rivalling Perseus and following in the footsteps of Dionysus, the ancestor of my line. I wish to bring the chorus of victorious Greeks to India once more, and to renew the memory of Bacchic revels among the wild mountainous peoples beyond the Caucasus. And there are said to be holy men in those parts who live under laws of their own, a rough and naked sect devoting their lives to the god. They are even more self-denying than Diogenes, in that they require no wallet, for they do not save any food since the land continually provides them with a fresh supply. Flowing rivers furnish them with drink, trees shed their foliage over them and herbs of the field serve them as a bed. Thanks to me they will come to know of Diogenes, and Diogenes of them. I, too, must coin money, and stamp the form of a Greek constitution on a barbarian mold."

Well, then, do his deeds appear to be primarily the result of chance? Power in war? Government by force? Do they not rather suggest the great courage and justice, the great self-control and mildness of one who does everything in an orderly and intelligent manner and in accordance with a sober and sagacious plan?

REVIEW QUESTIONS

1. How would you characterize Plutarch's view of Alexander?
2. Is it completely unbiased?
3. What kind of leader does Alexander appear to be?
4. Does he have any apparent flaws?
5. What, according to Plutarch, were the motives underlying Alexander's conquests?

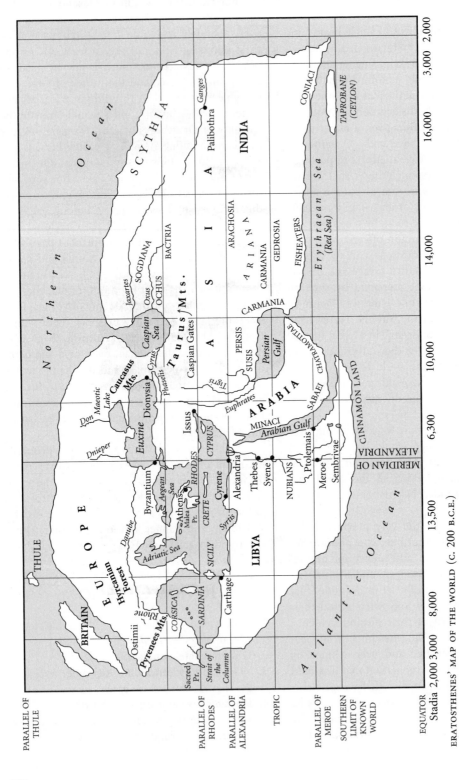

ERATOSTHENES' MAP OF THE WORLD (C. 200 B.C.E.)

As shown in this reconstruction, the world map created by the Hellenistic geographer Eratosthenes (c. 275–195 B.C.E.) shows the use of lines corresponding to latitude and longitude and is considerably advanced for its time. How might Eratosthenes' research have benefited from Alexander's campaigns? How well developed was the Hellenistic sense of Africa, Asia, and Europe?

206

HELLENISTIC ARCHITECTURE IN THE NEAR EAST (C. 175 C.E.)

In the wake of Alexander's conquests, Greek culture and tastes were adopted by many of the native elites in the Near East. This "treasury" (perhaps a royal mausoleum in actuality) was carved into the sandstone of the city of Petra, now in modern Jordan. In the third and second centuries B.C.E., Petra was the capital of the Nabataean kings, much of whose wealth and power derived from Petra's importance as a major hub for long-distance caravan trade. How does the style of the architecture compare with that of Greek public buildings? What would have inspired non-Greeks to adopt Greek styles?

FROM **The First Book of Maccabees**

There survive relatively few documents that provide evidence of the response of Near Eastern peoples to their conquest by Alexander's armies and their subsequent inclusion in the Ptolemid and Seleucid kingdoms. Perhaps the most eloquent and informative sources are from the Hebrew Bible. The following selection is from the First Book of Maccabees. Probably written around 100 B.C.E., it chronicles the rebellion begun in 167 B.C.E. by the priest Mattathias, and then continued by his sons Judas, Jonathan, and Simon (all of whom came to be known as Maccabee, possibly meaning "designated by God"), against the Seleucid rulers of Syria. After years of struggle, the rebels succeeded in securing the independent Hasmonean kingdom of Judea, which later was incorporated into the Roman Empire.

From *The Oxford Study Bible*, edited by M. Jack Suggs, Katharine Doob Sakenfeld, and James R. Mueller (Oxford, Eng.: Oxford University Press, 1992).

*   *   *

On his return from the conquest of Egypt in the year 143 Antiochus marched up with a strong force against Israel and Jerusalem. In his arrogance he entered the temple and carried off the gold altar, the lampstand with all its fittings, the table of the Bread of the Presence, the libation cups and bowls, the gold censers, the curtain, and the garlands. He stripped the gold plating from the front of the temple, seized the silver and gold, the precious vessels, and whatever secret treasures he found, and carried them all away when he left for his own country. He had caused much bloodshed, and he boasted arrogantly of what he had done.

Great was the mourning throughout
  Israel,
deep the groans of rulers and elders.
Girls and young men languished;
the beauty of our women was
  disfigured.
Every bridegroom took up the lament;
every bride sat mourning in her bridal
  chamber.
The land trembled for its inhabitants,
and all the house of Jacob was wrapped
  in shame.

Two years later, the king sent a governor to put the towns of Judaea under tribute. When he arrived at Jerusalem with a powerful force his language, though friendly, was full of guile, for once he had gained the city's confidence he launched a sudden and savage attack. Many of the Israelites were killed, and their city was sacked and set ablaze. On every side the houses and city walls were demolished; the women and children were captured, and the livestock seized.

The City of David was turned into a citadel, enclosed by a high, stout wall with strong towers, and garrisoned by impious foreigners and renegades. Having made themselves secure, they laid up a store of arms and provisions, and brought in the plunder they had collected from Jerusalem. They lurked there, a snare and threat to the temple and a perpetual menace to Israel.

*   *   *

The king issued an edict throughout his empire: his subjects were all to become one people and abandon their own customs. Everywhere the nations complied with the royal command, and many in Israel willingly adopted the foreign cult, sacrificing to idols and profaning the sabbath. The king sent agents to Jerusalem and the towns of Judaea with written orders that ways and customs foreign to the country should be introduced. Whole-offerings, sacrifices, and drink-offerings were forbidden in the temple; sabbaths and feast days were to be profaned, the temple and its ministers defiled. Pagan altars, idols, and sacred precincts were to be established, swine and other unclean beasts to be offered in sacrifice. The Jews were to leave their sons uncircumcised; they had to make themselves in every way abominable, unclean, and profane, and so forget the law and change all their statutes. The penalty for disobeying the royal command was death.

Such were the terms of the edict issued by the king throughout his realm. He appointed superintendents over all the people, and instructed the towns of Judaea to offer sacrifice, town by town. Those of the people who were ready to betray the law all thronged to their side in large numbers. Their wicked conduct throughout the land drove Israel into hiding in every possible place of refuge.

On the fifteenth day of the month of Kislev in the year 145, "the abomination of desolation" was set up on the altar of the Lord. In the towns throughout Judaea pagan altars were built; incense was offered at the doors of houses and in the streets. Every scroll of the law that was found was torn up and consigned to the flames, and anyone discovered in possession of a Book of the Covenant or conforming to the law was by sentence of the king condemned to die. Thus month after month these wicked men used their power against the Israelites whom they found in their towns. On the twenty-fifth day of each month they offered sacrifice on the pagan altar which was on top of the altar of whole-offering. In accordance with the royal decree, they put to death women who had had their children circumcised; their babies, their families, and those who had performed the circumcisions were hanged by the neck.

Yet many in Israel found strength to resist, taking a determined stand against the eating of any unclean food. They welcomed death and died rather than defile themselves and profane the holy covenant. Israel lay under a reign of terror.

*   *   *

At that time many who sought to maintain their religion and law went down to live in the desert, taking their children and their wives and their livestock with them, for their miseries were more than they could bear. Word soon reached the king's officers and the forces stationed in Jerusalem, the city of David, that Israelites who had defied the king's order had gone down into hiding-places in the desert. A large body of soldiers, setting off in pursuit, came upon them, and drew up in battle order ready to attack on the sabbath. "There is still time," they shouted; "come out, do as the king commands, and your lives will be spared." "We will not come out," was the reply; "we will not obey the king's command to profane the sabbath." Without more ado the attack was launched, but the Israelites did nothing in reply; they neither hurled stones, nor barricaded their caves. "Let us all meet death with a clear conscience," they said; "we call heaven and earth to witness it is contrary to all justice that you are making away with us." So on the sabbath they were attacked and massacred, men, women, and children, up to a thousand in all, along with their livestock.

When Mattathias and his friends learnt of it, their grief was very great, and they said to one another, "If we all do as our brothers have done and refuse to fight the Gentiles in defence of our lives as well as our laws and customs, then they will soon wipe us off the face of the earth." That day the decision was taken that if anyone came to fight against them on the sabbath, they would fight back, rather than all perish as their brothers in the caves had done.

*   *   *

Mattathias and his friends swept through the country, demolishing the pagan altars and forcibly circumcising all the uncircumcised boys found within the frontiers of Israel. They hunted down their arrogant enemies, and the cause prospered in their hands. Thus they came to the defence of the law against the Gentiles and their kings and withheld power from the wicked.

*   *   *

Judas Maccabaeus came forward to take his father's place. He had the support of all his brothers and his father's followers, obtained the sword of Apollonius, and for the rest of his life he used it in his campaigns.

*   *   *

Judas and his brothers came to be regarded with fear, and alarm spread among the Gentiles round about. His fame reached the ears of the king, and the story of his battles was told in every nation. Incensed by those reports, King Antiochus issued orders for the mobilization of all the forces of his empire, an immensely powerful army.

*   *   *

The following year Lysias mustered sixty thousand picked infantry and five thousand cavalry to bring the war with the Jews to an end. Marching into Idumaea, they encamped at Bethsura, where Judas opposed them with ten thousand men. When he saw the strength of the enemy's army, he prayed: "All praise to you, Saviour of Israel, who by the hand of your servant David broke the giant's onslaught and who delivered the Philistine army into the hands of Jonathan, Saul's son, and of his armour-bearer. Now let this army be hemmed in by the power of your people Israel, and let the enemy's pride in their troops and mounted men be humbled; fill them with cowardice, make their insolent strength melt away, let them reel under a crushing defeat; may they fall by the sword of those who love you. And let all who know your name praise you with songs of thanksgiving."

Battle was joined, and in the hand-to-hand fighting Lysias lost about five thousand men. When he saw his own army routed and Judas's army in fighting spirit, ready to live or to die nobly, he withdrew to Antioch, where he recruited a force of mercenaries, intending to return to Judaea with a much larger army.

Judas and his brothers said: "Now that our enemies have been crushed, let us go up to cleanse and rededicate the temple." When the whole army had assembled, they went up to Mount Zion, where they found the temple laid waste, the altar desecrated, the gates burnt down, the courts overgrown like a thicket or wooded hillside, and the priests' rooms in ruin. They tore their garments, lamented loudly, put ashes on their heads, and threw themselves face downwards on the ground. They cried aloud to Heaven, and the ceremonial trumpets were sounded.

Then Judas detailed men to engage the citadel garrison while the temple was being cleansed. He selected priests without blemish and faithful to the law, and they purified the temple, removing to an unclean place the stones which defiled it. They discussed what to do about the desecrated altar of whole-offerings, and rightly decided to demolish it, for fear it might become a lasting reproach to them because it had been defiled by the Gentiles. They therefore pulled down the altar, and stored away the stones in a suitable place on the temple hill, until there should arise a prophet to give a decision about them. They took unhewn stones, as the law directs, and built a new altar on the model of the previous one. They also repaired the temple and restored its interior, and they consecrated the temple courts. New sacred vessels were made; the lampstand, the altar of incense, and the table were brought into the temple. They burnt incense on the altar, and they lit the lamps on the lampstand to shine within the temple. When they had set the Bread of the Presence on the table and spread out the curtains, their work was completed.

Early on the twenty-fifth day of the ninth month, the month of Kislev, in the year 148, sacrifice was offered, as laid down by the law, on the newly constructed altar of whole-offerings. On the anniversary of the day of its desecration by the Gentiles, on that very day it was dedicated with hymns of thanksgiving, to the music of harps and lutes and cymbals. All the people prostrated themselves in worship and gave praise to Heaven for prospering their cause.

They celebrated the dedication of the altar for eight days; there was rejoicing as they brought whole-offerings and sacrificed shared-offerings and thank-offerings. They decorated the front of the temple with gold garlands and ornamental shields. They renovated the gates and restored the priests' rooms, fitting them with doors. At the lifting of the disgrace brought on them by the Gentiles there was very great rejoicing among the people.

Judas, his brothers, and the whole congregation of Israel decreed that, at the same season each year, the dedication of the altar should be observed with joy and gladness for eight days, beginning on the twenty-fifth of Kislev.

*   *   *

REVIEW QUESTIONS

1. According to the First Book of Maccabees, what was the impact of Greek conquest on the Jews of Israel?
2. What provoked them to resist Hellenistic domination?
3. Where lay the conflicts between the values of the Jews and those of their conquerors?
4. How does this account of Greek domination contrast with the ideals of Alexander as described by Plutarch?

THEOCRITUS

FROM *Idylls*

An often-noted aspect of Hellenistic literature and philosophy is an emphasis on escapism. This frequently involved turning one's concern away from the weighty issues of public life that had often characterized the culture of the Classical city-state era and focusing attention instead on more personal (and, some might say, less consequential) matters. This shift in focus is quite evident in the pastoral idylls of the third-century B.C.E. poet Theocritus.

From *The Norton Book of Classical Literature,* edited by Bernard Knox (New York: Norton, 1993), pp. 560–61.

Idyll III

I'm off to serenade Amaryllis.
Tityrus grazes my goats on the hill.
Feed them, good Tityrus, lead them to water.
And watch that ram, the yellow Libyan,
or he'll be butting you.

My Amaryllis, my beauty, why can it be
you no longer seek me out from your cave
and call me in? Me, your lover?
Do you hate me? Or is it, perhaps,
at closer range, I seem snub-nosed?
My chin's too long? I'll hang myself,
for you one day. I will, I know.
I've brought you, see, ten apples,

picked just where you asked me;
tomorrow I promise I'll fetch you some more.
But look, I'm in pain. My heart's in a turmoil.
How I wish I were that buzzing bee
that I might so easily fly into your cave
through the ivy and fern you hide behind.
Now I know Love. He's a formidable god.
A lioness suckled him, brought him up
deep in the woods. And now I'm tortured
to the very bones by his slow fires.
Your bewitching glances are solid stone,
my Nymph, my love, my dark-browed beauty;
come to my arms, your goatherd's arms,
for he longs, he longs to give you his kiss.
Even in empty kisses there is fond delight.
You will make me tear this garland to pieces,
Amaryllis, my love, this crown I made you
of ivy, of rosebuds and sweet celery.
What lies ahead for me? What but pain?
You are deaf to my every complaint.
At the cliff where Olpis the fisherman
watches for tunny, I shall bare my back
and throw myself off into the waves:
if I die, you at least will be satisfied.

    It was not long ago I learnt the truth.
You were on my mind; I was wondering
if you loved me, so I slapped the leaf
of love-in-absence firmly on my arm—
but no, it didn't stick; uselessly
it shrivelled up on my smooth skin.

Agroeo, too, the prophet of the sieve,
told me a truth the other day
as we were harvesting side by side:
I loved you, she said, with all my heart,
but you took not a moment's notice of me.
Look, I've kept you a snow-white goat,
with two kids, which Memnon's dusky girl
keeps asking for. And she shall have them
since you persist in showing me such disdain.
My right eye twitched. Can she be coming?
I'll lean here, beneath this pine, awhile,
and sing for her. Perhaps she'll notice me;
she cannot be made all of adamant.

*   *   *

My head aches, but that's nothing to you.
I will sing no more. I'll just lie here,
here where I've fallen, till the wolves devour me.
Let's hope you'll find that as sweet as honey.

REVIEW QUESTIONS

1. What kinds of people are the focus of this idyll, and what kinds of concerns dominate their actions?
2. How appealing do you find them when compared to a character like Antigone?
3. Were the actions of the Greeks always motivated by rational thinking?

EPICURUS

Principal Doctrines

With the exception of Stoicism, no Hellenistic philosophy has had more influence on the intellectual history of Western civilization than Epicureanism. Although later thinkers mistakenly perceived Epicureanism as a philosophy that espoused a hedonistic pleasure seeking, in fact its founder, the Athenian philosopher Epicurus (341–270 B.C.E.) advocated a prudent pursuit of pleasure in the quest for peace of mind. Attaining that state entailed, among other things, an avoidance of excessive involve-

ment in public affairs—very much in keeping with the escapism that in so many ways characterized the Hellenistic approach to life. The following selection provides the principal doctrines of his teaching.

From *Greek and Roman Philosophy after Aristotle*, by Jason L. Saunders (New York: Free Press, 1994).

1. A blessed and eternal being has no trouble himself and brings no trouble upon any other being; hence he is exempt from movements of anger and partiality, for every such movement implies weakness.

2. Death is nothing to us; for the body, when it has been resolved into its elements, has no feeling, and that which has no feeling is nothing to us.

3. The magnitude of pleasure reaches its limit in the removal of all pain. When pleasure is present, so long as it is uninterrupted, there is no pain either of body or of mind or of both together.

4. Continuous pain does not last long in the flesh; on the contrary, pain, if extreme, is present a very short time, and even that degree of pain which barely outweighs pleasure in the flesh does not last for many days together. Illnesses of long duration even permit of an excess of pleasure over pain in the flesh.

5. It is impossible to live a pleasant life without living wisely and well and justly, and it is impossible to live wisely and well and justly without living pleasantly. Whenever any one of these is lacking, when, for instance, the man is not able to live wisely, though he lives well and justly, it is impossible for him to live a pleasant life.

6. In order to obtain security from other men any means whatsoever of procuring this was a natural good.

7. Some men have sought to become famous and renowned, thinking that thus they would make themselves secure against their fellow-men. If, then, the life of such persons really was secure, they attained natural good; if, however, it was insecure, they have not attained the end which by nature's own prompting they originally sought.

8. No pleasure is in itself evil, but the things which produce certain pleasures entail annoyances many times greater than the pleasures themselves.

9. If all pleasure had been capable of accumulation, if this had gone on not only by recurrence in time, but all over the frame or, at any rate, over the principal parts of man's nature, there would never have been any difference between one pleasure and another, as in fact there is.

10. If the objects which are productive of pleasures to profligate persons really freed them from fears of the mind,—the fears, I mean, inspired by celestial and atmospheric phenomena, the fear of death, the fear of pain; if, further, they taught them to limit their desires, we should never have any fault to find with such persons, for they would then be filled with pleasures to overflowing on all sides and would be exempt from all pain, whether of body or mind, that is, from all evil.

11. If we had never been molested by alarms at celestial and atmospheric phenomena, nor by the misgiving that death somehow affects us, nor by neglect of the proper limits of pains and desires, we should have had no need to study natural science.

12. It would be impossible to banish fear on matters of the highest importance, if a man did not know the nature of the whole universe, but lived in dread of what the legend tells us. Hence without the study of nature there was no enjoyment of unmixed pleasures.

13. There would be no advantage in providing security against our fellow-men, so long as we were alarmed by occurrences over our heads or beneath the earth or in general by whatever happens in the boundless universe.

14. When tolerable security against our fellow-men is attained, then on a basis of power sufficient to afford support and of material prosperity arises

in most genuine form the security of a quiet private life withdrawn from the multitude.

15. Nature's wealth at once has its bounds and is easy to procure; but the wealth of vain fancies recedes to an infinite distance.

16. Fortune but seldom interferes with the wise man; his greatest and highest interests have been, are, and will be, directed by reason throughout the course of his life.

17. The just man enjoys the greatest peace of mind, while the unjust is full of the utmost disquietude.

18. Pleasure in the flesh admits no increase when once the pain of want has been removed; after that it only admits of variation. The limit of pleasure in the mind, however, is reached when we reflect on the things themselves and their congeners which cause the mind the greatest alarms.

19. Unlimited time and limited time afford an equal amount of pleasure, if we measure the limits of that pleasure by reason.

20. The flesh receives as unlimited the limits of pleasure; and to provide it requires unlimited time. But the mind, grasping in thought what the end and limit of the flesh is, and banishing the terrors of futurity, procures a complete and perfect life, and has no longer any need of unlimited time. Nevertheless it does not shun pleasure, and even in the hour of death, when ushered out of existence by circumstances, the mind does not lack enjoyment of the best life.

21. He who understands the limits of life knows how easy it is to procure enough to remove the pain of want and make the whole of life complete and perfect. Hence he has no longer any need of things which are not to be won save by labor and conflict.

22. We must take into account as the end all that really exists and all clear evidence of sense to which we refer our opinions; for otherwise everything will be full of uncertainty and confusion.

23. If you fight against all your sensations, you will have no standard to which to refer, and thus no means of judging even those judgments which you pronounce false.

24. If you reject absolutely any single sensation without stopping to discriminate with respect to that which awaits confirmation between matter of opinion and that which is already present, whether in sensation or in feelings or in any presentative perception of the mind, you will throw into confusion even the rest of your sensations by your groundless belief and so you will be rejecting the standard of truth altogether. If in your ideas based upon opinion you hastily affirm as true all that awaits confirmation as well as that which does not, you will not escape error, as you will be maintaining complete ambiguity whenever it is a case of judging between right and wrong opinion.

25. If you do not on every separate occasion refer each of your actions to the end prescribed by nature, but instead of this in the act of choice or avoidance swerve aside to some other end, your acts will not be consistent with your theories.

26. All such desires as lead to no pain when they remain ungratified are unnecessary, and the longing is easily got rid of, when the thing desired is difficult to procure or when the desires seem likely to produce harm.

27. Of all the means which are procured by wisdom to ensure happiness throughout the whole of life, by far the most important is the acquisition of friends.

28. The same conviction which inspires confidence that nothing we have to fear is eternal or even of long duration, also enables us to see that even in our limited conditions of life nothing enhances our security so much as friendship.

29. Of our desires some are natural and necessary; others are natural, but not necessary; others, again, are neither natural nor necessary, but are due to illusory opinion.

30. Those natural desires which entail no pain when not gratified, though their objects are vehemently pursued, are also due to illusory opinion; and when they are not got rid of, it is not because of their own nature, but because of the man's illusory opinion.

31. Natural justice is a symbol or expression of expediency, to prevent one man from harming or being harmed by another.

32. Those animals which are incapable of making

covenants with one another, to the end that they may neither inflict nor suffer harm, are without either justice or injustice. And those tribes which either could not or would not form mutual covenants to the same end are in like case.

33. There never was an absolute justice, but only an agreement made in reciprocal intercourse in whatever localities now and again from time to time, providing against the infliction or suffering of harm.

34. Injustice is not in itself an evil, but only in its consequence, viz. the terror which is excited by apprehension that those appointed to punish such offences will discover the injustice.

35. It is impossible for the man who secretly violates any article of the social compact to feel confident that he will remain undiscovered, even if he has already escaped ten thousand times; for right on to the end of his life he is never sure he will not be detected.

36. Taken generally, justice is the same for all, to wit, something found expedient in mutual intercourse; but in its application to particular cases of locality or conditions of whatever kind, it varies under different circumstances.

37. Among the things accounted just by conventional law, whatever in the needs of mutual intercourse is attested to be expedient, is thereby stamped as just, whether or not it be the same for all; and in case any law is made and does not prove suitable to the expediencies of mutual intercourse, then this is no longer just. And should the expediency which is expressed by the law vary and only for a time correspond with the prior conception, nevertheless for the time being it was just, so long as we do not trouble ourselves about empty words, but look simply at the facts.

38. Where without any change in circumstances the conventional laws, when judged by their consequences, were seen not to correspond with the notion of justice, such laws were not really just; but wherever the laws have ceased to be expedient in consequence of a change in circumstances, in that case the laws were for the time being just when they were expedient for the mutual intercourse of the citizens, and subsequently ceased to be just when they ceased to be expedient.

39. He who best knew how to meet fear of external foes made into one family all the creatures he could; and those he could not, he at any rate did not treat as aliens; and where he found even this impossible, he avoided all intercourse, and, so far as was expedient, kept them at a distance.

40. Those who were best able to provide themselves with the means of security against their neighbors, being thus in possession of the surest guarantee, passed the most agreeable life in each other's society; and their enjoyment of the fullest intimacy was such that, if one of them died before his time, the survivors did not lament his death as if it called for commiseration.

REVIEW QUESTIONS

1. What is Epicurus's view of the gods' role in the cosmos?
2. What is the role of human senses?
3. Does his view conflict with that of Plato?

LUCRETIUS

FROM *On the Nature of Things*

Among the chief tenets of Epicureanism was the belief in a completely materialistic interpretation of the cosmos. Thus, human beings had nothing to fear from non-existent supernatural powers or from eternal misery after this life. The epitaph of the otherwise obscure philosopher Diogenes of Oenoanda sums up the Epicurean creed with marvelous succinctness: "Nothing to fear in God, nothing to feel in death, good can be attained, evil can be endured." A much more eloquent discourse on the Epicurean view of death and of Epicurean beliefs in general is to be found in On the Nature of Things, *by the first-century* B.C.E. *Roman poet Lucretius.*

From *The Way Things Are,* translated by Rolfe Humphries (Bloomington: Indiana University Press, 1968), pp. 596–603.

*   *   *

Death
Is nothing to us, has no relevance
To our condition, seeing that the mind
Is mortal. Just as, long ago, we felt
Not the least touch of trouble when the wars
Were raging all around the shaken earth
And from all sides the Carthaginian hordes
Poured forth to battle, and no man ever knew
Whose subject he would be in life or death,
Which doom, by land or sea, would strike him
    down,
So, when we cease to be, and body and soul,
Which joined to make us one, have gone their
    ways,
Their separate ways, nothing at all can shake
Our feelings, not if earth were mixed with sea
Or sea with sky. Perhaps the mind or spirit,
After its separation from our body,
Has some sensation; what is that to us?
Nothing at all, for what we knew of being,
Essence, identity, oneness, was derived
From body's union with spirit, so, if time,
After our death, should some day reunite
All of our present particles, bring them back

To where they now reside, give us once more
The light of life, this still would have no meaning
For us, with our self-recollection gone.
As we are now, we lack all memory
Of what we were before, suffer no wound
From those old days. Look back on all that
    space
Of time's immensity, consider well
What infinite combinations there have been
In matter's ways and groupings. How easy, then,
For human beings to believe we are
Compounded of the very selfsame motes,
Arranged exactly in the selfsame ways
As once we were, our long-ago, our now
Being identical. And yet we keep
No memory of that once-upon-a-time,
Nor can we call it back; somewhere between
A break occurred, and all our atoms went
Wandering here and there and far away
From our sensations. If there lies ahead
Tough luck for any man, he must be there,
Himself, to feel its evil, but since death
Removes this chance, and by injunction stops
All rioting of woes against our state,
We may be reassured that in our death
We have no cause for fear, we cannot be

Wretched in nonexistence. Death alone
Has immortality, and takes away
Our mortal life. It does not matter a bit
If we once lived before.
                              So, seeing a man
Feel sorry for himself, that after death
He'll be a rotting corpse, laid in a tomb,
Succumb to fire, or predatory beasts,
You'll know he's insincere, just making noise,
With rancor in his heart, though he believes,
Or tries to make us think so, that death ends all.

*   *   *

Some older man, a senior citizen,
Were plaintiff, wretcheder than he ought to be,
Lamenting death, would Nature not be right
To cry him down, with even sharper voice,
"Why, you old scoundrel, take those tears of yours
Somewhere away from here, cut out the whining.
You have had everything from life, and now
You find you're going to pieces. You desire,
Always, what isn't there; what is, you scorn,
So life has slipped away from you, incomplete,
Unsatisfactory, and here comes death,
An unexpected summoner, to stand
Beside you, long before you want to leave,
Long, long, before you think you've had enough.
Let it all go, act as becomes your age,
Be a great man, composed; give in; you must."
Such a rebuke from Nature would be right,
For the old order yields before the new,
All things require refashioning from others.
No man goes down to Hell's black pit; we need
Matter for generations yet to come,
Who, in their turn, will follow you, as men
Have died before you and will die hereafter.
So one thing never ceases to arise
Out of another; life's a gift to no man
Only a loan to him. Look back at time—
How meaningless, how unreal!—before our birth.
In this way Nature holds before our eyes
The mirror of our future after death.
Is this so grim, so gloomy? Is it not
A rest more free from care than any sleep?
Now all those things which people say exist
In Hell, are really present in our lives.

The story says that Tantalus, the wretch,
Frozen in terror, fears the massive rock
Balanced in air above him. It's not true.
What happens is that in our lives the fear,
The silly, vain, ridiculous fear of gods,
Causes our panic dread of accident.
No vultures feed on Tityos, who lies
Sprawled out for them in Hell; they could not find
In infinite eternities of time
What they are searching for in that great bulk,
Nine acres wide, or ninety, or the spread
Of all the globe. No man can ever bear
Eternal pain, nor can his body give
Food to the birds forever. We do have
A Tityos in ourselves, and lie, in love,
Torn and consumed by our anxieties,
Our fickle passions. Sisyphus, too, is here
In our own lives; we see him as the man
Bent upon power and office, who comes back
Gloomy and beaten after every vote.
To seek for power, such an empty thing,
And never gain it, suffering all the while,
This is to shove uphill the stubborn rock
Which over and over comes bouncing down again
To the flat levels where it started from.
Or take another instance: when we feed
A mind whose nature seems unsatisfied,
Never content, with all the blessings given
Through season after season, with all the charms
And graces of life's harvest, this, I'd say,
Is to be like those young and lovely girls,
The Danaids, trying in vain to fill
Their leaky jars with water. Cerberus,
The Furies, and the dark, and the grim jaws
Of Tartarus, belching blasts of heat—all these
Do not exist at all, and never could.
But here on earth we do fear punishment
For wickedness, and in proportion dread
Our dreadful deeds, imagining all too well
Being cast down from the Tarpeian Rock,
Jail, flogging, hangmen, brands, the rack, the knout;
And even though these never touch us, still
The guilty mind is its own torturer

With lash and rowel, can see no end at all
To suffering and punishment, and fears
These will be more than doubled after death.
Hell does exist on earth—in the life of fools.

You well might think of saying to yourself:
"Even good Ancus closed his eyes on the light—
A better man than you will ever be,
You reprobate—and many lords and kings
Rulers of mighty nations, all have died.
Even that monarch, who once paved the way
Making the sea a highway for his legions
Where foot and horse alike could march dry-
    shod
While the deep foamed and thundered at the
    outrage,
Even he, great Xerxes, died and left the light,
And Scipio, the thunderbolt of war,
Terror of Carthage, gave his bones to earth
As does the meanest lackey. Add to these
Philosophers and artists, all the throng
Blessed by the Muses; Homer's majesty
Lies low in the same sleep as all the rest.
Democritus, warned by a ripe old age
That, with his memory, his powers of mind
Were also failing, gave himself to death;
And Epicurus perished, that great man
Whose genius towered over all the rest,
Making their starry talents fade and die
In his great sunlight. Who are you, forsooth,
To hesitate, resent, protest your death?
Your life is death already, though you live
And though you see, except that half your time
You waste in sleep, and the other half you snore
With eyes wide open, forever seeing dreams,
Forever in panic, forever lacking wit
To find out what the trouble is, depressed,
Or drunk, or drifting aimlessly around."

Men seem to feel some burden on their souls,
Some heavy weariness; could they but know
Its origin, its cause, they'd never live
The way we see most of them do, each one
Ignorant of what he wants, except a change,
Some other place to lay his burden down.
One leaves his house to take a stroll outdoors

Because the household's such a deadly bore,
And then comes back, in six or seven minutes—
The street is every bit as bad. Now what?
He has his horses hitched up for him, drives,
Like a man going to a fire, full-speed,
Off to his country-place, and when he gets there
Is scarcely on the driveway, when he yawns,
Falls heavily asleep, oblivious
To everything, or promptly turns around,
Whips back to town again. So each man flees
Himself, or tries to, but of course that pest
Clings to him all the more ungraciously.
He hates himself because he does not know
The reason for his sickness; if he did,
He would leave all this foolishness behind,
Devote his study to the way things are,
The problem being his lot, not for an hour,
But for all time, the state in which all men
Must dwell forever and ever after death.
Finally, what's this wanton lust for life
To make us tremble in dangers and in doubt?
All men must die, and no man can escape.
We turn and turn in the same atmosphere
In which no new delight is ever shaped
To grace our living; what we do not have
Seems better than everything else in all the world
But should we get it, we want something else.
Our gaping thirst for life is never quenched.
We have to know what luck next year will bring,
What accident, what end. But life, prolonged,
Subtracts not even one second from the term
Of death's continuance. We lack the strength
To abbreviate that eternity. Suppose
You could contrive to live for centuries,
As many as you will. Death, even so,
Will still be waiting for you; he who died
Early this morning has as many years
Interminably before him, as the man,
His predecessor, has, who perished months
Or years, or even centuries ago.

*   *   *

REVIEW QUESTIONS

1. From an Epicurean standpoint, what is an appropriate attitude toward death?

2. Should death hold any terror for humans?
3. Can you discern from this selection something of the Epicurean view concerning matter and the composition of the cosmos?

EPICTETUS

FROM *The Manual:* Stoicism

The school of philosophy known as Stoicism, founded by Zeno of Citium, undoubtedly has had a more profound impact on the Western intellectual tradition than any other of the Hellenistic schools. In particular, its emphasis on a universal natural order governed by a divine plan greatly influenced the later development of both Roman imperial law and Christian thought. The literary remains of the early development of Stoic philosophy are quite fragmentary. Much better preserved is the systematic presentation of Stoic principles in The Manual of Epictetus *(60 C.E.–?), as set down probably by his student Arrian.*

From *The Manual of Epictetus,* translated by P. E. Matheson (Oxford, Eng.: Clarendon Press).

1. Of all existing things some are in our power, and others are not in our power. In our power are thought, impulse, will to get and will to avoid, and, in a word, everything which is our own doing. Things not in our power include the body, property, reputation, office, and, in a word, everything which is not our own doing. Things in our power are by nature free, unhindered, untrammelled; things not in our power are weak, servile, subject to hindrance, dependent on others. Remember then that if you imagine that what is naturally slavish is free, and what is naturally another's is your own, you will be hampered, you will mourn, you will be put to confusion, you will blame gods and men; but if you think that only your own belongs to you, and that what is another's is indeed another's, no one will ever put compulsion or hindrance on you, you will blame none, you will accuse none, you will do nothing against your will, no one will harm you, you will have no enemy, for no harm can touch you.

Aiming then at these high matters, you must remember that to attain them requires more than ordinary effort; you will have to give up some things entirely, and put off others for the moment. And if you would have these also—office and wealth—it may be that you will fail to get them, just because your desire is set on the former, and you will certainly fail to attain those things which alone bring freedom and happiness.

Make it your study then to confront every harsh impression with the words, "You are but an impression, and not at all what you seem to be." Then test it by those rules that you possess; and first by this—the chief test of all—"Is it concerned with what is in our power or with what is not in our power?" And if it is concerned with what is not in our power, be ready with the answer that it is nothing to you.

2. Remember that the will to get promises attainment of what you will, and the will to avoid promises escape from what you avoid; and he who fails to get what he wills is unfortunate, and he who does not escape what he wills to avoid is miserable. If then you try to avoid only what is unnatural in the region within your control, you will escape from all that you avoid; but if you try to avoid disease or death or poverty you will be miserable.

Therefore let your will to avoid have no concern with what is not in man's power; direct it only to things in man's power that are contrary to nature. But for the moment you must utterly remove the will to get; for if you will to get something not in man's power you are bound to be unfortunate; while none of the things in man's power that you could honourably will to get is yet within your reach. Impulse to act and not to act, these are your concern; yet exercise them gently and without strain, and provisionally.

3. When anything, from the meanest thing upwards, is attractive or serviceable or an object of affection, remember always to say to yourself, "What is its nature?" If you are fond of a jug, say you are fond of a jug; then you will not be disturbed if it be broken. If you kiss your child or your wife, say to yourself that you are kissing a human being, for then if death strikes it you will not be disturbed.

4. When you are about to take something in hand, remind yourself what manner of thing it is. If you are going to bathe put before your mind what happens in the bath—water pouring over some, others being jostled, some reviling, others stealing; and you will set to work more securely if you say to yourself at once: "I want to bathe, and I want to keep my will in harmony with nature," and so in each thing you do; for in this way, if anything turns up to hinder you in your bathing, you will be ready to say, "I did not want only to bathe, but to keep my will in harmony with nature, and I shall not so keep it, if I lose my temper at what happens."

5. What disturbs men's minds is not events but their judgements on events. For instance, death is nothing dreadful, or else Socrates would have thought it so. No, the only dreadful thing about it is men's judgement that it is dreadful. And so when we are hindered, or disturbed, or distressed, let us never lay the blame on others, but on ourselves, that is, on our own judgements. To accuse others for one's own misfortunes is a sign of want of education; to accuse oneself shows that one's education has begun; to accuse neither oneself nor others shows that one's education is complete.

6. Be not elated at an excellence which is not your own. If the horse in his pride were to say, "I am handsome," we could bear with it. But when you say with pride, "I have a handsome horse," know that the good horse is the ground of your pride. You ask then what you can call your own. The answer is—the way you deal with your impressions. Therefore when you deal with your impressions in accord with nature, then you may be proud indeed, for your pride will be in a good which is your own.

7. When you are on a voyage, and your ship is at anchorage, and you disembark to get fresh water, you may pick up a small shellfish or a truffle by the way, but you must keep your attention fixed on the ship, and keep looking towards it constantly, to see if the Helmsman calls you; and if he does, you have to leave everything, or be bundled on board with your legs tied like a sheep. So it is in life. If you have a dear wife or child given you, they are like the shellfish or the truffle, they are very well in their way. Only, if the Helmsman call, run back to your ship, leave all else, and do not look behind you. And if you are old, never go far from the ship, so that when you are called you may not fail to appear.

8. Ask not that events should happen as you will, but let your will be that events should happen as they do, and you shall have peace.

9. Sickness is a hindrance to the body, but not to the will, unless the will consent. Lameness is a hindrance to the leg, but not to the will. Say this to yourself at each event that happens, for you

shall find that though it hinders something else it will not hinder you.

10. When anything happens to you, always remember to turn to yourself and ask what faculty you have to deal with it. If you see a beautiful boy or a beautiful woman, you will find continence the faculty to exercise there; if trouble is laid on you, you will find endurance; if ribaldry, you will find patience. And if you train yourself in this habit your impressions will not carry you away.

11. Never say of anything, "I lost it," but say, "I gave it back." Has your child died? It was given back. Has your wife died? She was given back. Has your estate been taken from you? Was not this also given back? But you say, "He who took it from me is wicked." What does it matter to you through whom the Giver asked it back? As long as He gives it you, take care of it, but not as your own; treat it as passers-by treat an inn.

12. If you wish to make progress, abandon reasonings of this sort: "If I neglect my affairs I shall have nothing to live on;" "If I do not punish my son, he will be wicked." For it is better to die of hunger, so that you be free from pain and free from fear, than to live in plenty and be troubled in mind. It is better for your son to be wicked than for you to be miserable. Wherefore begin with little things. Is your drop of oil spilt? Is your sup of wine stolen? Say to yourself, "This is the price paid for freedom from passion, this is the price of a quiet mind." Nothing can be had without a price. When you call your slave-boy, reflect that he may not be able to hear you, and if he hears you, he may not be able to do anything you want. But he is not so well off that it rests with him to give you peace of mind.

*   *   *

14. It is silly to want your children and your wife and your friends to live for ever, for that means that you want what is not in your control to be in your control, and what is not your own to be yours. In the same way if you want your servant to make no mistakes, you are a fool, for you want vice not to be vice but something different. But if

you want not to be disappointed in your will to get, you can attain to that.

Exercise yourself then in what lies in your power. Each man's master is the man who has authority over what he wishes or does not wish, to secure the one or to take away the other. Let him then who wishes to be free not wish for anything or avoid anything that depends on others; or else he is bound to be a slave.

*   *   *

16. When you see a man shedding tears in sorrow for a child abroad or dead, or for loss of property, beware that you are not carried away by the impression that it is outward ills that make him miserable. Keep this thought by you: "What distresses him is not the event, for that does not distress another, but his judgement on the event." Therefore do not hesitate to sympathize with him so far as words go, and if it so chance, even to groan with him; but take heed that you do not also groan in your inner being.

17. Remember that you are an actor in a play, and the Playwright chooses the manner of it: if he wants it short, it is short; if long, it is long. If he wants you to act a poor man you must act the part with all your powers; and so if your part be a cripple or a magistrate or a plain man. For your business is to act the character that is given you and act it well; the choice of the cast is Another's.

18. When a raven croaks with evil omen, let not the impression carry you away, but straightway distinguish in your own mind and say, "These portents mean nothing to me; but only to my bit of a body or my bit of property or name, or my children or my wife. But for me all omens are favourable if I will, for, whatever the issue may be, it is in my power to get benefit therefrom."

19. You can be invincible, if you never enter on a contest where victory is not in your power. Beware then that when you see a man raised to honour or great power or high repute you do not let your impression carry you away. For if the reality of good lies in what is in our power, there is no room for envy or jealousy. And you will not wish to be praetor, or prefect or consul, but to be free;

and there is but one way to freedom—to despise what is not in our power.

20. Remember that foul words or blows in themselves are no outrage, but your judgement that they are so. So when any one makes you angry, know that it is your own thought that has angered you. Wherefore make it your first endeavour not to let your impressions carry you away. For if once you gain time and delay, you will find it easier to control yourself.

21. Keep before your eyes from day to day death and exile and all things that seem terrible, but death most of all, and then you will never set your thoughts on what is low and will never desire anything beyond measure.

*   *   *

26. It is in our power to discover the will of Nature from those matters on which we have no difference of opinion. For instance, when another man's slave has broken the wine-cup we are very ready to say at once, "Such things must happen." Know then that when your own cup is broken, you ought to behave in the same way as when your neighbour's was broken. Apply the same principle to higher matters. Is another's child or wife dead? Not one of us but would say, "Such is the lot of man;" but when one's own dies, straightway one cries, "Alas! miserable am I." But we ought to remember what our feelings are when we hear it of another.

27. As a mark is not set up for men to miss it, so there is nothing intrinsically evil in the world.

*   *   *

29. . . . Man, consider first what it is you are undertaking; then look at your own powers and see if you can bear it. Do you want to compete in the pentathlon or in wrestling? Look to your arms, your thighs, see what your loins are like. For different men are born for different tasks. Do you suppose that if you do this you can live as you do now—eat and drink as you do now, indulge desire and discontent just as before? Nay, you must sit up late, work hard, abandon your own people, be looked down on by a mere slave, be ridiculed

by those who meet you, get the worst of it in everything—in honour, in office, in justice, in every possible thing. This is what you have to consider: whether you are willing to pay this price for peace of mind, freedom, tranquillity. If not, do not come near; do not be, like the children, first a philosopher, then a tax-collector, then an orator, then one of Caesar's procurators. These callings do not agree. You must be one man, good or bad; you must develop either your Governing Principle, or your outward endowments; you must study either your inner man, or outward things—in a word, you must choose between the position of a philosopher and that of a mere outsider.

*   *   *

31. For piety towards the gods know that the most important thing is this: to have right opinions about them—that they exist, and that they govern the universe well and justly—and to have set yourself to obey them, and to give way to all that happens, following events with a free will, in the belief that they are fulfilled by the highest mind. For thus you will never blame the gods, nor accuse them of neglecting you. But this you cannot achieve, unless you apply your conception of good and evil to those things only which are in our power, and not to those which are out of our power. For if you apply your notion of good or evil to the latter, then, as soon as you fail to get what you will to get or fail to avoid what you will to avoid, you will be bound to blame and hate those you hold responsible. For every living creature has a natural tendency to avoid and shun what seems harmful and all that causes it, and to pursue and admire what is helpful and all that causes it. It is not possible then for one who thinks he is harmed to take pleasure in what he thinks is the author of the harm, any more than to take pleasure in the harm itself. That is why a father is reviled by his son, when he does not give his son a share of what the son regards as good things; thus Polynices and Eteocles were set at enmity with one another by thinking that a king's throne was a good thing. That is why the farmer, and the sailor, and the merchant, and those who

lose wife or children revile the gods. For men's religion is bound up with their interest. Therefore he who makes it his concern rightly to direct his will to get and his will to avoid, is thereby making piety his concern. But it is proper on each occasion to make libation and sacrifice and to offer first-fruits according to the custom of our fathers, with purity and not in slovenly or careless fashion, without meanness and without extravagance.

*   *   *

32. ✶ ✶ ✶ Lay down for yourself from the first a definite stamp and style of conduct, which you will maintain when you are alone and also in the society of men. Be silent for the most part, or, if you speak, say only what is necessary and in a few words. Talk, but rarely, if occasion calls you, but do not talk of ordinary things—of gladiators, or horse-races, or athletes, or of meats or drinks—these are topics that arise everywhere—but above all do not talk about men in blame or compliment or comparison. If you can, turn the conversation of your company by your talk to some fitting subject; but if you should chance to be isolated among strangers, be silent. Do not laugh much, nor at many things, nor without restraint.

Refuse to take oaths, altogether if that be possible, but if not, as far as circumstances allow.

Refuse the entertainments of strangers and the vulgar. But if occasions arise to accept them, then strain every nerve to avoid lapsing into the state of the vulgar. For know that, if your comrade has a stain on him, he that associates with him must needs share the stain, even though he be clean in himself.

For your body take just so much as your bare need requires, such as food, drink, clothing, house, servants, but cut down all that tends to luxury and outward show.

Avoid impurity to the utmost of your power before marriage, and if you indulge your passion, let it be done lawfully. But do not be offensive or censorious to those who indulge it, and do not be always bringing up your own chastity. If some one tells you that so and so speaks ill of you, do not

defend yourself against what he says, but answer, "He did not know my other faults, or he would not have mentioned these alone."

It is not necessary for the most part to go to the games; but if you should have occasion to go, show that your first concern is for yourself; that is, wish that only to happen which does happen, and him only to win who does win, for so you will suffer no hindrance. But refrain entirely from applause, or ridicule, or prolonged excitement. And when you go away do not talk much of what happened there, except so far as it tends to your improvement. For to talk about it implies that the spectacle excited your wonder.

Do not go lightly or casually to hear lectures; but if you do go, maintain your gravity and dignity and do not make yourself offensive. When you are going to meet any one, and particularly some man of reputed eminence, set before your mind the thought, "What would Socrates or Zeno have done?" and you will not fail to make proper use of the occasion.

When you go to visit some great man, prepare your mind by thinking that you will not find him in, that you will be shut out, that the doors will be slammed in your face, that he will pay no heed to you. And if in spite of all this you find it fitting for you to go, go and bear what happens and never say to yourself, "It was not worth all this"; for that shows a vulgar mind and one at odds with outward things.

In your conversation avoid frequent and disproportionate mention of your own doings or adventures; for other people do not take the same pleasure in hearing what has happened to you as you take in recounting your adventures.

Avoid raising men's laughter; for it is a habit that easily slips into vulgarity, and it may well suffice to lessen your neighbour's respect.

It is dangerous too to lapse into foul language; when anything of the kind occurs, rebuke the offender, if the occasion allow, and if not, make it plain to him by your silence, or a blush or a frown, that you are angry at his words.

34. When you imagine some pleasure, beware that it does not carry you away, like other imagi-

nations. Wait a while, and give yourself pause. Next remember two things: how long you will enjoy the pleasure, and also how long you will afterwards repent and revile yourself. And set on the other side the joy and self-satisfaction you will feel if you refrain. And if the moment seems come to realize it, take heed that you be not overcome by the winning sweetness and attraction of it; set in the other scale the thought how much better is the consciousness of having vanquished it.

35. When you do a thing because you have determined that it ought to be done, never avoid being seen doing it, even if the opinion of the multitude is going to condemn you. For if your action is wrong, then avoid doing it altogether, but if it is right, why do you fear those who will rebuke you wrongly?

* * *

37. If you try to act a part beyond your powers, you not only disgrace yourself in it, but you neglect the part which you could have filled with success.

38. As in walking you take care not to tread on a nail or to twist your foot, so take care that you do not harm your Governing Principle. And if we guard this in everything we do, we shall set to work more securely.

39. Every man's body is a measure for his property, as the foot is the measure for his shoe. If you stick to this limit, you will keep the right measure; if you go beyond it, you are bound to be carried away down a precipice in the end; just as with the shoe, if you once go beyond the foot, your shoe puts on gilding, and soon purple and embroidery. For when once you go beyond the measure there is no limit.

40. Women from fourteen years upwards are called "madam" by men. Wherefore, when they see that the only advantage they have got is to be marriageable, they begin to make themselves smart and to set all their hopes on this. We must take pains then to make them understand that they are really honoured for nothing but a modest and decorous life.

41. It is a sign of a dull mind to dwell upon the cares of the body, to prolong exercise, eating, drinking, and other bodily functions. These things are to be done by the way; all your attention must be given to the mind.

42. When a man speaks evil or does evil to you, remember that he does or says it because he thinks it is fitting for him. It is not possible for him to follow what seems good to you, but only what seems good to him, so that, if his opinion is wrong, he suffers, in that he is the victim of deception. In the same way, if a composite judgement which is true is thought to be false, it is not the judgement that suffers, but the man who is deluded about it. If you act on this principle you will be gentle to him who reviles you, saying to yourself on each occasion, "He thought it right."

* * *

44. It is illogical to reason thus, "I am richer than you, therefore I am superior to you," "I am more eloquent than you, therefore I am superior to you." It is more logical to reason, "I am richer than you, therefore my property is superior to yours," "I am more eloquent than you, therefore my speech is superior to yours." You are something more than property or speech.

* * *

46. On no occasion call yourself a philosopher, nor talk at large of your principles among the multitude, but act on your principles. For instance, at a banquet do not say how one ought to eat, but eat as you ought. Remember that Socrates had so completely got rid of the thought of display that when men came and wanted an introduction to philosophers he took them to be introduced; so patient of neglect was he. And if a discussion arise among the multitude on some principle, keep silent for the most part; for you are in great danger of blurting out some undigested thought. And when someone says to you, 'You know nothing', and you do not let it provoke you, then know that you are really on the right road. For sheep do not bring grass to their shepherds and show them how much they have eaten, but they digest their fodder and then produce it in the form of wool and milk.

Do the same yourself; instead of displaying your principles to the multitude, show them the results of the principles you have digested.

* * *

The signs of one who is making progress are: he blames none, praises none, complains of none, accuses none, never speaks of himself as if he were somebody, or as if he knew anything. And if any one compliments him he laughs in himself at his compliment; and if one blames him, he makes no defence. He goes about like a convalescent, careful not to disturb his constitution on its road to recovery, until it has got firm hold. He has got rid of the will to get, and his will to avoid is directed no longer to what is beyond our power but only to what is in our power and contrary to nature. In all things he exercises his will without strain. If men regard him as foolish or ignorant he pays no heed. In one word, he keeps watch and guard on himself as his own enemy, lying in wait for him.

* * *

REVIEW QUESTIONS

1. As presented in this work, according to what principles is the practitioner of Stoicism to live his life?
2. Why do things happen as they do, and what should the proper Stoic's attitude be?
3. How do the principles of Stoicism contrast with those of Epicureanism?

HELLENISTIC AUTHORS

Short Poems

Many short poems by various, often (for us, at least) obscure authors survive from the Hellenistic era. As the selections provided below reveal, the concerns that they reflect are not limited to the human beings of two thousand years ago.

Asclepiades of Samos

Although she's a girl, Dorkion
Is wise to the ways of the boys.
Like a chubby kid, she knows how
To throw over her shoulder, from
Under her broadbrimmed hat, the quick
Glance of Public Love, and let her
Cape show a glimpse of her bare butt.

Didyme waved her wand at me.
I am utterly enchanted.
The sight of her beauty makes me

Melt like wax before the fire. What
Is the difference if she is black?
So is coal, but alight, it shines like roses.

Leonidas of Tarentum

These were my end: a fierce down-squall from
   the east,
And night, and the waves of Oriôn's stormy
   setting:
And I, Kallaischros, yielded my life
Far on the waste of the lonely Libyan sea.

And now I roll with drifting currents, the prey
Of fishes:
                            and this gravestone lies
If it says that it marks the place of my burial.

Anonymous

Boy, hold my wreath for me.
The night is black,
                            the path is long,
And I am completely and beautifully drunk.
Nevertheless I will go
To Themison's house and sing beneath his
     window.
You need not come with me:
                            though I may
     stumble,
He is a steady lamp for the feet of love.

Philodemos

          In the middle of the night
          I stole from my husband's bed
          And came to you, soaked with rain.
          And now, are we going to
          Sit around, and not get down
          To business, and not bill and coo,
          And love like lovers ought to love?

Here it's rose-time again, chick-peas in season,
cabbages, Sosylus, first heads of the year,
fillets of smelt, fresh-salted cheese,
tender and furled up lettuce leaves . . .
but we don't go way out to the point, Sosylus,
or picnic, as we used to, on the overlook.
Antigenes and Bacchios had the old party spirit,
but today we dump them in their graves.

Anonymous

At sixty I, Dionysios of Tarsos, lie here,
Never having married:
                            and I wish my father had
     not.

Marcus Argentarius

1

Welcome, old friend, long-necked bottle,
Dearest companion of my table
And of the winejar, with your soft gurgle
And your sweetly chuckling mouth: welcome;
You secret witness of my poverty
(Which you've done little enough to aid)
At last I hold you in my hand again.
But I wish you had come to me undiluted,
Pure as a virgin to her bridegroom's bed.

2

Lately thumbing the pages of *Works and Days,*
I saw my Pyrrhè coming.
                            Goodbye book!
"Why in the world should I cobweb my days," I
     cried,
"With the works of Old Man Hesiod?"

3

It was this way:

I'd been going for weeks with this girl,
Alkippè her name was; well, so
One night I manage to get her up to my room.
That's all right,
Though our hearts are cloppety-clopping like
     mad

Anonymous, from *Poems from the Greek Anthology,* translated and edited by Peter Jay (London: Allen Lane, 1973).

Marcus Argentarius, from *Poems from the Greek Anthology,* translated by Fleur Adcock, edited by Peter Jay (London: Allen Lane, 1973).

Leonidas of Tarentum, Anonymous and *Philodemos,* from *Poems from the Greek Anthology,* translated by Dudley Fitts (New York: New Directions, 1946), p. 588.

For fear we'll be caught together.
                                    Well,
Everything's fine, you know what I mean, when
All of a sudden the door pops
And in pokes her old mother's sheep-head:
"Remember, daughter," she bleats, "you and I
    go halves!"

Dioskorides

Hiero's former Nurse
Silenis, who liked wine
Straight & plentiful
Rests in these vine-fields,
May her old body
Buried amid vines
Feed in death the vats
She loved in life.

Meleager

Whose the hand unloosed Clearista's zone
at bride-night, in her bride-room?
Death, in guise of the bridegroom.

Evening, & flutes & clapping hands
clamour at bridal door.
At dawn the funeral wail. No more
the Hymen song. The very lights
    that lit the bridal bed
light now Clearista's journey to the dead.

Glaukos

Time was when once upon a time, such toys
As balls or pet birds won a boy, or dice.

Now it's best china, or cash. Lovers of boys,
Try something else next time. Toys cut no ice.

Krinagoras

Back from the west, back from the war, Marcellus,
carrying his loot, at the rocky frontier post
first shaved his tawny beard—as the fatherland
had wished: it sent a boy, got back a man.

Lucilius

Doubly unfortunate are those who dwell in
    Hell—
    Eutychides the Lyric Poet,
out of breath at last, has had burned with him
    twelve lyres and twenty-five
albums of songs, which poor Charon will have to
    ferry over the charcoal waters.
Alas, where will music-lovers take refuge now
    Eutychides will be singing for eternity?

Nikarchos

Agelaus was kind to Acestorides,
    who, if he'd lived, would have been lame.
Agelaus decided to operate.

REVIEW QUESTION

1. To what extent do the themes of these brief
   poems echo the concerns expressed in the writings of Epicurean and Stoic philosophers?

Dioskordes and *Melanger*, from *Poems from the Greek Anthology*, translated by Peter Wigham, edited by Peter Jay (London: Allen Lane, 1973).

Glaukos, from *Poems from the Greek Anthology*, translated and edited by Peter Jay (London: Allen Lane, 1973).

Krinagoras, from *Poems from the Greek Anthology*, translated by Alistair Elliot, edited by Peter Jay (London: Allen Lane, 1973).

Lucilius, from *Poems from the Greek Anthology*, translated by Peter Porter, edited by Peter Jay (London: Allen Lane, 1973).

Nikarchos, from *Poems from the Greek Anthology*, translated by Peter Porter, edited by Peter Jay (London: Allen Lane, 1973).

6 ∽ ROMAN CIVILIZATION

During the same period that the Greeks and Persians were doing battle at Marathon and Thermopylae and Alexander was launching his invasion of the Near East, a new power that in time was to supersede them both had begun gradually to emerge in the west. The rise of Rome is one of the most compelling stories of Western civilization: an insignificant settlement, confronted by dangerous enemies and often wracked by internal turmoil, succeeds not only in surviving but also in becoming first the master of Italy, then of the Mediterranean. In only a few centuries, Rome fashioned an empire that extended from Spain to Mesopotamia.

During the march to empire, of course, the Romans sustained casualties. Among them were their early system of government, a republic, and a society that was regulated by a strict code of law and by a tradition that emphasized respect for paternal authority and duty to family, state, and gods. In time, however, the republican system that had brought Rome to greatness was ripped apart by the demands of overseas dominion, to be replaced by rival, power-hungry generals and, eventually, by an emperor whose status, in time, went from that of princeps *("first citizen") to* dominus et deus *("lord and god"). As Roman government was inexorably changed, so Roman society and values were transformed by the massive infusion of luxury brought by imperial possessions and the influence of Greek culture and philosophical ideas on venerable Roman traditions and behavior. Indeed, of the many parallels that have been drawn between the rise of Rome and the rise of the United States to global domination two millennia later, none has been more jarring, and perhaps more potentially instructive, than the perception of decline brought by the transformation of traditional values in the wake of involvement with the outside world. For both Rome and the United States, one can discern changes brought by the influence of foreign cultures and ideas as their respective dominions expanded; in both cases, the challenge of such changes brought a response, in the form of attempts to reassert the primacy of traditional values and attitudes. This process is no-where more evident in the Roman world than in the introduction and rapid spread of Christianity and the official Roman response to it. For both Roman and U.S. societies, the balance sheet of benefits and liabilities will surely be discussed for years to come.*

Whatever the conclusions historians and others may reach in such matters, it remains indisputable that the Pax Romana (Roman peace) over which the Roman emperors presided gave Western civilization the longest period of continuous peace and stability that it had ever seen or has seen since. In the names of our months and the nine planets of our solar system, in the names of some of our important governmental institutions (senate, consulate, diocese), in the architectural style and grandeur of some of our most important public buildings, we find constant reminders that, even with its slavery, gladiatorial games, and vomitoria, the age of imperial Rome remains the great golden age of Western civilization.

FROM **The Twelve Tables**

Issued by a commission of Roman magistrates in 449 B.C.E., this codification of early Roman law was originally inscribed on twelve bronze plaques that were set up in the Forum in Rome. Our single most important source on the society and economy of early Rome, the Twelve Tables reflect, in relatively unvarnished fashion, the values that dominated life during the early years of the Roman Republic. (To borrow a modern expression, there was not much "kidding around.")

From *Roman Civilization: Selected Readings,* vol. 2, edited by Naphtali Lewis and Meyer Reinhold (New York: Columbia University Press, 1953), pp. 54–67.

Table I
Preliminaries to and Rules for a Trial

If plaintiff summons defendant to court, he shall go. If he does not go, plaintiff shall call witness thereto. Then only shall he take defendant by force.

If defendant shirks or takes to his heels, plaintiff shall lay hands on him.

If disease or age is an impediment, he [who summons defendant to court] shall grant him a team; he shall not spread with cushions the covered carriage if he does not so desire.

For a landowner, a landowner shall be surety; but for a proletarian person, let any one who is willing be his protector. . . .

When parties make a settlement of the case, the judge shall announce it. If they do not reach a settlement, they shall state the outline of their case in the meeting place or Forum before noon.

They shall plead it out together in person. After noon, the judge shall adjudge the case to the party present. If both be present, sunset shall be the time limit [of proceedings].

Table II
Further Enactments on Trials

Action under solemn deposit: 500 *as* pieces is the sum when the object of dispute under solemn deposit is valued at 1,000 in bronze or more, fifty pieces when less. Where the controversy concerns the liberty of a human being, fifty pieces shall be the solemn deposit under which the dispute should be undertaken.

If any of these be impediment for judge, referee, or party, on that account the day of trial shall be broken off.

Whoever is in need of evidence, he shall go on every third day to call out loudly before witness' doorway.

Table III
Execution; Law of Debt

When a debt has been acknowledged, or judgment about the matter has been pronounced in court, thirty days must be the legitimate time of grace. After that, the debtor may be arrested by laying on of hands. Bring him into court. If he does not satisfy the judgment, or no one in court offers himself as surety in his behalf, the creditor may take the defaulter with him. He may bind him either in stocks or in fetters; he may bind him with a weight no more than fifteen pounds, or with less if he shall so desire. The debtor, if he wishes, may live on his own. If he does not live on his own, the person who shall hold him in bonds shall give him one pound of grits for each day. He may give more if he so desires.

Unless they make a settlement, debtors shall be held in bonds for sixty days. During that time they shall be brought before the praetor's court in the meeting place on three successive market days,

and the amount for which they are judged liable shall be announced; on the third market day they shall suffer capital punishment or be delivered up for sale abroad, across the Tiber.

On the third market day creditors shall cut pieces. Should they have cut more or less than their due, it shall be with impunity.

Against a stranger, title of ownership shall hold good forever.

Table IV
Patria Potestas: Rights of Head of Family

Quickly kill . . . a dreadfully deformed child.

If a father thrice surrender a son for sale, the son shall be free from the father.

A child born ten months after the father's death will not be admitted into a legal inheritance.

Table V
Guardianship; Succession

Females shall remain in guardianship even when they have attained their majority . . . except Vestal Virgins.

Conveyable possessions of a woman under guardianship of agnates cannot be rightfully acquired by *usucapio*, save such possessions as have been delivered up by her with a guardian's sanction.

According as a person shall will regarding his [household], chattels, or guardianship of his estate, this shall be binding.

If a person dies intestate, and has no self-successor, the nearest agnate kinsman shall have possession of deceased's household.

If there is no agnate kinsman, deceased's clansmen shall have possession of his household.

To persons for whom a guardian has not been appointed by will, to them agnates are guardians.

If a man is raving mad, rightful authority over his person and chattels shall belong to his agnates or to his clansmen.

A spendthrift is forbidden to exercise administration over his own goods. . . . A person who, being insane or a spendthrift, is prohibited from administering his own goods shall be under trusteeship of agnates.

The inheritance of a Roman citizen-freedman shall be made over to his patron if the freedman has died intestate and without self-successor.

Items which are in the category of debts are not included in the division when they have with automatic right been divided into portions of an inheritance.

Debt bequeathed by inheritance is divided proportionally amongst each heir with automatic liability when the details have been investigated.

Table VI
Acquisition and Possession

When a party shall make bond or conveyance, the terms of the verbal declaration are to be held binding. ✶ ✶ ✶

A person who has been ordained a free man [in a will, on condition] that he bestow a sum of 10,000 pieces on the heir, though he has been sold by the heir, shall win his freedom by giving the money to the purchaser.

It is sufficient to make good such faults as have been named by word of mouth, and that for any flaws which the vendor had expressly denied, he shall undergo penalty of double damage. ✶ ✶ ✶

Any woman who does not wish to be subjected in this manner to the hand of her husband should be absent three nights in succession every year, ✶ ✶ ✶

A person shall not dislodge from a framework a [stolen] beam which has been fixed in buildings or a vineyard. . . . Action [is granted] for double damages against a person found guilty of fixing such [stolen] beam.

Table VII
Rights Concerning Land

Ownership within a five-foot strip [between two pieces of land] shall not be acquired by long usage.

The width of a road [extends] to eight feet where it runs straight ahead, sixteen round a bend. . . .

Persons shall mend roadways. If they do not keep them laid with stone, a person may drive his beasts where he wishes.

If rainwater does damage . . . this must be restrained according to an arbitrator's order.

If a water course directed through a public place shall do damage to a private person, he shall have right of suit to the effect that damage shall be repaired for the owner.

Branches of a tree may be lopped off all round to a height of more than 15 feet. . . . Should a tree on a neighbor's farm be bent crooked by a wind and lean over your farm, action may be taken for removal of that tree.

It is permitted to gather up fruit falling down on another man's farm.

Table VIII
Torts or Delicts

If any person has sung or composed against another person a song such as was causing slander or insult to another, he shall be clubbed to death.

If a person has maimed another's limb, let there be retaliation in kind unless he makes agreement for settlement with him.

If he has broken or bruised a freeman's bone with his hand or a club, he shall undergo penalty of 300 *as* pieces; if a slave's, 150.

If he has done simple harm [to another], penalties shall be 25 *as* pieces.

If a four-footed animal shall be said to have caused loss, legal action . . . shall be either the surrender of the thing which damaged, or else the offer of assessment for the damage.

For pasturing on, or cutting secretly by night, another's crops acquired by tillage, there shall be capital punishment in the case of an adult malefactor . . . he shall be hanged and put to death as a sacrifice to Ceres. In the case of a person under the age of puberty, at the discretion of the praetor either he shall be scourged or settlement shall be made for the harm done by paying double damages.

Any person who destroys by burning any building or heap of corn deposited alongside a house shall be bound, scourged, and put to death by burning at the stake, provided that he has committed the said misdeed with malice aforethought; but if he shall have committed it by accident, that is, by negligence, it is ordained that he repair the damage, or, if he be too poor to be competent for such punishment, he shall receive a lighter chastisement.

Any person who has cut down another person's trees with harmful intent shall pay 25 *as* pieces for every tree.

If theft has been done by night, if the owner kill the thief, the thief shall be held lawfully killed.

It is forbidden that a thief be killed by day . . . unless he defend himself with a weapon; even though he has come with a weapon, unless he use his weapon and fight back, you shall not kill him. And even if he resists, first call out.

In the case of all other thieves caught in the act, if they are freemen, they should be flogged and adjudged to the person against whom the theft has been committed, provided that the malefactors have committed it by day and have not defended themselves with a weapon; slaves caught in the act of theft should be flogged and thrown from the Rock; boys under the age of puberty should, at the praetor's discretion, be flogged, and the damage done by them should be repaired.

If a person pleads on a case in theft in which the thief has not been caught in the act, the thief must compound for the loss by paying double damages. * * *

No person shall practice usury at a rate more than one twelfth . . . A usurer is condemned for quadruple amount. * * *

If a patron shall have defrauded his client, he must be solemnly forfeited.

Whosoever shall have allowed himself to be called as witness or shall have been scales-balancer, if he does not as witness pronounce his testimony, he must be deemed dishonored and incapable of acting as witness.

Penalty . . . for false witness . . . a person who has been found guilty of giving false witness shall be hurled down from the Tarpeian Rock. . . .

No person shall hold meetings by night in the city.

Members [of associations] . . . are granted . . . the right to pass any binding rule they like for themselves provided that they cause no violation of public law.

Table IX
Public Law

*   *   *

The penalty shall be capital punishment for a judge or arbiter legally appointed who has been found guilty of receiving a bribe for giving a decision.

He who shall have roused up a public enemy, or handed over a citizen to a public enemy, must suffer capital punishment.

Putting to death . . . of any man who has not been convicted, whosoever he might be, is forbidden.

Table X
Sacred Law

A dead man shall not be buried or burned within the city.

One must not do more than this [at funerals]; one must not smooth the pyre with an axe. * * *

Women must not tear cheeks or hold chorus of "Alas!" on account of funeral.

When a man is dead one must not gather his bones in order to make a second funeral. An exception [in the case of] death in war or in a foreign land. . . .

Anointing by slaves is abolished, and every kind of drinking bout.

Let there be no costly sprinkling . . . no long garlands . . . no incense boxes. . . .

When a man wins a crown himself or through a chattel or by dint of valor, the crown bestowed on him . . . [may be laid in the grave] with impunity [on the man who won it] or on his father.

To make more than one funeral for one man and to make and spread more than one bier for him . . . this should not occur . . . and a person must not add gold. . . .

But him whose teeth shall have been fastened together with gold, if a person shall bury or burn him along with that gold, it shall be with impunity.

No new pyre or personal burning-mound must be erected nearer than sixty feet to another person's buildings without consent of the owner * * *

Table XI
Supplementary Laws

Intermarriage shall not take place between plebeians and patricians.

* * *

REVIEW QUESTIONS

1. What can you deduce from this selection about early Roman justice?
2. What are the roles and the rights of the family in early Roman law?
3. How important was corporal punishment in Roman law?

PLUTARCH

FROM *Lives*

By the early second century B.C.E., Rome's conquests outside Italy, along with its increased exposure to Greek culture, began to have a significant impact on Rome's traditional values. In particular, there began to emerge leaders whose individualistic behavior challenged ancient traditions that subjugated the interests of the individual to those of family and state. Plutarch's biography of Cato the Elder (234–149 B.C.E.), however, presents the life of a Roman leader steeped in traditional values and opposed to the inroads that Greek culture was making into Roman society.

From *Lives*, by Plutarch, translated by Bernadotte Perrin, vol. 2 (Cambridge, Mass.: Harvard University Press, 1914).

* * *

FROM Marcus Cato the Elder

The family of Marcus Cato, it is said, was of Tusculan origin, though he lived, previous to his career as soldier and statesman, on an inherited estate in the country of the Sabines. His ancestors commonly passed for men of no note whatever, but Cato himself extols his father, Marcus, as a brave man and good soldier. He also says that his grandfather, Cato, often won prizes for soldierly valour, and received from the state treasury, because of his bravery, the price of five horses which had been killed under him in battle. The Romans used to call men who had no family distinction, but were coming into public notice through their own achievements, "new men," and such they called Cato. But he himself used to say that as far as office and distinction went, he was indeed new, but having regard to ancestral deeds of valour, he was oldest of the old. His third name was not Cato at first, but Priscus. Afterwards he got the surname of Cato for his great abilities. The Romans call a man who is wise and prudent, *catus.*

* * *

His physical body—since he laboured from the very first with his own hands, held to a temperate way of life, and performed military duties —was very serviceable, vigorous, and healthy. His eloquence—a second body, as it were, and an instrument with which to perform not only necessary, but also high and noble services—he developed and perfected in the villages and towns about Rome. There he served as advocate for all who needed him, and got the reputation of being, first a zealous pleader, and then a capable orator. Thenceforth the weight and dignity of his character revealed themselves more and more to those who had dealings with him; they saw that he was bound to be a man of great affairs, and have a leading place in the state. For he not only gave his services in legal contests without fee of any sort, but did not appear to cherish even the reputation won in such contests. For he was more desirous of high reputation in battles and campaigns against the enemy, and while he was yet a mere youth had his breast covered with honourable wounds. He says himself that he made his first campaign when he was seventeen years old, at the time when Hannibal was consuming Italy with the flames of his successes.

In battle, he showed himself effective in hand combat, sure and steadfast of foot, and with a fierce expression. With threatening speech and harsh cries he would advance upon the foe, for he rightly thought, and tried to show others, that often-times such action terrifies the enemy more than does the sword. On the march, he carried his own armour on foot, while a single servant followed in charge of his camp provisions. With this man, it is said, he was never angry, and never scolded him when he served up a meal; he actually assisted in most of such preparations, provided he was free from his military duties. Water was what he drank on his campaigns, except that once in a while, in a raging thirst, he would call for vinegar, or, when his strength was failing, would add a little wine.

Near his fields was the cottage which had once belonged to Manius Curius, a hero of three triumphs. To this he would often go, and the sight of the small farm and the simple dwelling led him to think of their former owner, who, though he had become the greatest of the Romans, had subdued the most warlike nations, and driven Pyrrhus out of Italy. Nevertheless, he tilled this little patch of ground with his own hands and occupied this cottage, after three triumphs. Here it was that the ambassadors of the Samnites once found him seated at his hearth cooking turnips, and offered him much gold; but he dismissed them, saying that a man whom such a meal satisfied had no need of gold, and for his part he thought that a more honourable thing than the possession of gold was the conquest of its possessors. Cato would go away with his mind full of these things, and on viewing again his own house and lands and servants and way of life, would increase the labours of his hands and reduce his extravagances.

* * *

The influence which Cato's oratory won for him increased, and men called him a Roman Demosthenes; but his manner of life was even more talked about and carried abroad. For his oratorical ability set before young men not only a goal which many already were striving eagerly to attain, but a man who worked with his own hands, as his fathers did, and was contented with a cold breakfast, a frugal dinner, simple clothing, and a humble dwelling—one who thought more of rejecting the extras of life than of possessing them. The Roman commonwealth had now grown too large to keep its earlier integrity. The conquest of many kingdoms and peoples had brought a large mixture of customs, and the adoption of ways of life of every sort. It was natural, therefore, that men should admire Cato, when they saw that, whereas other men were broken down by labors and weakened by pleasures, he was victor over both. And this too, not only while he was still young and ambitious, but even in his old age, after consulship and triumph. Then, like some victorious athlete, he persisted in the regimen of his training, and kept his mind unaltered to the last.

He tells us that he never wore expensive clothing; that he drank the same wine as his slaves; that as for fish and meats, he would buy enough for his dinner from the public stalls—and even this for Rome's sake, that he might strengthen his body for military service. He once inherited an embroidered Babylonian robe, but sold it at once; not a single one of his farm-houses had plastered walls; he never paid much for a slave, since he did not want them to be delicately beautiful, but sturdy workers, such as grooms and herdsmen. And these he thought it his duty to sell when they got old, instead of feeding them when they were useless; and that in general, he thought nothing cheap that one could do without. He said also that he bought lands where crops were raised and cattle herded, not those where lawns were sprinkled and paths swept for pleasure.

These things were thought by some to be the result of the man's stinginess; but others excused them in the belief that he lived in this way only to correct and moderate the extravagance of others. However, for my part, I regard his treatment of his slaves like beasts of burden, using them to the utmost, and then, when they were old, driving them off and selling them, as the mark of a very mean nature, which recognizes no tie between man and man but that of profit. . . . A kindly man will take good care even of his horses when they are worn out with age, and of his dogs, too, not only in their puppyhood, but when their old age needs nursing. . . .

We should not treat living creatures like shoes or pots and pans, casting them aside when they are bruised and worn out with service; but, if for no other reason, than for the sake of practice in kindness to our fellow men, we should accustom ourselves to mildness and gentleness in our dealings with other creatures. I certainly would not sell even an ox that had worked for me, just because he was old, much less an elderly man, removing him from his habitual place and customary life, as it were from his native land, for a paltry price, useless as he is to those who sell him and as he will be to those who buy him. But Cato, boasting of such things, says that he left in Spain even the horse which had carried him through his military campaign, that he might not tax the city with the cost of its transportation home. Whether these things should be set down to greatness of spirit or littleness of mind, is an open question.

But in other matters, his self-restraint was beyond measure admirable. For instance, when he was in command of an army, he took for himself and his staff not more than three bushels of wheat a month, and for his beasts of burden, less than a bushel and a half of barley a day. He received Sardinia to govern as his province; and whereas his predecessors used to charge the public treasury for their tents, couches, and clothing, . . . his simple economy stood out in an incredible contrast. He made no demands whatever upon the public treasury, and made his circuit of the cities on foot, followed by a single public officer, who carried his robe and cup for libations to the gods. And yet, though in such matters he showed himself mild and lenient to those under his authority, in other ways he displayed a dignity and severity proper to the administration of justice. He carried out the edicts of the government in a direct and masterful way so that the Roman power never inspired its subjects with greater fear or affection.

*   *   *

He dealt with the Athenians through an interpreter. He could have spoken to them directly, but he always clung to his native ways, and mocked at those who were lost in admiration of anything that was Greek.

* * *

Ten years after his consulship, Cato was a candidate for the censorship. This office towered, as it were, above every other civic honour, and was, in a way, the high point of a political career. The variety of its powers was great, including that of examining into the lives and manners of the citizens. Its creators thought that no one should be left to his own ways and desires, without inspection and review, either in his marrying, having children, ordering his daily life, or in the entertainment of his friends. Thinking that these things revealed a man's real character more than did his public and political career, they set men in office to watch, warn, and chastise, that no one should turn to vices and give up his native and customary way of life. They chose to this office one of the so-called patricians, and one of the plebeians. These officers were called censors, and they had authority to degrade a knight, or to expel a senator who led a wild and disorderly life. They also revised the assessments of property, and arranged the citizens in lists [for military service] according to their social and political classes. There were other great powers also connected with the office.

Therefore, when Cato became a candidate, nearly all the best known and most influential men of the senatorial party united to oppose him. The men of noble parentage among them were moved by jealousy, thinking that nobility of birth would be trampled if men of lowly origin forced their way up to the summits of honour and power; while those who were conscious of base practices and of a departure from ancestral customs, feared the severity of the man, which was sure to be harsh and unyielding in the exercise of power. Therefore, after due consultation and preparation, they put up in opposition to Cato seven candidates for the office, who sought the favour of the people with promises of mild conduct in office, supposing that they wanted to be ruled with a lax and indulgent hand. Cato, on the contrary, showed no inclination to be agreeable whatever, but plainly threatened wrong-doers in his speeches, and loudly cried that the city had need of a great purification. He urged the people, if they were wise, not to choose the most agreeable physician, but the one who was most in earnest. He himself, he said, was such a physician, and so was Valerius Flaccus, of the patricians. With him as colleague, and him alone, he thought he could cut the excessive luxury and effeminacy of the time. As for the rest of the candidates, he saw that they were all trying to force their way into the office in order to administer it badly, since they feared those who would administer it well. And so truly great were the Roman voters, and so worthy of great leaders, that they did not fear Cato's rigour and haughty independence, but rejected those candidates who, it was believed, would do everything to please them, and elected Flaccus to the office along with Cato.

* * *

As censor, Cato paid not the slightest heed to his accusers, but grew still more strict. He cut off the pipes by which people conveyed part of the public water supply into their private houses and gardens; he upset and demolished all buildings that encroached on public land; he reduced the cost of public works to the lowest, and forced the rent of public lands to the highest possible figure. All these things brought much hatred upon him.

* * *

Still, it appears that the people approved of his censorship to an amazing extent. At any rate, after erecting a statue to his honour in the temple of Health, they commemorated in the inscription upon it, not the military commands nor the triumph of Cato, but, as the inscription may be translated, the fact "that when the Roman state was tottering to its fall, he was made censor, and by helpful guidance, wise restraints, and sound teachings, restored it again." . . .

* * *

He was also a good father, a considerate husband, and a household manager of no little talent;

nor did he give only a fitful attention to this, as a matter of little or no importance. Therefore, I think I ought to give suitable instances of his conduct in these relations. He married a wife who was of higher birth than she was rich, thinking that, although the rich and the high-born may be alike given to pride, still, women of high birth have such a horror of what is disgraceful that they are more obedient to their husbands in all that is honourable. He used to say that the man who struck his wife or child, laid violent hands on the holiest of holy things. Also that he thought it more praiseworthy to be a good husband than a great senator, and there was nothing more to admire in Socrates of old than that he was always kind and gentle with his shrewish wife and stupid sons. After the birth of his own son, no business could be so urgent, unless it had a public character, as to prevent him from being present when his wife bathed and wrapped the babe. For the mother nursed it herself, and often gave her breast also to the infants of her slaves, that so they might come to cherish a brotherly affection for her son. As soon as the boy showed signs of understanding, his father took him under his own charge and taught him to read, although he had an accomplished slave, Chilo by name, who was a school-teacher, and taught many boys. Still, Cato thought it not right, as he tells us himself, that his son should be scolded by a slave, or have his ears tweaked when he was slow to learn, still less that he should be indebted to his slave for such a priceless thing as education. He was therefore himself not only the boy's reading-teacher, but his tutor in law, and his athletic trainer, and he taught his son not merely to hurl the javelin and fight in armour and ride the horse, but also to box, to endure heat and cold, and to swim strongly through the eddies and billows of the Tiber. His "History of Rome," as he tells us himself, he wrote out with his own hand and in large characters, that his son might have in his own home an aid to acquaintance with his country's ancient traditions. He declares that his son's presence put him on guard against making indecencies of speech as if in the presence of the Vestal Virgins, and that he never bathed with him.

This, indeed, would seem to have been a general taboo with the Romans, for even fathers-in-law avoided bathing with their sons-in-law, because they were ashamed to uncover their nakedness. Afterwards, however, when they had learned from the Greeks their freedom in going naked before men, they in their turn infected the Greeks with the practice of doing so even before women.

* * *

He owned many slaves, and usually bought those prisoners of war who were young and still capable of being reared and trained. Not one of his slaves ever entered another man's house unless sent there by Cato or his wife, and when any of them was asked what Cato was doing, he always answered that he did not know. A slave of his was expected either to be busy about the house, or to be asleep, and he preferred the sleepy ones. He thought these gentler than the wakeful ones, and that those who had enjoyed the gift of sleep were better for any kind of service than those who lacked it. In the belief that his slaves were led into most mischief by their sexual passions, he required that the males should have sex with the female slaves of the house at a fixed price, but should never approach any other woman.

At the outset, when Cato was still poor and in military service, he found no fault at all with what was served up to him, declaring that it was shameful for a man to quarrel with a servant over food and drink. But afterwards, when his circumstances were improved and he used to entertain his friends and colleagues at table, no sooner was the dinner over than he would flog those slaves who had been unsatisfactory in preparing or serving it. He was always arranging that his slaves should have feuds and disagreements among themselves; harmony among them made him suspicious and fearful of them. He had those who were suspected of some capital offence brought to trial before all their fellow servants, and, if convicted, put to death.

* * *

He used to lend money also to those of his slaves who wished it, and they would buy boys with it, and after training and teaching them for a year, at Cato's expense, would sell them again. Many of these boys Cato would retain for himself, counting to the credit of the slave the highest price bid for his boy by outsiders. He tried to persuade his son also to such investments, by saying that it was not the part of a man, but of a widow woman, to lessen his property. But surely Cato was going too far when he said that a man should be admired and glorified like a god if the final inventory of his property showed that he had added to it more than he had inherited.

When he was now well on in years, there came as delegates from Athens to Rome, Carneades the Academic, and Diogenes the Stoic philosopher, to beg the reversal of a certain decision against the Athenian people, which imposed upon them a heavy fine. Upon the arrival of these philosophers, the most studious of the city's youth hastened to wait upon them, and became their devoted and admiring listeners. The charm of Carneades especially, which had boundless power, and a fame not inferior to its power, won large and sympathetic audiences, and filled the city, like a rushing mighty wind, with the noise of his praises. Report spread far and wide that a Greek of amazing talent, who disarmed all opposition by the magic of his eloquence, had infused a tremendous passion into the youth of the city—in consequence of which they gave up their other pleasures and pursuits and were "possessed" about philosophy. The other Romans were pleased at this, and glad to see their young men lay hold of Greek culture and associate with such admirable men. But Cato, at the very outset, when this zeal for discussion came into the city, was distressed—fearing that the young men, by giving this direction to their ambition, should come to love a reputation based on mere words more than one achieved by military deeds. And when the fame of the visiting philosophers rose yet higher in the city, and their first

speeches before the Senate were interpreted, at his own instance and request, by so conspicuous a man as Gaius Acilius, Cato determined, on some excuse or other, to rid the city of them all. So he rose in the Senate and condemned the city officials for keeping for so long a time a delegation composed of men who could easily secure anything they wished, so persuasive were they. "We ought," he said, "to make up our minds one way or another, and vote on what the delegation proposes, in order that these men may return to their schools and lecture to the sons of Greece, while the youth of Rome give ear to their laws and officials, as before."

This he did, not, as some think, out of personal hostility to Carneades, but because he was wholly opposed to philosophy, and made mock of all Greek culture and training, out of patriotic Roman zeal. He says, for instance, that Socrates was a mighty talker, who attempted, as best he could, to be his country's tyrant, by abolishing its customs, and by enticing his fellow citizens into opinions contrary to the laws. * * * And seeking to prejudice his son against Greek culture, he declared, in the tone of a prophet or a seer, that Rome would lose her empire when she had become infected with Greek literature. But time has certainly shown the emptiness of this pessimistic declaration, for while the city was at the height of its empire, she made every form of Greek learning and culture her own.

*   *   *

REVIEW QUESTIONS

1. What were the virtues that Cato prized most highly?
2. What were his reasons for opposing the spread of Greek culture?
3. How did he treat his slaves?
4. What were his attitudes toward women?

DIODORUS SICULUS

FROM *On Slavery in the Later Republic*

Rome's imperial conquests, besides exposing Roman values to alien influences, also produced a huge supply of captives who generally were reduced to slavery. The following selection describes the conditions of slaves set to work in the silver and gold mines of Spain, and then describes an especially destructive slave revolt on Sicily between 135 and 132 B.C.E.

From *On Slavery in the Later Republic, The Library of History*, vol. 3, by Diodorus Siculus, translated by C. H. Oldfather (Cambridge, Mass.: Harvard University Press, 1939), pp. 114–16.

*   *   *

. . . After the Romans had made themselves masters of Iberia, a multitude of Italians have swarmed to the mines and taken great wealth away with them, such was their greed. For they purchase a multitude of slaves whom they turn over to the overseers of the working of the mines; and these men, opening shafts in a number of places and digging deep into the ground, seek out the seams of earth which are rich in silver and gold; and not only do they go into the ground a great distance, but they also push their diggings many stades in depth and run galleries off at every angle, turning this way and that, in this manner bringing up from the depths the ore which gives them the profit they are seeking. . . .

But to continue with the mines, the slaves who are engaged in the working of them produce for their masters revenues in sums defying belief, but they themselves wear out their bodies both by day and by night in the diggings under the earth, dying in large numbers because of the exceptional hardships they endure. For no respite or pause is granted them in their labours, but compelled beneath blows of the overseers to endure the severity of their plight, they throw away their lives in this wretched manner, although certain of them who

can endure it, by virtue of their bodily strength and their persevering souls, suffer such hardships over a long period; indeed death in their eyes is more to be desired than life, because of the magnitude of the hardships they must bear.

There was never a sedition of slaves so great as that which occurred in Sicily, whereby many cities met with grave calamities, innumerable men and women, together with their children, experienced the greatest misfortunes, and all the island was in danger of falling into the power of fugitive slaves. . . .

. . . The Servile War broke out for the following reason. The Sicilians, having shot up in prosperity and acquired great wealth, began to purchase a vast number of slaves, to whose bodies, as they were brought in droves from the slave markets, they at once applied marks and brands. The young men they used as cowherds, the others in such ways as they happened to be useful. But they treated them with a heavy hand in their service, and granted them the most meagre care, the bare minimum for food and clothing. . . .

The slaves, distressed by their hardships, and frequently outraged and beaten beyond all reason, could not endure their treatment. Getting together as opportunity offered, they discussed the possibility of revolt, until at last they put their plans into action. . . . The beginning of the whole revolt took place as follows.

There was a certain Damophilus of Enna, a man of great wealth but insolent of manner; he had abused his slaves to excess, and his wife Megallis vied even with her husband in punishing the slaves and in her general inhumanity towards them. The slaves, reduced by this degrading treatment to the level of brutes, conspired to revolt and to murder their masters. Going to Eunus they asked him whether their resolve had the favour of the gods. He, resorting to his usual mummery, promised them the favour of the gods, and soon persuaded them to act at once. Immediately, therefore, they brought together four hundred of their fellow slaves and, having armed themselves in such ways as opportunity permitted, they fell upon the city of Enna, with Eunus at their head and working his miracle of the flames of fire for their benefit. When they found their way into the houses they shed much blood, sparing not even suckling babes. Rather they tore them from the breast and dashed them to the ground, while as for the women—and under their husbands' very eyes—but words cannot tell the extent of their outrages and acts of lewdness! By now a great multitude of slaves from the city had joined them, who, after first demonstrating against their own masters their utter ruthlessness, then turned to the slaughter of others. When Eunus and his men learned that Damophilus and his wife were in the garden that lay near the city, they sent some of their band and dragged them off, both the man and his wife, fettered and with hands bound behind their backs, subjecting them to many outrages along the way. Only in the case of the couple's daughter were the slaves seen to show consideration throughout, and this was because of her kindly nature, in that to the extent of her power she was always compassionate and ready to succour the slaves. Thereby it was demonstrated that the others were treated as they were, not because of some "natural savagery of slaves," but rather in revenge for wrongs previously received.

The men appointed to the task, having dragged Damophilus and Megallis into the city, as we said, brought them to the theatre, where the crowd of rebels had assembled. But when Damophilus attempted to devise a plea to get them off safe and was winning over many of the crowd with his words, Hermeias and Zeuxis, men bitterly disposed towards him, denounced him as a cheat, and without waiting for a formal trial by the assembly the one ran him through the chest with a sword, the other chopped off his head with an axe. Thereupon Eunus was chosen king, not for his manly courage or his ability as a military leader, but solely for his marvels and his setting of the revolt in motion. . . .

Established as the rebels' supreme commander, he called an assembly and put to death all the citizenry of Enna except for those who were skilled in the manufacture of arms: these he put in chains and assigned them to this task. He gave Megallis to the maidservants to deal with as they might wish; they subjected her to torture and threw her over a precipice. He himself murdered his own masters, Antigenes and Pytho. Having set a diadem upon his head, and arrayed himself in full royal style, he proclaimed his wife queen (she was a fellow Syrian and of the same city) and appointed to the royal council such men as seemed to be gifted with superior intelligence. . . .

. . . In three days Eunus had armed, as best he could, more than six thousand men, besides others in his train who had only axes and hatchets, or slings, or sickles, or fire-hardened stakes, or even kitchen spits; and he went about ravaging the countryside. Then, since he kept recruiting untold numbers of slaves, he ventured even to do battle with Roman generals, and on joining combat repeatedly overcame them with his superior numbers, for he now had more than ten thousand soldiers.

Soon after, engaging in battle with a general arrived from Rome, Lucius Hypsaeus, who had eight thousand Sicilian troops, the rebels were victorious, since they now numbered twenty thousand. Before long their band reached a total of two hundred thousand, and in numerous battles with the Romans they acquitted themselves well, and failed but seldom. As word of this was bruited about, a revolt of one hundred and fifty slaves, banded together, flared up in Rome, of more than a thousand in Attica, and of yet others in Delos and many other places. But thanks to the speed with which forces were brought up and to the severity of their punitive measures, the magistrates of these communities at once disposed of the rebels and brought to their senses any who were wavering on the verge of revolt. In Sicily, however, the trouble grew. Cities were captured with all their inhabitants, and many armies were cut to pieces by the rebels, until Rupilius, the Roman commander, recovered Tauromenium for the Romans by placing it under strict siege and confining the rebels under conditions of unspeakable duress and famine: conditions such that, beginning by eating the children, they progressed to the women, and did not altogether abstain even from eating one another. . . .

Finally, after Sarapion, a Syrian, had betrayed the citadel, the general laid hands on all the runaway slaves in the city, whom, after torture, he threw over a cliff. From there he advanced to Enna, which he put under siege in much the same manner, bringing the rebels into extreme straits and frustrating their hopes. . . . Rupilius captured this city also by betrayal, since its strength was impregnable to force of arms. Eunus, taking with him his bodyguards, a thousand strong, fled in unmanly fashion. . . .

. . . He met such an end as befitted his knavery, and died at Morgantina. Thereupon Rupilius, traversing the whole of Sicily with a few picked troops, sooner than had been expected rid it of every nest of robbers.

* * *

REVIEW QUESTIONS

1. According to Diodorus, to what kinds of treatment were slaves subjected in the second century B.C.E.?
2. How does Cato the Elder's treatment of his slaves compare with the conditions of slaves in the mines?

CICERO

FROM *On the Laws*

Whereas Cato the Elder epitomizes the traditionalists' resistance to the advances of Greek culture in the late Roman Republic, Cicero (106–43 B.C.E.) is that era's foremost representative of Greek ideals. A foremost legal expert and compelling orator, he was a leading political figure during the era of the rise of Julius Caesar and was eventually executed after Caesar's assassination for advocating the restoration of the power of the Roman Senate. His most significant influence on the later Western intellectual tradition, however, lies in his prolific production as a writer. It was largely through his works that Greco-Roman thought was transmitted to later eras. The fol-

lowing selection is from Cicero's On the Laws, *in which, through the mechanism of dialogue that was used so well by earlier Greek philosophers, he propounds his concept of the ideal state.*

From *De Legibus* (*On the Laws*), by Cicero, translated by Clinton W. Keyes (Cambridge, Mass.: Harvard University Press, 1928), pp. 311–91.

*   *   *

ATTICUS. Yet if you ask what I expect of you, I consider it a logical thing that, since you have already written a treatise on the constitution of the ideal State, you should also write one on its laws. For I note that this was done by your beloved Plato, whom you admire, revere above all others, and love above all others.

MARCUS. Is it your wish, then, that, as he discussed the institutions of States and the ideal laws, . . . sometimes walking about, sometimes resting —you recall his description—we, in like manner, strolling or taking our ease among these stately poplars on the green and shady river bank, shall discuss the same subjects along somewhat broader lines than the practice of the courts calls for? * * *

MARCUS. And you are wise, for you must understand that in no other kind of discussion can one bring out so clearly what Nature's gifts to man are, what a wealth of most excellent possessions the human mind enjoys, what the purpose is, to strive after and accomplish which we have been born and placed in this world, what it is that unites men, and what natural fellowship there is among them. For it is only after all these things have been made clear that the origin of Law and Justice can be discovered.

ATTICUS. Then you do not think that the science of law is to be derived from the praetor's edict, as the majority do now, or from the Twelve Tables, as people used to think, but from the deepest mysteries of philosophy?

MARCUS. Quite right; for in our present conversation, Pomponius, we are not trying to learn how to protect ourselves legally, or how to answer clients' questions. Such problems may be important, and in fact they are; for in former times

many eminent men made a specialty of their solution, and at present one person performs this duty with the greatest authority and skill. But in our present investigation we intend to cover the whole range of universal Justice and Law in such a way that our own civil law, as it is called, will be confined to a small and narrow corner. For we must explain the nature of Justice, and this must be sought for in the nature of man; we must also consider the laws by which States ought to be governed; then we must deal with the enactments and decrees of nations which are already formulated and put in writing; and among these the civil law, as it is called, of the Roman people will not fail to find a place. * * *

MARCUS. . . . now let us investigate the origins of Justice.

Well then, the most learned men have determined to begin with Law, and it would seem that they are right, if, according to their definition, Law is the highest reason, implanted in Nature, which commands what ought to be done and forbids the opposite. This reason, when firmly fixed and fully developed in the human mind, is Law. And so they believe that Law is intelligence, whose natural function it is to command right conduct and forbid wrongdoing. . . . Now if this is correct, as I think it to be in general, then the origin of Justice is to be found in Law, for Law is a natural force; it is the mind and reason of the intelligent man, the standard by which Justice and Injustice are measured. But since our whole discussion has to do with the reasoning of the populace, it will sometimes be necessary to speak in the popular manner, and give the name of law to that which in written form decrees whatever it wishes, either by command or prohibition. For such is the crowd's definition of law. But in determining what

Justice is, let us begin with that supreme Law which had its origin ages before any written law existed or any State had been established. ⁎ ⁎ ⁎

⁎   ⁎   ⁎

MARCUS. I will not make the argument long. Your admission leads us to this: that animal which we call man, endowed with foresight and quick intelligence, complex, keen, possessing memory, full of reason and prudence, has been given a certain distinguished status by the supreme God who created him; for he is the only one among so many different kinds and varieties of living beings who has a share in reason and thought, while all the rest are deprived of it. But what is more divine, I will not say in man only, but in all heaven and earth, than reason? And reason, when it is full grown and perfected, is rightly called wisdom. Therefore, since there is nothing better than reason, and since it exists both in man and God, the first common possession of man and God is reason. But those who have reason in common must also have right reason in common. And since right reason is Law, we must believe that men have Law also in common with the gods. Further, those who share Law must also share Justice; and those who share these are to be regarded as members of the same commonwealth. If indeed they obey the same authorities and powers, this is true in a far greater degree; but as a matter of fact they do obey this celestial system, the divine mind, and the God of transcendent power. Hence we must now conceive of this whole universe as one commonwealth of which both gods and men are members.

⁎   ⁎   ⁎

MARCUS. The points which are now being briefly touched upon are certainly important; but out of all the material of the philosophers' discussions, surely there comes nothing more valuable than the full realization that we are born for Justice, and that right is based, not upon men's opinions, but upon Nature. This fact will immediately be plain if you once get a clear conception of man's fellowship and union with his fellow-men. For no single thing is so like another, so exactly its counterpart, as all of us are to one another. Nay, if bad habits and false beliefs did not twist the weaker minds and turn them in whatever direction they are inclined, no one would be so like his own self as all men would be like all others. And so, however we may define man, a single definition will apply to all. This is a sufficient proof that there is no difference in kind between man and man; for if there were, one definition could not be applicable to all men; and indeed reason, which alone raises us above the level of the beasts and enables us to draw inferences, to prove and disprove, to discuss and solve problems, and to come to conclusions, is certainly common to us all, and, though varying in what it learns, at least in the capacity to learn it is invariable. For the same things are invariably perceived by the senses, and those things which stimulate the senses, stimulate them in the same way in all men; and those rudimentary beginnings of intelligence to which I have referred, which are imprinted on our minds, are imprinted on all minds alike; and speech, the mind's interpreter, though differing in the choice of words, agrees in the sentiments expressed. In fact, there is no human being of any race who, if he finds a guide, cannot attain to virtue.

⁎   ⁎   ⁎

MARCUS. The next point, then, is that we are so constituted by Nature as to share the sense of Justice with one another and to pass it on to all men. And in this whole discussion I want it understood that what I shall call Nature is that which is implanted in us by Nature; that, however, the corruption caused by bad habits is so great that the sparks of fire, so to speak, which Nature has kindled in us are extinguished by this corruption, and the vices which are their opposites spring up and are established. But if the judgments of men were in agreement with Nature, so that . . . they considered "nothing alien to them which concerns mankind," then Justice would be equally observed by all. For those creatures who have received the gift of reason from Nature have also received right reason, and therefore they have also received the gift of Law, which is right reason applied to command and prohibition. And if they have received Law, they have received Justice also. Now all men have received reason; therefore all men have received Justice. . . .

Now all this is really a preface to what remains to be said in our discussion, and its purpose is to make it more easily understood that Justice is inherent in Nature. After I have said a few words more on this topic, I shall go on to the civil law, the subject which gives rise to all this discourse. . . .

But you see the direction this conversation is to take; our whole discourse is intended to promote the firm foundation of States, the strengthening of cities, and the curing of the ills of peoples. For that reason I want to be especially careful not to lay down first principles that have not been wisely considered and thoroughly investigated. Of course I cannot expect that they will be universally accepted, for that is impossible; but I do look for the approval of all who believe that everything which is right and honourable is to be desired for its own sake, and that nothing whatever is to be accounted a good unless it is praiseworthy in itself, or at least that nothing should be considered a great good unless it can rightly be praised for its own sake.

* * *

MARCUS. Once more, then, before we come to the individual laws, let us look at the character and nature of Law, for fear that, though it must be the standard to which we refer everything, we may now and then be led astray by an incorrect use of terms, and forget the rational principles on which our laws must be based.

QUINTUS. Quite so, that is the correct method of exposition.

MARCUS. Well, then, I find that it has been the opinion of the wisest men that Law is not a product of human thought, nor is it any enactment of peoples, but something eternal which rules the whole universe by its wisdom in command and prohibition. Thus they have been accustomed to say that Law is the primal and ultimate mind of God, whose reason directs all things either by

compulsion or restraint. Wherefore that Law which the gods have given to the human race has been justly praised; for it is the reason and mind of a wise lawgiver applied to command and prohibition.

* * *

MARCUS. So in the very beginning we must persuade our citizens that the gods are the lords and rulers of all things, and that what is done, is done by their will and authority; that they are likewise great benefactors of man, observing the character of every individual, what he does, of what wrong he is guilty, and with what intentions and with what piety he fulfils his religious duties; and that they take note of the pious and the impious. For surely minds which are imbued with such ideas will not fail to form true and useful opinions. Indeed, what is more true than that no one ought to be so foolishly proud as to think that, though reason and intellect exist in himself, they do not exist in the heavens and the universe, or that those things which can hardly be understood by the highest reasoning powers of the human intellect are guided by no reason at all? In truth, the man that is not driven to gratitude by the orderly courses of the stars, the regular alternation of day and night, the gentle progress of the seasons, and the produce of the earth brought forth for our sustenance—how can such an one be accounted a man at all? And since all things that possess reason stand above those things which are without reason, and since it would be sacrilege to say that anything stands above universal Nature, we must admit that reason is inherent in Nature. Who will deny that such beliefs are useful when he remembers how often oaths are used to confirm agreements, how important to our well-being is the sanctity of treaties, how many persons are deterred from crime by the fear of divine punishment, and how sacred an association of citizens becomes when the immortal gods are made members of it, either as judges or as witnesses?

REVIEW QUESTIONS

1. According to Cicero, what is the source of all law?

2. What is the relationship of civil law to law as Cicero defines it?

3. Do you find in this selection any evidence of a Stoic concept of universal human brotherhood and equality?

JUVENAL

FROM *The Sixteen Satires*

As Rome's power and wealth increased, the values and concerns of its people were affected and transformed. The next three readings testify, in one way or another, to that transformation. The first selection, which is drawn from the "Third" and "Sixth Satires" of Juvenal (ca. 55–130 C.E.), sharply criticizes the excessive wealth and growing corruption of Roman society.

From *The Sixteen Satires,* by Juvenal, translated by Peter Green (New York: Penguin Books, 1974), pp. 87–91, 142–44.

*   *   *

Yet a musical wife's not so bad as some presumptuous
Flat-chested busybody who rushes around the town
Gate-crashing all-male meetings, talking back straight-faced
To a uniformed general—*and* in her husband's presence.
She knows all the news of the world, what's cooking in Thrace
Or China, just what the stepmother did with her stepson
Behind closed doors, who's fallen in love, which gallant
Is all the rage. She'll tell you who got the widow
Pregnant, and in which month; she knows each woman's
Pillow endearments, and all the positions she favors.

She's the first to spot any comet presaging trouble
For some eastern prince, in Armenia, maybe, or Parthia.
She's on to the latest gossip and rumors as soon as
They reach the city-gates, or invents her own, informing
Everyone she meets that Niphates has overflowed
And is inundating whole countries—towns are cut off,
She says, and the land is sinking: flood and disaster!
    Yet even this is not so insufferable
As her habit, when woken up, of grabbing some poor-class
Neighbor and belting into him with a whip. If her precious
Sleep is broken by barking, "Fetch me the cudgels,"
She roars, "and be quick about it!" The dog gets a thrashing,
But its master gets one first. She's no joke to cross,

A SCENE FROM A ROMAN-ERA ITALIAN HARBOR (C. 80 C.E.)

This scene is from a wall painting discovered at the small town of Stabiae, near Pompeii, which was destroyed by the eruption of Mt. Vesuvius in 79 C.E. What does this reflect about the organization and sophistication of maritime trade in the Roman Empire? Was much expense devoted to the construction and decoration of the harbor's facilities? Why might such a painting have been commissioned?

And her face is a grisly fright. Not till the evening
Does she visit the baths: only then are her oil-
    jars and
The rest of her clobber transferred there. First
    she works out
With the weights and dumb-bells. Then, when
    her arms are aching,
The masseur takes over, craftily slipping one hand
Along her thigh, and tickling her up till she comes.
Lastly she makes for the sweat-room. She loves
    to sit there
Amid all that hubbub, perspiring. Meanwhile at
    home
Her unfortunate guests are nearly dead with
    hunger.
At last she appears, all flushed, with a three-
    gallon thirst,
Enough to empty the brimming jar at her
    feet
Without assistance. She knocks back two straight
    pints
On an empty stomach, to sharpen her appetite:
    then
Throws it all up again, souses the floor with
    vomit
That flows in rivers across the terrazzo. She
    drinks
And spews by turns, like some big snake that's
    tumbled
Into a wine-vat, till her gilded jordan brims
Right over with sour and vinous slops. Quite
    sickened,
Eyes shut, her husband somehow holds down his
    bile.
    Worse still is the well-read menace, who's
    hardly settled for dinner
Before she starts praising Virgil, making a moral
    case
For Dido (death justifies all), comparing,
    evaluating
Rival poets, Virgil and Homer suspended
In opposite scales, weighed up one against the
    other.
Critics surrender, academics are routed, all
Fall silent, not a word from lawyer or
    auctioneer—

Or even another woman. Such a rattle of talk,
You'd think all the poets and bells were being
    clashed together
When the moon's in eclipse. . . .
                    So avoid a dinner-partner
With an argumentative style, who hurls well-
    rounded
Syllogisms like slingshots, who has all history
    pat:
Choose someone rather who doesn't understand
    all she reads.
I hate these authority-citers, the sort who are
    always thumbing
Some standard grammatical treatise, whose every
    utterance
Observes all the laws of syntax, who with
    antiquarian zeal
Quote poets I've never heard of. Such matters
    are men's concern.
If she wants to correct someone's language, she
    can always
Start with her unlettered girl-friends.

                    *   *   *

From here we strolled down
To the nymph's new, modernized grotto. (What
    a gain in sanctity
And atmosphere there would be if grassy banks
Surrounded the pool, if no flash marble
    affronted
Our native limestone!) Here Umbricius stood,
    and
Opened his heart to me.
"There's no room in this city,"
He said, "for the decent professions: they don't
    show any profit.
My resources have shrunk since yesterday, and
    tomorrow
Will eat away more of what's left. So I am going
Where Daedalus put off his weary wings, while
    as yet
I'm in vigorous middle age, while active years
    are left me,
While my white hairs are still few, and I need no
    stick

To guide my tottering feet. So farewell Rome, I
 leave you
To sanitary engineers and municipal architects,
 men
Who by swearing black is white land all the juicy
 contracts
Just like that—a new temple, swamp-drainage,
 harbour-works,
River-clearance, undertaking, the lot—then
 pocket the cash
And fraudulently file their petition in
 bankruptcy.
Once these fellows were horn-players, stumping
 the provinces
In road-shows, their puffed-out cheeks a familiar
 sight
To every country village. But now they stage
 shows themselves,
Of the gladiatorial sort, and at the mob's
 thumbs-down
Will butcher a loser for popularity's sake, and
Pass on from that to erecting public privies.
 Why not?
These are such men as Fortune, by way of a
 joke,
Will sometimes raise from the gutter and make
 Top People.
What can I do in Rome? I never learnt how
To lie. If a book is bad, I cannot puff it, or
 bother
To ask around for a copy; astrological clap-trap
Is not in my stars. I cannot and will not promise
To encompass any man's death by way of
 obliging his son.
I have never meddled with frogs' guts; the task
 of carrying
Letters and presents between adulterous lovers
I resign to those who know it. I refuse to
 become
An accomplice in theft—which means that no
 governor
Will accept me on his staff. It's like being a
 cripple
With a paralysed right hand. Yet who today is
 favoured

Above the conspirator, his head externally
 seething
With confidential matters, never to be revealed?
Harmless secrets carry no obligations, and he
Who shares them with you feels no great call
 thereafter
To keep you sweet. But if Verres promotes a
 man
You can safely assume that man has the screws
 on Verres
And could turn him in tomorrow. Not all the
 gold
Washed seaward with the silt of tree-lined Tagus
Is worth the price you pay, racked by insomnia,
 seeing
Your high-placed friends all cringe at your
 approach—and
For what? Too-transient prizes, unwillingly
 resigned."
    "Now let me turn to that race which goes
    down so well
With our millionaires, but remains *my* special
 pet aversion,
And not mince my words. I cannot, citizens,
 stomach
A Greek-struck Rome. Yet what fraction of these
 sweepings
Derives, in fact, from Greece? For years now
 Syrian
Orontes has poured its sewerage into our native
 Tiber—
Its lingo and manners, its flutes, its outlandish
 harps
With their transverse strings, its native
 tambourines,
And the whores who hang out round the race-
 course. (That's where to go
If you fancy a foreign piece in one of those
 saucy toques.)
Our beloved Founder should see how his
 homespun rustics
Behave today, with their dinner-pumps—
 trechedipna
They call them—not to mention their
 niceteria

(Decorations to you) hung round their *ceromatic* (that's
Well-greased) wrestlers' necks. Here's one from Sicyon,
Another from Macedonia, two from Aegean islands—
Andros, say, or Samos—two more from Caria,
All of them lighting out for the City's classiest districts
And burrowing into great houses, with a long-term plan
For taking them over. Quick wit, unlimited nerve, a gift
Of the gab that outsmarts a professional public speaker—
These are their characteristics. What do you take
That fellow's profession to be? He has brought a whole bundle
Of personalities with him—schoolmaster, rhetorician,
Surveyor, artist, masseur, diviner, tightrope-walker,
Magician or quack, your versatile hungry Greekling
Is all by turns. Tell him to fly—he's airborne.
The inventor of wings was no Moor or Slav, remember,
Or Thracian, but born in the very heart of Athens."
  "When such men as these wear the purple, when some creature
Blown into Rome along with the figs and damsons
Precedes me at dinner-parties, or for the witnessing
Of manumissions and wills—*me,* who drew my first breath
On these Roman hills, and was nourished on Sabine olives!—
Things have reached a pretty pass. What's more, their talent
For flattery is unmatched. They praise the conversation
Of their dimmest friends; the ugly they call handsome,

So that your scrag-necked weakling finds himself compared
To Hercules holding the giant Antaeus aloft
Way off the earth. They go into ecstasies over
Some shrill and scrannel voice that sounds like a hen
When the cock gets at her. We can make the same compliments, but
It's they who convince. On the stage they remain supreme
In female parts, courtesan, matron or slave-girl,
With no concealing cloak: you'd swear it was a genuine
Woman you saw, and not a masked performer.
Look there, beneath that belly: no bulge, all smooth, a neat
Nothingness—even a hint of the Great Divide. Yet back home
These queens and dames pass unnoticed. Greece is a nation
Of actors. Laugh, and they split their sides. At the sight
Of a friend's tears, they weep too—though quite unmoved.
If you ask for a fire in winter, the Greek puts on his cloak;
If you say 'I'm hot,' *he* starts sweating. So you see
We are not on an equal footing: he has the great advantage
Of being able on all occasions, night and day,
To take his cue, his mask, from others. He's always ready
To throw up his hands and applaud when a friend delivers
A really resounding belch, or pisses right on the mark,
With a splendid drumming sound from the upturned golden basin."
  "Besides, he holds nothing sacred, not a soul is safe
From his randy urges, the lady of the house, her
Virgin daughter, her daughter's still unbearded
Husband-to-be, her hitherto virtuous son—

And if none of these are to hand, he'll cheerfully
    lay
His best friend's grandmother. (Anything to
    ferret
Domestic secrets out, and get a hold over
    people.)"
    "And while we are on the subject of Greeks,
    let us consider
Academics and their vices—not the gymnasium
    crowd
But big philosophical wheels, like that Stoic
    greybeard
Who narked on his friend and pupil, and got
    him liquidated.
He was brought up in Tarsus, by the banks of
    that river
Where Bellerophon fell to earth from the
    Gorgon's flying nag.
No room for honest Romans when Rome's ruled
    by a junta
Of Greek-born secret agents, who—like all their
    race—
Never share friends or patrons. One small dose
    of venom
(Half Greek, half personal) dropped in that
    ready ear
And I'm out, shown the back-door, my years of
    obsequious
Service all gone for nothing. Where can a
    hanger-on
Be ditched with less fuss than in Rome?

       *   *   *

               Here a citizen, free-born,
Must stand aside on the pavement for some
    wealthy tycoon's slave:
He can afford to squander a senior officer's
    income
On classy amateur harlots, just for the privilege
Of laying them once or twice. But when *you*
    fancy
A common-or-garden tart, you dither and
    hesitate:
Can I afford to accost her?

       *   *   *

The poor man's an eternal
Butt for bad jokes, with his torn and dirt-caked
    top-coat,
His grubby toga, one shoe agape where the
    leather's
Split—those clumsy patches, that coarse and tell-
    tale stitching
Only a day or two old. The hardest thing to bear
In poverty is the fact that it makes us ridiculous.
"Out of those front-row seats," we're told. "You
    ought to be
Ashamed of yourselves—your incomes are far
    too small, and
The law's the law. Make way for some pander's
    son,
Spawned in an unknown brothel, let your place
    be occupied
By that natty auctioneer's offspring, with his
    high-class companions
The trainer's brat and the son of the gladiator
Applauding beside him." Such were the fruits of
    that pinhead
Otho's Reserved Seat Act. What prospective son-
    in-law
Ever passed muster here if he was short on cash
To match the girl's dowry? What poor man ever
    inherits
A legacy, or is granted that meanest of
    sinecures—
A job with the Office of Works? All lower-
    income citizens
Should have marched out of town, in a body,
    years ago.
Nobody finds it easy to get to the top if meagre
Resources cripple his talent. But in Rome the
    problem's worse
Than anywhere else. Inflation hits the rental
Of your miserable apartment, inflation distends
The ravenous maws of your slaves; your humble
    dinner
Suffers inflation too. You feel ashamed to eat
Off earthenware dishes—yet if you were
    transported

To some rural village, you'd be content enough
And happily wear a cloak of coarse blue
　　broadcloth
Complete with hood. Throughout most of Italy
　　—we
Might as well admit it—no one is seen in a toga
Till the day he dies. Even on public holidays,
When the same old shows as last year are
　　cheerfully staged
In the grassgrown theatre, when peasant
　　children, sitting
On their mothers' laps, shrink back in terror at
　　the sight
Of those gaping, whitened masks, you will still
　　find the whole
Audience—top row or bottom—dressed exactly
　　alike;
Even the magistrates need no better badge of
　　status
Than a plain white tunic. But here in Rome we
　　must toe
The line of fashion, living beyond our means,
　　and
Often on borrowed credit: every man jack of us
Is keeping up with his neighbours. To cut a long
　　story short,
Nothing's for free in Rome. ∗ ∗ ∗
　　"What countryman ever bargained, besides,
　　　for his house collapsing
About his ears? Such things are unheard-of in
　　cool
Praeneste, or rural Gabii, or Tivoli perched on
　　its hillside,
Or Volsinii, nestling amid its woodland ridges.
　　But here
We live in a city shored up, for the most part,
　　with gimcrack
Stays and props: that's how our landlords arrest
The collapse of their property, papering over
　　great cracks
In the ramshackle fabric, reassuring the
　　tenants
They can sleep secure, when all the time the
　　building

Is poised like a house of cards. I prefer to live
　　where
Fires and midnight panics are not quite such
　　common events.
By the time the smoke's got up to your third-
　　floor apartment
(And you still asleep) your downstairs neighbour
　　is roaring
For water, and shifting his bits and pieces to
　　safety.
If the alarm goes at ground-level, the last to fry
Will be the attic tenant, way up among the
　　nesting
Pigeons, with nothing but tiles between himself
　　and the weather.
What did friend Cordus own? One truckle bed,
　　too short
For even a midget nympho; one marble-topped
　　sideboard
On which stood six little mugs; beneath it, a
　　pitcher
And an up-ended bust of Chiron; one ancient
　　settle
Crammed with Greek books (though by now
　　analphabetic mice
Had gnawed their way well into his texts of the
　　great poets).
Cordus could hardly be called a property-owner,
　　and yet
What little the poor man had, he lost. Today the
　　final
Straw on his load of woe (clothes worn to
　　tatters, reduced
To begging for crusts) is that no one will offer
　　him lodging
Or shelter, not even stand him a decent meal.
　　But if
Some millionaire's mansion is gutted, women
　　rend their garments,
Top people put on mourning, the courts go into
　　recess:
Then you hear endless complaints about the
　　hazards
Of city life, these deplorable outbreaks of fire;

Then contributions pour in while the shell is still
  ash-hot—
Construction materials, marble, fresh-gleaming
  sculptured nudes.
Up comes A with bronzes (genuine antique
  works
By a real Old Master) acquired, as part of his
  booty,
From their hallowed niche in some Asiatic
  temple;
B provides bookshelves, books, and a study bust
  of Minerva;
C a sackful of silver. So it goes on, until
This dandified bachelor's losses are all
  recouped—
And more than recouped—with even rarer
  possessions,
And a rumour (well-founded) begins to circulate
That he fired the place himself, a deliberate piece
  of arson."

*   *   *

"Insomnia causes more deaths amongst
  Roman invalids
Than any other factor (the most common
  complaints, of course,
Are heartburn and ulcers, brought on by over-
  eating.)
How much sleep, I ask you, can one get in
  lodgings here?
Unbroken nights—and this is the root of the
  trouble—
Are a rich man's privilege. The waggons
  thundering past
Through those narrow twisting streets, the oaths
  of draymen
Caught in a traffic-jam—these alone would
  suffice
To jolt the doziest sea-cow of an Emperor into
Permanent wakefulness. If a business
  appointment
Summons the tycoon, *he* gets there fast, by litter,
Tacking above the crowd. There's plenty of
  room inside:

He can read, or take notes, or snooze as he jogs
  along—
Those drawn blinds are most soporific. Even so
He outstrips us: however fast we pedestrians
  hurry
We're blocked by the crowds ahead, while those
  behind us
Tread on our heels. Sharp elbows buffet my ribs,
Poles poke into me; one lout swings a crossbeam
Down on my skull, another scores with a barrel.
My legs are mud-encrusted, big feet kick me, a
  hobnailed
Soldier's boot lands squarely on my toes. Do you
  see
All that steam and bustle? The great man's
  hangers-on
Are getting their free dinner, each with his own
Kitchen-boy in attendance. Those outsize dixies,
And all the rest of the gear one poor little slave
Must balance on his head, while he trots along
To keep the charcoal glowing, would tax the
  strength
Of a musclebound general. Recently-patched
  tunics
Are ripped to shreds. Here's the great trunk of a
  fir-tree
Swaying along on its waggon, and look, another
  dray
Behind it, stacked high with pine-logs, a nodding
  threat
Over the heads of the crowd. If that axle
  snapped, and a
Cartload of marble avalanched down on them,
  what
Would be left of their bodies? Who could
  identify bits
Of ownerless flesh and bone? The poor man's
  flattened corpse
Would vanish along with his soul. And
  meanwhile, all unwitting,
The folk at home are busily scouring dishes,
Blowing the fire to a glow, clattering over
  greasy
Flesh-scrapers, filling up oil-flasks, laying out
  clean towels.

But all the time, as his houseboys hasten about
   their chores,
Himself is already sitting—the latest arrival—
By the bank of the Styx, and gawping in holy
   terror
At its filthy old ferryman. No chance of a
   passage over
That mud-thick channel for him, poor devil,
   without so much
As a copper stuck in his mouth to pay for the
   ride."
   "There are other nocturnal perils, of various
   sorts,
Which you should consider. It's a long way up
   to the rooftops,
And a falling tile can brain you—not to
   mention all
Those cracked or leaky pots that people toss out
   through windows.
Look at the way they smash, the weight of them,
   the damage
They do to the pavement! You'll be thought
   most improvident,
A catastrophe-happy fool, if you don't make
   your will before
Venturing out to dinner. Each open upper
   casement
Along your route at night may prove a death-
   trap:
So pray and hope (poor you!) that the local
   housewives
Drop nothing worse on your head than a pailful
   of slops."
   Then there's the drunken bully, in an
   agonized state
For lack of a victim, who lies there tossing and
   turning
The whole night through, like Achilles after the
   death
Of his boy-friend Patroclus. [This lout is
   doomed to insomnia
Unless he gets a fight.] Yet however flown with
   wine
Our young hothead may be, he carefully keeps
   his distance

From the man in a scarlet cloak, the man
   surrounded
By torches and big brass lamps and a numerous
   bodyguard.
But for me, a lonely pedestrian, trudging home
   by moonlight
Or with hand cupped round the wick of one
   poor guttering candle,
He has no respect whatever. This is the way the
   wretched
Brawl comes about (if you can term it a brawl
When you do the fighting and I'm just cast as
   punchbag).
He blocks my way. "Stop," he says. I have no
   option
But to obey—what else can one do when
   attacked
By a huge tough, twice one's size and fighting-
   mad as well?
   "Where have *you* sprung from?" he shouts.
   "Ugh, what a stench
Of beans and sour wine! I know your sort,
   you've been round
With some cobbler-crony, scoffing a boiled
   sheep's head
And a dish of spring leeks. What? Nothing to
   say for yourself?
Speak up, or I'll kick your teeth in! Tell me,
   where's your pitch?
What synagogue do you doss in?" It makes not
   a jot of difference
Whether you try to answer, or back away from
   him
Without saying a word, you get beaten up just
   the same—
And then your irate "victim" takes *you* to court
   on a charge
Of assault and battery. Such is the poor man's
   "freedom":
After being slugged to a pulp, he may beg, as a
   special
Favour, to be left with his last few remaining
   teeth.

*   *   *

REVIEW QUESTIONS

1. On the basis of this selection, what were some of the major dangers and irritations of life in Rome?

2. What is Juvenal's attitude toward the bearers of Greek culture?

3. What kinds of women do his satires deal with?

OVID

FROM *The Loves*

Written in a style in distinct contrast to Juvenal's biting satires, Ovid's works about love (or lust) reflect what some might regard as a certain shallowness in Roman social relations. Eventually, Emperor Augustus found his work so morally repugnant that he banished Ovid from Rome.

From *Amores*, by Ovid, translated by Guy Lee (London: John Murray, 1968), pp. 728–31.

*   *   *

Your husband? Going to the same dinner as us?
I hope it chokes him.

So I'm only to gaze at you, darling? Play
     gooseberry
while another man enjoys your touch?

You'll lie there snuggling up to him? He'll put
     his arm
round your neck whenever he wants?

No wonder Centaurs fought over Hippodamia
when the wedding wine began to flow.

I don't live in the forest nor am I part horse
but I find it hard to keep my hands off you.

However here's my plan. Listen carefully.
Don't throw my words of wisdom to the winds.

Arrive before him—not that I see what good
arriving first will do but arrive first all the same.

When he takes his place on the couch and you
     go to join him
looking angelic, secretly touch my foot.

Watch me for nods and looks that talk
and unobserved return my signals

in the language of eyebrows and fingers
with annotations in wine.

Whenever you think of our love-making
stroke that rosy cheek with your thumb.

If you're cross with me, darling,
press the lobe of your ear

but turn your ring round if you're pleased
with anything I say or do.

When you feel like cursing your fool of a
    husband
touch the table as if you were praying.

If he mixes you a drink, beware—tell him to
    drink it himself,
then quietly ask the waiter for what you want.

I'll intercept the glass as you hand it back
and drink from the side you drank from.

Refuse all food he has tasted first—
it has touched his lips.

Don't lean your gentle head against his shoulder
and don't let him embrace you

or slide a hand inside your dress
or touch your breasts. Above all don't kiss him.

If you do I'll cause a public scandal,
grab you and claim possession.

I'm bound to see all this. It's what I shan't see
that worries me—the goings on under your
    cloak.

Don't press your thigh or your leg against his
or touch his coarse feet with your toes.

I know all the tricks. That's why I'm worried.
I hate to think of him doing what I've done.

We've often made love under your cloak,
    sweetheart,
in a glorious race against time.

You won't do that, I know. Still,
to avoid all doubt don't wear one.

Encourage him to drink but mind—no kisses.
Keep filling his glass when he's not looking.

If the wine's too much for him and he drops off
we can take our cue from what's going on
    around us.

When you get up to leave and we all follow
move to the middle of the crowd.

You'll find me there—or I'll find you
so touch me anywhere you can.

But what's the good? I'm only temporizing.
Tonight decrees our separation.

Tonight he'll lock you in and leave me
desolated at your door.

Then he'll kiss you, then go further,
forcing his right to our secret joy.

But you *can* show him you're acting under
    duress.
Be mean with your love—give grudgingly—in
    silence.

He won't enjoy it if my prayers are answered.
And if they're not, at least assure me you won't.

But whatever happens tonight tell me tomorrow
you didn't sleep with him—and stick to that
    story.

*   *   *

REVIEW QUESTIONS

1. Does Ovid seem to have any moral scruples
   about adultery?
2. Would Cato the Elder have approved?

PETRONIUS

FROM *The Satyricon*

Petronius's novel The Satyricon *is one of the bawdier and most entertaining literary works of imperial Roman culture. Few other works give us such a vivid sense of the more everyday concerns of the era. In the following selection, the men conversing are attending a banquet hosted by a rather wealthy man named Trimalchio, who has just left to use the bathroom.*

From *The Satyricon*, by Petronius, translated by William Arrowsmith (Ann Arbor: University of Michigan Press, 1959), pp. 39–45.

*   *   *

At this point Trimalchio heaved himself up from his couch and waddled off to the toilet. Once rid of our table tyrant, the talk began to flow more freely. Damas called for larger glasses and led off himself. "What's one day? Bah, nothing at all. You turn round and it's dark. Nothing for it, I say, but jump right from bed to table. Brrrr. Nasty spell of cold weather we've been having. A bath hardly warmed me up. But a hot drink's the best overcoat of all; that's what I always say. Whoosh, I must have guzzled gallons. I'm tight and no mistake. Wine's gone right to my head . . ."

"As for me," Seleucus broke in, "I don't take a bath every day. Your bath's a fuller; the water's got teeth like a comb. Saps your vital juices. But once I've had a slug of mead, then bugger the cold. Couldn't have had a bath today anyway. Had to go to poor old Chrysanthus' funeral. Yup, he's gone for good, folded his tent forever. And a grand little guy he was; they don't make 'em any better these days. I might almost be talking to him now. Just goes to show you. What are men anyway but balloons on legs, a lot of blown-up bladders? Flies, that's what we are. No, not even flies. Flies have something inside. But a man's a bubble, all air, nothing else. And, you know, Chrysanthus might still be with us if he hadn't tried that star-vation diet. Five days and not a crumb of bread, not a drop of water, passed his lips. Tch, tch. And now he's gone, joined the great majority. Doctors killed him. Maybe not doctors, call it fate. What good's a doctor but for peace of mind? But the funeral was fine, they did it up brown: nice bier, fancy drapes, and a good bunch of mourners turned out too. Mostly slaves he'd set free, of course. But his old lady was sure stingy with the tears. Not that he didn't lead her a hard life, mind. But women, they're a race of kites. Don't deserve love. You might as well drop it down a well. And old love's a real cancer . . ."

He was beginning to be tiresome and Phileros shouted him down. "Whoa there," he cut in, "let's talk about the living. He got what was coming to him. He lived well, he died well. What the hell more did he want? And got rich from nothing too. And no wonder, I say. That boy would have grubbed in the gutter for a coin and picked it out with his teeth too. God knows what he had salted away. Just got fatter and fatter, bloated with the stuff. Why, that man oozed money the way a honeycomb oozes honey. But I'll give you the low-down on him, and no frills either. He talked tough, sure, but he was a born gabber. And a real scrapper too, regular pair of fists on legs. But you take his brother: now that's a real man for you, friendly and generous as they come, and what's more, he knows how to put on a spread. Anyway, as I was saying, what does our boy do but flop on his first big deal and end up eating crow? But come the vintage and he got right back on his feet and sold his wine at his own figure. What really gave him a boost was some legacy he got. And I don't mind telling you, he milked that legacy for all it was worth and then some. So what does the sap do next but pick a fight with his own brother and leave everything to a total stranger? I mean, it just shows you. Run from your kin and you run a damn long ways, as the saying goes. Well, you know, he had some slaves and he listened to them as though they were a lot of oracles, so naturally they took him in the end. It's like I always say, a sucker gets screwed. And that goes double when a man's in business. But there's a saying, it isn't what you're given, but what you can get that counts. Well, he got the meat out of that one all his life. He was Lady Luck's fair-haired boy and no mistake. Lead turned to gold in his hand. Of course, it's easy when the stuff comes rolling in on its own. And you know how old he was when he died? Seventy and then some. But carried it beautifully, hard as nails and his hair as black as a crow. I knew him for ages, and he was horny, right to the end. By god, I'll bet he even pestered the dog. Boys were what he really liked, but he wasn't choosy: he'd jump anything with legs. I don't blame him a bit, you understand. He won't have any fun where he's gone now."

But Ganymedes struck in, "Stuff like that doesn't matter a bit to man or beast. But nobody mentions the real thing, the way the price of bread is pinching. God knows, I couldn't buy a mouthful of bread today. And this damn drought goes on and on. Nobody's had a bellyful for years now. It's those rotten officials, you take my word for it. They're in cahoots with the bakers: you scratch me and I'll scratch you. So the little people get it in the neck, but in the rich man's jaws it's jubilee all year. By god, if we only had the kind of men we used to have, the sort I found here when I arrived from Asia. Then life was something like living. Man, milk and honey day in and day out, and the way they'd wallop those blood-sucking officials,

you'd have thought old Jupiter was having himself a tantrum. I remember old Safinius now. He used to live down by the old arch when I was a boy. More peppercorn than man. Singed the ground wherever he went. But honest and square and a real friend! Why, you could have matched coins with him in the dark. And in the townhall he'd lay it right on the line, no frills at all, just square on the target. And when he made a speech in the main square, he'd let loose like a bugle blowing. But neat as a pin all the time, never ruffled, never spat: there was something Asiatic about him. And you know, he always spoke to you, even remembered your name, just as though he were one of us. And bread was dirt-cheap in his day. For a penny you got a loaf that two men couldn't finish. Nowadays bulls' eyes come bigger than bread. But that's what I mean, things are just getting worse and worse. Why, this place is running downhill like a heifer's ass. You tell me, by god, the good of this three-fig official of ours who thinks more of his graft than what's happening to us. Why, that boy's just living it up at home and making more in a day than most men ever inherit. If we had any balls, let me tell you, he'd be laughing out of the other side of his face. But not us. Oh no, we're big lions at home and scared foxes in public. Why, I've practically had to pawn my clothes and if bread prices don't drop soon, I'll have to put my houses on the market. Mark my words, we're in for bad times if some man or god doesn't have a heart and take pity on this place. I'll stake my luck on it, the gods have got a finger in what's been happening here. And you know why? Because no one believes in the gods, that's why. Who observes the fast days any more, who cares a rap for Jupiter? One and all, bold as brass, they sit there pretending to pray, but cocking their eyes on the chances and counting up their cash. Once upon a time, let me tell you, things were different. The women would dress up in their best and climb barefoot up to the temple on the hill. Their hair was unbound and their hearts were pure and they went to beg Jupiter for rain. And you know what happened? Then or never, the rain would come sloshing down by the bucket, and they'd all stand

first century C.E. It describes in considerable detail how an agricultural estate should be organized and managed.

From *Roman Civilization: Selected Readings,* vol. 2, edited by Naphtali Lewis and Meyer Reinhold (New York: Columbia University Press, 1953), pp. 54–67.

The size of the villa and the number of its parts should be proportioned to the whole enclosure, and it should be divided into three groups: the *villa urbana,* the *villa rustica,* and the *villa fructuaria.* The manor house should be divided in turn into winter apartments and summer apartments, in such a way that the winter bedrooms face the southeast, and the winter dining room faces the west. The summer bedrooms, on the other hand, should look toward the south, but the dining rooms of that season should look toward the southeast. The baths should face the northwest, that they may be lighted from midday up to evening. The promenades should have a southern exposure, so as to receive both the maximum of sun in winter and the minimum in summer. But in the part devoted to farm uses there will be placed a spacious and high kitchen, that the rafters may be free from the danger of fire, and that it may offer a convenient place for the slave household to stop in at every season of the year. It will be best that cubicles for unfettered slaves be built facing the south; for those who are in chains there should be an underground prison, as wholesome as possible, receiving light through a number of narrow windows built so high from the ground that they cannot be reached with the hand.

For cattle there should be stables which will not be troubled by either heat or cold; for animals broken to work, two sets of stalls—one for winter, another for summer; and for the other animals which it is proper to keep within the farmstead there should be places partly covered, partly open to the sky, and surrounded with high walls so that the animals may rest in the one place in winter, in the other in summer, secure against attacks by wild animals. But stables should be roomy and so arranged that no moisture can flow in and that whatever is made there may run off quickly, to prevent the rotting of either the bases of the walls or the hoofs of the cattle. Ox stalls should be ten feet wide, or nine at least—a size which will allow room for the animal to lie down and for the ox-herd to move around in it when performing his duties. The feedracks should not be too high for the ox or pack animal to feed from without inconvenience while standing. Quarters should be provided for the overseer alongside the entrance, so that he may have oversight of all who come in and go out; and for the steward over the entrance for the same reason, and also so that he may keep close watch on the overseer; and near both of these there should be a storehouse in which all farm gear may be collected, and within it a closet for the storing of the iron implements.

Cells for the herdsmen and shepherds should be adjacent to their animals, so that they may conveniently run out to care for them. And yet all should be quartered as close as possible to one another, so that the diligence of the overseer may not be overtaxed in making the rounds of the several places, and also that they may be witnesses of one another's industry and diligence.

The storehouse part is divided into rooms for oil, for presses, for wine, for the boiling down of must; lofts for hay and chaff; and storerooms and grain bins—in such a manner that those on the ground floor take care of liquid products, such as oil and wine for marketing, while dry products, such as grain, hay, leaves, chaff, and other fodder, should be stored in lofts. But the grain lofts, as I have said, should be reached by ladders and should receive ventilation through small openings on the north side; for that exposure is the coolest and the least humid, and both these factors contribute to the preservation of stored grain. The same reason holds true in the placing of the wine room on the ground floor; and it should be far removed from the baths, oven, dunghill, and other filthy places which give off a foul odor, and no less so from cisterns and running water, from which is derived a moisture that spoils the wine. . . .

The press rooms especially and the storerooms for oil should be warm, because every liquid is more readily thinned with heat and thickened by great cold; and if oil freezes, which seldom happens, it becomes rancid. But as it is natural heat that is wanted, arising from the climate and the exposure, there is no need of fire or flame, as the taste of oil is spoiled by smoke and soot. For this reason the pressing room should be lighted from the southern side, so that we may not find it necessary to employ fires and lamps when the olives are being pressed.

The cauldron room, in which boiled wine is made, should be neither narrow nor dark, so that the attendant who is boiling down the must may move around without inconvenience. The smoke room, too, in which timber not long cut may be seasoned quickly, can be built in a section of the farmhouse adjoining the farmhouse baths (it is important also that there be such places in which the household may bathe—but only on holidays; for the frequent use of baths is not conducive to physical vigor). Storerooms for wine will be situated to advantage over these places from which smoke is usually rising, for wines age more rapidly when they are brought to an early maturity by a certain kind of smoke. For this reason there should be another loft to which they may be removed, to keep them from becoming tainted, on the other hand, by too much smoking.

As for the situation of the farmhouse and the arrangement of its several parts, enough has been said. It will be necessary, next, that the farmhouse have the following near it: an oven and a mill, of such size as may be required by the number of tenant farmers; at least two ponds, one to serve for geese and cattle, the other in which we may soak lupines, elm withes, twigs, and other things suitable for our needs. There should also be two manure pits, one to receive the fresh dung and

keep it for a year, and a second from which the old is hauled; but both of them should be built shelving with a gentle slope, in the manner of fish ponds, and built up and packed hard with earth, so as not to let the moisture drain away. . . .

The threshing floor is to be placed, if possible, in such manner that it can be viewed from above by the master, or at least by the farm manager. Such a floor is best when paved with hard stone, because the grain is thus threshed out quickly, since the ground does not give way under the beating of the hoofs and threshing sledges, and the winnowed grain is cleaner and is free from small stones and clods, which a dirt floor nearly always casts up during the threshing. . . .

The orchards, too, and the gardens should be fenced all around and should lie close by, in a place to which there may flow all manure-laden seepage from barnyard and baths, and the watery lees squeezed from olives; for both vegetables and trees thrive on nutriment of this sort, too.

After all these things have been obtained or constructed, the master must give special attention, among other things, to laborers; and these are either tenant farmers or slaves. He should be civil in dealing with his tenant farmers, should show himself affable, and should be more exacting in the matter of work than of payments, as this gives less offense yet is, generally speaking, more profitable. For when land is carefully tilled, it usually brings a profit, and never a loss except when it is assailed by unusually severe weather or robbers; and therefore the tenant does not venture to ask for reduction of his rent. But the master should not be insistent on his rights in every particular to which he has bound his tenant, such as the exact day for payment of money, or the matter of demanding firewood and other trifling contributions; attention to such matters causes country folk more trouble than expense. . . . I myself remember having heard Publius Volusius, an old man who had been consul and was very wealthy, declare that estate to be most fortunate which had natives of the place as tenant farmers and which held them by reason of long association, even from the cradle, as if born on their own father's property. So I am decidedly of the opinion that repeated re-letting of a farm is a bad thing, but that a worse thing is the tenant farmer who lives in town and prefers to till the land through his slaves rather than by his own hand. Saserna used to say that from a man of this sort the return was usually a lawsuit instead of income, and that for this reason we should take pains to keep with us tenants who are country-bred and at the same time diligent farmers, when we are not able to till the land ourselves or when it is not feasible to cultivate it with our own household; though this does not happen except in districts which are desolated by the severity of the climate and the barrenness of the soil. But when the climate is moderately healthful and the soil moderately good, a man's personal attention never fails to yield a larger return from his land than does that of a tenant. Even reliance on an overseer yields a larger return, except in the event of extreme carelessness or greed on the part of that slave. There is no doubt that in general both these offenses are either committed or fostered through the fault of the master, inasmuch as he has the authority to prevent such a person from being placed in charge of his affairs or to see to it that he is removed if so placed. On far-distant estates, however, which it is not easy for the owner to visit, it is better for every kind of land to be under free farmers than under slave overseers, but this is particularly true of grain land. To such land a tenant farmer can do no great harm, as he can to vineyards and trees, while slaves do it tremendous damage: they let out oxen for hire, and they keep them and other animals poorly fed; they do not plow the ground carefully, and they charge the account with far more seed than they have actually sown; what they have committed to the earth they do not foster so that it will make the proper growth; and when they have brought it to the threshing floor, every day during the threshing they lessen the quantity either by trickery or by carelessness. For they themselves steal it and do not guard against the thieving of others, and even when it is stored away, they do not enter it honestly in their accounts. The result is that both manager and hands

are offenders, and the land pretty often gets a bad name. Therefore my opinion is that an estate of this sort should be leased if, as I have said, it cannot have the presence of the owner.

The next point is with regard to slaves—over what duty it is proper to place each, and to what sort of tasks to assign them. So my advice at the start is not to appoint an overseer from the sort of slaves who are physically attractive, and certainly not from that class which has been engaged in the voluptuous occupations of the city. This lazy and sleepy-headed class of slaves, accustomed to idling, to the Field of Mars, the circus and the theaters, to gambling, to taverns, to bawdy houses, never ceases to dream of these follies; and when they carry them over into their farming, the master suffers not so much loss in the slave himself as in his whole estate. A man should be chosen who has been hardened by farm work from his infancy, one who has been tested by experience. . . . He should be of middle age and of strong physique, skilled in farm operations or at least very painstaking, so that he may learn the more readily; for it is not in keeping with this business of ours for one man to give orders and another to give instruction, nor can a man properly exact work when he is being tutored by an underling as to what is to be done and in what way. Even an illiterate person, if only he have a retentive mind, can manage affairs well enough. Cornelius Celsus says that an overseer of this sort brings money to his master oftener than he does his book, because, being illiterate, he is either less able to falsify accounts or is afraid to do so through a second party, because that would make another aware of the deception.

But be the overseer what he may, he should be given a woman companion to keep him within bounds and moreover in certain matters to be a help to him. . . . He must be urged to take care of the equipment and the iron tools, and to keep in repair and stored away twice as many as the number of slaves requires, so that there will be no need of borrowing from a neighbor; for the loss in slave labor exceeds the cost of articles of this sort. In the care and clothing of the slave household he should have an eye to usefulness rather than appearance, taking care to keep them fortified against wind, cold, and rain, all of which are warded off with long-sleeved leather tunics, garments of patchwork, or hooded cloaks. If this be done, no weather is so unbearable but that some work may be done in the open. He should be not only skilled in the tasks of husbandry but should also be endowed, as far as the servile disposition allows, with such qualities of mind that he may exercise authority without laxness and without cruelty, and always humor some of the better hands, at the same time being forbearing even with those of lesser worth, so that they may rather fear his sternness than detest his cruelty. . . .

In the case of the other slaves, the following are, in general, the precepts to be observed, and I do not regret having held to them myself: to talk rather familiarly with the country slaves, provided only that they have not conducted themselves unbecomingly, more frequently than I would with town slaves; and when I perceived that their unending toil was lightened by such friendliness on the part of the master, I would even jest with them at times and allow them also to jest more freely. Nowadays I make it a practice to call them into consultation on any new work, as if they were more experienced, and to discover by this means what sort of ability is possessed by each of them and how intelligent he is. Furthermore, I observe that they are more willing to set about a piece of work on which they think that their opinions have been asked and their advice followed. Again, it is the established custom of all men of caution to inspect the slaves in the prison, to find out whether they are carefully chained, whether the places of confinement are quite safe and properly guarded, whether the overseer has put anyone in fetters or removed his shackles without the master's knowledge. . . . And the investigation of the householder should be the more painstaking in the interest of slaves of this sort, that they may not be treated unjustly in the matter of clothing or other allowances, inasmuch as, being subject to a greater number of people, such as overseers, taskmasters, and jailers, they are the more liable to

unjust punishment, and again, when smarting under cruelty and greed, they are more to be feared. Accordingly, a careful master inquires not only of them, but also of those who are not in bonds, as being more worthy of belief, whether they are receiving what is due them under his instructions. He also tests the quality of their food and drink by tasting it himself and examines their clothing, mittens, and foot covering. In addition, he should give them frequent opportunities for making complaints against those persons who treat them cruelly or dishonestly. In fact, I now and then avenge those who have just cause for grievance, as well as punish those who incite the slaves to revolt or who slander their taskmasters; and, on the other hand, I reward those who conduct themselves with energy and diligence. Also, to women who are unusually prolific, and who ought to be rewarded for the bearing of a certain number of offspring, I have granted exemption from work and sometimes even freedom after they have reared many children: a mother of three children received exemption from work, a mother of more, her freedom as well. Such justice and consideration on the part of the master contributes greatly to the increase of his estate. . . .

This, too, I believe: that the duties of the slaves should not be confused to the point where all take a hand in every task. For this is by no means to the advantage of the husbandman, either because no one regards any particular task as his own or because, when he does make an effort, he is performing a service that is not his own but common to all, and therefore shirks his work to a great extent; and yet fault cannot be fastened upon any one man because many have a hand in it. For this reason plowmen must be distinguished from vine dressers, and vine dressers from plowmen, and both of these from men of all work. Furthermore, squads should be formed, not to exceed ten men each, which the ancients called *decuriae* and approved of highly, because that limited number was most conveniently guarded while at work and the size was not disconcerting to the person in charge as he led the way. Therefore, if the field is of considerable extent, such squads should be distributed over sections of it and the work should be so apportioned that men will not be by ones or twos, because they are not easily watched when scattered; and yet they should not number more than ten, lest, on the other hand, when the band is too large, each individual may think that the work does not concern him. This arrangement not only stimulates rivalry, but also discloses the slothful; for, when a task is enlivened by competition, punishment inflicted on the laggards appears just and free from censure.

REVIEW QUESTIONS

1. What kinds of crops are produced on the estate?
2. Who performs most of the work?
3. How are the workers to be managed and treated?
4. How does the treatment of slaves on this estate compare with the treatment of slaves in the mines of Spain (as described in the earlier selection by Diodorus Siculus)?
5. How do living conditions on a country estate compare with those in Rome?

FROM The Gospel of Matthew

Among the eastern religions that gained popularity during the early empire was Judaism, especially that version of it espoused by the Nazarenes, followers of the teachings of an itinerant Jewish preacher named Yeshua (in Latin, Jesus), whose career in Judaea ended with his death by crucifixion sometime around 30 C.E. The chief records of his life and teachings are contained in the gospels, a number of which were composed in the decades after his death (including a gospel of James and a gospel of Thomas) but only four of which, those of Mark, Matthew, Luke, and John, were later accepted as authoritative.

From *The Oxford Study Bible*, edited by M. Jack Suggs, Katharine Doob Sakenfeld, and James R. Mueller (Oxford, Eng.: Oxford University Press, 1992).

*　　*　　*

IN the course of time John the Baptist appeared in the Judaean wilderness, proclaiming this message: "Repent, for the kingdom of Heaven is upon you!" It was of him that the prophet Isaiah spoke when he said,

A voice cries in the wilderness,
"Prepare the way for the Lord;
clear a straight path for him."

John's clothing was a rough coat of camel's hair, with a leather belt round his waist, and his food was locusts and wild honey. Everyone flocked to him from Jerusalem, Judaea, and the Jordan valley, and they were baptized by him in the river Jordan, confessing their sins.

When he saw many of the Pharisees and Sadducees coming for baptism he said to them: "Vipers' brood! Who warned you to escape from the wrath that is to come? Prove your repentance by the fruit you bear; and do not imagine you can say, 'We have Abraham for our father.' I tell you that God can make children for Abraham out of these stones. The axe lies ready at the roots of the trees; every tree that fails to produce good fruit is cut down and thrown on the fire. I baptize you with water, for repentance; but the one who comes after me is mightier than I am, whose sandals I am not worthy to remove. He will baptize you with the Holy Spirit and with fire. His winnowing-shovel is ready in his hand and he will clear his threshing-floor; he will gather the wheat into his granary, but the chaff he will burn on a fire that can never be put out."

Then Jesus arrived at the Jordan from Galilee, and came to John to be baptized by him. John tried to dissuade him. "Do you come to me?" he said. "It is I who need to be baptized by you." Jesus replied, "Let it be so for the present; it is right for us to do all that God requires." Then John allowed him to come. No sooner had Jesus been baptized and come up out of the water than the heavens were opened and he saw the Spirit of God descending like a dove to alight on him.

And there came a voice from heaven saying, "This is my beloved Son, in whom I take delight."

*   *   *

WHEN he saw the crowds he went up a mountain. There he sat down, and when his disciples had gathered round him he began to address them. And this is the teaching he gave:

"Blessed are the poor in spirit;
the kingdom of Heaven is theirs.
Blessed are the sorrowful;
they shall find consolation.
Blessed are the gentle;
they shall have the earth for their
    possession.
Blessed are those who hunger and
    thirst to see right prevail;
they shall be satisfied.
Blessed are those who show mercy;
mercy shall be shown to them.
Blessed are those whose hearts are
    pure;
they shall see God.

Blessed are the peacemakers;
they shall be called God's children.
Blessed are those who are persecuted in
    the cause of right;
the kingdom of Heaven is theirs.

"Blessed are you, when you suffer insults and persecution and calumnies of every kind for my sake. Exult and be glad, for you have a rich reward in heaven; in the same way they persecuted the prophets before you.

"You are salt to the world. And if salt becomes tasteless, how is its saltness to be restored? It is good for nothing but to be thrown away and trodden underfoot.

"You are light for all the world. A town that stands on a hill cannot be hidden. When a lamp is lit, it is not put under the meal-tub, but on the lampstand, where it gives light to everyone in the house. Like the lamp, you must shed light among your fellows, so that, when they see the good you do, they may give praise to your Father in heaven.

"DO NOT suppose that I have come to abolish the law and the prophets; I did not come to abolish, but to complete. Truly I tell you: so long as heaven and earth endure, not a letter, not a dot, will disappear from the law until all that must happen has happened. Anyone therefore who sets aside even the least of the law's demands, and teaches others to do the same, will have the lowest place in the kingdom of Heaven, whereas anyone who keeps the law, and teaches others to do so, will rank high in the kingdom of Heaven. I tell you, unless you show yourselves far better than the scribes and Pharisees, you can never enter the kingdom of Heaven.

"You have heard that our forefathers were told, 'Do not commit murder; anyone who commits murder must be brought to justice.' But what I tell you is this: Anyone who nurses anger against his brother must be brought to justice. Whoever calls his brother "good for nothing" deserves the sentence of the court, whoever calls him "fool" deserves hell-fire. So if you are presenting your gift at the altar and suddenly remember that your brother has a grievance against you, leave your gift where it is before the altar. First go and make your peace with your brother; then come back and offer your gift. If someone sues you, come to terms with him promptly while you are both on your way to court; otherwise he may hand you over to the judge, and the judge to the officer, and you will be thrown into jail. Truly I tell you: once you are there you will not be let out until you have paid the last penny.

"You have heard that they were told, 'Do not commit adultery.' But what I tell you is this: If a man looks at a woman with a lustful eye, he has already committed adultery with her in his heart. If your right eye causes your downfall, tear it out and fling it away; it is better for you to lose one part of your body than for the whole of it to be thrown into hell. If your right hand causes your downfall, cut it off and fling it away; it is better for you to lose one part of your body than for the whole of it to go to hell.

"They were told, 'A man who divorces his wife must give her a certificate of dismissal.' But what I tell you is this: If a man divorces his wife for any cause other than unchastity he involves her in adultery; and whoever marries her commits adultery.

"Again, you have heard that our forefathers were told, 'Do not break your oath,' and 'Oaths sworn to the Lord must be kept.' But what I tell you is this: You are not to swear at all—not by heaven, for it is God's throne, nor by the earth, for it is his footstool, nor by Jerusalem, for it is the city of the great King, nor by your own head, because you cannot turn one hair of it white or black. Plain 'Yes' or 'No' is all you need to say; anything beyond that comes from the evil one.

"You have heard that they were told, "An eye for an eye, a tooth for a tooth." But what I tell you is this: Do not resist those who wrong you. If anyone slaps you on the right cheek, turn and offer him the other also. If anyone wants to sue you and takes your shirt, let him have your cloak as well. If someone in authority presses you into service for one mile, go with him two. Give to anyone who asks; and do not turn your back on anyone who wants to borrow.

"You have heard that they were told, 'Love your neighbour and hate your enemy.' But what I tell you is this: Love your enemies and pray for your persecutors; only so can you be children of your heavenly Father, who causes the sun to rise on good and bad alike, and sends the rain on the innocent and the wicked. If you love only those who love you, what reward can you expect? Even the tax-collectors do as much as that. If you greet only your brothers, what is there extraordinary about that? Even the heathen do as much. There must be no limit to your goodness, as your heavenly Father's goodness knows no bounds.

"BE careful not to parade your religion before others; if you do, no reward awaits you with your Father in heaven.

"So, when you give alms, do not announce it with a flourish of trumpets, as the hypocrites do in synagogues and in the streets to win the praise of others. Truly I tell you: they have their reward already. But when you give alms, do not let your left hand know what your right is doing; your good deed must be secret, and your Father who sees what is done in secret will reward you.

"Again, when you pray, do not be like the hypocrites; they love to say their prayers standing up in synagogues and at street corners for everyone to see them. Truly I tell you: they have their reward already. But when you pray, go into a room by yourself, shut the door, and pray to your Father who is in secret; and your Father who sees what is done in secret will reward you.

"In your prayers do not go babbling on like the heathen, who imagine that the more they say the more likely they are to be heard. Do not imitate them, for your Father knows what your needs are before you ask him.

"This is how you should pray:

Our Father in heaven,
may your name be hallowed;
your kingdom come,
your will be done,

on earth as in heaven.
Give us today our daily bread.
Forgive us the wrong we have done,
  as we have forgiven those who have
    wronged us.
And do not put us to the test,
  but save us from the evil one.

"For if you forgive others the wrongs they have done, your heavenly Father will also forgive you; but if you do not forgive others, then your Father will not forgive the wrongs that you have done.

"So too when you fast, do not look gloomy like the hypocrites: they make their faces unsightly so that everybody may see that they are fasting. Truly I tell you: they have their reward already. But when you fast, anoint your head and wash your face, so that no one sees that you are fasting, but only your Father who is in secret; and your Father who sees what is done in secret will give you your reward.

"Do NOT store up for yourselves treasure on earth, where moth and rust destroy, and thieves break in and steal; but store up treasure in heaven, where neither moth nor rust will destroy, nor thieves break in and steal. For where your treasure is, there will your heart be also.

"The lamp of the body is the eye. If your eyes are sound, you will have light for your whole body; if your eyes are bad, your whole body will be in darkness. If then the only light you have is darkness, how great a darkness that will be.

"No one can serve two masters; for either he will hate the first and love the second, or he will be devoted to the first and despise the second. You cannot serve God and Money.

"This is why I tell you not to be anxious about food and drink to keep you alive and about clothes to cover your body. Surely life is more than food, the body more than clothes. Look at the birds in the sky; they do not sow and reap and store in barns, yet your heavenly Father feeds them. Are you not worth more than the birds? Can anxious thought add a single day to your life? And why be anxious about clothes? Consider how the lilies

grow in the fields; they do not work, they do not spin; yet I tell you, even Solomon in all his splendour was not attired like one of them. If that is how God clothes the grass in the fields, which is there today and tomorrow is thrown on the stove, will he not all the more clothe you? How little faith you have! Do not ask anxiously, 'What are we to eat? What are we to drink? What shall we wear?' These are the things that occupy the minds of the heathen, but your heavenly Father knows that you need them all. Set your mind on God's kingdom and his justice before everything else, and all the rest will come to you as well. So do not be anxious about tomorrow; tomorrow will look after itself. Each day has troubles enough of its own.

"Do NOT judge, and you will not be judged. For as you judge others, so you will yourselves be judged, and whatever measure you deal out to others will be dealt to you. Why do you look at the speck of sawdust in your brother's eye, with never a thought for the plank in your own? How can you say to your brother, "Let me take the speck out of your eye," when all the time there is a plank in your own? You hypocrite! First take the plank out of your own eye, and then you will see clearly to take the speck out of your brother's.

"Do not give dogs what is holy; do not throw your pearls to the pigs: they will only trample on them, and turn and tear you to pieces.

"Ask, and you will receive; seek, and you will find; knock, and the door will be opened to you. For everyone who asks receives, those who seek find, and to those who knock, the door will be opened.

"Would any of you offer his son a stone when he asks for bread, or a snake when he asks for a fish? If you, bad as you are, know how to give good things to your children, how much more will your heavenly Father give good things to those who ask him!

"Always treat others as you would like them to treat you: that is the law and the prophets.

"Enter by the narrow gate. Wide is the gate and broad the road that leads to destruction, and many enter that way; narrow is the gate and constricted the road that leads to life, and those who find them are few.

"Beware of false prophets, who come to you dressed up as sheep while underneath they are savage wolves. You will recognize them by their fruit. Can grapes be picked from briars, or figs from thistles? A good tree always yields sound fruit, and a poor tree bad fruit. A good tree cannot bear bad fruit, or a poor tree sound fruit. A tree that does not yield sound fruit is cut down and thrown on the fire. That is why I say you will recognize them by their fruit.

"Not everyone who says to me, 'Lord, Lord' will enter the kingdom of Heaven, but only those who do the will of my heavenly Father. When the day comes, many will say to me, 'Lord, Lord, did we not prophesy in your name, drive out demons in your name, and in your name perform many miracles?' Then I will tell them plainly, 'I never knew you. Out of my sight; your deeds are evil!' "

"So whoever hears these words of mine and acts on them is like a man who had the sense to build his house on rock. The rain came down, the floods rose, the winds blew and beat upon that house; but it did not fall, because its foundations were on rock. And whoever hears these words of mine and does not act on them is like a man who was foolish enough to build his house on sand. The rain came down, the floods rose, the winds blew and battered against that house; and it fell with a great crash."

When Jesus had finished this discourse the people were amazed at his teaching; unlike their scribes he taught with a note of authority.

*   *   *

REVIEW QUESTIONS

1. As expressed in the Sermon on the Mount, what were the chief features of Jesus's teaching?
2. How does he offer his teachings as a break from earlier traditions?

TACITUS

FROM *Germania*

As the Romans' empire expanded, they came into contact with various peoples. None of them was to have a more significant or enduring influence on the shaping of Western civilization than the Germans, whose chieftains eventually would supplant Roman authority in western Europe. That at least some Romans had an inkling of the Germans' later importance is evident in the Germania *of the Roman historian Tacitus, who wrote this work at the end of the first century C.E.*

From *The Agricola and Germany of Tacitus,* translated by A. J. Church and W. J. Brodribb (Basingstoke, Eng.: Macmillan Publishers, 1877).

A MUMMY FROM THE TIME OF THE ROMAN EMPIRE (100 C.E.)

This painted and gilded case contains the mummy of a man with the very un-Egyptian name Artemidorus, who died evidently in his early twenties, shortly after 100 C.E. To what extent are classical and Egyptian artistic elements and symbolism mixed in the decoration of this case? Do you see evidence for the survival of ancient Egyptian religious beliefs and traditions under Roman rule? What is your assessment of the skill of the artist who painted Artemidorus's portrait?

*   *   *

For my own part, I agree with those who think that the tribes of Germany are free from all taint of intermarriages with foreign nations, and that they appear as a distinct, unmixed race, like none but themselves. Hence, too, the same physical peculiarities throughout so vast a population. All have fierce blue eyes, red hair, huge frames, fit only for a sudden exertion. They are less able to bear laborious work. Heat and thirst they cannot in the least endure; to cold and hunger their climate and their soil inure them.

Their country, though somewhat various in appearance, yet generally either bristles with forests or reeks with swamps; it is more rainy on the side of Gaul, bleaker on that of Noricum and Pannonia. It is productive of grain, but unfavourable to fruit-bearing trees; it is rich in flocks and herds, but these are for the most part undersized, and even the cattle have not their usual beauty or noble head. It is number that is chiefly valued; they are in fact the most highly prized, indeed the only riches of the people. Silver and gold the gods have refused to them, whether in kindness or in anger I cannot say. I would not, however, affirm that no vein of German soil produces gold or silver, for who has ever made a search? They care but little to possess or use them. You may see among them vessels of silver, which have been presented to their envoys and chieftains, held as cheap as those of clay. The border population, however, value gold and silver for their commercial utility, and are familiar with, and show preference for, some of our coins. The tribes of the interior use the simpler and more ancient practice of the barter of commodities. They like the old and well-known money, coins milled, or showing a two-horse chariot. They likewise prefer silver to gold, not from any special liking, but because a large number of silver pieces is more convenient for use among dealers in cheap and common articles.

Even iron is not plentiful with them, as we infer from the character of their weapons. But few use swords or long lances. They carry a spear with a narrow and short head, but so sharp and easy to wield that the same weapon serves, according to circumstances, for close or distant conflict. As for the horse-soldier, he is satisfied with a shield and spear; the foot-soldiers also scatter showers of missiles, each man having several and hurling them to an immense distance, and being naked or lightly clad with a little cloak. There is no display about their equipment: their shields alone are marked with very choice colours. A few only have corslets, and just one or two here and there a metal or leathern helmet. Their horses are remarkable neither for beauty nor for fleetness. Nor are they taught various evolutions after our fashion, but are driven straight forward, or so as to make one wheel to the right in such a compact body that none is left behind another. On the whole, one would say that their chief strength is in their infantry, which fights along with the cavalry; admirably adapted to the action of the latter is the swiftness of certain foot-soldiers, who are picked from the entire youth of their country, and stationed in front of the line. Their number is fixed,—a hundred from each canton; and from this they take their name among their countrymen, so that what was originally a mere number has now become a title of distinction. Their line of battle is drawn up in a wedge-like formation. To give ground, provided you return to the attack, is considered prudence rather than cowardice. The bodies of their slain they carry off even in indecisive engagements. To abandon your shield is the basest of crimes; nor may a man thus disgraced be present at the sacred rites, or enter their council; many, indeed, after escaping from battle, have ended their infamy with the halter.

They choose their kings by birth, their generals for merit. These kings have not unlimited or arbitrary power, and the generals do more by example than by authority. If they are energetic, if they are conspicuous, if they fight in the front, they lead because they are admired. But to reprimand, to imprison, even to flog, is permitted to the priests alone, and that not as a punishment, or at the general's bidding, but, as it were, by the mandate of the god whom they believe to inspire the warrior. They also carry with them into battle certain figures and images taken from their sacred groves. And what most stimulates their courage is, that their squadrons or battalions, instead of being formed by chance or by a fortuitous gathering, are composed of families and clans. Close by them, too, are those dearest to them, so that they hear the shrieks of women, the cries of infants. *They are to every man the most sacred witnesses of his bravery—they* are his most generous applauders. The soldier brings his wounds to mother and wife, who shrink not from counting or even demanding them and who administer both food and encouragement to the combatants.

Tradition says that armies already wavering and giving way have been rallied by women who, with earnest entreaties and bosoms laid bare, have vividly represented the horrors of captivity, which the Germans fear with such extreme dread on behalf of their women, that the strongest tie by which a state can be bound is the being required to give, among the number of hostages, maidens of noble birth. They even believe that the sex has a certain sanctity and prescience, and they do not despise their counsels, or make light of their answers. In Vespasian's days we saw Veleda, long regarded by many as a divinity. In former times, too, they venerated Aurinia, and many other women, but not with servile flatteries, or with sham deification.

*   *   *

Augury and divination by lot no people practise more diligently. The use of the lots is simple. A little bough is lopped off a fruit-bearing tree, and cut into small pieces; these are distinguished by certain marks, and thrown carelessly and at random over a white garment. In public questions the priest of the particular state, in private the father of the family, invokes the gods, and, with his eyes towards heaven, takes up each piece three times, and finds in them a meaning according to the mark previously impressed on them. If they prove unfavourable, there is no further consultation that day about the matter; if they sanction it, the confirmation of augury is still required. For they are also familiar with the practice of consult-ing the notes and the flight of birds. It is peculiar to this people to seek omens from horses. Kept at the public expense, in these same woods and groves, are white horses, pure from the taint of earthly labour; these are yoked to a sacred car, and accompanied by the priest and the king, or chief of the tribe, who note their neighings and snortings. No species of augury is more trusted, not only by the people and by the nobility, but also by the priests, who regard themselves as the ministers of the gods, and the horses as acquainted with their will. They have also another method of observing auspices, by which they seek to learn the result of an important war. Having taken, by whatever means, a prisoner from the tribe with whom they are at war, they pit him against a picked man of their own tribe, each combatant using the weapons of their country. The victory of the one or the other is accepted as an indication of the issue.

About minor matters the chiefs deliberate, about the more important the whole tribe. Yet even when the final decision rests with the people, the affair is always thoroughly discussed by the chiefs. They assemble, except in the case of a sudden emergency, on certain fixed days, either at new or at full moon; for this they consider the most auspicious season for the transaction of business. Instead of reckoning by days as we do, they reckon by nights, and in this manner fix both their ordinary and their legal appointments. Night they regard as bringing on day. Their freedom has this disadvantage, that they do not meet simultaneously or as they are bidden, but two or three days are wasted in the delays of assembling. When the multitude think proper, they sit down armed. Silence is proclaimed by the priests, who have on these occasions the right of keeping order. Then the king or the chief, according to age, birth, distinction in war, or eloquence, is heard, more because he has influence to persuade than because he has power to command. If his sentiments displease them, they reject them with murmurs; if they are satisfied, they brandish their spears. The most complimentary form of assent is to express approbation with their weapons.

In their councils an accusation may be preferred or a capital crime prosecuted. Penalties are distinguished according to the offence. Traitors and deserters are hanged on trees; the coward, the unwarlike, the man stained with abominable vices, is plunged into the mire of the morass, with a hurdle put over him. This distinction in punishment means that crime, they think, ought, in being punished, to be exposed, while infamy ought to be buried out of sight. Lighter offences, too, have penalties proportioned to them; he who is convicted, is fined in a certain number of horses or of cattle. Half of the fine is paid to the king or to the state, half to the person whose wrongs are avenged and to his relatives. In these same councils they also elect the chief magistrates, who administer law in the cantons and the towns. Each of these has a hundred associates chosen from the people, who support him with their advice and influence.

They transact no public or private business without being armed. It is not, however, usual for anyone to wear arms till the state has recognised his power to use them. Then in the presence of the council one of the chiefs, or the young man's father, or some kinsman, equips him with a shield and a spear. These arms are what the "toga" is with us, the first honour with which youth is invested. Up to this time he is regarded as a member of a household, afterwards as a member of the commonwealth. Very noble birth or great services rendered by the father secure for lads the rank of a chief; such lads attach themselves to men of mature strength and of long approved valour. It is no shame to be seen among a chief's followers. Even in his escort there are gradations of rank, dependent on the choice of the man to whom they are attached. These followers vie keenly with each other as to who shall rank first with his chief, the chiefs as to who shall have the most numerous and the bravest followers. It is an honour as well as a source of strength to be thus always surrounded by a large body of picked youths; it is an ornament in peace and a defence in war. And not only in his own tribe but also in the neighbouring states it is the renown and glory of a chief to be distinguished for the number and valour of his followers, for such a man is courted by embassies, is honoured with presents, and the very prestige of his name often settles a war.

When they go into battle, it is a disgrace for the chief to be surpassed in valour, a disgrace for his followers not to equal the valour of the chief. And it is an infamy and a reproach for life to have survived the chief, and returned from the field. To defend, to protect him, to ascribe one's own brave deeds to his renown, is the height of loyalty. The chief fights for victory; his vassals fight for their chief. If their native state sinks into the sloth of prolonged peace and repose, many of its noble youths voluntarily seek those tribes which are waging some war, both because inaction is odious to their race, and because they win renown more readily in the midst of peril, and cannot maintain a numerous following except by violence and war. Indeed, men look to the liberality of their chief for their war-horse and their blood-stained and victorious lance. Feasts and entertainments, which, though inelegant, are plentifully furnished, are their only pay. The means of this bounty come from war and rapine. Nor are they as easily persuaded to plough the earth and to wait for the year's produce as to challenge an enemy and earn the honour of wounds. Nay, they actually think it tame and stupid to acquire by the sweat of toil what they might win by their blood.

Whenever they are not fighting, they pass much of their time in the chase, and still more in idleness, giving themselves up to sleep and to feasting, the bravest and the most warlike doing nothing, and surrendering the management of the household, of the home, and of the land, to the women, the old men, and all the weakest members of the family. They themselves lie buried in sloth, a strange combination in their nature that the same men should be so fond of idleness, so averse to peace. It is the custom of the states to bestow by voluntary and individual contribution on the chiefs a present of cattle or of grain, which, while accepted as a compliment, supplies their wants. They are particularly delighted by gifts from neighbouring tribes, which are sent not only by individuals but also by the state, such as choice steeds, heavy armour, trappings, and neckchains. We have now taught them to accept money also.

It is well known that the nations of Germany have no cities, and that they do not even tolerate closely contiguous dwellings. They live scattered and apart, just as a spring, a meadow, or a wood has attracted them. Their villages they do not arrange in our fashion, with the buildings connected and joined together, but every person surrounds his dwelling with an open space, either as a precaution against the disasters of fire, or because they do not know how to build. No use is made by them of stone or tile; they employ timber for all purposes, rude masses without ornament or attractiveness. Some parts of their buildings they stain more carefully with a clay so clear and bright that it resembles painting, or a coloured design. They are wont also to dig out subterranean caves, and pile on them great heaps of dung, as a shelter from winter and as a receptacle for the year's produce, for by such places they mitigate the rigour of the cold. And should an enemy approach, he lays waste the open country, while what is hidden and buried is either not known to exist, or else escapes him from the very fact that it has to be searched for.

They all wrap themselves in a cloak which is fastened with a clasp, or, if this is not forthcoming, with a thorn, leaving the rest of their persons bare. They pass whole days on the hearth by the fire. The wealthiest are distinguished by a dress which is not flowing, like that of the Sarmatae and Parthi, but is tight, and exhibits each limb. They also wear the skins of wild beasts; the tribes on the Rhine and Danube in a careless fashion, those of the interior with more elegance, as not obtaining other clothing by commerce. These select certain animals, the hides of which they strip off and vary them with the spotted skins of beasts, the produce of the outer ocean, and of seas unknown to us. The women have the same dress as the men, except that they generally wrap themselves in linen garments, which they embroider with purple, and do not lengthen out the upper part of their clothing into sleeves. The upper and lower arm is thus bare, and the nearest part of the bosom is also exposed.

Their marriage code, however, is strict, and indeed no part of their manners is more praiseworthy. Almost alone among barbarians they are content with one wife, except a very few among them, and then not from sensuality, but because their noble birth procures for them many offers of alliance. The wife does not bring a dower to the husband, but the husband to the wife. The parents and relatives are present, and pass judgment on the marriage-gifts, gifts not meant to suit a woman's taste, nor such as a bride would deck herself with, but oxen, a caparisoned steed, a shield, a lance, and a sword. With these presents the wife is espoused, and she herself in her turn brings her husband a gift of arms. This they count their strongest bond of union, these their sacred mysteries, these their gods of marriage. Lest the woman should think herself to stand apart from aspirations after noble deeds and from the perils of war, she is reminded by the ceremony which inaugurates marriage that she is her husband's partner in toil and danger, destined to suffer and to dare with him alike both in peace and in war. The yoked oxen, the harnessed steed, the gift of arms, proclaim this fact. She must live and die with the feeling that she is receiving what she must hand down to her children neither tarnished nor depreciated, what future daughters-in-law may receive, and may be so passed on to her grandchildren.

Thus with their virtue protected they live uncorrupted by the allurements of public shows or the stimulant of feastings. Clandestine correspondence is equally unknown to men and women. Very rare for so numerous a population is adultery, the punishment for which is prompt, and in the husband's power. Having cut off the hair of the adulteress and stripped her naked, he expels her from the house in the presence of her kinsfolk, and then flogs her through the whole village. The loss of chastity meets with no indulgence; neither beauty, youth, nor wealth will procure the culprit a husband. No one in Germany laughs at vice, nor do they call it the fashion to corrupt and to be corrupted. Still better is the condition of those states in which only maidens are given in marriage, and where the hopes and expectations of a bride are then finally terminated. They receive one husband, as having one body and one life, that they may have no thoughts beyond, no further-reaching desires, that they may love not so much the husband as the married state. To limit the number of their children or to destroy any of their subsequent offspring is accounted infamous, and good habits are here more effectual than good laws elsewhere.

In every household the children, naked and filthy, grow up with those stout frames and limbs which we so much admire. Every mother suckles her own offspring, and never entrusts it to servants and nurses. The master is not distinguished from the slave by being brought up with greater delicacy. Both live amid the same flocks and lie on the same ground till the freeborn are distinguished by age and recognised by merit. The young men marry late, and their vigour is thus unimpaired. Nor are the maidens hurried into marriage; the same age and a similar stature is required; well-matched and vigorous they wed, and the offspring reproduce the strength of the parents. Sisters' sons are held in as much esteem by their uncles as by their fathers; indeed, some regard the relation as even more sacred and binding, and prefer it in receiving hostages, thinking thus to secure a stronger hold on the affections and a wider bond for the family. But every man's own children are his heirs and successors, and there are no wills. Should there be no issue, the next in succession to the property are his brothers and his uncles on either side. The more relatives he has, the more numerous his connections, the more honoured is his old age; nor are there any advantages in childlessness.

It is a duty among them to adopt the feuds as well as the friendships of a father or a kinsman. These feuds are not implacable; even homicide is expiated by the payment of a certain number of cattle and of sheep, and the satisfaction is accepted by the entire family, greatly to the advantage of

the state, since feuds are dangerous in proportion to a people's freedom.

No nation indulges more profusely in entertainments and hospitality. To exclude any human being from their roof is thought impious; every German, according to his means, receives his guest with a well-furnished table. When his supplies are exhausted, he who was but now the host becomes the guide and companion to further hospitality, and without invitation they go to the next house. It matters not; they are entertained with like cordiality. No one distinguishes between an acquaintance and a stranger, as regards the rights of hospitality. It is usual to give the departing guest whatever he may ask for, and a present in return is asked with as little hesitation. They are greatly charmed with gifts, but they expect no return for what they give, nor feel any obligation for what they receive.

On waking from sleep, which they generally prolong to a late hour of the day, they take a bath, oftenest of warm water, which suits a country where winter is the longest of the seasons. After their bath they take their meal, each having a separate seat and table of his own. Then they go armed to business, or no less often to their festal meetings. To pass an entire day and night in drinking disgraces no one. Their quarrels, as might be expected with intoxicated people, are seldom fought out with mere abuse, but commonly with wounds and bloodshed. Yet it is at their feasts that they generally consult on the reconciliation of enemies, on the forming of matrimonial alliances, on the choice of chiefs, finally even on peace and war, for they think that at no time is the mind more open to simplicity of purpose or more warmed to noble aspirations. A race without either natural or acquired cunning, they disclose their hidden thoughts in the freedom of the festivity. Thus the sentiments of all having been discovered and laid bare, the discussion is renewed on the following day, and from each occasion its own peculiar advantage is derived. They deliberate when they have no power to dissemble; they resolve when error is impossible.

A liquor for drinking is made out of barley or

other grain, and fermented into a certain resemblance to wine. The dwellers on the river-bank also buy wine. Their food is of a simple kind, consisting of wild-fruit, fresh game, and curdled milk. They satisfy their hunger without elaborate preparation and without delicacies. In quenching their thirst they are not equally moderate. If you indulge their love of drinking by supplying them with as much as they desire, they will be overcome by their own vices as easily as by the arms of an enemy.

One and the same kind of spectacle is always exhibited at every gathering. Naked youths who practise the sport bound in the dance amid swords and lances that threaten their lives. Experience gives them skill, and skill again gives grace; profit or pay are out of the question; however reckless their pastime, its reward is the pleasure of the spectators. Strangely enough they make games of hazard a serious occupation even when sober, and so venturesome are they about gaining or losing, that, when every other resource has failed, on the last and final throw they stake the freedom of their own persons. The loser goes into voluntary slavery; though the younger and stronger, he suffers himself to be bound and sold. Such is their stubborn persistency in a bad practice; they themselves call it honour. Slaves of this kind the owners part with in the way of commerce, and also to relieve themselves from the scandal of such a victory.

The other slaves are not employed after our manner with distinct domestic duties assigned to them, but each one has the management of a house and home of his own. The master requires from the slave a certain quantity of grain, of cattle, and of clothing, as he would from a tenant, and this is the limit of subjection. All other household functions are discharged by the wife and children. To strike a slave or to punish him with bonds or with hard labour is a rare occurrence. They often kill them, not in enforcing strict discipline, but on the impulse of passion, as they would an enemy, only it is done with impunity. The freedmen do not rank much above slaves, and are seldom of any weight in the family, never in the state, with the exception of those tribes which are ruled by kings. There indeed they rise above the freedborn and the noble; elsewhere the inferiority of the freedman marks the freedom of the state.

Of lending money on interest and increasing it by compound interest they know nothing—a more effectual safeguard than if it were prohibited.

Land proportioned to the number of inhabitants is occupied by the whole community in turn, and afterwards divided among them according to rank. A wide expanse of plains makes the partition easy. They till fresh fields every year, and they have still more land than enough; with the richness and extent of their soil, they do not laboriously exert themselves in planting orchards, inclosing meadows, and watering gardens. Corn is the only produce required from the earth; hence even the year itself is not divided by them into as many seasons as with us. Winter, spring, and summer have both a meaning and a name; the name and blessings of autumn are alike unknown.

In their funerals there is no pomp; they simply observe the custom of burning the bodies of illustrious men with certain kinds of wood. They do not heap garments or spices on the funeral pile. The weapons of the dead man and in some cases his horse are consigned to the fire. A turf mound forms the tomb. Monuments with their lofty elaborate splendour they reject as oppressive to the dead. Tears and lamentations they soon dismiss; grief and sorrow but slowly. It is thought becoming for women to bewail, for men to remember, the dead.

Such on the whole is the account which I have received of the origin and manners of the entire German people.

*   *   *

REVIEW QUESTIONS

1. As described by Tacitus, what were some of the principal values that governed German society?
2. How did those values compare with those of imperial Roman society as evidenced in some of the preceding readings?

7 ❧ CHRISTIANITY AND THE TRANSFORMATION OF THE ROMAN WORLD

By 300 C.E., the emperor Diocletian and his colleagues had reorganized the Roman Empire, which now appeared more prosperous and stable than it had been for decades. Paganism, a convenient but misleading name for the broad spectrum of ancient, nonmonotheistic beliefs, remained dominant, and Diocletian soon began a vigorous persecution of the Christian sect. By about 600 C.E., this world had profoundly changed. The Roman Empire had disappeared in the West, replaced by numerous barbarian kingdoms. Starting with the conversion of the emperor Constantine in 312 C.E., Christianity gradually triumphed over paganism in the Roman Empire, becoming the official religion before the collapse of the empire. Missionary work among the barbarian tribes succeeded in bringing new peoples like the Goths and Franks into the Christian fold. The barbarian kingdoms and the Christian Church, through its bishops and monasteries, transformed the legacies of the ancient world, religion, and classical culture and created the new society of early medieval Europe.

Constantine's conversion remains one of the most important events in late antiquity. The emperor's understanding of his new faith included the idea that he was an authority in religious matters and a leader of the church in this world. As emperor and high priest of the Roman state cult, Constantine retained the same legal rights over Christianity that earlier rulers had exercised over pagan cults. Of all the aspects of Roman culture, its legal system, based on imperial decrees and legal commentaries, was one of the main bequests to subsequent societies. The fifth-century C.E. Theodosian Code and the great compilations made under Emperor Justinian in the next century show the Christian Roman emperors trying to incorporate the recently tolerated (313 C.E.) and soon-enough only official religion (391 C.E.) into a legal system originally attuned to pagan values.

In the centuries before Christianity emerged from persecution, the new faith found adherents because of its promise of salvation, the supportive and caring nature of early Christian communities, and the witnessing of generations of *martyrs. For nearly three centuries Christianity existed in a context of bouts of persecution and indifference, as Rome's pagan subjects, Christians, and Jews were in conflict over the most basic beliefs. In addition to the texts collected into the New Testament and approved by church leaders, many other documents reveal both the spirit of the early martyrs and the effects of martyrdom on the people who witnessed it.*

One of Christianity's distinctive institutions was the monastery, and the Benedictine Rule demonstrates how a community dedicated to poverty, chastity, and obedience organized a common life for people wanting to escape the secular world and its temptations. Not everyone was called to be a nun or monk, but her or his style of life, as well as that of the more-isolated hermits, defined perfection, especially after the opportunities for martyrdom waned. The late empire's internal decay encouraged people to abandon the world, but it also attracted its most serious external threat, the waves of barbarians from the north and east. Tribes like the Franks and Visigoths, seeking protection inside the frontiers from more fearsome peoples like the Huns, ended up wrecking an empire they probably wanted to preserve for their own benefit. But as Rome was unable to defend its western frontiers, more doubts surfaced about the vitality and meaning of classical values.

Saint Augustine of Hippo in North Africa was perhaps the most significant voice of the late Roman world. His many books continued to influence theologians in the medieval and early modern periods and beyond. Augustine tried to account for the sack of Rome in 410 C.E. in terms that strengthened Christian beliefs and denied pagans the chance to blame the new religion for the empire's defeats. Augustine, laying the foundations for doctrines on original sin and predestination of the saved and damned, also took on one of the empire's most important social and economic institutions, slavery, and fit it into Christian belief. The Christian Church preserved some of the traditions and texts of ancient culture as most of this world crumbled.

CONSTANTINE

FROM An Oration

Constantine the Great (ruled 312–337 C.E.) converted to Christianity in 312 C.E., unified the empire under his rule by 324 C.E., and began the process of turning the Roman Empire into a Christian state. He also founded its new eastern capital at Constantinople and summoned the first great ecumenical council of the church at

Nicaea in 325 c.e. This document is the final part of a speech Constantine probably gave to a local church council in Antioch in the spring of 325 c.e. This oration displays the emperor's bombastic style and his opinions about the new religion and God he chose to adopt.

From *Eusebius,* vol. 1, *Nicene and Post-Nicene Fathers of the Christian Church,* edited by Henry Wace and Philip Schaff (1890), pp. 578–80.

*   *   *

Chapter XXII

To thee, Piety, I ascribe the cause of my own prosperity, and of all that I now possess. To this truth the happy issue of all my endeavors bears testimony: brave deeds, victories in war, and triumphs over conquered foes. This truth the great city itself allows with joy and praise. The people, too, of that much-loved city accord in the same sentiment, though once, deceived by ill-grounded hopes, they chose a ruler unworthy of themselves, a ruler who speedily received the chastisement which his audacious deeds deserved. But be it far from me now to recall the memory of these events, while holding converse with thee, Piety, and essaying with earnest endeavor to address thee with holy and gentle words. Yet will I say one thing, which haply shall not be unbefitting or unseemly. A furious, a cruel, and implacable war was maintained by the tyrants against thee, Piety, and thy holy churches: nor were there wanting some in Rome itself who exulted at a calamity so grievous to the public weal. Nay, the battlefield was prepared; when thou didst stand forth, and present thyself a voluntary victim, supported by faith in God. Then indeed it was that the cruelty of ungodly men, which raged incessantly like a devouring fire, wrought for thee a wondrous and ever memorable glory. Astonishment seized the spectators themselves, when they beheld the very executioners who tortured the bodies of their holy victims wearied out, and disgusted at the cruelties; the bonds loosened, the engines of torture powerless, the flames extinguished, while the sufferers preserved their constancy unshaken even for a moment. What, then,

hast thou gained by these atrocious deeds, most impious of men? And what was the cause of thy insane fury? Thou wilt say, doubtless, these acts of thine were done in honor of the gods. What gods are these? or what worthy conception hast thou of the Divine nature? Thinkest thou the gods are subject to angry passions as thou art? Were it so indeed, it had been better for thee to wonder at their strange determination than obey their harsh command, when they urged thee to the unrighteous slaughter of innocent men. Thou wilt allege, perhaps, the customs of thy ancestors, and the opinion of mankind in general, as the cause of this conduct. I grant the fact: for those customs are very like the acts themselves, and proceed from the self-same source of folly. Thou thoughtest, it may be, that some special power resided in images formed and fashioned by human art; and hence thy reverence, and diligent care lest they should be defiled: those mighty and highly exalted gods, thus dependent on the care of men!

Chapter XXIII

Compare our religion with your own. Is there not with us genuine concord, and unwearied love of others? If we reprove a fault, is not our object to admonish, not to destroy; our correction for safety, not for cruelty? Do we not exercise, not only sincere faith towards God, but fidelity in the relations of social life? Do we not pity the unfortunate? Is not ours a life of simplicity, which disdains to cover evil beneath the mask of fraud and hypocrisy? Do we not acknowledge the true God, and his undivided sovereignty? This is real godliness: this is religion sincere and truly undefiled: this is the life of wisdom; and they who have it are travelers, as it were, on a noble road which leads to eternal life. For he who has entered on such a course, and keeps his soul pure from the pollutions of the body, does not wholly die: rather may he be said to complete the service appointed him by God, than to die. Again, he who confesses allegiance to God is not easily overborne by insolence or rage, but nobly stands under the pressure of necessity and the trial of his constancy is, as it were, a passport to the favor of God. For we cannot doubt that the Deity is pleased with excellence in human conduct. For it would be absurd indeed if the powerful and the humble alike acknowledge gratitude to those from whose services they receive benefit, and repay them by services in return, and yet that he who is supreme and sovereign of all, nay, who is Good itself, should be negligent in this respect. Rather does he follow us throughout the course of our lives, is near us in every act of goodness, accepts, and at once rewards our virtue and obedience; though he defers the full recompense to that future period, when the actions of our lives shall pass under his review, and when those who are clear in that account shall receive the reward of everlasting life, while the wicked shall be visited with the penalties due to their crimes.

Chapter XXIV

To thee, Decius, I now appeal, who has trampled with insult on the labors of the righteous: to thee, the hater of the Church, the punisher of those who lived a holy life: what is now thy condition after death? How hard and wretched thy present circumstances! Nay, the interval before thy death gave proof enough of thy miserable fate, when, overthrown with all thine army on the plains of Scythia, thou didst expose the vaunted power of Rome to the contempt of the Goths. Thou, too, Valerian, who didst manifest the same spirit of cruelty towards the servants of God, hast afforded an example of righteous judgment. A captive in the enemies' hands, led in chains while yet arrayed in the purple and imperial attire, and at last thy skin stripped from thee, and preserved by com-

mand of Sapor the Persian king, thou hast left a perpetual trophy of thy calamity. And thou, Aurelian, fierce perpetrator of every wrong, how signal was thy fall, when, in the midst of thy wild career in Thrace, thou wast slain on the public highway, and didst fill the furrows of the road with thine impious blood!

Chapter XXV

Diocletian, however, after the display of relentless cruelty as a persecutor, evinced a consciousness of his own guilt, and, owing to the affliction of a disordered mind, endured the confinement of a mean and separate dwelling. What, then, did he gain by his active hostility against our God? Simply this, I believe, that he passed the residue of his life in continual dread of the lightning's stroke. Nicomedia attests the fact; eyewitnesses, of whom I myself am one, declare it. The palace, and the emperor's private chamber were destroyed, consumed by lightning, devoured by the fire of heaven. Men of understanding hearts had indeed predicted the issue of such conduct; for they could not keep silence, nor conceal their grief at such unworthy deeds; but boldly and openly expressed their feeling, saying one to another: "What madness is this? and what an insolent abuse of power, that man should dare to fight against God; should deliberately insult the most holy and just of all religions; and plan, without the slightest provocation, the destruction of so great a multitude of righteous persons? O rare example of moderation to his subjects! Worthy instructor of his army in the care and protection due to their fellow-citizens! Men who had never seen the backs of a retreating army plunged their swords into the breasts of their own countrymen!" So great was the effusion of blood shed, that if shed in battle with barbarian enemies, it had been sufficient to purchase a perpetual peace. At length, indeed, the providence of God took vengeance on these unhallowed deeds; but not without severe damage to the state. For the entire army of the emperor of whom I have just spoken, becoming subject to the authority of a worthless person, who had violently usurped the supreme authority at Rome (when the providence of God restored freedom to that great city), was destroyed in several successive battles. And when we remember the cries with which those who were oppressed, and who ardently longed for their native liberty, implored the help of God; and their praise and thanksgiving to him on the removal of the evils under which they had groaned, when that liberty was regained, and free and equitable intercourse restored: do not these things every way afford convincing proofs of the providence of God, and his affectionate regard for the interests of mankind?

Chapter XXVI

When men commend my services, which owe their origin to the inspiration of Heaven, do they not clearly establish the truth that God is the cause of the exploits I have performed? Assuredly they do: for it belongs to God to do whatever is best, and to man, to perform the commands of God. I believe, indeed, the best and noblest course of action is, when, before an attempt is made, we provide as far as possible for a secure result: and surely all men know that the holy service in which these hands have been employed has originated in pure and genuine faith towards God; that whatever has been done for the common welfare has been effected by active exertion combined with supplication and prayer; the consequence of which has been as great an amount of individual and public benefit as each could venture to hope for

himself and those he holds most dear. They have witnessed battles, and have been spectators of a war in which the providence of God has granted victory to this people: they have seen how he has favored and seconded our prayers. For righteous prayer is a thing invincible; and no one fails to attain his object who addresses holy supplication to God: nor is a refusal possible, except in the case of wavering faith; for God is ever favorable, ever ready to approve of human virtue. While, therefore, it is natural for man occasionally to err, yet God is not the cause of human error. Hence it becomes all pious persons to render thanks to the Saviour of all, first for our own individual security, and then for the happy posture of public affairs: at the same time intreating the favor of Christ with holy prayers and constant supplications, that he would continue to us our present blessings. For he is the invincible ally and protector of the righteous: he is the supreme judge of all things, the prince of immortality, the Giver of everlasting life.

REVIEW QUESTIONS

1. How does Constantine account for his own successes?
2. Describe Constantine's understanding of Christianity.
3. What difference did the emperor's conversion make to the ordinary men and women of the empire?

FROM The Theodosian Code: Roman Law

The Theodosian Code is a collection of imperial decrees put together in the early fifth century C.E. to arrange by topic the Roman legal tradition. The Roman Empire had no formal constitution, and its legal system depended on senatorial laws and precedent-setting decisions by emperors in particular cases. The selections here

SAN PAOLO FUORI LE MURI, ROME (C. 385 C.E.)

Interior of a classic late Roman nave. The building was begun in 385; it was largely rebuilt after a fire in 1823. The Christian Roman emperors intended to make a statement about their church. What were they trying to say?

from Book 16 are decisions on how the Christian Church and its officials should function in the empire's legal and tax policies. Both Church and state were also concerned about the heretics, people who believed the "wrong" things.

From *The Theodosian Code and Novels and the Sirmondian Constitutions,* by Claude Pharr (Princeton, N.J.: Princeton University Press, 1980), pp. 440–51.

Book 16

TITLE 1
THE CATHOLIC FAITH

1. Emperors Valentinian and Valens Augustuses to Symmachus, Prefect of the City

If any judge or apparitor should appoint men of the Christian religion as custodians of temples, he shall know that neither his life nor his fortunes will be spared.

Given on the fifteenth day before the kalends of December at Milan in the year of the consulship of Valentinian and Valens Augustuses.—November 17, 365; 364.

2. Emperors Gratian, Valentinian, and Theodosius Augustuses: An Edict to the People of the City of Constantinople

It is Our will that all the peoples who are ruled by the administration of Our Clemency shall practice that religion which the divine Peter the Apostle transmitted to the Romans, as the religion which he introduced makes clear even unto this day. It is evident that this is the religion that is followed by the Pontiff Damasus and by Peter, Bishop of Alexandria, a man of apostolic sanctity; that is, according to the apostolic discipline and the evangelic doctrine, we shall believe in the single Deity of the Father, the Son, and the Holy Spirit, under the concept of equal majesty and of the Holy Trinity.

We command that those persons who follow this rule shall embrace the name of Catholic Christians. The rest, however, whom We adjudge demented and insane, shall sustain the infamy of heretical dogmas, their meeting places shall not receive the name of churches, and they shall be smitten first by divine vengeance and secondly by the retribution of Our own initiative, which We shall assume in accordance with the divine judgment.

Given on the third day before the kalends of March at Thessalonica in the year of the fifth consulship of Gratian Augustus and the first consulship of Theodosius Augustus.—February 28, 380.

3. The same Augustuses to Auxonius, Proconsul of Asia

We command that all churches shall immediately be surrendered to those bishops who confess that the Father, the Son, and the Holy Spirit are of one majesty and virtue, of the same glory, and of one splendor; to those bishops who produce no dissonance by unholy distinction, but who affirm the concept of the Trinity by the assertion of three Persons and the unity of the Divinity; to those bishops who appear to have been associated in the communion of Nectarius, Bishop of the Church of Constantinople, and of Timotheus, Bishop of the City of Alexandria in Egypt; to those bishops also who, in the regions of the Orient, appear to be communicants with Pelagius, Bishop of Laodicea, and with Diodorus, Bishop of Tarsus; also, in the Proconsular Province of Asia and in the Diocese of Asia, with Amphilochius, Bishop of Iconium, and with Optimus, Bishop of Antioch; in the Diocese of Pontus, with Helladius, Bishop of Caesarea, and with Otreius of Melitene, and with Gregorius, Bishop of Nyssa; with Terennius, Bishop of Scythia, and with Marmarius, Bishop of Martianopolis. Those bishops who are of the communion and fellowship of such acceptable priests must be permitted to obtain the Catholic churches. All, however, who dissent from the communion of the faith of those who have been expressly mentioned in this special enumeration shall be expelled from their churches as manifest heretics and hereafter shall be altogether denied the right and power to obtain churches, in order that the priesthood of the true Nicene faith may remain pure, and after the clear regulations of Our law, there shall be no opportunity for malicious subtlety.

Given on the third day before the kalends of August at Heraclea in the year of the consulship of Eucherius and Syagrius.—July 30, 381.

4. Emperors Valentinian, Theodosius, and Arcadius Augustuses to Eusignius, Praetorian Prefect

We bestow the right of assembly upon those persons who believe according to the doctrines which in the times of Constantius of sainted memory were decreed as those that would endure forever, when the priests had been called together from all the Roman world and the faith was set forth at the Council of Ariminum by these very persons who are now known to dissent, a faith which was also confirmed by the Council of Constantinople. The right of voluntary assembly shall also be open to those persons for whom We have so ordered. If those persons who suppose that the right of assembly has been granted to them alone should attempt to provoke any agitation against the regulation of Our Tranquillity, they shall know that, as authors of sedition and as disturbers of the peace of the Church, they shall also pay the penalty of high treason with their life and blood. Punishment shall no less await those persons who may attempt to supplicate Us surreptitiously and secretly, contrary to this Our regulation.

Given on the tenth day before the kalends of February at Milan in the year of the consulship of Emperor Designate Honorius and of Evodius.—January 23, 386.

TITLE 2
BISHOPS, CHURCHES, AND CLERICS

1. Emperor Constantine Augustus
We have learned that clerics of the Catholic Church are being so harassed by a faction of heretics that they are being burdened by nominations and by service as tax receivers, as public custom demands, contrary to the privileges granted them. It is Our pleasure, therefore, that if Your Gravity should find any person thus harassed, another person shall be chosen as a substitute for him and that henceforward men of the aforesaid religion shall be protected from such outrages.

Given on the day before the kalends of November in the year of the third consulship of Constantine Augustus and of Licinius Caesar.—October 31, 313(?).

2. The same Augustus to Octavianus, Governor of Lucania and of Bruttium

Those persons who devote the services of religion to divine worship, that is, those who are called clerics, shall be exempt from all compulsory public services whatever, lest, through the sacrilegious malice of certain persons, they should be called away from divine services.

Given on the twelfth day before the kalends of November in the year of the fifth consulship of Constantine Augustus and the consulship of Licinius Caesar.—October 21, 319; 313.

INTERPRETATION: This law by special ordinance directs that no person whatsoever by sacrilegious ordinance shall presume to make tax collectors or tax gatherers of clerics. The law commands that such clerics shall be free from every compulsory public service, that is, from every duty and servitude, and shall zealously serve the Church.

3. The same Augustus to Bassus, Praetorian Prefect

A constitution was issued which directs that thenceforth no decurion or descendant of a decurion or even any person provided with adequate resources and suitable to undertake compulsory public services shall take refuge in the name and the service of the clergy, but that in the place of deceased clerics thereafter only those persons shall be chosen as substitutes who have slender fortunes and who are not held bound to such compulsory municipal services. But We have learned that those persons also are being disturbed who became associated with the clergy before the promulgation of the aforesaid law. We command, therefore, that the latter shall be freed from all annoyance, and that the former, who in evasion of public duties have taken refuge in the number of the clergy after the issuance of the law, shall be completely separated from that body, shall be restored to their orders and to the municipal councils, and shall perform their municipal duties.

Posted on the fifteenth day before the kalends of August in the year of the sixth consulship of Constantine Augustus and the consulship of Constantius Caesar.—July 18, 320; 329.

4. The same Augustus to the People

Every person shall have the liberty to leave at his death any property that he wishes to the most holy and venerable council of the Catholic Church. Wills shall not become void. There is nothing which is more due to men than that the expression of their last will, after which they can no longer will anything, shall be free and the power of choice, which does not return again, shall be unhampered.

Posted on the fifth day before the nones of July at Rome in the year of the second consulship of Crispus and Constantine Caesars.—July 3, 321.

5. The same Augustus to Helpidius

Whereas We have learned that certain ecclesiastics and others devoting their services to the Catholic sect have been compelled by men of different religions to the performance of lustral sacrifices, We decree by this sanction that, if any person should suppose that those who devote their services to the most sacred law may be forced to the ritual of an alien superstition, he shall be beaten publicly with clubs, provided that his legal status so permits. If, however, the consideration of his honorable rank protects him from such an outrage, he shall sustain the penalty of a very heavy fine, which shall be vindicated to the municipalities.

Given on the eighth day before the kalends of June at Sirmium in the year of the consulship of Severus and Rufinus.—May (December) 25, 323.

6. The same Augustus to Ablavius, Praetorian Prefect

Exemption from compulsory public services shall not be granted by popular consent, nor shall it be granted indiscriminately to all who petition under the pretext of being clerics, nor shall great numbers be added to the clergy rashly and beyond measure, but rather, when a cleric dies, another shall be selected to replace the deceased, one who has no kinship with a decurion family and who has not the wealth of resources whereby he may very easily support the compulsory public services. Thus, if there should be a dispute about the name of any person between a municipality and the clergy, if equity claims him for public service and if he is adjudged suitable for membership in the municipal council through either lineage or wealth, he shall be removed from the clergy and shall be delivered to the municipality. For the wealthy must assume secular obligations, and the poor must be supported by the wealth of the churches.

Posted on the kalends of June in the year of the seventh consulship of Constantine Augustus and the consulship of Constantius Caesar.—June 1, 326; 329.

7. The same Augustus to Valentinus, Governor of Numidia

Lectors of the divine scriptures, subdeacons, and the other clerics who through the injustice of heretics have been summoned to the municipal councils shall be absolved, and in the future, according to the practice of the Orient, they shall by no means be summoned to the municipal councils, but they shall possess fullest exemption.

Given on the nones of February at Sofia (Serdica) in the year of the consulship of Gallicanus and Symmachus.—February 5, 330.

8. Emperor Constantius Augustus to the Clergy, Greetings

According to the sanction which you are said to have obtained previously, no person shall obligate you and your slaves to new tax payments, but you shall enjoy exemption. Furthermore, you shall not be required to receive quartered persons, and if any of you, for the sake of a livelihood, should wish to conduct a business, they shall possess tax exemption.

Given on the sixth day before the kalends of September in the year of the consulship of Placidus and Romulus.—August 27, 343.

9. The same Augustus to Severianus, Proconsul of Achaea

All clerics must be exempt from compulsory services as decurions and from every annoyance of municipal duties. Their sons, moreover, must continue in the Church, if they are not held obligated to the municipal councils.

Given on the third day before the ides of April in the year of the consulship of Limenius and Catullinus.—April 11, 349.

10. Emperors Constantius and Constans Augustuses to all the Bishops throughout the various provinces.

In order that organizations in the service of the churches may be filled with a great multitude of people, tax exemption shall be granted to clerics and their acolytes, and they shall be protected from the exaction of compulsory public services of a menial nature. They shall by no means be subject to the tax payments of tradesmen, since it is manifest that the profits which they collect from stalls and workshops will benefit the poor. We decree also that their men who engage in trade shall be exempt from all tax payments. Likewise, the exaction of services for the maintenance of the supplementary postwagons shall cease. This indulgence We grant to their wives, children, and servants, to males and females equally, for We command that they also shall continue exempt from tax assessments.

Given on the seventh day before the kalends of June at Constantinople in the year of the sixth consulship of Constantius and the consulship of Constans.—May 26, 353; 320; 346.

11. The same Augustuses to Longinianus, Prefect of Egypt

We formerly sanctioned that bishops and clerics of the Catholic faith who possess nothing at all and are useless with respect to patrimony shall not be summoned to compulsory public services as decurions. But We learn that they are being disturbed in their life of perfection, to no public advantage. Therefore, We direct that their sons also who are not financially responsible and who are found to be below the legal age shall sustain no molestation.

Given on the fourth day before the kalends of March in the year of the seventh consulship of Constantius Augustus and the consulship of Constans Augustus.—February 26, 354; 342.

12. The same Augustuses to their dear friend Severus, Greetings

By a law of Our Clemency We prohibit bishops to be accused in the courts, lest there should be an unrestrained opportunity for fanatical spirits to accuse them, while the accusers assume that they will obtain impunity by the kindness of the bishops. Therefore, if any person should lodge any complaint, such complaint must unquestionably be examined before other bishops, in order that an opportune and suitable hearing may be arranged for the investigation of all concerned.

Given as a letter on the ninth day before the kalends of October.—September 23. Received on the nones of October in the year of the consulship of Arbitio and Lollianus.—October 7, 355.

INTERPRETATION: It is specifically prohibited that any person should dare to accuse a bishop before secular judges, but he shall not delay to submit to the hearing of bishops whatever he supposes may be due him according to the nature of the case, so that the assertions which he makes against the bishop may be decided in a court of other bishops.

13. The same Augustus and Julian Caesar to Leontius

We command that the privileges granted to the Church of the City of Rome and to its clerics shall be firmly guarded.

Given on the fourth day before the ides of November at Milan in the year of the ninth consulship of Constantius Augustus and the second consulship of Julian Caesar.—November 10, 357; 356.

14. The same Augustus and Julian Caesar to Bishop Felix

Clerics shall be protected from every injustice of an undue suit and from every wrong of an unjust exaction, and they shall not be summoned to compulsory public services of a menial nature. Moreover, when tradesmen are summoned to some legally prescribed tax payment, all clerics shall cease to be affected by such a disturbance; for if they have accumulated anything by thrift, foresight, or trading, but still in accordance with honesty, this must be administered for the use of the poor and needy, and whatever they have been able to acquire and collect from their workshops and stalls they shall regard as having been collected for the profit of religion.

(1) Moreover, with respect to their men who are employed in trade, the statutes of the sainted Emperor, that is, of Our father, provided with manifold regulations that the aforesaid clerics should abound in numerous privileges. (2) Therefore, with respect to the aforesaid clerics, the requirement of extraordinary services and all molestation shall cease. (3) Moreover, they and their resources and substance shall not be summoned to furnish supplementary postwagons.

(4) All clerics shall be assisted by the prerogative of this nature, namely, that wives of clerics and also their children and attendants, males and females equally, and their children, shall continue to be exempt forever from tax payments and free from such compulsory public services.

Given on the eighth day before the ides of De-

cember at Milan—December 6. Read into the records on the fifth day before the kalends of January in the year of the ninth consulship of Constantius Augustus and the second consulship of Julian Caesar.—December 28, 357; 356. Or: Read in court proceedings, acta, 2, 8, 1, n. 4.

*   *   *

16. The same Augustuses to the inhabitants of Antioch

If in any city, town, village, hamlet, or municipality, any person by a vow of the Christian faith should show to all persons the merit of exceptional and extraordinary virtue, he shall enjoy perpetual security. For it is Our will that he shall rejoice and glory always in the faith, since We are aware that Our State is sustained more by religion than by official duties and physical toil and sweat.

Given on the sixteenth day before the kalends of March at Antioch in the year of the consulship of Taurus and Florentius.—February 14, 361.

17. Emperors Valentinian and Valens Augustuses to the inhabitants of Byzacium

We forbid altogether that wealthy plebeians shall be received as clerics by the Church.

Given on the fourth day before the ides of September at Aquileia in the year of the consulship of the sainted Jovian and of Varronianus.—September 10 (12), 364.

*   *   *

20. Emperors Valentinian, Valens, and Gratian Augustuses to Damasus, Bishop of the City of Rome

Ecclesiastics, ex-ecclesiastics, and those men who wish to be called by the name of Continents shall not visit the homes of widows and female wards, but they shall be banished by the public courts, if hereafter the kinsmen, by blood or marriage, of the aforesaid women should suppose that such men ought to be reported to the authorities.

We decree, further, that the aforesaid clerics shall be able to obtain nothing whatever, through any act of liberality or by a last will of those women to whom they have attached themselves privately under the pretext of religion. Everything that may have been left by the aforesaid women to any one of the aforesaid ecclesiastics shall be ineffective to such an extent that they shall not be able, even through an interposed person, to obtain anything either by gift or by testament. Furthermore, if by chance after the admonition of Our law the aforesaid women should suppose that anything ought to be bestowed on the aforesaid men, either by gift or by last will, such property shall be appropriated by the fisc. If, on the other hand, the aforesaid men should receive anything through the will of the aforesaid women, to whose succession or property they are assisted either by the civil law or by benefit of the edict, they shall take it as near kinsmen.

Read in the churches at Rome on the third day before the kalends of August in the year of the consulship of Valentinian Augustus and the third consulship of Valens Augustus.—July 30, 370.

21. The same Augustuses to Ampelius, Prefect of the City

Those persons who have continuously served the Church shall be held exempt from service in the municipal councils, provided, however, that it shall be established that they have devoted themselves to the cult of Our law before the beginning of Our reign. All others who have joined the ecclesiastics after this time shall be recalled.

Given on the sixteenth day before the kalends of June in the year of the second consulship of Gratian Augustus and the consulship of Probus.—May 17, 371.

22. The same Augustuses to Paulinus, Governor of New Epirus

The general rule of the foregoing decree shall be valid and shall extend also to the persons of bishops and virgins as well as to the other persons who are included in the foregoing statute.

Given on the kalends of December at Trier in the year of the consulship of Modestus and Arintheus.—December 1, 372.

*   *   *

25. Emperors Gratian, Valentinian, and Theodosius Augustuses

Those persons who through ignorance confuse or through negligence violate and offend the sanctity of the divine law commit sacrilege.

Given on the third day before the kalends of March at Thessalonica in the year of the fifth consulship of Gratian Augustus and the first consulship of Theodosius Augustus.—February 28, 380.

*   *   *

29. Emperors Arcadius and Honorius Augustuses to Hierius, Vicar of Africa

We direct that whatever statutes were enacted by Our Fathers at different times with respect to the sacrosanct churches shall remain inviolate and unimpaired. None of their privileges, therefore, shall be altered, and protection shall be granted to all those persons who serve the churches, for We desire that reverence shall be increased in Our time rather than that any of the privileges which were formerly granted should be altered.

Given on the tenth day before the kalends of April at Milan in the year of the consulship of Olybrius and Probinus.—March 23, 395.

30. The same Augustuses to Theodorus, Praetorian Prefect

We decree nothing new by the present sanction; rather, We confirm those privileges that appear to have been granted formerly. We prohibit, therefore, under threat of punishment, that privileges which were formerly obtained through reverence for religion shall be curtailed, so that those who serve the Church may also enjoy fully those special benefits which the Church enjoys.

Given on the day before the kalends of February at Milan in the year of the consulship of Caesarius and Atticus.—January 31, 397.

31. The same Augustuses to Theodorus, Praetorian Prefect

If any person should break forth into such sacrilege that he should invade Catholic churches and

tened by a due sentence, he is deserving of deportation.

Given on the fifteenth day before the kalends of August at Constantinople in the year of the second consulship of Arcadius Augustus and the consulship of the Most Noble Rufinus.—July 18, 392.

4. Emperors Arcadius, Honorius, and Theodosius Augustuses to Anthemius, Master of Offices

All members of the office staffs shall be warned to abstain from participation in tumultuous conventicles, and if any persons with sacrilegious intent should dare to violate the authority of Our Imperial Divinity, they shall be deprived of their cincture of office and punished with the proscription of their goods.

Given on the fourth day before the kalends of February at Constantinople in the year of the sixth consulship of Honorius Augustus and the consulship of Aristaenetus.—January 29, 404.

*   *   *

TITLE 5
HERETICS

1. Emperor Constantine Augustus to Dracilianus

The privileges that have been granted in consideration of religion must benefit only the adherents of the Catholic faith. It is Our will, moreover, that heretics and schismatics shall not only be alien from these privileges but shall also be bound and subjected to various compulsory public services.

Posted on the kalends of September at Gerastus in the year of the seventh consulship of Constantine Augustus and the consulship of Constantius Caesar.—September 1, 326.

2. The same Augustus to Bassus

We have not found that the Novatians were precondemned to such an extent that We should suppose that those things which they sought ought not to be granted to them. We direct, therefore, that they shall firmly possess, without disquietude,

their own church buildings and places suitable for burial: that is, those properties which they have held for a long time either through purchase or through acquisition in any manner whatsoever. Of course, due provision must be made that they shall not attempt to appropriate to themselves any of the property which manifestly belonged to the Church of perpetual sanctity before the schism.

Given on the seventh day before the kalends of October at Spoleto in the year of the seventh consulship of Constantine Augustus and the consulship of Constantius Caesar.—September 25, 326.

*   *   *

5. Emperors Gratian, Valentinian, and Theodosius Augustuses to Hesperius, Praetorian Prefect

All heresies are forbidden by both divine and imperial laws and shall forever cease. If any profane man by his punishable teachings should weaken the concept of God, he shall have the right to know such noxious doctrines only for himself but shall not reveal them to others to their hurt. If any person by a renewed death should corrupt bodies that have been redeemed by the venerable baptismal font, by taking away the effect of that ceremony which he repeats, he shall know such doctrines for himself alone, and he shall not ruin others by his nefarious teaching. All teachers and ministers alike of this perverse superstition shall abstain from the gathering places of a doctrine already condemned, whether they defame the name of bishop by the assumption of such priestly office, or, that which is almost the same, they belie religion with the appellation of priests, or also if they call themselves deacons, although they may not even be considered Christians. Finally, the rescript that was recently issued at Sirmium shall be annulled, and there shall remain only those enactments pertaining to Catholic doctrine which were decreed by Our father of eternal memory and which We ourselves commanded by an equally manifold order, which will survive forever.

Given on the third day before the nones of August at Milan.—August 3. Received on the thir-

teenth day before the kalends of September in the year of the consulship of Auxonius and Olybrius.—August 20, 379.

6. The same Augustuses to Eutropius, Praetorian Prefect

No place for celebrating their mysteries, no opportunity for exercising the madness of their excessively obstinate minds shall be available to the heretics. All men shall know also that even if some concession has been impetrated by that kind of men through any special rescript whatever, if it has been fraudulently elicited, it shall not be valid.

1. Crowds shall be kept away from the unlawful congregations of all the heretics. The name of the One and Supreme God shall be celebrated everywhere; the observance, destined to remain forever, of the Nicene faith, as transmitted long ago by Our ancestors and confirmed by the declaration and testimony of divine religion, shall be maintained. The contamination of the Photinian pestilence, the poison of the Arian sacrilege, the crime of the Eunomian perfidy, and the sectarian monstrosities, abominable because of the ill-omened names of their authors, shall be abolished even from the hearing of men.

2. On the other hand, that man shall be accepted as a defender of the Nicene faith and as a true adherent of the Catholic religion who confesses that Almighty God and Christ the Son of God are One in name, God of God, Light of Light, who does not violate by denial the Holy Spirit which we hope for and receive from the Supreme Author of things; that man who esteems, with the perception of inviolate faith, the undivided substance of the incorrupt Trinity, that substance which those of the orthodox faith call, employing a Greek word, *ousia.* The latter beliefs are surely more acceptable to Us and must be venerated.

3. Those persons, however, who are not devoted to the aforesaid doctrines shall cease to assume, with studied deceit, the alien name of true religion, and they shall be branded upon the disclosure of their crimes. They shall be removed and completely barred from the threshold of all churches, since We forbid all heretics to hold unlawful assemblies within the towns. If factions should attempt to do anything, We order that their madness shall be banished and that they shall be driven away from the very walls of the cities, in order that Catholic churches throughout the whole world may be restored to all orthodox bishops who hold the Nicene faith.

Given on the fourth day before the ides of January at Constantinople in the year of the consulship of Eucherius and Syagrius.—January 10, 381.

REVIEW QUESTIONS

1. What did the emperors and their officials want from the church?
2. What benefits did the church expect from the state?
3. What are the assumptions and logic of Roman legal thought?

IGNATIUS OF ANTIOCH

Letter to the Romans

Around the year 110 C.E. Ignatius of Antioch in Syria wrote a series of letters to communities of Christians. In these letters he argued against heretics and the Gnostics; in this one to the Romans, he made a personal statement about his approaching martyrdom. The letter shows the Christian community immediately after the age of the Apostles and is a precious early source, not much later than the New Testament.

From *Early Christian Fathers,* by Cyril C. Richardson (Basingstoke, Eng.: Macmillan Publishers, 1970), pp. 102–6.

Greetings in Jesus Christ, the Son of the Father, from Ignatius, the "God-inspired," to the church that is in charge of affairs in Roman quarters and that the Most High Father and Jesus Christ, his only Son, have magnificently embraced in mercy and love. You have been granted light both by the will of Him who willed all that is, and by virtue of your believing in Jesus Christ, our God, and of loving him. You are a credit to God: you deserve your renown and are to be congratulated. You deserve praise and success and are privileged to be without blemish. Yes, you rank first in love, being true to Christ's law and stamped with the Father's name. To you, then, sincerest greetings in Jesus Christ, our God, for you cleave to his every commandment—observing not only their letter but their spirit—being permanently filled with God's grace and purged of every stain alien to it.

Since God has answered my prayer to see you godly people, I have gone on to ask for more. I mean, it is as a prisoner for Christ Jesus that I hope to greet you, if indeed it be God's will that I should deserve to meet my end. Things are off to a good start. May I have the good fortune to meet my fate without interference! What I fear is your generosity which may prove detrimental to me. For you can easily do what you want to, whereas it is hard for me to get to God unless you let me alone. I do not want you to please men, but to please God, just as you are doing. For I shall never again have such a chance to get to God, nor can you, if you keep quiet, get credit for a finer deed. For if you quietly let me alone, people will see in me God's Word. But if you are enamored of my mere body, I shall, on the contrary, be a meaningless noise. Grant me no more than to be a sacrifice for God while there is an altar at hand. Then you can form yourselves into a choir and sing praises to the Father in Jesus Christ that God gave the bishop of Syria the privilege of reaching the sun's setting when he summoned him from its rising. It is a grand thing for my life to set on the world, and for me to be on my way to God, so that I may rise in his presence.

You never grudged anyone. You taught others. So I want you to substantiate the lessons that you bid them heed. Just pray that I may have strength of soul and body so that I may not only talk about martyrdom, but really want it. It is not that I want merely to be called a Christian, but actually to *be* one. Yes, if I prove to be one, then I can have the name. Then, too, I shall be a convincing Christian only when the world sees me no more. Nothing you can see has real value. Our God Jesus Christ, indeed, has revealed himself more clearly by returning to the Father. The greatness of Christianity lies in its being hated by the world, not in its being convincing to it.

I am corresponding with all the churches and bidding them all realize that I am voluntarily dying for God—if, that is, you do not interfere. I plead with you, do not do me an unseasonable kindness. Let me be fodder for wild beasts—that is how I can get to God. I am God's wheat and I am being ground by the teeth of wild beasts to make a pure loaf for Christ. I would rather that you fawn on the beasts so that they may be my tomb and no scrap of my body be left. Thus, when I have fallen asleep, I shall be a burden to no one. Then I shall be a real disciple of Jesus Christ when the world sees my body no more. Pray Christ for me that by these means I may become God's sacrifice. I do not give you orders like Peter and Paul. They were apostles: I am a convict. They were at liberty: I am still a slave. But if I suffer, I shall be emancipated by Jesus Christ; and united to him, I shall rise to freedom.

Even now as a prisoner, I am learning to forgo my own wishes. All the way from Syria to Rome I am fighting with wild beasts, by land and sea, night and day, chained as I am to ten leopards (I mean to a detachment of soldiers), who only get worse the better you treat them. But by their injustices I am becoming a better disciple, "though not for that reason am I acquitted." What a thrill I shall have from the wild beasts that are ready for me! I hope they will make short work of me. I shall coax them on to eat me up at once and not to hold off, as sometimes happens, through fear. And if they are reluctant, I shall force them to it. Forgive me—I know what is good for me. Now is the moment I am beginning to be a disciple. May nothing seen or unseen begrudge me making my way to Jesus Christ. Come fire, cross, battling with wild beasts, wrenching of bones, mangling of limbs, crushing of my whole body, cruel tortures of the devil—only let me get to Jesus Christ! Not the wide bounds of earth nor the kingdoms of this world will avail me anything. "I would rather die" and get to Jesus Christ, than reign over the ends of the earth. That is whom I am looking for—the One who died for us. That is whom I want—the One who rose for us. I am going through the pangs

of being born. Sympathize with me, my brothers! Do not stand in the way of my coming to life—do not wish death on me. Do not give back to the world one who wants to be God's; do not trick him with material things. Let me get into the clear light and manhood will be mine. Let me imitate the Passion of my God. If anyone has Him in him, let him appreciate what I am longing for, and sympathize with me, realizing what I am going through.

The prince of this world wants to kidnap me and pervert my godly purpose. None of you, then, who will be there, must abet him. Rather be on my side—that is, on God's. Do not talk Jesus Christ and set your heart on the world. Harbor no envy. If, when I arrive, I make a different plea, pay no attention to me. Rather heed what I am now writing to you. For though alive, it is with a passion for death that I am writing to you. My Desire has been crucified and there burns in me no passion for material things. There is living water in me, which speaks and says inside me, "Come to the Father." I take no delight in corruptible food or in the dainties of this life. What I want is God's bread, which is the flesh of Christ, who came from David's line; and for drink I want his blood: an immortal love feast indeed!

I do not want to live any more on a human plane. And so it shall be, if you want it to. Want it to, so that you will be wanted! Despite the brevity of my letter, trust my request. Yes, Jesus Christ will clarify it for you and make you see I am really in earnest. He is the guileless mouth by which the Father has spoken truthfully. Pray for me that I reach my goal. I have written prompted, not by human passion, but by God's will. If I suffer, it will be because you favored me. If I am rejected, it will be because you hated me.

Remember the church of Syria in your prayers. In my place they have God for their shepherd. Jesus Christ alone will look after them—he, and your love. I blush to be reckoned among them, for I do not deserve it, being the least of them and an afterthought. Yet by his mercy I shall be something, if, that is, I get to God.

With my heart I greet you; and the churches which have welcomed me, not as a chance passerby, but in the name of Jesus Christ, send their love. Indeed, even those that did not naturally lie on my route went ahead to prepare my welcome in the different towns. I am sending this letter to you from Smyrna by those praiseworthy Ephesians. With me, along with many others, is Crocus—a person very dear to me. I trust you have had word about those who went ahead of me from Syria to Rome for God's glory. Tell them I am nearly there. They are all a credit to God and to you; so you should give them every assistance. I am writing this to you on the twenty-fourth of August. Farewell, and hold out to the end with the patience of Jesus Christ.

REVIEW QUESTIONS

1. What did Ignatius hope to accomplish by his death?
2. How does he describe his attitude toward death?
3. How might a contemporary pagan react to the sentiments in this letter?

The Martyrdom of Polycarp

Around the year 156 C.E. Polycarp, a leader of the church in Smyrna in Asia Minor, was martyred. A group of his followers composed the following account of his arrest, trial, and execution. This is one of the earliest documents on martyrdom, which was experienced by many men and women in the phases of persecution in the Roman Empire. Authentic texts on martyrdom were an important means by which the early churches kept alive the memory of martyrs, especially for those who did not see the actual events described in the acts.

From *Early Christian Fathers*, by Cyril C. Richardson (Basingstoke, Eng.: Macmillan Publishers, 1970), pp. 149–58.

The church of God that sojourns at Smyrna to the church of God that sojourns at Philomelium, and to all those of the holy and Catholic Church who sojourn in every place: may mercy, peace, and love be multiplied from God the Father and our Lord Jesus Christ.

We write you, brethren, the things concerning those who suffered martyrdom, especially the blessed Polycarp, who put an end to the persecution by sealing it, so to speak, through his own witness. For almost everything that led up to it happened in order that the Lord might show once again a martyrdom conformable to the gospel. For he waited to be betrayed, just as the Lord did, to the end that we also might be imitators of him, "not looking only to that which concerns ourselves, but also to that which concerns our neighbors." For it is a mark of true and steadfast love for one not only to desire to be saved oneself, but all the brethren also.

Blessed and noble, indeed, are all the martyrdoms that have taken place according to God's will; for we ought to be very reverent in ascribing to God power over all things. For who would not admire their nobility and patient endurance and love of their Master? Some of them, so torn by scourging that the anatomy of their flesh was visible as far as the inner veins and arteries, endured with such patience that even the bystanders took pity and wept; others achieved such heroism that not one of them uttered a cry or a groan, thus showing all of us that at the very hour of their tortures the most noble martyrs of Christ were no longer in the flesh, but rather that the Lord stood by them and conversed with them. And giving themselves over to the grace of Christ they despised the tortures of this world, purchasing for themselves in the space of one hour the life eternal. To them the fire of their inhuman tortures was cold; for they set before their eyes escape from the fire that is everlasting and never quenched, while with the eyes of their heart they gazed upon the good things reserved for those that endure patiently, "which things neither ear has heard nor eye has seen, nor has there entered into the heart of man." But they were shown to them by the Lord, for they were no longer men, but were already angels. Similarly, those condemned to the wild beasts endured fearful punishments, being made to lie on sharp shells and punished with other forms of various torments, in order that the devil might bring them, if possible, by means of the prolonged punishment, to a denial of their faith.

Many, indeed, were the machinations of the devil against them. But, thanks be to God, he did not prevail against them all. For the most noble Germanicus encouraged their timidity through his own patient endurance—who also fought with the beasts in a distinguished way. For when the proconsul, wishing to persuade him, bade him have pity on his youth, he forcibly dragged the wild beast toward himself, wishing to obtain more quickly a release from their wicked and lawless life. From this circumstance, all the crowd, marveling at the heroism of the God-loving and God-fearing race of the Christians, shouted: "Away with the atheists! Make search for Polycarp!"

But a Phrygian, named Quintus, lately arrived from Phrygia, took fright when he saw the wild beasts. In fact, he was the one who had forced himself and some others to come forward voluntarily. The proconsul by much entreaty persuaded him to take the oath and to offer the sacrifice.

For this reason, therefore, brethren, we do not praise those who come forward of their own accord, since the gospel does not teach us so to do.

The most admirable Polycarp, when he first heard of it, was not perturbed, but desired to remain in the city. But the majority induced him to withdraw, so he retired to a farm not far from the city and there stayed with a few friends, doing nothing else night and day but pray for all men and for the churches throughout the world, as was his constant habit. And while he was praying, it so happened, three days before his arrest, that he had a vision and saw his pillow blazing with fire, and turning to those who were with him he said, "I must be burned alive."

And while those who were searching for him continued their quest, he moved to another farm, and forthwith those searching for him arrived. And when they did not find him, they seized two young slaves, one of whom confessed under torture. For it was really impossible to conceal him, since the very ones who betrayed him were of his own household. And the chief of the police, who chanced to have the same name as Herod, was zealous to bring him into the arena in order that he might fulfill his own appointed lot of being made a partaker with Christ; while those who betrayed him should suffer the punishment of Judas himself.

Taking, therefore, the young slave on Friday about suppertime, the police, mounted and with their customary arms, set out as though "hasting after a robber." And late in the evening they came up with him and found him in bed in the upper room of a small cottage. Even so he could have escaped to another farm, but he did not wish to do so, saying, "God's will be done." Thus, when he heard of their arrival, he went downstairs and talked with them, while those who looked on marveled at his age and constancy, and at how there should be such zeal over the arrest of so old a man. Straightway he ordered food and drink, as much as they wished, to be set before them at that hour, and he asked them to give him an hour so that he might pray undisturbed. And when they consented, he stood and prayed—being so filled with the grace of God that for two hours he could not hold his peace, to the amazement of those who heard. And many repented that they had come to get such a devout old man.

When at last he had finished his prayer, in which he remembered all who had met with him at any time, both small and great, both those with and those without renown, and the whole Catholic Church throughout the world, the hour of departure having come, they mounted him on an ass and brought him into the city. It was a great Sabbath. And there the chief of the police, Herod, and his father, Nicetas, met him and transferred him to their carriage, and tried to persuade him, as they sat beside him, saying, "What harm is there to say 'Lord Caesar,' and to offer incense and all that sort of thing, and to save yourself?"

At first he did not answer them. But when they persisted, he said, "I am not going to do what you advise me."

Then when they failed to persuade him, they uttered dire threats and made him get out with such speed that in dismounting from the carriage he bruised his shin. But without turning around, as though nothing had happened, he proceeded swiftly, and was led into the arena, there being such a tumult in the arena that no one could be heard. But as Polycarp was entering the arena, a voice from heaven came to him, saying, "Be strong, Polycarp, and play the man." No one saw the one speaking, but those of our people who were present heard the voice.

And when finally he was brought up, there was a great tumult on hearing that Polycarp had been arrested. Therefore, when he was brought before him, the proconsul asked him if he were Polycarp. And when he confessed that he was, he tried to persuade him to deny the faith, saying, "Have respect to your age"—and other things that customarily follow this, such as, "Swear by the fortune of Caesar; change your mind; say, 'Away with the atheists!'"

But Polycarp looked with earnest face at the whole crowd of lawless heathen in the arena, and

motioned to them with his hand. Then, groaning and looking up to heaven, he said, "Away with the atheists!"

But the proconsul was insistent and said: "Take the oath, and I shall release you. Curse Christ."

Polycarp said: "Eighty-six years I have served him, and he never did me any wrong. How can I blaspheme my King who saved me?"

And upon his persisting still and saying, "Swear by the fortune of Caesar," he answered, "If you vainly suppose that I shall swear by the fortune of Caesar, as you say, and pretend that you do not know who I am, listen plainly: I am a Christian. But if you desire to learn the teaching of Christianity, appoint a day and give me a hearing."

The proconsul said, "Try to persuade the people."

But Polycarp said, "You, I should deem worthy of an account; for we have been taught to render honor, as is befitting, to rulers and authorities appointed by God so far as it does us no harm; but as for these, I do not consider them worthy that I should make defense to them."

But the proconsul said: "I have wild beasts. I shall throw you to them, if you do not change your mind."

But he said: "Call them. For repentance from the better to the worse is not permitted us; but it is noble to change from what is evil to what is righteous."

And again he said to him, "I shall have you consumed with fire, if you despise the wild beasts, unless you change your mind."

But Polycarp said: "The fire you threaten burns but an hour and is quenched after a little; for you do not know the fire of the coming judgment and everlasting punishment that is laid up for the impious. But why do you delay? Come, do what you will."

And when he had said these things and many more besides he was inspired with courage and joy, and his face was full of grace, so that not only did it not fall with dismay at the things said to him, but on the contrary, the proconsul was astonished, and sent his own herald into the midst of the arena to proclaim three times: "Polycarp has confessed himself to be a Christian."

When this was said by the herald, the entire crowd of heathen and Jews who lived in Smyrna shouted with uncontrollable anger and a great cry: "This one is the teacher of Asia, the father of the Christians, the destroyer of our gods, who teaches many not to sacrifice nor to worship."

Such things they shouted and asked the Asiarch Philip that he let loose a lion on Polycarp. But he said it was not possible for him to do so, since he had brought the wild-beast sports to a close. Then they decided to shout with one accord that he burn Polycarp alive. For it was necessary that the vision which had appeared to him about his pillow should be fulfilled, when he saw it burning while he was praying, and turning around had said prophetically to the faithful who were with him, "I must be burned alive."

Then these things happened with such dispatch, quicker than can be told—the crowds in so great a hurry to gather wood and faggots from the workshops and the baths, the Jews being especially zealous, as usual, to assist with this. When the fire was ready, and he had divested himself of all his clothes and unfastened his belt, he tried to take off his shoes, though he was not heretofore in the habit of doing this because each of the faithful always vied with one another as to which of them would be first to touch his body. For he had always been honored, even before his martyrdom, for his holy life. Straightway then, they set about him the material prepared for the pyre. And when they were about to nail him also, he said: "Leave me as I am. For he who grants me to endure the fire will enable me also to remain on the pyre unmoved, without the security you desire from the nails."

So they did not nail him, but tied him. And with his hands put behind him and tied, like a noble ram out of a great flock ready for sacrifice, a burnt offering ready and acceptable to God, he looked up to heaven and said:

Lord God Almighty, Father of thy beloved and blessed Servant Jesus Christ, through whom we have received full knowledge of thee, "the God of angels and powers and all creation" and of the whole race of the righteous who live in thy presence: I bless thee, because thou hast deemed me worthy of this day and hour, to take my part in the number of the martyrs, in the cup of thy Christ, for "resurrection to eternal life" of soul and body in the immortality of the Holy Spirit; among whom may I be received in thy presence this day as a rich and acceptable sacrifice, just as thou hast prepared and revealed beforehand and fulfilled, thou that art the true God without any falsehood. For this and for everything I praise thee, I bless thee, I glorify thee, through the eternal and heavenly High Priest, Jesus Christ, thy beloved Servant, through whom be glory to thee with him and Holy Spirit both now and unto the ages to come. Amen.

And when he had concluded the Amen and finished his prayer, the men attending to the fire lighted it. And when the flame flashed forth, we saw a miracle, we to whom it was given to see. And we are preserved in order to relate to the rest what happened. For the fire made the shape of a vaulted chamber, like a ship's sail filled by the wind, and made a wall around the body of the martyr. And he was in the midst, not as burning flesh, but as bread baking or as gold and silver refined in a furnace. And we perceived such a sweet aroma as the breath of incense or some other precious spice.

At length, when the lawless men saw that his body could not be consumed by the fire, they commanded an executioner to go to him and stab him with a dagger. And when he did this a dove and a great quantity of blood came forth, so that the fire was quenched and the whole crowd marveled that there should be such a difference between the unbelievers and the elect. And certainly the most admirable Polycarp was one of these elect, in whose times among us he showed himself an apostolic and prophetic teacher and bishop of the Catholic Church in Smyrna. Indeed, every utterance that came from his mouth was accomplished and will be accomplished.

But the jealous and malicious evil one, the adversary of the race of the righteous, seeing the greatness of his martyrdom and his blameless life from the beginning, and how he was crowned with the wreath of immortality and had borne away an incontestable reward, so contrived it that his corpse should not be taken away by us, although many desired to do this and to have fellowship with his holy flesh. He instigated Nicetas, the father of Herod and brother of Alce, to plead with the magistrate not to give up his body, "else," said he, "they will abandon the Crucified and begin worshiping this one." This was done at the instigation and insistence of the Jews, who also watched when we were going to take him from the fire, being ignorant that we can never forsake Christ, who suffered for the salvation of the whole world of those who are saved, the faultless for the sinners, nor can we ever worship any other. For we worship this One as Son of God, but we love the martyrs as disciples and imitators of the Lord, deservedly so, because of their unsurpassable devotion to their own King and Teacher. May it be also our lot to be their companions and fellow disciples!

The captain of the Jews, when he saw their contentiousness, set it [his body] in the midst and burned it, as was their custom. So we later took up his bones, more precious than costly stones and more valuable than gold, and laid them away in a suitable place. There the Lord will permit us, so far as possible, to gather together in joy and gladness to celebrate the day of his martyrdom as a birthday, in memory of those athletes who have gone before, and to train and make ready those who are to come hereafter.

Such are the things concerning the blessed Polycarp, who, martyred at Smyrna along with twelve others from Philadelphia, is alone remembered so much the more by everyone, that he is even spoken of by the heathen in every place. He was not only a noble teacher, but also a distinguished martyr, whose martyrdom all desire to imitate as one according to the gospel of Christ. By his patient endurance he overcame the wicked magistrate and so received the crown of immortality; and he rejoices with the apostles and all the righteous to glorify God the Father Almighty and to bless our Lord Jesus Christ, the Saviour of our souls and Helmsman of our bodies and Shepherd of the Catholic Church throughout the world.

You requested, indeed, that these things be related to you more fully, but for the present we have briefly reported them through our brother Marcion. When you have informed yourselves of these things, send this letter to the brethren elsewhere, in order that they too might glorify the Lord, who makes his choices from his own servants. To him who is able by his grace and bounty to bring us to his everlasting Kingdom, through his Servant, the only-begotten Jesus Christ, be glory, honor, might, majesty, throughout the ages. Greet all the saints. Those with us greet you and also Evarestus, who wrote this, with his whole household.

The blessed Polycarp was martyred on the second day of the first part of the month Xanthicus, the seventh day before the kalends of March, a great Sabbath, at two o'clock P.M. He was arrested by Herod, when Philip of Tralles was high priest, and Statius Quadratus was proconsul, but in the everlasting reign of our Lord Jesus Christ. To him be glory, honor, majesty, and the eternal throne, from generation to generation. Amen.

We bid you farewell, brethren, as you live by the word of Jesus Christ according to the gospel, with whom be glory to God the Father and Holy Spirit, unto the salvation of his holy elect; just as the blessed Polycarp suffered martyrdom, in whose footsteps may it be our lot to be found in the Kingdom of Jesus Christ.

These things Gaius copied from the papers of Irenaeus, a disciple of Polycarp; he also lived with Irenaeus. And Isocrates, wrote it in Corinth from the copy of Gaius. Grace be with all.

I, Pionius, again wrote it from the aforementioned copy, having searched for it according to a revelation of the blessed Polycarp, who appeared to me, as I shall explain in the sequel. I gathered it together when it was almost worn out with age, in order that the Lord Jesus Christ might bring me also with his elect unto his heavenly Kingdom. To him be glory with the Father and Holy Spirit unto the ages of ages. Amen.

Another Epilogue from the Moscow Manuscript

These things Gaius copied from the papers of Irenaeus. He also lived with Irenaeus, who had been a disciple of the holy Polycarp. For this Irenaeus, at the time of the martyrdom of Bishop Polycarp, was in Rome and taught many; and many of his excellent and orthodox writings are in circulation, in which he mentions Polycarp, for he was taught by him. He ably refuted every heresy and handed down the ecclesiastical and Catholic rule, as he had received it from the saint. He says this also: that once when Marcion, after whom the Marcionites are called, met the holy Polycarp and said, "Do you know us, Polycarp?" he said to Marcion, "I know you; I know the first-born of Satan." And

this fact is also found in the writings of Irenaeus, that on the day and at the hour when Polycarp was martyred in Smyrna, Irenaeus, being in the city of Rome, heard a voice like a trumpet saying, "Polycarp has suffered martyrdom."

From these papers of Irenaeus, then, as was said above, Gaius made a copy, and from Gaius' copy Isocrates made another in Corinth. And I, Pionius, again from the copies of Isocrates wrote according to the revelation of holy Polycarp, when I searched for it, and gathered it together when it was almost worn out with age, in order that the Lord Jesus Christ might bring me with his elect unto his heavenly Kingdom. To whom be glory with the Father and the Son and the Holy Spirit unto the ages of ages. Amen.

REVIEW QUESTIONS

1. What threat did Polycarp pose to the Roman state?
2. What does this document reveal about relations among Christians, Jews, and pagans?
3. How did Polycarp's friends portray him as the ideal martyr?

ST. BENEDICT

FROM *The Rule*

St. Benedict (ca. 480–547 C.E.), the author of The Rule of Saint Benedict *and founder of the monastery of Monte Cassino in southern Italy, drew on Egyptian and Syrian practices for his guidelines for a religious community. By withdrawing from the world and its temptations, the monks wanted to fight the devil and secure their own salvation. The monastery was in theory a self-sustaining community where all members prayed and worked. The following sections of the rule discuss some central values: obedience, silence, and humility.*

From *The Rule of Saint Benedict,* by Cardinal Gasquet (Whitestone: Cooper Square, 1966).

Chapter V
On Obedience

The first degree of humility is prompt obedience. This is required of all who, whether by reason of the holy servitude to which they are pledged, or through fear of hell, or to attain to the glory of eternal life, hold nothing more dear than Christ. Such disciples delay not in doing what is ordered by their superior, just as if the command had come from God. Of such our Lord says, *At the hearing of the ear he hath obeyed me.* And to the teachers He likewise says, *He that heareth you, heareth me.*

For this reason such disciples, surrendering forthwith all they possess, and giving up their own will, leave unfinished what they were working at, and with the ready foot of obedience in their acts follow the word of command. Thus, as it were, at the same moment comes the order of the master and the finished work of the disciple: with the speed of the fear of God both go jointly forward and are quickly effected by such as ardently desire to walk in the way of eternal life. These take the narrow way, of which the Lord saith, *Narrow is the way which leads to life.* That is, they live not as they themselves will, neither do they obey their own desires and pleasures; but following the command and direction of another and abiding in their monasteries, their desire is to be ruled by an abbot. Without doubt such as these carry out that saying of our Lord, *I came not to do my own will, but the will of Him Who sent me.*

This kind of obedience will be both acceptable to God and pleasing to men, when what is ordered is not done out of fear, or slowly and coldly, grudgingly, or with reluctant protest. Obedience shown to superiors is indeed given to God, Who Himself hath said, *He that heareth you, heareth Me.* What is commanded should be done by those under obedience, with a good will, since *God loveth a cheerful giver.* If the disciple obey unwillingly and murmur in word as well as in heart, it will not be accepted by God, Who considereth the heart of a murmurer, even if he do what was ordered. For a work done in this spirit shall have no reward; rather shall the doer incur the penalty appointed for murmurers if he amend not and make not satisfaction.

Chapter VI
On Silence

Let us do as the prophet says, *I have said, I will keep my ways, that I offend not with my tongue. I have been watchful over my mouth: I held my peace and humbled myself and was silent from speaking even good things.* Here the prophet shows that, for the sake of silence, we are at times to abstain even from good talk. If this be so, how much more needful is it that we refrain from evil words, on account of the penalty of the sin! Because of the importance of silence, therefore, let leave to speak be seldom given, even to perfect disciples, although their talk be of good and holy matters and tending to edification, since it is written, *In much speaking, thou shalt not escape sin.* The master, indeed, should speak and teach: the disciple should hold his peace and listen.

Whatever, therefore, has to be asked of the prior, let it be done with all humility and with reverent submission. But as to coarse, idle words, or such as move to laughter, we utterly condemn and ban them in all places. We do not allow any disciple to give mouth to them.

Chapter VII
On Humility

Brethren, Holy Scripture cries out to us, saying, *Every one who exalteth himself shall be humbled, and he who humbleth himself shall be exalted.* In this it tells us that every form of self-exaltation is a kind of pride, which the prophet declares he carefully avoided, where he says, *Lord, my heart is not exalted, neither are my eyes lifted up; neither have I walked in great things, nor in wonders above myself. And why? If I did not think humbly, but exalted my soul: as a child weaned from his mother, so wilt Thou reward my soul.*

Wherefore, brethren, if we would scale the

summit of humility, and swiftly gain the heavenly height which is reached by our lowliness in this present life, we must set up a ladder of climbing deeds like that which Jacob saw in his dream, whereon angels were descending and ascending. Without doubt that descending and ascending is to be understood by us as signifying that we descend by exalting ourselves and ascend by humbling ourselves. But the ladder itself thus set up is our life in this world, which by humility of heart is lifted by our Lord to heaven. Our body and soul we may indeed call the sides of the ladder in which our divine vocation has set the divers steps of humility and discipline we have to ascend.

The first step of humility, then, is reached when a man, with the fear of God always before his eyes, does not allow himself to forget, but is ever mindful of all God's commandments. He remembers, moreover, that such as contemn God fall into hell for their sins, and that life eternal awaits such as fear Him. And warding off at each moment all sin and defect in thought and word, of eye, hand or foot, of self-will, let such a one bestir himself to prune away the lusts of the flesh.

Let him think that he is seen at all times by God from heaven; and that wheresoever he may be, all his actions are visible to the eye of God and at all times are reported by the angels. The prophet shows us this when he says that God is ever present to our thoughts: *God searcheth the hearts and reins.* And again, *The Lord knoweth the thoughts of men that they are vain.* He also saith, *Thou hast understood my thoughts afar off;* and again, *The thought of man shall confess Thee.* In order, then, that the humble brother may be careful to avoid wrong thoughts let him always say in his heart, *Then shall I be without spot before Him, if I shall keep me from my iniquity.*

We are forbidden to do our own will, since Scripture tells us, *Leave thy own will and desire.* And again, *We beg of God in prayer that His will may be done in us.*

Rightly are we taught therefore not to do our own will, if we take heed of what the Scripture teaches: *There are ways which to men seem right, the end whereof plungeth even into the deep pit of*

hell. And again, when we fear what is said about the negligent, *They are corrupted, and made abominable in their pleasures.* But in regard of the desires of the flesh we ought to believe that God is present with us; as the prophet says, speaking to the Lord, *O Lord, all my desire is before Thee.*

We have therefore to beware of evil desires, since death stands close at the door of pleasure. It is for this reason that Scripture bids us, *Follow not thy concupiscences.* If, therefore, the eyes of the Lord behold both the good and the bad; if He be ever looking down from heaven upon the sons of men to find one who thinks of God or seeks Him; and if day and night what we do is made known to Him—for these reasons, by the angels appointed to watch over us, we should always take heed, brethren, lest God may sometime or other see us, as the prophet says in the Psalm, *inclined to evil and become unprofitable servants.* Even though He spare us for a time, because He is loving and waits for our conversion to better ways, let us fear that He may say to us hereafter, *These things thou hast done and I held my peace.*

The second step of humility is reached when any one not loving self-will takes no heed to satisfy his own desires, but copies in his life what our Lord said, *I came not to do My own will, but the will of Him Who sent Me.* Scripture likewise proclaims that self-will engendereth punishment, and necessity purchaseth a crown.

The third step of humility is reached when a man, for the love of God, submits himself with all obedience to a superior, imitating our Lord, of whom the apostle saith, *He was made obedient even unto death.*

The fourth step of humility is reached when any one in the exercise of his obedience patiently and with a quiet mind bears all that is inflicted on him, things contrary to nature, and even at times unjust, and in suffering all these he neither wearies nor gives over the work, since the Scripture says, *He only that persevereth to the end shall be saved;* also *Let thy heart be comforted, and expect the Lord.* And in order to show that for our Lord's sake the faithful man ought to bear all things, no matter how contrary to nature they may be, in the person of the sufferers, says, *For thee we suffer death all the day long; we are esteemed as sheep for the slaughter.* Secure in the hope of divine reward they rejoice, saying, *But in all things we overcome by the help of Him Who hath loved us.*

Elsewhere also Scripture says, *Thou hast proved us, O Lord; Thou hast tried us, as silver is tried, with fire. Thou hast brought us into the snare; Thou hast laid tribulation upon our backs.* And to show that we ought to be subject to a prior it goes on, *Thou hast placed men over our heads.* And, moreover, they fulfil the Lord's command by patience in adversity and injury, who, *when struck on one cheek, offer the other;* when one *taketh away their coat leave go their cloak also,* and who being compelled to carry a burden one mile, go two; who, with Paul the apostle, suffer false brethren, and bless those who speak ill of them.

The fifth step of humility is reached when a monk manifests to his abbot, by humble confession, all the evil thoughts of his heart and his secret faults. The Scripture urges us to do this where it says, *Reveal thy way to the Lord and hope in Him.* It also says, *Confess to the Lord, because He is good, because His mercy endureth for ever.* And the prophet also says, *I have made known unto Thee mine offence, and mine injustices I have not hidden. I have said, I will declare openly against myself mine injustices to the Lord; and Thou hast pardoned the wickedness of my heart.*

The sixth step of humility is reached when a monk is content with all that is mean and vile; and in regard to everything enjoined him accounts himself a poor and worthless workman, saying with the prophet, *I have been brought to nothing, and knew it not. I have become as a beast before Thee, and I am always with Thee.*

The seventh step of humility is reached when a man not only confesses with his tongue that he is most lowly and inferior to others, but in his inmost heart believes so. Such a one, humbling himself, exclaims with the prophet, *I am a worm and no man, the reproach of men and the outcast of the people. I have been exalted and am humbled and confounded* And again, *It is good for me that*

Thou hast humbled me, that I may learn Thy commandments.

The eighth step of humility is reached when a monk does nothing but what the common rule of the monastery, or the example of his seniors, enforces.

The ninth step of humility is reached when a monk restrains his tongue from talking, and, practising silence, speaks not till a question be asked him, since Scripture says, *In many words thou shalt not avoid sin,* and *a talkative man shall not be directed upon the earth.*

The tenth step of humility is attained to when one is not easily and quickly moved to laughter, for it is written, *The fool lifteth his voice in laughter.*

The eleventh step of humility is reached when a monk, in speaking, do so quietly and without laughter, humbly, gravely and in a few words and not with a loud voice, for it is written, *A wise man is known by a few words.*

The twelfth step of humility is reached when a monk not only has humility in his heart, but even shows it also exteriorly to all who behold him. Thus, whether he be in the oratory at the "Work of God," in the monastery, or in the garden, on a journey, or in the fields, or wheresoever he be, sitting, standing or walking, always let him, with head bent and eyes fixed on the ground, bethink himself of his sins and imagine that he is arraigned before the dread judgment of God. Let him be ever saying to himself, with the publican in the Gospel, *Lord, I a sinner am not worthy to lift mine eyes to heaven;* and with the prophet, *I am bowed down and humbled on every side.*

When all these steps of humility have been mounted the monk will presently attain to that love of God which is perfect and casteth out fear. By means of this love everything which before he had observed not without fear, he shall now begin to do by habit, without any trouble and, as it were, naturally. He acts now not through fear of hell, but for the love of Christ, out of a good habit and a delight in virtue. All this our Lord will vouchsafe to work by the Holy Ghost in His servant, now cleansed from vice and sin.

REVIEW QUESTIONS

1. What did we learn about the lives of the women and men who lived according to this rule?

2. Why is humility such a central monastic value?

3. How does the monastic life define sin and struggle against it?

AMMIANUS MARCELLINUS

FROM *The History*

Ammianus Marcellinus (ca. 330–after 392 C.E.) was the last of a series of Roman authors whose vigorous classical style shaped a distinctive imperial history centered on Rome and the frontiers. In these passages Ammianus describes a powerful politician, Petronius Probus, whose career typified late Roman imperial administration. Ammianus was also an early source on the new threats the barbarians posed to the Empire.

From *Ammianus Marcellinus: The Later Roman Empire,* edited by Walter Hamilton (New York: Penguin Books, 1986), pp. 345–46, 410–16.

*   *   *

Career and Character of Probus (A.D. 368)

During this period Vulcatius Rufinus died in office, and Probus was recalled from Rome to succeed him as praetorian prefect. Probus was known all over the Roman world for his high birth, powerful influence, and vast riches; he owned estates in almost every part of the empire, but whether they were honestly come by or not is not for a man like me to say. In his case Fortune, who, to use the language of poetry, carried him on her swift wings, took a double form. Sometimes she exhibited him as a benevolent man engaged in promoting the careers of his friends; at others he appeared as a pernicious schemer who worked off his deadly grudges by inflicting injury. Through-out his life he exercised enormous influence owing to the gifts he bestowed and the constant succession of offices he filled. There were times when he showed fear of those who stood up to him, but he took a high line with those who were afraid of him. When he felt that he was on strong ground he hectored in the elevated style of tragedy, but in panic he could be more abject than any down-at-heel comedian. Probus languished like a fish out of water if he was not in office. This he was driven to seek by the lawless behaviour of his countless dependants, whose excessive greed could never be satisfied in an innocent way, and who thrust their master into public life so as to be able to gain their ends with impunity. It must be admitted that he had sufficient principle never to order a client or slave to break the law, but if he heard that any had committed a crime he would defend him in the teeth of justice itself, without any investigation of the matter or regard for right and honour. This is a fault reprobated by Cicero when he says: 'What is the difference between prompting a deed and approving it when it is done? Or what difference does it make whether I wished it to happen or am glad that it has happened?'

Probus was by nature suspicious and petty. He could wear a sour smile, and sometimes employed flattery when he meant to injure. He had a common defect of characters of his type that is conspicuously bad, especially when its possessor believes that he can conceal it: he was so implacable and inflexible that once he had decided to injure a man he was deaf to all entreaties. Nothing could induce him to pardon an offence, and his ears seemed stopped with lead rather than the proverbial wax.

Even at the height of wealth and honour he was nervous and worried, and in consequence always subject to slight ailments. This was the course of events in the western part of the empire.

*   *   *

Omens of the Death of Valens and of the Imminent Gothic Disaster

Meanwhile a rapid turn of fortune's wheel, which is perpetually alternating adversity and prosperity, was arming Bellona and her attendant Furies and bringing sad calamity upon the East. Its approach was plainly foreshadowed by omens and portents. Besides many true predictions from seers and augurs, dogs howled in answer to wolves, night-birds burst into doleful shrieks, and gloomy dawns dimmed the bright light of morning. At Antioch, where quarrels and riots among the populace were common, it became the habit for anyone who thought himself wronged to shout boldly: 'Burn Valens alive.' Criers could be heard constantly urging people to collect combustibles to set fire to the Baths of Valens, which had been built at the instance of the emperor himself. This indicated almost in so many words the manner of his death. In addition, the ghostly likeness of the king of Ar-

menia and the pathetic shades of the victims in the recent affair of Theodorus made the night hideous with dirge-like howls, and inspired dire terror. A heifer was found lying dead with its throat cut, and this was a sign of widespread misery and death among the public. Lastly, when the old walls of Chalcedon were being taken down to provide material for a bath at Constantinople, the removal of the stone revealed a square block hidden in the fabric, on which were inscribed in Greek the following verses, a clear indication of what was to come:

When through the city's street with garlands
    crowned
Fresh maidens whirl rejoicing in the dance,
And what was once a city wall shall serve—
O what a mournful change—to guard a bath,
Then countless hordes of men from lands afar
Shall cross fair Ister's river, lance in hand,
And lay all Scythia and Mysia waste;
Next on Paeonia turn their mad career,
To spread there likewise nought but death and
    strife.

The Nature of the Huns and Alans

The seed-bed and origin of all this destruction and of the various calamities inflicted by the wrath of Mars, which raged everywhere with unusual fury, I find to be this. The people of the Huns, who are mentioned only cursorily in ancient writers and who dwell beyond the Sea of Azov (Palus Maeotis) near the frozen ocean, are quite abnormally savage. From the moment of birth they make deep gashes in their children's cheeks, so that when in due course hair appears its growth is checked by the wrinkled scars; as they grow older this gives them the unlovely appearance of beardless eunuchs. They have squat bodies, strong limbs, and thick necks, and are so prodigiously ugly and bent that they might be two-legged animals, or the figures crudely carved from stumps which are seen on the parapets of bridges. Still, their shape, however disagreeable, is human; but their way of life is so rough that they have no use for fire or seasoned food, but live on the roots of wild plants and the half-raw flesh of any sort of animal, which they warm a little by placing it between their thighs and the backs of their horses. They have no buildings to shelter them, but avoid anything of the kind as carefully as we avoid living in the neighbourhood of tombs; not so much as a hut thatched with reeds is to be found among them. They roam at large over mountains and forests, and are inured from the cradle to cold, hunger, and thirst. On foreign soil only extreme necessity can persuade them to come under a roof, since they believe that it is not safe for them to do so. They wear garments of linen or of the skins of field-mice stitched together, and there is no difference between their clothing whether they are at home or abroad. Once they have put their necks into some dingy shirt they never take it off or change it till it rots and falls to pieces from incessant wear. They have round caps of fur on their heads, and protect their hairy legs with goatskins. Their shapeless shoes are not made on a last and make it hard to walk easily. In consequence they are ill-fitted to fight on foot, and remain glued to their horses, hardy but ugly beasts, on which they sometimes sit like women to perform their everyday business. Buying or selling, eating or drinking, are all done by day or night on horseback, and they even bow forward over their beasts' narrow necks to enjoy a deep and dreamy sleep. When they need to debate some important matter they conduct their conference in the same posture. They are not subject to the authority of any king, but break through any obstacle in their path under the improvised command of their chief men.

They sometimes fight *by challenging their foes to single combat,* but when they join battle they advance in packs, uttering their various warcries. Being lightly equipped and very sudden in their movements they can deliberately scatter and gallop about at random, inflicting tremendous slaughter; their extreme nimbleness enables them to force a rampart or pillage an enemy's camp before one catches sight of them. What makes them the most formidable of all warriors is that they shoot from a distance arrows tipped with sharp splinters of bone instead of the usual heads; these are joined to the shafts with wonderful skill. At close quarters they fight without regard for their lives, and while their opponents are guarding against sword-thrusts they catch their limbs in lassos of twisted cloth which make it impossible for them to ride or walk. None of them ploughs or ever touches a plough-handle. They have no fixed abode, no home or law or settled manner of life, but wander like refugees with the wagons in which they live. In these their wives weave their filthy clothing, mate with their husbands, give birth to their children, and rear them to the age of puberty. No one if asked can tell where he comes from, having been conceived in one place, born somewhere else, and reared even further off. You cannot make a truce with them, because they are quite unreliable and easily swayed by any breath of rumour which promises advantage; like unreasoning beasts they are entirely at the mercy of the maddest impulses. They are totally ignorant of the distinction between right and wrong, their speech is shifty and obscure, and they are under no restraint from religion or superstition. Their greed for gold is prodigious, and they are so fickle and prone to anger that often in a single day they will quarrel with their allies without any provocation, and then make it up again without anyone attempting to reconcile them.

This wild race, moving without encumbrances and consumed by a savage passion to pillage the property of others, advanced robbing and slaughtering over the lands of their neighbours till they reached the Alans. The Alans are the ancient Massagetae, and at this point it is relevant to discuss their origin and situation. This is a problem that has perplexed geographers, who have, however, *after much discussion found a reliable solution.*

The Danube, swollen by the waters of a number of tributaries, flows past the territory of the Sarmatians, which extends as far as the river Don (Tanais), the boundary between Europe and Asia. Beyond this the Alans inhabit the immense deserts of Scythia, deriving their name from the mountains. By repeated victories they gradually wore down the people next to them, and, like the Per-

on which they now congratulate themselves. The barbarians spared them for Christ's sake; and now these Romans assail Christ's name. The sacred places of the martyrs and the basilicas of the apostles bear witness to this, for in the sack of Rome they afforded shelter to fugitives, both Christian and pagan. The bloodthirsty enemy raged thus far, but here the frenzy of butchery was checked; to these refuges the merciful among the enemy conveyed those whom they had spared outside, to save them from encountering foes who had no such pity. Even men who elsewhere raged with all the savagery an enemy can show, arrived at places where practices generally allowed by laws of war were forbidden and their monstrous passion for violence was brought to a sudden halt; their lust for taking captives was subdued.

In this way many escaped who now complain of this Christian era, and hold Christ responsible for the disasters which their city endured. But they do not make Christ responsible for the benefits they received out of respect for Christ, to which they owed their lives. They attribute their deliverance to their own destiny; whereas if they had any right judgement they ought rather to attribute the harsh cruelty they suffered at the hands of their enemies to the providence of God. For God's providence constantly uses war to correct and chasten the corrupt morals of mankind, as it also uses such afflictions to train men in a righteous and laudable way of life, removing to a better state those whose life is approved, or else keeping them in this world for further service.

Moreover, they should give credit to this Christian era for the fact that these savage barbarians showed mercy beyond the custom of war —whether they so acted in general in honour of the name of Christ, or in places specially dedicated to Christ's name, buildings of such size and capacity as to give mercy a wider range. For this clemency our detractors ought rather to give thanks to God; they should have recourse to his name in all sincerity, so as to escape the penalty of everlasting fire, seeing that so many of them assumed his name dishonestly, to escape the penalty of immediate destruction. Among those whom you see insulting Christ's servants with such wanton insolence there are very many who came unscathed through that terrible time of massacre only by passing themselves off as Christ's servants. And now with ungrateful pride and impious madness they oppose his name in the perversity of their hearts, so that they may incur the punishment of eternal darkness; but then they took refuge in that name, though with deceitful lips, so that they might continue to enjoy this transitory light.

2. THAT VICTORS SHOULD SPARE THE VANQUISHED OUT OF RESPECT FOR THEIR GODS IS SOMETHING UNEXAMPLED IN HISTORY.

We have the records of many wars, both before the foundation of Rome and after its rise to power. Let our enemies read their history, and then produce instances of the capture of any city by foreign enemies when those enemies spared any whom they found taking refuge in the temples of their gods. Let them quote any barbarian general who gave instructions, at the storming of a town, that no one should be treated with violence who was discovered in this temple or that. Aeneas saw Priam at the altar,

> polluting with his blood
> The fire which he had consecrated.

And Diomedes and Ulysses

> Slew all the warders of the citadel
> And snatched with bloody hands the sacred
>   image;
> Nor shrank to touch the chaplets virginal
> Of the dread goddess.

And there is no truth in the statement that comes after,

> The Grecian hopes then failed, and ebbed away.

For what in fact followed was the Greek victory, the destruction of Troy by fire and sword, the slaughter of Priam at the altar.

And it was not because Troy lost Minerva that Troy perished. What loss did Minerva herself first incur, that led to her own disappearance? Was it, perhaps, the loss of her guards? There can be no doubt that their death made her removal possible—the image did not preserve the men; the men were preserving the image. Why then did they worship her, to secure her protection for their country and its citizens? She could not guard her own keepers.

3. THE FOLLY OF THE ROMANS IN CONFIDING THEIR SAFETY TO THE HOUSEHOLD GODS WHO HAD FAILED TO PROTECT TROY.

There you see the sort of gods to whom the Romans gladly entrusted the preservation of their city. Pitiable folly! Yet the Romans are enraged by such criticisms from us, while they are not incensed at the authors of such quotations; in fact they pay money to become acquainted with their works, and they consider that those who merely instruct them in these works merit an official salary and an honoured position in the community. Virgil certainly is held to be a great poet; in fact he is regarded as the best and the most renowned of all poets, and for that reason he is read by children at an early age—they take great draughts of his poetry into their unformed minds, so that they may not easily forget him, for, as Horace remarks,

New vessels will for long retain the taste
Of what is first poured into them.

Now in Virgil Juno is introduced as hostile to the Trojans, and when she urges Aeolus, king of the winds, against them, she says,

A race I hate sails the Etruscan sea
Bringing to Italy Troy's vanquished gods,
And Troy itself.

Ought the Romans, as prudent men, to have entrusted the defence of Rome to gods unable to defend themselves? Juno no doubt spoke like a woman in anger, heedless of what she was saying.

But consider what is said by Aeneas himself, who is so often called "the pious."

Panthus, the priest of Phoebus and the citadel,
Snatching his conquered gods and his young
    grandson
Rushes in frenzy to the door.

He does not shrink from calling the gods "conquered," and he speaks of them as being entrusted to him, rather than the other way round, when he is told, "To thee, Troy now entrusts her native gods."

If Virgil speaks of such gods as "vanquished," and tells how, after their overthrow, they only succeeded in escaping because they were committed to the care of a man, what folly it is to see any wisdom in committing Rome to such guardians, and in supposing that it could not be sacked while it retained possession of them. To worship "vanquished" gods as protectors and defenders is to rely not on divinities but on defaulters. It is not sensible to assume that Rome would have escaped this disaster had these gods not first perished; the sensible belief is that those gods would have perished long before, had not Rome made every effort to preserve them. Anyone who gives his mind to it can see that it is utter folly to count on invincibility by virtue of the possession of defenders who have been conquered and to attribute destruction to the loss of such guardian deities as these. In fact, the only possible cause of destruction was the choice of such perishable defenders. When the poets wrote and sang of "vanquished gods," it was not because it suited their whim to lie—they were men of sense, and truth compelled them to admit the facts.

But I must deal with this subject in fuller detail in a more convenient place. For the present I will return to the ingratitude of those who blasphemously blame Christ for the disasters which their moral perversity deservedly brought upon them, and I will deal with the subject as briefly as I can. They were spared for Christ's sake, pagans though they were; yet they scorn to acknowledge this. With the madness of sacrilegious perversity they use their tongues against the name of Christ; yet with those same tongues they dishonestly claimed that name in order to save their lives, or else, in places sacred to him, they held their tongues through fear. They were kept safe and protected there where his name stood between them and the enemy's violence. And so they issue from that shelter to assail him with curses of hate.

*   *   *

15. MAN'S NATURAL FREEDOM; AND THE SLAVERY CAUSED BY SIN.

This relationship is prescribed by the order of nature, and it is in this situation that God created man. For he says, "Let him have lordship over the fish of the sea, the birds of the sky . . . and all the reptiles that crawl on the earth." He did not wish the rational being, made in his own image, to have dominion over any but irrational creatures, not man over man, but man over the beasts. Hence the first just men were set up as shepherds of flocks, rather than as kings of men, so that in this way also God might convey the message of what was required by the order of nature, and what was demanded by the deserts of sinners—for it is understood, of course, that the condition of slavery is justly imposed on the sinner. That is why we do not hear of a slave anywhere in the Scriptures until Noah, the just man, punished his son's sin with this word; and so that son deserved this name because of his misdeed, not because of his nature. The origin of the Latin word for slave, *servus,* is believed to be derived from the fact that those who by the laws of war could rightly be put to death by the conquerors, became *servi,* slaves, when they were preserved, receiving this name from their preservation. But even this enslavement could not have happened, if it were not for the deserts of sin. For even when a just war is fought it is in defence of his sin that the other side is contending; and victory, even when the victory falls to the wicked, is a humiliation visited on the conquered by divine judgement, either to correct or to punish their sins. We have a witness to this in Daniel, a

man of God, who in captivity confesses to God his own sins and the sins of his people, and in devout grief testifies that they are the cause of that captivity. The first cause of slavery, then, is sin, whereby man was subjected to man in the condition of bondage; and this can only happen by the judgement of God, with whom there is no injustice, and who knows how to allot different punishments according to the deserts of the offenders.

Now, as our Lord above says, "Everyone who commits sin is sin's slave," and that is why, though many devout men are slaves to unrighteous masters, yet the masters they serve are not themselves free men; 'for when a man is conquered by another he is also bound as a slave to his conqueror.' And obviously it is a happier lot to be slave to a human being than to a lust; and, in fact, the most pitiless domination that devastates the hearts of men, is that exercised by this very lust for domination, to mention no others. However, in that order of peace in which men are subordinate to other men, humility is as salutary for the servants as pride is harmful to the masters. And yet by nature, in the condition in which God created man, no man is the slave either of man or of sin. But it remains true that slavery as a punishment is also ordained by that law which enjoins the preservation of the order of nature, and forbids its disturbance; in fact, if nothing had been done to contravene that law, there would have been nothing to require the discipline of slavery as a punishment. That explains also the Apostle's admonition to slaves, that they should be subject to their masters, and serve them loyally and willingly. What he means is that if they cannot be set free by their masters, they themselves may thus make their slavery, in a sense, free, by serving not with the slyness of fear, but with the fidelity of affection, until all injustice disappears and all human lordship and power is annihilated, and God is all in all.

16. EQUITY IN THE RELATION OF MASTER AND SLAVE.

This being so, even though our righteous fathers had slaves, they so managed the peace of their households as to make a distinction between the situation of children and the condition of slaves in respect of the temporal goods of this life; and yet in the matter of the worship of God—in whom we must place our hope of everlasting goods—they were concerned, with equal affection, for all the members of their household. This is what the order of nature prescribes, so that this is the source of the name *paterfamilias,* a name that has become so generally used that even those who exercise unjust rule rejoice to be called by this title. On the other hand, those who are genuine "fathers of their household" are concerned for the welfare of all in their households in respect of the worship and service of God, as if they were all their children, longing and praying that they may come to the heavenly home, where it will not be a necessary duty to give orders to men, because it will no longer be a necessary duty to be concerned for the welfare of those who are already in the felicity of that immortal state. But until that home is reached, the fathers have an obligation to exercise the authority of masters greater than the duty of slaves to put up with their condition as servants.

However, if anyone in the household is, through his disobedience, an enemy to the domestic peace, he is reproved by a word, or by a blow, or any other kind of punishment that is just and legitimate, to the extent allowed by human society; but this is for the benefit of the offender, intended to readjust him to the domestic peace from which he had broken away. For just as it is not an act of kindness to help a man, when the effect of the help is to make him lose a greater good, so it is not a blameless act to spare a man, when by so doing you let him fall into a greater sin. Hence the duty of anyone who would be blameless includes not only doing no harm to anyone but also restraining a man from sin or punishing his sin, so that either the man who is chastised may be corrected by his experience, or others may be deterred by his example. Now a man's house ought to be the beginning, or rather a small component part of the city, and every beginning is directed to some end of its own kind, and every component part contributes to the completeness of the whole of which it forms a part. The implication is quite apparent, that domestic peace contributes to the peace of the city—that is, the ordered harmony of those who live together in a house in the matter of giving and obeying orders, contributes to the ordered harmony concerning authority and obedience obtaining among the citizens. Consequently it is fitting that the father of a household should take his rules from the law of the city, and govern his household in such a way that it fits in with the peace of the city.

REVIEW QUESTIONS

1. How does Augustine interpret the meaning of the sack of Rome?
2. How does he justify slavery?
3. What light does he shed on the daily life of Roman slaves?

MOSAICS OF JUSTINIAN (TOP) AND THEODORA (BOTTOM), CHURCH OF SAN VITA, RAVENNA (C. 500 C.E.)

Justinian holds a communion dish, Theodora a chalice. The emperor commissioned these mosaics for an important church in Ravenna, capital of a part of Byzantine Italy. What does this mosaic suggest about the position of the imperial family in the church?

8 ⁓ ROME'S THREE HEIRS: THE BYZANTINE, ISLAMIC, AND EARLY MEDIEVAL WORLDS

Roman control over most of the western Mediterranean collapsed in the fifth century, and soon Rome itself became the capital of an Ostrogothic kingdom in Italy. A world formerly centered on the Middle Sea began to take a different shape. In the eastern Mediterranean the Roman Empire endured. This state, smaller after the rise of Islam and the loss of North Africa, Egypt, Syria, and the Holy Land, became the Byzantine Empire, a largely Greek kingdom on the shores of the Aegean Sea. Ancient culture continued to evolve here in the setting of Eastern Orthodox Christianity and a nearly incessant struggle for survival against Slavic, Muslim, and eventually western Christian neighbors.

The Arabian Peninsula, largely neglected by the neighboring Roman and Persian Empires, unified in the seventh century under the influence of Muhammed of Mecca. The new religion of Islam, partially drawing on and extending Jewish and Christian traditions but containing a specific revelation and message for the Arabian peoples, unified Arabia with a mission. Armies spread the new faith as they quickly extended Muslim conquests across Africa to the west and crossed to the Iberian Peninsula, and the religion spread through Mesopotamia, Persia, and northern India to the east eventually to the Philippines. The collected revelations of Muhammed, in the form of the Quran, brought a knowledge of the religion as well as Arabic language to all the new peoples converted into the world of Islam. Islamic scholars and schools preserved much of ancient Greek, Syrian, and Persian culture and soon contributed new insights in the sciences and history. Much of the West's knowledge of ancient Greek thought came through translations of Arabic sources.

In northwestern Europe the barbarian kingdoms, converted to Christianity, became the center of a third culture, not Greek Christian or Muslim, but eventually a Latin Christendom, shaped by the Roman heritage and Germanic culture. European monasteries preserved and copied classical Latin and early Christian texts that became the core of early medieval culture. The religious

319

frontiers between the Eastern Orthodox, Roman Catholic, and Muslim worlds in Europe masked deep ethnic divisions and eventual splits in the unity of the faiths. All three cultures preserved parts of the classical legacy, while despising paganism and some ancient values not suited to the newer religions.

For a time in the sixth century the Emperor Justinian seemed poised to restore imperial authority in large parts of the West, but his failures and the rise of Islam resulted in a more compact Byzantine state. For nearly a thousand years Byzantine culture produced distinctive artistic works and writers. In the West there was no longer a Roman emperor until the coronation of Charlemagne in 800. The resurgent Frankish state in the West helped to halt the advance of Islam in Europe and extended the frontiers of Christendom into pagan Germanic and Slavic lands to the east. Government depended on the personality of individual rulers, and in Charlemagne the Franks benefited from the rule of an ideal king who was also interested in sponsoring the revival of learning and the arts. Anglo-Saxon England, remaining outside the Carolingian Empire, also contributed monks and missionaries, as well as a distinctive literature, to this early medieval culture. A renewed wave of Viking, Hungarian, and Muslim attacks in the late eighth and ninth centuries disrupted the Carolingian and Anglo-Saxon states.

In the Muslim world the caliphate of Baghdad presided over a golden age of Arabic culture under Harun al Rashid (786–809). This ruler established contacts with the Christian West and sent Charlemagne an elephant, an animal not seen in Europe since the Romans and a marvel of the age, and a clock, which did not last as long as the elephant. By about the year 1000 three centers of power had replaced the Roman Empire of late antiquity. Islamic rulers held sway over the southern and eastern shores of the Mediterranean, and in the East a Greek state calling itself a Roman Empire still endured. In the West a Latin Christendom emerged from the end of Rome and the subsequent barbarian kingdoms, but this world was insecure and beset by powerful enemies on all sides.

PROCOPIUS

FROM *Secret History*

Procopius, a sixth century Byzantine writer active in the reign of Justinian (527–565), suppressed some of his true opinions from the public by including them in his lively Secret History. *In these selections Procopius explains his purpose in writing history and attacks Justinian, whose ambitions to reestablish Roman authority in the West exhausted his empire.*

From *Procopius: Secret History,* edited by Richard Atwater (Ann Arbor: University of Michigan Press, 1978), pp. 40–44.

*   *   *

In what I have written on the Roman wars up to the present point, the story was arranged in chronological order and as completely as the times then permitted. What I shall write now follows a different plan, supplementing the previous formal chronicle with a disclosure of what really happened throughout the Roman Empire. You see, it was not possible, during the life of certain persons, to write the truth of what they did, as a historian should. If I had, their hordes of spies would have found out about it, and they would have put me to a most horrible death. I could not even trust my nearest relatives. That is why I was compelled to hide the real explanation of many matters glossed over in my previous books.

These secrets it is now my duty to tell and reveal the remaining hidden matters and motives. Yet when I approach this different task, I find it hard indeed to have to stammer and retract what I have written before about the lives of Justinian and Theodora. Worse yet, it occurs to me that what I am now about to tell will seem neither probable nor plausible to future generations, especially as time flows on and my story becomes ancient history. I fear they may think me a writer of fiction, and even put me among the poets.

However, I have this much to cheer me, that my account will not be unendorsed by other testimony: so I shall not shrink from the duty of completing this work.

*   *   *

Character and Appearance of Justinian

Now this went on not only in Constantinople, but in every city: for like any other disease, the evil, starting there, spread throughout the entire Roman Empire. But the Emperor was undisturbed by the trouble, even when it went on continually under his own eyes at the hippodrome. For he was very complacent and resembled most the silly ass, which follows, only shaking its ears, when one drags it by the bridle. As such Justinian acted, and threw everything into confusion.

As soon as he took over the rule from his uncle, his first measure was to spend the public money without restraint, now that he had control of it. He gave much of it to the Huns who, from time to time, entered the state; and in consequence the Roman provinces were subject to constant incursions, for these barbarians, having once tasted Roman wealth, never forgot the road that led to it. And he threw much money into the sea in the form of moles, as if to master the eternal roaring of the breakers. For he jealously hurled stone breakwaters far out from the mainland against the onset of the sea, as if by the power of wealth he could outmatch the might of ocean.

He gathered to himself the private estates of Roman citizens from all over the Empire: some by accusing their possessors of crimes of which they were innocent, others by juggling their owners' words into the semblance of a gift to him of their property. And many, caught in the act of murder and other crimes, turned their possessions over to him and thus escaped the penalty for their sins.

Others, fraudulently disputing title to lands happening to adjoin their own, when they saw they had no chance of getting the best of the argument, with the law against them, gave him their equity in the claim so as to be released from court. Thus, by a gesture that cost him nothing, they gained his favor and were able illegally to get the better of their opponents.

I think this is as good a time as any to describe the personal appearance of the man. Now in physique he was neither tall nor short, but of average height; not thin, but moderately plump; his face was round, and not bad looking, for he had good color, even when he fasted for two days. To make a long description short, he much resembled Domitian, Vespasian's son. He was the one whom the Romans so hated that even tearing him into pieces did not satisfy their wrath against him, but a decree was passed by the Senate that the name of this Emperor should never be written, and that no statue of him should be preserved. And so this name was erased in all the inscriptions at Rome and wherever else it had been written, except only where it occurs in the list of emperors; and nowhere may be seen any statue of him in all the Roman Empire, save one in brass, which was made for the following reason.

Domitian's wife was of free birth and otherwise noble; and neither had she herself ever done wrong to anybody, nor had she assented in her husband's acts. Wherefore she was dearly loved; and the Senate sent for her, when Domitian died, and commanded her to ask whatever boon she wished. But she asked only this: to set up in his memory one brass image, wherever she might desire. To this the Senate agreed. Now the lady, wishing to leave a memorial to future time of the savagery of those who had butchered her husband, conceived this plan: collecting the pieces of Domitian's body, she joined them accurately together and sewed the body up again into its original semblance. Taking this to the statue makers, she ordered them to produce the miserable form in brass. So the artisans forthwith made the image, and the wife took it, and set it up in the street which leads to the Capitol, on the right hand side as one goes there from the Forum: a monument to Domitian and a revelation of the manner of his death until this day.

Justinian's entire person, his manner of expression and all of his features might be clearly pointed out in this statue.

Now such was Justinian in appearance; but his character was something I could not fully describe. For he was at once villainous and amenable; as people say colloquially, a moron. He was never truthful with anyone, but always guileful in what he said and did, yet easily hoodwinked by any who wanted to deceive him. His nature was an unnatural mixture of folly and wickedness. What in olden times a peripatetic philosopher said was also true of him, that opposite qualities combine in a man as in the mixing of colors. I will try to portray him, however, insofar as I can fathom his complexity.

This Emperor, then, was deceitful, devious, false, hypocritical, two-faced, cruel, skilled in dissembling his thought, never moved to tears by either joy or pain, though he could summon them artfully at will when the occasion demanded, a liar always, not only offhand, but in writing, and when he swore sacred oaths to his subjects in their very hearing. Then he would immediately break his agreements and pledges, like the vilest of slaves, whom indeed only the fear of torture drives to confess their perjury. A faithless friend, he was a treacherous enemy, insane for murder and plunder, quarrelsome and revolutionary, easily led to anything evil, but never willing to listen to good counsel, quick to plan mischief and carry it out, but finding even the hearing of anything good distasteful to his ears.

How could anyone put Justinian's ways into words? These and many even worse vices were disclosed in him as in no other mortal: nature seemed to have taken the wickedness of all other men combined and planted it in this man's soul. And besides this, he was too prone to listen to accusations; and too quick to punish. For he decided such cases without full examination, naming the punishment when he had heard only the accuser's side of the matter. Without hesitation he wrote decrees for the plundering of countries, sacking of cities, and slavery of whole nations, for no cause whatever. So that if one wished to take all the calamities which had befallen the Romans before this time and weigh them against his crimes, I think it would be found that more men had been murdered by this single man than in all previous history.

He had no scruples about appropriating other people's property, and did not even think any excuse necessary, legal or illegal, for confiscating what did not belong to him. And when it was his, he was more than ready to squander it in insane display, or give it as an unnecessary bribe to the barbarians. In short, he neither held on to any money himself nor let anyone else keep any: as if his reason were not avarice, but jealousy of those who had riches. Driving all wealth from the country of the Romans in this manner, he became the cause of universal poverty.

Now this was the character of Justinian, so far as I can portray it.

* * *

REVIEW QUESTIONS

1. What difference does Procopius see between official and secret history?
2. How does this account square with the version of Justinian's reign in the textbook?

SEBEOS

The Armenian History

The Armenian History Attributed to Sebeos is a contemporary account from the Armenian perspective of the period from the late sixth to the early seventh century. The value of this work, of uncertain authorship, is that it describes the effects the rise of Islam had on the Byzantine and Persian states. Armenia, a Christian land set between the great powers, struggled to survive in a changing world.

From *Translated Texts for Historians,* vol. 31, translated by R. W. Thomson (Liverpool, Eng.: Liverpool University Press, 1999), pp. 95–103.

* * *

I shall speak of the stock of Abraham, not of the free one but of that born from the hand-maiden, concerning which the unerring divine word was fulfilled: "His hands on all, and the hands of all on him."

Then the twelve tribes of all the clans of the

Jews went and gathered at the city of Edessa. When they saw that the Persian army had departed from them and had left the city in peace, they shut the gate and fortified themselves within. They did not allow the army of the Roman empire to enter among them. Then the Greek king Heraclius ordered it to be besieged. When they realized that they were unable to resist him in battle, they parleyed for peace with him. Opening the gates of the city, they went and stood before him. Then he ordered them to go and remain in each one's habitation, and they departed. Taking desert roads, they went to Tachkastan, to the sons of Ismael, summoned them to their aid and informed them of their blood relationship through the testament of scripture. But although the latter were persuaded of their close relationship, yet they were unable to bring about agreement within their great number, because their cults were divided from each other.

At that time a certain man from among those same sons of Ismael whose name was Mahmet, a merchant, as if by God's command appeared to them as a preacher [and] the path of truth. He taught them to recognize the God of Abraham, especially because he was learned and informed in the history of Moses. Now because the command was from on high, at a single order they all came together in unity of religion. Abandoning their vain cults, they turned to the living God who had appeared to their father Abraham. So Mahmet legislated for them: not to eat carrion, not to drink wine, not to speak falsely, and not to engage in fornication. He said. "With an oath God promised this land to Abraham and his seed after him for ever. And he brought about as he promised during that time while he loved Israel. But now you are the sons of Abraham, and God is accomplishing his promise to Abraham and his seed for you. Love sincerely only the God of Abraham, and go and seize your land which God gave to your father Abraham. No one will be able to resist you in battle, because God is with you."

Then they all gathered in unison "from Ewila as far as Sur, which is opposite Egypt"; and they went from the desert of P'aṙan, 12 tribes according to the tribes of the families of their patriarchs. They divided the 12,000 men, like the sons of Israel, into their tribes—a thousand men from each tribe—to lead them into the land of Israel. They set off, camp by camp according to each one's patriarchal line: "Nabēutʿ, Kedar, Abdiwł, Mabsam, Masmay, Iduma, Masē, Kʿołdad, Tʿeman, Yetur, Napʿēs and Kedmay. These are the tribes of Ismael." They reached Ěrbovtʿ of Moab in the territory of Ṙuben, for the Greek army had camped in Arabia. Falling on them unexpectedly, they put them to the sword, and put to flight Tʿēodos the brother of the emperor Heraclius. Then they returned and camped in Arabia.

All the remnants of the people of the sons of Israel gathered and united together; they formed a large army. Following that they sent messages to the Greek king, saying: "God gave that land to our father Abraham as a hereditary possession and to his seed after him. We are the sons of Abraham. You have occupied our land long enough. Abandon it peacefully and we shall not come into your territory. Otherwise, we shall demand that possession from you with interest."

But the emperor did not agree. He did not respond appropriately to their message, but said: 'This land is mine, your lot of inheritance is the desert. Go in peace to your land.' He began to collect troops, about 70,000, appointed as general over them one of his trusted eunuchs, and ordered them to go to Arabia. He commanded them not to fight with them, but to look to their own defence until he should have gathered other troops to send to their assistance. But when they reached the Jordan and crossed into Arabia, they left their camps on the river bank and went on foot to attack their army. The latter posted part of their force in ambush on either side, and arranged the multitude of their tents around their camp. Bringing up the herds of camels, they tethered them around the camp and their tents, and bound their feet with cords. This was the fortification of their camp. The others, though wearied from their march, were able at certain places to penetrate the fortification of the camp, and began to slaughter them. Unexpectedly, those lying in ambush rose up from their places and attacked them. Fear of the Lord fell on the Greek army, and they turned in flight before them. But they could not flee, because of the density of the sand, since their feet sank in up to their shins; and there was great distress from the heat of the sun, and the enemy's sword pursued them. So all the generals fell and were slain. The number of the fallen was more than 2,000. A few of them escaped and fled to a place of refuge.

They [the Ismaelites] crossed the Jordan and camped at Jericho. Then dread of them fell on all the inhabitants of the land, and they all submitted to them. That night the people of Jerusalem took in flight the Lord's Cross and all the vessels of the churches of God. Setting sail on the sea in ships, they brought them to the palace of Constantinople. Then, having requested an oath from them, they submitted to them.

But the Greek king could raise no more troops to oppose them. So they divided their forces into three parts. One part went to Egypt and seized [the country] as far as Alexandria. One part was in the north, opposing the Greek empire. And in the twinkling of an eye they occupied [the land] from the edge of the sea as far as the bank of the great river Euphrates; and on the other side of the river [they occupied] Urha and all the cities of Mesopotamia. The third part [went] to the east, against the kingdom of Persia.

The Persian kingdom was eclipsed at that time, and their army was divided into three parts. Then the army of Ismael, which had gathered in the regions of the east, went and besieged Ctesiphon, because there the Persian king was residing. The army of the land of the Medes gathered under the command of their general Řostom, 80,000 armed men, and marched to do battle with them. Then they left the city and crossed to the other side of the river Tigris. The others also crossed the river and pursued them closely, but the former did not stop until they reached their own borders, the village called Hertʻichan. The latter pressed hard behind them, and they camped on the plain. The Armenian general Musheł Mamikonean, son of Dawitʻ, was also there with 3,000 fully-armed men;

and prince Grigor, lord of Siwnikʻ, with a thousand. A mutual attack ensued. The Persian army fled before them, but they pursued them and put them to the sword. All the leading nobles were killed, and the general Řostom was also killed. They also slew Musheł with his two nephews, and Grigor lord of Siwnikʻ with one son. The others escaped in flight to their own country.

When the survivors of the Persian army reached Atrpatakan, they gathered together in one place and installed Khořokhazat as their general. He hastened to Ctesiphon, took all the treasures of the kingdom, the inhabitants of the cities, and their king, and made haste to bring them to Atrpatakan. After they had set out and had gone some distance, unexpectedly the Ismaelite army attacked them. Terrified, they abandoned the treasures and the inhabitants of the city, and fled. Their king also fled and took refuge with the army of the south. But these [the Ismaelites] took all the treasure and returned to Ctesiphon, taking also the inhabitants of the cities, and they ravaged the whole land.

Then the blessed Heraclius completed his life at a good old age. The days of his reign were 30 years. He made his son Constantine swear to exercise [mercy] on all the transgressors whom he had ordered to be exiled, and to restore them to each one's place. He also made him swear regarding the *aspet* that he would bring him and his wife and children back, and establish him in his former rank. "If he should wish to go to his own country, I have [so] sworn to him. Let not my oath be false. Release him, and let him go in peace."

Heraclius died, and his son Constantine reigned. And no one was chosen as general in the land of Armenia, because the princes were disunited and had separated from each other.

A destructive army came from Asorestan along the road of Dzor to the land of Taron; they seized it and Bznunikʻ and Ałiovit. Continuing their march to the valley of Berkri through Ordspoy and Gogovit, they debouched in Ayrarat. None of the Armenian troops was able to bring the grievous news to the town of Dvin, save three of the princes who went to gather the scattered army—

T'ēodoros Vahewuni, Khach'ean Aṙawełean, and Shapuh Amatuni. They fled to Dvin, and on reaching the bridge of the Metsamawr destroyed it, having crossed to spread the news in the town. They brought together in the citadel all the people of the province who had come for the vintage of the vineyards. But T'ēodoros went to the city of Nakhchawan.

When the enemy reached the Metsamawr bridge, he was unable to cross. But they had as their guide Vardik, prince of Mokk', who was called Aknik. Then crossing by the bridge of the Metsamawr they inflicted the whole land with raiding, and gathered very much booty and many captives. They came and camped at the edge of the forest of Khosrovakert.

On the fifth day they attacked the city. It was delivered into their hands because they surrounded it with smoke. By means of the smoke and the shooting of arrows they pushed back the defenders of the wall. Having set up ladders, they mounted the wall, entered inside, and opened the city gate. The enemy army rushed within and put the multitude of the city's population to the sword. Having plundered the city, they came out and camped in the same encampment. It was the 20th of the month Trē, a Friday. After staying a few days, they left by the same route that they had come, leading away the host of their captives, 35,000 souls. Now the prince of Armenia, the lord of Ṙshtunik', was lying in ambush in the province of Gogovit, and he attacked them with a few men. But he was unable to resist them and fled before them. They pursued him and slew most of them. Then they proceeded to Asorestan. This happened in the years of the Catholicos Ezr.

On account of this battle a command came from the emperor [bestowing] the command of the army on T'ēodoros, lord of Ṙshtunik', with the rank of *patrik*. This all was brought about through the Catholicos Nersēs, who in that same year succeeded to the throne of the Catholicosate in place of the Catholicos Ezr.

Now when the sons of Ismael went to the east from the desert of Sin, their king Amṙ did not go with them. Being victorious in battle, they defeated both kingdoms; they occupied [the land] from Egypt as far as the great Taurus mountain, and from the western sea as far as Media and Khuzhastan. Then they penetrated with royal armies into the original borders of the territory of Ismael. The king commanded ships and many sailors to be gathered, to cross the sea to the south-east: to Pars, Sakastan, Sind, Krman, [and] the land of Kuran and Makuran as far as the borders of India. So the troops rapidly made preparations and carried out their orders. They burned the whole land; and taking booty and plunder they returned. After making raids over the waves of the sea, they came back to their own places.

This we heard from men who had been taken as captives to Khuzhastan, [from] Tachkastan. Having been themselves eyewitnesses of these events, they gave this account to us.

*   *   *

REVIEW QUESTIONS

1. How does the rise of Islam appear from this Armenian perspective?
2. How does this source account for the speedy Arab successes against the Byzantines and Persians?
3. *Catholicos* is the word used here for the head of the Armenian church. Where is Armenia? What does this text reveal about its circumstances in the early 600s?

MUHAMMED

FROM The Quran

The prophet Muhammed (ca. 570–632) brought the message of Islam first to the Arab peoples of his home city, Mecca. Muslims, those who submitted to the will of the one God, Allah, believe that the revelations committed to Muhammed and the prophet's teachings were collected shortly after his death and compose the Quran. The following selections are two suras (chapters) from the Quran, number 29, the Spider, and number 47, Muhammed, and are typical of the style and content of the Quran.

From Al-Quran: A Contemporary Translation, by Ahmed Ali (Princeton, N.J.: Princeton University Press, 1984), pp. 337–42, 435–38.

*   *   *

The Spider

In the name of Allah, most benevolent, ever-merciful.

ALIF LĀM MĪM
Do men think they will get away by saying: "We believe,"
and will not be tried?
We had tried those who were before them
so that God knew who spoke the truth, and who were liars.
Do those who do evil think
that they will get the better of Us?
How bad is the judgement that they make!
He who hopes to meet God (should know)
that God's appointed time will surely come.
He is all-hearing and all-knowing.
He who strives does so for himself.
Verily God is independent of the creatures of the world.
We shall pardon the sinful deeds of those
who believe and do the right,
and give them a reward better than their deeds.

We have enjoined on man to be good to his parents;
but if they try to make you associate with Me
that of which you have no knowledge, then do not obey them.
You have to come back to Us, when I will tell you
what you used to do.
We shall admit those who believe and do the right
among the righteous.
There are among men those who say: "We believe in God;"
yet if they happen to suffer in the cause of God
they take oppression by men as punishment from God.
And if help comes to them from your Lord,
they say: "We were with you."
Does not God know what is hidden in the hearts of men?
God will surely know the believers
and know the hypocrites.
Those who deny say to those who affirm:
"Follow our way; we shall carry the burden of your sins."
But they cannot carry the burden of their sins in the least.

They are liars indeed.
They will carry their own loads
and other loads besides their own;
and will surely be questioned
on the Day of Resurrection
about what they contrived.

We sent Noah to his people, and he lived with
them
a thousand years minus fifty.
Then they were caught by the deluge
for they were evil.
But We saved him and those with him in the
ark,
and made it a sign for the creatures of the
world.
And (remember) Abraham who said to his
people:
"Worship God and be obedient to Him.
This is better for you if you understand.
You worship idols in place of God
and invent lies.
Surely those you worship other than God
have no power over your means of livelihood.
So seek your sustenance from God,
and worship Him and give Him thanks.
To Him will you be brought back in the end.
But if you deny,
then many a people have denied before you.
The duty of the apostle is to convey
the message clearly."
Do they not see how God originates
creation,
then reverts it back?
This is indeed how inevitably the law of God
works;
Say: "Travel on the earth and see
how He originated creation.
Then (you will know) how God will raise the
last raising
(of the dead). Surely God has power over every
thing,
Punish whom He will,
and have mercy on whom He please.

And to Him will you be brought back in the
end.
Escape Him you cannot either in the earth or in
the sky;
and you have no friend or helper apart from
God.

Those who deny the signs of God
and the meeting with Him,
cannot have hope of My mercy.
There is a painful punishment for them.
The people (of Abraham) had no answer except:
"Kill him or burn him;"
but God saved him from the fire.
There are lessons in this for those who believe.
He said: "You have taken to idols
through mutual affection in this life, in place of
God,
but on the Day of Resurrection you will disown
and curse each other,
and your abode will be Hell,
and you will have none to help you."
Then Lot believed in him; and (Abraham) said:
"I will separate myself and take refuge in my
Lord.
Surely He is all-mighty and all-wise."
So We bestowed on him Isaac and Jacob
and gave his progeny prophethood and scripture,
and rewarded him in this world,
and in the next he will be among the upright.
And (remember) Lot when he said to his people:
"You indulge in lecherous acts
which none of the creatures had done before
you.
You commit unnatural acts with men
and cut off the way (of procreation),
and commit obscenities in your gatherings."
The only answer his people made was: "Bring
the punishment of God, if you are truthful."
"O Lord, help me against the wicked people,"
(Lot) prayed.

When Our messengers came to Abraham with
good news,
they said: "We have to destroy this city

as its inhabitants have become sinful."
He said: "Surely Lot is there."
They answered: "We know who is there.
We are to save him and his family except his
     wife,
for she is one of those who will stay behind."
So, when Our messengers came to Lot,
he was worried on their account
as he was unable to protect them.
They said: "Have no fear or regret.
We will certainly save you and your family
     except your wife,
for she is one of those who will stay behind.
We have to bring a scourge from the heavens
on the people of this city as they are depraved."
Verily We have left a clear sign of this
for people of sense to see.
To Midian We sent their brother Shu'aib.
He said: "O people, worship God
and be ready for the Day of Resurrection.
Do no evil, and create no mischief in the land."
But they denied him and were seized
by an earthquake, and lay overturned
in their homes in the morning.
And (remember) 'Ad and Thamud.
It will be clear to you from their habitations
(how they were destroyed),
for Satan had made their deeds look attractive to
     them,
and turned them away from the path;
and yet they were a people of acumen.
(Remember) Qarun, Pharaoh and Haman
to whom Moses came with clear signs;
but they were haughty (and oppressed) the land.
Yet they could not run away from Us;
And We seized all of them for their crimes.
Against some We sent a violent wind hurling
     stones,
and some We seized with a mighty blast,
and some We submerged under the earth,
and some We drowned.
It was not for God to wrong them,
they wronged themselves.
The semblance of those who take protectors
     besides God

is that of the spider.
She arranges a house for herself,
but the flimsiest of houses is the spider's.
If only they had sense!
Verily God knows what they invoke in His place,
for He is all-mighty and all-wise.
These are precepts of wisdom We offer to men,
but only those who are rational understand.
God has created the heavens and the earth
with reason.
Surely in this is a sign for those who believe.

Recite what has been revealed to you of this
     Book,
and be constant in devotion. Surely prayer
keeps you away from the obscene and detestable,
but the remembrance of God is greater far;
and God knows what you do.
Do not argue with the people of the Book
unless in a fair way, apart from those
who act wrongly, and say to them:
"We believe what has been sent down to us,
and we believe what has been sent down to you.
Our God and your God is one,
and to Him we submit."
That is how We have revealed this Book to you;
and those to whom We have sent down the
     Book
will believe in it.
Only those who are infidels will deny it.
You did not read any Scripture before this,
nor wrote one with your right hand,
or else these dissemblers would have found a
     cause to doubt it.
In fact, in the minds of those who have
     intelligence
these are clear signs.
No one denies Our revelations except those who
     are unjust.
For they say: "How is it no signs
were sent down to him from his Lord?"
Say: "The signs are with God.
I am only a warner, plain and simple."
Is it not sufficient for them that We have
     revealed

the Book to you which is read out to them?
It is indeed a grace and reminder
for people who believe.

Say: "God is sufficient as witness between me
      and you."
He knows what is in the heavens and the
      earth.
It is those who believe in falsehood and
      disbelieve in God
who will perish.
They want you to hasten the punishment:
But for a time already determined
the punishment would have come upon them.
It will come upon them all too suddenly,
and they will be caught unawares.
They want you to hasten the punishment:
Hell will indeed surround the unbelievers.
The day the punishment comes upon them
from above and underneath their feet,
(God will) say: "And now taste of what you had
      done."
O My creatures who believe,
surely My earth has plenty of scope and
so worship only Me.
Every soul has to know the taste of death.
You will then be sent back to Us.
We shall admit those who believe and do the
      right
to empyreal gardens with rivers rippling by,
where they will abide for ever.
How excellent the guerdon of those who toil,
Who persevere and place their trust in their
      Lord.
How many living things there are on the earth
that do not store their food;
God provides them as well as you.
He is all-hearing and all-knowing.
If you ask them: "Who created the heavens and
      the earth,
and who set the sun and the moon to work?"
They will answer: "God."
Why then do they vacillate?
God increases the means of those of His
      creatures as He please,
or limits them for whomsoever He will.

He is certainly cognisant of every thing.
If you ask them: "Who sends down rain from
      the sky
and quickens the earth when it is dead?"
They will answer: "God."
Say: "All praise be to God."
But most of them do not understand.

The life of this world is only a sport and play.
It is surely the home of the Hereafter
that will indeed be life extended and new,
if only they knew!
When they board a ship they call on God,
placing their faith wholly in Him.
But when He brings them safely back to shore,
they begin to associate others with Him,
And deny what We had given them,
in order to go on enjoying themselves.
They will come to know soon.
Do they not see that We have given them a safe
      sanctuary,
while all around them men are being despoiled?
Do they then believe what is false,
and deny the bounty of God?
Who is more unjust than he
who fabricates a lie about God,
or denies the truth when it has come to him?
Is there not an abode for unbelievers in Hell?
We shall guide those who strive in Our cause
to the paths leading straight to Us.
Surely God is with those who do good.

*   *   *

Muhammad

In the name of Allah, most benevolent, ever-
      merciful.

THOSE WHO DISBELIEVE
and obstruct (others) from the way of God
will have wasted their deeds.
But those who believe and do the right,
and believe what has been revealed to
      Muhammad,
which is the truth from their Lord,

will have their faults condoned by Him
and their state improved.
That is because those who refuse to believe
only follow what is false; but those who believe
follow the truth from their Lord.
That is how God gives men precepts of wisdom.
So, when you clash with the unbelievers,
smite their necks until you overpower them,
then hold them in bondage.
Then either free them graciously
or after taking a ransom,
until war shall have come to end.
If God had pleased
He could have punished them (Himself),
but He wills to test some of you through some
    others.
He will not allow the deeds
of those who are killed in the cause of God
to go waste.
He will show them the way,
and better their state,
And will admit them into gardens
with which he has acquainted them.
O you who believe, if you help (in the cause of)
    God
He will surely come to your aid,
and firmly plant your feet.
As for the unbelievers, they will suffer
    misfortunes,
and their deeds will be rendered ineffective.
That is so as they were averse
to what has been revealed by God,
and their actions will be nullified.
Have they not journeyed in the land
and seen the fate of those before them?
Destroyed they were utterly by God;
and a similar (fate) awaits the unbelievers.
This is so for God is the friend of those who
    believe
while the unbelievers have no friend.

Verily God will admit those who believe and do
    the right
into gardens with streams of water running
    by.
But the unbelievers revel and carouse

and subsist like beasts, and Hell will be their
    residence.
How many were the habitations,
mightier than your city which has turned you
    out,
which We destroyed;
and they did not have a helper.
Can one who stands on a clear proof from his
    Lord,
be like one enamoured of his evil deeds
and follows his inane desires?
The semblance of Paradise promised the pious
    and devout
(is that of a garden) with streams of water that
    will not go rank,
and rivers of milk whose taste will not undergo
    a change,
and rivers of wine delectable to drinkers,
and streams of purified honey,
and fruits of every kind in them, and forgiveness
    of their Lord.
Are these like those who will live for ever in the
    Fire
and be given boiling water to drink
which will cut their intestines to shreds?
There are some who listen to you; but as soon
    as they go
from you they say to those who were given
    knowledge:
"What is this he is saying now?"
They are those whose hearts
have been sealed by God, and they follow their
    own lusts.
But those who are rightly guided will be given
greater guidance by Him, and they will have
    their intrinsic piety.
Do they wait for any thing but the Hour (of
    change),
that it may come upon them suddenly?
Its signs have already appeared.
How then will they be warned when it has come
    upon them?
Know then, therefore, there is no god but He,
and ask forgiveness for your sins
and those of believing men and women.

God knows your wanderings
and your destination.

Those who believe say: "How is it no Surah was
    revealed?"
But when a categorical Surah is revealed
that mentions war, you should see those
who are sceptical
staring at you like a man in the swoon of death.
Alas the woe for them!
Obedience and modest speech (would have been
    more becoming).
And when the matter has been determined
it is best for them to be true to God.
Is it possible that if placed in authority
you will create disorder in the land
and sever your bonds of relationship?
They are those who were condemned by God,
whose ears were blocked by Him and their eyes
    blinded.
Do they not ponder
on what the Qur'an says?
Or have their hearts been sealed with locks?
Those who turn their backs
after the way of guidance has been opened to
    them,
have been surely tempted by Satan
and beguiled by illusory hopes.
This was so because they said to those
who disdain what God has revealed:
"We shall obey you in some things."
But God knows their secret intentions well.
How will it be when the angels draw out their
    souls
striking their faces and their backs?
Because they followed what displeases God,
and they were averse to pleasing Him.
So We nullified their deeds.

Do they whose minds are filled with doubt,
    think
that God will not expose their malice?
Had We pleased We could have shown them to
    you
that you could know them by their marks,
and recognise them from the way

they twist their words.
Yet God knows all your deeds.
We shall try you in order to know
who are the fighters among you,
and who are men of fortitude,
and verify your histories.
Surely those who do not believe, and obstruct
    others
from the path of God, and oppose the Prophet
after the way of guidance has been opened to
    them,
will not hurt God in the least,
and He will nullify all that they have done.
O you who believe, obey God and the Prophet,
and do not waste your deeds.
Those who do not believe and obstruct others
from the way of God, and die disbelieving,
will not be pardoned by God.
So do not become weak-kneed and sue for
    peace,
for you will have the upper hand
as God is with you and will not overlook your deeds.
Verily the life of this world
is no more than a sport and frivolity.
If you believe and fear God,
He will give you your reward,
and will not ask for your possessions.
If He asks for all you possess and insist upon it,
you will become niggardly,
and it will bring out your malevolence.
Beware! You are called to spend in the way of
    God,
yet some among you close their fists.
But he who is niggardly is so for his own self:
God is above need, and it is you who are
    needy.
If you turn away then God
will bring other people in your place
who, moreover, will not be like you.

*   *   *

Review Questions

1. What aspects of Muslim belief are the most important in these suras?

2. What seems to be the relationship between Islam and the peoples of the Book, Christians and Jews?

3. What are the rewards of the faithful?

AL-ṬABARĪ

The History

al-Ṭabarī (?838–923) was one of the most-respected scholars in early Islam. This prolific author, who worked and taught in Baghdad, wrote on Islamic law and religion as well as producing his monumental history, an immense work covering the subject from its beginnings to his own times. al-Ṭabarī's history carefully noted the sources he used. This excerpt describes the conquest of Jerusalem by the Caliph ʿUmar in 637.

From *The History of al-Ṭabarī*, vol. 12, translated by Yohanan Friedmann (New York: State University of New York Press, 1992), pp. 189–99.

*   *   *

The Conquest of Jerusalem

According to Sālim b. ʿAbdallāh: When ʿUmar reached al-Jābiyah, a Jew said to him: "O Commander of the Faithful, you will not return to your country before God has granted you victory over Jerusalem." While in al-Jābiyah ʿUmar b. al-Khaṭṭāb saw an approaching detachment of horsemen. When they came close, they drew their swords, but ʿUmar said: "These are people who are coming to seek an assurance of safety. Grant it to them." They drew near and it became clear that they were people from Jerusalem. They made peace with ʿUmar on the condition that they would pay the poll tax and opened up Jerusalem for him. When ʿUmar was granted victory over Jerusalem, he summoned that same Jew, and it was said to him: "He is, indeed, in possession of knowledge." ʿUmar asked the Jew about the false Messiah, for he was wont to ask about him a great deal. The Jew said to him: "What are you asking about him, O Commander of the Faithful? You, the Arabs, will kill him ten odd cubits in front of the gate of Lydda."

According to Sālim: When ʿUmar entered Syria, a Jew from Damascus met him and said: "Peace be upon you, O Fārūq! You are the master of Jerusalem. By God, you will not return before God conquers Jerusalem!"

[The people of Jerusalem] caused distress to ʿAmr and he caused distress to them, but he could not conquer Jerusalem, nor could he conquer al-Ramlah.

While ʿUmar was camping in al-Jābiyah, the Muslims seized their weapons in alarm. ʿUmar asked: "What is it?", and they replied: "Do you not see the horsemen and the swords?" ʿUmar looked and saw a detachment of horsemen brandishing their swords. He said: "They are seeking

DOME OF THE ROCK, JERUSALEM (C. 690 C.E.)

Built in the 690s and restored in the sixteenth century, the dome sits over the traditional site where Abraham nearly sacrificed Isaac and where the prophet Muhammad on his horse began his ascent to Paradise. The building is on the Temple Mount, the traditional location of Solomon's Temple, and is near the Church of the Holy Sepulchre. What is distinctive about Muslim art? What does the building imply about the connections between Islam and Jerusalem?

an assurance of safety. Do not be afraid, but grant it to them." They granted them an assurance of safety and [it became clear that] these were people from Jerusalem. They gave to ᶜUmar . . . and asked him to give them in writing [the peace terms] for Jerusalem and its region and for al-Ramlah and its region. Palestine was divided into two parts: one part was with the people of Jerusalem, and the other with the people of al-Ramlah. The people of Palestine were [organized in] ten provinces, and Palestine was equal to Syria in its entirety.

The Jew witnessed the conclusion of the peace treaty. ᶜUmar asked him about the false Messiah. The Jew said: "He is from the sons of Benjamin. By God, you Arabs will kill him ten odd cubits from the gate of Lydda."

According to Khālid and ᶜUbādah: The peace treaty concerning Palestine was concluded by the populace of Jerusalem and al-Ramlah. The reason for this was that Arṭabūn and al-Tadhāriq had left for Egypt when ᶜUmar came to al-Jābiyah; they were subsequently killed in one of the summer expeditions.

It was said that the reason for ᶜUmar's coming to Syria was the following: Abū ᶜUbaydah besieged Jerusalem. Its people asked him to conclude peace with them on the conditions of the Syrian cities and asked that ᶜUmar b. al-Khaṭṭāb be responsible for the treaty. Abū ᶜUbaydah wrote to ᶜUmar about it, and ᶜUmar made the journey from Medina.

According to ᶜAdī b. Sahl: When the Muslims of Syria asked ᶜUmar to help them against the people of Palestine, he appointed ᶜAlī as his deputy and set out to reinforce them. ᶜAlī said: "Where are going by yourself? You are heading toward a rabid enemy." ᶜUmar said: "I hasten to fight the enemy before the death of al-ᶜAbbās. If you lose al-ᶜAbbās, evil will untwist you like the ends of a rope." ᶜAmr and Shuraḥbīl joined ᶜUmar in al-Jābiyah when the peace [with the people of Palestine] was concluded. They witnessed the writing [of the treaty].

According to Khālid and ᶜUbādah: ᶜUmar made peace with the people of Jerusalem in al-Jābiyah. He wrote for them the peace conditions. He wrote one letter to all the provinces (of Palestine) except to the people of Jerusalem:

In the name of God, the Merciful, the Compassionate. This is the assurance of safety (*amān*) which the servant of God, ᶜUmar, the Commander of the Faithful, has granted to the people of Jerusalem. He has given them an assurance of safety for themselves, for their property, their churches, their crosses, the sick and the healthy of the city, and for all the rituals that belong to their religion. Their churches will not be inhabited [by Muslims] and will not be destroyed. Neither they, nor the land on which they stand, nor their cross, nor their property will be damaged. They will not be forcibly converted. No Jew will live with them in Jerusalem. The people of Jerusalem must pay the poll tax like the people of the [other] cities, and they must expel the Byzantines and the robbers. As for those who will leave the city, their lives and property will be safe until they reach their place of safety; and as for those who remain, they will be safe. They will have to pay the poll tax like the people of Jerusalem. Those of the people of Jerusalem who want to leave with the Byzantines, take their property, and abandon their churches and their crosses will be safe until they reach their place of safety. Those villagers (*ahl al-arḍ*) who were in Jerusalem before the killing of so-and-so may remain in the city if they wish, but they must pay the poll tax like the people of Jerusalem. Those who wish may go with the Byzantines, and and those who wish may return to their families. Nothing will be taken from them before their harvest is reaped. If they pay the poll tax according to their obligations, then the contents of this letter are under the covenant of God, are the responsibility of His Prophet, of the caliphs, and of the faithful. The persons who attest to it are Khālid b. al-Walīd, ᶜAmr b. al-ᶜĀṣī, ᶜAbd al-Raḥmān b. ᶜAwf, and Muᶜāwiyah b. Abī Sufyān. This letter was written and prepared in the year 15/636–37.

The rest of the letters were identical to the letter of Lydda [which follows]:

In the name of God, the Merciful, the Compassionate. This is what the servant of God, ʿUmar, the Commander of the Faithful, awarded to the people of Lydda and to all the people of Palestine who are in the same category. He gave them an assurance of safety for themselves, for their property, their churches, their crosses, their sick and their healthy, and all their rites. Their churches will not be inhabited [by the Muslims] and will not be destroyed. Neither their churches, nor the land where they stand, nor their rituals, nor their crosses, nor their property will be damaged. They will not be forcibly converted, and none of them will be harmed. The people of Lydda and those of the people of Palestine who are in the same category must pay the poll tax like the people of the Syrian cities. The same conditions, in their entirety, apply to them if they leave (Lydda).

He then sent to them [an army] and divided Palestine between two men; he put ʿAlqamah b. Ḥakīm in charge of one half and stationed him in al-Ramlah, and he put ʿAlqamah b. Mujazziz in charge of the other half and stationed him in Jerusalem. Each of them stayed in his province with the soldiers who were with him.

According to Sālim: [ʿUmar] appointed ʿAlqamah b. Mujazziz governor of Jerusalem and appointed ʿAlqamah b. al-Ḥakīm governor of al-Ramlah. He placed the soldiers who were with ʿAmr (b. al-ʿĀṣī) at their disposal. He ordered ʿAmr and Shuraḥbīl to join him in al-Jābiyah. When they reached al-Jābiyah, they found ʿUmar riding. They kissed his knee, and ʿUmar embraced them, holding them to his chest.

According to ʿUbādah and Khālid: Having sent the assurance of safety to the people of Jerusalem and having stationed the army there, ʿUmar set out from al-Jābiyah to Jerusalem. He saw that his horse had injuries on its hooves. So he dismounted, and a jade was brought to him and he rode it. The jade shook him, however, so ʿUmar dismounted, hit the jade's face with his mantle, and said: "May God make ugly him who taught you this!" Then he called for his horse to be brought to him, after he had left him unridden for a few days, and treated his hooves. He mounted his horse and rode until he reached Jerusalem.

According to Abū Ṣafiyyah, an elder from Banū Shaybān: When ʿUmar came to Syria, he was brought a jade and rode it. The jade moved in an unstable manner, inclining from side to side. ʿUmar dismounted, hit the jade's face, and said: "May God not teach him who taught you this sort of pride!" He had not ridden a jade before that or after that.

Jerusalem and its entire region were conquered by ʿUmar, except for Ajnādayn, which was conquered by ʿAmr (b. al-ʿĀṣi), and Caesarea, which was conquered by Muʿāwiyah (b. Abī Sufyān).

According to Abū ʿUthmān and Abū Ḥārithah: Jerusalem and its region were conquered in the month of Rabīʿ al-Ākhir of the year 16/May 637.

According to Abū Maryam, the client of Salāmah, who said: I witnessed the conquest of Jerusalem with ʿUmar: He set out from al-Jābiyah, leaving it behind until he came to Jerusalem. He then went on and entered the mosque. Then he went on toward the miḥrāb of David, while we were with him; he entered it, recited the prostration of David, and prostrated himself, and we prostrated ourselves with him.

According to Rajāʾ b. Ḥaywah—persons who were present at the event: When ʿUmar came from al-Jābiyah to Jerusalem and drew near the gate of the mosque, he said: "Watch out for Kaʿb on my behalf!" When the gate was opened for him, he said: "O God, I am ready to serve you in what you love most." Then he turned to the miḥrāb, the miḥrāb of David, peace be upon him. It was at night, and he prayed there. It was not long before dawn broke, and then ʿUmar ordered the muʾadhdhin to sound the call for prayer. Then he moved forward, led the prayer, and recited Sūrat Ṣād with the people. During the prayer he prostrated himself. Then he stood up and read with them in the second (rakʿah) the beginnning of Sūrat Banī Isrāʾīl. Then he prayed another rakʿah and went away. He said: "Bring Kaʿb to me." Kaʿb was brought to him. ʿUmar said: "Where do you think we should establish the place of prayer?" Kaʿb said: "Toward the Rock." ʿUmar said: "O Kaʿb, you are imitating the Jewish religion! I have seen you taking off your shoes." Kaʿb said: "I wanted to touch this ground with my feet." ʿUmar said: "I have seen you. Nay, we shall place the *qiblah* in the front of it; the Messenger of God likewise made the front part of our mosques the *qiblah*. Take care of your own affairs; we were not commanded to venerate the Rock, but we were commanded to venerate the Kaʿbah."

ʿUmar made the front part of the mosque its *qiblah*. Then he stood up from his place of prayer and went to the rubbish in which the Romans buried the temple (*bayt al-maqdis*) at the time of the sons of Israel. (When he came to the Byzantines, they had uncovered a part but left the rest [under the rubbish].) He said: "O people, do what I am doing." He knelt in the midst of the rubbish and put it by the handful into the lower part of his mantle. He heard behind him the proclamation "God is most great!" He disliked improper behavior in any matter and said: "What is this?" The people said: "Kaʿb proclaimed 'God is most great!' and the people proclaimed it following him." ʿUmar said: "Bring him to me!" Kaʿb said: "O Commander of the Faithful, five hundred years ago a prophet predicted what you have done today." ʿUmar asked: "In what way?" Kaʿb said:

The Byzantines (*Rūm*) attacked the sons of Israel, were given victory over them, and buried the temple. Then they were given another victory, but they did not attend to the temple until the Persians attacked them. The Persians oppressed the sons of Israel. Later the Byzantines were given victory over the Persians. Then you came to rule. God sent a prophet to the [city buried in] rubbish and said: "Rejoice O Jerusalem (*Ūrī shalam*)! Al-Fārūq will come to you and cleanse you." Another prophet was sent to Constantinople. He stood on a hill belonging to the city and said: "O Constantinople, what did your people do to My House? They ruined it, presented you as if you were similar to My

throne and made interpretations contrary to My purpose. I have determined to make you one day unfortified (and defenseless). Nobody will seek shelter from you, nor rest in your shade. [I shall make you unfortified] at the hands of Banū al-Qādhir, Sabā, and Waddān."

By the time it was evening nothing remained of the rubbish.

An identical tradition was transmitted according to Rabīʿah al-Shāmī. He added: "Al-Fārūq came to you with my obedient army. They will take revenge upon the Byzantines on behalf of your people." Regarding Constantinople he said: "I shall leave you unfortified and exposed to the sun; nobody will seek shelter from you, and you will not cast your shade on anyone."

According to Anas b. Mālik:

I was present in Jerusalem with ʿUmar. While he was giving food to the people one day, a monk from Jerusalem came to him without knowing that wine had been prohibited. The monk said: "Do you want a drink which will be permissible according to our books [even] when wine is prohibited?"

ʿUmar asked him to bring it and said: "From what has it been prepared?" The monk informed him that he had cooked it from juice until only one-third of it remained. ʿUmar dipped his finger into it, then stirred it in the vessel, divided it into two halves, and said: "This is syrup (*ṭilāʾ*)." He likened it to resin (*qaṭirān*), drank from it, and ordered the amīrs of the Syrian provinces to prepare it. He wrote to the newly established garrison towns (*amṣār*), saying: "I have been brought a beverage cooked from juice until two-thirds of it were gone and one-third remained. It is like syrup. Cook it and provide it to the Muslims."

According to Abū ʿUthmān and Abū Ḥārithah: Arṭabūn went to Egypt when ʿUmar came to al-Jābiyah. Those who rejected the peace agreement and wanted [to go with him] joined him. Then, when the people of Egypt made a peace agreement [with the Muslims] and defeated the Byzantines, he took to the sea and survived afterward. He commanded the summer expeditions of the Byzantines and confronted the commander of the Muslim summer expeditions. Arṭabūn and a man from the tribe of Qays, whose name was Ḍurays, exchanged blows, and Arṭabūn cut the Qaysī's hand. The Qaysī killed him and recited:

Though Arṭabūn of the Byzantines maimed my
    hand,
there is still some use to it, praise be to God.
Two fingers and a stump, with which I hold
    straight
the front part of the spear when people are
    struck with fear.
Though Arṭabūn of the Byzantines cut my
    hand,
I left his limbs cut to pieces, in return.

Ziyād b. Ḥanẓalah recited:

I remembered the long wars against the
Byzantines,
when we spent a year full of journeys.
When we were in the land of Ḥijāz and
a month's journey separated us, with anxieties
    in between;
When Arṭabūn of the Byzantines defended his
    country,
a noble chieftain tackled him here and struggled
    with him;
When al-Fārūq saw that the time [was right] for
    the conquest of Arṭabūn's land,

he brought forward God's soldiers to attack
    him.
When they became aware of al-Fārūq and
    feared his assault,
they came to him and said: "You are of those
    whom we shall befriend."
Syria threw its buried treasures at his feet,
as well as a life of abundance with countless
    gains.
He put whatever was between east and west at
    our disposal,
as inheritance for posterity, gathered by his two-
    humped camels.
Many a beast of burden that had been unable
    to carry its load,
[now] carried a burden while being well into
    pregnancy.

*   *   *

REVIEW QUESTIONS

1. How do you explain ʿUmar's easy success in conquering Syria and Palestine?
2. What role does Jerusalem play for Muslims, Christians, and Jews in the region?
3. What are al-Ṭabarī's strengths and weaknesses as a historian?

BEDE

FROM *A History of the English Church and People*

The Venerable Bede (died 735), to use his common name, was an Anglo-Saxon monk who wrote on many religious, scientific, and historical subjects. He was especially interested in problems of chronology and time, in an age when an accurate calendar was a considerable accomplishment. In this selection from his most famous book, A History of the English Church and People, *Bede describes the conversion of Edwin of Northumbria.*

From *Bede: A History of the English Church and People,* edited by Leo Serley-Price (New York: Penguin Books, 1968), pp. 126–29.

*   *   *

Chapter 13

When he heard this, the king answered that it was his will as well as his duty to accept the Faith that Paulinus taught, but said that he must still discuss the matter with his principal advisers and friends, so that, if they were in agreement with him, they might all be cleansed together in Christ the Fount of Life. Paulinus agreed, and the king kept his promise. He summoned a council of the wise men, and asked each in turn his opinion of this strange doctrine and this new way of worshipping the godhead that was being proclaimed to them.

Coifi, the Chief Priest, replied without hesitation: "Your Majesty, let us give careful consideration to this new teaching; for I frankly admit that, in my experience, the religion that we have hitherto professed seems valueless and powerless. None of your subjects has been more devoted to the service of our gods than myself; yet there are many to whom you show greater favour, who receive greater honours, and who are more successful in all their undertakings. Now, if the gods had any power, they would surely have favoured myself, who have been more zealous in their service. Therefore, if on examination you perceive that these new teachings are better and more effectual, let us not hesitate to accept them."

Another of the king's chief men signified his agreement with this prudent argument, and went on to say: "Your Majesty, when we compare the present life of man on earth with that time of which we have no knowledge, it seems to me like the swift flight of a single sparrow through the banqueting-hall where you are sitting at dinner on a winter's day with your thanes and counsellors. In the midst there is a comforting fire to warm the hall; outside, the storms of winter rain or snow are raging. This sparrow flies swiftly in through one door of the hall, and out through another. While he is inside, he is safe from the winter storms; but after a few moments of comfort, he vanishes from sight into the wintry world from which he came. Even so, man appears on earth for a little while; but of what went before this life or of what follows, we know nothing. Therefore, if this new teaching has brought any more certain knowledge, it seems only right that we should follow it." The other elders and counsellors of the king, under God's guidance, gave similar advice.

Coifi then added that he wished to hear Paulinus' teaching about God in greater detail; and when, at the king's bidding, this had been given, he exclaimed: "I have long realized that there is nothing in our way of worship; for the more diligently I sought after truth in our religion, the less I found. I now publicly confess that this teaching clearly reveals truths that will afford us the blessings of life, salvation, and eternal happiness. Therefore, Your Majesty, I submit that the temples and altars that we have dedicated to no advantage be immediately desecrated and burned." In short, the king granted blessed Paulinus full permission to preach, renounced idolatry, and professed his acceptance of the Faith of Christ. And when he asked the Chief Priest who should be the first to profane the altars and shrines of the idols, together with the enclosures that surrounded them, Coifi replied: "I will do this myself; for now that the true God has granted me knowledge, who more suitably than I can set a public example and destroy the idols that I worshipped in ignorance?" So he formally renounced his empty superstitions and asked the king to give him arms and a stallion—for hitherto it had not been lawful for the Chief Priest to carry arms or to ride anything but a mare—and, thus equipped, he set out to destroy the idols. Girded with a sword and with a spear in his hand, he mounted the king's stallion and rode up to the idols. When the crowd saw him, they thought he had gone mad; but without hesitation, as soon as he reached the temple, he cast into it the spear he carried and thus profaned it. Then, full of joy at his knowledge of the worship of the true God, he told his companions to set fire to the temple and its enclosures and destroy them. The site where these idols once stood is still shown, not far east of York, beyond the river Derwent, and is known today as Goodmanham. Here it was that the Chief Priest, inspired by the true God, desecrated and destroyed the altars that he had himself dedicated.

Chapter 14

So King Edwin, with all the nobility of his kingdom and a large number of humbler folk, accepted the Faith and were washed in the cleansing waters of Baptism in the eleventh year of his reign, which was the year of our Lord 627, and about one hundred and eighty years after the first arrival of the English in Britain. The king's Baptism took place at York on Easter Day, the 12th of April, in the church of Saint Peter the Apostle, which the king had hastily built of timber during the time of his instruction and preparation for Baptism; and in this city he established the see of his teacher and bishop Paulinus. Soon after his Baptism, at Paulinus' suggestion, he gave orders to build on the same site a larger and more noble basilica of stone, which was to enclose the little oratory he had built before. The foundations were laid, and the walls of a square church began to rise around this little oratory; but before they reached their appointed height, the cruel death of the king left the work to be completed by Oswald his successor. Thenceforward for six years, until the close of Edwin's reign, Paulinus preached the word in that province with the king's full consent and approval, and as many as were predestined to eternal life believed and were baptized. Among these were Osfrid and Eadfrid, sons of King Edwin, who were both born to him in exile of Coenburg, daughter of Cearl, King of the Mercians.

At a later date, other children of his by Queen Ethelberga were also baptized: these included a son, Ethelhun; a daughter, Ethelthryd; and another son, Wuscfrea. The two former were snatched from life while still wearing their white baptismal robes, and were buried in the church at York. Yffi, son of Osfrid, was also baptized, and many others of noble and princely rank. Indeed, so great was the fervour of faith and desire for baptism among the Northumbrian people that Paulinus is said to have accompanied the king and queen to the royal residence at Ad-Gefrin and remained there thirty-six days constantly occupied in instructing and baptizing. During this period, he did nothing from dawn to dusk but proclaim Christ's saving message to the people, who gathered from all the surrounding villages and countryside; and when he had instructed them, he washed them in the cleansing waters of Baptism in the nearby River Glen. This residence was abandoned by the later kings, who built another at a place called Maelmin.

These events took place in the province of Bernicia.

*   *   *

REVIEW QUESTIONS

1. Is there a core of credible pagan belief in the story of the sparrow?
2. If so, what is it?
3. How does Edwin's conversion compare to that of Clovis?

FROM The Lombard Laws: Rothair's Edict

*In 568 the Lombards, another Germanic tribe, invaded Italy and overthrew the Os-
trogothic kingdom, and also took some areas away from Byzantine control. The
Lombards settled down to rule a complex peninsula with Roman, Gothic, and Greek
laws still in place, and the papacy in Rome with its own developing sense of canon
law. Rothair's Edict (643) is the earliest legal text from the Lombard kingdom in
Italy. These sections of the law outline some of the most serious crimes and
punishments.*

From *The Lombard Laws,* edited by Katherine Fischer Drew (Philadelphia: University of
Pennsylvania Press, 1973).

*   *   *

9. If in the presence of the king one man accuses another of an offense which would involve the loss of his life, then the accused may offer satisfactory oath and clear himself. If in such a case the man accused is present together with him who accused him of the offense, then the accused may refute the charge, if he can, by means of the *camfio,* that is, by judicial duel. If the accusation is proved against him, he shall lose his life or pay such an amount as composition as pleases the king. If the charge is not proved against him, and it is recognized that he has been accused wrongfully, then he who accused him and was not able to prove it shall pay the amount of his wergeld as composition, half to the king and half to him charged with the offense.

10. If any freeman plots against another man's life and that one does not die as a result, then the plotter shall pay twenty solidi as composition.

11. On plots involving death. If freemen without the king's consent plot another man's death, but that one does not die as a result of the agreement, then each of them shall pay twenty solidi as composition, as stated above. But if that one conspired against dies as a result of the plot, then the doer of the deed shall pay the victim's wergeld,[1] according as he is valued, as composition.

12. If two or three or more freemen commit a homicide together, and wish to associate themselves so that as one they may pay composition for that one the man killed according as he is valued, such an agreement is permitted to them. If one of them separates himself from the others and is not able to clear himself as the law provides, namely, he is not able to prove that he inflicted none of the blows against that man who was killed, then he is as guilty as the others who paid the composition. If he does clear himself, however, he shall be free of blame in connection with the homicide. If he is accused of being in the counsel of the conspirators, he shall pay twenty solidi as composition, as stated above, unless he can clear himself of involvement in the conspiracy.

13. He who kills his lord, shall be killed himself. The man who tries to defend this murderer who killed his lord shall pay 900 solidi as composition, half to the king and half to the relatives of the dead man. And he who refuses aid in avenging the man's death, if his aid is sought, shall pay fifty solidi as composition, half to the king and half to the man to whom he refused aid.

14. On murder. If anyone secretly kills a freeman or a man or woman slave, if one or two persons

---

[1]Wergeld is the value of human life, based on rank, and
paid as compensation. [Editor.]

commit the homicide, he or they shall pay 900 solidi as composition. If more than two were involved, each shall pay the wergeld of the man killed, if he was a native-born freeman, according to his rank. If it was a slave or freedman who was killed, each shall pay composition according to his value. If they plunder the dead body, that is, if they commit *plodraub,* each shall pay eighty solidi as composition for this.

15. On grave breaking. He who breaks into the grave of a dead man and despoils the body and throws it out shall pay 900 solidi to the relatives of the dead. And if there are no near relatives, then the king's gastald or schultheis shall exact this penalty and collect it for the king's court.

16. On despoiling the dead. He who finds a human corpse in a river or beside it and despoils the body and hides it shall pay eighty solidi as composition to the relatives of the dead man. If he found and stripped the body, however, and immediately after made it known to those in the vicinity that he did it for the sake of reward and not for the purpose of robbery, then he shall return those things which he had found on the body and no further guilt shall be imputed to him.

17. If one of our men wishes to come to us, let him come in safety and return to his home unharmed; let none of his enemies presume to cause any injury or harm to him on the journey. It shall be done thus in order that he who hastens to come to the king may come openly and receive no injury or damage of any sort on that journey while coming to the king and returning. He who does cause such injury shall pay compensation as is provided below in this code.

18. He who, in order to avenge some injury or damage, attacks with arms one of his enemies who is on his way to the king, shall pay 900 solidi, half to the king and half to him who bore the injury.

19. He who falls upon another with armed hand in order to vindicate some injury, or who leads an armed band containing up to four men into a village, shall die for his unlawful presumption or shall at least pay 900 solidi as composition, half to the king and half to him who was wronged. Each

of those with him, if freemen, shall pay eighty solidi as composition, half to the king and half to him who was wronged. And, in addition, if they have burned houses in that village or killed any man there, then they shall pay composition, according as the damage is assessed, to him whose houses were burned or whose relative or slave was killed.

20. If any soldier refuses to go to his duke for justice, he shall pay twenty solidi as composition to the king and to his duke.

21. Anyone who refuses to go out with the army or with the guard shall pay twenty solidi as composition to the king and to his duke.

22. Any soldier who refuses aid to his duke when that one is pursuing justice, shall pay twenty solidi as composition to the king and to the duke.

23. If a duke treats his men unjustly, the gastald shall aid the injured man. The gastald shall find out the truth and bring the case to justice in the presence of the king or at least before the duke.

24. If any gastald treats his man contrary to reason, then the duke shall aid the injured man and find out the truth.

25. If anyone attempts to obtain his property from another soldier, and that one does not return it to him, then he shall go to his duke. And if the duke or the judge appointed for that place by the king will not serve him with truth and justice, then he the duke or judge shall pay twenty solidi as composition to the king and to him who brought the case, and the case shall continue.

26. On road-blocking, that is *orbitaria.* Anyone who places himself in the road before a free woman or girl, or inflicts some injury upon her, shall pay 900 solidi as composition, half to the king and half to her who suffered the injury or to him who is her legal guardian.

27. Anyone who blocks the road to a freeman shall pay him twenty solidi as composition, provided no physical injury was caused. But he who causes injury shall pay twenty solidi as composition to him before whom the road was blocked and he shall also pay compensation for any wounds or injuries

that he inflicted according to the schedule provided below.

28. Anyone who blocks the road to another's man or woman slave or to his *aldius* or freedman shall pay twenty solidi as composition to that one's lord.

29. He who in defense closes his field or meadow or other enclosure to any man by placing himself so that it cannot be entered is not guilty as is that one who blocks the road to a man simply walking along, because in this particular case he is protecting his own property.

30. On throwing someone from his horse. He who intentionally throws a freeman from his horse to the ground by any means shall pay the aggrieved party eighty solidi as composition. And if he causes that one some injury, he shall in addition pay composition for the injuries as is provided in this code.

31. Concerning him who in disguise does violence. He who unjustly does violence to a freeman as a walopaus shall pay the injured party eighty solidi as composition. A walopaus is one who secretly puts on another's clothing or disguises his head or face.

32. If a freeman is found in someone else's courtyard at night and does not willingly give his hands to be bound, he may be killed and no compensation may be sought by his relatives. But if he gives his hands to be bound and they have been bound, he still must pay eighty solidi for himself, because it is not consistent with reason that a man should silently or secretly enter someone else's courtyard at night; if he has some useful purpose, he should call out before he enters.

33. If a slave is found at night in someone else's courtyard and does not give his hands to be bound he may be killed and no compensation may be sought by his lord. But if the slave holds out his hands and they have been bound, he may free himself with a payment of forty solidi.

34. That one who in anger shoots an arrow or hurls a lance into another's courtyard from outside of the wall and wounds someone within the yard shall pay twenty solidi as composition. In addition, he must pay composition for any wounds or injuries inflicted as provided in this code.

35. On breach of the peace. He who creates a disturbance in a church shall pay forty solidi to that venerable place in addition to him who suffered the wounds or injuries. The abovementioned forty solidi shall be collected by the schultheis or judge of the district and laid on the holy altar of that church where the offense occurred.

36. He who dares to create a disturbance within the king's palace when the king is present shall lose his life unless he can redeem his life from the king.

37. The freeman who creates a disturbance in that district where the king is present, although he does not strike a blow, shall pay twelve solidi to the king's palace. But he who raises a disturbance and also strikes a blow, shall pay twenty-four solidi to the fisc. In addition, he shall pay composition for any wounds or injuries which he caused as provided below.

*   *   *

REVIEW QUESTIONS

1. What is the Lombard conception of justice?
2. How does this style of punishment help to keep the peace?
3. What are the assumptions of Lombard legal reasoning?

EINHARD

FROM *The Life of Charlemagne*

Einhard's biography of Charlemagne, composed shortly after the emperor's death in 814, is an excellent source on this remarkable ruler's career. Charlemagne's numerous accomplishments made him a fitting subject for the first biography of a secular ruler since the fall of the Roman Empire. Although Einhard patterned his biography on Roman models, he presents an accurate portrait of his friend the emperor. This chapter covers Charlemagne's private life, which the author distinguishes from the accomplishments of his father, Pepin, and his wars, mainly against the Muslims in Spain and the Saxons in Germany, and also against the Avars around what is today Austria and Hungary.

From *Two Lives of Charlemagne*, edited by Lewis Thorpe (New York: Penguin Books, 1969), pp. 73–82.

*   *   *

The Emperor's Private Life

What has gone before is a fair picture of Charlemagne and all that he did to protect and enlarge his kingdom, and indeed to embellish it. I shall now speak of his intellectual qualities, his extraordinary strength of character, whether in prosperity or adversity, and all the other details of his personal and domestic life.

After the death of his father, at the time when he was sharing the kingship with Carloman, Charlemagne bore with such patience this latter's hatred and jealousy that everyone was surprised that he never lost his temper with his brother.

Then, at the bidding of his mother, he married the daughter of Desiderius, the King of the Longobards. Nobody knows why, but he dismissed this wife after one year. Next he married Hildigard, a woman of most noble family, from the Swabian race. By her he had three sons, Charles, Pepin and Lewis, and the same number of daugh-

ters, Rotrude, Bertha and Gisela. He had three more daughters, Theoderada, Hiltrude and Rothaide, two of these by his third wife, Fastrada, who was from the race of Eastern Franks or Germans, and the last by a concubine whose name I cannot remember. Fastrada died and he married Luitgard, from the Alamanni, but she bore him no children. After Luitgard's death, he took four concubines: Madelgard, who bore him a daughter Ruothilde; Ger svinda, of the Saxon race, by whom he had a daughter Adaltrude; Regina, who bore him Drogo and Hugo; and Adallinda, who became the mother of Theodoric.

Charlemagne's own mother, Bertrada, lived with him in high honour to a very great age. He treated her with every respect and never had a cross word with her, except over the divorce of King Desiderius' daughter, whom he had married on her advice. Bertrada died soon after Hildigard, living long enough to see three grandsons and as many granddaughters in her son's house. Charlemagne buried her with great honour in the church of Saint Denis, where his father lay.

He had a single sister, Gisela by name, who from her childhood onwards had been dedicated to the religious life. He treated her with the same respect which he showed his mother. She died a few years before Charlemagne himself, in the nunnery where she had spent her life.

Charlemagne was determined to give his children, his daughters just as much as his sons, a proper training in the liberal arts which had formed the subject of his own studies. As soon as they were old enough he had his sons taught to ride in the Frankish fashion, to use arms and to hunt. He made his daughters learn to spin and weave wool, use the distaff and spindle, and acquire every womanly accomplishment, rather than fritter away their time in sheer idleness.

Of all his children he lost only two sons and one daughter prior to his own death. These were his eldest son Charles, Pepin whom he had made King of Italy, and Rotrude, the eldest of his daughters, who had been engaged to Constantine, the Emperor of the Greeks. Pepin left one son, called Bernard, and five daughters, Adelhaid, Atula, Gundrada, Berthaid and Theoderada. Charlemagne gave clear proof of the affection which he bore them all, for after the death of Pepin he ordered his grandson Bernard to succeed and he had his granddaughters brought up with his own girls. He bore the death of his two sons and his daughter with less fortitude than one would have expected, considering the strength of his character; for his emotions as a father, which were very deeply rooted, made him burst into tears.

When the death of Hadrian, the Pope of Rome and his close friend, was announced to him, he wept as if he had lost a brother or a dearly loved son. He was firm and steady in his human relationships, developing friendship easily, keeping it up with care and doing everything he possibly could for anyone whom he had admitted to this degree of intimacy.

He paid such attention to the upbringing of his sons and daughters that he never sat down to table without them when he was at home, and never set out on a journey without taking them with him. His sons rode at his side and his daughters followed along behind. Hand-picked guards watched over them as they closed the line of march. These girls were extraordinarily beautiful and greatly loved by their father. It is a remarkable fact that, as a result of this, he kept them with him in his household until the very day of his death, instead of giving them in marriage to his own men or to foreigners, maintaining that he could not live without them. The consequence was that he had a number of unfortunate experiences, he who had been so lucky in all else that he undertook. However, he shut his eyes to all that happened, as if no suspicion of any immoral conduct had ever reached him, or as if the rumour was without foundation.

I did not mention with the others a son called Pepin who was born to Charlemagne by a concubine. He was handsome enough, but a hunchback. At a moment when his father was wintering in Bavaria, soon after the beginning of his campaign against the Huns, this Pepin pretended to be ill and conspired with certain of the Frankish leaders who had won him over to their cause by pretending to offer him the kingship. The plot was discovered and the conspirators were duly punished. Pepin was tonsured and permitted to take up, in the monastery of Prüm, the life of a religious for which he had already expressed a vocation.

Earlier on there had been another dangerous conspiracy against Charlemagne in Germany. All the plotters were exiled, some having their eyes put out first, but the others were not maltreated physically. Only three of them were killed. These resisted arrest, drew their swords and started to defend themselves. They slaughtered a few men in the process and had to be destroyed themselves, as there was no other way of dealing with them.

The cruelty of Queen Fastrada is thought to have been the cause of both these conspiracies, since it was under her influence that Charlemagne seemed to have taken actions which were fundamentally opposed to his normal kindliness and good nature. Throughout the remainder of his life he so won the love and favour of all his fellow human beings, both at home and abroad, that no one ever levelled against him the slightest charge of cruelty or injustice.

He loved foreigners and took great pains to make them welcome. So many visited him as a result that they were rightly held to be a burden not only to the palace, but to the entire realm. In his magnanimity he took no notice at all of this criticism, for he considered that his reputation for hospitality and the advantage of the good name which he acquired more than compensated for the great nuisance of their being there.

The Emperor was strong and well built. He was tall in stature, but not excessively so, for his height was just seven times the length of his own feet. The top of his head was round, and his eyes were piercing and unusually large. His nose was slightly longer than normal, he had a fine head of white hair and his expression was gay and good-humoured. As a result, whether he was seated or standing, he always appeared masterful and dignified. His neck was short and rather thick, and his stomach a trifle too heavy, but the proportions of the rest of his body prevented one from noticing these blemishes. His step was firm and he was manly in all his movements. He spoke distinctly, but his voice was thin for a man of his physique. His health was good, except that he suffered from frequent attacks of fever during the last four years of his life, and towards the end he was lame in one foot. Even then he continued to do exactly as he wished, instead of following the advice of his doctors, whom he came positively to dislike after they advised him to stop eating the roast meat to which he was accustomed and to live on stewed dishes.

He spent much of his time on horseback and out hunting, which came naturally to him, for it would be difficult to find another race on earth who could equal the Franks in this activity. He took delight in steam-baths at the thermal springs, and loved to exercise himself in the water whenever he could. He was an extremely strong swimmer and in this sport no one could surpass him. It was for this reason that he built his palace at Aachen and remained continuously in residence there during the last years of his life and indeed until the moment of his death. He would invite not only his sons to bathe with him, but his nobles and friends as well, and occasionally even a crowd of his attendants and bodyguards, so that sometimes a hundred men or more would be in the water together.

He wore the national dress of the Franks. Next to his skin he had a linen shirt and linen drawers; and then long hose and a tunic edged with silk. He wore shoes on his feet and bands of cloth wound round his legs. In winter he protected his chest and shoulders with a jerkin made of otter skins or ermine. He wrapped himself in a blue cloak and always had a sword strapped to his side, with a hilt and belt of gold or silver. Sometimes he would use a jewelled sword, but this was only on great feast days or when ambassadors came from foreign peoples. He hated the clothes of other countries, no matter how becoming they might be, and he would never consent to wear them. The only exception to this was one day in Rome when Pope Hadrian entreated him to put on a long tunic and a Greek mantle, and to wear shoes made in the Roman fashion; and then a second time, when Leo, Hadrian's successor, persuaded him to do the same thing. On feast days he walked in procession in a suit of cloth of gold, with jewelled shoes, his cloak fastened with a golden brooch and with a crown of gold and precious stones on his head. On ordinary days his dress differed hardly at all from that of the common people.

He was moderate in his eating and drinking, and especially so in drinking; for he hated to see drunkenness in any man, and even more so in himself and his friends. All the same, he could not go long without food, and he often used to complain that fasting made him feel ill. He rarely gave banquets and these only on high feast days, but then he would invite a great number of guests. His main meal of the day was served in four courses, in addition to the roast meat which his hunters used to bring in on spits and which he enjoyed more than any other food. During his meal he would listen to a public reading or some other entertainment. Stories would be recited for him, or the doings of the ancients told again. He took great pleasure in the books of Saint Augustine and especially in those which are called *The City of God*.

He was so sparing in his use of wine and every other beverage that he rarely drank more than three times in the course of his dinner. In summer, after his midday meal, he would eat some fruit and take another drink; then he would remove his shoes and undress completely, just as he did at night, and rest for two or three hours. During the night he slept so lightly that he would wake four or five times and rise from his bed. When he was dressing and putting on his shoes he would invite his friends to come in. Moreover, if the Count of the Palace told him that there was some dispute which could not be settled without the Emperor's personal decision, he would order the disputants to be brought in there and then, hear the case as if he were sitting in tribunal and pronounce a judgement. If there was any official business to be transacted on that day, or any order to be given to one of his ministers, he would settle it at the same time.

He spoke easily and fluently, and could express with great clarity whatever he had to say. He was not content with his own mother tongue, but took the trouble to learn foreign languages. He learnt Latin so well that he spoke it as fluently as his own tongue; but he understood Greek better than he could speak it. He was eloquent to the point of sometimes seeming almost garrulous.

He paid the greatest attention to the liberal arts; and he had great respect for men who taught them, bestowing high honours upon them. When he was learning the rules of grammar he received tuition from Peter the Deacon of Pisa, who by then was an old man, but for all other subjects he was taught by Alcuin, surnamed Albinus, another Deacon, a man of the Saxon race who came from Britain and was the most learned man anywhere to be found. Under him the Emperor spent much time and effort in studying rhetoric, dialectic and especially astrology. He applied himself to mathematics and traced the course of the stars with

great attention and care. He also tried to learn to write. With this object in view he used to keep writing-tablets and notebooks under the pillows on his bed, so that he could try his hand at forming letters during his leisure moments; but, although he tried very hard, he had begun too late in life and he made little progress.

Charlemagne practised the Christian religion with great devotion and piety, for he had been brought up in this faith since earliest childhood. This explains why he built a cathedral of such great beauty at Aachen, decorating it with gold and silver, with lamps, and with lattices and doors of solid bronze. He was unable to find marble columns for his construction anywhere else, and so he had them brought from Rome and Ravenna.

As long as his health lasted he went to church morning and evening with great regularity, and also for early-morning Mass, and the late-night hours. He took the greatest pains to ensure that all church ceremonies were performed with the utmost dignity, and he was always warning the sacristans to see that nothing sordid or dirty was brought into the building or left there. He donated so many sacred vessels made of gold and silver, and so many priestly vestments, that when service time came even those who opened and closed the doors, surely the humblest of all church dignitaries, had no need to perform their duties in their everyday clothes.

He made careful reforms in the way in which the psalms were chanted and the lessons read. He was himself quite an expert at both of these exercises, but he never read the lesson in public and he would sing only with the rest of the congregation and then in a low voice.

He was most active in relieving the poor and in that form of really disinterested charity which the Greeks call *eleemosyna*. He gave alms not only in his own country and in the kingdom over which he reigned, but also across the sea in Syria, Egypt, Africa, Jerusalem, Alexandria and Carthage. Wherever he heard that Christians were living in want, he took pity on their poverty and sent them money regularly. It was, indeed, precisely for this reason that he sought the friendship of kings beyond the sea, for he hoped that some relief and alleviation might result for the Christians living under their domination.

Charlemagne cared more for the church of the holy Apostle Peter in Rome than for any other sacred and venerable place. He poured into its treasury a vast fortune in gold and silver coinage and in precious stones. He sent so many gifts to the Pope that it was impossible to keep count of them. Throughout the whole period of his reign nothing was ever nearer to his heart than that, by his own efforts and exertion, the city of Rome should regain its former proud position. His ambition was not merely that the church of Saint Peter should remain safe and protected thanks to him, but that by means of his wealth it should be more richly adorned and endowed than any other church. However much he thought of Rome, it still remains true that throughout his whole reign of forty-seven years he went there only four times to fulfil his vows and to offer up his prayers.

These were not the sole reasons for Charlemagne's last visit to Rome. The truth is that the inhabitants of Rome had violently attacked Pope Leo, putting out his eyes and cutting off his tongue, and had forced him to flee to the King for help. Charlemagne really came to Rome to restore the Church, which was in a very bad state indeed, but in the end he spent the whole winter there. It was on this occasion that he received the title of Emperor and Augustus. At first he was far from wanting this. He made it clear that he would not have entered the cathedral that day at all, although it was the greatest of all the festivals of the Church, if he had known in advance what the Pope was planning to do. Once he had accepted the title, he endured with great patience the jealousy of the so-called Roman Emperors, who were most indignant at what had happened. He overcame their hostility only by the sheer strength of his personality, which was much more powerful than theirs. He was for ever sending messengers to them, and in his dispatches he called them his brothers.

Now that he was Emperor, he discovered that there were many defects in the legal system of his own people, for the Franks have two separate codes of law which differ from each other in many points. He gave much thought to how he could best fill the gaps, reconcile the discrepancies, correct the errors and rewrite the laws which were ill-expressed. None of this was ever finished; he added a few sections, but even these remained incomplete. What he did do was to have collected together and committed to writing the laws of all the nations under his jurisdiction which still remained unrecorded.

At the same time he directed that the age-old narrative poems, barbarous enough, it is true, in which were celebrated the warlike deeds of the kings of ancient times, should be written out and so preserved. He also began a grammar of his native tongue.

*   *   *

REVIEW QUESTIONS

1. According to Einhard, what are the qualities of a strong Germanic king?
2. What do we learn about the role of women at the upper levels of Carolingian society?
3. Einhard does not want to reveal the emperor's weaknesses, but what might they be?

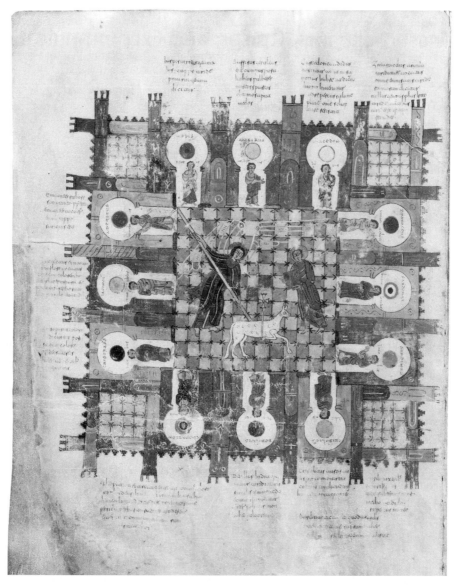

VISION OF THE HEAVENLY JERUSALEM (C. 900)   Maius

An illumination by Maius for a manuscript by Beatus of Liébana, tenth-century Spain. Beatus of Liébana wrote a commentary on the Apocalypse for which the illuminator/artist Maius did 110 miniatures. This page shows the Heavenly Jerusalem as an early medieval city, surrounded by the twelve apostles. Inside the city are St. John the Evangelist with his book, the Lamb of God, and an angel measuring the city. Do any features of this miniature connect it to Christian Spain? Illustrating a book by hand was an immense labor. Why did medieval monks and nuns go to all this trouble?

Monastic Clamors, Curses, and Excommunications

Monastic culture relied on prayer and God's help to protect its people and posses-sions in an increasingly violent world. The spiritual weapons at the church's disposal consisted mainly of words, in the form of ritual cursing and excommunication of enemies. These short excerpts illustrate a clamor, a collective plea to God for help against troubles and enemies, a curse on enemies, an excommunication, and an-other curse.

From *Benedictine Maledictions: Liturgical Cursing in Romanesque France,* by Lester Little (Ithaca, N.Y.: Cornell University Press, 1993), pp. 25, 36, 41, 43.

A Clamor from Chartres, about 1020

*   *   *

In the spirit of humility and with contrite soul we come before your sacred altar and your most holy body and blood, Lord Jesus, redeemer of the world, and we acknowledge ourselves guilty against you on account of our sins, for which we are justly afflicted. To you, Lord Jesus, we come; to you, prostrate, we clamor, because iniquitous and proud men, emboldened by their own follow-ers, invade, plunder, and lay waste the lands of this your sanctuary and of other churches subject to it. They compel your poor ones who till these lands to live in pain and hunger and nakedness; they kill both by the sword and by torment. And our belongings as well, by which we are supposed to live and which blessed souls bequeathed to this place for their own salvation, they seize and vio-lently take away from us. This your church, Lord, which in ancient times you founded and raised up in honor of the blessed and glorious ever-virgin Mary, sits in sadness. There is no one who can console it or liberate it except you, our God. So rise up, Lord Jesus, in support of us. Comfort us and help us. Attack those who are attacking us, and break the pride of those who afflict your place and us. You know, Lord, who they are and what their names are; their bodies and their hearts have been known to you alone from before they

were born. Wherefore, Lord, judge them as you know how in your strength. Make them aware, to the extent that it pleases you, of their misdeeds, and free us by your mercy. Do not despise us, Lord, who call out to you in affliction, but because of the glory of your name and the mercy with which you founded this place and dedicated it in honor of your mother, visit us in peace and bring us out of our present distress.

*   *   *

A Curse from Reims, about 900

In the name of the Lord and by the power of the Holy Spirit and the authority divinely granted bishops by blessed Peter, prince of the apostles, we separate them from the bosom of holy mother church and we condemn them with an anathema of perpetual malediction, that they might not have help from any man or contact with any Christian. May they be cursed in town and cursed in the fields. May their barns be cursed and may their bones be cursed. May the fruit of their loins be cursed as well as the fruit of their lands, their herds of cattle and their flocks of sheep. May they be cursed going in and coming out. May they be cursed at home and may they be fugitives outside their homes. May they drain out through their bowels, like the faithless and unhappy Arius. May there come upon them all those maledictions by which the Lord through Moses threatened transgressors of the divine law.

*   *   *

A Curse by Pope Benedict VIII in 1014

May they be cursed in the four corners of the earth. May they be cursed in the East, disinherited in the West, interdicted in the North, and excommunicated in the South. May they be cursed in the day and excommunicated at night. May they be cursed at home and excommunicated while away, cursed in standing and excommunicated in sitting, cursed in eating, drinking and sleeping, excommunicated in waking, cursed when they work and excommunicated when they rest. May they be cursed in the spring and excommunicated in the summer, cursed in the autumn and excommunicated in the winter.

*   *   *

An Excommunication from Compiègne

By the authority of the Father and of the Son and of the Holy Spirit and of the Blessed Mary ever virgin and of the blessed apostles Peter and Paul and of the holy martyrs Cornelius and Cyprianus, we excommunicate them from the company of all Christians, and we bar them from the thresholds of the holy church of God so that they undergo eternal punishments with Dathan and Abiron and with those who said to the Lord God: "Stay away from us, we do not wish to know of your ways." And so may their lights be extinguished forever and ever unless they come forward and make amends.

*   *   *

REVIEW QUESTIONS

1. What type of justice is at work here?
2. What is the church trying to accomplish through these rituals?
3. How might the targets have responded?

"The Wanderer": Anglo-Saxon Poetry

"The Wanderer," known from a copy made about 975, is an example of an Anglo-Saxon elegiac lament, a poem in which a warrior must search for a new lord to follow. Like the great epic Beowulf, *this poem illustrates some of the spirit of Germanic culture with a thin or nonexistent veneer of Christianity.*

"The Wanderer" translated by E. Talbot Donaldson (New York: Norton, 1993).

He who is alone often lives to find favor, mildness of the Lord, even though he has long had to stir with his arms the frost-cold sea, troubled in heart over the water-way had to tread the tracks of exile. Fully-fixed is his fate."

So spoke the earth-walker, remembering hardships, fierce war-slaughters—the fall of dear kinsmen.

"Often before the day dawned I have had to speak of my cares, alone: there is now none among the living to whom I dare clearly express the thought of my heart. I know indeed that it is a fine custom for a man to lock tight his heart's coffer, keep closed the hoard-case of his mind, whatever his thoughts may be. Words of a weary heart may not withstand fate, nor those of an angry spirit bring help. Therefore men eager for fame shut sorrowful thought up fast in their breast's coffer.

"Thus I, wretched with care, removed from my homeland, far from dear kinsmen, have had to fasten with fetters the thoughts of my heart—ever since the time, many years ago, that I covered my gold-friend in the darkness of the earth; and from there I crossed the woven waves, winter-sad, downcast for want of a hall, sought a giver of treasure—a place, far or near, where I might find one in a mead-hall who should know of my people, or would comfort me friendless, receive me with gladness. He who has experienced it knows how cruel a companion sorrow is to the man who has no beloved protectors. Exile's path awaits him, not twisted gold—frozen thoughts in his heart-case, no joy of earth. He recalls the hall-warriors and the taking of treasure, how in youth his gold-friend made him accustomed to feasting. All delight has gone.

"He who has had long to forgo the counsel of a beloved lord knows indeed how, when sorrow and sleep together bind the poor dweller-alone, it will seem to him in his mind that he is embracing and kissing his liege lord and laying his hands and his head on his knee, as it some times was in the old days when he took part in the gift-giving.

Then he wakens again, the man with no lord, sees the yellow waves before him, the sea-birds bathe, spread their feathers, frost and snow fall, mingled with hail.

"Then the wounds are deeper in his heart, sore for want of his dear one. His sorrow renews as the memory of his kinsmen moves through his mind: he greets them with glad words, eagerly looks at them, a company of warriors. Again they fade, moving off over the water; the spirit of these fleeting ones brings to him no familiar voices. Care renews in him who must again and again send his weary heart out over the woven waves.

"Therefore I cannot think why the thoughts of my heart should not grow dark when I consider all the life of men through this world—with what terrible swiftness they forgo the hall-floor, bold young retainers. So this middle-earth each day fails and falls. No man may indeed become wise before he has had his share of winters in this world's kingdom. The wise man must be patient, must never be too hot-hearted, nor too hasty of speech, nor too fearful, nor too glad, nor too greedy for wealth, nor ever too eager to boast before he has thought clearly. A man must wait, when he speaks in boast, until he knows clearly, sure-minded, where the thoughts of his heart may turn.

"The wise warrior must consider how ghostly it will be when all the wealth of this world stands waste, just as now here and there through this middle-earth wind-blown walls stand covered with frost-fall, storm-beaten dwellings. Wine-halls totter, the lord lies bereft of joy, all the company has fallen, bold men beside the wall. War took away some, bore them forth on their way; a bird carried one away over the deep sea; a wolf shared one with Death; another a man sad of face hid in an earth-pit.

"So the Maker of mankind laid waste this dwelling-place until the old works of giants stood idle, devoid of the noise of the stronghold's keepers. Therefore the man wise in his heart considers carefully this wallplace and this dark life, remembers the multitude of deadly combats long ago, and speaks these words: 'Where has the horse gone? Where the young warrior? Where is the giver of treasure? What has become of the feasting seats? Where are the joys of the hall? Alas, the bright cup! Alas, the mailed warrior! Alas, the prince's glory! How that time has gone, vanished beneath night's cover, just as if it never had been! The wall, wondrous high, decorated with snake-likenesses, stands now over traces of the beloved company. The ash-spears' might has borne the earls away—weapons greedy for slaughter, Fate the mighty; and storms beat on the stone walls, snow, the herald of winter, falling thick binds the earth when darkness comes and the night-shadow falls, sends harsh hailstones from the north in hatred of men. All earth's kingdom is wretched, the world beneath the skies is changed by the work of the fates. Here wealth is fleeting, here friend is fleeting,

here man is fleeting, here woman is fleeting—all this earthly habitation shall be emptied.' "

So spoke the man wise in heart, sat apart at the council. He is good who keeps his word; a man must never utter too quickly his breast's passion, unless he knows first how to achieve remedy, as a leader with his courage. It will be well with him who seeks favor, comfort from the Father in heaven, where for us all stability resides.

REVIEW QUESTIONS

1. What are the values of this warrior society?
2. What are the qualities of a good follower?
3. If the dominant tone is pessimistic, then what human or supernatural powers can counteract the gloomy side of life?

FROM *Egil's Saga:* Viking Literature

Egil's Saga is one of the best examples of Viking literature. This tale is about Egil Skallagrimson and his life in Norway and Iceland in the ninth and tenth centuries. The great Icelandic historian Snorri Sturluson (1179–1241) is the probable composer of the saga. Egil's life, however, contains many realistic adventures that illustrate Scandinavian life before 1000 C.E. The first excerpt concerns Egil's friend Einar, and the second describes Egil's old age and death. Both episodes take place in Iceland.

From *The Sagas of Icelanders,* by Paul Kellogg and Jane Smiley, translated by Bernard Scudder (New York: Viking Penguin, 2000), pp. 165–67, 180–84.

*   *   *

81

There was a man named Einar, the son of Helgi Ottarsson and the great-grandson of Bjorn the Easterner who settled in Breidafjord. Einar was the brother of Osvif the Wise. Even at an early age, Einar was large and strong and a man of great

accomplishments. He began composing poetry when he was young and was fond of learning.

One summer at the Althing, Einar went to Egil Skallagrimsson's booth and they began talking. The conversation soon turned to poetry and they both took great delight in the discussion.

After that, Einar made a habit of talking to Egil and a great friendship developed between them. Einar had just come back from a voyage abroad.

on the king's guard.

> *king's guard*: his back? a bed? his chest?
> My legs are two
> frigid widows,
> those women
> need some flame.

This was at the start of Earl Hakon the Powerful's reign. Egil Skallagrimsson was in his eighties then and still active apart from his blindness.

In the summer, when everyone was preparing to ride to the Thing, Egil asked Grim to ride there with him. Grim was reluctant.

When Grim spoke to Thordis, he told her what Egil had asked of him.

"I want you to find out what lies behind this request of his," he said.

Thordis went to see her kinsman Egil, who by that time had no greater pleasure in life than talking to her.

When she saw him she asked, "Is it true that you want to ride to the Thing, kinsman? I'd like you to tell me what you're planning."

"I will tell you what I've been thinking," he said. "I want to go to the Thing with the two chests full of English silver that King Athelstan gave to me. I'm going to have the chests carried to the Law Rock when the crowd there is at its biggest. Then I'll toss the silver at them and I'll be very much surprised if they all share it out fairly amongst themselves. I expect there'll be plenty of pushing and shoving. It might even end with the whole Thing breaking out in a brawl."

Thordis said, "That sounds like a brilliant plan. It will live for as long as people live in Iceland."

Then Thordis went to talk to Grim and tell him about Egil's plan.

"He must never be allowed to get away with such a mad scheme," said Grim.

When Egil brought up the subject of riding to the Thing with Grim he would have none of it, so Egil stayed at home while the Thing was held. He was displeased and wore a rather grumpy look.

The cattle at Mosfell were kept in a shieling, and Thordis stayed there while the Thing took place.

One evening when everyone was going to bed at Mosfell, Egil called in two of Grim's slaves.

He told them to fetch him a horse, "because I want to go to bathe in the pool."

When he was ready he went out, taking his chests of silver with him. He mounted the horse, crossed the hayfields to the slope that begins there and disappeared.

In the morning, when all the people got up, they saw Egil wandering around on the hill east of the farm, leading a horse behind him. They went over to him and brought him home.

But neither the slaves nor the chests of treasure ever returned, and there are many theories about where Egil hid his treasure. East of the farm is a gully leading down from the mountain. It has been noticed that English coins have been found in the gully when the river recedes after floods caused by sudden thaws. Some people believe Egil must have hidden his treasure there. Then there are large and exceptionally deep marshes below the hayfields at Mosfell, and it is claimed that Egil threw his treasure into them. On the south side of the rivers are hot springs with big pits nearby, where some people believe Egil must have hidden his treasure, because a will-o'-the-wisp is often seen there. Egil himself said he had killed Grim's slaves and hidden his treasure somewhere, but he never told a single person where it was.

In the autumn Egil caught the illness that eventually led to his death. When he died, Grim had his body dressed in fine clothes and taken over to Tjaldanes, where a mound was made that Egil was buried in, along with his weapons and clothes.

89

Grim from Mosfell was baptized when Christianity was made the law in Iceland and he had a church built at Mosfell. It is said that Thordis had Egil's bones moved to the church. This is supported by the fact that when a cemetery was dug, after the church that Grim had had built at Hrisbru was taken down and set up at Mosfell, human bones were found under the site of the altar. They were much larger than normal human bones, and on the basis of old accounts people are certain they must have belonged to Egil.

Skafti Thorarinsson the Priest, a wise man, was there at the time. He picked up Egil's skull and put it on the wall of the churchyard. The skull was astonishingly large and even more incredible for its weight. It was all ridged on the outside, like a scallop shell. Curious to test its thickness, Skafti took a fair-sized hand-axe in one hand and struck the skull with it as hard as he could, to try to break it. A white mark was left where he struck the skull, but it neither dented nor cracked. This goes to prove that such a skull would not have been easy for weak men to damage when it was covered with hair and skin. Egil's bones were buried by the edge of the churchyard at Mosfell.

90

Thorstein, Egil's son, was baptized when Christianity came to Iceland and he had a church built at Borg. He was a devout and orderly man. He grew to an old age, died of illness and was buried at Borg in the church he had had built there.

A great family is descended from Thorstein which includes many prominent men and poets. Thorstein's descendants belong to the Myrar clan, as do all other descendants of Skallagrim. For a long time it was a family trait to be strong and warlike, and some members were men of great wisdom. It was a family of contrasts. Some of the best-looking people ever known in Iceland belonged to it, such as Thorstein Egilsson, his nephew Kjartan Olafsson, Hall Gudmundarson and Thorstein's daughter Helga the Fair, whose love Gunnlaug Serpent-tongue and Hrafn the Poet contested. But most members of the Myrar clan were exceptionally ugly.

Of Thorstein's sons, Thorgeir was the strongest but Skuli was the greatest. He lived at Borg after his father's day and spent a long time on Viking raids. He was at the stem of Earl Eirik's ship Iron-prow in the battle where King Olaf Tryggvason was killed. Skuli fought seven battles on his Viking raids and was considered to be outstandingly resolute and brave. He went to Iceland afterwards and farmed at Borg, where he lived until his old age, and many people are descended from him. And here this saga ends.

REVIEW QUESTIONS

1. What are the roles of poetry and poets in Icelandic society?
2. What attitudes toward wealth and gifts emerge from this saga?
3. These excerpts reveal a society in transition from traditional Norse religious beliefs to Christianity. What does the saga show about these two systems of belief?

9 ∽ THE EXPANSION OF EUROPE: ECONOMY, SOCIETY, AND POLITICS IN THE HIGH MIDDLE AGES, 1000–1300

The centuries of the High Middle Ages witnessed tremendous economic growth, which began in agriculture, the basis of the medieval economy. All societies in Europe, North Africa, and the Middle East remained overwhelmingly rural and depended on villages of peasants to produce the food and supplies needed to sustain urban life and to pay the taxes for the emerging national governments. Better technology for vital tools like plows and harnesses, accurate record keeping and attention to land, and perhaps benign weather, all contributed to the improved yields in crops and flocks. Great landowners, especially the bishops and monasteries, kept records of their manors, the great estates where peasants lived and worked. Manors did not exist everywhere and were not uniform across Europe, but they were a widespread feature of rural life. Rulers and landowners needed to mix coercion and incentives to keep their serfs, peasants tied to the land, in the countryside and to recruit farmers for the new lands being reclaimed from the forests, swamps, and even the sea. The feudal warrior class and the church depended on the peasantry for subsistence and in return were supposed to protect peasants in this world and the next and to keep the peace necessary for growth.

About the year 1000, Christian Europe had only a few small cities, while the Muslim world contained many large ones in Spain, Sicily, and elsewhere. Most European cities rapidly increased in population in the following centuries, a growth that depended on adequate food supplies, either produced locally or acquired through trade. People living in towns also needed certain rights and liberties to transact business, and urban people wanted secure land ownership; personal liberty, including freedom of travel; and a sound coinage. Merchants did not want to resort to feuds and vendettas to settle their disputes. Kings and lords were prepared to grant some liberties to towns in exchange for money. Urban wealth largely resulted from trade and a modest level of artisan manufactures, especially cloth. The most lucrative trade with the Muslim world required reliable contracts in order to encourage merchants to invest or risk their lives in overseas trade. These contracts rested on a legal framework partly inherited from the Romans but also invented in the new trading centers. As certain families amassed fortunes in trade and the rest benefited from a general increase in prosperity, the use of written documents in business and family life became more common throughout urban society. Literacy, once mainly useful to the church, became a valuable money-making skill and produced jobs for copyists and notaries who provided the written word to a basically illiterate society still dependant on memory. An ability to manipulate numbers was also valuable in a world where rationality about words or sums was remaking the older, simpler society of those who prayed, fought, and farmed.

Monarchs ruled over states that contained proud and quarrelsome nobles tied to kings by reciprocal feudal links of vassalage, urban people engaged in a variety of businesses and crafts, and the great majority of the population which remained as peasants working the land. States became more bureaucratic and had laws, taxes, and courts, all of which required written records. The personality and energy of individual rulers, however, were still important, as the career of the saintly Louis IX of France illustrates. A bad or simply weak ruler, like John of England, had to yield rights to other centers of power—a process described in the Magna Carta. Fighting wars and dispensing justice remained the main tasks of medieval government, and good outcomes in them the best measures of its success. Whether a free city or an emerging kingdom, a government was above all expected to defend its existence. Good tax records and laws were the best means to accomplish this goal. Better-organized states and the reformed church had the authority to define more closely all liberties and duties, and this was not usually good news for women or for religious or ethnic minorities. The origins of persecution and subjugation rested in the better records and bureaucracies produced by the improving economy.

The Statutes of Lorris

The statutes of Lorris, from the twelfth century, show the kings of France as great landowners and feudal lords providing incentives for peasants to remain on the land and not run away to other lords or the cities. Peasants tied to the land, true serfs, did not have all the rights enjoyed by the free farmers of Lorris. Establishing direct relations with peasants was an unusual step for a monarch, but the policy succeeded in providing incentives for the peasants to work hard on their own lands. In the *long run it was in the crown's interest to have taxpayers rather than serfs, but not all lords perceived this advantage.*

From *Medieval Culture and Society,* by David Herlihy (New York: HarperCollins, 1968), pp. 178–84.

* * *

1. We concede that whoever owns a house in the parish of Lorris shall pay for his house and for each arpent of land, if he should hold it in the same parish, six pennies of quitrent only. And if he should acquire property by clearing wastelands he shall hold it for the same quitrent as his house.

2. No man of the parish of Lorris shall pay either a tariff or other tax upon his food. Nor shall he pay any tax for measuring the grain which he obtains from his own labor or that of his animals. Nor shall he pay any tax on the wine which he obtains from his own vineyards.

3. No man need go on an expedition on foot or by horse unless he can return if he wishes the same day.

4. No man shall pay tolls as far as Etamps nor as far as Orléans, nor as far as Milly, which is in the Gâtinais.

5. Whoever has his farm in the parish of Lorris, shall lose none of it by fines, unless he has been fined for offense against us or any of our new settlers.

6. No one going to or coming from the fairs or the market of Lorris shall be arrested or disturbed, unless he committed an offense on that same day. No one, on the day of the market or fair of Lorris, shall confiscate a bond put up as security, unless the pledge was made for such a day.

7. Fines of sixty solidi shall be reduced to five solidi, those of five solidi to twelve pennies, and the fee of the prévôt to four pennies.

8. No man need leave Lorris in order to plead in the court of the king.

9. No one, neither we ourselves nor any one else, shall demand of the men of Lorris a taille or requisition or aid.

10. No one shall sell wine at Lorris with a proclamation, except the king, who may sell his own wine in his cellar with such a proclamation.

11. We shall have at Lorris credit in food for our own need and that of the queen for fifteen full days. And if anyone have a pledge belonging to the lord king, he shall not keep it more than eight days, unless by our will.

* * *

15. No man of Lorris should labor for us except once a year, to bring our wine to Orléans. Nor are others to do this, but only those who have horses and wagons and have been summoned. They shall not receive lodging from us. The villeins shall bring wood for our kitchen.

16. No one of them should be kept in prison if he is able to furnish bail.

17. If any of them wish to sell their belongings, he may sell them, and with the payments from the sales, may freely and quietly leave the village, if he wishes to leave, unless he has committed a crime in the village.

18. Whoever lives in the parish of Lorris one year and a day with no demand having been made for him, if he was not denied the right by us or by our prévôt, from that time he shall remain free and undisturbed.

* * *

20. And when the men of Lorris shall go to Orléans with their goods to be sold, they should pay for their wagon only one coin when they leave the city, that is, when they shall go not for reason of the fair. And when for reason of the fair they go in March, in leaving Orléans they should pay four pennies for their wagon, and in entering the city two pennies.

21. In weddings at Lorris, neither the herald nor the watchman shall receive a payment.

22. No peasant of the parish of Lorris who cultivates the land with a plow shall give more than one mina of rye to the sergeants of Lorris at harvest.

23. And if any knight or sergeant shall find horses or other animals of the men of Lorris in our forests, he should bring them only to the prévôt of Lorris.

If any animal of the parish of Lorris, fleeing from bulls or incited by flies, should enter our forest or grove, he whose animal it is shall pay nothing to the prévôts, if he is able to swear that the animal entered against the will of the guard. And if it entered with the knowledge of the guard, he shall give twelve pennies for this. And if there were several animals, he should pay so much for each.

24. At the furnaces of Lorris there shall be no tax for porters.

25. There shall be no tax for the guard at Lorris.

26. If anyone from Lorris brings salt or wine to Orléans, he shall give one penny for his wagon only.

27. No man of Lorris shall make payment to the prévôt of Etamps, nor to the prévôt of Pithiviers, nor in all the Gâtinais.

28. No one of them shall pay a toll at Ferrières, nor Château-Landon, nor Piuseaux nor Nibelle.

29. The men of Lorris may take dead wood outside the forest for their own use.

30. Whoever in the market of Lorris should buy or sell anything and in forgetfulness retain the toll, let him pay it after eight days, without any prosecution, if he can swear that he did not knowingly retain it.

*   *   *

32. And if any man of Lorris should be accused of anything, and it cannot be proved by a witness, he shall purge himself by his own oath against the affirmation of the accuser.

33. No one of the same parish from what he may sell or buy over the week, and from what he may buy on Wednesdays in the market for his own use, shall pay a tax.

34. These customs have been conceded to the men of Lorris, and they are the same as those granted to the men who live at Courtpalais, at Chanteloup and in the bailiwick of Harpard.

35. Finally we ordain that every time the prévôt is changed in the village, he shall swear to observe faithfully these customs, and the new sergeants shall do the same every time they are installed.

*   *   *

REVIEW QUESTIONS

1. In the statutes of Lorris, what rights does it appear were most important to the peasants?
2. How did rural people use money and its equivalents?
3. What rights did the kings retain?

The Charter of Liberties for St. Omer

William of Normandy, count of Flanders, issued this famous charter of liberties to the citizens of St. Omer in 1127. Such charters were the foundations of urban free-dom, and they reveal what city people needed to conduct their businesses. William also benefited from this arrangement, and the charter embodies the results of some hard bargaining between the merchants and their lord.

From *Medieval Culture and Society,* by David Herlihy (New York: HarperCollins, 1968), pp. 178–84.

I, William, by the grace of God, Count of the Flemings, not wishing to reject the petition of the citizens of St. Omer—especially as they have willingly received my petition about the con-sulate of Flanders, and because they have always been more honest and faithful than other Flem-ings to me—grant them the laws and customs written below in perpetuity, and command that these laws remain inviolate.

1. First, that to every man I will show peace, and I will maintain and defend them as my own men without deceit. And I concede that their aldermen can make right judgment concerning all men, in-cluding myself. I grant liberty to those aldermen such as the most favored aldermen of my lands enjoy.

2. If any citizen of St. Omer lend money to any-one, and the borrower freely acknowledges this in the presence of lawful men who hold inheri-tances in the city, if the debt is unpaid on the agreed date, he or his goods may be detained until all is paid. If he is unwilling to pay, or denies the agreement, he shall be detained until he pays the debt, if he is convicted on the testimony of two aldermen or two sworn men.

3. If anyone is accused under the law of the Church, he need not leave St. Omer to do justice elsewhere, but may do what is right in the city, in the presence of the bishop or his archdeacon or his priest, and by the judgment of the clerics and aldermen. He need answer to no one, except for these three reasons: that is, desecration of a church or temple, an injury of a cleric, or rape and vio-lation of a woman. If a complaint is lodged against him for other reasons, the case should be heard in the presence of the judges and my prévôt. Thus it was decreed in the presence of Count K. Charles and Bishop John.

4. I concede to them the liberty which they en-joyed at the time of my ancestors, that is, that they never must leave their territory on campaign, sav-ing only if a hostile army invade Flanders. Then they must defend me and my land.

5. All those who have their guild and belong to it and reside within the circle of the city, I free from all tolls at the port of Dixmude and Grave-lines; and throughout all the land of Flanders I free them of the tax called *sewerp.* I grant them the toll which the men of Arras pay at Bapaume.

6. If any of them go into the land of the emperor for trading, he shall not be required by any of my men to pay the tax known as *hansa.*

7. If it should happen that at any time I should acquire land outside of Flanders, or if a treaty of peace should be made between me and my uncle Henry, king of England, I shall free them of all tolls in the land acquired or in the entire realm of the English, or I shall make them free of all cus-toms by the terms of such a treaty.

8. In every market of Flanders, if anyone raises a complaint against them, they shall undergo the judgment of the aldermen concerning every com-plaint without a duel. They shall henceforth be free from the duel.

9. All who live within the walls of St. Omer, or who shall live there in the future, I make free from the *cavagium,* that is, from the head tax, and from payments to the court officials.

10. Their money which after the death of Count K. was taken from them, and which because of the fidelity which they hold towards me is still not given them, I shall repay within the year, or I shall have justice done for them according to the judgment of the aldermen.

11. Moreover, they have asked the king of France and Ralph of Péronne that wherever they go in their lands they should be free from all toll, transit duties and passage; this I too wish to grant them.

12. I command that their commune remain undisturbed, just as they created it by oath. I shall let it be dissolved by no one. I concede to them all right and right justice, as it is best available in my land, that is, in Flanders. I wish them to be free henceforth of all customary taxes, as the best and freer townsmen of Flanders. I shall ask of them no scot, no taille, and make no request for their money.

13. I give my mint at St. Omer, from which I have had 30 pounds per year, and whatever I ought to have from it, for the repayment of their losses and the sustenance of their guild. These townsmen should keep the money for all my life stable and good, so that their city may be improved.

14. The guards who every night in the year protect the castle of St. Omer, and who, besides their salary and support as was established in olden times in oats and cheese and in goatskins, are accustomed to demand unjustly and violently one loaf and one or two pennies from each house in the city, at the feasts of St. Omer and St. Bertin and at Christmas, should dare no longer to take anything besides their salary and support.

15. Whoever comes to Nieuport from any place should have permission to come to St. Omer with his goods in whatever ship he pleases.

16. If I make peace with Stephan count of Boulogne, I shall in that peace make them free from toll and *sewerp* at Wissant and in all his lands.

17. I grant for their use the pasture adjacent to the city of St. Omer in the forest which is called Lo and in the marshes and meadows, moors and uncultivated lands, except in the land of the lepers, as it was at the time of Count Robert the Bearded.

18. I make free from all tolls the houses which are under the supervision of the advocate of the abbey of St. Bertin, namely those which are inhabited. Each one shall give 12 pennies at the feast of St. Michael, 12 pennies as bread tax, and 12 pennies as beer tax. Deserted houses shall pay nothing.

19. If any stranger should attack any citizen of St. Omer and bring injury or insult upon him or violently rob him of his property, and with this injury should escape his hands, and is afterwards summoned by the castellan or by his wife or by his steward, if he disdains to come to make satisfaction within three days or should neglect to do so, the commune shall together take the injury of their brother upon themselves. In taking vengeance, if a home should be destroyed or burned, or if anyone should be injured or killed, he who accomplished the vengeance should not incur any danger of person or property nor should he know or fear my displeasure concerning this. If however, whoever made the injury should soon be taken, he shall be judged according to the laws and customs of the city and shall be punished according to the degree of the crime, that is, he shall render an eye for eyes, a tooth for a tooth, and a head for a head.

20. Concerning the death of Eustache of Steenvoorde, whoever may disturb and molest any citizen of St. Omer should be held guilty of the betrayal and death of Count K., since whatever was done was done out of fidelity to me. And as I swore and gave faith, thus I wish them to be reconciled and hold peace towards his relatives.

The following persons under oath promised to uphold this commune and to observe the abovementioned customs and agreements: Louis, the king of the French; William, the count of Flanders; Ralph of Péronne; Hugh Oatfield; Osto the castellan and William his brother; Robert of Béthune and William his son; Anselm of Hesdin; Stephan, the count of Boulogne; Masasses, the count of Guines; Walter of Lillers; Balduin of Ghent; Ywain his brother; Roger the castellan of Lille, and Robert his son; Rasse of Gavere; Daniel of Termonde;

Helias of Saint-Saens; Henry of Bourbourg; Eustache the advocate and Arnulf his son; the castellan of Ghent, Gervais; Peter the steward; Stephan of Steninghem.

This privilege was confirmed by Count William and the abovementioned barons, by faith and oath approved and accepted. In the year of the Lord's Incarnation 1127, 18 kalends of May, the fifth day of the week, the feast of the saints Tiburtius and Valerian.

REVIEW QUESTIONS

1. From this charter, what liberties appear to be the crucial ones to urban people?
2. What did William get from this charter?
3. How did St. Omer govern itself?

The Last Will and Testament of Oberto Lomellino

Oberto Lomellino was a wealthy merchant and warrior, not an unusual combination for an Italian noble in this period, in the port city of Genoa. The last will and testament, dictated to a notary and recorded in Latin in the year 1252, was the legal way to ensure that one's last wishes were recorded and carried out. The procedures for drawing up wills and enforcing their provisions were another means by which literacy benefited society. The will is a form of contract with one's family, as well as an important means for a person to benefit his or her soul through charitable acts.

From *Will and Wealth in Medieval Genoa*, by Steven Epstein (Cambridge, Mass.: Harvard University Press, 1984), pp. 1150–250.

I, Oberto Lomellino, of good and sound mind, fearing the judgment of God, with contemplation of my last will thus make disposition of my goods. I order my body to be buried at the Church of San Teodoro. For my soul I leave L.25 gen., of which I leave one-tenth to the works of San Lorenzo. Of the rest I leave to the said church L.10 for annual and monthly masses for my soul. The rest should be distributed by my in-law Ugone Grillo, my in-law Simone Spinola, and my wife, Simona. Item: I wish and order that my wife Simona should and ought to have from my goods L.500 gen. of her dowry and the L.100 gen. of her marriage gift in cash. Item: I leave the said Simona, my wife, beyond her said rights of dowry and *antefactum*, my land with a house that I have in Castelleto, and the instruments and everything on it, and all her garments and jewelry and clothes that she uses or has used, with all the furnishings and with all the accessories of her suite and also of the house, and with all the possessions, utensils, and all the rest of the things which may be in my house that I have, except my arms and pieces of armor made of iron. Of these I leave to Miroaldo de Turca a hauberk with a pair of metal greaves and a mail doublet with sleeves, which he himself shall choose from those I have. Item: I leave to Gavino and Petrino, sons of my wife, Simona, whom she had with her late husband, Daniele Doria, L.50 gen. to each of them from my goods, to be invested in Sardinia in livestock for their benefit, with the counsel and by the wish of my in-laws Pietro Grillo and Ingone Grillo, according to how it seems best to them. Item: I leave to the said Gavino and Petrino for my soul whatever is owed to me and whatever I should receive from them for their support, if I should die of this illness, and I want the decrees which I have against them for their support to be returned to them after my death. Item: I leave to each of them a mail doublet which they shall choose from those I have, minus the hauberk and mail doublet that I left the said Miroaldo. Item: I leave to my sister Adalasia, wife of my in-law Simone Spinola, my house in which the said Adalasia, my sister, lives with the said Simone Spinola, my in-law. Item: I leave to Amico Lomellino, my blood relative, my house which I have in the Furrier district, and land which I have in Pegli, in such a way, namely, that the said Amico cannot sell nor alienate nor obligate to any end, for himself or for others, the said house and land, and if the said Amico shall die without a legitimate male heir born in wedlock, I wish and order that Simone Lomellino, Tommaso Lomellino, Giovanni Lomellino, and Ansaldo Lomellino, or their heirs, each succeed Amico for one-fourth of the said house and land in Pegli, and I order that I substitute them for the said heir in the above. Item: I leave the said Amico all my armor of iron and my arms, saving what I left above to the said Miroaldo, Gavino, and Petrino. Item: I leave to Andriola, sister of the said Amico, for my soul in clothes L.5. Item: to Simona, sister of the said Amico, I leave for my soul in clothes L.5. Item: to Montanaria, sister of the said Amico and wife of Enrico de Nigrone, I leave for my soul L.5, and I remit to Montanaria for my soul twenty solidi which she owes me, beyond the L.5 I left her above. Item: I acknowledge that I ought to give Enrico Florentino de Castello L.9 gen. which remain to be paid for the dowry of his wife, my niece Simona. Item: I acknowledge that Brother Marino, preceptor of San Giovanni, owes the said Enrico Florentino L.3 gen. which he promised to give the said Simona, his wife, for her dowry, which I want to be paid from my goods if the said Brother Marino will not pay. Item: I decide and order that my father-in-law, Federigo Grillo, have

and ought to have after my death the house I live in for a price and under the estimate of the price of L.300 gen., saving all, that my wife have an apartment in that house for her lifetime while she will stay and does stay in the house without a husband. If, however, she marries, the said Federigo, my father-in-law, should have the house for the said L.300 as is said above. Item: I remit to Enriceto Spinola, son of Simone Spinola, after my death whatever I have against him concerning a *commenda* which I made with him, and let there be a satisfactory end to this. Item: I leave to Rosso de Turca and his son Miroaldo L.37 s.14 which they owe me, and also, concerning the question and controversy that I have with the said Rosso, let there be a finish and an end and nothing further, and my heirs should not bother him on account of this dispute. Item: I acknowledge that I owe my servant Raimundeta for her pay thirty-six solidi, which I want her to have from my goods, and I leave her for my soul L.3 from my goods. Item: I leave the Church of Santa Maria delle Vigne for masses for my soul forty solidi. I acknowledge that I owe Lord Rosso, prior of the Monastery of Santa Maria delle Vigne, L.150 gen. for a loan, as contained and written in my cartulary, and this sum belongs to Gerardo and Jacobino, sons of the late Fulcone Muasgerio, and I want them to have this amount from my goods. Item: I leave Altilia and Barbarina, daughters of the late Guglielmo Lomellino, in clothes L.5 each. Item: to the works of the harbor mole forty solidi. Item: to Jacoba, wife of Guglielmo de Baiamonte, L.5. Item: I leave to my sister Adalasia, wife of Simone Spinola, whatever right I have or can be sought for me against anyone or whatever persons concerning cases or sentences that I have pursued, and whatever right I have against all persons, except for the above-mentioned land. Item: I acknowledge that I owe Simone Spinola, my in-law, L.10 gen. which he loaned me. I make as my heir the said Amico Lomellino for the rest of all my goods, minus my said debts and legacies. I name Simone Spinola and my wife, Simona, as distributors and payers of my legacies and my debts from my goods, saving always the loans, obligations, and assessments of the commune of Genoa, and the rest of the loans from them. I order and decide that those to whom some movable property has been left ought to record the movables in writing in a cartulary of the commune of Genoa before they take possession of them, in order to make expenditures from them in the commune of Genoa. This is my last will, which if it does not hold by the law of the testament, at least I wish it by the law of codicils of another last will to hold and have force. Done in Genoa in the chambers of the said Lord Oberto, 8 June 1252, after nones. Witnesses: Pietro Grillo, Simone Lomellino, Tom-maso Lomellino, Marino Usodimare, Jacopo de Vivaldo, Nicola *baracerius*, Jacopo Grillo, and Andriolo de Turca.

REVIEW QUESTIONS

1. What does this will reveal about Oberto's family and the ways he treats women and men?
2. What was on Oberto's mind as he faced death?
3. What are the strengths and weaknesses of wills as historical sources?
4. Why is the will dated to the hour it was made?

Medieval Commercial Contracts and Reports

Urban society and trade required reliable contracts. These documents, mostly from Genoa, illustrate five basic types of contract. The exchange contract allowed people to change currencies and be paid in different places. In a sea loan a merchant acquired capital for overseas commerce. A hybrid sea loan and exchange combined features of the first two contracts. The famous commenda and societas contracts were partnerships in which the parties contributed varying amounts of capital and labor to a joint enterprise and divided the profits accordingly. The letter from an Italian merchant in France to his colleagues back in Siena reveals the work and worries of a merchant.

From *Medieval Trade in the Mediterranean World,* by Robert S. Lopez and Irving W. Raymond (New York: Columbia University Press, 1955), pp. 165–66, 170–73, 179, 181, 190–93, 388–92.

*   *   *

A Standard Contract of Exchange

Genoa, September 12, 1191

Oberto Falzone acknowledges that he shall give to Ricerio Caviglia £50 Genoese by the next octave of Saint Andrew. And if he does not pay then, he promises to give Provisine currency at the rate of 12 deniers Provisine for every 15 deniers Genoese at the next fair of Lagny. And if the coins be deteriorated by alloy or by weight or be debased, he promises to give a mark of good silver for every 48 shillings up to the total of the entire debt. And he promises to accept the word of the creditor without oath in regard to expenses, losses, and capital of the loan, and he pledges his goods as security.

And Ottolino of San Martino and Rufino Belardengo constitute themselves as debtors and payers, and pledge, both liable for the whole amount, their goods as security, waiving exemptions under the legislation on joint liability and the legislation by which it is provided that the principal debtor be sued first.

Witnesses: Gandolfo of Acqui; Firmino, draper. Under the *volta* of the Fornari, on September 12.

"Dry Exchange" Contracts

Genoa, April 19, 1188

We, Girardo de Valle and Tommaso de Valle, acknowledge that we have received from you, Beltrame Bertaldo, banker, a number of deniers Genoese for which we promise to pay £4 Provisine to you or your accredited messenger at the next May fair of Provins. And if we do not do this, we promise to pay you on our next return from the same fair for every 12 deniers Provisine 16 deniers Genoese until you are fully paid. Otherwise we promise you, making the stipulation, the penalty of the double, and in addition we promise to restore to you the entire expense you may have incurred through it, trusting in regard to the debt your word without oath. And for this we pledge to you all our goods as security, waiving, etc. Witnesses: Thibaud Abortateur of Troyes; Bertramo, son of Arduino of Comazzo. In the new shop of the Malocelli, on April 19, between prime and terce.

*   *   *

Sea Loan

Marseilles, April 2, 1227

In the name of the Lord. In the year of the Incarnation of the Same 1227, fifteenth indiction, the fourth day before the Nones of April. Be it known to all that I, al-Hakim, Saracen of Alexandria, acknowledge and recognize that I have had and have received, by virtue of a purchase from you, Bernard Manduel, 2 quintals of Socotran aloes and 1 quintal 80 pounds of cassia bark, and 2 *centenaria* of coral, for all of which I owe you 135 bezants of good *miliarisia,* old and of correct

weight, waiving, with my full knowledge, the exception that the goods have not been delivered to me. And these 135 bezants of good *miliarisia,* old and of correct weight, net of duty and of all customs, I promise by stipulation to pay fully and to deliver peacefully to you, said Bernard, or to your accredited messenger, in Ceuta within a space of twenty days after the ship 'The Falcon' arrives there. And for these I pledge to you as security all the aforesaid goods which I bought from you, and these goods are to go and remain at your risk for the said value of 135 bezants and any surplus value to be at my risk. This is to be so done that if I do not pay you the said 135 bezants by the established time limit, you are then to be permitted on your own authority to sell all said security or to pledge it as security, and to do what you want with it, until you have been fully paid of the aforesaid 135 bezants of good *miliarisia,* old, just as has been stated above. And I also promise in good faith, under pledge of all my goods, to restore to you the whole of what may be lacking. And I waive in regard to all this the period of grace of twenty days and four months and any other delay and any legal rights. This was done in a certain house of the late Anselme, in which Januaire, notary, lives. Witnesses called and invited for this purpose were Guy of Aix, Peire de Cardeilhac, Guillem de Conchis, Hermengaud of Narbonne, Guirard Beguin; and I, Januaire, public notary of Marseilles, by commission of both parties, wrote this.

The Mating of the Sea Loan with Exchange

Ayas, February 27, 1274

In the name of the Lord, amen. I, Riccomanno, son of the late Camissario, Pisan, acknowledge to you, Bandenaco, son of the late Bandenaco of Casa Orlandi, Pisan, that I have had and have received from you a number of your new dirhams of Armenia, waiving the exception that the dirhams have not been had and received, the exception that there has been fraud in the act, and the claim [that may be made for] a thing given without any ground, and waiving every other legal right. Wherefore and for which I promise to give and to pay by reason of correct and true exchange, personally or through my messenger, to you or to your accredited messenger, 300 gold bezants, old of Cairo, good and lawful and of correct weight at the common weight of the country of Egypt, net and cleared of all duties and customs of sea and land, within twenty days after the arrival at Damietta of the ship which is named 'Saint Nicholas,' belonging to me and to my partner, without any change in the route. This, however, is to be done provided that the said ship arrives safely at the risk and fortune of God, the sea, and hostile people, and at the risk of the security written below. Otherwise the penalty of the double. . . .

And for this penalty and for the observing of this I pledge to you as security in particular 420 chests of iron, which weigh 38 *cantaria* according to the *cantarium* of Acre, loaded in the said ship belonging to me and to my partner. And I acknowledge that this security was bought with your own dirhams, which I have had and have received from you, as I have acknowledged above. And if perchance I do not pay the said 300 bezants to you or to your accredited messenger within the aforesaid time limit, I give and concede to you the power of selling and obligating the said security, so that you may obtain payment of the said bezants out of the same security and out of my goods if the security be insufficient, without objection by me nor by any magistrate in my behalf; and this under the said penalty and pledge of all my goods, existing and future.

Done in Ayas, under the portico of the house of the late Giovanni Clarea, in the year of the Nativity of the Lord, 1274, first indiction, February 27, between prime and terce. Witnesses: Guglielmo, son of Pietro; Pietro Riccio, Pisan, resident of Ayas; and Paolo Dedi, Pisan.

"Dry" Sea Exchange

Genoa, June 23, 1271

In the name of the Lord, amen. We—namely, I, Guglielmo Streiaporco, and I, Porchetto Streia-

porco, his emancipated son acting in the presence of my said father and by his order and will—both of us liable for the whole amount, acknowledge to you, Benedetto Zaccaria, that we have had and have received from you a number of Genoese deniers, waiving the exception that the Genoese deniers have not been received and every legal right and exception. Wherefore and for which we promise, both of us liable for the whole amount, to give and to pay to you or to your accredited messenger 53 gold hyperpers, good and of correct weight, in the Byzantine Empire *Romania* by the Kalends of September. If, however, we do not give you these hyperpers within the said time limit, we promise for each of the said hyperpers 11 shillings Genoese in Genoa whenever you wish. Otherwise we promise, both of us liable for the whole amount, to give you, making the stipulation, the penalty of the double of the said amount, the aforesaid conditions remaining as settled. And we pledge to you as security for the aforesaid promises all our goods, existing and future; and we promise the return of the expenses, waiving the legislation on joint liability, the Epistle of the divine Hadrian, and every legal right.

And the said Porchetto acknowledges that he is eighteen years old, and swears that he will undertake, fulfill, and observe everything as above. And the said Porchetto does all this in the presence and by order, will, and authorization of the said father, and by advice of Pietro Streiaporco and Vivaldo Bello, whom he chose and declared to be his relatives and advisors.

Done in Genoa, in the street of the Nepitella, in front of the house where Giovanni Guercio lives. Witnesses: the said Pietro Streiaporco and Vivaldo Bello and Federico, servant of the said Benedetto. In the year of the Nativity of the Lord 1271, thirteenth indiction, June 23, after vespers.

*   *   *

The Genoese Commenda and Societas

Genoa, September 29, 1163

Witnesses: Simone Bucuccio, Ogerio Peloso, Ribaldo di Sauro, and Genoardo Tasca. Stabile and Ansaldo Garraton have formed a *societas* in which, as they mutually declared, Stabile contributed £88 Genoese and Ansaldo £44. Ansaldo carries this *societas,* in order to put it to work, to Tunis or to wherever goes the ship in which he shall go—namely, [the ship] of Baldizzone Grasso and Girardo. On his return he will place the proceeds in the power of Stabile or of his messenger for [the purpose of] division. After deducting the capital, they shall divide the profits in half. Done in the chapter house, September 29, 1163, eleventh indiction.

In addition, Stabile gave his permission to send that money to Genoa by whatever ship seems most convenient to him to Ansaldo.

*   *   *

Genoa, October 7, 1163

Witnesses: Bernizone Serra, Raimondo, Crispino and Pietro Vinattiere. I, Ingo Bedello, declare publicly that I am carrying £41 s.6 Genoese of goods belonging to Guglielmotto Ciriolo invested in silk and paper to Tunis, and from there to Genoa where I shall place the proceeds in the power of Guglielmotto or of his messenger. And he is not under obligation to contribute toward expenses in regard to them except in furnishing the original money. Ingo on his return will place the proceeds in the power of Guglielmotto or of his messenger and, after deducting the capital, he is to have one fourth of the profit. And Guglielmotto himself reserved as his right that there will be no expense for him in it. Done in the chapter house, October 7, 1163, eleventh indiction.

*   *   *

Barcelona, August 9, 1252

Be it known to all that I, Arnau Fabriz, am carrying in *comanda* from you, Bernat Fuentes, though you are absent, and from your partners in this present voyage which I am making in the ship of Ferrer Descoll and partners to Overseas Territory or wherever the said ship shall make port in this present voyage for the purpose of commerce, £140 s.4 d.5 Barcelonese invested in five pieces of cloth of Saint-Quentin and in six Saracens. And I promise you to sell all of this well and faithfully there, and to invest in good faith the proceeds obtained from it in useful merchandise just as I see and understand best. And after this voyage is made I promise to return into your possession and into that of your partners said merchandise, that is, the capital and the profit, just as God shall have granted to preserve them, so acting, however, that after deducting your said capital for you I am to have one fourth of all the profit that God shall have granted in this *comanda* of yours. But you are to have the three remaining parts of the said profit in addition to your said capital, your *comanda* itself, however, going and being held there and returning anywhere at your risk and fortune. This was done on the fifth day before the Ides of August, in the year of the Lord, 1252.

*   *   *

Intermediate Forms of Partnership

Marseilles, May 8, 1248

The same day and place. Bonenfant, son of the late Jacob, and Bonseigneur, son of Astruc, and Bonafous, son of the late Chaim, wishing to go on a voyage to Valencia in the vessel of Bertram Belpel, which is named 'Leopard,' have formed a *societas* among themselves in the manner written below, to wit, that the profits of all *comandae* made by the three of them or by one of them, no matter how many the *comandae* are, are to be common to them in equal shares in the aforesaid voyage; and all investments of the said *comandae* made by them or by one of them, and the investments of those amounts of money which any one of them shall carry in the aforesaid voyage, are to be common to them: with this reservation, that whoever of them shall have extra money of his own in the said *companhia* is to receive that extra share of the profits, according as it is coming to him, by the solidus and by the pound. And all the aforesaid men have promised, by stipulation, each of them to the others, to be faithful and law-abiding one to the other, and to tell each other the truth, and to keep faith throughout the voyage mentioned above, pledging to each other, etc., waiving, etc. And for greater security they all swore on the Mosaic Law, touched by them physically with the hand, to undertake and to fulfill all the aforesaid. Witnesses: R. Boneti, Jehan Gauselin, G. Peire Salvi.

*   *   *

Genoa, January 19, 1308

In the name of the Lord, amen. Percivalle Grillo, son of Andreolo; Daniele Grillo; Meliano Grillo; Benedetto Contardo and Nicola Contardo, brothers, sons of the late Luchetto Contardo; Manuele Bonifacio; Antonino Grillo, son of Andreolo, acknowledge to each other that they have formed and made a *societas* for the purpose of maintaining a bank in the city of Genoa and of engaging in commerce and business in Genoa and throughout other and different parts of the world, according to what shall seem proper and shall be the pleasure of the partners themselves, to continue, God willing, for the next two succeeding years. This *societas* they acknowledge to be of £9,450 Genoese, in which sum they acknowledge to each other that each of them has or has deposited as below, viz.: said Percivalle, £3,500; said Daniele, £2,000; said Meliano, £1,000; the aforesaid Benedetto Contardo and Nicola, his brother, £2,000; said Manuele Bonifacio, £450; and said Antonio Grillo, £500. This capital they acknowledge to be in the hands of said Percivalle in money, in credits, in exchange to be received in France, and in a vein of iron in Elba. And the aforesaid partners have waived the exception and legal right by which they could speak against or oppose the aforesaid. And said Percivalle is to use this money in business and commerce in Genoa in said bank which he maintains, in the buying and selling of wares, and in exchange both in France and throughout other and different parts

of the world, by sea and by land, personally and through his factors and messengers, according as God may dispose better for him, up to the time limit mentioned above, at the risk and fortune of the partners. And he has promised said partners of his to act in good faith and efficiently for the increase and preservation of said *societas*. And the aforesaid partners promised each other to guard and to preserve the goods and wares and money which may come into the hands of any one of them from the aforesaid *societas*, and not to defraud one another in anything. The profit which God may grant in the aforesaid *societas* shall be allocated to each of them pro rata to his capital; and if any accident befall said *societas* or the goods of said *societas*—may God be our help—it shall be allocated similarly to each of them pro rata to his capital. And they have promised each other in good faith to come to the accounting of the capital and profit of said *societas* at the end of the time limit; and each of them is to deduct his capital and to divide among them the profit pro rata to the capital of each one. The aforesaid *societas* and each and all of the above conditions the aforesaid partners promised each other, etc. Firm, etc., and for it, etc. And said Benedetto acknowledges that he is more than twenty-four years old, and said Nicola acknowledges that he is more than nineteen years old, and said Antonio acknowledges that he is more than nineteen years old, and said Antonio acknowledges that he is more than nineteen years old. And they swore by the sacred Gospels of God, putting their hands on the Scriptures, to undertake and to observe everything as above stated and not to do anything or to act contrary in any way by reason of their being minors or by any other cause. And they made the aforesaid agreement with the counsel of the witnesses written below, whom for this purpose they call their relatives, neighbors, and counselors. Done in Genoa in the Church of Santa Maria delle Vigne, in the year of the Nativity of the Lord 1308, fifth indiction, January 19, about nones. Witnesses: Arnaldo of Spigno, dealer in poultry; Manfredo; and Pagano of Moneglia, dealer in poultry.

*   *   *

Reports from the Fairs of Champagne

Siena, July 5, 1260

In the name of the Lord, amen. Reply to the letters from France brought by the first messenger of the May fair of Provins, year 1260.

Dear Giacomo di Guido Cacciaconti:

Giacomo and Giovannidi Gregorio, Vincente di Aldobrandino Vincenti and the other partners send you greetings. And we are informing you that we have safely received the letters which you sent us by the messenger of the gild merchant from the May fair of Provins of this year. And through these letters we perfectly understand what were your instructions, and we shall get busy on what will be our business here. Therefore we beg you to be on the alert and to make it your concern to work and get busy on what you have to do. And especially we beg you to be careful in investing and in lending what you have in your hands and what you will have in the future to good and reliable payers, so that we can have it back at any time we may need it or we may want it back. And to do this we ask from God our Lord mercy, that He grant you the grace to do it so that honor may come to you personally and that the partnership may come out in good standing. Amen.

You ought to know, Giacomo, that we shall write accurately all that we have to write, and especially what you will instruct us by your letters, such as your receipts, your payments, and the loans you will make. Just as you will instruct us by your letters at each fair, so at each fair shall we write and enter it in our book. The receipts we shall post to your receipts, the payments we shall post to your payments, and the loans we shall write to the loans, just as we have always done up to the present time. Therefore, any money which you collect or which comes into your hands, when you have instructed us once by letter about it, do not repeat it any more; for as soon as you have instructed us about it, we post it at once—whatever you tell us are receipts among the receipts, and we post the payments to the payments, and

the loans to the loans. And we do so for every letter. Therefore, if you should instruct us through more than one letter, you see that it would not be a good thing to do; for just as many times as you instruct us, so many times we shall post it in the book in our customary way. Therefore do take care. And we mention this in connection with the £3 Provisine, which Testa Tebaldi takes and Tederigo Lei gives. For you received out of them 34 soldi less 4 deniers, and you have sent me instructions about this through several letters. For if we had not remembered that we had posted them once to your receipts, we certainly would have posted them a second time. Therefore take care—do not instruct us about it more than once.

And just as we instructed you in the other letter, so we repeat in this that you must not be astonished that we have sold and are selling Provisines; for you ought to know, Giacomo, that we are under great expense and extremely busy because of the war we are having against Florence. And you ought to know that we have to have money to spend and to make war; on account of this, we see that we cannot raise money from any source more advantageous for us than by selling Provisines. And should you say that we ought to obtain a loan here, it would do us no good: for you ought to know that money costs from 5 to 6 deniers a pound from one merchant to another, and it costs those who are not merchants from 10 to 12 deniers a pound in *corsa,* although it is in the same state. Now you see what the conditions of lending are here. Therefore do not feel too badly that we are selling Provisines, since we had rather be in debt in France than be in debt here or sell sterling. For it is worth far more to us so long as we can get Provisines at the price they cost you today than it would be to sell the sterling or to borrow here; because we draw greater interest in England than we would in France, and in order to raise a loan here today we should have to pay a price greater than would be any profit that we could get in France. Therefore be satisfied with what we are doing, and do not be astonished at all about it. And you ought to know, Giacomo, that if in the country of France one could profit more than one can profit there today, we should do well, since you would have a great many Provisines, so that you would well get whatever arrangement you may wish, and we would certainly get our share of whatever profit might be made in that land; and about that be of good cheer.

And we understand from you through your letter that you have gone, both without and with Tolomeo Pelacane, to see the dean of Saint Etienne of Troyes about the business of Lyons-on-the-Rhone, and that you spoke and argued a good deal with the procurator of that archbishop of Lyons-on-the-Rhone, and you could not persuade him to come to any conclusion or agreement that was good for us; nor could you persuade him unless we sent you a letter from the papal Curia against him. In this matter you ought to know that we have had and are still having a great deal of trouble, because of the war and making expeditions and cavalry raids, so that we have not been able to devote our attention to obtaining the letter. Therefore you ought to know that as soon as we have a breathing spell to devote our attention to it we shall do so, and we shall see to it that you get the said letter against them.

And we also understand from you through that letter of yours that you and Tolomeo Pelacane had been to see Bonico Maniardi and had told him that you wanted to go to Lyons to learn if you could get any agreement at all from that person, and the said Bonico answered that you could go all right but that he would not pay one bit of the expenses unless Mino Pieri instructed him to do so; for he told you that Mino had not sent a word of instruction about the matter. This astonishes us, for we were in agreement about it here with Mino Pieri, and Mino told us he would instruct him to pay us whatever was his share of our expenses. And in this letter we cannot tell you anything further about it, because Mino Pieri is with the army at Montepulciano while we are writing this letter. Through other letters we shall get in touch with him; and if he has not instructed about it, we certainly shall tell him to instruct him, and we shall communicate to you what he will answer us.

And we also understand from you through a note of yours that we are expected to beg Orlando Bonsignore that he should instruct his partners over there that whenever you wish to borrow from his partners they should consent to it, for that would be a great boon to us. In this regard we tell you that the said Orlando Bonsignore was not in Siena when this letter was written, but he was with the army at Montepulciano. Therefore, when he returns, we shall get in touch with him and remind him about it; and we definitely believe that he will do what we wish about it.

You ought to know, Giacomo, that I, Vincente, will give 60 to Madonna Pacina, just as you have instructed me. And Niccolò, son of Messer Nicola, wants us to beg you for his love that if you have not sold for him his Kirkoswald *biffa*, you get it sold. He would have instructed you about this in a letter if he had not been with the army at Montepulciano; for he went there before the letters were written, and he begged me, Vincente, that I should write you about it in this letter.

And also we let you know that we have sold £106 Provisine to Giacomo Ubertini, changer, to be paid at the fair of Saint John, year 1260; and we sold them at the rate of s.33 a dozen, and we have been paid. Therefore you shall pay them at his order to Rimbotto Buonaiuti at the latter's pleasure; and when you make the payment to him, have a record made of it in the book of the Officials of the Merchants, as is customary to do.

And also we have sold £24 Provisine to Accorso Guarguaglia and his partnership, to be paid at the said fair of Saint John, at the rate of 31 a dozen, and we have been paid. Therefore you shall pay them to Gregorio Rigoli at his pleasure at that fair; and when you pay them, have a record made of it in the book of the Officials of the Merchants, as is customary to do.

On the other hand, we want to let you know about the developments in Tuscany. For you ought to know, Giacomo, that we are today under great expense and extremely busy because of the war we are having against Florence. And you ought to know that it will take plenty out of our pocket; but we shall lick Florence so badly that we shall never have to guard ourselves from her any more, if God protects from evil the lord King Manfred, to whom may God grant long life, amen. . . .

You ought to know, Giacomo, that after this letter was written up to this point we had news that Montepulciano had come to terms and had pledged loyalty to the lord king—King Manfred—and to Siena. And she will make expeditions and cavalry raids against whomever we wish, will hold our friends as friends, and our enemies as enemies. And when that was done, lord Count Giordano left Montepulciano with all the expedition he had and went against Arezzo; and we believe that he will have the town at his will. Well, things up to now have been like this; for the future they will be the same and better, if it please God.

Dispatched Monday, the fifth day of July.

To Giacomo di Guido Cacciaconti, and let it not be given to anyone else.

*   *   *

REVIEW QUESTIONS

1. What is a contract?
2. What were the levels of risks and rewards in the various styles of medieval partnerships?
3. Which ones required the most trust, and which did the law help to enforce?
4. How did merchants make money?

ANNA COMNENA

FROM *The Alexiad*

Anna Comnena (1083–after 1148), an imperial princess, wrote an admiring biography of her father, the Alexiad. *In this selection she is describing how Emperor Alexius engaged his mother, Anna Dalassena, in the governance of the Byzantine Empire, and there is also a digression on Anna Dalassena's own qualities. Byzantine royal families allowed a wide scope for women to participate in government. Alexius spent much of his reign defending the empire from Turkish advances in Asia Minor, and his request for help from the West was one of the motivations for the First Crusade, the centerpiece of Anna's history.*

From *The Alexiad of Anna Commena*, edited by E. R. A. Stewter (New York: Penguin Books, 1969), pp. 116–23.

*   *   *

Gradually and surreptitiously he involved her more and more in state affairs; on occasions he even declared openly that without her brains and good judgement the Empire would not survive. By these means he bound her more closely to himself, but prevented her from attaining her own goal and frustrated it. She had in mind the last stage of life and dreamed of monasteries in which she would drag out her remaining years in the contemplation of wisdom. Such was her intention, the constant aim of her prayers. Despite this longing in her heart, despite the total preoccupation with a higher life, she also loved her son to a quite exceptional degree and wished somehow to bear with him the storms that buffeted the Empire (if I may apply seafaring metaphor to the manifold troubles and tumults to which it was exposed). She desired to guide the ship of state on the best possible course, in fair weather or in tempest (when waves crashed on to it from all sides), especially since the young man had only just taken his seat in the stern and put his hand to the tiller, with no previous experience of storms, winds and waves of such violence. She was constrained, therefore, by a mother's affection for her son, and governed with him, sometimes even grasping the reins (to change the metaphor) and alone driving the chariot of power—and without accident or error. The truth is that Anna Dalassena was in any case endowed with a fine intellect and possessed besides a really first-class aptitude for governing. On the other hand, she was distracted from it by her love for God. When in the month of August (in the same indiction) Robert's crossing to Epirus compelled Alexius to leave the capital, he brought to light and put into operation his cherished plan: the whole executive power was entrusted to his mother alone and the decision was confirmed publicly in a chrysobull. As it is the historian's duty not merely to summarize the deeds and decrees of good men, but as far as he can to give some details of the former and transmit the latter in full, I myself will set out the terms of this document, omitting only the subtle refinements of the scribe. It ran thus: "When danger is foreseen or some other dreadful occurrence is expected, there is no safeguard stronger than a mother who is understanding and loves her son, for if she gives counsel, her advice will be reliable; if she offers prayers, they will confer strength and certain protection. Such at any rate has been the experience of myself, your emperor, in the case of my own revered mother, who has taught and guided and sustained me throughout, from my earliest years. She had a place in aristocratic society, but her first concern was for her son and his faith in her was preserved intact. It was well known that one soul animated us, physically separated though we were,

and by the grace of Christ that happy state has persisted to this day. Never were those cold words, 'mine' and 'yours,' uttered between us, and what was even more important, the prayers she poured out during all that time reached the ears of the Lord and have raised me now to the imperial throne. After I took in my hand the imperial sceptre, she found it intolerable that she was not bearing an equal share in my labours, to the interests both of your emperor and of the whole people. But now I am preparing with God's help to do battle with Rome's enemies; with much forethought an army is being recruited and thoroughly equipped; not the least of my cares, however, has been the provision of an efficient organization in financial and civil affairs. Fortunately, an impregnable bulwark for good government has been found—in the appointment of my revered mother, of all women most honoured, as controller of the entire administration. I, your emperor, therefore decree explicitly in this present chrysobull the following: because of her vast experience of secular affairs (despite the very low value she sets upon such matters), whatever she decrees in writing (whether the case be referred to her by the logothete, or by his subordinate officers, or by any other person who prepares memoranda or requests or judgements concerning remissions of public debts) shall have permanent validity as if I myself, your Serene Emperor, had issued them or after dictating them had had them committed to writing. Whatever decisions or orders are made by her, written or unwritten, reasonable or unreasonable, provided that they bear her seal (the Transfiguration and the Assumption), shall be regarded as coming from myself, by the fact that they carry the 'In the month . . .' of the current logothete. Moreover, with regard to promotions and successions to the tribunals and fiscs, and in the matter of honours, offices and donations of immovable property, my saintly mother shall have full power to take whatever action shall seem good to her. Further, if any persons are promoted to the tribunals or succeed to the fiscs and are honoured with the highest or medium or lowest dignities, they shall thereafter retain these positions on a permanent basis. Again, increases of salary, additional gifts, reductions of tax, economies and diminution of payments shall be settled by her without question. In brief, nothing shall be reckoned invalid which she commands either in writing or by word of mouth, for her words and her decisions shall be reckoned as my own and none of them shall be annulled. In years to come they shall have the force of law permanently. Neither now nor in the future shall my mother be subjected to inquiry or undergo any examination whatsoever at the hands of anybody, whoever he may be. The same provision shall also hold good for her ministers and the chancellor of the time, whether their actions seem to be reasonable or ridiculous. It shall be absolutely impossible in the future to demand account of any action taken by them under the terms of this present chrysobull."

The reader may be surprised by the honour conferred on his mother by the emperor in this matter, since he yielded her precedence in everything, relinquishing the reins of government, as it were, and running alongside as she drove the imperial chariot; only in the title of emperor did he share with her the privileges of his rank. And this despite the fact that he had already passed his boyhood years and was of an age which in the case of men like him is particularly susceptible to the lust for power. Wars against the barbarians, with all their attendant trials and tribulations he was prepared to face himself, but the entire administration of affairs, the choice of civil magistrates, the accounts of the imperial revenues and expenditure he left to his mother. At this point the reader may well censure him for transferring the government of the Empire to the gynaeconitis, but had he known this woman's spirit, her surpassing virtue, intelligence and energy, his reproaches would soon have turned to admiration. For my grandmother had an exceptional grasp of public affairs, with a genius for organization and government; she was capable, in fact, of managing not only the Roman Empire, but every other empire under the sun as well. She had vast experience and a wide understanding of the motives, ultimate

consequences, interrelations good and bad of various courses of action, penetrating quickly to the right solution, adroitly and safely carrying it out. Her intellectual powers, moreover, were paralleled by her command of language. She was indeed a most persuasive orator, without being verbose or long-winded. Nor did the inspiration of the argument readily desert her, for if she began on a felicitous note, she was also most successful in ending her speeches with just the right words. She was already a woman of mature years when she was called upon to exercise imperial authority, at a time of life when one's mental powers are at their best, when one's judgement is fully developed and knowledge of affairs is widest—all qualities that lend force to good administration and government. It is natural that persons of this age should not merely speak with greater wisdom than the young (as the tragic playwright says), but also act in a more expedient way. In the past, when Anna Dalassena was still looked upon as a younger woman, she had impressed everyone as "having an old head on young shoulders"; to the observant her face alone revealed Anna's inherent virtue and gravity. But, as I was saying, once he had seized power my father reserved for himself the struggles and hard labour of war, while she became so to speak an onlooker, but he made her sovereign and like a slave said and did whatever she commanded. He loved her exceedingly and depended on her for advice (such was his affection for her). His right hand he devoted to her service; his ears listened for her bidding. In all things he was entirely subservient, in fact, to her wishes. I can sum up the whole situation thus: he was in theory the emperor, but she had real power. She was the legislator, the complete organizer and governor, while he confirmed her arrangements, written and unwritten, the former by his signature, the latter by his spoken approval. One might say that he was indeed the instrument of her power—he was not emperor, for all the decisions and ordinances of his mother satisfied him, not merely as an obedient son, but as an attentive listener to her instruction in the art of ruling. He was convinced that she had attained perfection in everything and easily excelled all men of that generation in prudence and understanding of affairs.

Such were the events that marked the beginning of the reign. One could hardly at that stage call Alexius emperor once he had entrusted to her the supreme authority. Another person might yield here to the claims of panegyric and extol the native land of this remarkable woman; he might trace her descent from the Adriani Dalasseni and Charon, while he embarked on the ocean of their achievements. But I am writing history and my fitting task is not to describe her through the family and kinsmen, but by reference to her character, her virtue, and the events which form the proper subject of history. To return once more to my grandmother, I must add this: not only was she a very great credit to her own sex, but to men as well; indeed, she contributed to the glory of the whole human race. The women's quarters in the palace had been the scene of utter depravity ever since the infamous Constantine Monomachos had ascended the throne and right up to the time when my father became emperor had been noted for foolish love intrigues, but Anna effected a reformation; a commendable decorum was restored and the palace now enjoyed a discipline that merited praise. She instituted set times for the singing of sacred hymns, stated hours for breakfast; there was now a special period in which magistrates were chosen. She herself set a firm example to everybody else, with the result that the palace assumed the appearance rather of a monastery under the influence of this really extraordinary woman and her truly saintly character; for in self-control she surpassed the famous women of old, heroines of many a legend, as the sun outshines all stars. As for her compassion for the poor and her generosity to the needy, no words could do justice to them. Her house was a refuge for penniless relatives, but no less for strangers. Priests and monks she honoured in particular: they shared her meals and no one ever saw her at table without some of them as guests. Her outward serenity, true reflection of character, was respected by angels but terrorized even the demons, and pleasure-loving fools, victims of their own passions, found a single glance from her more than they could bear; yet to the chaste she seemed gentle and gay. She knew exactly how to temper reserve and dignity; her own reserve never gave the impression of harshness or cruelty, nor did her tenderness seem too soft or unrestrained—and this, I fancy, is the true definition of propriety: the due proportion of warm humanity and strict moral principle. She was by nature thoughtful and was always evolving new ideas, not, as some folk whispered, to the detriment of the state; on the contrary, they were wholesome schemes which restored to full vigour the already corrupted empire and revived, as far as one could, the ruined fortunes of the people. In spite of her preoccupation with matters of government, she by no means neglected the duties incumbent on a religious woman, for the greater part of the night was spent by her in the chanting of sacred hymns and she wore herself out with continual prayers and vigils. Nevertheless, at dawn or even at second cock-crow, she was applying herself anew to state business, attending to the choice of magistrates and answering the petitions of suppliants with the help of her secretary Gregory Genesius. Now if some orator had decided to make this the subject of a panegyric, he would no doubt have exalted her and praised her to the skies (as is the way of encomiasts) for her deeds and thoughts and superiority to all others; the famous ones of old, both men and women, who were renowned for their virtue would certainly have been thrown into the shade. But such licence is not for the writer of history. Those who know her virtue, therefore, her dignified character, her never-failing sagacity and the loftiness and sublimity of her spirit, must not blame my history, if I have done less than justice to her great qualities.

*   *   *

REVIEW QUESTIONS

1. What do we learn about the role of women at the highest levels of Byzantine society?

2. How does their position compare to their role in the West?

3. What are Anna Comnena's skills as a historian and writer?

JEAN DE JOINVILLE

FROM *The Life of Saint Louis*

Jean de Joinville was a French noble who knew King Louis IX of France and went on a crusade to Egypt with him in 1248. Long after the king's death in 1270 while on a crusade in North Africa, Joinville dictated these reminiscences as part of a successful campaign to have the church canonize Louis as a saint. Joinville admired his king and stressed his outstanding qualities as a king and warrior. In this section of the biography, Joinville is remembering the holiness that the king displayed during his lifetime, but there is much more here about Louis's character.

From *Joinville and Villehardouin: Chronicles of the Crusades,* edited by M. R. B. Shaw (New York: Penguin Books, 1963), pp. 167–75.

Chapter 1
The Servant of God

In the name of God Almighty, I, Jean, Lord of Joinville, Seneschal of Champagne, dictate the life of our good King, Saint Louis, in which I shall record what I saw and heard both in the course of the six years in which I was on pilgrimage in his company oversea, and after we returned to France. But before I speak to you of his great deeds and his outstanding valour, I will tell you what I myself observed of his good teaching and his saintly conversation, so that it may be set down in due order for the edification of those to whom this book is read.

This saintly man loved our Lord with all his heart, and in all his actions followed His example. This is apparent from the fact that as our Lord died for the love he bore His people, even so King Louis put his own life in danger, and that several times, for the very same reason. It was danger too that he might well have avoided, as I shall show you later.

The great love King Louis bore his people is shown by what he said, as he lay dangerously ill at Fontainebleau, to his eldest son, my Lord Louis. "My dear son," he said, "I earnestly beg you to make yourself loved by all your people. For I would rather have a Scot come from Scotland to govern the people of this kingdom well and justly than that you should govern them ill in the sight of all the world." This upright king, moreover, loved truth so well that, as I shall show you later, he would never consent to lie to the Saracens with regard to any covenant he made with them.

He was so temperate in his appetite that I never heard him, on any day of my life, order a special dish for himself, as many men of wealth and standing do. On the contrary, he would always eat with good grace whatever his cooks had prepared to set before him. He was equally temperate in his speech. I never, on any single occasion, heard him speak evil of any man; nor did I ever hear him utter the name of the Devil—a name in very common use throughout the kingdom—which practice, so I believe, is not pleasing to God.

He used to add water to his wine, but did so reasonably, according as the strength of the wine allowed it. While we were in Cyprus he asked me why I did not mix my wine with water. I replied that this was on the advice of my doctors, who had told me that I had a strong head and a cold stomach, so that I could not get drunk. He answered that they had deceived me; for if I did not learn to mix my wine with water while I was still young, and wished to do so in my old age, gout and stomach troubles would take hold on me, and I should never be in good health. Moreover, if I went on drinking undiluted wine when I was old, I should get drunk every night, and it was too revolting a thing for any brave man to be in such a state.

The king once asked me if I wished to be honoured in this world, and to enter paradise when I died. I told him I did. "If so," said he, "you should avoid deliberately saying or doing anything which, if it became generally known, you would be ashamed to acknowledge by saying 'I did this,' or 'I said that.'" He also told me not to contradict or call in question anything said in my presence —unless indeed silence would imply approval of something wrong, or damaging to myself, because harsh words often lead to quarrelling, which has ended in the death of countless numbers of men.

He often said that people ought to clothe and arm themselves in such a way that men of riper age would never say they had spent too much on dress, or young men say they had spent too little. I repeated this remark to our present king when speaking of the elaborately embroidered tabards that are in vogue today. I told him that, during the whole of our voyage oversea, I had never seen such embroidered tabards, either on the king or

on any one else. He said to me that he had several such garments, with his own arms embroidered on them, and they had cost him eight hundred *livres parisis*. I told him that he would have put his money to better use if he had given it to God, and had his clothes made of good plain taffeta bearing his arms, as his father had done.

King Louis once sent for me and said: "You have such a shrewd and subtle mind that I hardly dare speak to you of things concerning God. So I have summoned these two monks to come here, because I want to ask you a question." Then he said: "Tell me, seneschal, what is your idea of God?" "Your Majesty," I replied, "He is something so good that there cannot be anything better." "Indeed," said he, "you've given me a very good answer; for it's precisely the same as the definition given in this book I have here in my hand.

"Now I ask you," he continued, "which you would prefer: to be a leper or to have committed some mortal sin?" And I, who had never lied to him, replied that I would rather have committed thirty mortal sins than become a leper. The next day, when the monks were no longer there, he called me to him, and making me sit at his feet said to me: "Why did you say that to me yesterday?" I told him I would still say it. "You spoke without thinking, and like a fool," he said. "You ought to know there is no leprosy so foul as being in a state of mortal sin; for the soul in that condition is like the Devil; therefore no leprosy can be so vile. Besides, when a man dies his body is healed of its leprosy; but if he dies after committing a mortal sin, he can never be sure that, during his lifetime, he has repented of it sufficiently for God to forgive him. In consequence, he must be greatly afraid lest that leprosy of sin should last as long as God dwells in paradise. So I beg you," he added, "as earnestly as I can, for the love of God, and for love of me, to train your heart to prefer any evil that can happen to the body, whether it be leprosy or any other disease, rather than let mortal sin take possession of your soul."

At another time King Louis asked me if I washed the feet of the poor on Maundy Thursday. "Your Majesty," I exclaimed, "what a terrible idea!

I will never wash the feet of such low fellows." "Really," said he, "that is a very wrong thing to say; for you should never scorn to do what our Lord Himself did as an example for us. So I beg you, first for the love of God and then for love of me, to accustom yourself to washing the feet of the poor."

This good king so loved all manner of people who believed in God and loved Him that he appointed Gilles le Brun, who was not a native of his realm, as High Constable of France, because he was held in such high repute for his faith in God and devotion to His service. For my part, I believe he well deserved that reputation. Another man, Maître Robert de Sorbon, who was famed for his goodness and his learning, was invited, on that account, to dine at the royal table.

It happened one day that this worthy priest was sitting beside me at dinner, and we were talking to each other rather quietly. The king reproved us and said: "Speak up, or your companions may think you are speaking ill of them. If at table you talk of things that may give us pleasure, say them aloud, or else be silent."

When the king was feeling in a mood for fun, he would fire questions at me, as for instance: "Seneschal, can you give me reasons why a wise and upright layman is better than a friar?" Thereupon a discussion would begin between Maître Robert and myself. When we had disputed for some length of time the king would pronounce judgement. "Maître Robert," he would say, "I would willingly be known as a wise and upright man, provided I were so in reality—and you can have all the rest. For wisdom and goodness are such fine qualities that even to name them leaves a pleasant taste in the mouth."

On the other hand, he always said that it was a wicked thing to take other people's property. "To 'restore,' " he would say, "is such a hard thing to do that even in speaking of it the word itself rasps one's throat because of the r's that are in it. These r's are, so to speak, like the rakes of the Devil, with which he would draw to himself all those who wish to 'restore' what they have taken from others. The Devil, moreover, does this very

subtly; for he works on great usurers and great robbers in such a way that they give to God what they ought to *restore* to men."

On one occasion the king gave me a message to take to King Thibaut, in which he warned his son-in-law to beware lest he should lay too heavy a burden on his soul by spending an excessive amount of money on the house he was building for the Predicants of Provins. "Wise men," said the king, "deal with their possessions as executors ought to do. Now the first thing a good executor does is to settle all debts incurred by the deceased and restore any property belonging to others, and only then is he free to apply what money remains to charitable purposes."

One Whitsunday the saintly king happened to be at Corbeil, where all the knights had assembled. He had come down after dinner into the court below the chapel, and was standing at the doorway talking to the Comte de Bretagne, the father of the present count—may God preserve him!—when Maître Robert de Sorbon came to look for me, and taking hold of the hem of my mantle led me towards the king. So I said to Maître Robert: "My good sir, what do you want with me?" He replied: "I wish to ask you whether, if the king were seated in this court and you went and sat down on his bench, at a higher place than he, you ought to be severely blamed for doing so?" I told him I ought to be. "Then," he said "you certainly deserve a reprimand for being more richly dressed than the king, since you are wearing a fur-trimmed mantle of fine green cloth, and he wears no such thing." "Maître Robert," I answered, "I am, if you'll allow me to say so, doing nothing worthy of blame in wearing green cloth and fur, for I inherited the right to such dress from my father and mother. But you, on the other hand, are much to blame, for though both your parents were commoners, you have abandoned their style of dress, and are now wearing finer woollen cloth than the king himself." Then I took hold of the skirt of his surcoat and of the surcoat worn by the king, and said to Maître Robert: "See if I'm not speaking the truth." At this the king began to take Maître Robert's part, and say all in his power to defend him.

A little later on the king beckoned to his son, the Prince Philippe—the father of our present king—and to King Thibaut. Then, seating himself at the entrance to his oratory, he patted the ground and said to the two young men: "Sit down here, quite close to me, so that we shan't be overheard." "But, my lord," they protested, "we should not dare to sit so close to you." Then the king said to me, "Seneschal, you sit here." I obeyed, and sat down so close to him that my clothes were touching his. He made the two others sit down next, and said to them: "You have acted very wrongly, seeing you are my sons, in not doing as I commanded the moment I told you. I beg you to see this does not happen again." They assured him it would not.

Then the king said to me that he had called us together to confess that he had wrongly defended Maître Robert against me. "But," said he, "I saw he was so taken aback that he greatly needed my help. All the same you must not attach too great importance to anything I may have said in his defence. As the seneschal rightly says, you ought to dress well, and in a manner suited to your condition, so that your wives will love you all the more and your men have more respect for you. For, as a wise philosopher has said, our clothing and our armour ought to be of such a kind that men of mature experience will not say that we have spent too much on them, nor younger men say we have spent too little."

I will tell you here of one of the lessons King Louis taught me on our voyage back from the land oversea. It so happened that our ship was driven on to the rocks off the island of Cyprus by a wind known as the *garbino,* which is not one of the four great winds. At the shock our ship received the sailors were so frantic with despair that they rent their clothes and tore their beards. The king sprang out of bed barefoot—for it was night— and with nothing on but his tunic went and lay with arms outstretched to form a cross before the body of Our Lord on the altar, as one who expected nothing but death.

The day after this alarming event, the king called me aside to talk with him alone, and said to me: "Seneschal, God has just shown us a glimpse of His great power; for one of these little winds, so little indeed that it scarcely deserves a name, came near to drowning the King of France, his children, his wife, and his men. Now Saint Anselm says that such things are warnings from our Lord, as if God meant to say to us: 'See how easily I could have brought about your death if that had been My will.' 'Lord God,' says the saint, 'why dost Thou thus threaten us? For when Thou dost, it is not for Thy own profit, nor for Thy advantage— seeing that if Thou hadst caused us all to be lost Thou wouldst be none the poorer, nor any the richer either if Thou hadst caused us to be saved. Therefore the warning Thou sendest us is not for Thy own benefit, but for ours, if so be we know how to profit by it.'

"Let us therefore," said the king, "take this warning God has sent us in such a way that if we feel there is anything in our hearts or our bodies that is displeasing to Him, we shall get rid of it without delay. If, on the other hand, we can think of anything that will please Him, we ought to see about doing it with equal speed. If we act thus our Lord will give us blessings in this world, and in the next greater bliss than we can tell. But if we do not act as we ought, He will deal with us as a good lord deals with his unfaithful servant. For if the latter will not amend his ways after he has been given warning, then his lord punishes him with death, or with penalties even harder to bear."

So I, Jean de Joinville, say: "Let the king who now reigns over us beware; for he has escaped from perils as great as those to which we were then exposed, or even greater. Therefore, let him turn from doing wrong, and in such a way that God will not smite him cruelly, either in himself or in his possessions."

In the conversations he had with me, this saintly king did every thing in his power to give me a firm belief in the principles of Christianity as given us by God. He used to say that we ought to have such an unshaken belief in all the articles of faith that neither fear of death nor of any harm that might happen to our bodies should make us willing to go against them in word or deed. "The

Enemy," he would add, "works so subtly that when people are at the point of death he tries all he can to make them die with some doubt in their minds on certain points of our religion. For this cunning adversary is well aware that he cannot take away the merit of any good works a man has done; and he also knows that a man's soul is lost to him if he dies in the true faith.

"Therefore," the king would say, "it is our duty so to defend and guard ourselves against this snare as to say to the Enemy, when he sends us such a temptation: 'Go away! You shall not lure me from my steadfast belief in the articles of my faith. Even if you had all my limbs cut off, I would still live and die a true believer.' Whoever acts thus overcomes the Devil with the very same weapons with which this enemy of mankind had proposed to destroy him."

King Louis would also say that the Christian religion as defined in the creed was something in which we ought to believe implicitly, even though our belief in it might be founded on hearsay. On this point he asked me what was my father's name. I told him it was Simon. So he asked me how I knew it, and I replied that I thought I was certain of it, and believed it without question, because I had my mother's word for it. "Then," said he, "you ought to have a sure belief in all the articles of our faith on the word of the Apostles, which you hear sung of a Sunday in the Creed."

On one occasion the king repeated to me what Guillaume, Bishop of Paris, had told him about a certain eminent theologian who had come to see him. This man told the bishop that he wished to speak with him. "Speak as freely as you like, sir," said the bishop. However, when the theologian tried to speak to him he only burst into tears. So the bishop said: "Say what you have to say, sir; don't be disheartened; no one can be such a sinner that God can no longer forgive him." "Indeed, my lord," said the theologian, "I cannot control my tears. For I fear I must be an apostate, since I cannot compel my heart to believe in the sacrament of the altar, in the way that Holy Church teaches. Yet I know very well that this is a temptation of the Enemy."

"Pray tell me, sir," said the bishop, "do you feel any pleasure when the Enemy exposes you to this temptation?" "On the contrary, my lord," said the theologian, "it worries me as much as anything can." "Now," said the bishop, "I will ask you whether you would accept any gold or silver if it were offered you on condition you allowed your mouth to utter anything derogatory to the sacrament of the altar, or the other sacraments of Holy Church?" "My lord," said the other, "I can assure you that nothing in the world would induce me to do so. I would rather have one of my limbs torn from my body than consent to say such a thing."

"I will now," said the bishop, "take a different approach. You know that the King of France is at war with the King of England; you also know that the castle nearest the boundary-line between their two domains is the castle of Rochelle in Poitou. So I will ask you a question: Suppose the king had set you to guard the castle of Rochelle, and had put me in charge of the castle of Montlhéri, which is in the very centre of France, where the land is at peace, to which of us do you think the king would feel most indebted at the end of the war—to you who had guarded La Rochelle without loss, or to me who had remained in safety at Montlhéri?" "Why, in God's name, my lord," cried the theologian, "to me, who had guarded La Rochelle, and not lost it to the enemy."

"Sir," said the bishop, "my heart is like the castle of Montlhéri; for I have neither temptation nor doubts concerning the sacrament of the altar. For this reason I tell you that if God owes me any grace because my faith is secure and untroubled, He owes four times as much to you, who have kept your heart from defeat when beset by tribulations, and have moreover such good-will towards Him that neither worldly advantage, nor fear of any harm that might be done to your body, could tempt you to renounce Him. So I tell you to be comforted; for your state is more pleasing to Our Lord than mine." When the theologian heard this, he knelt before the bishop, at peace with himself, and well satisfied.

The king once told me how several men from

ILLUMINATED BIBLE, FRANCE (C. 1230)

This illuminated page from a Bible shows Queen Blanche and her son Louis IX of France. Below are an editor who is selecting texts and dictating and a scribe who is writing. How does this picture complement Joinville's description of King Louis IX of France? What do the figures at the bottom of the page suggest about literacy in thirteenth-century France?

among the Albigenses had gone to the Comte de Montfort, who at the time was guarding their land for his Majesty, and asked him to come and look at the body of our Lord, which had become flesh and blood in the hands of the priest. The count had answered: "Go and see it for yourselves, you who do not believe it. As for me, I believe it firmly, in accordance with Holy Church's teaching on the sacrament of the altar. And do you know," he added, "what I shall gain for having, in this mortal life, believed what Holy Church teaches us? I shall have a crown in heaven, and a finer one than the angels, for they see God face to face and consequently cannot but believe."

King Louis also spoke to me of a great assembly of clergy and Jews which had taken place at the monastery of Cluny. There was a poor knight there at the time to whom the abbot had often given bread for the love of God. This knight asked the abbot if he could speak first, and his request was granted, though somewhat grudgingly. So he rose to his feet, and leaning on his crutch, asked to have the most important and most learned rabbi among the Jews brought before him. As soon as the Jew had come, the knight asked him a question. "May I know, sir," he said, "if you believe that the Virgin Mary, who bore our Lord in her body and cradled Him in her arms, was a virgin at the time of His birth, and is in truth the Mother of God?"

The Jew replied that he had no belief in any of those things. Thereupon the knight told the Jew that he had acted like a fool when—neither believing in the Virgin, nor loving her—he had set foot in that monastery which was her house. "And by heaven," exclaimed the knight, "I'll make you pay for it!" So he lifted his crutch and struck the Jew such a blow with it near the ear that he knocked him down. Then all the Jews took to flight, and carried their sorely wounded rabbi away with them. Thus the conference ended.

The abbot went up to the knight and told him he had acted most unwisely. The knight retorted that the abbot had been guilty of even greater folly in calling people together for such a conference, because there were many good Christians there who, before the discussion ended, would have gone away with doubts about their own religion through not fully understanding the Jews. "So I tell you," said the king, "that no one, unless he is an expert theologian, should venture to argue with these people. But a layman, whenever he hears the Christian religion abused, should not attempt to defend its tenets, except with his sword, and that he should thrust into the scoundrel's belly, and as far as it will enter."

*   *   *

REVIEW QUESTIONS

1. According to Joinville, what kind of man was Louis?
2. How did his personality shape the way he ruled?
3. Why does Joinville admire Louis?
4. What do we learn of the king's attitudes toward his social inferiors and Jews?

The Magna Carta: English Constitutional Law

The Magna Carta, or Great Charter of Liberties, is one of the most famous of medieval documents. Various disasters, including the loss of almost all his possessions in France, placed King John in a weak position by 1215, when his bishops, nobles, and other powerful men, all in revolt, extracted this contract from him. The charter is a curious mix of lofty ideals and practical details about how John should govern his realm and not infringe on the liberties of his subjects, who were by no means all equal.

From *Select Documents of English Constitutional History,* edited by George Burton Adams and H. Morse Stephens (Basingstoke, Eng.: Macmillan Publishers, 1901).

John, by the grace of God, king of England, lord of Ireland, duke of Normandy and Aquitaine, count of Anjou, to the archbishops, bishops, abbots, earls, barons, justiciars, foresters, sheriffs, reeves, servants, and all bailiffs and his faithful people greeting. Know that by the suggestion of God and for the good of our soul and those of all our predecessors and of our heirs, to the honor of God and the exaltation of holy church, and the improvement of our kingdom, by the advice of our venerable fathers Stephen, archbishop of Canterbury, primate of all England and Cardinal of the Holy Roman Church, Henry, archbishop of Dublin, William of London, Peter of Winchester, Joscelyn of Bath and Glastonbury, Hugh of Lincoln, Walter of Worcester, William of Coventry, and Benedict of Rochester, bishops; of Master Pandulf, subdeacon and member of the household of the lord Pope, of Brother Aymeric, master of the Knights of the Temple in England; and of the noblemen William Marshall, earl of Pembroke, William, earl of Salisbury, William, earl Warren, William, earl of Arundel, Alan of Galloway, constable of Scotland, Warren Fitz-Gerald, Peter Fitz-Herbert, Hubert de Burgh, seneschal of Poitou, Hugh de Nevil, Matthew Fitz-Herbert, Thomas Bassett, Alan Bassett, Philip d'Albini, Robert de Ropesle, John Marshall, John Fitz-Hugh, and others of our faithful.

1. In the first place we have granted to God, and by this our present charter confirmed, for us and our heirs forever, that the English church shall be free, and shall hold its rights entire and its liberties uninjured; and we will that it thus be observed; which is shown by this, that the freedom of elections, which is considered to be most important and especially necessary to the English church, we, of our pure and spontaneous will, granted, and by

our charter confirmed, before the contest between us and our barons had arisen; and obtained a confirmation of it by the lord Pope Innocent III.; which we will observe and which we will shall be observed in good faith by our heirs forever.

We have granted moreover to all free men of our kingdom for us and our heirs forever all the liberties written below, to be had and holden by themselves and their heirs from us and our heirs.

2. If any of our earls or barons, or others holding from us in chief by military service shall have died, and when he has died his heir shall be of full age and owe relief, he shall have his inheritance by the ancient relief; that is to say, the heir or heirs of an earl for the whole barony of an earl a hundred pounds; the heir or heirs of a baron for a whole barony a hundred pounds; the heir or heirs of a knight, for a whole knight's fee, a hundred shillings at most; and who owes less let him give less according to the ancient custom of fiefs.

3. If moreover the heir of any one of such shall be under age, and shall be in wardship, when he comes of age he shall have his inheritance without relief and without a fine.

4. The custodian of the land of such a minor heir shall not take from the land of the heir any except reasonable products, reasonable customary payments, and reasonable services, and this without destruction or waste of men or of property; and if we without destruction or waste of men or of property; and if we shall have committed the custody of the land of any such a one to the sheriff or to any other who is to be responsible to us for its proceeds, and that man shall have caused destruction or waste from his custody we will recover damages from him, and the land shall be committed to two legal and discreet men of that

fief, who shall be responsible for its proceeds to us or to him to whom we have assigned them; and if we shall have given or sold to any one the custody of any such land, and he has caused destruction or waste there, he shall lose that custody, and it shall be handed over to two legal and discreet men of that fief who shall be in like manner responsible to us as is said above.

5. The custodian moreover, so long as he shall have the custody of the land, must keep up the houses, parks, warrens, fish ponds, mills, and other things pertaining to the land, from the proceeds of the land itself; and he must return to the heir, when he has come to full age, all his land, furnished with ploughs and implements of husbandry according as the time of wainage requires and as the proceeds of the land are able reasonably to sustain.

6. Heirs shall be married without disparity, so nevertheless that before the marriage is contracted, it shall be announced to the relatives by blood of the heir himself.

7. A widow, after the death of her husband, shall have her marriage portion and her inheritance immediately and without obstruction, nor shall she give anything for her dowry or for her marriage portion, or for her inheritance which inheritance her husband and she held on the day of the death of her husband; and she may remain in the house of her husband for forty days after his death, within which time her dowry shall be assigned to her.

8. No widow shall be compelled to marry so long as she prefers to live without a husband, provided she gives security that she will not marry without our consent, if she holds from us, or without the consent of her lord from whom she holds, if she holds from another.

9. Neither we nor our bailiffs will seise any land or rent, for any debt, so long as the chattels of the debtor are sufficient for the payment of the debt; nor shall the pledges of a debtor be distrained so long as the principal debtor himself has enough for the payment of the debt; and if the principal debtor fails in the payment of the debt, not having the wherewithal to pay it, the pledges shall be responsible for the debt; and if they wish, they shall have the lands and the rents of the debtor until they shall have been satisfied for the debt which they have before paid for him, unless the principal debtor shall have shown himself to be quit in that respect towards those pledges.

10. If any one has taken anything from the Jews, by way of a loan, more or less, and dies before that debt is paid, the debt shall not draw interest so long as the heir is under age, from whomsoever he holds; and if that debt falls into our hands, we will take nothing except the chattel contained in the agreement.

11. And if any one dies leaving a debt owing to the Jews, his wife shall have her dowry, and shall pay nothing of that debt; and if there remain minor children of the dead man, necessaries shall be provided for them corresponding to the holding of the dead man; and from the remainder shall be paid the debt, saving the service of the lords. In the same way debts are to be treated which are owed to others than the Jews.

12. No scutage or aid shall be imposed in our kingdom except by the common council of our kingdom, except for the ransoming of our body, for the making of our oldest son a knight, and for once marrying our oldest daughter, and for these purposes it shall be only a reasonable aid; in the same way it shall be done concerning the aids of the city of London.

13. And the city of London shall have all its ancient liberties and free customs, as well by land as by water. Moreover, we will and grant that all other cities and boroughs and villages and ports shall have all their liberties and free customs.

14. And for holding a common council of the kingdom concerning the assessment of an aid otherwise than in the three cases mentioned above, or concerning the assessment of a scutage we shall cause to be summoned the archbishops, bishops, abbots, earls, and greater barons by our letters individually; and besides we shall cause to be summoned generally, by our sheriffs and bailiffs all those who hold from us in chief, for a certain day,

that is at the end of forty days at least, and for a certain place; and in all the letters of that summons, we will express the cause of the summons, and when the summons has thus been given the business shall proceed on the appointed day, on the advice of those who shall be present, even if not all of those who were summoned have come.

15. We will not grant to any one, moreover, that he shall take an aid from his free men, except for ransoming his body, for making his oldest son a knight, and for once marrying his oldest daughter; and for these purposes only a reasonable aid shall be taken.

16. No one shall be compelled to perform any greater service for a knight's fee, or for any other free tenement than is owed from it.

17. The common pleas shall not follow our court, but shall be held in some certain place.

18. The recognition of *novel disseisin, mort d'ancestor,* and *darrein presentment* shall be held only in their own counties and in this manner: we, or if we are outside of the kingdom our principal justiciar, will send two justiciars through each county four times a year, who with four knights of each county, elected by the county, shall hold in the county, and on the day and in the place of the county court, the aforesaid assizes of the county.[1]

19. And if the aforesaid assizes cannot be held within the day of the county court, a sufficient number of knights and free-holders shall remain from those who were present at the county court on that day to give the judgments, according as the business is more or less.

20. A free man shall not be fined for a small offence, except in proportion to the measure of the offence; and for a great offence he shall be fined in proportion to the magnitude of the offence, saving his freehold; and a merchant in the same way, saving his merchandise; and the villain shall

be fined in the same way, saving his wainage, if he shall be at our mercy; and none of the above fines shall be imposed except by the oaths of honest men of the neighborhood.

21. Earls and barons shall only be fined by their peers, and only in proportion to their offence.

22. A clergyman shall be fined, like those before mentioned, only in proportion to his lay holding, and not according to the extent of his ecclesiastical benefice.

23. No vill or man shall be compelled to make bridges over the rivers except those which ought to do it of old and rightfully.

24. No sheriff, constable, coroners, or other bailiffs of ours shall hold pleas of our crown.

25. All counties, hundreds, wapentakes, and trithings shall be at the ancient rents and without any increase, excepting our demesne manors.

26. If any person holding a lay fief from us shall die, and our sheriff or bailiff shall show our letters-patent of our summons concerning a debt which the deceased owed to us, it shall be lawful for our sheriff or bailiff to attach and levy on the chattels of the deceased found on his lay fief, to the value of that debt, in the view of legal men, so nevertheless that nothing be removed thence until the clear debt to us shall be paid; and the remainder shall be left to the executors for the fulfilment of the will of the deceased; and if nothing is owed to us by him, all the chattels shall go to the deceased, saving to his wife and children their reasonable shares.

27. If any free man dies intestate, his chattels shall be distributed by the hands of his near relatives and friends, under the oversight of the church, saving to each one the debts which the deceased owed to him.

28. No constable or other bailiff of ours shall take any one's grain or other chattels, without immediately paying for them in money, unless he is able to obtain a postponement at the goodwill of the seller.

29. No constable shall require any knight to give money in place of his ward of a castle if he is willing to furnish that ward in his own person or through another honest man, if he himself is

[1]Note that *novel disseisin* is the recovery of recently seized land; *mort d'ancestor* is an inheritance claim; and *darrein presentment* is a last nomination to a church office. [Editor.]

not able to do it for a reasonable cause; and if we shall lead or send him into the army he shall be free from ward in proportion to the amount of time during which he has been in the army through us.

30. No sheriff or bailiff of ours or any one else shall take horses or wagons of any free man for carrying purposes except on the permission of that free man.

31. Neither we nor our bailiffs will take the wood of another man for castles, or for anything else which we are doing, except by the permission of him to whom the wood belongs.

32. We will not hold the lands of those convicted of a felony for more than a year and a day, after which the lands shall be returned to the lords of the fiefs.

33. All the fish-weirs in the Thames and the Medway, and throughout all England shall be done away with, except those on the coast.

34. The writ which is called *præcipe* shall not be given for the future to any one concerning any tenement by which a free man can lose his court.

35. There shall be one measure of wine throughout our whole kingdom, and one measure of ale, and one measure of grain, that is the London quarter, and one width of dyed cloth and of russets and of halbergets, that is two ells within the selvages; of weights, moreover it shall be as of measures.

36. Nothing shall henceforth be given or taken for a writ of inquisition concerning life or limbs, but it shall be given freely and not denied.

37. If any one holds from us by fee farm or by socage or by burgage, and from another he holds land by military service, we will not have the guardianship of the heir or of his land which is of the fief of another, on account of that fee farm, or socage, or burgage; nor will we have the custody of that fee farm, or socage, or burgage, unless that fee farm itself owes military service. We will not have the guardianship of the heir or of the land of any one, which he holds from another by military service on account of any petty serjeanty which he holds from us by the service of paying to us knives or arrows, or things of that kind.

38. No bailiff for the future shall put any one to his law on his simple affirmation, without credible witnesses brought for this purpose.

39. No free man shall be taken or imprisoned or dispossessed, or outlawed, or banished, or in any way destroyed, nor will we go upon him, nor send upon him, except by the legal judgment of his peers or by the law of the land.

40. To no one will we sell, to no one will we deny, or delay right or justice.

41. All merchants shall be safe and secure in going out from England and coming into England and in remaining and going through England, as well by land as by water, for buying and selling, free from all evil tolls, by the ancient and rightful customs, except in time of war, and if they are of a land at war with us; and if such are found in our land at the beginning of war, they shall be attached without injury to their bodies or goods, until it shall be known from us or from our principal justiciar in what way the merchants of our land are treated who shall be then found in the country which is at war with us; and if ours are safe there, the others shall be safe in our land.

42. It is allowed henceforth to any one to go out from our kingdom, and to return, safely and securely, by land and by water, saving their fidelity to us, except in time of war for some short time, for the common good of the kingdom; excepting persons imprisoned and outlawed according to the law of the realm, and people of a land at war with us, and merchants, of whom it shall be done as is before said.

43. If any one holds from any escheat, as from the honor of Wallingford, or Nottingham, or Boulogne, or Lancaster, or from other escheats which are in our hands and are baronies, and he dies, his heir shall not give any other relief, nor do to us any other service than he would do to the baron, if that barony was in the hands of the baron; and we will hold it in the same way as the baron held it.

44. Men who dwell outside the forest shall not henceforth come before our justiciars of the forest, on common summons, unless they are in a plea

of, or pledges for any person or persons who are arrested on account of the forest.

45. We will not make justiciars, constables, sheriffs or bailiffs except of such as know the law of the realm and are well inclined to observe it.

46. All barons who have founded abbeys for which they have charters of kings of England, or ancient tenure, shall have their custody when they have become vacant, as they ought to have.

47. All forests which have been afforested in our time shall be disafforested immediately; and so it shall be concerning river banks which in our time have been fenced in.

48. All the bad customs concerning forests and warrens and concerning foresters and warreners, sheriffs and their servants, river banks and their guardians shall be inquired into immediately in each county by twelve sworn knights of the same county, who shall be elected by the honest men of the same county, and within forty days after the inquisition has been made, they shall be entirely destroyed by them, never to be restored, provided that we be first informed of it, or our justiciar, if we are not in England.

49. We will give back immediately all hostages and charters which have been liberated to us by Englishmen as security for peace or for faithful service.

50. We will remove absolutely from their bailiwicks the relatives of Gerard de Athyes, so that for the future they shall have no bailiwick in England; Engelard de Cygony, Andrew, Peter and Gyon de Chancelles, Gyon de Cygony, Geoffrey de Martin and his brothers, Philip Mark and his brothers, and Geoffrey his nephew and their whole retinue.

51. And immediately after the reëstablishment of peace we will remove from the kingdom all foreign-born soldiers, cross-bow men, serjeants, and mercenaries who have come with horses and arms for the injury of the realm.

52. If any one shall have been dispossessed or removed by us without legal judgment of his peers, from his lands, castles, franchises, or his right we will restore them to him immediately; and if contention arises about this, then it shall be done according to the judgment of the twenty-five barons, of whom mention is made below concerning the security of the peace. Concerning all those things, however, from which any one has been removed or of which he has been deprived without legal judgment of his peers by King Henry our father, or by King Richard our brother, which we have in our hand, or which others hold, and which it is our duty to guarantee, we shall have respite till the usual term of crusaders; excepting those things about which the suit has been begun or the inquisition made by our writ before our assumption of the cross; when, however, we shall return from our journey or if by chance we desist from the journey, we will immediately show full justice in regard to them.

53. We shall, moreover, have the same respite and in the same manner about showing justice in regard to the forests which are to be disafforested or to remain forests, which Henry our father or Richard our brother made into forests; and concerning the custody of lands which are in the fief of another, custody of which we have until now had on account of a fief which any one has held from us by military service; and concerning the abbeys which have been founded in fiefs of others than ourselves, in which the lord of the fee has asserted for himself a right; and when we return or if we should desist from our journey we will immediately show full justice to those complaining in regard to them.

54. No one shall be seised nor imprisoned on the appeal of a woman concerning the death of any one except her husband.

55. All fines which have been imposed unjustly and against the law of the land, and all penalties imposed unjustly and against the law of the land are altogether excused, or will be on the judgment of the twenty-five barons of whom mention is made below in connection with the security of the peace, or on the judgment of the majority of them, along with the aforesaid Stephen, archbishop of Canterbury, if he is able to be present, and others whom he may wish to call for this purpose along with him. And if he should not be able to be present, nevertheless the business shall go on without him, provided that if any one or more of the aforesaid twenty-five barons are in a similar suit

they should be removed as far as this particular judgment goes, and others who shall be chosen and put upon oath, by the remainder of the twenty-five shall be substituted for them for this purpose.

56. If we have dispossessed or removed any Welshmen from their lands, or franchises, or other things, without legal judgment of their peers, in England, or in Wales, they shall be immediately returned to them; and if a dispute shall have arisen over this, then it shall be settled in the borderland by judgment of their peers, concerning holdings of England according to the law of England, concerning holdings of Wales according to the law of Wales, and concerning holdings of the borderland according to the law of the borderland. The Welsh shall do the same to us and ours.

57. Concerning all those things, however, from which any one of the Welsh shall have been removed or dispossessed without legal judgment of his peers, by King Henry our father, or King Richard our brother, which we hold in our hands, or which others hold, and we are bound to warrant to them, we shall have respite till the usual period of crusaders, those being excepted about which suit was begun or inquisition made by our command before our assumption of the cross. When, however, we shall return or if by chance we shall desist from our journey, we will show full justice to them immediately, according to the laws of the Welsh and the aforesaid parts.

58. We will give back the son of Lewellyn immediately, and all the hostages from Wales and the charters which had been liberated to us as a security for peace.

59. We will act toward Alexander, king of the Scots, concerning the return of his sisters and his hostages, and concerning his franchises and his right, according to the manner in which we shall act toward our other barons of England, unless it ought to be otherwise by the charters which we hold from William his father, formerly king of the Scots, and this shall be by the judgment of his peers in our court.

60. Moreover, all those customs and franchises mentioned above which we have conceded in our kingdom, and which are to be fulfilled, as far as pertains to us, in respect to our men; all men of our kingdom as well clergy as laymen, shall observe as far as pertains to them, in respect to their men.

61. Since, moreover, for the sake of God, and for the improvement of our kingdom, and for the better quieting of the hostility sprung up lately between us and our barons, we have made all these concessions; wishing them to enjoy these in a complete and firm stability forever, we make and concede to them the security described below; that is to say, that they shall elect twenty-five barons of the kingdom, whom they will, who ought with all their power to observe, hold, and cause to be observed, the peace and liberties which we have conceded to them, and by this our present charter confirmed to them; in this manner, that if we or our justiciar, or our bailiffs, or any one of our servants shall have done wrong in any way toward any one, or shall have transgressed any of the articles of peace or security; and the wrong shall have been shown to four barons of the aforesaid twenty-five barons, let those four barons come to us or to our justiciar, if we are out of the kingdom, laying before us the transgression, and let them ask that we cause that transgression to be corrected without delay. And if we shall not have corrected the transgression or, if we shall be out of the kingdom, if our justiciar shall not have corrected it within a period of forty days, counting from the time in which it has been shown to us or to our justiciar, if we are out of the kingdom; the aforesaid four barons shall refer the matter to the remainder of the twenty-five barons, and let these twenty-five barons with the whole community of the country distress and injure us in every way they can; that is to say by the seizure of our castles, lands, possessions, and in such other ways as they can until it shall have been corrected according to their judgment, saving our person and that of our queen, and those of our children; and when the correction has been made, let them devote themselves to us as they did before. And let whoever in the country wishes take an oath that in all the above-mentioned measures he will obey

the orders of the aforesaid twenty-five barons, and that he will injure us as far as he is able with them, and we give permission to swear publicly and freely to each one who wishes to swear, and no one will we ever forbid to swear. All those, moreover, in the country who of themselves and their own will are unwilling to take an oath to the twenty-five barons as to distressing and injuring us along with them, we will compel to take the oath by our mandate, as before said. And if any one of the twenty-five barons shall have died or departed from the land or shall in any other way be prevented from taking the above-mentioned action, let the remainder of the aforesaid twenty-five barons choose another in his place, according to their judgment, who shall take an oath in the same way as the others. In all those things, moreover, which are committed to those five and twenty barons to carry out, if perhaps the twenty-five are present, and some disagreement arises among them about something, or if any of them when they have been summoned are not willing or are not able to be present, let that be considered valid and firm which the greater part of those who are present arrange or command, just as if the whole twenty-five had agreed in this; and let the aforesaid twenty-five swear that they will observe faithfully all the things which are said above, and with all their ability cause them to be observed. And we will obtain nothing from any one, either by ourselves or by another by which any of these concessions and liberties shall be revoked or diminished; and if any such thing shall have been obtained, let it be invalid and void, and we will never use it by ourselves or by another.

62. And all ill-will, grudges, and anger sprung up between us and our men, clergy and laymen, from the time of the dispute, we have fully renounced and pardoned to all. Moreover, all transgressions committed on account of this dispute, from Easter in the sixteenth year of our reign till the restoration of peace, we have fully remitted to all, clergy and laymen, and as far as pertains to us, fully pardoned. And moreover we have caused to be made for them testimonial letters-patent of lord Stephen, archbishop of Canterbury, lord Henry, archbishop of Dublin, and of the aforesaid bishops and of Master Pandulf, in respect to that security and the concessions named above.

63. Wherefore we will and firmly command that the Church of England shall be free, and that the men in our kingdom shall have and hold all the aforesaid liberties, rights and concessions, well and peacefully, freely and quietly, fully and completely, for themselves and their heirs, from us and our heirs, in all things and places, forever, as before said. It has been sworn, moreover, as well on our part as on the part of the barons, that all these things spoken of above shall be observed in good faith and without any evil intent. Witness the above named and many others. Given by our hand in the meadow which is called Runnymede, between Windsor and Staines, on the fifteenth day of June, in the seventeenth year of our reign.

REVIEW QUESTIONS

1. What liberties were most important to English nobles?
2. What rights did the church and the English people get from this charter?
3. What powers remained to the king?

EKKEHARD AND UTA, NAUMBERG CATHEDRAL STATUES (C. 1250)

The Naumberg Master, an unknown artist of the first rank, created a series of statues for the interior of Naumberg Cathedral in Germany. The noble couple Ekkehard and Uta, patrons of the church, were not sculpted from life, but they represent marvelous, idealized yet distinctive portraits of believable people. How do the characteristics of the noble class emerge from these statues?

FROM *Las Siete Partidas:* Castilian Law Code

Las Siete Partidas *is a great law code compiled for the kingdom of Castile early in the reign of Alfonso the Wise (1252–1284), a learned ruler interested in history, science, and the law. This selection concerns how the law regulated the Jews, who were a small minority of the population in Castile but much more numerous there than in most other parts of Christian Europe.*

From *Las Siete Partidas*, edited by Samuel Parsons Scott (1931).

*   *   *

Title XXIV
Concerning the Jews

Jews are a people who, although they do not believe in the religion of Our Lord Jesus Christ, yet, the great Christian sovereigns have always permitted them to live among them. Wherefore, since in the preceding Title we spoke of Diviners, and other men who allege that they know things that are to come, which is a kind of contempt of God, since they desire to make themselves equal to Him by learning his acts and his secrets; we intend to speak here of the Jews, who insult His name and deny the marvelous and holy acts which He performed when he sent His Son, Our Lord Jesus Christ, into the world to save sinners. We shall explain what the word Jew means; whence it derived this name; for what reasons the Church and the great Christian world permitted the Jews to live among them; in what way Jews should pass their lives among Christians; what things they should not use, or do, according to our religion; and what Jews those are who can be subjected to force on account of the wicked acts that they have performed, or the debt which they owe. Also why Jews who become Christians should not be subject to compulsion; what advantage a Jew, by becoming a Christian obtains over other Jews who do not; what penalty those deserve who cause him injury or dishonor; and to what punishment Christians, who become Jews, and also Jews who force their Moorish slaves to embrace their religion, are liable.

LAW I
WHAT THE WORD JEW MEANS, AND WHENCE THIS TERM IS DERIVED.

A party who believes in, and adheres to the law of Moses is called a Jew, according to the strict signification of the term, as well as one who is circumcised, and observes the other precepts commanded by his religion. This name is derived from the tribe of Judah which was nobler and more powerful than the others, and, also possessed another advantage, because the king of the Jews had to be selected from that tribe, and its members always received the first wounds in battle. The reason that the church, emperors, kings and princes, permitted the Jews to dwell among them and with Christians, is because they always lived, as it were, in captivity, as it was constantly in the minds of men that they were descended from those who crucified Our Lord Jesus Christ.

LAW II
IN WHAT WAY JEWS SHOULD PASS THEIR LIVES AMONG CHRISTIANS; WHAT THINGS THEY SHOULD NOT MAKE USE OF OR PRACTICE, ACCORDING TO OUR RELIGION; AND WHAT PENALTY THOSE DESERVE WHO ACT CONTRARY TO ITS ORDINANCES.

Jews should pass their lives among Christians quietly and without disorder, practicing their own religious rites, and not speaking ill of the faith of Our Lord Jesus Christ, which Christians acknowledge. Moreover, a Jew should be very careful to avoid preaching to, or converting any Christian, to the end that he may become a Jew, by exalting his own belief and disparaging ours. Whoever violates this law shall be put to death and lose all his property. And because we have heard it said that in some places Jews celebrated, and still celebrate Good Friday, which commemorates the Passion of Our Lord Jesus Christ, by way of contempt; stealing children and fastening them to crosses, and making images of wax and crucifying them, when they cannot obtain children; we order that, hereafter, if in any part of our dominions anything like this is done, and can be proved, all persons who were present when the act was committed shall be seized, arrested and brought before the king; and after the king ascertains that they are guilty, he shall cause them to be put to death in a disgraceful manner, no matter how many there may be.

We also forbid any Jew to dare to leave his house or his quarter on Good Friday, but they must all remain shut up until Saturday morning; and if they violate this regulation, we decree that they shall not be entitled to reparation for any injury or dishonor inflicted upon them by Christians.

LAW III
NO JEW CAN HOLD ANY OFFICE OR EMPLOYMENT BY WHICH HE MAY BE ABLE TO OPPRESS CHRISTIANS.

Jews were formerly highly honored, and enjoyed privileges above all other races, for they alone were called the People of God. But for the reason that they disowned Him who had honored them and given them privileges; and instead of showing Him reverence humiliated Him, by shamefully putting Him to death on the cross; it was proper and just that, on account of the great crime and wickedness which they committed, they should forfeit the honors and privileges which they enjoyed; and therefore from the day when they crucified Our Lord Jesus Christ they never had either king or priests among themselves, as they formerly did. The emperors, who in former times were lords of all the world, considered it fitting and right that, on account of the treason which they committed in killing their lord, they should lose all said honors and privileges, so that no Jew could ever afterwards hold an honorable position, or a public office by means of which he might, in any way, oppress a Christian.

LAW IV
HOW JEWS CAN HAVE A SYNAGOGUE AMONG CHRISTIANS.

A synagogue is a place where the Jews pray, and a new building of this kind cannot be erected in any part of our dominions, except by our order. Where, however, those which formerly existed there are torn down, they can be built in the same spot where they originally stood; but they cannot be made any larger or raised to any greater height, or be painted. A synagogue constructed in any other manner shall be lost by the Jews, and shall belong to the principal church of the locality where it is built. And for the reason that a synagogue is a place where the name of God is praised, we forbid any Christian to deface it, or remove anything from it, or take anything out of it by force; except where some malefactor takes refuge there; for they have a right to remove him by force in order to bring him before the judge. Moreover, we forbid Christians to put any animal into a synagogue, or loiter in it, or place any hindrance in the way of the Jews while they are there performing their devotions according to their religion.

LAW V
NO COMPULSION SHALL BE BROUGHT TO BEAR UPON THE JEWS ON SATURDAY, AND WHAT JEWS CAN BE SUBJECT TO COMPULSION.

Saturday is the day on which Jews perform their devotions, and remain quiet in their lodgings, and do not make contracts or transact any business; and for the reason that they are obliged by their religion, to keep it, no one should on that day summon them or bring them into court. Wherefore we order that no judge shall employ force or any constraint upon Jews on Saturday, in order to bring them into court on account of their debts; or arrest them; or cause them any other annoyance; for the remaining days of the week are sufficient for the purpose of employing compulsion against them, and for making demands for things which can be demanded of them, according to law. Jews are not bound to obey a summons served upon them on that day; and, moreover, we decree that any decision rendered against them on Saturday shall not be valid; but if a Jew should wound, kill, rob, steal, or commit any other offense like these for which he can be punished in person and property, then the judge can arrest him on Saturday.

We also decree that all claims that Christians have against Jews, and Jews against Christians, shall be decided and determined by our judges in the district where they reside, and not by their old men. And as we forbid Christians to bring Jews into court or annoy them on Saturday; so we also decree that Jews, neither in person, nor by their attorneys, shall have the right to bring Christians into court, or annoy them on this day. And in addition to this, we forbid any Christian, on his own responsibility, to arrest or wrong any Jew either in his person or property, but where he has any complaint against him he must bring it before our judges; and if anyone should be so bold as to use violence against the Jews, or rob them of anything, he shall return them double the value of the same.

LAW VI
JEWS WHO BECOME CHRISTIANS SHALL NOT BE SUBJECT TO COMPULSION; WHAT ADVANTAGE A JEW HAS WHO BECOMES A CHRISTIAN; AND WHAT PENALTY OTHER JEWS DESERVE WHO DO HIM HARM.

No force or compulsion shall be employed in any way against a Jew to induce him to become a Christian; but Christians should convert him to the faith of Our Lord Jesus Christ by means of the texts of the Holy Scriptures, and by kind words, for no one can love or appreciate a service which is done him by compulsion. We also decree that if any Jew or Jewess should voluntarily desire to become a Christian, the other Jews shall not interfere with this in any way, and if they stone, wound, or kill any such person, because they wish to become Christians, or after they have been baptized, and this can be proved; we order that all the murderers, or the abettors of said murder or attack, shall be burned. But where the party was not killed, but wounded, or dishonored; we order that the judges of the neighborhood where this took place shall compel those guilty of the attack, or who caused the dishonor, to make amends to him for the same; and also that they be punished for the offence which they committed, as they think they deserve; and we also order that, after any Jews become Christians, all persons in our dominions shall honor them; and that no one shall dare to reproach them or their descendants, by way of insult, with having been Jews; and that they shall possess all their property, sharing the same with their brothers, and inheriting it from their fathers and mothers and other relatives, just as if they were Jews; and that they can hold all offices and dignities which other Christians can do.

LAW VII
WHAT PENALTY A CHRISTIAN DESERVES WHO BECOMES A JEW.

Where a Christian is so unfortunate as to become a Jew, we order that he shall be put to death just as if he had become a heretic; and we decree that his property shall be disposed of in the same way that we stated should be done with that of heretics.

LAW VIII
NO CHRISTIAN, MAN OR WOMAN SHALL LIVE WITH A JEW.

We forbid any Jew to keep Christian men or women in his house, to be served by them; although he may have them to cultivate and take care of his lands, or protect him on the way when he is compelled to go to some dangerous place. Moreover, we forbid any Christian man or woman to invite a Jew or a Jewess, or to accept an invitation from them, to eat or drink together, or to drink any wine made by their hands. We also order that no Jews shall dare to bathe in company with Christians, and that no Christian shall take any medicine or cathartic made by a Jew; but he can take it by the advice of some intelligent person, only where it is made by a Christian, who knows and is familiar with its ingredients.

LAW IX
WHAT PENALTY A JEW DESERVES WHO HAS INTERCOURSE WITH A CHRISTIAN WOMAN.

Jews who live with Christian women are guilty of great insolence and boldness, for which reason we decree that all Jews who, hereafter, may be convicted of having done such a thing shall be put to death. For if Christians who commit adultery with married women deserve death on that account, much more do Jews who have sexual intercourse with Christian women, who are spiritually the wives of Our Lord Jesus Christ because of the faith and the baptism which they receive in His name; nor do we consider it proper that a Christian woman who commits an offense of this kind shall escape without punishment. Wherefore we order that, whether she be a virgin, a married woman, a widow, or a common prostitute who gives herself to all men, she shall suffer the same penalty which we mentioned in the last law in the Title concerning the Moors, to which a Christian woman is liable who has carnal intercourse with a Moor.

LAW X
WHAT PENALTY JEWS DESERVE WHO HOLD CHRISTIANS AS SLAVES.

A Jew shall not purchase, or keep as a slave a Christian man or woman, and if anyone violates this law the Christian shall be restored to freedom and shall not pay any portion of the price given for him, although the Jew may not have been aware when he bought him, that he was a Christian; but if he knew that he was such when he purchased him, and makes use of him afterwards as a slave, he shall be put to death for doing so. Moreover, we forbid any Jew to convert a captive to his religion, even though said captive may be a Moor, or belong to some other barbarous race. If anyone violates this law we order that the said slave who has become a Jew shall be set at liberty, and removed from the control of the party to whom he or she belonged. If any Moors who are the captives of Jews become Christians, they shall at once be freed, as is explained in the Fourth Partida of this book, in the Title concerning Liberty, in the laws which treat of this subject.

LAW XI
JEWS SHALL BEAR CERTAIN MARKS IN ORDER THAT THEY MAY BE KNOWN.

Many crimes and outrageous things occur between Christians and Jews because they live together in cities, and dress alike; and in order to avoid the offenses and evils which take place for this reason, we deem it proper, and we order that all Jews male and female living in our dominions shall bear some distinguishing mark upon their heads so that people may plainly recognize a Jew, or a Jewess; and any Jew who does not bear such a mark, shall pay for each time he is found without it ten maravedis of gold; and if he has not the means to do this he shall publicly receive ten lashes for his offence.

REVIEW QUESTIONS

1. In *Las Siete Partidas,* what aspects of Jewish life were Christians most eager to control?
2. What does it tell us about Christian-Jewish interactions?
3. In what ways does it both protect and oppress Jews?

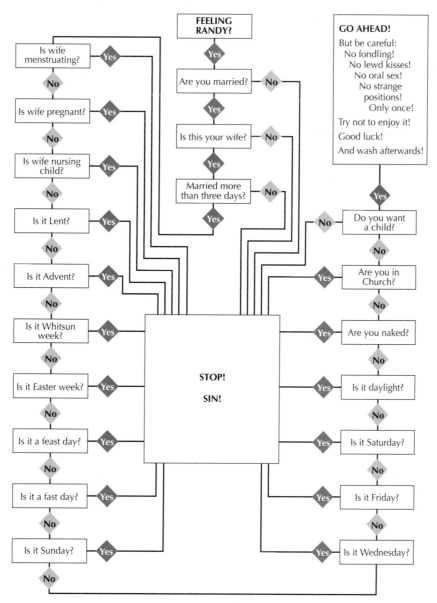

THE MEDIEVAL SEXUAL DECISION-MAKING PROCESS (C. 1275)

Medieval penitentials were manuals that described penances for transgressions against the teachings of the church. Canon law, the rules of the Catholic Church across Christendom, contained an increasingly elaborate set of laws regulating sexual conduct. The following chart is a decision tree that a modern historian has constructed to show the kinds of questions a believer was supposed to ask himself or herself before engaging in sexual relations. What attitudes toward human sexuality emerge from this decision tree? What is the purpose of sex? What is the most positive interpretation that can be placed on the chart? Whom does it protect? Is the chart taking a too cynical approach to this important moral matter?

10 ❧ THE HIGH MIDDLE AGES: RELIGIOUS AND INTELLECTUAL DEVELOPMENTS, 1000–1300

As the economic and social vitality of the High Middle Ages strengthened the institutions of church, monarchy, and city governments, medieval people faced the problem of determining the right relationship between these different centers of power. The processes of crusade, mission, and colonization expanded the frontiers of Western Christendom and brought Europeans into conflicts with their neighbors. In the early eleventh century the papacy was a weak institution and no universities existed in Europe. By 1300 the pope in Rome had become the center of a huge ecclesiastical bureaucracy, and new religious orders like the Franciscans and Dominicans and an intricate system of canon law buttressed the church's authority. The university, perhaps the most distinctive and certainly the most durable legacy of the Middle Ages, supplied the church with an educated clergy trained in the new disciplines of theology and canon law. Medicine and civil law also benefited from the birth of higher education. Faith and logic and civil and canon law occupied university professors and their students, while across Europe millions of women and men looked to their local churches and traditions for answers on how they should live.

The movement for reforming the church in the eleventh century, instigated by monastic spirituality and a few dutiful German emperors, raised the issues of clerical celibacy, simony, and the proper relations between the church and the secular world of warriors and kings. Pope Gregory VII, a leader of the reform movement, began the investiture controversy with the emperor Henry IV. This dispute concerned the appointment of church officials and their investiture with the symbols of office, and the limits of their duties to secular lords. A series of powerful popes like Urban II, Innocent III, and Gregory IX increased the church's authority by successfully claiming that the church should not be subordinate to any earthly power. The church's jurisdiction over sin gave the clergy wide authority over many familial, moral, and even economic activities. Pope Boniface VIII's papacy (1294–1303) represents the most extreme claim of papal supremacy in the world. One of the papacy's best tools for uniting Western Christendom behind its teachings was the crusades, a series of holy wars the popes proclaimed and attempted to direct against Muslims and others. Eventually, the church used the crusades as a way to fight heretics and even the political opponents of the church.

As Europeans fought against Muslims in Spain, North Africa, and the Middle East, some church leaders and kings also tried to foster the conversion of non-Christians and to find allies against the Muslims. (The journeys of the Venetian Polo family to China later in the century were motivated by a desire for profits from the eastern trade.) The church also accepted new styles of religious life that some charismatic teachers offered. St. Francis is the best-known founder of a new order, but other spiritual leaders like St. Clare and St. Dominic attracted followers. The older Benedictine monasteries and convents remained centers of learning and reform. St. Elizabeth of Hungary's life embodied many of the new styles of thirteenth-century piety.

At the local level creative minds were also finding new answers to old questions about faith, health, and miracles. What was happening at the universities often seemed remote from the daily lives of peasants. St. Thomas Aquinas, the most-accomplished theologian of the thirteenth century, applied the recently revived tools of Aristotelian logic to the same basic concerns in order to harmonize faith and reason, the goal of scholasticism. Many artistic developments accompanied all this religious and intellectual fervor, and the great cathedrals and churches rising across Europe are testimony to the society's prosperity and values. In literature the transition from epic to romance reflects changing noble tastes; the new courtly literature reflects both the older heroic tastes and some of the new refinements and complex attitudes toward women.

GREGORY VII

"To Herman of Metz, in Defense of the Papal Policy toward Henry IV"

Pope Gregory VII (1073–1085) wrote this letter to Herman of Metz to justify his decision to excommunicate Emperor Henry IV of Germany and to explain his views on the role of the church in the world. The pope's dispute with Henry IV concerned the emperor's claim to appoint bishops and abbots. The pope considered these ap-

pointments to be in the church's jurisdiction, and other reformers were also troubled by churchmen who became vassals of a secular lord. Homage and fealty for fiefs gave the appearance that the secular power was superior to the spiritual. This letter is a concise statement of the reform movement's position.

From *The Correspondence of Pope Gregory VII,* edited by Ephriam Emerton (New York: Columbia University Press, 1969), pp. 166–75.

Gregory . . . to his beloved brother in Christ, Hermann, bishop of Metz, greeting . . .

We know you to be ever ready to bear labor and peril in defense of the truth, and doubt not that this is a gift from God. It is a part of his unspeakable grace and his marvelous mercy that he never permits his chosen ones to wander far or to be completely cast down; but rather, after a time of persecution and wholesome probation, makes them stronger than they were before. On the other hand, just as among cowards one who is worse than the rest is broken down by fear, so among the brave one who acts more bravely than the rest is stirred thereby to new activity. We remind you of this by way of exhortation that you may stand more joyfully in the front ranks of the Christian host, the more confident you are that they are the nearest to God the conqueror.

You ask us to fortify you against the madness of those who babble with accursed tongues about the authority of the Holy Apostolic See not being able to excommunicate King Henry as one who despises the law of Christ, a destroyer of churches and of the empire, a promoter and partner of heresies, nor to release anyone from his oath of fidelity to him; but it has not seemed necessary to reply to this request, seeing that so many and such convincing proofs are to be found in Holy Scripture. Nor do we believe that those who abuse and contradict the truth to their utter damnation do this as much from ignorance as from wretched and desperate folly. And no wonder! It is ever the way of the wicked to protect their own iniquities by calling upon others like themselves; for they think it of no account to incur the penalty of falsehood.

To cite but a few out of the multitude of proofs: Who does not remember the words of our Lord and Savior Jesus Christ: "Thou art Peter and on this rock I will build my Church, and the gates of hell shall not prevail against it. And I will give thee the keys of the kingdom of heaven and whatsoever thou shalt bind on earth shall be bound in heaven and whatsoever thou shalt loose on earth shall be loosed in heaven." Are kings excepted here? Or are they not of the sheep which the Son of God committed to St. Peter? Who, I ask, thinks himself excluded from this universal grant of the power of binding and loosing to St. Peter unless, perchance, that unhappy man who, being unwilling to bear the yoke of the Lord, subjects himself to the burden of the Devil and refuses to be numbered in the flock of Christ? His wretched liberty shall profit him nothing; for if he shakes off from his proud neck the power divinely granted to Peter, so much the heavier shall it be for him in the day of judgment.

This institution of the divine will, this foundation of the rule of the Church, this privilege granted and sealed especially by a heavenly decree to St. Peter, chief of the Apostles, has been accepted and maintained with great reverence by the holy fathers, and they have given to the Holy Roman Church, as well in general councils as in their other acts and writings, the name of "universal mother." They have not only accepted her expositions of doctrine and her instructions in our holy religion, but they have also recognized her judicial decisions. They have agreed as with one spirit and one voice that all major cases, all especially important affairs and the judgments of all churches ought to be referred to her as to their head and mother, that from her there shall be no appeal, that her judgments may not and cannot be reviewed or reversed by anyone.

Thus Pope Gelasius, writing to the emperor Anastasius, gave him these instructions as to the right theory of the principate of the Holy and Apostolic See, based upon divine authority:

Although it is fitting that all the faithful should submit themselves to all priests who perform their sacred functions properly, how much the more should they accept the judgment of that prelate who has been appointed by the supreme divine ruler to be superior to all priests and whom the loyalty of the whole later Church has recognized as such. Your Wisdom sees plainly that no human capacity whatsoever can equal that of him whom the word of Christ raised above all others and whom the reverend Church has always confessed and still devotedly holds as its Head.

So also Pope Julius, writing to the eastern bishops in regard to the powers of the same Holy and Apostolic See, says:

You ought, my brethren, to have spoken carefully and not ironically of the Holy Roman and Apostolic Church, seeing that our Lord Jesus Christ addressed her respectfully, saying, "Thou art Peter and upon this rock I will build my church, and the gates of hell shall not prevail against it; and I will give thee the keys of the kingdom of heaven." For it has the power, granted by a unique privilege, of opening and shutting the gates of the celestial kingdom to whom it will.

To whom, then, the power of opening and closing Heaven is given, shall he not be able to judge the earth? God forbid! Do you remember what the most blessed Apostle Paul says: "Know ye not that we shall judge angels? How much more things that pertain to this life?"

So Pope Gregory declared that kings who dared to disobey the orders of the Apostolic See should forfeit their office. He wrote to a certain senator and abbot in these words:

If any king, priest, judge or secular person shall disregard this decree of ours and act contrary to it, he shall be deprived of his power and his office and shall learn that he stands condemned at the bar of God for the wrong that he has done. And unless he shall restore what he has wrongfully taken and shall have done fitting penance for his unlawful acts he shall be excluded from the sacred body and blood of our Lord and Savior Jesus Christ and at the last judgment shall receive condign punishment.

Now then, if the blessed Gregory, most gentle of doctors, decreed that kings who should disobey his orders about a hospital for strangers should be not only deposed but excommunicated and condemned in the last judgment, how can anyone blame us for deposing and excommunicating Henry, who not only disregards apostolic judgments, but so far as in him lies tramples upon his mother the Church, basely plunders the whole kingdom and destroys its churches—unless indeed it were one who is a man of his own kind?

As we know also through the teaching of St. Peter in his letter touching the ordination of Clement, where he says: "If any one were friend to those with whom he is not on speaking terms, that man is among those who would like to destroy the Church of God and, while he seems to be with us in the body, he is against us in mind and heart, and he is a far worse enemy than those who are without and are openly hostile. For he, under the forms of friendship, acts as an enemy and scatters and lays waste the Church." Consider then, my best beloved, if he passes so severe a judgment upon him who associates himself with those whom the pope opposes on account of their actions, with what severity he condemns the man himself to whom the pope is thus opposed.

But now, to return to our point: Is not a sovereignty invented by men of this world who were ignorant of God subject to that which the providence of Almighty God established for his own glory and graciously bestowed upon the world? The Son of God we believe to be God and man, sitting at the right hand of the Father as High

Priest, head of all priests and ever making intercession for us. He despised the kingdom of this world wherein the sons of this world puff themselves up and offered himself as a sacrifice upon the cross.

Who does not know that kings and princes derive their origin from men ignorant of God who raised themselves above their fellows by pride, plunder, treachery, murder—in short, by every kind of crime—at the instigation of the Devil, the prince of this world, men blind with greed and intolerable in their audacity? If, then, they strive to bend the priests of God to their will, to whom may they more properly be compared than to him who is chief over all the sons of pride? For he, tempting our High Priest, head of all priests, son of the Most High, offering him all the kingdoms of this world, said: "All these will I give thee if thou wilt fall down and worship me."

Does anyone doubt that the priests of Christ are to be considered as fathers and masters of kings and princes and of all believers? Would it not be regarded as pitiable madness if a son should try to rule his father or a pupil his master and to bind with unjust obligations the one through whom he expects to be bound or loosed, not only on earth but also in heaven? Evidently recognizing this the emperor Constantine the Great, lord over all kings and princes throughout almost the entire earth, as St. Gregory relates in his letter to the emperor Mauritius, at the holy synod of Nicaea took his place below all the bishops and did not venture to pass any judgment upon them but, even addressing them as gods, felt that they ought not to be subject to his judgment but that he ought to be bound by their decisions.

Pope Gelasius, urging upon the emperor Anastasius not to feel himself wronged by the truth that was called to his attention said: "There are two powers, O august Emperor, by which the world is governed, the sacred authority of the priesthood and the power of kings. Of these the priestly is by so much the greater as they will have to answer for kings themselves in the day of divine judgment;" and a little further: "Know that you are subject to their judgment, not that they are to be subjected to your will."

In reliance upon such declarations and such authorities, many prelates have excommunicated kings or emperors. If you ask for illustrations: Pope Innocent excommunicated the emperor Arcadius because he consented to the expulsion of St. John Chrysostom from his office. Another Roman pontiff deposed a king of the Franks, not so much on account of his evil deeds as because he was not equal to so great an office, and set in his place Pippin, father of the emperor Charles the Great, releasing all the Franks from the oath of fealty which they had sworn to him. And this is often done by Holy Church when it absolves fighting men from their oaths to bishops who have been deposed by apostolic authority. So St. Ambrose, a holy man but not bishop of the whole Church, excommunicated the emperor Theodosius the Great for a fault which did not seem to other prelates so very grave and excluded him from the Church. He also shows in his writings that the priestly office is as much superior to royal power as gold is more precious than lead. He says: "The honor and dignity of bishops admit of no comparison. If you liken them to the splendor of kings and the diadem of princes, these are as lead compared to the glitter of gold. You see the necks of kings and princes bowed to the knees of priests, and by the kissing of hands they believe that they share the benefit of their prayers." And again: "Know that we have said all this in order to show that there is nothing in this world more excellent than a priest or more lofty than a bishop."

Your Fraternity should remember also that greater power is granted to an exorcist when he is made a spiritual emperor for the casting out of devils, than can be conferred upon any layman for the purpose of earthly dominion. All kings and princes of this earth who live not piously and in their deeds show not a becoming fear of God are ruled by demons and are sunk in miserable slavery. Such men desire to rule, not guided by the love of God, as priests are, for the glory of God and the profit of human souls, but to display their intolerable pride and to satisfy the lusts of their mind. Of these St. Augustine says in the first book of his Christian doctrine: "He who tries to rule over men—who are by nature equal to him—acts with intolerable pride." Now if exorcists have power over demons, as we have said, how much more over those who are subject to demons and are limbs of demons! And if exorcists are superior to these, how much more are priests superior to them!

Furthermore, every Christian king when he approaches his end asks the aid of a priest as a miserable suppliant that he may escape the prison of hell, may pass from darkness into light and may appear at the judgment seat of God freed from the bonds of sin. But who, layman or priest, in his last moments has ever asked the help of any earthly king for the safety of his soul? And what king or emperor has power through his office to snatch any Christian from the might of the Devil by the sacred rite of baptism, to confirm him among the sons of God and to fortify him by the holy chrism? Or—and this is the greatest thing in the Christian religion—who among them is able by his own word to create the body and blood of the Lord? or to whom among them is given the power to bind and loose in Heaven and upon earth? From this it is apparent how greatly superior in power is the priestly dignity.

Or who of them is able to ordain any clergyman in the Holy Church—much less to depose him for any fault? For bishops, while they may ordain other bishops, may in no wise depose them except by authority of the Apostolic See. How, then, can even the most slightly informed person doubt that priests are higher than kings? But if kings are to be judged by priests for their sins, by whom can they more properly be judged than by the Roman pontiff?

In short, all good Christians, whosoever they may be, are more properly to be called kings than are evil princes; for the former, seeking the glory of God, rule themselves rigorously; but the latter, seeking their own rather than the things that are of God, being enemies to themselves, oppress oth-

ers tyrannically. The former are the body of the true Christ; the latter, the body of the Devil. The former rule themselves that they may reign forever with the supreme ruler. The power of the latter brings it to pass that they perish in eternal damnation with the prince of darkness who is king over all the sons of pride.

It is no great wonder that evil priests take the part of a king whom they love and fear on account of honors received from him. By ordaining any person whomsoever, they are selling their God at a bargain price. For as the elect are inseparably united to their Head, so the wicked are firmly bound to him who is head of all evil—especially against the good. But against these it is of no use to argue, but rather to pray God with tears and groans that he may deliver them from the snares of Satan, in which they are caught, and after trial may lead them at last into knowledge of the truth.

So much for kings and emperors who, swollen with the pride of this world, rule not for God but for themselves. But since it is our duty to exhort everyone according to his station, it is our care with God's help to furnish emperors, kings and other princes with the weapons of humility that thus they may be strong to keep down the floods and waves of pride. We know that earthly glory and the cares of this world are wont especially to cause rulers to be exalted, to forget humility and, seeking their own glory, strive to excel their fellows. It seems therefore especially useful for emperors and kings, while their hearts are lifted up in the strife for glory, to learn how to humble themselves and to know fear rather than joy. Let them therefore consider carefully how dangerous, even awesome is the office of emperor or king, how very few find salvation therein, and how those who are saved through God's mercy have become far less famous in the Church by divine judgment than many humble persons. From the beginning of the world to the present day we do not find in all authentic records emperors or kings whose lives were as distinguished for virtue and piety as were those of a countless multitude of men who despised the world—although we believe that many of them were saved by the mercy of God. Not to speak of Apostles and Martyrs, who among emperors and kings was famed for his miracles as were St. Martin, St. Antony and St. Benedict? What emperor or king ever raised the dead, cleansed lepers or opened the eyes of the blind? True, Holy Church praises and honors the emperor Constantine, of pious memory, Theodosius and Honorius, Charles and Louis, as lovers of justice, champions of the Christian faith and protectors of churches, but she does not claim that they were illustrious for the splendor of their wonderful works. Or to how many names of kings or emperors has Holy Church ordered churches or altars to be dedicated or masses to be celebrated?

Let kings and princes fear lest the higher they are raised above their fellows in this life, the deeper they may be plunged in everlasting fire. Wherefore it is written: "The mighty shall suffer mighty torments." They shall render unto God an account for all men subject to their rule. But if it is no small labor for the pious individual to guard his own soul, what a task is laid upon princes in the care of so many thousands of souls! And if Holy Church imposes a heavy penalty upon him who takes a single human life, what shall be done to those who send many thousands to death for the glory of this world? These, although they say with their lips, *mea culpa,* for the slaughter of many, yet in their hearts they rejoice at the increase of their glory and neither repent of what they have done nor regret that they have sent their brothers into the world below. So that, since they do not repent with all their hearts and will not restore what they have gained by human bloodshed, their penitence before God remains without the fruits of a true repentance.

Wherefore they ought greatly to fear, and they should frequently be reminded that, as we have said, since the beginning of the world and throughout the kingdoms of the earth very few kings of saintly life can be found out of an innumerable multitude, whereas in one single chair of successive bishops—the Roman—from the time of the blessed Apostle Peter nearly a hundred are counted among the holiest of men. How can

this be, except because the kings and princes of the earth, seduced by empty glory, prefer their own interests to the things of the Spirit, whereas pious pontiffs, despising vainglory, set the things of God above the things of the flesh. The former readily punish offenses against themselves but are not troubled by offenses against God; the latter quickly forgive those who sin against them but do not easily pardon offenders against God. The former, far too much given to worldly affairs, think little of spiritual things; the latter, dwelling eagerly upon heavenly subjects, despise the things of this world.

All Christians, therefore, who desire to reign with Christ are to be warned not to reign through ambition for worldly power. They are to keep in mind the admonition of that most holy pope Gregory in his book on the pastoral office: "Of all these things what is to be followed, what held fast, except that the man strong in virtue shall come to his office under compulsion? Let him who is without virtue not come to it even though he be urged thereto." If, then, men who fear God come under compulsion with fear and trembling to the Apostolic See where those who are properly ordained become stronger through the merits of the blessed Apostle Peter, with what awe and hesitation should men ascend the throne of a king where even good and humble men like Saul and David become worse! What we have said above is thus stated in the decrees of the blessed pope Symmachus—though we have learned it by experience: "He, that is St. Peter, transmitted to his successors an unfailing endowment of merit together with an inheritance of innocence;" and again: "For who can doubt that he is holy who is raised to the height of such an office, in which if he is lacking in virtue acquired by his own merits, that which is handed down from his predecessor is sufficient. For either he raises men of distinction to bear this burden or he glorifies them after they are raised up."

Wherefore let those whom Holy Church, of its own will and with deliberate judgment, not for fleeting glory but for the welfare of multitudes, has called to royal or imperial rule—let them be obedient and ever mindful of the blessed Gregory's declaration in that same pastoral treatise: "When a man disdains to be the equal of his fellow men, he becomes like an apostate angel. Thus Saul, after his period of humility, swollen with pride, ran into excess of power. He was raised in humility, but rejected in his pride, as God bore witness, saying: 'Though thou wast little in thine own sight, wast thou not made the head of the tribes of Israel?' " and again: "I marvel how, when he was little to himself he was great before God, but when he seemed great to himself he was little before God." Let them watch and remember what God says in the Gospel: "I seek not my own glory," and, "He who would be first among you, let him be the servant of all." Let them ever place the honor of God above their own; let them embrace justice and maintain it by preserving to everyone his right; let them not enter into the counsels of the ungodly, but cling to those of religion with all their hearts. Let them not seek to make Holy Church their maid-servant or their subject, but recognizing priests, the eyes of God, as their masters and fathers, strive to do them becoming honor.

If we are commanded to honor our fathers and mothers in the flesh, how much more our spiritual parents! If he that curseth his father or his mother shall be put to death, what does he deserve who curses his spiritual father or mother? Let not princes, led astray by carnal affection, set their own sons over that flock for whom Christ shed his blood if a better and more suitable man can be found. By thus loving their own son more than God they bring the greatest evils upon the Church. For it is evident that he who fails to provide to the best of his ability so great and necessary an advantage for our holy mother, the Church, does not love God and his neighbor as befits a Christian man. If this one virtue of charity be wanting, then whatever of good the man may do will lack all saving grace.

But if they do these things in humility, keeping their love for God and their neighbor as they ought, they may count upon the mercy of him who said: "Learn of me, for I am meek and lowly of heart." If they humbly imitate him, they shall pass from their servile and transient reign into the kingdom of eternal liberty.

*   *   *

REVIEW QUESTIONS

1. What does Pope Gregory VII think is the right relationship between the church and secular authority?
2. How effectively does he use evidence to support his case?
3. How might a supporter of Henry IV answer the pope's arguments?

POPE BONIFACE VIII

Papal Bull *Unam Sanctam*

Pope Boniface VIII (1294–1303) quarreled with Philip IV of France about papal authority over the French church and the crown's power to tax the church. In this papal bull, November 1302, the pope reformulated the church's view on the sources and extent of its authority. Ultimately, the king of France accused the pope of her-

*esy and sent officials to arrest Boniface, who narrowly escaped, with his health and
prestige severely damaged.*

From *The Crisis of Church and State 1050–1300*, edited by Brian Tierney (Upper Saddle
River, N.J.: Prentice-Hall, 1964), pp. 188–89.

That there is one holy, Catholic and apostolic church we are bound to believe and to hold, our faith urging us, and this we do firmly believe and simply confess; and that outside this church there is no salvation or remission of sins, as her spouse proclaims in the Canticles, "One is my dove, my perfect one. She is the only one of her mother, the chosen of her that bore her"; which represents one mystical body whose head is Christ, while the head of Christ is God. In this church there is one Lord, one faith, one baptism. At the time of the Flood there was one ark, symbolizing the one church. It was finished in one cubit and had one helmsman and captain, namely Noah, and we read that all things on earth outside of it were destroyed. This church we venerate and this alone, the Lord saying through his prophet, "Deliver, O God, my soul from the sword, my only one from the power of the dog." He prayed for the soul, that is himself, the head, and at the same time for the body, which he called the one church on account of the promised unity of faith, sacraments and charity of the church. This is that seamless garment of the Lord which was not cut but fell by lot. Therefore there is one body and one head of this one and only church, not two heads as though it were a monster, namely Christ and Christ's vicar, Peter and Peter's successor, for the Lord said to this Peter, "Feed my sheep." He said "My sheep" in general, not these or those, whence he is understood to have committed them all to Peter. Hence, if the Greeks or any others say that they were not committed to Peter and his successors, they necessarily admit that they are not of Christ's flock, for the Lord says in John that there is one sheepfold and one shepherd.

We are taught by the words of the Gospel that in this church and in her power there are two swords, a spiritual one and a temporal one. For when the apostles said "Here are two swords," meaning in the church since it was the apostles who spoke, the Lord did not reply that it was too many but enough. Certainly anyone who denies that the temporal sword is in the power of Peter has not paid heed to the words of the Lord when he said, "Put up thy sword into its sheath." Both then are in the power of the church, the material sword and the spiritual. But the one is exercised for the church, the other by the church, the one by the hand of the priest, the other by the hand of kings and soldiers, though at the will and suffrance of the priest. One sword ought to be under the other and the temporal authority subject to the spiritual power. For, while the apostle says, "There is no power but from God and those that are ordained of God," they would not be ordained unless one sword was under the other and, being inferior, was led by the other to the highest things. For, according to the blessed Dionysius, it is the law of divinity for the lowest to be led to the highest through intermediaries. In the order of the universe all things are not kept in order in the same fashion and immediately but the lowest are ordered by the intermediate and inferiors by superiors. But that the spiritual power excels any earthly one in dignity and nobility we ought the more openly to confess in proportion as spiritual things excel temporal ones. Moreover we clearly perceive this from the giving of tithes, from benediction and sanctification, from the acceptance of this power and from the very government of things. For, the truth bearing witness, the spiritual power has to institute the earthly power and to judge it if it has not been good. So is verified the prophecy of Jeremias concerning the church and the power of the church, "Lo, I have set thee this day over the nations and over kingdoms" etc.

Therefore, if the earthly power errs, it shall be judged by the spiritual power, if a lesser spiritual power errs it shall be judged by its superior, but if the supreme spiritual power errs it can be judged only by God not by man, as the apostle witnesses, "The spiritual man judgeth all things and he himself is judged of no man." Although this authority was given to a man and is exercised by a man it is not human but rather divine, being given to Peter at God's mouth, and confirmed to him and to his successors in him, the rock whom the Lord acknowledged when he said to Peter himself "Whatsoever thou shalt bind" etc. Whoever therefore resists this power so ordained by God resists the ordinance of God unless, like the Manicheans, he imagines that there are two beginnings, which we judge to be false and heretical, as Moses witnesses, for not "in the beginnings" but "in the beginning" God created heaven and earth. Therefore we declare, state, define and pronounce that it is altogether necessary to salvation for every human creature to be subject to the Roman Pontiff.

REVIEW QUESTIONS

1. What does Pope Boniface VII see as the right relation between the church and secular power?
2. How do his arguments and evidence differ from those of his predecessor Gregory VII?
3. What, in practice, did the last sentence of this bull mean?

OTTO OF FREISING

FROM *The Deeds of Frederick Barbarossa*

The Deeds of Frederick Barbarossa *is a history by a German bishop, Otto of Freising, and concerns the origins of the Second Crusade. Pope Eugenius III (1145–1153) summoned this Crusade in response to Turkish victories over the Latin states established in the East after the victorious First Crusade and the conquest of Jerusalem (1099). The Crusades to the Holy Land, as well as the wars against the Muslims in the Iberian Peninsula, were holy wars that benefited the souls of the participants, whose motives were often mixed.*

From *The Deeds of Frederick of Barbarossa*, by Otto of Freising, translated by Charles Mierow (New York: Columbia University Press, 1953), pp. 70–73.

*   *   *

While Eugenius was pope in Rome, Conrad reigning there and Louis in France, Manuel being emperor in the royal city, and Fulk ruling at Jerusalem, Louis was impelled by a secret desire to go to Jerusalem because his brother Philip had bound himself by the same vow but had been prevented by death. He was unwilling further to postpone this resolve; he therefore summoned certain of his princes and revealed what he was turning over in his mind.

There was at that time in France a certain abbot of the monastery of Clairvaux named Bernard, venerable in life and character, conspicuous in his religious order, endowed with wisdom and a

SALISBURY CATHEDRAL (1258, SPIRE 1330)

Salisbury Cathedral is a classic example of English Gothic architecture. What are the characteristic features of Gothic architecture? What possible connections are there between these features and the messages the medieval church tried to communicate to the laity?

knowledge of letters, renowned for signs and wonders. The princes decided to have him summoned and to ask of him, as of a divine oracle, what ought to be done with reference to this matter. The aforesaid abbot was called and his advice requested regarding the wish of the prince I have mentioned. As he judged it unbecoming to give answer concerning so weighty a matter on the sole basis of his own opinion, he replied that it was best to refer the question to the hearing and the consideration of the Roman pontiff. Therefore an embassy was sent to Eugenius, and the whole matter was set before him. And he, pondering upon the example set by his predecessor—namely, the fact that Urban, upon an occasion of this sort, had won back into the unity of peace the Church across the water and two patriarchal sees (of Antioch and Jerusalem) that had cut themselves off from obedience to the Roman see—gave his assent to the wishes of the aforesaid king for extending the observance of the Christian faith. He granted to the abbot previously named, who was looked upon by all the peoples of France and Germany as a prophet and apostle, the authority to preach and to move the hearts of all thereto. Whence there is extant his letter directed to the king and his princes, as follows:

"Bishop Eugenius, the servant of the servants of God, to his very dear son in Christ, Louis, the illustrious and glorious king of the Franks, and to his beloved sons, the princes, and to all God's faithful people that dwell throughout France, greeting and apostolic benediction.

"How greatly our predecessors, the Roman popes, have labored for the liberation of the Eastern Church we have learned from the recital of men of old and have found written in their histories. For our predecessor of blessed memory, Pope Urban, sent forth a voice like a heavenly trumpet and undertook to summon sons of the Holy Roman Church from the ends of the earth to deliberate about this. At his call those beyond the mountains, and in particular the most valiant and vigorous warriors of the kingdom of the Franks, and those also from Italy that were on fire with the flame of love, flocked together and— when a very great host had assembled—not without great shedding of their own blood, and accompanied by divine aid, freed from the defilement of the heathen that city in which our Savior willed to suffer for us and left behind for us as a memorial of his passion his glorious sepulcher—and how many other cities that, to avoid prolixity, we forbear to mention. These, by the grace of God and the zeal of your fathers, who in the intervening years have striven mightily to defend them and to spread abroad the name of Christ in those parts, have been held by the Christians down to our own times; and other cities of the infidels have been courageously stormed by them. But now, because of our own sins and those of the people, the city of Edessa—which we cannot mention without great grief and lamentation—the city of Edessa, called in our tongue *Rohais,* and which, it is said, alone served the Lord under the sway of the Christians when formerly all the land in the Orient was held by pagans, has been taken by the enemies of the cross of Christ, and many strongholds of the Christians have been seized by them. The archbishop of that city, with his clergy and many other Christians, has been slain there, and the relics of the saints have been given over to infidels to be trampled upon and scattered.

"How great a peril thereby threatens the Church of God and all Christendom we ourselves realize and, we believe, is not hid from Your Prudence. For it is evident that it will be the greatest proof of nobility and integrity if that which the might of the fathers won is mightily defended by you, their sons. But should it be otherwise—which God forbid—the valor of the fathers is shown to be diminished in their sons.

"Therefore we warn, we beseech, and we command every one of you and enjoin it for the forgiveness of your sins, that they that are God's, and in particular the more mighty and the noble, gird themselves manfully and strive thus to oppose the multitude of the infidels which is rejoicing at having secured a period of victory over us, and so to defend the Eastern Church, freed as we have said from their tyranny by the shedding of so much blood of your fathers, and to rescue out of their hands the many thousands of captives, our brothers, that the honor of the Christian name may be increased in your time and that your valor, which is praised throughout the entire world, may be kept whole and unimpaired.

"Let that good man Mattathias serve as an example for you, who hesitated not at all to expose himself, with his sons and his parents, to death in order to preserve the laws of his fathers, and to relinquish all that he possessed in the world; and at last by the assistance of divine aid, though only after many labors, both he and his descendants triumphed manfully over their enemies.

"But we, making provision with a father's solicitude both for the peace of your people and the destitution of that Church, by the authority vouchsafed unto us by God grant and confirm, to those who in religious zeal have decided to undertake and to perform so holy and so very necessary a work and task, that forgiveness of sins which our aforesaid predecessor, Pope Urban, instituted. And we decree that their wives and their sons, their goods also and their possessions, shall remain under the protection of Holy Church, and under our own protection and that of the archbishops, bishops, and other prelates of the Church of God. Moreover we forbid, by apostolic authority, that any legal procedure be set in motion touching any property within their peaceful possession at the time when they accepted the cross, until there is sure knowledge concerning their return or their decease.

"Furthermore, since those who are soldiers of the Lord should by no means give attention to costly clothing or personal adornment or dogs or falcons or other things which proclaim luxurious living, we admonish Your Prudence, in the Lord, that they who have reached a decision to undertake so holy a task give no heed to these things,

but devote all their zeal and care, with all their might, to arms, horses, and other things whereby they may vanquish the infidels.

"Moreover, all they that are burdened by debt and have, with pure heart, undertaken so holy a journey need not pay the interest past due, and if they themselves or others for them have been bound by oath and pledge, by reason of such interest, by apostolic authority we absolve them. It is to be permitted them also, in case their relatives or the lords to whom they are feudatory, upon being asked, are unwilling or unable to provide funds, to pledge their lands or other possessions to churches or ecclesiastical personages or others of the faithful freely and without any refusal.

"Forgiveness of sins and absolution we grant, in accordance with the precedent established by our aforesaid predecessor, by the authority of Almighty God and the blessed Peter, chief of the apostles, granted unto us by God; so that he who has devoutly undertaken so holy a journey and finished it or died there shall obtain absolution for all his sins of which he has made confession with broken and contrite heart and shall obtain, from the Rewarder of all, the fruit of an eternal recompense.

"Given at Vetralla on the Kalends of December 1145."

*　　*　　*

REVIEW QUESTIONS

1. How did the pope motivate people to go on a Crusade?
2. What benefits did he promise them?
3. What attitudes toward warfare are imbedded in this letter?

FROM *Carmina Burana*

Carmina Burana ("Songs of Beuren," the place in Bavaria where the manuscript was found) is a collection of about 350 songs and poems on a variety of subjects. This thirteenth-century manuscript preserves the greatest collection of medieval Latin poetry. The texts reflect the world of late-twelfth-century university and courtly life. All the works in the manuscript are anonymous, though some authors have been identified from other sources. The poems are a window on many aspects of medieval social history. The first piece here, attributed by some to Walter of Châtillon, concerns the decline in morals, and the second the game of chess.

From *Selections from the Carmina Burana*, translated by David Parlett (New York: Penguin Books, 1986), pp. 56–57, 169–72.

*   *   *

CB3 Mouldering Morals

Ecce torpet probitas,
virtus sepelitur . . .

Morals lie a-mouldering,
  virtue's all a-tatter,
liberality grows lean,
  parsimony fatter,
only lies are genuine—
  truth's another matter.
    Laws are for the breaking:
all illicitly allow
    any undertaking.

Mammon lords it over all,
  misers run the nation—
none but wouldn't gladly crawl
  for a small donation,
counting on their wherewithal
  for their reputation.
    Laws are for the breaking:
understanding underwrites
    any undertaking.

What's the hardest verb to learn?
  G I V E is. Give—gave—given.
Few words are of less concern
  to those who have striven

after wealth—who, more they earn,
  more to crave are driven.
    Laws are for the breaking:
moneymakers can't keep count
    of the amount they're making.

Self-control is on the wane,
  prurience uprears:
faithless vows are poured in vain
  into faithless ears:
Jove to Juno's found to feign,
  Dido to Aeneas.
    Laws are for the breaking:
who forsake fidelity
    are themselves forsaking.

If you seek to be precise
  don't describe as 'living'
fools who, once involved in vice,
  sin without misgiving.
Life? The word must ill suffice
  for their self-deceiving.
    Laws are for the breaking—
all overtly overlook
    any undertaking.

*   *   *

CB210 Verses on Chess

Qui cupit egregium   scachorum noscere ludum,
  Audiat: ut potui   carmine composui . . .

All who desire instruction
in chess, most noble distraction,
   hark: I've written you these
   ditties of expertise.

First, a few lines to settle
the scene of this sportive battle.
   The board measures eight by eight
   and bi-coloured squares alternate.

White is the usual colour
of one, and red is the other—
   failing red, black or blue
   or any old colour will do.

Rooks in the first position
threaten their warlike commission:
   on each next square, a knight
   champs at the bit for a fight.

On the third square stands a bishop
on guard against royal mishap:
   king on the fourth is seen
   standing next to his queen.

Then follow, up to the border,
the same men but in reverse order—
   and on the subsequent row
   little pawns, raring to go.

They proceed down the wide ways
capturing, right or left, sideways,
   adverse pieces that stand
   on each diagonal hand.

Should any pawn's expedition
reach to the eighthmost position
   it drops the pawn's routine,
   takes on that of a queen.

Having thus changed its sex, it
fights for its monarch—protects it,

orders and regulates:
   here conquers, and there abates.

Pawns, as the first to engage in
battle, fall first to its raging,
   leaving a pathway clear
   for those in wait at the rear.

Rooks, let loose by their slaughter,
roam over every quarter,
   marching wherever they may
   if nothing stands in their way.

Major pieces take major,
threaten the minor with danger—
   yet even they may fall
   prey to the weakest of all.

Bearing the signs of his knighting,
swift, wise, and clever at fighting,
   see the bold knight advance
   seizing his every chance.

Capturing innocent pieces
who lack his subtle caprices:
   worrying this way and that,
   here lays low—there is laid flat.

As for the bishop, his three-pointed
headgear leaves courage disjointed:
   hither and thither he goes
   felling invigilant foes.

Dominant pieces put paid to
minor pieces—yet they, too,
   yield to the weakest of all.
   Pawns are the quickest to fall.

No king can ever be taken
although by his partner forsaken:
   queenless, her king and lord
   has to remain on the board.

Often a king, though surrounded
by aides, is 'checkmated' or grounded:
   if he has nowhere to flee
   that is the finish of he.

*   *   *

REVIEW QUESTIONS

1. How is the rise of a money economy affecting the traditional values of this society?

2. How do the rules of chess reflect the social realities of medieval Europe?

ST. FRANCIS

FROM *The Rule of 1223* and *The Testament*

Francis of Assisi (1182–1226) was an inspired preacher whose famous conversion from secular life put him on the path to founding the Friars Minor (the Little Brothers), the Franciscans. Francis abandoned the worlds of commerce and warfare and devoted himself to preaching and acts of charity toward the sick and poor. Supported by Pope Innocent III, Francis tried to imitate the life of Christ through preaching, poverty, and humility. The Rule of 1223 and his Testament show the charismatic Francis trying to take his small band of followers into the institutional world of the organized church so that his community would outlive him.

From *St. Francis of Assisi: Writings and Early Biographies,* edited by Raphael Brown (Quincy: Franciscan Herald Press, 1973), pp. 57–64, 67–70.

FROM *The Rule of 1223*

CHAPTER 1
IN THE NAME OF THE LORD BEGINS THE LIFE OF THE FRIARS MINOR

The Rule and life of the Friars Minor is this, namely, to observe the Holy Gospel of our Lord Jesus Christ by living in obedience, without property, and in chastity. Brother Francis promises obedience and reverence to his holiness Pope Honorius and his lawfully elected successors and to the Church of Rome. The other friars are bound to obey Brother Francis and his successors.

CHAPTER 2
OF THOSE WHO WISH TO TAKE UP THIS LIFE AND HOW THEY ARE TO BE RECEIVED

If anyone wants to profess our Rule and comes to the friars, they must send him to their provincial minister, because he alone, to the exclusion of others, has permission to receive friars into the Order. The ministers must carefully examine all candidates on the Catholic faith and the sacraments of the Church. If they believe all that the Catholic faith teaches and are prepared to profess it loyally, holding by it steadfastly, to the end of their lives, and if they are not married; or if they are married and their wives have already entered a convent or after taking a vow of chastity have by the authority of the bishop of the diocese been granted this permission; and the wives are of such an age that no suspicion can arise concerning them: let the ministers tell them what the holy Gospel says, that they should go and sell all that belongs to them and endeavour to give it to the poor. If they cannot do this, their good will is sufficient.

The friars and their ministers must be careful not to become involved in the temporal affairs of newcomers to the Order, so that they may dispose of their goods freely, as God inspires them. If they ask for advice, the ministers may refer them to some God-fearing persons who can advise them how to distribute their property to the poor.

When this has been done, the ministers should clothe the candidates with the habit of probation, namely, two tunics without a hood, a cord and trousers, and a caperon reaching to the cord, unless the ministers themselves at any time decide that something else is more suitable. After the year of the novitiate, they should be received to obedience, promising to live always according to this life and Rule. It is absolutely forbidden to leave the Order, as his holiness the Pope has laid down. For the Gospel tells us, *No one, having put his hand to the plough and looking back, is fit for the kingdom of God.*

The friars who have already vowed obedience may have one tunic with a hood and those who wish may have another without a hood. Those who are forced by necessity may wear shoes. All the friars are to wear poor clothes and they can use pieces of sackcloth and other material to mend them, with God's blessing.

I warn all the friars and exhort them not to condemn or look down on people whom they see wearing soft or gaudy clothes and enjoying luxuries in food or drink; each one should rather condemn and despise himself.

CHAPTER 3
OF THE DIVINE OFFICE AND FASTING, AND HOW THE FRIARS ARE TO TRAVEL ABOUT THE WORLD

The clerics are to recite the Divine Office according to the rite of the Roman Curia, except the psalter; and so they may have breviaries. The lay brothers are to say twenty-four *Our Fathers* for Matins and five for Lauds; for Prime, Terce, Sext, and None, for each of these, they are to say seven; for Vespers twelve and for Compline seven. They should also say some prayers for the dead.

All the friars are to fast from the feast of All Saints until Christmas. Those who voluntarily fast for forty days after Epiphany have God's blessing, because this is the period our Lord sanctified by his holy fast. However, those who do not wish to do so, should not be forced to it. All the friars are bound to keep the Lenten fast before Easter, but they are not bound to fast at other times, except on Fridays. However, in case of manifest necessity, they are not obliged to corporal fasting.

And this is my advice, my counsel, and my earnest plea to my friars in our Lord Jesus Christ that, when they travel about the world, they should not be quarrelsome or take part in disputes with words or criticize others; but they should be gentle, peaceful, and unassuming, courteous and humble, speaking respectfully to everyone, as is expected of them. They are forbidden to ride on horseback, unless they are forced to it by manifest necessity or sickness. *Whatever house* they *enter,* they should *first say, "Peace to this house,"* and in the words of the Gospel they *may eat what is set before* them.

CHAPTER 4
THE FRIARS ARE FORBIDDEN TO ACCEPT MONEY

I strictly forbid all the friars to accept money in any form, either personally or through an intermediary. The ministers and superiors, however, are bound to provide carefully for the needs of the sick and the clothing of the other friars, by having recourse to spiritual friends, while taking into account differences of place, season, or severe climate, as seems best to them in the circumstances. This does not dispense them from the prohibition of receiving money in any form.

CHAPTER 5
THE MANNER OF WORKING

The friars to whom God has given the grace of working should work in a spirit of faith and devotion and avoid idleness, which is the enemy of the soul, without however extinguishing the spirit of prayer and devotion, to which every temporal consideration must be subordinate. As wages for their labour they may accept anything necessary for their temporal needs, for themselves or their brethren, except money in any form. And they should accept it humbly as is expected of those who serve God and strive after the highest poverty.

CHAPTER 6
THAT THE FRIARS ARE TO APPROPRIATE NOTHING FOR THEMSELVES; ON SEEKING ALMS; AND ON THE SICK FRIARS

The friars are to appropriate nothing for themselves, neither a house, nor a place, nor anything else. As *strangers and pilgrims* in this world, who serve God in poverty and humility, they should beg alms trustingly. And there is no reason why they should be ashamed, because God made himself poor for us in this world. This is the pinnacle of the most exalted poverty, and it is this, my dearest brothers, that has made you heirs and kings of the kingdom of heaven, poor in temporal things, but rich in virtue. This should be your portion, because it leads to the land of the living. And to this poverty, my beloved brothers, you must cling with all your heart, and wish never to have anything else under heaven, for the sake of our Lord Jesus Christ.

Wherever the friars meet one another, they should show that they are members of the same family. And they should have no hesitation in making known their needs to one another. For if a mother loves and cares for her child in the flesh, a friar should certainly love and care for his spiritual brother all the more tenderly. If a friar falls ill, the others are bound to look after him as they would like to be looked after themselves.

CHAPTER 7
OF THE PENANCE TO BE IMPOSED ON FRIARS WHO FALL INTO SIN

If any of the friars, at the instigation of the enemy, fall into mortal sin, they must have recourse as soon as possible, without delay, to their provincial ministers, if it is a sin for which recourse to them has been prescribed for the friars. If the ministers are priests, they should impose a moderate penance on such friars; if they are not priests, they should see that a penance is imposed by some priest of the Order, as seems best to them before God. They must be careful not to be angry or upset because a friar has fallen into sin, because anger or annoyance in themselves or in others makes it difficult to be charitable.

CHAPTER 8
THE ELECTION OF THE MINISTER GENERAL OF THE ORDER AND THE PENTECOST CHAPTER

The friars are always bound to have a member of the Order as Minister General, who is the servant of the whole fraternity, and they are strictly bound to obey him. At his death the provincial ministers and the custodes are to elect a successor at the Pentecost Chapter, at which the provincial ministers are bound to assemble in the place designated by the Minister General. This chapter should be held once every three years, or at a longer or shorter interval, if the Minister General has so ordained.

If at any time it becomes clear to all the provincial ministers and custodes that the Minister General is incapable of serving the friars and can be of no benefit to them, they who have the power to elect must elect someone else as Minister General.

After the Pentecost Chapter, the provincial ministers and custodes may summon their subjects to a chapter in their own territory once in the same year, if they wish and it seems worthwhile.

CHAPTER 9
OF PREACHERS

The friars are forbidden to preach in any diocese, if the bishop objects to it. No friar should dare to preach to the people unless he has been examined and approved by the Minister General of the Order and has received from him the commission to preach.

Moreover, I advise and admonish the friars that in their preaching, their words should be examined and chaste. They should aim only at the advantage and spiritual good of their listeners, telling them briefly about vice and virtue, punishment and glory, because our Lord himself kept his words short on earth.

CHAPTER 10
ON ADMONISHING AND CORRECTING THE FRIARS

The ministers, who are the servants of the other friars, must visit their subjects and admonish them, correcting them humbly and charitably, without commanding them anything that is against their conscience or our Rule. The subjects, however, should remember that they have renounced their own wills for God's sake. And so I strictly command them to obey their ministers in everything that they have promised God and is not against their conscience and our Rule. The friars who are convinced that they cannot observe the Rule spiritually, wherever they may be, can and must have recourse to their ministers. The ministers, for their part, are bound to receive them kindly and charitably, and be so sympathetic towards them that the friars can speak and deal with them as employers with their servants. That is the way it ought to be; the ministers should be the servants of all the friars.

With all my heart, I beg the friars in our Lord Jesus Christ to be on their guard against pride, boasting, envy, and greed, against the cares and anxieties of this world, against detraction and complaining. Those who are illiterate should not be anxious to study. They should realize instead that the only thing they should desire is to have

the spirit of God at work within them, while they pray to him unceasingly with a heart free from self-interest. They must be humble, too, and patient in persecution or illness, loving those who persecute us by blaming us or bringing charges against us, as our Lord tells us, *Love your enemies, pray for those who persecute and calumniate you. Blessed are those who suffer persecution for justice' sake, for theirs is the kingdom of heaven. He who has persevered to the end will be saved.*

CHAPTER 11
THE FRIARS ARE FORBIDDEN TO ENTER THE MONASTERIES OF NUNS

I strictly forbid all the friars to have suspicious relationships or conversations with women. No one may enter the monasteries of nuns, except those who have received special permission from the Apostolic See. They are forbidden to be sponsors of men or women lest scandal arise amongst or concerning the friars.

CHAPTER 12
OF THESE WHO WISH TO GO AMONG THE SARACENS AND OTHER UNBELIEVERS

If any of the friars is inspired by God to go among the Saracens or other unbelievers, he must ask permission from his provincial minister. The ministers, for their part, are to give permission only to those whom they see are fit to be sent.

The ministers, too, are bound to ask the Pope for one of the cardinals of the holy Roman Church to be governor, protector, and corrector of this fraternity, so that we may be utterly subject and submissive to the Church. And so, firmly established in the Catholic faith, we may live always according to the poverty, and the humility, and the Gospel of our Lord Jesus Christ, as we have solemnly promised.

*   *   *

The Testament

This is how God inspired me, Brother Francis, to embark upon a life of penance. When I was in sin, the sight of lepers nauseated me beyond measure; but then God himself led me into their company, and I had pity on them. When I had once become acquainted with them, what had previously nauseated me became a source of spiritual and physical consolation for me. After that I did not wait long before leaving the world.

And God inspired me with such faith in his churches that I used to pray with all simplicity, saying, "We adore you, Lord Jesus Christ, here and in all your churches in the whole world, and we bless you, because by your holy cross you have redeemed the world."

God inspired me, too, and still inspires me with such great faith in priests who live according to the laws of the holy Church of Rome, because of their dignity, that if they persecuted me, I should still be ready to turn to them for aid. And if I were as wise as Solomon and met the poorest priests of the world, I would still refuse to preach against their will in the parishes in which they live. I am determined to reverence, love and honour priests and all others as my superiors. I refuse to consider their sins, because I can see the Son of God in them and they are better than I. I do this because in this world I cannot see the most high Son of God with my own eyes, except for his most holy Body and Blood which they receive and they alone administer to others.

Above everything else, I want this most holy Sacrament to be honoured and venerated and reserved in places which are richly ornamented. Whenever I find his most holy name or writings containing his words in an improper place, I make a point of picking them up, and I ask that they be picked up and put aside in a suitable place. We should honour and venerate theologians, too, and the ministers of God's word, because it is they who give us spirit and life.

When God gave me some friars, there was no one to tell me what I should do; but the Most High himself made it clear to me that I must live the life of the Gospel. I had this written down briefly and simply and his holiness the Pope confirmed it for me. Those who embraced this life gave everything they had to the poor. They were satisfied with one habit which was patched inside and outside, and a cord, and trousers. We refused to have anything more.

Those of us who were clerics said the Office like other clerics, while the lay brothers said the *Our Father,* and we were only too glad to find shelter in abandoned churches. We made no claim to learning and we were submissive to everyone. I worked with my own hands and I am still determined to work; and with all my heart I want all the other friars to be busy with some kind of work that can be carried on without scandal. Those who do not know how to work should learn, not because they want to get something for their efforts, but to give good example and to avoid idleness. When we receive no recompense for our work, we can turn to God's table and beg alms from door to door. God revealed a form of greeting to me, telling me that we should say, "God give you peace."

The friars must be very careful not to accept churches or poor dwellings for themselves, or anything else built for them, unless they are in harmony with the poverty which we have promised in the Rule; and they should occupy these places only as strangers and pilgrims.

In virtue of obedience, I strictly forbid the friars, wherever they may be, to petition the Roman Curia, either personally or through an intermediary, for a papal brief, whether it concerns a church or any other place, or even in order to preach, or because they are being persecuted. If they are not welcome somewhere, they should flee to another country where they can lead a life of penance, with God's blessing.

I am determined to obey the Minister General of the Order and the guardian whom he sees fit to give me. I want to be a captive in his hands so that I cannot travel about or do anything against his command or desire, because he is my superior. Although I am ill and not much use, I always want to have a cleric with me who will say the Office for me, as is prescribed in the Rule.

All the other friars, too, are bound to obey their guardians in the same way, and say the Office according to the Rule. If any of them refuse to say the Office according to the Rule and want to change it, or if they are not true to the Catholic faith, the other friars are bound in virtue of obedience to bring them before the custos nearest the place where they find them. The custos must keep any such friar as a prisoner day and night so that he cannot escape from his hands until he personally hands him over to his minister. The minister, then, is strictly bound by obedience to place him in the care of friars who will guard him day and night like a prisoner until they present him before his lordship the Bishop of Ostia, who is the superior, protector, and corrector of the whole Order.

The friars should not say, this is another Rule. For this is a reminder, admonition, exhortation, and my testament which I, Brother Francis, worthless as I am, leave to you, my brothers, that we may observe in a more Catholic way the Rule we have promised to God. The Minister General and all the other ministers and custodes are bound in virtue of obedience not to add anything to these words or subtract from them. They should always have this writing with them as well as the Rule and at the chapters they hold, when the Rule is read, they should read these words also.

In virtue of obedience, I strictly forbid any of my friars, clerics or lay brothers, to interpret the Rule or these words, saying, "This is what they mean." God inspired me to write the Rule and these words plainly and simply, and so you too must understand them plainly and simply, and live by them, doing good to the last.

And may whoever observes all this be filled in heaven with the blessing of the most high Father, and on earth with that of his beloved Son, together with the Holy Spirit, the Comforter, and all the powers of heaven and all the saints. And I, Brother Francis, your poor worthless servant, add my share internally and externally to that most holy blessing. Amen.

REVIEW QUESTIONS

1. How did Francis expect the brothers to live without property?
2. In what ways are his teachings a support or a threat to the organized church?
3. What was Francis worried about as he dictated his last will and testament?

HILDEGARD OF BINGEN

Letter to the Clergy of Mainz

Hildegard of Bingen (1098–1179) was a German abbess whose creative genius extended to preaching, founding convents, and above all writing down her visionary prophesies. She was also a prolific composer of sacred songs and plays. Hildegard's remarkable career as an abbess demonstrates one of the few opportunities women

GOLD AND SILVER JEWELED BOOK COVER,
WEINGARTEN ABBEY, GERMANY (C. 1200–1232)

*This binding or book cover has the Virgin and Child at the center, the apostles in the corners
(with their distinctive creatures), and other saints and angels. The cover protected the monastery's sacramentary. The binding also contains relics of the Virgin Mary and Saints George,
Oswald, Bartholomew, Thomas, Peter, Paul, and James, as the writing along the edges
reveals. This book cover is also a reliquary—an object containing pieces of the saints. What
is the significance and power of a relic? Can you tell a book by its cover? What does this
cover say?*

had to be in charge of an institution in the medieval world. In this letter to the male clergy of Mainz, Hildegard is objecting to the interdict her convent is experiencing because of a dispute over a burial.

From *The Letters of Hildegard of Bingen,* edited by Joseph L. Baird (Oxford, Eng.: Oxford University Press, 1994), pp. 76–79.

By a vision, which was implanted in my soul by God the Great Artisan before I was born, I have been compelled to write these things because of the interdict by which our superiors have bound us, on account of a certain dead man buried at our monastery, a man buried without any objection, with his own priest officiating. Yet only a few days after his burial, these men ordered us to remove him from our cemetery. Seized by no small terror, as a result, I looked as usual to the True Light, and, with wakeful eyes, I saw in my spirit that if this man were disinterred in accordance with their commands, a terrible and lamentable danger would come upon us like a dark cloud before a threatening thunderstorm.

Therefore, we have not presumed to remove the body of the deceased inasmuch as he had confessed his sins, had received extreme unction and communion, and had been buried without objection. Furthermore, we have not yielded to those who advised or even commanded this course of action. Not, certainly, that we take the counsel of upright men or the orders of our superiors lightly, but we would not have it appear that, out of feminine harshness we did injustice to the sacraments of Christ, with which this man had been fortified while he was still alive. But so that we may not be totally disobedient we have, in accordance with their injunction, ceased from singing the divine praises and from participation in Mass, as had been our regular monthly custom.

As a result, my sisters and I have been greatly distressed and saddened. Weighed down by this burden, therefore, I heard these words in a vision: It is improper for you to obey human words ordering you to abandon the sacraments of the Garment of the Word of God, Who, born virgin-

ally of the Virgin Mary, is your salvation. Still, it is incumbent upon you to seek permission to participate in the sacraments from those prelates who laid the obligation of obedience upon you. For ever since Adam was driven from the bright region of paradise into the exile of this world on account of his disobedience, the conception of all people is justly tainted by that first transgression. Therefore, in accordance with God's inscrutable plan, it was necessary for a man free from all pollution to be born in human flesh, through whom all who are predestined to life might be cleansed from corruption and might be sanctified by the communion of his body so that he might remain in them and they in him for their fortification. That person, however, who is disobedient to the commands of God, as Adam was, and is completely forgetful of Him must be completely cut off from participation in the sacrament of His body, just as he himself has turned away from Him in disobedience. And he must remain so until, purged through penitence, he is permitted by the authorities to receive the communion of the Lord's body again. In contrast, however, a person who is aware that he has incurred such a restriction not as a result of anything that he has done, either consciously or deliberately, may be present at the service of the life-giving sacrament, to be cleansed by the Lamb without sin, Who, in obedience to the Father, allowed Himself to be sacrificed on the altar of the cross that he might restore salvation to all.

In that same vision I also heard that I had erred in not going humbly and devoutly to my superiors for permission to participate in the communion, especially since we were not at fault in receiving that dead man into our cemetery. For, after all, he had been fortified by his own priest with proper Christian procedure, and, without objection from anyone, was buried in our cemetery, with all Bingen joining in the funeral procession. And so God has commanded me to report these things to you, our lords and prelates. Further, I saw in my vision also that by obeying you we have been celebrating the divine office incorrectly, for from the time of your restriction up to the present, we have ceased to sing the divine office, merely reading it instead. And I heard a voice coming from the Living Light concerning the various kinds of praises, about which David speaks in the psalm: "Praise Him with sound of trumpet: praise Him with psaltery and harp," and so forth up to this point: "Let every spirit praise the Lord." These words use outward, visible things to teach us about inward things. Thus the material composition and the quality of these instruments instruct us how we ought to give form to the praise of the Creator and turn all the convictions of our inner being to the same. When we consider these things carefully, we recall that man needed the voice of the living Spirit, but Adam lost this divine voice through disobedience. For while he was still innocent, before his transgression, his voice blended fully with the voices of the angels in their praise of God. Angels are called spirits from that Spirit which is God, and thus they have such voices by virtue of their spiritual nature. But Adam lost that angelic voice which he had in paradise, for he fell asleep to that knowledge which he possessed before his sin, just as a person on waking up only dimly remembers what he had seen in his dreams. And so when he was deceived by the trick of the devil and rejected the will of his Creator, he became wrapped up in the darkness of inward ignorance as the just result of his iniquity.

God, however, restores the souls of the elect to that pristine blessedness by infusing them with the light of truth. And in accordance with His eternal plan, He so devised it that whenever He renews the hearts of many with the pouring out of the prophetic spirit, they might, by means of His interior illumination, regain some of the knowledge which Adam had before he was punished for his sin.

And so the holy prophets, inspired by the Spirit which they had received, were called for this purpose: not only to compose psalms and canticles (by which the hearts of listeners would be inflamed) but also to construct various kinds of musical instruments to enhance these songs of praise with melodic strains. Thereby, both through the form and quality of the instruments, as well as through the meaning of the words which accompany them, those who hear might be taught, as we said above, about inward things, since they have been admonished and aroused by outward things. In such a way, these holy prophets get beyond the music of this exile and recall to mind that divine melody of praise which Adam, in company with the angels, enjoyed in God before his fall.

Men of zeal and wisdom have imitated the holy prophets and have themselves, with human skill, invented several kinds of musical instruments, so that they might be able to sing for the delight of their souls, and they accompanied their singing with instruments played with the flexing of the fingers, recalling, in this way, Adam, who was formed by God's finger, which is the Holy Spirit. For, before he sinned, his voice had the sweetness of all musical harmony. Indeed, if he had remained in his original state, the weakness of mortal man would not have been able to endure the power and the resonance of his voice.

But when the devil, man's great deceiver, learned that man had begun to sing through God's inspiration and, therefore, was being transformed to bring back the sweetness of the songs of heaven, mankind's homeland, he was so terrified at seeing his clever machinations go to ruin that he was greatly tormented. Therefore, he devotes himself continually to thinking up and working out all kinds of wicked contrivances. Thus he never ceases from confounding confession and the sweet beauty of both divine praise and spiritual hymns, eradicating them through wicked suggestions, impure thoughts, or various distractions from the heart of man and even from the mouth of the Church itself, wherever he can, through dissension, scandal, or unjust oppression.

Therefore, you and all prelates must exercise

the greatest vigilance to clear the air by full and thorough discussion of the justification for such actions before your verdict closes the mouth of any church singing praises to God or suspends it from handling or receiving the divine sacraments. And you must be especially certain that you are drawn to this action out of zeal for God's justice, rather than out of indignation, unjust emotions, or a desire for revenge, and you must always be on your guard not to be circumvented in your decisions by Satan, who drove man from celestial harmony and the delights of paradise.

Consider, too, that just as the body of Jesus Christ was born of the purity of the Virgin Mary through the operation of the Holy Spirit so, too, the canticle of praise, reflecting celestial harmony, is rooted in the Church through the Holy Spirit. The body is the vestment of the spirit, which has a living voice, and so it is proper for the body, in harmony with the soul, to use its voice to sing praises to God. Whence, in metaphor, the prophetic spirit commands us to praise God with clashing cymbals and cymbals of jubilation, as well as other musical instruments which men of wisdom and zeal have invented, because all arts pertaining to things useful and necessary for mankind have been created by the breath that God sent into man's body. For this reason it is proper that God be praised in all things.

And because sometimes a person sighs and groans at the sound of singing, remembering, as it were, the nature of celestial harmony, the prophet, aware that the soul is symphonic and thoughtfully reflecting on the profound nature of the spirit, urges us in the psalm to confess to the Lord with the harp and to sing a psalm to Him with the ten-stringed psaltery. His meaning is that the harp, which is plucked from below, relates to the discipline of the body; the psaltery, which is plucked from above, pertains to the exertion of the spirit; the ten chords, to the fulfillment of the law.

Therefore, those who, without just cause, impose silence on a church and prohibit the singing of God's praises and those who have on earth unjustly despoiled God of His honor and glory will lose their place among the chorus of angels, unless they have amended their lives through true penitence and humble restitution. Moreover, let those who hold the keys of heaven beware not to open those things which are to be kept closed nor to close those things which are to be kept open, for harsh judgment will fall upon those who rule, unless, as the apostle says, they rule with good judgment.

And I heard a voice saying thus: Who created heaven? God. Who opens heaven to the faithful? God. Who is like Him? No one. And so, O men of faith, let none of you resist Him or oppose Him, lest He fall on you in His might and you have no helper to protect you from His judgment. This time is a womanish time, because the dispensation of God's justice is weak. But the strength of God's justice is exerting itself, a female warrior battling against injustice, so that it might fall defeated.

REVIEW QUESTIONS

1. What role does Hildegard assign to music in worship?
2. Why is music such a big part of her argument about the interdict?
3. What are the sources of Hildegard's authority to challenge the decisions of the Mainz clergy?

STEPHEN OF BOURBON

FROM *On the Seven Gifts of the Holy Spirit*

The Dominican preacher and author Stephen of Bourbon (?1180–1262) preserves in a theological work this account of what he learned while hearing confessions in the diocese of Lyons in southern France. Only from an educated and observant friar do we learn the story of St. Guinefort. The official, institutional church still did not control the variety of religious practices on the local level.

From *The Holy Greyhound,* by Jean Claude Schmitt (Cambridge, Eng.: Cambridge University Press, 1983), pp. 4–6.

*   *   *

On the Worship of the Dog Guinefort

Sixthly, I should speak of offensive superstitions, some of which are offensive to God, others to our fellow men. Offensive to God are those which honour demons or other creatures as if they were divine: it is what idolatry does, and it is what the wretched women who cast lots do, who seek salvation by worshipping elder trees or making offerings to them; scorning churches and holy relics, they take their children to these elder trees, or to anthills, or to other things in order that a cure may be effected.

This recently happened in the diocese of Lyons where, when I preached against the reading of oracles, and was hearing confession, numerous women confessed that they had taken their children to Saint Guinefort. As I thought that this was some holy person, I continued with my enquiry and finally learned that this was actually a greyhound, which had been killed in the following manner.

In the diocese of Lyons, near the enclosed nuns' village called Neuville, on the estate of the Lord of Villars, was a castle, the lord of which and his wife had a baby boy. One day, when the lord and lady had gone out of the house, and the nurse had done likewise, leaving the baby alone in the cradle, a huge serpent entered the house and approached the baby's cradle. Seeing this, the greyhound, which had remained behind, chased the serpent and, attacking it beneath the cradle, upset the cradle and bit the serpent all over, which defended itself, biting the dog equally severely. Finally, the dog killed it and threw it well away from the cradle. The cradle, the floor, the dog's mouth and head were all drenched in the serpent's blood. Although badly hurt by the serpent, the dog remained on guard beside the cradle. When the nurse came back and saw all this she thought that the dog had devoured the child, and let out a scream of misery. Hearing it the child's mother also ran up, looked, thought the same thing and screamed too. Likewise the knight, when he arrived, thought the same thing and drew his sword and killed the dog. Then, when they went closer to the baby they found it safe and sound, sleeping peacefully. Casting around for some explanation, they discovered the serpent, torn to pieces by the dog's bites, and now dead. Realising then the true facts of the matter, and deeply regretting having unjustly killed so useful a dog they threw it into a well in front of the manor door, threw a great pile of stones on top of it, and planted trees beside it, in memory of the event. Now, by divine will, the manor was destroyed and the estate, reduced to a desert, was abandoned by its inhabitants. But the peasants, hearing of the dog's conduct and of how it had been killed, although innocent, and for a deed for which it might have expected praise, visited the place, honoured the dog as a martyr, prayed to it when they were sick or in need of something, and many there fell victim to the enticements and illusions of the devil, who in this way used to lead men into error. Above all, though, it was women with sick or weak children who took them to this place. They would go and seek out an old woman in a fortified town a league distant, and she taught them the rituals they should enact in order to make offerings to demons, and in order to invoke them, and she led them to the place. When they arrived, they would make offerings of salt and other things; they would hang their babies' swaddling-clothes on the bushes roundabout; they would drive nails into the trees which had grown in this place; they would pass the naked babies between the trunks of two trees —the mother, on one side, held the baby and threw it nine times to the old woman, who was on the other side. Invoking the demons, they called upon the fauns in the forest of Rimite to take the sick, feeble child which, they said, was theirs, and to return their child that the fauns had taken away, fat and well, safe and sound.

Having done this, the infanticidal mothers took their children and laid them naked at the foot of the tree on straw from the cradle; then, using the light they had brought with them, they lit two candles, each an inch long, one on each side of the child's head and fixed them in the trunk above it. Then they withdrew until the candles had burnt out, so as not to see the child or hear him crying.

Several people have told us that while the candles were burning like this they burnt and killed several babies. One woman also told me that she had just invoked the fauns and was withdrawing from the scene when she saw a wolf come out of the forest towards the baby. If maternal love had not made her feel pity and go back for him, the wolf, or as she put it, the devil in the shape of a wolf, would have devoured the baby.

When a mother returned to her child and found it still alive, she carried it out into the fast-flowing waters of a nearby river, called the Chalaronne, and plunged it in nine times; if it came through without dying on the spot, or shortly afterwards, it had a very strong constitution.

We went to this place, we called together all the people on the estate, and we preached against everything that had been said. We had the dead dog disinterred, and the sacred wood cut down and burnt, along with the remains of the dog. And I had an edict passed by the lords of the estate, warning that anyone going thenceforth to that place for any such reason would be liable to have his possessions seized and then sold.

*   *   *

REVIEW QUESTIONS

1. How could these people believe that a dog could be a saint?
2. What was the social meaning of the ritual of leaving sick children in the forest?
3. Does Stephen really understand what the mothers were doing with their sick children?

JACOBUS DE VORAGINE

FROM *The Golden Legend*

Jacopo de Voragine's The Golden Legend *was the most widely known collection of medieval saints' lives. Jacopo (c. 1226–1298) was a well-educated Dominican friar who eventually became archbishop of Genoa. Most of the saints in the collection were martyrs and heroes of the early church, but a few, like St. Elizabeth, lived in Jacopo's century. The author borrowed and adapted these biographies of the saints from numerous sources, but his plain and vivid style made the collection accessible across Europe. St. Elizabeth's life reveals the opportunities and constraints facing women in thirteenth-century society.*

From *The Golden Legend*, by Jacobus de Voragine, translated by William Granger Ryan (Princeton, N.J.: Princeton University Press, 1993), vol. 2, pp. 306–13.

Life of St. Elizabeth of Hungary

*   *   *

Elizabeth, illustrious daughter of the king of Hungary, was noble by birth and still more noble by her faith and her devotion to religion. She ennobled her already noble lineage by her example, shed light on it by her miracles, and embellished it with the grace of her holiness. The Author of nature somehow raised her above nature. As a child growing up surrounded by regal privileges and pleasures, she either spurned the things children love, or directed them to God's service, showing how much her tender childhood was strengthened by her simplicity, and how sweet was the devotion of her earliest years. As a child she applied herself to serious concerns, shunning idle games, avoiding worldly success and prosperity, and advancing always in reverence toward God. When she was only five years old, she spent so much time praying in church that her companions and her maids could hardly get her out to play. Her servants and playmates noticed that when one of them in the course of a game went into the chapel, Elizabeth followed her, profiting by the opportunity to get into the church; and when she entered, she would kneel down or lie full length on the floor. She had not yet learned to read but often spread the Psalter open before her, pretending to read so that no one would disturb her. Sometimes she stretched herself on the ground beside other girls, playing at measuring herself against them, but also to display reverence for God. When playing the game of rings or any other game, she put her whole trust in God. When as a little girl she won something in a game or acquired a new possession in some other way, she divided it among poor children, urging them to say frequently the Our Father and the Hail Mary.

Elizabeth grew in age and even more in the intensity of her devotion. She chose the Blessed Virgin, mother of God, as her patroness and advocate, and Saint John the Evangelist as the guardian of her chastity. When papers with the names of the several apostles written on them were placed on the altar and then distributed at random among the girls, Elizabeth prayed three times and always received the paper with Saint Peter's name on it as she wanted to, because her devotion to that saint was so fervent that she would never deny anything to anyone who asked in his name. For fear that worldly successes might attract flattery to her, she daily gave away some token of her prosperity. When she won in some game, she called a halt and said: "I don't want to play any more! I leave the rest for the sake of God!" When invited to dance with other girls she would dance one round, then would say: "Let's let one round be enough and give up the rest for God," thus tempering the girls' taste for such vain pastimes. She abhorred too much show in dress and loved modesty in all such matters.

Elizabeth imposed upon herself the daily recitation of a certain number of prayers, and if she was too busy to complete the number during the day and was put to bed by her maids, she stayed awake until she had fulfilled her promise to her heavenly spouse. She observed solemn feast days with so much devotion that she would not allow her long sleeves to be stitched on her dress under any pretext until after the celebration of mass. She forbade herself the wearing of gloves before noon on Sunday, wishing thereby both to defer to the sacred solemnity and to satisfy her own devotion. For this same purpose it was her custom to impose such practices upon herself by vow, so that no one would be able to dissuade her from carrying out her intention. She assisted at liturgical services with such reverence that when the gospel was read, or the host consecrated, she removed her sleeves if they had been stitched on, and put aside her necklaces and any ornaments she was wearing on her head.

She lived out her state of virginity prudently and innocently, but was compelled to enter the state of marriage in obedience to her father's order. Thus she gained the thirtyfold fruit, keeping the faith of the Trinity and obeying the Ten Commandments. She consented to conjugal intercourse, not out of libidinous desire but out of respect for her father's command, and in order to procreate and raise children for the service of God. Thus, while bound by the law of the conjugal bed, she was not bound to enjoyment. This is obvious from the fact that she made a vow in Master Conrad's hands, that if she survived her husband she would practice continence for the rest of her life.

Elizabeth therefore was married to the landgrave of Thuringia, as befitted her royal dignity but also as God's providence ordained, namely, that she might thus lead many to the love of God and might give instruction to the ignorant.[1] Although her state of life was changed, there was no change in the way she intended to live. How great her devotion and humility toward God was, how strict her austerity and self-denial, how abundant her generosity and compassion for the poor, it will be the purpose of what follows to demonstrate.

She was so fervently devoted to prayer that she sometimes hurried to arrive in church ahead of her maids, as if wishing by some secret prayer to win a particular favor from God. She often rose during the night to pray, though her husband begged her to spare herself and give her body some rest. She had an arrangement with one of her maids who was closer to her than the others, that if by chance she overslept, the maid would wake her up by touching her foot. Once by mistake she touched the landgrave's foot. He woke up with a start but understood what had happened, and patiently put up with it and pretended not to have noticed anything. In order to make her prayers a rich sacrifice to God, Elizabeth often sprinkled them with a profusion of tears, but she shed her tears happily and without any unseemly change of countenance, weeping with sorrow and rejoicing at the sorrow; and this beautified her visage with gladness.

So profound was her humility that for the love of God she never shunned menial or lowly work, but did it with unbounded devotion. She once took an ugly sick man and clasped his filthy head to her bosom, then cut his hair and washed his head, while her maids stood by laughing. On Rogation Days she always walked in the procession barefoot and wearing a plain woolen garment. At the station churches she sat among the poorest women to hear the sermon, as if she too were poor and of low estate. When she went to be churched after childbirth, she never made a show of jewelry

---

[1]Landgrave was a title equivalent to "count."

or gold-embroidered gowns, as other women did.[2] Following the example of Mary the immaculate mother, she carried her child in her arms and humbly offered him at the altar with a lamb and a candle, thus showing her distaste for wordly pomp and modeling her behavior after that of the Blessed Mother. Then, when she returned to her house, she gave the clothing she had worn in church to some poor woman.

As a further manifestation of her humility, Elizabeth, unsurpassed though she was in freedom and high station, submitted herself in obedience to a priest called Master Conrad. Conrad was a very poor man but was known for his knowledge and piety. With her husband's consent and the marriage right safeguarded, she pledged herself to obey Master Conrad so unreservedly that she would fulfill any order of his with reverence and joy. Her purpose was to gain merit and to imitate the example of her Savior, who became obedient even unto death. For instance, on one occasion Master Conrad had ordered her to attend a service at which he was to preach, but the marchioness of Meissen came to visit and Elizabeth missed the service. Conrad took her disobedience so amiss that he would not forgive it until, stripped to her shift, she was soundly flogged, along with some of her servants who had committed some fault.

Elizabeth took on herself so much abstinence and privation that her body was wasted with vigils and disciplines and fasting. Frequently she avoided her husband's bed and went without sleep in order to spend the night in contemplation and to pray to her heavenly Father in secret. When sleep overcame her, she slept on mats strewn on the floor. When her husband was away she passed the whole night in prayer with her heavenly spouse. Often, too, she had her serving women flog her in her bedroom, in return for the scourging her Savior had borne for her and to quell all carnal desire. Such was Elizabeth's temperance in matters of

food and drink that at her husband's table, laden as it was with a variety of tasty dishes, she sometimes ate nothing but a bit of bread. Master Conrad forbade her to eat any food about which she had the slightest qualm of conscience, and she obeyed this behest so meticulously that however abundant the delicious foods might be, she and her servingmaids partook of coarser fare. At other times she sat at table and divided and moved the food around on her plate, so as to seem to be eating and to ward off any notion that she was superstitious: thus, by her urbanity, she put all the guests at their ease. When they were traveling and she was worn out with the length and labors of the journey, and she and her husband were offered foods that might not have been honestly acquired, she accepted none of them and patiently ate stale black bread soaked in hot water, as her maids did. For this reason, indeed, her husband had assigned funds to her, sufficient to provide for her living and that of some few of her women, who chose to follow her example in everything. Frequently, too, she refused what was served at the royal table and asked for the provisions of ordinary people. The landgrave was tolerant of all of this and said that he would gladly do the same himself if he were not afraid of upsetting the whole household.

Elizabeth's position was one of the highest dignity, but her whole desire was to share poverty with the poor, so that she might make return to Christ for his poverty and the world might have no claim on her. Sometimes, when she was alone with her servingwomen, she put on cheap, dingy clothing, covered her head with a shabby kerchief, and said to them: "This is how I will go about when I have attained the state of poverty." She checked her own appetite with a tight rein of abstinence but was openhanded in her generosity to the poor, never letting anyone go hungry and supplying the needs of all so liberally that she was acclaimed as the mother of the poor.

Blessed Elizabeth put her utmost effort into the performance of the seven works of mercy, hoping to inherit the everlasting kingdom and to reign there perpetually, and to possess the Father's

---

[2]"To be churched" refers to the practice in which after giving birth, a woman came to the church to offer thanksgiving and to receive a special blessing.

blessing with the saints gathered at his right hand. She clothed the naked and provided raiment for the burial of poor people and strangers, as well as for infants at their christening. Often she lifted children of the poor from the baptismal font and sewed clothing for them with her own hands: having become their godmother, she then did more for them. On one occasion she gave a rather elegant dress to a poor woman, who was so overwhelmed with joy at the sight of such a magnificent gift that she fell to the ground and was thought to be dead. Blessed Elizabeth, seeing her lying there, was sorry she had given her so fine a present, fearing that she had thus been the cause of her death, but she prayed for her and the woman stood up fully recovered. Often, too, she spun wool in company with her servants, in order to receive the glorious fruit of these good labors, giving an example of true humility, and an alms to God out of the toil of her own body.

She fed the hungry. Once, when the landgrave had gone to the court of Emperor Frederick, then being held at Cremona, Elizabeth collected the whole year's crop from his barns, called in the poor from all sides, and provided for their daily needs, because the cost of living had risen and they were threatened with famine. When poor people ran out of money, she often sold her jewelry in order to help them. Indeed she regularly drew from her own resources and those of her faithful servingwomen to have something put aside for the poor.

She gave drink to the thirsty. Once she was serving beer to poor people, and after everyone had been served, the jug was still as full as it had been before she started.

She provided shelter for pilgrims and poor people. She had a very large house built at the foot of the high hill on which her castle stood, and there took care of numbers of the ill and infirm despite the difficulty of getting up and down the hill. While with them she saw to all their needs and exhorted them to patience. Bad air always distressed her, but for God's love, even in the heat of summer, she did not shrink from the smells and sores of the sick, but applied remedies to their wounds, dried them with the veil from her head,

and treated them with her own hands, although her maids could hardly bear to watch her.

In this same house Elizabeth saw to it that children of poor women were well fed and cared for. She was so gentle and kind to them that they all called her Mother and, when she came into the house, followed her around as if she were in fact their mother, and crowded about her to be as close to her as possible. She also bought some small dishes and cups and rings and other glass toys for the children to play with. She was riding up the hill, carrying these things in the fold of her cloak, when they came loose and fell to the rocks below, but not one of the toys was broken.

Elizabeth visited the sick. Her compassion for their sufferings ruled her heart so much that she often went looking for their lodgings and visited them solicitously, entering their poor abodes as if she were at home, not deterred by the strangeness of the locale or bothered by the distance she had to go. She provided for their needs and spoke words of consolation to them, thus earning reward in five ways, namely, by honoring them with her visit, by the fatigues of the journey, by the warmth of her compassion, by her words of consolation, and by the generosity of her donations.

She concerned herself with the burial of the poor, devotedly going to their funerals, covering their bodies with clothes that she herself had made, and on one occasion cutting up the large linen veil she was wearing and wrapping the corpse of a poor person with part of it. She prepared them for interment with her own hands and piously stayed for the rites at the grave.

The piety of her husband deserves praise for his part in all these doings. He had many interests to attend to but was devout in honoring God, and, since he could not personally get involved in such activities, gave his wife the freedom and the means to do whatever served the honor of God and made for the salvation of his soul. Blessed Elizabeth wanted very much to see her husband turn the use of his arms to the defense of the faith, and by her salutary exhortations persuaded him to go to the Holy Land. There the landgrave, a faithful prince, devout and renowned for the integrity and sincerity of his faith, lost his life and received the reward of his good works.

Elizabeth now piously embraced the state of widowhood, taking care not to be defrauded of the reward of a widow's continence and to gain the sixtyfold fruit by observing the Decalogue together with the seven works of mercy. But as soon as the news of her husband's death spread throughout Thuringia, she was denounced by some of the landgrave's vassals as a prodigal, wasteful woman and was shamefully banned from her country. Thus her patience was brought fully to light, and her long-standing desire for poverty was fulfilled.

She went by night to the house of an innkeeper and was given shelter where the pigs usually rested, and for this she gave thanks to God. In the morning she went to the house of the Friars Minor and asked them to sing a *Te Deum,* in thanksgiving for the troubles that had befallen her. The following day she was ordered to go with her children into the house of one of her enemies, where she was given a very small room to live in. The man and woman whose house it was treated her so meanly that she bade farewell only to the walls, saying: "I would gladly give my good wishes to these people, if they had been kind to me." Having no place else to go she went back to the innkeeper's house, sending her children to various places to be cared for. She had to go along a path filled with mud, with only stepping-stones to walk on, and came face to face with an old woman whom she had befriended many times; but the old woman would not let her pass and she fell into the mud. Nothing daunted, she came up rejoicing and laughing, and shook the mud out of her clothes.

Now her aunt, who was an abbess, took pity on Elizabeth's poverty and brought her to the bishop of Bamberg, who was her uncle. He received her with due honor and shrewdly gave her hospitality in his house, planning to get her married again. The servingwomen who had vowed continence with her learned of the bishop's intention and wept as they reported it to blessed Elizabeth; but she reassured them, saying: "I trust in the Lord, for love of whom I have vowed perpetual continence. He will keep my resolution firm, will ward off all violence, and will defeat the schemes of men. If perchance my uncle wishes to wed me to another, I will set my mind against him and contradict him verbally; and if no other way of escape is left to me, I will cut off my nose, because no one would have me, thus disfigured."

By the bishop's order she was taken against her will to a castle, to stay there until she consented to marry, and she wept and commended her chastity to the Lord. But now, by God's will, her husband's bones were returned from overseas, and the bishop had Elizabeth brought back to give loving welcome to her spouse's remains. The bishop met the landgrave's bones in a procession of honor, and blessed Elizabeth gave them welcome with devotion and much shedding of tears. She then turned to the Lord and said: "I give you thanks, O God, for deigning to console miserable me by the reception of the bones of my spouse whom you loved. You know, O Lord, that I loved him dearly, as he loved you, yet for love of you I deprived myself of his presence and sent him to relieve your Holy Land. Delightful as it would be for me to live with him still, even were we reduced to go begging through the whole world, yet I would not give one hair of my head to have him back against your will, nor to recall him to this mortal life. I commend him and me to your grace."

Now, lest she lose the hundredfold fruit which is given to those who strive for evangelical perfection and are transferred from the left hand of misery to the right hand of glory, Elizabeth put on religious dress, namely, robes of plain gray, low-grade material. She observed perpetual continence after her husband's death, embraced voluntary poverty, and would have begged from door to door had not Master Conrad forbidden her. Her habit was so shabby that her gray cloak had to be lengthened and the holes in the sleeves of her tunic patched with cloth of a different color. When her father, the king of Hungary, heard of the destitution in which she was living, he sent a knight to persuade her to return to her paternal home. When the knight saw her dressed in such poor attire, sitting humbly and spinning thread, he was overcome with confusion and wonder, and exclaimed: "Never has a king's daughter been seen in such tawdry clothes, nor any royal personage spinning wool!"

Blessed Elizabeth absolutely refused to return with the knight, preferring to live in poverty with the poor rather than to be surrounded with riches with the rich. Then in order that her spirit might move totally to God and her devotion be unhampered by distraction or impediment, she prayed the Lord to fill her with contempt for all temporal goods, to take from her heart her love for her children, and to grant her indifference and constancy in the face of every insult. When she had finished her prayer, she heard the Lord saying to her: "Your prayer has been favorably heard." Elizabeth told her women: "The Lord has heard my voice graciously, because I regard all temporal things as dung, I care for my children no more than for others around me, I make light of all contempt and disrespect, and it seems to me that I no longer love any but God alone."

Master Conrad often imposed disagreeable and contrary things upon her, and separated from her company any persons to whom she seemed to feel a particular attachment. Thus he sent away from her two servingmaids who had grown up with her and were her loyal and dear friends: many tears were shed on both sides over this separation. The holy man took these measures in order to break her will and allow her to direct her whole desire to God, and to guard her from being reminded of her past glory by any of her servants. In all these matters she was quick in obedience and steadfast in patience, in order to possess her own soul by patience, and by obedience to be crowned with victory.

Blessed Elizabeth also said: "For God's sake I fear mortal man as much as I ought to fear the heavenly judge. Therefore I choose to give my obedience to Master Conrad, a poor, undistinguished man, rather than to some bishop, so that every occasion of worldly consolation may be taken away from me." Once when she had yielded to the earnest request of some nuns and had visited their convent without obtaining permission from her spiritual master, he had her flogged so severely that the marks of the lashes were still visible three weeks later. To her women she said, for their consolation as well as for her own: "The sedge grass lies flat when the river is in flood, and when the water recedes, the sedge straightens up. So, when some affliction befalls us, we should bow to it humbly and, when it passes, be lifted up by spiritual joy to God." Her humility was such that she would not allow her servants to address her as "lady" but insisted that they use the singular forms, as is usual when speaking to inferiors.[3] She washed the dishes and other kitchen utensils, and, lest her maids prevent her from doing so, had them carried to different places. She also said: "Could I have found a more menial way of life, I would have chosen it."

For the rest, in order to possess the best part with Mary, Elizabeth gave herself diligently to contemplative prayer. In this prayer she had special graces to shed tears, to have frequent visions of heaven, and to light the fire of love in others. At times when she was happiest she shed tears of joyous devotion, so that happy tears seemed to flow from her eyes as from a serene fountain. She seemed to be weeping and rejoicing at the same time, never letting tears change or mar her face. She said of those who looked gloomy when they wept: "Do they want to frighten the Lord away? Let them give to God what they have to give him with joy and good cheer!"

*   *   *

Elizabeth, having reached the summit of perfection through Mary's contemplative prayer, did not give up Martha's laborious activity, as we have shown by her devotion to the seven works of mercy. Indeed, after taking the veil of religion, she practiced those works as assiduously as before. She had received two thousand marks for her dowry. Now she gave some of that to the poor and with the rest built a large hospital at Marburg. This made people regard her as a prodigal spendthrift, and many called her insane. When she gladly ac-

---

[3]Singular forms are thou, thee, thy, etc.

cepted these insults, they accused her of being so happy because she had put the memory of her husband out of her heart too quickly.

After the hospital was built, she committed herself to serving the poor like a simple serving-woman. She ministered solicitously to their needs, bathing them, putting them to bed, covering them, and cheerfully saying to her own maids: "How fortunate we are, to be able to bathe our Lord and cover him!" In waiting on the sick she humbled herself so completely that when a poor child who had only one eye and was covered with scabs came into the hospital, she took him in her arms to the privy seven times in one night and willingly washed his bedclothes. Again there was a woman with a horrible leprosy whom she bathed and put to bed, cleansing and bandaging her sores, applying remedies, trimming her fingernails, and kneeling at her feet to loosen her shoes. She prevailed upon the sick to confess their sins and to receive holy communion, and when one old woman flatly refused, she had her whipped to change her mind.

When Elizabeth was not busy with caring for the sick, she spun wool that was sent to her from a monastery, and divided the money she earned among the needy. At a time when everyone was poor, Elizabeth received five hundred marks from her dowry and set about distributing the money to those in need. She lined them all up, tied an apron on, and began the distribution, having made a rule that if anyone changed place in the line in order to receive a second time, that person's hair would be cut off. It happened that a girl named Radegund, who was admired for the beauty of her tresses, came to the hospital, not to receive an alms but to visit her sister who was ill. Since she did not get on line, she was brought to blessed Elizabeth for breaking the rule, and Elizabeth ordered her hair cut off, despite her sobs and her struggles. Then some of those present said that the girl was not at fault, but Elizabeth said: "At least from now on she won't be able to flaunt her curls at dances or indulge in similar vanities." She asked Radegund if she had ever thought of entering the religious life, and the girl answered that she would have done so long since if she were

not so proud of her hair. Elizabeth: "It is dearer to me that you have lost your hair than if my son had been raised to the Empire!" Radegund took the religious habit and stayed on with Elizabeth, leading a praiseworthy life.

A poor woman gave birth to a daughter, and blessed Elizabeth lifted the baby from the sacred font and gave her her own name. Then she saw to the mother's needs and gave her the sleeves taken from her maid's coat to keep the infant warm. She also gave her shoes to the mother. Three weeks later the woman deserted her child and secretly went off with her husband. When Elizabeth got word of this, she had recourse to prayer, and the man and wife were unable to go a step farther, but had to come back to her and beg her forgiveness. She reproached them for their ingratitude, as they deserved, then turned the baby over to them to be cared for, and provided them with the necessary means.

The time was drawing near when the Lord intended to call his beloved out of the prison of this world, and to receive her, who had despised the kingdom of mortals, into the kingdom of the angels. Christ appeared to her and said: "Come, my beloved, to the eternal dwelling prepared for you!" She was brought low with fever and lay with her face turned toward the wall, and those who stood around her heard her humming a sweet melody. When one of her maids asked her what this meant, she answered: "A little bird perched between me and the wall, and sang so sweetly that I too had to sing." Throughout her illness she was always cheerful and prayed all the time. The day before she died she said to her attendants: "What would you do if the devil came near you?" After an interval she cried out three times: "Go away!" as if chasing the devil. Then she said: "It is almost midnight, the hour when Christ chose to be born and when he lay in his crib." And as the moment of her departure drew near, she said: "Now is the time when almighty God calls those who are his friends to the celestial nuptials!" Another interval, and she breathed her last and slept in peace, in the year of our Lord 1231.

Although her venerable body lay unburied for

four days, no unpleasant odor came from it, but rather a pleasant aroma that refreshed everyone. Then flocks of small birds that had never been seen there before clustered on the roof of the church. Their melodies were so sweet and their harmonies so varied that their music, which, as it were, accompanied the saint's obsequies, won the admiration of all who heard it. Loud was the mourning of the poor, deep the devotion of all the people. Some cut off wisps of her hair; others clipped shreds from her graveclothes, to be kept as precious relics. Her body was placed in a monument from which oil is said to have flowed afterwards.

*   *   *

REVIEW QUESTIONS

1. What are the characteristic attributes of a thirteenth-century female saint?
2. What were the signs that Elizabeth was in fact a saint?
3. Elizabeth was a member of the nobility. How did her social status determine the opportunities she had, as opposed to women from other social classes?

ST. THOMAS AQUINAS

FROM *Summa Theologica*

Thomas Aquinas (ca. 1225–1274) was a Dominican theologian, university professor, and author of the Summa Theologica, *the most influential theological work of the Middle Ages. Theology was a new term devised to define the recent academic subject of applying the tools of reason to religious truths. This confidence in human ability to understand a reasonable universe working according to God's logical plans and laws is central to the values of medieval humanism. In these sections of the* Summa Theologica *Thomas is analyzing proofs of God's existence, and the meaning of humanity's creation. This translation, faithful to the content of the original, rearranges for a modern audience a very formal style of scholastic argument.*

From *St. Thomas Aquinas: Summa Theologica,* edited by Timothy McDermott (1989), pp. 12–13, 144–49.

*   *   *

There Is a God. There are Five Ways of Proving There is a God:

The first and most obvious way is based on change. We see things changing. Now anything changing is being changed by something else. (For things changing are on the way to realization, whereas things causing change are already realized: they are realizing something else's potential, and for that they must themselves be real. The actual heat of a fire causes wood, already able to be hot, to become actually hot, and so causes change in the wood. Now the actually hot cannot at the same time be potentially hot, but only potentially cold. So what changes cannot as such be causing the change, but must be being changed by something else.) This something else, if itself changing, is being changed by yet another thing; and this last by another. Now we must stop somewhere, otherwise there will be no first cause of the change, and, as a result, no subsequent causes. (Only when acted upon by a first cause do intermediate causes produce a change; if a hand does not move the stick, the stick will not move anything else.) We arrive then at some first cause of change not itself being changed by anything, and this is what everybody understands by *God.*

The second way is based on the very notion of cause. In the observable world causes derive their causality from other causes; we never observe, nor ever could, something causing itself, for this would mean it preceded itself, and this is not possible. But the deriving of causality must stop somewhere; for in the series of causes an earlier member causes an intermediate and the intermediate a last (whether the intermediate be one or many). Now eliminate a cause and you also eliminate its effects: you cannot have a last cause, nor an intermediate one, unless you have a first. Given no stop in the series of causes, no first cause, there will be no intermediate causes and no last effect; which contradicts observation. So one is forced to suppose some first cause, to which everyone gives the name *God.*

The third way is based on what need not be and on what must be, and runs as follows. Some of the things we come across can be but need not be, for we find them springing up and dying away, thus sometimes in being and sometimes not. Now everything cannot be like this, for a thing that need not be, once was not; and if everything need not be, once upon a time there was nothing. But if that were true there would be nothing even now, because something that does not exist can only be brought into being by something already existing. If nothing was in being nothing could be brought into being, and nothing would be in being now, which

contradicts observation. Not everything therefore is the sort of thing that need not be; some things must be, and these may or may not owe this necessity to something else. But just as a series of causes must have a stop, so also a series of things which must be and owe this to other things. One is forced to suppose something which must be, and owes this to nothing outside itself; indeed it itself is the cause that other things must be.

The fourth way is based on the gradation observed in things. Some things are better, truer, more excellent than others. Such comparative terms describe varying degrees of approximation to a superlative; for example, things are hotter and hotter the nearer they approach what is hottest. Something therefore is the truest and best and most excellent of things, and hence the most fully in being; for Aristotle says that the truest things are the things most fully in being. Now *when many things possess some property in common, the one most fully possessing it causes it in the others: fire,* as Aristotle says, *the hottest of all things, causes all other things to be hot.* Something therefore causes in all other things their being, their goodness, and whatever other perfection they have. And this is what we call *God.*

The fifth way is based on the guidedness of nature. Goal-directed behaviour is observed in all bodies obeying natural laws, even when they lack awareness. Their behaviour hardly ever varies and practically always turns out well, showing that they truly tend to goals and do not merely hit them by accident. But nothing lacking awareness can tend to a goal except it be directed by someone with awareness and understanding; the arrow, for example, requires an archer. Everything in nature, therefore, is directed to its goal by someone with understanding, and this we call *God.*

*   *   *

month of May, in the year of Our Lord 1207. [The poem has been read out, give us some wine; if you have no pennies, throw down some pledges there, for you will get a good return on them.]

REVIEW QUESTIONS

1. In this poem, what assumptions about justice are behind trial by combat?
2. What values of the warrior aristocracy are apparent in this poem?

11 ⌾ THE LATER MIDDLE AGES, 1300–1500

By about 1300 Europe's economic and demographic growth seemed to stall. Medieval society reached limits on its geographic frontiers, could not count on increased agricultural yields from depleted soils, and no longer experienced big productivity gains from improved technologies in artisan manufacturing. Signs of trouble, famines and increased mortality, appeared long before the devastating plague of 1348, which killed one-third of the population in Europe and the Middle East and was especially lethal in the great cities like Cairo and Florence. The long fourteenth century, calamitous for its repeated epidemics and wars like the century-long episodic conflict between France and England, is a bridge between the confident thirteenth century and the first signs of recovery in the late fifteenth century The Later Middle Ages *is an awkward but necessary term for the period roughly from 1300 to 1500. The new values and artistic tastes associated with the Renaissance in Italy usually stand apart from the wider world of feudal monarchies and lingering medieval culture in northern Europe.*

Yet basic similarities in religion and the economy united this world, and above all the bubonic plague was no respecter of historical periods. Much of Europe experienced the same religious, economic, social, and psychological responses to repeated outbreaks of plague. The basic institutions of late medieval life—the family, papacy, monarchies, and universities—endured the shocks of high levels of mortality, proving the strength of late medieval people and their culture. These same institutions offered few practical explanations for the new killer, leading to a crisis in belief and a search for scapegoats that focused on traditional targets, the Jews and the lepers.

Giovanni Boccaccio, an eye witness to the plague's course through Florence where it killed more than half the population, recorded in his introduction to the Decameron *the impressions of a survivor. Whether the disease was the one known to modern biologists as bubonic plague, its effects on society, movingly described by Boccaccio, occurred in a setting where the economic shocks of high mortality led to declining prices and rents, and the paradox of higher wages for the remaining workers. The mood of the survivors—a strange mix of hyperconsumerism, greed, fear, and suspicion—produced a culture more preoccupied with piety, melancholy, and death. The plague struck down priests, students, monks, and nuns in higher than average numbers, and the church, with the papacy in Avignon and on the verge of schism, faced new challenges to its authority. Theologians like John Wyclif and Jan Hus raised fundamental questions about the sacraments and how the church functioned in the world. The papacy itself was usually at the center of controversies, especially when the great schism resulted in three competing popes by 1409. Pius II's account of his election as pope in 1458 shows the strengths and weaknesses of the mid-fifteenth-century church.*

In the eastern Mediterranean the Ottoman state was advancing into the Balkans and finally destroyed the last remnant of the Byzantine Empire by taking Constantinople in 1453. The Russian church and people came to see themselves as the third Rome, heirs to the Greek world and bulwark against the Muslims and Tartars. Another distinctive feature of this period is the rise of a vernacular culture, as more literature appeared outside the traditional Latin of the universities. Authors like Dante in Italian, Chaucer in English, and Christine de Pisan in French captured the spirit of late medieval society. The small reading audience and the larger numbers who were read to wanted literature and art that responded to the crises and questions of late medieval life. The old epics and courtly romances still appealed to many, but so much death required new approaches and explanations.

In the last phase of the Hundred Years' War, the dramatic career of France's heroic Jeanne d'Arc reveals a complex mix of the miraculous, nationalism, and misogyny at work as a teenage woman saved the French cause but paid a great price. The Later Middle Ages witnessed the irony of destructive wars fought by smaller armies and navies in the midst of continued devastating outbreaks of plague.

IBN KHALDUN

FROM *The Muqaddimah*

The North African scholar Ibn Khaldun (1332–1406) wrote The Muqaddimah, *the first systematic explanation of history as a useful subject for research and analytical writing. In these excerpts Ibn Khaldun discusses the complex subject of history and truth, and the even more difficult topic of interpreting the Quran in its historical context.*

From *Ibn Khaldun: The Muqaddimah,* vol. 1, by Franz Rosenthal (Princeton, N.J.: Princeton University Press, 1967), pp. 6–17.

History is a discipline widely cultivated among nations and races. It is eagerly sought after. The men in the street, the ordinary people, aspire to know it. Kings and leaders vie for it.

Both the learned and the ignorant are able to understand it. For on the surface history is no more than information about political events, dynasties, and occurrences of the remote past, elegantly presented and spiced with proverbs. It serves to entertain large, crowded gatherings and brings to us an understanding of human affairs. It shows how changing conditions affect human affairs, how certain dynasties came to occupy an ever wider space in the world, and how they settled the earth until they heard the call and their time was up.

The inner meaning of history, on the other hand, involves speculation and an attempt to get at the truth, subtle explanation of the causes and origins of existing things, and deep knowledge of the how and why of events. History, therefore, is firmly rooted in philosophy. It deserves to be accounted a branch of philosophy.

The outstanding Muslim historians made exhaustive collections of historical events and wrote them down in book form. But, then, persons who had no right to occupy themselves with history introduced into those books untrue gossip which they had thought up or freely invented, as well as false, discredited reports which they had made up or embellished. Many of their successors followed in their steps and passed that information on to us as they had heard it. They did not look for, or pay any attention to, the causes of events and conditions, nor did they eliminate or reject nonsensical stories.

Little effort is being made to get at the truth. The critical eye, as a rule, is not sharp. Errors and unfounded assumptions are closely allied and familiar elements in historical information. Blind trust in tradition is an inherited trait in human beings. Occupation with the scholarly disciplines on the part of those who have no right is widespread. But the pasture of stupidity is unwholesome for mankind. No one can stand up against the authority of truth, and the evil of falsehood is to be fought with enlightening speculation. The reporter merely dictates and passes on the material. It takes critical insight to sort out the hidden truth; it takes knowledge to lay truth bare and polish it so that critical insight may be applied to it.

Many systematic historical works have been composed, and the history of nations and dynasties in the world has been compiled and written down. But there are very few historians who have become so well known as to be recognized as authorities, and who have replaced the products of their predecessors by their own works. They can almost be counted on the fingers of the hands; they are hardly more numerous than the vowels in grammatical constructions which are just three. There are, for instance, Ibn Ishâq; at-Tabarî; Ibn al-Kalbî; Muhammad b. 'Umar al-Wâqidî; Sayf b. 'Umar al-Asadî; al-Mas'ûdî, and other famous historians who are distinguished from the general run of historians.

It is well known to competent persons and reliable experts that the works of al-Mas'ûdî and al-Wâqidî are suspect and objectionable in certain respects. However, their works have been distinguished by universal acceptance of the information they contain and by adoption of their methods and their presentation of material. The discerning critic is his own judge as to which part of their material he finds spurious, and which he gives credence to. Civilization, in its different conditions, contains different elements to which historical information may be related and with which reports and historical materials may be checked.

Most of the histories by these authors cover everything because of the universal geographical extension of the two earliest Islamic dynasties and because of the very wide selection of sources of which they did or did not make use. Some of these authors, such as al-Mas'ûdî and historians of his type, gave an exhaustive history of the pre-Islamic dynasties and nations and of other pre-Islamic affairs in general. Some later historians, on the other hand, showed a tendency toward greater restriction, hesitating to be so general and comprehensive. They brought together the happenings of their own period and gave exhaustive historical information about their own part of the world. They restricted themselves to the history of their own dynasties and cities. This was done by Ibn Hayyân, the historian of Spain and the Spanish Umayyads, and by Ibn ar-Raqîq, the historian of Ifrîqiyah and the dynasty in Kairouan (al-Qayra-wân).

The later historians were all tradition-bound and dull of nature and intelligence, or did not try not to be dull. They merely copied the older historians and followed their example. They disregarded the changes in conditions and in the customs of nations and races that the passing of time had brought about. Thus, they presented historical information about dynasties and stories of events from the early period as mere forms without substance, blades without scabbards, as knowledge that must be considered ignorance, because it is not known what of it is extraneous and what is genuine. Their information concerns happenings the origins of which are not known. It concerns species the genera of which are not taken into consideration, and whose specific differences are not verified. With the information they set down they merely repeated historical material which is, in any case, widely known, and followed the earlier historians who worked on it. They neglected the importance of change over the generations in their treatment of the historical material, because they had no one who could interpret it for them. Their works, therefore, give no explanation for it. When they then turn to the description of a particular dynasty, they report the historical information about it mechanically and take care to preserve it as it had been passed on down to them, be it imaginary or true. They do not turn to the beginning of the dynasty. Nor do they tell why it unfurled its banner and was able to give prominence to its emblem, or what caused it to come to a stop when it had reached its term. The student, thus, has still to search for the beginnings of conditions and for the principles of organization of the various dynasties. He must himself investigate why the various dynasties brought pressures to bear upon each other and why they succeeded each other. He must search for a convincing explanation of the elements that made for mutual separation or contact among the dynasties. All this will be dealt with in the Introduction to this work.

Other historians, then, came with too brief a presentation of history. They went to the extreme of being satisfied with the names of kings, without any genealogical or historical information, and with only a numerical indication of the length of reigns. This was done by Ibn Rashîq in the *Mîzân al-camal*, and by those lost sheep who followed his method. No credence can be given to what they say. They are not considered trustworthy, nor is their material considered worthy of transmission, for they caused useful material to be lost and damaged the methods and customs acknowledged as sound and practical by historians.

When I had read the works of others and probed into the recesses of yesterday and today, I shook myself out of that drowsy complacency and sleepiness. Although not much of a writer, I exhibited my own literary ability as well as I could, and, thus, composed a book on history. In this book I lifted the veil from conditions as they arise in the various generations. I arranged it in an orderly way in chapters dealing with historical facts and reflections. In it I showed how and why dynasties and civilization originate. I based the work on the history of the two races that constitute the population of the Maghrib at this time and people its various regions and cities, and on that of their ruling houses, both long- and short-lived, including the rulers and allies they had in the past. These two races are the Arabs and the Berbers. They are the two races known to have resided in the Maghrib for such a long time that one can hardly imagine they ever lived elsewhere, for its inhabitants know no other human races.

I corrected the contents of the work carefully and presented it to the judgment of scholars and the elite. I followed an unusual method of arrangement and division into chapters. From the various possibilities, I chose a remarkable and original method. In the work, I commented on civilization, on urbanization, and on the essential characteristics of human social organization, in a way that explains to the reader how and why things are as they are, and shows him how the men who constituted a dynasty first came upon the historical scene. As a result, he will wash his hands of any blind trust in tradition. He will become aware of the conditions of periods and races that were before his time and that will be after it.

I divided the work into an introduction and three books:

The Introduction deals with the great merit of historiography, offers an appreciation of its various methods, and cites errors of the historians.

The First Book deals with civilization and its essential characteristics, namely, royal authority, government, gainful occupations, ways of making a living, crafts, and sciences, as well as with the causes and reasons thereof.

The Second Book deals with the history, races, and dynasties of the Arabs, from the beginning of creation down to this time. This will include references to such famous nations and dynasties contemporaneous with them, as the Nabataeans, the Syrians, the Persians, the Israelites, the Copts, the Greeks, the Byzantines, and the Turks.

The Third Book deals with the history of the Berbers and of the Zanâtah who are part of them; with their origins and races; and, in particular, with the royal authority and dynasties in the Maghrib.

Later on, there was my trip to the East, in order to find out about the manifold illumination it offers and to fulfill the religious duty and custom of circumambulating the Kaʿbah and visiting Medina, as well as to study the systematic works and tomes on Eastern history. As a result, I was able to fill the gaps in my historical information about the non-Arab (Persian) rulers of those lands, and about the Turkish dynasties in the regions over which they ruled. I added this information to what I had written here before in this connection. I inserted it into the treatment of the nations of the various districts and rulers of the various cities and regions that were contemporary with those Persian and Turkish races. In this connection I was brief and concise and preferred the easy goal to the difficult one. I proceeded from general genealogical tables to detailed historical information.

Thus, this work contains an exhaustive history of the world. It forces stubborn stray wisdom to return to the fold. It gives causes and reasons for happenings in the various dynasties. It turns out to be a vessel for philosophy, a receptacle for historical knowledge. The work contains the history of the Arabs and the Berbers, both the sedentary groups and the nomads. It also contains references to the great dynasties that were contemporary with them, and, moreover, clearly indicates memorable lessons to be learned from early conditions and from subsequent history. Therefore, I called the work "Book of Lessons and Archive of Early and Subsequent History, Dealing with the Political Events Concerning the Arabs, Non-Arabs, and Berbers, and the Supreme Rulers Who Were Contemporary with Them."

I omitted nothing concerning the origin of races and dynasties, concerning the synchronism of the earliest nations, concerning the reasons for change and variation in past periods and within religious groups, concerning dynasties and religious groups, towns and hamlets, strength and humiliation, large numbers and small numbers, sciences and crafts, gains and losses, changing general conditions, nomadic and sedentary life, actual events and future events, all things expected to occur in civilization. I treated everything comprehensively and exhaustively and explained the arguments for and causes of its existence.

As a result, this book has become unique, as it contains unusual knowledge and familiar if hidden wisdom. Still, after all has been said, I am conscious of imperfection when I look at the scholars of past and contemporary times. I confess my inability to penetrate so difficult a subject. I wish that men of scholarly competence and wide knowledge would look at the book with a critical, rather than a complacent eye, and silently correct and overlook the mistakes they come upon. The capital of knowledge that an individual scholar has to offer is small. Admission of one's shortcomings saves from censure. Kindness from colleagues is hoped for. It is God whom I ask to make our deeds acceptable in His sight. He suffices me. He is a good protector.

Introduction

It should be known that history is a discipline that has a great number of different approaches. Its useful aspects are very many. Its goal is distinguished.

History makes us acquainted with the conditions of past nations as they are reflected in their national character. It makes us acquainted with the biographies of the prophets and with the dynasties and policies of rulers. Whoever so desires may thus achieve the useful result of being able to imitate historical examples in religious and worldly matters.

The writing of history requires numerous sources and greatly varied knowledge. It also requires a good speculative mind and thoroughness. Possession of these two qualities leads the historian to the truth and keeps him from slips and errors. If he trusts historical information in its plain transmitted form and has no clear knowledge of the principles resulting from custom, the fundamental facts of politics, the nature of civilization, or the conditions governing human social organization, and if, furthermore, he does not evaluate remote or ancient material through comparison with near or contemporary material, he often cannot avoid stumbling and slipping and deviating from the highroad of truth. Historians, Qur'ân commentators and leading transmitters have committed frequent errors in the stories and events they reported. They accepted them in the plain transmitted form, without regard for its value. They did not check them with the principles underlying such historical situations, nor did they compare them with similar material. Also, they did not probe more deeply with the yardstick of philosophy, with the help of knowledge of the nature of things, or with the help of speculation and historical insight. Therefore, they strayed from the truth and found themselves lost in the desert of baseless assumptions and errors.

This is especially the case with figures, either of sums of money or of soldiers, whenever they occur in stories. They offer a good opportunity for false information and constitute a vehicle for nonsensical statements. They must be controlled and checked with the help of known fundamental facts.

For example, al-Masʿûdî and many other historians report that Moses counted the army of the Israelites in the desert. He had all those able to carry arms, especially those twenty years and older, pass muster. There turned out to be 600,000 or more. In this connection, al-Masʿûdî forgets to take into consideration whether Egypt and Syria could possibly have held such a number of soldiers. Every realm may have as large a militia as it can hold and support, but no more. This fact is attested by well-known customs and familiar conditions. Moreover, an army of this size cannot march or fight as a unit. The whole available territory would be too small for it. If it were in battle formation, it would extend two, three, or more times beyond the field of vision. How, then, could two such parties fight with each other, or one battle formation gain the upper hand when one flank does not know what the other flank is doing! The situation at the present day testifies to the correctness of this statement. The past resembles the future more than one drop of water another.

Furthermore, the realm of the Persians was much greater than that of the Israelites. This fact is attested by Nebuchadnezzar's victory over them. He swallowed up their country and gained complete control over it. He also destroyed Jerusalem, their religious and political capital. And he was merely one of the officials of the province of Fârs. It is said that he was the governor of the western border region. The Persian provinces of the two ʿIrâqs, Khurâsân, Transoxania, and the region of Derbend on the Caspian Sea were much larger than the realm of the Israelites. Yet, the Persian army did not attain such a number or even approach it. The greatest concentration of Persian troops, at al-Qâdisîyah, amounted to 120,000 men, all of whom had their retainers. This is according to Sayf who said that with their retainers they amounted to over 200,000 persons. According to ʿAʾishah and az-Zuhrî, the troop concentration with which Rustum advanced against Saʿd at al-Qâdisîyah amounted to only 60,000 men, all of whom had their retainers.

*   *   *

It should be known that the Qurʾân was revealed in the language of the Arabs and according to their rhetorical methods. All Arabs understood it and knew the meaning of the individual words and composite statements. It was revealed in chapters and verses, in order to explain the oneness of God and the religious duties according to the various occasions.

Some passages of the Qurʾân concern articles of faith. Others concern the duties of the limbs of the body. Some are early and are followed by other, later passages that abrogate the earlie ones.

The Prophet used to explain these things, as it is said: "So that you may explain to the people that which was revealed to them." He used to explain the unclear statements in the Qurʾân and to distinguish the abrogating statements from those abrogated by them, and to inform the men around him in this sense. The men around him, thus, became acquainted with the subject. They knew why individual verses had been revealed, and the situation that had required them, directly on Muhammad's authority. Thus, the verse of the Qurʾân, "When God's help comes and the victory," refers to the announcement of the Prophet's death, and similar things.

These explanations were transmitted on the authority of the men around Muhammad and were circulated by the men of the second generation after them on their authority. They continued to be transmitted among the early Muslims, until knowledge became organized in scholarly disciplines and systematic scholarly works were written. At that time, most of these explanations were committed to writing. The traditional information concerning them, which had come down from the men around Muhammad and the men of the second generation, was transmitted farther. That material reached at-Tabarî, al-Wâqidî, ath-Thaʾâlibî, and other Qurʾân interpreters. They committed to writing as much of the traditional information as God wanted them to do.

The linguistic sciences then became technical discussions of the lexicographical meaning of words, the rules governing vowel endings, and style in word combinations. Systematic works were written on these subjects. Formerly, these subjects had been habits with the Arabs. No recourse to oral and written transmission had been necessary with respect to them. Now, that state of affairs was forgotten, and these subjects were learned from the books of philologists. They were needed for the interpretation of the Qur'ân, because the Qur'ân is in Arabic and follows the stylistic technique of the Arabs. Qur'ân interpretation thus came to be handled in two ways.

One kind of Qur'ân interpretation is traditional. It is based upon information received from the early Muslims. It consists of knowledge of the abrogating verses and of the verses that are abrogated by them, of the reasons why a given verse was revealed, and of the purposes of individual verses. All this can be known only through traditions based on the authority of the men around Muhammad and the men of the second generation. The early scholars had already made complete compilations on the subject. However, their works and the information they transmit contain side by side important and unimportant matters, accepted and rejected statements. The reason is that the Arabs had no books or scholarship. The desert attitude and illiteracy prevailed among them. When they wanted to know certain things that human beings are usually curious to know, such as the reasons for the existing things, the beginning of creation, and the secrets of existence, they consulted the earlier People of the Book about it and got their information from them. The People of the Book were the Jews who had the Torah, and the Christians who followed the religion of the Jews. Now, the people of the Torah who lived among the Arabs at that time were themselves Bedouins. They knew only as much about these matters as is known to ordinary People of the Book in contrast to learned rabbis. The majority of those Jews were Himyarites who had adopted Judaism. When they became Muslims, they clung to the information they possessed, such as information about the beginning of creation and information of the type of forecasts and predictions. That information had no connection with the Jewish or Christian religious laws they were preserving as theirs. Such men were Ka'b al-aḥbâr, Wahb b. Munabbih, 'Abdallâh b. Sallâm,

and similar people. The Qur'ân commentaries were filled with material of such tendencies transmitted on their authority. It is information that entirely depends on them. It has no relation to religious laws, such that one might claim for it the soundness that would make it necessary to act in accordance with it. The Qur'ân interpreters were not very rigorous in this respect. They filled the Qur'ân commentaries with such material, which originated, as we have stated, with the people of the Torah who lived in the desert and were not capable of verifying the information they transmitted. However, they were famous and highly esteemed, because they were people of rank in their religion and religious group. Therefore, their interpretation has been accepted from that time onwards.

Later, scholars applied themselves to verification and critical investigation. Abû Muhammad b. 'Aṭîyah, a recent Maghribî scholar, made his appearance. He abridged all the commentaries and selected the most likely interpretations. He set that material down in a good book, which is in general circulation among the inhabitants of the Maghrib and of Spain. Al-Qurṭubî adopted his method in this respect in another work, which is well known in the East.

The other kind of Qur'ân interpretation has recourse to linguistic knowledge, such as lexicography and the stylistic form used for conveying meaning through the appropriate means and methods. This kind of Qur'ân interpretation rarely appears separately from the first kind. The first kind is the one that is wanted essentially. The second kind made its appearance only after language and the philological sciences had become crafts. However, it has become preponderant, as far as certain Qur'ân commentaries are concerned.

The commentary in which this discipline is best represented is the *Kitâb al-Kashshâf* by az-Zamakhsharî, of Khuwârizm in the 'Irâq. However, its author is a Mu'tazilah in his dogmatic views. Therefore, he uses the various methods of rhetoric, arguing in favor of the pernicious doctrines of the Mu'tazilah, wherever he believed they occurred in the verses of the Qur'ân. Competent orthodox scholars have, therefore, come to disregard his work and to warn everyone against its pitfalls. However, they admit that he is on firm ground in everything relating to language and style. If the student of the work is acquainted with the orthodox dogmas and knows the arguments in their defense, he is no doubt safe from its fallacies. Therefore, he should seize the opportunity to study it, because it contains remarkable and varied linguistic information.

Recently, a work by an ʿIrâqî scholar, Sharaf-ad-dîn aṭ-Ṭîbî, of Tabrîz in the non-Arab ʿIrâq, has reached us. It is a commentary on the work of az-Zamakhsharî. Aṭ-Ṭîbî follows az-Zamakh-sharî's work literally, but opposes its Muʿtazilah dogmas and arguments, showing their lack of validity and always explaining that an eloquent style exists in a given verse but it reflects the opinions of orthodox Muslims, and not the dogmas of the Muʿtazilah. He does that very well, and he also possesses all the various disciplines of rhetoric *balâghah*.

"And He knows more than any scholar."

*   *   *

REVIEW QUESTIONS

1. On the basis of Ibn Khaldun's principles, how can we determine the truth and accuracy of a historical work?
2. Is there a difference between truth and accuracy in history?
3. How does Ibn Khaldun handle his chief religious text, the Quran?

GIOVANNI BOCCACCIO

FROM *The Decameron*

Giovanni Boccaccio (1313–1374), a poet, scholar, and humanist, put together by 1351 this collection of one hundred tales, The Decameron, *to entertain the survivors of the plague and divert them from their troubles. The framework of these stories is the ten Florentines who fled the city to escape death and passed the time by telling stories on set themes. In the introduction Boccaccio describes how his home city, Florence, experienced and survived the first terrible outbreak of plague in the spring of 1348.*

From *The Decameron*, edited by Giovanni Boccaccio, translated by G. H. McWilliams (New York: Penguin Books, 1995), pp. 5–13.

FROM Introduction

I say, then, that the sum of thirteen hundred and forty-eight years had elapsed since the fruitful Incarnation of the Son of God, when the noble city of Florence, which for its great beauty excels all others in Italy, was visited by the deadly pestilence. Some say that it descended upon the human race through the influence of the heavenly bodies, others that it was a punishment signifying God's righteous anger at our iniquitous way of life. But whatever its cause, it had originated some years

THE TRIUMPH OF DEATH (C. 1340)   FRANCESCO TRAINI (?)

This painting is part of a series of frescos decorating the Camposanto, the famous cemetery of Pisa. The frescos are by local tradition attributed to the Pisan painter Francesco Traini. This fresco about death was probably painted just before the arrival of the bubonic plague in Pisa in 1348, and it incorporates images of death formed in the years of famine and epidemics of the early fourteenth century. What overall impression of death does this fresco convey? In particular, find the image of Death and consider her role in the fresco. One of the many striking parts of this fresco is the detail in which the three riders confront the three corpses. What can we learn about the mentality of a people who commissioned this fresco to decorate a cemetery?

earlier in the East, where it had claimed countless lives before it unhappily spread westward, growing in strength as it swept relentlessly on from one place to the next.

In the face of its onrush, all the wisdom and ingenuity of man were unavailing. Large quantities of refuse were cleared out of the city by officials specially appointed for the purpose, all sick persons were forbidden entry, and numerous instructions were issued for safeguarding the people's health, but all to no avail. Nor were the countless petitions humbly directed to God by the pious, whether by means of formal processions or in all other ways, any less ineffectual. For in the early spring of the year we have mentioned, the plague began, in a terrifying and extraordinary manner, to make its disastrous effects apparent. It did not take the form it had assumed in the East, where if anyone bled from the nose it was an obvious portent of certain death. On the contrary, its earliest symptom, in men and women alike, was the appearance of certain swellings in the groin or the armpit, some of which were egg-shaped whilst others were roughly the size of the common apple. Sometimes the swellings were large, sometimes not so large, and they were referred to by the populace as *gavòccioli*. From the two areas already mentioned, this deadly *gavòcciolo* would begin to spread, and within a short time it would appear at random all over the body. Later on, the symptoms of the disease changed, and many people began to find dark blotches and bruises on their arms, thighs, and other parts of the body, sometimes large and few in number, at other times tiny and closely spaced. These, to anyone unfortunate enough to contract them, were just as infallible a sign that he would die as the *gavòcciolo* had been earlier, and as indeed it still was.

Against these maladies, it seemed that all the advice of physicians and all the power of medicine were profitless and unavailing. Perhaps the nature of the illness was such that it allowed no remedy: or perhaps those people who were treating the illness (whose numbers had increased enormously because the ranks of the qualified were invaded by

people, both men and women, who had never received any training in medicine), being ignorant of its causes, were not prescribing the appropriate cure. At all events, few of those who caught it ever recovered, and in most cases death occurred within three days from the appearance of the symptoms we have described, some people dying more rapidly than others, the majority without any fever or other complications.

But what made this pestilence even more severe was that whenever those suffering from it mixed with people who were still unaffected, it would rush upon these with the speed of a fire racing through dry or oily substances that happened to come within its reach. Nor was this the full extent of its evil, for not only did it infect healthy persons who conversed or had any dealings with the sick, making them ill or visiting an equally horrible death upon them, but it also seemed to transfer the sickness to anyone touching the clothes or other objects which had been handled or used by its victims.

It is a remarkable story that I have to relate. And were it not for the fact that I am one of many people who saw it with their own eyes, I would scarcely dare to believe it, let alone commit it to paper, even though I had heard it from a person whose word I could trust. The plague I have been describing was of so contagious a nature that very often it visibly did more than simply pass from one person to another. In other words, whenever an animal other than a human being touched anything belonging to a person who had been stricken or exterminated by the disease, it not only caught the sickness, but died from it almost at once. To all of this, as I have just said, my own eyes bore witness on more than one occasion. One day, for instance, the rags of a pauper who had died from the disease were thrown into the street, where they attracted the attention of two pigs. In their wonted fashion, the pigs first of all gave the rags a thorough mauling with their snouts, after which they took them between their teeth and shook them against their cheeks. And within a short time they began to writhe as though they had been poisoned, then they both dropped dead to the ground, spread-eagled upon the rags that had brought about their undoing.

These things, and many others of a similar or even worse nature, caused various fears and fantasies to take root in the minds of those who were still alive and well. And almost without exception, they took a single and very inhuman precaution, namely to avoid or run away from the sick and their belongings, by which means they all thought that their own health would be preserved.

Some people were of the opinion that a sober and abstemious mode of living considerably reduced the risk of infection. They therefore formed themselves into groups and lived in isolation from everyone else. Having withdrawn to a comfortable abode where there were no sick persons, they locked themselves in and settled down to a peaceable existence, consuming modest quantities of delicate foods and precious wines and avoiding all excesses. They refrained from speaking to outsiders, refused to receive news of the dead or the sick, and entertained themselves with music and whatever other amusements they were able to devise.

Others took the opposite view, and maintained that an infallible way of warding off this appalling evil was to drink heavily, enjoy life to the full, go round singing and merrymaking, gratify all of one's cravings whenever the opportunity offered, and shrug the whole thing off as one enormous joke. Moreover, they practised what they preached to the best of their ability, for they would visit one tavern after another, drinking all day and night to immoderate excess; or alternatively (and this was their more frequent custom), they would do their drinking in various private houses, but only in the ones where the conversation was restricted to subjects that were pleasant or entertaining. Such places were easy to find, for people behaved as though their days were numbered, and treated their belongings and their own persons with equal abandon. Hence most houses had become common property, and any passing stranger could make himself at home as naturally as though he were the rightful owner. But for all their riotous

manner of living, these people always took good care to avoid any contact with the sick.

In the face of so much affliction and misery, all respect for the laws of God and man had virtually broken down and been extinguished in our city. For like everybody else, those ministers and executors of the laws who were not either dead or ill were left with so few subordinates that they were unable to discharge any of their duties. Hence everyone was free to behave as he pleased.

There were many other people who steered a middle course between the two already mentioned, neither restricting their diet to the same degree as the first group, nor indulging so freely as the second in drinking and other forms of wantonness, but simply doing no more than satisfy their appetite. Instead of incarcerating themselves, these people moved about freely, holding in their hands a posy of flowers, or fragrant herbs, or one of a wide range of spices, which they applied at frequent intervals to their nostrils, thinking it an excellent idea to fortify the brain with smells of that particular sort; for the stench of dead bodies, sickness, and medicines seemed to fill and pollute the whole of the atmosphere.

Some people, pursuing what was possibly the safer alternative, callously maintained that there was no better or more efficacious remedy against a plague than to run away from it. Swayed by this argument, and sparing no thought for anyone but themselves, large numbers of men and women abandoned their city, their homes, their relatives, their estates and their belongings, and headed for the countryside, either in Florentine territory or, better still, abroad. It was as though they imagined that the wrath of God would not unleash this plague against men for their iniquities irrespective of where they happened to be, but would only be aroused against those who found themselves within the city walls; or possibly they assumed that the whole of the population would be exterminated and that the city's last hour had come.

Of the people who held these various opinions, not all of them died. Nor, however, did they all survive. On the contrary, many of each different persuasion fell ill here, there, and everywhere, and having themselves, when they were fit and well, set an example to those who were as yet unaffected, they languished away with virtually no one to nurse them. It was not merely a question of one citizen avoiding another, and of people almost invariably neglecting their neighbours and rarely or never visiting their relatives, addressing them only from a distance; this scourge had implanted so great a terror in the hearts of men and women that brothers abandoned brothers, uncles their nephews, sisters their brothers, and in many cases wives deserted their husbands. But even worse, and almost incredible, was the fact that fathers and mothers refused to nurse and assist their own children, as though they did not belong to them.

Hence the countless numbers of people who fell ill, both male and female, were entirely dependent upon either the charity of friends (who were few and far between) or the greed of servants, who remained in short supply despite the attraction of high wages out of all proportion to the services they performed. Furthermore, these latter were men and women of coarse intellect and the majority were unused to such duties, and they did little more than hand things to the invalid when asked to do so and watch over him when he was dying. And in performing this kind of service, they frequently lost their lives as well as their earnings.

As a result of this wholesale desertion of the sick by neighbours, relatives and friends, and in view of the scarcity of servants, there grew up a practice almost never previously heard of, whereby when a woman fell ill, no matter how gracious or beautiful or gently bred she might be, she raised no objection to being attended by a male servant, whether he was young or not. Nor did she have any scruples about showing him every part of her body as freely as she would have displayed it to a woman, provided that the nature of her infirmity required her to do so; and this explains why those women who recovered were possibly less chaste in the period that followed.

Moreover a great many people died who would perhaps have survived had they received some assistance. And hence, what with the lack of appropriate means for tending the sick, and the virulence of the plague, the number of deaths reported in the city whether by day or by night was so enormous that it astonished all who heard tell of it, to say nothing of the people who actually witnessed the carnage. And it was perhaps inevitable that among the citizens who survived there arose certain customs that were quite contrary to established tradition.

It had once been customary, as it is again nowadays, for the women relatives and neighbours of a dead man to assemble in his house in order to mourn in the company of the women who had been closest to him; moreover his kinsfolk would forgather in front of his house along with his neighbours and various other citizens, and there would be a contingent of priests, whose numbers varied according to the quality of the deceased; his body would be taken thence to the church in which he had wanted to be buried, being borne on the shoulders of his peers amidst the funeral pomp of candles and dirges. But as the ferocity of the plague began to mount, this practice all but disappeared entirely and was replaced by different customs. For not only did people die without having many women about them, but a great number departed this life without anyone at all to witness their going. Few indeed were those to whom the lamentations and bitter tears of their relatives were accorded; on the contrary, more often than not bereavement was the signal for laughter and witticisms and general jollification—the art of which the women, having for the most part suppressed their feminine concern for the salvation of the souls of the dead, had learned to perfection. Moreover it was rare for the bodies of the dead to be accompanied by more than ten or twelve neighbours to the church, nor were they borne on the shoulders of worthy and honest citizens, but by a kind of gravedigging fraternity, newly come into being and drawn from the lower orders of society. These people assumed the title of sexton, and demanded a fat fee for their services, which consisted in taking up the coffin and hauling it swiftly away, not to the church specified by the dead man in his will, but usually to the nearest at hand. They would be preceded by a group of four or six clerics, who between them carried one or two candles at most, and sometimes none at all. Nor did the priests go to the trouble of pronouncing solemn and lengthy funeral rites, but, with the aid of these so-called sextons, they hastily lowered the body into the nearest empty grave they could find.

As for the common people and a large proportion of the bourgeoisie, they presented a much more pathetic spectacle, for the majority of them were constrained, either by their poverty or the hope of survival, to remain in their houses. Being confined to their own parts of the city, they fell ill daily in their thousands, and since they had no one to assist them or attend to their needs, they inevitably perished almost without exception. Many dropped dead in the open streets, both by day and by night, whilst a great many others, though dying in their own houses, drew their neighbours' attention to the fact more by the smell of their rotting corpses than by any other means. And what with these, and the others who were dying all over the city, bodies were here, there and everywhere.

Whenever people died, their neighbours nearly always followed a single, set routine, prompted as much by their fear of being contaminated by the decaying corpse as by any charitable feelings they may have entertained towards the deceased. Either on their own, or with the assistance of bearers whenever these were to be had, they extracted the bodies of the dead from their houses and left them lying outside their front doors, where anyone going about the streets, especially in the early morning, could have observed countless numbers of them. Funeral biers would then be sent for, upon which the dead were taken away, though there were some who, for lack of biers, were carried off on plain boards. It was by no means rare for more than one of these biers to be seen with two or three bodies upon it at a time; on the contrary, many were seen to contain a husband and wife, two or three brothers and sisters, a father and son, or some other pair of close relatives. And times

without number it happened that two priests would be on their way to bury someone, holding a cross before them, only to find that bearers carrying three or four additional biers would fall in behind them; so that whereas the priests had thought they had only one burial to attend to, they in fact had six or seven, and sometimes more. Even in these circumstances, however, there were no tears or candles or mourners to honour the dead; in fact, no more respect was accorded to dead people than would nowadays be shown towards dead goats. For it was quite apparent that the one thing which, in normal times, no wise man had ever learned to accept with patient resignation (even though it struck so seldom and unobtrusively), had now been brought home to the feeble-minded as well, but the scale of the calamity caused them to regard it with indifference.

Such was the multitude of corpses (of which further consignments were arriving every day and almost by the hour at each of the churches), that there was not sufficient consecrated ground for them to be buried in, especially if each was to have its own plot in accordance with long-established custom. So when all the graves were full, huge trenches were excavated in the churchyards, into which new arrivals were placed in their hundreds, stowed tier upon tier like ships' cargo, each layer of corpses being covered over with a thin layer of soil till the trench was filled to the top.

But rather than describe in elaborate detail the calamities we experienced in the city at that time, I must mention that, whilst an ill wind was blowing through Florence itself, the surrounding region was no less badly affected. In the fortified towns, conditions were similar to those in the city itself on a minor scale; but in the scattered hamlets and the countryside proper, the poor unfortunate peasants and their families had no physicians or servants whatever to assist them, and collapsed by the wayside, in their fields, and in their cottages at all hours of the day and night, dying more like animals than human beings. Like the townspeople, they too grew apathetic in their ways, disregarded their affairs, and neglected their possessions. Moreover they all behaved as though each day was to be their last, and far from making provision for the future by tilling their lands, tending their flocks, and adding to their previous labours, they tried in every way they could think of to squander the assets already in their possession. Thus it came about that oxen, asses, sheep, goats, pigs, chickens, and even dogs (for all their deep fidelity to man) were driven away and allowed to roam freely through the fields, where the crops lay abandoned and had not even been reaped, let alone gathered in. And after a whole day's feasting, many of these animals, as though possessing the power of reason, would return glutted in the evening to their own quarters, without any shepherd to guide them.

But let us leave the countryside and return to the city. What more remains to be said, except that the cruelty of heaven (and possibly, in some measure, also that of man) was so immense and so devastating that between March and July of the year in question, what with the fury of the pestilence and the fact that so many of the sick were inadequately cared for or abandoned in their hour of need because the healthy were too terrified to approach them, it is reliably thought that over a hundred thousand human lives were extinguished within the walls of the city of Florence? Yet before this lethal catastrophe fell upon the city, it is doubtful whether anyone would have guessed it contained so many inhabitants.

Ah, how great a number of splendid palaces, fine houses, and noble dwellings, once filled with retainers, with lords and with ladies, were bereft of all who had lived there, down to the tiniest child! How numerous were the famous families, the vast estates, the notable fortunes, that were seen to be left without a rightful successor! How many gallant gentlemen, fair ladies, and sprightly youths, who would have been judged hale and hearty by Galen, Hippocrates and Aesculapius (to say nothing of others), having breakfasted in the morning with their kinsfolk, acquaintances and friends, supped that same evening with their ancestors in the next world!

The more I reflect upon all this misery, the deeper my sense of personal sorrow; hence I shall refrain from describing those aspects which can suitably be omitted, and proceed to inform you that these were the conditions prevailing in our city, which was by now almost emptied of its inhabitants. ⋆ ⋆ ⋆

⋆ ⋆ ⋆

REVIEW QUESTIONS

1. According to Boccaccio, how did contemporaries explain the nature of the plague?
2. What were the worst social effects of the plague in Florence?
3. How were the unafflicted and the survivors likely to respond to their own continued life in the face of so much death?

GEOFFREY CHAUCER

FROM *The Canterbury Tales*

The English poet Geoffrey Chaucer (ca. 1340–1400) never completed his famous late work, The Canterbury Tales, *a collection of stories in verse form told by a group of pilgrims on their way to the shrine of St. Thomas Beckett in Canterbury. This format gave Chaucer the chance to retell some old stories, including a few from Boc-*

caccio. "The Pardoner's Tale," the story by a minor church official, is one of Chaucer's best and most revealing pieces.

From *The Canterbury Tales: Nine Tales and the General Prologue*, by Geoffrey Chaucer, edited by V. A. Kolve and Glending Olson, A Norton Critical Edition (New York: Norton, 1989), pp. 192–207.

The Prologue

"Lordinges," quod he, "in chirches whan I preche,
I peyne me° to han an hauteyn° speche,   *take pains / elevated*
And ringe it out as round as gooth° a belle,   *sounds*
For I can al by rote° that I telle.   *know all by memory*
My theme° is alwey oon,° and evere was—   *text / always the same*
Radix malorum est Cupiditas.[1]
    First I pronounce° whennes° that I come,   *proclaim / whence, from where*
And thanne my bulles[2] shewe I, alle and somme.°   *one and all*
Oure lige lordes seel[3] on my patente,°   *license*
That shewe I first, my body° to warente,°   *person / authorize*
That no man be so bold, ne preest ne clerk,°   *neither priest nor scholar*
Me to destourbe of Cristes holy werk;
And after that thanne telle I forth my tales.
Bulles of popes and of cardinales,
Of patriarkes,° and bishoppes I shewe,   *heads of churches*
And in Latyn I speke a wordes fewe
To saffron with my predicacioun,[4]
And for to stire° hem to devocioun.   *stir*
Thanne shewe I forth my longe cristal stones,°   *glass cases*
Y-crammed ful of cloutes° and of bones—   *rags*
Reliks been they, as wenen they echoon.[5]
Thanne have I in latoun[6] a sholder-boon
Which that was of an holy Jewes shepe.
'Goode men,' seye I, 'tak of my wordes kepe:°   *heed*
If that this boon be wasshe° in any welle,   *washed, dunked*
If cow, or calf, or sheep, or oxe swelle,°   *swell (up)*

---

[1] "Avarice (the love of money) is the root of all evil."
[2] Bulls, writs of indulgence for sin, purchasable in lieu of other forms of penance.
[3] Bishop's seal.
[4] "With which to season my preaching." (Saffron is a yellow spice.)
[5] "They are (saints') relics, or so they all suppose."
[6] Latten, a metal like brass.

That any worm hath ete, or worm y-stonge,[7]
Tak water of that welle, and wash his tonge,
And it is hool° anon;° and forthermore,   *healed / at once*
Of pokkes° and of scabbe and every sore   *pox*
Shal every sheep be hool,° that of this welle   *healed*
Drinketh a draughte. Tak kepe° eek° what I telle: *heed / also*
If that the good-man that the bestes° oweth°   *animals / owns*
Wol every wike,° er° that the cok him croweth,   *week / before*
Fastinge,° drinken of this welle a draughte—   *(While) fasting*
As thilke° holy Jewe[8] bure eldres taughte—   *that same*
His bestes and his stoor° shal multiplye.   *stock*
     And, sires, also it heleth° jalousye: *heals*
For though a man be falle in jalous rage,
Let maken with this water his potage,[9]
And nevere shal he more his wyf mistriste,°   *mistrust*
Though he the sooth° of hir defaute° wiste°—   *truth / erring / should know*
Al° had she taken° preestes two or three.   *Even if / taken (as lovers)*
     Heer is a miteyn° eek, that ye may see: *mitten*
He that his hond wol putte in this miteyn,
He shal have multiplying of his greyn°   *grain*
Whan he hath sowen, be it whete° or otes,°   *wheat / oats*
So that he offre pens, or elles grotes.[10]
     Good men and wommen, o° thing warne° I yow: *one / tell*
If any wight° be in this chirche now,   *person*
That hath doon sinne horrible, that he
Dar° nat for shame of it y-shriven[11] be,   *Dare*
Or any womman, be she yong or old,
That hath y-maked hir housbonde cokewold,°   *a cuckold*
Swich° folk shul have no power ne no grace   *Such*
To offren° to my reliks in this place.   *To offer (money)*
And whoso findeth him out of swich blame,°   *not deserving such blame*
He wol com up and offre a° Goddes name,   *make an offering in*
And I assoille° him by the auctoritee°   *(will) absolve / authority*
Which that by bulle y-graunted was to me.'
     By this gaude° have I wonne,° yeer° by yeer,   *trick / earned / year*
An hundred mark sith I was pardoner.[12]

---

[7]"Who has eaten any (poisonous) worm, or whom a snake has stung (bitten)."
[8]Jacob.
[9]"Have his soup made with this water."
[10]"Provided that he offers (to me) pennies or else groats (coins worth fourpence)."
[11]Confessed and absolved.
[12]"A hundred marks (coins worth thirteen shillings fourpence) since I became a pardoner."

I stonde lyk a clerk° in my pulpet,   *scholar*
And whan the lewed° peple is doun y-set,   *ignorant, unlearned*
I preche, so as ye han herd bifore,
And telle an hundred false japes° more.   *tricks, stories*
Thanne peyne I me° to strecche forth the nekke,   *I take pains*
And est and west upon the peple I bekke°   *nod*
As doth a dowve,° sittinge on a berne.°   *dove / in a barn*
Myn hondes and my tonge goon so yerne°   *rapidly*
That it is joye to see my bisinesse.
Of avaryce and of swich° cursednesse   *such*
Is al my preching, for° to make hem free°   *in order / generous*
To yeven hir pens, and namely unto me.[13]
For myn entente° is nat but for to winne,°   *intention / profit*
And nothing° for correccioun of sinne: *not at all*
I rekke° nevere, whan that they ben beried,°   *care / buried*
Though that hir soules goon a-blakeberied![14]
For certes,° many a predicacioun°   *certainly / sermon*
Comth ofte tyme of yvel° entencioun: *evil*
Som for plesaunce° of folk and flaterye,   *the entertainment*
To been avaunced by ypocrisye,[15]
And som for veyne glorie,° and som for hate.   *vainglory*
For whan I dar non other weyes debate,[16]
Than wol I stinge him[17] with my tonge smerte°   *sharp*
In preching, so that he shal nat asterte°   *leap up (to protest)*
To been° defamed falsly, if that he   *At being*
Hath trespased to° my brethren[18] or to me.   *wronged*
For, though I telle noght his propre° name,   *own*
Men shal wel knowe that it is the same
By signes and by othere circumstances.
Thus quyte° I folk that doon us displesances;°   *requite / offenses*
Thus spitte I out my venim under hewe°   *hue, coloring*
Of holynesse, to semen° holy and trewe.   *seem*
  But shortly° myn entente I wol devyse:°   *briefly / describe*
I preche of no thing but for coveityse.°   *out of covetousness*
Therfore my theme is yet, and evere was,
Radix malorum est cupiditas.
Thus can I preche agayn° that same vyce   *against*
Which that I use,° and that is avaryce.   *practice*

---

[13]"In giving their pence, and particularly to me."

[14]Blackberrying, i.e., wandering.

[15]To seek advancement through hypocrisy.

[16]"For when I dare enter into contest (argument) no other
  way."

[17]Some enemy.

[18]Fellow pardoners.

But though myself be gilty in that sinne,
Yet can I maken other folk to twinne°   *part*
From avaryce, and sore° to repente.   *ardently*
But that is nat my principal entente:
I preche nothing but for coveityse.
Of this matere° it oughte y-nogh suffyse.   *subject*
   Than telle I hem ensamples many oon°   *examples many a one*
Of olde stories longe tyme agoon,°   *past*
For lewed° peple loven tales olde;   *unlearned*
Swich° thinges can they wel reporte° and holde.°   *Such / repeat / remember*
What, trowe ye, the whyles I may preche[19]
And winne° gold and silver for° I teche,   *obtain / because*
That I wol live in povert° wilfully?°   *poverty / willingly*
Nay, nay, I thoghte° it nevere, trewely!   *considered*
For I wol preche and begge in sondry° londes;   *various*
I wol nat do no labour with myn hondes,
Ne make baskettes,[20] and live therby,
By cause I wol nat beggen ydelly.°   *without profit*
I wol non of the Apostles counterfete:°   *imitate*
I wol have money, wolle,° chese, and whete,   *wool*
Al° were it yeven of° the povereste page,°   *Even if / given by / servant*
Or of° the povereste widwe° in a village,   *by / poorest widow*
Al sholde hir children sterve for famyne.[21]
Nay! I wol drinke licour° of the vyne,   *liquor, wine*
And have a joly wenche in every toun.
But herkneth,° lordinges, in conclusioun: *listen*
Youre lyking is that I shall telle a tale.
Now have I dronke a draughte of corny° ale,   *malty*
By God, I hope I shal yow telle a thing
That shal by resoun° been at° youre lyking.   *with reason / to*
For though myself be a ful vicious° man,   *evil, vice-ridden*
A moral tale yet I yow telle can,

Which I am wont to preche for to winne.[22]
Now holde youre pees,° my tale I wol beginne."   *peace*

The Tale

In Flaundres whylom was° a compaignye   *once (there) was*
Of yonge folk, that haunteden folye—

---

[19]"What? do you believe (that) as long as I can preach."
[20]St. Paul was said to have been a basket maker.
[21]"Even though her children should die of hunger."
[22]"Which I am in the habit of preaching, in order to make some money."

As ryot, hasard, stewes, and tavernes,[23]
Where as° with harpes, lutes, and giternes,°
They daunce and pleyen at dees° bothe day and night,
And eten also and drinken over hir might,°
Thurgh which they doon the devel sacrifyse°
Withinne that develes temple,[24] in cursed wyse,°
By superfluitee° abhominable.
Hir othes° been so grete and so dampnable,°
That it is grisly for to here hem swere.
Our blissed Lordes body they totere°—
Hem thoughte° Jewes rente° him noght y-nough—
And ech° of hem at otheres sinne lough.°
And right anon thanne comen tombesteres°
Fetys and smale, and yonge fruytesteres,[25]
Singeres with harpes, baudes,° wafereres,°
Whiche been the verray° develes officeres
To kindle and blowe the fyr of lecherye
That is annexed° unto glotonye:
The Holy Writ take I to my witnesse
That luxurie° is in wyn and dronkenesse.
　　Lo, how that dronken Loth° unkindely°
Lay by his doghtres two, unwitingly;°
So dronke he was, he niste° what he wroghte.°
　　Herodes,° whoso wel the stories soghte,°
Whan he of wyn was repleet° at his feste,
Right at his owene table he yaf° his heste°
To sleen the Baptist John ful giltelees.°
　　Senek° seith a good word doutelees:
He seith, he can no difference finde
Bitwix a man that is out of his minde
And a man which that is dronkelewe,°
But that woodnesse, y-fallen in a shrewe,[26]
Persevereth lenger° than doth dronkenesse.
O glotonye,° ful of cursednesse!
O cause first° of oure confusioun!°
O original° of oure dampnacioun,
Til Crist had boght us with his blood agayn!

There where / guitars
dice
beyond their capacity
make sacrifice to the devil
way
excess
oaths, curses / condemnable

tear apart
It seemed to them / tore
each / laughed
female tumblers, dancers

bawds / girls selling cakes
the very

joined (as a sin)

lechery
Lot / unnaturally
unknowingly
knew not / did
Herod / should seek out
replete, full
gave / command
guiltless (innocent)
Seneca

drunken

Continues longer
gluttony
first cause / ruin
origin

---

[23]"Of young folk who gave themselves up to folly—(such)
as excessive revelry, gambling with dice, (visiting) brothels
and taverns."

[24]The tavern.

[25]"Shapely and slender, and young girls selling fruit."

[26]"Except that madness, having afflicted a miserable man."

Lo, how dere,° shortly for to sayn,°   *costly / to speak briefly*
Aboght was thilke cursed vileinye;[27]
Corrupt° was al this world for glotonye!   *Corrupted*
Adam oure fader and his wyf also
Fro Paradys to labour and to wo
Were driven for that vyce, it is no drede.°   *doubt*
For whyl that Adam fasted, as I rede,°   *read*
He was in Paradys; and whan that he
Eet of the fruyt defended° on the tree,   *forbidden*
Anon° he was outcast to wo and peyne.°   *Immediately / pain*
O glotonye, on thee wel oghte us pleyne![28]
    O, wiste a man° how manye maladyes   *(if) a man knew*
Folwen of° excesse and of glotonyes,   *Follow on*
He wolde been the more mesurable°   *measured, temperate*
Of his diete, sittinge at his table.
Allas! the shorte throte, the tendre mouth,[29]
Maketh that,° est and west, and north and south,   *Causes*
In erthe, in eir,° in water, men to swinke°   *air / labor*
To gete a glotoun deyntee° mete and drinke!   *dainty*
Of this matere,° O Paul, wel canstow trete:°   *subject / canst thou treat*
"Mete° unto wombe,° and wombe eek unto mete,   *Meat / belly*
Shal God destroyen bothe," as Paulus seith.[30]
Allas! a foul thing is it, by my feith,
To seye this word, and fouler is the dede,
Whan man so drinketh of the whyte and rede[31]
That of his throte he maketh his privee,°   *privy (toilet)*
Thurgh thilke° cursed superfluitee.°   *that same / excess*
    The apostel,[32] weping, seith ful pitously,
"Ther walken manye of whiche yow told have I"—
I seye it now weping with pitous voys—
"They been enemys of Cristes croys,°   *cross*
Of which the ende is deeth: wombe° is her° god!"   *belly / their*
O wombe! O bely! O stinking cod,[33]
Fulfild of donge and of corrupcioun![34]
At either ende of thee foul is the soun.°   *sound*

---

[27]"Bought was that same cursed, evil deed."
[28]"Oh, gluttony, we certainly ought to complain against you."
[29]"The brief pleasure of swallowing, the mouth accustomed to delicacies."
[30]1 Corinthians 6:13.
[31]Wines.
[32]St. Paul. See Philippians 3:18–19.
[33]"Bag," i.e., the stomach.
[34]"Filled up with dung and with decaying matter."

How° greet labour and cost is thee to finde!°   *What / to provide for*

Thise cookes, how they stampe,° and streyne,° and
  grinde,   *pound / strain*

And turnen substaunce into accident,[35]

To fulfille al thy likerous talent!°   *lecherous (here, gluttonous) appetite*

Out of the harde bones knokke they

The mary,° for they caste noght° awey   *marrow / nothing*

That may go thurgh the golet° softe and swote;°   *gullet / sweet*

Of spicerye° of leef, and bark, and rote°   *spices / root(s)*

Shal been his sauce y-maked by delyt,°   *to give pleasure*

To make him yet a newer° appetyt.   *renewed*

But certes, he that haunteth swich delyces[36]

Is deed, whyl that° he liveth in tho° vyces.   *while / those*

   A lecherous thing is wyn, and dronkenesse

Is ful of stryving° and of wrecchednesse.   *quarreling*

O dronke man, disfigured is thy face,

Sour is thy breeth, foul artow° to embrace,   *art thou*

And thurgh thy dronke nose semeth the soun°   *sound*

As though thou seydest ay° "Sampsoun, Sampsoun";[37]   *ever*

And yet, God wot,° Sampsoun drank nevere no wyn.   *knows*

Thou fallest,[38] as it were a stiked swyn;°   *stuck pig*

Thy tonge is lost, and al thyn honest cure,°   *care for decency*

For dronkenesse is verray sepulture°   *the true tomb*

Of mannes wit° and his discrecioun.°   *understanding / discretion*

In whom that° drinke hath dominacioun,   *In him whom*

He can no conseil° kepe, it is no drede.°   *secrets / doubt*

Now kepe yow fro the whyte and fro the rede—

And namely° fro the whyte wyn of Lepe[39]   *especially*

That is to selle° in Fishstrete° or in Chepe.°   *for sale / Fish Street / Cheapside*

This wyn of Spaigne crepeth subtilly

In othere wynes growinge faste by,[40]

Of° which ther ryseth swich fumositee,°   *From / vapor*

That whan a man hath dronken draughtes three

And weneth° that he be at hoom in Chepe,   *thinks*

He is in Spaigne, right at the toune of Lepe,

---

[35]"And turn substance into accident" (a scholastic joke: *sub-staunce* means "essence, essential qualities"; *accident*, "external appearances").

[36]"But truly, he that gives himself up to such pleasures."

[37]A witty kind of onomatopoeia—the snoring sound seems to say "Samson," who was betrayed.

[38]Down.

[39]Near Cadiz.

[40]The wines sold as French are often mixed with the cheaper wines of Spain.

Nat at The Rochel,° ne at Burdeux toun;°   *La Rochelle / Bordeaux*
And thanne wol he seye, "Sampsoun, Sampsoun."
    But herkneth,° lordinges, o° word I yow preye,   *listen / one*
That alle the sovereyn actes,° dar I seye,   *supreme deeds*
Of victories in the Olde Testament,
Thurgh verray° God, that is omnipotent,   *true*
Were doon in abstinence and in preyere:
Loketh the Bible, and ther ye may it lere.°   *learn*
    Loke Attila,[41] the grete conquerour,
Deyde° in his sleep, with shame and dishonour,   *Died*
Bledinge ay° at his nose in dronkenesse: *continually*
A capitayn shoulde live in sobrenesse.
And over al this, avyseth yow right wel°   *be well advised*
What was comaunded unto Lamuel°—   *Lemuel*
Nat Samuel, but Lamuel, seye I—
Redeth the Bible, and finde it expresly
Of wyn-yeving to hem that han justyse.[42]
Namore of this, for it may wel suffyse.
    And now that I have spoke of glotonye,
Now wol I yow defenden° hasardrye.°   *forbid / gambling at dice*
Hasard is verray moder° of lesinges,°   *the true mother / lies*
And of deceite and cursed forsweringes,°   *perjuries*
Blaspheme of Crist, manslaughtre, and wast° also   *waste*
Of catel° and of tyme; and forthermo,   *goods*
It is repreve° and contrarie of honour   *a reproach*
For to ben holde a commune hasardour.°   *gambler*
And ever the hyer° he is of estaat°   *higher / in social rank*
The more is he y-holden desolaat:°   *considered debased*
If that a prince useth° hasardrye,   *practices*
In alle governaunce and policye
He is, as by commune opinioun,
Y-holde the lasse in reputacioun.
    Stilbon, that was a wys° embassadour,   *wise*
Was sent to Corinthe in ful greet honour,
For Lacidomie° to make hire alliaunce.°   *Lacedaemon (Sparta) / their alliance*
And whan he cam, him happede par chaunce°   *it happened by chance*
That alle the grettest° that were of that lond,   *greatest (men)*
Pleyinge atte° hasard he hem fond.   *at (the)*
For which, as sone as it mighte be,°   *could be*
He stal him° hoom agayn to his contree,   *stole away*
And seyde, "Ther wol I nat lese° my name,°   *lose / (good) name*
Ne I wol nat take on me so greet defame,°   *dishonor*

---

[41]The Hun.
[42]Concerning the giving of wine to those responsible for the
  law (see Proverbs 31.4–5).

Yow for to allye° unto none hasardours.°   *to ally / gamblers*
Sendeth othere wyse embassadours—
For by my trouthe, me were levere dye°   *I would rather die*
Than I yow sholde to hasardours allye.
For ye that been so glorious in honours
Shul nat allyen yow with hasardours
As by my wil, ne as by my tretee.”°   *negotiations*
This wyse philosophre, thus seyde he.
    Loke eek° that to the king Demetrius   *also*
The king of Parthes,° as the book seith us,[43]   *Parthia*
Sente him a paire of dees° of gold in scorn,   *dice*
For he hadde used hasard ther-biforn;
For which he heeld his glorie or his renoun°   *renown*
At no value or reputacioun.
Lordes may finden other maner pley
Honeste° y-nough to dryve the day awey.   *Honorable*
    Now wol I speke of othes° false and grete   *oaths, curses*
A word or two, as olde bokes trete.
Gret swering° is a thing abhominable,   *cursing*
And false swering[44] is yet more reprevable.°   *reproachable*
The heighe° God forbad swering at al—   *high*
Witnesse on Mathew—but in special
Of swering seith the holy Jeremye,°   *Jeremiah*
“Thou shalt swere sooth° thyn othes° and nat lye,   *truly / oaths*
And swere in dome,° and eek in rightwisnesse;”°   *(good) judgment / righteousness*
But ydel° swering is a cursednesse.°   *vain / wickedness*
Bihold and see, that in the first table°   *tablet (of Moses)*
Of heighe Goddes hestes° honurable,   *commandments*
How that the seconde heste of him is this:
“Tak nat my name in ydel° or amis.”°   *in vain / amiss (wrongly)*
Lo, rather° he forbedeth swich° swering   *earlier (in the list) / such*
Than homicyde or many a cursed thing—
I seye that, as by ordre,° thus it stondeth—   *in terms of the order*
This knoweth, that his hestes understondeth,[45]
How that the second heste of God is that.
And further over,° I wol thee telle al plat°   *moreover / flatly*
That vengeance shal nat parten° from his hous   *depart*
That° of his othes is to° outrageous.   *Who / too*
“By Goddes precious herte,” and “By his nayles,”

---

[43]The *Policraticus* of John of Salisbury, which also contains
  the preceding story.
[44]I.e., Of oaths.
[45]“[He] knows this, who understands His commandments.”

Thus walke I, lyk
And on the grou
I knokke with my
And seye, 'Leve°
Lo, how I vanish,
Allas! whan shul
Moder, with yow
That in my cham
Ye, for an heyre
But yet to me she
For which ful pal
    But sires, to yo
To speken to an
But° he trespasse°
In Holy Writ ye r
'Agayns° an old r
Ye sholde aryse.'
Ne dooth unto an
Namore than that
In age, if that ye s
And God be with
I moot° go thider
    "Nay, olde cher
Seyde this other h
"Thou partest° nat
Thou spak right n
That in this contre
Have heer my trou
Telle wher he is, o
By God, and by th
For soothly thou a
To sleen us yonge
    "Now, sires," qu
To finde Deeth, tu
For in that grove I
Under a tree, and t
Nat for youre boos
See ye that ook?° ri
God save yow, that
    And yow amend
And everich° of thi

And "By the blode of Crist that is in Hayles,[46]
Seven is my chaunce,[47] and thyn is cink° and treye;"°   *five / three*
"By Goddes armes, if thou falsly pleye,
This dagger shal thurghout thyn herte go!"
This fruyt cometh of the bicched bones two—[48]
Forswering,° ire,° falsnesse, homicyde.   *Perjury / anger*
Now for the love of Crist that for us dyde,
Lete° youre othes, bothe grete and smale.   *Cease*
But, sires, now wol I telle forth my tale.
    Thise ryotoures° three of which I telle,   *rioters, revelers*
Longe erst er° pryme° rong of any belle,   *before / 9 A.M.*
Were set hem° in a taverne for to drinke;   *Had set themselves down*
And as they sat, they herde a belle clinke
Biforn a cors° was° caried to his grave.   *corpse / (which) was (being)*
That oon of hem gan callen to his knave,
"Go bet," quod he, "and axe redily,[49]
What cors is this that passeth heer forby;°   *by here*
And looke that thou reporte his name wel."[50]
    "Sire," quod this boy, "it nedeth never-a-del.°   *it isn't at all necessary*
It was me told, er° ye cam heer two houres.   *before*
He was, pardee,[51] an old felawe° of youres;   *companion*
And sodeynly he was y-slayn to-night,
For-dronke,° as he sat on his bench upright.   *Dead drunk*
Ther cam a privee° theef men clepeth° Deeth,   *secret / call*
That in this contree° al the peple sleeth,°   *region / kills*
And with his spere he smoot his herte atwo,[52]
And wente his wey withouten wordes mo.°   *more*
He hath a thousand slayn this pestilence.°   *(during) this plague*
And maister, er° ye come in his presence,   *before*
Me thinketh° that it were necessarie   *It seems to me*
For to be war° of swich an adversarie: *aware, careful*
Beth redy for to mete him everemore.°   *always*

---

[46]An abbey in Gloucestershire supposed to possess (as a high relic) some of Christ's blood.

[47]Throw.

[48]This fruit, i.e., result, comes from the two cursed dice. (Dice were made of bone; hence "bones" here.)

[49]The one of them proceeded to call to his servant-boy, "Go quickly," he said, "and ask straightway."

[50]Correctly.

[51]A weak form of the oath "by God," based on the French *par dieu.*

[52]"And with his spear he struck his heart in two." (Death was often shown in the visual arts as a hideous skeleton menacing men with a spear or arrow.)

---

[54]"But, sirs, it is not c
[55]" 'You should stand
    (this) advice."
[56]"He won't conceal h

Thus taughte
"By Seinte M
"The child se
Henne° over
Bothe man ai
I trowe° his h
To been avys
Er that° he di
"Ye,° Godd
"Is it swich p
I shal him sel
I make avow
Herkneth, fela
Lat ech° of us
And ech of us
And we wol s
He shal be sla
By Goddes di
Togidres° h
To live and d
As though he
And up they s
And forth the
Of which the
And many a g
And Cristes bl
Deeth shal be
Whan they
Right° as they
An old man a
This olde man
And seyde thu
The proude
Answerde agay
Why artow al
Why livestow°
This olde man
And seyde t
A man, though
Neither in cite
That wolde ch:
And therfore r
As longe time
Ne Deeth, allas

53"Why art thou

ing to her, there was a light, she answered that there was a great deal of light on all sides, as was most fitting. She added to the examiner that not all the light came to him alone!

* * *

Asked whether, when she went to Orleans, she had a standard or banner, in French *estandart ou banière*, and what colour it was, she answered she had a banner, with a field sown with lilies; the world was depicted on it, and two angels, one at each side; it was white, of white linen or boucassin, and on it were written, she thought, these names, JHESUS MARIA; and it was fringed with silk.

Asked if these names JHESUS MARIA were written above, or below, or at the side, she answered, at the side, she believed.

Asked which she preferred, her standard or her sword, she answered she much preferred her standard to her sword.

Asked who persuaded her to have this painting on her standard, she answered: "I have told you often enough that I have done nothing but by God's command." She said also that she herself bore the standard, when attacking the enemy, so as not to kill anyone; she never has killed anyone, she said.

Asked what force her king gave her when he set her to work, she answered that he gave her 10 or 12,000 men; and she went first to Orleans, to the fortress of Saint-Loup, and then to the fortress of the Bridge.

Asked to which fortress she ordered her men to retire, she says she does not remember. She added that she was confident of raising the siege of Orleans, for it had been revealed to her, and she had told the king so before going there.

Asked whether, when the assault was to be made, she did not tell her men that she would receive arrows, crossbolts and stones hurled by catapults or cannons, she answered no; there were a hundred wounded, or more. But she had indeed told her men not to fear and they would raise the siege. She said also that at the assault upon the fortress of the Bridge she was wounded in the neck by an arrow or crossbolt; but she received great comfort from St. Margaret, and was better in a fortnight. But she did not on account of that give up her riding or work.

Asked if she knew beforehand that she would be wounded, she answered that she did indeed, and she had told her king so; but that notwithstanding she would not give up her work. And it was revealed to her by the voices of the two saints, namely the blessed Catherine and Margaret. She added that she herself was the first to plant the ladder against the said fortress of the Bridge; and as she was raising the ladder she was wounded in the neck with the crossbolt, as she had said.

* * *

Asked on the subject of the woman's dress offered her so that she might hear Mass, she answered that she would not put it on till it should please Our Lord. And if it be that she must be brought to judgment she requests the Lords of the Church to grant her the mercy of a woman's dress and a hood for her head; she would die rather than turn back from what Our Lord commanded her; she firmly believed God would not let her be brought so low, or be presently without His help or miracle.

Asked why, if she wore man's dress at God's bidding, she asked for a woman's robe in the event of her death, she answered: "It is enough for me that it be long."

Asked if her godmother, who saw the fairies, was held to be a wise woman, she answered that she was held and reputed to be an honest woman, and not a witch or sorceress.

Asked whether her saying she would take a woman's dress if they would let her go would please God, she answered that if she were given permission to go in woman's dress she would immediately put on man's dress and do what Our Lord bade her. So she had formerly answered: and nothing would induce her to swear not to take up arms or to wear man's dress, to accomplish our Lord's will.

Asked about the age of the garments worn by St. Catherine and St. Margaret, she answered:

"You already have my reply on this matter, and you will get none other from me. I have answered you as best I can."

Asked if she did not believe heretofore that the fairies were evil spirits, she answered she knew nothing of that.

Asked how she knew that St. Catherine and St. Margaret hated the English, she answered: "They love those whom God loves, and hate whom He hates."

Asked if God hated the English, she answered that of God's love or His hatred for the English, or of what He would do to their souls, she knew nothing, but she was certain that, excepting those who died there, they would be driven out of France, and God would send victory to the French and against the English.

Asked if God was for the English when they were prospering in France, she answered that she knew not whether God hated the French, but she believed it was His will to suffer them to be beaten for their sins, if they were in a state of sin.

*   *   *

The Trial for Relapse

On Monday following, the day after Holy Trinity Sunday, we the said judges repaired to Jeanne's prison to observe her state and disposition. * * *

Now because the said Jeanne was wearing a man's dress, a short mantle, a hood, a doublet and other garments used by men (which at our order she had recently put off in favour of woman's dress), we questioned her to find out when and for what reason she had resumed man's dress and rejected woman's clothes. Jeanne said she had but recently resumed man's dress and rejected woman's clothes.

Asked why she had resumed it, and who had compelled her to wear it, she answered that she had taken it of her own will, under no compulsion, as she preferred man's to woman's dress.

She was told that she had promised and sworn not to wear man's dress again, and answered that she never meant to take such an oath.

Asked for what reason she had assumed male costume, she answered that it was more lawful and convenient for her to wear it, since she was among men, than to wear woman's dress. She said she had resumed it because the promises made to her had not been kept, which were to permit her to go to Mass and receive her Saviour, and to take off her chains.

Asked whether she had not abjured and sworn in particular not to resume this male costume, she answered that she would rather die than be in chains, but if she were allowed to go to Mass, if her chains were taken off and she were put in a gracious prison and were given a woman as companion, she would be good and obey the Church.

As we her judges had heard from certain people that she had not yet cut herself off from her illusions and pretended revelations, which she had previously renounced, we asked her whether she had not since Thursday heard the voices of St. Catherine and St. Margaret. She answered yes.

Asked what they told her, she answered that they told her God had sent her word through St. Catherine and St. Margaret of the great pity of this treason by which she consented to abjure and recant in order to save her life; that she had damned herself to save her life. She said that before Thursday they told her what to do and say then, which she did. Further her voices told her, when she was on the scaffold or platform before the people, to answer the preacher boldly. The said Jeanne declared that he was a false preacher, and had accused her of many things she had not done. She said that if she declared God had not sent her she would damn herself, for in truth she was sent from God. She said that her voices had since told her that she had done a great evil in declaring that what she had done was wrong. She said that what she had declared and recanted on Thursday was done only for fear of the fire.

Asked if she believed her voices to be St. Catherine and St. Margaret, she answered yes, and they came from God.

Asked to speak truthfully of the crown which is mentioned above, she replied: "In everything, I told you the truth about it in my trial, as well as I could."

*   *   *

REVIEW QUESTIONS

1. Why do the prosecutors seem preoccupied with the issues of Jeanne's dress and appearance?
2. How can she be tried for heresy?
3. How can we explain Jeanne's effect on contemporaries?

POPE PIUS II

FROM *Commentaries*

Aeneas Silvio Piccolomini (1405–1464) was born into an important aristocratic family in Siena. He received a fine humanist education and pursued a career in the church, where he rose in the ranks of papal diplomats. He became archbishop of Siena in 1450, a cardinal in 1456, and to his surprise was elected pope in 1458, taking the name Pius II. He spent most of his pontificate in a fruitless and very frustrating effort to organize a Crusade against the Ottoman Turks. This excerpt from his autobiography, the Commentaries—*a work not published in his lifetime —is a unique account of a papal election—his own. In this work the pope writes about himself in the third person, as Aeneas.*

From *Memoirs of a Renaissance Pope*, edited by Leona C. Gabel, translated by Florence A. Gragg (New York: Capricorn Books, 1955), pp. 79–88.

*   *   *

Ten days after Calixtus's death the other eighteen cardinals entered the conclave, while the whole city waited in suspense for the outcome; though indeed it was common talk that Aeneas, Cardinal of Siena, would be pope, since no one was held in higher esteem.

The conclave was held in the apostolic palace at St. Peter's, where two halls and two chapels were set apart for it. In the larger chapel were constructed cells in which the cardinals might eat and sleep; the smaller, called the chapel of San Niccolò, was reserved for discussion and the election of the pope. The halls were places where all might walk about freely.

On the day of their entrance nothing was done about the election. On the next day certain capitulations were announced, which they agreed should be observed by the new pope, and each swore that he would abide by them, should the lot fall on him. On the third day after mass, when they came to the scrutiny, it was found that Filippo, Cardinal of Bologna, and Aeneas, Cardinal of Siena, had an equal number of votes, five apiece. No one else had more than three. On that ballot, whether from strategy or dislike, no one voted for Guillaume, Cardinal of Rouen.

The cardinals were accustomed, after the result of the scrutiny was announced, to sit and talk together in case any wished to change his mind and transfer the vote he had given one to another (a method called "by accession"), for in this way they more easily reach an agreement. This procedure was omitted after the first scrutiny owing to the opposition of those who had received no votes and therefore could not now be candidates for accession. They adjourned for luncheon and then there were many private conferences. The richer and more influential members of the college summoned the rest and sought to gain the papacy for themselves or their friends. They begged, promised, threatened, and some, shamelessly casting aside all decency, pleaded their own causes and claimed the papacy as their right. Among these were Guillaume, Cardinal of Rouen, Pietro, Cardinal of San Marco, and Giovanni, Cardinal of Pavia; nor did the Cardinal of Lerida neglect his own interests. Each had a great deal to say for himself. Their rivalry was extraordinary, their energy unbounded. They took no rest by day or sleep by night.

Rouen, however, did not fear these men so much as he did Aeneas and the Cardinal of Bologna, toward whom he saw the majority of the votes inclining. But he was especially afraid of Aeneas, whose silence he had no doubt would prove far more effective than the barkings of the rest. Therefore he would summon now some, now others, and upbraid them as follows: "What is Aeneas to you? Why do you think him worthy of the papacy? Will you give us a lame, poverty-stricken pope? How shall a destitute pope restore a destitute church, or an ailing pope an ailing church? He has but recently come from Germany. We do not know him. Perhaps he will even transfer the Curia thither. And look at his writings! Shall we set a poet in Peter's place? Shall we govern the Church by the laws of the heathen? Or do you think Filippo of Bologna is to be preferred?—a stiff-necked fellow, who has not the wit to rule himself, and will not listen to those who show him the right course. I am the senior cardinal. You know I am not without wisdom. I am learned in

pontifical law and can boast of royal blood. I am rich in friends and resources with which I can succor the impoverished Church. I hold also not a few ecclesiastical benefices, which I shall distribute among you and the others, when I resign them."

He would then add many entreaties and if they had no effect, he would resort to threats. If anyone brought up his past simony as an indication that in his hands the papacy would be for sale, he did not deny that his past life had been tainted with that stain but swore that in the future his hands should be clean. He was supported by Alain, Cardinal of Avignon, who lent him every assistance in his power, not so much because he was a Frenchman siding with a Frenchman as because, at the elevation of Guillaume, he expected to obtain his house in Rome, the church of Rouen, and the vice-chancellorship. Not a few were won over by Rouen's splendid promises and were caught like flies by their gluttony. And the tunic of Christ without Christ was being sold.

Many cardinals met in the privies as being a secluded and retired place. Here they agreed as to how they might elect Guillaume pope and they bound themselves by written pledges and by oath. Guillaume trusted them and was presently promising benefices and preferment and dividing provinces among them. A fit place for such a pope to be elected! For where could one more appropriately enter into a foul covenant than in privies? Guillaume could certainly count on the two Greeks, the Cardinals of Genoa, San Sisto, Avignon, Colonna, and Pavia. The Vice-Chancellor, the Cardinals of Bologna, Orsini, and Sant' Anastasia were doubtful and seemed likely to accede to him if pushed a little. Indeed they had almost given him definite grounds for hope. Since it now appeared that eleven were agreed, they did not doubt that they would at once get the twelfth. For when it has come to this point, some one is always at hand to say, "I too make you pope," to win the favor that utterance always brings. They thought therefore that the thing was as good as done and were only waiting for daylight to go to the scrutiny.

Some time after midnight the Cardinal of Bologna went hurriedly to Aeneas's cell and waking him said, "Look here, Aeneas! Don't you know that we already have a pope? Some of the cardinals have met in the privies and decided to elect Guillaume. They are only waiting for daylight. I advise you to get up and go and offer him your vote before he is elected, for fear that if he is elected with you against him, he will make trouble for you. I intend to take care not to fall into the old trap. I know what it means to have the pope your enemy. I have had experience with Calixtus, who never gave me a friendly look, because I had not voted for him. It seems to me expedient to curry favor beforehand with the man who is going to be pope. I offer you the advice I am taking myself."

Aeneas answered, "Filippo, away with you and your advice! No one shall persuade me to vote for a man I think utterly unworthy to be the successor of St. Peter. Far from me be such a sin! I will be clean of that crime and my conscience shall not prick me. You say it is hard not to have the pope well-disposed to you. I have no fears on that score. I know he will not murder me because I have not voted for him. 'But,' you say, 'he will not love you, will not make you presents, will not help you. You will feel the pinch of poverty.' Poverty is not hard for one accustomed to it. I have led a life of indigence heretofore; what matter if I die indigent? He will not take from me the Muses, who are all the sweeter in humble fortunes.

"But I am not the man to believe that God will allow the Church, His Bride, to perish in the hands of the Cardinal of Rouen. For what is more alien to the profession of Christ than that His Vicar should be a slave to simony and lewdness? The Divine Mercy will not endure that this palace, which has been the dwelling of so many Holy Fathers, shall become a den of thieves or a brothel of whores. The apostleship is bestowed by God, not by men. Those who have conspired to commit the papacy to Rouen are men; and men's schemes are vain—who does not know it? Well has their conspiracy been made in the privies! Their plots too will have to retire and, like the Arian heresy, their most foul contrivings will end in a most foul place. Tomorrow will show that the Bishop of

Rome is chosen by God not by men. As for you, if you are a Christian, you will not choose as Christ's Vicar him whom you know to be a limb of the devil." With these words he frightened Filippo from going over to Rouen.

Next Aeneas went at daybreak to Rodrigo, the Vice-Chancellor, and asked whether he had sold himself to Rouen. "What would you have me do?" he answered. "The thing is settled. Many of the cardinals have met in the privies and decided to elect him. It is not for my advantage to remain with a small minority out of favor with a new pope. I am joining the majority and I have looked out for my own interests. I shall not lose the chancellorship; I have a note from Rouen assuring me of that. If I do not vote for him, the others will elect him anyway and I shall be stripped of my office." Aeneas said to him, "You young fool! Will you then put an enemy of your nation in the Apostle's chair? And will you put faith in the note of a man who is faithless? You will have the note; Avignon will have the chancellorship. For what has been promised you has been promised him also and solemnly affirmed. Will faith be kept with him or with you? Will a Frenchman be more friendly to a Frenchman or to a Catalan? Will he be more concerned for a foreigner or for his own countryman? Take care, you inexperienced boy! Take care, you fool! And if you have no thought for the Church of Rome, if you have no regard for the Christian religion and despise God, for Whom you are preparing such a vicar, at least take thought for yourself, for you will find yourself among the hindmost, if a Frenchman is pope."

The Vice-Chancellor listened patiently to these words of his friend and completely abandoned his purpose.

After this Aeneas, meeting the Cardinal of Pavia, said to him, "I hear that you too are with those who have decided to elect Rouen. Is this true?" He replied, "You have heard correctly. I have agreed to give him my vote so that I may not be left alone. For his victory is already certain; so many have declared for him." Aeneas said, "I thought you a different man from what I find you. Only see how much you have degenerated from your ancestors! Your father's brother (or was he your mother's?), Branda, Cardinal of Piacenza, when the papacy was beyond the mountains in Germany (for John XXIII, when he appointed the Council of Constance, had carried the Roman Curia across the Alps) never rested till he brought the Holy See back to Italy. It was owing to his diplomacy, devotion, and genius that on the withdrawal of the contestants for the papacy, Martin V, a Roman of the house of Colonna, was elected pope. Branda brought the Apostolic Curia back from Germany to Italy; you, his nephew, are going to transfer it from Italy to France. But Rouen will prefer his own nation to Italy and a Frenchman will be off to France with the supreme office.

"You say, 'He is under oath. He will not go outside this province without the decree of the senate and if he wishes to go, we will not consent.' What cardinal will dare oppose him when he is once seated on the apostolic throne? You will be the first, when you have secured some rich benefice, to say, 'Go where you will, Holy Father.' And what is our Italy without the Bishop of Rome? We still have the Apostleship though we have lost the Imperium, and in this one light we see light. Shall we be deprived of this with your sympathy, persuasion, help? A French pope will either go to France—and then our dear country is bereft of its splendor; or he will stay among us—and Italy, the queen of nations, will serve a foreign master, while we shall be the slaves of the French. The kingdom of Sicily will come into the hands of the French. The French will possess all the cities and strongholds of the Church. You might have taken warning from Calixtus, during whose papacy there was nothing the Catalans did not get. After trying the Catalans are you so eager to try the French? You will soon be sorry if you do! You will see the college filled with Frenchmen and the papacy will never again be wrested from them. Are you so dull that you do not realize that this will lay a yoke upon your nation forever?

"And what shall I say of this man's life? Are you not ashamed to entrust Christ's office to a slippery fellow who would sell his own soul? A fine bridegroom you are planning for the bride of Christ! You are trusting a lamb to a wolf. Where is your conscience? your zeal for justice? your common sense? Have you so far fallen below your true self? I suppose we have not often heard you say that it would be the Church's ruin if it fell into Rouen's hands? and that you would rather die than vote for this very man? What is the reason for this change? Has he suddenly been transformed from a demon to an angel of light? Or have you been changed from an angel of light to the devil, that you love his lust and filth and greed? What has become of your love for your country and your continual protestations that you preferred Italy above all other nations? I used to think that if everyone else fell away from devotion to her, you never would. You have failed me; nay, more, you have failed yourself and Italy, your country, unless you come to your senses."

The Cardinal of Pavia was stunned by these words and, overcome alike with grief and shame, he burst into tears. Then stifling his sobs he said, "I am ashamed, Aeneas. But what am I to do? I have given my promise. If I do not vote for Rouen, I shall be charged with treachery." Aeneas answered, "So far as I can see, it has come to the point where you will be guilty of treachery whichever way you turn. You now have to choose whether you prefer to betray Italy, your country, and the Church or the Bishop of Rouen." Convinced by these arguments Pavia decided it was less shameful to fail Rouen.

When Pietro, Cardinal of San Marco, learned of the conspiracy of the French and had lost hope of getting the papacy himself, actuated alike by patriotism and hatred of Rouen, he began to go to the Italian cardinals urging and warning them not to abandon their country; and he did not rest until he had gathered all the Italians except Colonna in the cell of the Cardinal of Genoa, revealed the conspiracy that had been made in the privies, and showed them that the Church would be ruined and Italy a slave forever, if Rouen should obtain the papacy. He implored them individually to show themselves men, to consult for the good of Mother Church and unhappy Italy, to put aside their enmities for one another and choose an Italian rather than a foreigner for pope. If they listened to him, they would prefer Aeneas to all others. There were present seven cardinals: Genoa, Orsini, Bologna, San Marco, Pavia, Siena, and Sant' Anastasia. All approved Pavia's words except Aeneas, who thought himself unworthy of so exalted an office.

The next day they went as usual to mass and then began the scrutiny. A golden chalice was placed on the altar and three cardinals, the Bishop of Ruthen, the Presbyter of Rouen, and the Deacon of Colonna, were set to watch it and see that there should be no cheating. The other cardinals took their seats and then, rising in order of rank and age, each approached the altar and deposited in the chalice a ballot on which was written the name of his choice for pope. When Aeneas came up to put in his ballot, Rouen, pale and trembling, said, "Look, Aeneas! I commend myself to you" —certainly a rash thing to say when it was not allowable to change what he had written. But ambition overcame prudence. Aeneas said, "Do you commend yourself to a worm like me?" and without another word he dropped his ballot in the cup and went back to his place.

When all had voted, a table was placed in the middle of the room and the three cardinals mentioned above turned out upon it the cupful of votes. Then they read aloud the ballots one after another and noted down the names written on them. And there was not a single cardinal who did not likewise make notes of those named, that there might be no possibility of trickery. This proved to be to Aeneas's advantage, for when the votes were counted and the teller, Rouen, announced that Aeneas had eight, though the rest said nothing about another man's loss, Aeneas did not allow himself to be defrauded. "Look more carefully at the ballots," he said to the teller, "for I have nine votes." The others agreed with him. Rouen said nothing, as if he had merely made a mistake.

This was the form of the ballot: The voter wrote with his own hand, "I, Peter (or John or whatever his name was) choose for pope Aeneas, Cardinal of Siena, and Jaime, Cardinal of Lisbon"; for it is permitted to vote for one or two or more,

on the understanding that the one first named is the one preferred, but if he does not have enough votes to be elected, the next is to be counted in his place, that an agreement may more easily be reached. But a thing advantageous in itself some men pervert to base ends, as Latino Orsini did on that day. He named seven in the hope that those he named might be influenced by that good turn either to accede to him in that scrutiny or to vote for him in another; although he who has the reputation of a cheat does not gain much by tricks.

When the result of the scrutiny was made known, it was found, as we have said before, that nine cardinals (Genoa, Orsini, Lerida, Bologna, San Marco, Santi Quattro Coronati, Zamora, Pavia, and Portugal) had voted for Aeneas; the Cardinal of Rouen had only six votes, and the rest were far behind. Rouen was petrified when he saw himself so far outstripped by Aeneas and all the rest were amazed, for never within the memory of man had anyone polled as many as nine votes by scrutiny. Since no one had received enough votes for election, they decided to resume their seats and try the method that is called "by accession," to see if perhaps it might be possible to elect a pope that day. And here again Rouen indulged in empty hopes. All sat pale and silent in their places as if entranced. For some time no one spoke, no one opened his lips, no one moved any part of his body except the eyes, which kept glancing all about. It was a strange silence and a strange sight, men sitting there like their own statues; no sound to be heard, no movement to be seen. They remained thus for some moments, those inferior in rank waiting for their superiors to begin the accession.

Then Rodrigo, the Vice-Chancellor, rose and said, "I accede to the Cardinal of Siena," an utterance which was like a dagger in Rouen's heart, so pale did he turn. A silence followed and each man looking at his neighbor, began to indicate his sentiments by gestures. By this time it looked as if Aeneas would be pope and some, fearing this result, left the conclave, pretending physical needs, but really with the purpose of escaping the fate of that day. Those who thus withdrew were the

Cardinals of Ruthen and San Sisto. However, as no one followed them, they soon returned. Then Jacopo, Cardinal of Sant' Anastasia, said, "I accede to the Cardinal of Siena." At this all appeared even more stunned, like people in a house shaken by unprecedented earthquakes, and lost the power of speech.

Aeneas now lacked but one vote, for twelve would elect a pope. Realizing this, Cardinal Prospero Colonna thought that he must get for himself the glory of announcing the pope. He rose and was about to pronounce his vote with the customary dignity, when he was seized by the Cardinals of Nicaea and Rouen and sharply rebuked for wishing to accede to Aeneas. When he persisted in his intention, they tried to get him out of the room by force, resorting even to such means to snatch the papacy from Aeneas. But Prospero, who, though he had voted for the Cardinal of Rouen on his ballot, was nevertheless bound to Aeneas by ties of old friendship, paid no attention to their abuse and empty threats. Turning to the other cardinals, he said, "I too accede to the Cardinal of Siena and I make him pope." When they heard this, the courage of the opposition failed and all their machinations were shattered.

All the cardinals immediately fell at Aeneas's feet and saluted him as Pope. Then they resumed their seats and ratified his election without a dissenting vote. At this point Bessarion, Cardinal of Nicaea, speaking for himself and for the others who had voted for the Cardinal of Rouen, said, "Your Holiness, we approve your election, which we do not doubt is of God. We thought before and still think that you are worthy of this office. The reason we did not vote for you was your infirmity. We thought your gout the one thing against you; for the Church needs an active man who has the physical strength to take long journeys and meet the dangers which we fear threaten us from the Turks. You on the contrary need rest. It was this consideration that won us to the side of the Cardinal of Rouen. If you were physically strong, there is no one we should have preferred. But, since God is satisfied, we must needs be satisfied too. God Himself, who has chosen you, will

make good the defect in your feet and will not punish our ignorance. We revere you as Pope, we elect you again, so far as is in our power, and we will serve you faithfully."

Aeneas answered, "Your Eminence of Nicaea, your opinion of us, as we understand it, is much higher than our own, when you attribute to us no defect except that in our feet. We are not ignorant that our imperfection is more general and we realize that our failings, which might justly have caused us to be rejected as pope, are almost innumerable. As to any virtues which might raise us to this post, we know of none; and we should declare ourselves utterly unworthy and should refuse the honor offered us, if we did not fear the judgment of Him Who has called us. For what is done by two thirds of the sacred college, that is surely of the Holy Ghost, which may not be resisted. Therefore we obey the divine summons and we praise you, Your Eminence of Nicaea, and those who voted with you. If, following the dictates of your conscience, you thought we ought not to be elected as being inadequate, you will still be welcomed by us, who attribute our calling not to this man or that but to the whole college and to God Himself, from Whom cometh every good and perfect gift."

With these words he took off the garments he was wearing and put on the white tunic of Christ. When asked by what name he wished to be called, he answered, "Pius," and he was at once addressed as Pius II. Then after swearing to observe the capitulations that had been announced in the college two days before, he took his place by the altar and was again reverenced by the cardinals, who kissed his feet, hands, and cheek. After that the election of a pope was proclaimed to the people from a high window and it was announced that he who had been Cardinal of Siena was now Pope Pius II.

*   *   *

REVIEW QUESTIONS

1. What were the divisions among the eighteen cardinals, and who were the ones with a chance of becoming pope?

2. Are there any signs in this candid account of the election that Aeneas is hiding something about his own ambitions?

3. In the end, what factors counted the most in Aeneas's election?

The Distribution of Wealth in Tuscany in 1427

In 1427 the republic of Florence instituted a new and complex system of taxation that assessed payment not on income but on wealth, minus some deductions. The records from this tax, called the catasto, *provide a very detailed portrait of households in Florence, as well as the towns, smaller cities, and countryside of Tuscany. The following table breaks down wealth by real property, mainly land; movables, things like animals and furniture; and shares in the public debt, minus the deductions for items like the family's house, tools, and a per capita exemption. This table provides a snapshot of the households of Florence; nowhere else in Europe provides such a detailed look at its population. The historians David Herlihy and Christiane Klapisch-Zuber created computer files for the individual returns and produced this table.*

From *Tuscans and Their Families,* by David Herlihy and Christiane Klapisch-Zuber (New Haven, Conn.: Yale University Press, 1985), p. 94.

Regional Distribution of Wealth in Tuscany according to Residence, 1427*

	Florence	Six Large Cities	Fifteen Towns	Countryside	Total
Nmbr Hhlds	9,946	6,724	5,994	37,266	59,890
Percent	16.2	11.2	10.0	62.2	100.0
Nmbr Persons	37,245	26,315	24,809	175,840	264,210
Percent	14.1	10.0	9.4	66.5	100.0
Real Property	4,128,024	1,137,466	614,446	2,178,253	8,058,189
Percent	51.2	14.1	7.6	17.0	100.0
Movables	3,467,707	585,357	170,245	223,792	4,447,101
Percent	78.0	13.2	3.8	5.0	100.0
Public Debt	2,573,378	3,438	1,888	1,337	2,580,041
Percent	99.7	0.1	0.1	0.1	100.0
Total Wealth	10,169,109	1,726,261	786,579	2,403,382	15,085,331
Percent	67.4	11.4	5.2	15.0	100.0
Deductions	2,504,041	332,763	135,341	321,205	3,293,350

Percent	76.0	10.1	4.1	9.8	100.0
Taxable Wealth	7,665,068	1,393,498	651,238	2,082,177	11,791,981
Percent	65.0	11.8	5.5	17.1	100.0

*Values are in gold florins. Figures do not include the personal deduction of 200 florins per person allowed at Florence and 50 florins at Pisa.

REVIEW QUESTIONS

1. Where was wealth concentrated, and what trends might have accounted for this distribution?

2. All of Florentine Tuscany contained about a quarter of a million people, and Renaissance Florence itself less than 40,000. What do these numbers reveal about the bubonic plague and its consequences?

3. Florence, with one-sixth of the households, had over three-quarters of the deductions. What might have accounted for this disparity?

12   Commerce, Conquest, and Colonization, 1300–1600

The commercial revolution of the Middle Ages built on and fostered a desire by Europeans to extend trading networks beyond their homelands. Trade was not the only motive for travel. Religious pilgrimages and missions, Crusades, and a desire to pillage their neighbors still motivated some people to venture beyond the frontiers of Western Christendom—their Europe. Successful trade depended on reliable knowledge about the world. Better maps and accounts of travels made it possible for people to find their way over the vast stretches of Asia to China or across the Atlantic to Vinland. The most adventurous travel was by sea, and better ships, sails, ropes, compasses, and astrolabes made it easier to sail long distances out of the sight of land. Traveling by galleys in the Mediterranean was a little easier than sailing in the Atlantic. The great inland sea, the Mediterranean, whose waters touched Africa, Asia, and Europe, witnessed the first advances in sailing techniques, and also the first experiments in European colonization on islands like Crete and Cyprus.

After 1250 Europeans increasingly visited, traded with, and eventually colonized the various "new worlds" that lay in all directions. These places were, of course, not new to their indigenous inhabitants. Northern travel was the least promising because of the difficult Arctic climate, yet the Scandinavians had established around 1000 a precarious settlement on Greenland that lasted until about 1450. Plague, climatic changes, and the hardships of making a living in the Arctic may explain the eventual retreat of the Vikings from parts of the north. Yet memories persisted about the mysterious Vinland. Modern excavations have proved that Vikings visited and for a time lived on North American soil. English and French fishing ships continued to visit the Grand Banks for its wonderful supplies of cod. In the 1490s both states resumed efforts to explore the North Atlantic. English kings supported the voyages of John and Sebastian Cabot out of Bristol to find a northern passage to China and the fabled riches of the East.

Beginning in the mid–thirteenth century, missionaries like William of Rubruck and intrepid merchants like the Polos of Venice followed the Silk Road
across central Asia to China, "the east beyond the east." A small trade continued along this route to Europe until the mid–fourteenth century, when plague
and changes in the Mongol Empire made travel across Asia more difficult. Accounts of the East and its immense riches in spices, precious gems and gold, and
silk continued to intrigue Europeans. Muslim travelers like Ibn Battuta displayed
a similar curiosity about Muslim states across Asia. In the fifteenth century,
Chinese explorers made it all the way to Madagascar off the coast of southern
Africa. The impulse to explore so far from home waned when the emperors
stopped supporting these trading voyages. If Europeans wanted regular trade
with China, they needed to find new, safe routes not controlled by the emerging
Islamic Ottoman and Mamluk Empires in the East. The Ottoman conquest of
Constantinople in 1453 choked off trade routes to the East and encouraged west-
ern Europeans like Columbus to look for new ways of reaching Asia. When the
Turks absorbed the Mamluk state in 1517, they became an important presence
in the Indian Ocean and found the Portuguese already there.

The Portuguese, facing the Atlantic, the Ocean Sea, began to explore the
west coast of Africa in search of gold. In the fourteenth century, Portuguese and
Italian sailors found the islands—the Azores and Madeira, both uninhabited,
and the Canaries, peopled by the Canarians. Spanish and French traders and
explorers also took an interest in the opportunities for trade and settlement, but
only the Portuguese continued to sail south beyond the Saharan coast. Merchants and sailors from Lisbon hoped to confirm ancient speculations that it was
possible to circumnavigate Africa and find a way to the Indian Ocean. Explorations of the West African coast opened up a lucrative trade in gold and slaves
that made tiny Portugal a world power. The patronage of the infante Henry the
Navigator (1394–1460) established a seafaring tradition that enabled Bartolo-
meu Dias to round the Cape of Good Hope in 1488. Vasco de Gama in 1497
sailed for India and eventually rewarded his investors with fabulous profits in
spices. The opening up of sub-Saharan Africa to trade was not yet followed by
significant colonization, as Europeans did not thrive in the tropics.

Only after reaching the "new worlds" of Asia and Africa did Europeans
again "discover" the last new world, the Americas. It is important to recognize
that Europeans had some previous experiences with colonies and new peoples before Columbus. The Italian-born Christopher Columbus (c. 1450–1506) convinced Isabella of Castile and Ferdinando of Aragon to gamble on a sea route
across the perilous Atlantic to the East. Until his dying day Columbus remained
convinced that the people he called Indians lived off the coast of Asia, though he
must have been puzzled by his repeated failures to reach the Chinese and Japa-
nese. Still, Columbus's accomplishments as a sailor were striking. His search for
wealth and trade was frustrated, however, and he laid the foundations for trad-

ing in slaves and exploiting the Indians and their lands in the search for gold that reached its bloody conclusion with Hernando Cortéz in Mexico in 1519 and and the Pizarros in Peru in 1533. In the sixteenth century the Spanish, and soon the Portuguese in Brazil, began to establish permanent colonies in their new territories. Soon other European powers, notably the Dutch, English, and French, would follow in their wake, first as explorers, traders, pirates, and slave traders.

At the same time a demographic catastrophe occurred in the Americas as the new diseases like smallpox which the Europeans brought with them wiped out a high percentage, in some places perhaps as much as 90 percent, of the Indians. As the Indians completely disappeared in some places and were greatly reduced in numbers in others, colonists planning to make money in the mines or the newly established sugar plantations increasingly relied on African slaves for labor. Supplying slaves to the last new world became an increasingly lucrative trade for the Portuguese, and soon enough for the Dutch and English as well. This first global economy, involving trade networks that stretched from Lisbon to Nanking, from the Senegal River in Africa to Vera Cruz in Mexico, enriched some Europeans and laid the foundations for colonial empires on which the sun never set.

WILLIAM OF RUBRUCK

FROM *On the Mongols*

William of Rubruck, a Franciscan monk from Flanders, was sent in 1253 to the Mongols by Louis IX of France, then on crusade in the East. The Mongol Empire, established by Chingis, or Genghis, Chan (1167–1227) and extended by successors like Mangu (1251–1259), had sent scouting parties as far west as Poland and Hungary. In the first section of this account, William describes Mongol culture to the French king. In the second section he is at the Mongol capital of Caracorum in Mongolia, seeking another audience with Mangu.

From *Mission to Asia*, edited by Christopher Dawson (Cambridge, Mass.: Medieval Academy of America, 1980), pp. 95–98, 100–6, 194–97.

*   *   *

Commerce and Conquest

The married women make for themselves really beautiful carts which I would not know how to describe for you except by a picture; in fact I would have done you paintings of everything if I only knew how to paint. A wealthy Mongol or Tartar may well have a hundred or two hundred such carts with chests. Baatu has twenty-six wives and each of these has a large house, not counting the other small ones which are placed behind the large one and which are, as it were, chambers in which their attendants live; belonging to each of these houses are a good two hundred carts. When they pitch their houses the chief wife places her dwelling at the extreme west end and after her the others according to their rank, so that the last wife will be at the far east end, and there will be the space of a stone's throw between the establishment of one wife and that of another. And so the orda of a rich Mongol will look like a large town and yet there will be very few men in it.

One woman will drive twenty or thirty carts, for the country is flat. They tie together the carts, which are drawn by oxen or camels, one after the other, and the woman will sit on the front one driving the ox while all the others follow in step. If they happen to come on a bad bit of track they loose them and lead them across it one by one. They go at a very slow pace, as a sheep or an ox might walk.

When they have pitched their houses with the door facing south, they arrange the master's couch at the northern end. The women's place is always on the east side, that is, on the left of the master of the house when he is sitting on his couch looking towards the south; the men's place is on the west side, that is, to his right.

On entering a house the men would by no means hang up their quiver in the women's section. Over the head of the master there is always an idol like a doll or little image of felt which they call the master's brother, and a similar one over the head of the mistress, and this they call the mistress's brother; they are fastened on to the wall. Higher up between these two is a thin little one which is, as it were, the guardian of the whole house. The mistress of the house places on her right side, at the foot of the couch, in a prominent position, a goat-skin stuffed with wool or other material, and next to it a tiny image turned towards her attendants and the women. By the entrance on the women's side is still another idol with a cow's udder for the women who milk the cows, for this is the women's job. On the other side of the door towards the men is another image with a mare's udder for the men who milk the mares.

When they have foregathered for a drink they first sprinkle with the drink the idol over the master's head, then all the other idols in turn; after this an attendant goes out of the house with a cup and some drinks; he sprinkles thrice towards the south, genuflecting each time; this is in honour of fire; next towards the east in honour of the air, and after that to the west in honour of water; they cast it to the north for the dead. When the master is holding his cup in his hand and is about to drink, before he does so he first pours some out on the earth as its share. If he drinks while seated on a horse, before he drinks he pours some over the neck or mane of the horse. And so when the attendant has sprinkled towards the four quarters of the earth he returns into the house; two servants with two cups and as many plates are ready to carry the drink to the master and the wife sitting beside him upon his couch. If he has several wives, she with whom he sleeps at night sits next to him during the day, and on that day all the others have to come to her dwelling to drink, and the court is held there, and the gifts which are presented to the master are placed in the treasury of that wife. Standing in the entrance is a bench with a skin of milk or some other drink and some cups.

In the winter they make an excellent drink from rice, millet, wheat and honey, which is clear like wine. Wine, too, is conveyed to them from distant regions. In the summer they do not bother about anything except cosmos. Cosmos is always to be found inside the house before the entrance door, and near it stands a musician with his instrument. Our lutes and viols I did not see there but many other instruments such as are not known among us. When the master begins to drink, then one of the attendants cries out in a loud voice "Ha!" and the musician strikes his instrument. And when it is a big feast they are holding, they all clap their hands and also dance to the sound of the instrument, the men before the master and the women before the mistress. After the master has drunk, then the attendant cries out as before and the instrument-player breaks off. Then they drink all round, the men and the women, and sometimes vie with each other in drinking in a really disgusting and gluttonous manner.

When they want to incite anyone to drink they seize him by the ears and pull them vigorously to make his gullet open, and they clap and dance in front of him. Likewise when they want to make a great feast and entertainment for anyone, one man takes a full cup and two others stand, one on his right and one on his left, and in this manner the three, singing and dancing, advance right up to him to whom they are to offer the cup, and they sing and dance before him; when he stretches out his hand to take the cup they suddenly leap back, and then they advance again as before; and in this way they make fun of him, drawing back the cup three or four times until he is in a really lively mood and wants it: then they give him the cup and sing and clap their hands and stamp with their feet while he drinks.

The Food of the Tartars

As for their food and victuals I must tell you they eat all dead animals indiscriminately and with so many flocks and herds you can be sure a great many animals do die. However, in the summer as long as they have any cosmos, that is mare's milk, they do not care about any other food. If during that time an ox or a horse happens to die, they dry the flesh by cutting it into thin strips and

hanging it in the sun and the wind, and it dries immediately without salt and without any unpleasant smell. Out of the intestines of horses they make sausages which are better than pork sausages and they eat these fresh; the rest of the meat they keep for the winter. From the hide of oxen they make large jars which they dry in a wonderful way in the smoke. From the hind part of horses' hide they make very nice shoes.

They feed fifty or a hundred men with the flesh of a single sheep, for they cut it up in little bits in a dish with salt and water, making no other sauce; then with the point of a knife or a fork especially made for this purpose—like those with which we are accustomed to eat pears and apples cooked in wine—they offer to each of those standing round one or two mouthfuls, according to the number of guests. Before the flesh of the sheep is served, the master first takes what pleases him; and also if he gives anyone a special portion then the one receiving it has to eat it himself and may give it to no one else. But if he cannot eat it all he may take it away with him or give it to his servant, if he is there, to keep for him; otherwise he may put it away in his *captargac*, that is, a square bag which they carry to put all such things in: in this they also keep bones when they have not the time to give them a good gnaw, so that later they may gnaw them and no food be wasted.

*   *   *

The Animals They Eat, Their Clothes and Their Hunting

The great lords have villages in the south from which millet and flour are brought to them for the winter; the poor provide for themselves by trading sheep and skins; and the slaves fill their bellies with dirty water and are content with this. They also catch mice, of which many kinds abound there; mice with long tails they do not eat but give to their birds; they eat dormice and all kinds of mice with short tails. There are also many marmots there which they call *sogur* and these congregate in one burrow in the winter, twenty or thirty of them together, and they sleep for six months; these they catch in great quantities.

Also to be found there are conies with a long tail like a cat and having at the tip of the tail black and white hairs. They have many other little animals as well which are good to eat, and they are very clever at knowing the difference. I saw no deer there, I saw few hares, many gazelles; wild asses I saw in great quantities and these are like mules. I also saw another kind of animal which is called *arcali* and which has a body just like a ram's and horns twisted like a ram's but of such a size that I could scarce lift the two horns with one hand; and they make large cups out of these horns.

They have hawks, gerfalcons and peregrine falcons in great numbers and these they carry on their right hand, and they always put a little thong round the hawk's neck. This thong hangs down the middle of its breast and by it they pull down with the left hand the head and breast of the hawk when they cast it at its prey, so that it is not beaten back by the wind or carried upwards. They procure a large part of their food by the chase.

When they want to hunt wild animals they gather together in a great crowd and surround the district in which they know the animals to be, and gradually they close in until between them they shut in the animals in a circle and then they shoot at them with their arrows.

I will tell you about their garments and their clothing. From Cathay and other countries to the east, and also from Persia and other districts of the south, come cloths of silk and gold and cotton materials which they wear in the summer. From Russia, Moxel, Great Bulgaria and Pascatu, which is Greater Hungary, and Kerkis, which are all districts towards the north, and full of forests, and from many other regions in the north which are subject to them, valuable furs of many kinds are brought for them, such as I have never seen in our part of the world; and these they wear in winter. In the winter they always make at least two fur garments, one with the fur against the body, the other with the fur outside to the wind and snow,

and these are usually of the skins of wolves or foxes or monkeys, and when they are sitting in their dwelling they have another softer one. The poor make their outer ones of dog and goat.

They also make trousers out of skins. Moreover, the rich line their garments with silk stuffing which is extraordinarily soft and light and warm. The poor line their clothes with cotton material and with the softer wool which they are able to pick out from the coarser. With the coarse they make felt to cover their dwellings and coffers and also for making bedding. Also with wool mixed with a third part horse-hair they make their ropes. From felt they make saddle pads, saddle cloths and rain cloaks, which means they use a great deal of wool. You have seen the men's costume.

How the Men Shave and the Women Adorn Themselves

The men shave a square on the top of their heads and from the front corners of this they continue the shaving in strips along the sides of the head as far as the temples. They also shave their temples and neck to the top of the cervical cavity and their forehead in front to the top of the frontal bone, where they leave a tuft of hair which hangs down as far as the eyebrows. At the sides and the back of the head they leave the hair, which they make into plaits, and these they braid round the head to the ears.

The costume of the girls is no different from that of the men except that it is somewhat longer. But on the day after she is married a woman shaves from the middle of her head to her forehead, and she has a tunic as wide as a nun's cowl, and in every respect wider and longer, and open in front, and this they tie on the right side. Now in this matter the Tartars differ from the Turks, for the Turks tie their tunics on the left, but the Tartars always on the right.

They also have a head-dress which they call *bocca*, which is made out of the bark of a tree or of any other fairly light material which they can find; it is large and circular and as big as two hands can span around, a cubit and more high and square at the top like the capital of a column. This *bocca* they cover with costly silk material, and it is hollow inside, and on the capital in the middle or on the side they put a rod of quills or slender canes, likewise a cubit and more in length; and they decorate this rod at the top with peacock feathers and throughout its length all round with little feathers from the mallard's tail and also with precious stones. The wealthy ladies wear such an ornament on the top of their head and fasten it down firmly with a hood which has a hole in the top for this purpose, and in it they stuff their hair, gathering it up from the back on to the top of the head in a kind of knot and putting over it the *bocca* which they then tie firmly under the chin. So when several ladies ride together and are seen from a distance, they give the appearance of soldiers with helmets on their heads and raised lances; for the *bocca* looks like a helmet and the rod on top like a lance.

All the women sit on their horses like men, astride, and they tie their cowls with a piece of sky-blue silk round the waist, and with another strip they bind their breasts, and they fasten a piece of white stuff below their eyes which hangs down to the breast.

The women are wondrous fat and the less nose they have the more beautiful they are considered. They disfigure themselves hideously by painting their faces. They never lie down on a bed to give birth to their children.

The Duties of the Women and Their Work

It is the duty of the women to drive the carts, to load the houses on to them and to unload them, to milk the cows, to make the butter and *grut*, to dress the skins and to sew them, which they do with thread made out of tendons. They split the tendons into very thin threads and then twist these into one long thread. They also sew shoes and socks and other garments. They never wash their clothes, for they say that that makes God angry

and that it would thunder if they hung them out to dry; they even beat those who do wash them and take them away from them. They are extraordinarily afraid of thunder. At such a time they turn all strangers out of their dwellings and wrap themselves in black felt in which they hide until it has passed over. They never wash their dishes, but when the meat is cooked, they wash out the bowl in which they are going to put it with some boiling broth from the cauldron which they afterwards pour back. The women also make the felt and cover the houses.

The men make bows and arrows, manufacture stirrups and bits and make saddles; they build the houses and carts, they look after the horses and milk the mares, churn the cosmos, that is the mares' milk, and make the skins in which it is kept, and they also look after the camels and load them. Both sexes look after the sheep and goats, and sometimes the men, sometimes the women, milk them. They dress skins with the sour milk of ewes, thickened and salted.

When they want to wash their hands or their head, they fill their mouth with water and, pouring this little by little from their mouth into their hands, with it they wet their hair and wash their head.

As for their marriages, you must know that no one there has a wife unless he buys her, which means that sometimes girls are quite grown up before they marry, for their parents always keep them until they sell them. They observe the first and second degrees of consanguinity, but observe no degrees of affinity; they have two sisters at the same time or one after the other. No widow among them marries, the reason being that they believe that all those who serve them in this life will serve them in the next, and so of a widow they believe that she will always return after death to her first husband. This gives rise to a shameful custom among them whereby a son sometimes takes to wife all his father's wives, except his own mother; for the orda of a father and mother always falls to the youngest son and so he himself has to provide for all his father's wives who come to him with his father's effects; and then, if he so wishes, he uses them as wives, for he does not consider an injury has been done to him if they return to his father after death.

And so when anyone has made an agreement with another to take his daughter, the father of the girl arranges a feast and she takes flight to relations where she lies hid. Then the father declares: "Now my daughter is yours; take her wherever you find her." Then he searches for her with his friends until he finds her; then he has to take her by force and bring her, as though by violence, to his house.

Of Their Justice and Judgments, Death and Burial

Concerning their penal laws I can tell you that when two men fight no one dares to interfere, even a father dare not help his son, but he who comes off the worse may appeal to the court of the lord and if the other touches him after the appeal, he is put to death. But he must go immediately without any delay and the one who has suffered the injury leads the other like a captive.

They inflict capital punishment on no one unless he has been caught in the act or confesses; but when a man is accused by a number of people, they torture him well, so that he confesses. Murder they punish by the death sentence, and also cohabiting with a woman not one's own. By one's own I mean wife or servant, for it is lawful for a man to use his slave as he will. Robbery on a grand scale they likewise punish by death. For a petty theft, such as one sheep, so long as a man has not been caught doing it often, they beat him cruelly, and if they deal him a hundred strokes, then they have to have a hundred rods. I am speaking of those who are beaten as a result of the court's sentence. Similarly they put to death false ambassadors, that is to say men who pretend they are ambassadors but are not; also sorceresses, of whom however I will tell you more later, for they consider them to be witches.

When anyone dies they mourn, wailing in a loud voice, and then they are free from paying taxes until the year is up. And if anyone is present at the death of an adult, he does not enter the dwelling of Mangu Chan for a year; if it is a child who dies he does not enter it for a month.

Near the grave of a dead man they always leave a dwelling, if he is of the nobility, that is of the family of Chingis, who was their first father and lord. The burial place of him who dies is not known; and always around those places where they bury their nobles there is a camp of men who guard the tombs. It has not come to my knowledge that they bury treasure with the dead. The Comans make a great mound over the dead man and set up a statue to him, facing the east and holding a cup in its hand in front of its navel. They also make pyramids for the rich, that is, little pointed houses; and in some places I saw large towers of baked tiles, and in others stone houses, although stones are not to be found there. I saw a man recently dead for whom they had hung up, between tall poles, the skins of sixteen horses, four facing each quarter of the earth, and they had put cosmos there for him to drink and meat for him to eat, and in spite of this they said of him that he had been baptised. Further east I saw other tombs, namely large areas strewn with stones, some round, some square and then four tall stones upright round the plot facing the four quarters of the earth.

When anyone is ill he takes to his bed and places a sign above his dwelling that there is a sick person there and that no one may enter. And so nobody visits the invalid except the one who looks after him. When anyone from one of the great ordas is sick, they place guards at a distance round the orda and they do not allow anyone to cross these bounds, for they are afraid an evil spirit or wind may come in with those entering. They summon their soothsayers as if they were their priests.

*　　*　　*

Friar William's Last Audience with Mangu

On the day of Pentecost Mangu Chan summoned me and the *tuin* with whom I had debated to his presence; before I went in the interpreter, Master William's son, told me we would have to return to our own country and that I was not to offer any objection for he had learned this was settled. When I came before the Chan I had to kneel down with the *tuin* beside me together with his interpreter. Then the Chan said to me: "Tell me if it is true that the other day when I sent my scribes to you, you said I was a *tuin*." I replied: "My lord, I did not say that, but, if you allow me, I will tell you the words I used." I then repeated to him what I had said and he answered: "I well thought you had not said it, for that was not the sort of thing you ought to say, but your interpreter translated badly." And he stretched out towards me the staff on which he was leaning, saying "Fear not." I smiled and said quietly: "If I were afraid I would not have come here." He enquired of the interpreter what I had said and he repeated it to him.

He then began to make a profession of his faith to me. "We Mongols," said he, "believe that there is but one God, by Whom we live and by Whom we die and towards Him we have an upright heart." I said, "God Himself will grant this for it cannot come about but by His gift." He asked what I had said and the interpreter told him. Afterwards the Chan continued: "But just as God gave different fingers to the hand so has He given different ways to men. To you God has given the Scriptures and you Christians do not observe them. You do not find in the Scriptures that a man ought to disparage another, now do you?" he said. "No," I replied, "but from the beginning I made it clear to you that I had no wish to wrangle with anyone." "My words do not apply to you," said he. "Similarly you do not find that a man ought to turn aside from justice for the sake of money." "No, my Lord," I said, "and for a truth I have not come to these parts in order to gain money, rather have I refused that which was offered to me." There was a scribe present, who bore witness to

the fact that I had refused a *iascot* and some pieces of silk. "My words do not apply to you," he said. "As I was saying, God has given you the Scriptures and you do not keep them; to us, on the other hand, He has given soothsayers, and we do what they tell us, and live in peace." He drank four times, I believe, before he finished saying these things.

And while I was listening closely to hear if there was still more he wished to declare concerning his faith, he began to speak of my return saying: "You have stayed here a long time, it is my wish that you go back. You have said that you dare not take my envoys with you; are you willing to take a message and letter from me?"

From then onwards I had neither the opportunity nor the time to put the Catholic Faith before him, for a man may not say more in his presence than he desires, unless he be an envoy; an envoy can say whatever he will, and they always enquire whether he wishes to say still more. I, however, was not allowed to continue speaking, but had to listen to him and reply to the questions he put.

I then answered him that if he would have his message explained to me and put down in writing, I would gladly take it to the best of my ability. He next asked if I desired gold or silver or costly garments. I said: "Such things we do not accept, but we have no provisions and without your aid cannot leave your country." He answered: "I will arrange for you to have all that you need as far as my territory stretches, do you wish for more?" I replied, "That is sufficient for me." He then enquired: "How far do you wish to be conducted?" I said: "We can manage for ourselves when we reach the land of the King of Armenia. If I were given a guide as far as that I would be satisfied." He answered: "I will have you accompanied thus far, after that you can fend for yourselves." And he added, "There are two eyes in a head, yet although they are two, nevertheless they have but one sight, and whither the vision of one is directed so is that of the other; you came from Baatu, it therefore behoves you to return by way of him."

When he had said this I asked his leave to say

a few words. "You may speak," he answered. Then I said: "My Lord, we are not warlike men, we would like to see those holding dominion over the world who would govern it most justly according to the will of God. Our duty is to teach men to live according to the will of God; for this reason did we come to these parts and we would gladly have remained here if you had allowed it. Since it is your good pleasure that we return, it must needs be; I will go back and carry your letter to the best of my ability in accordance with your commands. I would like to ask of your Eminence that, when I have taken your letter, I may be granted your permission to return to you, especially as you have some poor serfs at Bolac who speak our language and need a priest to teach them and their children their faith, and I would gladly abide with them." He replied: "Provided your masters send you back to me." I then said: "My Lord, I do not know what my masters have in mind, but I have permission from them to go wherever I will, where there is need to preach the word of God; and it seems to me that it is most necessary in these parts, therefore whether he send back an envoy to you or not, given your permission I would return."

He kept silent and sat for a long time as if turning things over in his mind, and the interpreter told me not to speak any more. However, I anxiously awaited his reply. At last he spoke: "You have a long journey ahead of you, fortify yourself with food so that you may be strong enough to reach your own country." And he had me given something to drink. I then left his presence, and never afterwards returned. If I had had the power of working miracles like Moses, he might have humbled himself.

*   *   *

REVIEW QUESTIONS

1. If William were a spy or an anthropologist, what valuable insights would he offer about Mongol culture?
2. In particular, according to William, how does the role of women in Mongol society compare with that of European women?
3. What ideas about religion determine the ways Mangu and William think about it?

IBN BATTUTA

FROM *The Travels*

Ibn Battuta (1304–c. 1377), from Tangier in Morocco, was an extraordinary traveler whose journeys took him as far as China and India. He wrote extensive accounts of his travels; here he describes Muslim Cairo in its prime before the plague.

From *The Travels of Ibn Battuta,* edited by H. A. R. Gibb (Cambridge, Mass.: Harvard University Press, 1958), pp. 41–53.

*   *   *

Commerce

I arrived at length at the city of Miṣr, mother of cities and seat of Pharaoh the tyrant, mistress of broad provinces and fruitful lands, boundless in multitude of buildings, peerless in beauty and splendour, the meeting-place of comer and goer, the stopping-place of feeble and strong. Therein is what you will of learned and simple, grave and gay, prudent and foolish, base and noble, of high estate and low estate, unknown and famous; she surges as the waves of the sea with her throngs of folk and can scarce contain them for all the capacity of her situation and sustaining power. Her youth is ever new in spite of length of days, and the star of her horoscope does not move from the mansion of fortune; her conquering capital (al-Qāhira) has subdued the nations, and her kings have grasped the forelocks of both Arab and non-Arab. She has as her peculiar possession the majestic Nile, which dispenses her district from the need of entreating the distillation [of the rain]; her territory is a month's journey for a hastening traveller, of generous soil, and extending a friendly welcome to strangers.

Ibn Juzayy remarks: Of Cairo the poet says—

No common town is Cairo, by thy life! Nay, she
Is heaven on earth for those with eyes to see;
Her youth those boys and maids with lustrous eyes,
Kawthar her Nile, her Rawḍa Paradise.

*   *   *

It is said that in Cairo there are twelve thousand water-carriers who transport water on camels, and thirty thousand hirers of mules and donkeys, and that on its Nile there are thirty-six thousand vessels belonging to the Sultan and his subjects, which sail upstream to Upper Egypt and downstream to Alexandria and Damietta, laden with goods and commodities of all kinds. On the bank of the Nile opposite Cairo is the place known as al-Rawḍa ['the Garden'], which is a pleasure park and promenade, containing many beautiful gardens. The people of Cairo are fond of pleasure and amusement. I once witnessed a fête there which was held for al-Malik al-Nāṣir's recovery from a fracture which he had suffered in his hand. All the merchants decorated their bazaars and had rich stuffs, ornaments, and silken fabrics hung up in their shops for several days.

The Mosque of 'Amr b. al-'Āṣ, and the Colleges, Hospital, and Convents

The Mosque of 'Amr b. al-'Āṣ is a noble mosque, highly venerated and widely celebrated. The Friday service is held in it, and the road runs right through it from east to west. To the west of it is the cell where the Imām Abū 'Abdallāh al-Shāfi'ī used to teach. As for the madrasas in Cairo, they are too many for anyone to count; and as for the Māristān, which is "between the two castles" near the mausoleum of al-Malik al-Manṣūr Qalā'ūn, no description is adequate to its beauties. It is equipped with innumerable conveniences and medicaments, and its revenue is reported to be a thousand dinars a day. The convents too are numerous. The people there call them khawāniq, the singular being khānqa, and the amīrs in Cairo vie with one another in building them.

Each convent in Cairo is affected to the use of a separate congregation of poor brethren, most of whom are Persians, men of good education and adepts in the 'way' of Sufism. Each has a shaikh and a warden, and the organization of their affairs is admirable. It is one of their customs in the matter of their food that the steward of the house comes in the morning to the faqīrs, each of whom then specifies what food he desires. When they assemble for meals, each person is given his bread and soup in a separate dish, none sharing with another. They eat twice a day. They receive winter clothing and summer clothing and a monthly allowance varying from twenty to thirty dirhams each. Every Thursday night they are given sugar cakes, soap to wash their clothes, the price of admission to the bath-house, and oil to feed their lamps. These men are celibate; the married men have separate convents. Amongst the stipulations required of them are attendance at the five daily prayers, spending the night in the convent, and assembly in mass in a chapel within the convent. Another of their customs is that each one of them sits upon a prayer-carpet reserved for his exclusive use. When they pray the dawn prayer they recite the chapters of *Victory,* of *the Kingdom,* and of *'Amma.* After this copies of the Holy Qur'ān are brought, divided into sections, and each faqīr takes a section. After 'sealing' the Qur'ān and reciting a *dhikr,* the Qur'ān-readers give a recital according to the custom of the Easterners. They hold a similar service following the mid-afternoon prayer.

They have a regular ritual for the admission of newcomers. The applicant comes to the gate of the convent and takes up his stand there, with his waist girt, a prayer mat on his shoulder, the staff in his right hand and the jug in his left. The gate-keeper informs the steward of the convent that he is there. The steward then comes out to him and asks him from what country he has come, what convents he has stayed in on his way, and who was his spiritual director (*shaikh*). When he has ascertained the truth of his answers, he admits him into the convent, spreads his prayer-mat for him in a place befitting his station, and shows him the lavatory. The newcomer renews his ablutions and, returning to his mat, ungirds his waist, and prays two prostrations, then he clasps the hand of the shaikh and those of the others present, and takes his seat amongst them. Another custom of theirs is that on Fridays the servant collects all their prayer-mats and takes them to the mosque, where he spreads them in readiness for their coming. The faqīrs come out in a body, accompanied by their shaikh, proceed to the mosque, and pray each on his own mat. When they have finished the prayer they recite the Qur'ān according to their

custom, and thereafter return in a body to the convent, accompanied by their shaikh.

The Qarāfa of Cairo and Its Sanctuaries

At [Old] Cairo too is [the cemetery called] al-Qarāfa, a place of vast repute for blessed power, whose special virtue is affirmed in a tradition related by al-Qurtubī amongst others, for it is a part of the amount al-Muqattam, of which God has promised that it shall be one of the gardens of Paradise. These people build in the Qarāfa beautiful domed chapels and surround them by walls, so that they look like houses, and they construct chambers in them and hire the services of Qur'ān-readers, who recite night and day in beautiful voices. There are some of them who build a religious house or a madrasa by the side of the mausoleum. They go out every Thursday evening to spend the night there with their children and womenfolk and make a circuit of the famous sanctuaries. They go out also to spend the night there on the night of mid-Sha'bān, and the market-people take out all kinds of eatables.

Among the celebrated sanctuaries is the imposing holy shrine where rests the head of al-Husain b. 'Alī * * *. Beside it is a vast convent, of wonderful workmanship, on the doors of which there are silver rings, and plates also on them of the same metal. This shrine is paid its full meed of respect and veneration.

Amongst the monuments is the tomb of the Lady (*Sayyida*) Nafīsa, daughter of Zaid b. 'Alī b. al-Husain b. 'Alī (upon them be peace). She was a woman answered in prayer and zealous in her devotions. This mausoleum is of elegant construction and resplendent brightness, and beside it is a convent which is visited by a great concourse during the days of the feast dedicated to her. Another is the tomb of the Imām Abū 'Abdallāh Muhammad b. Idrīs al-Shāfi'ī, close by which is a large convent. The mausoleum enjoys an immense revenue and is surmounted by the famous dome, of admirable workmanship and marvellous construction, an exceedingly fine piece of architecture and exceptionally lofty, the diameter of which exceeds thirty cubits. The Qarāfa of Cairo contains also an incalculable number of graves of men eminent for learning and religion, and in it lie a goodly number of the Companions and of the leading figures of both earlier and later generations (God be pleased with them). * * *

*   *   *

The Egyptian Nile

The Egyptian Nile surpasses all rivers of the earth in sweetness of taste, breadth of channel and magnitude of utility. Cities and villages succeed one another along its banks without interruption and have no equal in the inhabited world, nor is any river known whose basin is so intensively cultivated as that of the Nile. There is no river on earth but it which is called a sea; God Most High has said "If thou fearest for him, cast him into the *yamm*," thus calling it *yamm*, which means "sea" (*bahr*). It is related in an unimpeachable Tradition that the Prophet of God (God's blessing and peace upon him) reached on the night of his Ascension the Lote-Tree of the Extremity, and lo, at its base were four streams, two outer streams and two inner streams. He asked Gabriel (peace be upon him) what streams these were, and he replied 'The two inner streams flow through Paradise, and as for the two outer streams they are the Nile and Euphrates'. It is also related in the Traditions of the Prophet that the Nile, Euphrates, Saiḥān and Jaiḥān are, each one, rivers of Paradise. The course of the Nile is from south to north, contrary to all the great rivers. One extraordinary thing about it is that it begins to rise in the extreme hot weather, at the time when rivers generally diminish and dry up, and begins to subside at the time when rivers increase in volume and overflow. The river of Sind [Indus] resembles it in this respect, and will be mentioned later. The first beginning of the Nile flood is in Ḥazīrān, that is June; and when its rise

amounts to sixteen cubits, the land-tax due to the Sultan is payable in full. If it rises another cubit, there is plenty in that year, and complete well-being. But if it reaches eighteen cubits it does damage to the cultivated lands and causes an outbreak of plague. If it falls short of sixteen by a cubit, the Sultan's land-tax is diminished, and if it is two cubits short the people make solemn prayers for rain and there is the greatest misery.

The Nile is one of the five great rivers of the world, which are the Nile, Euphrates, Tigris, Saiḥūn [Syr Darya] and Jaiḥūn [Amu Darya]; five other rivers rival these, the river of Sind, which is called Panj Ab [i.e. Five Rivers], the river of Hindustān which is called the Kank [or Gang, i.e. Ganges]—to it the Hindus go on pilgrimage, and when they burn their dead they throw the ashes of them into it, and they say that it comes from Paradise—the river Jūn, also in Hindustān, the river Itil [Volga] in the Qifjaq [Kipchak] steppe, on the shore of which is the city of al-Sarā, and the river Sarū in the land of al-Khitā [Cathay], on the banks of which is the city of Khān-Bāliq [Peking], whence it descends to the city of al-Khansā [Hang-chow] and from there to the city of al-Zaitūn [Zayton] in the land of China. We shall speak of all these in their proper places, if God will. Some distance below Cairo the Nile divides into three sections, and none of these streams can be crossed except by boat, winter or summer. The inhabitants of every township have canals led off the Nile; when it is in flood it fills these and they inundate the cultivated fields.

The Pyramids and Berbās

These are among the marvels which have been celebrated through the course of ages, and there is much talk and theorizing amongst men about them, their significance and the origin of their construction. They aver that all branches of knowledge which came into existence before the Deluge were derived from Hermes the Ancient, who lived in the remotest part of the Ṣaʿīd [Upper Egypt]; he is also called by the name of Khanūkh

[Enoch] that is Idrīs (on him be peace). It is said that he was the first to speculate on the movements of the spheres and the celestial bodies, and the first to construct temples and glorify God in them; and that he warned men of the coming of the Deluge, and fearing for the disappearance of knowledge and destruction of the practical arts built the pyramids and berbas, in which he depicted all the practical arts and their tools, and made diagrams of the sciences, in order that they might remain immortalized. It is said also that the seat of learning and kingship in Egypt was the city of Manūf [Memphis], which is one *barīd* from al-Fusṭāṭ. When Alexandria was built, the people removed to it, and it became the seat of learning and kingship until the coming of Islām, when ʿAmr b. al-ʿĀṣ (God be pleased with him) laid out the city of al-Fusṭāṭ, which remains the capital of Egypt to this day.

The pyramids is an edifice of solid hewn stone, of immense height and circular plan, broad at the base and narrow at the top, like the figure of a cone. They have no doorways and the manner of their erection is unknown. One of the tales related about them is that a certain king of Egypt before the Flood dreamed a dream which filled him with terror and determined him to build these pyramids on the western side of the Nile, as a depository for the sciences and for the bodies of the kings. He asked the astrologers whether they would be opened in the future at any spot, and they told him that an opening would be made on the north side, and informed him of the exact spot where the opening would begin, and of the sum of money which would be expended in making the opening. He then ordered to be deposited in that place the sum of money which they had told him would be spent in breaching it. By pressing forward its construction, he completed it in sixty years, and wrote this inscription upon them: "We erected these pyramids in the space of sixty years; let him who will, pull them down in the space of six hundred years; yet to pull down is easier than to build." Now when the Caliphate devolved upon the Commander of the Faithful al-Maʾmūn, he proposed to pull them down, and although one of the Egyptian shaikhs advised him not to do so he persisted in his design and ordered that they should be breached from the north side. So they set about lighting fires up against them and then sprinkling them with vinegar and battering them with a mangonel, until the breach which is still to be seen in them was opened up. There they found, facing the hole, a sum of money which the Commander of the Faithful ordered to be weighted. He then calculated what had been spent on making the breach, and finding the two sums equal, was greatly astonished. At the same time they found the breadth of the wall to be twenty cubits.

The Sultan of Egypt

The Sultan of Egypt at the time of my entry was al-Malik al-Nāṣir Abuʾl-Fatḥ Muḥammad, son of al-Malik al-Manṣūr Saif al-Dīn Qalāʾūn al-Ṣāliḥī. Qalāʾūn was known as al-Alfī ['the Thousandman'] because al-Malik al-Ṣāliḥ bought him for a thousand dinars of gold. He came originally from Qifjaq [Kipchak]. Al-Malik al-Nāṣir (God's mercy upon him was a man of generous character and great virtues, and sufficient proof of his nobility is furnished by his devotion to the service of the two holy sanctuaries of Mecca and Madīna and the works of beneficence which he does every year to assist the pilgrims, in furnishing camels loaded with provisions and water for those without means and the helpless, and for carrying those who cannot keep up with the caravan or are too weak to walk on foot, both on the Egyptian pilgrim-road and on that from Damascus. He also built a great convent at Siryāqus, in the outskirts of Cairo. But the convent built by our lord the Commander of the Faithful and Defender of the Faith, the refuge of the poor and needy, Caliph of God upon earth, whose zeal in the Holy War transcends its obligations, Abū ʿInān (God be his strength and aid, and grant him the signal victory, and prosper him), in the outskirts of his sublime residence, the luminous city (God guard it), has no equal to it in the inhabited world for perfection of architec-

thedral of Holy Sophia, the Wisdom of God. There he put them in the middle of the church in an honorable place, and ordered that the patriarchal epistles be read aloud. When the Orthodox people, who were in the cathedral, heard these writings read aloud, they rendered glory to God and rejoiced with great joy. Archbishop Vasily opened one of the arks and removed the cover. And a wonderful fragrance and miraculous radiance spread through the church. Archbishop Vasily and all present were in wonderment, witnessing these happenings. And Bishop Eumeny, who was sent by the patriarch, wondered about these blessed deeds of God that he had witnessed. And they all rendered glory to God, and celebrated the service of thanksgiving.

Archbishop Vasily took the White Cowl from the ark and saw that it appeared exactly like the one he had seen on the angel's head in his vision. And he kissed it with reverence. At that same moment there came a sonorous voice from the icon of the Lord, which was in the cupola of the church, saying, "Holy, holy." And after a moment of silence there came the same voice, which thrice announced, "Ispola eti despota." And when the archbishop and all those present heard these voices, they were seized with awe and joy. And they said, "The Lord have mercy upon us!" And the archbishop then ordered that all present in the church be silent, and he revealed to them his vision of the angel and his words concerning the White Cowl. And he told of his vision as it had happened and in detail, even as it was told to him by the angel in the night.

Giving thanks to God for sending this cowl, the archbishop went forth from the church, preceded by the deacons in holy vestments carrying tapers and singing hymns. And they proceeded with serenity and piety. And the people crowded round, jostling each other and jumping so that they might see the White Cowl on the arch-

bishop's head. And all were in wonderment. Thus, in this way, thanks to the Grace of our Lord, Jesus Christ, and to the blessing of his Holiness Philotheus, Patriarch of of Constantinople, the White Cowl became a symbol upon the heads of the archbishops of Novgorod. And Archbishop Vasily was overcome with great joy, and for seven days he feasted all priests, deacons, and clerics of the city of Novgorod the Great. And he also offered food and drink to the poor, to monks, and to prisoners. And he asked that the prisoners be released. During the divine service he placed the holy and venerable gifts of the patriarch in the Cathedral of Holy Sophia and with the blessings of all clerics. And the golden salver, on which the White Cowl was placed, was also deposited in the Cathedral of Holy Sophia during the Mass.

The messengers of the patriarch who brought the Holy White Cowl were also shown great honor and they received many gifts. The archbishop sent gifts to the Emperor and Patriarch of Constantinople and sent the messengers forth with great honors. Thereafter, multitudes arrived from many cities and kingdoms to look upon, as if it were a miracle, the archbishop in the White Cowl. And they were in wonderment about it, and told of it in many lands. This Holy White Cowl was created by the first pious Christian Emperor, Constantine, for Blessed Pope Sylvester in the year 297. And this is the history of the Holy White Cowl up to this day.

REVIEW QUESTIONS

1. What were the Russian attitudes toward the Roman Catholic Church, the Muslims, and the Eastern Orthodox Church?
2. Given these attitudes, why is anyone in Russia interested in portraying it as a third Rome?

ALVISE DA MOSTO

Voyage to Africa

Alvise da Mosto (died 1483), also known as Cadamosto, was a member of a promi-
nent family in the Venetian nobility. Alvise passed his early years as a merchant,
visiting Flanders and Portugal. In 1454 he accompanied a Portuguese expedition en-
gaged in trade and exploration south of the Sahara. The account of this voyage and
another one the following year constitutes one of the earliest European descriptions
of black Africa. This excerpt contains Alvise's first impressions of the empire of Mali
(here called Melli) in central Africa, inhabited by the people he called the Azanegi
(Tuaregs) and the Wolof people, a large tribe south of the Senegal River.

From *The Voyages of Cadamosto,* translated and edited by G. R. Crone (London: Hakluyt
Society, 1937), pp. 20–33.

*   *   *

You should know that these people have no
knowledge of any Christians except the Portuguese, against whom they have waged war for
[thirteen or] fourteen years, many of them having
been taken prisoners, as I have already said, and
sold into slavery. It is asserted that when for the
first time they saw sails, that is, ships, on the sea
(which neither they nor their forefathers had ever
seen before), they believed that they were great
sea-birds with white wings, which were flying, and
had come from some strange place: when the sails
were lowered for the landing, some of them,
watching from far off, thought that the ships were
fishes. Others again said that they were phantoms
that went by night, at which they were greatly terrified. The reason for this belief was because these
caravels within a short space of time appeared at
many places, where attacks were delivered, especially at night, by their crews. Thus one such assault might be separated from the next by a
hundred or more miles, according to the plans of
the sailors, or as the winds, blowing hither and
thither, served them. Perceiving this, they said
amongst themselves, "If these be human creatures,

how can they travel so great a distance in one
night, a distance which we could not go in three
days?" Thus, as they did not understand the art of
navigation, they all thought that the ships were
phantoms. This I know is testified to by many
Portuguese who at that time were trading in caravels on this coast, and also by those who were
captured on these raids. And from this it may be
judged how strange many of our ways appeared
to them, if such an opinion could prevail.

Beyond the said mart of Edon [Oden], six days
journey further inland, there is a place called
Tagaza, that is to say in our tongue "cargador,"
where a very great quantity of rock-salt is mined.
Every year large caravans of camels belonging to
the above mentioned Arabs and Azanaghi, leaving
in many parties, carry it to Tanbutu [Timbuktu];
thence they go to Melli, the empire of the Blacks,
where, so rapidly is it sold, within eight days of its
arrival all is disposed of at a price of two to three
hundred *mitigalli* a load, according to the quantity
[a *mitigallo* is worth about a ducat]: then with the
gold they return to their homes.

In this empire of Melli it is very hot, and the
pasturage is very unsuitable for fourfooted animals: so that of the majority which come with the

caravans no more than twenty-five out of a hundred return. There are no quadrupeds in this country, because they all die, and many also of the Arabs and Azanaghi sicken in this place and die, on account of the great heat. It is said that on horseback it is about forty days from Tagaza to Tanbutu, and thirty from Tanbutu to Melli.

I enquired of them what the merchants of Melli did with this salt, and was told that a small quantity is consumed in their country. Since it is below the meridional and on the equinoctial, where the day is constantly about as long as the night, it is extremely hot at certain seasons of the year: this causes the blood to putrefy, so that were it not for this salt, they would die. The remedy they employ is as follows: they take a small piece of the salt, mix it in a jar with a little water, and drink it every day. They say that this saves them. The remainder of this salt they carry away on a long journey in pieces as large as a man can, with a certain knack, bear on his head.

You must know that when this salt is carried to Melli by camel it goes in large pieces [as it is dug out from the mines], of a size most easily carried on camels, two pieces on each animal. Then at Melli, these blacks break it in smaller pieces, in order to carry it on their heads, so that each man carries one piece, and thus they form a great army of men on foot, who transport it a great distance. Those who carry it have two forked sticks, one in each hand: when they are tired, they plant them in the ground, and rest their load upon them. In this way they carry it until they reach certain waters: I could not learn from them whether it is fresh or sea water, so that I do not know if it is a river or the sea, though they consider it to be the sea. [I think however it must be a river, for if it were the sea, in such a hot country there would be no lack of salt.] These Blacks are obliged to carry it in this way, because they have no camels or other beasts of burden, as these cannot live in the great heat. It may be imagined how many men are required to carry it on foot, and how many are those who consume it every year. Having reached these waters with the salt, they

proceed in this fashion: all those who have the salt pile it in rows, each marking his own. Having made these piles, the whole caravan retires half a day's journey. Then there come another race of blacks who do not wish to be seen or to speak. They arrive in large boats, from which it appears that they come from islands, and disembark. Seeing the salt, they place a quantity of gold opposite each pile, and then turn back, leaving salt and gold. When they have gone, the negroes who own the salt return: if they are satisfied with the quantity of gold, they leave the salt and retire with the gold. Then the blacks of the gold return, and remove those piles which are without gold. By the other piles of salt they place more gold, if it pleases them, or else they leave the salt. In this way, by long and ancient custom, they carry on their trade without seeing or speaking to each other. Although it is difficult to believe this, I can testify that I have had this information from many merchants, Arab as well as Azanaghi, and also from persons in whom faith can be placed.

How the Emperor Sought to Take One of These Traders Prisoner

Reflecting upon this, I asked the merchants how it came to be that the Emperor of Melli, who, they said, was so great a lord, had not wished so to proceed as to find out by love or by other means what people these were who did not wish to speak or to be seen. They replied that, not many years previously, an Emperor of Melli determined at all costs to get one of them in his power, and having taken counsel about it, ordered some of his men to leave a few days before the salt caravan, and proceed to the place where it was customary to pile the salt, to dig trenches near by, in which to conceal themselves. When the Blacks returned to set the gold by the salt, they were to attack them and to take two or three, whom they were to convey under close guard to Melli. To be brief, this was done. They seized four, the others taking to flight: of the four they released three, surmising that one would satisfy the desires of the lord, and not wishing to anger these Blacks more. They spoke to this man in several Negro languages, but he would not reply, or speak at all, neither would he eat. He lived four days and then died. For this reason these blacks of Melli are of the opinion, after the experience they had with him who would not speak, that they are dumb. Others think that they behave thus from disdain [of doing what their ancestors had never done]. This death vexed all the blacks of Melli, for on account of it their lord could not achieve his intention. On returning to him they related the incident in due order.

Then the lord was very displeased with them, and asked what the blacks looked like. They replied they were very black in colour, with well-formed bodies, a span higher than they themselves. The lower lip, more than a span in width, hung down, huge and red, over the breast, displaying the inner part glistening like blood.[1] The upper lip was as small as their own. This form of the lips displayed the gums and teeth, the latter, they said, being bigger than their own: they had two large teeth on each side, and large black eyes. Their appearance is terrifying, and the gums exude blood, as do the lips.

Because of this incident, none of the emperor's men have since been willing to embroil themselves in similar affairs, since, as a result of the capture and death of this one Negro, it was three years before the others would resume the customary exchange of gold for salt. It was thought that their lips became putrid, being in a warmer country than ours: so that these blacks, having borne much sickness and death [for this space of time], and having no other way of obtaining the salt to cure themselves, resumed the accustomed trade. On this account, it is our opinion, being unable to live without salt, they set off their plight against our action, just as the Emperor did not care whether these blacks spoke or not, so long as he had the profit of the gold. This is what I understood from this incident, and since it is related by so many we

can accept it. Because I have seen and understood such things in the world, I am one of those who are willing to believe this and other matters to be possible.

The gold thus brought to Melli is divided in three parts: one portion goes with the caravan which takes the road from Melli to a place that is called Cochia. This is the route which runs towards Soria [and il Cairo]: the second and third portions go with a caravan from Melli to Tanbutu. There they are separated: one portion goes to Atoet, whence it is carried to Tunis in Barbary through all the coast beyond: the other part goes to the above mentioned Hoden, whence it spreads towards Orā and Hona, towns in Barbary within the Strecto de Zibelterra, Afezes, Amarochos, Arzib, Azafi, and Amessa, towns in Barbary beyond the Straits. In these places it is bought by us Italians and other Christians from the Moors with the various merchandize we give them.

To return to my first subject, this is the best thing that is brought from the said land and country of the Azanaghi, that is, the brown men. Of that portion of the gold which is brought every year to Hoden, as described already, some quantity is carried to the sea coast, and sold to the Spaniards who are continuously stationed on the said island of Argin for the trade of merchandize, in exchange for other things.

In this land of the brown men, no money is coined, and they have never used it. Nor, formerly, was money to be found in any of their towns. Their sole method is to barter article for article, or two articles for one, and by such means they live. It is true that I understand that inland these Azanaghi, and also the Arabs in some of their districts, are wont to employ white cowries, of those small kinds which are brought to Venice from the Levant. They give certain numbers of these according to the things they have to buy. I should explain that the gold they sell they give by the weight of a *mitigallo;* according to the practice in Barbary, this *mitigallo* is of the value of a ducat, more or less.

---

[1]This suggests the use of the labret, which is still worn by the Lobi women.

*   *   *

The Rio de Senega, Which Divides the Desert from the Fertile Land

When we had passed in sight of this Cauo Bianco, we sailed on our journey to the river called the Rio de Senega, the first river of the Land of the Blacks, which debouches on this coast. This river separates the Blacks from the brown people called Azanaghi, and also the dry and arid land, that is, the above mentioned desert, from the fertile country of the Blacks. The river is large; its mouth being over a mile wide, and quite deep. There is another mouth a little distance beyond, with an island between. Thus it enters the sea by two mouths, and before each of them about a mile out to sea are shoals and broad sand-banks. In this place the water increases and decreases every six hours, that is, with the rise and fall of the tide. The tide ascends the river more than sixty miles, according to the information I have had from Portuguese who have been [many miles] up it [in caravels]. He who wishes to enter this river must go in with the tide, on account of the shoals and banks at the mouth. From Cauo Bianco it is 380 miles to the river: all the coast is sandy to within about twenty miles of the mouth. It is called Costa de Antte rotte, and is of the Azanaghi, or brown men.

It appears to me a very marvellous thing that beyond the river all men are very black, tall and big, their bodies well formed; and the whole country green, full of trees, and fertile: while on this side, the men are brownish, small, lean, ill-nourished, and small in stature: the country sterile and arid. This river is said to be a branch of the river Nile, of the four royal rivers: it flows through all Ethiopia, watering the country as in Egypt: passing through "lo caiero," it waters all the land of Egypt. This river has many other very large branches, in addition to that of Senega, and they are great rivers on this coast of Ethiopia, of which more will be related later.

The Lords Who Rule on the Coast of Capo Verde

The country of these first blacks of the Kingdom of Senega is at the beginning of the first Kingdom of Ethiopia. It is all low-lying country, and many people live on the banks of this river. They are called Zilofi. For a great distance beyond, it is low country, and beyond the river likewise, except for Cauo Verde, which is the highest land on all this coast, for 400 miles beyond this Cauo Verde, and for 900 miles on this side of the said cape, the whole coast is flat. [And the people who dwell along its banks are called Gilofi. And all this coast and the known country behind is all lowland as far as the river, and also beyond this river to Capo Verde. This Cape is the highest land on the whole coast, that is for four hundred miles beyond the said Cape.]

The King of Senega in my time was called Zuchalin [Zucolin—a youth of twenty-two years. This Kingdom does not descend by inheritance] but in this land there are divers lesser lords, who [three or four of whom] through jealousy, at times agree among themselves, and set up a King of their own, if he is in truth of noble parentage. This King rules as long as is pleasing to the said lords [that is, according to the treatment they receive from him]. Frequently [they banish him by force: and as frequently] the King makes himself so powerful that he can defend himself against them. Thus his position is not stable and firm, as is that of the Soldan of Babilonia: but he is always in dread of deposition [death or exile].

You must know that this King is lord of a very poor people, and has no city in his country, but villages with huts of straw only. [They do not know how to build houses with walls:] they have no lime with which to build walls, and there is great lack of stones. This Kingdom, also, is very small; it extends no more than two hundred miles along the coast, and, from the information I had, about the same distance inland or a little more. The king lives thus: he has no fixed income [from taxes]: save that each year the lords of the country, in order to stand well with him, present him with horses, which are much esteemed owing to their scarcity, forage, beasts such as cows and goats, vegetables, millet, and the like. The King supports himself by raids, which result in many slaves from his own as well as neighbouring countries. He employs these slaves [in many ways, mainly] in cultivating the land allotted to him: but he also sells many to the Azanaghi [and Arab] merchants in return for horses and other goods, and also to Christians, since they have begun to trade with these blacks.

The King is permitted to have as many wives as he wishes, as also are all the chiefs and men of this country, that is, as many as they can support. Thus this King has always thirty of them, though he favours one more than another, according to those from whom they are descended. This is his manner of living with his wives: he has certain villages and places, in some of which he keeps eight or ten of them. Each has a house of her own, with young servants to attend her, and slaves to cultivate the possessions and lands assigned by the lord, [with the fruits of which they are able to support themselves]. They have also a certain number of beasts, such as cows and goats, for their use; in this way his wives have the land sown and the beasts tended, and so gain a living. When the King arrives at one of these villages, he goes to the house of one of his wives, for they are obliged to provide, out of this produce, for him and those accompanying him. Every morning, at sunrise, each prepares three or four dishes of various foods, either meat, fish, or other Moorish foods according to their practice. These are sent by their slaves to be put at the disposal of their lord, so that within an hour forty or fifty dishes are assembled; when the time at which the lord wishes to eat has arrived, he picks out whatever tempts him, and gives the remainder to those in his train. But he never gives his people abundance to eat, so that they are always hungry. In this fashion he journeys from place to place without giving any thought to his victuals, and lodges sometimes with one wife, sometimes with another, so that he begets nu-

merous sons, for when one is pregnant he leaves her alone. All the other chiefs of this country live in this same fashion.

The Customs of the Blacks, and Their Beliefs

The faith of these first Blacks is Muhammadanism: they are not however, as are the white Moors, very resolute in this faith, especially the common people. The chiefs adhere to the tenets of the Muhammadans because they have around them priests of the Azanaghi or Arabs, [who have reached this country]. These give them some instruction in the laws of Muhammad, enlarging upon the great disgrace of being rulers and yet living without any divine law, and behaving as do their people and lowly men, who live without laws; and since they have converse with none but these Azanaghi and Arab priests, they are converted to the law of Muhammad. But since they have had converse with Christians, they believe less in it, for our customs please them, and they also realise our wealth and ingenuity in everything as compared with theirs. They say that the God, who has bestowed so many benefits, has shown his great love for us, which could only be if his law were good—but that, none the less, theirs is still the law of God, through which they will find salvation, as we through ours.

These people dress thus: almost all constantly go naked, except for a goatskin fashioned in the form of drawers, with which they hide their shame. But the chiefs and those of standing wear a cotton garment—for cotton grows in these lands. Their women spin it into cloth of a span in width. They are unable to make wider cloth because they do not understand how to card it for weaving. When they wish to make a larger piece, they sew four or five of these strips together. These garments are made to reach half way down the thigh, with wide sleeves to the elbow. They also wear breeches of this cotton, which are tied across, and reach to the ankles, and are otherwise so large as to be from thirty to thirty-five, or even forty *palmi* round the top; when they are girded round the waist, they are much crumpled and form a sack in front, and the hinder part reaches to the ground, and waggles like a tail—the most comical thing to be seen in the world. They would come in these wide petticoats with these tails and ask us if we had ever seen a more beautiful dress or fashion: for they hold it for certain that they are the most beautiful garments in the world. Their women, both married and single, all go covered with girdles, below which they wear a sheet of these cotton strips bound across, half way down their legs. Men and women always go barefoot. They wear nothing on their heads: the hair of both sexes is fashioned into neat tresses arranged in various styles, though their hair by nature is no longer than a span. You must know also that the men of these lands perform many women's tasks, such as spinning, washing clothes and such things. It is always very hot there, and the further one goes inland, the greater the heat: by comparison, it is no colder in these parts in January than it is in April in our country of Italy.

Men Clean in Their Persons and Filthy in Eating

The men and women are clean in their persons, since they wash themselves all over four or five times a day: but in eating they are filthy, and ill-mannered. In matters of which they have no experience they are credulous and awkward, but in those to which they are accustomed they are the equal of our skilled men. They are talkative, and never at a loss for something to say: in general they are great liars and cheats: but on the other hand, charitable, receiving strangers willingly, and providing a night's lodging and one or two meals without any charge.

*   *   *

REVIEW QUESTIONS

1. What does da Mosto's account reveal about the earliest phases of the African slave trade?
2. His description of the silent trade is the first extended account we have of this remarkable type of barter. How plausible is this account, and what might it teach the economic historian about markets?
3. Alvise da Mosto was also the first European ethnographer of the Wolof. What types of bias and questions did he bring to his view of the Wolof? What contrasts are there in the way he described them to the way William of Rubruck described the Mongols?

CHRISTOPHER COLUMBUS

Letter on His First Voyage

Christopher Columbus (c. 1450–1506) was born somewhere around Genoa and from an early age made his living as a sailor. Columbus saw much of the Mediterranean and Atlantic world and acquired real skill as a mapmaker and navigator. Self-taught in geography, Columbus developed a theory of the globe's size that made sailing across the Atlantic to China and Japan a daring but plausible adventure. After spending years looking for a patron among the rulers of Europe, at last in

SAPI-PORTUGUESE SALT CELLAR, IVORY (C. 1500)

Portuguese traders in West Africa commissioned art works from the indigenous Sapi people. Merchants then sold these imaginative ivory carvings across Europe; this salt cellar ended up in Italy. Why would a European collector have purchased this object? How does the style of Sapi art differ from contemporary works of art created by Europeans?

1492 Isabella of Castile took the lead along with her husband Ferdinando of Aragon in sponsoring Columbus's first voyage. This letter is one of his earliest accounts of this trip—but we do not know to whom the letter was sent.

From *Selected Documents Illustrating the Four Voyages of Christopher Columbus,* translated and edited by Cecil Jane (London: Hakluyt Society, 1930), pp. 3–18.

Sir, As I know that you will be pleased at the great victory with which Our Lord has crowned my voyage, I write this to you, from which you will learn how in thirty-three days, I passed from the Canary Islands to the Indies with the fleet which the most illustrious king and queen, our sovereigns, gave to me. And there I found very many islands filled with people innumerable, and of them all I have taken possession for their highnesses, by proclamation made and with the royal standard unfurled, and no opposition was offered to me. To the first island which I found, I gave the name *San Salvador,* in remembrance of the Divine Majesty, Who has marvellously bestowed all this; the Indians call it "Guanahani." To the second, I gave the name *Isla de Santa María de Concepción;* to the third, *Fernandina;* to the fourth, *Isabella;* to the fifth, *Isla Juana,* and so to each one I gave a new name.

When I reached Juana, I followed its coast to the westward, and I found it to be so extensive that I thought that it must be the mainland, the province of Catayo. And since there were neither towns nor villages on the seashore, but only small hamlets, with the people of which I could not have speech, because they all fled immediately, I went forward on the same course, thinking that I should not fail to find great cities and towns. And, at the end of many leagues, seeing that there was no change and that the coast was bearing me northwards, which I wished to avoid, since winter was already beginning and I proposed to make from it to the south, and as moreover the wind was carrying me forward, I determined not to wait for a change in the weather and retraced my path as far as a certain harbour known to me. And from that point, I sent two men inland to learn if there were a king or great cities. They travelled three days' journey and found an infinity of small hamlets and people without number, but nothing of importance. For this reason, they returned.

I understood sufficiently from other Indians, whom I had already taken, that this land was nothing but an island. And therefore I followed its coast eastwards for one hundred and seven leagues to the point where it ended. And from that cape, I saw another island, distant eighteen leagues from the former, to the east, to which I at once gave the name "Española." And I went there and followed its northern coast, as I had in the case of Juana, to the eastward for one hundred and eighty-eight great leagues in a straight line. This island and all the others are very fertile to a limitless degree, and this island is extremely so. In it there are many harbours on the coast of the sea, beyond comparison with others which I know in Christendom, and many rivers, good and large, which is marvellous. Its lands are high, and there are in it very many sierras and very lofty mountains, beyond comparison with the island of Teneriffe. All are most beautiful, of a thousand shapes, and all are accessible and filled with trees of a thousand kinds and tall, and they seem to touch the sky. And I am told that they never lose their foliage, as I can understand, for I saw them as green and as lovely as they are in Spain in May, and some of them were flowering, some bearing fruit, and some in another stage, according to their nature. And the nightingale was singing and other birds of a thousand kinds in the month of November there where I went. There are six or eight kinds of palm, which are a wonder to behold on account of their beautiful variety, but so are the other trees and fruits and plants. In it are marvellous pine groves, and there are very large tracts of cultivatable lands, and there is honey, and there are birds of many kinds and fruits in great diversity. In the interior are mines of metals, and the population is without number. Española is a marvel.

The sierras and mountains, the plains and arable lands and pastures, are so lovely and rich for planting and sowing, for breeding cattle of every kind, for building towns and villages. The harbours of the sea here are such as cannot be believed to exist unless they have been seen, and so with the rivers, many and great, and good waters, the majority of which contain gold. In the trees and fruits and plants, there is a great difference from those of Juana. In this island, there are many spices and great mines of gold and of other metals.

The people of this island, and of all the other islands which I have found and of which I have information, all go naked, men and women, as their mothers bore them, although some women cover a single place with the leaf of a plant or with a net of cotton which they make for the purpose. They have no iron or steel or weapons, nor are they fitted to use them, not because they are not well built men and of handsome stature, but because they are very marvellously timorous. They have no other arms than weapons made of canes, cut in seeding time, to the ends of which they fix a small sharpened stick. And they do not dare to make use of these, for many times it has happened that I have sent ashore two or three men to some town to have speech, and countless people have come out to them, and as soon as they have seen my men approaching they have fled, even a father not waiting for his son. And this, not because ill has been done to anyone; on the contrary, at every point where I have been and have been able to have speech, I have given to them of all that I had, such as cloth and many other things, without receiving anything for it; but so they are, incurably timid. It is true that, after they have been reassured and have lost their fear, they are so guileless and so generous with all they possess, that no one would believe it who has not seen it. They never refuse anything which they possess, if it be asked of them; on the contrary, they invite anyone to share it, and display as much love as if they would

give their hearts, and whether the thing be of value or whether it be of small price, at once with whatever trifle of whatever kind it may be that is given to them, with that they are content. I forbade that they should be given things so worthless as fragments of broken crockery and scraps of broken glass, and ends of straps, although when they were able to get them, they fancied that they possessed the best jewel in the world. So it was found that a sailor for a strap received gold to the weight of two and a half *castellanos,* and others much more for other things which were worth much less. As for new *blancas,* for them they would give everything which they had, although it might be two or three *castellanos'* weight of gold or an *arroba* or two of spun cotton. . . . They took even the pieces of the broken hoops of the wine barrels and, like savages, gave what they had, so that it seemed to me to be wrong and I forbade it. And I gave a thousand handsome good things, which I had brought, in order that they might conceive affection, and more than that, might become Christians and be inclined to the love and service of their highnesses and of the whole Castilian nation, and strive to aid us and to give us of the things which they have in abundance and which are necessary to us. And they do not know any creed and are not idolaters; only they all believe that power and good are in the heavens, and they are very firmly convinced that I, with these ships and men, came from the heavens, and in this belief they everywhere received me, after they had overcome their fear. And this does not come because they are ignorant; on the contrary, they are of a very acute intelligence and are men who navigate all those seas, so that it is amazing how good an account they give of everything, but it is because they have never seen people clothed or ships of such a kind.

And as soon as I arrived in the Indies, in the first island which I found, I took by force some of them, in order that they might learn and give me information of that which there is in those parts, and so it was that they soon understood us, and we them, either by speech or signs, and they have been very serviceable. I still take them with me, and they are always assured that I come from Heaven, for all the intercourse which they have had with me; and they were the first to announce this wherever I went, and the others went running from house to house and to the neighbouring towns, with loud cries of, 'Come! Come to see the people from Heaven!' So all, men and women alike, when their minds were set at rest concerning us, came, so that not one, great or small, remained behind, and all brought something to eat and drink, which they gave with extraordinary affection. In all the island, they have very many canoes, like rowing *fustas,* some larger, some smaller, and some are larger than a *fusta* of eighteen benches. They are not so broad, because they are made of a single log of wood, but a *fusta* would not keep up with them in rowing, since their speed is a thing incredible. And in these they navigate among all those islands, which are innumerable, and carry their goods. One of these canoes I have seen with seventy and eighty men in her, and each one with his oar.

In all these islands, I saw no great diversity in the appearance of the people or in their manners and language. On the contrary, they all understand one another, which is a very curious thing, on account of which I hope that their highnesses will determine upon their conversion to our holy faith, towards which they are very inclined.

I have already said how I have gone one hundred and seven leagues in a straight line from west to east along the seashore of the island Juana, and as a result of that voyage, I can say that this island is larger than England and Scotland together, for, beyond these one hundred and seven leagues, there remain to the westward two provinces to which I have not gone. One of these provinces they call "Avan," and there the people are born with tails; and these provinces cannot have a length of less than fifty or sixty leagues, as I could understand from those Indians whom I have and who know all the islands.

The other, Española, has a circumference greater than all Spain, from Colibre, by the sea-coast, to Fuenterabia in Vizcaya, since I voyaged along one side one hundred and eighty-eight great

leagues in a straight line from west to east. It is a land to be desired and, seen, it is never to be left. And in it, although of all I have taken possession for their highnesses and all are more richly endowed than I know how, or am able, to say, and I hold them all for their highnesses, so that they may dispose of them as, and as absolutely as, of the kingdoms of Castile, in this Española, in the situation most convenient and in the best position for the mines of gold and for all intercourse as well with the mainland here as with that there, belonging to the Grand Khan, where will be great trade and gain, I have taken possession of a large town, to which I gave the name *Villa de Navidad,* and in it I have made fortifications and a fort, which now will by this time be entirely finished, and I have left in it sufficient men for such a purpose with arms and artillery and provisions for more than a year, and a *fusta,* and one, a master of all sea-craft, to build others, and great friendship with the king of that land, so much so, that he was proud to call me, and to treat me as, a brother. And even if he were to change his attitude to one of hostility towards these men, he and his do not know what arms are and they go naked, as I have already said, and are the most timorous people that there are in the world, so that the men whom I have left there alone would suffice to destroy all that land, and the island is without danger for their persons, if they know how to govern themselves.

In all these islands, it seems to me that all men are content with one woman, and to their chief or king they give as many as twenty. It appears to me that the women work more than the men. And I have not been able to learn if they hold private property; what seemed to me to appear was that, in that which one had, all took a share, especially of eatable things.

In these islands I have so far found no human monstrosities, as many expected, but on the contrary the whole population is very well-formed, nor are they Negroes as in Guinea, but their hair is flowing, and they are not born where there is intense force in the rays of the sun; it is true that the sun has there great power, although it is distant from the equinoctial line twenty-six degrees. In these islands, where there are high mountains, the cold was severe this winter, but they endure it, being used to it and with the help of meats which they eat with many and extremely hot spices. As I have found no monsters, so I have had no report of any, except in an island "Quaris," the second at the coming into the Indies, which is inhabited by a people who are regarded in all the islands as very fierce and who eat human flesh. They have many canoes with which they range through all the islands of India and pillage and take as much as they can. They are no more malformed than the others, except that they have the custom of wearing their hair long like women, and they use bows and arrows of the same cane stems, with a small piece of wood at the end, owing to lack of iron which they do not possess. They are ferocious among these other people who are cowardly to an excessive degree, but I make no more account of them than of the rest. These are those who have intercourse with the women of "Matinino," which is the first island met on the way from Spain to the Indies, in which there is not a man. These women engage in no feminine occupation, but use bows and arrows of cane, like those already mentioned, and they arm and protect themselves with plates of copper, of which they have much.

In another island, which they assure me is larger than Española, the people have no hair. In it, there is gold incalculable, and from it and from the other islands, I bring with me Indians as evidence.

In conclusion, to speak only of that which has been accomplished on this voyage, which was so hasty, their highnesses can see that I will give them as much gold as they may need, if their highnesses will render me very slight assistance; moreover, spice and cotton, as much as their highnesses shall command; and mastic, as much as they shall order to be shipped and which, up to now, has been found only in Greece, in the island of Chios, and the Seignory sells it for what it pleases; and aloe wood, as much as they shall order to be shipped, and slaves, as many as they shall order to be

shipped and who will be from the idolaters. And I believe that I have found rhubarb and cinamon, and I shall find a thousand other things of value, which the people whom I have left there will have discovered, for I have not delayed at any point, so far as the wind allowed me to sail, except in the town of Navidad, in order to leave it secured and well established, and in truth, I should have done much more, if the ships had served me, as reason demanded.

This is enough . . . and the eternal God, our Lord, Who gives to all those who walk in His way triumph over things which appear to be impossible, and this was notably one; for, although men have talked or have written of these lands, all was conjectural, without suggestion of ocular evidence, but amounted only to this, that those who heard for the most part listened and judged it to be rather a fable than as having any vestige of truth. So that, since Our Redeemer has given this victory to our most illustrious king and queen, and to their renowned kingdoms, in so great a matter, for this all Christendom ought to feel delight and make great feasts and give solemn thanks to the Holy Trinity with many solemn prayers for the great exaltation which they shall have, in the turning of so many peoples to our holy faith, and afterwards for temporal benefits, for not only Spain but all Christians will have hence refreshment and gain.

This, in accordance with that which has been accomplished, thus briefly.

Done in the caravel, off the Canary Islands, on the fifteenth of February, in the year one thousand four hundred and ninety-three.

At your orders.   El Almirante.

After having written this, and being in the sea of Castile, there came on me so great a south-south-west wind, that I was obliged to lighten ship. But I ran here to-day into this port of Lisbon, which was the greatest marvel in the world, whence I decided to write to their highnesses. In all the Indies, I have always found weather like May; where I went in thirty-three days and I had returned in twenty-eight, save for these storms which have detained me for fourteen days, beating about in this sea. Here all the sailors say that never has there been so bad a winter nor so many ships lost.

Done on the fourth day of March.

REVIEW QUESTIONS

1. What can we learn about Columbus's personality and motives from this letter?
2. Columbus also provided here the first Western account of the people he called Indians. What do we learn about his interests and abilities as an ethnographer?

MANUEL I

"The Letter Which the King, Our Lord, Wrote to the King and Queen of Castile, His Kin, Concerning the News of India"

In 1501 King Manuel I of Portugal wrote this letter to his relatives Isabella of Castile and Ferdinando of Aragon. The king was clearly proud of the journey Pedro Alvarez Cabral made to India the previous year. As this letter explains, Cabral's fleet also "discovered" Brazil (here called Santa Cruz) during this voyage. The letter describes Cabral's visit to Kilwa (here Quilon) in East Africa as well. But most of the letter concerns Cabral's long stay in Calicut in India.

From *The Voyage of Pedro Álvares Cabral to Brazil and India,* translated by William Brooks Greenlee (London: Hakluyt Society, 1937), pp. 43–52.

Most high and most excellent and most powerful Sovereigns, Father and Mother: During these past days, after the first news arrived from India, I did not write at once to Your Majesties concerning the matters there because Pedro Alvarez Cabral, my chief captain of the fleet, which I had sent there, had not yet returned. And after his arrival I also delayed in doing so because two ships of his company had not yet come. One of these he had sent to Çofalla, a gold-mine which was discovered recently, not to establish trade, but only to have true information of what was there; because of the two ships which went there for this purpose, one was lost at sea, and the other was separated from the fleet in stormy weather and did not go there. And after the aforesaid ships had arrived, and I was on the point of notifying Your Majesties, Pero Lopes de Padilha told me that you would be glad to have news of what had happened there. The following is briefly everything which took place. My aforesaid captain with thirteen ships departed from Lisboa the 9th of March of last year, and during the octave of Easter he reached a land which he newly discovered, to

CONQUEST OF MEXICO, FLORENTINE CODEX (C. 1555)

The Franciscan friar Bernardino de Sahagún (d. 1590) directed a team of Nahua aides who produced the Florentine Codex. This book is an account of Cortéz's expedition of 1519, which resulted in the destruction of the Aztec Empire. The book is in Nahuatl and is accompanied by over 100 illustrations. Scholars have debated the extent to which the text and pictures allowed the Nahua to express their own views on these events. Sahagún began collecting information in the 1540s, and this chapter may have been composed around 1555. The illustrations accompanying the text may also have been sketched by Nahua people. These six pictures show characteristic battle scenes; in the last one the Mexica have captured a Spanish cannon. Guns and steel certainly played a role in the Spanish conquest of Mexico. What evidence do these pictures provide of this? Perhaps even more striking were the roles of horses and large dogs (not pictured here). What advantages did these animals provide the Spaniards?

which he gave the name of Santa Cruz. In it he found the people nude as in the first innocence, gentle, and peaceable. It seemed that Our Lord miraculously wished it to be found, because it is very convenient and necessary for the voyage to India, because he repaired his ships and took water there. And on account of the long voyage which he had to make, he did not stop to obtain information about the said land; he only sent me a ship from there to notify me how he found it; and he pursued his route by way of the Cape of Good Hope. In that gulf, before arriving at it, he encountered great storms, in which, during one single day, four ships foundered together before his eyes, of which not a single person escaped. At this time, also, another of his ships disappeared, of which no news has been received up to this time. And that in which he went, with the others which remained, passed through great danger. And thus he went his way to make port at the kingdom of Quiloa, which belongs to the Moors, under whose sovereignty is the said mine of Ço-falla, because he carried my letters and messages for its king, to establish peace with him, and a treaty concerning purchases and trade at the said mine. And before reaching the aforesaid kingdom, he found two ships with a great quantity of gold, which he took possession of, and because they belonged to the said King of Quiloa, after doing them much honour, he let them go. He was very well received by that king, who came in person to converse with my said captain on the sea, and entered with him in his boat, and he sent him presents; and after receiving my letters and messages, he agreed to the treaty. And since the ships which were destined for that mine were among those which were lost, no trade was begun there at that time, because the merchandise which the other ships carried was not suitable for what was needed for that land. And he departed from there and went to another kingdom, Melinde, for which he also was carrying my letters and messages, because its king, who likewise is a Moor, had done good deeds to Dom Vasco, who first went there to discover it. This king likewise visited him on the sea and also sent him presents, and confirmed and established peace and friendship with him, and gave him the pilots whom he needed for his voyage. These kingdoms extend from the Red Sea in this direction, and in the interior they border on Gentiles, and these Gentiles border on the land of Prester John, whom they call the *abechy*. In their language this means "branded with iron," because, as a matter of fact, they do this, and they are branded with iron as a sign that they are baptized in water. From there he departed for Calecut, which is seven hundred leagues beyond. This city, as I believe you must already know, is of the Gentiles who worship many things and believe that there is only one God. And it is very populous, and there are in it many Moors who, until now, always traded there in spices, because it is thus like Bruges in Flanders, the principal trading place for the things of India, which come to it from outside; and in it there are only cassiafistula and ginger. He arrived at this city five months after having departed from Lisbon. And he was very honourably received by the king, who came to a house beside the sea to speak to him, with all his lords and many other people. And there he gave him my messages and established with him my peace and concord. Concerning this agreement the aforesaid king ordered a letter written on a sheet of silver with his seal inlaid in gold, for this is the custom in his land in matters of great importance, and other letters written on leaves of trees which resemble palms, on which they ordinarily write. And from these trees and their fruit are made the following things: sugar, honey, oil, wine, water, vinegar, charcoal, and cordage for ships, and for everything else, and matting of which they make some sails for ships, and it serves them for everything which they need. And the aforesaid fruit, in addition to what is thus made of it, is their chief food, particularly at sea. After the agreement had thus been made with the said king, my factor sent on shore the entire establishment which I had ordered for the above-mentioned factory, and at once he began to trade with his merchandise and to load the ships with spices. In the meantime, the King of Calecut sent word to my captain that a very large and well-armed ship which had annoyed him on previous occasions, belonging to another king, his enemy, had sent word to him that it was passing before his port, without any fear of him, and he begged him to order it to be captured, enlarging on the matter, as it greatly concerned his estate and honour.

And the said captain, in view of the good treatment which he and also my factor were beginning to receive, and in order to confirm further peace and friendship, agreed to do it. And in order to show him the strength of our people in ships and artillery, he sent against it only the smallest ship which he had, with a large bombard. And it overtook them within the harbour of another king, his neighbour, and before his eyes and those of all his people he captured it, and brought it to Calecut with 400 bowmen and some artillery and with seven elephants, trained in warfare, on board (there these would be worth thirty thousand cruzados, for they gave five thousand for only one of them), and with other merchandise of spices. This ship my captain ordered to be presented to him, and he gave it to him with everything which came in it, and he came to the shore with all his state and pomp to see it, since it was to them a very great surprise that so small a ship with so few men should take so large a ship with so many people, and to receive the message which the said captain was sending him concerning it. And the Moors, especially those of Mecca, who were there, seeing that they were in this concord and friendship, and that two ships were already loaded with spices, and seeing also the great loss which they were suffering, sought all the means that they could to put discord between my factor and the king. And they stirred up a tumult on land to hinder them; and because all the merchandise was in the hands of the Moors they hid it, and secretly sent it elsewhere. When he learned this, the aforesaid captain sent word to the King of Calecut, complaining to him and asking him to fulfil what he had agreed, which was that in twenty days he would give him merchandise with which to load the said ships, and that until they were loaded, he would not give authority to load to any others. And the king answered him that he would at once order all the

merchandise which there was in the land to be given to him, and that if any ship should be loaded in his harbour without the knowledge of his officials, he gave him the authority and power to detain it until he sent his said officials, so that they might arrange to turn it over to him. As soon as the Moors learned of this, they agreed to load a ship publicly with great diligence, using still greater care in hiding the merchandise than they had previously done, and this, in order to give an excuse for an outbreak to begin, for they are powerful. And the city is of many nationalities and of extensive population, in which the king can, with difficulty, attend to the tumults of the populace. And when my factor saw that the ship was being loaded, he asked the said captain to detain it, as the king had agreed. And the said captain, fearing an outbreak, hesitated to do it; and the said factor again asked him to detain it, telling him that the chief Moors and also some Gentiles told him that if the said ship were not held they could in no way load their ships. According to what followed it appears that they were doing it in order to give rise to the said outbreak. And my captain, after hesitating many times, fearing what followed, ordered the people of that ship to be told that, because of the authority which he had for this, it should not leave; but they were not willing to agree to this. And then it was necessary to order it to be held. And he commanded his boats to bring it inside the harbour, where it surely could not leave without his permission. And as soon as the Moors saw this, since it was the end which they desired, at that very moment they came quickly with all the rest of the population, whom they had already stirred up, to attack the said factor and his house, and fought with him. And he with those few whom he had with him, defended themselves for some time, and leaving the house, rallied at the sea. And my captain, who was then ill, as soon as he was told of the uprising on land, ordered all his boats to aid him, and although the sea was very rough he nevertheless gathered up some of the people. They killed the factor and with him fifty people were lost, either dead or captives. After this was done, when my captain saw that the king had not come to help and that he sent no message and was providing himself with some equipment implying war, and also had taken possession of my property which had remained on shore, he waited one day to see if he would make amends for the said matter. When he saw that he was sending him no message, fearing that he was arming himself effectively, as he afterwards did, to prevent him from taking the vengeance he could take at that time, he decided to act at once, and he took ten large ships which were in the harbour, and ordered all the people who were on them to be put to the sword, with the exception of a few who, concealing themselves, escaped death, and whom afterwards he did not wish to kill, but brought captive to me. And he ordered the said ships to be burned in front of the port, which caused great horror to the king and to the people of the land. On the ships there were three elephants which died there. In this manner he spent the entire day; and as soon as it was night, he went with all the ships, and placed himself as near land as he could in front of the city; and as soon as it was dawn, he began to fire with artillery, and bombarded it until night, especially the houses of the king. In this he did much damage, and killed many of his people, as he learned afterwards, and he killed one of the chief men who was near the king. On account of this, the king immediately departed from the city, for it seemed to him that he was not safe anywhere. And he sailed from there to another port of his, which was called Fandarene [Pandarani], which he also damaged with artillery, and killed people. And from there he sailed to the kingdom of Cochim, which is the region from which spices come, 30 leagues beyond Calecut, and on the way, he found two other ships of Calecut, which he also captured and ordered to be burned. And when he reached Cochim, after having informed the king of what had happened in Calecut, he was very well received by him, and made an agreement with him in the same manner which he had done in Calecut. Then he immediately sent my factor and certain men with him on shore, for whom they gave him honourable men as hostages, whom he brought to me; and they

loaded his ships in 16 days; and the merchandise they brought to him in their boats was brought with so much greater friendliness and security that it appeared that Our Lord permitted the outbreak at Calecut in order that this other agreement might take place, which is of greater profit and security, because the harbour is much better and of much more extensive trade, since, of almost all the merchandise which goes to Calecut, most of it is to be found in that land, and because others go there first without going to Calecut. In this city of Cochim there are many ships, and he learned that two merchants alone had as many as 50 ships. In that kingdom there are many true Christians of the conversion of Saint Thomas, and their priests follow the manner of life of the apostles with much strictness, having nothing of their own except what is given them as alms. And they practise celibacy, and have churches in which they say mass, and they consecrate unleavened bread, and wine which they make from dried fruit with water, for they cannot make other. In their churches they have no images save the cross, and all the Christians wear the apostolic garments, and never cut their beards and hair. And there he found definite information concerning where the body of Saint Thomas lies, which is 150 leagues from there, on the sea coast, in a city which is called Maliapor [Mailapur], of a small population; and he brought me earth from his tomb. And all the Christians and also the Moors and Gentiles, on account of the great miracles which are performed, go to his house on pilgrimage. He also brought us two Christians who came of their own accord and with the permission of their prelate, so that we might send them to Rome and to Jerusalem, to see the things of the Church there, and to be informed about them, for they consider that they are better ruled by being ordained by Saint Peter, who, they believe, was the chief of the apostles. And he also learned certain news of great Christian nations which are on the other side of that kingdom, who come on pilgrimage to the aforesaid house of Saint Thomas, and have very great kings who obey One only. They are white men of fair hair, and are considered strong. The land is called Malchima, and from it come porcelain, and musk and amber, and aloe-wood, which they bring from the river Ganges, which is on this side of them. And there are such fine vases of porcelain there, that a single one of them is worth a hundred cruzados. And while he was in the kingdom of Cochim, when the treaty had been agreed to and the ships loaded, there came to him messages from the King of Cananor, and from the King of Colum [Quilon] who are near by, requesting him to come to them because they would make more profitable trade with him, but, because he had already made the treaty, he declined to go. At this time, as he was about to depart from Cochim, the same king sent word to him that a large fleet from Calecut was coming against him, and that as many as 15,000 men were in it. It did not seem well to my captain to fight with it, because he had his ships loaded, and had few men, and it did not seem to him that there was time or necessity for taking the risk, since he feared that they might kill or disable some of them, and on account of the length of the journey which he had to go, which was 4,000 leagues from here. But he set sail, with them following him, and as they did not dare to go far out to sea, they turned back, because they feared to go against him. From there he went his way, which was to the kingdom of Cananor, [ruled by] one of those kings who invited him. And as he was passing, as soon as those on land caught sight of him, they sent him another message, asking him to stop there, because the king wanted to send a messenger to me by him, whom he brought me. And in the single day that he was there, he ordered so much spicery to be brought to the ships that he might have entirely filled them, had they been empty; and they gave what they might carry free, as a present to win my friendship. And all his chief men came also to my captain, telling him on behalf of the king that they would see to it that he was treated there in a different manner than in Calecut, assuring him that if he wanted to make war on Calecut they would help him, and that he in person would go on land, and all his fleet on the sea. And after thanking him greatly in my name, he took leave of him, saying to him that in

the other fleet which I was to send soon, I would send him my answer regarding everything. He went his way, and in the middle of that crossing he took a very large ship loaded with merchandise. It appeared to him that it was a ship of Mecca which was just coming from Calecut. And finding that the aforesaid ship belonged to the King of Cambaia [Cambay], he abandoned it, sending word by it to the said king that he had released it because he did not intend to make war with any one; he had made it only on those who had broken the word which they had given to him in my name. Continuing farther on his way, he lost one of the ships which was laden, for it ran aground during the night. Its people were saved, and he ordered the ship to be burned because it could not be dislodged safely. From this place he sent a ship to obtain news of the mine of Çofalla which I have mentioned before. This has just arrived, and brought me definite information of it and also concerning the trade and the merchandise of the country and of the great quantity of gold which is there; and there he found news, that among the men who carry gold from there to the coasts, they saw many who have four eyes, namely, two in front and two behind. The men are small of body and strong, and it is said that they are cruel, and that they eat the men with whom they have war, and that the cows of the king wear collars of heavy gold around their necks. Near this mine there are two islands on which they gather much pearl and amber. My aforesaid captain departed from there, and reached Lisboa 16 months from the day he had left it, and, blessed be Our Lord, in all this voyage he lost only three men from sickness, and all the others are healthy and of good spirits.[1] And now a certain message comes to me saying that one of the ships that was going to Çoffala which he believed lost, is coming, and will be here shortly. They say that it entered the Red Sea, and that it is bringing from there some silver and also some information concerning matters there, although I am already informed in detail concerning

---

[1]This is a mistake, since many had died of scurvy.

the said Red Sea, having been informed thereof by my above-mentioned captain, who had information concerning it in many ways. I leave the other details of this matter to Pero Lopes, who was present at everything. Very exalted and very excellent and very puissant Sovereigns, Father and Mother, may Our Lord have your life and royal estate in His holy care.

Written in Santarem the 29th of July, 1501.

El Rey.

REVIEW QUESTIONS

1. One theme here concerns Portuguese rivalry with the Moors—Muslims in East Africa and India. What were these relationships like?
2. What types of trade did the Portuguese hope to conduct in India?
3. Even though the information in the letter is at second hand, we still have an extensive view of the people of Calicut. What image of India has Manuel constructed for his readers?

13 ❧ THE CIVILIZATION OF THE RENAISSANCE, C. 1350–1550

The Renaissance began as an Italian phenomenon, occurring between c. 1300 and 1520, that spread to the rest of Europe over the course of the 1500s and early 1600s. Its principal manifestations were the revival of classicism and naturalism in arts and literature, the rise of the modern dynastic state as the dominant political structure, and an economic crisis fueled by industrial change and economic contraction.

Until recently, scholars have traditionally viewed the Renaissance as a period of great change. Contemporaries used the term rinascita *to express their sense of a rebirth, a perfection in the arts. Many modern scholars view the period as one of fundamental change, an abrupt departure from the past, and have identified the following several characteristics that set the Renaissance apart as a discrete period of history. Scholars and artists revived classical antiquity as a subject of study and emulation. The state emerged as a work of art, that is, as a calculated design by persons in pursuit of power. The universal man, well rounded in physical and intellectual endeavors, became the political and pedagogical ideal of the age. The social mobility born of a rapidly changing economy led to an aristocracy of merit, a fusion of nobility and bourgeoisie in which achievement mattered more than lineage.*

All of these characteristics have been criticized and reviewed by latter-day historians of the Renaissance, most of whom would emphasize its continuity with the Middle Ages. Few, however, would disagree that the age was unusually self-conscious—aware of its achievements, intrigued by its potential, and impatient of its limits. The following selections capture something of this mentality.

LEON BATTISTA ALBERTI

FROM *I Libri della Famiglia*

Leon Battista Alberti (1404–1474) embodied the Renaissance universal man. Born the illegitimate son of a Florentine merchant, he was an athlete, polymath, and artist. He earned a degree in canon law at the University of Bologna in 1428, and migrated to Rome and entered papal service. It was there, in 1438, that he began to write On the Family. *Written in the form of a dialogue among the members of the Alberti family, gathered at the deathbed of Leon Battista's father in 1421, it examines the ideal family as a unit for the begetting and rearing of children, for the amassing and maintaining of fortunes, and for the accumulation and exercise of power. It was also a sly exercise in satire, insofar as it indirectly criticizes his brothers and uncles for violating his father's dying wish that Leon Battista be treated as a legitimate member of the family.*

From *I Libri della Famiglia,* translated by Renee New Watkins (Columbia: University of South Carolina Press, 1969).

*   *   *

XIII

Lionardo: If I had children, you may be sure I should think about them, but my thoughts would be untroubled. My first consideration would only be to make my children grow up with good character and virtue. Whatever activities suited their taste would suit me. Any activity which is not dishonest is not displeasing to an honorable mind. The activities which lead to honor and praise belong to honorable and wellborn men. Certainly I will admit that every son cannot achieve all that his father might wish. If he does something he is able to do, however, I like that better than to have him strike out in a direction where he cannot follow through. I also think it is more praiseworthy for a man, even if he does not altogether succeed, to do his best in some field rather than sit inactive, inert, and idle. There is an old saying which our ancestors often repeated: "Idleness is the mother of vice." It is an ugly and hateful thing to see a

man keep himself forever useless, like that idle fellow who when they asked him why he spent all day as if condemned to sit or lie on public benches, answered "I am waiting to get fat." The man who heard him was disgusted, and asked him rather to try to fatten up a pig, since at least something useful might come of it. Thus quite correctly he showed him what an idle fellow amounts to, which is less than a pig.

I'll go further, Adovardo. However rich and noble a father may be, he should try to have his son learn, besides the noble skills, some occupation which is not degrading. By means of this occupation in case of misfortune he can live honestly by his own labor and the work of his hands. Are the vicissitudes of this world so little or so infrequent that we can ignore the possibility of adverse circumstances? Was not the son of Perseus, king of Macedonia, seen sweating and soiled in a Roman factory, employed in making his living with heavy and painful labor? If the instability of things could thus transport the son of a famous and powerful king to such depths of poverty and need, it is right for us private citizens as well as for men of higher station to provide against every misfortune. If none in our house ever had to devote himself to such laboring occupations, thank fortune for it, and let us make sure that none will have to in the future. A wise and foresightful pilot, to be able to survive in adverse storms, carries more rope, anchors, and sheets than he needs for good weather. So let the father see that his sons enjoy some praiseworthy and useful activity. In this matter let him consider first of all the honesty of the work, and then adapt his course to what he knows his son can actually accomplish, and finally try to choose a field in which, by applying himself, the young man can hope to earn a reputation.

*   *   *

Battista: Whatever you think. The only question we have is what are the things that make a family fortunate. Go on with what you have to say and we shall listen.

*   *   *

Lionardo: In our discussion we may establish four general precepts as sound and firm foundation for all the other points to be developed or added. I shall name them. In the family the number of men must not diminish but augment; possessions must not grow less, but more; all forms of disgrace are to be shunned—a good name and fine reputation is precious and worth pursuing; hatreds, enmities, rancor must be carefully avoided, while good will, numerous acquaintances, and friendships are something to look for, augment, and cultivate.

*   *   *

If a family is not to fall for these reasons into what we have described as the most unfortunate condition of decline, but is to grow, instead, in fame and in the prosperous multitude of its youth, we must persuade our young men to take wives. We must use every argument for this purpose, offer incentive, promise reward, employ all our wit, persistence, and cunning. A most appropriate reason for taking a wife may be found in what we

were saying before, about the evil of sensual indulgence, for the condemnation of such things may lead young men to desire honorable satisfactions. As other incentives, we may also speak to them of the delights of this primary and natural companionship of marriage. Children act as pledges and securities of marital love and kindness. At the same time they offer a focus for all a man's hopes and desires. Sad, indeed, is the man who has labored to get wealth and power and lands, and then has no true heir and perpetuator of his memory. No one can be more suited than a man's true and legitimate sons to gain advantages by virtue of his character, position, and authority, and to enjoy the fruits and rewards of his labor. If a man leaves such heirs, furthermore, he need not consider himself wholly dead and gone. His children keep his own position and his true image in the family. Dido, the Phoenician, when Aeneas left her, his mistress, cried out with tears, among her great sorrows no desire above this one: "Ah, had I but a small Aeneas now, to play beside me." As you were first poisoned, wretched and abandoned woman, by that man whose fatal and consuming love you did embrace, so another little Aeneas might by his similar face and gestures have offered you some consolation in your grief and anguish.

*   *   *

When, by the urging and counsel of their elders and of the whole family, young men have arrived at the point of marriage, their mothers and other female relatives and friends, who have known the virgins of the neighborhood from earliest childhood and know the way their upbringing has formed them, should select all the well-born and well-brought-up girls and present that list to the new groom-to-be. He can then choose the one who suits him best. The elders of the house and all of the family shall reject no daughter-in-law unless she is tainted with the breath of scandal or bad reputation. Aside from that, let the man who will have to satisfy her satisfy himself. He should act as do wise heads of families before they acquire some property—they like to look it over several times before they actually sign a contract. It is good in the case of any purchase and contract to inform oneself fully and to take counsel. One should consult a good number of persons and be very careful in order to avoid belated regrets. The man who has decided to marry must be still more cautious. I recommend that he examine and anticipate in every way, and consider for many days, what sort of person it is he is to live with for all his years as husband and companion. Let him be minded to marry for two purposes: first to perpetuate himself in his children, and second to have a steady and constant companion all his life. A woman is needed, therefore, who is likely to bear children and who is desirable as a perpetual mate.

*   *   *

To sum up this whole subject in a few words, for I want above all to be brief on this point, let a man get himself new kinsmen of better than plebeian blood, of a fortune more than diminutive, of a decent occupation, and of modest and respectable habits. Let them not be too far above himself, lest their greatness overshadow his own honor and position. Too high a family may disturb his own and his family's peace and tranquillity, and also, if one of them falls, you cannot help to support him without collapsing or wearing yourself out as you stagger under a weight too great for your arms and your strength. I also do not want the new relatives to rank too low, for while the first error puts you in a position of servitude, the second causes expense. Let them be equals, then, and, to repeat, modest and respectable people.

*   *   *

We have, as I said, made the house numerous and full of young people. It is essential to give them something to do now, and not let them grow lazy. Idleness is not only useless and generally despised in young men, but a positive burden and danger to the family. I do not need to teach you to shun idleness, when I know you are hard workers and active. I do encourage you to continue as

you are doing in every sort of activity and hard discipline that you may attain excellence and deserve fame. Only think this matter over and consider whether any man, even if he is not necessarily ambitious of gaining glory but merely a little shy of falling into disgrace, can ever be, in actuality or even if we merely try to imagine him, a man not heartily opposed to idleness and to mere sitting. Who has ever dreamed he might reach any grace or dignity without hard work in the noblest arts, without assiduous efforts, without plenty of sweat poured out in manly and strenuous exertions? Certainly a man who would wish for the favor of praise and fame must avoid and resist idleness and inertia just as he would do major and hateful enemies. There is nothing that leads more quickly to dishonor and disgrace than idleness. The lap of the idler has always been the nest and lair of vice. Nothing is so harmful and pestilent in public and private life as the lazy and passive citizen. From idleness springs lasciviousness; from lasciviousness comes a contempt for the law; from disobedience to law comes ruin and the destruction of the country itself. To the extent that men tolerate the first resistance of men's will to the customs and ways of the country, their spirits soon turn to arrogance, pride, and the harmful power of avarice and greed. Thieves, murderers, adulterers, and all sorts of criminals and evil men run wild.

*   *   *

To this I might add that man ought to give some reward to God, to satisfy him with good works in return for the wonderful gifts which He gave to the spirit of man exalting and magnifying it beyond that of all other earthly beings. Nature, that is, God, made man a composite of two parts, one celestial and divine, the other most beautiful and noble among mortal things. He provided him with a form and a body suited to every sort of movement, so as to enable him to perceive and to flee from that which threatened to harm and oppose him. He gave him speech and judgment so that he would be able to seek after and to find what he needed and could use. He gave him movement and sentiment, desire and the power of excitement, so that he might clearly appreciate and pursue useful things and shun those harmful and dangerous to him. He gave him intelligence, teachability, memory and reason, qualities divine in themselves and which enable man to investigate, to distinguish, to know what to avoid and what to desire in order best to preserve himself. To these great gifts, admirable beyond measure, God added still another power of the spirit and mind of man, namely moderation. As a curb on greed and on excessive lusts, he gave him modesty and the desire for honor. Further, God established in the human mind a strong tie to bind together human beings in society, namely justice, equity, liberality, and love. These are the means by which a man can gain the favor and praise of other men, as well as the mercy and grace of the creator. Beyond this, God filled the manly breast with powers that make man able to bear fatigue, adversity, and the hard blows of fortune. He is able to undertake what is difficult, to overcome sorrow, not even to fear death—such are his qualities of strength, of endurance and fortitude, such can be his contempt for transitory things. These are qualities which enable us to honor and serve God as fully as we should, with piety, with moderation, and with every other perfect and honorable deed. Let us agree, then, that man was not born to languish in idleness but to labor and create magnificent and great works, first for the pleasure and glory of God, and second for his own enjoyment of that life of perfect virtue and its fruit, which is happiness.

*   *   *

Let men seek their own happiness first, and they will obtain the happiness of their family also. As I have said, happiness cannot be gained without good works and just and righteous deeds. Works are just and good which not only do no harm to anyone, but which benefit many. Works are righteous if they are without a trace of the dishonorable or any element of dishonesty. The best works are those which benefit many people. Those are most virtuous, perhaps, which cannot

be pursued without strength and nobility. We must give ourselves to manly effort, then, and follow the noblest pursuits.

It seems to me, before we dedicate ourselves to any particular activity, it would be wise to think over and examine the question of what is our easiest way to reach or come near to happiness. Not every man easily attains happiness. Nature did not make all men of the same humor, or of the same intelligence or will, or equally endowed with skill and power. Rather nature planned that where I might be weak, you would make good the deficiency, and in some other way you would lack the virtue found in another. Why this? So that I should have need of you, and you of him, he of another, and some other of me. In this way one man's need for another serves as the cause and means to keep us all united in general friendship and alliance. This may, indeed, have been the source and beginning of republics. Laws may have begun thus rather than as I was saying before; fire and water alone may not have been the cause of so great a union among men as society gives them. Society is a union sustained by laws, by reason, and by custom.

Let us not digress. To decide which is the most suitable career for himself, a man must take two things into account: the first is his own intelligence, his mind and his body, everything about himself; and the second, the question requiring close consideration, is that of outside supports, the help and resources which are necessary or useful and to which he must have early access, welcome, and free right of use if he is to enter the field for which he seems more suited than for any other. Take an example: if a man wished to perform great feats of arms while he knew he was himself but a weak fellow, not very robust, incapable of bearing up through dust and storm and sun, this would not be the right profession for him to pursue. If I, being poor, longed to devote my life to letters, though I had not the money to pay the considerable expenses attached to such a career, again this would be a poor choice of career. If you are equipped with numerous relatives, plenty of friends, abundant wealth, and if you possess within yourself intelligence, eloquence, and such tact as to keep you out of any rough or awkward situations, and you decide to dedicate yourself to civic affairs, you might do extremely well.

*   *   *

We should also consider at this point how much reward and profit, how much honor and fame, you can gain from any work or achievement you undertake to perform. The only condition is that you surpass everyone else in the field. In every craft the most skilled master, as you know, gains most riches and has the best position and the greatest stature among his companions. Think how even in so humble a profession as shoemaking men search out the best among the cobblers. If it is true of the humblest occupations that the most skilled practitioners are ever most in demand and so become most famous, consider whether in the highest professions the opposite suddenly holds true. In fact you will find it still more to the point to be the best in these, or at least one of the best. If you succeed in these fields, you know that you have been given a greater portion of happiness than other men. If you are learned, you realize the misfortune of the ignorant. You know, in addition, that the unhappiest lot falls to those who, being ignorant, desire still to appear learned.

*   *   *

Consider in your own mind what a boon to know more than others and to put the knowledge to good use at the right time and place. If you think it over, I am sure you will realize that in every field a man who would appear to be valuable must be valuable in fact. Now we have stated this much: that youth should not be wasted but should be directed to some honorable kind of work, that a man should do his utmost in that work, and that he should choose the field which will be most helpful to his family and bring him most fame. A career should suit our own nature and the state of our fortunes, and should be pursued in such a way that we may never, by our own fault at least, fall short of the first rank.

Riches, however, are for nearly everyone the primary reason for working at all. They are also most useful in making it possible to persevere in our undertakings until we win approval and attain public favor, position, and fame. This is the time, therefore, to explain how wealth is acquired and how it is kept. It was also one of the four things which we said were necessary to bring about and to preserve contentment in a family. Now, then, let us begin to accumulate wealth. Perhaps the present moment, as the evening grows dark, is just right for this subject, for no occupation seems less attractive to a man of large and liberal spirit than the kind of labor by which wealth is in fact gathered. If you will count over in your imagination the actual careers that bring great profits, you will see that all basically concern themselves with buying and selling or with lending and collecting the returns. Having neither petty nor vulgar minds, I imagine you probably find these activities, which are solely directed to making a profit, somewhat below you. They seem entirely to lack honor and distinction.

*   *   *

Those who thus dismiss all mercenary activities are wrong, I believe. If the pursuit of wealth is not as glorious as are other great pursuits, yet a man is not contemptible if, being unsuited by nature to achieve anything much in other finer fields of work, he devotes himself to this kind of activity. Here, it may be, he knows he is not inadequately equipped to do well. Here everyone admits he is very useful to the republic and still more to his own family. Wealth, if it is used to help the needy, can gain a man esteem and praise. With wealth, if it is used to do great and noble things and to show a fine magnanimity and splendor, fame and dignity can be attained. In emergencies and times of need we see every day how useful is the wealth of private citizens to the country itself. From public funds alone it is not always possible to pay the wages of those whose arms and blood defend the country's liberty and dignity. Nor can republics increase their glory and their might without enormous expenditure.

*   *   *

Why have I gone on at length on these topics? Only to show you that, among occupations, there are quite a few, both honorable and highly esteemed, by means of which wealth in no small measure may be gained. One of these occupations, as you know, is that of merchant. You can easily call to mind other similar careers which are both honorable and highly profitable. You want to know, then, what they are. Let us run through them. We shall spread out all the occupations before us and choose the best among them, then we shall try to define how they make us wealthy and prosperous. Occupations that do not bring profit and gain will never make you rich. Those that bring frequent and large profits are the ones that make you rich. The only system for becoming rich, by our own industry and by the means that luck, friends, or anyone's favor can give us, is to make profits. And how do men grow poor? Ill fortune certainly plays a part, this I admit, but excluding fortune, let us speak here of industry. If riches come through profits, and these through labor, diligence, and hard work, then poverty, which is the reverse of profit, will follow from the reverse of these virtues, namely from neglect, laziness, and sloth. These are the fault neither of fortune nor of others, but of oneself. One grows poor, also, by spending too much. Prodigality dissipates wealth and throws it away. The opposite of prodigality, the opposite of neglect, are carefulness and conscientiousness, in short, good management. Good management is the means to preserve wealth. Thus we have found out that to become rich one must make profits, keep what one has gained, and exercise rational good management.

*   *   *

REVIEW QUESTIONS

1. What, according to Alberti, is the role and nature of a father?
2. How is his authority different from other kinds of authority?
3. What is the role of education in the formation of human nature?
4. How does this view differ from that of other authors?
5. What is honor?
6. What is its relationship to the family and why is it so important to Alberti?
7. How might Alberti define the family?

BENVENUTO CELLINI

FROM *The Autobiography*

Benvenuto Cellini (1500–1571) was a native of Florence. Apprenticed as a young man to a goldsmith, he eventually wandered to Rome, where he established himself as an independent craftsman and artist. Supported by the patronage of merchants, aristocrats, and prelates, his success knew no bounds, at least in his own telling. Indeed, Cellini's individualism, self-confidence, and talent, expressed in both art and violence, are recorded in his autobiography. It is both a fascinating portrait of the Renaissance artist and a valuable window on the era.

From *The Autobiography of Benvenuto Cellini,* translated by John Addington Symonds (New York: Modern Library, 1995).

*   *   *

All the while I was at Florence, I studied the noble manner of Michel Agnolo, and from this I have never deviated. About that time I contracted a close and familiar friendship with an amiable lad of my own age, who was also in the goldsmith's trade. He was called Francesco, son of Filippo, and grandson of Fra Lippo Lippi, that most excellent painter. Through intercourse together, such love grew up between us that, day or night, we never stayed apart. The house where he lived was still full of the fine studies which his father had made, bound up in several books of drawings by his hand, and taken from the best antiquities of Rome. The sight of these things filled me with passionate enthusiasm; and for two years or thereabouts we lived in intimacy. At that time I fashioned a silver bas-relief of the size of a little child's hand. It was intended for the clasp to a man's belt; for they were then worn as large as that. I carved on it a knot of leaves in the antique style, with figures of children and other masks of great beauty. This piece I made in the workshop of one Francesco Salimbene; and on its being exhibited to the trade, the goldsmiths praised me as the best young craftsman of their art.

There was one Giovan Battista, surnamed Il Tasso, a wood-carver, precisely of my own age, who one day said to me that if I was willing to go to Rome, he should be glad to join me. Now we had this conversation together immediately after dinner; and I being angry with my father for the same old reason of the music, said to Tasso: "You are a fellow of words, not deeds." He answered: "I too have come to anger with my mother; and if I had cash enough to take me to Rome, I would not turn back to lock the door of that wretched little workshop I call mine." To these words I re-

plied that if that was all that kept him in Florence I had money enough in my pockets to bring us both to Rome. Talking thus and walking onwards, we found ourselves at the gate San Piero Gattolini without noticing that we had got there; whereupon I said: "Friend Tasso, this is God's doing that we have reached this gate without either you or me noticing that we were there; and now that I am here, it seems to me that I have finished half the journey." And so, being of one accord, we pursued our way together, saying, "Oh, what will our old folks say this evening?" We then made an agreement not to think more about them till we reached Rome. So we tied our aprons behind our backs, and trudged almost in silence to Siena. When we arrived at Siena, Tasso said (for he had hurt his feet) that he would not go farther, and asked me to lend him money to get back. I made answer: "I should not have enough left to go forward; you ought indeed to have thought of this on leaving Florence; and if it is because of your feet that you shirk the journey, we will find a return horse for Rome, which will deprive you of the excuse." Accordingly I hired a horse; and seeing that he did not answer, I took my way toward the gate of Rome. When he knew that I was firmly resolved to go, muttering between his teeth, and limping as well as he could, he came on behind me very slowly and at a great distance. On reaching the gate, I felt pity for my comrade, and waited for him, and took him on the crupper, saying: "What would our friends speak of us to-morrow, if, having left for Rome, we had not pluck to get beyond Siena?" Then the good Tasso said I spoke the truth; and as he was a pleasant fellow, he began to laugh and sing; and in this way, always singing and laughing, we travelled the whole way to Rome. I had just nineteen years then, and so had the century.

When we reached Rome, I put myself under a master who was known as Il Firenzuola. His name was Giovanni, and he came from Firenzuola in Lombardy, a most able craftsman in large vases and big plate of that kind. I showed him part of the model for the clasp which I had made in Florence at Salimbene's. It pleased him exceedingly; and turning to one of his journeymen, a Florentine called Giannotto Giannotti, who had been several years with him, he spoke as follows: "This fellow is one of the Florentines who knows something, and you are one of those who know nothing." Then I recognised the man, and turned to speak with him; for before he went to Rome, we often went to draw together, and had been very intimate comrades. He was so put out by the words his master flung at him, that he said he did not recognise me or know who I was; whereupon I got angry, and cried out: "O Giannotto, you who were once my friend—for have we not been together in such and such places, and drawn, and ate, and drunk, and slept in company at your house in the country? I don't want you to bear witness on my behalf to this worthy man, your master, because I hope my hands are such that without aid from you they will declare what sort of a fellow I am."

XIV

When I had thus spoken, Firenzuola, who was a man of hot spirit and brave, turned to Giannotto, and said to him: "You vile rascal, aren't you ashamed to treat a man who has been so intimate a comrade with you in this way?" And with the same movement of quick feeling, he faced round and said to me: "Welcome to my workshop; and do as you have promised; let your hands declare what man you are."

He gave me a very fine piece of silver plate to work on for a cardinal. It was a little oblong box, copied from the porphyry sarcophagus before the door of the Rotonda. Beside what I copied, I enriched it with so many elegant masks of my invention, that my master went about showing it through the art, and boasting that so

good a piece of work had been turned out from his shop. It was about half a cubit in size, and was so constructed as to serve for a salt-cellar at table. This was the first earning that I touched at Rome, and part of it I sent to assist my good father; the rest I kept for my own use, living upon it while I went about studying the antiquities of Rome, until my money failed, and I had to return to the shop for work. Battista del Tasso, my comrade, did not stay long in Rome, but went back to Florence.

After undertaking some new commissions, I took it into my head, as soon as I had finished them, to change my master; I had indeed been worried into doing so by a certain Milanese, called Pagolo Arsago. My first master, Firenzuola, had a great quarrel about this with Arsago, and abused him in my presence; whereupon I took up speech in defence of my new master. I said that I was born free, and free I meant to live, and that there was no reason to complain of him, far less of me, since some few crowns of wages were still due to me; also that I chose to go, like a free journeyman, where it pleased me, knowing I did wrong to no man. My new master then put in with his excuses, saying that he had not asked me to come, and that I should gratify him by returning with Firenzuola. To this I replied that I was not aware of wronging the latter in any way, and as I had completed his commissions, I chose to be my own master and not the man of others, and that he who wanted me must beg me of myself. Firenzuola cried: "I don't intend to beg you of yourself; I have done with you; don't show yourself again upon my premises." I reminded him of the money he owed me. He laughed me in the face; on which I said that if I knew how to use my tools in handicraft as well as he had seen, I could be quite as clever with my sword in claiming the just payment of my labour. While we were exchanging these words, an old man happened to come up, called Maestro Antonio, of San Marino. He was the chief among the Roman goldsmiths, and had been Firenzuola's master. Hearing what I had to say, which I took good care that he should understand, he immediately espoused my cause, and bade Firenzuola pay me. The dispute waxed warm, because Firenzuola was an admirable swordsman, far better than he was a goldsmith. Yet reason made itself heard; and I backed my cause with the same spirit, till I got myself paid. In course of time Firenzuola and I became friends, and at his request I stood godfather to one of his children.

*   *   *

REVIEW QUESTIONS

1. What distinguishes the artist according to Cellini?
2. How is genius dependent on wealth?
3. What does Cellini tell us about patronage and its effects on art?
4. In what ways is the artist like a courtier?

GIORGIO VASSARI

FROM *The Lives of the Artists*

Giorgio Vassari (1511–1574) was one of the most fashionable and prolific painters of his age. He spent most of his life traveling about Italy on various commissions. During these travels, he gathered specific information about artists and their works that he later incorporated into The Lives of the Artists *(1500). Its biographical sketches reveal not only fascinating insights into the practice of art in the Renaissance but also the taste and perspective of an accomplished artist. As a young man, Vassari studied painting under Michelangelo Buonarotti (1475–1564) and remained a lifelong disciple and admirer. Michelangelo began his career in 1492 under the patronage of Lorenzo de Medici. In 1505 he moved to Rome to design the tomb of Pope Julius II (1502–1513). Among his more famous commissions are the ceiling of the Sistine Chapel and the Basilica of St. Peter's. His career stretched to the middle of the sixteenth century, "bringing to perfection" (in Vassari's words) the three branches of the fine arts.*

From *The Lives of the Artists*, by Giorgio Vassari, translated by George Bull (New York: Penguin Books, 1965), pp. 325–26, 349–54.

*   *   *

Enlightened by what had been achieved by the renowned Giotto and his school, all artists of energy and distinction were striving to give the world proof of the talents with which fortune and their own happy temperaments had endowed them.

They were all anxious (though their efforts were in vain) to reflect in their work the glories of nature and to attain, as far as possible, perfect artistic discernment or understanding. Meanwhile, the benign ruler of heaven graciously looked down to earth, saw the worthlessness of what was being done, the intense but utterly fruitless studies, and the presumption of men who were farther from true art than night is from day, and resolved to save us from our errors. So he decided to send into the world an artist who would be skilled in each and every craft, whose work alone would teach us how to attain perfection in design (by correct drawing and by the use of contour and light and shadows, so as to obtain relief in painting) and how to use right judgment in sculpture and, in architecture, create buildings which would be comfortable and secure, healthy, pleasant to look at, well-proportioned and richly ornamented. Moreover, he determined to give this artist the knowledge of true moral philosophy and the gift of poetic expression, so that everyone might admire and follow him as their perfect exemplar in life, work, and behaviour and in every endeavour, and he would be acclaimed as divine. He also saw that in the practice of these exalted disciplines and arts, namely, painting, sculpture, and architecture, the Tuscan genius has always been preeminent, for the Tuscans have devoted to all the various branches of art more labour and study than all the other Italian peoples. And therefore he chose to have Michelangelo born a Florentine, so that one of her own citizens might bring to absolute perfection the achievements for which Florence was already justly renowned.

So in the year 1474 in the Casentino, under a fateful and lucky star, the virtuous and noble wife of Lodovico di Leonardo Buonarroti gave birth to a baby son. That year Lodovico (who was said to be related to the most noble and ancient family of the counts of Canossa) was visiting magistrate at the township of Chiusi and Caprese near the Sasso della Vernia (where St. Francis received the stigmata) in the diocese of Arezzo. The boy was born on Sunday, 6 March, about the eighth hour of the night; and without further thought his father decided to call him Michelangelo, being inspired by heaven and convinced that he saw in him something supernatural and beyond human experience. This was evident in the child's horoscope which showed Mercury and Venus in the house of Jupiter, peaceably disposed; in other words, his mind

and hands were destined to fashion sublime and magnificent works of art.

*   *   *

Meanwhile, the Pope had returned to Rome while Michelangelo remained in Bologna to finish the statue. In his absence Bramante was constantly plotting with Raphael of Urbino to remove from the Pope's mind the idea of having Michelangelo finish the tomb on his return. Bramante did this (being a friend and relation of Raphael and therefore no friend of Michelangelo's) when he saw the way his holiness kept praising and glorifying Michelangelo's work as a sculptor. He and Raphael suggested to Pope Julius that if the tomb were finished it would bring nearer the day of his death, and they said that it was bad luck to have one's tomb built while one was still alive. Eventually they persuaded his holiness to get Michelangelo on his return to paint, as a memorial for his uncle, Pope Sixtus IV, the ceiling of the chapel that he had built in the Vatican. In this way Bramante and Michelangelo's other rivals thought they would divert his energies from sculpture, in which they realized he was supreme. This, they argued, would make things hopeless for him, since as he had no experience of colouring in fresco he would certainly, they believed, do less creditable work as a painter. Without doubt, they thought, he would be compared unfavourably with Raphael, and even if the work were a success, being forced to do it would make him angry with the Pope; and thus one way or another they would succeed in their purpose of getting rid of him. So when Michelangelo returned to Rome he found the Pope resolved to leave the tomb as it was for the time being, and he was told to paint the ceiling of the chapel. Michelangelo, being anxious to finish the tomb, and considering the magnitude and difficulty of the task of painting the chapel, and his lack of experience, tried in every possible way to shake the burden off his shoulders. But the more he refused, the more determined he made the Pope, who was a wilful man by nature and who in any case was again being prompted by Michelangelo's rivals, and especially Bramante. And finally, being the hot-tempered man he was, his holiness was all ready to fly into a rage.

However, seeing that his holiness was persevering, Michelangelo resigned himself to doing what he was asked. Then the Pope ordered Bramante to make the ceiling ready for painting, and he did so by piercing the surface and supporting the scaffolding by ropes. When Michelangelo saw this he asked Bramante what he should do, when the painting was finished, to fill up the holes. Bramante said: "We'll think of it when it's time." And he added that there was no other way. Michelangelo realized that Bramante either knew nothing about the matter or else was no friend of his, and he went to the Pope and told him that the scaffolding was unsatisfactory and that Bramante had not known how to make it; and the Pope replied, in the presence of Bramante, that Michelangelo should do it himself in his own way. So he arranged to have the scaffolding erected on props which kept clear of the wall, a method for use with vaults (by which many fine works have been executed) which he subsequently taught to various people, including Bramante. In this instance he enabled a poor carpenter, who rebuilt the scaffolding, to dispense with so many of the ropes that when Michelangelo gave him what was over he sold them and made enough for a dowry for his daughter.

Michelangelo then started making the cartoons for the vaulting; and the Pope also decided that the walls that had been painted by previous artists in the time of Sixtus should be scraped clean and that Michelangelo should have fifteen thousand ducats for the cost of the work, the price being decided through Giuliano da Sangallo. Then being forced reluctantly, by the magnitude of the task, to take on some assistants, Michelangelo sent for help to Florence. He was anxious to show that his paintings would surpass the work done there earlier, and he was determined to show modern artists how to draw and paint. Indeed, the circumstances of this undertaking encouraged Michelangelo to aim very high, for the sake both of his own reputation and the art of painting; and in this mood he started and finished the cartoons. He was then ready to begin the frescoes, but he lacked the necessary experience. Meanwhile, some of his friends, who were painters, came to Rome from Florence in order to assist him and let him see their technique. Several of them were skilled painters in fresco, and they included Granaccio, Giuliano Bugiardini, Jacopo di Sandro, the elder Indaco, Angelo di Donnino, and Aristotile. Having started the work, Michelangelo asked them to produce some examples of what they could do. But when he saw that these were nothing like what he wanted he grew dissatisfied, and then one morning he made up his mind to scrap everything they had done. He shut himself up in the chapel, refused to let them in again, and would never let them see him even when he was at home. So, when they thought the joke was wearing thin, they accepted their dismissal and went back ashamed to Florence.

Thereupon, having arranged to do all the work by himself, Michelangelo carried it well on the way to completion; working with the utmost solicitude, labour, and study he refused to let anyone see him in case he would have to show what he was painting. As a result every day the people became more impatient.

Pope Julius himself was always keen to see whatever Michelangelo was doing, and so naturally he was more anxious than ever to see what was being hidden from him. So one day he resolved to go and see the work, but he was not allowed in, as Michelangelo would never have consented. (This was the cause of the quarrel described earlier, when Michelangelo had to leave Rome as he would not let the Pope see what he was painting.) Now when a third of the work was completed (as I found out from Michelangelo himself, to clear up any uncertainty) during the winter when the north wind was blowing several spots of mould started to appear on the surface. The reason for this was that the Roman lime, which is white in colour and made of travertine, does not dry very quickly, and when mixed with pozzolana, which is a brownish colour, forms a dark mixture which is very watery before it sets; then after the wall has been thoroughly soaked, it often effloresces when it is drying. Thus this salt efflorescence appeared in many places, although in time the air dried it up. When Michelangelo saw what was happening he despaired of the whole undertaking and was reluctant to go on. However, his holiness sent Giuliano da Sangallo to see him and explain the reason for the blemishes. Sangallo explained how to remove the moulds and encouraged him to continue. Then, when the work was half finished, the Pope who had subsequently gone to inspect it several times (being helped up the ladders by Michelangelo) wanted it to be thrown open to the public. Being hasty and impatient by nature, he simply could not bear to wait until it was perfect and had, so to say, received the final touch.

As soon as it was thrown open, the whole of Rome flocked to see it; and the Pope was the first, not having the patience to wait till the dust had settled after the dismantling of the scaffolds. Raphael da Urbino (who had great powers of imitation) changed his style as soon as he had seen Michelangelo's work and straight away, to show his skill, painted the prophets and sibyls of Santa Maria della Pace; and Bramante subsequently tried to persuade the Pope to let Raphael paint the other half of the chapel. When Michelangelo heard about this he complained of Bramante and revealed to the Pope, without reserve, many faults in his life and in his architectural works. (He himself, as it happened, was later to correct the mistakes made by Bramante in the fabric of St. Peter's.) However, the Pope recognized Michelangelo's genius more clearly every day and wanted him to carry on the work himself; and after he had seen it displayed he was of the opinion that Michelangelo would do the other half even better. And so in twenty months Michelangelo brought the project to perfect completion without the assistance even of someone to grind his colours. Michelangelo at times complained that because of the haste the Pope imposed on him he was unable to finish it in the way he would have liked; for his

holiness was always asking him importunately when it would be ready. On one of these occasions Michelangelo retorted that the ceiling would be finished "when it satisfies me as an artist."

And to this the Pope replied: "And we want you to satisfy us and finish it soon."

Finally, the Pope threatened that if Michelangelo did not finish the ceiling quickly he would have him thrown down from the scaffolding. Then Michelangelo, who had good reason to fear the Pope's anger, lost no time in doing all that was wanted; and after taking down the rest of the scaffolding he threw the ceiling open to the public on the morning of All Saints' Day, when the Pope went into the chapel to sing Mass, to the satisfaction of the entire city.

Michelangelo wanted to retouch some parts of the painting *a secco,* as the old masters had done on the scenes below, painting backgrounds, draperies, and skies in ultramarine, and in certain places adding ornamentation in gold, in order to enrich and heighten the visual impact. The Pope, learning that this ornamentation was lacking, and hearing the work praised so enthusiastically by all who saw it, wanted him to go ahead. However, he lacked the patience to rebuild the scaffolding, and so the ceiling stayed as it was. His holiness used to see Michelangelo often and he would ask him to have the chapel enriched with colours and gold, since it looked impoverished. And Michelangelo would answer familiarly:

"Holy Father, in those days men did not bedeck themselves in gold and those you see painted there were never very rich. They were holy men who despised riches."

For this work Michelangelo was paid by the Pope three thousand crowns in several instalments, of which he had to spend twenty-five on colours. He executed the frescoes in great discomfort, having to work with his face looking upwards, which impaired his sight so badly that he could not read or look at drawings save with his head turned backwards; and this lasted for several months afterwards. I can talk from personal experience about this, since when I painted five rooms in the great apartments of Duke Cosimo's palace if I had not made a chair where I could rest my head and relax from time to time I would never have finished; even so this work so ruined my sight and injured my head that I still feel the effects, and I am astonished that Michelangelo bore all that discomfort so well. In fact, every day the work moved him to greater enthusiasm, and he was so spurred on by his own progress and improvements that he felt no fatigue and ignored all the discomfort.

*   *   *

REVIEW QUESTIONS

1. What distinguishes the artist according to Vassari?
2. What is the source of artistic genius?
3. What does the experience of Michelangelo tell us about human art and human nature as viewed by Vassari?

LEONARDO DA VINCI

FROM *The Notebooks*

Leonardo da Vinci (1452–1519) was born in the countryside of Florence, the illegitimate son of a notary in the town of Vinci. He was self-taught and could read Latin poorly. He was left-handed, a condition viewed by contemporaries as a deformity. Sometime around 1481 he moved to Milan, where his patrons were the Dukes Gian Galeazzo (1476–94) and Ludovico Sforza (1494–1500). During the French invasion of 1499 Leonardo fled Milan and led a peripatetic existence until 1508, when he returned to the city. In 1513 he was taken to France, where he lived the remainder of his days. He is widely acclaimed as a genius, the designer of futuristic machines of many sorts. Among these was a device for grinding concave mirrors and lenses that made possible the invention of the telescope in 1509. He was a great artist in many media as well as a keen observer of nature. His interests ranged from aerodynamics to physics to biology to anatomy to optics. His writings on perspective are drawn from his notebooks, which he wrote backward, in a mirror hand, and in no particular order, and which were never published in his lifetime.

From *The Notebooks of Leonardo da Vinci*, translated by Edward MacCurdy (London: Cape, 1958).

*   *   *

Principle of Perspective

All things transmit their image to the eye by means of pyramids; the nearer to the eye these are intersected the smaller the image of their cause will appear.

If you should ask how you can demonstrate these points to me from experience, I should tell you, as regards the vanishing point which moves with you, to notice as you go along by lands ploughed in straight furrows, the ends of which start from the path where you are walking, you will see that continually each pair of furrows seem to approach each other and to join at their ends.

As regards the point that comes to the eye, it may be comprehended with greater ease; for if you look in the eye of anyone you will see your own image there; consequently if you suppose two lines to start from your ears and proceed to the ears of the image which you see of yourself in the eye of the other person, you will clearly recognise that these lines contract so much that when they have continued only a little way beyond your image as mirrored in the said eye they will touch one another in a point.

The thing that is nearer to the eye always appears larger than another of the same size which is more remote.

Perspective is of such a nature that it makes what is flat appear in relief, and what is in relief appear flat.

The perspective by means of which a thing is represented will be better understood when it is seen from the view-point at which it was drawn.

If you wish to represent a thing near, which should produce the effect of natural things, it is impossible for your perspective not to appear false, by reason of all the illusory appearances and errors in proportion of which the existence may be assumed in a mediocre work, unless whoever is looking at this perspective finds himself surveying it from the exact distance, elevation, angle of vision or point at which you were situated to make this perspective. Therefore it would be necessary to make a window of the size of your face or in truth a hole through which you would look at the said work. And if you should do this, then without any doubt your work will produce the effect of nature if the light and shade are correctly rendered, and you will hardly be able to convince yourself that these things are painted. Otherwise do not trouble yourself about representing anything, unless you take your view-point at a distance of at least twenty times the maximum width and height of the thing that you represent; and this will satisfy every beholder who places himself in front of the work at any angle whatever.

If you wish to see a proof of this quickly, take a piece of a staff like a small column eight times as high as its width without plinth or capital, then measure off on a flat wall forty equal spaces which are in conformity with the spaces; they will make between them forty columns similar to your small column. Then let there be set up in front of the middle of these spaces, at a distance of four braccia from the wall, a thin band of iron, in the centre of which there is a small round hole of the size of a large pearl; place a light beside this hole so as to touch it, then go and place your column above each mark of the wall and draw the outline of the shadow, then shade it and observe it through the hole in the iron.

In Vitolone there are eight hundred and five conclusions about perspective.

Perspective

No visible body can be comprehended and well judged by human eyes, except by the difference of the background where the extremities of this body terminate and are bounded, and so far as its contour lines are concerned no object will seem to be separated from this background. The moon, although far distant from the body of the sun, when by reason of eclipses it finds itself between our eyes and the sun, having the sun for its background will seem to human eyes to be joined and attached to it.

Perspective comes to aid us where judgment fails in things that diminish.

It is possible to bring about that the eye does not see distant objects as much diminished as they are in natural perspective, where they are diminished by reason of the convexity of the eye, which is obliged to intersect upon its surface the pyramids of every kind of image that approach the eye at a right angle. But the method that I show here in the margin cuts these pyramids at right angles near the surface of the pupil. But whereas the convex pupil of the eye can take in the whole of our hemisphere, this will show only a single star; but where many small stars transmit their images to the surface of the pupil these stars are very small; here only one will be visible but it will be large; and so the moon will be greater in size and its spots more distinct. You should place close to the eye a glass filled with the water mentioned in chapter four of book 113 'Concerning Natural Things', water which causes things congealed in balls of crystalline glass to appear as though they were without glass.

Of the eye. Of bodies less than the pupil of the eye that which is nearest to it will be least discerned by this pupil—and from this experience it follows that the power of sight is not reduced to a point.

But the images of objects which meet in the pupil of the eye are spread over this pupil in the same way as they are spread about in the air; and the proof of this is pointed out to us when we look at the starry heavens without fixing our gaze more upon one star than upon another, for then the sky shows itself to us strewn with stars, and they bear to the eye the same proportions as in the sky, and the spaces between them also are the same.

Natural perspective acts in the opposite way, for the greater the distance the smaller does the thing

seen appear, and the less the distance the larger it appears. But this invention constrains the beholder to stand with his eye at a small hole, and then with this small hole it will be seen well. But since many eyes come together to see at the same time one and the same work produced by this art, only one of them will have a good view of the function of this perspective and all the others will only see it confusedly. It is well therefore to shun this compound perspective, and to keep to the simple which does not purport to view planes foreshortened but as far as possible in exact form.

And of this simple perspective in which the plane intersects the pyramid that conveys the images to the eye that are at an equal distance from the visual faculty, an example is afforded us by the curve of the pupil of the eye upon which these pyramids intersect at an equal distance from the visual faculty.

Of Equal Things the More Remote Appears Smaller

The practice of perspective is divided into two parts, of which the first treats of all the things seen by the eye at whatsoever distance, and this in itself shows all these things diminished as the eye beholds them, without the man being obliged to stand in one place rather than in another, provided that the wall does not foreshorten it a second time.

But the second practice is a combination of perspective made partly by art and partly by nature, and the work done according to its rules has no part that is not influenced by natural and accidental perspective. Natural perspective I understand has to do with the flat surface on which this perspective is represented; which surface, although it is parallel to it in length and height, is constrained to diminish the distant parts more than its near ones. And this is proved by the first of what has been said above, and its diminution is natural.

Accidental perspective, that is that which is created by art, acts in the contrary way; because it causes bodies equal in themselves to increase on the foreshortened plane, in proportion as the eye is more natural and nearer to the plane, and as the part of this plane where it is represented is more remote from the eye.

*   *   *

REVIEW QUESTIONS

1. According to da Vinci, what is the relationship between perspective in nature and perspective in the human eye?
2. What is the relationship between perspective and mathematical principles?
3. Is perspective a constant or contingent?
4. What implications does this have for painting?
5. How might it shape the enterprise of reading?

BALDESAR CASTIGLIONE

FROM *The Book of the Courtier*

Baldesar Castiglione (1478–1529) was born near Mantua and educated in Milan. He entered the service of the duke of Milan in 1496. After the duke was carried prisoner to France, Castiglione returned to Mantua. In 1504, he entered the court of Guidobaldo of Montefeltro, duke of Urbino, where he remained until 1524; this is the setting of The Book of the Courtier. *Although he wrote elegant verse in Latin and Italian, this reflection on courtly life was Castiglione's claim to fame. Fashioned as a discourse among courtiers and courtesans, it described the ideal courtier and presented the Renaissance man.*

From *The Book of the Courtier*, by Baldesar Castiglione, translated by Charles S. Singleton (New York: Bantam Doubleday Dell, 1959), pp. 29–30, 32–34, 70–72, 205–8, 289–90.

*   *   *

"Thus, I would have our Courtier born of a noble and genteel family; because it is far less becoming for one of low birth to fail to do virtuous things than for one of noble birth, who, should he stray from the path of his forebears, stains the family name, and not only fails to achieve anything but loses what has been achieved already. For noble birth is like a bright lamp that makes manifest and visible deeds both good and bad, kindling and spurring on to virtue as much for fear of dishonor as for hope of praise. And since this luster of nobility does not shine forth in the deeds of the lowly born, they lack that spur, as well as that fear of dishonor, nor do they think themselves obliged to go beyond what was done by their forebears; whereas to the wellborn it seems a reproach not to attain at least to the mark set them by their ancestors. Hence, it almost always happens that, in the profession of arms as well as in other worthy pursuits, those who are most distinguished are men of noble birth, because nature has implanted in everything that hid-

LAST SUPPER (1498)　　　　　　　　　　　　　　　　　　　　　　　　LEONARDO DA VINCI

Perhaps da Vinci's greatest painting, the Last Supper *captures the drama of the moment in which Jesus reveals to his disciples that one of them will betray him. For all its moment, however, it remains compellingly intimate in the individuality of expressions and gestures and in the conversational groupings of three. What do you think makes the* Last Supper *representative of Renaissance art in general? How might the artistic device of perspective be said to be an extension of urban, mercantile culture, the very culture that gave rise to the Renaissance? What does the* Last Supper *reveal about religious faith during the Renaissance?*

den seed which gives a certain force and quality of its own essence to all that springs from it, making it like itself: as we can see not only in breeds of horses and other animals, but in trees as well, the shoots of which nearly always resemble the trunk; and if they sometimes degenerate, the fault lies with the husbandman. And so it happens with men, who, if they are tended in the right way, are almost always like those from whom they spring, and often are better; but if they lack someone to tend them properly, they grow wild and never attain their full growth.

* * *

"But, to return to our subject, I say that there is a mean to be found between such supreme grace on the one hand and such stupid ineptitude on the other, and that those who are not so perfectly endowed by nature can, with care and effort, polish and in great part correct their natural defects. Therefore, besides his noble birth, I would wish the Courtier favored in this other respect, and endowed by nature not only with talent and with beauty of countenance and person, but with that certain grace which we call an 'air,' which shall make him at first sight pleasing and lovable to all who see him; and let this be an adornment informing and attending all his actions, giving the promise outwardly that such a one is worthy of the company and the favor of every great lord."

* * *

"But to come to some particulars: I hold that the principal and true profession of the Courtier must be that of arms; which I wish him to exercise with vigor; and let him be known among the others as bold, energetic, and faithful to whomever he serves. And the repute of these good qualities will be earned by exercising them in every time and place, inasmuch as one may not ever fail therein without great blame. And, just as among women the name of purity, once stained, is never restored, so the reputation of a gentleman whose profession is arms, if ever in the least way he sullies himself through cowardice or other disgrace, always remains defiled before the world and cov-

ered with ignominy. Therefore, the more our Courtier excels in this art, the more will he merit praise; although I do not deem it necessary that he have the perfect knowledge of things and other qualities that befit a commander, for since this would launch us on too great a sea, we shall be satisfied, as we have said, if he have complete loyalty and an undaunted spirit, and be always seen to have them. For oftentimes men are known for their courage in small things rather than in great. And often in important perils and where there are many witnesses, some men are found who, although their hearts sink within them, still, spurred on by fear of shame or by the company of those present, press forward with eyes shut, as it were, and do their duty, God knows how; and in things of little importance and when they think they can avoid the risk of danger, they are glad to play safe. But those men who, even when they think they will not be observed or seen or recognized by anyone, show courage and are not careless of anything, however slight, for which they could be blamed, such have the quality of spirit we are seeking in our Courtier.

"However, we do not wish him to make a show of being so fierce that he is forever swaggering in his speech, declaring that he has wedded his cuirass, and glowering with such dour looks as we have often seen Berto do; for to such as these one may rightly say what in polite society a worthy lady jestingly said to a certain man (whom I do not now wish to name) whom she sought to honor by inviting him to dance, and who not only declined this but would not listen to music or take any part in the other entertainments offered him, but kept saying that such trifles were not his business. And when finally the lady said to him: 'What then is your business?' he answered with a scowl: 'Fighting.' Whereupon the lady replied at once: 'I should think it a good thing, now that you are not away at war or engaged in fighting, for you to have yourself greased all over and stowed away in a closet along with all your battle harness, so that you won't grow any rustier than you already are'; and so, amid much laughter from those present, she ridiculed him in his stupid presumption.

Therefore, let the man we are seeking be exceedingly fierce, harsh, and always among the first, wherever the enemy is; and in every other place, humane, modest, reserved, avoiding ostentation above all things as well as that impudent praise of himself by which a man always arouses hatred and disgust in all who hear him."

*   *   *

"I would have him more than passably learned in letters, at least in those studies which we call the humanities. Let him be conversant not only with the Latin language, but with Greek as well, because of the abundance and variety of things that are so divinely written therein. Let him be versed in the poets, as well as in the orators and historians, and let him be practiced also in writing verse and prose, especially in our own vernacular; for, besides the personal satisfaction he will take in this, in this way he will never want for pleasant entertainment with the ladies, who are usually fond of such things. And if, because of other occupations or lack of study, he does not attain to such a perfection that his writings should merit great praise, let him take care to keep them under cover so that others will not laugh at him, and let him show them only to a friend who can be trusted; because at least they will be of profit to him in that, through such exercise, he will be capable of judging the writing of others. For it very rarely happens that a man who is unpracticed in writing, however learned he may be, can ever wholly understand the toils and industry of writers, or taste the sweetness and excellence of styles, and those intrinsic niceties that are often found in the ancients.

These studies, moreover, will make him fluent, and (as Aristippus said to the tyrant) bold and self-confident in speaking with everyone. However, I would have our Courtier keep one precept firmly in mind, namely, in this as in everything else, to be cautious and reserved rather than forward, and take care not to get the mistaken notion that he knows something he does not know.

*   *   *

"Let us leave these blind ones to their error, and let us have our Courtier be of such good judgment that he will not let himself be persuaded that black is white, or presume of himself more than he clearly knows to be true; and especially in those points which (if your memory serves you) messer Cesare said we had often used as the means of bringing to light the folly of many persons. Indeed, even if he knows that the praises bestowed upon him are true, let him avoid error by not assenting too openly to them, nor concede them without some protest; but let him rather disclaim them modestly, always showing and really esteeming arms as his chief profession, and the other good accomplishments as ornaments thereto; and do this especially when among soldiers, in order not to act like those who in studies wish to appear as soldiers, and, when in the company of warriors, wish to appear as men of letters. In this way, for the reasons we have stated, he will avoid affectation and even the ordinary things he does will appear to be very great things."

*   *   *

Then said the Duchess: "Do not exceed bounds, signor Magnifico, but hold to the order given, and describe the Court Lady so that such a noble lady may have someone capable of serving her worthily."

The Magnifico continued: "Then, Madam, in order to show that your commands can induce me to attempt what I do not even know how to do, I will speak of this excellent Lady as I would wish her to be; and when I have fashioned her to my taste, and since then I may not have another, like Pygmalion I will take her for my own. And, though signor Gasparo has said that the same rules which serve for the Courtier serve also for the Lady, I am of a different opinion; for although some qualities are common to both and are as necessary for a man as for a woman, there are yet others that befit a woman more than a man, and others that befit a man and to which a woman ought to be a complete stranger. I say this of bodily exercises; but above all I think that in her ways, manners, words, gestures, and bearing, a woman ought to be very unlike a man; for just as he must show a certain solid and sturdy manliness, so it is seemly for a woman to have a soft and delicate tenderness, with an air of womanly sweetness in her every movement, which, in her going and staying, and in whatever she says, shall always make her appear the woman without any resemblance to a man.

"Now, if this precept be added to the rules which these gentlemen have taught the Courtier, then I think she ought to be able to follow many such and adorn herself with the best accomplishments, as signor Gasparo says. For I hold that many virtues of the mind are as necessary to a woman as to a man; also, gentle birth; to avoid affectation, to be naturally graceful in all her actions, to be mannerly, clever, prudent, not arrogant, not envious, not slanderous, not vain, not contentious, not inept, to know how to gain and hold the favor of her mistress and of all others, to perform well and gracefully the exercises that are suitable for women. And I do think that beauty is more necessary to her than to the Courtier, for truly that woman lacks much who lacks beauty. Also she must be more circumspect, and more careful not to give occasion for evil being said of her, and conduct herself so that she may not only escape being sullied by guilt but even by the suspicion of it, for a woman has not so many ways of defending herself against false calumnies as a man has. But since Count Ludovico has set forth in great detail the chief profession of the Courtier, and has insisted that this be arms, I think it is also fitting to state what I judge that of the Court Lady to be, and when I have done this I shall think to have discharged the greater part of my assignment.

"Leaving aside, then, those virtues of the mind which she is to have in common with the Courtier (such as prudence, magnanimity, continence, and many others), as well as those qualities that befit all (such as kindness, discretion, ability to manage her husband's property and house and children, if she is married, and all qualities that are requisite in a good mother), I say that, in my opinion, in a Lady who lives at court a certain pleasing affability is becoming above all else, whereby she will be able to entertain graciously every kind of man with agreeable and comely conversation suited to the time and place and to the station of the person with whom she speaks, joining to serene and modest manners, and to that comeliness that ought to inform all her actions, a quick vivacity of spirit whereby she will show herself a stranger to all boorishness; but with such a kind manner as to cause her to be thought no less chaste, prudent, and gentle than she is agreeable, witty, and discreet: thus, she must observe a certain mean (difficult to achieve and, as it were, composed of contraries) and must strictly observe certain limits and not exceed them.

"Now, in her wish to be thought good and pure, this Lady must not be so coy, or appear so to abhor gay company or any talk that is a little loose, as to withdraw as soon as she finds herself involved, for it might easily be thought that she was pretending to be so austere in order to hide something about herself which she feared others might discover; for manners so unbending are always odious. Yet, on the other hand, for the sake of appearing free and amiable she must not utter unseemly words or enter into any immodest and unbridled familiarity or into ways such as might cause others to believe about her what is perhaps not true; but when she finds herself present at such talk, she ought to listen with a light blush of shame.

"Likewise, she must avoid an error into which I have seen many women fall, which is to gossip and eagerly listen to evil spoken of other women. For those women who, when they hear of the unchaste ways of other women, bristle and pretend that the thing is incredible and that a woman so immodest is a monster, in making so much of the fault give cause to think that they might be guilty of it themselves. And those others who continually go about prying into other women's love affairs, relating them in such detail and with such glee,

The other hours of the day, when they are not working, eating, or sleeping, are left to each man's individual discretion, provided he does not waste them in roistering or sloth, but uses them busily in some occupation that pleases him. Generally these periods are devoted to intellectual activity. For they have an established custom of giving public lectures before daybreak; attendance at these lectures is required only of those who have been specially chosen to devote themselves to learning, but a great many other people, both men and women, choose voluntarily to attend. Depending on their interests, some go to one lecture, some to another. But if anyone would rather devote his spare time to his trade, as many do who don't care for the intellectual life, this is not discouraged; in fact, such persons are commended as especially useful to the commonwealth.

*   *   *

But in all this, you may get a wrong impression, if we don't go back and consider one point more carefully. Because they allot only six hours to work, you might think the necessities of life would be in scant supply. This is far from the case. Their working hours are ample to provide not only enough but more than enough of the necessities and even the conveniences of life. You will easily appreciate this if you consider how large a part of the population in other countries exists without doing any work at all. In the first place, hardly any of the women, who are a full half of the population, work; or, if they do, then as a rule their husbands lie snoring in the bed. Then there is a great lazy gang of priests and so-called religious men. Add to them all the rich, especially the landlords, who are commonly called gentlemen and nobility. Include with them their retainers, that mob of swaggering bullies. Finally, reckon in with these the sturdy and lusty beggars, who go about feigning some disease as an excuse for their idleness. You will certainly find that the things which satisfy our needs are produced by far fewer hands than you had supposed.

And now consider how few of those who do work are doing really essential things. For where money is the standard of everything, many superfluous trades are bound to be carried on simply to satisfy luxury and licentiousness. Suppose the multitude of those who now work were limited to a few trades, and set to producing more and more of those conveniences and commodities that nature really requires. They would be bound to produce so much that the prices would drop, and the workmen would be unable to gain a living. But suppose again that all the workers in useless trades were put to useful ones, and that all the idlers (who now guzzle twice as much as the working-men who make what they consume) were assigned to productive tasks—well, you can easily see how little time each man would have to spend working, in order to produce all the goods that human needs and conveniences require—yes, and human pleasure too, as long as it's true and natural pleasure.

*   *   *

Their Gold and Silver

For these reasons, therefore, they have accumulated a vast treasure, but they do not keep it like a treasure. I'm really quite ashamed to tell you how they do keep it, because you probably won't believe me. I would not have believed it myself if someone had just told me about it; but I was there, and saw it with my own eyes. It is a general rule that the more different anything is from what people are used to, the harder it is to accept. But, considering that all their other customs are so unlike ours, a sensible man will not be surprised that they use gold and silver quite differently than we do. After all, they never do use money among themselves, but keep it only for a contingency which may or may not actually arise. So in the meanwhile they take care that no one shall overvalue gold and silver, of which money is made, beyond what the metals themselves deserve. Anyone can see, for example, that iron is far superior to either; men could not live without iron, by heaven, any more than without fire or water. But gold and silver have, by nature, no function that we cannot easily dispense with. Human folly has made them precious because they are rare. Like a most wise and generous mother, nature has placed the best things everywhere and in the open, like air, water, and the earth itself; but she has hidden away in remote places all vain and unprofitable things.

If in Utopia gold and silver were kept locked up in some tower, foolish heads among the common people might well concoct a story that the prince and the senate were out to cheat ordinary folk and get some advantage for themselves. They might indeed put the gold and silver into beautiful plate-ware and rich handiwork, but then in case of necessity the people would not want to give up such articles, on which they had begun to fix their hearts, only to melt them down for soldiers' pay. To avoid all these inconveniences, they thought of a plan which conforms with their institutions as clearly as it contrasts with our own. Unless we've actually seen it working, their plan may seem ridiculous to us, because we prize gold so highly and are so careful about protecting it. With them it's just the other way. While they eat from pottery dishes and drink from glass cups, well made but inexpensive, their chamber pots and stools—all their humblest vessels, for use in the common halls and private homes—are made of gold and silver. The chains and heavy fetters of slaves are also made of these metals. Finally, criminals who are to bear through life the mark of some disgraceful act are forced to wear golden rings on their ears, golden bands on their fingers, golden chains around their necks, and even golden crowns on their heads. Thus they hold gold and silver up to scorn in every conceivable way. As a result, when they have to part with these metals, which other nations give up with as much agony as if they were being disemboweled, the Utopians feel it no more than the loss of a penny.

*   *   *

Slaves

The Utopians enslave prisoners of war only if they are captured in wars fought by the Utopians themselves. The children of slaves are not automatically enslaved, nor are any men who were enslaved in a foreign country. Most of their slaves are either their own former citizens, enslaved for some heinous offense, or else men of other nations who were condemned to death in their own land. Most are of the latter sort. Sometimes the Utopians buy them at a very modest rate, more often they ask for them, get them for nothing, and bring them home in considerable numbers. These kinds of slaves are kept constantly at work, and are always fettered. The Utopians deal with their own people more harshly than with others, feeling that their crimes are worse and deserve stricter punishment because, as it is argued, they had an excellent education and the best of moral training, yet still couldn't be restrained from wrongdoing. A third class of slaves consists of hardworking penniless drudges from other nations who voluntarily choose to become slaves in Utopia. Such people are treated well, almost as well as citizens, except that they are given a little extra work, on the score that they're used to it. If one of them wants to leave, which seldom happens, no obstacles are put in his way, nor is he sent off empty-handed.

*   *   *

REVIEW QUESTIONS

1. Why did More choose to call the place *Utopia*, literally "Nowhere"?
2. What possibilities created by the discovery of a new world does More explore in *Utopia*?

3. How are More's Utopians different from what medieval Europeans would have considered Christian?
4. How does More's attitude toward the people of Utopia reflect attitudes of the Renaissance?

5. How might *Utopia* be critical of Renaissance society?
6. What do More's Utopians have in common with the kind of Christians Erasmus described in his colloquy "Cyclops, the Gospel-Bearer"?

14 ✤ THE PROTESTANT REFORMATION

The year 1492 marks both the end of the expansion of Christianity in Europe, with the final expulsion of the Jews and Muslims from the Iberian Peninsula, and the beginning of the expansion of European Christianity across the globe. So, too, it marks the nadir of papal ambition, venality, and corruption, and thereby the medieval Christian hierarchy. In that year the Borgia pope, Alexander VI, whom contemporaries such as Machiavelli knew to be rapacious, murderous, treacherous, and ambitious, was elected.

Within a generation of the Reconquista of Spain, the German lands of the grandson of Ferdinando and Isabella of Spain would be split between two very different understandings of Christianity: what it meant to be a Christian, what the Church was and how it was to be constituted, and what the nature of worship was. In part, the Reformation arose in response to perceptions of papal bellicosity and immorality; it belonged to an older tradition of reformatio. Equally, however, the Reformation was heir to the Renaissance: the philological skills and discoveries of fifteenth-century humanists enabled new approaches to the study of the Bible, and the humanist emphasis on historical accuracy led to a call for a return to apostolic Christianity. That return to the text of Scripture, along with a new sensitivity to historical periods, brought theologians such as Martin Luther to reconsider not only devotional practices but the very structure of authority of medieval Christendom—the papal hierarchy—and others, such as John Calvin, to return to the Acts of the Apostles for a vision of the true church.

Even as Christendom divided against itself in Europe, it expanded through the persons of conquistadores to create worlds unimagined in the European tradition. Reformation and expansion both came through bloodshed. In Germany, peasants and artisans fought lords and emperor to institute the godly law they *found in the Bible, only to be massacred. In France, the Low Countries, and England, as well as the Holy Roman Empire, Christians executed Christians over questions of the Eucharist, the place of images in worship, and the cult of the saints. Churches divided from one another, each defining itself against the others, even as all confronted worlds for which neither the Bible nor the classical tradition had prepared them.*

GIOVANNI MICHIEL

FROM A Venetian Ambassador's Report on the St. Bartholomew's Day Massacre

The struggle for supremacy in northern Italy, which marked the last half of the fifteenth century, gave rise to a new form of diplomacy, including structures and procedures that would be fundamental to relations among all modern states. Requiring continuous contact and communication, Renaissance states turned to permanent diplomacy, distinguished by the use of accredited resident ambassadors rather than ad hoc missions of medieval legates. The tasks of a permanent ambassador were to represent his government at state ceremonies, to gather information, and, occasionally, to enter into negotiations. Nowhere was this system more fully and expertly articulated than by the Republic of Venice in the late fifteenth and sixteenth centuries. Its ambassadors were chosen with unusual care from the most prominent families of the city. They were highly educated, and their duties were carefully defined. Among the latter were weekly dispatches reporting all matters of any interest to Venice. These reports were regularly read and debated in the senate, which replied with questions, instructions, and information of its own. As a result, Venetian ambassadors were among the most skilled and respected in early modern Europe. In this report, Giovanni Michiel interprets the events of St. Bartholomew's Day in 1572. The massacre of Huguenots, instigated by the Queen Mother, Catherine de Medici, outraged Protestant Europe and dashed all hopes for peace in France. Of particular interest is the ambassador's harshly realistic account of the political motives for so violent an act of statecraft.

From *Pursuit of Power: Venetian Ambassadors' Reports on Spain, Turkey and France in the Age of Phillip II, 1560–1600,* by James C. Davis (New York: HarperCollins, 1970), pp. 72–76, 78–79.

*   *   *

Turning to the queen, Admiral de Coligny said, "Madame, the king refuses to involve himself in one war. God grant that he may not be caught up in another which he cannot avoid."

By these words he meant, some say, that if they abandoned the prince of Orange things might go badly for him, and there would be a danger that if the prince failed to win or was actually driven out by the Spanish or for some other reason, then he might enter France with his French and German followers and it might be necessary to drive him out by force. However, everyone understood his words in a very different sense, namely that he was giving notice that he planned to stir up new storms and renew the rioting and civil war. When the queen carefully pondered this it became the chief reason, taken together with the other considerations, why she hurried to prepare that fate for him which he eventually met.

*   *   *

Then, at the dinner hour on Friday, while the admiral was returning on foot from the court to his lodgings and reading a letter, someone fired an arquebus at him. The shot came from a window which faced a bit obliquely on the street, near the royal palace called the Louvre. But it did not strike him in the chest as intended because it so happened that the admiral was wearing a pair of slippers which made walking difficult and, wanting to take them off and hand them to a page, he had just started to turn around. So the arquebus shot tore off a finger on his left hand and then hit his right arm near the wrist and passed through it to the other side near the elbow. If he had simply walked straight ahead it would have hit him in the chest and killed him.

As you can imagine, news of the event caused great excitement, especially at court. Everyone supposed it had been done by order of the duke of Guise to avenge his family, because the window from which the shot was fired belonged to his mother's house, which had purposely been left empty after she had gone to stay in another. When the news was reported to the king, who happened to be playing tennis with the duke of Guise, they say he turned white and looked thunderstruck. Without saying a word he withdrew into his chambers and made it obvious that he was extremely angry.

*   *   *

On Saturday the admiral's dressings were changed and the word was given out—which may or may not have been true—that the wound was not a mortal one and that there was no danger even that he would lose the arm. The Huguenots only blustered all the more, and everyone waited to see what would happen next. The duke of Guise knew he might be attacked, so he armed himself and stuck close to his uncle, the duke of Aumale, and as many relatives, friends and servants as possible.

But before long the situation changed. Late Saturday night, just before the dawn of Saint Bartholomew's Day, the massacre or slaughter was carried out. The French say the king ordered it. How wild and terrifying it was in Paris (which has a larger population than any other city in Europe), no one can imagine. Nor can one imagine the rage and frenzy of those who slaughtered and sacked, as the king ordered the people to do. Nor what a marvel, not to say a miracle, it was that the common people did not take advantage of this freedom to loot and plunder from Catholics as well as Huguenots, and ravenously take whatever they could get their hands on, especially since the city is incredibly wealthy. No one would ever imagine that a people could be armed and egged on by their ruler, yet not get out of control once they were worked up. But it was not God's will that things should reach such a pass.

The slaughter went on past Sunday for two or three more days, despite the fact that edicts were issued against it and the duke of Nevers was sent riding through the city along with the king's natural brother to order them to stop the killing. The massacre showed how powerfully religion can affect men's minds. On every street one could see the barbarous sight of men cold-bloodedly outraging others of their own people, and not just men who had never done them any harm but in most cases people they knew to be their neighbors and even their relatives. They had no feeling, no mercy on anyone, even those who kneeled before them and humbly begged for their lives. If one man hated another because of some argument or lawsuit all he had to say was "This man is a Huguenot" and he was immediately killed. (That happened to many Catholics.) If their victims threw themselves in the river as a last resort and tried to swim to safety, as many did, they chased them in boats and then drowned them. There was a great deal of looting and pillaging and they say the goods taken amounted to two million because many Huguenots, including some of the richest of them, had come to live in Paris after the most recent edict of pacification. Some estimate the number who were killed as high as four thousand, while others put it as low as two thousand.

The killing spread to all the provinces and most of the major cities and was just as frenzied there, if not more so. They attacked anyone, even the gentry, and as a result all the leaders who did not escape have been killed or thrown in prison. It is true that Montgomery and some others who were pursued by the duke of Guise escaped to England, but they are not major figures. And the king has terrified them enough so they won't make any trouble.

*   *   *

REVIEW QUESTIONS

1. According to the report, at what level of society did the St. Bartholomew's Day Massacre originate?
2. Who was said to have initiated it?
3. How was a person identified as Huguenot or Catholic?
4. What does that say about religious identity in early modern France?
5. Do we know from this report who ordered the assassination?
6. Who caused the massacre?
7. What do we learn about the relation of religion to politics and political action?

ST. IGNATIUS OF LOYOLA

FROM *The Spiritual Exercises*

St. Ignatius of Loyola (1491–1556), the great mystic and founder of the Society of Jesus, was born into a hidalgo family and spent his early manhood in military service to the king of Spain. Wounded in battle, he spent his convalescence reading the lives of saints, which awoke in him a sense of spiritual inadequacy not unlike those which fired the religious engagements of Martin Luther and John Calvin. His early attempts at reconciliation, in the form of physical austerities practiced on pilgrimage to Montserrat and in the hermitage at Manresa, failed to reassure him of his soul's salvation, just as they failed to ease the spiritual torments of the young Luther. The scholastically trained Luther sought solace in the systematic study of the Bible; the uneducated Loyola found it in visions of God. Loyola spent the next decade educating himself and seeking his mission. After a pilgrimage to the Holy Land in 1523, Loyola began his formal education by studying elementary Latin with schoolboys in Barcelona. He attended the universities in Alcala and Salamanca, preached in the streets, and was arrested by the Inquisition on suspicion of heresy. He attended the University of Paris from 1528 to 1535 and began to gather around him the companions who would form the initial core of the Society of Jesus. In 1534, he and nine companions swore an oath of poverty and chastity and promised either to undertake a crusade to the Holy Land or, failing that, to offer absolute obedience to the pope. At the center of this group was not only the man Loyola but his series of devotions and meditations that would later be published as The Spiritual Exercises *(1548). These exercises offered a practical and ascetic meditation on the life and death of Christ that drew much from the systematic meditations of the* devotio moderna *("modern devotions"). It instructed those who made or directed a religious retreat in order to stimulate an imitation of Christ that would be expressed in apostolic action as well as religious devotion. In 1535, Loyola and his company left for Italy. He was ordained in Venice in 1537. Finding no passage to the Holy Land, they continued to Rome, where they preached in the streets and ministered to the poor. Introduced to Pope Paul III by Gasparo Contarini, a great advocate of monastic reform, the company received a charter of foundation as the Society of Jesus in 1540. Constituted an order of clerks regular, devoted to educating the young and propagating the faith, sworn to poverty and obedience, the Jesuits grew quickly to become one of the most influential Catholic orders of the early modern period, a model of piety, discipline, education, and service.*

From *The Spiritual Exercises of St. Ignatius,* translated by Anthony Molho (New York: Bantam Doubleday Dell, 1989), pp. 139–42.

Rules for Thinking with the Church

In order to have the proper attitude of mind in the Church Militant we should observe the following rules:

1. Putting aside all private judgment, we should keep our minds prepared and ready to obey promptly and in all things the true spouse of Christ our Lord, our Holy Mother, the hierarchical Church.

2. To praise sacramental confession and the reception of the Most Holy Sacrament once a year, and much better once a month, and better still every week, with the requisite and proper dispositions.

3. To praise the frequent hearing of Mass, singing of hymns and psalms, and the recitation of long prayers, both in and out of church; also the hours arranged for fixed times for the whole Divine Office, for prayers of all kinds and for the canonical hours.

4. To praise highly religious life, virginity, and continence; and also matrimony, but not as highly as any of the foregoing.

5. To praise the vows of religion, obedience, poverty, chastity, and other works of perfection and supererogation. It must be remembered that a vow is made in matters that lead to evangelical perfection. It is therefore improper to make a vow in matters that depart from this perfection; as, for example, to enter business, to get married, and so forth.

6. To praise the relics of the saints by venerating them and by praying to these saints. Also to praise the stations, pilgrimages, indulgences, jubilees, Crusade indulgences, and the lighting of candles in the churches.

7. To praise the precepts concerning fasts and abstinences, such as those of Lent, Ember Days, Vigils, Fridays, and Saturdays; likewise to praise acts of penance, both interior and exterior.

8. To praise the adornments and buildings of churches as well as sacred images, and to venerate them according to what they represent.

9. Finally, to praise all the precepts of the Church, holding ourselves ready at all times to find reasons for their defense, and never offending against them.

10. We should be more inclined to approve and praise the directions and recommendations of our superiors as well as their personal behavior. Although sometimes these may not be or may not have been praiseworthy, to speak against them when preaching in public or in conversation with people would give rise to murmuring and scandal rather than to edification. As a result, the people would be angry with their superiors, whether temporal or spiritual. Still, while it does harm to our superiors in their absence to speak ill of them in the presence of the people, it might be useful to speak of their bad conduct to those who can apply a remedy.

11. To praise both positive and scholastic theology, for as it is more characteristic of the positive doctors, such as St. Augustine, St. Jerome, St. Gregory, and others, to encourage the affections to greater love and service of God our Lord in all things, so it also is more characteristic of the scholastic doctors, such as St. Thomas, St. Bonaventure, and the Master of the Sentences, etc., to define and explain for our times the things necessary for eternal salvation, and to refute and expose all errors and fallacies. Also, the scholastic doctors, being of more recent date, not only have a clearer understanding of the Holy Scripture and of the teachings of the positive and holy doctors, but also, being enlightened and inspired by the Divine Power, they are helped by the Councils,

Canons, and Constitutions of our Holy Mother Church.

12. We must be on our guard against making comparisons between the living and those who have already gone to their reward, for it is no small error to say, for example: "This man knows more than St. Augustine"; "He is another St. Francis, or even greater"; "He is another St. Paul in goodness, holiness, etc."

13. If we wish to be sure that we are right in all things, we should always be ready to accept this principle: I will believe that the white that I see is black, if the hierarchical Church so defines it. For, I believe that between the Bridegroom, Christ our Lord, and the Bride, His Church, there is but one spirit, which governs and directs us for the salvation of our souls, for the same Spirit and Lord, who gave us the Ten Commandments, guides and governs our Holy Mother Church.

14. Although it be true that no one can be saved unless it be predestined and unless he have faith and grace, still we must be very careful of our manner of discussing and speaking of these matters.

15. We should not make predestination an habitual subject of conversation. If it is sometimes mentioned we must speak in such a way that no person will fall into error, as happens on occasion when one will say, "It has already been determined whether I will be saved or lost, and in spite of all the good or evil that I do, this will not be changed." As a result, they become apathetic and neglect the works that are conducive to their salvation and to the spiritual growth of their souls.

16. In like manner, we must be careful lest by speaking too much and with too great emphasis on faith, without any distinction or explanation, we give occasion to the people to become indolent and lazy in the performance of good works, whether it be before or after their faith is founded in charity.

17. Also in our discourse we ought not to emphasize the doctrine that would destroy free will. We may therefore speak of faith and grace to the extent that God enables us to do so, for the greater praise of His Divine Majesty. But, in these dan-

gerous times of ours, it must not be done in such a way that good works or free will suffer any detriment or be considered worthless.

18. Although the generous service of God for motives of pure love should be most highly esteemed, we should praise highly the fear of His Divine Majesty, for filial fear and even servile fear are pious and most holy things. When one cannot attain anything better or more useful, this fear is of great help in rising from mortal sin, and after this first step one easily advances to filial fear which is wholly acceptable and pleasing to God our Lord, since it is inseparable from Divine Love.

*   *   *

REVIEW QUESTIONS

1. What do you suppose Loyola means by the *church militant?*
2. How might the Jesuits have been soldiers of Christ?
3. Loyola asks the members of his order to "praise" in order to be "thinking with the Church." How does this serve the Church?
4. What specifically does Loyola ask the Jesuits to praise?
5. What do the "Rules for Thinking with the Church" tell us about the Church?

FROM *The Trial of Klaus Hottinger of Zurich:* Iconoclasm

Among the most dramatic manifestations of reformation in the sixteenth century were instances of iconoclasm. Traditionally understood as a direct response to reformed teaching against the veneration of saints and the reliance on images, occasionally leavened with social and economic antagonism, iconoclasm has more recently been interpreted as a popular form of reformation, a point at which the common folk put into action the religious ideals of an educated elite. The following is a transcription of one of the earliest trials of iconoclasts, which occurred in the Swiss city of Zurich in September 1523. Three men pulled down and broke up a large crucifix that stood at a crossing in the suburb of Stadelhofen, just outside the city walls of Zurich. Such crosses were often quite tall; this one is described variously as eight to ten feet tall. This account retains some of the legal distinctions that would have been important to the iconoclasts, not only the ownership of the crucifix but the nature of that ownership. It also gives evidence of the common interpretation of images, an issue at the heart of the Reformation.

From *The Trial of Klaus Hottinger of Zurich,* translated by L. P. Wandel (Zurich: Staatsarchiv).

*   *   *

Witnesses

1. Hans Ockenfuss stated: Klaus Hottinger came to him and asked a favor of him, to help Hottinger remove a crucifix at Stadelhofen. The miller had given it free and clear to Hottinger to do with as he pleased. Since one hears daily, that such crucifixes and all other images of God, our Savior, are forbidden, Ockenfuss was of the opinion, that he had not behaved inappropriately or done anything illegal.

2. Heini Hirt, the miller of Stadelhofen, stated: days past, this witness, with his brothers, had gone out from the lower grainary, planning to have a drink together, when Klaus Hottinger ran after him and spoke: Hey, Hirt, when are you going to put away your idols? Hirt answered him, they did not bother him; he simply must not pray to them. He wished to leave this issue to his Lords (the magistrate of Zurich), for he was not learned in scripture and had no understanding of the matter. To this, Hottinger replied, if he (Hirt) were a good Christian man, he would remove them, because he had been informed from God's Word, that such idols should not be. When Hirt heard this, as he did not want trouble, he said to Hottinger, in so far as Hirt had the power and right to put away such idols, he transferred them and his jurisdiction over them, such as he had, to Hottinger for his own. Hottinger then told Hirt he must also help him to do this. But Hirt wanted nothing more to do with it, to be nowhere near it. Hottinger said, he would certainly find others who would help him. Hirt did not note, that Hottinger was so agitated. Hottinger came to him again after had been to Ulrich Trinkler, a magistrate, and said, "I have removed the idols," and further, he had not done it without involving my honorable Lords. He had namely sought counsel from Claus Setzstab, a magistrate, telling him what he wished to do. Furthermore, as my Lords had acknowledged, when they arrested the said Hottinger and his associates, Hottinger had come to him and said, would he

do so well as to go to Mr. Setzstab, and ask him not to put the case behind him, that he had talked with him. Hirt did not go to Setzstab—he did not wish to bring the whole matter upon himself. Hottinger also said that he had sold the woodwork and given out the money that had been "released" from it to the poor.

3. Lorenz Hochruetiner stated: He had already been imprisoned, along with Wolf the cabinetmaker, on account of the oil lamps, which the two had broken two weeks earlier in Our Lady's Church in Zurich, and was therefore, entirely of the opinion that he should steer clear of this; my Lords would not wish him to take part in such a case anymore. Then Claus Hottinger came up to him and told him of the crucifix in Stadelhofen, how he and Hans Ockenfuss had removed it, and asked him that he would help them tomorrow, for Ockenfuss had something else to do and could not help him anymore. He also said to him, how the miller had transferred the crucifix to him freely, to have as his own, with my Lord Ulrich Trinkler as witness. Finally upon his word, and because other people carried images of saints and crucifixes out of the churches, and no one marked it, he opined that it was not illegal, and he did as Hottinger wished, and unearthed the said sul.

The Accused

Klaus Hottinger gave his answer concerning the crucifix: A few days ago he talked over a lot of things with Heini Hirt, the miller from Stadelhofen, namely about images and other things. And the same Hirt said, if it were not right, then he would suffer to have his crucifix in Stadelhofen removed. And the two talked so much with one another, that he (Hirt) gave him the crucifix as a gift, free and clear, with Mr. Ulrich Trinkler as witness. And along with Hans Ockenfuss, he then removed that crucifix and in the morning, Lorenz Hochruetiner helped him to unearth the sul. And it was their opinion and their agreement that the best course would be to sell the wood from it, and give the money from it to the poor. He had not done this without the knowledge and will of certain lords of the Great and Small Councils, Mr. Claus Setzstab, Mr. Thoma Spruengli, and Heinrich Trueben. They did not warn him away, but instead said that by their understanding, they held and acknowledged it to be a good work, that such images come away. And namely, Mr. Stezstab said he had been there when Hans Huobers of Augsburg gave it to him to remove as he pleased. And he thought, no one talked him out of it.

And, so that no one thought, he sought counsel only after he had done the deed, he went in that very hour, in which Hirt had given him the crucifix, to Mr. Ulrich Trinkler, and understood nothing else from him, than that he held it for a good work. And had the forementioned either all together or singly warned him away with a single word, he would not have taken this on and would have away quietly. The said Mr. Trinkler also showed him certain images, which stood under the stairs in his house, and said, though it had cost him a great deal, he had them carried out of the church, so that no one would pray to them.

Further finding of the court: It was put before him, that he had said, he would give as a gift either to my Lords or to the poor in the hospice a measure of wine. He answered, not to his knowledge and he could not make sense of it, that he would have said such a thing. In so far as they nonetheless found this true of him, he could say nothing contrary, he would lie to no one. On the contrary, if an honest man said it of him, he could well believe it and not oppose it. Further: he went to Heini Hirt afterwards, and informed him, he had to go to the tower, and told him, he lied and contradicted to my Lords how he had given the crucifix as a gift.

Upon this Hirt became outraged and said, he had given it to him to do with as he wished insofar as he had the power and right, but gave it to me free and clear, as my own to do with as I pleased. And he reminded the said Hirt so much that Hirt said, it had occurred as Hottinger said, and if it came to that, he would also tell my Lords that.

Judgment

1. Klaus Hottinger, by his sworn oath to God and the Saints, is banned for two years and all costs are bound over to him. To have the oath lifted, he must return to the authorities. 2. Lorenz Hochruetiner, the weaver, had to swear "an oath out of my Lords' city and country" and to assume the costs. 3. Hans Ockenfuss is allowed to leave prison on parole, but should keep cognizance of my Lords and assume the costs. The latter two men were penalized for being participants in Hottinger's transgression.

REVIEW QUESTIONS

1. Why does this trial indicate iconoclasts appear before the city council, a civil authority?
2. What does that tell you about the nature of the crime of iconoclasm?
3. What does Hottinger tell us about the crucifix?
4. Why does he tear it down?
5. What does he turn it into?
6. What do we learn about the meaning of images and the process of reformation for ordinary Christians?

St. Teresa of Avila

FROM *The Life of Teresa of Jesus*

St. Teresa of Avila (1515–1582) was a Spanish mystic, spiritual author, and monastic reformer. Her worldly achievements were great, to which the Discalced Carmelites still bear witness; in addition, the beauty of her inner life, as revealed in her writings, earned her recognition as one of the world's great female religious authors. Teresa was born in central Spain, the daughter of a wealthy hidalgo. At age fourteen, she was sent to a boarding school, where she became ill and began to consider her life's vocation. Despite paternal opposition, Teresa became a novice in a Carmelite convent around 1535. Her health collapsed again, leaving her an invalid for three years. During her convalescence she began the series of meditations that would establish her reputation as a mystic. It took fifteen years to perfect the prayers and meditations that would lead to her ecstatic visions and conversations with God. Her most celebrated work, The Life, *written in obedience to her confessors and directors, captured this process as the history of a soul, much like Augustine's* Confessions. *They combine religious ardor with human candor, an insistence that her experiences were a gift of God with an unwillingness to claim any spiritual distinction.*

In 1558, Teresa began to consider the restoration of Carmelite life to its original observance of austerity. It required complete separation from the world to promote prayerful meditation, such as was enjoined in the Primitive Carmelite Rule of 1247. In 1562, with the authorization of Pope Pius IV, Teresa and four companions opened the first convent of the Carmelite reform. Despite intense opposition from secular and ecclesiastical officials, her efforts eventually won the approval of the Carmelite general as well as his mandate to extend her reform to men. In 1567, she met a young Carmelite priest, Juan de Yepes, later canonized as St. John of the Cross, a brilliant friar who helped her initiate the Carmelite reform for men. In her lifetime, she saw sixteen convents and twelve monasteries established. The last decades of her life were given to this work. Forty years after her death, she was canonized; in 1970 she was made a doctor of the Church.

From *The Life of Theresa of Jesus: The Autobiography of Teresa of Avila,* translated by E. Allison Peters (New York: Bantam Doubleday Dell, 1991), pp. 68–71.

*   *   *

I have strayed far from any intention, for I was trying to give the reasons why this kind of vision cannot be the work of the imagination. How could we picture Christ's Humanity by merely studying the subject or form any impression of His great beauty by means of the imagination? No little time would be necessary if such a reproduction was to be in the least like the original. One can indeed make such a picture with one's imagination, and spend time in regarding it, and considering the form and the brilliance of it; little by little one may even learn to perfect such an image and store it up in the memory. Who can prevent this? Such a picture can undoubtedly be fashioned with the understanding. But with regard to the vision which we are discussing there is no way of doing this: we have to look at it when the Lord is pleased to reveal it to us—to look as He wills and at whatever He wills. And there is no possibility of our subtracting from it or adding to it, or any way in which we can obtain it, whatever we may do, or look at it when we like or refrain from looking at it. If we try to look at any particular part of it, we at once lose Christ.

For two years and a half things went on like this and it was quite usual for God to grant me this favour. It must now be more than three years since He took it from me as a continually recurring favour, by giving me something else of a higher kind, which I shall describe later. Though I saw that He was speaking to me, and though I was looking upon that great beauty of His, and experiencing the sweetness with which He uttered those words—sometimes stern words—with that most lovely and Divine mouth, and though, too, I was extremely desirous of observing the colour of His eyes, or His height, so that I should be able to describe it, I have never been sufficiently worthy to see this, nor has it been of any use for me to attempt to do so; if I tried, I lost the vision altogether. Though I sometimes see Him looking at me compassionately, His gaze has such power that my soul cannot endure it and remains in so sublime a rapture that it loses this beauteous vision in order to have the greater fruition of it all. So there is no question here of our wanting or not wanting to see the vision. It is clear that the Lord wants of us only humility and shame, our acceptance of what is given us and our praise of its Giver.

This refers to all visions, none excepted. There is nothing that we can do about them; we cannot see more or less of them at will; and we can neither call them up nor banish them by our own efforts. The Lord's will is that we shall see quite clearly that they are produced, not by us but by His Majesty. Still less can we be proud of them: on the contrary, they make us humble and fearful, when we find that, just as the Lord takes from us the power of seeing what we desire, so He can also take from us these favours and His grace, with the result that we are completely lost. So while we live in this exile let us always walk with fear.

Almost invariably the Lord showed Himself to me in His resurrection body, and it was thus, too, that I saw Him in the Host. Only occasionally, to strengthen me when I was in tribulation, did He show me His wounds, and then He would appear sometimes as He was on the Cross and sometimes as in the Garden. On a few occasions I saw Him wearing the crown of thorns and sometimes He would also be carrying the Cross—because of my necessities, as I say, and those of others—but always in His glorified flesh. Many are the affronts and trials that I have suffered through telling this and many are the fears and persecutions that it has brought me. So sure were those whom I told of it that I had a devil that some of them wanted to exorcize me. This troubled me very little, but I was sorry when I found that my confessors were afraid to hear my confessions or when I heard that people were saying things to them against me. None the less, I could never regret having seen these heavenly visions and I would not exchange them for all the good things and delights of this world. I always considered them a great favour from the Lord, and I think they were the greatest of treasures; often the Lord Himself would reassure me about them. I found my love for Him growing exceedingly: I used to go to Him and tell Him about all these trials and I always came away from prayer comforted and with new strength. I did not dare to argue with my critics, because I saw that that made things worse, as they thought me lacking in humility. With my confessor, however, I did discuss these matters; and whenever he saw that I was troubled he would comfort me greatly.

As the visions became more numerous, one of those who had previously been in the habit of helping me and who used sometimes to hear my confessions when the minister was unable to do so, began to say that it was clear I was being deceived by the devil. So, as I was quite unable to resist it, they commanded me to make the sign of the Cross whenever I had a vision, and to snap my fingers at it so as to convince myself that it came from the devil, whereupon it would not come again: I was not to be afraid, they said, and God would protect me and take the vision away. This caused me great distress: as I could not help believing that my visions came from God, it was a terrible thing to have to do; and, as I have said, I could not possibly wish them to be taken from me. However, I did as they commanded me. I besought God often to set me free from deception; indeed, I was continually doing so and with many tears. I would also invoke Saint Peter and Saint Paul, for the Lord had told me (it was on their festival that He had first appeared to me) that they would prevent me from being deluded; and I used often to see them very clearly on my left hand, though not in an imaginary vision. These glorious Saints were in a very real sense my lords.

To be obliged to snap my fingers at a vision in which I saw the Lord caused me the sorest distress. For, when I saw Him before me, I could not have believed that the vision had come from the devil even if the alternative were my being cut to pieces. So this was a kind of penance to me, and a heavy one. In order not to have to be so continually crossing myself, I would carry a cross in my hand. This I did almost invariably; but I was not so particular about snapping my fingers at the vision, for it hurt me too much to do that. It reminded me of the way the Jews had insulted Him, and I would beseech Him to forgive me, since I did it out of obedience to him who was in His own place, and not to blame me, since he was one of the ministers whom He had placed in His Church. He told me not to worry about it and said I was quite right to obey, but He would see that my confessor learned the truth. When they made me stop my prayer He seemed to me to have become angry, and He told me to tell them that this was tyranny. He used to show me ways of knowing that the visions were not of the devil; some of these I shall describe later.

*   *   *

REVIEW QUESTIONS

1. What distinguishes Teresa's spirituality from that of Ignatius Loyola?
2. Might we call her spirituality feminine?
3. Is Teresa's piety private or public? In what ways?
4. Are visions portable?
5. Are they entirely private?
6. How does language fail Teresa?

SEBASTIAN LOTZER

The Twelve Articles of the Peasants of Swabia

The Twelve Articles of the Peasants of Swabia, adopted at the free imperial city of Memmingen in 1525, is one of the signal documents of the great agrarian revolt known as the Peasants' War of 1525. More than any other such document, it specifically linked the social and political grievances of the peasants with the evangelical principles of the Reformation. Ironically, the Twelve Articles of the Peasants of Swabia was not composed by a peasant but by a townsman, the journeyman furrier and lay preacher Sebastian Lotzer. To do so, he summarized and condensed the long

THE ECSTASY OF ST. TERESA (1652)   GIAN LORENZO BERNINI

Bernini's masterful rendering of the spiritual transport of St. Teresa is considered one of the great works of the Catholic Reformation. It captures all the inarticulate emotional and mystical elements of worship that were thought to be a counterpoint to the Protestant emphasis on the spoken word. How might art of this sort be considered an effective response to the propagandistic content of broadsides such as The Godly Mill? *What does the rendering of the angel reveal about the artist's conception of God's love? What does the rendering of St. Teresa reveal about the artist's conception of religious truth?*

599

(several hundred articles) list of demands put forward by the peasants of Baltringen. The Memmingen preacher Christoph Schappeler added a preamble and supplied biblical references in the margins. The document acquired its importance because it was quickly printed and widely disseminated. In many areas of the revolt, it was adopted as the basis for lists of grievances and proposals for settlement.

From *The Revolution of 1525: The German Peasants from a New Perspective,* translated by Thomas A. Brady Jr. (Baltimore: Johns Hopkins University Press, 1981), pp. 195–201.

The Just and Fundamental Articles of All the Peasantry and Tenants of Spiritual and Temporal Powers by Whom They Think Themselves Oppressed

To the Christian reader, the peace and grace of God through Jesus Christ.

There are many antichrists who, now that the peasants are assembled together, seize the chance to mock the gospel, saying, "Is this the fruit of the new gospel: to band together in great numbers and plot conspiracies to reform and even topple the spiritual and temporal powers—yes, even to murder them?" The following articles answer all these godless, blasphemous critics. We want two things: first, to make them stop mocking the word of God; and second, to establish the Christian justice of the current disobedience and rebellion of all the peasants.

First of all, the gospel does not cause rebellions and uproars, because it tells of Christ, the promised Messiah, whose words and life teach nothing but love, peace, patience, and unity. And all who believe in this Christ become loving, peaceful, patient, and one in spirit. This is the basis of all the articles of the peasants (as we will clearly show): to hear the gospel and to live accordingly. How then can the antichrists call the gospel a cause of rebellion and of disobedience? It is not the gospel that drives some antichrists and foes of the gospel to resist and reject these demands and requirements, but the devil, the deadliest foe of the gos-

pel, who arouses through unbelief such opposition in his own followers. His aim is to suppress and abolish the word of God, which teaches love, peace, and unity.

Second, it surely follows that the peasants, whose articles demand this gospel as their doctrine and rule of life, cannot be called "disobedient" or "rebellious." For if God deigns to hear the peasants' earnest plea that they may be permitted to live according to his word, who will dare deny his will? Who indeed will dare question his judgment? Who will dare oppose his majesty? Did he not hear the children of Israel crying to him and deliver them out of Pharaoh's hand? And can he not save his own today as well? Yes, he will save them, and soon! Therefore, Christian reader, read these articles diligently, and then judge for yourself.

These are the Articles.

THE FIRST ARTICLE

First of all, we humbly ask and beg—and we all agree on this—that henceforth we ought to have the authority and power for the whole community to elect and appoint its own pastor. We also want authority to depose a pastor who behaves improperly. This elected pastor should preach to us the holy gospel purely and clearly, without human additions or human doctrines or precepts. For constant preaching of the true faith impels us to beg God for his grace, that he may instill in us and confirm in us that same true faith. Unless we have his grace in us, we remain mere, useless flesh and blood. For the Scripture clearly teaches that we may come to God only through true faith and can be saved only through His mercy. This is why we need such a guide and pastor; and thus our demand is grounded in Scripture.

THE SECOND ARTICLE

Second, although the obligation to pay a just tithe prescribed in the Old Testament is fulfilled in the New, yet we will gladly pay the large tithe on grain—but only in just measure. Since the tithe should be given to God and distributed among his servants, so the pastor who clearly preaches the word of God deserves to receive it. From now on we want to have our church wardens, appointed by the community, collect and receive this tithe and have our elected pastor draw from it, with the whole community's consent, a decent and adequate living for himself and his. The remainder should be distributed to the village's own poor, again with the community's consent and according to need. What then remains should be kept in case some need to be called up to defend the country; and then the costs can be met from this reserve, so that no general territorial tax will be laid upon the poor folk.

Wherever one or more villages have sold off the tithe to meet some emergency, those purchasers who can show that they bought the tithe with the consent of the whole village shall not be simply expropriated. Indeed we hope to reach fair compromises with such persons, according to the facts of the case, and to redeem the tithe in installments. But wherever the tithe holder—be he clergyman or layman—did not buy the tithe from the whole village but has it from ancestors who simply seized it from the village, we will not, ought not, and do not intend to pay it any longer, except (as we said above) to support our elected pastor. And we will reserve the rest or distribute it to the poor, as the Bible commands. As for the small tithe, we will not pay it at all, for the Lord God created cattle for man's free use; and it is an unjust tithe

invented by men alone. Therefore, we won't pay it anymore.

THE THIRD ARTICLE

Third, it has until now been the custom for the lords to own us as their property. This is deplorable, for Christ redeemed and bought us all with his precious blood, the lowliest shepherd as well as the greatest lord, with no exceptions. Thus the Bible proves that we are free and want to be free. Not that we want to be utterly free and subject to no authority at all; God does not teach us that. We ought to live according to the commandments, not according to the lusts of the flesh. But we should love God, recognize him as our Lord in our neighbor, and willingly do all things God commanded us at his Last Supper. This means we should live according to his commandment, which does not teach us to obey only the rulers, but to humble ourselves before everyone. Thus we should willingly obey our elected and rightful ruler, set over us by God, in all proper and Christian matters. Nor do we doubt that you, as true and just Christians, will gladly release us from bondage or prove to us from the gospel that we must be your property.

THE FOURTH ARTICLE

Fourth, until now it has been the custom that no commoner might catch wild game, wildfowl, or fish in the running waters, which seems to us altogether improper, unbrotherly, selfish, and contrary to God's Word. In some places the rulers protect the game to our distress and great loss, for we must suffer silently while the dumb beasts gobble up the crops God gave for man's use, although this offends both God and neighbor. When the Lord God created man, he gave him dominion over all animals, over the birds of the air, and the fish in the waters. Thus we demand that if someone owns a stream, lake, or pond, he should have to produce documentary proof of ownership and show that it was sold to him with the consent of the whole village. In that case we do not want to seize it from him with force but only to review the matter in a Christian way for the sake of brotherly love. But whoever cannot produce adequate proof of ownership and sale should surrender the waters to the community, as is just.

THE FIFTH ARTICLE

Fifth, we have another grievance about woodcutting, for our lords have seized the woods for themselves alone; and when the poor commoner needs some wood, he has to pay twice the price for it. We think that those woods whose lords, be they clergymen or laymen, cannot prove ownership by purchase should revert to the whole community. And the community should be able to allow in an orderly way each man to gather firewood for his home and building timber free, though only with permission of the community's elected officials. If all the woods have been fairly purchased, then a neighborly and Christian agreement should be reached with their owners about their use. Where the woods were simply seized and then sold to a third party, however, a compromise should be reached according to the facts of the case and the norms of brotherly love and Holy Writ.

THE SIXTH ARTICLE

Sixth, there is our grievous burden of labor services, which the lords daily increase in number and kind. We demand that these obligations be properly investigated and lessened. And we should be allowed, graciously, to serve as our forefathers did, according to God's word alone.

THE SEVENTH ARTICLE

Seventh, in the future we will not allow the lords to oppress us any more. Rather, a man shall have his holding on the proper terms on which it has been leased, that is, by the agreement between lord and peasant. The lord should not force or press the tenant to perform labor or any other service without pay, so that the peasant may use and en-

joy his land unburdened and in peace. When the lord needs labor services, however, the peasant should willingly serve his own lord before others; yet a peasant should serve only at a time when his own affairs do not suffer and only for a just wage.

THE EIGHTH ARTICLE

Eighth, we have a grievance that many of us hold lands that are overburdened with rents higher than the land's yield. Thus the peasants lose their property and are ruined. The lords should have honorable men inspect these farms and adjust the rents fairly, so that the peasant does not work for nothing. For every laborer is worthy of his hire.

THE NINTH ARTICLE

Ninth, we have a grievance against the way serious crimes are punished, for they are constantly making new laws. We are not punished according to the severity of the case but sometimes out of great ill will and sometimes out of favoritism. We think that punishments should be dealt out among us according to the ancient written law and the circumstances of the case, and not according to the judge's bias.

THE TENTH ARTICLE

Tenth, we have a grievance that some people have seized meadows and fields belonging to the community. We shall restore these to the community, unless a proper sale can be proved. If they were improperly bought, however, then a friendly and brotherly compromise should be reached, based on the facts.

THE ELEVENTH ARTICLE

Eleventh, we want the custom called death taxes totally abolished. We will not tolerate it or allow widows and orphans to be so shamefully robbed of their goods, as so often happens in various ways, against God and all that is honorable. The very ones who should be guarding and protecting our goods have skinned and trimmed us of them instead. Had they the slightest legal pretext, they would have grabbed everything. God will suffer this no longer but will wipe it all out. Henceforth no one shall have to pay death taxes, whether small or large.

CONCLUSION

Twelfth, we believe and have decided that if any one or more of these articles is not in agreement with God's Word (which we doubt), then this should be proved to us from Holy Writ. We will abandon it, when this is proved by the Bible. If some of our articles should be approved and later found to be unjust, they shall be dead, null, and void from that moment on. Likewise, if Scripture truly reveals further grievances as offensive to God and a burden to our neighbor, we will reserve a place for them and declare them included in our list. We, for our part, will live and exercise our-

selves in all Christian teachings, for which we will pray to the Lord God. For he alone, and no other, can give us the truth. The peace of Christ be with us all.

REVIEW QUESTIONS

1. What does the Twelve Articles tell you about relations between the common man and his lords?
2. What are the priorities of the Twelve Articles?
3. What is most important to the petitioners?
4. Why is a pastor so important?
5. What is second in importance?
6. What changes are the petitioners asking for the tithe?
7. What is Godly Law?
8. What might be its applications?
9. What are the implications of Godly Law for the lords?

FROM *Canons and Decrees of the Council of Trent*

The great centerpiece of Catholic reform and reaction was the ecumenical Council of Trent, held in several sessions between 1545 and 1563. From the beginning of the sixteenth century, Catholic clergy, secular leaders, and Protestant reformers had called for an ecumenical council to heal the inadequacies of the Catholic Church. Popes had resisted the tactic just as insistently for fear that such a council might be used to limit papal authority, as, indeed, had been the case in the fifteenth century. Pope Paul III, however, realized that a council might serve the cause of papal authority as well as that of church reform and accordingly called a council to meet in the city of Trent, located in imperial territory but still close to Rome. Agreements on procedures and the leadership of papal legates assured that the council remained firmly under papal direction and set a tone of doctrinal and disciplinary conservatism. Its deliberations and decisions divide themselves into three great periods. The first period, 1545–1547, was devoted to dogma. The council rejected the Protestant teaching on scripture as the sole source of religious truth and insisted that scripture and tradition were equally authoritative. It retained the traditional seven sacra-

ments. Most important, it rejected the Protestant doctrine of justification. During the second period, 1551–1552, the council reasserted the traditional Catholic teaching on the Eucharist, rejecting the interpretations of Luther, Zwingli, and Calvin. Long delayed by political events and papal indifference, the council reconvened for the third and last time in 1562. In its final year, the council defined the Mass, addressed various liturgical issues, and resolved disciplinary issues such as clerical residency and training. Viewed in its entirety, the Council of Trent strengthened the authority of the papacy in the Catholic Church. If its decrees and canons were largely conservative, they were also unmistakable in their clarity and uniformity. In its pronouncements on discipline, it laid the foundations for a better-educated, more conscientious clergy. The Council of Trent clearly defined Catholic Christianity in opposition to Protestantism.

From *Canons and Decrees of the Council of Trent,* translated by H. J. Schroeder (London: Herder, 1941).

*   *   *

Fourth Session
Celebrated on the Eighth Day
of April 1546

DECREE CONCERNING THE CANONICAL SCRIPTURES

The holy, ecumenical and general Council of Trent, lawfully assembled in the Holy Ghost, the same three legates of the Apostolic See presiding, keeps this constantly in view, namely, that the purity of the Gospel may be preserved in the Church after the errors have been removed. This, of old promised through the Prophets in the Holy Scriptures, our Lord Jesus Christ, the Son of God, promulgated first with His own mouth, and then commanded it to be preached by His Apostles to every creature as the source at once of all saving truth and rules of conduct. It also clearly perceives that these truths and rules are contained in the written books and in the unwritten traditions, which, received by the Apostles from the mouth of Christ Himself, or from the Apostles themselves, the Holy Ghost dictating, have come down to us, transmitted as it were from hand to hand. Following, then, the examples of the orthodox Fathers, it receives and venerates with a feeling of

piety and reverence all the books both of the Old and New Testaments, since one God is the author of both; also the traditions, whether they relate to faith or to morals, as having been dictated either orally by Christ or by the Holy Ghost, and preserved in the Catholic Church in unbroken succession. It has thought it proper, moreover, to insert in this decree a list of the sacred books, lest a doubt might arise in the mind of someone as to which are the books received by this council. They are the following: of the Old Testament, the five books of Moses, namely, Genesis, Exodus, Leviticus, Numbers, Deuteronomy; Josue, Judges, Ruth, the four books of Kings, two of Paralipomenon, the first and second of Esdras, the latter of which is called Nehemias, Tobias, Judith, Esther, Job, the Davidic Psalter of 150 Psalms, Proverbs, Ecclesiastes, the Canticle of Canticles, Wisdom, Ecclesiasticus, Isaias, Jeremias, with Baruch, Ezechiel, Daniel, the twelve minor Prophets, namely, Osee, Joel, Amos, Abdias, Jonas, Micheas, Nahum, Habacuc, Sophonias, Aggeus, Zacharias, Malachias; two books of Machabees, the first and second. Of the New Testament, the four Gospels, according to Matthew, Mark, Luke and John; the Acts of the Apostles written by Luke the Evangelist; fourteen Epistles of Paul the Apostle, to the Romans, two to the Corinthians, to the Galatians, to the Ephesians, to the Philippians, to the Colossians, two to the Thessalonians, two to Timothy, to Titus, to Philemon, to the Hebrews; two of Peter the Apostle, three of John the Apostle, one of James the Apostle, one of Jude the Apostle, and the Apocalypse of John the Apostle. If anyone does not accept as sacred and canonical the aforesaid books in their entirety and with all their parts, as they have been accustomed to be read in the Catholic Church and as they are contained in the old Latin Vulgate Edition, and knowingly and deliberately rejects the aforesaid traditions, let him be anathema. Let all understand, therefore, in what order and manner the council, after having laid the foundation of the confession of faith, will proceed, and who are the chief witnesses and supports to whom it will appeal in confirming dogmas and in restoring morals in the Church.

DECREE CONCERNING THE EDITION AND USE OF THE SACRED BOOKS

Moreover, the same holy council considering that not a little advantage will accrue to the Church of God if it be made known which of all the Latin editions of the sacred books now in circulation is to be regarded as authentic, ordains and declares that the old Latin Vulgate Edition, which, in use for so many hundred years, has been approved by the Church, be in public lectures, disputations, sermons and expositions held as authentic, and that no one dare or presume under any pretext whatsoever to reject it.

Furthermore, to check unbridled spirits, it decrees that no one relying on his own judgment shall, in matters of faith and morals pertaining to the edification of Christian doctrine, distorting the Holy Scriptures in accordance with his own conceptions, presume to interpret them contrary to that sense which holy mother Church, to whom it belongs to judge of their true sense and interpretation, has held and holds, or even contrary to the unanimous teaching of the Fathers, even though such interpretations should never at any time be published. Those who act contrary to this shall be made known by the ordinaries and punished in

accordance with the penalties prescribed by the law.

And wishing, as is proper, to impose a restraint in this matter on printers also, who, now without restraint, thinking what pleases them is permitted them, print without the permission of ecclesiastical superiors the books of the Holy Scriptures and the notes and commentaries thereon of all persons indiscriminately, often with the name of the press omitted, often also under a fictitious press-name, and what is worse, without the name of the author, and also indiscreetly have for sale such books printed elsewhere, this council decrees and ordains that in the future the Holy Scriptures, especially the old Vulgate Edition, be printed in the most correct manner possible, and that it shall not be lawful for anyone to print or to have printed any books whatsoever dealing with sacred doctrinal matters without the name of the author, or in the future to sell them, or even to have them in possession, unless they have first been examined and approved by the ordinary, under penalty of anathema and fine prescribed by the last Council of the Lateran. If they be regulars they must in addition to this examination and approval obtain permission also from their own superiors after these have examined the books in accordance with their own statutes. Those who lend or circulate them in manuscript before they have been examined and approved, shall be subject to the same penalties as the printers, and those who have them in their possession or read them, shall, unless they make known the authors, be themselves regarded as the authors. The approbation of such books, however, shall be given in writing and shall appear authentically at the beginning of the book, whether it be written or printed, and all this, that is, both the examination and approbation, shall be done gratuitously, so that what ought to be approved may be approved and what ought to be condemned may be condemned.

Furthermore, wishing to repress that boldness whereby the words and sentences of the Holy Scriptures are turned and twisted to all kinds of profane usages, namely, to things scurrilous, fabulous, vain, to flatteries, detractions, superstitions, godless and diabolical incantations, divinations, the casting of lots and defamatory libels, to put an end to such irreverence and contempt, and that no one may in the future dare use in any manner the words of Holy Scripture for these and similar purposes, it is commanded and enjoined that all people of this kind be restrained by the bishops as violators and profaners of the word of God, with the penalties of the law and other penalties that they may deem fit to impose.

*   *   *

Twenty-third Session
Which Is the Seventh under the Supreme Pontiff, Pius IV, Celebrated on the Fifteenth Day of July 1563
The True and Catholic Doctrine Concerning the Sacrament of Order, Defined and Published by the Holy Council of Trent in the Seventh Session in Condemnation of Current Errors

FROM CHAPTER I
THE INSTITUTION OF THE PRIESTHOOD OF THE NEW LAW

Sacrifice and priesthood are by the ordinance of God so united that both have existed in every law. Since therefore in the New Testament the Catholic Church has received from the institution of Christ the holy, visible sacrifice of the Eucharist, it must also be confessed that there is in that Church a new, visible and external priesthood, into which the old has been translated. That this was instituted by the same Lord our Savior, and that to the Apostles and their successors in the priesthood was given the power of consecrating, offering and administering His body and blood, as also of forgiving and retaining sins, is shown by the Sacred Scriptures and has always been taught by the tradition of the Catholic Church.

CHAPTER II
THE SEVEN ORDERS

But since the ministry of so holy a priesthood is something divine, that it might be exercised in a more worthy manner and with greater veneration, it was consistent that in the most well-ordered arrangement of the Church there should be several distinct orders of ministers, who by virtue of their office should minister to the priesthood, so distributed that those already having the clerical tonsure should ascend through the minor to the major orders. For the Sacred Scriptures mention unmistakably not only the priests but also the deacons, and teach in the most definite words what is especially to be observed in their ordination; and from the very beginning of the Church the names of the following orders and the duties proper to each one are known to have been in use, namely, those of the subdeacon, acolyte, exorcist, lector and porter, though these were not of equal rank; for the subdiaconate is classed among the major orders by the Fathers and holy councils, in which we also read very often of other inferior orders.

CHAPTER III
THE ORDER OF THE PRIESTHOOD IS TRULY A SACRAMENT

Since from the testimony of Scripture, Apostolic tradition and the unanimous agreement of the Fathers it is clear that grace is conferred by sacred ordination, which is performed by words and outward signs, no one ought to doubt that order is truly and properly one of the seven sacraments of holy Church. For the Apostle says: *I admonish thee that thou stir up the grace of God which is in thee by the imposition of my hands. For God has not given us the spirit of fear, but of power and of love and of sobriety.*

CHAPTER IV
THE ECCLESIASTICAL HIERARCHY
AND ORDINATION

But since in the sacrament of order, as also in baptism and confirmation, a character is imprinted which can neither be effaced nor taken away, the holy council justly condemns the opinion of those who say that the priests of the New Testament have only a temporary power, and that those who have once been rightly ordained can again become laymen if they do not exercise the ministry of the word of God. And if anyone should assert that all Christians without distinction are priests of the New Testament, or that they are all *inter se* endowed with an equal spiritual power, he seems to do nothing else than derange the ecclesiastical hierarchy, which is *an army set in array*; as if, contrary to the teaching of St. Paul, all are apostles, all prophets, all evangelists, all pastors, all doctors. Wherefore, the holy council declares that, besides the other ecclesiastical grades, the bishops, who have succeeded the Apostles, principally belong to this hierarchical order, and have been placed, as the same Apostle says, by the Holy Ghost to rule the Church of God; that they are superior to priests, administer the sacrament of confirmation, ordain ministers of the Church, and can perform many other functions over which those of an inferior order have no power. The council teaches furthermore, that in the ordination of bishops, priests and the other orders, the consent, call or authority, whether of the people or of any civil power or magistrate is not required in such wise that without this the ordination is invalid; rather does it decree that all those who, called and instituted only by the people or by the civil power or magistrate, ascend to the exercise of these offices, and those who by their rashness assume them, are not ministers of the Church, but are to be regarded as thieves and robbers, who have not entered by the door. These are the things which in general it has seemed good to the holy council to teach to the faithful of Christ regarding the sacrament of order. The contrary, however, it has resolved to condemn in definite and appro-

priate canons in the following manner, in order that all, making use with the help of Christ of the rule of faith, may in the midst of the darkness of so many errors recognize more easily the Catholic truth and adhere to it.

CANONS ON THE SACRAMENT OF ORDER

Canon 1. If anyone says that there is not in the New Testament a visible and external priesthood, or that there is no power of consecrating and offering the true body and blood of the Lord and of forgiving and retaining sins, but only the office and bare ministry of preaching the Gospel; or that those who do not preach are not priests at all, let him be anathema.

Canon 2. If anyone says that besides the priesthood there are not in the Catholic Church other orders, both major and minor, by which, as by certain steps, advance is made to the priesthood, let him be anathema.

Canon 3. If anyone says that order or sacred ordination is not truly and properly a sacrament instituted by Christ the Lord, or that it is some human contrivance devised by men unskilled in ecclesiastical matters, or that it is only a certain rite for choosing ministers of the word of God and of the sacraments, let him be anathema.

Canon 4. If anyone says that by sacred ordination the Holy Ghost is not imparted and that therefore the bishops say in vain: *Receive ye the Holy Ghost*, or that by it a character is not imprinted, or that he who has once been a priest can again become a layman, let him be anathema.

Canon 5. If anyone says that the holy unction which the Church uses in ordination is not only not required but is detestable and pernicious, as also are the other ceremonies of order, let him be anathema.

Canon 6. If anyone says that in the Catholic Church there is not instituted a hierarchy by divine ordinance, which consists of bishops, priests and ministers, let him be anathema.

Canon 7. If anyone says that bishops are not superior to priests, or that they have not the power to confirm and ordain, or that the power which they have is common to them and to priests, or that orders conferred by them without the consent or call of the people or of the secular power are invalid, or that those who have been neither rightly ordained nor sent by ecclesiastical and canonical authority, but come from elsewhere, are lawful ministers of the word and of the sacraments, let him be anathema.

Canon 8. If anyone says that the bishops who are chosen by the authority of the Roman pontiff are not true and legitimate bishops, but merely human deception, let him be anathema.

* * *

Twenty-fifth Session Which Is the Ninth and Last under the Supreme Pontiff, Pius IV, Begun on the Third and Closed on the Fourth Day of December 1563

DECREE CONCERNING PURGATORY

Since the Catholic Church, instructed by the Holy Ghost, has, following the sacred writings and the ancient tradition of the Fathers, taught in sacred councils and very recently in this ecumenical council that there is a purgatory, and that the souls there detained are aided by the suffrages of the faithful and chiefly by the acceptable sacrifice of the altar, the holy council commands the bishops that they strive diligently to the end that the sound doctrine of purgatory, transmitted by the Fathers and sacred councils, be believed and maintained by the faithful of Christ, and be everywhere taught and preached. The more difficult and subtle questions, however, and those that do not make for edification and from which there is for the most part no increase in piety, are to be excluded from popular instructions to uneducated people. Likewise, things that are uncertain or that have the appearance of falsehood they shall not permit to be made known publicly and discussed. But those things that tend to a certain kind of curiosity or superstition, or that savor of filthy lucre, they shall prohibit as scandals and stumbling

blocks to the faithful. The bishops shall see to it that the suffrages of the living, that is, the sacrifice of the mass, prayers, alms and other works of piety which they have been accustomed to perform for the faithful departed, be piously and devoutly discharged in accordance with the laws of the Church, and that whatever is due on their behalf from testamentary bequests or other ways, be discharged by the priests and ministers of the Church and others who are bound to render this service not in a perfunctory manner, but diligently and accurately.

ON THE INVOCATION, VENERATION, AND RELICS OF SAINTS, AND ON SACRED IMAGES

The holy council commands all bishops and others who hold the office of teaching and have charge of the *cura animarum*, that in accordance with the usage of the Catholic and Apostolic Church, received from the primitive times of the Christian religion, and with the unanimous teaching of the holy Fathers and the decrees of sacred councils, they above all instruct the faithful diligently in matters relating to intercession and invocation of the saints, the veneration of relics, and the legitimate use of images, teaching them that the saints who reign together with Christ offer up their prayers to God for men, that it is good and beneficial suppliantly to invoke them and to have recourse to their prayers, assistance and support in order to obtain favors from God through His Son, Jesus Christ our Lord, who alone is our redeemer and savior; and that they think impiously who deny that the saints who enjoy eternal happiness in heaven are to be invoked, or who assert that they do not pray for men, or that our invocation of them to pray for each of us individually is idolatry, or that it is opposed to the word of God and inconsistent with the honor of the *one mediator of God and men, Jesus Christ,* or that it is foolish to pray vocally or mentally to those who reign in heaven. Also, that the holy bodies of the holy martyrs and of others living with Christ, which were the living members of Christ and the temple of the Holy Ghost, to be awakened by Him to eternal life and to be glorified, are to be venerated by the faithful, through which many benefits are bestowed by God on men, so that those who maintain that veneration and honor are not due to the relics of the saints, or that these and other memorials are honored by the faithful without profit, and that the places dedicated to the memory of the saints for the purpose of obtaining their aid are visited in vain, are to be utterly condemned, as the Church has already long since condemned and now again condemns them. Moreover, that the images of Christ, of the Virgin Mother of God, and of the other saints are to be placed and retained especially in the churches, and that due honor and veneration is to be given them; not, however, that any divinity or virtue is believed to be in them by reason of which they are to be venerated, or that something is to be asked of them, or that trust is to be placed in images, as was done of old by the Gentiles who placed their hope in idols; but because the honor which is shown them is referred to the prototypes which they represent, so that by means of the images which we kiss and before which we uncover the head and prostrate ourselves, we adore Christ and venerate the saints whose likeness they bear. That is what was defined by the decrees of the councils, especially of the Second Council of Nicaea, against the opponents of images.

Moreover, let the bishops diligently teach that by means of the stories of the mysteries of our redemption portrayed in paintings and other representations the people are instructed and confirmed in the articles of faith, which ought to be borne in mind and constantly reflected upon; also that great profit is derived from all holy images, not only because the people are thereby reminded of the benefits and gifts bestowed on them by Christ, but also because through the saints the miracles of God and salutary examples are set before the eyes of the faithful, so that they may give God thanks for those things, may fashion their own life and conduct in imitation of the saints and be moved to adore and love God and cultivate piety. But if anyone should teach or maintain anything contrary to these decrees, let him be anathema. If any abuses shall have found their way into these holy and salutary observances, the holy council desires earnestly that they be completely removed, so that no representation of false doctrines and such as might be the occasion of grave error to the uneducated be exhibited. And if at times it happens, when this is beneficial to the illiterate, that the stories and narratives of the Holy Scriptures are portrayed and exhibited, the people should be instructed that not for that reason is the divinity represented in picture as if it can be seen with bodily eyes or expressed in colors or figures. Furthermore, in the invocation of the saints, the veneration of relics, and the sacred use of images, all superstition shall be removed, all filthy quest for gain eliminated, and all lasciviousness avoided, so that images shall not be painted and adorned with a seductive charm, or the celebration of saints and the visitation of relics be perverted by the people into boisterous festivities and drunkenness, as if the festivals in honor of the saints are to be celebrated with revelry and with no sense of decency. Finally, such zeal and care should be exhibited by the bishops with regard to these things that nothing may appear that is disorderly or unbecoming and confusedly arranged, nothing that is profane, nothing disrespectful, since holiness becometh the house of God. That these things may be the more faithfully observed, the holy council decrees that no one is permitted to erect or cause to be erected in any place or church, howsoever exempt, any unusual image unless it has been approved by the bishop; also that no new miracles be accepted and no relics recognized unless they have been investigated and approved by the same bishop, who, as soon as he has obtained any knowledge of such matters, shall, after consulting theologians and other pious men, act thereon as he shall judge consonant with truth and piety. But if any doubtful or grave abuse is to be eradicated, or if indeed any graver question concerning these matters should arise, the bishop, before he settles the controversy, shall await the decision of the metropolitan and of the bishops of the province in a provincial synod; so, however, that nothing new or anything that has not hitherto been in use in the Church, shall be decided upon without having first consulted the most holy Roman pontiff.

*   *   *

REVIEW QUESTIONS

1. How does the Council of Trent approach the question of the authority of Scripture?

2. Why did it set that discussion in terms of a list of books the council recognized as sacred?

3. On what basis might the council claim the authority to name the books of the Bible and determine the correct translation?

4. What are the seven orders? What is their place in Christianity and their function? What is the nature of their authority?

5. What do these decrees suggest about the practice of Catholicism in the years following the Reformation?

JOHN CALVIN

FROM Draft Ecclesiastical Ordinances, September and October 1541

John Calvin (1509–1564) was born of bourgeois parents in the city of Noyon in Picardy. Destined by his father for an ecclesiastical career, he received several benefices to finance his education as early as 1521. In 1523, he transferred to the University of Paris, where he imbibed the spirit of humanism from such teachers as Mathurin Cordier and Guillaume Bude. Calvin earned a master of arts degree at Paris and, without abandoning his study of classical languages and literature, turned to law at Orleans in 1528. By 1532, he had earned a doctorate of law. Sometime during his legal training or shortly thereafter, Calvin converted to Protestantism. The year 1534 was decisive for Calvin. Forced to flee Paris because of the proscription of Protestantism, he made his way to Basel, where he began work on his great systematic theology, Institutes of the Christian Religion *(1536). It was immediately recognized as a superb normative statement of reformed theology and established Calvin's stature as a leader among Protestants despite his youth. As the first edition went to press, Calvin made his way to Geneva, where Guillaume Farel enlisted his aid in the reform of the city. The early years of the Reformation in Geneva were stormy, and there was considerable opposition to the doctrines advocated by Calvin. In a dispute over church discipline, the city council banished the Protestant pastors. Calvin made his way to Strasbourg, where he remained as a colleague of Martin Bucer and minister to the French refugee church until 1541. Meanwhile, political and religious chaos in Geneva eventually forced the government to seek the return of Calvin. He reluctantly consented, but only with the assurance that his entire original scheme of church polity would be instituted. The ecclesiastical ordinance adopted in 1541 encapsulated that polity and became influential for reformed churches throughout Europe. Calvin remained in Geneva from 1541 until his death in 1564, by which time the city that had accepted reform so reluctantly had been transformed into the center of an international Reformation.*

From *Calvin: Theological Treatises,* translated by J. K. S. Reid (Louisville: Westminster John Knox Press, 1954).

There are four orders of office instituted by our Lord for the government of his Church. First, pastors; then doctors; next elders; and fourth deacons.

Hence if we will have a Church well ordered and maintained we ought to observe this form of government.

As to the pastors, whom Scripture also sometimes calls elders and ministers, their office is to proclaim the Word of God, to instruct, admonish, exhort and censure, both in public and private, to administer the sacraments and to enjoin brotherly corrections along with the elders and colleagues.

Now in order that nothing happen confusedly in the Church, no one is to enter upon this office without a calling. In this it is necessary to consider three things, namely: the principal thing is the examination; then what belongs to the institution of the ministers; third, what ceremony or method of procedure it is good to observe in introducing them to office.

The examination contains two parts, of which the first concerns doctrine—to ascertain whether the candidate for ordination has a good and holy knowledge of Scripture; and also whether he be a fit and proper person to communicate it edifyingly to the people.

Further to avoid all danger of the candidate holding some false opinion, it will be good that he profess his acceptance and maintenance of the doctrine approved by the Church.

To know whether he is fit to instruct, it would be necessary to proceed by interrogation and by hearing him discuss in private the doctrine of the Lord.

The second part concerns life, to ascertain whether he is of good habits and conducts himself always without reproach. The rule of procedure in this matter which it is needful to follow is very well indicated by Paul.

There Follows, to Whom It Belongs to Institute Pastors

It will be good in this connection to follow the order of the ancient Church, for it is the only practice which is shown us in Scripture. The order is that ministers first elect such as ought to hold office; afterwards that he be presented to the Council; and if he is found worthy the Council receive and accept him, giving him certification to produce finally to the people when he preaches, in order that he be received by the common consent of the company of the faithful. If he be found unworthy, and show this after due probation, it is necessary to proceed to a new election for the choosing of another.

As to the manner of introducing him, it is good to use the imposition of hands, which ceremony was observed by the apostles and then in the ancient Church, providing that it take place without superstition and without offence. But because there has been much superstition in the past and scandal might result, it is better to abstain from it because of the infirmity of the times.

When he is elected, he has to swear in front of the Seigneury. Of this oath there will be a prescribed form, suitable to what is required of a minister.

Now as it is necessary to examine the ministers well when they are to be elected, so also it is necessary to have good supervision to maintain them in their duty.

First it will be expedient that all the ministers, for conserving purity and concord of doctrine among themselves, meet together one certain day each week, for discussion of the Scriptures; and none are to be exempt from this without legitimate excuse. If anyone be negligent, let him be admonished.

As for those who preach in the villages, throughout the Seigneury, they are to be exhorted to come as often as they are able. For the rest, if they default an entire month, it is to be held to be very great negligence, unless it is a case of illness or other legitimate hindrance.

If there appear difference of doctrine, let the ministers come together to discuss the matter. Afterwards, if need be, let them call the elders to assist in composing the contention. Finally, if they are unable to come to friendly agreement because of the obstinacy of one of the parties, let the case be referred to the magistrate to be put in order.

To obviate all scandals of living, it will be proper that there be a form of correction to which all submit themselves. It will also be the means by which the ministry may retain respect, and the Word of God be neither dishonoured nor scorned because of the ill reputation of the ministers. For as one is to correct those who merit it, so it will be proper to reprove calumnies and false reports which are made unjustly against innocent people.

But first it should be noted that there are crimes which are quite intolerable in a minister, and there are faults which may on the other hand be endured while direct fraternal admonitions are offered.

Of the first sort are:

heresy, schism, rebellion against ecclesiastical order, blasphemy open and meriting civil punishment, simony and all corruption in presentations, intrigue to occupy another's place, leaving one's Church without lawful leave or just calling, duplicity, perjury, lewdness, larceny, drunkenness, assault meriting punishment by law, usury, games forbidden by the law and scandalous, dances and similar dissoluteness, crimes carrying with them loss of civil rights,

crime giving rise to another separation from the Church.

Of the second sort are:

strange methods of treating Scripture which turn to scandal, curiosity in investigating idle questions, advancing some doctrine or kind of practice not received in the Church, negligence in studying and reading the Scriptures, negligence in rebuking vice amounting to flattery, negligence in doing everything required by his office, scurrility, lying, slander, dissolute words, injurious words, foolhardiness and evil devices, avarice and too great parsimony, undisciplined anger, quarrels and contentions, laxity either of manner or of gesture and like conduct improper to a minister.

In the case of the crimes which cannot at all be tolerated, if some accusation and complaint arise, let the assembly of ministers and elders investigate it, in order to proceed reasonably and according to whatever is discovered in judging the case, and then report judgment to the magistrate in order that if required the delinquent be deposed.

In the case of the lesser vices which may be corrected by simple admonition, one is to proceed according to the command of our Lord, so that as a last step it come for ecclesiastical judgment.

To keep this discipline in operation, let the ministers every three months take special notice whether there be anything to discuss among themselves, to remedy it as is reasonable.

Of the Number, Place and Time of Preachings

Each Sunday, there is to be sermon at St. Peter and St. Gervais at break of day, and at the usual hour at the said St. Peter and St. Gervais.

At midday, there is to be catechism, that is, instruction of little children in all the three churches, the Magdalene, St. Peter and St. Gervais.

At three o'clock second sermon in St. Peter and St. Gervais.

For bringing children to catechism, and for receiving the sacraments, the boundaries of the parishes should as far as possible be observed; that is, St. Gervais embracing what it had in the past, the Magdalene similarly, St. Peter what belonged formerly to St. Germain, St. Cross, Our Lady the New, and St. Legier.

Besides the two preachings which take place, on working days there will be a sermon at St. Peter three times a week, on Monday, Tuesday and Friday one hour before beginning is made at the other places.

To maintain these charges and others pertaining to the ministry, it will be necessary to have five ministers and three coadjutors who will also be ministers, to aid and assist as necessity requires.

Concerning the Second Order, Which We Have Called Doctors

The office proper to doctors is the instruction of the faithful in true doctrine, in order that the purity of the Gospel be not corrupted either by ignorance or by evil opinions. As things are disposed today, we always include under this title aids and instructions for maintaining the doctrine of God and defending the Church from injury by the fault of pastors and ministers. So to use a more intelligible word, we will call this the order of the schools.

The degree nearest to the minister and most closely joined to the government of the Church is the lecturer in theology, of which it will be good to have one in Old Testament and one in New Testament.

But because it is only possible to profit from such lectures if first one is instructed in the languages and humanities, and also because it is necessary to raise offspring for time to come, in order not to leave the Church deserted to our children, a college should be instituted for instructing children to prepare them for the ministry as well as for civil government.

For the first, a proper place ought to be assigned for both doing lessons and accommodating the children and others who would profit. There must be a man learned and expert in arranging both the house and the instruction, who is able also to lecture. He is to be chosen and remunerated on condition that he have under his charge lecturers both in languages and in dialectic, if it can be done. Likewise there should be some matriculated persons to teach the little children; and these we hope shortly to appoint to assist the master.

All who are there will be subject like ministers to ecclesiastical discipline.

There need be no other school in the city for the little children, but let the girls have their school apart, as has hitherto been the case.

Let no one be received if he is not approved by the ministers on their testimony, for fear of impropriety.

Concerning the Third Order Which Is That of Elders

Their office is to have oversight of the life of everyone, to admonish amicably those whom they see to be erring or to be living a disordered life, and, where it is required, to enjoin fraternal corrections themselves and along with others.

In the present condition of the Church, it would be good to elect two of the Little Council, four of the Council of Sixty, and six of the Council of Two Hundred, men of good and honest life, without reproach and beyond suspicion, and above all fearing God and possessing spiritual prudence. These should be so elected that there be some in every quarter of the city, to keep an eye on everybody.

The best way of electing them seems to be this, that the Little Council suggest the nomination of the best that can be found and the most suitable; and to do this, summon the ministers to confer with them; after this they should present those whom they would commend to the Council of Two Hundred, which will approve them. If it find them worthy, let them take the special oath, whose form will be readily drawn up. And at the end of the year, let them present themselves to the Seigneury for consideration whether they ought to be continued or changed. It is inexpedient that they be changed often without cause, so long as they discharge their duty faithfully.

The Fourth Order of Ecclesiastical Government, That Is, the Deacons

There were always two kinds in the ancient Church, the one deputed to receive, dispense and hold goods for the poor, not only daily alms, but also possessions, rents and pensions; the other to tend and care for the sick and administer allowances to the poor. This custom we follow again now for we have procurators and hospitallers.

The number of procurators appointed for this hospital seems to us to be proper; but we wish that there be also a separate reception office, so that not only provisions be in time made better, but that those who wish to do some charity may be more certain that the gift will not be employed otherwise than they intend. And if the revenue assigned by their Lordships be insufficient, or should extraordinary necessity arise, the Seigneury will advise about adjustment, according to the need they see.

The election of both procurators and hospitallers is to take place like that of the elders; and in electing them the rule proposed by Paul for deacons is to be followed.

With regard to the office of procurator, we think the rules which have already been imposed on them by us are good, by means of which, in urgent affairs, and where there is danger in deferment, and chiefly when there is no grave difficulty or question of great expense, they are not obliged always to be meeting, but one or two can do what is reasonable in the absence of the others.

It will be their duty to watch diligently that the public hospital is well maintained, and that this be so both for the sick and the old people unable to work, widowed women, orphaned children and other poor creatures. The sick are always to be lodged in a set of rooms separate from the other people who are unable to work, old men, widowed women, orphaned children and the other poor.

Moreover, care for the poor dispersed through the city should be revived, as the procurators may arrange it.

Moreover, besides the hospital for those passing through which must be maintained, there should be some attention given to any recognized as worthy of special charity. For this purpose, a special room should be set aside to receive those who ought to be assisted by the procurators, which is to be reserved for this business.

It should above all be demanded that the families of the hospitallers be honourably ruled in accordance with the will of God, since they have to govern houses dedicated to God.

The ministers must on their side enquire whether there be any lack or want of anything, in order to ask and desire the Seigneury to put it in order. To do this, some of their company with the procurators should visit the hospital every three months, to ascertain if all is in order.

It would be good, not only for the poor of the hospital, but also for those of the city who cannot help themselves, that they have a doctor and a surgeon of their own who should still practise in the city, but meanwhile be required to have care of the hospital and to visit the other poor.

As for the hospital for plague, it should be wholly separate and apart, and especially if it happen that the city be visited by this scourge of God.

For the rest, to discourage mendicancy which is contrary to good order, it would be well, and we have so ordered it, that there be one of our officials at the entrance of the churches to remove from the place those who loiter; and if there be any who give offence or offer insolence to bring them to one of the Lords Syndic. Similarly for the rest of the time, let the Overseers of Tens take care that the total prohibition of begging be well observed.

*   *   *

REVIEW QUESTIONS

1. What is the church according to Calvin?
2. What is its structure?
3. What do the four offices tell us about the function of the church?
4. What is the purpose of the church?
5. What are its goals?
6. What are the practices of the church and the relation of those practices to the process of becoming a Christian?
7. What is the relation between the church and salvation?

MARTIN LUTHER

FROM "Appeal to the Christian Nobility of the German Nation"

Martin Luther (1483–1546), the founder of Protestantism, was born of peasant stock. His father had left his fields for the copper mines of Mansfeld in Saxony, where he flourished economically and rose to the status of town councillor. His son Martin received a primary education from the Brethren of the Common Life and enrolled at the University of Erfurt in 1501, where he earned his bachelor of arts in 1502 and his master of arts in 1505. His father hoped that his son would continue the family's rise to prominence by pursuing a legal career. These aspirations were shattered when Luther unexpectedly entered a monastery in 1505. As a member of the order of Augustinian Hermits, Luther began formal training in theology. Selected for advanced training in theology, he made his way to the University of Wittenberg, where he received his doctorate in 1512 and occupied the chair of biblical theology. Even as his academic career prospered, his inner life suffered. Luther was beset by doubts about his own salvation, the result of a consciousness both of his own weakness and of divine righteousness. Long study and meditation led him to a resolution that became the basis for his theology of justification. Salvation was the result of divine grace, freely given; the forgiven conscience could be at peace; the soul could serve God joyfully. Given this new conviction, it is not surprising that the extravagant claims surrounding the sale of indulgences in 1517 provoked Luther to public protest. His objection to the notion that the pope could remit the temporal punishment for sins led him deeper and deeper into controversy and ultimately to schism. By 1520, the rift between Luther and the Catholic Church had become irreparable and extended to far more issues than papal power. In that year, he published three manifestos of reform, the first of which, "Appeal to the Christian Nobility of the German Nation," is excerpted below. It addressed the princes and rulers of Germany, recited the many grievances against the Church, and urged them to call a council for the reform of religion. It found a deep response in the nation and mobilized the forces of the Reformation.

From *The American Edition of Luther's Works,* edited by Jaroslav Pelikan (Minneapolis, Minn.: Augsburg Press, 1943), pp. 7–12, 18–24.

Jesus

To the Esteemed and Reverend Master, Nicholas von Amsdorf, Licentiate of Holy Scripture, and Canon of Wittenberg, my special and kind friend, from Doctor Martin Luther.

The grace and peace of God be with you, esteemed, reverend, and dear sir and friend.

The time for silence is past, and the time to speak has come, as Ecclesiastes says. I am carrying out our intention to put together a few points on the matter of the reform of the Christian estate, to be laid before the Christian nobility of the German nation, in the hope that God may help his church through the laity, since the clergy, to whom this task more properly belongs, have grown quite indifferent. I am sending the whole thing to you, reverend sir, that you may give an opinion on it and, where necessary, improve it.

I know full well that I shall not escape the charge of presumption because I, a despised, inferior person, venture to address such high and great estates on such weighty matters, as if there were nobody else in the world except Doctor Luther to take up the cause of the Christian estate and give advice to such high-ranking people. I make no apologies no matter who demands them. Perhaps I owe my God and the world another work of folly. I intend to pay my debt honestly. And if I succeed, I shall for the time being become a court jester. And if I fail, I still have one advantage—no one need buy me a cap or put scissors to my head. It is a question of who will put the bells on whom. I must fulfil the proverb, "Whatever the world does, a monk must be in the picture, even if he has to be painted in. More than once a fool has spoken wisely, and wise men have often been arrant fools. Paul says, "He who wishes to be wise must become a fool." Moreover, since I am not only a fool, but also a sworn doctor of Holy Scripture, I am glad for the opportunity to fulfil my doctor's oath, even in the guise of a fool.

I beg you, give my apologies to those who are moderately intelligent, for I do not know how to earn the grace and favor of the superintelligent. I have often sought to do so with the greatest pains, but from now on I neither desire nor value their favor. God help us to seek not our own glory but his alone. Amen.

At Wittenberg, in the monastery of the Augustinians, on the eve of St. John Baptist in the year fifteen hundred and twenty.

To His Most Illustrious, Most Mighty, and Imperial Majesty, and to the Christian Nobility of the German Nation, from Doctor Martin Luther.

Grace and power from God, Most Illustrious Majesty, and most gracious and dear lords.

It is not from sheer impertinence or rashness that I, one poor man, have taken it upon myself to address your worships. All the estates of Christendom, particularly in Germany, are now oppressed by distress and affliction, and this has stirred not only me but everybody else to cry out time and time again and to pray for help. It has even compelled me now at this time to cry aloud that God may inspire someone with his Spirit to lend a helping hand to this distressed and wretched nation. Often the councils have made some pretense at reformation, but their attempts have been cleverly frustrated by the guile of certain men, and things have gone from bad to worse. With God's help I intend to expose the wiles and wickedness of these men, so that they are shown up for what they are and may never again be so obstructive and destructive. God has given us a young man of noble birth as head of state, and in him has awakened great hopes of good in many hearts. Presented with such an opportunity we ought to apply ourselves and use this time of grace profitably.

The first and most important thing to do in this matter is to prepare ourselves in all seriousness. We must not start something by trusting in great power or human reason, even if all the power in the world were ours. For God cannot and will not suffer that a good work begin by relying upon one's own power and reason. He dashes such works to the ground, they do no good at all. As it says in Psalm 33, "No king is saved by his great might and no lord is saved by the greatness of his strength." I fear that this is why the good emperors Frederick I and Frederick II and many other German emperors were in former times shamefully oppressed and trodden underfoot by the popes, although all the world feared the emperors. It may be that they relied on their own might more than on God, and therefore had to fall. What was it in our own times that raised the bloodthirsty Julius II to such heights? Nothing else, I fear, except that France, the Germans, and Venice relied upon themselves. The children of Benjamin slew forty-two thousand Israelites because the latter relied on their own strength, Judges 30.

That it may not so fare with us and our noble Charles, we must realize that in this matter we are not dealing with men, but with the princes of hell. These princes could fill the world with war and bloodshed, but war and bloodshed do not overcome them. We must tackle this job by renouncing trust in physical force and trusting humbly in God. We must seek God's help through earnest prayer and fix our minds on nothing else than the misery and distress of suffering Christendom without regard to what evil men deserve. Otherwise, we may start the game with great prospects of success, but when we get into it the evil spirits will stir up such confusion that the whole world will swim in blood, and then nothing will come

of it all. Let us act wisely, therefore, and in the fear of God. The more force we use, the greater our disaster if we do not act humbly and in the fear of God. If the popes and Romanists have hitherto been able to set kings against each other by the devil's help, they may well be able to do it again if we were to go ahead without the help of God on our own strength and by our own cunning.

The Romanists have very cleverly built three walls around themselves. Hitherto they have protected themselves by these walls in such a way that no one has been able to reform them. As a result, the whole of Christendom has fallen abominably.

In the first place, when pressed by the temporal power they have made decrees and declared that the temporal power had no jurisdiction over them, but that, on the contrary, the spiritual power is above the temporal. In the second place, when the attempt is made to reprove them with the Scriptures, they raise the objection that only the pope may interpret the Scriptures. In the third place, if threatened with a council, their story is that no one may summon a council but the pope.

In this way they have cunningly stolen our three rods from us, that they may go unpunished. They have ensconced themselves within the safe stronghold of these three walls so that they can practice all the knavery and wickedness which we see today. Even when they have been compelled to hold a council they have weakened its power in advance by putting the princes under oath to let them remain as they were. In addition, they have given the pope full authority over all decision of a council, so that it is all the same whether there are many councils or no councils. They only deceive us with puppet shows and sham fights. They fear terribly for their skin in a really free council! They have so intimidated kings and princes with this technique that they believe it would be an offense against God not to be obedient to the Romanists in all their knavish and ghoulish deceits.

May God help us, and give us just one of those trumpets with which the walls of Jericho were overthrown to blast down these walls of straw and paper in the same way and set free the Christian rods for the punishment of sin, and bring to light the craft and deceit of the devil, to the end that through punishment we may reform ourselves and once more attain God's favor.

Let us begin by attacking the first wall. It is pure invention that pope, bishop, priests, and monks are called the spiritual estate while princes, lords, artisans, and farmers are called the temporal estate. This is indeed a piece of deceit and hypocrisy. Yet no one need be intimidated by it, and for this reason: all Christians are truly of the spiritual estate, and there is no difference among them except that of office. Paul says in I Corinthians 12 that we are all one body, yet every member has its own work by which it serves the others. This is because we all have one baptism, one gospel, one faith, and are all Christians alike; for baptism, gospel, and faith alone make us spiritual and a Christian people.

*   *   *

The second wall is still more loosely built and less substantial. The Romanists want to be the only masters of Holy Scripture, although they never learn a thing from the Bible all their life long. They assume the sole authority for themselves, and, quite unashamed, they play about with words before our very eyes, trying to persuade us that the pope cannot err in matters of faith, regardless of whether he is righteous or wicked. Yet they cannot point to a single letter. This is why so many heretical and unChristian, even unnatural, ordinances stand in the canon law. But there is no need to talk about these ordinances at present. Since these Romanists think the Holy Spirit never leaves them, no matter how ignorant and wicked they are, they become bold and decree only what they want. And if what they claim were true, why have Holy Scripture at all? Of what use is Scripture? Let us burn the Scripture and be satisfied with the unlearned gentlemen at Rome who possess the Holy Spirit! And yet the Holy Spirit can be possessed only by pious hearts. If I had not read the words with my own eyes, I would not have believed it possible for the devil to have made such

stupid claims at Rome, and to have won supporters for them.

But so as not to fight them with mere words, we will quote the Scriptures. St. Paul says in I Corinthians 14, "If something better is revealed to anyone, though he is already sitting and listening to another in God's word, then the one who is speaking shall hold his peace and give place." What would be the point of this commandment if we were compelled to believe only the man who does the talking, or the man who is at the top? Even Christ said in John 6 that all Christians shall be taught by God. If it were to happen that the pope and his cohorts were wicked and not true Christians, were not taught by God and were without understanding, and at the same time some obscure person had a right understanding, why should the people not follow the obscure man? Has the pope not erred many times? Who would help Christendom when the pope erred if we did not have somebody we could trust more than him, somebody who had the Scriptures on his side?

Therefore, their claim that only the pope may interpret Scripture is an outrageous fancied fable. They cannot produce a single letter of Scripture to maintain that the interpretation of Scripture or the confirmation of its interpretation belongs to the pope alone. They themselves have usurped this power. And although they allege that this power was given to St. Peter when the keys were given him, it is clear enough that the keys were not given to Peter alone but to the whole community. Further, the keys were not ordained for doctrine or government, but only for the binding or loosing of sin. Whatever else or whatever more they arrogate to themselves on the basis of the keys is a mere fabrication. But Christ's words to Peter, "I have prayed for you that your faith fail not," cannot be applied to the pope, since the majority of the popes have been without faith, as they must themselves confess. Besides, it is not only for Peter that Christ prayed, but also for all apostles and Christians, as he says in John 17, "Father, I pray for those whom thou hast given me, and not for these only, but for all who believe on me through their word." Is that not clear enough?

Just think of it! The Romanists must admit that there are among us good Christians who have the true faith, spirit, understanding, word, and mind of Christ. Why, then, should we reject the word and understanding of good Christians and follow the pope, who has neither faith nor the Spirit? To follow the pope would be to deny the whole faith as well as the Christian church. Again, if the article, "I believe in one holy Christian church," is correct, then the pope cannot be the only one who is right. Otherwise, we would have to confess, "I believe in the pope at Rome." This would reduce the Christian church to one man, and be nothing else than a devilish and hellish error.

Besides, if we are all priests, as was said above, and all have one faith, one gospel, one sacrament, why should we not also have the power to test and judge what is right or wrong in matters of faith? What becomes of Paul's words in I Corinthians 2, "A spiritual man judges all things, yet he is judged by no one"? And II Corinthians 4, "We all have one spirit of faith"? Why, then, should not we perceive what is consistent with faith and what is not, just as well as an unbelieving pope does?

We ought to become bold and free on the authority of all these texts, and many others. We ought not to allow the Spirit of freedom (as Paul calls him) to be frightened off by the fabrications of the popes, but we ought to march boldly forward and test all that they do, or leave undone, by our believing understanding of the Scriptures. We must compel the Romanists to follow not their own interpretation but the better one. Long ago Abraham had to listen to Sarah, although she was in more complete subjection to him than we are to anyone on earth. And Balaam's ass was wiser than the prophet himself. If God spoke then through an ass against a prophet, why should he not be able even now to speak through a righteous man against the pope? Similarly, St. Paul rebukes St. Peter as a man in error in Galatians 2. Therefore, it is the duty of every Christian to espouse the cause of the faith, to understand and defend it, and to denounce every error.

The third wall falls of itself when the first two are down. When the pope acts contrary to the Scriptures, it is our duty to stand by the Scriptures, to reprove him and to constrain him, according to the word of Christ, Matthew 18, "If your brother sins against you, go and tell it to him, between you and him alone; if he does not listen to you, then take one or two others with you; if he does not listen to them, tell it to the church; if he does not listen to the church, consider him a heathen." Here every member is commanded to care for every other. How much more should we do this when the member that does evil is responsible for the government of the church, and by his evil-doing is the cause of much harm and offense to the rest! But if I am to accuse him before the church, I must naturally call the church together.

The Romanists have no basis in Scripture for their claim that the pope alone has the right to call or confirm a council. This is just their own ruling, and it is only valid as long as it is not harmful to Christendom or contrary to the laws of God. Now when the pope deserves punishment, this ruling no longer obtains, for not to punish him by authority of a council is harmful to Christendom.

Thus we read in Acts 15 that it was not St. Peter who called the Apostolic Council but the apostles and elders. If then that right had belonged to St. Peter alone, the council would not have been a Christian council, but a heretical *conciliabulum*. Even the Council of Nicaea, the most famous of all councils, was neither called nor confirmed by the bishop of Rome, but by the emperor Constantine. Many other emperors after him have done the same, and yet these councils were the most Christian of all. But if the pope alone has the right to convene councils, then these councils would all have been heretical. Further, when I examine the councils the pope did summon, I find that they did nothing of special importance.

Therefore, when necessity demands it, and the pope is an offense to Christendom, the first man who is able should, as a true member of the whole body, do what he can to bring about a truly free council. No one can do this so well as the temporal authorities, especially since they are also fellow-Christians, fellow-priests, fellow-members of the spiritual estate, fellow-lords over all things. Whenever it is necessary or profitable they ought to exercise the office and work which they have received from God over everyone. Would it not be unnatural if a fire broke out in a city and everybody were to stand by and let it burn on and on and consume everything that could burn because nobody had the authority of the mayor, or because, perhaps, the fire broke out in the mayor's house? In such a situation is it not the duty of every citizen to arouse and summon the rest? How much more should this be done in the spiritual city of Christ if a fire of offense breaks out, whether in the papal government, or anywhere else! The same argument holds if an enemy were to attack a city. The man who first roused the others deserves honor and gratitude. Why, then, should he not deserve honor who makes known the presence of the enemy from hell and rouses Christian people and calls them together?

*　　*　　*

REVIEW QUESTIONS

1. Why does Luther address the German nobility?
2. How is Luther redefining temporal and spiritual authorities?
3. What is their relation to one another?
4. Where does Luther locate true authority?

"Statement of Grievances," Diet of Worms, 1521

The Diet of Worms in 1521, the first meeting of Emperor Charles V with the representatives of the German Estates and the occasion of Martin Luther's appearance before the emperor, is a dramatic moment in the history of the Reformation. It provided the setting for Luther's declaration of faith in Scripture and freedom of conscience: "Here I stand." It also provided the opportunity for an official statement of grievances concerning the state of the church. Thus, even as it condemned Luther, the diet reminded Charles both of the reformer's extraordinary popular support and of the necessity of addressing the "burdens and abuses" placed on the empire by Rome. Charles asked the representatives to submit a catalogue of these abuses for consideration and action. A committee of electors and princes, both secular and spiritual, drew up the following list, probably using complaints submitted by individual representatives. Though no formal action was taken at Worms, the "Statement of Grievances" provided the basis of a document sent to Rome after the Diet of Nuremberg in 1523.

From *Manifestations of Discontent in Germany on the Eve of the Reformation*, edited by Gerald Strauss (Bloomington: Indiana University Press, 1971), pp. 52–63.

Hᴵꜱ Rᴏᴍᴀɴ Iᴍᴘᴇʀɪᴀʟ Mᴀᴊᴇꜱᴛʏ desiring the electors, princes, and General Estates of the Empire to acquaint him with the burdens placed on the German nation by His Holiness the Pope and other ecclesiastics, and to make known to him our counsel and opinions as to how these burdens might be lifted from us, we have in all haste set down the following points, begin-

THE GODLY MILL (1521)

Church reformers—both Protestant and Catholic—made full use of the new technology of printing to broadcast their ideological message to the common folk. Often, a printed image was worth a thousand words to a still largely illiterate population. The Godly Mill distills the early Lutheran message of reliance on Scripture as the sole source of religious truth: As the truth of the Gospel is disseminated, as in the workings of a mill, those institutions and traditions not explicitly established in it are banished. What is the significance of the grouping of the four figures: Christ, Erasmus, Luther, and Karsthans, the common man? Why would Lutherans choose a mill as their symbol for the dissemination of the Gospel? Given the year in which it was printed, 1521, how might this image be directly related to significant political events?

ning with matters touching His Holiness the Pope.

1. *Secular cases are transferred to Rome for trial in the first instance.* Our Most Holy Father the Pope, heeding the clamor of his priests, causes numerous persons to be summoned for trial in Rome in matters of inheritance, mortgage and similar worldly concerns, a practice conducive to the curtailment of the competence of secular authorities. We ask that Your Imperial Majesty undertake to ensure that no person, spiritual or worldly, be summoned to Rome for first trial in any matter, spiritual or worldly, but that he be allowed instead to appear in the first instance before the bishop or archdeacon of his province or, if he is a layman and the matter at issue is secular, before the prince, government, or ordinary judge with appropriate competence.

*   *   *

7. *Rome often grants benefices to unworthy persons.* Rome awards German benefices to unqualified, unlearned, and unfit persons such as gunners, falconers, bakers, donkey drivers, stable grooms, and so on, most of whom know not a word of German and never assume the duties connected with their benefices, shifting them instead to worthless vicars who are content with a pittance in pay. Thus the German laity receives neither spiritual care nor worldly counsel from the Church, while a hoard of money flows yearly to Italy with no return to us, least of all gratitude. We think that German benefices should be awarded to native Germans only and that beneficed persons ought to be required to reside in the place to which they are assigned.

*   *   *

9. *Concerning annates.* In former times emperors granted annates to Rome for a limited term of years only and for no purpose other than to enable the Church to hold back the Turk and support Christendom. In the course of time, however, the payment of annates grew into a regular custom, and, as is generally known, the German nation has been excessively burdened with them. . . .

10. *Annates are constantly increased in amount.* Not only are annates almost daily raised in amount, but they are also being extended from archbishoprics and bishoprics to abbeys, priories, parishes, and other ecclesiastical prebends. . . . Although the old regulations placed a pallium fee of not more than ten thousand gulden upon the bishoprics of Mainz, Cologne, Salzburg, and others, the pallium cannot now be fetched home for less than twenty thousand to twenty-four thousand gulden.

11. *Concerning new devices employed by Rome.* The main reason for the constant rise in the cost of episcopal confirmations and pallium fees is the proliferation of offices in Rome, such as chamberlains, shield-bearers, and others, for whose emoluments our bishops' subjects must pay taxes and tributes. Furthermore, Rome obtains money by means of a number of cunning and novel devices, especially the following: a certain newly elected bishop has been given papal leave to pay his pallium fees not in cash but instead in the form of a pledge from certain sponsors to make payment at a given time. Suddenly, and for no reason, these sponsors are excommunicated and, almost at once, absolved again, for which absolution the bishop-elect must pay from three to five hundred ducats. It has been made known to us that His Holiness has this year created several new offices and is now personally served by more than 150 retainers who make their living off the proceeds of ecclesiastical benefices, for which the German nation furnishes the money.

*   *   *

19. *Concerning papal dispensation and absolution.* Popes and bishops reserve to themselves certain sins and offenses from which, they say, only they can absolve us. Whenever such a "case" occurs and a man wishes absolution, he discovers that only money can procure it for him. Nor does Rome give out a dispensation except on payment of gold. A poor man without money will not see his matter despatched. A rich man can, moreover, for a sum, obtain papal letters of indult, which entitle him to priestly absolution for any sin he might commit in the future, murder, for example, or perjury. All this shows how Roman greed and covetousness cause sins and vices to multiply in the world.

20. *Concerning the depredations of papal courtiers.* The German nation also suffers exceedingly from the greed of papal and curial hangers-on who are bent on occupying ecclesiastical benefices in our land. These courtiers compel honorable old clerics, long established and blameless in their offices, to go to Rome, where they are subjected to humiliating chicaneries. There they must wait until Rome gets what it wants through reservations and pensions obtained by means of so-called Chancellery Rules, setting aside old agreements and replacing them with new ones. In this way, honorable old clerics who are not schooled in courtiers' tricks are defrauded of their benefices *lite pendente,* no matter what the outcome of their case will be.

* * *

22. *Concerning indulgences.* We also regard it in the highest degree objectionable that His Holiness should permit so many indulgences to be sold in Germany, a practice through which simple-minded folk are misled and cheated of their savings. When His Holiness sends nuncios or emissaries to a country, he empowers them to offer indulgences for sale and retain a portion of the income for their traveling expenses and salaries. . . . Bishops and local secular authorities also get their share for helping with the arrangements for the sale. All this money is obtained from poor and simple people who cannot see through the curia's cunning deceptions.

23. *Concerning mendicants, relic hawkers, and miracle healers.* These riffraff go back and forth through our land, begging, collecting, offering indulgences, and extracting large sums of money from our people. We think these hawkers ought to be kept out of our country. . . .

* * *

31. *How some clerics escape punishment for their misdeeds.* If an ordained cleric going about in the world on secular business and in secular clothes is brought before a secular court on some charge and is detained by it, he need only say "I am ordained" and demand to be transferred to an ecclesiastical court, and he will go free. His bishop will support him, notwithstanding the fact that the man was apprehended without tonsure and wearing worldly dress. And if the secular court does not release him within twenty-four hours, its judges are excommunicated. Are not such practices bound to encourage clerics to wicked acts, the more since ecclesiastical courts let them go scot-free, no matter what their offense? . . .

32. *How secular property comes into ecclesiastical hands.* Seeing that the spiritual estate is under papal instructions never to sell or otherwise transfer the Church's real estate and immobilia to the laity, we think it advisable for His Roman Imperial Majesty to cause a corresponding law to be made for the secular estate, to wit, that no secular person be allowed to make over any part of his real property to any ecclesiastical person or institution, and that this proscription apply to inheritance as well. If such a law is not introduced without delay, it is possible that the secular estate will, in the course of time, be altogether bought out by the Church . . . and the secular estate of the Holy Roman Empire eventually be entirely beholden to the Church.

* * *

37. *Ecclesiastical courts give support to Jewish usury.* Everyone knows that the Jews' usury in Germany pauperizes and corrupts Christian society. But whenever a secular authority sets out to curb the Jews, the latter call upon an ecclesiastical court for help and cause the Christians to be excommunicated. For although the debtors swear that the money owed the Jews was not procured on terms of usury, the court knows that Jews do not lend except usuriously and that the poor, in their great need, perjure themselves. Canon and civil law forbids the rendering of judicial or other aid in matters of usury, but bishops and prelates permit it nonetheless.

* * *

39. *Sinners are given fines to pay rather than spiritual penance to do.* Although spiritual penance ought to be imposed upon sinners for one reason only, to gain salvation for their souls, ecclesiastical judges tend nowadays to make penalties so formidable that the sinner is obliged to buy his way out of them, through which practice untold

amounts of money flow into the Church's treasury . . . .

*   *   *

43. *Excommunication is used indiscriminately, even in trivial matters.* Notwithstanding the original and true purpose of spiritual censure and excommunication, namely, to aid and direct Christian life and faith, this weapon is now flung at us for the most inconsequential debts—some of them amounting to no more than a few pennies—or for non-payment of court or administrative costs after the principal sum has already been returned. With such procedures the very life blood is sucked out of the poor, untutored laity, who are driven to distraction by the fear of the Church's ban. . . .

*   *   *

54. *There are too many vagrant mendicants in our land.* The poor in Germany are sorely oppressed by the extraordinary number of mendicant monks, especially by begging friars maintained by mendicant orders in violation of their own rules. Some villages and towns have two, three, or four of these begging brothers going about with hands outstretched, and the alms that should go to old and indigent householders who can no longer support themselves fill the monks' pouches instead. Bishops condone this practice in return for a portion of the collection.

*   *   *

56. *Too many priests are ordained, many of them unlearned and unfit.* Archbishops and bishops have been ordaining base and uneducated persons whose only claim to the priesthood is that they are needy. Such people, either because of their low estate or because of some native inclination to wickedness, lead reckless and dishonorable lives, bringing the whole spiritual estate into disrepute and setting the common folk a bad example. Before making ordination, the bishop is obliged to consult six witnesses on the candidate's fitness for the priestly office; but as things are now, the witnesses have, likely as not, never seen or heard of the candidate. Thus our Christian laws are nothing but pretense and sham to them.

*   *   *

58. *Bishops ought to hold frequent synods.* All the above shortcomings would doubtless be alleviated if bishops fulfilled their obligation to meet in synods with their prelates and ecclesiastical subjects in order to seek the aid and counsel of all the clergy present, as the law of the Church obliges them to do.

*   *   *

66. *Certain clerics behave like laymen and are even seen brawling in taverns.* The majority of parish priests and other secular clerics mingle with the common people at inns and taverns. They frequent public dances and walk about the streets in lay garments, brandishing long knives. They engage in quarrels and arguments, which usually lead to blows, whereupon they fall upon poor folk, wound or even kill them, and then excommunicate them unless the innocently injured parties agree to offer money for a settlement with the offending priest.

67. *Clerics set bad examples by cohabiting with their serving women.* Most parish priests and other clerics have established domestic relations with women of loose morals. They dwell openly with the women and with their children. It is a dishonest, detestable life for priests and a wretched example to set for their parishioners.

*   *   *

69. *Many clerics have turned to tavern keeping and gambling.* Clerics can frequently be seen setting themselves up as inn keepers. On holidays, in places where they have proprietary rights, priests put up tables for dice, bowls, or cards and invite people to play. Then they take the winnings, shamelessly claiming that these belong to them by rights of sovereignty. . . .

*   *   *

85. *They try to gain exclusive jurisdiction over legal matters, which should be heard in secular courts.* Much legal business that, according to law, may be settled in either ecclesiastical or secular courts, has in fact been usurped by the clergy. For when a secular judge claims a case, it often happens that a spiritual judge steps forward and threatens the other with excommunication unless he lets go of

the case. Thus the clergy take over what they wish. According to our laws, offenses like perjury, adultery, and black magic may be handled by either spiritual or lay courts, depending on who first claimed the case. But the clergy make bold to grasp all such cases, thus undercutting secular authority.

* * *

88. *How they take over secular jurisdiction by falsely pleading prescription.* Some experts hesitate to call attention to the Church's practice of acquiring rights by possession, that is, by pleading prescriptive rights to gain legal jurisdiction over lay matters, though His Imperial Majesty's and the empire's highest dignities and jurisdictions are thereby being steadily eroded. But we know it to be according to right and law that no one may prescribe, or claim to have acquired by possession, against the high sovereignty of pope and emperor, no matter how many years he has held on to something or used it without interference.

* * *

91. *Money can buy tolerance of concubinage and usury.* If a man and a woman cohabit without being married, they may pay an annual fee to the clergy and be left to live in shame and sin. The same is done with usurers. . . . A married person whose spouse has disappeared but might still be living is, without any further search for the missing partner, allowed to take up cohabitation with another. This they call *"toleramus,"* and it serves to bring contempt upon the holy sacrament of marriage.

* * *

95. *Innocent people who happen to live near an excommunicated person are themselves excommunicated.* In some towns and villages ten or twelve neighbors of an excommunicate are placed under the ban along with him, although they have nothing to do with his offense. And this is done for no reason other than the clergy's eagerness to establish its authority and to have it obeyed. Because of this practice, poor and innocent people are forced to buy their way out of the ban, or else to remove their families and belongings from their homes. No distinction is made in these indiscrim-

inate excommunications. No one asks: Is the man poor or not? Did he associate voluntarily with the excommunicated sinner? And even though their own canon law forbids declarations of interdict for debts or other money matters, they impose the ban on whole towns and villages, alleging disobedience as the cause in order to mask their illegal and unjust action.

* * *

97. *They demand a weekly tribute from artisans.* In many places the clergy demand a weekly tax or tribute from millers, inn keepers, bakers, shoe makers, smiths, tailors, shepherds, cowherds, and other craftsmen. If this tribute is refused, they enforce their demand with the threat of excommunication.

* * *

101. *They withhold the sacraments for trivial offenses.* If a man owes a small debt to the priest or to the parish, and if he is too poor to repay it on time and asks for a short extension of the loan, the priest often withholds the sacraments from him and nags and intimidates him, although the matter ought by rights to be brought before a secular judge.

REVIEW QUESTIONS

1. What are the general categories into which the grievances may be organized?
2. How would you characterize the list as a whole?
3. On the basis of the statement, what was the nature of discontent with the Roman Church on the eve of the Reformation?
4. What kind of action or reforms did the representatives at Worms hope to prompt from the pope in Rome?
5. To what extent does the statement reflect the spiritual yearnings of Christians like Luther?

The Oath of Allegiance

The "Form or Example of the Profession and Oath Exhibited to Henry VIII, King of England, by the Bishops and Clergy Assembled in the Convocation in Parliament Held Anno Domini 1534," indicates clearly the state of the Reformation in England during that year. The doctrinal split with Rome had not reached a crucial stage, but the political schism was nearly complete. In March Pope Clement VII pronounced Henry's marriage to Catherine of Aragon to be valid and declared the king excommunicate if he did not accept the decision. Thus ended Henry's hope for an annulment and remarriage within the Church. Yet, his desire for an heir drove him to defiance. The Oath of Allegiance effectively severed all ecclesiastical ties to Rome and established the monarch as the head of the Anglican Church.

From *Selections from the Sources of English History*, edited by Charles W. Colby (New York: Longmans, Green, 1899), pp. 145–47.

To the most invincible and our most pious Lord in Christ, the Lord Henry the eighth, by the grace of God, king of England and France, defender of the faith, lord of Ireland, and on earth, under Christ, supreme head of the Church of England, your humble subjects and most obliged supplicants.

Reverence and obedience due to, and worthy of so excellent and mighty a prince, with all honour of subjection.

We, not constrained by force or fear, not hereunto induced or seduced by any deceit or other sinister machination, but out of our own certain knowledge, deliberate minds and mere and spontaneous wills, do, purely of our own accord, and absolutely in the word of our priesthood, profess, promise and swear, unto your most illustrious majesty, our singular and most high lord and patron, Henry the eighth, by the grace of God King of England and France, defender of the faith, lord of Ireland, and on earth of the English Church, immediately under Christ, supreme head: That from henceforth we will promise or give, or cause to be given, to no foreign emperor, king, prince, or prelate, nor to the bishop of Rome (whom they call Pope) fidelity or obedience in word or writing, simple or by oath; but at all times, in every case

and condition, we will follow and observe, and to our power defend the parts of your royal majesty, and of your successors, against every man whom we shall know or suspect to be an adversary to your majesty, or to your successors: and we will sincerely and heartily perform fidelity and obedience to your royal majesty alone, as to our supreme prince, and head of the English Church: we profess that the papacy of Rome is not ordained by God in holy writ, but that it is of human tradition; we constantly affirm, and openly do declare, and will declare, and will diligently take care that others shall so publish the same. Neither will we privately or publicly treat with any mortal man, or give our consent, that the bishop of Rome may here have, or exercise any longer, any authority or jurisdiction, or that he may hereafter be restored to any. And we do knowingly, publicly aver the modern bishop of Rome or his successor in that bishopric whosoever, not to be pope, nor high priest, nor universal bishop, nor the most high lord, but only bishop or prelate of Rome, as by our ancestors used: and the laws and statutes of this realm, at any time set forth and enacted, for the extirpation and taking away of popery, and of the authority and jurisdiction of the said bishop of Rome, we will, after our strength, knowledge and wit, firmly observe ourselves, and, as much as in us lies, will take care, and cause the same to be in like manner observed by others: neither will we henceforth appeal to the said bishop of Rome, or consent to any that shall appeal: neither will we act in his court for right or justice, nor will answer to any that there doth act, nor will there take upon us the person of a plaintiff or defendant: and if the said bishop, by message, or by his letters, shall signify anything unto us, whatsoever it be, we will, as soon as conveniently we may, signify or cause the same to be signified, either to your royal majesty, or to your privy council, or to your successors, or to their privy council; and we will neither send, or cause to be sent, any letters or message to the said bishop of Rome, or to his court, unless your majesty or your successor first know or consent that such letter or message shall be sent to him. We will not procure any bulls, briefs or rescripts whatsoever, for ourselves or others, from the bishop of Rome or his court, neither will we counsel any such to be procured by any other. And if any such shall be procured generally or specially for us without our knowledge, or any otherwise shall be granted, we will renounce the same, nor will we consent thereto, nor any way use the same, but will take care that the same be delivered to your majesty, or to your successors. And we do by this writing expressly renounce all exemption whereby, mediately or immediately, we are or have been subject to the bishop of Rome, highest prelate (as they call him), or to him by what name soever he is called, or to his church of Rome, and all his grants, privileges, gifts, whatsoever conferred; and we profess ourselves to be subjects and vassals to your majesty alone, and we do thereto submit ourselves, and promise only to be subject thereunto. Neither will we by ourselves, or by any other interposed person or persons, pay or cause to be paid, to the said bishop of Rome,

or to his messengers, orators, collectors, or legates, any procuration, pension, portion, taxes, or any other sum of moneys, by what name soever it be called. Moreover, to confirm this our covenant, we profess and undertake, and in the word of a priest, and under the fidelity due to your majesty and our own conscience before God, we promise, that, against this our aforesaid profession and undertaking, we will use no dispensation, no exception, no appellation or provocation, and no remedy of law or of fact; and if we have made any profession to the hindrance of this our profession and undertaking, we do revoke the same, for the time present, and for all time to come, and to renounce the same by these present letters; whereunto we have subscribed our names, either under our own hands, or the hands of our procurators at our request: and the same we have caused to be confirmed by the fixing of our common seal thereto, and by the mark and subscription of the public notary under written. Dated and acted in our Chapter-House.

REVIEW QUESTIONS

1. What are the implications of declaring Henry "on earth of the Church of England, immediately under Christ, supreme head"?
2. What did it mean to declare the papacy a "human tradition"?
3. How might the prohibition of appeals "to the said bishop of Rome" influence the lives of the common folk?
4. What economic motives might have inspired the Oath of Allegiance?
5. How does the Oath of Allegiance compare with the "Statement of Grievances" presented to the Diet of Worms in 1521?

15 ❧ RELIGIOUS WARS AND STATE BUILDING, 1540–1660

The challenge to the authority of classical culture that the new worlds posed, combined with the fragmentation of the medieval Christian Church, the "body of all believers," laid the foundation in the second half of the sixteenth century for profound crises of political and social order and of epistemology, the very foundation of human knowledge. In their efforts to describe what they saw in the Americas, European conquistadores and clergy were forced to adopt analogies: hundreds of species of plants and animals were not to be found in Pliny, the great and trusted botanist and zoologist of the ancient world, or in the Bible. The cultures of the Americas posed new models of social and political relations, opening new possibilities for the ordering of political relations and calling into question the very nature of political authority.

Within Europe, civil wars arose in the wake of the fragmentation of the Christian Church. The wars of religion in France, 1562–1598, led astute observers such as Montaigne to question the claim of each side to know the truth, and to question whether human reason was sufficient to discern the truth. In all the religious wars, beginning with the German Peasants' War of 1525 and culminating in the Thirty Years' War, 1618–1648, the social order was overthrown, as peasant killed lord, brother killed brother, son killed father, and neighbor killed neighbor. What was it to be human? To be savage? And where was God as Christian slaughtered Christian?

The crisis of the seventeenth century was not simply intellectual and spiritual but had real material aspects. The expansion of Europe into new worlds changed patterns of consumption and production, thus contributing to the overthrow of traditional work processes and lifestyles. It created a tremendous influx of wealth that aided the rise of new economic and political powers, both social groups and nation-states, and that contributed to chronic inflation. Changes in society, economy, and politics created tensions that found expression in the violence of the period. Religious wars were seldom entirely religious in cause or in consequence. The almost constant march and countermarch of armies not only destroyed life and property but also disrupted agriculture and spread disease. The struggle for existence, difficult under the best of circumstances in the early modern period, became much more difficult in the age of crisis.

By 1660, peasants had risen in unprecedented numbers against their lords; common Englishmen had executed their king; Europeans had witnessed multiple incidents of cannibalism in their own villages; and the medieval epistemology, that very base by which Europeans could be certain of the veracity of what they knew, had collapsed. New formulations were being tentatively put forward, but they did not yet replace the old certainties that had been irrecoverably lost.

JEAN BODIN

FROM *On Sovereignty*

Jean Bodin (1529–1596) was born a bourgeois in Angers. He entered a Carmelite monastery in 1545, apparently set on an ecclesiastical career, but obtained release from his vows around 1549. He pursued a course of study at the royal Collège de Quatre Langues in Paris. By 1550, he was well trained in humanist studies and went on to become one of the greatest scholars of his day. His continual search for religious truth placed him repeatedly under suspicion of heresy, but no clear evidence exists to support a conversion to Calvinism. Bodin continued his studies and attended the University of Toulouse, where he studied law during the 1550s. In 1561, he launched his public career by serving as an advocate before the parlement in Paris. Bodin soon rose to the attention of high officials and dignitaries and received special commissions from the king as early as 1570. In 1571, he entered the service of Francis, Duke of Alençon, a prince of the blood. During his service to Alençon, and in the aftermath of the St. Bartholomew's Day massacre, Bodin published his great work, Six livres de la république (1576), a systematic exposition of public law. It included an absolutist theory of royal government, from which the following selection is drawn. Bodin's theory was based on the controversial notion, which proved highly influential in the development of royal absolutism, that sovereignty was indivisible and that high powers of government could not be shared by separate agents or agencies. His notion that all governmental powers were concentrated in the king of France, can be seen as a direct response to the anarchy of civil war that gripped the kingdom during the second half of the sixteenth century. In 1576, Bodin was chosen as a deputy for the Third Estate of the Estates-General of Blois. Though a royalist, Bodin opposed the civil wars that raged in France and became a leading spokesperson against royal requests for increased taxation and religious uniformity. It cost him royal favor and high office. With the death in 1584 of his patron, the duke of Alençon, Bodin's career in high politics ended. He retired to Laon, where he died.

From *On Sovereignty,* by Jean Bodin, edited by Julian H. Franklin (Cambridge, Eng.: Cambridge University Press, 1992), pp. 46–50.

Book I

*   *   *

CHAPTER 8
ON SOVEREIGNTY

Sovereignty is the absolute and perpetual power of a commonwealth, which the Latins call *maiestas;* the Greeks *akra exousia, kurion arche,* and *kurion politeuma;* and the Italians *segnioria,* a word they use for private persons as well as for those who have full control of the state, while the Hebrews call it *to-mech shévet*—that is, the highest power of command. We must now formulate a definition of sovereignty because no jurist or political philosopher has defined it, even though it is the chief point, and the one that needs most to be explained, in a treatise on the commonwealth. Inasmuch as we have said that a commonwealth is a just government, with sovereign power, of several households and of that which they have in common, we need to clarify the meaning of sovereign power.

*   *   *

We shall conclude, then, that the sovereignty of the monarch is in no way altered by the presence of the Estates. On the contrary, his majesty is all the greater and more illustrious when all his people publicly acknowledge him as sovereign, even though, in an assembly like this, princes, not wishing to rebuff their subjects, grant and pass many things that they would not consent to had they not been overcome by the requests, petitions, and just complaints of a harassed and afflicted people which has most often been wronged without the knowledge of the prince, who sees and hears only through the eyes, ears, and reports of others.

We thus see that the main point of sovereign majesty and absolute power consists of giving the law to subjects in general without their consent. Not to go to other countries, we in this kingdom have often seen certain general customs repealed by edicts of our kings without hearing from the Estates when the injustice of the rules was obvious. Thus the custom concerning the inheritance by mothers of their children's goods, which was observed in this kingdom throughout the entire region governed by customary law, was changed without assembling either the general or local estates. Nor is this something new. In the time of King Philip the Fair, the general custom of the entire kingdom, by which the losing party in a case could not be required to pay expenses, was suppressed by an edict without assembling the Estates.

*   *   *

CHAPTER 10
ON THE TRUE MARKS OF SOVEREIGNTY

Since there is nothing greater on earth, after God, than sovereign princes, and since they have been established by Him as His lieutenants for commanding other men, we need to be precise about their status so that we may respect and revere their majesty in complete obedience, and do them honor in our thoughts and in our speech. Contempt for one's sovereign prince is contempt toward God, of whom he is the earthly image. That is why God, speaking to Samuel, from whom the people had demanded a different prince, said "It is me that they have wronged."

To be able to recognize such a person—that is, a sovereign—we have to know his attributes, which are properties not shared by subjects. For if they were shared, there would be no sovereign prince. Yet the best writers on this subject have not treated this point with the clarity it deserves, whether from flattery, fear, hatred, or forgetfulness.

We read that Samuel, after consecrating the king that God had designated, wrote a book about the rights of majesty. But the Hebrews have written that the kings suppressed his book so that they could tyrannize their subjects. Melanchthon thus went astray in thinking that the rights of majesty were the abuses and tyrannical practices that Samuel pointed out to the people in a speech. "Do you wish to know," said Samuel, "the ways of tyrants? It is to seize the goods of subjects to dispose of at his pleasure, and to seize their women and their children in order to abuse them and to make them slaves." The word *mishpotim* as it is used in this passage does not mean rights, but rather practices and ways of doing things. Otherwise this good prince, Samuel, would have contradicted himself. For when accounting to the people for the stewardship that God had given him, he said, "Is there anyone among you who can say that I ever took gold or silver from him, or any present whatsoever?" And thereupon the whole people loudly praised him for never having done a wrong or taken anything from anyone no matter who.

*   *   *

We may thus conclude that the first prerogative of a sovereign prince is to give law to all in general and each in particular. But this is not sufficient. We have to add "without the consent of any other, whether greater, equal, or below him." For if the prince is obligated to make no law without the consent of a superior, he is clearly a subject; if of an equal, he has an associate; if of

subjects, such as the senate or the people, he is not sovereign. The names of grandees that one finds affixed to edicts are not put there to give the law its force, but to witness it and to add weight to it so that the enactment will be more acceptable. For there are very ancient edicts, extant at Saint Denys in France, issued by Philip I and Louis the Fat in 1060 and 1129 respectively, to which the seals of their queens Anne and Alix, and of Robert and Hugh, were affixed. For Louis the Fat, it was year twelve of his reign; for Adelaide, year six.

When I say that the first prerogative of sovereignty is to give law to all in general and to each in particular, the latter part refers to privileges, which are in the jurisdiction of sovereign princes to the exclusion of all others. I call it a privilege when a law is made for one or a few private individuals, no matter whether it is for the profit or the loss of the person with respect to whom it is decreed. Thus Cicero said, *Privilegium de meo capite latum est.* "They have passed," he said, "a capital privilege against me." He is referring to the authorization to put him on trial decreed against him by the commoners at the request of the tribune Clodius. He calls this the *lex Clodia* in many places, and he bitterly protests that privileges could be decreed only by the great Estates of the people as it was laid down by the laws of the Twelve Tables in the words: *Privilegia, nisi comitiis centuriatis irroganto, qui secus faxit capital esto.*[1] And all those who have written of regalian rights agree that only the sovereign can grant privileges, exemptions, and immunities, and grant dispensations from edicts and ordinances. In monarchies, however, privileges last only for the lifetime of the monarchs, as the emperor Tiberius, Suetonius reports, informed all those who had received privileges from Augustus.

*   *   *

[1] "Let no privileges be imposed except in the *comita centuriata;* let him who has done otherwise be put to death."

Book II

CHAPTER 5

WHETHER IT IS LAWFUL TO MAKE AN ATTEMPT UPON THE TYRANT'S LIFE AND TO NULLIFY AND REPEAL HIS ORDINANCES AFTER HE IS DEAD

Ignorance of the exact meaning of the term "tyrant" has led many people astray, and has been the cause of many inconveniences. We have said that a tyrant is someone who makes himself into a sovereign prince by his own authority—without election, or right of succession, or lot, or a just war, or a special calling from God. This is what is understood by tyrant in the writings of the ancients and in the laws that would have him put to death. Indeed, the ancients established great prizes and rewards for those who killed tyrants, offering titles of nobility, prowess, and chivalry to them along with statues and honorific titles, and even all the tyrant's goods, because they were taken as true liberators of the fatherland, or of the motherland, as the Cretans say. In this they did not distinguish, between a good and virtuous prince and a bad and wicked one, for no one has the right to seize the sovereignty and make himself the master of those who had been his companions, no matter what pretenses of justice and virtue he may offer. In strictest law, furthermore, use of the prerogatives reserved to sovereignty is punishable by death. Hence if a subject seeks, by whatever means, to invade the state and steal it from his king or, in a democracy or aristocracy, to turn himself from a fellow-citizen into lord and master, he deserves to be put to death. In this respect our question does not pose any difficulty.

*　　*　　*

At this point there are many questions one may ask, such as whether a tyrant, who I said may be justly killed without form or shape of trial, becomes legitimate if, after having encroached upon sovereignty by force or fraud, he has himself elected by the Estates. For it seems that the solemn act of election is an authentic ratification of the tyranny, an indication that the people have found it to their liking. But I say that it is nevertheless permissible to kill him, and to do so by force unless the tyrant, stripping off his authority, has given up his arms and put power back into the hands of the people in order to have its judgment. What tyrants force upon a people stripped of power cannot be called consent. Sulla, for example, had himself made dictator for eighty years by the Valerian law, which he got published with a powerful army camped inside the city of Rome. But Cicero said that this was not a law. Another example is Caesar, who had himself made permanent dictator by the Servian law; and yet another is Cosimo de Medici who, having an army inside Florence, had himself elected duke. When objections were raised, he set off a volley of gunfire in front of the palace, which induced the lords and magistrates to get on with it more quickly.

*　　*　　*

So much then for the tyrant, whether virtuous or wicked, who makes himself a sovereign lord on his own authority. But the chief difficulty arising from our question is whether a sovereign prince who has come into possession of the state by way of election, or lot, or right of succession, or just war, or by a special calling from God, can be killed if he is cruel, oppressive, or excessively wicked. For that is the meaning given to the word tyrant. Many doctors and theologians, who have touched upon this question, have resolved that it is permissible to kill a tyrant without distinction, and some, putting two words together that are incompatible, have spoken of a king-tyrant (*roi tyran*), which has caused the ruin of some very fine and flourishing monarchies.

But to decide this question properly we need to distinguish between a prince who is absolutely sovereign and one who is not, and between subjects and foreigners. It makes a great difference whether we say that a tyrant can be lawfully killed by a foreign prince or by a subject. For just as it is glorious and becoming, when the gates of justice have been shut, for someone, whoever he may be, to use force in defense of the goods, honor, and life of those who have been unjustly oppressed— as Moses did when he saw his brother being beaten and mistreated and had no way of getting justice—so is it a most beautiful and magnificent thing for a prince to take up arms in order to avenge an entire people unjustly oppressed by a tyrant's cruelty, as did Hercules, who traveled all over the world exterminating tyrant-monsters and was deified for his great feats. The same was done by Dion, Timoleon, Aratus, and other generous princes, who obtained the title of chastisers and correctors of tyrants. This, furthermore, was the sole cause for which Tamerlane, prince of the Tartars, declared war on Bajazet, who was then besieging Constantinople, Tamerlane saying that he had come to punish him for tyranny and to deliver the afflicted peoples. He defeated Bajazet in a battle fought on the plateau of Mount Stella, and after he had killed and routed three hundred thousand Turks, he had the tyrant chained inside a cage until he died. In this case it makes no difference whether this virtuous prince proceeds against a tyrant by force, deception, or judicial means. It is however true that if a virtuous prince has seized a tyrant, he will obtain more honor by putting him on trial and punishing him as a murderer, parricide, and thief, rather than acting against him by the common law of peoples (*droit des gens*).

But as for subjects, and what they may do, one has to know whether the prince is absolutely sovereign, or is properly speaking not a sovereign. For if he is not absolutely sovereign, it follows necessarily that sovereignty is in the people or the aristocracy. In this latter case there is no doubt that it is permissible to proceed against the tyrant either by way of law if one can prevail against him, or else by way of fact and open force, if one cannot otherwise have justice. Thus the Senate took the first way against Nero, the second against Maximinus inasmuch as the Roman emperors were no more than princes of the republic, in the sense of first persons and chief citizens, with sovereignty remaining in the people and the Senate.

* * *

But if the prince is sovereign absolutely, as are the genuine monarchs of France, Spain, England, Scotland, Ethiopia, Turkey, Persia, and Moscovy —whose power has never been called into question and whose sovereignty has never been shared with subjects—then it is not the part of any subject individually, or all of them in general, to make an attempt on the honor or the life of the monarch, either by way of force or by way of law, even if he has committed all the misdeeds, impieties, and cruelties that one could mention. As to the way of law, the subject has no right of jurisdiction over his prince, on whom all power and authority to command depends; he not only can revoke all the power of his magistrates, but in his presence, all the power and jurisdiction of all magistrates, guilds and corporations, Estates and communities, cease, as we have said and will say again even more elaborately in the proper place. And if it is not permissible for a subject to pass judgment on his prince, or a vassal on his lord, or a servant on his master—in short, if it is not permissible to proceed against one's king by way of law—how could it be licit to do so by way of force? For the question here is not to discover who is the strongest, but only whether it is permissible in law, and whether a subject has the power to condemn his sovereign prince.

A subject is guilty of treason in the first degree not only for having killed a sovereign prince, but also for attempting it, advising it, wishing it, or even thinking it. And the law finds this so monstrous [as to subject it to a special rule of sentencing]. Ordinarily, if someone who is accused, seized, and convicted dies before he has been sentenced, his personal status is not diminished, no matter what his crime, even if it was treason. But treason in the highest degree can never be purged by the death of the person accused of it, and even someone who was never accused is considered in law as having been already sentenced. And although evil thoughts are not subject to punishment, anyone who has thought of making an attempt on the life of his sovereign prince is held to be guilty of a capital crime, no matter whether he repented of it. In fact there was a gentleman from Normandy who confessed to a Franciscan friar that he had wanted to kill King Francis I but had repented of this evil wish. The Franciscan gave him absolution, but still told the king about it; he had the gentleman sent before the Parlement of Paris to stand trial, where he was condemned to death by its verdict and thereupon executed. And one cannot say that the court acted from fear, in view of the fact that it often refused to verify edicts and letters patent even when the king commanded it. And in Paris a man, named Caboche, who was completely mad and out of his senses, drew a sword against King Henry II without any effect or even attempt. He too was condemned to die without consideration of his insanity, which the law ordinarily excuses no matter what murder or crime the madman may have committed.

*　　*　　*

As for Calvin's remark that if there existed in these times magistrates especially constituted for the defense of the people and to restrain the licentiousness of kings, like the ephors in Sparta, the tribunes in Rome, and the demarchs in Athens, then those magistrates should resist, oppose, and prevent their licentiousness and cruelty—it clearly shows that it is never licit, in a proper monarchy, to attack a sovereign king, or defend one's self against him, or to make an attempt upon his life or honor, for he spoke only of democratic and aristocratic states. I have shown above that the kings of Sparta were but simple senators and captains. And when he speaks of the Estates, he says "possible," not daring to be definite. In any event there is an important difference between attacking the honor of one's prince and resisting his tyranny, between killing one's king and opposing his cruelty.

We thus read that the Protestant princes of Germany, before taking up arms against the emperor, asked Martin Luther if it were permissible. He frankly replied that it was not permissible no matter how great the charge of impiety or tyranny.

But he was not heeded; and the outcome of the affair was miserable, bringing with it the ruin of some great and illustrious houses of Germany. *Quia nulla iusta causa videri potest,* said Cicero, *adversus patriam arma capiendi.*[2] Admittedly, it is quite certain that the sovereignty of the German Empire does not lie in the person of the emperor, as we shall explain in due course. But since he is the chief, they could have taken up arms against him only with the consent of the Estates or its majority, which was not obtained. It would have been even less permissible against a sovereign prince.

I can give no better parallel than that of a son with respect to his father. The law of God says that he who speaks evil of his father or his mother shall be put to death. If the father be a murderer, a thief, a traitor to his country, a person who has committed incest or parricide, a blasphemer, an atheist, and anything else one wants to add, I confess that the entire gamut of penalties will not suffice for his punishment; but I say that it is not for his son to lay hands on him, *quia nulla tanta impietas, nullum tantum factum est quod sit parricidio vindicandum,*[3] as it was put by an orator of ancient times. And yet Cicero, taking up this question, says that love of country is even greater. Hence the prince of our country, being ordained and sent by God, is always more sacred and ought to be more inviolable than a father.

I conclude then that it is never permissible for a subject to attempt anything against a sovereign prince, no matter how wicked and cruel a tyrant he may be. It is certainly permissible not to obey him in anything that is against the law of God or nature—to flee, to hide, to evade his blows, to suffer death rather than make any attempt upon his life or honor. For oh, how many tyrants there would be if it were lawful to kill them! He who taxes too heavily would be a tyrant, as the vulgar understand it; he who gives commands that the

[2]"Because there can never be a just cause to take up arms against one's country."

[3]"Because there is no impiety so great, and no crime so great that it ought to be avenged by patricide."

people do not like would be a tyrant, as Aristotle defined a tyrant in the *Politics;* he who maintains guards for his security would be a tyrant; he who punishes conspirators against his rule would be a tyrant. How then should good princes be secure in their lives? I would not say that it is illicit for other princes to proceed against tyrants by force of arms, as I have stated, but it is not for subjects.

* * *

REVIEW QUESTIONS

1. What, according to Bodin, is the definition of sovereignty?
2. In describing its prerogatives, would Bodin have agreed with Machiavelli?
3. Can sovereignty be mixed? Why?
4. Is it permissible to resist a tyrant?
5. Can a sovereign ruler be a tyrant?
6. May one resist a sovereign?

FROM "Instructions of the Magistracy of Health in Florence for Justices in the Countryside * * *"

In 1348, an epidemic of bubonic plague erupted in the city of Genoa and swept across Europe. The effects were catastrophic. Population dropped sharply, especially in crowded cities. Without the advantages of medical science or even the rudiments of public hygiene, nothing could be done to control or resist the contagion. In Florence, the number of inhabitants dropped from about 100,000 in 1348 to less than 50,000 by 1351. Population loss translated into lost production and lost consumption. Markets shrank, industries declined, and firms went bankrupt. Serious social upheavals accompanied economic decline. Antagonism and violence followed disease and deprivation. France was shaken by the peasant revolt known as the Jacquerie (1358). Recovery proved slow and sporadic. Plague recurred intermittently and remained a threat, especially to cities, until the seventeenth century, and contributed notably to the general crisis of that period. In 1630, when plague raged in Florence and the surrounding countryside once again, the administration of the Grand Duchy of Tuscany released the following "Instructions of the Health Board of Florence for the Justices of the Countryside in Case of Infectious Sicknesses that Might be Discovered in the Areas under Their Jurisdiction." These were guidelines for fighting the disease. They reflect the seriousness with which the authorities viewed

THE SURRENDER OF BREDA (1635)

DIEGO VELÁZQUEZ

One of a series of marshal portraits by Velázquez, The Surrender of Breda *records the moment in which Dutch governor Justin de Nassau symbolically surrendered the keys of the Brabantine fortress town of Breda to Ambrosio de Spinola, commander of the besieging Spanish forces. The actual capitulation took place three days earlier. Spinola had offered honorable terms in order to end twelve months of determined resistance. The depiction of peaceful amity and order between bitter foes contrasted sharply with the harsh realities of warfare in early modern Europe. What might have been Velázquez's purpose, as a painter at the court of Spain, in capturing the surrender of Breda? What might be the symbolic intent of Spinola's (figure receiving key, right center) graceful smile and the peaceful attitudes of the* tercios *(soldiers with vertical lances, extreme right)? How and why does* The Surrender of Breda *describe and distort the realities of statecraft and warfare in the seventeenth century?*

epidemic disease, as a threat to the political, social, and economic order, and the altogether insufficient measures they took against it.

From *Faith, Reason, and the Plague,* by Carlo Cipolla (Ithaca, N.Y.: Cornell University Press, 1981), pp. 87–92.

It being the task of all justices, criminal as well as civil, to watch over everything that concerns good government, they shall in particular, above all else, have an eye to good regulations regarding the interests of the Public Health, and for this purpose shall make shift to have notice of all cases of sickness believed to be infectious that should chance to occur in their jurisdictions and as soon as they come by news of any case whether of sickness or death, they shall observe the following and proceed to carry out the orders herein described against any persons whatsoever, even if they should be Florentine citizens or others in other ways privileged.

First, they shall give orders to whomever is concerned that those dead of suspected plague are not to be buried in the churches but in the countryside far from the high roads, and a hundred armslengths from the houses, and in a grave at least three armslengths deep with the benediction that will seem fit to the priests of the parish church where such deaths may be, and if there are no gravediggers, have the corpse put on a ladder and handling it as little as possible, carried to the grave, and, where possible, put on the said corpse lime and then earth.

As soon as the news arrives of the sickness being discovered in whatsoever house, the Justice shall give orders that the sick man be carried to the pesthouse, if it is near enough for him to be carried there.

Then he will have orders given to the occupants of the house where the sickness has been, if they are tenants, that they must not leave the house and the fields where they are, that they must not associate with anybody, and must not give away anything from their house or fields under pain, as transgressors, of their lives and confiscation of their goods.

If the sick of the said houses should be far from the pesthouses so that they could not with ease be carried thither, give in any case orders that none must leave home or fields, as above, being tenants.

If the said sick are subtenants or live in houses without land the order must be given to all the occupants, with the said penalty, not to leave the house.

As the said persons under orders need to be sustained with victuals, if they are tenants, give orders to the owners of the land that they supply the said victuals, giving them credit to repay at the harvests or in some other way.

If they are farmworkers, or occupants of houses without land, or poor, give order to the Chamberlain of the Council that he supply them with the necessary victuals from some innkeeper or shopkeeper nearby to the amount of eight *soldi* a day per head.

If the landlords of the said sick tenants should not live in the same jurisdiction so that the order cannot be given to them, then have the Chamberlain of the Council supply the said expenses for victuals for the said eight *soldi* a day for each one of those under orders as above.

And they shall give orders that the victuals be brought to those under orders, not in money, but in bread and eatables by the nearest innkeepers or shopkeepers or others they deem suitable, and such things should be delivered through the windows or in some other way such that whoever brings them does not approach and does not converse with the suspect cases and those under orders, and for this debt they must be reimbursed by the owners of the land who in turn shall reimburse themselves from the peasants on whom the money is being spent.

The said Justices will give order to the Health

Deputies nearest the dwelling of the suspects, or to other of their officials, who will from time to time go and inspect the affected areas and ensure that victuals are supplied them as above and that they do not leave the house and land respectively assigned to them as the place of disinfection, which they must do, proceeding against transgressors with every rigour, having them isolated and the doors of their houses nailed up; and then after the usual disinfection have them put into prison and advise the Magistrate of the Health Board of Florence and await orders from him, which will be given.

The quarantine and disinfection that are to be carried out in each house must be of twenty-two days at least from the day that the last person sick with the suspect sickness had died or recovered; after this period the said houses can be opened and freed.

It must be noted that before the houses closed or under orders are opened even where none of the occupants is left, it is very fitting and necessary that first the said houses be perfumed and purified in the following manner and with the diligence described, to wit:

First, whoever enters the house to perfume it should carry in his hand brushwood, or something like it, lighted and burning and should go upstairs with it and make fire with flames in the rooms. Then shut the windows tight and make smoke with sulphur all through the house.

Sweep the floors, benches, and walls well, and if possible, whitewash the house or, at least, wash the walls down with alkaline solution using a whitewashing brush. The woodwork should also be washed down with alkaline solution. Put the linen cloths to soak in water and wash the mattresses and put other cloths where they can get air, and keep them aired for many, many days before they are used again. And those that were used directly by the infected person are to be burnt if they be woollens or linen. The room where the dead or sick person had been must, for three days after it has come empty, be washed out with vinegar, and have it swept thoroughly every day, and the first time, scatter lime around the room and throw vinegar over it until it has smoked and burnt itself out.

And since it often chances that the sick are peasants far away from lands and castles and from the advantage of being able to have physicians and medicines, make very sure that they know of some easy medicines proposed to the Magistrates of the Health Board as being easy by their physicians, with which the occupants of the said houses under orders and the sick themselves may make their own medicines.

And they shall do their utmost to save those, above all, who are healthy in the said closed houses; and for this purpose the latter, every morning, shall take some Venice treacle, oil themselves with oil against the poison, and other like preservatives, and if they have none of these, shall take nuts, and dried figs, and rue and, early in the morning, eat them or other things that are meant for the purpose.

Every morning the sick shall take a five-ounce glass of very hot chick-pea or goat's-rue juice, and shall cover themselves well so as to sweat; they must be informed that sweating is an excellent remedy for the infectious sickness that is latent. That they strive to bring out this sweat, however, with fire or with putting cloths on or as best they can.

Oil the swellings that appear with oil of white lilies or of camomile or flax seeds and place upon them a little wool soaked in one of these oils.

If these swellings do not come out, go about to make them do so with a cupping glass or by putting on them white onion roasted on the embers and mixed with Venice treacle.

If a blister or small carbuncle be found, put upon it devil's bit or scabious grass crushed between two stones, and, to remove the scab, put a little chicken fat on it and slit with a razor and then put a little Venice treacle on it. Around the small carbuncle put pomegranate juice together with the pomegranate seeds, well peeled and crushed together.

The sick must take good care of themselves, eating meat, eggs, and good things; they must abstain from wine, and drink boiled water with the soft part of a loaf and a few coriander seeds in it.

Note must be taken of these medicines for the use of those who cannot have, as above, the services of physicians or other medicines, those, that is, like the poor peasants who live in the countryside, etc.

REVIEW QUESTIONS

1. Why should those concerned with good government pay particular attention to public health?
2. What might be the relation of civic order to health?
3. What effect do you suppose quarantining had on civic order and public health?
4. What do you learn about the understanding of disease in early modern Europe?
5. How is illness a social issue?

GIANFRANCESCO MOROSINI

FROM A Venetian Ambassador's Report on Spain

The struggle for supremacy in northern Italy, which marked the last half of the fifteenth century, gave rise to a new form of diplomacy, structures and procedures that would be fundamental to relations among all modern states. Requiring continuous contact and communication, Renaissance states turned to permanent diplomacy, distinguished by the use of accredited resident ambassadors rather than ad hoc missions of medieval legates. The tasks of a permanent ambassador were to represent his government at state ceremonies, to gather information, and, occasionally, to enter into negotiations. Nowhere was this system more fully and expertly articulated than by the Republic of Venice in the late fifteenth and sixteenth centuries. Ambassadors were chosen with unusual care from the most prominent families of the city. They were highly educated, and their duties were carefully defined.

Among the ambassadors' duties were weekly dispatches reporting all matters of any interest to Venice. These reports were regularly read and debated in the senate, which replied with questions, instructions, and information of its own. As a result, Venetian ambassadors were among the most skilled and respected in early modern Europe. Their reports remain a singularly important source for the history of that period. Gianfrancesco Morosini is, perhaps, not typical among Venetian ambassadors. He had a particularly sharp eye for social structures and details. His reports to his principals, therefore, are unusually rich in observations on the states, in this case Spain, to which he was posted. He documented the distribution of wealth in Spain, the wealth and feebleness of its aristocrats, and the poverty and incompetence of its commoners. By so doing, he offers a firsthand account of the Spanish paradox, its power and its impotence.

From *Pursuit of Power: Venetian Ambassadors' Reports on Spain, Turkey and France in the Age of Phillip II, 1560–1600*, by James C. Davis (New York: HarperCollins, 1970), pp. 72–76, 78–79.

Most of the men in this country are small in stature and dark in complexion, haughty if they belong to the upper classes or prudently humble if they are common people, and unsuited for any kind of work. As farmers they are the most lackadaisical in the world, and as artisans they are so lazy and slow that work that would be done anywhere else in one month in Spain requires four. They are such stupid craftsmen that in all their provinces you can hardly find a building or anything else of interest except for antiquities done in Roman times or works built by the Moorish kings. Most of the Spanish live in houses so ineptly built of inferior materials that it is remarkable if one lasts as long as the man who built it. The cities are badly run and dirty; they throw all their refuse into the public streets instead of having the conveniences in their houses which are used in Italy and other parts of the world. They give no thought to food supplies; as a result the common people often have to fight each other to get bread, not so much because there is a shortage of grain as because there is no official whose job it is to make sure that there is bread. ✶ ✶ ✶

✶   ✶   ✶

Spain might be quick to rebel if there were a leader courageous enough to direct a revolt. All of the people are discontented with their king and his current ministers. The nobles are dissatisfied because they are virtually ignored, and everyone else because they pay such unbearably heavy taxes; no other people in the world carry such a tax burden as the Castilians. True, the Aragonese and Castilians have ended their quarrels and there have been no more of those rebellions of the cities against the kings which happened in the reign of the emperor Charles V, and earlier during the reign of King Ferdinand. But when the king dies —or if he should get into serious problems— these and even more unpleasant humors might recur in the body politic. There would be a special danger if the rebels used religion as a battle standard, since religious faith lends itself very well to subverting and destroying monarchies. Spain would be particularly susceptible because there are so many there who are Moors at heart, many others who secretly remain Jews, and even some heretics. They are all very cautious because they fear the Inquisition, a high tribunal so powerful and harsh that everyone is terrified of it. Without the Inquisition Spain would be more lost than Germany and England, even though the Spanish look at first glance like the most devout Catholics in the world.

Most Spaniards are either very rich or very poor, and there would seem to be a cause-and-effect relationship between the wealth of some and the poverty of the rest. It is as if four men had to divide this chamber among them. If one man took three-quarters there would be very little to divide among the other three. The Spanish clergy is very rich; the church in Toledo alone has revenues of 400,000 ducats a year, and all the other fifty-seven bishoprics are also very wealthy. The incomes of the churches have been estimated at four million in gold per year. Then there are twenty-two dukes, forty-seven counts, and thirty-six marquises in those lands, and their incomes total nearly three million in gold a year. The richest of all is said to be the duke of Medina Sidonia, the governor-elect of Milan, whose income exceeds 150,000 ducats a year.

*   *   *

Because the king does not use them in his service, very few of the grandees know anything about running a government, nor do they know anything else. They consider it beneath them to leave their estates unless to take major government positions; on the other hand, they are not suited for life on their own estates. They do not read; they do not discuss anything of value; they simply live in ignorance. The only noteworthy thing about them is a certain loftiness and dignity which in Italy we call "Spanish composure" and which makes all foreigners hate them. They let it be understood that not only is there no other people which bears comparison with them, but that everyone should be grateful to be ruled by them. And they do not forget to use this haughtiness even among themselves. Before addressing a person as "*Señor,*" "*Vuestra Merced,*" "you," . . . or "*el,*" they give the matter a great deal of thought, because they believe that any distinction they confer on someone else reduces their own importance.

Because they remain on their own lands they have seen and they know nothing about the world. Their lack of schooling makes them ignorant and their lack of contacts with others makes them arrogant. This arrogance is very common among the young people, especially those who are surrounded by great wealth. Revered and deferred to by their own domestic servants, they soon come to believe that everyone should behave that way toward them, and that no one is so important as they. The result is that they look down on others —indeed, they often despise them—and only late or never do they realize their error, when they have been damaged and shamed.

The Spanish grandees consider attending to business matters just as ridiculous as book reading; both pursuits are detestable, or at least completely at odds with the life of a knight. And yet they do not take much pleasure in horsemanship. Instead they pass the time idly, even depravedly. The reasons for this are that they have been poorly brought up and they believe that exercise in Spain is "unhealthy," and also that the king lives in great seclusion and has no interest in watching tournaments.

*   *   *

The nobles and other aristocrats are all tax exempt; they pay the king no head or property tax at all. Their only obligation is to serve in his army at their own expense, and even then only when it is a question of defending Spain from attack. They are very firm and determined about guarding their tax immunity, just as the Aragonese defend all of their liberties. Once when the government tried to impose a very light tax on them they raised such an uproar that the matter was dropped.

The nobles and grandees of Castile have so little legal authority in their own jurisdictions that most of them have courts only of the first instance; and few of their courts may hear appeals. All appeals eventually go to the chancelleries and the royal council. Their own vassals can have them summoned to these higher courts on the slightest of grounds, and they are often treated worse there than the lowliest subjects. This happens both because such is the king's wish and because the judges usually come from the lower classes. The reason for this is that judges have to be university graduates; since the nobles consider it beneath them to study anything, the power of the courts goes by default into the hands of plebeians. Professional learning is the only route by which men from the lower classes can rise to important posts. This explains why not only the law courts but almost all of the bishoprics are also in the hands of commoners, who are enemies of the nobility. This in turn is another of the grudges the upper classes have against the present regime. At one time most of the bishoprics were given as a matter of course to younger sons of the grandees, as a way of compensating them for not being the heirs. Despite all I have said, however, the king still has ample means to gratify the nobles, since he has many knighthoods in the military orders to distribute, all of which may be conferred only on nobles.

Some of these have incomes of up to twelve thousand ducats.

*   *   *

REVIEW QUESTIONS

1. What were the sources of Spain's declining power according to Morosini?

2. How does Morosini depict the nobility?
3. What are their values?
4. What does Morosini suggest is significantly undervalued by the Spanish nobility? Why?
5. What do we learn about the distribution of authority in Spain?
6. How are political decisions made?

REGINALD SCOT

FROM *Discoverie of Witchcraft*

Reginald Scot (1538–1599) was a Kentish squire who witnessed a number of fraudulent accusations of witchcraft in the villages of his shire during the reign of Elizabeth I. In 1584 he wrote his Discoverie of Witchcraft, *which contains a remarkable exposition of magical elements in medieval Catholicism and a protest against the persecution of harmless old women. Scot doubted that God could ever have allowed witches to exercise supernatural powers, much less demand that they be persecuted for it. In this regard, he deserves to be ranked among the skeptics on the question of witchcraft, although he never denied the existence of witches. According to Scot, all "witches" fell into one of four categories. First were the innocent, those falsely accused. Second were the deluded, those convinced through their own misery that they were witches. Third were the malefactors, those who harmed people and damaged property, though not by supernatural means. Fourth were imposters, those who posed as witches and conjurers. Scot denied that any of these "witches" had access to supernatural powers. Malefactors and imposters were, in fact, the witches named in the Bible as not being suffered to live. They were the only witches Scot admitted. His work is said to have made a great impression in the magistracy and clergy of his day. Nonetheless, his remained a minority opinion. Most contemporaries understood as tantamount to atheism any denial of the reality of spirits or the possibility of the supernatural. The persecution of witches continued unabated into the eighteenth century; many thousands, mostly harmless old women, fell victim to the rage.*

From *Discoverie of Witchcraft, 1584*, edited by Hugh Ross Wilkinson (Carbondale: Southern Illinois Press, 1962).

*   *   *

The inconvenience growing by mens credulitie herein, with a reproofe of some churchmen, which are inclined to the common conceived opinion of witches omnipotencie, and a familiar example thereof. But the world is now so bewitched and over-run with this fond error, that even where a man shuld seeke comfort and counsell, there shall hee be sent (in case of necessitie) from God to the divell; and from the Physician, to the coosening witch, who will not sticke to take upon hir, by wordes to heale the lame (which was proper onelie to Christ: and to them whom he assisted with his divine power) yea, with hir familiar & charmes she will take upon hir to cure the blind: though in the tenth of S. *Johns* Gospell it be written, that the divell cannot open the eies of the blind. And they attaine such credit as I have heard (to my greefe) some of the ministerie affirme, that they have had in their parish at one instant, xvii. or xviii. witches: meaning such as could worke miracles supernaturallie. Whereby they manifested as well their infidelitie and ignorance, in conceiving Gods word; as their negligence and error in instructing their flocks. For they themselves might understand, and also teach their parishoners, that God onelie worketh great woonders; and that it is he which sendeth such punishments to the wicked, and such trials to the elect: according to the saieng of the Prophet *Haggai*, I smote you with blasting and mildeaw, and with haile, in all the labours of your hands; and yet you turned not unto me, saith the Lord. And therefore saith the same Prophet in another place; You have sowen much, and bring in little. And both in *Joel* and *Leviticus,* the like phrases and proofes are used and made. But more shalbe said of this hereafter.

*   *   *

At the assises holden at *Rochester,* Anno 1581, one *Margaret Simons,* the wife of *John Simons,* of *Brenchlie* in *Kent,* was araigned for witchcraft, at the instigation and complaint of divers fond and malicious persons; and speciallie by the meanes of one *John Ferrall* vicar of that parish: with whom I talked about that matter, and found him both fondlie assotted in the cause, and enviouslie bent towards hir: and (which is worse) as unable to make a good account of his faith, as shee whom he accused. That which he, for his part, laid to the poore womans charge, was this.

His sonne (being an ungratious boie, and prentise to one *Robert Scotchford* clothier, dwelling in that parish of *Brenchlie*) passed on a daie by hir house; at whome by chance hir little dog barked. Which thing the boie taking in evill part, drewe his knife, & pursued him therewith even to hir doore: whom she rebuked with some such words as the boie disdained, & yet neverthelesse would not be persuaded to depart in a long time. At the last he returned to his maisters house, and within five or sixe daies fell sicke. Then was called to mind the fraie betwixt the dog and the boie: insomuch as the vicar (who thought himselfe so privileged, as he little mistrusted that God would visit his children with sicknes) did so calculate; as he found, partlie through his owne judgement, and partlie (as he himselfe told me) by the relation of other witches, that his said sonne was by hir bewitched. Yea, he also told me, that this his sonne (being as it were past all cure) received perfect health at the hands of another witch.

He proceeded yet further against hir, affirming, that alwaies in his parish church, when he desired to read most plainelie, his voice so failed him, as he could scant be heard at all. Which hee could impute, he said, to nothing else, but to hir inchantment. When I advertised the poore woman hereof, as being desirous to heare what she could saie for hir selfe; she told me, that in verie deed his voice did much faile him, speciallie when he strained himselfe to speake lowdest. How beit, she said that at all times his voice was hoarse and lowe: which thing I perceived to be true. But sir, said she, you shall understand, that this our vicar is diseased with such a kind of hoarsenesse, as divers of our neighbors in this parish, not long since, doubted that he had the French pox; & in that respect utterly refused to communicate with him: untill such time as (being therunto injoined by M. D. *Lewen* the Ordinarie) he had brought frō

London a certificat, under the hands of two physicians, that his hoarsenes proceeded from a disease in the lungs. Which certificat he published in the church, in the presence of the whole congregation: and by this meanes hee was cured, or rather excused of the shame of his disease. And this I knowe to be true by the relation of divers honest men of that parish. And truelie, if one of the Jurie had not beene wiser than the other, she had beene condemned thereupon, and upon other as ridiculous matters as this. For the name of a witch is so odious, and hir power so feared among the common people, that if the honestest bodie living chance to be arraigned thereupon, she shall hardlie escape condemnation.

A Confutation of the Common Conceived Opinion of Witches and Witchcraft, and How Detestable a Sinne It Is to Repaire to Them for Counsell or Helpe in Time of Affliction

But whatsoever is reported or conceived of such manner of witchcrafts, I dare avow to be false and fabulous (coosinage, dotage, and poisoning excepted:) neither is there any mention made of these kind of witches in the Bible. If Christ had knowne them, he would not have pretermitted to invaie against their presumption, in taking upon them his office: as, to heale and cure diseases; and to worke such miraculous and supernaturall things, as whereby he himselfe was speciallie knowne, beleeved, and published to be God; his actions and cures consisting (in order and effect) according to the power of our witchmongers imputed to witches. Howbeit, if there be any in these daies afflicted in such strange sort, as Christs cures and patients are described in the new testament to have beene: we flie from trusting in God to trusting in witches, who doo not onelie in their coosening art take on them the office of Christ in this behalfe; but use his verie phrase of speech to such idolators, as com to seeke divine assistance at their hands, saieng; Go thy waies, thy sonne or thy daughter, &c. shall doo well, and be whole.

*   *   *

In like manner I say, he that attributeth to a witch, such divine power, as dulie and onelie apperteineth unto GOD (which all witchmongers doo) is in hart a blasphemer, an idolater, and full of grosse impietie, although he neither go nor send to hir for assistance.

A Further Confutation of Witches Miraculous and Omnipotent Power, by Invincible Reasons and Authorities, with Dissuasions from Such Fond Credulitie

If witches could doo anie such miraculous things, as these and other which are imputed to them, they might doo them againe and againe, at anie time or place, or at anie mans desire: for the divell is as strong at one time as at another, as busie by daie as by night, and readie enough to doo all mischeefe, and careth not whom he abuseth. And in so much as it is confessed, by the most part of witchmongers themselves, that he knoweth not the cogitation of mans heart, he should (me thinks) sometimes appeere unto honest and credible persons, in such grosse and corporall forme, as it is said he dooth unto witches: which you shall never heare to be justified by one sufficient witnesse. For the divell indeed entreth into the mind, and that waie seeketh mans confusion.

The art alwaies presupposeth the power; so as, if they saie they can doo this or that, they must shew how and by what meanes they doo it; as neither the witches, nor the witchmongers are able to doo. For to everie action is required the facultie and abilitie of the agent or dooer; the aptnes of the patient or subject; and a convenient and possible application. Now the witches are mortall, and their power dependeth upon the analogie and consonancie of their minds and bodies; but with their minds they can but will and understand; and with their bodies they can doo no more, but as the bounds and ends of terrene sense will suffer: and therefore their power extendeth not to doo such miracles, as surmounteth their owne sense, and the understanding of others which are wiser than they; so as here wanteth the vertue and power of the efficient. And in reason, there can be no more vertue in the thing caused, than in the cause, or that which proceedeth of or from the benefit of the cause. And we see, that ignorant and impotent women, or witches, are the causes of incantations and charmes; wherein we shall perceive there is none effect, if we will credit our owne experience and sense unabused, the rules of philosophie, or the word of God. For alas! What an unapt instrument is a toothles, old, impotent, and unweldie woman to flie in the aier? Truelie, the divell little needs such instruments to bring his purposes to passe.

It is strange, that we should suppose, that such persons can worke such feates: and it is more strange, that we will imagine that to be possible to be doone by a witch, which to nature and sense is impossible; speciallie when our neighbours life dependeth upon our credulitie therein; and when we may see the defect of abilitie, which alwaies is an impediment both to the act, and also to the presumption thereof. And bicause there is nothing possible in lawe, that in nature is impossible; therefore the judge dooth not attend or regard what the accused man saith; or yet would doo: but what is prooved to have beene committed, and naturallie falleth in mans power and will to doo. For the lawe saith, that To will a thing unpossible, is a signe of a mad man, or of a foole, upon whom no sentence or judgement taketh hold. Furthermore, what Jurie will condemne, or what Judge will give sentence or judgement against one for killing a man at *Berwicke;* when they themselves, and manie other sawe that man at *London,* that verie daie, wherein the murther was committed; yea though the partie confesse himself guiltie therein, and twentie witnesses depose the same? But in this case also I saie the judge is not to weigh their testimonie, which is weakened by lawe; and the judges authoritie is to supplie the imperfection of the case, and to mainteine the right and equitie of the same.

Seeing therefore that some other things might naturallie be the occasion and cause of such calamities as witches are supposed to bring; let not us that professe the Gospell and knowledge of Christ, be bewitched to beleeve that they doo such things, as are in nature impossible, and in sense and reason incredible. If they saie it is doone through the divels helpe, who can work miracles; whie doo not theeves bring their busines to passe miraculouslie, with whom the divell is as conversant as with the other? Such mischeefes as are imputed to witches, happen where no witches are; yea and continue when witches are hanged and burnt: whie then should we attribute such effect to that cause, which being taken awaie, happeneth neverthelesse?

*   *   *

What Testimonies and Witnesses Are Allowed to Give Evidence against Reputed Witches, by the Report and Allowance of the Inquisitors Themselves, and Such as Are Speciall Writers Heerein

Excommunicat persons, partakers of the falt, infants, wicked servants, and runnawaies are to be admitted to beare witnesse against their dames in this mater of witchcraft: bicause (saith *Bodin* the champion of witchmoongers) none that be honest are able to detect them. Heretikes also and witches shall be received to accuse, but not to excuse a witch. And finallie, the testimonie of all infamous persons in this case is good and allowed. Yea, one lewd person (saith *Bodin*) may be received to accuse and condemne a thousand suspected witches. And although by lawe, a capitall enimie may be challenged; yet *James Sprenger,* and *Henrie Institor,* (from whom *Bodin,* and all the writers that ever I have read, doo receive their light, authorities and arguments) saie (upon this point of lawe) that The poore frendlesse old woman must proove, that hir capitall enimie would have killed hir, and that hee hath both assalted & wounded hir; otherwise she pleadeth all in vaine. If the judge aske hir, whether she have anie capitall enimies; and she rehearse other, and forget hir accuser; or else answer that he was hir capital enimie, but now she hopeth he is not so: such a one is nevertheles admitted for a witnes. And though by lawe, single witnesses are not admittable; yet if one depose she hath bewitched hir cow; another, hir sow; and the third, hir butter: these saith (saith *M. Mal.* and *Bodin*) are no single witnesses; bicause they agree that she is a witch.

The Fifteene Crimes Laid to the Charge of Witches, by Witchmongers, Speciallie by Bodin, in Dæmonomania

They denie God, and all religion.

Answere. Then let them die therefore, or at the least be used like infidels, or apostataes.

They cursse, blaspheme, and provoke God with all despite.

Answere. Then let them have the law expressed in *Levit.* 24. and *Deut.* 13 & 17.

They give their faith to the divell, and they worship and offer sacrifice unto him.

Ans. Let such also be judged by the same lawe.

They doo solemnelie vow and promise all their progenie unto the divell.

Ans. This promise proceedeth from an unsound mind, and is not to be regarded; bicause they cannot performe it, neither will it be prooved true. Howbeit, if it be done by anie that is sound of mind, let the cursse of *Jeremie,* 32.36. light upon them, to wit, the sword, famine and pestilence.

They sacrifice their owne children to the divell before baptisme, holding them up in the aire unto him, and then thrust a needle into their braines.

Ans. If this be true, I maintaine them not herein: but there is a lawe to judge them by. Howbeit, it is so contrarie to sense and nature, that it were follie to beleeve it; either upon *Bodins* bare word, or else upon his presumptions; speciallie when so small commoditie and so great danger

and inconvenience insueth to the witches thereby.

They burne their children when they have sacrificed them.

Ans. Then let them have such punishment, as they that offered their children unto *Moloch: Levit.* 20. But these be meere devises of witchmoongers and inquisitors, that with extreame tortures have wroong such confessions from them; or else with false reports have beelied them; or by flatterie & faire words and promises have woon it at their hands, at the length.

They sweare to the divell to bring as manie into that societie as they can.

Ans. This is false, and so prooved elsewhere.

They sweare by the name of the divell.

Ans. I never heard anie such oth, neither have we warrant to kill them that so doo sweare; though indeed it be verie lewd and impious.

They use incestuous adulterie with spirits.

Ans. This is a stale ridiculous lie, as is prooved apparentlie hereafter.

They boile infants (after they have murthered them unbaptised) untill their flesh be made potable.

Ans. This is untrue, incredible, and impossible.

They eate the flesh and drinke the bloud of men and children openlie.

Ans. Then are they kin to the *Anthropophagi* and *Canibals.* But I beleeve never an honest man in *England* nor in *France,* will affirme that he hath seene any of these persons, that are said to be witches, do so; if they shuld, I beleeve it would poison them.

They kill men with poison.

Ans. Let them be hanged for their labour.

They kill mens cattell.

Ans. Then let an action of trespasse be brought against them for so dooing.

They bewitch mens corne, and bring hunger and barrennes into the countrie; they ride and flie in the aire, bring stormes, make tempests, &c.

Ans. Then will I worship them as gods; for those be not the works of man nor yet of witch: as I have elsewhere prooved at large.

They use venerie with a divell called *Iucubus,*

even when they lie in bed with their husbands, and have children by them, which become the best witches.

Ans. This is the last lie, verie ridiculous, and confuted by me elsewhere.

Of Foure Capitall Crimes Objected against Witches, All Fullie Answered and Confuted as Frivolous

First therefore they laie to their charge idolatrie. But alas without all reason: for such are properlie knowne to us to be idolaters, as doo externall worship to idols or strange gods. The furthest point that idolatrie can be stretched unto, is, that they, which are culpable therein, are such as hope for and seeke salvation at the hands of idols, or of anie other than God; or fixe their whole mind and love upon anie creature, so as the power of God be neglected and contemned thereby. But witches neither seeke nor beleeve to have salvation at the hands of divels, but by them they are onlie deceived; the instruments of their phantasie being corrupted, and so infatuated, that they suppose, confesse, and saie they can doo that, which is as farre beyond their power and nature to doo, as to kill a man at *Yorke* before noone, when they have beene seene at *London* in that morning, &c. But if these latter idolaters, whose idolatrie is spirituall, and committed onelie in mind, should be punished by death; then should everie covetous man, or other, that setteth his affection anie waie too much upon an earthlie creature, be executed, and yet perchance the witch might escape scotfree.

Secondlie, apostasie is laid to their charge, whereby it is inferred, that they are worthie to die. But apostasie is, where anie of sound judgement forsake the gospell, learned and well knowne unto them; and doo not onelie embrace impietie and infidelitie; but oppugne and resist the truth erstwhile by them professed. But alas these poore women go not about to defend anie impietie, but after good admonition repent.

Thirdlie, they would have them executed for seducing the people. But God knoweth they have small store of Rhetorike or art to seduce; except to tell a tale of Robin good-fellow be to deceive and seduce. Neither may their age or sex admit that opinion or accusation to be just: for they themselves are poore seduced soules. I for my part (as else-where I have said) have prooved this point to be false in most apparent sort.

Fourthlie, as touching the accusation, which all the writers use herein against them for their carnall copulation with *Incubus:* the follie of mens credulitie is as much to be woondered at and derided, as the others vaine and impossible confessions. For the divell is a spirit, and hath neither flesh nor bones, which were to be used in the performance of this action. And since he also lacketh all instruments, substance, and seed ingendred of bloud; it were follie to staie overlong in the confutation of that, which is not in the nature of things. And yet must I saie somewhat heerein, bicause the opinion hereof is so stronglie and universallie received, and the fables thereupon so innumerable; wherby *M. Mal. Bodin, Hemingius, Hyperius, Danaeus, Erastus,* and others that take upon them to write heerein, are so abused, or rather seeke to abuse others; as I woonder at their fond credulitie in this behalfe. For they affirme undoubtedlie, that the divell plaieth *Succubus* to the man, and carrieth from him the seed of generation, which he delivereth as *Incubus* to the woman, who manie times that waie is gotten with child; which will verie naturallie (they saie) become a witch, and such one they affirme *Merline* was.

*   *   *

By What Meanes the Common People Have Beene Made Beleeve in the Miraculous Works of Witches, a Definition of Witchcraft, and a Description Thereof

The common people have beene so assotted and bewitched, with whatsoever poets have feigned of witchcraft, either in earnest, in jest, or else in derision; and with whatsoever lowd liers and couseners for their pleasures heerein have invented, and with whatsoever tales they have heard from old doting women, or from their mothers maids, and with whatsoever the grandfoole their ghostlie father, or anie other morrow masse preest had informed them; and finallie with whatsoever they have swallowed up through tract of time, or through their owne timerous nature or ignorant conceipt, concerning these matters of hagges and witches: as they have so settled their opinion and credit thereupon, that they thinke it heresie to doubt in anie part of the matter; speciallie bicause they find this word witchcraft expressed in the scriptures; which is as to defend praieng to saincts, bicause *Sanctus, Sanctus, Sanctus* is written in *Te Deum*.

And now to come to the definition of witchcraft, which hitherto I did deferre and put off purposelie: that you might perceive the true nature thereof, by the circumstances, and therefore the rather to allow of the same, seeing the varietie of other writers. Witchcraft is in truth a cousening art, wherin the name of God is abused, prophaned and blasphemed, and his power attributed to a vile creature. In estimation of the vulgar people, it is a supernaturall worke, contrived betweene a corporall old woman, and a spirituall divell. The maner thereof is so secret, mysticall, and strange, that to this daie there hath never beene any credible witnes thereof. It is incomprehensible to the wise, learned or faithfull; a probable matter to children, fooles, melancholike persons and papists. The trade is thought to be impious. The effect and end thereof to be sometimes evill, as when thereby man or beast, grasse, trees, or corne, &c; is hurt: sometimes good, as whereby sicke folkes are healed, theeves bewraied, and true men come to their goods, &c. The matter and instruments, wherewith it is accomplished, are words, charmes, signes, images, characters, &c; the which words although any other creature do pronounce, in manner and forme as they doo, leaving out no circumstance requisite or usually for that action: yet none is said to have the grace or gift to performe the matter, except she

be a witch, and so taken either by hir owne consent, or by others imputation.

Reasons to Proove That Words and Characters Are But Bables, and That Witches Cannot Doo Such Things as the Multitude Supposeth They Can, Their Greatest Woonders Prooved Trifles, of a Yoong Gentleman Cousened

That words, characters, images, and such other trinkets, which are thought so necessarie instruments for witchcraft (as without the which no such thing can be accomplished) are but bables, devised by couseners, to abuse the people withall; I trust I have sufficientlie prooved. And the same maie be further and more plainelie perceived by these short and compendious reasons following.

First, in that *Turkes* and infidels, in their witchcraft, use both other words, and other characters than our witches doo and also such as are most contrarie. In so much as, if ours be bad, in reason theirs should be good. If their witches can doo anie thing, ours can doo nothing. For as our witches are said to renounce Christ, and despise his sacraments: so doo the other forsake *Mahomet*, and his lawes, which is one large step to christianitie.

It is also to be thought, that all witches are couseners; when mother *Bungie*, a principall witch, so reputed, tried, and condemned of all men, and continuing in that exercise and estimation manie yeares (having cousened & abused the whole realme, in so much as there came to hir, witchmongers from all the furthest parts of the land, she being in diverse bookes set out with authoritie, registred and chronicled by the name of the great witch of *Rochester*, and reputed among all men for the cheefe ringleader of all other witches) by good proofe is found to be a meere cousener; confessing in hir death bed freelie, without compulsion or inforcement, that hir cunning consisted onlie in deluding and deceiving the people: saying that she had (towards the maintenance of hir credit in that cousening trade) some sight in physicke and surgerie, and the assistance of a freend of hirs, called *Heron,* a professor thereof. And this I know, partlie of mine owne knowledge, and partlie by the testimonie of hir husband, and others of credit, to whome (I saie) in hir death bed, and at sundrie other times she protested these things; and also that she never had indeed anie materiall spirit or divell (as the voice went) nor yet knew how to worke anie supernaturall matter, as she in hir life time made men beleeve she had and could doo.

*   *   *

Againe, who will mainteine, that common witchcrafts are not cousenages, when the great and famous witchcrafts, which had stolne credit not onlie from all the common people, but from men of great wisdome and authoritie, are discovered to be beggerlie slights of cousening varlots? Which otherwise might and would have remained a perpetuall objection against me. Were there not three images of late yeeres found in a doonghill, to the terror & astonishment of manie thousands? In so much as great matters were thought to have beene pretended to be doone by witchcraft. But if the Lord preserve those persons (whose destruction was doubted to have beene intended thereby) from all other the lewd practises and attempts of their enimies; I feare not, but they shall easilie withstand these and such like devises, although

they should indeed be practised against them. But no doubt, if such bables could have brought those matters of mischeefe to passe, by the hands of traitors, witches, or papists; we should long since have beene deprived of the most excellent jewell and comfort that we enjoy in this world. Howbeit, I confesse, that the feare, conceipt, and doubt of such mischeefous pretenses may breed inconvenience to them that stand in awe of the same. And I wish, that even for such practises, though they never can or doo take effect, the practisers be punished with all extremitie: bicause therein is manifested a traiterous heart to the Queene, and a presumption against God.

*   *   *

REVIEW QUESTIONS

1. What is witchcraft?
2. How does Scot depict it?
3. According to Scot, what characterizes witches and witchcraft?
4. How does Scot confound the very notion of witchcraft?
5. Where does he locate the source of all power to override the laws of nature?
6. What sort of power is left to witches?
7. What, according to Scot, is the relation of witches to the natural world?

BLAISE PASCAL

FROM *Pensées*

Blaise Pascal (1623–1662) was born the son of a French official. During his life, he dabbled in many subjects, including science, religion, and literature. His conversion to Jansenism plunged him into controversy with the Jesuits, giving rise to his Lettres provinciales. *These, along with his* Pensées, *from which the current selection is drawn, established his literary fame. His thought contains a fascinating blend of confidence in human reason and consciousness of its limits. René Descartes viewed Pascal as the embodiment of a mentality of intellectual and spiritual crisis. Be that as it may, Pascal is also considered one of the great stylists of the French language.*

From *Pensées*, by Blaise Pascal, translated by A. J. Krailsheimer (New York: Penguin Books, 1995), pp. 58–64, 121–25.

The Wager

*　　*　　*

Infinity—nothing. Our soul is cast into the body where it finds number, time, dimensions; it reasons about these things and calls them natural, or necessary, and can believe nothing else.

Unity added to infinity does not increase it at all, any more than a foot added to an infinite measurement: the finite is annihilated in the presence of the infinite and becomes pure nothingness. So it is with our mind before God, with our justice before divine justice. There is not so great a disproportion between our justice and God's as between unity and infinity.

God's justice must be as vast as his mercy. Now his justice towards the damned is less vast and ought to be less startling to us than his mercy towards the elect.

We know that the infinite exists without knowing its nature, just as we know that it is untrue that numbers are finite. Thus it is true that there is an infinite number, but we do not know what it is. It is untrue that it is even, untrue that it is odd, for by adding a unit it does not change its nature. Yet it is a number, and every number is even or odd. (It is true that this applies to every finite number.)

Therefore we may well know that God exists without knowing what he is.

Is there no substantial truth, seeing that there are so many true things which are not truth itself?

Thus we know the existence and nature of the finite because we too are finite and extended in space.

We know the existence of the infinite without

knowing its nature, because it too has extension but unlike us no limits.

But we do not know either the existence or the nature of God, because he has neither extension nor limits.

But by faith we know his existence, through glory we shall know his nature.

Now I have already proved that it is quite possible to know that something exists without knowing its nature.

Let us now speak according to our natural lights.

If there is a God, he is infinitely beyond our comprehension, since, being indivisible and without limits, he bears no relation to us. We are therefore incapable of knowing either what he is or whether he is. That being so, who would dare to attempt an answer to the question? Certainly not we, who bear no relation to him.

Who then will condemn Christians for being unable to give rational grounds for their belief, professing as they do a religion for which they cannot give rational grounds? They declare that it is a folly, *stultitiam,* in expounding it to the world, and then you complain that they do not prove it. If they did prove it they would not be keeping their word. It is by being without proof that they show they are not without sense. "Yes, but although that excuses those who offer their religion as such, and absolves them from the criticism of producing it without rational grounds, it does not absolve those who accept it." Let us then examine this point, and let us say: "Either God is or he is not." But to which view shall we be inclined? Reason cannot decide this question. Infinite chaos separates us. At the far end of this infinite distance a coin is being spun which will come down heads or tails. How will you wager? Reason cannot make you choose either, reason cannot prove either wrong.

Do not then condemn as wrong those who have made a choice, for you know nothing about it. "No, but I will condemn them not for having made this particular choice, but any choice, for, although the one who calls heads and the other one are equally at fault, the fact is that they are both at fault: the right thing is not to wager at all."

Yes, but you must wager. There is no choice, you are already committed. Which will you choose then? Let us see: since a choice must be made, let us see which offers you the least interest. You have two things to lose: the true and the good; and two things to stake: your reason and your will, your knowledge and your happiness; and your nature has two things to avoid: error and wretchedness. Since you must necessarily choose, your reason is no more affronted by choosing one rather than the other. That is one point cleared up. But your happiness? Let us weigh up the gain and the loss involved in calling heads that God exists. Let us assess the two cases: if you win you win everything, if you lose you lose nothing. Do not hesitate then; wager that he does exist. "That is wonderful. Yes, I must wager, but perhaps I am wagering too much." Let us see: since there is an equal chance of gain and loss, if you stood to win only two lives for one you could still wager, but supposing you stood to win three?

You would have to play (since you must necessarily play) and it would be unwise of you, once you are obliged to play, not to risk your life in order to win three lives at a game in which there is an equal chance of losing and winning. But there is an eternity of life and happiness. That being so, even though there were an infinite number of chances, of which only one were in your favour, you would still be right to wager one in order to win two; and you would be acting wrongly, being obliged to play, in refusing to stake one life against three in a game, where out of an infinite number of chances there is one in your favour, if there were an infinity of infinitely happy life to be won.

But here there is an infinity of infinitely happy life to be won, one chance of winning against a finite number of chances of losing, and what you are staking is finite. That leaves no choice; wherever there is infinity, and where there are not infinite chances of losing against that of winning, there is no room for hesitation, you must give everything. And thus, since you are obliged to play, you must be renouncing reason if you hoard your life rather than risk it for an infinite gain, just as likely to occur as a loss amounting to nothing.

For it is no good saying that it is uncertain whether you will win, that it is certain that you are taking a risk, and that the infinite distance between the certainty of what you are risking and the uncertainty of what you may gain makes the finite good you are certainly risking equal to the infinite good that you are not certain to gain. This is not the case. Every gambler takes a certain risk for an uncertain gain, and yet he is taking a certain finite risk for an uncertain finite gain without sinning against reason. Here there is no infinite distance between the certain risk and the uncertain gain: that is not true. There is, indeed, an infinite distance between the certainty of winning and the certainty of losing, but the proportion between the uncertainty of winning and the certainty of what is being risked is in proportion to the chances of winning or losing. And hence if there are as many chances on one side as on the other you are playing for even odds. And in that case the certainty of what you are risking is equal to the uncertainty of what you may win; it is by no means infinitely distant from it. Thus our argument carries infinite weight, when the stakes are finite in a game where there are even chances of winning and losing and an infinite prize to be won.

This is conclusive and if men are capable of any truth this is it.

"I confess, I admit it, but is there really no way of seeing what the cards are?"—"Yes. Scripture and the rest, etc."—"Yes, but my hands are tied and my lips are sealed; I am being forced to wager and I am not free; I am being held fast and I am so made that I cannot believe. What do you want me to do then?"—"That is true, but at least get it into your head that, if you are unable to believe, it is because of your passions, since reason impels you to believe and yet you cannot do so. Concentrate then not on convincing yourself by multiplying proofs of God's existence but by diminishing your passions. You want to find faith and you do not know the road. You want to be cured of unbelief and you ask for the remedy: learn from those who were once bound like you and who now wager all they have. These are people who know the road you wish to follow, who have been cured of the affliction of which you wish to be cured: follow the way by which they began. They behaved just as if they did believe, taking holy water, having masses said, and so on. That will make you believe quite naturally, and will make you more docile."—"But that is what I am afraid of."—"But why? What have you to lose? But to show you that this is the way, the fact is that this diminishes the passions which are your great obstacles. . . ."

End of this address.

"Now what harm will come to you from choosing this course? You will be faithful, honest, humble, grateful, full of good works, a sincere, true friend. . . . It is true you will not enjoy noxious pleasures, glory and good living, but will you not have others?

"I tell you that you will gain even in this life, and that at every step you take along this road you will see that your gain is so certain and your risk so negligible that in the end you will realize that you have wagered on something certain and infinite for which you have paid nothing."

"How these words fill me with rapture and delight!—"

"If my words please you and seem cogent, you must know that they come from a man who went down upon his knees before and after to pray this infinite and indivisible being, to whom he submits his own, that he might bring your being also to submit to him for your own good and for his glory: and that strength might thus be reconciled with lowliness."

*   *   *

REVIEW QUESTIONS

1. How does Pascal conceive of the human condition?
2. What does it mean for him to have a body?
3. How does he differ in this respect from Montaigne?
4. How does Pascal construct his proof for the existence of God?
5. Why does he begin with infinity, a mathematical concept?
6. What is he saying about the limits of human knowledge?
7. For whom might this essay have been written?
8. Why must we wager?

JOHN DONNE

FROM "The First Anniversarie"

John Donne (1572–1631) was esteemed by his contemporary Ben Jonson as "the first poet in the world in some things." He was born in London, the son of a prosperous merchant. His father died while Donne was still an infant, and he was raised by his mother, the daughter of the playwright John Heywood and grand-

daughter of Sir Thomas More's sister. His family was devoutly Roman Catholic. Donne matriculated at Hart Hall, Oxford, in 1584 but left without a degree because it was impossible for Catholics to take the oath of supremacy required at graduation. He entered Thavies Inn, London, as a law student in 1591 and transferred to Lincoln's Inn in 1592. At this point he began to write poetry. In 1596, he joined the earl of Essex's Cadiz expedition and on his return became secretary to Sir Thomas Egerton, the lord keeper of the Great Seal of England. Donne abjured his Catholic faith to join the Church of England and was about to embark on a diplomatic career when he secretly married Ann More, the niece of his employer's wife. He was imprisoned for marrying a minor without her guardian's consent, and the girl's father secured his dismissal from Egerton's service. On his release, Donne found himself without employment and his wife without a dowry. Years of poverty and dependence turned the poet toward religion and reflection, both of which found ready expression in his writing. His first published work, The Pseudo-Martyr *(1610), written to persuade Catholics to take the oath of allegiance, earned him an honorary master of arts degree from Oxford and the notice of the king. In 1614, he was elected to Parliament and, in 1615, became an Anglican priest. During these middle years, Donne wrote his "anniversaries," the first of which was published in 1611. The subject was Elizabeth Drury, who died in 1610 at the age of fourteen. The poem captures something of the weariness and insecurity that accompanied the crisis of the seventeenth century. His subsequent career was divided between the poet and the priest. When he died, as dean of St. Paul's, Donne had earned another reputation as the greatest preacher of his age.*

From *The Complete English Poems of John Donne,* edited by C. A. Patrides (New York: Everyman's Library, 1985).

An Anatomy of the World.
Wherein, By occasion of the untimely
death of Mistris
Elizabeth Drury the frailty and the decay of his whole
World is represented.

To The Praise of the Dead, and the Anatomy.
[by Joseph Hall?]

Wel dy'de the world, that we might live to see
This world of wit, in his Anatomee:
No evill wants his good: so wilder heyres
Bedew their fathers Toombs with forced teares,
Whose state requites their los: whils thus we
  gain
Well may wee walk in blacks, but not com-
  plaine.

*   *   *

She, of whom th'Auncients seem'd to prophesie,
When they call'd vertues by the name of shee;
She in whom vertue was so much refin'd,
That for Allay unto so pure a minde
Shee tooke the weaker Sex, she that could drive
The poysonous tincture, and the stayne of *Eve,*
Out of her thoughts, and deeds; and purifie
All, by a true religious Alchimy;
Shee, shee is dead; shee's dead: when thou
  knowest this,
Thou knowest how poore a trifling thing man is.
And learn'st thus much by our Anatomee,
The heart being perish'd, no part can be free.
And that except thou feed (not banquet) on
The supernaturall food, Religion,
Thy better Grouth growes withered, and scant;

Be more then man, or thou'rt lesse then an Ant.
Then, as mankinde, so is the worlds whole frame
Quite out of joynt, almost created lame:
For, before God had made up all the rest,
Corruption entred, and deprav'd the best:
It seis'd the Angels, and then first of all
The world did in her Cradle take a fall,
And turn'd her braines, and tooke a generall
    maime
Wronging each joynt of th'universall frame.
The noblest part, man, felt it first; and than
Both beasts and plants, curst in the curse of
    man.
So did the world from the first houre decay,
The evening was beginning of the day,
And now the Springs and Sommers which we
    see,
Like sonnes of women after fifty bee.
And new Philosophy cals all in doubt,
The Element of fire is quite put out;
The Sun is lost, and th'earth, and no mans wit
Can well direct him, where to looke for it.
And freely men confesse, that this world's spent,
When in the Planets, and the Firmament
They seeke so many new; they see that this
Is crumbled out againe to his Atomis.
'Tis all in pieces, all cohærence gone;
All just supply, and all Relation:
Prince, Subject, Father, Sonne, are things forgot,
For every man alone thinkes he hath got
To be a Phœnix, and that there can bee
None of that kinde, of which he is, but hee.
This is the worlds condition now, and now
She that should all parts to reunion bow,
She that had all Magnetique force alone,
To draw, and fasten sundred parts in one;
She whom wise nature had invented then
When she observ'd that every sort of men
Did in their voyage in this worlds Sea stray,
And needed a new compasse for their way;
Shee that was best, and first originall
Of all faire copies; and the generall
Steward to Fate; shee whose rich eyes, and brest,
Guilt the West Indies, and perfum'd the East;
Whose having breath'd in this world, did bestow
Spice on those Isles, and bad them still smell so,

And that rich Indie which doth gold interre,
Is but as single money, coyn'd from her:
She to whom this world must it selfe refer,
As Suburbs, or the Microcosme of her,
Shee, shee is dead; shee's dead: when thou
    knowst this,
Thou knowst how lame a cripple this world is.
And learnst thus much by our Anatomy,
That this worlds generall sickenesse doth not lie
In any humour, or one certaine part;
But, as thou sawest it rotten at the hart,
Thou seest a Hectique fever hath got hold
Of the whole substance, not to be contrould,
And that thou hast but one way, not t'admit
The worlds infection, to be none of it.
For the worlds subtilst immateriall parts
Feele this consuming wound, and ages darts.
For the worlds beauty is decayd, or gone,
Beauty, that's colour, and proportion.
We thinke the heavens enjoy their Spherical
Their round proportion embracing all.
But yet their various and perplexed course,
Observ'd in divers ages doth enforce
Men to finde out so many Eccentrique parts,
Such divers downe-right lines, such overthwarts,
As disproportion that pure forme. It teares
The Firmament in eight and fortie sheeres,
And in those constellations there arise
New starres, and old do vanish from our eyes:
As though heav'n suffred earth-quakes, peace or
    war,
When new Townes rise, and olde demolish'd
    are.
They have empayld within a Zodiake
The free-borne Sunne, and keepe twelve signes
    awake
To watch his steps; the Goat and Crabbe
    controule,
And fright him backe, who els to eyther Pole,
(Did not these Tropiques fetter him) might
    runne:
For his course is not round; nor can the Sunne
Perfit a Circle, or maintaine his way
One inche direct; but where he rose to day
He comes no more, but with a cousening line,
Steales by that point, and so is Serpentine:

And seeming weary with his reeling thus,
He meanes to sleepe, being now falne nearer us.
So, of the stares which boast that they do runne
In Circle still, none ends where he begunne.
All their proportion's lame, it sinks, it swels.
For of Meridians, and Parallels,
Man hath weav'd out a net, and this net
    throwne
Upon the Heavens, and now they are his owne.
Loth to goe up the hill, or labor thus
To goe to heaven, we make heaven come to us.
We spur, we raine the stars, and in their race
They're diversly content t'obey our pace.
But keepes the earth her round proportion still?
Doth not a Tenarif, or higher Hill
Rise so high like a Rocke, that one might thinke
The floating Moone would shipwracke there, and
    sink?
Seas are so deepe, that Whales being strooke to
    day,
Perchance to morrow, scarse at middle way
Of their wish'd journeys end, the bottom, dye.
And men, to sound depths, so much line untie,
As one might justly thinke, that there would rise
At end thereof, one of th'Antipodes:
If under all, a Vault infernall be,

(Which sure is spacious, except that we
Invent another torment, that there must
Millions into a strait hote roome be thrust)
Then solidnes, and roundnes have no place.
Are these but warts, and pock-holes in the face
Of th'earth? Thinke so: But yet confesse, in this
The worlds proportion disfigured is,
That those two legges whereon it doth relie,
Reward and punishment are bent awrie.
And, Oh, it can no more be questioned,
That beauties best, proportion, is dead,
Since even griefe it selfe, which now alone
Is left us, is without proportion.

*   *   *

REVIEW QUESTIONS

1. Of the changes in the early modern period that Donne catalogues, which does he highlight?
2. Why do you suppose he chose these?
3. What has been lost according to Donne?
4. How might he understand Pascal's notion of infinity?

HANS JAKOB CHRISTOPH VON GRIMMELSHAUSEN

FROM *Simplicissimus*

Hans Jakob Christoph von Grimmelshausen (1621–1676), author of Simplicissimus, *the greatest German novel of the seventeenth century and one of the great works of all German literature, was born at Gelnhausen, near Hanau in Hesse Kassel. The troubled times of the Thirty Years' War (1618–1648) that found eloquent considera- tion in his writing are reflected by his life. He lost his parents early, probably in the 1634 sack of Gelnhausen by troops under Ferdinand, general infanta of Spain, and was himself kidnapped by marauding Hessian troops the following year. His experi- ences became the stuff of his novel. In 1636 he joined the Imperial army. In 1639 he became secretary to Reinhard von Schauenburg, the commandant at Offenburg, on whose staff he served until 1647. At the end of the war, he was commandant on the Inn. Soon after the war he became steward of the Schauenburg estates, married, and converted to Catholicism. In 1667, Grimmelshausen was appointed magistrate and tax collector at Renchen, a town belonging to the Bishopric of Strasbourg. His duties evidently left him free to write; he published his masterpiece,* Simplicissimus, *in 1669. Modeled on the Spanish picaresque romance,* Simplicissimus *sketched the development of a human soul measured against the background of a land riven by warfare. It gave free reign to its authors narrative gifts: his realist detail, coarse humor, and social criticism.* Simplicissimus *is widely considered a historical document for its vivid picture of seventeenth-century Germany. Grimmelshausen's life ended as it began, in the shadow of war. In 1674, Rechen was occupied by French troops and his household was broken up. He died in 1676, once more in military service.*

From *Simplicissimus,* by Hans Jakob Christoph von Grimmelshausen, translated by S. Goodrich (San Francisco: Daedalus Press, 1995).

Book I

CHAPTER I
TREATS OF SIMPLICISSIMUS'S RUSTIC DESCENT AND OF HIS UPBRINGING ANSWERING THERETO

There appeareth in these days of ours (of which many do believe that they be the last days) among the common folk, a certain disease which causeth those who do suffer from it (so soon as they have either scraped and higgled together so much that they can, besides a few pence in their pocket, wear a fool's coat of the new fashion with a thousand bits of silk ribbon upon it, or by some trick of fortune have become known as men of parts) forthwith to give themselves out gentlemen and nobles of ancient descent. Whereas it doth often happen that their ancestors were day-labourers, carters, and porters, their cousins donkey-drivers, their brothers turnkeys and catchpolls, their sisters harlots, their mothers bawds—yea, witches even: and in a word, their whole pedigree of thirty-two quarterings as full of dirt and stain as ever was the sugarbakers' guild of Prague. Yea, these new sprigs of nobility be often themselves as black as if they had been born and bred in Guinea.

With such foolish folk I desire not to even myself, though 'tis not untrue that I have often fancied I must have drawn my birth from some great lord or knight at least, as being by nature disposed to follow the nobleman's trade had I but the means and the tools for it. 'Tis true, moreover, without jesting, that my birth and upbringing can be well compared to that of a prince if we overlook the one great difference in degree. How! did not my dad (for so they call fathers in the Spessart) have his own palace like any other, so fine as no king could build with his own hands, but must let that alone for ever. 'Twas painted with lime, and in place of unfruitful tiles, cold lead and red copper, was roofed with that straw whereupon the noble corn doth grow, and that he, my dad, might make a proper show of nobility and riches, he had his wall round his castle built, not of stone, which men do find upon the road or dig out of the earth in barren places, much less of miserable baked bricks that in a brief space can be made and burned (as other great lords be wont to do), but he did use oak, which noble and profitable tree, being such that smoked sausage and fat ham doth grow upon it, taketh for its full growth no less than a hundred years; and where is the monarch that can imitate him therein? His halls, his rooms, and his chambers did he have thoroughly blackened with smoke, and for this reason only, that 'tis the most lasting colour in the world, and doth take longer to reach to real perfection than an artist will spend on his most excellent paintings. The tapestries were of the most delicate web in the world, wove for us by her that of old did challenge

Minerva to a spinning match. His windows were dedicated to St. Papyrius for no other reason than that that same paper doth take longer to come to perfection, reckoning from the sowing of the hemp or flax whereof 'tis made, than doth the finest and clearest glass of Murano: for his trade made him apt to believe that whatever was produced with much paint was also more valuable and more costly; and what was moss costly was best suited to nobility. Instead of pages, lackeys, and grooms, he had sheep, goats, and swine, which often waited upon me in the pastures till I drove them home. His armoury was well furnished with ploughs, mattocks, axes, hoes, shovels, pitchforks, and hayforks, with which weapons he daily exercised himself; for hoeing and digging he made his military discipline, as did the old Romans in time of peace. The yoking of oxen was his generalship, the piling of dung his fortification, tilling of the land his campaigning, and the cleaning out of stables his princely pastime and exercise. By this means did he conquer the whole round world so far as he could reach, and at every harvest did draw from it rich spoils. But all this I account nothing of, and am not puffed up thereby, lest any should have cause to jibe at me as at other newfangled nobility, for I esteem myself no higher than was my dad, which had his abode in a right merry land, to wit, in the Spessart, where the wolves do howl good-night to each other. But that I have as yet told you nought of my dad's family, race and name is for the sake of precious brevity, especially since there is here no question of a foundation for gentlefolks for me to swear myself into; 'tis enough if it be known that I was born in the Spessart.

Now as my dad's manner of living will be perceived to be truly noble, so any man of sense will easily understand that my upbringing was like and suitable thereto: and whoso thinks that is not deceived, for in my tenth year had I already learned the rudiments of my dad's princely exercises: yet as touching studies I might compare with the famous Amphistides, of whom Suidas reports that he could not count higher than five: for my dad had perchance too high a spirit, and therefore followed the use of these days, wherein many persons of quality trouble themselves not, as they say with bookworms' follies, but have their hirelings to do their inkslinging for them. Yet was I a fine performer on the bagpipe, whereon I could produce most dolorous strains. But as to knowledge of things divine, none shall ever persuade me that any lad of my age in all Christendom could there beat me, for I knew nought of God or man, of Heaven or hell, of angel or devil, nor could discern between good and evil. So may it be easily understood that I, with such knowledge of theology, lived like our first parents in Paradise, which in their innocence knew nought of sickness or death or dying, and still less of the Resurrection. O noble life! (or, as one might better say, O noodle's life!) in which none troubles himself about medicine. And by this measure ye can estimate my proficiency in the study of jurisprudence and all other arts and sciences. Yea, I was so perfected in ignorance that I knew not that I knew nothing. So say I again, O noble life that once I led! But my dad would not suffer me long to enjoy such bliss, but deemed it right that as being nobly born, I should nobly act and nobly live: and therefore began to train me up for higher things and gave me harder lessons.

*   *   *

CHAPTER IV

HOW SIMPLICISSIMUS'S PALACE WAS STORMED, PLUNDERED, AND RUINATED, AND IN WHAT SORRY FASHION THE SOLDIERS KEPT HOUSE THERE

Although it was not my intention to take the peaceloving reader with these troopers to my dad's house and farm, seeing that matters will go ill therein, yet the course of my history demands that I should leave to kind posterity an account of what manner of cruelties were now and again practised in this our German war: yea, and moreover testify by my own example that such evils must often have been sent to us by the goodness of Almighty God for our profit. For, gentle reader, who would ever have taught me that there was a God in

Heaven if these soldiers had not destroyed my dad's house, and by such a deed driven me out among folk who gave me all fitting instruction thereupon? Only a little while before, I neither knew nor could fancy to myself that there were any people on earth save only my dad, my mother and me, and the rest of our household, nor did I know of any human habitation but that where I daily went out and in. But soon thereafter I understood the way of men's coming into this world, and how they must leave it again. I was only in shape a man and in name a Christian: for the rest I was but a beast. Yet the Almighty looked upon my innocence with a pitiful eye, and would bring me to a knowledge both of Himself and of myself. And although He had a thousand ways to lead me thereto, yet would He doubtless use that one only by which my dad and my mother should be punished: and that for an example to all others by reason of their heathenish upbringing of me.

The first thing these troopers did was, that they stabled their horses: thereafter each fell to his appointed task: which task was neither more nor less than ruin and destruction. For though some began to slaughter and to boil and to roast so that it looked as if there should be a merry banquet forward, yet others there were who did but storm through the house above and below stairs. Others stowed together great parcels of cloth and apparel and all manner of household stuff, as if they would set up a frippery market. All that they had no mind to take with them they cut in pieces. Some thrust their swords through the hay and straw as if they had not enough sheep and swine to slaughter: and some shook the feathers out of the beds and in their stead stuffed in bacon and other dried meat and provisions as if such were better and softer to sleep upon. Others broke the stove and the windows as if they had a never-ending summer to promise. Houseware of copper and tin they beat flat, and packed such vessels, all bent and spoiled, in with the rest. Bedsteads, tables, chairs, and benches they burned, though there lay many cords of dry wood in the yard. Pots and pipkins must all go to pieces, either because they would

eat none but roast flesh, or because their purpose was to make there but a single meal.

Our maid was so handled in the stable that she could not come out; which is a shame to tell of. Our man they laid bound upon the ground, thrust a gag into his mouth, and poured a pailful of filthy water into his body: and by this, which they called a Swedish draught, they forced him to lead a party of them to a another place where they captured men and beasts, and brought them back to our farm, in which company were my dad, my mother, and our Ursula.

And now they began: first to take the flints out of their pistols and in place of them to jam the peasants' thumbs in and so to torture the poor rogues as if they had been about the burning of witches: for one of them they had taken they thrust into the baking oven and there lit a fire under him, although he had as yet confessed no crime: as for another, they put a cord round his head and so twisted it tight with a piece of wood that the blood gushed from his mouth and nose and ears. In a word each had his own device to torture the peasants, and each peasant his several torture. But as it seemed to me then, my dad was the luckiest, for he with a laughing face confessed what others must out with in the midst of pains and miserable lamentations: and such honour without doubt fell to him because he was the householder. For they set him before a fire and bound him fast so that he could neither stir hand nor foot, and smeared the soles of his feet with wet salt, and this they made our old goat lick off, and so tickle him that he well nigh burst his sides with laughing. And this seemed to me so merry a thing that I must needs laugh with him for the sake of fellowship, or because I knew no better. In the midst of such laughter he must needs confess all that they would have of him, and indeed revealed to them a secret treasure, which proved far richer in pearls, gold, and trinkets than any would have looked for among peasants. Of the women, girls, and maidservants whom they took, I have not much to say in particular, for the soldiers would not have me see how they dealt with them.

Yet this I know, that one heard some of them scream most piteously in divers corners of the house; and well I can judge it fared no better with my mother and our Ursel than with the rest. Yet in the midst of all this miserable ruin I helped to turn the spit, and in the afternoon to give the horses drink, in which employ I encountered our maid in the stable, who seemed to me wondrously tumbled, so that I knew her not, but with a weak voice she called to me, "O lad, run away, or the troopers will have thee away with them. Look to it well that thou get hence: thou seest in what plight . . ." And more she could not say.

* * *

CHAPTER XV
HOW SIMPLICISSIMUS WAS PLUNDERED, AND HOW HE DREAMED OF THE PEASANTS AND HOW THEY FARED IN TIMES OF WAR

Now when I came home I found that my fireplace and all my poor furniture, together with my store of provisions, which I had grown during the summer in my garden and had kept for the coming winter, were all gone. "And whither now?" thought I. And then first did need teach me heartily to pray: and I must summon all my small wits together, to devise what I should do. But as my knowledge of the world was both small and evil, I could come to no proper conclusion, only that 'twas best to commend myself to God and to put my whole confidence in Him: for otherwise I must perish. And besides all this those things which I had heard and seen that day lay heavy on my mind: and I pondered not so much upon my food and my sustenance as upon the enmity which there is ever between soldiers and peasants. Yet could my foolish mind come to no other conclusion than this—that there must of a surety be two races of men in the world, and not one only, descended from Adam, but two, wild and tame, like other unreasoning beasts, and therefore pursuing one another so cruelly.

With such thoughts I fell asleep, for mere mis-ery and cold, with a hungry stomach. Then it seemed to me, as if in a dream, that all the trees which stood round my dwelling suddenly changed and took on another appearance: for on every treetop sat a trooper, and the trunks were garnished, in place of leaves, with all manner of folk. Of these, some had long lances, others musquets, hangers, halberts, flags, and some drums and fifes. Now this was merry to see, for all was neatly distributed and each according to his rank. The roots, moreover, were made up of folk of little worth, as mechanics and labourers, mostly, however, peasants and the like; and these nevertheless gave its strength to the tree and renewed the same when it was lost: yea more, they repaired the loss of any fallen leaves from among themselves to their own great damage: and all the time they lamented over them that sat on the tree, and that with good reason, for the whole weight of the tree lay upon them and pressed them so that all the money was squeezed out of their pockets, yea, though it was behind seven locks and keys: but if the money would not out, then did the commissaries so handle them with rods (which thing they call military execution) that sighs came from their heart, tears from their eyes, blood from their nails, and the marrow from their bones. Yet among these were some whom men call light o' heart; and these made but little ado, took all with a shrug, and in the midst of their torment had, in place of comfort, mockery for every turn.

CHAPTER XVI
OF THE WAYS AND WORKS OF SOLDIERS NOWADAYS, AND HOW HARDLY A COMMON SOLDIER CAN GET PROMOTION

So must the roots of these trees suffer and endure toil and misery in the midst of trouble and complaint, and those upon the lower boughs in yet greater hardship: yet were these last mostly merrier than the first named, yea and moreover, insolent and swaggering, and for the most part godless folk, and for the roots a heavy unbearable burden at all times. And this was the rhyme upon them:

> Hunger and thirst, and cold and heat, and work and woe, and all we meet;
> And deeds of blood and deeds of shame, all may ye put to the landsknecht's name.

Which rhymes were the less like to be lyingly invented in that they answered to the facts. For gluttony and drunkenness, hunger and thirst, wenching and dicing and playing, riot and roaring, murdering and being murdered, slaying and being slain, torturing and being tortured, hunting and being hunted, harrying and being harried, robbing and being robbed, frighting and being frighted, causing trouble and suffering trouble, beating and being beaten: in a word, hurting and harming, and in turn being hurt and harmed—this was their whole life. And in this career they let nothing hinder them: neither winter nor summer, snow nor ice, heat nor cold, rain nor wind, hill nor dale, wet nor dry; ditches, mountain-passes, ramparts and walls, fire and water, were all the same to them. Father nor mother, sister nor brother, no, nor the danger to their own bodies, souls, and consciences, nor even loss of life and of heaven itself, or aught else that can be named, will ever stand in their way, for ever they toil and moil at their own strange work, till at last, little by little, in battles, sieges, attacks, campaigns, yea, and in their winter quarters too (which are the soldiers' earthly paradise, if they can but happen upon fat peasants) they perish, they die, they rot and consume away, save but a few, who in their old age, unless they have been right thrifty rievers and robbers, do furnish us with the best of all beggars and vagabonds.

Next above these hard-worked folk sat old henroost-robbers, who, after some years and much peril of their lives, had climbed up the lowest branches and clung to them, and so far had had the luck to escape death. Now these looked more serious, and somewhat more dignified than the lowest, in that they were a degree higher ascended: yet above them were some yet higher, who had yet loftier imaginings because they had to command the very lowest. And these people did call coat-beaters, because they were wont to dust the jackets of the poor pikemen, and to give the musketeers oil enough to grease their barrels with.

Just above these the trunk of the tree had an interval or stop, which was a smooth place without branches, greased with all manner of ointments and curious soap of disfavour, so that no man save of noble birth could scale it, in spite of courage and skill and knowledge, God knows how clever he might be. For 'twas polished as smooth as a marble pillar or a steel mirror. Just over that smooth spot sat they with the flags: and of these some were young, some pretty well in years: the young folk their kinsmen had raised so far: the older people had either mounted on a silver ladder which is called the Bribery Backstairs or else on a step which Fortune, for want of a better client, had left for them. A little further up sat higher folk, and these had also their toil and care and annoyance: yet had they this advantage, that they could fill their pokes with the fattest slices which they could cut out of the roots, and that with a knife which they called "War-contribution." And these were at their best and happiest when there came a commissary-bird flying overhead, and shook out a whole panfull of gold over the tree to cheer them: for of that they caught as much as they could, and let but little or nothing at all fall to the lowest branches: and so of these last more died of hunger than of the enemy's attacks, from which danger those placed above seemed to be free. Therefore was there a perpetual climbing and swarming going on on those trees; for each would needs sit in those highest and happiest places: yet were there some idle, worthless rascals, not worth their commissariat-bread, who troubled themselves little about higher places, and only did their duty. So the lowest, being ambitious, hoped for the fall of the highest, that they might sit in their place, and if it happened to one among ten thousand of them that he got so far, yet would such good luck come to him only in his miserable old age when he was more fit to sit in the chimney-corner and roast apples than to meet the foe in the field. And if any man dealt honestly and carried himself well, yet was he ever envied by others, and perchance by reason of some unlucky chance of war deprived both of office and of life. And nowhere was this more grievous than at the before-mentioned smooth place on the tree: for there an officer who had had a good sergeant or corporal under him must lose him, however unwillingly, because he was now made an ensign. And for that reason they would take, in place of old soldiers, ink-slingers, footmen, overgrown pages, poor noblemen, and at times poor relations, tramps and vagabonds. And these took the very bread out of the mouths of those that had deserved it, and forthwith were made Ensigns.

*   *   *

REVIEW QUESTIONS

1. Who is Simplicissimus?
2. What is his relation to nature?
3. What does he consider noble and base?
4. What does Grimmelshausen tell us about the conduct of the Thirty Years' War?
5. What happens to the character of Simplicissimus when he witnesses the violence of war?
6. What did the Thirty Years' War do to the land and its occupants?

THOMAS HOBBES

FROM *Leviathan*

Thomas Hobbes (1588–1679) was an English philosopher whose mechanistic and deterministic theories of political life were highly controversial in his own time. Born in Malmesbury, Hobbes attended Magdalen Hall, Oxford, and became tutor to William Cavendish, later earl of Devonshire, in 1608. With his student, he undertook several tours of the continent where he met and spoke with leading intellectual lights of the day, including Galileo and Descartes. Around 1637, he became interested in the constitutional struggle between parliament and Charles I and set to work writing a "little treatise in English" in defense of the royal prerogative. Before its publication in 1650, the book circulated privately in 1640 under the title Elements of Law, Natural and Politic. *Fearing arrest by parliament, Hobbes fled to Paris, where he remained for the next eleven years. While in exile, he served as math tutor to the Prince of Wales, Charles II, from 1646–1648. His great work,* Leviathan *(1651), was a forceful argument for political absolutism. Its title, taken from the horrifying sea monster of the Old Testament, suggested the power and authority Hobbes thought necessary to compel obedience and order in human society. Strongly influenced by mechanical philosophy, he treated human beings as matter in motion, subject to certain physical, rational laws. People feared one another and lived in a state of constant competition and conflict. For this reason, they must submit to the absolute, supreme authority of the state, a social contract among selfish individuals moved by fear and necessity. Once delegated, that authority was irrevocable and indivisible. Ironically, these theories found favor neither with royalists nor with anti-royalists. Charles II believed that it was written in justification of the Commonwealth. The French feared its attacks on the papacy. After the Restoration, Parliament added* Leviathan *to a list of books to be investigated for atheistic tendencies. Despite frustrations over the reception of his political theories, Hobbes retained his intellectual vigor. At age eighty-four, he wrote an autobiography in Latin and translated the works of Homer into English. He died at age ninety-one.*

From *Leviathan,* by Thomas Hobbes, edited by E. Hershey Sneath (Needham: Ginn Press, 1898).

*   *   *

Of the Causes, Generation, and Definition of a Commonwealth

The final cause, end, or design of men, who naturally love liberty and dominion over others, in the introduction of that restraint upon themselves in which we see them live in commonwealths is the foresight of their own preservation, and of a more contented life thereby; that is to say, of getting themselves out from that miserable condition of war which is necessarily consequent . . . to the natural passions of men when there is no visible power to keep them in awe and tie them by fear of punishment to the performance of their covenants, and observation of the laws of nature. . . .

For the laws of nature, as "justice," "equity," "modesty," "mercy," and, in sum, "doing to others as we would be done to," of themselves, without the terror of some power to cause them to be observed, are contrary to our natural passions, that carry us to partiality, pride, revenge, and the like. And covenants without the sword are but words, and of no strength to secure a man at all. Therefore, notwithstanding the laws of nature, which every one has then kept when he has the will to keep them, when he can do it safely, if there be no power erected, or not great enough for our security; every man will, and may lawfully rely on

his own strength and art, for protection against all other men. And in all places where men have lived by small families, to rob and spoil one another has been a trade, and so far from being reputed against the law of nature that the greater spoils they gained, the greater was their honor; and men observed no other laws therein but the laws of honor; that is, to abstain from cruelty, leaving to men their lives and instruments of livelihood. And as small families did then, so now do cities and kingdoms, which are but greater families, for their own security enlarge their dominions upon all pretenses of danger and fear of invasion or assistance that may be given to invaders, and endeavor as much as they can to subdue or weaken their neighbors by open force and secret arts, for lack of other protection, justly; and are remembered for it in later ages with honor.

Nor is it the joining together of a small number of men that gives them this security, because in small numbers small additions on the one side or the other make the advantage of strength so great as is sufficient to carry the victory; and therefore gives encouragement to an invasion. The multitude sufficient to confide in for our security is not determined by any certain number but by comparison with the enemy we fear; and is then sufficient when the advantage of the enemy is not so visible and conspicuous to determine the event of war as to move him to attempt it.

And should there not be so great a multitude, even if their actions be directed according to their particular judgments and particular appetites, they can expect thereby no defense nor protection, neither against a common enemy nor against the injuries of one another. For being distracted in opinions concerning the best use and application of their strength, they do not help but hinder one another, and reduce their strength by mutual opposition to nothing; whereby they are easily not only subdued by a very few that agree together, but also, when there is no common enemy, they make war upon each other for their particular interests. For if we could suppose a great multitude of men to consent in the observation of justice and other laws of nature without a common power to keep them all in awe, we might as well suppose all mankind to do the same; and then there neither would be, nor need to be, any civil government or commonwealth at all, because there would be peace without subjection.

Nor is it enough for the security which men desire should last all the time of their life that they be governed and directed by one judgment for a limited time, as in one battle or one war. For though they obtain a victory by their unanimous endeavor against a foreign enemy, yet afterwards, when either they have no common enemy or he that by one group is held for an enemy is by another group held for a friend, they must needs, by the difference of their interests, dissolve, and fall again into a war among themselves.

It is true that certain living creatures, as bees and ants, live sociably one with another, which are therefore by Aristotle numbered among political creatures, and yet have no other direction, than their particular judgments and appetites; nor speech whereby one of them can signify to another what he thinks expedient for the common benefit; and therefore some man may perhaps desire to know why mankind cannot do the same. To which I answer:

First, that men are continually in competition for honor and dignity, which these creatures are not; and consequently among men there arises on the ground envy and hatred and finally war, but among these not so.

Secondly, that among these creatures the common good differ not from the private; and being by nature inclined to their private, they procure thereby the common benefit. But man, whose joy consists in comparing himself with other men, can relish nothing but what is eminent.

Thirdly, that these creatures, having not, as man, the use of reason, do not see nor think they see any fault, in the administration of their common business; whereas among men, there are very many that think themselves wiser and abler to govern the public better than the rest; and these strive to reform and innovate, one this way, another that way, and thereby bring it into distraction and civil war.

Fourthly, that these creatures, though they have some use of voice in making known to one another their desires and other affections, yet they lack that art of words by which some men can represent to others that which is good in the likeness of evil; and evil in the likeness of good; and augment or diminish the apparent greatness of good and evil, making men discontented and troubling their peace at their pleasure.

Fifthly, irrational creatures cannot distinguish between "injury" and "damage"; and, therefore, as long as they be at ease they are not offended with their fellows; whereas man is then most troublesome when he is most at ease; for then it is that he loves to show his wisdom and control the actions of them that govern the commonwealth.

Lastly, the agreement of these creatures is natural, that of men is by covenant only, which is artificial; and therefore, it is no wonder if there be somewhat else required besides covenant to make their agreement constant and lasting, which is a common power to keep them in awe and to direct their actions to the common benefit.

The only way to erect such a common power which may be able to defend them from the invasion of foreigners and the injuries of one another, and thereby to secure them in such sort so that by their own industry and by the fruits of the earth they may nourish themselves and live contentedly, is to confer all their power and strength upon one man, or upon one assembly of men that may reduce all their wills, by plurality of voices, unto one will; which is as much as to say, to appoint one man or assembly of men to bear their person; and every one to accept and acknowledge himself to be author of whatsoever he that so bears their person shall act or cause to be acted in those things which concern the common peace and safety, and therein to submit their wills every one to his will, and their judgments to his judgment. This is more than consent or concord; it is a real unity of them all in one and the same person, made by covenant of every man with every man, in such manner as if every man should say to every man, "I authorize and give up my right of governing myself to this man, or to this assembly of men, on this condition, that you give up your right to him and authorize all his actions in like manner." This done, the multitude so united in one person is called a "commonwealth," in Latin *civitas*. This is the generation of that great "leviathan," or rather, to speak more reverently, of that "mortal god," to which we owe, under the "immortal God," our peace and defense. For by this authority, given him by every particular man in the commonwealth, he has the use of so much power and strength conferred on him that, by terror thereof, he is enabled to form the wills of them all to peace at home and mutual aid against their enemies abroad. And in him consists the essence of the commonwealth, which, to define it, is "one person, of whose acts a great multitude, by mutual covenants one with another, have made themselves the author, to the end he may use the strength and means of them all as he shall think expedient for their peace and common defense."

And he that carries this person is called "sovereign" and said to have "sovereign power"; and every one besides, his "subject."

The attaining to this sovereign power is by two ways. One, by natural force, as when a man makes his children to submit themselves and their children to his government, as being able to destroy them if they refuse; or by war subdues his enemies to his will, giving them their lives on that condition. The other is when men agree among themselves to submit to some man or assembly of men voluntarily, on confidence that they will be protected by him against all others. This latter, may

be called a political commonwealth, or commonwealth by "institution," and the former, a commonwealth by "acquisition." ✶ ✶ ✶

Of the Office of the Sovereign Representative

The office of the sovereign, be it a monarch or an assembly, consists in the end for which he was trusted with the sovereign power, namely, the securing of "the safety of the people"; to which he is obliged by the law of nature, and to render an account thereof to God, the author of that law, and to none but him. But by safety here is not meant a bare preservation but also all other contentments of life which every man by lawful industry, without danger or hurt to the commonwealth, shall acquire to himself.

And this is to be done, not by care applied to individuals further than their protection from injuries when they shall complain, but by a general provision contained in public instruction, both of doctrine and example, and in the making and executing of good laws to which individual persons may apply their own cases.

And because, if the essential rights of sovereignty . . . be taken away, the commonwealth is thereby dissolved and every man returns into the condition and calamity of a war with every other man, which is the greatest evil that can happen in this life; it is the office of the sovereign, to maintain those rights entire, and consequently against his duty, first, to transfer to another or to lay from himself any of them. For he that deserts the means deserts the ends; and he deserts the means when, being the sovereign, he acknowledges himself subject to the civil laws and renounces the power of supreme judicature, or of making war or peace by his own authority; or of judging of the necessities of the commonwealth; or of levying money and soldiers when and as much as in his own conscience he shall judge necessary; or of making officers and ministers both of war and peace; or of appointing teachers and examining what doctrines are conformable or contrary to the defense, peace, and good of the people. Secondly, it is against his duty to let the people be ignorant or misinformed of the grounds and reasons of those his essential rights, because thereby men are easy to be seduced and drawn to resist him when the commonwealth shall require their use and exercise.

And the grounds of these rights have the need to be diligently and truly taught, because they cannot be maintained by any civil law or terror of legal punishment. For a civil law that shall forbid rebellion (and such is all resistance to the essential rights of the sovereignty), is not, as a civil law, any obligation, but by virtue only of the law of nature that forbids the violation of faith; which natural obligation if men know not, they cannot know the right of any law the sovereign makes. And for the punishment, they take it but for an act of hostility which when they think they have strength enough, they will endeavor by acts of hostility, to avoid. ＊ ＊ ＊

To the care of the sovereign belongs the making of good laws. But what is a good law? By a good law I mean not a just law; for no law can be unjust. The law is made by the sovereign power, and all that is done by such power is warranted and owned by every one of the people; and that which every man will have so, no man can say is unjust. It is in the laws of a commonwealth as in the laws of gaming; whatsoever the gamesters all agree on is injustice to none of them. A good law is that which is "needed" for the "good of the people" and "perspicuous."

For the use of laws, which are but rules authorized, is not to bind the people from all voluntary actions but to direct and keep them in such a motion as not to hurt themselves by their own impetuous desires, rashness, or indiscretion; as hedges are set not to stop travellers, but to keep them in their way. And, therefore, a law that is not needed, having not the true end of a law, is not good. A law may be conceived to be good when it is for the benefit of the sovereign, though it be not necessary for the people, but it is not so. For the good of the sovereign and people cannot be separated. It is a weak sovereign, that has weak subjects, and a weak people, whose sovereign lacks power to rule them at his will. Unnecessary laws are not good laws but traps for money; which, where the right of sovereign power is acknowledged, are superfluous, and where it is not acknowledged, insufficient to defend the people. ＊ ＊ ＊

It belongs also to the office of the sovereign to make a right application of punishments and rewards. And seeing the end of punishing is not revenge and discharge of anger, but correction, either of the offender, or of others by his example; the severest punishments are to be inflicted for those crimes that are of most danger to the public; such as are those which proceed from malice to the government established; those that spring from contempt of justice; those that provoke indignation in the multitude; and those which, unpunished, seem authorized, as when they are committed by sons, servants, or favorites of men in authority. For indignation carries men not only against the actors and authors of injustice, but against all power that is likely to protect them; as in the case of Tarquin, when for the insolent act of one of his sons he was driven out of Rome and the monarchy itself dissolved. But crimes of infirmity, such as are those which proceed from great provocation, from great fear, great need, or from ignorance, whether the fact be a great crime or not, there is place many times for leniency without prejudice to the commonwealth; and leniency, when there is such place for it, is required by the law of nature. The punishment of the leaders and teachers in a commotion, not the poor seduced people, when they are punished, can profit the commonwealth by their example. To be severe to the people is to punish that ignorance which may in great part be imputed to the sovereign, whose fault it was that they were no better instructed.

In like manner it belongs to the office and duty of the sovereign, to apply his rewards so that there may arise from them benefit to the commonwealth, wherein consists their use, and end; and is then done when they that have well served the commonwealth are, with as little expense of the common treasure as is possible, so well recompensed as others thereby may be encouraged both to serve the same as faithfully as they can and to study the arts by which they may be enabled to do it better. To buy with money or preferment from a popular ambitious subject to be quiet and desist from making ill impressions in the minds of the people has nothing of the nature of reward (which is ordained not for disservice, but for service past), nor a sign of gratitude, but of fear; nor does it tend to the benefit but to the damage of the public. It is a contention with ambition like that of Hercules with the monster Hydra which, having many heads, for every one that was vanquished there grew up three. For in like manner, when the stubbornness of one popular man is overcome with reward there arise many more, by the example, that do the same mischief in hope of like benefit; and as all sorts of manufacture, so also malice increases by being salable. And though sometimes a civil war may be deferred by such ways as that, yet the danger grows still the greater and the public ruin more assured. It is therefore against the duty of the sovereign, to whom the public safety is committed, to reward those that aspire to greatness by disturbing the peace of their country, and not rather to oppose the beginnings of such men with a little danger than after a longer time with greater. * * *

When the sovereign himself is popular, that is, revered and beloved of his people, there is no danger at all from the popularity of a subject. For soldiers are never so generally unjust as to side with their captain though they love him, against their sovereign, when they love not only his person but also his cause. And therefore those who by violence have at any time suppressed the power of their lawful sovereign, before they could settle themselves in his place have been always put to the trouble of contriving their titles to save the people from the shame of receiving them. To have a known right to sovereign power is so popular a quality as he that has it needs no more, for his

own part, to turn the hearts of his subjects to him but that they see him able absolutely to govern his own family; nor, on the part of his enemies, but a disbanding of their armies. For the greatest and most active part of mankind has never hitherto been well contented with the present.

Concerning the offices of one sovereign to another, which are comprehended in that law which is commonly called the "law of nations," I need not say anything in this place because the law of nations and the law of nature is the same thing. And every sovereign has the same right, in securing the safety of his people that any particular man can have in securing the safety of his own body. And the same law that dictates to men that have no civil government what they ought to do and what to avoid in regard of one another dictates the same to commonwealths, that is, to the consciences of sovereign princes and sovereign assemblies, there being no court of natural justice but in the conscience only; where not man but God reigns whose laws, such of them as oblige all mankind, in respect of God as he is the author of nature are "natural," and in respect of the same God as he is King of kings are "laws."

*   *   *

REVIEW QUESTIONS

1. What is Hobbes's view of human nature?
2. What motivates human beings?
3. What, according to Hobbes, is the purpose of the state?
4. Why do human beings come together to form a political society?
5. What are the responsibilities of the sovereign?
6. What is the sovereign's highest obligation?
7. Does Hobbes hold out any hope that the state can improve human nature?

MICHEL EYQUEM DE MONTAIGNE

FROM "It Is Folly to Measure the True and False by Our Own Capacity"

Michel Eyquem de Montaigne (1533–1592) introduced the essay as a literary form. Born of a wealthy family in the Château de Montaigne, near Libourne, he was first educated by a tutor who spoke Latin but no French. Until he was six years old, Montaigne learned the classical language as his native tongue. He was further educated at the Collège du Guyenne, where his fluency intimidated some of the finest Latinists in France, and studied law at Toulouse. In 1554, his father purchased an office in the Cour des Aides of Périgeaux, a fiscal court later incorporated into the Parlement of Bordeaux, a position he soon resigned to his son. Montaigne spent thirteen years in office at work he found neither pleasant nor useful. In 1571, he retired to the family estate. Apart from brief visits to Paris and Rouen, periods of travel, and two terms as mayor of Bordeaux (1581–1585), Montaigne spent the rest of his life as a country gentleman. His life was not all leisure. He became gentleman-in-ordinary to the king's chamber and spent the period 1572–1576 trying to broker a peace between Catholics and Huguenots. His first two books of the Essais *appeared in 1580; the third and last volume appeared in 1588. These essays are known for their discursive, conversational style, in which Montaigne undertook explorations of custom, opinion, and institutions. They gave voice to his opposition to all forms of dogmatism that were without rational basis. He observed life with a degree of skepticism, emphasizing the limits of human knowledge and the contradictions in human behavior. Indeed, Montaigne's essays are often cited as examples of an epistemological crisis born of the new discoveries, theological debates, and social tensions that marked the early modern period.*

From *The Complete Essays of Montaigne*, translated by Donald M. Frame (Stanford, Calif.: Stanford University Press, 1958), pp. 132–35.

Perhaps it is not without reason that we attribute facility in belief and conviction to simplicity and ignorance; for it seems to me I once learned that belief was a sort of impression made on our mind, and that the softer and less resistant the mind, the easier it was to imprint something on it. *As the scale of the balance must necessarily sink under the weight placed upon it, so must the mind yield to evident things.* The more a mind is empty and without counterpoise, the more easily it gives beneath the weight of the first persuasive argument. That is why children, common people, women, and sick people are most subject to being led by the ears. But then, on the other hand, it is foolish presumption to go around disdaining and condemning as false whatever does not seem likely to us; which is an ordinary vice in those who think they have more than common ability. I used to do so once; and if

I heard of returning spirits, prognostications of future events, enchantments, sorcery, or some other story that I could not swallow,

> Dreams, witches, miracles, magic alarms,
> Nocturnal specters, and Thessalian charms,
>
> Horace

I felt compassion for the poor people who were taken in by these follies. And now I think that I was at least as much to be pitied myself. Not that experience has since shown me anything surpassing my first beliefs, and that through no fault of my curiosity; but reason has taught me that to condemn a thing thus, dogmatically, as false and impossible, is to assume the advantage of knowing the bounds and limits of God's will and of the power of our mother Nature; and that there is no more notable folly in the world than to reduce these things to the measure of our capacity and competence. If we call prodigies or miracles whatever our reason cannot reach, how many of these appear continually to our eyes! Let us consider through what clouds and how gropingly we are led to the knowledge of most of the things that are right in our hands; assuredly we shall find that it is rather familiarity than knowledge that takes away their strangeness,

> But no one now, so tired of seeing are our eyes,
> Deigns to look up at the bright temples of the
> skies,
>
> Lucretius

and that if those things were presented to us for the first time, we should find them as incredible as any others, or more so.

> If they were here for the first time for men to
> see,
> If they were set before us unexpectedly,
> Nothing more marvelous than these things
> could be told,
> Nothing more unbelievable for men of old.
>
> Lucretius

He who had never seen a river thought that the first one he came across was the ocean. And the things that are the greatest within our knowledge we judge to be the utmost that nature can do in that category.

> A fair-sized stream seems vast to one who until
> then
> Has never seen a greater; so with trees, with
> men.
> In every field each man regards as vast in size
> The greatest objects that have come before his
> eyes.
>
> Lucretius

The mind becomes accustomed to things by the habitual sight of them, and neither wonders nor inquires about the reasons for the things it sees all the time.

The novelty of things incites us more than their greatness to seek their causes.

We must judge with more reverence the infinite power of nature, and with more consciousness of our ignorance and weakness. How many things of slight probability there are, testified to by trustworthy people, which, if we cannot be convinced of them, we should at least leave in suspense! For to condemn them as impossible is to pretend, with rash presumption, to know the limits of possibility. If people rightly understood the difference between the impossible and the unusual, and between what is contrary to the orderly course of nature and what is contrary to the common opinion of men, neither believing rashly nor disbelieving easily, they would observe the rule of "nothing too much," enjoined by Chilo.

When we find in Froissart that the count of Foix, in Béarn, learned of the defeat of King John of Castile at Juberoth the day after it happened, and the way he says he learned it, we can laugh at it; and also at the story our annals tell, that Pope Honorius performed public funeral rites for King Philip Augustus and commanded them to be performed throughout Italy on the very day he died at Mantes. For the authority of these witnesses has perhaps not enough rank to keep us in check. But if Plutarch, besides several examples that he cites from antiquity, says that he knows with certain knowledge that in the time of Domitian, the news of the battle lost by Antonius in Germany was published in Rome, several days' journey from there, and dispersed throughout the whole world, on the same day it was lost; and if Caesar maintains that it has often happened that the report has preceded the event—shall we say that these simple men let themselves be hoaxed like the common herd, because they were not clear-sighted like ourselves? Is there anything more delicate, clearer, and more alert than Pliny's judgment, when he sees fit to bring it into play, or anything farther from inanity? Leaving aside the excellence of his knowledge, which I count for less, in which of these qualities do we surpass him? However, there is no schoolboy so young but he will convict him of falsehood, and want to give him a lesson on the progress of nature's works.

When we read in Bouchet about the miracles done by the relics of Saint Hilary, let it go: his credit is not great enough to take away our right to contradict him. But to condemn wholesale all similar stories seems to me a singular impudence. The great Saint Augustine testifies that he saw a blind child recover his sight upon the relics of Saint Gervase and Saint Protasius at Milan; a woman at Carthage cured of a cancer by the sign of the cross that a newly baptized woman made over her; Hesperius, a close friend of his, cast out the spirits that infested his house with a little earth from the sepulcher of our Lord, and a paralytic promptly cured by this earth, later, when it had been carried to church; a woman in a procession, having touched Saint Stephen's shrine with a bouquet, and rubbed her eyes with this bouquet, recover her long-lost sight; and he reports many other miracles at which he says he himself was present. Of what shall we accuse both him and two holy bishops, Aurelius and Maximinus, whom he calls upon as his witnesses? Shall it be of ignorance, simplicity, and credulity, or of knavery and imposture? Is there any man in our time so impudent that he thinks himself comparable to them, either in virtue and piety, or in learning, judgment, and ability? *Who, though they brought forth no proof, might crush me by their mere authority.*

It is a dangerous and fateful presumption, be-sides the absurd temerity that it implies, to disdain what we do not comprehend. For after you have established, according to your fine understanding, the limits of truth and falsehood, and it turns out that you must necessarily believe things even stranger than those you deny, you are obliged from then on to abandon these limits. Now, what seems to me to bring as much disorder into our consciences as anything, in these religious troubles that we are in, is this partial surrender of their beliefs by Catholics. It seems to them that they are being very moderate and understanding when they yield to their opponents some of the articles in dispute. But, besides the fact that they do not see what an advantage it is to a man charging you for you to begin to give ground and withdraw, and how much that encourages him to pursue his point, those articles which they select as the most trivial are sometimes very important. We must either submit completely to the authority of our ecclesiastical government, or do without it completely. It is not for us to decide what portion of obedience we owe it.

Moreover, I can say this for having tried it. In other days I exercised this freedom of personal choice and selection, regarding with negligence certain points in the observance of our Church which seem more vain or strange than others; until, coming to discuss them with learned men, I found that these things have a massive and very solid foundation, and that it is only stupidity and ignorance that make us receive them with less reverence than the rest. Why do we not remember how much contradiction we sense even in our own judgment? How many things were articles of faith to us yesterday, which are fables to us today? Vainglory and curiosity are the two scourges of our soul. The latter leads us to thrust our noses into everything, and the former forbids us to leave anything unresolved and undecided.

REVIEW QUESTIONS

1. What are the limits of human knowledge?
2. What roles do authority and experience play in knowledge?
3. How does Montaigne's attitude toward prodigies or miracles compare with that of Reginald Scot?
4. How do their conceptions of nature differ?
5. How might Montaigne's reflection on knowledge indicate an intellectual crisis?

MICHEL EYQUEM DE MONTAIGNE

FROM "Of Cannibals"

From *The Complete Essays of Montaigne,* translated by Donald M. Frame (Stanford, Calif.: Stanford University Press, 1958).

When King Pyrrhus passed over into Italy, after he had reconnoitered the formation of the army that the Romans were sending to meet him, he said: "I do not know what barbarians these are" (for so the Greeks called all foreign nations), "but the formation of this army that I see is not at all barbarous." The Greeks said as much of the army that Flamininus brought into their country, and so did Philip, seeing from a knoll the order and distribution of the Roman camp, in his kingdom, under Publius Sulpicius Galba. Thus we should beware of clinging to vulgar opinions, and judge things by reason's way, not by popular say.

I had with me for a long time a man who had lived for ten or twelve years in that other world which has been discovered in our century, in the place where Villegaignon landed, and which he called Antarctic France. This discovery of a boundless country seems worthy of consideration. I don't know if I can guarantee that some other such discovery will not be made in the future, so many personages greater than ourselves having been mistaken about this one. I am afraid we have eyes bigger than our stomachs, and more curiosity than capacity. We embrace everything, but we clasp only wind.

*   *   *

This man I had was a simple, crude fellow—a character fit to bear true witness; for clever people observe more things and more curiously, but they interpret them; and to lend weight and conviction to their interpretation, they cannot help altering history a little. They never show you things as they are, but bend and disguise them according to the way they have seen them; and to give credence to their judgment and attract you to it, they are prone to add something to their matter, to stretch it out and amplify it. We need a man either very honest, or so simple that he has not the stuff to build up false inventions and give them plausibility; and wedded to no theory. Such was my man; and besides this, he at various times brought sailors and merchants, whom he had known on that trip, to see me. So I content myself with his information, without inquiring what the cosmographers say about it.

*   *   *

Now, to return to my subject, I think there is nothing barbarous and savage in that nation, from what I have been told, except that each man calls barbarism whatever is not his own practice; for indeed it seems we have no other test of truth and reason than the example and pattern of the opinions and customs of the country we live in. *There is always the perfect religion, the perfect government, the perfect and accomplished manners in all things.* Those people are wild, just as we call wild the fruits that Nature has produced by herself and in her normal course; whereas really it is those that we have changed artificially and led astray from the common order, that we should rather call wild. The former retain alive and vigorous their genuine, their most useful and natural, virtues and properties, which we have debased in the latter in adapting them to gratify our corrupted taste. And yet for all that, the savor and delicacy of some uncultivated fruits of those countries is quite as excellent, even to our taste, as that of our own. It is not reasonable that art should win the place of honor over our great and powerful mother Nature. We have so overloaded the beauty and richness of her works by our inventions that we have quite smothered her. Yet wherever her purity shines forth, she wonderfully puts to shame our vain and frivolous attempts:

Ivy comes readier without our care;
In lonely caves the arbutus grows more fair;
No art with artless bird song can compare.
                                        Propertius

All our efforts cannot even succeed in reproducing the nest of the tiniest little bird, its contexture, its beauty and convenience; or even the web of the puny spider. All things, says Plato, are produced by nature, by fortune, or by art; the greatest and most beautiful by one or the other of the first two, the least and most imperfect by the last.

These nations, then, seem to me barbarous in this sense, that they have been fashioned very little by the human mind, and are still very close to their original naturalness. The laws of nature still rule them, very little corrupted by ours; and they are in such a state of purity that I am sometimes vexed that they were unknown earlier, in the days when there were men able to judge them better than we. I am sorry that Lycurgus and Plato did not know of them; for it seems to me that what we actually see in these nations surpasses not only all the pictures in which poets have idealized the golden age and all their inventions in imagining a happy state of man, but also the conceptions and the very desire of philosophy. They could not imagine a naturalness so pure and simple as we see by experience; nor could they believe that our society could be maintained with so little artifice and human solder. This is a nation, I should say to Plato, in which there is no sort of traffic, no knowledge of letters, no science of numbers, no name for a magistrate or for political superiority, no custom of servitude, no riches or poverty, no contracts, no successions, no partitions, no occupations but leisure ones, no care for any but common kinship, no clothes, no agriculture, no metal, no use of wine or wheat. The very words that signify lying, treachery, dissimulation, avarice, envy, belittling, pardon—unheard of. How far from this perfection would he find the republic that he imagined: *Men fresh sprung from the gods.*

These manners nature first ordained.
                                        Virgil

For the rest, they live in a country with a very pleasant and temperate climate, so that according to my witnesses it is rare to see a sick man there; and they have assured me that they never saw one palsied, bleary-eyed, toothless, or bent with age. They are settled along the sea and shut in on the land side by great high mountains, with a stretch about a hundred leagues wide in between. They have a great abundance of fish and flesh which bear no resemblance to ours, and they eat them with no other artifice than cooking. The first man who rode a horse there, though he had had dealings with them on several other trips, so horrified them in this posture that they shot him dead with arrows before they could recognize him.

Their buildings are very long, with a capacity

of two or three hundred souls; they are covered with the bark of great trees, the strips reaching to the ground at one end and supporting and leaning on one another at the top, in the manner of some of our barns, whose covering hangs down to the ground and acts as a side. They have wood so hard that they cut with it and make of it their swords and grills to cook their food. Their beds are of a cotton weave, hung from the roof like those in our ships, each man having his own; for the wives sleep apart from their husbands.

They get up with the sun, and eat immediately upon rising, to last them through the day; for they take no other meal than that one. Like some other Eastern peoples, of whom Suidas tells us, who drank apart from meals, they do not drink then; but they drink several times a day, and to capacity. Their drink is made of some root, and is of the color of our claret wines. They drink it only lukewarm. This beverage keeps only two or three days; it has a slightly sharp taste, is not at all heady, is good for the stomach, and has a laxative effect upon those who are not used to it; it is a very pleasant drink for anyone who is accustomed to it. In place of bread they use a certain white substance like preserved coriander. I have tried it; it tastes sweet and a little flat.

The whole day is spent in dancing. The younger men go to hunt animals with bows. Some of the women busy themselves meanwhile with warming their drink, which is their chief duty. Some one of the old men, in the morning before they begin to eat, preaches to the whole barnful in common, walking from one end to the other, and repeating one single sentence several times until he has completed the circuit (for the buildings are fully a hundred paces long). He recommends to them only two things: valor against the enemy and love for their wives. And they never fail to point out this obligation, as their refrain, that it is their wives who keep their drink warm and seasoned.

There may be seen in several places, including my own house, specimens of their beds, of their ropes, of their wooden swords and the bracelets with which they cover their wrists in combats, and of the big canes, open at one end, by whose sound they keep time in their dances. They are close shaven all over, and shave themselves much more cleanly than we, with nothing but a wooden or stone razor. They believe that souls are immortal, and that those who have deserved well of the gods are lodged in that part of heaven where the sun rises, and the damned in the west.

They have some sort of priests and prophets, but they rarely appear before the people, having their home in the mountains. On their arrival there is a great feast and solemn assembly of several villages—each barn, as I have described it, makes up a village, and they are about one French league from each other. The prophet speaks to them in public, exhorting them to virtue and their duty; but their whole ethical science contains only these two articles: resoluteness in war and affection for their wives. He prophesies to them things to come and the results they are to expect from their undertakings, and urges them to war or holds them back from it; but this is on the condition that when he fails to prophesy correctly, and if things turn out otherwise than he has predicted, he is cut into a thousand pieces if they catch him, and condemned as a false prophet. For this reason, the prophet who has once been mistaken is never seen again.

*   *   *

They have their wars with the nations beyond the mountains, further inland, to which they go quite naked, with no other arms than bows or wooden swords ending in a sharp point, in the manner of the tongues of our boar spears. It is astonishing what firmness they show in their combats, which never end but in slaughter and bloodshed; for as to routs and terror, they know nothing of either.

Each man brings back as his trophy the head of the enemy he has killed, and sets it up at the entrance to his dwelling. After they have treated their prisoners well for a long time with all the hospitality they can think of, each man who has a prisoner calls a great assembly of his acquaintances. He ties a rope to one of the prisoner's arms, by the end of which he holds him, a few steps away, for fear of being hurt, and gives his dearest friend the other arm to hold in the same way; and these two, in the presence of the whole assembly, kill him with their swords. This done, they roast him and eat him in common and send some pieces to their absent friends. This is not, as people think, for nourishment, as of old the Scythians used to do; it is to betoken an extreme revenge. And the proof of this came when they saw the Portuguese, who had joined forces with their adversaries, inflict a different kind of death on them when they took them prisoner, which was to bury them up to the waist, shoot the rest of their body full of arrows, and afterward hang them. They thought that these people from the other world, being men who had sown the knowledge of many vices among their neighbors and were much greater masters than themselves in every sort of wickedness, did not adopt this sort of vengeance without some reason, and that it must be more painful than their own; so they began to give up their old method and to follow this one.

I am not sorry that we notice the barbarous horror of such acts, but I am heartily sorry that, judging their faults rightly, we should be so blind to our own. I think there is more barbarity in eating a man alive than in eating him dead; and in tearing by tortures and the rack a body still full of feeling, in roasting a man bit by bit, in having him bitten and mangled by dogs and swine (as we have not only read but seen within fresh memory, not among ancient enemies, but among neighbors and fellow citizens, and what is worse, on the pretext of piety and religion), than in roasting and eating him after he is dead.

*   *   *

So we may well call these people barbarians, in respect to the rules of reason, but not in respect to ourselves, who surpass them in every kind of barbarity.

Their warfare is wholly noble and generous, and as excusable and beautiful as this human disease can be; its only basis among them is their rivalry in valor. They are not fighting for the conquest of new lands, for they still enjoy that natural abundance that provides them without toil and trouble with all necessary things in such profusion that they have no wish to enlarge their boundaries. They are still in that happy state of desiring only as much as their natural needs demand; anything beyond that is superfluous to them.

They generally call those of the same age, brothers; those who are younger, children; and the old men are fathers to all the others. These leave to their heirs in common the full possession of their property, without division or any other title at all than just the one that Nature gives to her creatures in bringing them into the world.

If their neighbors cross the mountains to attack them and win a victory, the gain of the victor is glory, and the advantage of having proved the master in valor and virtue; for apart from this they have no use for the goods of the vanquished, and they return to their own country, where they lack neither anything necessary nor that great thing, the knowledge of how to enjoy their condition happily and be content with it. These men of ours do the same in their turn. They demand of their prisoners no other ransom than that they confess and acknowledge their defeat. But there is not one in a whole century who does not choose to die rather than to relax a single bit, by word or look, from the grandeur of an invincible courage; not one who would not rather be killed and eaten than so much as ask not to be. They treat them very freely, so that life may be all the dearer to them, and usually entertain them with threats of their coming death, of the torments they will have to suffer, the preparations that are being made for that purpose, the cutting up of their limbs, and the feast that will be made at their expense. All this is done for the sole purpose of extorting from their lips some weak or base word, or making them want to flee, so as to gain the advantage of having terrified them and broken down their firmness. For indeed, if you take it the right way, it is in this point alone that true victory lies:

It is no victory
Unless the vanquished foe admits your mastery.
Claudian

The Hungarians, very bellicose fighters, did not in olden times pursue their advantage beyond putting the enemy at their mercy. For having wrung a confession from him to this effect, they let him go unharmed and unransomed, except, at most, for exacting his promise never again to take up arms against them.

We win enough advantages over our enemies that are borrowed advantages, not really our own. It is the quality of a porter, not of valor, to have sturdier arms and legs; agility is a dead and corporeal quality; it is a stroke of luck to make our enemy stumble, or dazzle his eyes by the sunlight; it is a trick of art and technique, which may be found in a worthless coward, to be an able fencer. The worth and value of a man is in his heart and his will; there lies his real honor. Valor is the strength, not of legs and arms, but of heart and soul; it consists not in the worth of our horse or our weapons, but in our own. He who falls obstinate in his courage, *if he has fallen, he fights on his knees.* He who relaxes none of his assurance, no matter how great the danger of imminent death; who, giving up his soul, still looks firmly and scornfully at his enemy—he is beaten not by us, but by fortune; he is killed, not conquered.

*   *   *

To return to our story. These prisoners are so far from giving in, in spite of all that is done to them, that on the contrary, during the two or three months that they are kept, they wear a gay expression; they urge their captors to hurry and put them to the test; they defy them, insult them, reproach them with their cowardice and the number of battles they have lost to the prisoners' own people.

I have a song composed by a prisoner which contains this challenge, that they should all come boldly and gather to dine off him, for they will be eating at the same time their own fathers and grandfathers, who have served to feed and nourish his body. "These muscles," he says, "this flesh and these veins are your own, poor fools that you are. You do not recognize that the substance of your ancestors' limbs is still contained in them. Savor them well; you will find in them the taste of your own flesh." An idea that certainly does not smack of barbarity. Those that paint these people dying, and who show the execution, portray the prisoner spitting in the face of his slayers and scowling at them. Indeed, to the last gasp they never stop braving and defying their enemies by word and look. Truly here are real savages by our standards; for either they must be thoroughly so, or we must be; there is an amazing distance between their character and ours.

The men there have several wives, and the higher their reputation for valor the more wives they have. It is a remarkably beautiful thing about their marriages that the same jealousy our wives have to keep us from the affection and kindness of other women, theirs have to win this for them. Being more concerned for their husbands' honor than for anything else, they strive and scheme to have as many companions as they can, since that is a sign of their husbands' valor.

*   *   *

Three of these men, ignorant of the price they will pay some day, in loss of repose and happiness, for gaining knowledge of the corruptions of this side of the ocean; ignorant also of the fact that of this intercourse will come their ruin (which I suppose is already well advanced: poor wretches, to let themselves be tricked by the desire for new things, and to have left the serenity of their own sky to come and see ours!)—three of these men were at Rouen, at the time the late King Charles IX was there. The king talked to them for a long time; they were shown our ways, our splendor, the aspect of a fine city. After that, someone asked their opinion, and wanted to know what they had found most amazing. They mentioned three things, of which I have forgotten the third, and I am very sorry for it; but I still remember two of them. They said that in the first place they thought it very strange that so many grown men, bearded, strong, and armed, who were around the king (it is likely that they were talking about the Swiss of his guard) should submit to obey a child, and that one of them was not chosen to command instead. Second (they have a way in their language of speaking of men as halves of one another), they had noticed that there were among us men full and gorged with all sorts of good things, and that their other halves were beggars at their doors, emaciated with hunger and poverty; and they thought it strange that these needy halves could endure such an injustice, and did not take the others by the throat, or set fire to their houses.

I had a very long talk with one of them; but I had an interpreter who followed my meaning so badly, and who was so hindered by his stupidity in taking in my ideas, that I could get hardly any satisfaction from the man. When I asked him what profit he gained from his superior position among his people (for he was a captain, and our sailors called him king), he told me that it was to march foremost in war. How many men followed him? He pointed to a piece of ground, to signify as

many as such a space could hold; it might have been four or five thousand men. Did all his authority expire with the war? He said that this much remained, that when he visited the villages dependent on him, they made paths for him through the underbrush by which he might pass quite comfortably.

All this is not too bad—but what's the use? They don't wear breeches.

*   *   *

REVIEW QUESTIONS

1. What lessons does Montaigne draw from accounts of the new world?
2. Why do you suppose Montaigne chose cannibalism, of all possible topics, to compare European and American cultures?
3. How does he reflect the crisis of the Iron Century?
4. Are there any human constants for Montaigne?
5. Does he believe in a single human nature, a single ideal of virtue?

HENRY BLOUNT

FROM *A Voyage into the Levant*

The Englishman Henry Blount was an adventurer and traveler. His acute, sympathetic observations of the Turkish Empire render vividly the great power of the Ottomans. In the 1630s, after more than a century of invasion and conquest, the Ottoman Turks were still considered a menace—aggressive, hostile, and heathen— to the Christian West. This particular passage, concerning the organization of the

THE PLUNDERING AND BURNING OF A VILLAGE, A HANGING, AND
PEASANTS AVENGE THEMSELVES (1633)   JACQUES CALLOT

These three prints, often referred to as The Horrors of War, *powerfully reveal commonplace events of the early seventeenth century: the ravages of war on a small village, the punishment of unruly troops, and the violence of the violated. They reveal the underbelly of early modern warfare in a way that contrasts starkly with the stately, heroic images of Velázquez and others. How do the troopers depicted by Callot differ from those depicted by Velázquez? How do their representations of warfare differ? How does Callot portray rural life? What general aspects of the Iron Century does Callot capture in his images?*

676

Turkish army, suggests that the perception was not misplaced. At the same time, however, the 1634 publication of his A Voyage into the Levant *signals Blount's growing fascination with a wider, non-European world.*

From *Documentary History of Eastern Europe*, edited by Alfred J. Bannan and Achilles Edelenyi (New York: Twayne, 1970), pp. 100–4.

*   *   *

Turkish Power in the 1630s

At length we reached Vallivoh, a pretty little town upon the confines of Hungary; where the camp staying some days, we left them behind, and being to pass a wood near the Christian country, doubting it to be (as confines are) full of thieves, we divided our caravan of six score horse in two parts; half with the persons, and goods of least esteem, we sent a day before the rest, that so the thieves, having a booty, might be gone before we came, which happened accordingly; they were robbed; one thief, and two of ours slain; some hundred dollars worth of goods lost. The next day we passed, and found sixteen thieves in a narrow passage, before whom we set a good guard of harquebuzes and pistols, till the weaker fort passed by; so in three days we came safe to Belgrada.

The city, anciently called Taurunum, or Alba Graeca, was the metropolis of Hungary, till won by sultan Soliman the second, in the year 1525. It is one of the most pleasant, stately, and commodious situations that I have seen; it stands most in a bottom, encompassed eastward by gentle and pleasant ascents, employed in orchards or vines; southward is an easy hill, part possessed with buildings, the rest a burying-place of well nigh three miles in compass, so full of graves as one can be by another; the west end yields a right magnificient aspect, by reason of an eminency of land jetting out further than the rest, and bearing a goodly strong castle, whose walls are two miles about, excellently fortified with a dry ditch and out works. This castle on the west side is washed by the great river Sava, which on the north of the city loses itself in the Danubius, of old called Ister,

now Duny, and is held the greatest river in the world, deep and dangerous for navigation, runs eastward into the Euxine or Black Sea, in its passage receiving fifty and odd rivers, most of them navigable. Two rarities, I was told of this river, and with my own experience found true; one was, that at mid-day and mid-night, the stream runs slower by much than at other times; this they find by the noise of those boat-mills, whereof there are about twenty, like those upon the Rhoane at Lions; their clackers beat much slower at those times than else, which argues like difference in the motion of the wheel, and by consequence of the stream; the cause is neither any reflux, nor stop of current by wind or otherwise, for there is no increase of water observed. The other wonder is, that where those two great currents meet, their waters mingle no more than water and oil; not that either floats above other, but join unmixed; so that near the middle of the river, I have gone in a boat, and tasted of the Danuby as clear and pure as a well; then putting my hand not an inch further, I have taken of the Sava as troubled as a street channel, tasting the gravel in my teeth; yet it did not tast unctious, as I expected, but hath some others secret ground of the antipathy, which though not easily found out, is very effectual; for they run thus threescore miles together, and for a day's journey I have been an eye witness thereof.

The castle is excellently furnished with artillery, and at the entrance there stands an arsenal with some forty or fifty fair brass pieces, most bearing the arms and inscription of Ferdinand the emperor. That which to me seemed strangest in this castle (for I had free liberty to pry up and down) was a round tower called the Zindana, a cruelty not by them devised, and seldom practiced; it is like old Rome's Gemoniae: the tower is large and round, but within severed into many squares of long beams, set on end about four feet asunder; each beam was stuck frequently with great flesh hooks; the person condemned was naked, let fall amongst those hooks, which gave him a quick or lasting misery, as he chanced to light; then at the bottom the river is let in by grates, whereby all the putrefaction was washed away. Within this great castle is another little one, with works of its own; I had like to have miscarried with approaching the entrance, but the rude noise, and worse looks of the guard, gave me a timely apprehension with sudden passage, and humiliation, to sweeten them, and get off; for, as I after learned, there is kept great part of the Grand Seignior's treasure, to be ready when he wars on that side the empire: it is death for any Turk or Christian to enter; and the captain is never to go forth without particular license from the emperor. Here the bashaw of Temesuar, joining the people of Buda, and his own with those of Belgrade and Bosnah, they were held encamped on the south side of the town, yet not so severely, but the Spahies, Janisaaries, and Venturiers, had leave to go before to the general rendezvous, as they pleased, though most of them staid to attend the bashaws; they there expected Murath bashaw; he, five days after our arrival, came in with a few foot, but four thousand horse, of the Spahy Timariot's; such brave horses, and men so dexterous in the use of the launce, I had not seen. Then was made public proclamation to hang all such Janissaries as should be found behind these forces. With them the next day we set forward for Sophia, which in twelve days we reached. The bashaws did not go all in company, but setting forth about an hour one after another, drew out their troops in length without confusion, not in much exact order of file and rank, as near no enemy. In this and our former march, I much admired that we had a caravan loaded with clothes, silks, tissues, and other rich commodities, were so safe, not only in the main army, but in straggling troops, amongst whom we often wandered, by reason of recovering the Jews sabbath; but I found the cause to be the cruelty of justice;

for thieves upon the way are empaled without delay; or mercy; and there was a Saniack, with two hundred horse, who did nothing but coast up and down the country, and every man who could not give a fair account of his being where he found him, was presently strangled, though not known to have offended; for their justice, although not so rash as we suppose, yet will rather cut off two innocent men, than let one offender escape; for in the execution of an innocent, they think if he be held guilty, the example works as well as if he were guilty indeed; and where a constant denial makes the fact doubted, in that execution, the resentment so violent terrifies the more: therefore to prevent disorders sometimes, in the beginnings of war, colourable punishments are used, where just ones are wanting. This speedy and remorseless severity makes that when then their great armies lie about any town or pass, no man is endamaged or troubles to secure his goods; in which respect it pretends more effect upon a bad age than our Christian compassion, which is so easily abused, as we cannot raise two or three companies of soldiers, but they pilfer and rifle wheresoever they pass; wherein the want of cruelty upon delinquents, causes much more oppression of the innocent, which is the greatest cruelty of all. Yet without their army there want not scandals, for in the way we passed by a Palanga, which is a village fortified with mud walls against thieves, where we found a small caravan to have been assaulted the day before, and divers remaining sore wounded; for through all Turkey, especially in desart places, there are many mountaineers, or outlaws, like the Wild Irish, who live upon spoil, and are not held members of the state, but enemies, and used accordingly. In all our march, though I could not perceive much discipline, as not near an adverse party, yet I wondered to see such a multitude so clear of confusion, violence, want, sickness, or any other disorder; and, though we were almost three score thousand, and sometimes found not a town in seven or eight days, yet was there such plenty of good bisket, rice, and mutton, as wheresoever I passed up and down to view the Spahies and others in their tents, they would often make me sit and eat with them very plentifully and well. . . .

*   *   *

REVIEW QUESTIONS

1. What does Blount's account reveal about the perils of travel within Europe during the seventeenth century?

2. Why do you suppose Blount reserved so much of his attention for the Turkish military force?

3. What does he most admire?

4. How does his account of Turkish soldiers contrast with that of Christian soldiers by Grimmelshausen?

5. Does the description of Turkish society and military organization serve as a deliberate contrast to and criticism of those organizations ravaging much of central Europe in the 1630s?

LORENZO BERNARDO

FROM A Venetian Ambassador's Report on the Ottoman Empire

*The struggle for supremacy in northern Italy, which marked the last half of the fif-
teenth century, gave rise to a new form of diplomacy, structures and procedures that
would be fundamental to relations among all modern states. Requiring continuous
contact and communication, Renaissance states turned to permanent diplomacy, distinguished by the use of accredited resident ambassadors rather than ad hoc missions of medieval legates. The tasks of a permanent ambassador were to represent
his government at state ceremonies, to gather information, and, occasionally, to enter into negotiations. Nowhere was this system more fully and expertly articulated
than by the Republic of Venice in the late fifteenth and sixteenth centuries. Ambassadors were chosen with unusual care from the most prominent families of the city.
They were highly educated, and their duties were carefully defined.*

*Among the ambassadors' duties were weekly dispatches reporting all matters of
any interest to Venice. These reports were regularly read and debated in the Senate,
which replied with questions, instructions, and information of its own. As a result,
Venetian ambassadors were among the most skilled and respected in early modern
Europe. Their reports remain a singularly important source for the history of that
period. Lorenzo Bernardo had the distinction of serving as the Venetian ambassador
to a non-European state, Venice's chief rival in trade to the Middle East and the
great power of the Moslem world, the Ottoman Empire. Though his assignment to
Constantinople was brief (1591–1592), he offered the following analysis of the empire's strengths and weaknesses and of why Venice might expect its imminent decline. It offers insights into the political power in early modern Europe, as well as a
Western perspective on non-Western states and civilizations.*

From *Pursuit of Power: Venetian Ambassadors' Reports on Spain, Turkey and France in the
Age of Phillip II, 1560–1600,* by James C. Davis (New York: HarperCollins, 1970), pp. 72–
76, 78–79.

*   *   *

Three basic qualities have enabled the Turks
to make such remarkable conquests, and rise to
such importance in a brief period: religion, frugality, and obedience.

From the beginning it was religion that made
them zealous, frugality that made them satisfied
with little, and obedience that produced men
ready for any dangerous campaign.

In an earlier report I discussed at length these
three qualities, which were then and always had
been typical of the Turks. Now I plan to follow
the same order, but to discuss whether any
changes have taken place subsequently that might
lead us to hope that empire will eventually decline.

For nothing is more certain than that every living thing (including kingdoms and empires) has a beginning, a middle, and an end, or, you might say, a growth, maturity, and decline.

In former times, Serene Prince, all Turks held to a single religion, whose major belief is that it is "written" when and how a man will die, and that if he dies for his God and his faith he will go directly to Paradise. It is not surprising, then, that one reads in histories about Turks who vied for the chance to fill a ditch with their bodies, or made a human bridge for others to use crossing a river, going to their deaths without the slightest hesitation. But now the Turks have not a single religion, but three of them. The Persians are among the Turks like the heretics among us, because some of them hold the beliefs of Ali, and others those of Omar, both of whom were followers of Mohammed, but held different doctrines. Then there are the Arabs and Moors, who claim they alone preserve the true, uncorrupted religion and that the "Greek Turks" (as they call these in Constantinople) are bastard Turks with a corrupted religion, which they blame on their being mostly descended from Christian renegades who did not understand the Muslim religion. As a matter of fact, I have known many of these renegades who had no religious beliefs, and said religions were invented by men for political reasons. They hold that when the body dies the soul dies, just as it does with brute beasts, which they are.

The belief that one's death is "written" and that one has no free will to escape dangers is declining in Turkey with each passing day. Experience teaches them the opposite when they see that a man who avoids plague victims saves his life while one who has stayed with them catches plague and dies. During my time there as *bailo* I even saw their mufti flee Constantinople for fear of plague and go to the garden to live, and the Grand Signor himself took care to avoid all contacts with his generals. Having learned they can escape from plagues, they now apply the same lesson to wars. Everybody shirks war service as long as he can, and when he does go he hangs back from the front lines and concentrates on saving

his own life. When the authorities announce a campaign in Persia there are outcries and revolts, and if the sultan wants to send janissaries there he creates new ones who are so glad to have the higher pay that they are willing to risk dangers which the regulars dread and flee. In short, nowadays they all look out for their own safety.

As for frugality, which I said was the second of the three sources of the Turks' great power, this used to be one of their marked characteristics. At one time the Turks had no interest in fine foods or, if they were rich, in splendid decorations in their houses. Each was happy with bread and rice, and a carpet and a cushion; he showed his importance only by having many slaves and horses with which he could better serve his ruler. No wonder then that they could put up with the terrible effort and physical discomfort involved in conquering and ruling. What a shameful lesson to our own state, where we equate military glory with sumptuous banquets and our men want to live in their camps and ships as if they were back home at weddings and feasts!

But now that the Turks have conquered vast, rich lands they too have fallen victims to the corruption of wealth. They are beginning to appreciate fine foods and game, and most of them drink wine. They furnish their houses beautifully and wear clothes of gold and silver with costly linings. Briefly, then, they become fonder every day of luxury, comfort, and display. They are happy to follow the example provided by the sultan, who cares nothing about winning glory on the battlefield and prefers to stay at home and enjoy the countless pleasures of the seraglio. Modeling themselves on him, all the splendid pashas, governors, and generals, and the ordinary soldiers too, want to stay in *their* homes and enjoy *their* pleasures and keep as far as possible from the dangers and discomforts of war. The pashas make use of their wives, who are related to the Grand Signor, to persuade him to keep their husbands at home. They do this not only to satisfy the men but also because they know that if they stay in Constantinople their husbands can win more favor by serving and fawning on the Grand Signor. If they go to war their rivals down such particulars as may serve for the cause we have in hand.

1. First, although this Realm be already exceeding rich by nature, yet might it be much encreased by laying the waste grounds (which are infinite) into such employments as should no way hinder the present revenues of other manured lands, but hereby to supply our selves and prevent the importations of Hemp, Flax, Cordage, Tobacco, and divers other things which now we fetch from strangers to our great impoverishing.

2. We may likewise diminish our importations, if we would soberly refrain from excessive consumption of forraign wares in our diet and rayment, with such often change of fashions as is used, so much the more to encrease the waste and charge; which vices at this present are more notorious amongst us than in former ages. Yet might they easily be amended by enforcing the observation of such good laws as are strictly practised in other Countries against the said excesses; where likewise by commanding their own manufactures to be used, they prevent the coming in of others, without prohibition, or offence to strangers in their mutual commerce.

3. In our exportations we must not only regard our own superfluities, but also we must consider our neighbours necessities, that so upon the wares which they cannot want, nor yet be furnished thereof elsewhere, we may (besides the vent of the Materials) gain so much of the manufacture as we can, and also endeavour to sell them dear, so far forth as the high price cause not a less vent in the quantity. But the superfluity of our commodities which strangers use, and may also have the same from other Nations, or may abate their vent by the use of some such like wares from other places, and with little inconvenience; we must in this case strive to sell as cheap as possible we can, rather than to lose the utterance of such wares. For we have found of late years by good experience, that being able to sell our Cloth cheap in Turkey, we have greatly encreased the vent thereof, and the *Venetians* have lost as much in the utterance of theirs in those Countreys, because it is dearer. And on the other side a few years past, when by the

excessive price of Wools our Cloth was exceeding dear, we lost at the least half our clothing for forraign parts, which since is no otherwise (well neer) recovered again than by the great fall of price for Wools and Cloth. We find that twenty five in the hundred less in the price of these and some other Wares, to the loss of private mens revenues, may raise above fifty upon the hundred in the quantity vented to the benefit of the publique. For when Cloth is dear, other Nations doe presently practice clothing, and we know they want neither art nor materials to this performance. But when by cheapness we drive them from this employment, and so in time obtain our dear price again, then do they also use their former remedy. So that by these alterations we learn, that it is in vain to expect a greater revenue of our wares than their condition will afford, but rather it concerns us to apply our endeavours to the times with care and diligence to help our selves the best we may, by making our cloth and other manufactures without deceit, which will encrease their estimation and use.

4. The value of our exportations likewise may be much advanced when we perform it our selves in our own Ships, for then we get only not the price of our wares as they are worth here, but also the Merchants gains, the charges of ensurance, and fraight to carry them beyond the seas. As for example, if the *Italian* Merchants should come hither in their own shipping to fetch our Corn, our red Herrings or the like, in this case the Kingdom should have ordinarily but 25s. for a quarter of Wheat, and 20s. for a barrel of red herrings, whereas if we carry these wares our selves into *Italy* upon the said rates, it is likely that wee shall obtain fifty shillings for the first, and forty shillings for the last, which is a great difference in the utterance or vent of the Kingdoms stock. And although it is true that the commerce ought to be free to strangers to bring in and carry out at their pleasure, yet nevertheless in many places the exportation of victuals and munition are either prohibited, or at least limited to be done onely by the people and Shipping of those places where they abound.

5. The frugal expending likewise of our own nat-

ural wealth might advance much yearly to be exported unto strangers; and if in our rayment we will be prodigal, yet let this be done with our own materials and manufactures, as Cloth, Lace, Imbroderies, Cut-works and the like, where the excess of the rich may be the employment of the poor, whose labours notwithstanding of this kind, would be more profitable for the Commonwealth, if they were done to the use of strangers.

6. The Fishing in his Majesties seas of *England, Scotland,* and *Ireland* is our natural wealth, and would cost nothing but labour, which the *Dutch* bestow willingly, and thereby draw yearly a very great profit to themselves by serving many places of Christendom with our Fish, for which they return and supply their wants both of forraign Wares and Mony, besides the multitude of Mariners and Shipping, which hereby are maintain'd, whereof a long discourse might be made to show the particular manage of this important business. Our fishing plantation likewise in *New-England, Virginia, Groenland,* the *Summer Islands* and the *New-found-land,* are of the like nature, affording much wealth and employments to maintain a great number of poor, and to encrease our decaying trade.

7. A Staple or Magazin for forraign Corn, Indigo, Spices, Raw-silks, Cotton wool or any other commodity whatsoever, to be imported will encrease Shipping, Trade, Treasure, and the Kings customes, by exporting them again where need shall require, which course of Trading, hath been the chief means to raise *Venice, Genoa,* the *low-Countreys,* with some others; and for such a purpose *England* stands most commodiously, wanting nothing to this performance but our own diligence and endeavour.

8. Also wee ought to esteem and cherish those trades which we have in remote or far Countreys, for besides the encrease of Shipping and Mariners thereby, the wares also sent thither and receiv'd from thence are far more profitable unto the kingdom than by our trades neer at hand; As for example; suppose Pepper to be worth here two Shillings the pound constantly, if then it be brought from the *Dutch* at *Amsterdam,* the Merchant may give there twenty pence the pound, and gain well by the bargain; but if he fetch this Pepper from the *East-indies,* he must not give above three pence the pound at the most, which is a mighty advantage, not only in that part which serveth for our own use, but also for that great quantity which (from hence) we transport yearly unto divers other Nations to be sold at a higher price: whereby it is plain, that we make a far greater stock by gain upon these *Indian* Commodities, than those Nations doe where they grow, and to whom they properly appertain, being the natural wealth of their Countries. But for the better understanding of this particular, we must ever distinguish between the gain of the Kingdom, and the profit of the Merchant; for although the Kingdom payeth no more for this Pepper than is before supposed, nor for any other commodity bought in forraign parts more than the stranger receiveth from us for the same, yet the Merchant payeth not only that price, but also the fraight, ensurance, customes and other charges which are exceeding great in these long voyages; but yet all these in the Kingdoms accompt are but commutations among our selves, and no Privation of the Kingdoms stock, which being duly considered, together with the support also of our other trades in our best Shipping to *Italy, France, Turkey,* the *East Countreys* and other places, by transporting and venting the wares which we bring yearly from the *East Indies;* It may well stir up our utmost endeavours to maintain and enlarge this great and noble business, so much importing the Publique wealth, Strength, and Happiness. Neither is there less honour and judgment by growing rich (in this manner) upon the stock of other Nations, than by an industrious encrease of our own means, especially when this later is advanced by the benefit of the former, as we have found in the *East Indies* by sale of much of our Tin, Cloth, Lead and other Commodities, the vent whereof doth daily encrease in those Countreys which formerly had no use of our wares.

9. It would be very beneficial to export money as well as wares, being done in trade only, it would encrease our Treasure; but of this I write

more largely in the next Chapter to prove it plainly.

10. It were policie and profit for the State to suffer manufactures made of forraign Materials to be exported custome-free, as Velvets and all other wrought Silks, Fustians, thrown Silks and the like, it would employ very many poor people, and much encrease the value of our stock yearly issued into other Countreys, and it would (for this purpose) cause the more forraign Materials to be brought in, to the improvement of His Majesties Customes. I will here remember a notable increase in our manufacture of winding and twisting only of forraign raw Silk, which within 35. years to my knowledge did not employ more than 300. people in the City and suburbs of London, where at this present time it doth set on work above fourteen thousand souls, as upon diligent enquiry hath been credibly reported unto His Majesties Commissioners for Trade. And it is certain, that if the said forraign Commodities might be exported from hence, free of custome, this manufacture would yet encrease very much, and decrease as fast in *Italy* and in the *Netherlands*. But if any man allege the *Dutch* proverb, *Live and let others live;* I answer, that the Dutchmen notwithstanding their own Proverb, doe not onely in these Kingdoms, encroach upon our livings, but also in other forraign parts of our trade (where they have power) they do hinder and destroy us in our lawful course of living, hereby taking the bread out of our mouth, which we shall never prevent by plucking the pot from their nose, as of late years too many of us do practise to the great hurt and dishonour of this famous Nation; We ought rather to imitate former times in taking sober and worthy courses more pleasing to God and suitable to our ancient reputation.

11. It is needful also not to charge the native commodities with too great customes, lest by indearing them to the strangers use, it hinder their vent. And especially forraign wares brought in to be transported again should be favoured, for otherwise that manner of trading (so much importing the good of the Commonwealth) cannot prosper nor subsist. But the Consumption of such forraign wares in the Realm may be the more charged, which will turn to the profit of the kingdom in the *Ballance of the Trade,* and thereby also enable the King to lay up the more Treasure out of his yearly incomes, as of this particular I intend to write more fully in his proper place, where I shall shew how much money a Prince may conveniently lay up without the hurt of his subjects.

12. Lastly, in all things we must endeavour to make the most we can of our own, whether it be *Natural* or *Artificial;* And forasmuch as the people which live by the Arts are far more in number than they who are masters of the fruits, we ought the more carefully to maintain those endeavours of the multitude, in whom doth consist the greatest strength and riches both of King and Kingdom: for where the people are many, and the arts good, there the traffique must be great, and the Countrey rich. The *Italians* employ a greater number of people, and get more money by their industry and manufactures of the raw Silks of the Kingdom of *Cicilia,* than the King of *Spain* and his Subjects have by the revenue of this rich commodity. But what need we fetch the example so far, when we know that our own natural wares doe not yield us so much profit as our industry? For Iron oar in the Mines is of no great worth, when it is compared with the employment and advantage it yields being digged, tried, transported, bought, sold, cast into Ordnance, Muskets, and many other instruments of war for offence and defence, wrought into Anchors, bolts, spikes, nayles and the like, for the use of Ships, Houses, Carts, Coaches, Ploughs, and other instruments for Tillage. Compare our Fleece-wools with our Cloth, which requires shearing, washing, carding, spinning, Weaving, fulling, dying, dressing and other trimmings, and we shall find these Arts more profitable than the natural wealth, whereof I might instance other examples, but I will not be more tedious, for if I would amplify upon this and the other particulars before written, I might find matter sufficient to make a large volume, but my desire in all is only to prove what I propound with brevity and plainness.

THE SYNDICS OF THE DRAPERS' GUILD (1632)   REMBRANDT VAN RIJN

One of Rembrandt's most recognizable works, The Syndics *captures all the sober solidity and confidence of Calvinist merchants in the young Dutch Republic. Convinced that worldly success indicated divine election, they look out on the world with purposeful determination to make of their lives a testimonial to God's grace. The work is a penetrating psychological study of these members of the urban elite. What elements of Rembrandt's painting might be characterized as bourgeois? Insofar as the syndics were leaders in Amsterdam society, what does their portrait reveal of that society? Reading into the expressions on the faces and the composition of the portrait, what was Rembrandt's relationship to the artisanal and mercantile world of Amsterdam?*

REVIEW QUESTIONS

1. What does Mun consider trade to be?
2. Of what does it consist?
3. What is his chief concern regarding trade?
4. What is the relation of trade to the nation?
5. What are the foundations of successful trade for Mun?
6. Why does he emphasize moral values in a treatise on economic policy?
7. What are the goods to be found in commerce?

JEAN BAPTISTE POQUELIN (MOLIÈRE)

FROM *The Citizen Who Apes the Nobleman*

Molière (1622–1673) was baptized Jean Baptiste Poquelin. His life might be considered unorthodox from a very early stage. Though educated at the Collège de Clermont, which would number among its alumni such illustrious literati as Voltaire, and clearly intended for a career in royal service, he broke with tradition and joined a traveling company of players in 1643. He adopted his stage name, Molière, the following year and devoted the rest of his life to the stage. His rise to prominence began in 1658, when, playing on an improvised stage in a guardroom of the Louvre, he performed Corneille's Nicomède *as well as a play of his own,* Le docteur amoureux, *before Louis XIV.* Le bourgeois gentilhomme *appeared at the royal palace at Chambord in 1670. It satirized the ambition of contemporary bourgeois to compete in magnificence with the aristocracy. Yet, it was a double-edged satire. Though the theme must have pleased Molière's noble audience, the figure of Jourdain is no unpleasant, boorish climber but rather a delightfully good-natured soul, foolish but naive, fatuous but genuine. An unwillingness to subordinate his art to his audience may help explain why Molière frequently struggled in his lifetime. His actors often abandoned his company. Pensions went unpaid. His best works were not always well received. His fame spread only slowly. Though considered one of the greatest French writers, Molière was no writer in the strict sense. Little of his work was published; his comedies were written to be performed. Publication occurred only after several texts were pirated by Jean Ribou, and several remained unpublished long after Molière's death. This occurred in 1672, when Molière was taken ill during a performance of* Le malade imaginaire. *He died that same night, without receiving the sacraments or renouncing his stage life, and was buried unceremoniously in a common grave.*

From *The Dramatic Words of Molière,* vol. 5 (Barrie, n.d.).

FROM Act I

The overture is played by a great many instruments; and in the middle of the stage, the pupil of the music-master is busy composing a serenade, ordered by M. Jourdain.

SCENE I. A MUSIC-MASTER, A DANCING-MASTER, THREE MUSICIANS, TWO VIOLIN PLAYERS, FOUR DANCERS

Mus.-Mas. (*To the musicians*) Come, retire into that room, and rest yourselves until he comes.

Dan.-Mas. (*To the dancers*) And you also, on that side.

Mus.-Mas. (*To his pupil*) Is it done?

Pup. Yes.

Mus.-Mas. Let me look. . . . That is right.

Dan.-Mas. It is something new?

Mus.-Mas. Yes, it is an air for a serenade, which I made him compose here, while waiting till our gentleman is awake.

Dan.-Mas. May one have a look at it?

Mus.-Mas. You shall hear it by-and-by with the dialogue, when he comes; he will not be long.

Dan.-Mas. Our occupations, yours and mine, are no small matter just at present.

Mus.-Mas. True: we have both of us found here the very man whom we want. It is a nice little income for us this Mr. Jourdain, with his notions of nobility and gallantry, which he has taken into his head; and your dancing and my music might wish that everyone were like him.

Dan.-Mas. Not quite; and I should like him to be more of a judge than he is, of the things we provide for him.

Mus.-Mas. It is true that he knows little about them, but he pays well; and that is what our arts require just now above aught else.

Dan.-Mas. As for myself, I confess, I hunger somewhat after glory. I am fond of applause, and I think that, in all the fine arts, it is an annoying torture to have to exhibit before fools, to have one's compositions subjected to the barbarism of a stupid man. Do not argue; there is a delight in having to work for people who are capable of appreciating the delicacy of an art, who know how to give a sweet reception to the beauties of a work, and who, by approbations which tickle one's fancy, reward one for his labour. Yes, the most pleasant recompense one can receive for the things which one does, is to find them understood, and made much of by applause which does one honour, There is nothing in my opinion, that pays us better for all our troubles; and enlightened praises are exquisitely sweet.

Mus.-Mas. I quite agree with you, and I enjoy them as much as you do. Assuredly, there is nothing that tickles our fancy more than the applause you speak of; but such incense does not give us our livelihood. Praise pure and simple does not provide for a rainy day: there must be something solid mixed withal; and the best way to praise is to put one's hand in one's pocket. M. Jourdain is a man, it is true, whose knowledge is very small, who discourses at random upon all things, and never applauds but at the wrong time; but his money makes up for his bad judgment; he has discernment in his purse; his praises are minted, and this ignorant citizen is of more value to us, as you see, than the great lord who introduced us here.

Dan.-Mas. There is some truth in what you say; but I think you make a little too much of money; and the interest in it is something so grovelling, that no gentleman ought ever to show any attachment to it.

Mus.-Mas. You are glad enough, however, to receive the money which our gentleman gives you.

Dan.-Mas. Assuredly; but I do not make it my whole happiness; and I could wish that with all his wealth he had also some good taste.

Mus.-Mas. I could wish the same; and that is what we are aiming at both of us. But, in any case, he gives us the means of becoming known in the world; and he shall pay for others, and others shall applaud for him.

Dan.-Mas. Here he comes.

*   *   *

SCENE III. MRS. JOURDAIN,
M. JOURDAIN, TWO LACQUEYS

MRS. JOUR. Ha! ha! this is something new again! What is the meaning of this curious get-up, husband? Are you setting the world at nought to deck yourself out in this fashion? and do you wish to become a laughing-stock everywhere?

M. JOUR. None but he-fools and she-fools will make a laughing-stock of me, wife.

MRS. JOUR. In truth, they have not waited until now; and all the world has been laughing for a long while already at your vagaries.

M. JOUR. Who is all this world, pray?

MRS. JOUR. All this world is a world which is right, and which has more sense than you have. As for myself, I am disgusted with the life which you lead. I do not know whether this is our own house or not. One would think it is Shrove Tuesday every day; and from early morn, for fear of being too late, one hears nothing but the noise of fiddles and singers disturbing the whole neighbourhood.

NIC. The mistress is right. I shall never see the ship-shape again with this heap of people that you bring to your house. They have feet that pick up the mud in every quarter of the town to bring it in here afterwards; and poor Françoise is almost worked off her legs, with rubbing the floors which your pretty tutors come to dirty again regularly every day.

M. JOUR. Good gracious! Miss Nicole, your tongue is sharp enough for a country-lass!

MRS. JOUR. Nicole is right; and she has more sense than you have. I should much like to know what you want with a dancing-master, at your age.

NIC. And with a great hulking fencing-master, who shakes the whole house with his stamping, and uproots all the floor-tiles in our big room.

M. JOUR. Hold your tongues, you girl and my wife.

MRS. JOUR. Do you wish to learn dancing against the time when you shall have no longer any legs?

NIC. Do you want to kill any one?

M. JOUR. Hold your tongues, I tell you: you are ignorant women, both of you; and you do not know the benefits of all this.

MRS. JOUR. You ought rather to think of seeing your daughter married, who is of an age to be provided for.

M. JOUR. I shall think of seeing my daughter married when a suitable party shall present himself for her; but I shall also think of acquiring some polite learning.

NIC. I have also heard, Mistress, that for fear of shortcoming, he has taken a philosophy-master to-day.

M. JOUR. Very good. I wish to improve my mind, and to know how to argue about things amongst gentle-folks.

MRS. JOUR. Shall you not go, one of these days, to school, to get the birch, at your age?

M. JOUR. Why not? Would to heaven I could have the birch at this hour before everybody, and that I could know all that they teach at school!

NIC. Yes, indeed! that would improve your legs.

M. JOUR. No doubt it would.

MRS. JOUR. All this is highly necessary to manage your house!

M. JOUR. Assuredly. You both talk like fools, and I am ashamed at your ignorance. (*To Mrs. Jourdain.*) For instance, do you know what you are saying at this moment?

MRS. JOUR. Yes. I know that what I say is very well said, and that you ought to think of leading a different life.

M. JOUR. I am not speaking of that. I am asking you what these words are which you are speaking just now.

MRS. JOUR. They are very sensible words, and your conduct is scarcely so.

M. JOUR. I am not speaking of that, I tell you. I ask you, what I am speaking with you, what I am saying to you at this moment, what that is?

MRS. JOUR. Nonsense.

M. JOUR. He, no, that is not it. What we are saying

both of us, the language we are speaking at this moment?

MRS. JOUR. Well?

M. JOUR. What is it called?

MRS. JOUR. It is called whatever you like.

M. JOUR. It is prose, you stupid.

MRS. JOUR. Prose?

M. JOUR. Yes, prose. Whatever is prose is not verse, and whatever is not verse is prose. Eh? that comes from studying. (*To Nicole.*) And do you know what you are to do to say U?

NIC. How?

M. JOUR. Yes. What do you do when you say U?

NIC. What?

M. JOUR. Say U, just to see.

NIC. Well! U.

M. JOUR. What do you do?

NIC. I say U.

M. JOUR. Yes; but when you say U what do you do?

NIC. I do what you tell me to do.

M. JOUR. Oh! what a strange thing to have to do with fools? You pout the lips outwards, and bring the upper jaw near the lower one; U, do you see? I make a mouth, U.

NIC. Yes: that is fine.

MRS. JOUR. That is admirable!

M. JOUR. It is quite another thing, if you had seen O, and DA, DA, and FA, FA.

MRS. JOUR. But what is all this gibberish?

NIC. What are we the better for all this?

M. JOUR. It drives me mad when I see ignorant women.

MRS. JOUR. Go, you should send all these people about their business, with their silly stuff.

NIC. And above all, this great lout of a fencing-master, who fills the whole of my place with dust.

M. JOUR. Lord! this fencing-master sticks strangely in your gizzard! I will let you see your impertinence directly. (*After having had the foils brought, and giving one of them to Nicole.*) Stay, reason demonstrative. The line of the body. When one thrusts in carte, one has but to do so, and when one thrusts in tierce, one has but

to do so. This is the way never to be killed; and is it not very fine to be sure of one's game when one has to fight somebody? There, just thrust at me, to see.

(*Nicole thrusts several times at M. Jourdain.*)

NIC. Well, what!

M. JOUR. Gently! Hullo! ho! Softly! The devil take the hussy!

NIC. You tell me to thrust at you.

M. JOUR. Yes; but you thrust in tierce, before thrusting at me in carte, and you do not wait for me to parry.

MRS. JOUR. You are mad, husband, with all your fancies; and this has come to you only since you have taken it in your head to frequent the nobility.

M. JOUR. When I frequent the nobility, I show my judgment; and it is better than to frequent your citizens.

MRS. JOUR. Indeed! really there is much to gain by frequenting your nobles; and you have done a great deal of good with this beautiful count, with whom you are so smitten!

M. JOUR. Peace; take care what you say. Do you know, wife, that you do not know of whom you are speaking, when you speak of him? He is a personage of greater importance than you think, a nobleman who is held in great consideration at court, and who speaks to the King just as I speak to you. Is it not a great honour to me to see a person of such standing come so frequently to my house, who calls me his dear friend, and who treats me as if I were his equal? He has more kindness for me than one would ever imagine, and, before all the world, shows me such affection, that I am perfectly confused by it.

MRS. JOUR. Yes, he shows you kindness and affection; but he borrows your money.

M. JOUR. Well, is it not an honour to lend money to a man of that condition? and can I do less for a nobleman who calls me his dear friend?

MRS. JOUR. And this nobleman, what does he do for you?

M. JOUR. Things you would be astonished at, if you knew them.

Mrs. Jour. But what?

M. Jour. That will do! I cannot explain myself. It is enough that if I have lent him money, he will return it to me, and before long.

Mrs. Jour. Yes, you had better wait for it.

M. Jour. Assuredly. Has he not said so?

Mrs. Jour. Yes, yes, he will be sure not to fail in it.

M. Jour. He has given me his word as a nobleman.

Mrs. Jour. Stuff!

M. Jour. Good gracious, you are very obstinate, wife! I tell you that he will keep his word; I am sure of it.

Mrs. Jour. And I, I am sure that he will not, and that all the caresses he loads you with are only so much cajoling.

M. Jour. Hold your tongue. Here he comes.

Mrs. Jour. It wanted nothing but this. He comes perhaps to ask you for another loan; and the very sight of him spoils my dinner.

M. Jour. Hold your tongue, I tell you.

*   *   *

SCENE XII. CLÉONTE, M. JOURDAIN,
MRS. JOURDAIN, LUCILE, COVIELLE, NICOLE

Cle. Sir, I did not wish to depute any one else to prefer a request which I have long meditated. It concerns me sufficiently to undertake it in person; and without farther ado, I will tell you that the honour of being your son-in-law is a glorious favour which I beg of you to grant me.

M. Jour. Before giving you your answer, Sir, I pray you to tell me whether you are a nobleman.

Cle. Sir, most people, on this question, do not hesitate much; the word is easily spoken. There is no scruple in assuming that name, and present custom seems to authorize the theft. As for me, I confess to you, my feelings on this point are rather more delicate. I think that all imposture is unworthy of an honest man, and that it is cowardice to disguise what Heaven has made

us, to deck ourselves in the eyes of the world with a stolen title, and to wish to pass for what we are not. I am born of parents who, no doubt, have filled honourable offices; I have acquitted myself with honour in the army, where I served for six years; and I am sufficiently well to do to hold a middling rank in society; but with all this, I will not assume what others, in my position, might think they had the right to pretend to; and I will tell you frankly that I am not a nobleman.

M. Jour. Your hand, Sir; my daughter is not for you.

Cle. How.

M. Jour. You are not a nobleman: you shall not have my daughter.

Mrs. Jour. What is it you mean by your nobleman? Is it that we ourselves are descended from Saint Louis?

M. Jour. Hold your tongue, wife; I see what you are driving at.

Mrs. Jour. Are we two descended from aught else than from plain citizens?

M. Jour. If that is not a slander?

Mrs. Jour. And was your father not a tradesman as well as mine?

M. Jour. Plague take the woman, she always harps upon that. If your father was a tradesman, so much the worse for him; but as for mine, they are impertinent fellows who say so. All that I have to say to you, is that I will have a nobleman for a son-in-law.

Mrs. Jour. Your daughter wants a husband who is suited to her; and it is much better for her that she should have a respectable man, rich and handsome, than a beggarly and deformed nobleman.

Nic. That is true; we have the son of our village squire, who is the greatest lout and the most stupid nincompoop that I have ever seen.

M. Jour. (To Nicole). Hold your tongue, Miss Impertinence; you always thrust yourself into the conversation. I have sufficient wealth to give my daughter; I wish only for honours, and I will make her a marchioness.

Mrs. Jour. Marchioness?

M. Jour. Yes, marchioness.

Mrs. Jour. Alas! Heaven preserve me from it!

M. Jour. It is a thing I am determined on.

Mrs. Jour. It is a thing to which I shall never consent. Matches with people above one's own position are always subject to the most grievous inconvenience. I do not wish a son-in-law of mine to be able to reproach my daughter with her parents, or that she should have children who would be ashamed to call me their grand-mother. If she were to come and visit me with the equipage of a grand lady, and that, through inadvertency, she should miss curtseying to one of the neighbourhood, people would not fail to say a hundred silly things immediately. Do you see this lady marchioness, they would say, who is giving herself such airs? She is the daughter of M. Jourdain, who was only too glad, when she was a child, to play at ladyship with us. She has not always been so high up in the world, and her two grandfathers sold cloth near the St. Innocent gate. They amassed great wealth for their children, for which they are probably pay-ing very dearly in the other world; for people can scarcely become so rich by remaining hon-est folks. I will not have all this tittle-tattle, and in one word, I wish for a man who shall be grateful to me for my daughter, and to whom I shall be able to say: Sit down there, son-in-law, and dine with me.

M. Jour. These are the sentiments of a narrow mind, to wish to remain for ever in a mean condition. Do not answer me any more: my daughter shall be a marchioness in spite of all the world; and, if you put me in a passion, I shall make her a duchess.

* * *

REVIEW QUESTIONS

1. How are servants and masters, who operated in separate worlds, interdependent in Molière's comedy?
2. What is the relation between nobility and judgment?
3. Do women judge differently or according to different standards?

ROBERT FILMER

FROM *Patriarcha*

Robert Filmer (1588–1563), the English theorist of patriarchalism and absolutism, was born into the Kentish squirearchy. Filmer was educated at Trinity College, Cambridge, and at Lincoln's Inn and was knighted by Charles I. Though he never fought for the king, his house was sacked during the Civil War, and he was impris-oned in the royalist cause. He wrote many political tracts, but his most important work, Patriarcha *(1680), was not well received at the time. Common opinion seemed to follow that of John Locke, who wrote in his* Two Treatises of Govern-ment: *"There was never so much glib nonsense put together in well-sounding En-glish." Yet, Filmer remains interesting in his own right. He is the first English absolutist. Despite the publication date,* Patriarcha *was written before the Civil War and before publication of* Leviathan, *before the actions of Parliament prompted any*

THE MEETING IN LYONS (1625)   PETER PAUL RUBENS

The Meeting in Lyons *is part of a cycle of twenty-one paintings, the largest commission in Rubens's career, for Marie de Medici, dowager queen of France. Intended to hang in her palace in Paris, they describe the important events of her life. It was not easy work; she was a difficult subject, neither beautiful nor interesting nor agreeable. She had quarreled with her late husband, Henri IV, and her son, Louis XIII, had banished her from Paris. Still, Rubens managed to complete the commission to his patroness's satisfaction and created images glorifying the French monarchy. What do the two allegorical figures—Hera, Goddess of Marriage, joining the King and his Queen, and Lyons, driving a chariot—mean in relationship to the royal pair? Why would Rubens choose to represent Henri and Marie as mythological, semidivine figures? Considering the dates of the paintings, after a prolonged civil war and before a great international conflict, what might the allegorical representations of monarch and aristocracy suggest about their strength or weakness?*

696

defense of the monarchy and its prerogatives. Filmer believed that the state was a family, that the first king was a father, and that submission to patriarchal authority was the key to political obligation. Of particular interest is his interpretation of patriarchy, the social structure that characterized early modern Europe until the industrial revolution. Indeed, many scholars argue that Filmer's description of social relations is more realistic than the mechanical individualism put forward by Locke. His achievement notwithstanding, his historical significance rests solely on the fact that all of Locke's political thought was directed against him.

From *Patriarcha and Other Writings,* edited by Johann P. Sommerville (Cambridge, Eng.: Cambridge University Press, 1991), pp. 2–3, 5–12.

Since the time that school divinity began to flourish, there hath been a common opinion maintained as well by divines as by divers other learned men which affirms: "Mankind is naturally endowed and born with freedom from all subjection, and at liberty to choose what form of government it please, and that the power which any one man hath over others was at the first by human right bestowed according to the discretion of the multitude."

This tenet was first hatched in the schools, and hath been fostered by all succeeding papists for good divinity. The divines also of the reformed churches have entertained it, and the common people everywhere tenderly embrace it as being most plausible to flesh and blood, for that it prodigally distributes a portion of liberty to the meanest of the multitude, who magnify liberty as if the height of human felicity were only to be found in it—never remembering that the desire of liberty was the cause of the fall of Adam.

But howsoever this vulgar opinion hath of late obtained great reputation, yet it is not to be found in the ancient Fathers and doctors of the primitive church. It contradicts the doctrine and history of the Holy Scriptures, the constant practice of all ancient monarchies, and the very principles of the law of nature. It is hard to say whether it be more erroneous in divinity or dangerous in policy.

Yet upon the grounds of this doctrine both Jesuits and some over zealous favourers of the Geneva discipline have built a perilous conclusion, which is 'that the people or multitude have power to punish or deprive the prince if he transgress the laws of the kingdom'. Witness Parsons and Buchanan. The first, under the name of Doleman, in the third chapter of his first book labours to prove that kings have been lawfully chastised by their commonwealths. The latter in his book *De Jure Regni apud Scotos* maintains a liberty of the people to depose their prince. Cardinal Bellarmine and Mr Calvin both look asquint this way.

This desperate assertion, whereby kings are made subject to the censures and deprivations of their subjects, follows . . . as a necessary consequence of that former position of the supposed natural equality and freedom of mankind, and liberty to choose what form of government it please.

*   *   *

The rebellious consequence which follows this prime article of the natural freedom of mankind may be my sufficient warrant for a modest examination of the original truth of it. Much hath been said, and by many, for the affirmative. Equity requires that an ear be reserved a little for the negative.

*   *   *

To make evident the grounds of this question about the natural liberty of mankind, I will lay down some passages of Cardinal Bellarmine, that may best unfold the state of this controversy. "Secular or civil power," said he is instituted by men. It is in the people unless they bestow it on a prince. This power is immediately in the whole multitude, as in the subject of it. For this power is by the divine law, but the divine law hath given this power to no particular man. If the positive law be taken away, there is left no reason why amongst a multitude (who are equal) one rather than another should bear rule over the rest. Power is given by the multitude to one man, or to more by the same law of nature, for the commonwealth of itself cannot exercise this power, therefore it is bound to bestow it upon some one man, or some few. It depends upon the consent of the multitude to ordain over themselves a king, or consul, or other magistrate; and if there be a lawful cause, the multitude may change the kingdom into an aristocracy or democracy.

Thus far Bellarmine, in which passages are comprised the strength of all that ever I have read or heard produced for the natural liberty of the subject.

*   *   *

I come now to examine that argument which is used by Bellarmine, and is the one and only argument I can find produced by any author for the proof of the natural liberty of the people. It is thus framed: that God hath given or ordained power is evident by Scripture; but God hath given it to no particular man, because by nature all men are equal; therefore he hath given power to the people or multitude.

To answer this reason, drawn from the equality of mankind by nature, I will first use the help of Bellarmine himself, whose very words are these: 'if many men had been together created out of the earth, all they ought to have been princes over their posterity'. In these words we have an evident confession that creation made man prince of his posterity. And indeed not only Adam but the succeeding patriarchs had, by right of fatherhood, royal authority over their children. Nor dares Bel-

larmine deny this also. "That the patriarchs," saith he, "were endowed with kingly power, their deeds do testify." For as Adam was lord of his children, so his children under him had a command and power over their own children, but still with subordination to the first parent, who is lord paramount over his children's children to all generations, as being the grandfather of his people.

I see not then how the children of Adam, or of any man else, can be free from subjection to their parents. And this subjection of children is the only fountain of all regal authority, by the ordination of God himself. It follows that civil power not only in general is by divine institution, but even the assignment of it specifically to the eldest parent, which quite takes away that new and common distinction which refers only power universal as absolute to God, but power respective in regard of the special form of government to the choice of the people. Nor leaves it any place for such imaginary pactions between kings and their people as many dream of.

This lordship which Adam by creation had over the whole world, and by right descending from him the patriarchs did enjoy, was as large and ample as the absolutest dominion of any monarch which hath been since the creation. For power of life and death we find that Judah, the father, pronounced sentence of death against Thamar, his daughter-in-law, for playing the harlot. "Bring her forth," saith he, "that she may be burnt." Touching war, we see that Abraham commanded an army of 318 soldiers of his own family; and Esau met his brother Jacob with 400 men at arms. For matter of peace, Abraham made a league with Abimelech, and ratified the articles by an oath. These acts of judging in capital causes, of making war, and concluding peace, are the chiefest marks of sovereignty that are found in any monarch.

Not only until the Flood, but after it, this patriarchal power did continue—as the very name of patriarch doth in part prove. The three sons of Noah had the whole world divided amongst them by their father, for of them was the whole world overspread, according to the benediction given to him and his sons: "Be fruitful and multiply and replenish the earth." Most of the civillest nations in the world labour to fetch their original from some one of the sons or nephews of Noah, which were scattered abroad after the confusion of Babel. In this dispersion we must certainly find the establishment of regal power throughout the kingdoms of the world.

It is a common opinion that at the confusion of tongues there were seventy-two distinct nations erected. All which were not confused multitudes, without heads or governors, and at liberty to choose what governors or government they pleased, but they were distinct families, which had fathers for rulers over them. Whereby it appears that even in the confusion, God was careful to preserve the fatherly authority by distributing the diversity of languages according to the diversity of families.

*   *   *

In this division of the world, some are of opinion that Noah used lots for the distribution of it. Others affirm that he sailed about the Mediterranean sea in ten years and as he went about, pointed to each son his part, and so made the division of the then known world into Asia, Africa, and Europe, according to the number of his sons, the limits of which three parts are all found in that midland sea.

*   *   *

Some, perhaps, may think that these princes and dukes of families were but some pretty lords under some greater kings, because the number of them are so many that their particular territories could be but small, and not worthy the title of kingdoms. But they must consider that at first kings had no such large dominions as they have nowadays. We find in the time of Abraham, which was about 300 years after the Flood, that in a little corner of Asia nine kings at once met in battle, most of which were but kings of cities apiece, with the adjacent territories, as of Sodom, Gomorrha,

Shinar, etc. In the same chapter is mention of Melchisedek, king of Salem, which was but the city of Jerusalem. And in the catalogue of the kings of Edom, the name of each king's city is recorded as the only mark to distinguish their dominions. In the land of Canaan, which was but of a small circuit, Joshua destroyed thirty-one kings, and about the same time Adonibezek had seventy kings whose fingers and toes he had cut off, and made them feed under his table. A few ages after this, thirty-two kings came to Benhadad, king of Syria, and about seventy kings of Greece went to the wars of Troy. Caesar found more kings in France than there be now provinces there, and at his sailing over into this island he found four kings in our county of Kent. These heaps of kings in each nation are an argument that their territories were but small, and strongly confirm our assertion that erection of kingdoms came at first only by distinction of families.

By manifest footsteps we may trace this paternal government unto the Israelites coming into Egypt, where the exercise of supreme patriarchal jurisdiction was intermitted because they were in subjection to a stronger prince. After the return of these Israelites out of bondage, God, out of a special care of them, chose Moses and Joshua successively to govern as princes in the place and stead of the supreme fathers, and after them likewise for a time He raised up Judges to defend His people in times of peril. But when God gave the Israelites kings, He re-established the ancient and prime right of lineal succession to paternal government. And whensoever He made choice of any special person to be king, He intended that the issue also should have benefit thereof, as being comprehended sufficiently in the person of the father—although the father only were named in the grant.

It may seem absurd to maintain that kings now are the fathers of their people, since experience shows the contrary. It is true, all kings be not the natural parents of their subjects, yet they all either are, or are to be reputed as the next heirs to those progenitors who were at first the natural parents of the whole people, and in their right succeed to the exercise of supreme jurisdiction. And such heirs are not only lords of their own children, but also of their brethren, and all others that were subject to their fathers.

And therefore we find that God told Cain of his brother Abel: "His desires shall be subject unto thee, and thou shalt rule over him." Accordingly, when Jacob had bought his brother's birthright, Isaac blessed him thus: "Be lord over thy brethren, and let the sons of thy mother bow before thee." As long as the first fathers of families lived, the name of patriarchs did aptly belong unto them. But after a few descents, when the true fatherhood itself was extinct and only the right of the father descended to the true heir, then the title of prince or king was more significant to express the power of him who succeeds only to the right of that fatherhood which his ancestors did naturally enjoy. By this means it comes to pass that many a child, by succeeding a king, hath the right of a father over many a grey-headed multitude, and hath the title of *pater patriae*.

*   *   *

In all kingdoms or commonwealths in the world, whether the prince be the supreme father of the people or but the true heir of such a father, or whether he come to the crown by usurpation, or by election of the nobles or of the people, or by any other way whatsoever, or whether some few or a multitude govern the commonwealth, yet still the authority that is in any one, or in many, or in all of these, is the only right and natural authority of a supreme father. There is, and always shall be continued to the end of the world, a natural right of a supreme father over every multitude, although, by the secret will of God, many at first do most unjustly obtain the exercise of it.

To confirm this natural right of regal power, we find in the decalogue that the law which enjoins obedience to kings is delivered in the terms of "honour thy father" as if all power were originally in the father. If obedience to parents be immediately due by a natural law, and subjection to princes but by the mediation of an human ordinance, what reason is there that the law of nature should give place to the laws of men, as we see the power of the father over his child gives place and is subordinate to the power of the magistrate?

If we compare the natural duties of a father with those of a king, we find them to be all one, without any difference at all but only in the latitude or extent of them. As the father over one family, so the king, as father over many families, extends his care to preserve, feed, clothe, instruct and defend the whole commonwealth. His wars, his peace, his courts of justice and all his acts of sovereignty tend only to preserve and distribute to every subordinate and inferior father, and to their children, their rights and privileges, so that all the duties of a king are summed up in an universal fatherly care of his people.

*   *   *

REVIEW QUESTIONS

1. According to Filmer, what is the relation between the authority of a father and the authority of a king?
2. Why does Filmer link political authority to domestic authority?
3. What is the relation between authority and nature for Filmer?
4. How does political authority come into being?
5. What are the implications of Filmer's rejection of the natural liberty of humankind?
6. What are its implications for his conception of human nature?
7. What are its implications for economic relations?
8. What are its implications for social status?

JEAN BAPTISTE COLBERT

A Memorandum, 1669, AND
A Memorandum, 1670

Jean-Baptiste Colbert (1619–1683), the son of a merchant of Reims, rose above his mercantile roots to become a statesman and minister of finance to Louis XIV. His chief concern was the economic reconstruction of France. He reorganized the fiscal administration of the state and made it more efficient. He also promoted commerce and industry in ways consistent with mercantilist theory. To improve exports, he promoted industries that produced high-quality goods, increased the merchant fleet, attracted foreign artisans, and limited foreign competition. Indeed, the system of state sponsorship and regulation that arose under Colbert and soon bore his name was widely resented by entrepreneurs anxious to innovate and expand. In his capacity as secretary of state for the king's household, from 1669, he was also concerned with the arts and education in France. He founded schools and learned societies to foster these endeavors, including the Academy of Science in 1666 to promote science. All these activities served to expand the power and magnificence of the French state, in the service of which he remained his entire life. That service proved profitable on a private level as well. He died a very wealthy man, whose estate had risen to that of an aristocrat by dint of loyal service. Yet, he was a disappointed man. Though the state had become stronger and more prosperous through his policies, he saw his ambition to reform and expand the French economy frustrated by wars that pursued the ends of the king he had served.

From *Colbert and a Century of French Mercantilism*, by Charles W. Cole (New York: Columbia University Press, 1939), p. 320.

A Memorandum, 1669

The commerce of all Europe is carried on by ships of every size to the number of 20,000, and it is perfectly clear that this number cannot be increased, since the number of people in all the states remains the same and consumption likewise remains the same. . . .

Commerce is a perpetual and peaceable war of wit and energy among all nations. Each nation works incessantly to have its legitimate share of commerce or to gain an advantage over another nation. The Dutch fight at present, in this war, with 15,000 to 16,000 ships, a government of merchants, all of whose maxims and power are directed solely toward the preservation and increase of their commerce, and much more care, energy, and thrift than any other nation.

The English with 3,000 to 4,000 ships, less energy and care, and more expenditures than the Dutch.

The French with 500 to 600.

Those two last cannot improve their commerce save by increasing the number of their vessels, and cannot increase this number save from the 20,000 which carry all the commerce and consequently by making inroads on the 15,000 to 16,000 of the Dutch.

A Memorandum, 1670

Formerly the Dutch, English, Hamburgers, and other nations bringing into the realm a much greater quantity of merchandise than that which they carried away, withdrew the surplus in circulating money, which produced both their abundance and the poverty of the realm, and indisputably resulted in their power and our weakness.

We must next examine the means which were employed to change this destiny.

Firstly, in 1662 Your Majesty maintained his right to 50 sols per ton of freight from foreign vessels, which produced such great results that we have seen the number of French vessels increase yearly; and in seven or eight years the Dutch have been practically excluded from port-to-port commerce, which is carried on by the French. The advantages received by the state through the increase in the number of sailors and seamen, through the money which has remained in the realm by this means and an infinity of others, would be too long to enumerate.

At the same time, Your Majesty ordered work done to abolish all the tolls which had long been established on all the rivers of the kingdom, and he began from then on to have an examination made of the rivers which could be rendered navigable in order to facilitate the descent of commodities and merchandise from inside the realm toward the sea to be transported into foreign lands. Although everything that invites the universal admiration of men was still in disorder in these first years and although the recovery work was a sort of abyss, Your Majesty did not delay in beginning the examination of the tariffs of the *cinq grosses fermes* and scrutinized the fact that the regulation and levying of these sorts of duties concerning commerce had always been done with a great deal of ignorance on the basis of memoranda by tax farmers, who, being solely concerned with their own interests and the increase in the profits

from their tax farms while they possessed them, had always overvalued the commodities, merchandise, and manufactured items of the realm which they saw leaving in abundance, and favored the entrance of foreign merchandise and manufactured items, in order to have a greater quantity of them enter, without being concerned about whether money was as a result leaving the realm, for they were indifferent to this as long as their tax farms produced gain for them during the period of their possession.

Finally, after having thoroughly studied this matter, Your Majesty ordered the tariff of 1664, in which the duties are regulated on a completely different principle, that is to say, that all merchandise and manufactured items of the realm were markedly favored and the foreign ones priced out of the market, though not completely; for having as yet no established manufacturers in the realm, this increase in duties, had it been excessive, would have been a great burden for the *peuple,* because of their need for the aforesaid foreign merchandise and manufactured items; but this change began to provide some means of establishing the same manufactures in the realm; and to this end:

The fabric manufacture of Sedan has been reestablished, and enlarged to 62 from the 12 looms there were then.

The new establishments of Abbeville, Dieppe, Fécamp, and Rouen have been built, in which there are presently more than 200 looms.

The factory for barracan was next established at La Ferré-sous-Jouarre, which is made up of 120 looms;

That of little damasks from Flanders, at Meaux, consisting of 80 looms;

That for carpeting, in the same city, made up of 20 looms . . .

That for tin, in Nivernois;

That for French lace, in 52 cities and towns, in which more than 20,000 workers toil;

The manufacture of brass, or yellow copper, set up in Champagne;

That for camlet of Brussels, in Paris, which will become large and extensive;

Brass wire, in Burgundy;

Gold thread of Milan, at Lyons . . .

And since Your Majesty has wanted to work diligently at reestablishing his naval forces, and since for that it has been necessary to make very great expenditures, since all merchandise, munitions and manufactured items formerly came from Holland and the countries of the North, it has been absolutely necessary to be especially concerned with finding within the realm, or with establishing in it, everything which might be necessary for this great plan.

To this end, the manufacture of tar was established in Médoc, Auvergne, Dauphiné, and Provence;

Iron cannons, in Burgundy, Nivernois, Saintonge, and Périgord;

Large anchors, in Dauphiné, Nivernois, Brittany, and Rochefort;

Sailcloth for the Levant, in Dauphiné;

Coarse muslin, in Auvergne;

All the implements for pilots and others, at Dieppe and La Rochelle;

The cutting of wood suitable for vessels, in Burgundy, Dauphiné, Brittany, Normandy, Poitou, Saintonge, Provence, Guyenne, and the Pyrenees;

Masts, of a sort once unknown in this realm, have been found in Provence, Languedoc, Auvergne, Dauphiné, and in the Pyrenees.

Iron, which was obtained from Sweden and Biscay, is currently manufactured in the realm.

Fine hemp for ropes, which came from Prussia and from Piedmont, is currently obtained in Burgundy, Mâconnais, Bresse, Dauphiné; and markets for it have since been established in Berry and in Auvergue, which always provides money in these provinces and keeps it within the realm.

In a word, everything serving for the construction of vessels is currently established in the realm, so that Your Majesty can get along without foreigners for the navy and will even, in a short time, be able to supply them and gain their money in this fashion. And it is with this same objective of having everything necessary to provide abundantly for his navy and that of his subjects that he is working at the general reform of all the forests in his realm, which, being as carefully preserved as they are at present, will abundantly produce all the wood necessary for this.

REVIEW QUESTIONS

1. How does Colbert speak of commerce?
2. What does it entail?
3. What causes its success?
4. Why is commerce a war?
5. What does Colbert see as the source of Dutch and English power?
6. What has strengthened French commerce?
7. What goods does Colbert describe?
8. Why do you suppose he pays particular attention to them?

ANNE ROBERT JACQUES TURGOT

FROM *Reflections on the Accumulation and Distribution of Wealth*

Anne Robert Jacques Turgot, Baron de l'Aulne (1727–1781), was born in Paris and educated at the Sorbonne. His entire career was spent in state service. After holding numerous posts, he was appointed intendant *(chief administrative officer) of the district of Limoges in 1761. Influenced by physiocratic economic ideas that advocated the expansion of agriculture as the basis of all wealth, he instituted a number of fiscal reforms in his district, including the substitution of monetary payments for* corvée *(forced labor) service. While holding office in Limoges, Turgot published his economic treatise,* Reflections on the Accumulation and Distribution of Wealth *(1766), which began with the physiocratic notions of land as the sole source of wealth and agriculture as the most important kind of production but developed in its course a surprisingly modern notion of capital. It provides an interesting perspective on rural labor, productivity, and wealth before industrialization. In 1774, Turgot was appointed comptroller-general of finance. In this capacity he undertook a series of reforms aimed at controlling expenditures and taxation. He delivered his* Six Edicts, *which urged the abolition of forced labor, the suppression of monopolies, and the taxation of the nobility, to the royal council in 1776. These sweeping reforms provoked such resistance from the nobility that Turgot was forced into permanent retirement.*

From *Turgot on Progress, Sociology and Economics,* edited by Ronald L. Meek (Cambridge, Eng.: Cambridge University Press, 1973), pp. 119–28.

I

Impossibility of Commerce on the assumption of an equal division of land, where each man would have only what was necessary for his own support.

If the land were distributed among all the inhabitants of a country in such a way that each of them had precisely the quantity necessary for his support, and nothing more, it is evident that, all being equal, no one would be willing to work for others. Also no one would have the means of paying for the labour of another; for each man, having only as much land as was necessary to produce his own subsistence, would consume all that he had gathered in, and would have nothing which he could exchange for the labour of others.

II
The above hypothesis has never existed, and could not have continued to exist. The diversity of soils and the multiplicity of needs lead to the exchange of the products of the land for other products.

This hypothesis could never have existed, because the lands were cultivated before being divided, cultivation itself having been the only motive for the division and for the law which secures to every man his property. The first men who engaged in cultivation probably cultivated as much land as their resources would permit, and consequently more than was necessary for their own support.

Even if this state of affairs could have existed, it could not have been a lasting one. If each man drew no more than his subsistence from his land, and did not have the means of paying for the labour of others, he would not be able to meet his other needs for housing, clothing, etc. except by means of his own labour, and this would be virtually impossible, since *all land falls far short of producing everything.*

The man whose land was suitable only for corn, and would produce neither cotton nor hemp, would lack cloth with which to clothe himself. Another man would have land suitable for cotton which would produce no corn. One would lack wood to keep himself warm, while another would lack corn to feed himself. Experience would soon teach each man the kind of product for which his land was most suitable; and he would confine himself to cultivating this, in order to procure for himself the things which he lacked by means of exchange with his neighbours, who, having in their turn reasoned in the same way, would have cultivated the produce best suited to their land and abandoned the cultivation of all others.

III
The products of the land require long and difficult preparations in order to render them suitable to meet men's needs.

The produce which the land yields in order to satisfy the different needs of men cannot for the most part serve to do this in the state in which nature affords it; it must be subjected to various changes and be prepared by means of art. Wheat must be converted into flour and then into bread; hides must be tanned or dressed; wool and cotton must be spun; silk must be drawn from the cocoons; hemp and flax must be soaked, peeled, and spun; then different fabrics must be woven from them; and then they must be cut and sewn in order to make them into clothing, footwear, etc. If the same man who caused these different things to be produced from his land, and who used them to meet his needs, were also obliged to subject them to all these intermediate preparations, it is certain that the result would turn out very badly. The greater part of these preparations demand an amount of care, attention, and long experience which is acquired only by working continuously and on a great quantity of materials. Take for example the preparation of hides. Where is the husbandman who could attend to all the details involved in this operation, which goes on for several months and sometimes for several years? If he could, would he be able to do it for a single hide? What a loss of time, space, and materials, which could have served at the same time, or successively, to tan a great number of hides! And even if he did succeed in tanning one single hide, he needs only one pair of shoes: what would he make out of the remainder? Shall he kill an ox in order to have this pair of shoes? Shall he cut down a tree to make himself a pair of clogs? The same may be said of all the other needs of each man, who, if he were reduced to his own land and his own labour, would involve himself in a great deal of time and trouble in order to be very badly equipped in every respect, and would cultivate his land very badly.

IV

The necessity for these preparations leads to the exchange of products for labour.

The same motive which brought about the exchange of one kind of produce for another as between the Cultivators of soils of different qualities was bound to lead also to the exchange of produce for labour as between the Cultivators and another part of society, which had come to prefer the occupation of preparing and working up the products of the land to that of growing them. Everyone gained as a result of this arrangement, for each man by devoting himself to a single kind of work succeeded much better in it. The Husbandman obtained from his land the greatest possible quantity of products, and by means of the exchange of his surplus procured for himself all the other things he needed much more easily than he would have done by means of his own labour. The Shoemaker, by making shoes for the Husbandman, appropriated to himself a portion of the latter's harvest. Each Workman worked to meet the needs of the Workmen of all the other kinds, who in their turn all worked for him.

V

Pre-eminence of the Husbandman who produces over the Artisan who prepares. The Husbandman is the prime mover in the circulation of men's labour; it is he who causes the land to produce the wages of all the Artisans.

It must however be noted that the Husbandman, who supplies everyone with the most important and considerable objects of their consumption (I mean their food and also the materials of almost all manufactures), has the advantage of a greater degree of independence. His labour, among the various kinds of labour which are shared out be-

tween the different members of society, retains the same primacy and the same pre-eminence that the labour which provided for his subsistence possessed among the different kinds of labour which he was obliged, when he was in a solitary state, to devote to his needs of all kinds. What we have here is a primacy arising not from honour or dignity, but from *physical necessity*. The Husbandman, generally speaking, can get on without the labour of the other Workmen, but no Workman can labour if the Husbandman does not support him. In this circulation, which by means of the reciprocal exchange of needs renders men necessary to one another and constitutes the bond of society, it is therefore the labour of the Husbandman which is the prime mover. Whatever his labour causes the land to produce over and above his personal needs is the unique fund from which are paid the wages which all the other members of society receive in exchange for their labour. The latter, in making use of the consideration which they receive in this exchange to purchase in their turn the produce of the Husbandman, do no more than return to him exactly what they have received from him. Here we have a very basic difference between these two kinds of labour, and before we deal with the innumerable consequences which spring from it we must dwell upon it in order that we may be fully aware of how self-evident it is.

VI

The wage of the Workman is limited to his subsistence as a result of competition between Workmen. He earns no more than a living.

The simple Workman, who possesses only his hands and his industry, has nothing except in so far as he succeeds in selling his toil to others. He sells it more or less dear; but this higher or lower price does not depend upon himself alone; it results from the agreement which he makes with the man who pays for his labour. The latter pays him as little as he is able; since he has a choice between a great number of Workmen he prefers the one who works most cheaply. Thus the Workmen are obliged to vie with one another and lower their price. In every kind of work it is bound to be the case, and in actual fact is the case, that the wage of the Workman is limited to what is necessary in order to enable him to procure his subsistence.

VII

The Husbandman is the only one whose labour produces anything over and above the wage of the labour. He is therefore the unique source of all wealth.

The position of the Husbandman is quite different. The land, independently of any other man and of any agreement, pays him directly the price of his labour. Nature never bargains with him in order to oblige him to content himself with what is absolutely necessary. What she grants is proportionate neither to his needs nor to a contractual evaluation of the price of his working day. It is the physical result of the fertility of the soil, and of the correctness, much more than of the difficulty, of the means he has employed to render it fruitful. As soon as the labour of the Husbandman produces something over and above his needs, he is able, with this surplus over and above the reward for his toil which nature affords him as a pure gift, to purchase the labour of other members of the society. The latter, when they sell to him, earn no more than their living; but the Husbandman obtains, besides his subsistence, an independent and disposable form of wealth, which he has never purchased but which he sells. He is therefore the unique source of all wealth, which, through its circulation, animates all the industry of society; because he is the only one whose labour produces anything over and above the wage of the labour.

VIII

Primary division of society into two classes: first, the *productive class,* or the Cultivators; and second, the *stipendiary class,* or the Artisans.

Here then we have the whole society divided, as the result of a necessity founded on the nature of things, into two classes, both of which are occupied in work. But one of these, through its labour, produces or rather extracts from the land wealth which is continually renascent, and which provides the whole of society with subsistence and the materials for all its needs. The other, engaged in preparing the produced materials and giving them forms which render them suitable for men's use, sells its labour to the first, and receives its subsistence from it in exchange. The first may be called the *productive class,* and the second the *stipendiary class.*

IX

In the earliest times the Proprietor could not have been distinguished from the Cultivator.

Up to now we have made no distinction at all between the Husbandman and the Proprietor of the land; and in the beginning they were not in fact distinguished at all. It was as a result of the labour of those who first worked the fields, and who enclosed them, in order to make certain of securing the harvest, that all the land ceased to be common to all and that landed property was established. Until societies were consolidated, and until public power, or the law, having come to predominate over individual power, was able to guarantee everyone the peaceful possession of his property against all invasion from without, one could maintain one's ownership of a piece of land only in the way that one had acquired it, and by continuing to cultivate it. It would not have been safe to have one's fields worked by another who, having undergone all the toil involved, would have had difficulty in understanding that the whole of the harvest did not belong to him. Moreover, in these early times every industrious man would be able to find as much land as he wanted, and could thus not be induced to till the soil for others. Every proprietor was obliged either to cultivate his fields or to abandon them completely.

X
Progress of society; all land comes to have an owner.

But the land became populated, and was brought into cultivation to a greater and greater extent. In the course of time all the best land came to be occupied. There remained for the last comers only the infertile soils which had been rejected by the first. But in the end all land found its owner; and those who could not possess properties had at first no course open to them other than to exchange the labour of their hands in the occupations of the *stipendiary* class for the surplus produce of the cultivating Proprietor.

XI
It begins to be possible for the Proprietors to shift the labour of cultivation on to paid Cultivators.

But since the land rendered the owner who cultivated it not only his subsistence, not only the means of procuring for himself by way of exchange the other things he needed, but also a large surplus, he was able with this surplus to pay men to cultivate his land. And for men who live on wages, it is just as good to earn them in this occupation as in any other. Thus ownership could be separated from the labour of cultivation, and soon it was.

XII
Inequality in the division of property: causes which make this inevitable.

The original Proprietors, as has already been said, at first occupied as much land as their resources allowed them and their families to cultivate. A man of greater strength, more industrious, and more anxious about the future took more land than a man with the opposite character. He whose family was larger, having more needs and more hands, extended his possessions further; here was already a first form of inequality. All land is not equally fertile: two men with the same area of land and the same labour may obtain very different products from it: a second source of inequality. Properties, in passing from fathers to children, are divided up into portions which are more or less small according to whether the families are more or less numerous. As one generation succeeds another, the inheritances at one time are further subdivided, and at another time are brought together again through the dying out of branches of the family: a third source of inequality. The contrast between the intelligence, the activity, and above all the thrift of some with the indolence, inactivity, and extravagance of others, constituted a fourth cause of inequality, and the most powerful one of all. The negligent and improvident Proprietor, who cultivates badly, and who in abundant years consumes the whole of his surplus in frivolities, on the occurrence of the slightest accident finds himself reduced to asking for help from his more prudent neighbour, and to living on loans. If, as the result of new accidents or the continuation of his negligence, he finds that he is not in a position to pay, and if he is obliged to have recourse to new loans, there will in the end be nothing left for him to do but abandon a part or even the whole of his estate to his creditor, who will take it as an equivalent; or to part with it to another in exchange for other assets with which he will discharge his obligation to his creditor.

XIII
Consequence of this inequality: the Cultivator distinguished from the Proprietor.

So here we have landed estates as objects of commerce, being bought and sold. The portion of the Proprietor who is extravagant or unfortunate serves to increase that of the Proprietor who is luckier or more prudent; and in the midst of this infinitely varied inequality of possessions it is impossible that a great number of Proprietors should not possess more than they are able to cultivate. Moreover it is natural enough that a wealthy man should wish to enjoy his wealth in peace, and that instead of employing all his time in arduous labour he should prefer to give a part of his surplus to people who will work for him.

XIV
Division of the product between the Cultivator and the Proprietor. *Net product* or revenue.

According to this new arrangement, the product of the land is divided into two parts. One comprises the subsistence and profits of the Husbandman, which are the reward for his labour and the condition upon which he undertakes to cultivate the Proprietor's fields. What remains is that independent and disposable part which the land gives as a pure gift to the one who cultivates it, over and above his advances and the wages of his toil; and this is the share of the Proprietor, or the *revenue*, with which the latter is able to live without working and which he takes wherever he wishes.

XV
New division of the Society into three classes, the Cultivators, the Artisans, and the Proprietors, or the *'productive' class*, the *'stipendiary' class*, and the *'disposable' class*.

So now we have the Society divided into three classes: the class of Husbandmen, for which we may keep the name *productive class;* the class of Artisans and other *stipendiaries* supported by the product of the land; and the class of *Proprietors*, the only one which, not being bound by the need for subsistence to one particular kind of work, may be employed to meet the general needs of the Society, for example in war and the administration of justice, whether through personal service, or through the payment of a part of its revenue with which the State or the Society may hire men to discharge these functions. The name which for this reason suits it best is the *disposable class*.

XVI
Resemblance between the two industrious or non-disposable classes.

The two classes of Cultivators and Artisans resemble one another in many respects, and above all in the fact that those of whom they are composed do not possess any revenue and live equally on the wages which are paid to them out of the product of the land. Both also have this in common, that they earn nothing but the price of their labour and of their advances, and this price is almost the same in the two classes. The Proprietor beats down those who cultivate his land in order to give up to them the smallest possible portion of the product, in the same way as he haggles with his Shoemaker in order to buy his shoes as cheaply as possible. In a word, neither the Cultivator nor the Artisan receive more than a recompense for their labour.

XVII
Essential difference between the two industrious classes.

But there is this difference between these two kinds of labour, that the Cultivator's labour produces his own wage, and in addition the revenue which serves to pay the whole class of Artisans and other stipendiaries, whereas the Artisans receive simply their wages, that is, their share of the product of the land, in exchange for their labour, and do not produce any revenue. The Proprietor enjoys nothing except through the labour of the Cultivator; he receives from him his subsistence and the means of paying for the work of the other stipendiaries. He has need of the Cultivator because of a necessity which arises from the physical order of things, by virtue of which the land produces nothing at all without labour; but the Cultivator has need of the Proprietor only by virtue of human conventions and the civil laws which guaranteed to the original Cultivators and their heirs the ownership of the land which they had occupied, even after they ceased to cultivate it. But these laws could guarantee to the man who took no part in the work himself only that part of the product which the land yields over and above the recompense due to the Cultivators. The Proprietor is forced to abandon the latter, on pain of losing the whole. The Cultivator, completely restricted though he is to the recompense for his labour, thus retains that natural and physical primacy which renders him the prime mover of the whole machine of Society, and which causes not only his own subsistence, but also the wealth of the Proprietor and the wages for all other kinds of work,

to depend upon his labour alone. The Artisan, on the other hand, receives his wages, either from the Proprietor or from the Cultivator, and gives them, by the exchange of his labour, only the equivalent of these wages and nothing over and above this.

Thus, although neither the Cultivator nor the Artisan earn more than a recompense for their labour, the Cultivator generates over and above this recompense the revenue of the Proprietor, and the Artisan does not generate any revenue, either for himself or for others.

XVIII
This difference justifies their being distinguished as the *productive class* and the *sterile class*.

Thus we may distinguish the two non-disposable classes as the *productive class,* which is that of the Cultivators, and the *sterile class,* which includes all the other stipendiary members of the Society.

REVIEW QUESTIONS

1. What is different about Turgot's economic thought?
2. Have we seen constant principles applied to land and its use?
3. What might be the principles Turgot applies?
4. Why is labor of central importance to Turgot?
5. How is labor measured?
6. By what criteria does Turgot evaluate labor?
7. What is the source of wealth, according to Turgot?
8. What constitutes progress?

WILLIAM GOUDGE

FROM *Of Domesticall Duties*

William Goudge was a Puritan clergyman best remembered for his tract on family life, a conduct book entitled Of Domesticall Duties *(1634). It captured the common attitude toward domestic governance in early modern Europe. All authority rested in the hands of a pater familias, the husband-father-master, who possessed absolute control over the family's property and labor and to whom all members of the household owed unflinching obedience and loyalty. Though observed most often in the breach, this pattern of discipline was universally prescribed in early modern Europe.*

From *Western Societies*, edited by Brian Tierney and Joan Scott (New York: Knopf, 1984).

*   *   *

But what if a man of lewd and beastly conditions, as a drunkard, a glutton, a profane swaggerer, an impious swearer and blasphemer, be married to a wise, sober, religious matron, must she account him her superior and worthy of an husband's honor?

Surely she must. For the evil quality and disposition of his heart and life doth not deprive a man of that civil honor which God hath given unto him. Though an husband in regard of evil qualities may carry the image of the devil, yet in regard of his place and office; he beareth the Image of God: so do Magistrates in the Commonwealth, Ministers in the Church, Parents and Masters in the Family. Note for our present purpose, the exhortation of St Peter to Christian wives which have infidel husbands, 'Be in subjection to them: let your conversation be in fear'. If Infidels carry not the devil's image and are not, so long as they are Infidels, vassals of Satan, who are? Yet wives must be subject to them.

*   *   *

REVIEW QUESTIONS

1. What is the conflict between order and nature Goudge depicts?
2. Why should a wife stay with a brutal husband?
3. What sort of order does Goudge invoke?

Marquis de Vauban AND Curé of Rumegies

Much of our knowledge about the economy and society of early modern Europe comes from contemporary accounts. For many reasons, individuals described the life and times of which they were part. Some, like Sébastien Le Prestre, Marquis de Vauban (1633–1707), labored in the service of the state. A French military engineer and genius in the construction of fortifications under Louis XIV, he studied the society and economy of the Kingdom of France to determine its military capacity, the human and material resources that could be mobilized for war in pursuit of royal policy. The result was a series of sober, accurate descriptions of the French population. Others, like Henri Platelle, an obscure parish priest in the village of Rumegies, chronicled their own experiences and observations. The chance survival of Platelle's 1693 journal provides us with a firsthand account of the starkness of daily life in early modern Europe and the struggles of poor peasants simply to survive.

From *Ancien Regime: French Society, 1600–1750,* by Pierre Goubert (New York: Harper-Collins, 1973), pp. 116–18.

Marquis de Vauban

FROM *Description Geographique de l'Election de Vezelay*

*   *   *

. . . All the so-called *bas peuple* live on nothing but bread of mixed barley and oats, from which they do not even remove the bran, which means that bread can sometimes be lifted by the straw sticking out of it. They also eat poor fruits, mainly wild, and a few vegetables from their gardens, boiled up with a little rape- or nut-oil sometimes, but more often not, or with a pinch of salt. Only the most prosperous eat bread made of rye mixed with barley and wheat.

. . . The general run of people seldom drink, eat meat not three times a year, and use little salt . . . So it is no cause for surprise if people who are so ill-nourished have so little energy. Add to this what they suffer from exposure: winter and summer, three fourths of them are dressed in nothing but half-rotting tattered linen, and are shod throughout the year with *sabots,* and no other covering for the foot. If one of them does have shoes he only wears them on saints' days and Sundays: the extreme poverty to which they are reduced, owning as they do not one inch of land, rebounds against the more prosperous town and country bourgeois, and against the nobility and

the clergy. They lease their lands out to *métayage,* and the owner who wants a new *métayer* must begin by settling his obligations, paying his debts, stocking the holding with beasts and feeding him and his family for the coming year at his own expense . . .

The poor people are ground down in another manner by the loans of grain and money they take from the wealthy in emergencies, by means of which a high rate of usury is enforced, under the guise of presents which must be made after the debts fall due, so as to avoid imprisonment. After the term has been extended by only three or four months, either another present must be produced when the time is up, or they face the *sergent* who is sure to strip the house bare. Many others of these poor people's afflictions remain at my quill's tip, so as not to offend anybody.

Since hardship can hardly go much further, its normal effects are a matter of course: firstly, it makes people weak and unhealthy, especially the children, many of whom die for want of good food; secondly, the men become idle and apathetic, being persuaded that only the least and worst part of the fruit of their labours will turn to their own profit; thirdly, there are liars, robbers, men of bad faith, always willing to perjure themselves provided that it pays, and to get drunk as soon as they lay hands on the wherewithal . . .

. . . It only remains to take stock of two million men all of whom I suppose to be day-labourers or simple artisans scattered throughout the towns, *bourgs* and villages of the realm.

What I have to say about all these workers . . . deserves serious attention, for although this sector may consist of what are unfairly called the dregs of the people, they are nonetheless worthy of high consideration in view of the services which they render to the State. For it is they who undertake all the great tasks in town and country without which neither themselves nor others could live. It is they who provide all the soldiers and sailors and all the servants and serving women; in a word, without them the State could not survive. It is for this reason that they ought to be spared in the matter of taxes, in order not to burden them beyond their strength.

Let us begin with the town-dwellers. . . .

Among the smaller fry, particularly in the countryside, there are any number of people who, while they lay no claim to any special craft, are continually plying several which are most necessary and indispensable. Of such a kind are those whom we call *manoeuvriers*, who, owning for the most part nothing but their strong arms or very little more, do day- or piece-work for whoever wants to employ them. It is they who do all the major jobs such as mowing, harvesting, threshing, woodcutting, working the soil and the vineyards, clearing land, ditching, carrying soil to vineyards or elsewhere, labouring for builders and several other tasks which are all hard and laborious. These men may well find this kind of employment for part of the year, and it is true that they can usually earn a fair day's wage at haymaking, harvesting and grape-picking time, but the rest of the year is a different story . . .

It will not be inappropriate to give some particulars about what the country day-labourer can earn.

I shall assume that of the three hundred and sixty-five days in the year, he may be gainfully employed for one hundred and eighty, and earn nine *sols* a day. This is a high figure, and it is certain that except at harvest- and grape-picking time most earn not more than eight *sols* a day on average, but supposing we allow the nine *sols*, that

would amount to eighty-five *livres* and ten *sols*, call it ninety *livres*, from which we have to deduct his liabilities (taxes plus salt for a family of four say 14*l*. 16*s*) . . . leaving seventy-five *livres* four *sols*.

Since I am assuming that this family . . . consists of four people, it requires not less than ten *septiers* of grain, Paris measure, to feed them. This grain, half wheat, half rye . . . commonly selling at six *livres* per *septier* . . . will come to sixty *livres*, which leaves fifteen *livres* four *sols* out of the seventy-five *livres* four *sols*, out of which the labourer has to find the price of rent and upkeep for his house, a few chattels, if only some earthenware bowls, clothing and linen, and the needs of his entire family for one year.

But these fifteen *livres* four *sols* will not take him very far unless his industry or some particular business supervenes and his wife contributes to their income by means of her distaff, sewing, knitting hose or making small quantities of lace . . . also by keeping a small garden or rearing poultry and perhaps a calf, a pig or a goat for the better-off . . . ; by which means he might buy a piece of larding bacon and a little butter or oil for making soup. And if he does not additionally cultivate some small allotment, he will be hard pressed to subsist, or at least he will be reduced, together with his family, to the most wretched fare. And if instead of two children he has four, that will be worse still until they are old enough to earn their own living. Thus however we come at the matter, it is certain that he will always have the greatest difficulty in seeing the year out . . .

Curé of Rumegies

FROM *Journal*

. . . the final misfortune was the utter failure of the ensuing harvest, which caused grain to reach a tremendous price. And since the poor people were exhausted in like measure by the frequent demands of His Majesty and by these exorbitant taxes, they fell into such poverty as might just as well be called famine. Happy the man who could lay hands on a measure of rye to mix with oats, peas and beans and make bread to half fill his belly. I speak of two thirds of this village, if not more . . .

Throughout this time, the talk was all of thieves, murders and people dying of starvation. I do not know if it is to the credit of the *curé* of Rumegies to refer here to a death which occurred in his parish during that time: a man named Pierre du Gauquier, who lived by the statue of the Virgin, towards la Howardries. This poor fellow was a widower; people thought that he was not as poor as he was; he was burdened with three children. He fell ill, or rather he grew worn-out and feeble, but nobody informed the *curé*, until one Sunday, upon the final bell for mass, one of his sisters came and told the *curé* that her brother was dying of starvation, and that was all she said. The pastor gave her some bread to take to him forthwith, but perhaps the sister had need of it for herself, as seems likely to be the case. She did not take it to him, and at the second bell for vespers the poor man died of starvation. He was the only one to drop dead for want of bread, but several others died of that cause a little at a time, both here and in other villages, for that year saw a great mortality. In our parish alone, more people died than in several ordinary years . . . Truly men wearied of being of this world. Men of goodwill had their hearts wrung at the sight of the poor people's sufferings, poor people, without money while a measure of corn cost nine to ten *livres* at the end of the year, with peas and beans corresponding . . .

The ordinance made by His Majesty for the relief of his poor people cannot be forgotten here . . . Every community *had to* feed its poor. The pastors, mayors and men of law taxed the wealth-iest and the middling, each according to his capability, in order to succour the poor, whom it was also their duty to seek out. It was the right way to keep everybody provided . . . In this village, where there is no court and everybody is his own master, the *curé* read out and re-read that ordinance to no avail. The *mayeurs* and men of law, who were the richest and would therefore have to be taxed most, fought it with all their might. With much hardship, August was finally reached. A fortnight beforehand, people were harvesting the rye when it was still green, and putting it in ovens to dry it, and because this grain was unripe and unhealthy it caused several serious illnesses. May the Lord in his fatherly Providence vouchsafe us to be preserved henceforward from a like dearth . . .

REVIEW QUESTIONS

1. What does Vauban tell us about the lives of the great majority of French people?
2. How might they measure wealth?
3. How might they view taxes?
4. Would they be Turgot's workmen or husbandmen?
5. Who are the people Vauban describes?
6. What is their social place?
7. What is their economic function?
8. What services might they render to the state?
9. Who are the people Platelle describes as poor?
10. Do they cause their own poverty?
11. Does Platelle suggest any attributes that may have caused their poverty?
12. Whom do taxes serve in Platelle's parish?
13. What was the purpose of taxes?

ABBÉ GUILLAUME-THOMAS RAYNAL

FROM *A Philosophical and Political History of the Settlements and Trade of the Europeans in the East and West Indies*

The Abbé Guillaume-Thomas Raynal (1713–1796) was an author and propagandist, who helped set the intellectual climate for the French Revolution. Educated by the Jesuits, he initially joined the Society of Jesus but later left the religious life to concentrate on his writing. The author of several popular histories and the editor of the Mercure de France, *he established himself with the publication in 1770 of a six-volume history of the European colonies in the East Indies and North America, from which this passionate denunciation of slavery is drawn. The work's popularity can be measured by the fact that it went through thirty editions before the revolution. Elected to the Estates General in 1789, he refused to serve because of his opposition to violence. He later renounced radicalism in favor of a constitutional monarchy. His property was expropriated by the revolutionary regime he opposed, and Raynal died in poverty.*

From *A Philosophical and Political History of the Settlements and Trade of the Europeans in the East and West Indies,* by Abbé Raynal (Glasgow, Scot.: M'Kenzie, 1812), pp. 311–17.

*   *   *

Slavery is entirely contrary to humanity, reason, and justice.

We will not here so far demean ourselves, as to enlarge the ignominious list of those writers who devote their abilities to justify, by policy, what morality condemns. In an age where so many errors are boldly laid open, it would be unpardonable to conceal any truth that is interesting to humanity. If, whatever we have hitherto advanced, hath seemingly tended only to alleviate the burden of slavery, the reason is, that it was first necessary to give some comfort to those unhappy beings, whom we cannot set free; and convince their oppressors, that they are cruel, to the prejudice of real interests. But, in the meantime, until some great revolution makes the evidence of this great truth felt, it is proper to go on with the subject. We shall then first

prove, that there is no reason of state that can authorise slavery. We shall not be afraid to cite to the tribunal of reason and justice, those governments which tolerate this cruelty, or which even are not ashamed to make it the basis of their power.

Montesquieu could not resolve with himself to treat seriously the question concerning slavery. In reality it is degrading reason to employ it, I will not say in defending, but even in refuting an abuse so repugnant to it. Whoever justifies so odious a system, deserves the utmost contempt from a philosopher, and from the negro a stab with his dagger.

*   *   *

Will it be said, that he who wants to make me a slave does me no injury, but that he only makes use of his rights? Where are those rights? Who hath stamped upon them so sacred a character as to silence mine? From Nature I hold the right of self-defence; Nature, therefore, has not given to another the right of attacking me. If thou thinkest thyself authorised to oppress me, because thou art stronger and more ingenious than I am; do not complain if my vigorous arm shall plunge a dagger into thy breast; do not complain when in thy tortured entrails thou shalt feel the pangs of death conveyed by poison into thy food: I am stronger and more ingenious than thou; fall a victim, therefore, in thy, turn, and expiate the crime of having been an oppressor.

He who supports the system of slavery, is the enemy of the whole human race. He divides it into two societies of legal assassins; the oppressors, and the oppressed. It is the same thing as proclaiming to the world, if you would preserve your life, instantly take away mine, for I want to have yours.

But the right of slavery, you say, extends only to the right of labour and the privation of liberty, not of life. What! does not the master, who disposes of my strength at his pleasure, likewise dispose of my life, which depends on the voluntary and moderate use of my faculties. What is existence to him, who has not the disposal of it? I cannot kill my slave, but I can make him bleed under the whip of an excutioner; I can overwhelm him with sorrows, drudgery, and want; I can injure him every way, and secretly undermine the principles and springs of his life; I can smother, by slow punishments, the wretched infant, which a negro woman carries in her womb. Thus the laws protect the slave against violent death, only to leave to my cruelty the right of making him die by degrees.

Let us proceed a step farther: the right of slavery is that of perpetrating all sorts of crimes: those crimes which invade property; for slaves are not suffered to have any, even in their own persons: those crimes which destroy personal safety; for the slave may be sacrificed to the caprice of his master: those crimes, which make modesty shudder. My blood rises at these horrid images. I detest, I abhor the human species, made up only of victims and executioners; and, if it is never to become better, may it be anihilated!

*   *   *

But these negroes, say they, are a race of men born for slavery; their dispositions are narrow, treacherous, and wicked; they themselves allow the superiority of our understandings, and almost acknowledge the justice of our authority.

The minds of the negroes are contracted; because slavery spoils all the springs of the soul. They are wicked; but not half so wicked as you. They are treacherous, because they are under no obligation to speak truth to their tyrants. They acknowledge the superiority of our understandings, because we have abused their ignorance. They allow the justice of our authority, because we have abused their weakness. I might as well say, that the Indians are a species of men born to be crushed to death, because there are fanatics among them who throw themselves under the wheels of their idol's car, before the temple of Jaguernat.

But these negroes, it is farther urged, were born as slaves. Barbarians, will you persuade me, that a man can be the property of a sovereign, a son the property of a father, a wife the property of an husband, a domestic the property of a master, a negro the property of a planter?

But these slaves have sold themselves. Could ever a man, by compact, or by an oath, permit another to use and abuse him? If he assented to this compact, or confirmed it by an oath, it were a transport of ignorance or folly; and he is released from it, the moment that he either knows himself, or his reason returns.

But they had been taken in war. What have you to do with that? Suffer the conqueror to make what ill use he pleases of his own victory. Why do you make yourselves his accomplices?

But they were criminals, condemned in their own country to slavery. Who was it that condemned them? Do you not know, that in a despotic state there is no criminal but the despot?

The subject of a despotic prince is the same as the slave in a state repugnant to Nature. Every thing that contributes to keep a man in such a state, is an attempt against his person. Every power, which fixes him to the tyranny of one man, is the power of his enemies; and all those who are about him, are the authors or abettors of this violence. His mother, who taught him the first lessons of disobedience; his neighbour, who set him the example of it; his superiors, who compelled him into this state; and this equals, who led him into it by their opinion: All these are the ministers and instruments of tyranny. The tyrant can do nothing of himself; he is only the first mover of those efforts which all his subjects exert to their mutual oppression. He keeps them in a state of perpetual war, which renders robberies, treasons, and even assassinations, lawful. Thus, like the blood which flows in his veins, all crimes originate from his heart, and return thither, as to their primary source. Caligula used to say, that he wished the whole human race had but one head, that he might have the pleasure of cutting it off. Socrates would have said, that if all crimes were heaped upon one head, that should be the one which ought to be struck off.

Let us, therefore, endeavour to make the light of reason, and the sentiments of Nature, take place of the blind ferocity of our ancestors. Let us break the bonds of so many victims to our mercenary principles, should we even be obliged to discard a commerce which is founded only on injustice, and whose object is luxury.

But even this is not necessary. There is no occasion to give up those conveniences which custom hath so much endeared to us. We may draw them from our colonies, without peopling them with the slaves. These productions may be cultivated by the hands of free men, and then be reaped without remorse.

The islands are filled with blacks, whose fetters have been broken. They successfully clear the small plantations that have been given them, or which they have acquired by their industry. Such of these unhappy men, as should recover their independence, would live in quiet upon the same manual labours, that would then be free and advantageous to them. The vassals of Denmark, who have lately been made free, have not abandoned their ploughs.

Is it then apprehended, that the facility of acquiring subsistence without labour, on a soil naturally fertile, and of dispensing with the want of clothes under a burning sky, would plunge these men in idleness? Why then do not the inhabitants of Europe confine themselves to such labours as are of the first necessity? Why do they exhaust their powers in laborious employments, which tend only to the transient gratifications of a frivolous imagination? There are amongst us a thousand professions, some more laborious than others, which owe their origin to our institutions. Human laws have given rise to a variety of fictitious wants which otherwise would never have had an existence. By disposing of every species of property according to their capricious institutions, they have subjected an infinite number of people to the imperious will of their fellow-creatures, so far as even to make them sing and dance for a living. We have amongst us beings formed like ourselves, who have consented to inter themselves under mountains, to furnish us with metals and with copper, perhaps to poison us: Why do we imagine that the negroes are less dupes and less foolish than the Europeans?

At the time that we gradually confer liberty on these unhappy beings as a reward for their economy, their good behaviour, and their industry, we must be careful to subject them to our laws and manners, and to offer them our super fluities. We must give to them a country, give them interest to study, productions to cultivate, and an object adequate to their respective tastes, and our colonies will never want men, who, being eased of their chains, will be more active and robust.

To what tribunal shall we refer the cause of humanity, which so many men are in confederacy to betray, in order to over turn the whole system of slavery, which is supported by passions so universal, by laws so authentic, by the emulations of such powerful nations, and by prejudices still more powerful? Sovereigns of the earth, you alone can bring about this revolution. If you do not sport with the rest of mortals, if you do not regard the power of kings as the right of a successful plunder, and the obedience of subjects as artfully obtained from their ignorance, reflect on your own obligations. Refuse the sanction of your authority to the infamous and criminal traffic of men, turned into so many herds of cattle, and this trade will cease. For once unite, for the happiness of the world, those powers and designs which have been so often exerted for its ruin. If some one amongst you would venture to found the expectation of his opulence and grandeur on the generosity of all the rest, he instantly becomes an enemy of mankind, who ought to be destroyed. You may carry fire and sword into his territories. Your armies will soon be inspired with the sacred enthusiasm of humanity. You will then perceive what difference virtue makes between men who succour the oppressed, and mercenaries who serve tyrants.

But, what am I saying? Let the ineffectual calls of humanity be no longer pleaded with the people and their masters; perhaps they have never been consulted in any public transactions. If then, ye nations of Europe, interest alone can exert its influence over you, listen to me once more: Your slaves stand in no need either of your generosity or of your counsels, in order to break the sacrilegious yoke which oppresses them. Nature speaks a more powerful language than philosophy, or interest. Some white people, already massacred, have expiated a part of our crimes; already have two colonies of fugitive negroes been established, to whom treaties and power give a perfect security from your attempts. Poison hath at different times been the instrument of their vengeance. Several

have eluded your oppression by a voluntary death. These enterprizes are so many indications of the impending storm; and the negroes only want a chief, sufficiently courageous, to lead them on to vengeance and slaughter.

Where is this great man to be found, whom Nature, perhaps, owes to the honour of the human species? Where is this new Spartacus, who will not find a Crassus? Then will the *black code* be no more; and the *white code* will be dreadful, if the conqueror only regards the right of reprisals.

Till this revolution takes place, the negroes will groan under the yoke of oppression, the description of which cannot, but interest us more and more in their destiny.

*   *   *

REVIEW QUESTIONS

1. What is the philosophical basis of Raynal's condemnation of slavery?
2. According to Raynal, what abuses arise as a result of slavery?
3. What is the consequence of slavery for the enslaved?
4. What would be the consequence of emancipation for the colonial powers?

ADAM SMITH

FROM *The Wealth of Nations*

Though best remembered for his towering system of political economy, An Inquiry into the Nature and Causes of the Wealth of Nations *(1776), Adam Smith (1723–1790) was one of the towering social philosophers of the eighteenth century, whose economic writings constitute only a part of his larger view of social and political development. Born the son of a minor government official, he entered the University of Glasgow in 1737, already a center of what became known as the Scottish Enlightenment, where he was deeply influenced by another great moral and eco-*

nomic philosopher, Francis Hutcheson. After completing his education at Oxford, he returned to Scotland, where he embarked on a series of public lectures in Edinburgh. In 1752 he was appointed professor of logic at Glasgow, and in 1754 he assumed the chair in moral philosophy. He would look on his tenure as the happiest and most honorable of his life. It was certainly the most productive. There he made the acquaintance of some of the leading intellectual lights of his day: James Watt, of steam-engine fame; David Hume, the great philosopher; and Andrew Cochrane. The last was the founder of the Political Economy Club and the likely source of much of Smith's information on business and commerce. In 1759, Smith published his first important work, The Theory of Moral Sentiments, *in which he attempted to describe universal principles of human nature. His answer to the question of moral judgment was the thesis of the "inner man," or "impartial spectator," which is the conscience in each human being and whose pronouncements cannot be ignored. Thus, human beings can be driven by passions and self-interests and simultaneously capable of ethics and generosity. This principle foreshadowed the "invisible hand" that would guide economic behavior in* The Wealth of Nations. *He began work on the classic text after resigning his post at Glasgow to serve as tutor to the young duke of Buccleuch. When it finally appeared, it continued the themes first addressed in* The Theory of Moral Sentiments, *the resolution of passion and reason in human behavior, and now, human history. Society evolves through four broad stages, each with appropriate institutions: simple hunters, nomadic herders, feudal farmers, and commercial workers. The guiding force in this development is human nature, motivated by self-interest but guided by disinterested reason. Most of the book is given over to a discussion of the function of the invisible hand in the final, current stage. Whereas conscience provided the necessary guidance in* The Theory of Moral Sentiments, *competition assumes that function in* The Wealth of Nations. *Competition rendered markets self-regulating and ensured that prices and wages never stray far from their "natural" levels. Much of the book, especially Book IV, where he places his discussion of colonies, is given over to a polemic against restriction, through both regulation and monopoly, in economic life.* The Wealth of Nations *appeared to great acclaim and earned its author fame and fortune. He published nothing more.*

From *An Inquiry into the Nature and Causes of the Wealth of Nations,* by Adam Smith (New York: Modern Library, 1950), pp. 599–609, 638–49.

*   *   *

Of the Motives for Establishing New Colonies

The interest which occasioned the first settlement of the different European colonies in America and the West Indies, was not altogether so plain and distinct as that which directed the establishment of those of ancient Greece and Rome.

GREEK COLONIES WERE SENT OUT WHEN THE POPULATION GREW TOO GREAT AT HOME.

All the different states of ancient Greece possessed, each of them, but a very small territory, and when the people in any one of them multiplied beyond what that territory could easily maintain, a part of them were sent in quest of a new habitation in some remote and distant part of the world; the warlike neighbours who surrounded them on all sides, rendering it difficult for any of them to enlarge very much its territory at home. ＊ ＊ ＊

THE MOTHER CITY CLAIMED NO AUTHORITY.

The mother city, though she considered the colony as a child, at all times entitled to great favour and assistance, and owing in return much gratitude and respect, yet considered it as an emancipated child, over whom she pretended to claim no direct authority or jurisdiction.

The colony settled its own form of government, enacted its own laws, elected its own magistrates, and made peace or war with its neighbours as an independent state, which had no occasion to wait for the approbation or consent of the mother city. Nothing can be more plain and distinct than the interest which directed every such establishment.

ROMAN COLONIES WERE SENT OUT TO SATISFY THE DEMAND FOR LANDS AND TO ESTABLISH GARRISONS IN CONQUERED TERRITORIES.

Rome, like most of the other ancient republics, was originally founded upon an Agrarian law, which divided the public territory in a certain proportion among the different citizens who composed the state. The course of human affairs, by marriage, by succession, and by alienation, necessarily deranged this original division, and frequently threw the lands, which had been allotted for the maintenance of many different families into the possession of a single person. To remedy this disorder, for such it was supposed to be, a law was made, restricting the quantity of land which any citizen could possess to five hundred jugera, about three hundred and fifty English acres. This law, however, though we read of its having been executed upon one or two occasions, was either neglected or evaded, and the inequality of fortunes went on continually increasing. The greater part

of the citizens had no land, and without it the manners and customs of those times rendered it difficult for a freeman to maintain his independency. ＊ ＊ ＊ The people became clamorous to get land, and the rich and the great, we may believe, were perfectly determined not to give them any part of theirs. To satisfy them in some measure, therefore, they frequently proposed to send out a new colony.

THEY WERE ENTIRELY SUBJECT TO THE MOTHER CITY.

But conquering Rome was, even upon such occasions, under no necessity of turning out her citizens to seek their fortune, if one may say so, through the wide world, without knowing where they were to settle. She assigned them lands generally in the conquered provinces of Italy, where, being within the dominions of the republic, they could never form any independent state; but were at best but a sort of corporation, which, though it had the power of enacting bye-laws for its own government, was at all times subject to the correction, jurisdiction, and legislative authority of the mother city. The sending out a colony of this kind, not only gave some satisfaction to the people, but often established a sort of garrison too in a newly conquered province, of which the obedience might otherwise have been doubtful. A Roman colony, therefore, whether we consider the nature of the establishment itself, or the motives for making it, was altogether different from a Greek one. The words accordingly, which in the original languages denote those different establishments, have very different meanings. The Latin word (*Colonia*) signifies simply a plantation. The Greek word (αποιηια), on the contrary, signifies a separation of dwelling, a departure from home, a going out of the house. But, though the Roman colonies were in many respects different from the Greek ones, the interest which prompted to establish them was equally plain and distinct. Both institutions derived their origin either from irresistible necessity, or from clear and evident utility.

THE UTILITY OF THE AMERICAN COLONIES IS NOT SO EVIDENT.

The establishment of the European colonies in America and the West Indies arose from no necessity: and though the utility which has resulted from them has been very great, it is not altogether so clear and evident. It was not understood at their first establishment, and was not the motive either of that establishment or of the discoveries which gave occasion to it; and the nature, extent, and limits of that utility are not, perhaps, well understood at this day.

THE VENETIANS HAD A PROFITABLE TRADE IN EAST INDIA GOODS.

The Venetians, during the fourteenth and fifteenth centuries, carried on a very advantageous commerce in spiceries, and other East India goods, which they distributed among the other nations of Europe. They purchased them chiefly in Egypt, at that time under the dominion of the Mammeluks, the enemies of the Turks, of whom the Venetians were the enemies; and this union of interest, assisted by the money of Venice, formed such a connection as gave the Venetians almost a monopoly of the trade.

THIS WAS ENVIED BY THE PORTUGUESE AND LED THEM TO DISCOVER THE CAPE OF GOOD HOPE PASSAGE.

The great profits of the Venetians tempted the avidity of the Portuguese. They had been endeavouring, during the course of the fifteenth century, to find out by sea a way to the countries from which the Moors brought them ivory and gold dust across the Desart. They discovered the Madeiras, the Canaries, the Azores, the Cape de Verd islands, the coast of Guinea, that of Loango, Congo, Angola, and Benguela, and finally, the Cape of Good Hope. They had long wished to share in the profitable traffic of the Venetians, and this last discovery opened to them a probable prospect of doing so. In 1497, Vasco de Gama sailed from the port of Lisbon with a fleet of four ships, and, after a navigation of eleven months, arrived upon the coast of Indostan, and thus completed a course of discoveries which had been pursued with great steadiness, and with very little interruption, for near a century together.

COLUMBUS ENDEAVOURED TO REACH THE EAST INDIES BY SAILING WESTWARDS.

Some years before this, while the expectations of Europe were in suspense about the projects of the Portuguese, of which the success appeared yet to be doubtful, a Genoese pilot formed the yet more daring project of sailing to the East Indies by the West. The situation of those countries was at that time very imperfectly known in Europe. The few European travellers who had been there had magnified the distance; perhaps through simplicity and ignorance, what was really very great, appearing almost infinite to those who could not measure it; or, perhaps, in order to increase somewhat more the marvellous of their own adventures in visiting regions so immensely remote from Europe. The longer the way was by the East, Columbus very justly concluded, the shorter it would be by the West. He proposed, therefore, to take that way, as both the shortest and the surest, and he had the good fortune to convince Isabella of Castile of the probability of his project. He sailed from the port of Palos in August 1492, near five years before the expedition of Vasco de Gama set out from Portugal, and, after a voyage of between two and three months, discovered first some of the small Bahama or Lucayan islands, and afterwards the great island of St. Domingo.

COLUMBUS MISTOOK THE COUNTRIES HE FOUND FOR THE INDIES.

But the countries which Columbus discovered, either in this or in any of his subsequent voyages, had no resemblance to those which he had gone in quest of. Instead of the wealth, cultivation and populousness of China and Indostan, he found, in St. Domingo, and in all the other parts of the new world which he ever visited, nothing but a country quite covered with wood, uncultivated, and inhabited only by some tribes of naked and miserable savages. He was not very willing, however, to believe that they were not the same with some of the countries described by Marco Polo, the first European who had visited, or at least had left behind him any description of China or the East Indies; and a very slight resemblance, such as that which he found between the name of Cibao, a mountain in St. Domingo, and that of Cipango, mentioned by Marco Polo, was frequently sufficient to make him return to this favourite prepossession, though contrary to the clearest evidence. In his letters to Ferdinand and Isabella he called the countries which he had discovered, the Indies. He entertained no doubt but that they were the extremity of those which had been described by Marco Polo, and that they were not very distant from the Ganges, or from the countries which had been conquered by Alexander. Even when at last convinced that they were different, he still flattered himself that those rich countries were at no great distance, and in a subsequent voyage, accordingly, went in quest of them along the coast of Terra Firma, and towards the isthmus of Darien.

HENCE THE NAMES EAST AND WEST INDIES.

In consequence of this mistake of Columbus, the name of the Indies has stuck to those unfortunate countries ever since; and when it was at last clearly discovered that the new were altogether different from the old Indies, the former were called the West, in contradistinction to the latter, which were called the East Indies.

THE COUNTRIES DISCOVERED WERE NOT RICH.

It was of importance to Columbus, however, that the countries which he had discovered, whatever they were, should be represented to the court of Spain as of very great consequence; and, in what constitutes the real riches of every country, the animal and vegetable productions of the soil, there

was at that time nothing which could well justify such a representation of them.

*   *   *

SO COLUMBUS RELIED ON THE MINERALS.

Finding nothing either in the animals or vegetables of the newly discovered countries, which could justify a very advantageous representation of them, Columbus turned his view towards their minerals; and in the richness of the productions of this third kingdom, he flattered himself, he had found a full compensation for the insignificancy of those of the other two. The little bits of gold with which the inhabitants ornamented their dress, and which, he was informed, they frequently found in the rivulets and torrents that fell from the mountains, were sufficient to satisfy him that those mountains abounded with the richest gold mines. St. Domingo, therefore, was represented as a country abounding with gold, and upon that account (according to the prejudices not only of the present times, but of those times), an inexhaustible source of real wealth to the crown and kingdom of Spain. * * *

THE COUNCIL OF CASTILE WAS ATTRACTED BY THE GOLD, COLUMBUS PROPOSING THAT THE GOVERNMENT SHOULD HAVE HALF THE GOLD AND SILVER DISCOVERED.

In consequence of the representations of Columbus, the council of Castile determined to take possession of countries of which the inhabitants were plainly incapable of defending themselves. The pious purpose of converting them to Christianity sanctified the injustice of the project. But the hope of finding treasures of gold there, was the sole motive which prompted to undertake it; and to give this motive the greater weight, it was proposed by Columbus that the half of all the gold and silver that should be found there should belong to the crown. This proposal was approved of by the council.

*   *   *

THE SUBSEQUENT SPANISH ENTERPRISES WERE ALL PROMPTED BY THE SAME MOTIVE.

All the other enterprises of the Spaniards in the new world, subsequent to those of Columbus, seem to have been prompted by the same motive. It was the sacred thirst of gold that carried Oieda, Nicuessa, and Vasco Nugnes de Balboa, to the isthmus of Darien, that carried Cortez to Mexico, and Almagro and Pizzarro to Chile and Peru. When those adventurers arrived upon any unknown coast, their first enquiry was always if there was any gold to be found there; and according to the information which they received concerning this particular, they determined either to quit the country or to settle in it.

*   *   *

IN THIS CASE EXPECTATIONS WERE TO SOME EXTENT REALISED, SO FAR AS THE SPANIARDS WERE CONCERNED.

In the countries first discovered by the Spaniards, no gold or silver mines are at present known which are supposed to be worth the working. The quantities of those metals which the first adventurers are said to have found there, had probably been very much magnified, as well as the fertility of the mines which were wrought immediately after the first discovery. What those adventurers were reported to have found, however, was sufficient to inflame the avidity of all their countrymen. Every Spaniard who sailed to America expected to find an Eldorado. Fortune too did upon this what she has done upon very few other occasions. She realized in some measure the extravagant hopes of her votaries, and in the discovery and conquest of Mexico and Peru (of which the one happened about thirty, the other about forty years after the first expedition of Columbus), she presented them with something not very unlike that profusion of the precious metals which they sought for.

A project of commerce to the East Indies, therefore, gave occasion to the first discovery of the West. A project of conquest gave occasion to all the establishments of the Spaniards in those newly discovered countries. The motive which excited them to this conquest was a project of gold and silver mines; and a course of accidents, which no human wisdom could foresee, rendered this project much more successful than the undertakers had any reasonable grounds for expecting.

BUT THE OTHER NATIONS WERE NOT SO SUCCESSFUL.

The first adventures of all the other nations of Europe, who attempted to make settlements in America, were animated by the like chimerical views; but they were not equally successful. It was more than a hundred years after the first settlement of the Brazils, before any silver, gold, or diamond mines were discovered there. In the English, French, Dutch, and Danish colonies, none have ever yet been discovered; at least none that are at present supposed to be worth the working. The first English settlers in North America, however, offered a fifth of all the gold and silver which should be found there to the king, as a motive for granting them their patents. In the patents to Sir Walter Raleigh, to the London and Plymouth companies, to the council of Plymouth, &c. this fifth was accordingly reserved to the crown. To the expectation of finding gold and silver mines, those first settlers too joined that of discovering a northwest passage to the East Indies. They have hitherto been disappointed in both.

Causes of the Prosperity of New Colonies

The colony of a civilized nation which takes possession either of a waste country, or of one so thinly inhabited, that the natives easily give place to the new settlers, advances more rapidly to wealth and greatness than any other human society.

COLONISTS TAKE OUT KNOWLEDGE AND REGULAR GOVERNMENT.

The colonists carry out with them a knowledge of agriculture and of other useful arts, superior to what can grow up of its own accord in the course of many centuries among savage and barbarous nations. They carry out with them too the habit of subordination, some notion of the regular government which takes place in their own country, of the system of laws which supports it, and of a regular administration of justice; and they naturally establish something of the same kind in the new settlement. But among savage and barbarous nations, the natural progress of law and government is still slower than the natural progress of arts, after law and government have been so far established, as is necessary for their protection.

LAND IS PLENTIFUL AND CHEAP.

Every colonist gets more land than he can possibly cultivate. He has no rent, and scarce any taxes to pay. No landlord shares with him in its produce, and the share of the sovereign is commonly but a trifle. He has every motive to render as great as possible a produce, which is thus to be almost entirely his own. But his land is commonly so extensive, that with all his own industry, and with all the industry of other people whom he can get to employ, he can seldom make it produce the tenth part of what it is capable of producing.

WAGES ARE HIGH.

He is eager, therefore, to collect labourers from all quarters, and to reward them with the most liberal wages. But those liberal wages, joined to the plenty and cheapness of land, soon make those labourers leave him, in order to become landlords themselves, and to reward, with equal liberality, other labourers, who soon leave them for the same reason that they left their first master.

*   *   *

Of the Advantages Which Europe Has Derived from the Discovery of America, and from That of a Passage to the East Indies by the Cape of Good Hope

THE ADVANTAGES DERIVED BY EUROPE FROM AMERICA ARE (1) THE ADVANTAGES OF EUROPE IN GENERAL, AND (2) THE ADVANTAGES OF THE PARTICULAR COUNTRIES WHICH HAVE COLONIES.

Such are the advantages which the colonies of America have derived from the policy of Europe.

What are those which Europe has derived from the discovery and colonization of America?

Those advantages may be divided, first, into the general advantages which Europe, considered as one great country, has derived from those great events; and, secondly, into the particular advantages which each colonizing country has derived from the colonies which particularly belong to it, in consequence of the authority or dominion which it exercises over them.

(1) THE GENERAL ADVANTAGES TO EUROPE ARE (A) AN INCREASE OF ENJOYMENTS

The general advantages which Europe, considered as one great country, has derived from the discovery and colonization of America, consist, first, in the increase of its enjoyments; and secondly, in the augmentation of its industry.

The surplus produce of America, imported into Europe, furnishes the inhabitants of this great continent with a variety of commodities which they could not otherwise have possessed, some for conveniency and use, some for pleasure, and some for ornament, and thereby contributes to increase their enjoyments.

(B) AN AUGMENTATION OF INDUSTRY NOT ONLY IN THE COUNTRIES WHICH TRADE WITH AMERICA DIRECTLY, BUT ALSO IN OTHER COUNTRIES WHICH DO NOT SEND THEIR PRODUCE TO AMERICA OR EVEN RECEIVE ANY PRODUCE FROM AMERICA.

The discovery and colonization of America, it will readily be allowed, have contributed to augment the industry, first, of all the countries which trade to it directly; such as Spain, Portugal, France, and England; and, secondly, of all those which, without trading to it directly, send, through the medium of other countries, goods to it of their own produce; such as Austrian Flanders, and some provinces of Germany, which, through the medium of the countries before mentioned, send to it a considerable quantity of linen and other goods. All such countries have evidently gained a more extensive market for their surplus produce, and must consequently have been encouraged to increase its quantity.

*   *   *

Those great events may even have contributed to increase the enjoyments, and to augment the industry of countries which, not only never sent any commodities to America, but never received any from it. Even such countries may have received a greater abundance of other commodities from countries of which the surplus produce had been augmented by means of the American trade. This greater abundance, as it must necessarily have increased their enjoyments, so it must likewise have augmented their industry. A greater number of new equivalents of some kind or other must have been presented to them to be exchanged for the surplus produce of that industry. A more extensive market must have been created for that surplus produce, so as to raise its value, and thereby encourage its increase. The mass of commodities annually thrown into the great circle of European commerce, and by its various revolutions annually distributed among all the different nations comprehended within it, must have been augmented by the whole surplus produce of America. A greater share of this greater mass, therefore, is likely to have fallen to each of those nations, to have increased their enjoyments, and augmented their industry.

*   *   *

(2) THE PARTICULAR ADVANTAGES OF THE COLONISING COUNTRIES ARE (A) THE COMMON ADVANTAGES DERIVED FROM PROVINCES, (B) THE PECULIAR ADVANTAGES DERIVED FROM PROVINCES IN AMERICA.

The particular advantages which each colonizing country derives from the colonies which particularly belong to it, are of two different kinds; first, those common advantages which every empire derives from the provinces subject to its dominion; and, secondly, those peculiar advantages which are supposed to result from provinces of so very peculiar a nature as the European colonies of America.

The common advantages which every empire derives from the provinces subject to its dominion, consist, first, in the military force which they furnish for its defence; and, secondly, in the revenue which they furnish for the support of its civil government. *   *   *

(A) THE COMMON ADVANTAGES ARE CONTRIBUTIONS OF MILITARY FORCES AND REVENUE, BUT NONE OF THE COLONIES HAVE EVER FURNISHED MILITARY FORCE.

The European colonies of America have never yet furnished any military force for the defence of the mother country. Their military force has never yet been sufficient for their own defence; and in the different wars in which the mother countries have been engaged, the defence of their colonies has generally occasioned a very considerable distraction of the military force of those countries. In this respect, therefore, all the European colonies have, without exception, been a cause rather of weakness than of strength to their respective mother countries.

AND THE COLONIES OF SPAIN AND PORTUGAL ALONE HAVE CONTRIBUTED REVENUE.

The colonies of Spain and Portugal only have contributed any revenue towards the defence of the mother country, or the support of her civil government. The taxes which have been levied upon those of other European nations, upon those of England in particular, have seldom been equal to the expence laid out upon them in time of peace, and never sufficient to defray that which they occasioned in time of war. Such colonies, therefore, have been a source of expence and not of revenue to their respective mother countries.

(B) THE EXCLUSIVE TRADE IS THE SOLE PECULIAR ADVANTAGE.

The advantages of such colonies to their respective mother countries, consist altogether in those peculiar advantages which are supposed to result from provinces of so very peculiar a nature as the European colonies of America; and the exclusive trade, it is acknowledged, is the sole source of all those peculiar advantages.

THE EXCLUSIVE TRADE OF EACH COUNTRY IS A DISADVANTAGE TO THE OTHER COUNTRIES.

In consequence of this exclusive trade, all that part of the surplus produce of the English colonies, for example, which consists in what are called enumerated commodities, can be sent to no other country but England. Other countries must afterwards buy it of her. It must be cheaper therefore in England than it can be in any other country, and must contribute more to increase the enjoyments of England than those of any other country. It must likewise contribute more to encourage her industry. For all those parts of her own surplus

produce which England exchanges for those enumerated commodities, she must get a better price than any other countries can get for the like parts of theirs, when they exchange them for the same commodities. The manufactures of England, for example, will purchase a greater quantity of the sugar and tobacco of her own colonies, than the like manufactures of other countries can purchase of that sugar and tobacco. So far, therefore, as the manufactures of England and those of other countries are both to be exchanged for the sugar and tobacco of the English colonies, this superiority of price gives an encouragement to the former, beyond what the latter can in these circumstances enjoy. The exclusive trade of the colonies, therefore, as it diminishes, or, at least, keeps down below what they would otherwise rise to, both the enjoyments and the industry of the countries which do not possess it; so it gives an evident advantage to the countries which do possess it over those other countries.

*   *   *

REVIEW QUESTIONS

1. How, according to Smith, did the colonial empires of early modern Europe differ from those of the ancient world?
2. What was the motive force of empire?
3. How does Smith explain the eventual success of the colonies in America?
4. What benefits does he see derive from empire? What costs?
5. How does Smith's vision of labor in the colonies differ from Abbé Raynal's discussion of slavery? Why do they differ?
6. How do we explain Smith's apparent indifference to the exploitation of native or slave populations?

SAMUEL PEPYS

FROM *The Diary*

Samuel Pepys (1633–1703) was the son of a rural tailor. Despite this humble origin, he rose to become one of the great men of his day, England's first secretary of the Admiralty, a member of Parliament, president of the Royal Society, and a baron of the Cinque Ports. He was the confidant of kings, familiar with both Charles II and James II. Yet, he is best remembered as the author of his diary, which offers a lively and fascinating account of life in Restoration England from 1660 to 1669. Educated at Magdalene College, Cambridge, he entered the service of his cousin, Admiral Edward Montagu, a favorite of Lord Protector Cromwell. He sailed as his cousin's secretary with the fleet that brought Charles II home from exile, after which he was appointed a clerk in the Admiralty. He found his vocation attending to the business matters of the Royal Navy, studied shipbuilding, victualing, and accounting, and so began a distinguished career in the naval administration. He distinguished himself during the Second Dutch War (1665–1667), at which time plague and fire ravaged London. He eventually rose to a position that combined the authority of first lord and secretary for the Admiralty, a position he held until the end of James II's reign. He retired in 1689 and spent the remainder of his life amassing a library, corresponding with scholars, and preparing a history of the Royal Navy. Yet the work for which he is best remembered had been completed some twenty years prior. His diary is a singular combination of the small and large events that convey intimately and frankly the sense of a life and time.

From *The Diary of Samuel Pepys,* edited by Richard Le Gallienne (New York: Modern Library, 2001), pp. 142–68.

1665

*   *   *

JUNE 1ST. I took coach and to Westminster Hall, where I took the fairest flower, and by coach to Tothill Fields for the ayre till it was dark. I 'light, and in with the fairest flower to eat a cake, and there did do as much as was safe with my flower, and that was enough on my part. Broke up, and away without any notice, and, after delivering the rose where it should be, I to the Temple and 'light, and come to the middle door, and there took another coach, and so home to write letters, but very few, God knows, being by my pleasure made to forget everything that is. The coachman that carried [us] cannot know me again, nor the people at the house where we were. Home to bed, certain news being come that our fleete is in sight of the Dutch ships.

2ND. Up and to the Duke of Albemarle, but missed him. Thence to the Harp and Ball and to Westminster Hall, where I visited "the flowers" in each place, and so met with Mr. Creed, and he and I to Mrs. Croft's to drink and did, but saw not her daughter Borroughes.

3RD. All this day by all people upon the River, and almost every where else hereabout were heard the guns, our two fleets for certain being engaged; which was confirmed by letters from Harwich, but nothing particular: and all our hearts full of concernment for the Duke, and I particularly for my Lord Sandwich and Mr. Coventry after his Royall Highnesse.

4TH. (SUNDAY). Newes being come that our fleete is pursuing the Dutch, who, either by cunning, or by being worsted, do give ground, but nothing more for certain.

5TH. Thence home to dinner, after 'Change, where great talke of the Dutch being fled and we in pursuit of them, and that our ship Charity is lost upon our Captain's, Wilkinson, and Lieutenant's yielding, but of this there is no certainty.

7TH. This day, much against my will, I did in Drury Lane see two or three houses marked with a red cross upon the doors, and "Lord have mercy upon us" writ there; which was a sad sight to me, being the first of the kind that, to my remembrance, I ever saw. It put me into an ill conception of myself and my smell, so that I was forced to buy some roll-tobacco to smell to and chaw, which took away the apprehension.

8TH. Alone at home to dinner, my wife, mother, and Mercer dining at W. Joyce's; I giving her a caution to go round by the Half Moone to his house, because of the plague. I to my Lord Treasurer's by appointment of Sir Thomas Ingram's, to meet the Goldsmiths; where I met with the great news at last newly come, brought by Bab May from the Duke of Yorke, that we have totally routed the Dutch; that the Duke himself, the Prince, my Lord Sandwich and Mr. Coventry are all well which did put me into such joy, that I forgot almost all other thoughts. Admirall Opdam blown up, Trump killed, and said by Holmes; all the rest of their admiralls, as they say, but Everson are killed: we having taken and sunk, as is believed, about 24 of their best ships; killed and taken near 8 or 10,000 men, and lost, we think, not above 700. A great[er] victory never known in

the world. They are all fled, some 43 got into the Texell, and others elsewhere, and we in pursuit of the rest. Thence, when my heart full of joy, home, and to my office a little; then to my Lady Pen's, where they are all joyed and not a little puffed up at the good successe of their father; and good service indeed is said to have been done by him. Had a great bonfire at the gate; and I with my Lady Pen's people and others to Mrs. Turner's great room, and then down into the streete. I did give the boys 4s. among them, and mighty merry. So home to bed, with my heart at great rest and quiett, saving that the consideration of the victory is too great for me presently to comprehend.

9TH. Lay long in bed, my head akeing with too much thoughts I think last night.

10TH. In the evening home to supper; and there, to my great trouble, hear that the plague is come into the City (though it hath these three or four weeks since its beginning been wholly out of the City); but where should it begin but in my good friend and neighbour's, Dr. Burnett, in Fanchurch Street: which in both points troubles me mightily. To the office to finish my letters and then home to bed, being troubled at the sicknesse, and my head filled also with other business enough, and particularly how to put my things and estate in order, in case it should please God to call me away, which God dispose of to his glory.

11TH (LORD'S DAY). Up, and expected long a new suit; but, coming not, dressed myself in my late new black silke camelott suit; and, when fully ready, comes my new one of coloured ferrandin, which my wife puts me out of love with, which vexes me, but I think it is only my not being used to wear colours which makes it look a little unusual upon me. To my chamber and there spent the morning reading. I out of doors a little, to shew, forsooth, my new suit, and back again, and in going I saw poor Dr. Burnett's door shut; but he hath, I hear, gained great goodwill among his neighbours; for he discovered it himself first, and caused himself to be shut up of his own accord: which was very handsome.

15TH. The towne grows very sickly, and people to be afeard of it; there dying this last week of the plague 112, from 43 the week before, whereof but [one] in Fanchurch-streete, and one in Broad-streete, by the Treasurer's office.

16TH. I to White Hall, where the Court is full of the Duke and his courtiers returned from sea. All fat and lusty, and ruddy by being in the sun.

17TH. It struck me very deep this afternoon going with a hackney coach from my Lord Treasurer's down Holborne, the coachman I found to drive easily and easily, at last stood still, and come down hardly able to stand, and told me that he was suddenly struck very sicke, and almost blind, he could not see; so I 'light and went into another coach, with a sad heart for the poor man and trouble for myself, lest he should have been struck with the plague, being at the end of the towne that I took him up; but God have mercy upon us all!

20TH. This day I informed myself that there died four or five at Westminster of the plague in one alley in several houses upon Sunday last, Bell Alley, over against the Palace-gate; yet people do think that the number will be fewer in the towne than it was the last weeke.

21ST. So homewards and to the Cross Keys at Cripplegate, where I find all the towne almost going out of towne, the coaches and waggons being all full of people going into the country. Here I had some of the company of the tapster's wife a while, and so home to my office, and then home to supper and to bed.

23RD. So home by hackney coach, which is become a very dangerous passage now-a-days, the sickness increasing mightily, and to bed.

26TH. The plague encreases mightily, I this day seeing a house, at a bitt-maker's over against St.

Clement's Church, in the open street, shut up; which is a sad sight.

29TH. Up and by water to White Hall, where the Court full of waggons and people ready to go out of towne. To the Harp and Ball, and there drank and talked with Mary, she telling me in discourse that she lived lately at my neighbour's, Mr. Knightly, which made me forbear further discourse. This end of the towne every day grows very bad of the plague. The Mortality Bill is come to 267; which is about ninety more than the last: and of these but four in the City, which is a great blessing to us.

30TH. Thus this book of two years ends. Myself and family in good health, consisting of myself and wife, Mercer, her woman, Mary, Alice, and Susan our maids, and Tom my boy. In a sickly time of the plague growing on. Having upon my hands the troublesome care of the Treasury of Tangier, with great sums drawn upon me, and nothing to pay them with: also the business of the office great. Consideration of removing my wife to Woolwich; she lately busy in learning to paint, with great pleasure and successe. All other things well; especially a new interest I am making, by a match in hand between the eldest son of Sir G. Carteret, and my Lady Jemimah Montagu.

*   *   *

AUGUST 1ST. Slept, and lay long; then up and my Lord [Crew] and Sir G. Carteret being gone abroad, I first to see the bridegroom and bride, and found them both up, and he gone to dress himself. Both red in the face, and well enough pleased this morning with their night's lodging.

2ND. Up, it being a publique fast, as being the first Wednesday of the month, for the plague; I within doors all day, and upon my monthly accounts late, I did find myself really worth £1,900, for which the great God of Heaven and Earth be praised!

5TH. In the morning up, and my wife showed me several things of her doing, especially one fine woman's Persian head mighty finely done beyond what I could expect of her; and so away by water, having ordered in the yarde six or eight bargemen to be whipped, who had last night stolen some of the King's cordage from out of the yarde.

10TH. By and by to the office, where we sat all the morning; in great trouble to see the Bill this week rise so high, to above 4,000 in all, and of them above 3,000 of the plague. And an odd story of Alderman Bence's stumbling at night over a dead corps in the street, and going home and telling his wife, she at the fright, being with child, fell sicke and died of the plague. Thence to the office and, after writing letters, home, to draw over anew my will, which I had bound myself by oath to dispatch by to-morrow night; the town growing so unhealthy, that a man cannot depend upon living two days to an end.

11TH. Up, and all day long finishing and writing over my will twice, for my father and my wife, only in the morning a pleasant rencontre happened in having a young married woman brought me by her father, old Delkes, that carries pins always in his mouth, to get her husband off that he should not go to sea, *une contre pouvait avoir* done any *cose cum elle*, but I did nothing, *si ni baisser* her. After they were gone my mind run upon having them called back again, and I sent a messenger to Blackwall, but he failed. So I lost my expectation.

12TH. The people die so, that now it seems they are fain to carry the dead to be buried by day-light, the nights not sufficing to do it in. And my Lord Mayor commands people to be within at nine at night all, as they say, that the sick may have liberty to go abroad for ayre.

14TH. This night I did present my wife with the dyamond ring, awhile since given me by Mr. Dicke Vines's brother, for helping him to be a purser, valued at about £10, the first thing of that

nature I did ever give her. Great fears we have that the plague will be a great Bill this weeke.

15TH. Up by 4 o'clock and walked to Greenwich, where called at Captain Cocke's and to his chamber, he being in bed, where something put my last night's dream into my head, which I think is the best that ever was dreamt, which was that I had my Lady Castlemayne in my armes and was admitted to use all the dalliance I desired with her, and then dreamt that this could not be awake, but that it was only a dream; but that since it was a dream, and that I took so much real pleasure in it, what a happy thing it would be if when we are in our graves (as Shakespeere resembles it) we could dream, and dream but such dreams as this, that then we should not need to be so fearful of death, as we are this plague time. It was dark before I could get home, and so land at Churchyard stairs, where, to my great trouble, I met a dead corps of the plague, in the narrow ally just bringing down a little pair of stairs. But I thank God I was not much disturbed at it. However, I shall beware of being late abroad again.

19TH. Our fleete is come home to our great grief with not above five weeks' dry, and six days' wet provisions: however, must out again. Having read all this news, and received commands of the Duke with great content, he giving me the words which to my great joy he hath several times said to me that his greatest reliance is upon me. And my Lord Craven also did come out to talk with me, and told me that I am in mighty esteem with the Duke, for which I bless God.

28TH. Up, and being ready I out to Mr. Colvill, the goldsmith's, having not for some days been in the streets; but now how few people I see, and those looking like people that had taken leave of the world.

30TH. Up betimes and to my business of settling my house and papers, and then abroad and met with Hadley, our clerke, who, upon my asking how the plague goes, he told me it encreases much, and much in our parish; for, says he, there died nine this week, though I have returned but six: which is a very ill practice, and makes me think it is so in other places; and therefore the plague much greater than people take it to be. Thence, walked towards Moorefields to see (God forbid my presumption!) whether I could see any dead corps going to the grave; but, as God would have it, did not. But, Lord! how every body's looks, and discourse in the street is of death, and nothing else, and few people going up and down, that the towne is like a place distressed and forsaken.

31st. Up; and, after putting several things in order to my removal, to Woolwich; the plague having a great encrease this week, beyond all expectation of almost 2,000, making the general Bill 7,000, odd 100; and the plague above 6,000. Thus this month ends with great sadness upon the publick, through the greatness of the plague every where through the kingdom almost. Every day sadder and sadder news of its encrease. In the City died this week 7,496, and of them 6,102 of the plague. But it is feared that the true number of the dead this week is near 10,000; partly from the poor that cannot be taken notice of, through the greatness of the number, and partly from the Quakers and others that will not have any bell ring for them. Our fleete gone out to find the Dutch, we having about 100 sail in our fleete, and in them the Soveraigne one; so that it is a better fleete than the former with the Duke was.

*   *   *

REVIEW QUESTIONS

1. How would you characterize life in Restoration England as it is portrayed in Pepys's diary?
2. Why is Pepys so little moved by the suffering of Londoners during the plague?
3. What image of domestic life do we derive from Pepys's accounts?
4. What is Pepys's relationship with Lady Castlemayne?
5. What sense does he offer of the relationship between aristocrats and commoners? How does it differ from accounts of France in the mid–seventeenth century? How might you explain the surprising degree of familiarity?

Coffee House Society

Coffee is an example of the impact of overseas trade and colonial empire on the consumption and lifestyle of ordinary Europeans. The bean's historical origins are shrouded in legend. What seems clear is that they were taken to Arabia from Africa during the fifteenth century and placed under cultivation. Introduced into Europe during the sixteenth and seventeenth centuries, they gained almost immediate popularity. Served at coffeehouses, the first of which was established in London around 1650, coffee's consumption became an occasion for transacting political, social, commercial, or literary business. So great was the demand for coffee that European merchants took it from the Arabian Peninsula to Java, Indonesia, and the Americas.

The following description gives some sense of the ways in which colonial products shaped European culture in the seventeenth century.

From *Selections from the Sources of English History,* edited by Charles W. Colby (New York: Longmans, Green, 1899), pp. 208–12.

*   *   *

1673

A coffee-house is a lay conventicle, good-fellow-ship turned puritan, ill-husbandry in masquerade, whither people come, after toping all day, to purchase, at the expense of their last penny, the repute of sober companions: A Rota [club] room, that, like Noah's ark, receives animals of every sort, from the precise diminutive band, to the hectoring cravat and cuffs in folio: a nursery for training up the smaller fry of virtuosi in confident tattling, or a cabal of kittling [carping] critics that have only learned to spit and mew; a mint of intelligence, that, to make each man his pennyworth, draws out into petty parcels, what the merchant receives in bullion: he, that comes often, saves twopence a week in Gazettes, and has his news and his coffee for the same charge, as at a threepenny ordinary they give in broth to your chop of mutton; it is an exchange, where haberdashers of political small-wares meet, and mutually abuse each other, and the public, with bottomless stories, and head-less notions; the rendezvous of idle pamphlets, and persons more idly employed to read them; a high court of justice, where every little fellow in a cam-let cloak takes upon him to transpose affairs both in church and state, to show reasons against acts of parliament, and condemn the decrees of general councils.

•   •   •

As you have a hodge-podge of drinks, such too is your company, for each man seems a leveller, and ranks and files himself as he lists, without regard to degrees or order; so that often you may see a silly fop and a worshipful justice, a griping rook and a grave citizen, a worthy lawyer and an errant pickpocket, a reverend nonconformist and a canting mountebank, all blended together to compose an oglio [medley] of impertinence.

If any pragmatic, to show himself witty or eloquent, begin to talk high, presently the further tables are abandoned, and all the rest flock round (like smaller birds, to admire the gravity of the madge-howlet [barn-owl]). They listen to him awhile with their mouths, and let their pipes go out, and coffee grow cold, for pure zeal of attention, but on the sudden fall all a yelping at once with more noise, but not half so much harmony, as a pack of beagles on the full cry. To still this bawling, up starts Capt. All-man-sir, the man of mouth, with a face as blustering as that of Æolus and his four sons, in painting, and a voice louder than the speaking trumpet, he begins you the story of a sea-fight; and though he never were further, by water, than the Bear-garden, . . . yet, having pirated the names of ships and captains, he persuades you himself was present, and performed miracles; that he waded knee-deep in blood on the upper-deck, and never thought to serenade his mistress so pleasant as the bullets whistling; how he stopped a vice-admiral of the enemy's under full sail; till she was boarded, with his single arm, instead of grappling-irons, and puffed out with his breath a fire-ship that fell foul on them. All this he relates, sitting in a cloud of smoke, and belching so many common oaths to vouch it, you can scarce guess whether the real engagement, or his romancing account of it, be the more dreadful: however, he concludes with railing at the conduct of some eminent officers (that, perhaps, he never saw), and protests, had they taken his advice at the council of war, not a sail had escaped us.

He is no sooner out of breath, but another begins a lecture on the Gazette, where, finding several prizes taken, he gravely observes, if this trade hold, we shall quickly rout the Dutch, horse and foot, by sea: he nicknames the Polish gentlemen wherever he meets them, and enquires whether Gayland and Taffaletta be Lutherans or Calvinists? *stilo novo* he interprets a vast new stile, or turnpike, erected by his electoral highness on the borders of Westphalia, to keep Monsieur Turenne's cavalry from falling on his retreating troops: he takes words by the sound, without examining their sense: Morea he believes to be the country of the Moors, and Hungary a place where famine always keeps her court, nor is there anything more certain, than that he made a whole room full of fops, as wise as himself, spend above two hours in searching the map for Aristocracy and Democracy, not doubting but to have found them there, as well as Dalmatia and Croatia.

1675

Though the happy Arabia, nature's spicery, prodigally furnishes the voluptuous world with all kinds of aromatics, and divers other rarities; yet I scarce know whether mankind be not still as much obliged to it for the excellent fruit of the humble coffee-shrub, as for any other of its more specious productions: for, since there is nothing we here enjoy, next to life, valuable beyond health, certainly those things that contribute to preserve us in good plight and eucrasy, and fortify our weak bodies against the continual assaults and batteries of disease, deserve our regards much more than those which only gratify a liquorish palate, or otherwise prove subservient to our delights. As for this salutiferous berry, of so general a use through all the regions of the east, it is sufficiently known, when prepared, to be moderately hot, and of a very drying attenuating and cleansing quality; whence reason infers, that its decoction must contain many good physical properties, and cannot but be an incomparable remedy to dissolve crudities, comfort the brain, and dry up ill humours in the stomach. In brief, to prevent or redress, in those that frequently drink it, all cold drowsy rheumatic distempers whatsoever, that proceed from excess of moisture, which are so numerous,

that but to name them would tire the tongue of a mountebank.

. . . .

Lastly, for diversion. It is older than Aristotle, and will be true, when Hobbes is forgot, that man is a sociable creature, and delights in company. Now, whither shall a person, wearied with hard study, or the laborious turmoils of a tedious day, repair to refresh himself? Or where can young gentlemen, or shop-keepers, more innocently and advantageously spend an hour or two in the evening, than at a coffee-house? Where they shall be sure to meet company, and, by the custom of the house, not such as at other places, stingy and reserved to themselves, but free and communicative; where every man may modestly begin his story, and propose to, or answer another, as he thinks fit. Discourse is *pabulum animi, cos ingenii*; the mind's best diet, and the great whetstone and incentive of ingenuity; by that we come to know men better than by their physiognomy. *Loquere, ut te videam*, speak, that I may see thee, was the philosopher's adage. To read men is acknowledged more useful than books; but where is there a better library for that study, generally, than here, amongst such a variety of humours, all expressing themselves on divers subjects, according to their respective abilities?

. . . .

In brief, it is undeniable, that, as you have here the most civil, so it is, generally, the most intelligent society; the frequenting whose converse, and observing their discourses and department, cannot but civilise our manners, enlarge our understandings, refine our language, teach us a generous confidence and handsome mode of address, and brush off that *pudor rubrusticus* (as, I remember, Tully somewhere calls it), that clownish kind of modesty frequently incident to the best natures, which renders them sheepish and ridiculous in company.

So that, upon the whole matter, spite of the idle sarcasms and paltry reproaches thrown upon it, we may, with no less truth than plainness, give this brief character of a well-regulated coffee-house (for our pen disdains to be an advocate for any sordid holes, that assume that name to cloak the practice of debauchery), that it is the sanctuary of health, the nursery of temperance, the delight of frugality, an academy of civility, and free-school of ingenuity.

*   *   *

REVIEW QUESTIONS

1. How would you describe coffeehouse society in the late seventeenth century?
2. What is the attitude of each of our two anonymous authors? How and why do they differ?
3. What is the significance of reading the *Gazette?*
4. What are the virtues of coffee?
5. How can coffee drinking be a vice in early modern Europe?

17 ∾ THE AGE OF ABSOLUTISM, 1660–1789

Absolutism refers to a particular conception of political authority that emerged in the wake of the crises of the later sixteenth century. It asserted order, where Europeans felt order had been undermined in political and social relations, by positing a vision of a society which had its apex in the person of a single ruler. At the center of all conceptions of absolutism was the will of the ruler: for all theorists, that will was absolute, not merely sovereign but determinative of all political relations. The king stood at the peak of that pyramid, and the function of that pyramid was to realize his will. Theories of absolutism drew on an understanding of the will that had its origins in the writings of Italian humanists in the fifteenth century and its fullest expression in the writings of theologians such as John Calvin and Martin Luther. By the end of the period, there would be calls for enlightened absolutism, in which reason guided the will of the sovereign, but the will of the monarch was still the agent of political life.

Such an understanding of the nature and operation of political power required a number of developments, not the least of which was a military and a bureaucracy to carry out the king's will. In France and in Spain, over the course of some three centuries, elaborate machineries of rule had evolved: chanceries for the collection, supervision, management, and disbursement of various incomes; judiciaries to decide such diverse issues as disputes over property, relations between lords and servants, and, in some kingdoms, private relations among families; and the emergence of diplomatic professionals, as well as secretaries of various kinds for record-keeping, which increased exponentially in this period. Finally, certain theories that posited a hierarchy of human nature, from natural slavery to natural monarchy, supported an understanding of that pyramid as not only rational, but natural.

These developments did not go unopposed. Among theorists there arose several who countered the notion of absolute monarchy with that of sovereignty placed in the hands of property owners. Moreover, they argued persuasively that the exercise of sovereignty was limited in accordance with the principles of natural law. In practice as in theory, social groups, especially the aristocracy, struggled to limit the expanding powers of the monarch, whom they viewed as one of their own, and to preserve their own political prerogatives.

No monarch in this period was truly absolute—such an effective expression of the will of the ruler requires greater technological and military support than any ruler prior to the nineteenth century could have. Many, however, were largely successful in representing themselves as the center of all political life in their states, nurturing courts and bureaucracies that reflected images of omniscient and powerful rulers. These same courts provided both a milieu and the financial support for philosophes such as Voltaire and scientists such as Galileo, even as those intellectuals were calling into question the ethics of and the social bases for absolutism.

LOUIS XIV AND THE DUC DE SAINT-SIMON

Revocation of the Edict of Nantes

The Edict of Nantes, signed by Henry IV in 1598, granted a measure of religious liberty to his Protestant subjects, the Huguenots. It granted them freedom of conscience and the right to hold public worship services anywhere they had done so in 1576, including two towns in every administrative unit of France, the houses of aristocrats, and within 5 kilometers of Paris. It also granted French Protestants full civil rights: to enter trade, inherit property, attend universities, and hold offices. The edict included one crucial political concession: the Huguenots were permitted to retain such fortified places as they held in 1597 as garrisoned strongholds at the expense of the crown. The edict also restored Catholicism in all areas where it had been disrupted. Nonetheless, French Catholics resented it as being too tolerant of heresy. The monarchy soon came to view its political clause as a danger to the state. Cardinal Richilieu reduced the Protestant strongholds by force of arms, and the Edict of Alès rescinded the political agreement in 1629 Louis XIV revoked the edict in 1685 and deprived the Huguenots of all civil and religious liberties. Their clergy were forced into exile. Thousands of religious refugees fled France for the Protestant states of Europe and America, where their commercial and artisanal skills contributed significantly to economic prosperity. The revocation provoked a storm of outraged protest against an arbitrary act of state. The proclamation, extracted below, offers the monarch's justification, based on his absolute authority and its religious underpinnings. Entries from the Memoirs of the Duke of Saint-Simon, *an eyewit-*

ness at the royal court, The Declaration of the Gallican Church, *interested parties to the revocation, and from Louis's letter to his heir reflect on the political context and consequences of the deed.*

From *Readings in European History,* translated by J. H. Robinson (Oxford, Eng.: Ginn, 1906).

Louis XIV

FROM Revocation of the Edict of Nantes

1. Be it known that of our certain knowledge, full power, and royal authority, we have, by this present perpetual and irrevocable edict, suppressed and revoked, and do suppress and revoke, the edict of our said grandfather, given at Nantes in April 1598, in its whole extent. . . .

2. We forbid our subjects of the R.P.R. [Religion pretendue reformee, i.e., the so-called reformed religion] to meet any more for the exercise of the said religion in any place or private house, under any pretext whatever. . . .

3. We likewise forbid all noblemen, of what condition soever, to hold such religious exercises in their houses or fiefs, under penalty to be inflicted upon all our said subjects who shall engage in the said exercises, of imprisonment and confiscation.

4. We enjoin all ministers of the said R.P.R., who do not choose to become converts and to embrace the Catholic, apostolic, and Roman religion, to leave our kingdom and the territories subject to us within a fortnight of the publication of our present edict, without leave to reside therein beyond that period, or, during the said fortnight, to engage in any preaching, exhortation, or any other function, on pain of being sent to the galleys. . . .

*   *   *

7. We forbid private schools for the instruction of children of the said R.P.R., and in general all things whatever which can be regarded as a concession of any kind in favor of the said religion.

*   *   *

Duc de Saint-Simon

FROM *Memoirs*

*   *   *

The first-fruits of this dreadful plot were the wanton revocation of the Edict of Nantes, without a shadow of a pretext, and the proscriptions which followed it; its ultimate results were the depopulation of a fourth part of the kingdom and the ruin of our commerce. For a long time the country was given over to the authorised ravages of dragoons, which caused the deaths of, literally, thousands of innocent people of all ages and both sexes. Families were torn asunder; men of all classes, often old and infirm, highly respected for their piety and learning, were sent to toil in the galleys under the lash of the overseer; multitudes were driven penniless from their homes to seek refuge in foreign countries, to which they carried our arts and manufactures, enriching them and causing their cities to flourish at the expense of France.

*   *   *

I reminded the Regent of the disturbances and civil wars caused by the Huguenots from the reign of Henry II to that of Louis XIII; pointing out that even when they were comparatively quiet they had formed a body apart within the State, having their own chiefs, courts of justice specially appointed to deal with their affairs, even when they concerned Catholics, with strong places and garrisons at their disposal; corresponding with foreign Powers; always complaining and ready to take up arms: subjects, in short, merely in name, and yielding just as much or as little allegiance to their Sovereign as they thought fit. I recapitulated the heroic struggles by which his grandfather, Louis XIII, had at last beaten down this Hydra; thereby enabling his successor to get rid of it once for all by the mere expression of his will, without the slightest opposition.

I begged the Regent to reflect that he was now reaping the benefit of these struggles in a profound domestic tranquility; and to consider whether it was worth while, in time of peace when no foreign Power was thinking about the question, to make a concession which the late King had rejected with indignation when reduced to the utmost extremities by a long and disastrous war. I said, in conclusion, that if Louis XIV had made a mistake in revoking the Edict of Nantes it was not so much in the act itself as in the mode of carrying it out.

*   *   *

FROM Declaration of the Gallican Church

We, the archbishops and bishops assembled at Paris by order of the King, with other ecclesiastical deputies who represent the Gallican Church, have judged it necessary to make the regulations and the declaration which follows:

That St. Peter and his successors, Vicars of Jesus Christ, and the whole Church herself, have received power of God only in things spiritual, and pertaining to eternal salvation, not in things civil or temporal, the Lord Himself having said, "My kingdom is not of this world," and also "Render unto Caesar the things that be Caesar's, and unto God the things that are God's"; as also firmly declareth the Apostle, "Let every soul be subject unto the higher powers; for there is no power but of God; the powers that be are ordained of God; whosoever therefore resisteth the power, resisteth the ordinance of God."

Therefore kings and princes are in no wise subjected by God's appointment to any ecclesiastical power in temporal things; neither can the authority of the Keys of the Church directly or indirectly depose them, or their subjects be dis-

pensed from the obedience and fidelity of their oaths to the same; and this doctrine we affirm to be necessary for the maintenance of public peace, no less profitable to the Church than to the State, and to be everywhere and every way observed as agreeable to the Word of God, to the tradition of the Fathers and the example of the Saints. . . .

*   *   *

Louis XIV

FROM **Letter to His Heir**

*   *   *

I have never failed, when an occasion has presented itself, to impress upon you the great respect we should have for religion, and the deference we should show to its ministers in matters specially connected with their mission, that is to say, with the celebration of the Sacred Mysteries and the preaching of the doctrine of the Gospels. But because people connected with the Church are liable to presume a little too much on the advantages attaching to their profession, and are willing sometimes to make use of them in order to whittle down their most rightful duties, I feel obliged to explain to you certain points on this question which may be of importance.

The first is that Kings are absolute *seigneurs,* and from their nature have full and free disposal of all property both secular and ecclesiastical, to use it as wise dispensers, that is to say, in accordance with the requirements of their State.

The second is that those mysterious names, the Franchises and Liberties of the Church, with which perhaps people will endeavour to dazzle you, have equal reference to all the faithful whether they be laymen or tonsured, who are all equally sons of this common Mother; but that they exempt neither the one nor the other from subjection to Sovereigns, to whom the Gospel itself precisely enjoins that they should submit themselves.

*   *   *

REVIEW QUESTIONS

1. Why did Louis revoke the Edict of Nantes?
2. What does this tell us about his conception of royal authority?

3. Is there any aspect of life that is exempt from royal authority?
4. How does this contrast with the political theory of John Locke?
5. What, according the Duke of Saint-Simon, were the real consequences of the revocation?
6. How might Louis or his advisors have justified the act?
7. What, benefits might have been expected in the first place?

JOHN LOCKE

FROM *Two Treatises on Government*

John Locke (1632–1704) was an English philosopher whose thought contributed to the Enlightenment. He grew up in a liberal Puritan family, the son of an attorney who fought in the civil war against Charles I, and attended Christ's Church College, Oxford. He received his bachelor of arts in 1656, lectured in classical languages while earning his master of arts, and entered Oxford medical school to avoid being forced to join the clergy. In 1666, Locke attached himself to the household of the earl of Shaftesbury and his fortunes to the liberal Whig Party. Between 1675 and 1679, he lived in France, where he made contact with leading intellectuals of the late seventeenth century. On his return to England, he plunged into the controversy surrounding the succession of James II, an avowed Catholic with absolutist pretensions, to the throne of his brother, Charles II. Locke's patron, Shaftesbury, was imprisoned for his opposition, and Locke went into exile in 1683. Though he was involved to some extent in the Glorious Revolution of 1688, he returned to England in 1689, in the entourage of Mary, princess of Orange, who would assume the throne with her husband William. The Two Treatises on Government (1690) were published anonymously, although readers commonly assumed Locke's authorship. More interesting is the point in time at which they were written. Most scholars assume that they were written immediately before publication, as a justification of the revolution just completed. Many scholars believe, however, that the treatises were written from exile as a call to revolution, a much more inflammatory and risky project. The first treatise comprises a long attack on Robert Filmer's Patriarcha, *a denial of the patriarchal justification of the absolute monarch. The second treatise constructs in the place of patriarchy a theory of politics based on natural law, which provides the foundation of human freedom. The social contract creates a political structure by consent of the governed designed to preserve those freedoms established in natural law. Locke's treatises inspired the political theories of the Enlightenment.*

From *First Treatises* in *Two Treatises on Government*, edited by Ernst Rhys (New York: Dutton, 1993).

us in only from bogs and precipices. So that however it may be mistaken, the end of law is not to abolish or restrain, but to preserve and enlarge freedom. For in all the states of created beings, capable of laws, where there is no law there is no freedom. For liberty is to be free from restraint and violence from others, which cannot be where there is no law; and is not, as we are told, "a liberty for every man to do what he lists." For who could be free, when every other man's humour might domineer over him? But a liberty to dispose and order freely as he lists his person, actions, possessions, and his whole property within the allowance of those laws under which he is, and therein not to be subject to the arbitrary will of another, but freely follow his own.

The power, then, that parents have over their children arises from that duty which is incumbent on them, to take care of their offspring during the imperfect state of childhood. To inform the mind, and govern the actions of their yet ignorant nonage, till reason shall take its place and ease them of that trouble, is what the children want, and the parents are bound to. For God having given man an understanding to direct his actions, has allowed him a freedom of will and liberty of acting, as properly belonging thereunto within the bounds of that law he is under. But whilst he is in an estate wherein he has no understanding of his own to direct his will, he is not to have any will of his own to follow. He that understands for him must will for him too; he must prescribe to his will, and regulate his actions, but when he comes to the estate that made his father a free man, the son is a free man too.

This holds in all the laws a man is under, whether natural or civil. Is a man under the law of Nature? What made him free of that law? what gave him a free disposing of his property, according to his own will, within the compass of that law? I answer, an estate wherein he might be supposed capable to know that law, that so he might keep his actions within the bounds of it. When he has acquired that state, he is presumed to know how far that law is to be his guide, and how far he may make use of his freedom, and so comes to have it; till then, somebody else must guide him, who is presumed to know how far the law allows a liberty. If such a state of reason, such an age of discretion made him free, the same shall make his son free too. Is a man under the law of England? what made him free of that law—that is, to have the liberty to dispose of his actions and possessions, according to his own will, within the permission of that law? a capacity of knowing that law. Which is supposed, by that law, at the age of twenty-one, and in some cases sooner. If this made the father free, it shall make the son free too. Till then, we see the law allows the son to have no will, but he is to be guided by the will of his father or guardian, who is to understand for him. And if the father die and fail to substitute a deputy in this trust, if he hath not provided a tutor to govern his son during his minority, during his want of understanding, the law takes care to do it: some other must govern him and be a will to him till he hath attained to a state of freedom, and his understanding be fit to take the government of his will. But after that the father and son are equally free, as much as tutor and pupil, after nonage, equally subjects of the same law together, without any dominion left in the father over the life, liberty, or estate of his son, whether they be only in the state and under the law of Nature, or under the positive laws of an established government.

*   *   *

The freedom then of man, and liberty of acting according to his own will, is grounded on his having reason, which is able to instruct him in that law he is to govern himself by, and make him know how far he is left to the freedom of his own will. To turn him loose to an unrestrained liberty, before he has reason to guide him, is not the allowing him the privilege of his nature to be free, but to thrust him out amongst brutes, and abandon him to a state as wretched and as much beneath that of a man as theirs. This is that which puts the authority into the parents' hands to govern the minority of their children. God hath made it their business to employ this care on their offspring, and hath placed in them suitable inclinations of tenderness and concern to temper this power, to apply it as His wisdom designed it, to the children's good as long as they should need to be under it.

But what reason can hence advance this care of the parents due to their offspring into an absolute, arbitrary dominion of the father, whose power reaches no farther than by such a discipline as he finds most effectual to give such strength and health to their bodies, such vigour and rectitude to their minds, as may best fit his children to be most useful to themselves and others, and, if it be necessary to his condition, to make them work when they are able for their own subsistence; but in this power the mother, too, has her share with the father.

Nay, this power so little belongs to the father by any peculiar right of Nature, but only as he is guardian of his children, that when he quits his care of them he loses his power over them, which goes along with their nourishment and education, to which it is inseparably annexed, and belongs as much to the foster-father of an exposed child as to the natural father of another. So little power does the bare act of begetting give a man over his issue, if all his care ends there, and this be all the title he hath to the name and authority of a father. And what will become of this paternal power in that part of the world where one woman hath more than one husband at a time? or in those parts of America where, when the husband and wife part, which happens frequently, the children are all left to the mother, follow her, and are wholly under her care and provision? And if the father die whilst the children are young, do they not naturally everywhere owe the same obedience to their mother, during their minority, as to their father, were he alive? And will any one say that the mother hath a legislative power over her children that she can make standing rules which shall be of perpetual obligation, by which they ought to regulate all the concerns of their property, and bound their liberty all the course of their lives, and enforce the observation of them with capital punishments? For this is the proper power of the magistrate, of which the father hath not so much as

the shadow. His command over his children is but temporary, and reaches not their life or property. It is but a help to the weakness and imperfection of their nonage, a discipline necessary to their education. And though a father may dispose of his own possessions as he pleases when his children are out of danger of perishing for want, yet his power extends not to the lives or goods which either their own industry, or another's bounty, has made theirs, nor to their liberty neither, when they are once arrived to the enfranchisement of the years of discretion. The father's empire then ceases, and he can from thenceforward no more dispose of the liberty of his son than that of any other man. And it must be far from an absolute or perpetual jurisdiction from which a man may withdraw himself, having licence from Divine authority to "leave father and mother and cleave to his wife."

*   *   *

Chapter VII
Of Political or Civil Society

God, having made man such a creature that, in His own judgment, it was not good for him to be alone, put him under strong obligations of necessity, convenience, and inclination, to drive him into society, as well as fitted him with understanding and language to continue and enjoy it. The first society was between man and wife, which gave beginning to that between parents and children, to which, in time, that between master and servant came to be added. And though all these might, and commonly did, meet together, and make up but one family, wherein the master or mistress of it had some sort of rule proper to a family, each of these, or all together, came short of "political society," as we shall see if we consider the different ends, ties, and bounds of each of these.

Conjugal society is made by a voluntary compact between man and woman, and though it consist chiefly in such a communion and right in one another's bodies as is necessary to its chief end, procreation, yet it draws with it mutual support and assistance, and a communion of interests too, as necessary not only to unite their care and affection, but also necessary to their common offspring, who have a right to be nourished and maintained by them till they are able to provide for themselves.

For the end of conjunction between male and female being not barely procreation, but the continuation of the species, this conjunction betwixt male and female ought to last, even after procreation, so long as is necessary to the nourishment and support of the young ones, who are to be sustained by those that got them till they are able to shift and provide for themselves. This rule, which the infinite wise Maker hath set to the works of His hands, we find the inferior creatures steadily obey. In those vivaporous animals which feed on grass the conjunction between male and female lasts no longer than the very act of copulation, because the teat of the dam being sufficient to nourish the young till it be able to feed on grass, the male only begets, but concerns not himself for the female or young, to whose sustenance he can contribute nothing. But in beasts of prey the conjunction lasts longer, because the dam, not being able well to subsist herself and nourish her numerous offspring by her own prey alone (a more laborious as well as more dangerous way of living than by feeding on grass), the assistance of the male is necessary to the maintenance of their common family, which cannot subsist till they are able to prey for themselves, but by the joint care of male and female. The same is observed in all birds (except some domestic ones, where plenty of food excuses the cock from feeding and taking care of the young brood), whose young, needing food in the nest, the cock and hen continue mates till the young are able to use their wings and provide for themselves.

And herein, I think, lies the chief, if not the only reason, why the male and female in mankind are tied to a longer conjunction than other creatures—viz., because the female is capable of conceiving, and, *de facto*, is commonly with child

again, and brings forth too a new birth, long before the former is out of a dependency for support on his parents' help and able to shift for himself, and has all the assistance due to him from his parents, whereby the father, who is bound to take care for those he hath begot, is under an obligation to continue in conjugal society with the same woman longer than other creatures, whose young, being able to subsist of themselves before the time of procreation returns again, the conjugal bond dissolves of itself, and they are at liberty till Hymen, at his usual anniversary season, summons them again to choose new mates. Wherein one cannot but admire the wisdom of the great Creator, who, having given to man an ability to lay up for the future as well as supply the present necessity, hath made it necessary that society of man and wife should be more lasting than of male and female amongst other creatures, that so their industry might be encouraged, and their interest better united, to make provision and lay up goods for their common issue, which uncertain mixture, or easy and frequent solutions of conjugal society, would mightily disturb.

But though these are ties upon mankind which make the conjugal bonds more firm and lasting in a man than the other species of animals, yet it would give one reason to inquire why this compact, where procreation and education are secured and inheritance taken care for, may not be made determinable, either by consent, or at a certain time, or upon certain conditions, as well as any other voluntary compacts, there being no necessity, in the nature of the thing, nor to the ends of it, that it should always be for life—I mean, to such as are under no restraint of any positive law which ordains all such contracts to be perpetual.

But the husband and wife, though they have but one common concern, yet having different understandings, will unavoidably sometimes have different wills too. It therefore being necessary that the last determination (i.e., the rule) should be placed somewhere, it naturally falls to the man's share as the abler and the stronger. But this, reaching but to the things of their common interest and property, leaves the wife in the full and true possession of what by contract is her peculiar right, and at least gives the husband no more power over her than she has over his life; the power of the husband being so far from that of an absolute monarch that the wife has, in many cases, a liberty to separate from him where natural right or their contract allows it, whether that contract be made by themselves in the state of Nature or by the customs or laws of the country they live in, and the children, upon such separation, fall to the father or mother's lot as such contract does determine.

For all the ends of marriage being to be obtained under politic government, as well as in the state of Nature, the civil magistrate doth not abridge the right or power of either, naturally necessary to those ends—viz., procreation and mutual support and assistance whilst they are together, but only decides any controversy that may arise between man and wife about them. If it were otherwise, and that absolute sovereignty and power of life and death naturally belonged to the husband, and were necessary to the society between man and wife, there could be no matrimony in any of these countries where the husband is allowed no such absolute authority. But the ends of matrimony requiring no such power in the husband, it was not at all necessary to it. The condition of conjugal society put it not in him; but whatsoever might consist with procreation and support of the children till they could shift for themselves—mutual assistance, comfort, and maintenance—might be varied and regulated by that contract which first united them in that society, nothing being necessary to any society that is not necessary to the ends for which it is made.

*   *   *

Let us therefore consider a master of a family with all these subordinate relations of wife, children, servants and slaves, united under the domestic rule of a family, with what resemblance soever it may have in its order, offices, and number too, with a little commonwealth, yet is very far from it both in its constitution, power, and end; or if it must be thought a monarchy, and the paterfamilias the absolute monarch in it, absolute monarchy will have but a very shattered and short power, when it is plain by what has been said before, that the master of the family has a very distinct and differently limited power both as to time and extent over those several persons that are in it; for excepting the slave (and the family is as much a family, and his power as paterfamilias as great, whether there be any slaves in his family or no) he has no legislative power of life and death over any of them, and none too but what a mistress of a family may have as well as he. And he certainly can have no absolute power over the whole family who has but a very limited one over every individual in it. But how a family, or any other society of men, differ from that which is properly political society, we shall best see by considering wherein political society itself consists.

Man being born, as has been proved, with a title to perfect freedom and an uncontrolled enjoyment of all the rights and privileges of the law of Nature, equally with any other man, or number of men in the world, hath by nature a power not only to preserve his property—that is, his life, liberty, and estate, against the injuries and attempts of other men, but to judge of and punish the breaches of that law in others, as he is persuaded the offence deserves, even with death itself, in crimes where the heinousness of the fact, in his opinion, requires it. But because no political society can be, nor subsist, without having in itself the power to preserve the property, and in order thereunto punish the offences of all those of that society, there, and there only, is political society where every one of the members hath quitted this natural power, resigned it up into the hands of the community in all cases that exclude him not from appealing for protection to the law established by it. And thus all private judgment of every particular member being excluded, the community comes to be umpire, and by understanding indifferent rules and men authorised by the community for their execution, decides all the differences that may happen between any members of that society concerning any matter of right, and punishes those offences which any member hath committed against the society with such penalties as the law has established; whereby it is easy to discern who are, and are not, in political society together. Those who are united into one body, and have a common established law and judicature to appeal to, with authority to decide controversies between them and punish offenders, are in civil society one with another; but those who have no such common appeal, I mean on earth, are still in the state of Nature, each being where there is no other, judge for himself and executioner; which is, as I have before showed it, the perfect state of Nature.

And thus the commonwealth comes by a power to set down what punishment shall belong to the several transgressions they think worthy of it, committed amongst the members of that society (which is the power of making laws), as well as it has the power to punish any injury done unto any of its members by any one that is not of it (which is the power of war and peace); and all this for the preservation of the property of all the members of that society, as far as is possible. But though every man entered into society has quitted his power to punish offences against the law of Nature in prosecution of his own private judgment, yet with the judgment of offences which he has given up to the legislative, in all cases where he can appeal to the magistrate, he has given up a right to the commonwealth to employ his force for the execution of the judgments of the commonwealth whenever he shall be called to it, which, indeed, are his own judgments, they being made by himself or his representative. And herein we have the original of the legislative and executive power of civil society, which is to judge by standing laws how far offences are to be punished when committed within the commonwealth; and also by occasional judgments founded on the present circumstances of the fact, how far injuries from without are to be vindicated, and in both these to employ all the force of all the members when there shall be need.

Wherever, therefore, any number of men so unite into one society as to quit every one his executive power of the law of Nature, and to resign it to the public, there and there only is a political

or civil society. And this is done wherever any number of men, in the state of Nature, enter into society to make one people one body politic under one supreme government: or else when any one joins himself to, and incorporates with any government already made. For hereby he authorises the society, or which is all one, the legislative thereof, to make laws for him as the public good of the society shall require, to the execution whereof his own assistance (as to his own decrees) is due. And this puts men out of a state of Nature into that of a commonwealth, by setting up a judge on earth with authority to determine all the controversies and redress the injuries that may happen to any member of the commonwealth, which judge is the legislative or magistrates appointed by it. And wherever there are any number of men, however associated, that have no such decisive power to appeal to, there they are still in the state of Nature.

And hence it is evident that absolute monarchy, which by some men is counted for the only government in the world, is indeed inconsistent with civil society, and so can be no form of civil government at all. For the end of civil society being to avoid and remedy those inconveniencies of the state of Nature which necessarily follow from every man's being judge in his own case, by setting up a known authority to which every one of that society may appeal upon any injury received, or controversy that may arise, and which every one of the society ought to obey. Wherever any persons are who have not such an authority to appeal to, and decide any difference between them there, those persons are still in the state of Nature. And so is every absolute prince in respect of those who are under his dominion.

For he being supposed to have all, both legislative and executive, power in himself alone, there is no judge to be found, no appeal lies open to any one, who may fairly and indifferently, and with authority decide, and from whence relief and redress may be expected of any injury or inconveniency that may be suffered from him, or by his order. So that such a man, however entitled, Czar, or Grand Signior, or how you please, is as much in the state of Nature, with all under his dominion, as he is with the rest of mankind. For wherever any two men are, who have no standing rule and common judge to appeal to on earth, for the determination of controversies of right betwixt them, there they are still in the state of Nature, and under all the inconveniencies of it, with only this woeful difference to the subject, or rather slave of an absolute prince. That whereas, in the ordinary state of Nature, he has a liberty to judge of his right, according to the best of his power to maintain it; but whenever his property is invaded by the will and order of his monarch, he has not only no appeal, as those in society ought to have, but, as if he were degraded from the common state of rational creatures, is denied a liberty to judge of, or defend his right, and so is exposed to all the misery and inconveniencies that a man can fear from one, who being in the unrestrained state of Nature, is yet corrupted with flattery and armed with power.

*   *   *

Chapter VIII
Of the Beginning of Political Societies

Men being, as has been said, by nature all free, equal, and independent, no one can be put out of this estate and subjected to the political power of another without his own consent, which is done by agreeing with other men, to join and unite into a community for their comfortable, safe, and peaceable living, one amongst another, in a secure enjoyment of their properties, and a greater security against any that are not of it. This any number of men may do, because it injures not the freedom of the rest; they are left, as they were, in the liberty of the state of Nature. When any number of men have so consented to make one community or government, they are thereby presently incorporated, and make one body politic, wherein the majority have a right to act and conclude the rest.

For, when any number of men have, by the consent of every individual, made a community, they have thereby made that community one body, with a power to act as one body, which is only by the will and determination of the majority. For that which acts any community, being only the consent of the individuals of it, and it being one body, must move one way, it is necessary the body should move that way whither the greater force carries it, which is the consent of the majority, or else it is impossible it should act or continue one body, one community, which the consent of every individual that united into it agreed that it should; and so every one is bound by that consent to be concluded by the majority. And therefore we see that in assemblies empowered to act by positive laws where no number is set by that positive law which empowers them, the act of the majority passes for the act of the whole, and of course determines as having, by the law of Nature and reason, the power of the whole.

And thus every man, by consenting with others to make one body politic under one government, puts himself under an obligation to every one of that society to submit to the determination of the majority, and to be concluded by it; or else this original compact, whereby he with others incorporates into one society, would signify nothing, and be no compact if he be left free and under no other ties than he was in before in the state of Nature. For what appearance would there be of any compact? What new engagement if he were no farther tied by any decrees of the society than he himself thought fit and did actually consent to? This would be still as great a liberty as he himself had before his compact, or any one else in the state of Nature, who may submit himself and consent to any acts of it if he thinks fit.

*   *   *

Whosoever, therefore, out of a state of Nature unite into a community, must be understood to give up all the power necessary to the ends for which they unite into society to the majority of the community, unless they expressly agreed in any number greater than the majority. And this is done by barely agreeing to unite into one political society, which is all the compact that is, or needs be, between the individuals that enter into or make up a commonwealth. And thus, that which begins and actually constitutes any political society is nothing but the consent of any number of free-men capable of majority, to unite and incorporate into such a society. And this is that, and that only, which did or could give beginning to any lawful government in the world.

*   *   *

Every man being, as has been showed, natu-rally free, and nothing being able to put him into subjection to any earthly power, but only his own consent, it is to be considered what shall be un-derstood to be a sufficient declaration of a man's consent to make him subject to the laws of any government. There is a common distinction of an express and a tacit consent, which will concern our present case. Nobody doubts but an express con-sent of any man, entering into any society, makes him a perfect member of that society, a subject of that government. The difficulty is, what ought to be looked upon as a tacit consent, and how far it binds—*i.e.,* how far any one shall be looked on to have consented, and thereby submitted to any gov-ernment, where he has made no expressions of it at all. And to this I say, that every man that hath any possession or enjoyment of any part of the do-minions of any government doth hereby give his tacit consent, and is as far forth obliged to obedi-ence to the laws of that government, during such enjoyment, as any one under it, whether this his possession be of land to him and his heirs for ever, or a lodging only for a week; or whether it be barely travelling freely on the highway; and, in effect, it reaches as far as the very being of any one within the territories of that government.

To understand this the better, it is fit to con-sider that every man when he at first incorporates himself into any commonwealth, he, by his unit-ing himself thereunto, annexes also, and submits to the community those possessions which he has, or shall acquire, that do not already belong to any other government. For it would be a direct con-

tradiction for any one to enter into society with others for the securing and regulating of property, and yet to suppose his land, whose property is to be regulated by the laws of the society, should be exempt from the jurisdiction of that government to which he himself, and the property of the land, is a subject. By the same act, therefore, whereby any one unites his person, which was before free, to any commonwealth, by the same he unites his posses-sions, which were before free, to it also; and they become, both of them, person and possession, sub-ject to the government and dominion of that com-monwealth as long as it hath a being. Whoever therefore, from thenceforth, by inheritance, pur-chases permission, or otherwise enjoys any part of the land so annexed to, and under the government of that commonweal, must take it with the condi-tion it is under—that is, of submitting to the government of the commonwealth, under whose jurisdiction it is, as far forth as any subject of it.

But since the government has a direct juris-diction only over the land and reaches the posses-sor of it (before he has actually incorporated himself in the society) only as he dwells upon and enjoys that, the obligation any one is under by virtue of such enjoyment to submit to the govern-ment begins and ends with the enjoyment; so that whenever the owner, who has given nothing but such a tacit consent to the government will, by donation, sale or otherwise, quit the said posses-sion, he is at liberty to go and incorporate himself into any other commonwealth, or agree with oth-ers to begin a new one *in vacuis locis,* in any part of the world they can find free and unpossessed; whereas he that has once, by actual agreement and any express declaration, given his consent to be of any commonweal, is perpetually and indispensably obliged to be, and remain unalterably a subject to it, and can never be again in the liberty of the state of Nature, unless by any calamity the government he was under comes to be dissolved.

But submitting to the laws of any country, liv-ing quietly and enjoying privileges and protection under them, makes not a man a member of that society; it is only a local protection and homage due to and from all those who, not being in a state of war, come within the territories belonging to any government, to all parts whereof the force of its law extends. But this no more makes a man a member of that society, a perpetual subject of that commonwealth, than it would make a man a subject to another in whose family he found it convenient to abide for some time, though, whilst he continued in it, he were obliged to comply with the laws and submit to the government he found there. And thus we see that foreigners, by living all their lives under another government, and enjoying the privileges and protection of it, though they are bound, even in conscience, to submit to its administration as far forth as any denizen, yet do not thereby come to be subjects or members of that commonwealth. Nothing can make any man so but his actually entering into it by positive engagement and express promise and compact. This is that which, I think, concerning the beginning of political societies, and that consent which makes any one a member of any commonwealth.

Chapter IX
Of the Ends of Political Society and Government

If man in the state of Nature be so free as has been said, if he be absolute lord of his own person and possessions, equal to the greatest and subject to nobody, why will he part with his freedom, this empire, and subject himself to the dominion and control of any other power? To which it is obvious to answer, that though in the state of Nature he hath such a right, yet the enjoyment of it is very uncertain and constantly exposed to the invasion of others; for all being kings as much as he, every man his equal, and the greater part no strict observers of equity and justice, the enjoyment of the property he has in this state is very unsafe, very insecure. This makes him willing to quit this condition which, however free, is full of fears and continual dangers; and it is not without reason that he seeks out and is willing to join in society

with others who are already united, or have a mind to unite for the mutual preservation of their lives, liberties and estates, which I call by the general name—property.

The great and chief end, therefore, of men uniting into commonwealths, and putting themselves under government, is the preservation of their property; to which in the state of Nature there are many things wanting.

Firstly, there wants an established, settled, known law, received and allowed by common consent to be the standard of right and wrong, and the common measure to decide all controversies between them. For though the law of Nature be plain and intelligible to all rational creatures, yet men, being biased by their interest, as well as ignorant for want of study of it, are not apt to allow of it as a law binding to them in the application of it to their particular cases.

Secondly, in the state of Nature there wants a known and indifferent judge, with authority to determine all differences according to the established law. For every one in that state being both judge and executioner of the law of Nature, men being partial to themselves, passion and revenge is very apt to carry them too far, and with too much heat in their own cases, as well as negligence and unconcernedness, make them too remiss in other men's.

Thirdly, in the state of Nature there often wants power to back and support the sentence when right, and to give it due execution. They who by any injustice offended will seldom fail where they are able by force to make good their injustice. Such resistance many times makes the punishment dangerous, and frequently destructive to those who attempt it.

*   *   *

REVIEW QUESTIONS

1. According to Locke, what is the nature of political society?

2. How does political society come into being?

3. How does Locke's notion of a social contract compare with that of Hobbes?

4. What are the ends of political society?

5. What are the implications of Locke's reasoning for early modern economic thinking?

JACQUES-BENIGNE BOSSUET

FROM *Politics Drawn from the Very Words of Holy Scripture*

Jacques-Benigne Bossuet (1627–1704) was a French Roman Catholic clergyman and writer, considered by some to be the greatest French preacher in history. He was born in Dijon, and was educated at Jesuit schools and at the Collège de Navarre in Paris. Ordained a priest in 1652, he served at court as tutor to the dauphin, the son of Louis XIV, for whom he wrote his great Discourse on Universal History *(1681), in which he argued that all history is moved by providence. The same year he was elevated to bishop of Meaux, a dignity he possessed until his death. Though best remembered for his* Funeral Orations *(1689), panegyrics on important national figures, history records his theory of absolutism as well. Bossuet's* Politics Drawn from the Very Words of Holy Scripture *was published posthumously in 1708. It argued that because God created kingship, kings were answerable only to God. By so reasoning, Bossuet offered one of the most explicit and extreme arguments for the divine right of kings.*

From *Politics Drawn from the Very Words of Holy Scripture*, by Jacques Bossuet, translated by Patrick Riley (Cambridge, Eng.: Cambridge University Press, 1990), pp. 39–43, 46–69, 57–63, 81–83, 103–6.

* * *

Third Book
In Which One Begins to Explain the Nature and the Properties of Royal Authority

First Article
Taking Notice of the Essential Characteristics.

SOLE PROPOSITION
THERE ARE FOUR CHARACTERISTICS OR QUALITIES ESSENTIAL TO ROYAL AUTHORITY.

First, royal authority is sacred;
Secondly, it is paternal;
Thirdly, it is absolute;
Fourthly, it is subject to reason.
All of this must be established, in order, in the following articles.

Article II
Royal Authority Is Sacred.

1ST PROPOSITION
GOD ESTABLISHES KINGS AS HIS MINISTERS, AND REIGNS THROUGH THEM OVER THE PEOPLES.

We have already seen that all power comes from God.

"The prince, St. Paul adds, is God's minister to thee for good. But if thou do that which is evil, fear: for he beareth not the sword in vain. For he is God's minister: an avenger to execute wrath upon him that doth evil."

Thus princes act as ministers of God, and his lieutenants on earth. It is through them that he exercises his Empire. "And now say you that you are able to withstand the kingdom of the Lord, which he possesseth by the sons of David?"

It is in this way that we have seen that the royal throne is not the throne of a man, but the throne of God himself. "God hath chosen Solomon my son, to sit upon the throne of the kingdom of the Lord over Israel." And again: "Solomon sat on the throne of the Lord."

And in order that no one believe that it was peculiar to the Israelites to have kings established by God, here is what Ecclesiasticus says: "Over every nation he set a ruler. And Israel was made the manifest portion of God."

Thus he governs all peoples, and gives them, all of them, their kings; though he governs Israel in a more particular and announced fashion.

* * *

3RD PROPOSITION
ONE MUST OBEY THE PRINCE BY REASON OF RELIGION AND CONSCIENCE.

St. Paul, after having said that the prince is the minister of God, concludes thus: "wherefore be subject of necessity, not only for wrath, but also for conscience' sake."

This is why "one must serve, not to the eye, as it were pleasing men, but, as the servants of Christ doing the will of God, from the heart."

And again: "Servants, obey in all things your temporal masters, not serving to the eye, as pleasing men, but in simplicity of heart, fearing God. Whatsoever you do, do it from the heart, as to the Lord, and not to men; knowing that you shall receive of the Lord the reward of inheritance. Serve ye the Lord Christ."

If the apostle speaks thus of slavery, a condition contrary to nature, what must we think of legitimate subjection to princes and to magistrates, the protectors of public liberty?

This is why St. Peter says: "Be ye subject therefore to every human creature for God's sake: whether it be to the king as excelling; Or to governors as sent by him for the punishment of evildoers, and for the praise of the good."

Even if rulers do not acquit themselves of this duty, one must respect in them their charge and their ministry. "Servants, be subject to your masters with all fear, not only to the good and gentle, but also to the angry and unjust."

There is thus something religious in the respect one gives to the prince. The service of God and respect for kings are inseparable things, and St. Peter places these two duties together: "Fear God, Honor the King."

God, moreover, has put something divine into kings. "I have said: You are Gods, and all of you the sons of the most High." It is God himself whom David makes speak in this way.

This accounts for the fact that the servants of God swear by the life and health of the king, as by a divine and sacred thing. Uriah spoke to David: "By thy welfare and by the welfare of thy soul I will not do this thing."

Even if the king should be an infidel, from the respect one should have for the ordination of God. "By the health of Pharaoh, you shall not depart hence."

Here one must listen to the first Christians, and to Tertullian, who speaks as follows in the name of all of them: "We shall swear, not by the genius of the Caesars, but by their life and by their health, which is the most august of all geniuses. Do you not know that geniuses are demons? But we, who see in the emperors the choice and judgment of God, who gave them the command over all peoples, respect in them what God has placed there, and we uphold that through a great oath."

He adds: "What more can I say about our religion and about our piety for the emperor, whom we must respect as he whom our God has chosen: such that I can say that Caesar is more to us than to you, because it is our God who has established him?"

Thus it is the spirit of Christianity to make kings respected in a kind of religious way—which Tertullian (again) calls very well "the religion of the second majesty."

This second majesty simply flows out of the first, that is to say the divine, which, for the good of human affairs, has lent some of its brilliance to kings.

*   *   *

Article III
Royal Authority Is Paternal, and Its Proper Character Is Goodness.

After the things which have been said, this truth has no further need of proofs.

We have seen that kings hold the place of God, who is the true Father of the human race.

We have also seen that the first idea of power that there was among men, is that of paternal power; and that kings were fashioned on the model of fathers.

Moreover, all the world agrees that obedience, which is due to public power, is only found (in the Decalogue) in the precept which obliges one to honor his parents.

From all of this it appears that the name "king" is a father's name, and that goodness is the most natural quality in kings.

Let us, nonetheless, reflect particularly on so important a truth.

1ST PROPOSITION
GOODNESS IS A ROYAL QUALITY, AND THE TRUE PREROGATIVE OF GREATNESS.

"The Lord your God is the God of gods, and the Lord of lords, a great and mighty and terrible, who accepteth no person nor taketh bribes. He doth judgment to the fatherless, and the widow, loveth the stranger, and giveth him food and raiment."

Because God is great and self-sufficient, he turns (as it were) entirely to do good to men, in conformity to this word: "For according to his greatness, also is his mercy with him."

He places an image of his greatness in kings, in order to oblige them to imitate his goodness.

He raises them to a condition in which they have nothing more to desire for themselves. We have heard David saying: "What can David add more, seeing thou hast thus glorified thy servant, and known him?"

And at the same time he declares to them that he gives them this greatness for love of the nations. "Because the Lord hath loved his people, therefore, he hath made thee king over them." And again: "God, whom thou hast pleased, . . . hath set thee upon the throne of Israel, because the Lord hath loved Israel for ever, and hath appointed thee king, to do judgment and justice."

That is why, in those passages where we read that the kingdom of David was raised over the people, the Hebrew and the Greek use *for* the people. This shows that greatness has for its object the good of subject peoples.

Indeed God, who has made all men from the same earth, bodily, and has placed equally in their souls his image and resemblance, has not established between them so many distinctions as to make on one side the proud and on the other slaves and wretches. He made the great only to protect the small; he gave his power to kings only to procure the public good, and for the support of the people.

*   *   *

Fourth Book
On the Characteristics
of Royalty (continuation)

First Article
Royal Authority Is Absolute.

In order to make this term odious and insupportable, many pretend to confuse absolute government and arbitrary government. But nothing is more distinct, as we shall make clear when we speak of justice.

1ST PROPOSITION
THE PRINCE NEED ACCOUNT TO NO ONE FOR WHAT HE ORDAINS.

"Observe the mouth of the king, and the commandments of the oath of God. Be not hasty to depart from his face, and do not continue in an evil work: for he will do all that pleaseth him. And his word is full of power: neither can any man say to him: Why dost thou so? He that keepeth the commandment, shall find no evil."

Without this absolute authority, he can neither do good nor suppress evil: his power must be such that no one can hope to escape him; and, in fine, the sole defense of individuals against the public power, must be their innocence.

This doctrine is in conformity with the saying of St. Paul: "Wilt thou then not be afraid of the power? Do that which is good."

2ND PROPOSITION
WHEN THE PRINCE HAS DECIDED, THERE CAN BE NO OTHER DECISION.

The judgments of sovereigns are attributed to God himself. When Josaphat established judges to judge the people, he said: "It is not in the name of man that you judge, but in the name of God."

This is what Ecclesiasticus is made to say: "Judge not against a judge." For still stronger reasons against the sovereign judge who is the king. And the reason which is given is that, "he judgeth according to that which is just." It is not that he is always so judging, but that he is assumed to be so judging; and that no one has the right to judge or to review after him.

One must, then, obey princes as if they were justice itself, without which there is neither order nor justice in affairs.

They are gods, and share in some way in divine independence. "I have said: You are gods, and all of you the sons of the most High."

Only God can judge their judgments and their persons. "God hath stood in the congregation of gods, and being in the midst of them he judgeth gods."

It is for that reason that St. Gregory, Bishop of Tours, said to King Chilperic in a council: "We speak to you, but you listen to us only if you want to. If you do not want to, who will condemn you other than he who has said that he was justice itself?"

It follows from this that he who does not want to obey the prince, is not sent to another tribunal; but he is condemned irremissibly to death as an enemy of public peace and of human society. "Whoever will be proud and will not obey the command of the pontiff and the ordinance of the judge will die, and you will thus eradicate the evil from among you." And again: "Whosoever shall refuse to obey all your orders, may he die." It is the people who speak thus to Joshua.

The prince can correct himself when he knows that he has done badly; but against his authority there can be no remedy except his authority.

This is why he must take care of what he orders. "Take heed what you do; and whatsoever you judge, it shall rebound to you. Let the fear of the Lord be with you, and do all things with great care."

It is thus that Joseph instructed the judges, to whom he was entrusting his authority: how much of this he recollected when he himself had to judge!

*   *   *

Fifth Book
Fourth and Final Characteristic of Royal Authority

First Article
Royal Authority Is Subject to Reason.

1ST PROPOSITION
GOVERNMENT IS A WORK OF REASON AND INTELLIGENCE. "NOW, LISTEN, O KINGS, AND BE INSTRUCTED, JUDGES OF THE EARTH."

All men are created capable of understanding. But principally you upon whom reposes an entire nation, you who should be the soul and intelligence of a state, in whom must be found the first reason for all its movements: the less it is necessary for you to justify yourself to others, the more you must have justification and intelligence within yourself.

The contrary of acting from reason is to act out of passion or anger. To act out of anger, as Saul acted against David, driven by his jealousy or possessed by his black melancholy, entails all kinds of irregularities, inconsistencies, inequalities, anomalies, injustice, and confusion in one's conduct.

Though one has only a horse to lead and a flock to guide, one cannot do it without reason. How much more is needed for the leadership of men and a rational flock!

"The Lord took David from the care of his sheep to have him conduct Jacob, his servant, and Israel, his inheritance. And he led them in the innocence of his heart with an able and intelligent hand."

Everything among men is accomplished through intelligence and through counsel. "Houses are built out of wisdom and become solid through prudence. Ability fills the granaries and amasses riches. The wise man is courageous. The able man is robust and strong because war is waged by strategy and by industry, and salvation is found where there is much counsel."

Wisdom herself says: "It is through me that kings rule and through me that legislators prescribe what is just."

She is so born to command that she gives the empire even to those born in servitude. "The wise servant will command the children of the house who lack wisdom, and he will apportion their lots." And furthermore: "Free people will subject themselves to a judicious servant."

God, upon installing Joshua, orders him to study the law of Moses, which was the law of the kingdom, "in order," he says, "that you should understand all that you do." And furthermore: "and then you will carry out your designs and you will understand what to do." David said as much to Solomon in the last instructions he gave to him upon dying. "Take care to observe the laws of God so that you may understand all that you do and to which side you are to turn.

"So that you may not be turned, turn yourself knowingly. Let reason direct all your movements. Know what you do and why you are doing it."

Solomon had learned from God himself how much wisdom is necessary to govern a great people. "God appeared to him in a dream during the night, and said to him: Ask what thou wilt that I should give thee. And Solomon said: Thou hast shown great mercy to thy servant David my father, even as he walked before thee in truth, and justice, and an upright heart with thee: and thou hast kept thy great mercy for him, and hast given him a son to sit on his throne, as it is this day. And now, O Lord God, thou hast made thy servant king instead of David my father: and I am but a child, and know not how to go out and come in (that is to say, I do not know how to conduct myself: where to begin or to end matters). And thy servant is in the midst of the people which thou hast chosen, an immense people, which cannot be numbered nor counted for multitude. Give therefore to thy servant an understanding heart, to judge thy people, and discern between good and evil. For who shall be able to judge this people, thy people which is so numerous? And the word was pleasing to the Lord that Solomon had asked such a thing. And the Lord said to Solomon: Because thou hast asked this thing, and hast not asked for thyself long life, or riches, nor the lives of thy enemies, but hast asked for thyself wisdom to discern judgment, Behold I have done for thee according to thy words, and have given thee a wise and understanding heart, insomuch that there hath been no one like thee before thee, nor shall arise after thee. Yea and the things also which thou didst not ask, I have given thee: to wit riches and glory, so that no one hath been like thee among the kings in all days heretofore."

This dream of Solomon's was an ecstasy in which the mind of this great king, separated from the senses and united to God, enjoyed true knowledge. He saw, while in this state, that wisdom is the sole grace that a prince should ask of God.

He saw the weightiness of the affairs and the immense multitude of the people whom he had to lead. So many temperaments, so many interests, so many artifices, so many passions, so many surprises to fear, so many things to consider, so many people from every side to hear and know: what mind could be equal to it?

I am young, he said, and I still do not know how to conduct myself. He was not lacking in spirit, any more than in resolution. For he had already spoken in a masterly tone to his brother Adonias: and from the beginning of his reign he had done his part at a decisive juncture, with as much prudence as could be desired: and all the same he trembled still, when he saw this immense chain of cares and of matters that accompany royalty: and he saw well that he could only find his way out through consummate wisdom.

He asked it of God, and God gave it to him: but at the same time he gave him all the rest which he had not asked, that is to say riches and glory.

He teaches kings that they will lack nothing when they have wisdom, and that she alone draws all other goods to them.

We find a fine commentary on Solomon's prayer in the book of Wisdom, which makes this wise king speak as follows: "Wherefore I wished, and understanding was given me: and I called upon God, and the spirit of wisdom came upon me. And I preferred her before kingdoms and thrones, and esteemed riches nothing in comparison of her. Neither did I compare unto her any precious stone: for all gold in comparison of her, is as a little sand, and silver in respect to her shall be counted as clay. I loved her above health and beauty, and chose to have her instead of light: for her light cannot be put out. Now all good things came to me together with her, and innumerable riches through her hands."

*   *   *

DIEGO VELÁZQUEZ

Velázquez's final masterpiece, a famous and curious reflection on court life, has long intrigued art historians. Why paint a picture of the infanta Margarita, followed by her entourage of ladies, dwarves, and pets? As legend has it, she burst into the artist's studio while he was painting a portrait of the king and queen, whose only representation remains a mirrored reflection in the background. He offers a strikingly realistic portrait of some of the members of the court of Philip IV of Spain and, at the same time, a subtle commentary on life in that court. How might Las Meninas *be considered a critique of the court? If the painting was intended as a criticism of royal manners and monarchical rule, what was the criticism? How might events in Spain and Europe at the middle of the seventeenth century have inspired the artist to risk such a statement?*

REVIEW QUESTIONS

1. Why does Bossuet begin his consideration of political authority with God?
2. What are the implications of this point of departure?
3. How is absolutism understood by Bossuet?
4. How does conscience relate to obedience according to Bossuet?
5. How does Bossuet's discussion of paternal authority compare with Filmer's?
6. Why is monarchy natural?
7. How is Bossuet construing nature?

DUC DE SAINT-SIMON

FROM *Historical Memoirs*

Louis de Rouvroy, duc de Saint-Simon (1675–1755), was a French soldier and diplomat, best remembered for his memoirs of court life during the reign of Louis XIV. Born the son of an aged nobleman, a parvenu raised to the aristocracy by Louis XIII, he was a remarkable figure. Physically unattractive, Saint-Simon possessed a violent and vindictive temper as well as great wit and intelligence. His career at court can best be described as disappointing. As his memoirs make clear, he never achieved the rank he sought because of his open and tactless opposition to Louis XIV on minor points of precedence and ceremony. Saint-Simon managed to attach himself to Philippe, duc de Orléans in 1712 and so persevered on the edge of affairs until his patron's death in 1723. From that point until his death in 1755, Saint-Simon remained in private life and devoted himself to writing his memoirs. A composite narrative, drawn from his own memory and papers as well as witness testimony and manuscript sources, it offers a wealth of information on life at the court and a close analysis of state affairs under an absolute monarch.

From *Historical Memoirs of the Duc de Saint-Simon*, vol. 1, translated by Lucy Norton (New York: McGraw-Hill, 1967).

* * *

After ten days at Givry the two armies separated and marched away, and two days later the siege of Namur was proclaimed, the King having covered that journey in a five-day march. Monseigneur, Monsieur, Monsieur le Prince, and the Maréchal d'Humières, in order of rank, led the army under the King's command. The Maréchal de Luxembourg, in sole command of his army, covered the siege and took observations. Meantime the ladies removed to Dinant. On the third day of the King's march Monsieur le Prince was sent on ahead to invest Namur town, for Vauban, the famous organizer of the King's sieges, had insisted on there being separate attacks for the town and the fortress. Nothing very eventful happened during the ten days of the siege; on the eleventh day of open trenches they sounded for a parley and a surrender was arranged on the defenders' terms. During all this time the King was living under canvas in very hot weather, for it had not rained since we left Paris. The army moved camp in order to besiege the fortress, and whilst that was taking place the King's own regiment of infantry found its new position held by a small detachment of the enemy digging trenches. There was a brisk engagement in which the royal troops greatly distinguished themselves, with very few losses, and the enemy were soon routed. The King was delighted by this, for he was particularly devoted to that regiment which he liked to think of as being his personal property.

The King's tents and those of his courtiers were pitched in a pleasant meadow five hundred paces from the monastery of Marlagne. By this time the weather had changed to abundant and continuous rain, such as no one in the army could remember and had thus greatly increased the reputation of St. Médard, whose feast-day is 8 June. It had poured on that day and, according to the saying, whatever the weather is then it will continue so for the next forty days, as it happened in that year. The soldiers were driven nearly to desperation by the floods, so that they cursed the saint heartily, breaking and burning his images wherever they could lay hands on them. The rain was indeed a perfect plague, and the King's tents could only be reached by laying down paths of brushwood which had daily to be renewed. The other tents were not more easily accessible and the trenches were soon full of muddy water. It sometimes took as much as three days to move a cannon from one battery to another. The waggons were unusable, and shells, cannon-balls, etc., had to be transported on mules and horses, which became the sole support of every service to the army and the Court. Without them nothing would have been possible. The flooding of the roads also prevented the army of M. de Luxembourg from using their waggons. They were near starvation for lack of fodder and would have died had not the King issued orders that detachments of his *maison* should ride each day carrying sacks of grain to a

certain village where M. de Luxembourg's officers would receive and count them.

Although the *maison* had had little rest on account of carrying brushwood, mounting the various guards, and their other daily duties, they were given this additional fatigue because the cavalry also had been continuously on duty and were down to leaves for forage. That consideration aroused no sympathy in the hearts of the pampered *maison,* who were accustomed to special privileges. They complained. The King was obdurate. The task remained theirs. On the very first day, however, the lifeguards and light cavalry were openly murmuring when they reached the depot in the early morning, and they so worked upon one another that the men actually threw the sacks down and refused to pick them up again. Cresnay, my brigadier, had most courteously asked me whether I was willing to take a sack, saying that otherwise he would find me some different duty; but I had consented, hoping thus to please the King, especially in view of all the grumbling. It so happened that I arrived on the scene with my troop of musketeers at the precise moment when the red-coats were about to mutiny, and I took up my sack before them all. Thereupon Marin, a cavalry-brigadier, who was supervising the loading by the King's orders and raging at the mutineers, called out my name, exclaiming that if I did not think myself too good for such work, lifeguardsmen and the light horse need not be ashamed to copy me. That argument and his stern eye had their effect; there was a rush to pick up the sacks, and never afterwards the smallest objection. Marin watched us go and then went to tell the King what had happened and the influence of my good example. That kind office resulted in the King saying some gracious things to me, and throughout the remainder of the siege he never saw me without saying something civil. I was all the more obliged to Marin because I had no acquaintance with him socially.

*   *   *

1700

The year began with an economy. The King announced that he would no longer pay for the changes made by courtiers in their lodgings, which had cost him more than sixty thousand livres since Fontainebleau. Mme de Mailly was thought to be the cause, for she had changed hers annually in the past three or four years. The new arrangement was better in that one could get alterations made as one wished without first obtaining the King's consent; on the other hand one had to pay for everything.

From Candlemas to Lent there was a continual succession of balls and entertainments at the Court. The King gave several at Versailles and Marly, with wonderfully ingenious masquerades and tableaux, a form of diversion that vastly pleased him under the guise of amusing Mme la Duchesse de Bourgogne. There were concerts and private theatricals at Mme de Maintenon's; Monseigneur gave balls, and the most distinguished persons took pride in offering entertainment to Mme la Duchesse de Bourgogne. Monsieur le Prince, though his rooms were few and small, contrived to astonish the Court with the most elegant party in the world, a full-evening-dress ball, masks, tableaux, booths with foreign merchandise, and a supper most exquisitely staged. No one at the Court was refused admittance to any part of it, and there was no crowding nor any other inconvenience.

One evening when there was no ball Mme de Pontchartrain gave one at the Chancellery, and it turned out to be the gayest of them all. The Chancellor received Monseigneur, the three princes, and Mme la Duchesse de Bourgogne at the front entrance at ten o'clock and then immediately went off to sleep at the Château. There were different rooms provided for a full-evening-dress ball, masks, a splendid supper, and booths for the merchants of various countries, China, Japan, etc., offering vast quantities of objects of beauty and virtue, all chosen with exquisite taste. No money was taken; all were presents offered to Mme la Duchesse de Bourgogne and the other ladies.

There was also a concert in her honour, a play, and tableaux. Never was anything better conceived, more sumptuous, nor more perfectly organized, and Mme de Pontchartrain in the midst of it all was as gay, civil, and unruffled as though she had no responsibilities.

Everyone enjoyed themselves immensely, and we did not reach home until eight in the morning. Mme de Saint-Simon, who was always in Mme la Duchesse de Bourgogne's retinue (a great favour), and I never saw the light of day in the last three weeks before Lent. Certain dancers were not allowed to leave the ball-room before the princess, and once at Marly when I tried to escape early she sent orders for me to be confined within its doors. The same thing occurred to others also. I was truly thankful when Ash Wednesday came, and for a couple of days after felt quite stunned. As for Mme de Saint-Simon, she was worn out by Shrove Tuesday and did not manage to stay the full course. The King amused himself also in Mme de Maintenon's room with some selected ladies, playing *brelan, petite prime,* and *reversis* on the days when he had no ministers or little work to do, and those diversions continued well into Lent.

*   *   *

1702

*   *   *

When the promotion of generals was finally put into execution it proved to be very sweeping, comprising seventeen lieutenants-general, fifty brigadiers, forty-one colonels of infantry, and thirty-eight of cavalry. But before recounting the action which that promotion led me to take, I must first describe how during that winter I was received into the Parlement.

In dealing with his bastards the King always gave immediate effect to the honours which he granted them, without waiting for the usual warrants, letters patent, notifications, or decrees to be published. Yet, for many years past, he had made it a rule that peers might not be received into the

Parlement without his consent. That he never re-fused, but he had lately begun to withhold per-mission if the peer were not yet twenty-five years old, thus gradually instituting a custom which might later become the general rule. I was aware of this and accordingly deferred my own reception until a year after my twenty-fifth birthday, on the plea of forgetfulness.

My first action was to call on President Harlay, who was overwhelmingly polite. I was then obliged to call on the princes of the blood and finally on the bastards. M. du Maine, when I vis-ited him, asked me to repeat the date, then with a delight that appeared restrained only by modesty and good manners, he exclaimed, "I shall be most careful not to forget. Such an honour! So grati-fying that you desire my presence! You may be sure of me," and so saying he escorted me as far as the gardens, for this was at a Marly, and I was of the house-party. The Comte de Toulouse and M. de Vendôme replied less effusively but no less pleasantly, and were as polite as M. du Maine. Cardinal de Noailles had never once attended at the Parlement since he received the Roman crim-son because his hat did not entitle him to a seat higher than that of his rank as count and peer. I elected to visit him at one of his public audiences. "You are aware," said he, "that I no longer have a seat?" "On the contrary," I replied, "I know that you have a most splendid place, and I beg you to take it at my reception." He then smiled, and I smiled also, for we perfectly understood one an-other. Later he personally escorted me to the top of his staircase, both doors open wide, and we walked together side by side, I on his right hand. M. de Luxembourg was the only one not to hear from me on that occasion. I had never forgiven him those abominable warrants, but he was not my friend and I did him no wrong.

Dongeois was at that time acting as registrar of the Parlement. He was a man whose ability and constant attendance had made him very knowl-edgeable in the customs of that body. I knew him well, and therefore went to consult him about the correct procedure. Yet despite the honesty and kindness of his intentions the good man laid three

traps for me, but luckily I was on the watch and fell into none of them. He said that out of respect for the Parlement I should make my first appear-ance there in a plain black coat unadorned with gold lace; that out of respect for the princes of the blood, whose short mantles were worn longer than their coats, I should not allow mine to come below the level of my jacket, and that out of respect for the premier président I should call to thank him on the morning after my reception, still wearing parliamentary dress. He did not bluntly make these suggestions but tactfully hinted at them. I made no issue of it, but I did the exact opposite, and having been alerted I took care to warn all those who were received after me, and they de-fended themselves likewise. It is by such ruses that many humiliations have come upon the dukes, one after another, in a constant stream that almost passes belief.

The reforming of the army after the Peace of Ryswick was on a very large scale but very hap-hazard. The quality of the various regiments, es-pecially of the cavalry, and the merits of their commanding officers were ignored by Barbezieux, who was young and impulsive, and to whom the King gave a free hand. I myself had no acquain-tance with him; my regiment was re-formed, and as it was very good parts of it were allocated to the Royals and the rest incorporated in the Duras regiment. My company was added to that of Bar-bezieux's brother-in-law the Comte d'Uzès, of whom he took particular care. It was small con-solation to hear that others were being treated in the same way, and I was deeply disappointed. The colonels of regiments re-formed like mine were placed at the bottom of the list in their new reg-iments, and I was ordered to serve under Saint-Mauris, a gentleman of Franche-Comté and a complete stranger to me, although his brother was a lieutenant-general and well regarded. Shortly af-ter this, the petty discipline that runs alongside active service demanded two months' service from officers at the tail of new regiments. That seemed monstrous to me. I went, of course, but I had been indisposed for some time past, and having been recommended the waters of Plombières I asked for leave of absence and for the next three years spent there the two months when I should have been exiled to a strange regiment, with no troops to command and no work to do. The King did not seem to mind. I often went to Marly; he spoke to me sometimes, a very good sign that was much remarked upon; in a word he treated me kindly, indeed better than most of my age and rank.

From time to time officers junior to myself were promoted; but they were veterans who had earned regiments by long and distinguished service, and I could understand the reason. Talk of a general promotion did not excite me, for birth and rank counted for nothing. I was too junior to be made a brigadier; my entire ambition was to command a regiment and fight at its head in the coming war, thus avoiding the humiliation of having to serve as a supernumerary aide-de-camp to Saint-Mauris. The King had distinguished me after the Neerwinden campaign by giving me a regiment; and I had brought it up to strength, and, dare I say so, commanded it with care and honour in four successive campaigns until the war ended.

The promotion was announced; everyone was astonished at the numbers, for there had never been so large a list. I eagerly scanned the names of new cavalry brigadiers, hoping to find my own, and was mortified to see five junior to me mentioned. My pride was most deeply hurt but I kept silent for fear of saying something rash in my vexation. The Maréchal de Lorges was most indignant and his brother-in-law not less so, and they both insisted that I ought to quit the service. I myself felt so angry that I was much inclined to do so; but my youth, the war beginning, the thought of renouncing my ambitions in my chosen career, the boredom of being idle, the tedious summers when conversation would all turn on war and partings, the advancement that could be earned by distinguished conduct, were all powerful deterrents, and I spent two months in mental agony, resigning every morning and every night reversing my decision.

At last, driven to extremes and harried by the two marshals, I resolved to take advice from men on whom I could rely, and to choose them from different walks of life. I finally decided upon the Maréchal de Choiseul, M. de Beauvilliers, the Chancellor, and M. de La Rochefoucauld. They knew how I was placed and were indignant on my behalf, and, moreover, the three last were courtiers. This was most desirable, for what I wished to discover was what the best people would think, particularly the solid men about the King. Above all I sought for advice that would not leave me a prey to indecision, rash impulses, or afterthoughts. Their verdict, given unanimously and most firmly, was that I should leave the service. They all agreed that it would be both a shame and most unsuitable for a man of my rank who had served with honour at the head of a good regiment to return to fight without regiment, troops, or even a company to command. They added that no duke and peer, especially not one with an establishment, wife and children, should consent to be left a mere soldier of fortune, whilst others of lesser degree received employment and commands in a large-scale promotion.

I did not take them as my judges in order to ponder their advice. My course was clear; but though I knew they were right I still hesitated, and three months passed in a torment of doubt before I could bring myself to act. When I finally did so, I followed the advice of those same arbiters. I was very careful to display no hurt feelings, for I wished to leave public and especially military opinion to judge of my having been passed over. The King's anger was inevitable; my friends warned me of it, and I was fully prepared. Need I say how much I dreaded it? He invariably took offence when officers left the service, calling it desertion, especially where the nobility were concerned. What really nettled him, however, was that a man should leave him with a grudge, and anyone who did so felt his displeasure long afterwards, if not for ever. Yet my friends drew no comparison between the disadvantage of resigning, which, at my age, would soon cease to affect me, and the disgrace of continuing to serve under such humiliating conditions. At the same time they insisted on my taking all possible precautions.

I accordingly wrote a short letter to the King,

in which without complaining, or any sign of discontent, or mention of regiments or promotion, I stated my distress at being obliged to leave his service for reasons of health. I added that my consolation would be to attend on him assiduously, with the honour of seeing and paying my court to him all the time. My advisers approved my letter and on Tuesday in Holy Week I presented it myself, at the door of his study, as he returned from mass. I went thence to Chamillart, with whom I had little acquaintance at that time. He was leaving to go to the council, but I told him my story by word of mouth, showing no sign of discontent, and immediately set out for Paris. I had already put many of my friends, both men and women, on the alert, to report anything, no matter how trivial, that the King might say on the subject of my letter. I stayed away for a week; returning on Easter Tuesday, I learned that the Chancellor had found the King in the act of reading it, and that he had exclaimed angrily, 'Here is another deserter!' and had thereupon read my letter aloud word for word. On that same evening I attended on him for the first time since he had heard from me.

After that, for three consecutive years I received no sign of favour from him, and he never missed the smallest opportunity (for want of greater ones) to make me feel how deeply I had offended. He never spoke to or looked at me except by accident. He never mentioned my letter or the circumstances of my leaving his service. I was no longer invited to Marly, and after the first few visits I no longer gave him the satisfaction of refusing me. I must end this sorry tale. Fourteen or fifteen months later he paid a visit to Trianon and supped with the Princesses. The custom on those occasions was for him to make a list, a very short one, of the ladies whom he wished invited. This particular visit was from a Wednesday to a Saturday, and Mme de Saint-Simon and I were doing what we usually did when he went to Marly, that is to say, dining at L'Etang with the Chamillarts on our way to sleep in Paris. We were just sitting down to table when Mme de Saint-Simon

received a message to say that she was on the King's supper-list for that evening. We were astounded and returned at once to Versailles. She then discovered that she was to be the only lady of her age at the King's table; the rest were Mme de Chevreuse, Mme de Beauvilliers, the Comtesse de Gramont, three or four chaperones, the palace ladies, and no others. She was invited again on the Friday, and thereafter the King always nominated her on his rare excursions to Trianon. I soon learned the reason for this favour and it struck me as absurd. He never invited her to Marly, because husbands had the right to go there with their wives. His intention was to show me that his disfavour was towards me alone and did not extend to my wife.

We none the less persevered in waiting on him as usual, but we never sought for invitations to Marly. We lived a pleasant enough life among our friends, and Mme de Saint-Simon continued to enjoy all the pleasures to which the King and Mme la Duchesse de Bourgogne summoned her, even although she could not share them with me. I have dealt with this matter at length because it throws light upon the King's nature.

*   *   *

REVIEW QUESTIONS

1. According to Saint-Simon, what is the relation between political power and military power?
2. What is the relation between nature and political power?
3. What does Saint-Simon tell us about the king's social and fiscal relations with his nobility?
4. What is part of the royal obligation?
5. What do balls and other festivities have to do with political power?
6. Why would legitimacy be both an issue and not an issue at the French court?
7. What are the relations of lineage to political power?

FREDERICK II, THE GREAT

FROM *Antimachiavell*

Frederick II, the Great (1712–1786), king of Prussia, was the third son of Frederick William II of Prussia and Sophia Dorothea of Hanover, sister of George II of England. As a boy, Frederick showed little interest in the military matters that fascinated his father and, led by his tutor, the French Calvinist refugee Jacob E. Duhan de Jandun, discovered a world of art and literature instead. He mastered the flute, for which he composed a number of pieces, and adopted a free-thinking philosophy. His father's efforts at discipline had little effect on the young Frederick, who tried to evade his duties by escaping to England in 1730. The plan was discovered, Frederick imprisoned, and his best friend executed. This brutal encounter had its desired effect: Frederick threw himself on his father's mercy and dedicated himself to the arts of kingship. After a period of military service, in 1735 Frederick withdrew to the castle of Rheinsberg, where he undertook a systematic program of reading. He corresponded with Voltaire and, through French literature, read widely in the philosophical works of the Enlightenment. His ideal of government became enlightened but absolute, serving the people but limited only by the ruler's sensibilities. In this period Frederick wrote a number of treatises on politics, among which was the Antimachiavell (1740), published by Voltaire at The Hague. In it, he developed his ideal of the enlightened, absolute monarch in contrast to those of the Florentine statesman. The work was widely read in France and praised as a formula for enlightened rule. In the same year, Frederick succeeded his father and began a long and illustrious reign as king of Prussia. He distinguished himself as the greatest military genius of his day. In peacetime, he transformed Prussia into the model of an enlightened despotism. His policies expanded education, promoted industry, and reformed justice, all in the interest of state power.

From *Frederick the Great on the Art of War*, edited and translated by Jay Luvaas (New York: Free Press, 1966).

The Duty of Sovereigns

Since Machiavelli wrote his political *Prince*, the face of Europe has changed so much that it can no longer be recognized. If some great general in the age of Louis XII were to come back into the world he would find himself much at a loss. He would see war now carried on by bodies of men so numerous that they can hardly be subsisted in the field, yet are kept up in peace as well as war, whereas in his age, to execute great enterprises and strike decisive blows a handful of men sufficed, and these were disbanded as soon as the war was over. Instead of coats of mail, lances, and harquebusses with matches, he would find the army furnished with uniforms, firelocks, and bayonets. He would see new methods of encamping, besieging, and giving battle, and find the art of subsisting the troops as necessary now as that of conquering was before.

But what would Machiavelli himself say upon seeing this new political face of Europe, and so many princes who were scarcely known in his day now being ranked with the greatest monarchs? What would he say upon seeing the power and authority of sovereigns firmly established, the present manner of negotiating, and that balance settled in Europe by the alliance of many princes and states against the over-powerful and ambitious, a balance solely designed for securing the peace and tranquility of mankind?

All of these things have produced such universal change that Machiavelli's maxims cannot be applied to modern politics. . . . He assumes that a prince who has a large territory, a numerous army, and a full treasury may defend himself against his enemies without foreign supplies. I venture to contradict. . . . Let a sovereign be ever so formidable, he cannot defend himself against powerful enemies without the assistance of allies. If the most formidable prince in Europe, Louis XIV, was reduced to the greatest distress and was nearly ruined by the war of the Spanish Succession, if for want of foreign assistance he was unable to defend himself against the alliance of so many kings and princes, how should a sovereign who is less powerful be able to resist the joint attacks of his neighbors, to which he may often be exposed, without allies?

It is often said—and often repeated without much reflection—that treaties are useless because they are never observed in all points, and that the present age is no more scrupulous in keeping faith than any other. I answer that although many examples may be produced, ancient, modern, and some very recent of princes who have not fulfilled all their engagements, yet it is always prudent and necessary to make alliances. For your allies otherwise will be so many enemies; and if they refuse to send you supplies when you need them, you may at least expect them to observe an exact neutrality.

It is a known truth in politics that the most natural and consequently the best allies are those who have common interests and who are not such close neighbors as to be involved in any dispute over frontiers. Sometimes it happens that strange accidents give birth to extraordinary alliances. In our own time we have seen nations that had always been rivals and even enemies united under the same banners. But these are events that rarely occur and that never can serve as examples, for such connections can only be momentary, whereas the other kind, which are contracted from a unity of interests, alone are capable of execution. In the present situation in Europe, when all her princes are armed and preponderating powers rise up capable of crushing the feeble, prudence requires that alliances should be formed with other powers, as much to secure aid in case of attack as to repress the dangerous plans of enemies, and to sustain all just pretensions by the help of such allies. . . .

Nor is this sufficient. We must have eyes and ears among our neighbors, especially among our enemies, which shall be open to receive and faithfully report what they have seen and heard. Men are wicked. Care must be taken especially not to suffer surprise, because surprises intimidate and terrify. This never happens when preparations are made, however vexatious the event anticipated. European politics are so fallacious that the wisest men may become dupes if they are not always alert and on their guard.

*   *   *

The military system ought . . . to rest on good principles that experience has shown to be valid. The genius of the nation ought to be understood —what it is capable of, and how far its safety may be risked by leading it against the enemy. . . .

There are states which, from their situation and constitution, must be maritime powers: such are England, Holland, France, Spain, and Denmark. They are surrounded by the sea, and their distant colonies force them to keep a navy and to maintain communication and trade between the mother country and these detached members. There are other states such as Austria, Poland, Prussia, and even Russia, some of which may well do without shipping and others that would commit an unpardonable error in politics if they were to . . . employ a part of their troops at sea when they stand indispensably in need of their services on land.

The number of troops maintained by a state ought to be in proportion to the troops maintained by its enemies. Their forces should be equal, or the weakest is in danger of being oppressed. Perhaps it may be argued that a king ought to depend on the aid of his allies. This reasoning would be good if allies were what they ought to be, but their zeal is only lukewarm, and he who shall depend upon another as upon himself will most certainly be deceived. If frontiers can be defended by fortresses, there must be no neglect in building nor any expense spared in bringing them to perfection. France has provided an example of this, and she has realized its advantages on different occasions.

But neither politics nor the army can prosper if the finances are not kept in the greatest order and if the prince himself be not a prudent economist. Money is like the magician's wand, for by its aid miracles are performed. Great political views, the maintenance of the military, and the best conceived plans for the well-being of the people will all remain lethargic if not animated by money. The economy of the sovereign is useful to the public good because, if he does not have sufficient funds in reserve either to supply the expenses of war without burdening his people with extraordinary taxes or to give relief to citizens in times of public calamity, all these burdens will fall on the subject, who will be without the means he needs most in such unhappy times.

* * *

All branches of the state administration are intimately tied together in one bundle: finances, politics, and military affairs are inseparable. Not one, but all of these departments must be uniformly well administered. They must be steered in a straight line, head to head, as the team of horses in the Olympic contest which, pulling with equal weight and speed, covered the course and brought victory to their driver. A prince who rules independently and has fashioned his political system

himself will not find himself in difficulty when he must make a quick decision, for he directs everything toward his established goal.

Above all, he must have acquired the greatest knowledge conceivable in the details of military affairs. One produces poor campaign plans at the round table, and where do the best plans lead if they are wrecked through the ignorance of those entrusted with their execution? A King may be the most able man, the best economist, the most subtle statesman—he will still fail as commander in chief if he neither knows the needs of an army nor cares about the countless details of its maintenance, if he is unaware how an army is mobilized, remains ignorant of the rules of war, or understands nothing of training troops in the garrison and leading them in the field. . . .

* * *

So in Prussia the ruler must do that which is most useful for the good of the state and therefore he must place himself at the head of the army. In this way he gives esteem to the military profession and preserves our excellent discipline and the order introduced among the troops. . . . If he possesses no expert knowledge, how will the king judge order and discipline among the different regiments and units? How can he improve what he himself does not understand? How can he blame the colonels for their mistakes and indicate to them at once the way in which they have been wrong and instruct them how to put their regiments in good order? If the king himself understands nothing of regimental and company economy, of troop leading and the art of maneuver, will he be so imprudent as to interfere? In this event he would expose himself to ridicule just as much as he would through ordering false troop movements. All this knowledge demands constant exercise, which one can only acquire if he is a soldier and applies himself to military service with unbroken diligence.

Finally, I venture the assertion that only the ruler can introduce and maintain this admirable discipline in the army. For often he must summon his authority, strongly censure the individual without regard for person and rank, reward others generously, have the troops mustered whenever possible, and not overlook the slightest negligence. The king of Prussia therefore must of necessity be a soldier and commander in chief. This office, which is courted in all republics and monarchies with diligence and ambition, nevertheless is held in low regard by the kings of Europe, who believe that they lose some of their dignity if they lead their armies themselves. But the throne turns out to be a disgrace if effeminate and lazy princes abandon the leadership of their troops to generals, and thus implicitly avow their own cowardice or incapacity.

In Prussia it is certainly honorable to work with the flower of the nobility and the elite of the nation in strengthening discipline. For it is discipline that preserves the fame of the fatherland, gives it respect in peace, and produces victory in war. One would have to be a completely pitiful human being, bogged down in inertia and unnerved by high living, if he wished to shrink from the trouble and work that the maintenance of discipline in the army demands. But in exchange for his efforts, the king certainly would find his reward in victories and fame, which is even more valuable than the highest peak of grandeur or the pinnacle of power.

*   *   *

As for the manner in which a prince ought to make war, I agree entirely with Machiavelli. Indeed, a great king ought always to assume command of his troops and to regard the camp as his place of residence. This is what his interest, duty, and glory require. As he is the chief magistrate in distributing justice to his people in times of peace, so he ought to be their chief protector and defender in war. When a prince is his own general and present in the field, his orders are more easily suited to all sudden emergencies and are executed with greater dispatch. His presence prevents that misunderstanding among the generals which is so often prejudicial to the interests of the sovereign and fatal to the army. More care is taken of the magazines, ammunition, and provisions, without which Caesar himself at the head of 100,000 men would never be able to accomplish anything. As it is the prince himself who gives orders for the battle, it seems to be his province to direct the execution of these orders, and by his presence and example to inspire his troops with valor and confidence.

But it may be objected that every man is not born to be a soldier and that many princes have not the talents, experience, or courage necessary for commanding an army. This objection may be easily removed: a prince will always find generals skilful enough to advise him, and it is sufficient for him in this case to be directed by their advice. Besides, no war can be carried on with great success if the general is under the direction of a ministry which is not present in the camp and consequently is unable to judge of sudden occurrences and to give orders accordingly.

*   *   *

REVIEW QUESTIONS

1. According to Frederick, why does a state need allies?
2. What has the state become according to Frederick?
3. How does a ruler choose allies?
4. What is their relation to the state?
5. How do they reflect the state? Why does the state need a military?
6. What is the purpose of the military?
7. How is Frederick's idea different from Machiavelli's?

HUGO GROTIUS

FROM *On the Law of War and Peace*

Hugo Grotius (1583–1645) was a Dutch statesman, jurist, theologian, poet, philologist, and historian, a man of all-embracing knowledge, whose writings were of fundamental importance in the formulation of international law. He was born in Delft, the son of the burgomaster and curator at the University of Leiden. Grotius was precocious; he matriculated at the University of Leiden at age eleven. By age fifteen, he had edited the encyclopedia of Martianus Capella and accompanied a diplomatic mission to the king of France, who described Grotius as the "miracle of Holland." He earned his doctorate in law at the University of Orléans and became a distinguished jurist at The Hague. In 1601, he was appointed historiographer of the States of Holland.

He wrote a number of minor but memorable legal treatises before publishing his great work, On the Law of War and Peace, *in 1625. Grotius argued that the entire law of humankind was based on four fundamental precepts: neither state nor individual may attack another state or individual, neither state nor individual may appropriate what belongs to another state or individual, neither state nor individual may disregard treaties or contracts, and neither state nor individual may commit a crime. In the case of a violation of one of these precepts, compensation might be sought either by war or by individual action. These principles and the arguments that surrounded them significantly aided the development of a theory of state sovereignty and international relations in the early modern period. During the remainder of his life, Grotius remained involved in political as well as intellectual affairs of his day. Apart from the vast corpus of his written works, he participated in the government of the United Provinces of the Netherlands. He was eventually imprisoned for his support of Arminianism and managed to escape hidden in a trunk. He spent the rest of his life in exile, honored as one of the great intellectuals of the seventeenth century but unacknowledged by his own country.*

From *The Rights of War and Peace,* by M. Walter Dunn (1901).

*   *   *

VIII

And here is the proper place for refuting the opinion of those, who maintain that, every where and without exception, the sovereign power is vested in the people, so that they have a right to restrain and punish kings for an abuse of their power. However there is no man of sober wisdom, who does not see the incalculable mischiefs, which such opinions have occasioned, and may still occasion; and upon the following grounds they may be refuted.

From the Jewish, as well as the Roman Law, it appears that any one might engage himself in private servitude to whom he pleased. Now if an individual may do so, why may not a whole people, for the benefit of better government and more certain protection, completely transfer their sovereign rights to one or more persons, without reserving any portion to themselves? Neither can it be alledged that such a thing is not to be presumed, for the question is not, what is to be presumed in a doubtful case, but what may lawfully be done. Nor is it any more to the purpose to object to the inconveniences, which may, and actually do arise from a people's thus surrendering their rights. For it is not in the power of man to devise any form of government free from imperfections and dangers. As a dramatic writer says, "you must either take these advantages with those imperfections, or resign your pretensions to both."

Now as there are different ways of living, some of a worse, and some of a better kind, left to the choice of every individual; so a nation, "under certain circumstances, WHEN for instance, the succession to the throne is extinct, or the throne has by any other means become vacant," may choose what form of government she pleases. Nor is this right to be measured by the excellence of this or that form of government, on which there may be varieties of opinion, but by the will of the people.

There may be many reasons indeed why a people may entirely relinquish their rights, and surrender them to another: for instance, they may have no other means of securing themselves from the danger of immediate destruction, or under the pressure of famine it may be the only way, through which they can procure support. For if the Campanians, formerly, when reduced by necessity surrendered themselves to the Roman people in the following terms:—"Senators of Rome, we consign to your dominion the people of Campania, and the city of Capua, our lands, our temples, and all things both divine and human," and if another people as Appian relates, offered to submit to the Romans, and were refused, what is there to prevent any nation from submitting in the same manner to one powerful sovereign? It may also happen that a master of a family, having large possessions, will suffer no one to reside upon them on any other terms, or an owner, having many

slaves, may give them their liberty upon condition of their doing certain services, and paying certain rents; of which examples may be produced. Thus Tacitus, speaking of the German slaves, says, "Each has his own separate habitation, and his own household to govern. The master considers him as a tenant, bound to pay a certain rent in corn, cattle, and wearing apparel. And this is the utmost extent of his servitude."

Aristotle, in describing the requisites, which fit men for servitude, says, that "those men, whose powers are chiefly confined to the body, and whose principal excellence consists in affording bodily service, are naturally slaves, because it is their interest to be so." In the same manner some nations are of such a disposition that they are more calculated to obey than to govern, which seems to have been the opinion which the Cappadocians held of themselves, who when the Romans offered them a popular government, refused to accept it, because the nation they said could not exist in safety without a king. Thus Philostratus in the life of Apollonius, says, that it was foolish to offer liberty to the Thracians, the Mysians, and the Getae, which they were not capable of enjoying. The example of nations, who have for many ages lived happily under a kingly government, has induced many to give the preference to that form. Livy says, that the cities under Eumenes would not have changed their condition for that of any free state whatsoever. And sometimes a state is so situated, that it seems impossible it can preserve its peace and existence, without submitting to the absolute government of a single person, which many wise men thought to be the case with the Roman Republic in the time of Augustus Cæsar. From these, and causes like these it not only may, but generally does happen, that men, as Cicero observes in the second book of his offices, willingly submit to the supreme authority of another.

Now as property may be acquired by what has been already styled just war, by the same means the rights of sovereignty may be acquired. Nor is the term sovereignty here meant to be applied to monarchy alone, but to government by nobles, from any share in which the people are excluded. For there never was any government so purely popular, as not to require the exclusion of the poor, of strangers, women, and minors from the public councils. Some states have other nations under them, no less dependent upon their will, than subjects upon that of their sovereign princes. From whence arose that question, Are the Collatine people in their own power? And the Campanians, when they submitted to the Romans, are said to have passed under a foreign dominion. In the same manner Acarnania and Amphilochia are said to have been under the dominion of the Aetolians; Peraea and Caunus under that of the Rhodians; and Pydna was ceded by Philip to the Olynthians. And those towns, that had been under the Spartans, when they were delivered from their dominion, received the name of the free Laconians. The city of Cotyora is said by Xenophon to have belonged to the people of Sinope. Nice in Italy, according to Strabo, was adjudged to the people of Marseilles; and the island of Pithecusa to the Neapolitans. We find in Frontinus, that the towns of Calati and Caudium with their territories were adjudged, the one to the colony of Capua, and the other to that of Beneventum. Otho, as Tacitus relates, gave the cities of the Moors to the Province of Baetia. None of these instances, any more than the cessions of other conquered countries could be admitted, if it were a received rule that the rights of sovereigns are under the controul and direction of subjects.

Now it is plain both from sacred and profane history, that there are kings, who are not subject to the controul of the people in their collective body; God addressing the people of Israel, says, if thou shalt say, "I will place a king over me"; and to Samuel "Shew them the manner of the king, who shall reign over them." Hence the King is said to be anointed over the people, over the inheritance of the Lord, over Israel. Solomon is styled King over all Israel. Thus David gives thanks to God, for subduing the people under him. And Christ says, "the Kings of the nations bear rule over them." There is a well known passage in Horace, "Powerful sovereigns reign over their own

subjects, and the supreme being over sovereigns themselves." Seneca thus describes the three forms of government, "Sometimes the supreme power is lodged in the people, sometimes in a senate composed of the leading men of the state, sometimes this power of the people, and dominion over the people themselves is vested in a single person." Of the last description are those, who, as Plutarch says, exercise authority not according to the laws, but over the laws. And in Herodutus, Otanes describes a monarch as one whose acts are not subject to controul. Dion Prusaeensis also and Pausanias define a monarchy in the same terms.

Aristotle says there are some kings, who have the same right, which the nation elsewhere possesses over persons and property. Thus when the Roman Princes began to exercise regal power, the people it was said had transferred all their own personal sovereignty to them, which gave rise to the saying of Marcus Antoninus the Philosopher, that no one but God alone can be judge of the Prince. Dion. L. liii. speaking of such a prince, says, "he is perfectly master of his own actions, to do whatever he pleases, and cannot be obliged to do any thing against his will." Such anciently was the power of the Inachidae established at Argos in Greece. For in the Greek Tragedy of the Suppliants, Aeschylus has introduced the people thus addressing the King: "You are the state, you the people; you the court from which there is no appeal, you preside over the altars, and regulate all affairs by your supreme will." King Theseus himself in Euripides speaks in very different terms of the Athenian Republic; "The city is not governed by one man, but in a popular form, by an annual succession of magistrates." For according to Plutarch's explanation, Theseus was the general in war, and the guardian of the laws; but in other respects nothing more than a citizen. So that they who are limited by popular controul are improperly called kings. Thus after the time of Lycurgus, and more particularly after the institution of the Ephori, the Kings of the Lacedaemonians are said by Polybius, Plutarch, and Cornelius Nepos, to have been Kings more in name than in reality. An example which was followed by the rest of Greece.

Thus Pausanias says of the Argives to the Corinthians, "The Argives from their love of equality have reduced their kingly power very low; so that they have left the posterity of Cisus nothing more than the shadow of Kings." Aristotle denies such to be proper forms of government, because they constitute only a part of an Aristocracy or Democracy.

Examples also may be found of nations, who have not been under a perpetual regal form, but only for a time under a government exempt from popular controul. Such was the power of the Amimonians among the Cnidians, and of the Dictators in the early periods of the Roman history, when there was no appeal to the people, from whence Livy says, the will of the Dictator was observed as a law. Indeed they found this submission the only remedy against imminent danger, and in the words of Cicero, the Dictatorship possessed all the strength of royal power.

It will not be difficult to refute the arguments brought in favour of the contrary opinion. For in the first place the assertion that the constituent always retains a controul over the sovereign power, which he has contributed to establish, is only true in those cases where the continuance and existence of that power depends upon the will and pleasure of the constituent: but not in cases where the power, though it might derive its origin from that constituent, becomes a necessary and fundamental part of the established law. Of this nature is that authority to which a woman submits when she gives herself to a husband. Valentinian the Emperor, when the soldiers who had raised him to the throne, made a demand of which he did not approve, replied; "Soldiers, your election of me for your emperor was your own voluntary choice; but since you have elected me, it depends upon my pleasure to grant your request. It becomes you to obey as subjects, and me to consider what is proper to be done."

Nor is the assumption true, that all kings are made by the people, as may be plainly seen from the instances adduced above, of an owner admitting strangers to reside upon his demesnes on condition of their obedience, and of nations submitting by right of conquest. Another argument is derived from a saying of the Philosophers, that all power is conferred for the benefit of the governed and not of the governing party. Hence from the nobleness of the end, it is supposed to follow, that subjects have a superiority over the sovereign. But it is not universally true, that all power is conferred for the benefit of the party governed. For some powers are conferred for the sake of the governor, as the right of a master over a slave, in which the advantage of the latter is only a contingent and adventitious circumstance. In the same manner the gain of a Physician is to reward him for his labour; and not merely to promote the good of his art. There are other kinds of authority established for the benefit of both parties, as for instance, the authority of a husband over his wife. Certain governments also, as those which are gained by right of conquest, may be established for the benefit of the sovereign; and yet convey no idea of tyranny, a word which in its original signification, implied nothing of arbitrary power or injustice, but only the government or authority of a Prince. Again, some governments may be formed for the advantage both of subjects and sovereign, as when a people, unable to defend themselves, put themselves under the protection and dominion of any powerful king. Yet it is not to be denied, but that in most governments the good of the subject is the chief object which is regarded: and that what Cicero has said after Herodotus, and Herodotus after Hesiod, is true, that Kings were appointed in order that men might enjoy complete justice.

Now this admission by no means goes to establish the inference that kings are amenable to the people. For though guardianships were invented for the benefit of wards, yet the guardian has a right to authority over the ward. Nor, though a guardian may for mismanagement be removed from his trust, does it follow that a king may for the same reason be deposed. The cases are quite different, the guardian has a superior to judge him; but in governments, as there must be some dernier resort, it must be vested either in an individual, or in some public body, whose misconduct, as there is no superior tribunal before which they can be called, God declares that he himself will judge. He either punishes their offences, should he deem it necessary; or permits them for the chastisement of his people.

This is well expressed by Tacitus: he says, "you should bear with the rapacity or luxury of rulers, as you would bear with drought, or excessive rains, or any other calamities of nature. For as long as men exist there will be faults and imperfections; but these are not of uninterrupted continuance, and they are often repaired by the succession of better times." And Marcus Aurelius speaking of subordinate magistrates, said, that they were under the controul of the sovereign: but that the sovereign was amenable to God. There is a remarkable passage in Gregory of Tours, where that Bishop thus addresses the King of France, "If any of us, Sir, should transgress the bounds of justice, he may be punished by you. But if you exceed them, who can call you to account? For when we address you, you may hear us if you please; but if you will not, who can judge you, except him, who has declared himself to be righteousness?" Among the maxims of the Essenes, Porphyry cites a passage, that "no one can reign without the special appointment of divine providence." Irenaeus has expressed this well, "Kings are appointed by him at whose command men are created; and their appointment is suited to the condition of those, whom they are called to govern." There is the same thought in the Constitutions of Clement, "You shall fear the King, for he is of the Lord's appointment."

Nor is it an objection to what has been said, that some nations have been punished for the offences of their kings, for this does not happen, because they forbear to restrain their kings, but because they seem to give, at least a tacit consent to their vices, or perhaps, without respect to this, God may use that sovereign power which he has over the life and death of every man to inflict a punishment upon the king by depriving him of his subjects.

*　　*　　*

REVIEW QUESTIONS

1. What is the relation between political power and will according to Grotius?
2. What is the state? The sovereign state?
3. Where does Grotius locate sovereignty?
4. Does sovereignty have a moral component?
5. What is its relation to property? To the good of the people?

Credits

Images

Page 21: (*top*) Erich Lessing/Art Resource, NY; (*bottom*) Giraudon/Art Resource, NY; **p. 31:** Scala/Art Resource, NY; **p. 75:** *Amenhotep III and Queen Tiye Enthroned.* Copy of a wall painting from the Tomb of Anen, ca. 1380 b.c. The Metropolitan Museum of Art, Rogers Fund, 1933 (33.8.8). Photograph © 1978 The Metropolitan Museum of Art; **p. 85:** Bill Curtsinger/National Geographic Image Collection; **p. 89:** Erich Lessing/Art Resource, NY; **p. 106:** Erich Lessing/Art Resource, NY; **p. 180:** On loan from the Philadelphia Museum of Art; Bequest of William S. Vaux, 1882. Courtesy of The University of Pennsylvania Museum (neg. #S8-120800); **p. 207:** Art Resource, NY; **p. 246:** Erich Lessing/Art Resource, NY; **p. 269:** © Copyright The British Museum; **p. 281:** Scala/Art Resource, NY; **p. 318:** (*top*) Archivo Iconografico, S.A./Corbis; (*bottom*) Archivo Iconografico/Corbis; **p. 334:** Robert Holmes/Corbis; **p. 349:** The Pierpont Morgan Library/Art Resource, NY; **p. 382:** The Pierpont Morgan Library/Art Resource, NY; **p. 391:** Erich Lessing/Art Resource, NY; **p. 408:** Anatoly Pronin/Art Resource, NY; **p. 419:** The Pierpont Morgan Library/Art Resource, NY; **p. 452:** (*top*) Alinari/Art Resource, NY; (*bottom*) Alinari/Art Resource, NY; **p. 489:** Erich Lessing/Art Resource, NY; **p. 535:** Ministero per i Beni e le Attività Culturali, Soprintendenza Speciale al Museo Nazionale Preistorico ed Etnografico "L. Pigorini", Roma; **p. 541:** Courtesy of the University of Utah Press; **p. 564:** Scala/Art Resource, NY; **p. 569:** Scala/Art Resource, NY; **p. 599:** Scala/Art Resource, NY; **p. 621:** By permission of the British Library; **p. 636:** Giraudon/Art Resource, NY; **p. 676:** (*top*) Photo by Josie Piller and Debra Doty, University Art Gallery, University of Pittsburgh; (*middle*) Bettmann/Corbis; (*bottom*) Photo by Josie Piller and Debra Doty, University Art Gallery, University of Pittsburgh; **p. 689:** Rijksmuseum, Amsterdam; **p. 696:** Erich Lessing/Art Resource, NY; **p. 740:** Giraudon/Art Resource, NY; **p. 756:** Scala/Art Resource, NY.

Text Selections

Page 3: Atrahasis from "The Babylonian Account of the Great Flood" from *Myths from Mesopotamia: Creation, the Flood, Gilgamesh, and Others,* translated by Stephanie Dalley (1989). Re-

printed with permission of Oxford University Press. **p. 12:** "The Epic of Gilgamesh" from *Myths from Mesopotamia: Creation, the Flood, Gilgamesh, and Others,* translated by Stephanie Dalley (1989). Reprinted with permission of Oxford University Press. **p. 22:** "The Cursing of Akkade" from *The Harps that Once . . . : Sumerian Poetry in Translation* by Thorkild Jacobsen. Copyright © 1987, Yale University Press. Reprinted by permission of the publisher. **p. 29:** James B. Pritchard, editor, "The Hymn to the Nile" in *Ancient Near Eastern Texts Relating to the Old Testament, Third Edition.* Copyright © 1969 by Princeton University Press; renewed © 1983 by Princeton University Press. Reprinted by permission of Princeton University Press. **p. 32:** From "Songs to Senusert III" and "In Praise of Ramesses II as a Warrior" from *Hymns, Prayers, and Songs: An Anthology of Ancient Egyptian Lyric Poetry,* translated by John L. Foster, SBL Writings from the Ancient World Series, Volume 8, Scholars Press, 1995. **p. 34:** "The Instructions of Ptah-hotep" from *Ancient Egyptian Literature,* Volume 1: *The Old and Middle Kingdoms* by Miriam Lichtheim. Copyright © 1973, 1980 by Regents of the University of California. Used by permission of publisher. **p. 40:** From "Egyptian Love Poetry" from *Hymns, Prayers, and Songs: An Anthology of Ancient Egyptian Lyric Poetry,* translated by John L. Foster, SBL Writings from the Ancient World Series, Volume 8, Scholars Press, 1995. **p. 42:** James B. Pritchard, editor, "The Book of the Dead" in *Ancient Near Eastern Texts Relating to the Old Testament, Third Edition.* Copyright © 1969 by Princeton University Press; renewed © 1983 by Princeton University Press. Used by permission of Princeton University Press. **p. 46:** From "Harper's Songs" from *Hymns, Prayers, and Songs: An Anthology of Ancient Egyptian Lyric Poetry,* translated by John L. Foster, SBL Writings from the Ancient World Series, Volume 8, Scholars Press, 1995. **p. 50:** "The Laws of Hammurabi" and "Middle Assyrian Laws" from *Law Collections from Mesopotamia and Asia Minor* by Martha T. Roth, SBL Writings from the Ancient World Series, Volume 6, Scholars Press, Copyright © 1995. Reprinted with permission of the Society of Biblical Literature. **p. 58:** "The Righteous Sufferer" in *From Distant Days: Myths, Tales, and Poetry of Ancient Mesopotamia,* translated by Benjamin R. Foster, CDL Press, 1995. Reprinted with permission of the publisher. **p. 65:** "Letters of Royal Women of the Old Babylonian Period" from *Mari and Karana: Two Old Babylonian Cities* by

Doctrines" from *Greek and Roman Philosophy after Aristotle,* by Jason L Saunders (New York: Free Press, 1994). **p. 216:** From "On The Nature of Things" from *The Way Things Are,* translated by Rolfe Humphries, Indiana University Press, 1968. Reprinted by permission of the publisher. **p. 219:** From *The Manual of Epictetus,* translated by P. E. Matheson, The Clarendon Press. **p. 225:** Translated by Dudley Fitts, from POEMS FROM THE GREEK ANTHOLOGY, copyright © 1956 by New Directions Publishing Corp. Reprinted by permission of New Directions Publishing Corp. **p. 226:** "Marcus Argentarius" translation by Fleur Adcock, from *The Greek Anthology,* edited by Peter Jay (Allen Lane, 1973). Reprinted by permission of Fleur Adcock. **p. 227:** "Dioskorides" and "Meleager" taken from *The Poems of Meleager* translated by Peter Whigham published by Anvil Press Poetry in 1975. **p. 227:** "Glaukos" translated by Peter Jay, from *The Greek Anthology and Other Ancient Greek Epigrams* © 1973 by Peter Jay (Viking 1973). **p. 227:** "Krinagoras" translated by Alistair Elliot in *The Greek Anthology* edited by Peter Jay (Allen Lane, 1973). Reprinted by permission of Alistair Elliot. **p. 227:** "Lucilius" and "Nikarchos" trans. by Peter Porter in *The Greek Anthology* edited by Peter Jay (Allen Lane, 1973). **p. 229:** "Twelve Tables" in *Roman Civilization: Selected Readings,* Vol. II, by Naphtali Lewis and Meyer Reinhold. Copyright © 1953 by Columbia University Press. Reprinted with permission of the publisher. **p. 233:** From "The Life of Marcus Cato the Elder" from *Lives,* translated by Bernadotte Perrin, Volume II, Marcus Cato, 1914. **p. 239:** From "On Slavery in the Late Republic," by Diodorus Siculus in *On Slavery in the Later Republic in The Library of History, III,* translated by C. H. Oldfather, Cambridge, Mass. Harvard University Press, 1939. The Loeb Classical Library ® is a registered trademark of the President and Fellows of Harvard College. **p. 241:** From "On The Laws" by Cicero from *De Legibus (On the Laws),* translated by Clinton W. Keyes, Cambridge, Mass. Harvard University Press, 1928. The Loeb Classical Library ® is a registered trademark of the President and Fellows of Harvard College. **p. 245:** From "Satires" from *The Sixteen Satires* by Juvenal, translated by Peter Green, pp. 87–91, 92–98, 142–44. Copyright © Peter Green, 1967, 1974. Reproduced by permission of Penguin Books, Ltd. **p. 254:** From "The Loves" in *Amores* by Ovid, translated by Guy Lee, John Murray Publishers, Ltd., 1968. Reprinted with permission of the publisher. **p. 256:** From *The Satyricon* by Petronius, translated by William Arrowsmith, translation copyright © 1959 by the University of Michigan Press. Reprinted by permission of the publisher. **p. 259:** "Management of a Large Estate" by Columella in *Roman Civilization: Selected Readings,* Vol. II, by Naphtali Lewis and Meyer Reinhold. Copyright © 1953 by Columbia University Press. Reprinted with permission of the publisher. **p. 264:** "The Gospel of Matthew" from *The Oxford Study Bible: Revised English Bible with the Apocrypha,* edited by M. Jack Suggs, Katherine Doob Sakenfeld, and James R. Mueller, Oxford University Press, 1992. **p. 268:** Tacitus, from "Germania" from *The Agricola and Germany of Tacitus,* translated by A. J. Church and W. J. Brodribb, Macmillan and Co., 1868, rev. 1877. **p. 277:** Tacitus, from "Germania" from *he Agricola and Germany of Tacitus,* translated by A. J. Church and W. J. Brodribb, Macmillan and Co., 1868, rev. 1877. **p. 282:** From *The Theodosian Code and the Sirmondian Constitutions,* by Claude Pharr, Princeton University Press, 1980. **p. 292:** "Letters to the Ro-

mans" from *Early Christian Fathers,* by Cyril C. Richardson, Macmillan Publishers, 1970. **p. 294:** *"The Martyrdom of Polycarp"* from *Early Christian Fathers,* by Cyril C. Richardson, Macmillan Publishers, 1970. **p. 299:** From *The Rule of St. Benedict,* by Cardinal Gasquet, Cooper Square, 1966. **p. 303:** From *Ammianus Marcellus: The Later Roman Empire* translated by Walter Hamilton (Penguin Classics, 1986). Translation copyright © Walter Hamilton, 1986. Reprinted with the permission of the Penguin Group. **p. 308:** From *History of the Franks.* Copyright © Columbia University Press. Reprinted with the permission of the publisher. **p. 313:** From *City of God,* by St. Augustine, translated by Henry Bettenson. Copyright © Henry Bettenson, 1972. Reprinted with the permission of the Penguin Group. **p. 321:** From *Secret History,* by Procopius, University of Michigan Press, 1978. **p. 323:** "The Armenian History: From *Translated Texts for Historians,* vol. 31, Liverpool University Press, 1999. **p. 327:** From *Al-Quran: A Contemporary Translation,* Princeton University Press, 1984. **p. 333:** From *The History of al-Tabari,* vol. 12, State University of New York Press, 1992. **p. 338:** From *Bede: A History of the English Church and People,* Penguin Books, 1968. **p. 341:** From *The Lombard Laws,* University of Pennsylvania Press, 1973. **p. 344:** "Einhard: The Life of Charlemagne" from *Two Lives of Charlemagne* by Einhard & Notker the Stammerer, translated by Lewis Thorpe (Penguin Classics, 1969). Copyright © Lewis Thorpe, 1969. Reprinted with the permission of the Penguin Group. **p. 350:** From *Benedictine Maledictions: Liturgical Cursing in Romanesque France.* Copyright © 1993. Used by the permission of the publisher, Cornell University Press. **p. 351:** From *The Norton Anthology of English Literature,* Sixth Edition, Vol. 1, by M. H. Abrams, et al eds.. Copyright © 1993, 1986, 1979, 1974, 1968, 1962 by W. W. Norton & Company, Inc. Used by permission of W. W. Norton & Company, Inc. **p. 353:** From *The Sagas of Icelanders,* Viking Penguin, 2000. **p. 359:** *Statutes of Lorris/The Charter of Libertie for St. Omer* from MEDIEVAL CULTURE AND SOCIETY. Copyright © 1968 by David Herlihy. Reprinted by the permission of HarperCollins Publishers Inc. **p. 362:** *Statutes of Lorris/The Charter of Libertie for St. Omer* from MEDIEVAL CULTURE AND SOCIETY. Copyright © 1968 by David Herlihy. Reprinted by the permission of HarperCollins Publishers Inc. **p. 364:** From *Will and Wealth in Medieval Genoa.* Reprinted by permission of the publisher from "Last Will and Testament of Oberto Lomellono." Cambridge, Mass.: Harvard University Press. Copyright © 1984 by the Presidents and Fellows of Harvard College. **p. 366:** From *Medieval Trade in the Mediterranean World.* Copyright © Columbia University Press. Reprinted with the permission of the publisher. **p. 373:** From *The Alexiad of Anna Comnena* translated by E.R.A. Sewter (Penguin Classics, 1969) Copyright © E.R.A. Sewter, 1960. Reprinted with the permission of the Penguin Group. **p. 377:** From *Joinville and Villhardouin: Chronicles of the Crusades* translated by Margaret R. B. Shaw (Penguin Classics, 1963) Copyright © M. R. B. Shaw, 1963. Reprinted with the permission of the Penguin Group. **p. 399:** From *The Correspondence of Pope Gregory VII.* Copyright © Columbia University Press. Reprinted with the permission of the publisher. **p. 406:** From *The Crisis of Church and State, 1050–1300,* Prentice-Hall, 1964. **p. 407:** From The Deeds of Frederick Barbarossa. Copyright © Columbia University Press. Reprinted with the permission of the publisher. **p. 411:** From *Selections from the Carmina Bur-*

ana, translated by David Parlett (Penguin Classics, 1986). Copyright © David Parlett, 1986. Reprinted with the permission of the Penguin Group. **p. 413:** From *St. Francis of Assisi: Writings and Early Biographies,* edited by Raphael Brown. Copyright © 1973 Franciscan Herald Press. Reprinted with permission of the publisher. **p. 418:** From *The Letters of Hildegard of Bingen,* Vol. 1, edited by Joseph L. Baird and Radd K. Ehrman. Copyright © 1994 by Oxford University Press, Inc. Used by the permission of Oxford University Press, Inc. **p. 423:** From *The Holy Greyhound.* Copyright © 1983 by Cambridge University Press. Reprinted with the permission of Cambridge University Press. **p. 425:** From *The Golden Legend: Life of Saint Elizabeth of Hungary,* by Jacobus de Voraigne. Copyright © 1993 by Princeton University Press. Reprinted with permission of Princeton University Press. **p. 432:** From *St. Thomas Aquinas, Concise Translations.* Copyright © 1989 Christian Classics. Reprinted by permission of Christian Classics, 200 East Bethany Drive, Allen, TX 75002. **p. 439:** From *The Poem of the Cid,* translated by Rita Hamilton and Janet Perry (Penguin Classics, 1984). Copyright © Rita Hamilton and Janet Perry, 1984. Reprinted with the Permission of The Penguin Group. **p. 445:** From *The Muqaddimah.* Copyright © 1958 by Bollingen, 1967 by Princeton University Press. Reprinted by the permission of Princeton University Press. **p. 451:** From *The Decameron,* by Boccaccio, translated by G. H. McWilliam (Penguin Classics, 1986) Copyright © G. H. McWilliam, 1986. Reprinted with the permission of The Penguin Group. **p. 457:** From *The Canterbury Tales: Nine Tales and a General Prologue,* edited by V. A. Kolve and Glending Olson. Copyright © 1989 by W. W. Norton & Company, Inc. Used by the permission of W. W. Norton & Company, Inc. **p. 475:** From *The Church* by John Hus, Charles Scribner's Sons, 1915. **p. 479:** From *The Divine Comedy,* translated by John Ciardi. Copyright © 1954, 1957, 1959, 1960, 1961, 1965, 1967, 1970 by the Ciardi Family Publishing Trust. Used by permission of W. W. Norton & Company, Inc. **p. 484:** *The Book of the City of Ladies,* by Christine de Pizan, translated by Earl Jeffrey Richards. Copyright © 1982, 1998 by Persea Books. Reprinted by permission of Persea Books, Inc. (New York). **p. 490:** From *The Trail of Jeanne d'Arc.* Copyright © Taylor & Francis. Reprinted with the permission of the publisher. **p. 494:** From *Memoirs of a Renaissance Pope,* Capricorn Books, 1955. **p. 500:** From *Tuscans and Their Families,* Yale University Press, 1985. **p. 504:** From *Mission to Asia,* Medieval Academy of America, 1980. **p. 511:** From *The Travels of Ibn Battuta.* Copyright © 1958 Cambridge University Press. Reprinted with the permission of Cambridge University Press. **p. 516:** From *Decline and Fall of Byzantium to the Ottoman Turks.* Copyright © by permission of the Wayne State University Press. **p. 522:** From *Islam: From the Prophet Muhammad to the Capture of Constantinople,* vol. 1, Oxford University Press, 1987. **p. 524:** From *Medieval Russia's Epics, Chronicals and Tales,* edited by Serge A Zenkovsky, translated by Serge A. Zenkovsky. Copyright © 1963, 1974 by Serge A. Zenkovsky; renewed © 1991 by Betty Jean Zenkovsky. Used by permission of Dutton, a division of Penguin Putnam, Inc. **p. 529:** From *The Voyage of Cadamosto.* Copyright © The Hakluyt Society. Reprinted by the permission of the publisher. **p. 536:** From *Selected Documents Illustrating the Four Voyages of Columbus.* Copyright © The Hakluyt Society. Reprinted by the permission of the publisher. **p. 540:** From *The Voyage of Pedro Alvares*

Cabal to Brazil and India. Copyright © The Hakluyt Society. Reprinted by the permission of the publisher. **p. 548:** From *I Libri della Famiglia,* University of South Carolina Press, 1969. Reprinted by permission of the publisher. **p. 553:** From *The Autobiography of Benvenuto Cellini,* Modern Library, 1995. Reprinted by permission of the publisher. **p. 556:** From *The Lives of Artists,* Penguin Books, 1965. Reprinted by permission of the publisher. **p. 560:** From *The Notebooks of Leonardo da Vinci,* Cape, 1958. Reprinted by permission of the publisher. **p. 563:** From *The Book of the Courtier,* Bantam Doubleday Dell, 1959. Reprinted by permission of the publisher. **p. 570:** From *Philosophy of Man,* University of Chicago Press, 1948. Reprinted by permission of the publisher. **p. 572:** From *The Prince,* W. W. Norton, 1977. Reprinted by permission of the publisher. **p. 576:** From *Ten Colloquies,* Prentice-Hall, 1986. Reprinted by permission of the publisher. **p. 581:** From *Utopia,* W. W. Norton, 1975. Reprinted by permission of the publisher. **p. 588:** From *The Pursuit of Power: Venetian Ambassadors' Reports* by James C. Davis, editor & translator. English translation copyright © 1970 by James C. Davis. Reprinted by permission of HarperCollins Publishers Inc. **p. 590:** From *The Spiritual Exercises of St. Ignatius* by Anthony Mottola, copyright © 1964 by Doubleday, a division of Random House, Inc. Used by permission of Doubleday, a division of Random House, Inc. **p. 593:** From *The Trial of Klaus Hottinger of Zurich,* translated by L. P. Wandel, Staatsarchiv, Zurich. **p. 596:** From *The Life of Theresa of Jesus:* The Autobiography of Teresa Avila, Bantam Doubleday Dell, 1991. Reprinted by permission of the publisher. **p. 598:** From *The Revolution of 1525: The German Peasants from a New Perspective,* Johns Hopkins University Press, 1981. **p. 603:** From *Canons and Decrees of the Council of Trent,* translated by H. J. Schroeder, Herder, 1941. **p. 610:** From *Calvin: Theological Treatises,* edited by J. K. S. Reid (Library of Christian Classics Series). Used by permission of Westminster John Knox Press. **p. 615:** From The American Edition of Luther's Works, copyright © 1943 Muhlenberg Press, admin. Augsburg Fortress. Used by permission. **p. 620:** From *Manifestations of Discontent in Germany on the Eve of the Reformation* by Gerald Strauss. Published by Indiana University Press. Copyright © 1971. Used by permission of Indiana University Press. **p. 626:** From *Selections from the Sources of English History Being a Supplement to Text-Books of English History* B.C. 55– A.D. 1832 arranged and edited by Charles W. Colby, M.A., Ph.D. Longmans, Green and Co., 1899. **p. 629:** From *On Sovereignty,* edited by Julian Franklin. Copyright © 1952 by Cambridge University Press. Reprinted with the permission of Cambridge University Press. **p. 637:** From Carlo Cipolla, *Faith, Reason, and the Plague.* Copyright © 1981 by Cornell University Press. Used by permission of the publishers, Cornell University Press. **p. 640:** From *The Pursuit of Power: Venetian Ambassadors' Reports* by James C. Davis, Editor & Translator. English translation copyright © 1970 by James C. Davis. Reprinted by permission of HarperCollins Publishers Inc. **p. 642:** From *Discoverie of Witchcraft, 1584,* edited by Hugh Ross Wilkinson, Carbondale, Illinois, 1962. **p. 649:** From *Pensées* by Blaise Pascal, translated by A. J. Krailsheimer, pp. 58–64, 121– 25. Copyright © A. J. Krailsheimer, 1966, 1995. Reproduced by permission of Penguin Books Ltd. **p. 652:** From *The Complete English Poems of John Donne,* edited by C. A. Patrides, Everyman's Library, 1985. **p. 656:** From *Simplicissimus,* translated by